SSAGE edge™

GIVES STUDENTS AN EDGE THROUGH HIGH-POWERED STUDY TOOLS

SAGE edge offers a robust online environment students can access anytime, anywhere, and features an impressive array of free tools and resources to keep them on the cutting edge of their learning experience.

- Mobile-friendly **eFlashcards** strengthen understanding of key terms and concepts.
- Mobile-friendly practice **quizzes** allow students to independently assess their mastery of course material.
- A customized **action plan** allows students to individualize their learning experience and take advantage of the resources available to them.
- **Learning objectives** reinforce the most important material.
- **Multimedia content** including video, audio, and web resources help engage students' senses.

GIVES INSTRUCTORS AN EDGE THROUGH HIGH-QUALITY, RELIABLE TEACHING TOOLS

Through SAGE Edge, a full suite of high-quality instructor ancillaries are available to help instructors make the most of their time and create a highly-effective learning environment for their students.

- **Test banks** available in both **Microsoft Word** and **Respondus** provide a diverse range of pre-written options as well as the opportunity to edit any question and/or insert personalized questions to effectively assess students' progress and understanding.
- Editable, chapter-specific **PowerPoint slides** offer complete flexibility for creating a multimedia presentation for the course.
- **Discussion questions** help launch classroom conversation by prompting students to engage with the material and by reinforcing important content.
- In-text visuals such as **tables** and **figures** are provided online to use in teaching aids such as PowerPoint slides, handouts, and lecture notes.
- **Multimedia content** including video, audio, and web resources allow for even more in-depth research.

D0074380

EXCLUSIVE!

SAGE Edge provides students with access to full-text articles for every chapter, from sources like ASA's *Contexts* magazine, *Pacific Standard*, SAGE Knowledge, and selected SAGE journals. Each article supports and expands on the concepts presented in the chapter. This feature also provides questions to focus and guide student interpretation. Combine reputable reporting and scholarship with the topics in your course for a robust classroom experience.

VISIT edge.sagepub.com/trevino

INVESTIGATING SOCIAL PROBLEMS

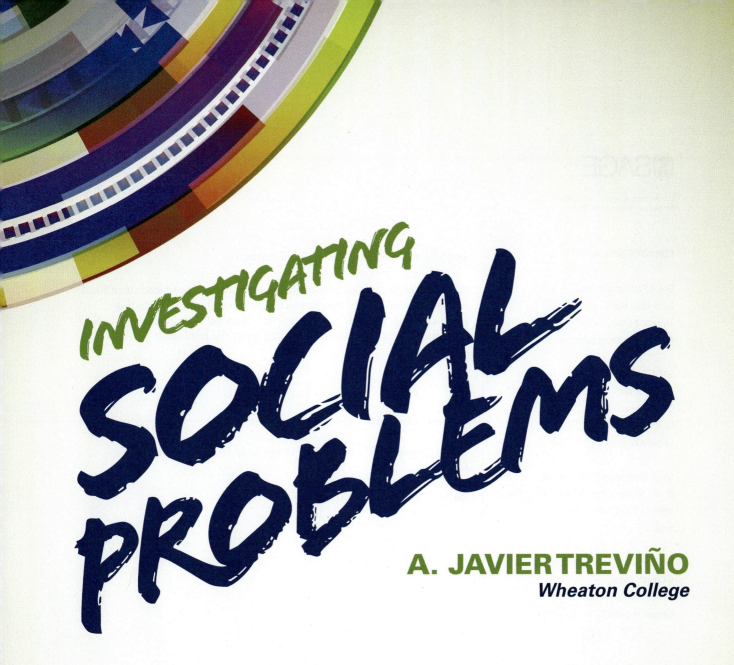

INVESTIGATING SOCIAL PROBLEMS

A. JAVIER TREVIÑO
Wheaton College

Chapter Authors

Wenda K. Bauchspies, Michael M. Bell, Michael Ian Borer,
Ryan W. Coughlan, Kathleen Currul-Dykeman, Susan Guarino-Ghezzi,
William Hoynes, Paul Joseph, Meg Wilkes Karraker, Brian C. Kelly,
Keith M. Kilty, Katharine A. Legun, Duane A. Matcha, Eileen O'Brien,
Dina Perrone, Rebecca F. Plante, Robyn Ryle, Alan R. Sadovnik,
Tyler S. Schafer, Susan F. Semel, Rudi Volti, Kevin White

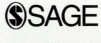

$SAGE

Los Angeles | London | New Delhi
Singapore | Washington DC

Los Angeles | London | New Delhi
Singapore | Washington DC

FOR INFORMATION:

SAGE Publications, Inc.
2455 Teller Road
Thousand Oaks, California 91320
E-mail: order@sagepub.com

SAGE Publications Ltd.
1 Oliver's Yard
55 City Road
London EC1Y 1SP
United Kingdom

SAGE Publications India Pvt. Ltd.
B 1/I 1 Mohan Cooperative Industrial Area
Mathura Road, New Delhi 110 044
India

SAGE Publications Asia-Pacific Pte. Ltd.
3 Church Street
#10-04 Samsung Hub
Singapore 049483

Acquisitions Editor: Jeff Lasser
Development Editor: Nathan Davidson
Editorial Assistant: Nick Pachelli
Production Editor: Olivia Weber-Stenis
Copy Editor: Judy Selhorst
Typesetter: C&M Digitals (P) Ltd.
Proofreader: Sally Jaskold
Indexer: Molly Hall
Cover Designer: Scott Van Atta
Layout Designer: Scott Van Atta
Marketing Manager: Erica DeLuca

Copyright © 2015 by SAGE Publications, Inc.

Printed in Canada.

Cataloging-in-Publication Data is available from the Library of Congress.

ISBN 978-1-4522-4203-3

This book is printed on acid-free paper.

14 15 16 17 18 10 9 8 7 6 5 4 3 2 1

ABOUT THE AUTHORS

1. SOCIOLOGY AND SOCIAL PROBLEMS

A. Javier Treviño is Jane Oxford Keiter Professor of Sociology at Wheaton College (Massachusetts). He is the author and editor of several books including *The Social Thought of C. Wright Mills*. He was a Research Fellow in Sociology at the University of Sussex, England (2006), and a Fulbright Scholar to the Republic of Moldova (2009). Treviño has served as president of the Justice Studies Association (2000–2002) and of the Society for the Study of Social Problems (2010–2011). He is editor of the SAGE Social Thinkers series.

2. POVERTY AND CLASS INEQUALITY

Keith M. Kilty is Professor Emeritus in the College of Social Work at The Ohio State University. His research interests focus on poverty and inequality in the United States, particularly for women and people of color. He co-founded, with Elizabeth A. Segal, *The Journal of Poverty: Innovations on Social, Political & Economic Inequalities*. He is the co-author, with Thomas M. Meenaghan and John McNutt, of *Social Policy Analysis and Practice*. He is co-editor, with Elizabeth A. Segal, of *Rediscovering the Other America: The Continuing Crisis of Poverty and Inequality in the United States*, of *Poverty and Inequality in the Latin American–U.S. Borderlands: Implications of U.S. Interventions*, and of *The Promise of Welfare Reform: Rhetoric or Reality?*

3. RACE AND ETHNICITY

Eileen O'Brien received her PhD in Sociology from University of Florida, focusing on race relations. She is the author of several books, including *Whites Confront Racism: Anti-racists and Their Paths to Action*; *White Men on Race: Power, Privilege, and the Shaping of Cultural Consciousness* (with Joe Feagin); and *The Racial Middle: Latinos and Asian Americans Living Beyond the Racial Divide*. Her upcoming and ongoing projects include interviews with Asian American participants in hip-hop culture, as well as a study of race and gender in military families.

4. GENDER

Robyn Ryle is an associate professor in the department of sociology and anthropology at Hanover College. Her research interests include gender as well as community and urban sociology. She teaches courses in the sociology of gender, environmental sociology, urban sociology, and sociology of food. She received her PhD from Indiana University Bloomington. She is the author of a sociology of gender textbook, *Questioning Gender: A Sociological Exploration*, which is in its second edition.

5. SEXUALITY

Rebecca F. Plante is associate professor of sociology at Ithaca College, where she studies gender, culture, and sexualities, particularly hooking up, relationships, and intimacy in the United States. She has been a Visiting Faculty Fellow at Cornell University in the Feminist, Gender, and Sexuality Studies program. Her books include *Sexualities in Context: A Social Perspective*, *Doing Gender Diversity: Readings in Theory and Real-World Experience*, and *Sexualities: Identities, Behaviors, and Society*. She has served as the book review editor of the *Journal of Sex Research* and is the winner of several student-generated awards for improving the campus sexual climate.

6. AGING

Duane A. Matcha is a professor of Sociology at Siena College. He received his PhD in Sociology from Purdue University in West Lafayette, Indiana. He is the author of a number of books including *Sociology of Aging: A Social*

Problems Perspective, Medical Sociology, and *Readings in Medical Sociology.* Other books include *Health Care Systems of the Developed World: How the United States' System Remains an Outlier* and *The Sociology of Aging: An International Perspective.* He is the recipient of two Fulbright teaching scholarships to the Jagiellonian University in Krakow, Poland, and Vilnius University in Vilnius, Lithuania. In 2012, he received the Kennedy Award for Scholarship at Siena College.

7. EDUCATION

Ryan W. Coughlan is completing his doctoral work in the Educational Policy track of the PhD program in Urban Systems at Rutgers University, Newark, New Jersey, as a Presidential Fellow. He also works as an adjunct professor in the Department of Secondary Education at the City College of New York. Previously, he taught environmental science at Validus Preparatory Academy, a small public high school in the Bronx.

Alan R. Sadovnik is Board of Governors Distinguished Service Professor of Education, Sociology and Public Administration and Affairs at Rutgers University, Newark, New Jersey. He is the author of *Equity and Excellence in Higher Education*; coauthor, with Susan F. Semel, of *Exploring Education: An Introduction to the Foundations of Education*; editor of *Knowledge and Pedagogy: The Sociology of Basil Bernstein* and *Sociology of Education: A Critical Reader*; and coeditor of *Sociology and Education: An Encyclopedia* and *No Child Left Behind and the Reduction of the Achievement Gap: Sociological Perspectives on Federal Educational Policy.*

Susan F. Semel is Chair of the Department of Leadership and Special Education and Professor of Education at the City College of New York and also Professor of Urban Education at the CUNY Graduate Center. She is the author of *The Dalton School: The Transformation of a Progressive School*; editor of *Foundations of Education: The Essential Texts;* coeditor (with Parlo Singh and Alan R. Sadovnik) of *Toolkits, Translation Devices and Conceptual Accounts: Essays on Basil Bernstein's Sociology of Knowledge*; and coeditor (with Alan R. Sadovnik) of *Founding Mothers and Others: Women Educational Leaders During the Progressive Era* and *International Handbook of Educational Reform.*

8. MEDIA

William Hoynes is Professor of Sociology and former Director of the Media Studies Program at Vassar College, where he teaches courses on media, culture, and social theory. He is the author of *Public Television for Sale: Media, the Market, and the Public Sphere;* and co-author, with David Croteau, of *Media/Society: Images, Industries, and Audiences,* now in its 5th edition, and *The Business of Media: Corporate Media and the Public Interest.*

9. FAMILY

Meg Wilkes Karraker is Professor of Sociology, Family Business Center Fellow, and University Scholar at the University of St. Thomas. She is the co-author of *Families with Futures: Family Studies into the 21st Century,* editor of *The Other People: Interdisciplinary Perspectives on Migration,* and author of *Global Families* and *Diversity and the Common Good: Civil Society, Religion, and Catholic Sisters in a Small City.* Her current research is "Middle Class in Middle America: Families, Neighbors, and a Good Society." Karraker was the recipient of the Midwest Sociological Society's Jane Addams Award for service to girls and women in 2012.

10. WORK AND THE ECONOMY

Rudi Volti is Emeritus Professor of Sociology at Pitzer College in Claremont, California. He has been a Senior Fellow at the Smithsonian Institution and a visiting scholar at the Universities Service Centre in Hong Kong, the University of Michigan, and the Autonomous University of Barcelona. He also has served as book editor for *Transfers: Interdisciplinary Journal of Mobility Studies.* His books include *The Encyclopedia of Science, Technology and Society; The Engineer in History; An Introduction to the Sociology of Work and Occupations; Society and Technological Change;* and *Technology Transfer and East Asian Economic Transformation.*

11. CRIME

Kathleen Currul-Dykeman is an expert on courtroom dynamics. A former prosecutor specializing in domestic violence, she has held the position of Suffolk Superior Court assistant district attorney; supervising assistant district attorney for the Dorchester, Massachusetts, Domestic Violence Court; and assistant district attorney in Worcester, Massachusetts. Currul-Dykeman combines her knowledge of criminal law with her research interests. She is the author of *Domestic Violence Case Processing: A Serious Crime or a Waste of Precious Time?*

Susan Guarino-Ghezzi is the former Chairperson and Professor of Sociology and Criminology at Stonehill College. Prior to that, she was Director of Research of the Massachusetts Department of Youth Services. A juvenile crime expert, she has been a frequent consultant on juvenile crime, and was Principal Investigator for research projects on juvenile sex offenders, ex-offender reintegration, deinstitutionalization, and staff-youth interactions. She is also the founder of the program Make Peace with Police for juvenile ex-offenders. Guarino-Ghezzi is co-author of the books *Balancing Juvenile Justice* and *Understanding Crime: A Multidisciplinary Approach*, in addition to numerous scholarly journal articles and technical reports.

12. ALCOHOL AND OTHER DRUGS

Brian C. Kelly is Associate Professor in the Department of Sociology and the Department of Anthropology at Purdue University. His areas of research interest include drug use, sexual health, HIV/AIDS, and youth cultures. The foci of his current research projects include prescription drug misuse and risk taking among young adults, methamphetamine abuse and HIV risk in China, neighborhood and network influences on HIV risk among gay men, club drug use among young adults, and the health outcomes for adolescent girls in age-discordant relationships. He has received several grants from the National Institute on Drug Abuse to pursue these projects.

Dina Perrone is an Assistant Professor in the School of Criminology, Criminal Justice, & Emergency Management at California State University, Long Beach. She earned her PhD in Criminal Justice from Rutgers University–Newark. Perrone's research and published works examine the patterns of use of emerging drugs, effects of drug policy, and factors associated with drug-related harm, particularly among hidden drug-using populations (i.e., those outside of the criminal justice system and drug treatment). She is the author of *The High Life: Club Kids, Harms, and Drug Policy*.

13. HEALTH

Kevin White is Reader in Sociology at The Australian National University, Canberra. He has previously held appointments at Flinders University of South Australia, Wollongong University, and The Victoria University of Wellington, New Zealand. He is the author of six books, including *Inequality in Australia* (with Frank Lewins and Alastair Greig) and *An Introduction to the Sociology of Health and Illness*. He teaches introductory courses on social psychology as well as advanced courses on classical social theory, qualitative research methods, and the sociology of health and illness.

14. THE ENVIRONMENT

Michael M. Bell is Vilas Distinguished Achievement Professor of Community and Environmental Sociology at the University of Wisconsin–Madison. He is principally an environmental sociologist and a social theorist, focusing on dialogics, the sociology of nature, and social justice. His books include *An Invitation to Environmental Sociology*, *Country Boys: Masculinity and Rural Life*, and *Walking Toward Justice: Democratization in Rural Life*.

Katharine A. Legun is Lecturer in Environmental Sociology at the University of Otago, New Zealand, and is affiliated with the Centre for Sustainability. She completed a PhD from the University of Wisconsin–Madison, where she did research on patented apple varieties owned by cooperatives. Her research looks at relationships between (biological) materials, social organization, and markets. Her work has been published in *Society and Natural Resources*.

15. SCIENCE AND TECHNOLOGY

Wenda K. Bauchspies is a sociologist specializing in science, technology, and gender in West Africa from a cultural perspective. She earned her PhD in science and technology studies from Rensselaer Polytechnic Institute. Bauchspies's research interests include science education, women and schooling, everyday technologies in a mid-sized West African city, and the adoption of new varieties of rice in West Africa. She has received a number of grants, including a Fulbright in Guinea where she taught at the University of Kankan and led a research team. This project involved household surveys and ethnographic research on the everyday technologies of water, electricity, transportation, communication, and waste disposal in an urban environment.

16. WAR AND TERRORISM

Paul Joseph was most recently the Distinguished Chair for the United States–India Education Foundation (Fulbright program) and based at Jawaharlal Nehru

University in New Delhi. His research specialty is the politics surrounding foreign and defense policy, especially the impact of public opinion and peace movements on policy outcomes. His latest book, *Are Americans Becoming More Peaceful?*, explores the influence of new public sensitivities to the costs of war on the George W. Bush administration's management of Operation Iraqi Freedom. His current project is an investigation of Human Terrain Systems, teams of social scientists embedded in combat brigades in Iraq and Afghanistan.

17. URBANIZATION

Michael Ian Borer is Associate Professor of Sociology at the University of Nevada, Las Vegas. His specializations include urban sociology, culture, and concepts of the sacred. He is the editor of *The Varieties of Urban Experience: The American City and the Practice of Culture*, the author of *Faithful to Fenway: Believing in Boston, Baseball, and America's Most Beloved Ballpark*, and co-author of *Urban People and Places: The Sociology of Cities, Suburbs, and Towns*. His work has been published in *City & Community*, the *Journal of Popular Culture*, *Religion & American Culture*, *Social Psychology Quarterly*, and *Symbolic Interaction*. Borer served as the 2011–2012 Vice President of the Society for the Study of Symbolic Interaction.

Tyler S. Schafer is a doctoral candidate at the University of Nevada, Las Vegas. He specializes in urban and community sociology, culture, alternative food movements, and sustainability discourse. His dissertation explores the intersection of these broad themes through a case study of a community garden in Las Vegas. His work has been published in the *Journal of Media and Religion*. He spent two years working in the UNLV Urban Sustainability Initiative and teaches undergraduate urban sociology.

BRIEF CONTENTS

DETAILED CONTENTS

PART I: The Sociological Study of Social Problems

1. SOCIOLOGY AND SOCIAL PROBLEMS   2

A. Javier Treviño

PART II: Problems of Inequality

2. POVERTY AND CLASS INEQUALITY   26

Keith M. Kilty

3. RACE AND ETHNICITY 54

Eileen O'Brien

4. GENDER 82

Robyn Ryle

5. SEXUALITY   108

Rebecca F. Plante

6. AGING   134

Duane A. Matcha

PART III: Problems of Institutions

7. EDUCATION 160

Ryan W. Coughlan, Alan R. Sadovnik,
and Susan F. Semel

9. FAMILY 218

Meg Wilkes Karraker

10. WORK AND THE ECONOMY 248

Rudi Volti

PART IV: Problems of Health and Safety

11. CRIME   278

Kathleen Currul-Dykeman and
Susan Guarino-Ghezzi

PART V: Problems of Global Impact

14. THE ENVIRONMENT — 366

Michael M. Bell and Katharine A. Legun

17. URBANIZATION 448

Michael Ian Borer and Tyler S. Schafer

PREFACE

"Introduction to sociology" courses and courses in "social problems" generally have a couple of things in common. First, they tend to serve as "gateway" courses that introduce students to sociology as a discipline and as a major; second, they teach students to think sociologically. But beyond that, these two kinds of courses are quite different, and the main difference has to do with the issues they cover. While general sociology courses acquaint students with fundamental concepts such as social structure and institutions, social problems courses go beyond this and focus on the troublesome situations endemic to social structures and institutions: poverty, social inequalities, crime, drug addiction, unemployment, environmental disasters, terrorism, and so on. Given the panoply of distressing, harmful, and threatening social situations and conditions—and their complexity—the study of social problems requires, indeed demands, specialized focus by experts.

Every social problems textbook currently on the market is written by one, two, or perhaps three authors who endeavor to cover a wide range of different social problems. This book is different: *it is written by a panel of twenty-two specialists.* As such, each chapter has been prepared by one or more scholars who specialize in that particular issue. All of them are sociologists who frame the problems in question within the sociological imagination and provide the most current theories, research, and examples. These experts teach at small liberal arts colleges and at large research universities; in departments of sociology, criminal justice, social work, and education; in ten U.S. states, from the Northeast to the West, from the Midwest to the South; and in two countries outside the United States. That said, this is *not* a specialized text that assumes foundational knowledge on the part of the student; rather, it is intended to service a general introductory class in social problems. Additionally, although this is an edited text, it is not a reader; every effort has been made to link themes and discussions between chapters. There is, in short, no other textbook like it. Below are descriptions of some of the other unique features of *Investigating Social Problems.*

THE MURAL MOTIF

The first page of each chapter presents a photo of a colorful mural or wall painting that depicts the social problem to be discussed. Students can examine these striking murals, from various countries and cultures, for their visual representations and interpret them for information they may reveal. Each of these images is accompanied by a statement that refers to the mural and that poses an initial question of relevance to the chapter topic.

LEARNING OBJECTIVES

Half a dozen or so learning objectives are listed at the beginning of each chapter. These alert students to the chapter's main themes and ask them to describe, explain, evaluate, or apply the information to be discussed. Each learning objective is repeated next to the first-level heading to which it corresponds, making it easier for students to keep track of the objectives as they read.

CRITICAL THINKING QUESTIONS

Interspersed throughout each chapter are critical thinking questions, flagged as "Ask Yourself." These help students apply the concepts discussed, get them to think about how the information provided relates to their everyday lives, and challenge them to think about what they would do in similar situations. In addition, all boxed features end with "Think about It" questions intended to spur classroom discussion.

OUR STORIES

Because each chapter is written by one or more sociologists who are expert in the social problem under discussion, chapter-opening "Investigating the social problem" boxes present the contributing authors' "stories" of how they came to be interested in their particular areas of expertise. These short bios personalize the chapters and help students to see that real people are involved in investigating real problems.

OPENING VIGNETTES

Every chapter begins with a brief opening vignette that sets the stage for the social problem to be discussed. The vignettes are summations of current news reports, documentary films, ethnographic accounts, or trade books that vividly describe provocative scenarios to introduce students to the social problems at hand. Along with each vignette, one or more questions are posed to get students to begin thinking about the topic.

THE USES OF GENERAL AND SPECIALIZED THEORIES

This textbook, more than any other on the market, takes seriously the application of sociological theory in investigating social problems. As such, each chapter considers the social problem in question from the point of view of the *three general theoretical approaches* of structural functionalism, conflict theory, and symbolic interactionism. These provide the student with distinct ways of making sense of the complex realities of the social problem. Beyond that, each chapter also provides greater in-depth analysis by employing particular *specialized theories* that the expert author or authors have specifically chosen to use in further investigating the social problem of concern. No other textbook employs specific theories. The utilization of both general and specialized theories shows students that conceptual analysis has an important place in the investigation of social problems.

A FOCUS ON SOCIAL POLICY

As a set of official strategies intended to manage specific social problems, *social policy* is given special consideration in every chapter. Each author proposes policy recommendations for social change that arise from the three main theoretical perspectives. This demonstrates to students that theory has a practical utility in addressing social problems.

BOXED FEATURES AND THREE KEY THEMES

Every chapter underscores three key themes that are of particular importance in the study of social problems. These are set off in boxes to illustrate their significance. "Beyond Our Borders" boxes demonstrate that social problems are global in scope. These help students, first, to understand the social problems of U.S. society in relationship to social problems in other countries. Second, the contents of these boxes show students that social problems are interconnected in that they affect many countries, cultures, and people around the world. "Experiencing" boxes pertain to intersectionality; that is, the problems in question are considered in the context of how individuals experience them in reference to their interrelated statuses of social class, race/ethnicity, gender, and so on. "Researching" boxes discuss recent studies or reports on particular aspects of the social problems under discussion and present quantitative or qualitative data on the topics. The boxed features also contain critical thinking questions to help students reflect on the information covered.

GENERAL SOCIAL SURVEY EXERCISES

Near the beginning of each chapter, students are presented with a set of questions under the rubric "What Do You Think?" These questions are related to the social problem under discussion, and students are invited to give their personal responses. At the end of each chapter, data from the General Social Survey pertaining to these questions is provided under the title "What Does America Think?" This allows students to compare the opinions and attitudes they held prior to reading the chapter with those of the general U.S. population after they have read the chapter.

PHOTOS AND OTHER VISUALS

Carefully selected photographs are strategically placed throughout the chapters. These are not merely stock photos used for visual interest; rather, they are intended to aid students in connecting personally with real-life situations. As such, all the photos are accompanied by informative captions, many of which impart the names of the real people, places, and events that are shown. This is another way in which the text reflects reality. Most of the photo captions also pose a question or questions. Other visuals include tables, figures, charts, and maps designed to help students better understand and remember the information provided in the chapter.

STUDENTS' ROLE IN SOCIAL CHANGE

After being informed about the problems that plague society, students frequently want to know what solutions are available. Indeed, they often want to know what *they* can do to make a difference. Another unique feature of this textbook is that the chapter authors provide suggestions on the opportunities available for students to involve themselves personally in practical efforts to ameliorate social problems.

GLOSSARIES

This text features marginal glossaries, offering students easy access to definitions and descriptions of concepts and other important terms and phrases. Key terms are bolded in the text on their first substantive use, and a comprehensive glossary appears at the end of the book.

CHAPTER REVIEW

Each chapter ends with a summary that encapsulates the main learning points and a set of discussion questions designed to help students review what they have learned and to foster critical thinking about the material.

ANCILLARIES

Instructor Teaching Site

http://edge.sagepub.com/trevino

A password-protected instructor teaching site provides one integrated source for all instructor materials, including the following key components for each chapter:

- A **test bank** offers a diverse set of test questions and answers for each chapter in the book. Multiple-choice, true/false, and short-answer/essay questions for every chapter will aid instructors in assessing students' progress and understanding.
- **PowerPoint presentations** are designed to assist with lecture and review, highlighting essential content, features, and artwork from the book.
- **Chapter-specific discussion questions** help launch classroom interaction by prompting students to engage with the material and by reinforcing important content.
- **Audio links** are related to important topics and designed to supplement key points within the text. Carefully selected, Web-based video links feature relevant interviews, lectures, personal stories, inquiries, and other content for use in independent or classroom-based explorations of key topics.

Student Study Site

http://edge.sagepub.com/trevino

- Mobile-friendly **eFlashcards** reinforce understanding of key terms and concepts that have been outlined in the chapters.
- Mobile-friendly **Web quizzes** allow for independent assessment of progress made in learning course material.
- **Web resources** direct students to relevant online sites for further research on important chapter topics.
- **Video and audio links** feature meaningful content for use in independent or classroom-based exploration of key topics.
- **General Social Survey questions** allow students to compare their answers to polling questions against how the general population answered.

Interactive eBook

Investigating Social Problems is also available as an interactive eBook, which can be packaged free with the book or purchased separately. The interactive eBook offers links to video cases and SAGE journal articles and reference articles, as well as additional audio, video, and Web resources.

ACKNOWLEDGMENTS

A small army of highly talented staff and editors at SAGE, most of them working "behind the scenes," made my job as this text's general editor that much easier and enjoyable. I very much appreciate their hard work and dedication to this project. I thank David Repetto for first conceiving the idea for *Investigating Social Problems* and appreciate his confidence in me to carry it out. I'm eternally grateful to Nathan Davidson for his gentle advice and kind wisdom, to say nothing of his hard work and organizational skills. Jeff Lasser inherited this project with good cheer and was supportive and encouraging every step of the way. Elisa Adams skillfully guided twenty-three authors to produce a coherent textbook. Catherine Gildae, my colleague at Wheaton College, prepared the end-of-chapter discussion questions with uncommon professionalism and reliability. I wish to thank Charlynn Devenny for contributing the data analysis exercises in each chapter. I'm also indebted to SAGE staff members Nick Pachelli, Erica DeLuca, Krysten Jones, Scott Van Atta, Catherine Forrest, and Olivia Weber-Stenis.

Above all, I'm especially grateful to each of the authors who wrote the various chapters presented here.

Simply put, without their industriousness, persistence, and expertise, the volume would not have been possible.

Thanks also to my wife, Nancy, and son, Myles, for their extraordinary patience while I spent many long hours at the computer and on the phone orchestrating the book's development.

Finally, I wish to thank all of the reviewers who contributed their many suggestions, critiques, and insights that helped make *Investigating Social Problems* a better text:

Evan Adelson, San Diego Mesa College

Brian Aldrich, Winona State University

Kristian Alexander, Zayed University

Annett Marie Allen, Troy University

Tammy L. Anderson, University of Delaware

Judith Andreasson, North Idaho College

Rebecca Bach, Duke University

Sam Elizabeth Baroni, Nova Southeastern University

Roberta Campbell, Miami University

Susan Eidson Claxton, Georgia Highlands College

Marian Colello, Bucks County Community College

Maia Cudhea, University of North Texas

Kristen De Vall, University of North Carolina Wilmington

Melanie Deffendall, Delgado Community College

Ricardo A. Dello Buono, Manhattan College

Sophia DeMasi, Mercer County Community College

Ione DeOllos, Ball State University

Andrew Dzurisin, Middlesex County College

Lois Easterday, Onondaga Community College

Kathy Edwards, Ashland Community and Technical College

Kathryn Feltey, University of Akron

Bethaney W. Ferguson, Cape Fear Community College

Sharman H. French, Capital Community College

Caren J. Frost, University of Utah

Albert Fu, Kutztown University

Brian Garavaglia, Macomb Community College

David Gauss, San Diego State University

Peggy Geddes, Trios College

Gary Gilles, Argosy University

Otis Grant, Indiana University South Bend

Lecia Gray, Belhaven University

Johnnie Griffin, Jackson State University

Stephen Groce, Western Kentucky University

William Gronfein, Indiana University–Purdue University Indianapolis

George Guay, Bridgewater State University

Gary Hamill, Lehigh Carbon Community College

Ayre J. Harris, Mountain View College

Franklin H. Harris, Roanoke Chowan Community College

Donna Haytko-Paoa, University of Hawaii Maui College

Gary Heidinger, Roane State Community College

Teresa Hibbert, University of Texas at El Paso

Sarah Hogue, Bridgewater State University

Kathryn Hovey, New Mexico State University

Hua-Lun Huang, University of Louisiana

Linda L. Jasper, Indiana University Southeast

Angela Lewellyn Jones, Elon University

Bennett Judkins, Lee University

Kyle Knight, University of Alabama in Huntsville

Rosalind Kopfstein, Western Connecticut State University

Charles Kusselow, River Valley Community College

Erma Lawson, University of North Texas

Debra LeBlanc, Bay Mills Community College

Laurie J. Linhart, Drake University

Jackie Logg, Cabrillo College

Dennis Loo, California State Polytechnic University Pomona

Steve Mabry, Cedar Valley College

Michael Macaluso, Grand Valley State University

Keith Mann, Cardinal Stritch University

Susan E. Mannon, Utah State University

Marguerite Marin, Gonzaga University

Vanessa Martinez, Holyoke Community College

Teresa Mayors, Curry College

Sheila McKinnon, HBI College

Neil McLaughlin, McMaster University

Pamela McMullin-Messier, Central Washington University

Stephanie Medley-Rath, Lake Land College

Sharon Methvin, Mt. Hood Community College

Kari Meyers, Moorpark College

Susan Nelson, University of South Alabama

Yvonne Newsome, Agnes Scott College

Erin Niclaus, Bucks County Community College

Michael J. O'Connor, Hawkeye Community College

David O'Donnell, Vermilion Community College

Josh Packard, University of Northern Colorado

Malcolm Potter, California State University Long Beach

Janice Kay Purk, Mansfield University

Susan Rahman, Santa Rose Junior College

Jean M. Raniseski, Alvin Community College

Abigail Richardson, Colorado Mesa University

Jacquelyn Robinson, Albany State University

Paulina X. Ruf, Lenoir-Rhyne University

Frank A. Salamone, Iona College

Baranda Sawyers, Lansing Community College

Luceal J. Simon, Wayne State University

Sheryl Skaggs, University of Texas at Dallas

Buffy Smith, University of St. Thomas

Stephen Soreff, Boston University

John R. Sterlacci, Broome Community College

Dennis J. Stevens, University of North Carolina Charlotte

Colin E. Suchland, St. Louis Community College

Sara C. Sutler-Cohen, Bellevue College

Susan Turner, Front Range Community College

Deidre Ann Tyler, Salt Lake Community College

Nicholas Vargas, Purdue University

Melissa D. Weise, Holyoke Community College

Bill Winders, Georgia Tech

Michael Woo, Bellevue University

Susan L. Wortmann, Nebraska Wesleyan University

Anat Yom-Tov, Haverford College

A. Javier Treviño
Norton, Massachusetts

SOCIOLOGY AND SOCIAL PROBLEMS

A. Javier Treviño

Frederic Soltan / Corbis

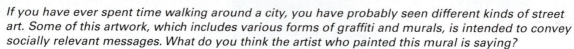

If you have ever spent time walking around a city, you have probably seen different kinds of street art. Some of this artwork, which includes various forms of graffiti and murals, is intended to convey socially relevant messages. What do you think the artist who painted this mural is saying?

Investigating Sociology and Social Problems: My Story

A. Javier Treviño

I took my first sociology course as a high school senior, and I knew I had found my calling. Although no one in my family had ever gone to college, I took both sociology courses offered at the local community college in Laredo, Texas, one of which was about social problems. My appetite whetted, I transferred to a state university to get a B.A. degree in sociology. After graduating and completing a year of substitute teaching at my former high school, I decided to get a master's degree in applied sociology, with an emphasis in social planning. Thinking this would be the end of my academic journey, I planned to work as a probation officer, a marriage counselor, or even a sociology teacher at a community college. But I soon realized I needed to know more about *theory* to gain a better understanding of the nature and causes of social problems. I enrolled in the Ph.D. sociology program at Boston College, concentrating on crime, deviance, and social control. I was fortunate to study and work with the preeminent criminologist Richard Quinney, who opened my eyes to a critical approach to the problem of crime. Since then I have looked at various issues—crime, deviance, legal matters—theoretically.

In 2011 I served as president of the Society for the Study of Social Problems and chose *service sociology* as the annual meeting's program theme. After a long career I believe it is time for scholars, practitioners, advocates, and students like you to become earnestly engaged in relieving the problems of our everyday life. To explore some ways in which service sociology is being done, see the book I edited with my colleague Karen M. McCormack, *Service Sociology and Academic Engagement in Social Problems* (2014).

LEARNING OBJECTIVES

1.1 Describe how working-class young adults are currently experiencing their lives.

1.2 Define what constitutes a social problem.

1.3 Explain the sociological imagination.

1.4 Discuss how sociological research can be used to study social problems.

1.5 Explain the three main sociological perspectives of structural functionalism, conflict theory, and symbolic interactionism.

1.6 Evaluate how each of the three theoretical perspectives can be applied to improve our understanding of social problems.

1.7 Discuss the role of social policy in managing social problems.

1.8 Explore the role of specialized theories in sociology.

1.9 Identify ways in which service sociology can make a difference.

 # WHAT DO YOU THINK?

Questions about Sociology and Social Problems from the General Social Survey

1. How scientific is sociology?
   - [ ] SCIENTIFIC
   - [ ] NOT SCIENTIFIC

2. People need not overly worry about others.
   - [ ] AGREE
   - [ ] DISAGREE
   - [ ] NEITHER AGREE NOR DISAGREE

3. Are people helpful or looking out for themselves?
   - [ ] HELPFUL
   - [ ] LOOKING OUT FOR THEMSELVES

4. People are treated with respect.
   - [ ] AGREE
   - [ ] DISAGREE

5. Can people be trusted?
   - [ ] YES
   - [ ] NO

Turn to the end of the chapter to view the results for the total population.

SOURCE: National Opinion Research Center, University of Chicago.

SETTLING FOR LESS

1.1 Describe how working-class young adults are currently experiencing their lives.

Jalen is a 24-year-old, single black man who works the baseball season as a nighttime security guard at a local stadium. He is living in the basement of his aunt and uncle's house. After graduating high school, with no clear plans for what to do next, Jalen impulsively joined the Marine Corps. After five years of service, which included three tours of duty in Afghanistan, he was honorably discharged. That was a year ago. Since then, his attempts to go to college and find a stable job have been thwarted again and again.

Wanting a career in firefighting, Jalen took the civil service exam. He made the city's hiring list and enrolled at the fire academy. However, on the second day of training Jalen tested positive for marijuana and was expelled. Although he does not consider himself "book smart," he knows a college degree will get him a good job, and, because he is a veteran, the G.I. Bill will pay for his schooling. He recently enrolled in a local community college, but two weeks into the semester, he still doesn't have his books because he has not yet received his G.I. Bill benefits check, which he needs to buy them. To make matters worse, he owes $18,000 in credit card debt and has no way to pay it off. He is now tentatively considering going back to the Marine Corps.

Jalen is one of 100 young working-class men and women whom sociologist Jennifer M. Silva interviewed for her book *Coming Up Short* (2013). Silva found that these young people's coming-of-age experiences—with education, work, relationships—have not measured up to their expectations. Although they continue to hold tight to the American Dream of realizing upward social mobility through hard work and well-paying jobs, they have achieved less than their parents were able to and feel permanently stuck in an extended adolescence. All the milestones that had previously marked adulthood in U.S. society—owning a home, getting married, having children, finding stable employment—remain hopelessly out of reach for these working-class young people.

What is the social problem in the scenario above? Let's see.

Due to their difficult situation, these young people experience a whole range of feelings: confusion, bitterness, regret, disappointment, betrayal, hope. In their interviews with Silva about their individual life experiences, they largely blame themselves for their inadequate education, unexpected layoffs, and failed relationships. They believe they are responsible for their own fates. They feel they can't trust **social institutions**—any set of persons cooperating together for the purpose of organizing stable patterns of human activity—such as the labor market, education, marriage, and government to help them attain a sense of dignity and well-being.

But let's look at the larger picture and consider these young adults not on a case-by-case basis but as a generational **cohort**—a group of individuals of similar age within a population who share a particular experience. Now we see that in 2012, 56% of the nation's 18- to 24-year-olds—the so-called millennial generation—were living with their parents (Fry 2013), compared to 35% of those in the same age group in 1960. They were also delaying marriage or not marrying at all. Consider that in the early 1960s the median age at first marriage was 20 for women and 22 for men. By 2010 it had increased to almost 26 for women and 28 for men (Silva 2013, 6).

Now, you may say that being single and living with parents is an unfortunate or undesirable situation for those twentysomethings who would rather be married and on their own, but these circumstances are not *social* problems. Fair enough. But let's also look at a situation in which many of the young people Silva interviewed found themselves, and that most of us would agree generally *is* regarded as a social problem: unemployment (the subject of Chapter 10). And let's consider unemployment on the basis of **demographic factors**, or social characteristics of a population—in particular race, age, and gender.

When we look at race (the subject of Chapter 3), we find that in 2011, black men like Jalen had the highest unemployment rate of any racial/ethnic group, 16.7%. Compare this to white men, who had a 7.7% unemployment rate (U.S. Bureau of Labor Statistics 2012c, 43). As for age, we know there is plenty of discrimination

....

Social institutions: Any set of persons, such as a family, economy, government, or religion, cooperating for the purpose of organizing stable patterns of human activity.

Cohort: Within a population, a group of individuals of similar age who share a particular experience.

Demographic factors: Social characteristics of a population, in particular those of race, age, and gender.

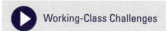 Working-Class Challenges

against older persons in the labor market (as we will see in Chapter 6), but we also know that in 2012, 13.3% of people around Jalen's age, 20–24, were unemployed, compared to 7% of people 25–54 years of age (U.S. Bureau of Labor Statistics 2012d, 1). Concerning gender (the subject of Chapter 4), we know that in 2011, women working full-time received 82 cents for every dollar earned by male workers (U.S. Bureau of Labor Statistics 2012b).

But what are we to make of all these statistics? For the moment, simply this: an awful lot of U.S. adults—tens of thousands, hundreds of thousands, even millions—are in the same predicament as those young men and women, like Jalen, whom Silva interviewed. And though they may have felt alone and isolated, these young people were not the only ones experiencing such circumstances. In other words, unemployment is not only a matter of these young people's *personal* troubles, it is, in fact, a *collective* problem.

Another important issue to consider briefly now, to which we will be paying greater attention in the rest of this textbook, is that some groups of people experience social conditions—like unemployment and its related issues of discrimination in hiring and wage earning—at higher levels than do other groups. It is for this reason that sociologists look at **intersectionality**, or the ways in which several demographic factors combine to affect people's experiences. In Jalen's case, we would consider how his age (young adult), race (black), gender (male), and social class (working class) combine to shape his life.

So let's now look at the demographic factor that, in addition to age, characterized all the 100 young people Silva spoke with: social class (discussed in more depth in Chapter 2). A **social class** is a category of people whose experiences in life are determined by the amount of income and wealth they own and control. Remember that the young adults Silva interviewed were from a *working-class* background. No doubt you have heard and read about the various social classes that exist in U.S. society. There is no agreement, even among social scientists, on how to distinguish among social classes, much less on how many there are. But we typically hear about the *upper class* (think here about such wealthy people as Amazon.com founder Jeff Bezos and investor Warren Buffet), the *middle classes* (usually referred to in the plural because there are several levels within this middle

David Ramos/Stinger, Getty

Sergi, 21, who lives in Spain, poses with his dog in his bedroom in his mother's apartment. Sergi is a college graduate and has been looking for a job for the past five months. According to the Spanish National Institute of Statistics, the youth unemployment rate is 54.37%, reaching 79% among 20- to 24-year-olds. What would you do if you were in Sergi's situation?

rank), and the *poor* (sometimes called the working poor, the homeless, or the indigent).

The working class, which we can place between the middle classes and the poor, generally consists of people who have a basic education (a high school diploma, vocational skills training, certification in a service occupation), modest income (earned from hourly wages), and jobs in manufacturing or the "service economy" (factory workers, truck drivers, cooks, waiters and waitresses, nurses, police officers). Thirty or so years ago, when the parents of the young men and women Silva spoke with were coming of age, young working-class adults were better able to get steady jobs and maintain relatively stable lives for themselves and their families. What has happened since then to lead thousands of working-class men and women in their 20s and 30s to increasingly remain unmarried, live at home with their parents, have children out of wedlock or not have children at all, divorce, and remain unemployed or stuck in low-paying jobs? We'll address this important question in due course, but first we turn to the discipline of sociology and its examination of social problems.

Intersectionality: The ways in which several demographic factors—especially social class, race, ethnicity, and gender—combine to affect people's experiences.

Social class: A category of people whose experiences in life are determined by the amount of income and wealth they own and control.

ASK YOURSELF: Think of a social issue about which you and your peers have expressed concern. How do you think this issue affects other people your age but from a social class different from yours? A different race or ethnicity? Think of the ways in which you do or do not identify with the young working-class adults Jennifer Silva interviewed.

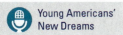

Young Americans' New Dreams

THE SOCIOLOGICAL STUDY OF SOCIAL PROBLEMS

1.2 Define what constitutes a social problem.

As the study of social behavior and human society, **sociology** is the field most likely to examine systematically social problems such as poverty, social discrimination (on the basis of race, ethnicity, gender, sexual identity, age), crime, drug abuse, immigration, climate change, terrorism, and more.

This textbook consists of 17 chapters on various social problems. They were written by more than two dozen sociologists who are experts in the social problems they discuss. While social problems may sometimes differ in their extent, and while we may research and analyze them differently, we define a **social problem** as a social condition, event, or pattern of behavior that negatively affects the well-being of a significant number of people (or a number of significant people) who believe that the condition, event, or pattern needs to be changed or ameliorated. Let's consider the various aspects of our definition, and some of their implications, in turn.

Patterns and Trends

To begin with, in discussing social problems we are talking about conditions, events, or behaviors that occur locally, nationally, or globally and cause or threaten to cause harm to all or some segment of the population. Consider the failure of U.S. schools to teach children basic literacy skills as a social *condition* that means many students (particularly poor and minority children) will not be well prepared to enter the job market, and that the United States will be less competitive in the world economy. Or consider an *event* like Hurricane Sandy, which, when it made landfall in New Jersey in 2012, left 2 million households without power, destroyed or damaged nearly 350,000 homes, and killed 37 people. Finally, consider as a social problem a *pattern of behavior* like the increased abuse of the prescription drugs OxyContin, Percocet, and Demerol by young adults, which in 2010 led to almost 3,000 deaths (National Institute on Drug Abuse 2013).

Because social problems affect large numbers of people, sociologists typically talk about them in terms of *patterns* and *trends* and use measures of *rates* to describe how frequent and pervasive their occurrence is. For example, we've all heard about how politicians, civic leaders, religious leaders, and average citizens are concerned about the crime rates in their cities and communities. In studying rates of crime, sociologists and criminologists rely on certain **data sources**, or collections of information, like the FBI's Uniform Crime Reports (UCR; to be discussed in Chapter 11). When we look at the UCR's percentage of violent crime by U.S. region we see that in 2012, the South had the highest rate of violent crime (murder, rape, robbery, aggravated assault) at 40.9%, compared to the Northeast region with 16% (Federal Bureau of Investigation 2013a).

Patterns and trends can be visually presented in a variety of formats, including charts, tables, and graphs. Throughout this textbook you will see data depicted in this way. Back in the 1920s and 1930s the sociologists at the University of Chicago were interested in studying the incidence and prevalence of alcoholism, suicide, mental illness, and prostitution in the city. Knowing that these problems tend to be more concentrated in some areas than in others, they wanted to identify their distribution throughout Chicago. For this they used maps. One of the most common types was the *spot map*, on which the researchers plotted the locations where a particular social problem was present. For example, Figure 1.1 is a map in which the spots indicate the home addresses of 8,591 alleged male juvenile delinquents during 1927.

TABLE 1.1 A Ranking of Social Problems

Rank	Problem	Percentage
1	Dissatisfaction with government	21
2	The economy	18
3	Health care	16
4	Unemployment	16
5	Federal budget deficit	8

In a public opinion poll conducted by Gallup in the period January 5–8, 2014, a random national sample of 1,000 adults were asked the question, "What do you think is the most important problem facing the country today?" Above are the top five results.

SOURCE: http://www.gallup.com/poll/1675/most-important-problem.aspx.

Sociology: The study of social behavior and human society.

Social problem: A social condition, event, or pattern of behavior that negatively affects the well-being of a significant number of people (or a number of significant people) who believe that the condition, event, or pattern needs to be changed or ameliorated.

Data sources: Collections of information.

FIGURE 1.1   Example of a Spot Map

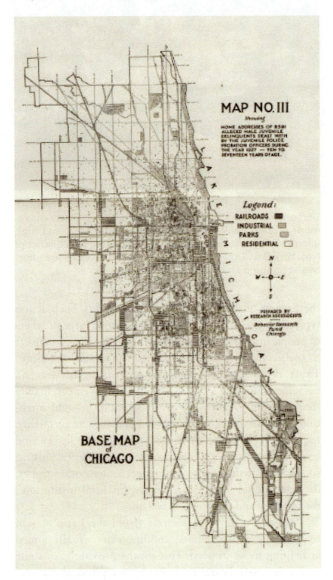

SOURCE: Originally published in *Delinquency Areas* by Clifford R. Shaw, with the collaboration of Frederick M. Zorbaugh, Henry D. McKay, Leonard S. Cottrell, 1929. Reprinted with permission from The University of Chicago Press.

The Objective and Subjective Aspects of Social Problems

We will come back to the way sociologists use and produce information about social problems when they do research, but for now notice that in measuring the rate of

Objective aspect of social problems: Those empirical conditions or facts that point to the concreteness of social problems "out there."

Subjective aspect of social problems: The process by which people define social problems.

crime—or, for that matter, of divorce, population growth, or sex trafficking—we are able to call attention to the **objective aspect of social problems**. In other words, data allow us to show, concretely, how much crime is really out there. Again, in looking at the UCR we can see that in 2012, 419 murders were reported in New York City compared to 515 the year before, and that there were 500 murders in Chicago in 2012 compared to 431 in 2011 (Federal Bureau of Investigation 2013b). These statistics tell us two things in straightforward terms: first, Chicago—with one-third the population of New York—had 81 *more* murders than New York, and second, the murder rate in Chicago *went up* from one year to the next.

More complicated, however, is the **subjective aspect of social problems**. Here we are talking about what people *define* as a social problem. There is often a close link between the objective and subjective aspects of a problem. For example, people are made objectively aware (usually through official data) that the murder rate in their community has doubled over the past five years, and, as a consequence, they become subjectively concerned about their safety and that of their community.

But even without a direct interaction between the objective and the subjective, people can be troubled about a particular social condition, event, or pattern of behavior. Consider that, on average, twice as many people in the United States die from injuries sustained in motor vehicle crashes as die from AIDS: in 2010 fatalities from these two causes were 32,885 and 15,529, respectively (National Highway Traffic Safety Administration 2012b; Centers for Disease Control and Prevention 2013c). Yet there are far more organizations and campaigns for AIDS awareness in the United States and worldwide—such as Acting on AIDS, ACT UP, the Stop AIDS Project, and the Elton John AIDS Foundation—than there are for car crashes. No doubt there are many justifiable reasons for this disproportionate focus, but while *objectively* the problem of auto fatalities causes twice as much harm to people and society, *subjectively* people are much more concerned about the problem of AIDS. In other words, if one troubling condition is more pervasive or more detrimental than another (and even if there's factual information indicating this), that doesn't necessarily mean people will perceive the condition as more problematic.

Another subjective aspect of social problems is the *relativity* with which people identify them. First, what is viewed as a social problem in one time and place may not be viewed as a social problem in another time and place. As we will see in Chapter 6, public attitudes toward the aged have fluctuated between positive and negative over the past 200 years. Currently politicians and policy makers worry that the rapidly growing segment of the U.S. population ages 65 and older will strain government programs like Social Security and Medicare; contrast this attitude with the past, when elderly people were more respected and were valued for their wisdom and insight. Second, relativity ensures that some segments of the population experience the social problem and others do not, or they experience it to a different extent. For example, the pervasiveness of assault rifles in U.S. society is a social problem to advocates of stricter gun laws, but not to supporters of gun ownership rights.

The subjective element of social problems is framed by a theoretical approach called **social constructionism**, which describes the social process by which people define a social problem into existence. Simply put, "social problems are what people think they are" (Spector and Kitsuse 1987, 73). Throughout the chapters in this textbook you will find many of the authors taking a constructionist approach in their analyses of various social phenomena.

Returning to our definition of a social problem, we've said that a sufficient or *significant number of people* must conceptualize the condition as problematic. This means enough people—a critical mass, in fact—must be concerned about the troubling or objectionable situation to call attention to it (in the chapters to follow they are generally called *stakeholders*). Because social problems are collective in nature, large collections of people are required to define them as such.

Sociologists also acknowledge that, when it comes to deciding which conditions are problematic, some people and groups are more significant or have greater influence than others. This speaks to the issue of political *power*. For example, as criminologist Richard Quinney (1970) notes, the more the powerful segments of society—such as politicians, bankers, and corporate executives—are concerned about crime, the greater the probability that laws will be created to prohibit such behaviors as muggings, store thefts, and drug use. Conversely, there will be fewer laws to prohibit behaviors like profiting from campaign financing, insider trading, and price-fixing. According to Quinney, definitions of crime align with the interests of those segments of society with the power to shape social policy. We will discuss the relationship between social problems and social policy shortly. But first let's consider why, once people perceive a social situation as detrimental to their well-being or that of others, they believe some sort of *action* must be taken to change or improve the situation.

Types of Action

The type of action needed to bring about large-scale *social change* is usually aimed at transforming the **social structure**,

AP Photo / Andrew Burton

Demonstrators affiliated with the Occupy Wall Street movement protest bank bailouts, home foreclosures, and high unemployment at an encampment in the financial district of New York City. Do you think these types of protests are effective at bringing about social change?

the pattern of interrelated social institutions. Such action typically includes organizing and mobilizing large numbers of people into **social movements**, which are collective efforts to realize social change in order to solve social problems. Think about how the civil rights movement, the women's movement, and the Occupy Wall Street movement, mainly through various forms of demonstration, brought attention to the issues of racial, gender, and income inequality, respectively. In order to bring about greater justice and equality for people of color, women, and the 99%, these social movements sought to change, among other things, the educational system, the family, financial institutions, the military, and the political system.

Actions meant to *ameliorate* (from the Latin *melior*, to improve) a problematic condition are usually aimed at helping those in need. This means providing, in some cases, the material relief necessary for physical survival (money, food, clothes); in most cases, however, it means providing nonmaterial services, such as counseling (employment, parenting), dispute resolution (peace talks, mediation), education (instruction and encouragement), and professional consultation (on specific troublesome issues). People hoping to take or support these kinds of actions typically engage in community service, civic

Social constructionism: The social process by which people define a social problem into existence.

Social structure: The pattern of interrelated social institutions.

Social movements: The collective efforts of people to realize social change in order to solve social problems.

Aging China

engagement, and advocacy. Think about organized forms of volunteerism and activism like AmeriCorps, the Red Cross, Big Brothers/Big Sisters, Do Something, Save the Children, Oxfam, and the United Way.

ASK YOURSELF: What troubling situations do you see in your community (neighborhood, campus)? How do these fit, or not fit, the definition of social problems given above? Do they have both objective and subjective aspects? Explain.

THE SOCIOLOGICAL IMAGINATION

 1.3 Explain the sociological imagination.

We now return to the question of what social structural changes have occurred during the past three decades to lead millions of working-class young adults like Jalen to join the military because they can't find jobs, to move back in with their parents, or to struggle to get through college, pay back their loans, and make their monthly car payments. Remember that these millennials—though they try hard to achieve the American Dream of finding stable jobs, getting married, and owning their own homes—largely blame themselves for having stopped "growing up." They feel insecure, powerless, and isolated. They feel trapped.

More than half a century ago, the American sociologist C. Wright Mills (1916–1962) wrote the following lines, which could easily be describing the lives of young working-class men and women today:

> Nowadays men [and women] often feel that their private lives are a series of traps. They sense that within their everyday worlds, they cannot overcome their troubles. . . . Underlying this sense of being trapped are seemingly impersonal changes in the very *structure* of continent-wide societies. . . . Neither *the life of an individual* nor the *history* of a society can be understood without understanding both. (Mills 1959, 3; emphases added)

Mills is saying that in order to understand our personal hardships and our own individual feelings, we must be

Sociological imagination: A form of self-consciousness that allows us to go beyond our immediate environments of family, neighborhood, and work and understand the major structural transformations that have occurred and are occurring.

aware of the larger forces of history and of social structure. To gain this awareness, he proposes, we should use a way of thinking that he calls the sociological imagination. The **sociological imagination** is a form of self-consciousness that allows us to go beyond our immediate environments (of family, neighborhood, work) and understand the major structural transformations that have occurred and are occurring. For working-class young men and women, some of these transformations have to do with family patterns, increased inequality of income and wealth, the rise of the service economy, declining social mobility, and depressed wages. These are some of the structural changes that have occurred during the past 30 years that in many ways operate against the working-class millennials' attempts to create stable and predictable adult lives.

The sociological imagination provides us with insight into the social conditions of our lives. It helps us understand why we feel trapped and insecure, isolated and powerless. The sociological imagination helps us make

C. Wright Mills was a leading critic of U.S. society in the 1950s and made contributions to the sociological perspective known as conflict theory. Mills taught at Columbia University and wrote about the power arrangements in U.S. society in such books as *White Collar* and *The Power Elite*. His most famous book, *The Sociological Imagination*, was published in 1959.

The Sociological Imagination Revisited

the connection between history and *biography,* between our own society and our private lives, and become aware of all individuals in similar circumstances. In short, the sociological imagination allows us to *see our personal troubles as social problems.* In this way we are not only able to confront social problems, but we are also aware of the social problems' origins. We come to understand that what we see and feel as personal misfortunes (for example, our inability to achieve the milestones of adulthood) are predicaments shared by many others and difficult for any one individual to solve.

But Mills (1959, 150) also asserts that the "problems of [our] societies are almost inevitably problems of the world." In other words, the sociological imagination requires that we take a **global perspective**, comparing our own society to other societies in all the world's regions. When we can understand the social problems of U.S. society in relationship to social problems in other countries, we are using the sociological imagination even more broadly. You will see that, in discussing social problems, the authors of the following chapters take a global perspective. In addition, each chapter contains a "Beyond Our Borders" box featuring discussion of the problem in a global context.

Also be aware that the expert authors writing on various social problems in these chapters have all been trained in sociology. And regardless of the fact that they specialize in one or a few social problems in their research and writing, as sociologists they have several things in common. First, they employ the sociological imagination, frequently from a global perspective. Second, they rely on sociological research. Third, they make use of sociological theory.

ASK YOURSELF: Do people you know feel trapped in their daily lives? How or why? Explain the sociological imagination in your own words. Explain how a social problem in the United States affects other areas of the world.

SOCIOLOGICAL RESEARCH

 1.4 Discuss how sociological research can be used to study social problems.

In discussing the *objective* aspect of social problems, we noted that sociologists look at patterns and trends in regard to crime, poverty, the AIDS epidemic, auto fatalities, and so on. In order to identify these patterns and trends they require numerical facts, like rates, percentages, and ratios. Sometimes these facts are available in data sources such as the Uniform Crime Reports.

Thousands of law enforcement agencies across the United States provide the FBI with statistics on local crime, and each year the FBI compiles these statistics and makes them available to law enforcement officials, policy makers, the news media, researchers, and the general public. Other data sources from which sociologists draw numerical facts for conducting social problems research include the ones listed in Table 1.2. Often, however, sociologists need to collect their own original data firsthand. In either case, we refer to these types of data collection as **quantitative research** because they rely on the empirical investigation of social problems through statistical analysis.

When it comes to the *subjective* aspects of social problems, sociologists tend to be less interested in facts and figures and more interested in the ways people define, experience, or understand problematic situations. In order to achieve this understanding, they engage in qualitative research, much as did Jennifer Silva when she talked with 100 young men and women of the working class to learn about their lives and feelings. When sociologists conduct studies of social problems, they can employ several **research methods** or techniques for obtaining information. Let's look at three of these research methods.

Survey Research

For quantitative research, the method most commonly used is the **survey**, a technique in which respondents are asked to answer questions on a written questionnaire. A *questionnaire* is a set of questions a researcher presents to respondents for their answers. Questionnaires typically ask questions that measure *variables,* such as attitudes (say, political affiliation), behaviors (church attendance), and statuses (ethnicity). Researchers may administer questionnaires in person or by telephone, or they can send them through the mail or use the Internet. Because it is often impractical to survey every subject in a population of interest—for example, every homeless person in a large city—the researcher selects a *sample* of subjects that represents that population. In this way the researcher tries to reach conclusions about all the homeless people in a city by studying a smaller number of them. In other

Global perspective: A viewpoint from which we compare our own society to other societies around the world.

Quantitative research: Research that studies social problems through statistical analysis.

Research methods: Techniques for obtaining information.

Survey: A research method that asks respondents to answer questions on a written questionnaire.

TABLE 1.2 Some Data Sources for Social Problems Research

Data source	Description
General Social Survey (GSS) http://www3.norc.org/GSS+Website	One of the largest sources for social scientific data in the United States; includes data on social trends, demographics, behaviors, opinions, and attitudes
U.S. Census Bureau http://www.census.gov	Government agency (a branch of the U.S. Department of Commerce) responsible for conducting the decennial U.S. Census; serves as a leading source of data about the American people and economy
U.S. Bureau of Labor Statistics http://www.bls.gov	Government agency (branch of the U.S. Department of Labor) responsible for collecting data about employment, unemployment, pay and benefits, consumer spending, work productivity, workplace injuries and fatalities, and employment productivity
National Center for Health Statistics http://www.cdc.gov/nchs/index.htm	Government agency (part of the Centers for Disease Control and Prevention) responsible for collecting data from birth and death records, medical records, nutrition records, and interview surveys, as well as through direct physical exams and laboratory testing, in order to provide information to help identify and address critical health problems in the United States
National Center for Education Statistics http://nces.ed.gov	Government agency (part of the U.S. Department of Education) that collects data on a variety of issues related to education, including academic achievement and performance, illiteracy, dropout rates, home schooling, adult learning, teacher qualifications, and public and private school comparisons

words, by measuring relationships between variables, survey research quantifies data and generalizes findings from the sample group to some larger population.

Although he employs several research methods, sociologist Steven J. Tepper (2011) relied extensively on survey research in his recent study examining controversies

---

Participant observation: A research method that includes observing and studying people in their everyday settings.

---

over cultural expressions. One of Tepper's hypotheses is that citizens are most likely to feel offended by certain forms of art, and will protest them, when they feel their lifestyles and values are being threatened. In other words, people will want to ban certain films, books, paintings, sculptures, clothing styles, popular music, and television programs when they have a fear or anxiety about social change. To test this hypothesis, Tepper consulted data from three national surveys that ask thousands of U.S. adults about their attitudes toward art, culture, and entertainment. He found that those most concerned about the rate of immigration into the country (an issue that relates to concerns about social change) were most likely to want to prohibit an unpopular speaker and remove an unpopular book from the library. And those who thought that "everything is changing too fast" were more likely to favor restrictions on television programming. These findings from large sample populations could have been obtained only from such large-scale surveys as the ones used by Tepper.

Participant Observation

Because qualitative researchers seek to understand the social world from the subject's point of view, they frequently employ **participant observation**, a method in which the researcher observes and studies people in their everyday settings. The researcher collects data through direct observation and in this way gains a deep understanding of and familiarity with the workings of a particular group, community, or social event. Groups and settings that sociologists observe include slum neighborhoods, emergency rooms, homeless shelters, religious groups, secret societies, gangs, welfare mothers, taxi drivers, and pregnant teens.

A good example of participant observation research is a study in which sociologist Shamus Rahman Khan (2011) examined how an elite New England boarding school educates students from wealthy families. Kahn spent a year as a researcher living and teaching at the school. During that time he observed much of the day-to-day life of the students, teachers, and members of the custodial and service staff. He also joined in their activities and talked with them in various places—his faculty office, the chapel, the dorms, and while eating in the dining halls, reading at the library, teaching and sitting in classes, and playing basketball. Khan learned that among the many things these students are taught at the school is how to display "ease"—the attitude of being comfortable in just about any social situation. This ease is not a style of living that nonelite students acquire, and that difference contributes to the increasing class divisions and inequalities in U.S. society. Khan could not have understood the attitude of ease and the many ways it is manifested by these wealthy students had he not spent long periods of time and fully embedded himself in their social world.

Interviewing

Quantitative research has the advantages of providing precise numerical data and of generalizing research findings. Qualitative research, on the other hand, has the advantage of providing in-depth information that describes complex phenomena in rich detail. One research method that may include both quantitative and qualitative elements is **interviewing,** the form of data collection in which the researcher asks respondents a series of questions. Interviews can be conducted face-to-face or on the phone, on a number of issues (sexual harassment, texting while driving, cutbacks to social welfare programs), and in a variety of settings (at home, on the street, outside a polling place). Researchers record the subjects' responses in writing or by audio recording. Once recorded, the responses can be treated quantitatively when researchers assign numerical values to them, enter the values into a data analysis program, and then run various statistical commands to identify patterns across responses. Researchers can use the patterns to make comparisons between different sample groups. Interviews can also be treated qualitatively, as guided conversations that let respondents talk at length and in detail. In this case the researcher listens carefully and may ask follow-up questions. Once the responses have been recorded, the researcher can identify categories or themes across them. This helps the researcher determine which issues from the interviews are significant.

One study that relied heavily on interviews was done by sociologist Susan Crawford Sullivan (2011). Wanting to find out about the role of religion in the day-to-day experiences of mothers in poverty, Sullivan conducted in-depth interviews with women who were on or had recently left welfare. She discovered that these poor mothers of young children found strength through religious faith to deal with challenging conditions such as searching for housing and decent jobs and raising their children in dangerous neighborhoods. In the interviews, the women spoke candidly about such painful subjects as domestic violence, drug abuse, incarceration, and the loss of children to protective services. As she listened carefully to what these women had to say, Sullivan realized that, for them, religious faith serves as a very important resource in making sense of their difficult lives.

A researcher interviews a young man in a poor township outside Cape Town, South Africa. She is attempting to find out how effective a program is in preventing children from joining gangs and engaging in criminal activity. What do you see as some of the merits of conducting interviews in doing research?

Mixed Methods

Because each method offers its own advantages, sociologists often combine quantitative and quantitative methods of research to achieve a fuller picture of the social problems they are studying. One example is Karolyn Tyson's (2011) research exploring why and how some black students associate academic achievement with whiteness. Tyson gathered data from 250 students in more than 30 schools and used a combination of daylong classroom observations, mail-in surveys of schools' gifted programs and advanced placement and honors courses, and interviews with students, teachers, principals, and parents. By employing these various research techniques, Tyson was able to show how students' equating school success with "acting white" grew from the institutional practice of curriculum tracking, which places very few black students in advanced and gifted classes. Her main finding is that academic achievement is racialized by the school's social structure.

In each of the chapters to follow you will find a "Researching" box feature that discusses a study or two done on a particular social problem, including information on methods and results.

ASK YOURSELF: Think of a social problem you would like to research. Which of the three research methods discussed above do you think is best suited for your purposes? Why?

Interviewing: A method of data collection in which the researcher asks respondents a series of questions.

THREE SOCIOLOGICAL THEORIES

 1.5 Explain the three main sociological perspectives of structural functionalism, conflict theory, and symbolic interactionism.

Once researchers have collected the information they need—whether through data sources, surveys, participant observation, interviewing, or other research methods—they must then *make sociological sense* of that information. In other words, they need to manage the data in a way that tells them something new or different about the social issue under consideration. In order to do this, they use **theory**, a collection of related concepts.

Concepts are ideas sociologists have about some aspect of the social world. They tend to be articulated as terms—words or phrases that make up the vocabulary of sociology. So far in this chapter, we have used and defined several sociological concepts, including "social institution," "social class," "social problem," "social constructionism," and "social structure." Throughout this textbook you will meet many concepts, introduced in boldface green type. These terms are defined at the bottom of the page, and the Glossary at the end of the book provides a comprehensive listing of these concepts and their definitions.

Concepts are also the building blocks of theory, and in this sense a theory is an attempt to articulate the relationship between concepts. Sociologists, for example, may want to examine the connection between certain types of social structure and certain types of social problems. Thus, they may pose such questions as the following: Does the kind of economic institution we have contribute to high levels of poverty? How does our political system prevent us from providing adequate health care to everyone? Why do some communities have higher rates of violent crime than others? Or sociologists may want to analyze the relationship between social problems and

certain behaviors and attitudes. In that case they might ask questions like these: How might sexist attitudes prevent the country from maximizing the numbers of scientists and engineers it produces? Why do students in some countries have uniformly high scores on math, science, and literacy exams, while in the United States there are large gaps in performance between the highest-scoring and the lowest-scoring students?

While sociology encompasses many theories, there are three main theories with which all sociologists, regardless of their specialty areas, are familiar: structural functionalism, conflict theory, and symbolic interactionism. Because they are very broad theories they are sometimes called **paradigms**, or theoretical perspectives. Let's get familiar with each of these in turn before we look at how policy makers can apply them to addressing social problems.

Structural Functionalism

Structural functionalism (or functionalism) is the sociological theory that considers how various social phenomena function, or work in a positive way, to maintain unity and order in society. The theory of structural functionalism dates back to the beginnings of sociology, and some of its ideas can be traced to several 19th-century sociologists, including Herbert Spencer.

Spencer viewed society as an organism, which is to say as an integrated *system* made up of different social institutions all working together to keep it going. Just as the human body (a biological organism) has many organs (the heart, brain, liver, kidneys, and so on), all of which are necessary to its survival, so too does society need the various institutions of the economy, the government, the family, religion, and so on to keep it orderly and cohesive. Each institution works in different ways to benefit society. For example, some of the **functions**—that is, positive consequences—of the family are that it provides an expedient way for humans to reproduce themselves biologically; it provides emotional support to family members; and it teaches, or *socializes*, children in the rules of society. Some of the functions of religion are that it provides answers to the larger questions of existence (What existed before the Big Bang? What happens after death?); it provides us with ideas about what is right and wrong; and it brings members of a particular religious group closer together in their shared beliefs. In short, social institutions have functions for society.

Talcott Parsons (1902–1979) was the most famous theorist of structural functionalism. His theory of the functions of social systems is very complex, but here we are concerned only with what he called "the problem of order." Simply put, Parsons believed that for society as a

---

Theory: A collection of related concepts.

Concepts: Ideas that sociologists have about some aspect of the social world.

Paradigms: Theoretical perspectives.

Structural functionalism (or functionalism): The sociological theory that considers how various social phenomena function, or work in a positive way, to maintain unity and order in society.

Functions: Positive consequences of social structures or social institutions.

Talcott Parsons was the leading American sociological theorist during the middle decades of the 20th century and did much to advance the theoretical perspective known as structural functionalism. Parsons, who taught at Harvard University, was most interested in knowing what contributes to order in society. His books include *The Social System* and *Toward a General Theory of Action*.

social system to keep functioning smoothly, it needs to maintain social order. And because the social institutions already provide functions for society, social order is common. However, sometimes strains and tensions threaten to disrupt social integration and stability. Think of wars, revolutions, high rates of crime, racial tensions, and terrorist attacks. Parsons believed that one way societies can prevent such disruptions is by encouraging people to conform to society's expectations. This is best achieved by having them abide by the same shared **norms**, or rules, and **values**, or beliefs. Thus, for Parsons, consensus produces social order.

Sociologist Robert K. Merton (1910–2003) agreed that social institutions and social structures can have functions. But he saw that they can also have **dysfunctions**, or negative consequences. Consider how the family can be a refuge from the larger world, where family members can get nurturance, love, and acceptance in ways that are not available to them in other institutional settings. But also consider how the family can be the setting where domestic violence, contentious divorce, and the sexual and emotional abuse of children may occur.

Merton would have us examine both the functions and the dysfunctions of social phenomena, and he would also have us ask about our social structures, "Functional for whom?" In other words, we must be aware that while a social phenomenon like income inequality in the social structure of U.S. society is dysfunctional for one group (the poor), it may be quite functional for another (the wealthy). This may be one reason that the rich, as stakeholders in the economic institution, may not define income inequality as a social problem or may not want to change the social structure that creates it.

Conflict Theory

Conflict theory is the sociological theory that focuses on dissent, coercion, and antagonism in society. In this sense we may see conflict theory as the opposite of structural functionalism. It too has its roots in the 19th century, particularly in the ideas of Karl Marx.

Karl Marx (1818–1883) was first and foremost engaged in critiquing **capitalism**, the economic system that includes the ownership of private property, the making of financial profit, and the hiring of workers. Marx saw two main antagonistic social classes in capitalist society. The first, the **capitalists** (or bourgeoisie), make up the economically dominant class that privately owns and controls human labor, raw materials, land, tools, machinery, technologies, and factories. The second social class consists of the **workers** (or proletariat), who own no property and must work for the capitalists in order to support themselves and their families financially. In their effort to maximize their profits, capitalists exploit workers by not paying them the full value of their work. Because their labor is bought and sold by the capitalists who hire and fire them, workers are treated as machines, not as human beings. Many sociologists have been influenced by Marx's conflict theory and examine the frictions that exist

Norms: Social rules.

Values: Social beliefs.

Dysfunctions: Negative consequences of social structures or social institutions.

Conflict theory: The sociological theory that focuses on dissent, coercion, and antagonism in society.

Capitalism: An economic system that includes the ownership of private property, the making of financial profit, and the hiring of workers.

Capitalists: The economically dominant class that privately owns and controls human labor, raw materials, land, tools, machinery, technologies, and factories.

Workers: Those who own no property and must work for the capitalists in order to support themselves and their families financially.

 Rising Minority Population

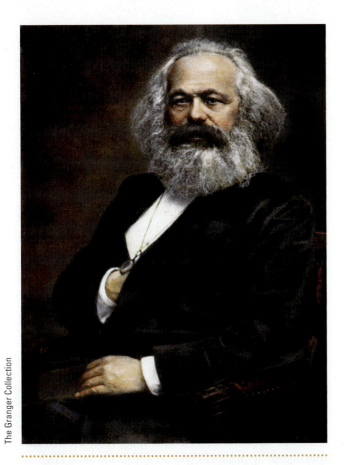

Karl Marx was a 19th-century revolutionary and critic of the economic institution known as capitalism. He believed that capitalist societies like England and the United States would eventually become communist societies. His best-known work, which he coauthored with Friedrich Engels, is *The Communist Manifesto*, first published in 1848.

between the powerful social classes (the rich, the 1%, the wealthy) and the powerless social classes (the working class, the 99%, the poor), and that give rise to a variety of social problems related to the unequal distribution of wealth.

Ralf Dahrendorf departed from Marx's focus on the conflict between social classes and looked instead to the conflict between **interest groups**, organized associations of people mobilized into action because of their membership in those associations. For Dahrendorf (1959), social

Interest groups: Organized associations of people mobilized into action because of their membership in those associations.

Social interaction: The communication that occurs between two or more people.

Symbolic interactionism: The sociological perspective that sees society as the product of symbols (words, gestures, objects) given meaning by people in their interactions with each other.

Mind: The internal conversations we have within ourselves.

Middle-Class Squeeze

inequalities have their basis not only in economic differences but also in *political power*. Simply put, those with power give orders and those without power take orders. Power relationships lead to the tensions between interests groups (also called advocacy groups or lobbying groups). Thus, for Dahrendorf, social conflict in relationship to social problems occurs among interests groups—such as Americans for Prosperity, Heritage Action for America, the Southern Poverty Law Center, and People for the American Way—some of which are politically liberal while others are politically conservative.

Those groups with sufficient political power use it, usually by influencing legislation, to protect their interests. Consider the politically powerful interest groups on opposite sides of the issue of gun control, such as those that support required background checks for all gun purchases (Mayors Against Illegal Guns) and those that oppose such checks (National Rifle Association). Or consider interest groups that favor abortion rights (Planned Parenthood and the National Organization for Women) and those that do not (Americans United for Life and the National Right to Life Committee).

In short, conflict theory looks at how one group or social class tries to dominate another in situations it perceives as threatening to its interests and well-being. In this sense, what one group considers to be a social problem (say, the sale of assault rifles), another group may not.

Symbolic Interactionism

As mentioned above, in the discussion of the subjective element of social problems, the *social constructionist* approach says that certain social conditions, events, or patterns of behavior are social problems because people *define* them as such. The third major sociological theory, symbolic interactionism, also takes a definitional approach to understanding social problems, but rather than looking at the social structure it tends to focus on **social interaction**, or the communication that occurs between two or more people. **Symbolic interactionism** is the sociological perspective that sees society as the product of symbols (words, gestures, objects) that are given meaning by people in their interactions with each other. Symbolic interactionism has its origins in the ideas of George Herbert Mead.

George Herbert Mead (1863–1931) was interested in understanding the relationship between mind, self, and society (Mead 1934). For Mead, **mind** refers to the internal conversations we have within ourselves. In other words, we continuously think about ourselves and about what is going on around us, and all this requires the use of language. Language is nothing more than a system

George Herbert Mead, who taught at the University of Chicago in the early 20th century, was one of the first scholars to take seriously the study of the social self. His most famous book, which was published by his students after he died, is *Mind, Self, and Society*. This book is regarded by many as the "bible" of symbolic interactionism.

of **symbols** (objects that represent something else) that we interpret. For example, you are reading the words on this page because you have learned to interpret the symbols (the written words) of the English language. But unless you can read Russian, the following words are not meaningful to you: Эти слова для вас не имеют никакого значения. In the same way you learned to read words, you learned to read or "define" a clock (symbolic of time), a map (symbolic of a particular physical place), a smile (symbolic of an emotion), and so on.

Just as important as our ability to define symbols is our ability to define our *self*. The **social self** is a process by which we are able to see ourselves in relationship to others. We are not born with a social self, which is why newborns do not have a sense of who they are. They have no self-consciousness. We can acquire the social self only after we have learned to consider who we are in relationship to the attitudes and expectations of others, of *society*.

Charles Horton Cooley (1864–1929) went further and proposed the concept of the **looking-glass self**, or the idea that we see ourselves as we think others see us (Cooley 1902).

For example, if our friends, family, and teachers continually tell us that we are clever, then we are likely to see ourselves as clever. If, on the other hand, teachers, police, and judges define, or "label," us as delinquent, we are likely to take on the identity of delinquent.

In addition to defining symbols (words, gestures, objects) and our social self (who we are), we define social situations. Long ago sociologist W. I. Thomas noted that *if people define a social situation as real, it will be real in its consequences* (Thomas and Thomas 1928). This means, for example, that if you and other students define what is going on in the classroom as a lecture, you will then listen closely to the speaker and take lecture notes. But if you define it as a funeral or a religious revival (admittedly harder to do), then it is that situation instead, and you will act appropriately. And if you define it as a party, then the consequences are that you stop taking notes and stop raising your hand to ask questions and instead mingle, talk to your friends, and have a good time.

As an extension of these ideas we may also propose a concept originated by Merton, the **self-fulfilling prophecy**, or the social process whereby a false definition of a situation brings about behavior that makes the false definition "come true." Let's combine and apply the self-fulfilling prophecy and the looking-glass self. Imagine a 5-year-old child, Pablo, who is a recent immigrant from Mexico and speaks only Spanish. His parents enroll him in an English-only school, and his teacher notices that Pablo does not say much in class, does not raise his hand to ask questions like the other students, and does not interact with playmates on the playground. After a while the teacher—and other teachers and students—may label Pablo as shy, introverted, a slow learner, asocial, and so on. Now, Pablo is actually none of these things, but he eventually starts to see himself that way and then becomes timid and unsure of himself. A couple of years later, Pablo is placed in a classroom for slow learners with interpersonal issues.

ASK YOURSELF: Think of a social problem you would like to research. Which of the three sociological theories discussed above do you think is best suited for your purposes? Why?

Symbols: Words, gestures, and objects to which people give meaning.

Social self: A process by which people are able to see themselves in relationship to others.

Looking-glass self: The idea that we see ourselves as we think others see us.

Self-fulfilling prophecy: The social process whereby a false definition of a situation brings about behavior that makes the false definition "come true."

APPLYING THE THREE THEORIES TO SOCIAL PROBLEMS

 1.6 Evaluate how each of the three theoretical perspectives can be applied to improve our understanding of social problems.

Let us now consider how we can apply each of the three main theoretical perspectives in sociology to gain a better understanding of social problems.

Structural Functionalism and Suicide

To illustrate how functionalism has been applied to the real world, we turn to the French sociologist Émile Durkheim (1858–1917) and his classic study on the social problem of suicide. Durkheim understood that all societies, in order to continue as they are, need two things. The first, **social integration**, describes a certain degree of unity. In order words, people need to come together and stay together. The opposite of social integration is *social disintegration*, which leads to the collapse of society. The second necessary condition, **social regulation**, means that to maintain social order, societies need to have a certain degree of control over the behavior of their members. This is typically achieved by having people follow social norms. The opposite of social regulation is *social disorder*, which may lead to what Durkheim called **anomie**, or a state of normlessness. Both social integration and social regulation are functional for society, but they can become dysfunctional and lead to social problems when there is too much or too little of them.

Turning to the differences in suicide rates among various groups, Durkheim (1979) found, for example, that suicide rates are higher among men than among women, higher for those who are single than for those who are married, and higher among Protestants than among Catholics or Jews. He explained these and other group differences by looking at the degree of social integration and social regulation and identified four types of social suicide.

Social integration: The unity or cohesiveness of society.

Social regulation: The control society has over the behavior of its members.

Anomie: A state of normlessness in society.

Altruistic suicide: Suicide that occurs as a result of too much social integration.

Egoistic suicide: Suicide that occurs as a result of too little social integration.

The French sociologist Émile Durkheim is regarded as one of the early founders of sociology. Working in the late 19th and early 20th centuries, he made many contributions to the topics of social solidarity, suicide, and religion. His most famous books include *The Division of Labor in Society, Suicide,* and *The Rules of Sociological Method.*

When a group has too much social integration, when it is overly cohesive, conditions lead to **altruistic suicide**. Here group members sacrifice their lives for the group. For example, although many complex reasons motivate suicide bombers, suicide bombing is a type of altruistic suicide because it requires that the bombers place less value on their own lives than on the group's honor, religion, or some other collective interest (Hassan 2011). By contrast, when a society has too little social integration, when its social bonds are weak, **egoistic suicide** may result. In this case, persons in certain populations kill themselves due to extreme isolation. For example, several studies indicate that while a number of risk factors cause older adults to commit suicide, one of the leading ones is social disconnectedness, which stems from living alone, losing a spouse, experiencing loneliness, or having low social support (Van Orden and Conwell 2011).

Too much social regulation, or excessive social control over people's behavior, can cause **fatalistic suicide**. Members of certain groups end their lives because they see no escape from their oppressive situation. For example, among women in Iranian society, fatalistic is the dominant type of suicide due to a traditional male-dominated social structure that, among other things, forces women into marriage at an early age and prohibits divorce, even in the case of domestic violence (Aliverdinia and Pridemore 2009). On the other hand, too little social regulation, which leads to the absence of norms, causes an increase in **anomic suicide**. This means that people kill themselves because they lack rules to give them social direction for meeting their needs. For example, a long-term causal relationship exists between the unemployment rate and men's suicide rate. One study explains that when men lose their jobs, society's regulating influence on their need to work is disrupted, causing an increase in their suicides (Riley 2010).

In sum, Durkheim demonstrates how an unbalanced degree of social integration and social regulation can be dysfunctional for society, thus resulting in high rates of suicide.

Conflict Theory and Alcohol Consumption

The use of conflict theory is demonstrated by Joseph R. Gusfield's (1986) examination of how a particular group—rural, middle-class evangelical Protestants—tried to preserve its own **culture**, or style of life, in U.S. society during the 19th and early 20th centuries. This cultural group, which Gusfield calls "the Dry forces," were reformers who wanted to correct what they saw as a major social problem: the drinking habits of ethnic immigrants. The ethnic immigrants who threatened the moral way of life of the Dry forces, and who therefore needed to be reformed and controlled, were mainly urban, lower-class Irish and Italian Catholics and German Lutherans whose cultures did not prohibit the consumption of alcohol. These ethnic groups were also generally ranked at the bottom of the U.S. social and economic ladder and thus had limited political power.

In order to retain the dominance of their way of life, the middle-class Protestants attempted to reform the ethnic drinkers. They did this, first, by trying to persuade them to stop their "immoral" drinking voluntarily and by inviting them to membership in the middle class. However, by the last quarter of the 19th century, as the United States was becoming more urban, secular, and Catholic, the Dry forces changed their tactics, substituting for persuasion a method that was more hostile and antagonistic: they tried to *coerce* reform through legislation. This coercive strategy culminated in a national policy of prohibition in 1919, when Congress ratified the 18th Amendment to the U.S. Constitution, which prohibited the manufacture, sale, and transportation of intoxicating liquors. This application of conflict theory clearly shows that the interest group with the most political power can prohibit behaviors it considers problematic.

Symbolic Interactionism and Depression

David A. Karp (1996) takes a symbolic interactionist perspective to explain how people with clinical depression make sense of their illness and their lives. In order to understand the behaviors and feelings of depression, Karp considers the subjective point of view of the person experiencing it. He thus sees depression as an illness not of the body or mind, but of the social self. This means there is a social process by which people gradually come to define themselves as depressed.

According to Karp, an individual develops a definition of him- or herself as depressed while moving through four distinct stages, each of which requires a redefinition of the self. The person experiences these stages as critical turning points in his or her identity that eventually lead the individual to say, "I am a depressed person."

In the first stage, the person feels different and ill at ease, and has emotional pain but can't put a name to what he or she is experiencing. The person believes that once certain life circumstances change, these ill feelings will change for the better. But when the person's life circumstances change and the same terrible feelings persist, the person moves to the second stage, concluding that something is "really" wrong with him or her. Here, the individual realizes that he or she possesses a sick self, one that works badly in *every* situation. The third stage is a period of crisis in which the person fully enters a therapeutic world of hospitals, psychiatric experts, and antidepressant medications. It is also the point where the person receives the "official" diagnosis of depression. Finally, the fourth stage in the transformation of the self of the depressed person consists of coming to grips with a mental illness identity.

Symbolic interactionism shows the critical turning points that people suffering from depression go through as they become caught up with assessing self, redefining self, and reinterpreting past selves in terms of the depression diagnosis.

ASK YOURSELF: Think of three different social problems. What are the strengths of each of the theoretical perspectives in helping you to understand each of the social problems? What are the weaknesses?

Fatalistic suicide: Suicide that occurs as a result of too much social regulation.

Anomic suicide: Suicide that occurs as a result of too little social regulation.

Culture: A style of life.

DeAgostini / Getty Images

Inspired by Marx's writings, Vladimir Lenin became the chief architect of the first successful socialist revolution, the Russian Revolution of 1917. Here he is addressing a meeting of workers and soldiers. Now that the Soviet Union has collapsed and communism is dead, do you think that Marx's ideas are still relevant today?

SOCIAL POLICY

 1.7 Discuss the role of social policy in managing social problems.

We've noted above that one possible way to deal with pervasive social problems like poverty is to change the social structure radically. However, short of a **social revolution**—a total and complete transformation in the social structure of society (such as the French Revolution of 1789, the Russian Revolution of 1917, the Chinese Revolution of 1948)—most social change is achieved piecemeal, and frequently reforms are begun through **social policy**, a more or less clearly articulated and usually written set of strategies for addressing a social problem.

Governmental implementation of social policy takes the form of **legislation** that makes some condition or pattern of behavior legal or illegal. The Civil Rights Act of 1964, a piece of legislation passed by Congress and signed by President Lyndon B. Johnson, made racial segregation in public accommodations illegal in the United States. Another type of social policy consists of an organization's guidelines about what ought to happen or not happen between members in regard to a particular issue, such as sexual harassment, bullying, smoking, infection control, and conflicts of interests. These guidelines are usually disseminated through handbooks, manuals, and official websites.

Although social policy has many goals, our concern here is with its role in managing social problems. Each chapter includes a section proposing policy recommendations for social change that arise from the three main theoretical perspectives.

Social revolution: A total and complete transformation in the social structure of society.

Social policy: A more or less clearly articulated and usually written set of strategies for addressing a social problem.

Legislation: Enacted laws that make some condition or pattern of behavior legal or illegal.

ASK YOURSELF: Think of some policies (rules and regulations) of a workplace where you have been employed. Do you think these policies may have prevented unacceptable or harmful behaviors in that workplace? How?

SPECIALIZED THEORIES

1.8 Explore the role of specialized theories in sociology.

Structural functionalism, conflict theory, and symbolic interactionism are the three most general theoretical frameworks in sociology. But given that the study of society and social behavior is a complicated business, and that there is a wide variety of social problems to consider, sociologists have constructed specialized theories to deal with this complexity and variety. Specialized concepts and theories examine narrower features of society (say, the institution of the family) or specific social problems (the rising rates of divorce). There are many such specialized concepts and theories within sociology—hundreds, in fact. We will not examine them all in this book, however.

All the chapter authors have expertise in particular areas of social problems research, and they employ specialized concepts and theories intended to address their concerns. You will see that some of these concepts and theories are interrelated across chapters, whereas others are more narrowly focused. In either event, the idea is to go beyond—deeper and further—what the three theoretical perspectives can offer.

ASK YOURSELF: Think of a social problem you would like to research. In what ways are the three sociological theories discussed above too broad to provide a specific understanding of that social problem? Imagine some characteristics of a specialized theory that might give you less breadth but more depth on the issue. What types of questions about your research area would it help you answer?

SERVICE SOCIOLOGY AND SOCIAL PROBLEMS

1.9 Identify ways in which service sociology can make a difference.

This is a textbook about social *problems,* which means we will be dealing with many issues that are troubling,

In 1889, Jane Addams cofounded Hull House, a settlement house in a poor neighborhood in Chicago. Hull House provided a wide variety of community services for poor immigrants, especially women and children. Addams received the Nobel Peace Prize in recognition of her work in 1931.

harmful, or just plain distressing. It is understandable that you may feel "it's all bad news," that something needs to be done, that things need to change. But how? If sociology is the discipline that studies social problems, you may want to know what solutions it has to offer. Indeed, you may be interested in finding out what *you* can do to make a difference.

Concerns about the problems of urban life and ways to alleviate them go back to the early days of U.S. sociology, at the beginning of the 20th century. As sociology became a more popular subject of study in colleges and universities around the country, it took two basic forms: the study of sociological theory and the practice of ameliorative reform and service. At that time, most people thought of sociology as a form of philanthropy (Ward 190 2), and courses with titles such as Methods of Social Amelioration, Charities and Corrections, and Preventive Philanthropy were common (Breslau 2007). Undergraduate sociology programs were even more focused on training in charity and social service work.

After its founding in 1892, the University of Chicago established the first full-fledged department of sociology in the country. At least initially, sociologists there were

 Great Society 2.0

Underwood & Underwood / Corbis

diligently engaged with applied social reform and philanthropy (Calhoun 2007). Indeed, the founder of the department, Albion W. Small (1903, 477), pointed out that sociology "is good for nothing unless it can enrich average life; our primary task is to work out correct statements of social problems and valid methods of solving them."

Along with the development of sociology at Chicago, between 1885 and 1930 a unique, active, and engaged sociology was being implemented in many of the **settlement houses**, neighborhood centers providing services to poor immigrants, that had been founded in major cities throughout the United States. Settlement sociologists considered the settlement an experimental effort in the solution of the social problems of the modern city. Jane Addams (1860–1935), who in 1889 cofounded the most famous of the settlement houses, Hull House, in one Chicago's poorest neighborhoods, was among them. Addams, and others like her, sought to compile empirical data on various social problems by gathering detailed descriptions of the conditions of groups living in poverty. In addition, Hull House provided a wide variety of community services, including securing support for deserted women, conducting a kindergarten and day nursery, implementing various enterprises for neighborhood improvement, and establishing a relief station.

A new type of sociology, devoted to the practical amelioration of social problems and with the early U.S. sociology of relief and reform as its heritage, is now emerging. **Service sociology** is a socially responsible and mission-oriented sociology of action and alleviation (Treviño 2011, 2012, 2103; Treviño and McCormack 2014). Motivated by care and compassion, service sociology is concerned with helping people to meet their pressing social needs. Its practitioners believe the personal needs of one individual are not so different from the collective needs of others in similar life circumstances. This belief is the reason service sociology treats individuals as people in community with each other. Its main goal is to help people by meeting their essential needs and concerns through service, including community counseling, coaching, mentoring, tutoring, conflict resolution, community gardening, friendly visiting, community cleanup, block activities, giving circles, crime prevention, community organizing, advocacy, voter registration, participatory action research, service learning, and mediation.

....

Settlement houses: Neighborhood centers that provide services to poor immigrants.

Service sociology: A socially responsible and mission-oriented sociology of action and alleviation.

Culture of service: A style of life that includes various forms of civic engagement, community service, and volunteerism intended to help alleviate social problems.

The time is now ripe for service sociology, and for student involvement in it. Consider that in the past few years there has been a renewed interest in volunteering and social service—a so-called compassion boom—particularly among the millennial generation. Today, more than one-quarter of all U.S. adults take part in some form of community service, with more than 64 million volunteers serving. In 2011 these volunteers dedicated nearly 8 billion hours to volunteer service, and the economic value of this service was $171 billion (Corporation for National and Community Service 2013). Across the country, millions of volunteers are engaged in a range of critical areas, including tutoring and teaching; participating in fund-raising activities or selling items to raise money for charitable or religious organizations; collecting, preparing, distributing, or serving food; and contributing general labor or providing transportation (Corporation for National and Community Service 2013).

What is more, no less than 26% of college students volunteered in 2010, and about 3 million of them dedicated more than 300 million hours of service to communities across the country, primarily in activities like youth mentoring, fund-raising, and teaching and tutoring (Corporation for National and Community Service 2011). In addition to community service, many citizens across the country are engaged civically. Indeed, in the period 2008 to 2010, about 8.4% of U.S. adults worked with neighbors to fix community problems, while 49.6% donated money, assets, or property with an average value of more than $25 to charitable or religious organizations. In 2010, 41.8% voted in the national election (Corporation for National and Community Service 2011).

In recent years we have also seen the emergence of several high-profile national service initiatives, such as President Obama's United We Serve campaign, the Edward M. Kennedy Serve America Act, the annual Martin Luther King Jr. National Day of Service, and the 9/11 National Day of Service and Remembrance. This service work is being done by many ordinary people who are picking up the slack for a city, a state, a nation unwilling or unable to attend to many critical matters that directly affect thousands, even millions, of people (Coles 1993). We have entered an era characterized by a **culture of service**—including various forms of civic engagement, community service, and volunteerism—that allows citizens to work together to ease or mitigate the predicaments and uncertainties created by poverty, hunger, racism, sexism, epidemics, calamities, and so on. It is in this current culture of service, with its numerous pressing needs and concerns, that we can consider the emergence of a sociology of social problems based on service. At the ends of the chapters to follow, the authors suggest ways in which you can get personally engaged in helping to alleviate social problems.

WHAT DOES AMERICA THINK?

Questions about Sociology and Social Problems from the General Social Survey*

 Turn to the beginning of the chapter to compare your answers to the total population.

1. How scientific is sociology?

   SCIENTIFIC: 55.4%

   NOT SCIENTIFIC: 44.6%

2. People need not overly worry about others.

   AGREE: 32.4%

   DISAGREE: 46.4%

   NEITHER AGREE NOR DISAGREE: 21.2%

3. Are people helpful or looking out for themselves?

   HELPFUL: 50.2%

   LOOKING OUT FOR THEMSELVES: 49.8%

4. People are treated with respect.

   AGREE: 90.1

   DISAGREE: 9.9%

5. Can people be trusted?

   YES: 33.75%

   NO: 66.25%

* Since 1972, the General Social Survey (GSS) has been monitoring the characteristics, behaviors, and attitudes of Americans on an annual basis. Along with data collected in the U.S. Census, GSS data play a vital role in helping researchers, journalists, policy makers, and educators understand our complex society.

 ## LOOK BEHIND THE NUMBERS

Go to **edge.sagepub.com/trevino** for a breakdown of these data across time and by race, sex, age, income, and other statuses.

1. Nearly one-third of respondents reported that people do not need to worry about others. What implications does this have for society? Examining age, who reported this most frequently? Income? Education?

2. When asked if people are helpful or looking out for themselves, just under half reported looking out for themselves. With regard to income, who reported this most frequently? Why do you think this is? Education?

SOURCE: National Opinion Research Center, University of Chicago.

3. What do you believe are the most pressing social problems? Do you think that the country is doing a good job addressing them? Why or why not?

4. Examine the General Social Survey data about whether or not people can be trusted from 1972 to 2012. The most frequent response does not change. Which response is given by the majority of respondents? Does this surprise you? Why or why not?

CHAPTER SUMMARY

1.1 Describe how working-class young adults are currently experiencing their lives.

When we look at young adults as a generational cohort and consider demographic factors, we get a larger picture of their life situation. Many people's personal troubles are, in fact, also collective problems. Because some groups of people experience social conditions differently than other groups, sociologists look at the intersectionality of several demographic factors.

1.2 Define what constitutes a social problem.

The objective aspect of social problems relies on statistical data and other empirical facts to identify patterns, trends, and rates of occurrence. The subjective aspect of social problems considers how people define a certain condition, event, or pattern of behavior as a social problem. Social constructionism states that social problems are social problems for no other reason than that people say they are. The type of action needed to bring about large-scale social change is usually aimed at transforming the social structure. The type of action needed to ameliorate a problematic condition is usually aimed at helping people in need.

1.3 Explain the sociological imagination.

The sociological imagination allows us to see personal troubles as social problems. When we take a global perspective, we compare our own society to other societies in all the world's regions. In this way we understand the social problems of U.S. society in relationship to social problems in other countries.

1.4 Discuss how sociological research can be used to study social problems.

Quantitative research investigates social problems through statistical analysis. Qualitative research explains how people define, experience, or understand problematic situations. Three common research methods are survey, participant observation, and interviewing. Using multiple methods gives sociologists a fuller picture of the social problems they are studying.

1.5 Explain the three main sociological perspectives of structural functionalism, conflict theory, and symbolic interactionism.

Functionalism is the sociological theory that considers how various social phenomena function, or work in a positive way, to maintain unity and order in society. Conflict theory is the sociological theory that focuses on dissent, coercion, and antagonism among groups in society. Symbolic interactionism sees society as the product of symbols (words, gestures, objects) that are given meaning by people in their interactions with each other.

1.6 Evaluate how each of the three theoretical perspectives can be applied to improve our understanding of social problems.

Durkheim's functionalism demonstrates how the degree of social integration and social regulation can result in high rates of suicide. Conflict theory shows how the interest group that has the most political power can prohibit behaviors it considers to be problematic. The symbolic interactionist perspective can help us explain how people with clinical depression make sense of their identity and illness.

1.7 Discuss the role of social policy in managing social problems.

Most social change happens piecemeal, and frequently the transformations are begun through social policy. Governmental implementation of social policy takes the form of legislation. Other forms are the delivery of services, the regulation of certain practices (such as drug use), and the establishment of welfare programs.

1.8 Explore the role of specialized theories in sociology.

Specialized concepts and theories examine particular aspects of society or specific social problems. They go beyond what the three theoretical perspectives can offer.

1.9 Identify ways in which service sociology can make a difference.

Service sociology is a socially responsible and mission-oriented sociology of action and alleviation. A culture of service—including various forms of civic engagement, community service, and volunteerism—allows citizens, including students, to work together to alleviate social problems.

DISCUSSION QUESTIONS

1. What is life like today for members of the millennial cohort? How is that life similar to and different from the lives of previous generational cohorts? What differences exist between members of the various racial and ethnic groups, social classes, and genders within the millennial cohort? Do the differences constitute a social problem?

2. How do sociologists understand a social problem? In what ways are the individual circumstances of people's lives connected to the larger patterns of problems that exist in society?

3. Why is the sociological imagination a useful tool for understanding social problems? How does understanding biography and history, and the connection between the two, lead to a richer understanding of problems and potential solutions? What examples of personal troubles do you see in your own life? How are these troubles connected, or not, to social problems?

4. What are the benefits of qualitative research for seeking an understanding of social problems? How do qualitative data compare with the data gathered through the use of quantitative research methods?

5. If you wanted to learn about poverty in the United States, which research method would produce the best results? Why? How would the data differ if you instead selected a different method?

6. What role does sociological theory play in making sense of the data collected by researchers? How does the focus of a structural functionalist compare with that of a conflict theorist when it comes to analyzing social problems such as violence in schools?

7. According to symbolic interactionism, why are some situations considered social problems and others not? How is the very definition of what constitutes a problem different in this perspective in comparison with the other two? What are the benefits and challenges to viewing social problems through this perspective?

8. Do you consider social policies ideal solutions to social problems? Does your response differ depending on the type of social policy, that is, if it is a government policy or an organization's policy? What are some other, nonpolicy sources for solutions to social problems?

9. How does sociology aim to make a difference in society with regard to addressing social problems? What role do individual sociologists play in bringing about positive social change? How can students of sociology engage in action to solve social problems?

10. Does service sociology appeal to you as a student and connect with your own reasons for taking a course about social problems? In what ways do the goals of service sociology connect with larger patterns of social responsibility and civic engagement in society? What does the move toward community service and volunteerism mean for our society as a whole when it comes to solving our various social problems?

KEY TERMS

altruistic suicide 17

anomic suicide 18

anomie 17

capitalism 14

capitalists 14

cohort 4

concepts 13

conflict theory 14

culture 18

culture of service 21

data sources 6

demographic factors 4

dysfunctions 14

egoistic suicide 17

fatalistic suicide 18

functions 18

global perspective 10

interest group 15

intersectionality 5

interviewing 12

legislation 19

looking-glass self 16

mind 15

norms 14

objective aspect of social problems 7

paradigm 13

participant observation 11

Sharpen your skills with SAGE edge at edge.sagepub.com/trevino

A personalized approach to help you accomplish your coursework goals in an easy-to-use learning environment.

2 POVERTY AND CLASS INEQUALITY

Keith M. Kilty

Reuters / John Kolesidis

A man pushes a shopping cart filled with scrap past a wall covered with street art in Athens, Greece. Dozens of poor scrap hunters can be spotted in rundown areas pushing carts stacked with metal, plastic, and paper. What do you think can be done for these people living on the margins of society?

Investigating Poverty and Class Inequality: My Story

Keith M. Kilty

Until I was 12 years old, I lived in a small town of conservative views and traditional U.S. values of self-reliance and hard work. I did not question these sentiments then and looked at the United States as the great hope of the world. Entering college in 1964, I joined Air Force ROTC and planned a military career. But that first year of college was eye-opening.

After taking a course on social psychology, I switched majors from aeronautical engineering to psychology. I experienced firsthand the turmoil of the civil rights movement and the beginning of anti–Vietnam War sentiment. I started grad school at Yale University, but, disenchanted, I dropped out and moved to New York to work in social service programs in prisons, where 60% of the inmates were black and 30% were Hispanic. Later I returned to school, committed to understanding how society functions in class, gender, race, and ethnic terms.

My research focused increasingly on poverty and inequality and my activities on progressive political activism. What I saw in prisons reflected the limits poverty puts on opportunities. To encourage more research on the connections among poverty, inequality, gender, race, and ethnicity, I cofounded, with Elizabeth A. Segal, the *Journal of Poverty: Innovations on Social, Political & Economic Inequalities*. To reach a broader audience, however, after retiring in 2007 I began work on a feature-length documentary film about poverty and inequality, with the goal of putting a human face back on poverty. We completed *Ain't I a Person?* in March 2011 and have been showing it in communities and on campuses around the country. (For more information, visit http://www.aintiaperson.com.)

LEARNING OBJECTIVES

2.1 Explain how poverty, class, and inequality are social constructions.

2.2 Discuss patterns and trends in defining and measuring poverty.

2.3 Describe social class and mobility.

2.4 Discuss income, wealth, and other dimensions of inequality.

2.5 Apply the functionalist, conflict, and symbolic interactionist perspectives to the problems of poverty, class, and inequality.

2.6 Apply specialized theories to poverty and inequality.

2.7 Identify steps toward social change in regard to poverty.

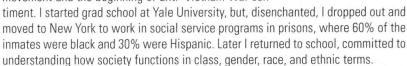

WHAT DO YOU THINK?

Questions about Poverty and Class Inequality from the General Social Survey

1. Your standard of living will improve.

☐ AGREE
☐ DISAGREE
☐ NEITHER AGREE NOR DISAGREE

2. How do people get ahead?

☐ HARD WORK
☐ LUCK OR HELP
☐ BOTH OF THE ABOVE

3. Should government reduce income differences?

☐ YES
☐ NO

4. People should help the less fortunate.

☐ AGREE
☐ DISAGREE
☐ NEITHER AGREE NOR DISAGREE

5. In the United States, do you think we're spending too much money on assistance to the poor, too little money, or about the right amount?

☐ TOO MUCH
☐ TOO LITTLE
☐ ABOUT THE RIGHT AMOUNT

▶▶ Turn to the end of the chapter to view the results for the total population.

SOURCE: National Opinion Research Center, University of Chicago.

WHO CAN AFFORD A COLLEGE DEGREE?

Kelsey Griffith, the daughter of a middle-class family, recently graduated from Ohio Northern University with a diploma and $120,000 in tuition debt. She has taken two restaurant jobs and moved back in with her parents. "I knew a private school would cost a lot of money," she told the *New York Times.* "But . . . I'm going to owe like $900 a month. No one told me that" (quoted in Martin and Lehren 2012).

Attending college, an avenue of upward mobility for generations of U.S. students, is increasingly a challenge for those at the bottom of society. Even middle-income students like Kelsey are facing rising debt that will take years to pay off. Nearly two-thirds of graduates with bachelor's degrees have student loans, and the total they owe on student loans has passed the $1 trillion mark. Economists even fear student debt is becoming a drag on the national economy (Stiglitz 2013).

Where did this problem come from? Education became a national priority following World War II, and the number of people with bachelor's degrees increased sixfold from 1940 to 2009. Recently, that trend appears to be reversing. Ohio State University, a typical example, now receives only 7% of its budget from the state, compared to 15% ten years ago, 25% in 1990, and more than 60% in the 1980s. Yet those figures do not really show how far the funding of education has receded as a public policy priority in this country. As state subsidies for higher education have dropped, tuition and fees have correspondingly jumped (Schmitt and Boushey 2010), while scholarships and grants have also declined, particularly as a percentage of tuition. What is left to finance college is mainly student loans.

In these circumstances, fewer people will be able to complete degrees without amassing staggering levels of debt. Many at the bottom will not qualify even to borrow the amount they need and will be locked out of the college opportunity. How will such limits on who can afford a college degree affect our idea of the American Dream?

ASK YOURSELF: Has public support for education changed in this country? Is college to become again mainly an option for the affluent? Is college a right or a privilege? Should it be open to anyone, regardless of personal or family resources? Why or why not?

POVERTY, CLASS, AND INEQUALITY ARE SOCIAL CONSTRUCTIONS

 2.1 Explain how poverty, class, and inequality are social constructions.

Some 46 million people in the United States live below the official poverty line, and millions more live barely above it, while those in the top 10% by income possess 90% of the wealth of the country. Class sharply divides who has access to which opportunities and resources, including a decent education and adequate health care. Inequality is growing, making it more difficult for those at the bottom to improve their lives or those of their children.

Poverty, class, and inequality are complex and intertwined concepts. They are also social constructions, yet they are more than just ideas, because they frame our everyday lives, the way we navigate through social space. Our ideas about poverty, class, and inequality are based not simply on facts but also on images and perceptions. Poverty is not just people with incomes below a certain level; it is also images of poorly dressed people begging on street corners. We know that we live in a society where some people have very little and others have immense wealth. But is that good or bad? Is inequality a useful incentive to spur people to work hard? Or is the gap between rich and poor unfair? That is what we mean by saying that concepts are socially constructed. Where do our ideas and images about poverty, class, and inequality come from?

What is social class? Are there only a few social classes, or is class in U.S. society represented by a continuum with many gradations? What is poverty? How is it related to inequality? Is poverty inevitable, or can we eradicate it? Should we define poverty exclusively in economic terms, or should we include social and political dimensions? Is inequality only an economic term, or does it too have

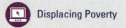
Displacing Poverty

other facets? These are the central issues on which we will focus in this chapter. As Gerhard Lenski (1966, 3) put it many years ago, the basic question is, "Who gets what and why?"

PATTERNS AND TRENDS

 2.2 Discuss patterns and trends in defining and measuring poverty.

Defining Poverty

More than 50 years ago, Michael Harrington published *The Other America* (1962), a book that opened the eyes of a complacent nation to deep poverty in the midst of affluence. Eradicating poverty, from Appalachia to inner cities, soon became a major focus of public policy. Critical legislation included the Economic Opportunity Act of 1964, the Civil Rights Act of 1964, and the Voting Rights Act of 1965 (Karger and Stoesz 2006). But to eradicate or even reduce poverty, we must be able to measure it. There are two ways.

An **absolute measure of poverty** sets a threshold, usually based on annual income. A person or family with an annual income at the line or below it is identified as being in **poverty.** If income is above the line—by even one dollar—the person or family is identified as not being in poverty.

The line is arbitrary but set by policy makers to help guide them in developing programs for the poor or in evaluating the effectiveness of antipoverty programs or in deciding who is eligible for some services. In 1963, Mollie Orshansky, an economist in the Social Security Administration, developed an absolute measure of poverty built on the cost of food. On the assumption that a family spends about one-third of its disposable income on food, Orshansky proposed a poverty threshold of three times the cost of a market basket of food, adjusted for family size. This standard has been used ever since, and the

A woman holds up her checkbook that shows "We're Broke!!" Many American families are in financial trouble. Do you think the government should help them get food, education, and full-time jobs?

federal government adjusts the rate for inflation each year so comparisons can be made across time. The poverty line in 2013 was $23,550 for a family of four.

There are many criticisms of this measure. For example, it uses a subsistence-level basket of food rather than a basket based on a more nutritionally sound diet, and the assumption that a family spends a third of its annual income on food is likely no longer accurate. In fact, most low-income families spend about half their income on rent (Karger and Stoesz 2006). Still, policy makers use the poverty line to guide them in developing and evaluating programs and in deciding who is eligible for certain services.

A **relative measure of poverty** looks at a person, or a group such as a family, in relationship to the rest of the community or society. Is the person or group far below or well above others in terms of income, quality of housing, educational levels or opportunities, household possessions? One common relative measure uses the *median* household income for a nation, the point that half the households are below and half are above. We might then consider poverty to be the income at half the median, indicating how some families compare to what is typical in their society. For example, the median U.S. household income for 2012 was $51,017. Half of that is $25,508.50. However, unlike an absolute measure, a relative measure is not a hard-and-fast line, so it changes depending on conditions in the society as a whole. The idea of a relative measure is that we see how individuals or families compare with others in their society; that is, are they relatively similar or more disadvantaged than most?

Absolute measure of poverty: A threshold or line (usually based on income) at or below which individuals or groups are identified as living in poverty.

Poverty: Deficiencies in necessary material goods or desirable qualities, including economic, social, political, and cultural.

Relative measure of poverty: A measure that looks at individuals or groups relative to the rest of their community or society rather than setting an absolute line.

FIGURE 2.1

The Poverty Threshold Calculation

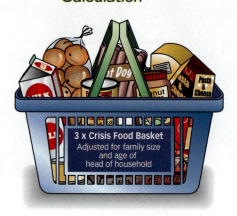

3 x Crisis Food Basket
Adjusted for family size
and age of
head of household

SOURCE: U.S. Census Bureau. (2010). Poverty: 2008 and 2009. American community survey briefs. Washington, DC: A. Bishaw & S. Macartney.

ASK YOURSELF: What advantages do you see in continuing to use the current method of calculating the poverty rate? What disadvantages? What other ways might poverty be measured? How do you feel poverty should be defined?

Poverty Rates over Time and among Different Social Groups

The U.S. Census Bureau releases an annual report on household income, poverty, and health insurance coverage, usually in the early fall. In the 2013 report, the poverty rate stood at 15% (DeNavas-Walt, Proctor, and Smith 2013). That is, more than 46.5 million U.S. men, women, and children fell below the official poverty line.

The Census Bureau takes into account age, family size, and the number of children in a household in counting the number of people below the poverty line. This creates a grid of what the Census Bureau calls the **poverty thresholds**, and a new set of thresholds is produced annually to take inflation into account. In 2012, the poverty threshold was $23,283 for a four-person household, which includes two children under age 18, and $18,498 for a three-person household including two children.

The U.S. Department of Health and Human Services uses a simplified version of the Census Bureau thresholds, called the **poverty guidelines**, which set what is known as the federal poverty level (FPL) (Table 2.1). The main difference is the Census Bureau's focus on the number of persons, including adults and children, in the household. The FPL, as developed by Orshansky, is the number generally referred to in the media when they mention the poverty line and also the guideline used to determine eligibility for many public services.

For many years, U.S. poverty rates declined (see Figure 2.2). The historic high was 1959, the first year for which figures were estimated. Nearly 40 million people were then in poverty, or about 23% of the U.S. population. Both absolute numbers and rates declined for most of the next two decades, especially among the elderly, since Social Security pensions were increasing not only in amount but also in extent of coverage. However, the Census Bureau uses a lower threshold for older people, so some of the decline in poverty among this group may be artificial.

By 1980, poverty rates began to grow again, peaking in the early 1990s and then dropping again until the 2000s. For the past several years of the Great Recession they have been increasing sharply, and the absolute number of people in poverty—13.3 million, or an increase of 40% from 2000 to 2010—is now higher than it was in 1959. The poverty rate went from 11.7% to 15.1%,

TABLE 2.1 Poverty Guidelines in the United States, 2013

Persons in family	Poverty guideline (annual income in $)
1	11,490
2	15,510
3	19,530
4	23,550
5	27,570
6	31,590
7	35,610
8	39,630

NOTE: For families with more than eight persons, add $4,020 for each additional person.

SOURCE: U.S. Department of Health and Human Services, "The 2011 HHS Poverty Guidelines" (ASPE.hhs.gov/poverty/11poverty.shtml).

Poverty thresholds: Measures of poverty used by the U.S. Census Bureau that take into account family size, number of children, and their ages.

Poverty guidelines: A simplified version of the U.S. Census Bureau poverty thresholds, which take into account only family size; the poverty guidelines are used to set the federal poverty level (FPL).

FIGURE 2.2 Poverty Levels in the United States, 1959–2012

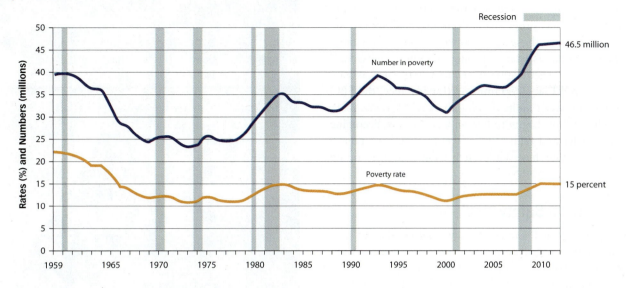

SOURCE: U.S. Census Bureau. (2012). Historical poverty tables: People.

an increase of 29%. Whether we look at absolute or relative numbers, poverty is clearly going in the wrong direction.

Some categories of people are more likely to be in poverty than others. The poverty rate for non-Hispanic whites was 9.7% in 2012, compared to 27.2% for African Americans, 25.6% of Hispanics (any race), and 11.7% of Asian Americans. If we look just at families, the rate for female-headed households is 30.9%, compared to 16.4% for male-headed households and 6.3% for married couples (see Table 2.2).

ASK YOURSELF: Why do you think poverty rates and numbers have increased in the past decade? Why are rates so much higher among female-headed households and lower among married-couple families?

"Extreme" Poverty and Low Income

It is not just the poverty rate or the number of people in poverty that is rising. The poor seem to be concentrated in particular neighborhoods, according to a recent report from the Brookings Institution (Kneebone, Nadeau, and Berube 2011). **Extreme poverty neighborhoods** are areas, usually U.S. census tracts, with poverty rates of 40%

Extreme poverty neighborhoods: Areas (usually based on census tracts) that have poverty rates of 40% or more.

TABLE 2.2 Poverty Rates of Selected U.S. Subgroups, 2012

Category	Percentage
White, non-Hispanic	9.7
Black	27.2
Hispanic	25.6
Asian	11.7
Female heads of household, no husband present	30.9
Male heads of household, no wife present	16.4
Married couples	6.3

SOURCES: DeNavas-Walt et al. 2011 for 2010; DeNavas-Walt et al. 2012 for 2011; and DeNavas-Walt et al. 2013 for 2012.

or more. The numbers of such neighborhoods declined throughout the 1990s but rose by a third between 2000 and 2005. According to Kneebone et al. (2011, 3): "Rather than spread evenly, the poor tend to cluster and concentrate in certain neighborhoods or groups of neighborhoods within a community. Very poor neighborhoods face a whole host of challenges that come from concentrated disadvantage—from higher crime rates and poorer health outcomes to lower-quality educational opportunities and weaker job networks."

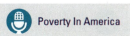
Poverty In America

Not only are more people falling into poverty, but their plight is also more severe now than in the past. Access to public assistance programs is declining, making the living conditions of those at the bottom of our society more difficult. Public assistance programs require individuals or families to meet eligibility requirements, such as having income below a certain level (for instance, the FPL) and meeting asset limits. During the past 15 years, more households have begun to live on less and less, becoming what Shaefer and Edin (2012) label the "extreme poor": households that have children present but little or no income.

The "Social Safety Net"

What we now call the **social safety net** consists of programs that emerged during the Great Depression. Until then, most charitable programs were either private, often church-based, or state and local in scope. Unfortunately, these social programs could not begin to alleviate the widespread suffering of the 1930s. The roots of the safety net are found in the Social Security Act of 1935. Most people probably think of Social Security as providing old-age pensions, but also included in this legislation were provisions for a number of additional programs: unemployment insurance; assistance to the aged, blind, and disabled; survivor benefits; and public assistance (originally for widows with children). Since its initial signing, the act has been amended, and some services have been modified or combined and others added.

A second period of expansion in federal programs occurred during the 1960s, when poverty emerged as a national concern. In addition, in response to the civil rights movement of the 1950s and 1960s, important federal legislation was enacted, including the Civil Rights Act of 1964 and the Voting Rights Act of 1965. Researchers focused not only on the problem of poverty but also on how minority status, including race and sex, was connected to poverty and being poor.

Some parts of the social safety net are social insurance programs, such as OASDI, or Old-Age, Survivors, and Disability Insurance, in which individuals pay into the system (or have spouses who pay into the system) and earn "entitlement" to services. One of the programs that has had the most impact on poverty is old-age insurance, or Social Security pensions for older people. By the 1960s, increasing numbers of workers were covered, and the level of payments helped to keep many older individuals and couples above the poverty line. Social Security pensions are now the most common form of income for older people, with more than 86% of older households receiving such income. In fact, more than half of all

Bettmann / Corbis

During the Great Depression, hundreds of hungry, homeless men lined up at the Municipal Lodging House in New York City for a free Thanksgiving Day dinner. The unemployment rate rose to 25% in the United States during the 1930s. Do you think this could happen again?

elderly households receive half their income from these benefits. The average monthly benefit at the beginning of 2012 was $1,230.

In 1965, Medicare was added to the Social Security program. This is a public health care program for people 65 and older, and most older people now participate in it. Medicaid is another important part of the social safety net. This is a public health insurance program for the poor, which now includes the State Children's Health Insurance Program (SCHIP). While most doctors and hospitals accept patients insured by Medicare, fewer are willing to accept Medicaid patients, making it difficult for many individuals who qualify for Medicaid to find physicians or hospitals who will treat them.

Some other social safety net elements, in contrast to social insurance programs, are means-tested programs for which people usually qualify by having a poverty-level income, as described earlier. For many years, the general public has had a negative image of means-tested public assistance programs, which are often associated with racial stereotypes. Some politicians have used images of "welfare cheats" and "welfare queens" to advance their careers,

Social safety net: Public programs intended to help those who are most vulnerable in a society.

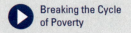
Breaking the Cycle of Poverty

The Social Safety Net

In 2005, a colleague went to Luxembourg to teach for a year, along with his wife and three sons. Luxembourg is typical of European Union countries in having a much more extensive social safety net than does the United States. For example, my friend's spouse received about 900 euros ($1,214) a month as a child benefit because of their three children. Such allowances in the EU are not the same as TANF; they are universal, not means-tested (that is, eligibility is not based on level of income). Workplaces in the EU must guarantee annual vacations of four weeks (some countries require up to six weeks). Housing allowances are also available, although generally the amounts are tied to income.

In Luxembourg, my colleague's family had access to national health insurance, which includes parental leave for both parents of up to six months with pay, whereas maternity leave in the United States is unpaid.

While in Luxembourg, my friend was diagnosed with chronic lymphocytic leukemia, which typically does not require immediate treatment. When he returned to the United States, his oncologist told him that his U.S. health insurance probably would not have covered the medical tests that were done in Luxembourg. Later, when my friend developed an acute leukemia, he found there were limits on where he could get treatment in the United States, unlike in Luxembourg.

Most European countries adhere more closely than the United States to the Universal Declaration of Human Rights (adopted by the General Assembly of the United Nations in 1948). Article 23 of the declaration focuses on employment rights, including equal pay. Article 24 deals with rest and leisure, including limits on work hours and paid holidays and vacations. Article 25 concerns the right to an adequate standard of living, regardless of unemployment, health disability, or old age, and gives special status to mothers and children. Article 26 focuses on education rights and gives parents the right to choose the type of education they feel is best for their children.

It should be no surprise, then, that poverty rates are much lower in the EU than in the United States. As Frances Fox Piven points out in the documentary *Ain't I a Person?* millions more who are not below the official federal poverty line would be considered poor in a country like Belgium.

▶ **THINK ABOUT IT:** What do you think it would be like to be a working woman in the United States who is about to have a baby? What about in Luxembourg? Why do you think the social safety net is so much more limited in the United States than in European countries?

though there has been little evidence of widespread cheating among welfare recipients (Segal and Kilty 2003).

Means-tested programs include Temporary Assistance for Needy Families (TANF), a program of cash assistance to poor families; and the **Supplemental Nutrition Assistance Program (SNAP)**, from which more than 46 million people receive benefits each month. (SNAP used to be known as the food stamp program.) Another important food-related program is the Special Supplemental Nutrition Program for Women, Infants, and Children (WIC), which provides nutrition education and a small amount

Supplemental Nutrition Assistance Program (SNAP): Federal program that provides low-income Americans with subsidies for food purchases; formerly known as the food stamp program.

of supplemental income that can be used with authorized vendors. In Ohio, for example, the average monthly WIC benefit per person is $38.75. Some means-tested programs allow recipients to have incomes somewhat higher than the official poverty line. The National School Lunch Program, for instance, provides reduced-cost meals for students whose family incomes are between 130% and 180% of the poverty line.

While the programs that make up the social safety net are valuable and help many people, especially the social insurance programs, fewer people are receiving benefits such as TANF, and the levels of benefits have dropped. In fact, the amount of help available for low-income individuals and families in the United States falls far short of what is available in many other countries, especially other industrialized nations (Waddan 2010).

Other Dimensions of Poverty

So far, we have looked at poverty in economic terms, focusing specifically on income. Are there other components to poverty?

We noted above that with a relative measure of poverty we are trying to get a picture of how individuals or families compare to their communities or societies. That suggests we should look at the extent to which particular individuals or families can actively participate in society. Are they accepted as legitimate members? Do they see themselves as legitimate members? When a child goes to school, can his or her family provide adequate resources, such as crayons? How does the child dress? Will he or she be accepted or shunned by peers?

People are unequal not just in income or wealth but also in desirable social and political qualities. Many now argue for considering certain "economic human rights" as part of our fundamental human rights. For instance, who can vote in the United States? Recent legislative efforts to limit voting rights have included restrictions on voter registration and the requirement to show photo identification at the polls. In some states, a person loses the right to vote if convicted of a felony, including simple drug possession. If you cannot vote, are you then deficient in a specific quality, in the same way as being below a certain income level? Should lack of political rights be included in a definition of poverty?

What about the right to marry? A majority of states now limit marriage to particular kinds of couples. What about the right to choose to be public or not about your sexual orientation? Should some people be so anxious about losing—or even getting—a job that they feel they must keep that part of their humanity hidden? Should we think of social conditions as a part of poverty?

···

ASK YOURSELF: What components do you think a definition of poverty should include? How would you define poverty?

···

SOCIAL CLASS

 Describe social class and mobility.

All societies are organized or stratified, most often into social classes, groups with different access to resources. In other words, inequalities in wealth, income, education, and occupation are common, and the system of social stratification we find in a particular society helps us to understand who gets what and why.

Many American citizens believe the United States is unique and that social class does not really exist here.

We tend to see our nation as egalitarian and open, a place where, through hard work and self-reliance, social mobility is not only possible but common. A majority claim "middle-class" status and about a quarter label themselves "working-class"; barely 1% identify as "upper-class" and only 7% as "lower-class" (Robinson 2003). More of us have recently come to acknowledge a conflict between rich and poor (Morin 2012), but few Americans seem to question the nature of the social class structure or whether it seriously affects opportunities. In fact, challenging whether the rich possess too much typically leads to charges of "class warfare"—especially from the rich and their conservative political allies.

Roots of the "Classless" Society

The roots of U.S. beliefs in egalitarianism and openness go back to colonial days. By the 17th century, when colonies in North America were firmly established, the English, French, and Dutch colonists found themselves in a vast expanse of open and what they perceived as unclaimed land. There was an indigenous population, but it was not as large as the one the Spanish and Portuguese found and subdued in South and Central America or the southern part of North America. For the hardy, the opportunities seemed boundless.

Yet opportunities were actually extremely limited for most European colonists. In the 13 English colonies, large landowners were generally given tracts of land by the English Crown, particularly in the southern colonies, where plantation farming and slavery were developing in the early 1600s. Most early colonists, and Africans brought to North America, were indentured servants obligated to work for landowners or merchants or craftsmen for set periods of time, usually 7 to 10 years. Chattel slavery developed between 1620 and 1660, when the rights and freedom of Africans were gradually taken away. However, in the early 1600s, black and white settlers were treated largely the same, and they lived lives of abject poverty. Since the average life expectancy then was only about 35 years, many indentured servants did not survive to become "free."

A class structure was developing, based on land and slave ownership in the southern colonies and on land and industry in the North. Opportunities were mainly reserved for those who arrived with advantage by birth. All the same, by the 19th century, a powerful narrative of success based on hard work, self-reliance, and perseverance had developed. This was the concept of the self-made man—the idea that anyone could rise from humble beginnings and become wealthy and successful simply by applying him- or herself (Miller and Lapham 2012). In this view, social position is a matter of individual achievement and has little or nothing to do with a person's origins in the social hierarchy.

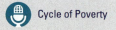

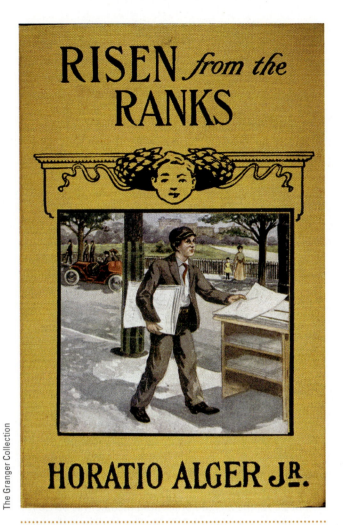

RISEN *from the* RANKS

HORATIO ALGER JR.

Horatio Alger's novel *Risen from the Ranks* was published in 1874. The book's protagonist is Harry Walton, who rises from the position of newsboy to newspaper editor. Alger's novels were hugely popular in their day. They followed the adventures of impoverished children who, through hard work, determination, courage, and honesty, were able to go from rags to riches. Can you think of other books or movies that serve to inspire people to financial success?

Self-made myth: The belief that anyone can rise from humble beginnings to become wealthy and successful simply by applying him- or herself.

Class: A person's social position relative to the economic sector.

Status: Social position, revolving around characteristics such as education, prestige, and religious affiliation.

Power: The aspect of social structure related to political affiliations and connections.

Socioeconomic status (SES): A conceptualization of social class in terms of a continuum or index based on social and economic factors.

Self-Made Myth

One of the major advocates of this **self-made myth** was the 19th-century author Horatio Alger (1832–1899), who wrote more than a hundred "rags to riches" novels and stories. Although his work had its critics even then, his vision became a central part of the American image. Later, the libertarian writer Ayn Rand (1905–1982) came to have a powerful influence on the continuing acceptance of the self-made myth, especially through her novel *Atlas Shrugged*. Her writings provided the foundation for the political philosophy and ethics of capitalism that lie behind modern conservative political thought and that advocate self-reliance and limited government influence on the economy. This is a powerful ideology that we hear expressed in the political rhetoric of such figures as Rand Paul, Sarah Palin, Paul Ryan, and Ted Cruz.

ASK YOURSELF: How do you feel about the self-made myth? Is a person's success based mainly on how hard that person works? Or does an individual succeed because of advantages received from family and social position? Does luck have anything to do with economic success? What about collective resources, such as schools, roads, and courts?

Class as a Social Science Concept

Two of the most important social scientists in the development of social class as a scientific concept were Karl Marx (1818–1883) and Max Weber (1881–1961). According to Marx, social position revolves around one important factor: ownership of the means of production. In essence, there are capitalists, who own the factories and other means of producing goods, and there are the working class, who sell their labor in order to survive. Many of Marx's critics, including Weber, have focused on this oversimplification of social stratification (Marx does identify other classes as well). In any case, Marx's view does bear an interesting similarity to the political slogan of the 1% versus the 99% championed by many advocates of the Occupy movement.

Marxist analysis of social structure has not been widely accepted in popular or academic circles in the United States because of the link between Marx and communist ideology. Much more acceptable have been the writings of Weber, who identifies three aspects of social structure: class, status, and power. **Class** refers to a person's position relative to the economic sector, such as proprietor, wage laborer, or renter. **Status** refers to social position in the context of characteristics like education, prestige, and religious affiliation. **Power** refers to political affiliations and connections.

Weber's ideas led to a conceptualization of U.S. social class as a continuum of **socioeconomic status (SES)**,

FIGURE 2.3   Class in the United States (Gilbert-Kahn Model)

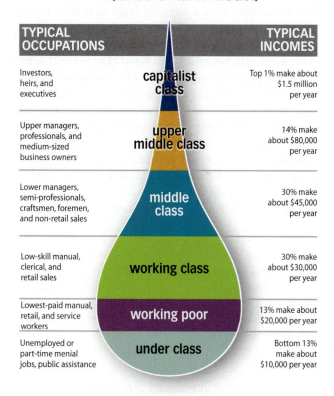

TYPICAL OCCUPATIONS		TYPICAL INCOMES
Investors, heirs, and executives	capitalist class	Top 1% make about $1.5 million per year
Upper managers, professionals, and medium-sized business owners	upper middle class	14% make about $80,000 per year
Lower managers, semi-professionals, craftsmen, foremen, and non-retail sales	middle class	30% make about $45,000 per year
Low-skill manual, clerical, and retail sales	working class	30% make about $30,000 per year
Lowest-paid manual, retail, and service workers	working poor	13% make about $20,000 per year
Unemployed or part-time menial jobs, public assistance	under class	Bottom 13% make about $10,000 per year

SOURCE: Gilbert, D. L. (2011). *The American class structure in an age of growing inequality*. Thousand Oaks, CA: Pine Forge Press.

rather than as a set of discrete categories that are easily distinguished from each other. Taking this perspective, we need to create an index of class based on a series of concepts, such as education, income, and occupation. That is how social science research generally treats class—by using a quantitative index or scale that measures several variables.

In many surveys and polls, in contrast, individuals are still often asked to self-identify as members of social classes using a subjective series of categories such as "upper class, middle class, working class, or lower class." As we have seen, a majority of respondents identify themselves as members of the middle class.

....

ASK YOURSELF: What is your social class? Why?

....

Social Mobility

Social mobility is upward or downward movement in social position over time in a society. That movement can be specific to individuals who change social positions or to categories of people, such as racial or ethnic groups.

As we saw earlier, the self-made myth suggests that social position in the United States is largely up to the individual, implying that mobility is quite common and easy to achieve for those who apply themselves. However, what people believe and what is fact are often not the same. While social mobility has always been limited in the United States, it has become even more so in the past three or four decades. Furthermore, it lags well behind mobility in most Western European nations—nations where many in the United States believe social class is much more entrenched (Miller and Lapham 2012).

Declining social mobility is a relevant issue for current college students. Not only will many graduate with considerable debt, but they are the first generation in U.S. history likely to end up at a lower social position than their parents (Ermisch et al. 2012).

An Alternate Way of Understanding the U.S. Class Structure

Focusing on income as an indicator of social class is an oversimplified way of looking at class. However, it may help us get a basic picture of the structure of our society. Table 2.3 presents the U.S. household income distribution for 2012 by quintile—that is, broken into five equal parts. The table shows the mean income for each quintile, as well as the share of the total income going to that group. Keep in mind that these income numbers are for *households*, not individuals.

For 2012, the median household income was $51,017, compared to a mean of $71,274. The median is the midpoint in a distribution where half the scores are above and half are below, while the mean is computed by adding all the scores together and dividing by the number of

TABLE 2.3   Annual Household Income in the U.S. by Quintile, 2012

Quintile	Mean ($)	Share of Total (%)
Top ($104,097 or more)	181,905	51
Fourth ($64,583–$104,096)	82,098	23
Third ($39,765–$64,582)	51,179	14.4
Second ($20,600–$39,764)	29,696	8.3
Bottom ($20,599 or less)	11,490	3.2

SOURCE: DeNavas-Walt et al. 2013.

....

Social mobility: Upward or downward movement in social position by groups or individuals over time.

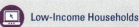 Low-Income Households

Social Mobility for Daughters and Sons in the United States and Sweden

To understand how mobility works in a particular society, it is often helpful to look at other countries. Comparing results from a study of mobility in Sweden with similar research in the United States, Lalaina Hirvonen (2008) found that intergenerational mobility, in terms of earnings, is greater in Sweden. That is, Sweden shows higher rates of mobility from one generation to another than does the United States, contrary to popular perceptions by Americans about mobility in their country.

The impact of family background on economic status is not as strong in Sweden as in the United States. Sweden is more egalitarian in that where someone comes from is much less of a determinant of where he or she ends up. In contrast, there is more likelihood of inheriting social position in the United States, contrary to what most U.S. adults believe. This likelihood is an important indicator of equality of opportunity in a society. When family background influences an individual's future social position, that means family background puts limits on mobility, especially for those lower in the social hierarchy. In other words, in such a society, opportunity for advancement is more limited than elsewhere.

Hirvonen also found that daughters in Sweden had somewhat greater mobility than sons; however, much of the research on U.S. social mobility has focused on sons and their fathers. That may have been appropriate in the past, when men's careers and earnings were more important than women's for family well-being, but more women have now entered the paid labor force and are remaining in it for longer periods, changing the dynamics of social mobility, especially for U.S. families or households. More research remains to be done.

▶ **THINK ABOUT IT:** Are you surprised there is more social mobility in Sweden than in the United States? Why or why not? What makes Sweden more egalitarian than the United States?

---

scores. The gap between the mean and median is important because it illustrates how unequal the distribution of household income is. Income is a skewed distribution, or a distribution in which a few values are at one extreme. In this case, the skewness is due to a few very high income values, compared to many more in the lower ranges.

Even more telling indicators of the depth of inequality in the United States are the upper limits for each of the quintiles. We saw in Table 2.1 that the 2013 poverty guideline for a family of two was $15,510, and for a family of three $19,530. Virtually the entire bottom quintile falls below those thresholds. The numbers for the second quintile are also striking, with many families barely above the FPL. In fact, the bottom 40% of all U.S. households received only 11.6% of all earned income in 2011. The top quintile, in contrast, received 51.1%. Average income of $178,020 in this group is just a little more than the $174,000 base salary for members of Congress. That salary alone puts every member of the U.S. Congress in the top quintile of household income—and nearly in the top 5%, where household income is $186,000 or greater.

....

Inequality: Differences between individuals or groups in the quantities of scarce resources they possess.

While income is useful as a metric variable, another way to consider social class is to use the quintiles as rough indicators. The bottom quintile represents the poor (with those below the mean for that group representing the extreme poor), the second quintile the near poor or working poor, the third the middle class, the fourth the upper-middle class, and the top quintile the upper class. We could also divide that top quintile into the affluent (the first 15%), the rich (the next 4%), and the super-rich (the top 1%).

....

ASK YOURSELF: Some in the Occupy movement distinguish the 99% from the 1%. Should such extreme differences exist among U.S. economic groups? Why or why not? Is that fair? Moral? Should we make distinctions among those who make up the 99%?

....

INEQUALITY

 Discuss income, wealth, and other dimensions of inequality.

When we ask who gets what and why, we are dealing with the issue of **inequality**—the fact that some in a society have more than others. Inequality is increasing throughout the world, but the gap between those at the top and those at the bottom is greater in the United States than in nearly all other industrialized societies, especially those in Europe. The same is true when we measure the proportion of the population below 50% of the median income (a measure of absolute poverty, as described earlier). Only Poland and Portugal come close to the United States.

We use the term *poverty* to depict the status of those at the very bottom. A good way to think of inequality, then, is as a continuum, with extreme poverty (or the poor) at one end and wealth (or the super-rich) at the other:

Poverty ⟵————————————⟶ Wealth

While income is an important aspect of this divide between top and bottom, it is not all there is to inequality.

What about housing? Or access to health care, good jobs, and education? What about assets (which we'll discuss below)? We also need to understand that no population or country is evenly distributed on this continuum—in fact, distribution is generally far from even. The continuum will not look like a flat line, such as we saw when we broke the income distribution into five equal parts or quintiles. It will not look like a bell curve, in which most of the population falls in the middle, with equal numbers of extreme cases on both sides. The continuum of inequality is a highly skewed distribution in which many more individuals fall toward the bottom than the top, as Figure 2.3 shows.

Income and Wealth

What is the difference between income and wealth? Each year, the Census Bureau releases a report on U.S. household income that defines **income** as the money that flows into a family or household from a variety of sources, such as earnings, unemployment compensation, Social Security benefits, interest and dividends, and rental income.

Wealth, in contrast, is often defined as a family's or household's assets or possessions, or as *net worth,* the difference between the value of these assets and the amount of the family's or household's debt. Many wealthy people may have high incomes as well as plentiful assets, but because income from investments often is subject to capital gains taxes rather than to income taxes, it is not included in surveys of household income. As a result, many wealthy people may not appear to have large incomes based on statistics from the Internal Revenue Service. But they still have plenty of money to spend and live very well compared to others. Currently, 10% of the population possesses nearly 90% of all the wealth in the United States, meaning the other 90% together share a meager 10% of everything there is to own. Even then, there are extremes among that top 10%, particularly between the top 5% and the others, and between the

top 1% and the top 4%. And the divide between those at the top and the rest of U.S. society has been growing rapidly in the past 30 years (Mishel, Bernstein, and Shierholz 2009).

We need to be careful, then, to distinguish between income and wealth when we are talking about the extent of inequality in a society. Typically, distributions of income and wealth will be similar, but they will not give identical depictions of the depth of inequality because the distribution of wealth is generally more unequal than the distribution of income.

We know that household or family income has stagnated or declined during the past decade. As we can see in Table 2.4, which uses income data from the Federal Reserve's triannual survey of consumer finances, median or mean family income stayed relatively even in the 2001, 2004, and 2007 surveys but dropped sharply in 2010, reflecting the impact of the Great Recession on U.S. families (Bricker et al. 2012). The difference between the median and the mean reflects the highly skewed distribution of income, with more families falling toward the bottom than toward the top. The decline in family income was most pronounced for families in the middle of the income distribution, partly because those at the bottom did not have nearly as far to fall.

We see similar results for net worth in Table 2.4. The median was at its peak in 2007, just before the impact of the Great Recession and falling home prices. In the years 2007 to 2010, median net worth fell by 38.8% (with mean net worth falling by 14.7%). According to the

TABLE 2.4 Mean and Median U.S. Family Income and Net Worth in Constant Dollars, 2001–2010

	2001	2004	2007	2010
Income				
Median	$48,900	$49,000	$49,600	$45,800
Mean	$83,300	$81,400	$88,300	$78,500
Net worth				
Median	$106,100	$107,200	$126,400	$77,300
Mean	$487,000	$517,100	$584,600	$498,800

SOURCE: Federal Reserve Survey of Consumer Finances.

Income: Money that comes into a family or household from a variety of sources, such as earnings, unemployment compensation, workers' compensation, Social Security, pension or retirement income, interest, and dividends.

Wealth: Assets (or possessions) or net worth (the difference between the value of assets and the amount of debt for an individual, family, or household).

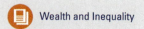
Wealth and Inequality

Federal Reserve, those in the top 10% were largely protected from declines felt by the remaining 90%, with respect not only to net worth but also to income. The share of the economic pie—whether in income or net worth—declined for everyone except those at the top.

These figures are striking, and the gap between rich and poor should actually be even more of a public concern. According to Chuck Collins (2012, 3):

- The 1 percent has 35.6 percent of all private wealth, more than the bottom 95 percent combined. The 1 percent has 42.4 percent of all financial wealth, more than the bottom 97 percent combined.
- The 400 wealthiest individuals on the Forbes 400 list have more wealth than the bottom 150 million Americans.
- In 2010, 25 of the 100 largest U.S. companies paid their CEO more than they paid in U.S. taxes. This is largely because corporations in the global 1 percent use offshore tax havens to dodge their U.S. taxes.
- In 2010, the 1 percent earned 21 percent of all income.
- Between 1983 and 2009, over 40 percent of all wealth gains flowed to the 1 percent and 82 percent of wealth gains went to the top 5 percent. The bottom 60 percent lost wealth over this same period.
- The world's 1 percent, almost entirely millionaires and billionaires, owns $42.7 trillion, more than the bottom 3 billion residents of Earth.
- While the middle-class standard of living implodes, sales of luxury items such as $10,000 wristwatches and Lamborghini sports cars are skyrocketing.
- Between 2001 and 2010, the United States borrowed over $1 trillion to give wealthy taxpayers with incomes over $250,000 substantial tax breaks, including the 2001 Bush-era tax cuts.

The way people believe wealth is distributed in the United States is very different from the way it is actually distributed. The middle bar in Figure 2.4 shows the way people believe wealth is distributed, while the bottom bar shows the way they would like it to be. Contrast both these views to the top bar, which shows the actual amount of wealth held by those at the very top of U.S. society.

It is not only in economic terms—in measures of income or the value of assets and possessions—that inequality is growing in our society. We can also see rising inequality in access to education, good jobs, health care, and education.

FIGURE 2.4 Wealth of the Top 20% of U.S. Residents: Popular Views versus Reality

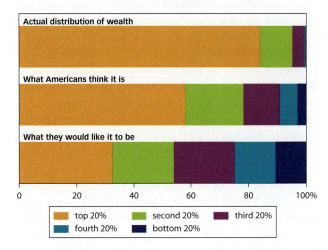

SOURCE: Michael I. Norton and Dan Ariely, "Building a Better America— One Wealth Quintile at a Time," *Perspectives on Psychological Science,* 2011, 6:1, pp. 9–12.

Other Dimensions of Inequality

Economic disparity is the central aspect of inequality, but many other social forces drive inequality in the United States and around the world. Two of the most significant of these are gender and race/ethnicity. It has been more than 50 years since the Civil Rights Act of 1964 was passed, but sexual and racial discrimination persist. While many hailed the election of Barack Obama to the U.S. presidency in 2008 as the beginning of a "postracial" era in the United States, for example, racial discrimination is still a fact of life. We also find major differences among racial and ethnic groups in income and wealth, particularly when we compare African Americans and Hispanics with whites (refer back to Table 2.2).

Another important dimension of inequality is access to health care. The number of people without health insurance in the United States has risen lately, partly because of the rise in unemployment and the loss of job-based health insurance for the newly unemployed. In 2011, 15.7% of the U.S. population was without health insurance coverage. African Americans and Hispanics fell well behind whites, and lower-income groups lagged higher-income groups (DeNavas-Walt, Proctor, and Smith 2012).

If we look at actual health conditions, we find that mortality, self-rated health, and specific serious illnesses are all associated with poverty. Some conditions may be due to occupations in which toxic conditions are more likely to be part of the environment. Others may occur or worsen because of inadequate or nonexistent health insurance. Lower-income workers are much more likely than higher-income workers to be underinsured or to have insurance that covers only themselves and not their spouses or dependent children. Chronic conditions often develop slowly, but with no or limited insurance they go untreated until they become much more serious. Preventive treatments and screenings are also often unavailable to many.

The likelihood of being imprisoned in the United States is directly related to race and ethnicity (Bonczar 2003). When we look at race and ethnicity, we find the incarceration rate per 100,000 men is 456 for whites, 1,252 for Hispanics, and 3,059 for African Americans (Guerino, Harrison, and Sabol 2011). Black men, then, are 6.7 times as likely as white men to be incarcerated, and Hispanic men are 2.7 times as likely as white men.

In 2010, almost 600,000 black men were in prisons across the United States, making up 38.0% of the total prison population, while 22.3% of all prisoners were Hispanic and 32.3% were white. Compare these numbers to the proportions of these groups in the general U.S. population: African Americans, 12.6%; Hispanics, 16.3%; and whites, 72.4%. Who commits crimes and who goes to prison? Are certain groups of people more likely to commit crimes, or are other factors, such as racial discrimination, at work in sending people to jail?

There are many other dimensions to inequality as well. We could look at educational rates, unemployment rates, quality and location of housing, likelihood of being hungry or participating in programs like SNAP, and many other measures. Clearly, however, despite what many believe about the extent of social mobility in the United States, especially in comparison to other countries, inequality is a fact of American life. For those who believe social change is possible and something to work toward, facing that reality is just the first step.

USING THEORY TO EXPLAIN POVERTY, CLASS, AND INEQUALITY: THE VIEWS FROM THE FUNCTIONALIST, SYMBOLIC INTERACTIONIST, AND CONFLICT PERSPECTIVES

 2.5 Apply the functionalist, conflict, and symbolic interactionist perspectives to the problems of poverty, class, and inequality.

Sociologists and other social scientists have grappled with the issues of poverty, class, and inequality for decades. Some theoretical explanations have focused on individual situations and characteristics, while others have looked at the structures of societies, institutions, and organizations. Still others have tried to bring the individual and the social together by describing how individuals manage within social contexts. We look at these three different perspectives in turn below.

Functionalism

Functionalism examines the nature of society and the way it is organized. **Functionalist theory** sees societies as complex systems whose various institutions and organizations work together to maintain a level of cohesion and stability. Society's norms, mores, values, traditions, and beliefs give individuals a sense of what to do and when to do it, as well as how to interact with others, particularly when they differ in social status. This shared awareness and acceptance of the structure of society is our particular culture, in which individual members accept their particular positions, whether at the top, in the middle, or at the bottom.

Drawing on the work of modern structural functionalist Talcott Parsons, the seminal work on functionalism and its application to poverty, class, and inequality is a 1945 article by Kingsley Davis and Wilbert E. Moore, "Some Principles of Stratification." Even though it has been 70 years since its publication, the principles outlined by Davis and Moore still largely reflect the functionalist view of poverty, class, and inequality: (a) some positions in a society are more valuable than others and require special skills to perform; (b) only a few people have the talent for the more important positions; (c) learning those skills requires sacrifices on the part of those who have the talent to learn; (d) to induce them to make the sacrifices requires that they receive more of society's scarce resources and rewards than others in less important positions; (e) access to scarce resources and rewards becomes attached to different positions in the social hierarchy. As a result, (f) different positions in the social hierarchy have different levels of prestige and esteem, and (g) social inequality among these positions is both inevitable and functional to society's maintenance.

Herbert J. Gans (1971) presents a clear application of these principles in "The Uses of Poverty," in which he described 15 "positive functions" for poverty. These include getting the "dirty work" of society done cheaply

....

Functionalist theory: The hypothesis that societies are complex systems whose parts work together to maintain cohesion and stability.

Experiencing Poverty and Class Inequality

From Middle-Class Citizens to Inmates in Poverty

Toyo Suyemoto Kawakami was 29 years old when she and her 6-month-old son were imprisoned because they were Japanese American. On February 19, 1942, not long after the United States entered World War II, President Franklin Delano Roosevelt issued Executive Order 9066, designating certain parts of the country "military areas" from which some unnamed people could be excluded. Though we like to think that all U.S. citizens are equal, that all have the right to "equal protection of the laws" under the 14th Amendment of the U.S. Constitution, such was not the case for Toyo, her family, and about 120,000 other Japanese Americans—many native-born U.S. citizens—who were rounded up and put into 10 concentration camps.

When we think of concentration camps, what usually comes to mind are the Nazi prisons. But there were also American concentration camps, and Toyo and her child spent more than three years in one.

When the trucks came to take them to the camp, they were allowed to take one suitcase per person. Toyo packed as much for her baby as she could in both her allotted suitcases, along with some precious books.

As the family left their home in Berkeley, California, Toyo's father told her he knew they would never see it again. Rather than locking the door, he simply put the keys in the mailbox for whoever would take possession. Throughout California, Oregon, and Washington, many whites took over homes and family businesses that had belonged to Japanese Americans, paying the owners nothing or pennies on the dollar.

Living situations in the camps were communal, with little privacy. Many older Japanese Americans became overwhelmed by shame at their situation and committed suicide. Toyo's son became ill. Medical treatment was not readily available, and weeks passed before he was taken to a hospital. He never fully recovered, and at age 16 he died of respiratory illness.

When Toyo and her family were released, none went back to California. Toyo went to the University of Michigan, where she earned a graduate degree in library science. An accomplished poet, she wrote about the internment experience, and she eventually became a librarian at Ohio State University, where she was director of the social work library when I arrived at the campus in 1978.

Social forces interact. When Toyo was growing up, her parents emphasized the importance of education and taught their children that value, providing them with a home filled with books and art. Her father, who had degrees in engineering and mining, worked as an insurance salesman. While Toyo's mother spoke limited English, she read widely in literature and philosophy. By the time of her internment, Toyo

Shortly after Japan's attack on Pearl Harbor in 1941, thousands of Japanese Americans were interned at camps like this one. Many U.S. soldiers of Japanese ancestry who were serving in the U.S. Army during World War II had families that were interned at home while they fought abroad.

herself had a college degree from the University of California, Berkeley, and was a published poet. Despite their education and social class, Toyo and her family were unable to escape mistreatment at the hands of the U.S. government. Upon their internment, everything they had worked so hard for was taken away from them. Because of their race, they went from being productive, middle-class citizens to being inmates, owning nothing more than a few personal items and the clothes on their backs.

Many people are clearly affected by being in multiple disadvantaged social categories. When we realize that more women, especially mothers, are in poverty, when we realize that more nonwhites than whites are living in poverty, when we see how age intersects with other social categories, then we can begin to appreciate why people who fall into certain overlapping categories are so terribly affected by poverty.

▶ **THINK ABOUT IT:** Do you think that today U.S. citizenship can protect people from having their homes and jobs taken away from them?

(garbage collection and working in farm fields), ensuring the purchase of low-quality products (wilting produce and day-old bread), and guaranteeing higher social status for those who are not poor, since someone has to be at the bottom. However, Gans goes on to demonstrate that these presumably positive functions can be quite costly for society and the affluent, not just financially but also in moral terms by requiring the toleration of exclusionary practices.

More recent theorists, including George Gilbert, Lawrence Mead, and Charles Murray, have continued to argue that social inequality is necessary and inevitable for the maintenance of any society, including the United States. To be a doctor or a banker requires much more training—which is time-consuming and arduous—than to be a janitor or a police officer. As a result, higher positions carry greater prestige and authority as well as access to scarce resources and rewards such as higher income and better housing. In *Coming Apart,* Murray (2012) argues that those in the top 5% of the population, particularly CEOs and policy makers, have extremely high IQs that lead to their success and for which they are rightly highly compensated.

....

ASK YOURSELF: Imagine yourself poor, and consider the functionalist provision that inequality is inevitable and functional. Would you accept your status as unavoidable and necessary?

....

Policy Implications of Functionalism

According to the functionalist perspective, inequality is not only inevitable but necessary for the functioning of society. Certain positions need higher levels of rewards because of the difficulty in acquiring the skills to perform them. Therefore, while some are advantaged, others should be disadvantaged, since anyone could perform the tasks of lower positions with minimal effort. In fact, society may need to threaten those at the bottom with sanctions simply to get them to do anything.

A good example of this approach in action is welfare reform. The welfare rights movement of the 1960s was successful in expanding both coverage and benefits provided by the Aid to Families with Dependent Children (AFDC) program. However, after the election of Richard M. Nixon to the presidency in 1968, critics of the War on Poverty began a concerted attack on public assistance, arguing that many recipients were merely unwilling to work and instead were taking advantage of public benefits. These arguments escalated during the years Ronald Reagan was in office, leading to a call for welfare reform based on the propositions that

many able-bodied individuals were avoiding work or job training, had become entrenched in a "culture of poverty," and needed to be pushed to learn appropriate work habits and values. Critics of welfare rejected structural explanations for poverty and believed that welfare recipients should take personal responsibility for their disadvantaged situation. By the 1990s, "welfare reform" had become policy at the federal level, leading to the **Personal Responsibility and Work Opportunity Reconciliation Act (PRWORA)** of 1996. Among this act's major provisions were time limits for receipt of benefits (no more than 60 months in a lifetime at the federal level, but less time at any state's discretion) and work requirements whereby individuals refusing to work could be sanctioned (including by losing monthly benefits).

Austerity programs—typically taking the form of cutbacks to social welfare programs that assist those at the bottom—are clearly reflections of functionalism. Many of the politicians and other commentators currently arguing for limiting the social safety net and reducing so-called entitlement programs (such as Social Security) take the functionalist approach. Other types of public assistance, such as SNAP and Medicaid, are also facing possible reductions by the U.S. Congress, even though they are vital to the health and well-being of many lower-income individuals and families. Austerity is proposed and often enacted for social safety net programs, while bailouts for banks, such as the Troubled Asset Relief Program (TARP), are not seen in the same light. In fact, those programs (which some would call corporate welfare) are seen as essential to the national economy, and no one—especially in the U.S. Congress—has raised the need for "personal responsibility" on the part of Wall Street bankers.

Symbolic Interactionism

Symbolic interactionism grew from George Herbert Mead's hypothesis that the meanings of social events emerge from the interactions among individuals, who are actors rather than reactors. An interaction is a negotiation, a learning process, in which the individuals involved absorb not only relevant norms and traditions but also beliefs and values—the core elements of a shared culture. In a sense, then, we learn culture or collective consciousness through the interaction process.

....

Personal Responsibility and Work Opportunity Reconciliation Act (PRWORA): U.S. federal legislation passed in 1996 that eliminated Assistance for Families with Dependent Children (AFDC) and established Temporary Assistance for Needy Families (TANF). Also known as welfare reform.

A homeless man sits on Fifth Avenue in New York City as shoppers pass him by. Have you ever given money to homeless people? Do you think your help can make a difference?

One of the most significant applications of interactionism to poverty, class, and inequality is the **culture of poverty thesis** proposed by Oscar Lewis (1969). Lewis believed people are poor not just because they lack resources but also because they hold a unique set of values that makes it difficult for them to escape poverty, including a sense of powerlessness that leads to feelings of helplessness and inferiority, and lack of a work ethic.

This thesis is similar to *labeling theory,* which applies interactionism to the understanding of deviance (Kilty and Meenaghan 1977). Individuals seen as deviant or as outsiders become labeled by others who are more advantaged because of their sex, race, ethnicity, class, or age. Labeling effectively reduces the options for both labeled and labelers. The poor are among the most disadvantaged in our society, and many are at further disadvantage because in addition they are women, are people of color, and/or have limited education and occupational histories.

Culture of poverty thesis: The idea that living in poverty leads to the acquisition of certain values and beliefs that perpetuate remaining in poverty.

These were the groups—poor women, poor blacks, poor Hispanics, poor American Indians, poor Appalachians—to whom the culture of poverty thesis was applied beginning in the 1960s. Many in these groups likely did feel powerless or appear to lack a work ethic. What were their options? Rather than looking at opportunity structures, the culture of poverty thesis focuses on the presumed failings of individuals—or, in William Ryan's (1976) words, on blaming the victim.

ASK YOURSELF: Why do some people get labeled in a positive way and others in a negative way? Why do certain ideas about some groups become widely accepted, such as who is good at certain sports or who is best able to work certain jobs?

Policy Implications of Symbolic Interactionism

The most striking application of symbolic interactionism to social policy is the continuing assault on public assistance—not only welfare but also other public services such as SNAP, Medicaid, and Head Start. A study of comments by members of the U.S. House of Representatives about PRWORA revealed that the legislators sounded certain themes, including personal responsibility, getting something for nothing, out-of-wedlock births, and fraud and abuse (Segal and Kilty 2003). The notion that only the "deserving" poor should get help was common, as was the idea that welfare encourages many to remain in a "cycle of dependency." Nearly all adult welfare recipients in 1996 were women, while 89% of the House were men. Male representatives were more likely to speak in favor of the "need" for welfare reform and to vote for the legislation than were women—although women representatives were certainly more privileged than women welfare recipients.

Labeling theory was not intended to be a mechanism for blaming the victim. In fact, it was meant to be quite the opposite: a means for identifying how power differentials marginalize particular groups, such as women or racial and ethnic minorities. To a large extent, it drew from the principles of *critical theory*, which argues that we need to examine cultural ideas in terms of which groups benefit from them and who then advocate their points of view. In this case, we need to examine carefully who was applying particular labels to the poor as a way of ostracizing them on the grounds that the poor are themselves responsible for their circumstances, rather than focusing on the systemic causes of poverty—who gets what and why.

Conflict Theory

At the heart of Marxist thought, from which conflict theory developed, is the division of class into two basic groups: the capitalists, or owners of the means of production, and the proletariat, or working class. Capitalists do not produce anything themselves. Rather, they extract surplus value from the work of those who make things the capitalists sell for a profit. The conflict is the struggle to control the means of production.

The point of capitalism is to make as much profit as possible forever. In the early days of capitalism, the profit extracted from the production of material goods or commodities was invested in the making of new goods. But profit can also be accumulated for its own sake, and money can be hoarded just like material goods. Furthermore, anything can be a commodity, including items essential for life, such as water, utilities, and food, which then are available only to those who can afford them. A modern commodity in the United States is health care. Those who can afford it (or who can afford health insurance) can have it, and those who cannot have to do without or rely on public and charitable programs. Even money can be a commodity, packaged and traded in various ways, as are home mortgages and other financial instruments that most of us need.

Reuters / Bobby Yip

Workers are seen at a factory operated by Foxconn, Apple's main supplier of iPhones, in Guangdong Province, China. In 2010 there was a series of suicides among Foxconn workers, which some attribute to long working hours and low pay. If you knew that your iPhone was manufactured at a labor camp, would you stop using it?

While anything can be a commodity, often the thing itself becomes what is of value rather than the human labor that makes it—what Marx referred to as a commodity fetish. Many of us are consumed with possessing "things," and we pay little attention to the labor that goes into them, or the conditions in which the laborers work, such as the Chinese sweatshops where iPhones are made.

Marx proposed the concept of **alienation** to describe the separation between the workers' labor to make something and the object itself, about which workers have little or no say. Workers sell their labor to capitalists and have little or no say in what they do as part of that production process. Alienation is not a psychological condition but rather a division between workers and their true human nature. Marx saw this as a key development in capitalist society, and it applies to all workers, whether laborers or farmworkers or professors. Marx believed in **dialectical materialism**—the idea that contradictions in an existing economic and social order, such as the conflict between owners and laborers, would create a push for change, eventually leading to new economic conditions and social relationships (Allan 2011).

Alienation: The separation of workers from their human nature in the capitalist production process—that is, the separation between the labor to make something and the object itself.

Dialectical materialism: The contradictions in an existing economic and social order that create a push for change, which eventually leads to new economic conditions and social relations.

From these ideas emerged conflict theory, which proposes that we need to examine the nature of power relationships in society. Do we actually have a shared acceptance or collective consciousness, or are different groups struggling to ensure that their positions and views remain predominant?

C. Wright Mills began an important tradition in U.S. social thought by examining how those in power assert themselves. In *The Power Elite*, originally published in 1956, Mills (2000) focused on the interconnections among corporate leaders, the military, and the government—what President Dwight D. Eisenhower would later term the military-industrial complex. By the late 20th century, academic leaders were also identified as part of this matrix, participating in a process in which individuals moved readily from one position to another in the corporate world, the academic world, and the government. Economists Timothy Geithner and Lawrence Summers, for instance, have both held powerful positions in corporations, the federal government, and higher education (see below). G. William Domhoff has published a series of studies identifying these "interlocking directorates," which show that the United States, like many other countries, is dominated by a powerful elite whose members are able to maintain their control based on their own or others' wealth and social positions.

Those concerned with poverty, class, and inequality have employed conflict theory to examine the dynamics of wealth and poverty (Piven and Cloward 1993). They have shown that poverty is systemic, rather than a function of the values or personal inclinations or attributes of the poor. As Gans (1971) has shown, poverty serves a "useful" function in society, in the sense that the threat of poverty hangs over the head of every working person. No matter how bad the situation is for a person with a job, it would be worse if he or she lost that job—a possibility that is part of everyday life for most of us. How many paychecks away from destitution are we? Are we willing to challenge our bosses and organize our coworkers, or are we afraid we will lose our jobs if we raise our voices? Those in power have the money to propagate their desired messages—that the poor are shiftless and lazy, that anyone who applies him- or herself and works hard enough will be successful—through what Frances Fox Piven calls the propaganda machine.

ASK YOURSELF: Can anything—not just material objects—be a commodity? Should we treat such necessities as food and health care as commodities? Should people have a right to necessities, whether they can afford them or not? Do you believe there is a "power elite" in the United States?

Minimum Wage

Policy Implications of Conflict Theory

From the conflict theory perspective, those at the bottom serve to keep wages for other workers low, since employers can fight efforts to raise wages by replacing outspoken workers with the unemployed. Who has the power is the critical element in the conflict theorist's view of society, and those with wealth have much more power than those at the bottom. Wealth not only buys influence through corporate leadership positions and access to the media for disseminating particular messages, but it also buys legislators and policy makers through campaign contributions and jobs outside government—as in the cases of Larry Summers, who became president of Harvard University after serving as secretary of the Treasury, and Tim Geithner, who was president of the Federal Reserve Bank of New York before becoming secretary of the Treasury.

Challenging the welfare "reform" of the 1990s means working with the poor as they struggle to organize. In the 1960s, it was not just federal legislation that created a War on Poverty but also the National Welfare Rights Union, which advocated for the plight of poor women and children, and the civil rights movement, which led to legislation that established voting rights and protected minorities and women from discrimination in the labor market. According to Frances Fox Piven (2006) and Mimi Abramovitz (2000), change is likely only when social movements like these are strong. Electoral politics can open possibilities, but political figures will advocate for the poor only when the poor themselves challenge authority in dramatic ways.

When the economic meltdown began in 2007, many blamed those who had overreached and taken on large, high-risk (subprime) mortgages. While that certainly happened, thousands were led by unscrupulous bankers into taking out risky loans for houses with inflated values, without being informed they had other options. Once again, those in power—the bankers, the corporate leaders, the media—chose to blame the victims rather than to accept any responsibility themselves.

SPECIALIZED THEORIES APPLIED TO POVERTY AND INEQUALITY

 2.6 Apply specialized theories to poverty and inequality.

Other theoretical frameworks have been used to understand the nature of poverty, class, and inequality. Theories concerned with social empathy, for example, focus on

Wheelock College student intern Meghan Kennedy gives information to Carlotta Martin, mother of five, at the Department of Transitional Assistance in Boston. Volunteers like Kennedy offer on-the-spot advocacy to families applying for emergency assistance. Do you think it is necessary for volunteers to have a certain degree of empathy with the people they are trying to help?

why some people seem more able than others to identify with the experiences of other people and on whether or not empathy can be learned. Frameworks that examine social inclusion look at how being marginalized and stigmatized affects people's interconnections. Distributive justice is concerned with the relationship between perceptions of inequality and the principle of fairness.

Social Empathy

According to Segal (2007, 75), many people lack **social empathy**—"the insights one has about other people's lives that allow one to understand the circumstances and realities of other people's living conditions." If people cannot appreciate the circumstances of others, social bonds are increasingly likely to weaken, and it may become very difficult for those at the top to act in a humane way toward those at the bottom. Social empathy is thus a crucial trait for policy makers who are responsible for developing and managing programs intended to respond to the needs of those in poverty. As Segal (2006) has documented, members of Congress and recipients of TANF benefits share few characteristics such as age, gender, race, ethnicity, or degree of wealth. The two groups come from very different worlds, and those in decision-making positions have little awareness of the lives of those at the bottom—a situation very different from the one that existed for the members of Congress who helped develop the New Deal programs of the Great Depression era.

Nickols and Nielsen (2011) have demonstrated that participation in a poverty simulation exercise can lead to greater understanding of the structural conditions

responsible for poverty and greater awareness of the difficult lives of the poor. Exercises like this are often used in classrooms and with volunteers and staff in social service programs and charitable organizations. Putting a human face on poverty is a necessary step in changing misconceptions about poverty.

Social Inclusion

How is it possible for someone on the margins of society to feel a sense of inclusion? Without **social inclusion**, individuals do not have a sense of interconnection with others, nor do they have incentives that may help them work toward changing their circumstances. We have seen that those at the top have not only high incomes but also considerable assets, unlike the poor. Social policies favoring these assets exclude the poor, and many public programs require the poor to have few or no assets in order to qualify for aid. Yet moving out of poverty requires not only an adequate income but also the development of assets, without which home and auto ownership, for instance, are not possible. According to Christy-McMullin and her associates (2010, 252), "This Catch-22 mentality, whereby the poor do not have access to the wealth accumulation they need to move out of poverty, contributes to the economic injustice and intergenerational poverty that is prevalent in this country."

The goal of the Individual Development Account (IDA) is to help people of limited means obtain and then accumulate assets in the form of personal savings (Lombe and Sherraden 2008). Usually, this takes the form of a structured social program that both matches an individual's savings and provides that person with information about the benefits of acquiring and maintaining savings or assets. IDAs have been shown to produce an increasing sense of social inclusion and economic participation.

Distributive Justice

One of the predominant principles of social welfare is **distributive justice**—relative equality in the distribution of society's social and economic resources (DiNitto 2005). Where inequalities exist, those who believe in distributive justice propose that government efforts be applied

Social empathy: The insights individuals have about other people's lives that allow them to understand the circumstances and realities of other people's living conditions.

Social inclusion: A sense of belonging to or membership in a group or a society.

Distributive justice: Relative equality in how social and economic resources are distributed in a society.

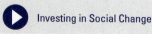 Investing in Social Change    Social Inclusion

to reduce or eliminate them. In political terms, this is the approach of liberals or progressives. On the other side, conservatives argue that inequality is not only necessary but essential for the maintenance of society—the functionalist perspective.

Appeals about fairness in public policy often focus on tax policy and whether the rich are paying their "fair share." Since the Reagan administration, the tax burden on the wealthiest Americans has been steadily reduced, on the grounds that low tax rates on the wealthy will increase the number of jobs. Jobs have not materialized, however, and at least three major recessions have occurred since Reagan left office—including the so-called Great Recession that began in 2007 (Mishel et al. 2013).

Another common argument for reducing taxes on the wealthy is that they pay the bulk of the income taxes collected by the federal government. This is true, but the reason is that they have very high incomes, and they have benefited the most from tax cuts over the past 30 years. At the same time, their after-tax incomes have escalated dramatically compared to everyone else's, with the top quintile's increasing more than 129% between 1979 and 2003, compared to 15.3% for the middle quintile (Kilty 2009).

Another tool of tax policy is the payroll or Social Security tax. Until recently this was a flat tax of 6.2% on earned income (with a temporary reduction in 2011 and 2012). A flat tax is an example of a *regressive tax*, one whose burden is greater on lower-income people. But the payroll tax is even more regressive because it has a cap, currently $113,700 for 2013. Income above the cap is not subject to the payroll tax, no matter how much higher that income may be. Table 2.5 shows how the Social Security payroll tax works. For incomes up to the cap, individuals pay a flat rate of 7.65% of their income. However, the maximum tax anyone pays is $8,698.05. If someone makes $125,000 in a year, that person still pays only that amount, which means his or her effective tax rate is no longer 7.65% but drops to 6.96% ($8,698/$125,000). If someone makes $250,000, his or her effective tax rate drops to 3.48% ($8,698/$250,000). As the table shows, the effective tax rate continues to shrink as income rises. The burden of the tax falls especially on those at the low end, since they must meet their basic expenses of housing, food, clothing, and transportation from a much smaller after-tax (or discretionary) income. Recently, Senator Sherrod Brown (D-OH) proposed legislation to eliminate the cap in order to make the payroll tax more equitable (Torry and Wehrman 2013).

Total tax burden is heavier on lower-income people who have less discretionary income, especially women and other minorities (Abramovitz and Morgen 2006). In addition to federal income and payroll taxes, they pay state income taxes, sales taxes, property taxes (which

TABLE 2.5 Social Security (Payroll) Tax at Various Income Levels, with Effective Tax Rate

Income ($)	Subject to Tax ($)	Actual Tax ($)	Less Paid ($)*	Effective Tax Rate (%)
20,000	20,000	1,530.00	0	7.65
50,000	50,000	3,825.00	0	7.65
70,000	70,000	5,355.00	0	7.65
95,000	95,000	7,267.50	0	7.65
113,700	113,700	8,698.05	0	7.65
125,000	**113,700**	**8,698.05**	**864.45**	**6.96**
150,000	113,700	8,698.05	2,776.95	5.80
250,000	**113,700**	**8,698.05**	**10,926.95**	**3.48**
500,000	113,700	8,698.05	29,551.95	1.74
1,000,000	113,700	8,698.05	67,801.95	0.87

NOTE: Lines in boldface show the maximum amount of income subject to the payroll tax in 2013.

*"Less paid" is the difference between what an individual paid and what he or she would have paid if Social Security taxes applied to total income.

SOURCE: Social Security Administration.

renters pay as part of their rent, but which owners can deduct from their taxes), and state and federal excise taxes and fees, such as on gasoline, cigarettes, and alcohol. In addition, deductions from income taxes for interest paid on mortgages benefit mostly the affluent, who realize about 60% of the $68 billion in savings this federal housing subsidy is worth. Those with incomes under $40,000 a year benefit little from such deductions (Kilty 2009).

Tax policy, then, has great potential for distributive purposes. While the principle of distributive justice is that we should reduce inequality, the policy question we face is whether we will reduce inequality or increase it. As it now stands, U.S. tax policy benefits those at the top while hurting those at the bottom (Marr and Huang 2012). Those who believe in distributive justice believe that that is unfair and needs to be changed. Taxing those at the top in a more equitable way would provide resources that could be used to help those at the bottom.

ASK YOURSELF: Do you feel that there is not enough social empathy? Why or why not? Why don't the poor save unless there are special programs to help them? What are your thoughts about distributive justice? What can we do to affect social policy? Should tax policy be used to reduce inequality?

SOCIAL CHANGE: WHAT CAN YOU DO?

 2.7 Identify steps toward social change in regard to poverty.

We all have a role in social change, yet taking action can be scary. What will our family and friends think? Will we get in trouble with school officials or the police? What can we actually achieve when the problems are so big? But we can take action; we all have the strength to change the way things are. Most of us probably won't live long enough to see all the changes we would like. But we can begin.

Many student groups are affiliated with national organizations and movements. The Social Welfare Action Alliance (SWAA), for example, is a national organization of progressive workers in social welfare with active chapters on a number of campuses and in local communities. SWAA works to make social change, sometimes in local communities and sometimes on a national level.

Some fraternities and sororities are service-oriented and stage various events to help their communities, from cleaning up local parks or neighborhoods to tutoring disadvantaged students in local schools. If your interest is the environment, you will likely find a student organization dealing with broad environmental concerns as well as specific local problems, such as helping low-income neighborhoods deal with toxic waste or other dump sites. Environmental racism affects many poor and near-poor neighborhoods.

Many colleges and universities now offer alternative activities during spring break and other breaks in the academic year, in which student volunteers take part in service immersion projects, working at homeless shelters, food and clothing banks, or soup kitchens, or participating in neighborhood cleanups.

Raising awareness is another meaningful action. Arranging screenings of relevant films, such as the documentary *Ain't I a Person?* (http://www.aintiaperson.com) about poverty in the United States, can help many see what they may never have experienced on a personal level. If a student group doesn't already exist that would be open to doing this, you might try creating one. Forums and panels where local experts provide information about community problems of poverty or inequality are also useful educational opportunities.

Many students who live off campus find themselves in low-income neighborhoods. What are the housing conditions like? Are food banks or clothing banks needed in your neighborhood? Is good-quality day care a problem? Is there a local public health clinic? Are community organizing groups or settlement houses active? Such agencies are always looking for volunteers.

Volunteers pitch in to feed the homeless at a Costa Mesa, California, soup kitchen. What acts of service can volunteers perform to deal with the social problem of poverty? If poverty has its origins in the social structure, what, if anything, can be done about it?

Other informal community groups may be trying to organize around such issues as renters' rights, quality of housing, availability of public transportation, and health care access. Unions sometimes provide legal or health services for their members and others in local communities.

Groups like Habitat for Humanity are looking for volunteers to help build new houses for low-income families. Other organizations, such as welfare rights unions and civil rights groups, may be more concerned with organizing people to challenge local, state, or federal authorities regarding the rights of the poor and near poor. Protest and social movements, such as the Occupy movement, exist in every community across the United States. Some may be large and highly visible, whereas others, such as Columbus Housing Justice (in Columbus, Ohio), are small but still provide essential services in their communities. Columbus Housing Justice works with residents of a housing project to help them organize around their legal right to live in good-quality, well-maintained public housing that meets local housing codes.

Members of state legislatures, city councils, and school boards sometimes engage in electoral politics from their commitment to public service. If you believe change can come through the electoral process, working with politicians who share your views is another option for bringing about change.

Change rarely happens as the result of the efforts of a solitary person. As individuals, we are limited in what we can do and whom we can reach. But when we join organizations—whether student clubs, local or national organizations like the NAACP or the Sierra Club, church-based groups, secular community groups, social service organizations, or professional organizations—we gain strength through numbers. Then we have the opportunity to try to change the world. What better legacy can we leave?

WHAT DOES AMERICA THINK?

Questions about Poverty and Class Inequality from the General Social Survey

 Turn to the beginning of the chapter to compare your answers to the total population.

1. Your standard of living will improve.

> **AGREE:** 54.9%
>
> **DISAGREE:** 28.3%
>
> **NEITHER AGREE NOR DISAGREE:** 16.8%

2. How do people get ahead?

> **HARD WORK:** 69.9%
>
> **LUCK OR HELP:** 9.8%
>
> **BOTH OF THE ABOVE:** 20.3%

3. Should government reduce income differences?

> **YES:** 60%
>
> **NO:** 40%

4. People should help the less fortunate.

> **AGREE:** 91.6%
>
> **DISAGREE:** 1.5%
>
> **NEITHER AGREE NOR DISAGREE:** 6.9%

5. In the United States, do you think we're spending too much money on assistance to the poor, too little money, or about the right amount?

> **TOO MUCH:** 62.8%
>
> **ABOUT THE RIGHT AMOUNT:** 26.5%
>
> **TOO LITTLE:** 10.7%

LOOK BEHIND THE NUMBERS

Go to **edge.sagepub.com/trevino** for a breakdown of these data across time and by race, sex, age, income, and other statuses.

1. More than 60% of respondents believe that we are spending too much money on assistance to the poor. What policy changes could that mean for the future?

2. Do you believe there is a relationship between education and an individual's response to the question concerning whether or not government should reduce income differences? Why do you think this is?

SOURCE: National Opinion Research Center, University of Chicago.

CHAPTER SUMMARY

 2.1 Explain how poverty, class, and inequality are social constructions.

Poverty, class, and inequality are complex and interconnected issues, and we cannot discuss one without the others. We often think of poverty in economic terms, but being in poverty means having deficiencies in necessary material goods or desirable qualities—not only in economic status but also in social, political, and cultural status. Class describes the positions in a society, usually based on a social, economic, and political hierarchy. We cannot have poverty or class without inequality, or differences in the quantities of scarce resources individuals or groups possess.

 2.2 Discuss patterns and trends in defining and measuring poverty.

We measure poverty in the United States using an absolute measure, an income threshold at or below which households or families are considered to be in poverty. During the 1960s and 1970s the U.S. poverty rate dropped, especially during the government's War on Poverty. Throughout the 1980s and 1990s it stayed relatively constant, but recently it has increased dramatically, to 15.1% in 2010. Poverty is also harsher now and more difficult to escape.

 2.3 Describe social class and mobility.

Social mobility is much more limited in the United States than most people believe, especially in comparison with social mobility in industrialized European countries. Those in the middle continue to fall further behind those at the top.

 2.4 Discuss income, wealth, and other dimensions of inequality.

Inequality in income and in wealth has been increasing steadily for the past 30 years. While the United States is one of the wealthiest nations in the world, it is also one of the most unequal. Inequality also exists in terms of race and ethnicity, gender, opportunity, and other social and political characteristics.

 2.5 Apply the functionalist, conflict, and symbolic interactionist perspectives to the problems of poverty, class, and inequality.

From the functionalist perspective, some positions in society (doctor, lawyer) are more valuable than others; the talented need to be motivated to make the sacrifices necessary to learn the skills to hold these positions; these positions deserve greater rewards than others; and there is a shared awareness and acceptance of social position. Symbolic interactionism focuses on interactions among individuals and the development of shared meaning. One approach here is labeling theory, originally applied to understanding why some groups become marginalized and learn to accept their disadvantaged position. It also led to the "culture of poverty" thesis, which argues that the poor learn a dysfunctional set of values that keeps them in poverty and thus are responsible for their own situation. Rather than arguing for a shared awareness and acceptance of social conditions, conflict theory focuses on power dynamics and the way those at the top of a social structure try to maintain their privileged position at the expense of those at the bottom. From this perspective, those at the bottom will try to change those conditions, often through social and protest movements challenging those in authority.

 2.6 Apply specialized theories to poverty and inequality.

We can apply many other theoretical frameworks to understanding poverty, class, and inequality. One is social empathy, which looks at why some people seem more able than others to identify with people in positions different from their own and how those who are less able to do so can be taught how to develop social empathy. Another is social inclusion, which is concerned with how being marginalized and stigmatized affects people's social connectivity. A last example is distributive justice, which is concerned with the relationship between perceptions of inequality and the principle of fairness.

 2.7 Identify steps toward social change in regard to poverty.

The Social Welfare Action Alliance has chapters that try to change the living conditions of the poor or broaden public awareness about poverty and other social problems. A wide variety of community groups also work to make change, such as settlement houses and organizations like Habitat for Humanity, which uses volunteer labor to build new homes for poor families. The important step is to get involved with groups. The actions of individuals are limited in their impacts, but when we put our energy together through groups and organizations, we can change the world.

DISCUSSION QUESTIONS

1. Where do ideas about poverty, social class, and inequality come from? How does one learn them and perpetuate them? How do sociologists describe the relationship between social class and inequality?

2. How does the dominant ideology in U.S. society, specifically, the focus on individual success over collective social good, contribute to the way we understand and explain poverty?

3. The United States uses a measure of absolute poverty derived from family size and the proportion of household income spent on food to determine if a household is poor or not. What would be an effective alternative measure for determining if a family is poor?

4. What are the social conditions today that have led to the increase in poverty in the United States, and how do these conditions make poverty more difficult to escape? Would a more complex understanding and definition of poverty make for a different description of how poverty has changed over time?

5. When asked to identify their own social class, most people in the United States claim to be members of the middle class. How does this self-identification contribute to the belief that social mobility is more possible in the United States than it actually is?

6. Social mobility was once more possible than it is today. What has changed to make it less likely that an individual will acquire a social class status higher than the one he or she was born into? What differences between the United States and Western European nations explain why social class mobility is more likely in the latter?

7. If we look at income as the measure of social class, what will we see and what will we miss? How is wealth different from income, and what are the implications of this difference for an understanding of inequality?

8. Why is inequality increasing? Why is inequality greater in the United States than in other Western nations? Along which lines is inequality increasing—only income and wealth? What about the other dimensions of inequality? Health? Education?

9. How did Marx and Weber understand social class differently? What are the resulting implications of their understandings of the class structure of society?

10. In what ways is poverty considered functional for society? How do social policies build on this perspective? What do other theories offer as alternative explanations for why poverty persists?

11. What aspects of our society make social empathy difficult? Is having social empathy more difficult for policy makers, as they are so often part of the upper classes?

12. How does distributive justice play a role in our existing social policies? What are the arguments against redistribution, and why do they have traction in U.S. society?

13. What motivates high school and college students to join efforts to alleviate poverty and help those who lack basic material goods? How do these individual efforts lead to larger social and political change?

KEY TERMS

absolute measure
  of poverty 29

alienation 44

class 35

culture of
  poverty thesis 43

dialectical
  materialism 44

distributive justice 46

extreme poverty
  neighborhoods 31

functionalist theory 40

income 38

inequality 37

Personal Responsibility
  and Work Opportunity
  Reconciliation Act
  (PRWORA) 42

poverty 29

poverty guidelines 30

poverty thresholds 30

power 35

Sharpen your skills with SAGE edge at edge.sagepub.com/trevino

A personalized approach to help you accomplish your coursework goals in an easy-to-use learning environment.

3 RACE AND ETHNICITY

Eileen O'Brien

Julie Dermansky / Corbis

The United States is becoming an increasingly multicultural society, with people from a variety of races and ethnicities. Given this great diversity, it is sometimes difficult for racial and ethnic groups to understand the ways of life of other racial and ethnic groups. How tolerant would you say you are of people from cultural groups very different from your own?

Investigating Race and Ethnicity: My Story

Eileen O'Brien

My eye-opener as a white girl dating across the color line in the American South drove my passion for racism education. As a sociology undergraduate at the College of William & Mary in Virginia, thousands of miles from Los Angeles, I saw students marching in protest after the not-guilty verdicts in the trial of the police officers accused of beating Rodney King. I experienced the college classroom as a space of transformative power and wanted to be part of that energy as my life's work.

As a doctoral student, I helped interview the proprietors of minority-owned businesses about the racism they faced in seeking government contracts. I've interviewed whites about their color-blind racism and Latinos and Asian Americans about their experiences with prejudice and discrimination (as reported in my book *The Racial Middle*, 2008). I've led workshops on confronting racism in local schools, churches, and community organizations. Recently, I've been studying hip-hop culture and race, and I'm investigating the U.S. military, both as a haven of racial open-mindedness and as the site of a persistent "brass ceiling."

A parent of two biracial children, I've been asked what I was doing with a dark-skinned baby. My son (who I'm told resembles Barack Obama) was delivered in a hospital where his own father could not be born because it did not serve black patients in the 1960s. My family is a constant reminder to me of how far we as a society have come and how far we have yet to go to achieve true racial equality.

LEARNING OBJECTIVES

3.1 Define race and ethnicity in the new millennium.

3.2 Discuss patterns and trends linking race and ethnicity to immigration, income, criminal justice, and health.

3.3 Apply the functionalist, symbolic interactionist, and conflict perspectives to social policy on racial inequality.

3.4 Apply specialized theories of racism.

3.5 Identify steps toward social change in racial inequality.

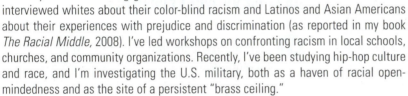

WHAT DO YOU THINK?
Questions about Race and Ethnicity from the General Social Survey

1. Do you feel discriminated against because of your race?

☐ YES
☐ NO

2. What is the racial makeup of your workplace?

☐ ALL WHITE
☐ MOSTLY WHITE
☐ HALF WHITE, HALF BLACK
☐ MOSTLY BLACK
☐ ALL BLACK

3. Should a homeowner be able to decide who they sell their house to based on race?

☐ OWNER DECIDES
☐ CAN'T DISCRIMINATE

4. Blacks overcome prejudice without favors.

☐ AGREE
☐ DISAGREE
☐ NEITHER AGREE NOR DISAGREE

5. Should the number of immigrants to America be increased, remain the same, or be decreased?

☐ INCREASED
☐ REMAIN THE SAME
☐ DECREASED

Turn to the end of the chapter to view the results for the total population.

SOURCE: National Opinion Research Center, University of Chicago.

WHITE RACIAL PRIVILEGE

In the aftermath of the Great Recession, when even a college degree cannot guarantee a job, many whites do not see themselves as particularly privileged. In fact, when Tim Wise first investigated his own background for signs of privilege, he knew his upbringing was humble at best. Wise grew up in a shabby Nashville apartment complex. His father was a stand-up comedian whose work was an irregular source of income. Even with his mother's job as a market researcher, there were times the family could have qualified for food stamps. However, Wise graduated from college, became the author of several successful books, and now lives a comfortably middle-class lifestyle. From his own research into the social problem of racism, he quickly discovered that many of his successes—while certainly due in part to his own hard work—were equally the product of white racial privilege.

Although she did not own a home, for example, his mother was able to use his grandmother's house as collateral to finance Wise's education at Tulane University. Due to open and legal discrimination in the real estate market, however, Wise's African American peers would not have had a relative with that kind of housing worth—no matter how hard or how long their families worked. In his book *White Like Me,* Wise reflects that his getting into college at all, and certainly his graduating, had everything to do with racial privilege.

Wise believes that white privilege and the double racial standards he witnessed among police allowed him to indulge in "boys will be boys" deviant behavior in college and emerge unscathed. When he interviewed scholar Michelle Alexander for his documentary film *White Like Me,* she said, "Part of white privilege is, to me, the freedom to make mistakes, and go on." Wise runs out of fingers on his hands to count all the breaks he has received as a white male in a persistently unequal society. He writes: "I am where I am today, doing what I am doing today, in large part because I was born white. I say this not to detract from whatever genuine abilities I may have, nor to take away from the hard work that helped my family in previous generations afford certain homes, but simply to say that ability and hard work alone could not have paved the way for me, just as they have not paved the way for anyone in isolation. . . . We always have help along the way, some of us a lot more than others. My help came color-coded, and that has made all the difference" (Wise 2008, 16).

DEFINING RACE AND ETHNICITY IN A NEW MILLENNIUM

 3.1 Define race and ethnicity in the new millennium.

Social scientists who study race, ethnicity, and immigration as social problems often document systematic patterns of racial and ethnic inequality. They also examine the way we develop racialized identities or create narratives or **ideologies** to rationalize and justify our positions. Ideologies can make it difficult for us to accept that racial inequality continues to exist centuries after slavery, in an age when it seems a person of color can do anything, even become president of the United States. Color-blind racism (Bonilla-Silva 2010; Frankenberg 1993), for instance, claims that race is irrelevant and racial discrimination is a thing of the past, so the problems minorities encounter must instead be the fault of individual inadequacies such as a poor work ethic. Clearly this view can hinder public policy efforts to curtail racial inequality. Yet as we'll see, **racism**—a system of advantage based on race (Tatum 2003)—plays a significant role in perpetuating racial inequalities in the United States and elsewhere.

Social scientists have reached near consensus that there is no biological basis for the separation of human

Ideologies: Belief systems that serve to rationalize/justify existing social arrangements.

Racism: A system that advantages the dominant racial group in a society.

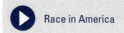 Race in America   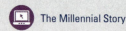 The Millennial Story

beings into "races" (Adelman 2003; Graves 2004). **Race** is now largely understood to be a social construction that uses certain traits—physical, religious, cultural, socioeconomic, or some combination—to organize people into hierarchical groups. Despite the lack of evidence that race exists, constructions of it are entrenched in social structures and organizations, leading scholars to view it as a "well-founded fiction" (Desmond and Emirbayer 2010, 21).

Asked to define race, students often begin with skin color. But suppose someone we classify as "white" (perhaps of Italian American descent) stands beside someone who identifies as Hispanic, and beside them is someone known as Asian American, a Native American, and finally a light-skinned African American. If we had them all hold out their arms, we might see that they all have exactly the same skin color. So clearly, there is something more to race.

Societies have also incorporated hair texture, nose shape, eye shape, religion, and socioeconomic status into their racial formulas. In Nazi Germany, Jews were considered a separate race, and for several decades the U.S. Census Bureau considered "Hindu" a race (Lee 1993). In some Latin American cultures, the saying "money whitens" reflects how mixed-race persons are perceived—the wealthier they are, the more likely they are to be considered "white" (O'Brien 2008). Under the "one-drop rule," a U.S. legacy that continued well after slavery's end, anyone identified with black ancestry (no matter how distant) was considered "Negro," even those with skin so light they could pass as white. Today, the U.S. Census Bureau considers Hispanic to be an origin, not a race, so those who identify as Hispanic must choose "some other race" on the census form. Various social and political arrangements thus shape what we know as race, but we treat it as a fixed biological reality rather than merely a human idea.

Race: A socially and politically constructed category of persons that is often created with certain physical traits (e.g., skin color, eye color, eye shape, hair texture) in mind but can also incorporate religion, culture, nationality, and social class, depending on the time, place, and political/economic structure of the society.

Ethnicity: Cultural background, often tied to nationality of origin and/or the culture practiced by the individual and his or her family of origin.

Symbolic ethnicity: An ethnicity that is not particularly salient in an individual's daily life and becomes relevant only at certain symbolic times or events.

Associated Press

Future U.S. president Barack Obama celebrates his high school graduation in Hawaii in 1979 with his maternal grandparents, Madelyn and Stanley Dunham. Many Americans identify themselves as multiracial, or as belonging to more than one race. Do you think that the racial tensions of the past will lessen as more people identify as multiracial?

How would you answer if asked, What is your ethnicity? The terms *race* and *ethnicity* often are used interchangeably, but **ethnicity** is a distinct concept that refers to a person's cultural heritage. Mary may be racially black, but ethnically Jamaican or Dominican. Bob may be racially white, but ethnically Irish or Italian. Cheryl may be racially Native American, but ethnically she is part of the Cherokee nation. Ethnicity is often connected to particular nation-states, but not always. It can also be associated with particular languages, surnames, holidays, clothing styles—anything we think of as culture. Further, ethnicity ranges on a continuum of strength from thick to thin, depending on how big a part ethnic practices play in everyday life (Vasquez 2011). Patrick O'Malley's name identifies him as ethnically Irish, but other than celebrating Saint Patrick's Day once a year, he may not take part in anything notably Irish during his daily activities. He participates largely in **symbolic ethnicity** (Gans 1979)—that is, ethnicity that derives more from the heritage of his distant relatives than from his own life.

Ethnicity affects the everyday lives of many, however. Social scientists who document racial segregation in housing or racialized poverty rates understand its influence, especially for Asian Americans and Hispanics. Japanese and Chinese Americans, on average, are much less likely to live in poverty than Vietnamese, Cambodian, Laotian,

▶ Who Is Black in America?

and Hmong Americans. Lighter-skinned Hispanics whose ethnicity is Argentinian or Peruvian are much less likely to be stuck in racially segregated housing than darker-skinned Dominican or Puerto Rican Americans (Desmond and Emirbayer 2010).

Notice that the way someone *personally* identifies racially or ethnically is only one piece of this puzzle. The way *society* perceives or categorizes that individual is equally, and sometimes more, influential. Karen may be ethnically Korean because of her parents and ancestors, but if she is adopted by a white U.S. family and lives the typical suburban lifestyle, she may feel culturally "white." However, in her daily life she is perceived as "Asian" and often stereotyped as such—people may call her names like "chink" and assume she cannot speak English well. Therefore, we refer to her race as Asian American (given that race is a social construction, and this is the societal response to her), but her ethnicity—the cultural heritage with which she identifies—is a bit more complicated. Some U.S. families with Korean adoptees incorporate Korean culture into their everyday lives, even visiting Korea on a regular basis. Other families choose to de-emphasize the ethnicity of foreign-born adoptees. But whether or not Karen feels connected to a Korean ethnicity, she cannot escape the racialized experience of being Asian in a nation that privileges whiteness.

Imagine that Karen was adopted by a family racially marked as "white" but culturally African American; they live in a black neighborhood, worship at a black church, eat "soul food," and listen to R&B music. If Karen exhibits black cultural styles and preferences at school, her teachers and peers may draw on racial stereotypes that depict African Americans (not Asian Americans) as academically unmotivated, and her school performance may suffer.

That we are even referring to a black culture here is significant, because many African Americans cannot trace their African nationality back to any particular ethnicity; a distinct African American culture emerged instead from rigid social divisions in the U.S. context. "Black" can also be both a race and an ethnicity. Some who are racially black but identify with Jamaican, Haitian, or Nigerian culture/ethnicity rather than African American may be more culturally similar to Europeans, due to European colonization. We can expect to find many ethnic groups within a particular race, but because any race is a social construction that varies with time and place, the ethnicities within it will vary too. Still, race and ethnicity matter when we analyze social problems, in part because social scientists have consistently measured disparities in social outcomes among racial and ethnic groups.

PATTERNS AND TRENDS

 3.2 Discuss patterns and trends linking race and ethnicity to immigration, income, criminal justice, and health.

Racial and Ethnic Groups

Social scientists' primary source of comprehensive data for the U.S. population by race, ethnicity, and Hispanic origin is the U.S. Bureau of the Census. Figure 3.1 shows two different questions from the census—race and Hispanic origin—and Table 3.1 shows the results. Why a separate question on Hispanic origin? As the Census Bureau says, "Hispanics can be of any race." According to 2010 figures, of the 16% of the U.S. population that is Hispanic, more than half (53%) identified as "white" and a third identified as "other" (36.7%) (Ennis, Ríos-Vargas, and Albert 2011). As Figure 3.1 shows, the 2010 form does not invite write-in answers about ethnicity from those who identify as white or black. Thus we have less census information on ethnicity for whites and blacks.

Whites still make up the numerical majority of the U.S. population. However, Hispanics have overtaken blacks as the largest minority group, and Asian Americans as a group grew by 43% between 2000 and 2010 (Humes, Jones, and Ramirez 2011). Asians and Hispanics are the two fastest-growing minority groups (see Figure 3.2).

For social scientists, the term **minority group** denotes not so much a group's size as the share of societal power and resources its members hold. Women are considered a minority group despite the fact that they represent a numerical majority of the population, because they lack the income and political power of men. People of color are the numerical majority globally, but they hold minority status within the United States due to their income, wealth, and health outcomes.

....

Minority group: A group that does not hold a sizable share of power and resources in a society; often the share of such resources is disproportionately small relative to the group's numerical presence in the overall population, and the group has a history of being systemically excluded from those resources.

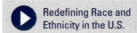
Redefining Race and Ethnicity in the U.S.

FIGURE 3.1 Race, Ethnicity, and Hispanic Origin Questions, U.S. Bureau of the Census Form, 2010

Please answer BOTH Question #5 about Hispanic origin and Question #6 about race. For this census, Hispanic origins are not races.

5. Is this person of Hispanic, Latino, or Spanish origin?

__ No, not of Hispanic, Latino, or Spanish origin

__ Yes, Mexican, Mexican American, Chicano

__ Yes, Puerto Rican

__ Yes, Cuban

__ Yes, another Hispanic, Latino, or Spanish origin
(Print origin—for example, Argentinian, Colombian, Dominican, Nicaraguan, Salvadorian, Spaniard, etc.)

_____

6. What is this person's race? *Mark one or more boxes.*

__ White

__ Black, African American, or Negro

__ American Indian or Alaskan Native *(Print name of enrolled or principal tribe.)* _____

__ Asian Indian   __ Japanese   __ Native Hawaiian

__ Chinese   __ Korean   __ Guamanian or Chamorro

__ Filipino   __ Vietnamese   __ Samoan

__ Other Asian *(Print race—for example Hmong, Laotian, Pakistani, Thai, and so on.)* _____

__ Other Pacific Islander *(Print race—for example, Fijian, Tongan, and so on.)* _____

__ Some other race _____

SOURCE: U.S. Census Bureau.

Though whites are a majority nationwide, in several U.S. states and about one-tenth of all counties, they are already a numerical minority. In 2010, Texas joined California, the District of Columbia, Hawaii, and New Mexico in having a "majority-minority" population—less than half the state's population is non-Hispanic whites. States approaching 50% minority populations in 2010 included Nevada, Maryland, Georgia, Arizona, and Florida (Humes et al. 2011, 19). Throughout U.S. history, anti-immigration sentiment has flared with fear and economic uncertainty, and law enforcement agencies in some states, including Arizona, have come down hard especially on Hispanic immigrants (Romero 2011). Minority population growth

Racialization: The process by which a society incorporates and clearly demarcates individuals who fit a certain profile into a particular racial group.

TABLE 3.1 Race and Hispanic Origin as Percentage of U.S. Population, 2010

Category	Percentage
White*	72
Non-Hispanic white	64
Hispanic/Latino (any race)	16
Black/African American*	13
Some other race*	6
Asian American	5
Native American	1

*These totals include Hispanics, who are also counted in the 16% figure, which is why the individual percentages add up to more than 100%.
SOURCE: Humes, Jones, and Ramirez (2011).

will intersect with race- and immigration-related social problems as these trends continue.

ASK YOURSELF: Beginning with the 2000 U.S. Census, respondents could choose to identify themselves as members of more than one race. When certain people identify as multiracial, why does society not see them as such? President Obama had a white mother and a black father, but he is often called the nation's first black president, while George Zimmerman (shooter of Trayvon Martin, 2012) has a white father and a Hispanic mother and has been variously described as white, Hispanic, or multiracial in the media. How does society decide whether persons of mixed-race parentage are white, people of color, or both, and is the logic consistent? What factors seem to affect these choices?

Immigration Patterns

The United States, often called a nation of immigrants, has regarded the influx of persons from other nations differently depending on the time and the immigrants' races or places of origin. The early settlers in North America were of Northern and Western European descent, followed by Germans in the 1830s, Irish in the 1840s, Chinese in the 1850s–1880s, and Southern and Eastern Europeans and Russian Jews in the early 20th century (see Figure 3.3) (Desmond and Emirbayer 2010). The Irish, Italians, and Jews were all subject to **racialization** in one way or another—caricatured with exaggerated features in popular

FIGURE 3.2 U.S. Population by Race and Hispanic Origin, 2012 and 2060 (projected)

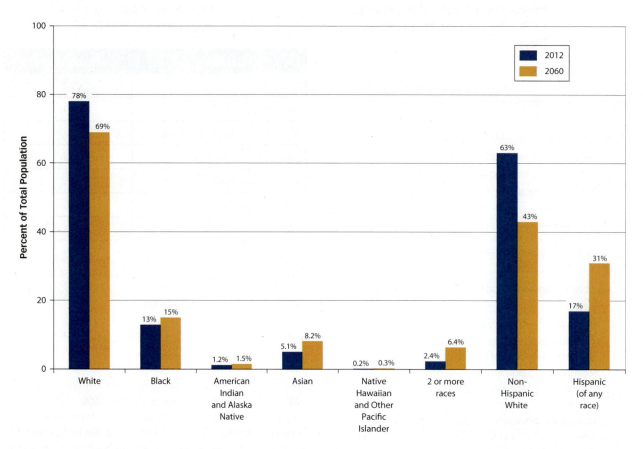

SOURCE: Based on data from the Census Bureau.

media—while signs posted by businesses saying things like "Irish need not apply" revealed the prejudice and discrimination of the period. The National Origins Act of 1924, which limited the number of immigrants allowed from each region of the world, is now regarded as among the more blatantly racist laws ever passed in the United States. With Asian and African quotas of zero, it clearly favored Northern and Western Europeans, yet it remained the basis of U.S. immigration law until 1965 (Healey 2009).

The 1965 Immigration and Nationality Act abolished racist quotas, and in 1980 the Refugee Act was passed. These reforms help explain why Hispanics and Asians are the fastest-growing U.S. groups (Desmond and Emirbayer 2010). Between 2009 and 2011, the most common country of origin for persons obtaining naturalized citizenship was Mexico, followed by India, China, the Philippines, Colombia, Cuba, Vietnam, Jamaica, Haiti, El Salvador, and South Korea (Lee 2012).

Whether we imagine an immigrant as a successful Cuban entrepreneur in Miami, a Korean student admitted to one of the nation's best universities, a struggling Mexican laborer,

or an impoverished Vietnamese refugee with no family in this country, we cannot overlook recurrent and troubling patterns. An average of one in three children of immigrants lives in poverty (Chitose 2005; Van Hook, Brown, and Kwenda 2004). Motivating supporters of the Dream Act is the worry that foreign-born children of illegal immigrants could spend their entire lives in the United States, graduate from high school, and even earn college degrees, yet be at risk for deportation to countries utterly foreign to them where they may have no connections. Even if they have college degrees, their employment opportunities are limited by their immigration status, and their socioeconomic status can remain as dismal as their parents' (Preston 2011).

The Dream Act

More than 2 million immigrant children in the "1.5 generation" (foreign-born but raised from childhood in the United States) could benefit from passage of the Development, Relief, and Education for Alien Minors Act, popularly known as the Dream Act. This legislation,

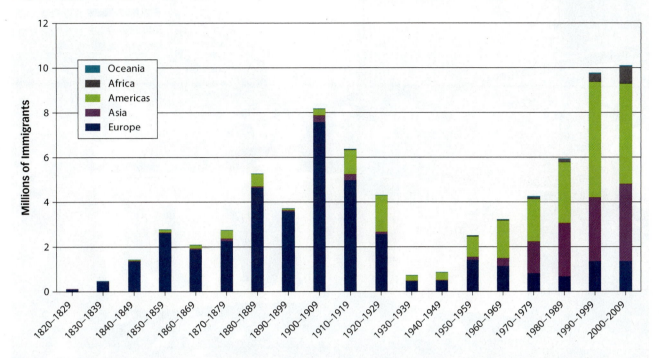

FIGURE 3.3   Legal Migration to the United States by Region of Origin, 1820–2009

SOURCE: Data from Table 2, Persons Obtaining Legal Permanent Resident Status by Region and Selected Country of Last Residence: Fiscal Years 1820 to 2012. *Yearbook of Immigration Statistics: 2012 Legal Permanent Residents.* U.S. Department of Homeland Security.

which Congress has not passed, would prevent their being deported, provided they meet certain requirements, and grant any who entered the United States before age 16 a six-year period during which they could either join the military or attend college, rights they are currently denied, provided they pass extensive background checks and refrain from all criminal activity.

Educators and military recruiters support the bill, but at this writing its passage remains uncertain. Critics say it goes too far; advocates of immigrant rights say it does not go far enough. In June 2012, President Obama signed an executive order freezing deportations of youth for two years, protecting about 800,000 children. But this temporary approach may not last beyond his term in office.

Income, Wealth, and Race

It is often difficult to disentangle class from race. When people speak of "at-risk" communities, "inner cities," and "welfare queens," without any mention of race, many imagine blacks and Hispanics (Bonilla-Silva 2010). While nonwhites in the United States are more likely to be poor and much less likely to be wealthy than whites, it is naive to assume that by addressing poverty we can also somehow eliminate racial inequality. Even among socioeconomically similar individuals, the U.S. white majority enjoys racial privilege in income and wealth. As Table 3.2 shows, among male high school graduates, a white non-Hispanic earns annual average income of $41,714, compared to $32,325 for blacks, $32,291 for Asians, and $31,668 for Hispanics. That's an advantage of nearly $10,000 per year for white males, even with the same education.

We see a similar pattern for college-educated folks. A white male with a bachelor's degree earns an annual average of $66,065, compared to a similarly educated black man's $51,504, an Asian man's $60,044, and a Hispanic man's $55,867. A black man has to earn an associate degree to make the same amount as a white male high school graduate, and a bachelor's degree to reach the earnings level of a white male with an associate degree. Only with postgraduate education do male Asians' earnings approach those of whites. Across every category, women earn substantially less than men, sometimes as much as $20,000 less per year, particularly women of color.

This is a cautionary tale against the **tokenistic fallacy**— the assumption that, because one or a few members of

Tokenistic fallacy: The common misunderstanding that when a small number of persons from a minority group become successful in a society there must no longer be racism in that society.

Jeff Topping / Reuters

Students march through downtown Phoenix, Arizona, in support of immigration reform and passage of the Dream Act. Many people who have entered the United States illegally see themselves as Americans and have contributed to U.S. society in various ways. Do you think these people should be given a chance to become U.S. citizens? What does it mean to be an American?

a minority group have achieved equality with majority counterparts, the group no longer experiences racial disadvantage or racism no longer exists (Desmond and Emirbayer 2010). Success stories notwithstanding, the data show a pattern of income inequality that lower levels of education cannot fully explain.

What, then, explains racial income inequality? Race discrimination in employment takes many forms, both overt and covert, and social scientists have used several innovative strategies to study it. Title VII of the Civil Rights Act of 1964 prohibits employment discrimination based on race, color, sex, religion, or national origin (U.S. Equal Employment Opportunity Commission 2009), so we might expect that since 1964 most such bias has operated covertly. However, recently settled civil rights cases reveal everyday situations where employees have been made to feel uncomfortable, denied promotions, or fired or never hired because of their race.

One Hispanic worker experienced so many racial/ethnic taunts that he finally complained to authorities. For retaliating against him, his employer, the township of Green Brook, New Jersey, had to pay him $35,000 in damages. The same year (2010), the Vanguard Group settled a suit for $300,000 by a black woman who was told she was not hired for lack of a training certificate, after it hired a white male without one (Pincus 2011). In the first example, the bias was overt—the employee knew he was singled out because of race. In the second example, the applicant needed to be a sleuth to uncover more subtle discrimination, because nonracial reasons were given to cover up the truth of why she was not hired.

A little critical thinking reveals that the number of cases of racial discrimination that are successfully fought in court far underrepresents the real extent of employment discrimination. Consider also that civil rights violations are just that—civil—and a victim's only recourse is to sue for monetary damages; there are no criminal penalties for racial discrimination. It takes time, energy, resources, and legal representation to file a successful lawsuit. Many victims simply take their talents elsewhere rather than invest in suing employers who discriminate against them. Thus social scientists cannot merely count successful court cases to reliably estimate the extent of

Immigration and Ethnic Diversity in Western Europe

The United States is not alone in struggling to manage resource and power imbalances in a diverse society. Germany, France, and the United Kingdom are among the top 10 nations in the world receiving international migrants (United Nations 2009), yet their unemployment rates for foreign-born residents are significantly higher than those for their native-born (Hansen 2012). Most of these immigrants are also European, but culturally distinct Muslims among them often draw anti-immigrant sentiment, and poor language skills and low earnings persist for two or three generations (Hansen 2012). Some analysts draw analogies between blacks in the United States and Muslims in Western Europe in that both suffer high unemployment and school dropout rates.

These and other economic concerns, coupled with fears among the public about security, crime, and terrorism, have raised *nativist* sentiment, which combines nationalism and xenophobia (fear of difference) to view the entry of foreign-born people as a threat to stability (Mudde 2012). Minority political parties can become viable forces in many European nations, and the Netherlands, Austria, Denmark, Switzerland, and Sweden have all seen a nativist political groundswell (Glazer 2010; Mudde 2012). Jimmie Akesson of the Swedish Democrats called immigration one of the most serious threats facing the nation and ran a campaign advertisement depicting Muslim women in burkas pushing strollers and overtaking an elderly white Swedish woman in a race to pension/welfare benefits (Glazer 2010). In Switzerland, once known for cultural tolerance, the Swiss People's Party (SVP) helped win 58% of the popular vote to ban minarets (spires) atop mosques, though Muslims make up less than 6% of the population (Glazer 2010; Papademetriou 2012). The SVP also advocated banning burkas; Belgium, France, and the Netherlands already have such bans in place (Mudde 2012).

▶ **THINK ABOUT IT:** Why is the perceived face of immigration for many Western Europeans a Muslim to be feared, when the data show the average immigrant is most likely from Europe?

A man walks past graffiti in central Athens. A major gateway for Asian and African immigrants trying to enter Europe, Greece has long struggled with illegal immigration. In the past few years, the problem exploded into a full-blown crisis as Greece sank into a deep recession, leaving one in four jobless and hardening attitudes toward migrants, who were blamed for a rise in crime. In what ways are Americans intolerant of immigrants coming into the United States?

Yannis Behrakis / Reuters

racial discrimination. They must adopt more innovative methods.

Because color-blind ideology makes some mistrust self-reporting about job discrimination, researchers have begun using experimental audit studies as an alternative. This methodology matches a group of testers on all relevant characteristics—résumé, qualifications, speaking patterns, and scripted answers for live interviews—except race (or gender). The researchers send the testers out to interview for jobs, find housing, or buy automobiles and then examine the results the testers report to assess whether black and white testers were treated differently. The federal government has long used this methodology to monitor housing discrimination (Feagin 2000), but it can also be used to explore employment discrimination, most notably hiring.

Economists Marianne Bertrand and Sendhil Mullainathan (2004) conducted a study in which they sent out 5,000 résumés in the Boston and Chicago areas, four to each employer. Two of the fictional job candidates (one white, one black) had weak work histories and experiences, while the other two (one white, one black) had stronger qualifications. As the title of their article reporting on the study suggests ("Are Emily and Greg More Employable than Lakisha and Jamal?"), they also wanted to test for the effects of names typically associated with

European Immigrants

TABLE 3.2 Median Annual Income of Year-Round Full-Time U.S. Workers by Race/ Ethnicity, Sex, and Education, 2009

Sex/Education	Median Annual Income ($)			
	White, Non-Hispanics	Blacks	Asians	Hispanics
Males				
Some high school	32,560	26,524	23,737	25,096
High school graduate	41,714	32,325	32,291	31,668
Some college	50,360	40,138	42,129	41,274
Associate degree	51,460	41,797	46,074	42,348
Bachelor's degree	66,065	51,504	60,044	55,867
Master's degree	80,362	61,101	89,472	72,180
Females				
Some high school	21,917	22,298	–	20,038
High school graduate	30,539	26,843	27,266	25,768
Some college	35,432	31,724	35,002	31,566
Associate degree	39,784	31,936	38,089	31,794
Bachelor's degree	46,863	46,224	51,089	44,085
Master's degree	61,034	55,875	72,415	55,187

SOURCE: US Census Bureau (2010).

blacks and whites. The applicants with white-sounding names got callbacks 1 in 10 times, while those with black-sounding names got callbacks only 1 in 15 times. Having a strong résumé had a bigger effect for whites (increasing callbacks by 30%) than for blacks (9%).

You might think a criminal record matters more than race, but sociologist Devah Pager (2003) found that a white male *with* a criminal record was more likely to get a callback from a prospective employer than a black male *without* such a record. By revealing employer preferences for hiring members of the majority/dominant group, these two studies help explain the racial differences in income shown in Table 3.2, as well as in unemployment rates—blacks have unemployment rates about twice as high as those of whites, especially in economic downturns. In June 2012, the white unemployment rate was 7.4%, while the black unemployment rate was 14.4% (U.S. Bureau of Labor Statistics 2012a) (see Figure 3.4).

Although these experiences happen in the context of economic institutions, sociologists consider them cases of **individual discrimination** (Yetman 1999) because individual employers are acting in discriminatory ways against individual applicants. However, **institutional discrimination**

is also partly to blame. Institutional discrimination happens as a matter of policy. It may not be racially intended, but regardless of intent, it has disparate impacts on members of minority groups. Consider the Baltimore City Fire Department, which raised eyebrows in 2004 by recruiting an entirely white incoming trainee class in a city that is 65% black. Although individual applicants were not turned away because of black-sounding names or appearances (individual discrimination), various institutional practices combined to result in a narrower pool of black applicants than white. Many rural areas where whites lived had volunteer fire department opportunities, where applicants gained insider knowledge that helped them achieve better entrance exam scores, and new positions were advertised internally and not predictably. Perhaps

Individual discrimination: Discrimination in which actors carry out their own intentions to exclude based on race, as opposed to being explicitly supported in doing so or directed to do so by an organization.

Institutional discrimination: Discrimination based in policies often written without overt racial language that nonetheless have disproportionately negative impacts on people of color.

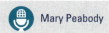 Mary Peabody

FIGURE 3.4   Unemployment Rates by Race, 2007–2012

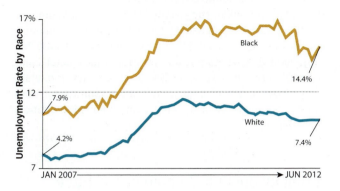

SOURCE: Bureau of Labor Statistics.

no one was thinking, "We'll do it this way so few black people will be able to apply successfully," but that was the result.

Sociologists who study racial economic inequality tend to look at either (1) dire unemployment and poverty faced by an inner-city black "underclass" whose members often do not complete high school or (2) glass ceilings faced by middle- to upper-class college-educated blacks. In her 2003 book *Race and the Invisible Hand*, Deirdre Royster reports on her study of 50 working-class men in Baltimore, in which she examined the overlooked middle between those two extremes. Royster studied some of the stronger students at a vocational and trade school she calls "Glendale" and found striking racial differences postgraduation. Among all male students, blacks were less likely than whites to be employed in the skilled trade in which they had been trained; blacks also earned less per hour, experienced fewer promotions, held lower-status positions, and experienced longer bouts of unemployment than whites.

Royster argues that lack of education or willingness to work hard cannot explain these outcomes. Rather, blue-collar networks function to privilege white workers and disadvantage blacks. White interviewees often talked about opportunities that "fell into their laps" because of family connections or contacts made in bars and other gathering places. Even white teachers at Glendale, who spoke highly of the black students, were much more likely to recommend white students for job openings. Black interviewees called the teachers "nice" and "fair," while whites called them instrumental in job placements—clearly a much more practical outcome than simply good grades.

Royster also explains that older men in hiring positions felt more comfortable recruiting employees who reminded them of themselves. She describes this dynamic

as the "invisible hand" because such networking privileges do not fit traditional definitions of racial discrimination. Nevertheless, they create white privilege and black disadvantage, however unintentional.

Institutional discrimination is often difficult to pinpoint because contemporary media and even courts of law focus our attention on discerning the "true intentions" of alleged discriminators, yet social scientists stress that the effect of discrimination remains harmful regardless of intent. We can think of racial discrimination as an iceberg, with the tip being cases such as that of the Hispanic worker in Green Brook, New Jersey—above the surface of the water, in plain view. Most racism occurs below the surface, and the untrained eye often struggles to identify it. This is due, in part, to our individualistic society's search for an individual to blame, when, in cases of institutional discrimination, such an individual does not exist.

An examination of wealth as opposed to income (see Chapter 2) further illustrates the consequences of institutional discrimination. It is difficult to save money when you are receiving less income than your counterparts; however, income differentials are only part of the story of wealth differences. As the PBS documentary *Race: The Power of an Illusion* explains, no statistic shows the extent of continuing racial inequality like the black/white wealth gap (Adelman 2003). The wealth of the average black family is one-tenth that of the average white family (Shapiro, Meschede, and Sullivan 2010) (see Figure 3.5). Sociologist Dalton Conley (1999, 26) used data from the Panel Study of Income Dynamics to show that this gap is "not a result of lower earnings among the black population. . . . [When income is controlled for,] at every income level, blacks have substantially fewer assets than whites." Conley also tested the hypothesis that blacks' savings rates are not as high as whites' (the "rampant consumerism" stereotype) and found no support for this explanation either.

Oliver and Shapiro (1995) coined the term "sedimentation of racial inequality" to describe how a history of institutional discrimination has reinforced the wealth gap. For example, when Social Security was established in 1935, it excluded virtually all blacks and Latinos— not by identifying specific racial groups as ineligible, but rather by excluding people in certain job categories, such as agricultural and domestic workers. As a result, this government-subsidized national savings and retirement program underserved nonwhites. Notably, however, a few exceptional nonwhites could "make it"—Madame C. J. Walker's hair-care products made her an 1880s black millionaire (Desmond and Emirbayer 2010). Institutional discrimination creates systematized patterns of racial exclusion, but it is not 100% exclusionary—it has always allowed for tokens. This is one reason some people find it difficult to realize that racism still exists.

FIGURE 3.5 U.S. Average Family Wealth by Race and Ethnicity, 1989–2010

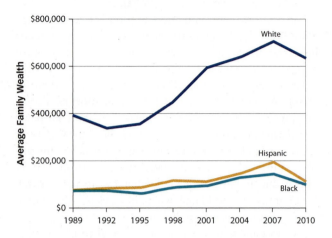

SOURCE: "The Racial Wealth Gap Is Not Improving," p. 3 in *Less Than Equal: Racial Disparities in Wealth Accumulation* by Signe-Mary McKernan, Caroline Ratcliff, Eugene Steuerie, and Sisi Zhang. The Urban Institute, April, 2013. Used by permission.

As Chapter 2 showed, wealth inequality is more severe than income inequality due to the intergenerational transmission of wealth. Homeownership forms the basis of most U.S. adults' net worth, but government policy on homeownership was racially biased for much of U.S. history. For example, the Federal Housing Authority played a major role in the sedimentation of racial inequality, particularly in the 1950s, when U.S. suburbia was created. Even now, the nest eggs that many middle- to upper-middle-class families depend on—the value of their homes—can be traced directly to parents' and grandparents' racialized experiences. Before the Fair Housing Act of 1969, banks and home insurance companies could legally charge higher mortgage and insurance rates for homes in black neighborhoods and exclude blacks from more prosperous white neighborhoods. This means, for example, that when President Barack Obama was attending college, many black families in the United States did not own homes with enough value against which to borrow to send their children to college.

Wealth makes the difference among various "middle-class" experiences. Even when their educations and incomes are comparable to those of their white counterparts, black middle-class families are often "asset poor" by comparison (Conley 1999), as are Asian American, Hispanic, and Native American families (Lui et al. 2006). Color-blind solutions like ensuring equal access to education and good jobs will not suffice—even with comparable income and education, racial inequality still persists.

ASK YOURSELF: When we think of media mogul Oprah Winfrey or President Barack Obama, it's often easy to succumb to a tokenistic fallacy. Why do so many people rely on this fallacy to assess the extent of racial inequality in today's society? What is so compelling about this argument despite its obvious flaws in logic? Color-blind racism uses cultural/nonbiological arguments to explain why more people of color aren't successful today. How might tokens like Winfrey and Obama be used to support this ideology?

Criminal Justice Outcomes and Race

Some researchers argue that a prison term is now a coming-of-age event for many poor nonwhite urban males, much as military service or college is for other young men. Among black males born from 1965 through 1969, 60% who did not graduate high school had been in prison by 1999 (Pettit and Western 2004).

Some argue that deindustrialization and the loss of jobs in urban centers led this jobless cohort to crime as a means of economic survival. Others point to the War on Drugs and differential enforcement of drug laws (1960–1990). Michelle Alexander (2012) contends that mass incarceration is the "new Jim Crow." The term **Jim Crow** refers to the system of racialized segregation that existed from the time of the Emancipation Proclamation of 1865 to the landmark civil rights legislations of the late 1960s. Blacks remained unable to own their own labor, testify as witnesses, obtain education equal to that available to whites, or vote (due to the Ku Klux Klan's reign of terror). Alexander argues that the criminal justice system is the major enforcer of Jim Crow today, locking predominantly nonwhites at the bottom of a racial caste system from which they cannot escape, even after they have completed their prison sentences. Pager's (2003) work supports this legal argument, demonstrating how the stigma of a criminal record disproportionately affects the lives of black adults.

On noting that prison populations consist mainly of blacks and Hispanics, some may assume that nonwhites are more likely than whites to commit crimes; even sympathetic observers who cite unfortunate lives of poverty as a cause may draw this conclusion. Sociological perspectives such as Robert K. Merton's strain theory (discussed

Jim Crow: The system of racialized segregation that existed in the United States from the Emancipation Proclamation of 1865 to the landmark civil rights legislation of the late 1960s. During this era, legal segregation was enforced by both law enforcement and white terror perpetrated by groups such as the Ku Klux Klan.

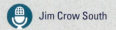
Jim Crow South

Bettmann / Corbis

The Memphis Sanitation Workers' Strike began on February 11, 1968, when some 1,300 black sanitation workers walked off the job to protest poor treatment, discrimination, and dangerous working conditions. Support for the black workers was divided along racial lines, and the strike became a major civil rights event, attracting the attention of the national news media and the Reverend Martin Luther King Jr. Why do you suppose the striking workers wore signs declaring "I *am* a man"?

in Chapter 11) may reinforce this view. However, most inmates in U.S. prisons are nonviolent drug offenders incarcerated for possession, not sale, despite yearly data from the U.S. Department of Health and Human Services showing nearly identical drug use rates for blacks and whites. When rates do differ, those for whites are slightly higher, particularly for cocaine and heroin (Alexander 2012). Thus evidence does not support the argument that more blacks and Hispanics are in jail because they commit more crimes.

We do know, however, that blacks and Hispanics are more likely than whites to be poor (Macartney, Bishaw, and Fontenot 2013), and socioeconomic status plays a role in criminal justice outcomes. A defendant who can hire a skillful and well-connected attorney might circumvent prison or probation altogether by negotiating for community service hours or treatment in a substance abuse program (Reiman 2001). A Seattle study found that white users of crack cocaine were more likely to be sentenced to

Manifest function: The intended positive outcome of social institutions or policies; the reason they were designed or created.

Latent function: An unintentional or unanticipated positive outcome of social institutions or policies.

Institutional racism: Policies and practices embedded in social institutions that consistently and disproportionately favor members of the dominant/majority group while systematically excluding/disadvantaging people of color.

Racial Profiling

treatment than to prison; only 25% were arrested, compared to 63% of black users (Beckett et al. 2005).

Most criminal cases are settled by plea bargain, not trial. Whether a defendant can afford bail has a major effect (Reiman 2001); those who cannot pay must wait in jail for a court date even if innocent. Thus they cannot assist in gathering evidence for their defense or provide for their families, circumstances that can make a plea bargain more alluring. A first-time offender may plead guilty and avoid jail, which in the short term returns him or her to job and family. In the long run, however, this person now has a criminal record. This disadvantages the person on the job market (particularly if he or she is not white), prevents him or her from voting, and makes avoiding prison highly unlikely for the individual in case of another arrest (Alexander 2012). While the intended or **manifest function** of plea bargains may be to facilitate quicker outcomes, their unintended or **latent function** is to create class and racial inequality in sentencing, even in identical cases. Sociologists find this feature of the system racist and classist because even if judges, juries, lawyers, and police officers are not prejudiced, racial inequality still results.

Institutional racism in the criminal justice system results not only from the way the court system is structured but also from the way policing works. First, it is easier for officers to patrol urban areas than it is for them to patrol in gated communities or other affluent areas, because in urban dwellings people are more densely packed and therefore criminal activities are more likely to occur outdoors, in easily visible spaces. Illegal activity is not more likely to occur in poorer areas; it is just easier to find. Second, police are rewarded for arrests that lead to convictions ("collars"), and they safely assume that poorer individuals (lacking high-quality counsel and vulnerable to plea bargain) are more likely to be convicted than affluent ones (Chambliss 1999). Thus, while individual officers may not be racially or class-biased, their workplace incentives make targeting poor people and minorities for law enforcement a logical choice to help them gain better pay and advancement.

Data from the 2005 Police Public Contact Survey reveal that black men were 2.5 times more likely to be arrested than white males and twice as likely to be searched during a routine traffic stop. Hispanic men were 1.5 times more likely to be stopped and three times more likely to be searched (Kansas State University 2012). Researchers in Minnesota who collected video data on 200,000 traffic stops in 2002 found that black, Hispanic, and American Indian drivers were more likely than whites to be stopped and searched. Searches of whites were more likely to uncover contraband, however, so the most serious offenders were not being targeted (Associated Press 2003).

Sometimes the "anything but race" (Bonilla-Silva 2010) argument emerges if a black officer targets an African American for surveillance. Is that racial profiling? **Internalized racism** happens when people of color buy into the dominant ideology and view themselves as inferior (Yamato 2001). Whether individual internalized racism motivates racial profiling or the structure of policing does so, officers of color are affected by the social forces supporting it. The study cited above that used data from the Police Public Contact Survey noted that the officer's race was not significant in the profiling patterns, demonstrating that institutionalized racism is powerful regardless of the individuals in the institution (Kansas State University 2012).

ASK YOURSELF: Analyze the complex interplay among public opinion, data on the causes of a social problem, and the creation of public policy about immigration. Why have politicians been successful at using the "immigrants cause crime" argument to garner support for recent changes in the law even when evidence suggests otherwise? Are average voters fact-checking their politicians? Is this even easy to do? What social changes might facilitate this process?

Health by Race and Ethnicity

In the United States, belonging to a racial minority increases a person's likelihood of being unemployed, of having lower income and net worth, of being subjected to racial profiling, and of spending time in prison. It also shortens a person's life. Health indicators such as mortality rates and mental health are positive for first-generation black and Latino immigrants, but these decline significantly by the third generation (Williams and Sternthall 2010). Asian Americans in counties that are predominantly white have markedly better life expectancy and lower death rates than all other Asian Americans (Murray et al. 2006). It is not biology that contributes to racial disparities in health. This is a profoundly *social* problem.

Some racial minorities live a "third world" existence in the United States in terms of health outcomes like mortality, life expectancy, and infant mortality. Table 3.3 shows that African American infants are more than twice as likely as white infants to die before reaching the age of 1 year, and an entire decade of life expectancy separates white females and black males. This table (compiled before President Obama's Affordable Care Act took effect) shows that nearly one-third of Hispanics lack health insurance coverage. But blacks and Native Americans are more likely than Hispanics to lag behind whites on life expectancy, death rate, and health care utilization (Murray et al. 2006; Williams and Sternthall 2010).

TABLE 3.3 U.S. Life Expectancy, Infant Mortality, and Lack of Health Insurance by Race and Ethnicity

Life expectancy (2009)	
White female	80.9
Black female	77.4
White male	76.2
Black male	70.9
Infant mortality rate* (2007)	
Black	13.3
American Indian	9.2
White	5.6
Mexican	5.4
Asian	4.8
No health insurance (2010) (%)	
Hispanic	30.4
Black	19.0
White	11.6

*Deaths before age 1 per 1,000 live births; black and white totals exclude Hispanics.
SOURCE: National Center for Health Statistics, Centers for Disease Control 2011.

Color-blind ideology might suggest that socioeconomic or cultural factors such as types of food, exercise rates, and other lifestyle behaviors explain these differences. However, sociological evidence points toward racial discrimination. In fact, some health disparities between blacks and whites manifest most strongly in the highest socioeconomic categories (Graves 2004). Figure 3.6 shows that the difference between whites and blacks in life expectancy at age 25 actually increases with education. Health researchers refer to a "diminishing returns" hypothesis, whereby African Americans receive fewer health advantages relative to whites with each step up in education (Williams and Sternthall 2010) because of increased stress from daily discrimination that contributes

Internalized racism: Feelings that occur in people of color when they buy into racist ideology that characterizes their own group as inferior—for example, when they believe that they themselves and/or other members of their group are not deserving of prestigious positions in society, or they assume that members of their group are prone to exhibiting stereotypical behaviors.

FIGURE 3.6 Life Expectancy at Birth, by Years of Education at Age 25, by Race and Sex, 2008

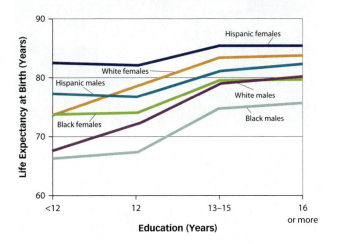

SOURCE: Reprinted with permission of the Center on Society and Health, Virginia Commonwealth University. *It Matters More to Health Than Ever Before*. Center on Society and Health Issue Brief, January 2014. Adapted from S. Jay Olshansky, et al., Differences In Life Expectancy Due To Race And Educational Differences Are Widening, And Many May Not Catch Up, *Health Affairs, 31*, no.8 (2012):1803-1813.

to hypertension and other health problems (Geronimus et al. 2006). Racial discrimination has as great or greater effect on blood pressure than smoking, lack of exercise, and diet combined (Krieger and Sidney 1996).

This is not to say that diet, exercise, and education do not matter, but we cannot ignore racial discrimination and segregation. Racial segregation has been linked to a host of health-related problems, due to its correlation with social disorder, concentration of poverty, lack of safe spaces for exercise, lack of infrastructure and trust in neighbors, and poor proximity to good-quality health care (Williams and Sternthall 2010). Native American reservations and predominantly black neighborhoods, regardless of income level, have also been routinely targeted for toxic waste dumping and strip mining (Desmond and Emirbayer 2010; Maher 1998), in a form of **environmental racism**. An area of Louisiana known as "Cancer Alley" holds more than a dozen toxic waste sites concentrated near poor, minority communities (Bullard 2000). Even the

Environmental racism: The process by which the dominant race in society is shielded from the most toxic/harmful environmental threats, while such health risks/hazards are located closest to neighborhoods where minority groups reside.

Race relations cycle: A pathway of incorporation into a host society that immigrants follow; includes four stages: contact, competition, accommodation, and eventual assimilation.

best diet, exercise, and health insurance offer little protection against the dangers posed by such sites.

Native American men have the highest rates of suicide, alcoholism, and death by automobile accident among all groups (Centers for Disease Control and Prevention [CDC] 2011). Because men in general are more likely to engage in risk taking, race and gender intersect in interesting ways in health. For example, while HIV diagnoses have been declining in white males, troubling increases in HIV are occurring among Native American and black men. Both black men and black women are more than twice as likely as their white counterparts to die from stroke and coronary heart disease as their white counterparts (CDC 2011). Thus, particularly for Native Americans, blacks, and Hispanics, racism can shave years, sometimes a decade or more, from a life. Better education and socioeconomic resources alone cannot remedy these problems.

USING THEORY TO EXPLAIN RACIAL INEQUALITY: THE VIEWS FROM THE FUNCTIONALIST, SYMBOLIC INTERACTIONIST, AND CONFLICT PERSPECTIVES

 3.3 Apply the functionalist, symbolic interactionist, and conflict perspectives to social policy on racial inequality.

Many theories seek to explain the causes of racial inequality. For particular groups or geographic areas, some may be more powerful explanatory tools than others. Below we sample work in the functionalist, conflict, and symbolic interactionist perspectives and a few others.

Structural Functionalism: Assimilation

Structural functionalism assumes that the structures of society function to produce stability. Thus in a healthy society, where resources and rewards are appropriately distributed, racial and ethnic minorities that are poorly integrated throw off the equilibrium. Minorities must therefore assimilate into the dominant culture and become like the dominant group.

Robert E. Park developed the theory of the **race relations cycle** to explain the incorporation of various groups (mainly Southern and Eastern European immigrants) into

Which Racism? Gender, Class, and Sexual Orientation Matter

It is impossible to review the data on racial inequality in income, health, criminal justice outcomes, and immigration policy without recognizing the ways gender, class, sexual orientation, and other forms of difference affect them. As Patricia Hill Collins (2008) argues, these statuses do not always interact with each other in predictable ways. While Hispanics are the racial/ethnic group most likely to be without health insurance in the United States, Hispanics do not face the same high infant mortality rates African Americans and Native Americans do (see Table 3.3). And at certain education levels, Asian American women are almost on par with or even outearn white women, but white men decisively dominate their Asian American counterparts (see Table 3.2).

Racial inequalities are conditioned not only by gender but also by social class. Particularly as measured by level of education, social class makes a tremendous difference in whether someone goes to prison (Pettit and Western 2004). Michelle Alexander (2012) argues that policies like affirmative action, aimed at reducing racial inequality in earnings, do little to help members of the black underclass, more of whom are under some form of correctional control today than the numbers of blacks ever affected by slavery in the United States.

The U.S. media identify "model minorities" to differentiate between highly skilled educated migrants like those from India (NBC News 2011) and unskilled laborers like those from Mexico, who conjure fear of crime even where data show it is unwarranted (Desmond and Emirbayer 2010). Ethnic hierarchies that emerge within racial groups often have a basis in social class (O'Brien 2008), leading some scholars to predict that certain ethnicities will soon be seen as "honorary whites" while others get left behind (Bonilla-Silva 2010).

Immigration policy debates also cannot ignore differences like sexual orientation. While marriage to a native-born citizen can smooth the path to citizenship, those in same-sex partnerships do not have access to those same privileges if their country does not legally extend them federal marriage benefits.

Despite the complexity of intersectionality, there is great potential for social change when women, labor unions, and LGBT rights groups unite with antiracist activists around issues such as police brutality, hate crimes, and immigration law to pursue legislation that benefits all groups.

Scott Houston / Corbis

These protesters of various races and ethnicities, many of whom are transgender, demand the end of profiling, harassment, and brutality at the hands of the New York City police. They also marched for access to restrooms, the legalization of all immigrants, prison reform, health care, and housing. Do you think that black, Hispanic, and Asian American gay, lesbian, and transgender people are doubly or triply stigmatized?

▶ **THINK ABOUT IT**

1. Is a woman always doubly disadvantaged if she is also a person of color? How are women affected differently from men by racism in criminal justice, income, and health?

2. Some propose that affirmative action policies in higher education should be altered to focus on social class and not race. Does your understanding of intersectionality suggest other options?

3. Social change advocacy groups fighting for racial equality are often diverse in class, gender, and sexual orientation. What strengths and challenges might such diversity present for these groups?

U.S. society (Park and Burgess 1924; Park, Burgess, and McKenzie 1925). He identified four steps in this cycle: contact, competition, accommodation, and eventual assimilation (Feagin and Feagin 2008). Park's model assumes that a society characterized by rules of law will eventually evaluate

Assimilation: The act of literally "becoming like" the dominant group of the host society; in its purest sense, when assimilation is complete an immigrant would be indistinguishable from the dominant group in society.

even a culturally different minority group fairly based on universal standards (Healey 2009). During the accommodation step, the minority group essentially proves itself by adapting as required, and the dominant culture rewards its efforts until **assimilation** occurs.

Milton Gordon (1964) proposed seven stages of assimilation and described the institutions and cultural practices that a minority group is required to accommodate for full assimilation; these are listed in Table 3.4. Gordon developed his theory before the 1965 Immigration and Nationality Act, based on groups whose members encountered fewer barriers to assimilation than the darker-skinned and refugee populations who came after. His "straight-line assimilation" theory has since been challenged and refined. Portes and Rumbaut (2006) describe **segmented assimilation**, whereby a minority group embeds itself within a particular segment of the host society on one of three pathways: assimilation to the white middle class (traditional), "downward assimilation" to an impoverished class (e.g., West Indian immigrants to New York City; Waters 1999), or a hybrid path combining economic/structural assimilation with strong cultural ties to the family of origin. In an increasingly globalized world, a second-generation immigrant following this third path might have advantages in a job market that values intercultural familiarity and bilingualism. Thus straight-line assimilation may not be the most functional in the modern context.

Herbert J. Gans (1992) proposed the idea of **bumpy-line assimilation**, in which individuals can have "thick" or "thin" ties to their parents' culture of origin. In her innovative study of three generations of Mexican American families, Jessica Vasquez (2011) identified two types that have "made it" by U.S. standards. Both were highly educated, fluent in English, and economically successful. "Thinned attachment" families had members who had intermarried and no longer spoke Spanish by the third generation, while "cultural maintenance" families were fluently bilingual, married within the group, and were visibly and culturally Hispanic. Vasquez's research shows that immigrants do not have to complete all seven of Gordon's stages to succeed in the dominant society.

Maintaining cultural heritage can even prevent some negative consequences of being a member of a minority

Segmented assimilation: A theory acknowledging different segments of the host society into which an immigrant can assimilate (not just the white middle class).

Bumpy-line assimilation: A modification of early 20th-century assimilation theory that challenges the traditional linear one-way progression; instead, immigrants can become full participating members of the host society while still retaining certain ties to their nationalities of origin (incorporates notion of "thick" versus "thin" ties).

TABLE 3.4   Gordon's Seven Stages of Assimilation

Cultural assimilation	Adopt language, surname, style of dress, foods, holidays/celebrations, leisure activities of the dominant group.
Structural assimilation	Fully participate in economic structure—labor market, unions—educational opportunities/training, and other voluntary associations of the dominant group.
Marital assimilation	Intermarry in significant numbers with the dominant group.
Identification assimilation	See self as "American" above other ethnic or nation-state identifiers.
Attitude-receptional assimilation	Adopt the stereotyping and prejudice of the dominant group, deflecting stereotyping of own group.
Behavior-receptional assimilation	Refrain from intentional discrimination.
Civic assimilation	Vote and participate in the political structures of citizenship; embrace values of the new nation-state.

group in an unequal society. Children who lack nurturing kinship ties, maintained primarily through shared language, have consistently lower educational and socioeconomic outcomes than fluently bilingual children (Fernandez-Kelly and Schauffler 1994; Rumburger and Larson 1998). Thus, while certain forms of assimilation are desirable, others may be detrimental, particularly in an increasingly global economy.

Policy Implications of Structural Functionalist Theories

Assimilation theory places the burden of avoiding racial/ethnic inequality on minority group members. Thus policy solutions that follow from it require immigrants to follow assimilation steps within a specified period. Citizenship tests that require English literacy and a basic knowledge of the U.S. political process reflect structural functionalist priorities, as do voluntary associations that teach English to immigrants and bilingual education programs. While nativist proposals to make English the official U.S. language have failed at the national level, many states have amended their constitutions to require "English only" (Costantini 2012), despite evidence that immigrants benefit from being fluently bilingual.

Franz-Marc Frei / Corbis

A mural in Philadelphia depicts black sociologist W. E. B. Du Bois. After graduating from Harvard, Du Bois conducted research in Philadelphia's black neighborhoods for his study *The Philadelphia Negro*. He is best known for *The Souls of Black Folk*, published in 1903, in which he famously proclaimed that "the problem of the Twentieth Century is the problem of the color-line."

Many critiques of assimilation theories rightly point out that even when minority groups play by all the rules, they face barriers erected by the dominant society (Feagin and Feagin 2008). We must look outside structural functionalist theory for a more complete understanding of the minority group experience.

Conflict Theory

Conflict theory sees society as characterized by an imbalance of power and resources that the group in control will maintain to its advantage. It is thus not the minority group that needs to be changed but rather the dominant/majority group's exclusionary practices, intentional or not. Conflict theorists study institutional discrimination and suggest ways to restructure society and public policy to reduce it.

In *The Philadelphia Negro* (1995), first published in 1899, W. E. B. Du Bois highlighted the poverty and unequal access to jobs and good health that African Americans experienced in the U.S. North. A highly educated black man (the first to receive a Ph.D. from Harvard) in the Jim Crow era, Du Bois understood firsthand that no matter how much a minority group attempted to assimilate, the majority group would resist its full inclusion. He demonstrated that unequal access to wealth and power gave blacks and whites vastly different understandings of the world and their place within it. The majority group's ideology, tied up in its sense of superiority, prevented it from seeing the disadvantaged group clearly. Du Bois (2003) used the concept of the **veil** to describe this psychic distance between unequal racial groups.

His idea of **double consciousness** suggests that blacks possess a dual understanding of (1) themselves as fully capable human beings and (2) the majority group's obscured perception of them. They use this double consciousness to negotiate their relationships with the majority group. For

Veil: A metaphor for the physical and psychic separation between the dominant/majority group and subordinate/minority groups.

Double consciousness: African Americans' ability to see themselves both as active agents with full humanity and as they are seen through the eyes of whites who view them as inferior and problematic.

Part II: Problems of Inequality

72

example, middle-class African Americans may adjust their dress and speech in commercial settings to minimize the possibility that they will be discriminated against during their transactions (Feagin and Sikes 1994). They know they are not going to shoplift, but they anticipate the assumptions of people in power and adjust their behavior accordingly. The modern concept of **white privilege** (McIntosh 2001)—whereby whites are unaware of the advantages their race gives them—owes an intellectual debt to Du Bois and his work. Other conflict theorists, such as Bob Blauner (1996), Andrew Hacker (2003), and Charles Gallagher (2003a), have examined how double consciousness creates "two worlds" that make it difficult to overcome majority group resistance to racial equality.

Contemporary conflict theorists also examine how rivalry between minority groups solidifies the dominant group's advantage. Edna Bonacich (1972) proposes a **split labor market theory** to describe how the (white) capitalist class divides the working class by race to keep workers from uniting to demand better pay and benefits. This analysis builds on Du Bois's concept of the **psychological wage**, whereby white capitalists simply make white workers feel superior to nonwhites to keep them from realizing they do not earn much more than the workers they look down upon (Roediger 1991).

In an analysis of Japanese Americans, Bonacich and Modell (1980) developed the concept of the **middleman minority** to show how certain minority groups act as a buffer when they are elevated in status (though not rivaling the majority), protecting the majority from those on the bottom and serving as a scapegoat for the aggression of those below. In 1992, blacks in Los Angeles were angry about their powerlessness in the aftermath of the so-called Rodney King trial, in which officers were acquitted of police brutality in the beating of King, an African American, and they

lashed out against the closest targets—Korean merchants in their own communities. From a conflict perspective, the tragedy of incidents like this is that the group on top, which makes money from both minority groups, remains unscathed. Middleman minority theory has implications for groups wanting to build alliances between minority groups in order to address their common interests.

Policy Implications of Conflict Theories

For conflict theorists, the focus is not on better training or cultural adaptation of minorities, but rather on adjusting institutional practices that have historically benefited whites so others who contribute to society can get greater access to society's benefits. Thus many related policy initiatives would benefit not only people of color but working-class and poor whites as well. Policy initiatives such as inheritance taxes and wealth creation accounts would seek to remedy the entrenched wealth inequalities that exist between whites and people of color (Oliver and Shapiro 1995; Conley 1999) but would also benefit asset-poor whites. Finding better solutions to drug offenses than prison would help to reduce the education and employment gap between whites and blacks. Conflict theorists since Du Bois have advocated for reduced criminalization of nonwhites, and groups like Books Not Bars and Let's Get Free, which organized a "Stop the Super-Jail" campaign in California, are multiracial coalitions that have worked toward this kind of change (Watkins 2005). The United States is unique among nations in that individual states can bar felons from voting indefinitely, even after release from prison. Not surprisingly, this disproportionately affects African Americans, who make up 40% of ex-felons (Enten 2012). Groups like Color of Change seek to address these and other racial power imbalances.

Symbolic Interactionist Theories

Symbolic interactionist theorists are interested in how the messages we internalize from socialization agents such as significant others and mass media affect the ways in which we, as everyday actors, maintain and perpetuate racial inequalities. Gordon Allport (1954) proposed the **contact hypothesis**, predicting that the more intergroup contact whites have with members of racial/ethnic minority groups, the less likely they are to be prejudiced. Empirical testing has consistently revealed that not just any contact is effective, however. Intergroup contact in which members are of equal status and contact is regular and sanctioned by an authority is more likely than other forms of contact to reduce racial prejudice (Jackman and Crane 1986).

The positive impact of interracial contact is increasingly muted by the dominance of color blindness, however. Cross-racial friends often ignore or joke about race, not

White privilege: The often unseen or unacknowledged benefits that members of the majority group receive in a society unequally structured by race.

Split labor market theory: The theory that white elites encourage divisions between working-class whites and blacks so that little unity can form between the two groups, preventing their coordinated revolt against exploitation.

Psychological wage: Feelings of racial superiority accorded to poor/working-class whites in the absence of actual monetary compensation for labor.

Middleman minority: A racial group that is not in the majority but is held up by the majority as a "positive" example of a minority and is used by those in power to pit minority groups against each other.

Contact hypothesis: The prediction that persons with greater degrees of cross-racial contact will have lower levels of racial prejudice than those with less contact.

Racial Prejudice

The Myth of the "Model Minority": An Interview with Rosalind Chou

Many adults in the United States perceive Asian Americans as the "model minority" and even admire and covet this group's perceived educational and economic successes.

In your book The Myth of the Model Minority *(Chou and Feagin 2008), what types of stigma, discrimination, and prejudice did your young interviewees report facing?* My interviewees each faced racial prejudice and discrimination that ranged from racialized verbal taunts and mocking to violent physical attacks. In some cases the discrimination was subtle and respondents felt excluded or invisible. Other times, they were overtly targeted for their race or ethnicity.

How did they manage the stress these incidents caused them, and in what ways did society's ignorance about Asian Americans make it difficult for them to manage that stress more effectively? Most of the Asian Americans I spoke with were ill equipped to manage the stress. Often their families preferred to not talk about it, discuss their feelings, or "rock the boat." They did not want to come off as "problem minorities." The stigma associated with African Americans and their collective resistance against racial oppression seemed undesirable to many Asian Americans, especially if they were first-generation Americans. Strikingly, many respondents suppressed memories, chose to turn off emotions, and/or internalized the mistreatment, with

alarming effects on emotional and psychological growth. On the rare occasions that my respondents did seek help, they were often misunderstood or brushed aside. Some who went to their teachers when they were bullied in school were asked to "toughen up." One student sought help from a school counselor to deal with overwhelming stress, but the counselor was more interested in the student's academic achievement, stereotyping her as a "model minority."

In your analysis, what are some of the root causes of anti-Asian racism and negative Asian American mental health outcomes as social problems? The root cause of anti-Asian racism is that racism is embedded in the foundation of our society. We are not in a "postracial" society. Anti-Asian sentiment continues because Asians are still stereotyped as "others," "foreign," and "alien." The "model minority" stereotyping has been used to create a hierarchy of people of color and Asians, and Asian Americans sometimes believe the stereotype, making it more difficult to form racial coalitions. Racial discrimination, stigma, and prejudice have solidly documented negative outcomes on mental health. Combined with a lack of services, reluctance to talk about racial discrimination within the Asian American community, and internalization of negative stereotypes, these effects produce alarming rates of depression and suicide for Asian Americans.

Sociologist Rosalind S. Chou is a native of Florida, where her parents settled after emigrating from Taiwan in the 1970s. She is coauthor, with Joe R. Feagin, of *The Myth of the Model Minority: Asian Americans Facing Racism.* She is also the author of *Asian American Sexual Politics: The Construction of Race, Gender, and Sexuality,* and of the upcoming *Yellow on a White Campus.*

What concrete solutions can be put into place to deal with anti-Asian racism and its victims more effectively? Multiracial coalitions are imperative to move forward. Many Asian Americans are not aware they share experiences of racial discrimination with each other and with other groups. We have to continue to educate all our citizens about our racial past and present. Awareness and understanding of the racist foundation of the United States will help combat the inequality and disparity related to discrimination. Asian Americans must also develop counternarratives to the racialized stereotypes that exist.

▶ **THINK ABOUT IT:** How can even seemingly positive stereotypes and prejudices (whether aimed at Asian Americans or other groups) create unintended negative consequences?

considering it a topic for serious exploration and leaving the white friend with the same beliefs as before (Korgen 2002). The contact hypothesis was also proposed before the expansion of mass media and the Internet. To the extent these venues substitute for face-to-face contacts, they can have both positive (O'Brien and Korgen 2007) and negative (Gallagher 2003b) effects on users' racial outlooks.

Symbolic interactionist theories examine how racial messages affect individual performance and how people view themselves. Claude Steele (1997; Steele and Aronson 1995) coined the term **stereotype threat** to describe how minorities' self-concepts and performance on tasks are harmed by societal stereotypes that portray them as less competent than other racial groups. Steele's test subjects were told either that their group tended to perform well on a test or that their group tended to perform poorly. Individual test scores reflected what subjects were told. Similarly, we saw above that internalized racism occurs when people of color come to believe they deserve mistreatment (Yamato 2001) or accept stereotypes about their own group (as when black police officers racially profile other people of color).

The symbolic interactionist perspective is also useful for considering the **costs of privilege** for the majority group. For example, despite substantial material advantages, whites lose out on the interactional benefits of being bicultural/multicultural and able to get along with diverse groups—a marketable skill in the global economy. Internalized superiority can also sometimes encourage excessive risk taking; whites are more likely than other racial groups to binge drink and to die from drug-related causes (CDC 2011). The advantages of racial privilege far outweigh the costs on the macro level, but looking at the micro level reveals the complex ways privilege and advantage interact in everyday lives. This vantage point also allows for optimism, because change can begin if we simply start the process of unlearning the detrimental aspects of our own racial/ethnic conditioning.

Policy Implications of the Symbolic Interactionist Perspective

The symbolic interactionist perspective suggests the need for more equal-status interracial contact with

Stereotype threat: The tendency of individuals to perform better or worse on standardized tests depending on what they have been told about their group's abilities.

Costs of privilege: Experiences that members of the majority group may miss out on due to racial isolation and limited worldviews.

Spatial mismatch theory: The theory that the movement of jobs away from central cities in the postindustrial era left many African Americans without employment.

open and honest dialogue about race and racism. Educational settings are ideal, and the earlier the better. Advocates of antiracist education face challenges in getting schools to do more than just "celebrate multiculturalism" or promote diversity in token ways. Publishers such as Rethinking Schools are trying to make this happen (Kailin 2002). Symbolic interactionist research also underscores the need to revamp media portrayals of people of color. Internalized racism is difficult to avoid when the news media are more likely to present African Americans in deviant criminal roles than as "Good Samaritan" figures (Feagin 2000). The NAACP and the Anti-Defamation League try to raise awareness about media biases, but consumers must exercise their buying power and send a message to media executives that they will not tolerate racially biased programming.

ASK YOURSELF: What are some common media messages about racial/ethnic minorities, such as Hispanics, African Americans, Asian Americans, and Native Americans, and how might internalized racism based on such stereotypes play out specifically for these groups in real life?

SPECIALIZED THEORIES ABOUT RACIAL INEQUALITY

 3.4 Apply specialized theories of racism.

Other theorists have approached racial inequality from more innovative vantage points, such as those discussed below.

Spatial Mismatch Theory

William Julius Wilson's (1978, 1987, 1996, 2009) research highlights the conditions faced by the worst-off African Americans. His **spatial mismatch theory** shows how deindustrialization left blacks without employment in the inner cities. With factory work, a man with barely a high school diploma could still do quite well for himself, but in the global transition from industry to a service/information-based economy, jobs moved to the suburbs, where many poor blacks could not afford to live. Such jobs also require education beyond high school, which poor blacks could also not easily afford. Further, Wilson shows how federal government housing and transportation policies upended previously

Iesha Leflore and her children, Jonquaill, 1, and Joreill, 5, sit on a bed, the only furniture they can sit on in their apartment in East Orange, New Jersey. Black and Hispanic single mothers are among those hit hardest by poverty in the United States. Do you think that the mainstream media ignore their situation?

stable low-income black communities, changing family structure and culture. The **feminization of poverty** occurs because of black men's joblessness rather than because of any characteristic of black culture. It becomes a rational choice for poor women to avoid marriage when pregnant (Edin and Kefalas 2005), yet children with one parent face disadvantages compounded by low socioeconomic status. And as long as work disappears, they will confront the same conditions as their parents, as the cycle continues (Wilson 1996).

Answering those who blame black culture for racial inequality, Wilson points to structural and economic factors. While many solutions flowing from his work as an adviser to the federal government and advocate for raising the minimum wage seem to mirror those of conflict theory (they benefit the poor as well as minorities), Wilson's focus is less on an oppressive dominant group and more on impersonal structural forces. Thus he believes his public policy framing will be more palatable to those weary of race-specific policies.

Color-Blind Racism

We have seen above that **color-blind racism**—the tendency to focus on "anything but race" to explain racial inequality—has actually made it increasingly difficult to address the problem. Bonilla-Silva (2001, 2010) innovatively combines quantitative data with in-depth interviews to demonstrate how whites avoid the appearance of being racially prejudiced on standard survey instruments, while in more candid interviews they reveal

troubling points of view conforming to a popular ideology increasingly resistant to antiracist public policy. He identifies four means by which people resist efforts to reduce racial inequalities: (1) abstract liberalism (blindly trusting that nation-states lean toward equity without any government interference), (2) cultural racism (blaming black culture's assumed values in regard to work ethic, education, and family structure), (3) naturalization (assuming people are hardwired to avoid other races, so public policy can achieve nothing), and (4) minimization (assuming people of color are exaggerating claims of discrimination). Common personal stories ("I didn't get that job because of a black man") and rhetorical strategies ("Some of my best friends are black") underlie this powerful racial ideology.

Bonilla-Silva also hypothesizes that as U.S. Hispanics and Asian Americans become a more sizable presence, some will be incorporated as "honorary whites" to support color-blind ideology. Other empirical analyses support this prediction (Yancey 2003; O'Brien 2008). Bonilla-Silva (2010, 267) calls on white people to "begin challenging color-blind nonsense from within" and to avoid language of "equal opportunity," demanding equality of results instead. Rather than avoiding "bad neighborhoods" and poor-quality schools, he asserts, whites should remain there and join people of color in refusing to accept substandard resources and conditions. Bonilla-Silva advocates **antiracism**, the active struggle against racism. As Tatum (2003) explains, antiracists are different from both active racists and passive racists (who allow racism to continue without confronting it). Antiracists actively walk against the flow of racism—obviously quite a challenge, yet necessary to combat the inertia of color blindness.

ASK YOURSELF: According to sociological definitions, is it "racist" for white families to move out of the city in pursuit of a better quality of education for their school-age children? What are some antiracist alternatives such families might be able to pursue instead? What would need to change to encourage more whites to do so?

Feminization of poverty: The trend of poverty being concentrated disproportionately in female-headed single-parent families.

Color-blind racism: A type of racism that avoids overt arguments of biological superiority/inferiority and instead uses ideologies that do not always mention race specifically.

Antiracism: The active struggle against racism in everyday life (micro) and/or institutionally (macro).

Identify steps toward social change in racial inequality.

There are a number of ways you can get involved in working to solve the social problem of racial inequality. Using **micropolitics**—that is, simply challenging friends and coworkers in everyday conversation—you can make a difference on a larger scale than you might expect (Pincus 2011). In addition, you might get involved with one or more of the many organizations devoted to addressing racial inequality, a few of which are described briefly below.

 ## Color of Change

Color of Change is an Internet-based organization founded in 2005 after the race and class atrocities of Hurricane Katrina's aftermath became known. Its e-mail alerts and blogs organize petitions to pressure organizations and political leaders to act on specific issues of concern to African Americans and their allies. This group favors many of the solutions discussed in the conflict theory section of this chapter. For instance, Color of Change asked its members to contact their legislators to end "stop and frisk" procedures and low-level marijuana arrests in Manhattan that disproportionately target people of color (and poor whites). It also exposes states and organizations trying to curtail voter registration among people of color, the very old, and the very young. You can sign up for e-mail alerts and participate in many petitions and citizen actions at http://www.colorofchange.org.

 ## National Association for the Advancement of Colored People (NAACP)

Founded in 1909, the NAACP is the world's oldest civil rights organization; one of its cofounders was sociologist W. E. B. Du Bois. Anyone can become a member. This organization takes stands on practically

Micropolitics: An individual's use of his or her own personal sphere of influence to affect social change.

Mario Tama / Staff / Getty Images

College students on the NAACP's "Vote Hard" bus tour encourage black residents of a housing project in Selma, Alabama, to vote. Why is it important to vote? How can voting in presidential elections help minority communities?

all the problems of racial inequality discussed in this chapter—health care, environmental racism, criminal justice, economics, and even the symbolic interactionist concern of media representation—and issues action alerts to encourage members to contact their legislative representatives. You can visit the website to join the national organization (http://www.naacp.org), but there are also more than 2,000 local chapters and an active college/youth division, so it is easy to get involved in regular meetings and actions.

 ## National Immigrant Solidarity Network (NISN)

Like Color of Change, National Immigrant Solidarity Network is a relatively new organization, founded in 2003, and does much of its work through e-mail action alerts to members. It is easy to get involved just by pointing and clicking (http://www.immigrantsolidarity .org). However, NISN also has four local offices in New York, Chicago, Los Angeles, and Washington, D.C., and it organizes marches and days of action in these and other areas. NISN supports the Dream Act and rejects militarization of the border, for example. Joining is a way to stay informed on issues of concern to immigrants, to get educated on your rights during a police stop, and to take action if you choose.

Community-Based Literacy Organizations

Most immigrants to the United States desperately want to learn English, yet there are not enough opportunities for them to do so with their grueling work schedules. Many adult literacy centers around the country are nonprofit, volunteer-based organizations looking for tutors to help immigrants with English-language skills as well as with civics education needed to pass citizenship tests. Using the Literacy Information and Communication System's literacy directory (http://www.literacydirectory.org), you can locate such a community-based center near you. Many towns and cities also have nonprofit community resource centers for refugees, where English-language and citizenship skills are taught by volunteers. If you are interested in hands-on social service and volunteer work, this would be a great place to start.

WHAT DOES AMERICA THINK?

Questions about Race from the General Social Survey

Turn to the beginning of the chapter to compare your answers to the total population.

1. Do you feel discriminated against because of your race?

    YES: 7%

    NO: 93%

2. What is the racial makeup of your workplace?

    ALL WHITE: 22.6%

    MOSTLY WHITE: 45.1%

    HALF WHITE, HALF BLACK: 26%

    MOSTLY BLACK: 5.6%

    ALL BLACK: 0.7%

3. Should a homeowner be able to decide who they sell their house to based on race?

    OWNER DECIDES: 26.5%

    CAN'T DISCRIMINATE: 73.5%

4. Blacks overcome prejudice without favors.

    AGREE: 69.5%

    DISAGREE: 15.8%

    NEITHER AGREE NOR DISAGREE: 14.7%

5. Should the number of immigrants to America be increased, remain the same, or be decreased?

    INCREASED: 13.9%

    REMAIN THE SAME: 40%

    DECREASED: 46.1%

LOOK BEHIND THE NUMBERS

Go to **edge.sagepub.com/trevino** for a breakdown of these data across time and by race, sex, age, income, and other statuses.

1. When respondents were asked about the number of immigrants to America, do you think whites and nonwhites gave similar responses? Why or why not? Examine the responses to the immigration question by whites and nonwhite. How do the data vary from your prediction?

2. Examine the gender data for the question about homeowners' ability to decide who they sell their homes to. Is there a difference in responses between males and females? Why do you think that is?

3. More than 20% of respondents reported working in exclusively white workplaces. Do you see this as a social problem? Explain.

SOURCE: National Opinion Research Center, University of Chicago.

CHAPTER SUMMARY

 3.1 Define race and ethnicity in the new millennium.

"Race" is a social construct that varies across time and place—it is a human invention tied to relationships of power and privilege and continues to have measurable consequences for minority groups worldwide. Groups that were once smaller minorities are now growing. Individual identities and experiences do not always fit neatly into socially defined racial and ethnic categories.

 3.2 Discuss patterns and trends linking race and ethnicity to immigration, income, criminal justice, and health.

Racial discrimination exists at both individual and institutional levels and can be overt or covert, intentional or unintentional. Large gaps in income, rates of imprisonment, and health exist between whites (the majority group) and people of color (minority groups) that are not attributable to differences in education, socioeconomic status, or criminal activities alone. Sociological evidence points us away from color-blind explanations for these differences and toward an examination of institutional structures that produce these racial inequalities. Immigration policies, the ways in which residents of the host society treat immigrants, and global political and economic changes affect racial and ethnic relationships in any society. The United States has had periods of openness and acceptance of immigrants as well as periods of repression and suspicion of them.

 3.3 Apply the functionalist, symbolic interactionist, and conflict perspectives to social policy on racial inequality.

Structural functionalists assume smoothly functioning societies characterized by balance, equilibrium, and meritocracy, and regard the assimilation process as the key for reducing racial/ethnic tensions. Assimilation theories better explain the experiences of pre-1965 European immigrants, however, and immigrants in today's globalized world often fare better when they both assimilate and retain some cultural traditions. Rather than focusing on minorities' efforts to assimilate, conflict theorists analyze the structures created and sustained by the dominant group that forestall equality, such as keeping workers divided by their own interethnic and interracial tensions. The policy solutions conflict theorists advocate thus benefit minorities as well as poor and working-class whites. Symbolic interactionists look on a micro level, explaining how racial ideology is socialized into the dominant group and internalized by minority groups, who may begin to believe in their own supposed inferiority.

 3.4 Apply specialized theories of racism.

Wilson's spatial mismatch theory identifies impersonal structural forces, like global shifts from industry to service economies, as the major cause of contemporary racial inequalities. Bonilla-Silva's focus on color-blind racism demonstrates how we rationalize racial inequality in the social structure by convincing ourselves that a certain degree of separation is "natural," and/or that minorities bring on their own problems. These seemingly nonracial ideologies perpetuate racism and prevent voters from supporting policies that explicitly address racial inequality.

 3.5 Identify steps toward social change in racial inequality.

Organizations such as Color of Change, the NAACP, NISN, and local literacy and other groups in need of tutors all offer opportunities to get involved. Simply practicing the micropolitics of change by opening up conversations about racial/ethnic inequalities and their sociological roots with friends, family, and coworkers can also have an indirect yet powerful impact.

DISCUSSION QUESTIONS

1. How do we understand race in a time when the genetic evidence fails to support a belief in distinct human races and when so many people see racism as a problem of the past? What benefits are there to learning to see race as a social construction instead of a biological reality?

2. Ethnicity is generally related to culture, but which culture? The culture of one's ancestors or of one's parents? How might one resolve a conflict between one's own personal identity and how one is seen by society?

3. How and why do social scientists use the term *minority group* differently than it may be understood by the general population? Why is an increasing population not significant enough to tip the balance of power between groups?

4. How do policies like the Dream Act and affirmative action deal with inequalities that exist in relation to race, ethnicity, and/or national origin? How do such policies fail to address inequality as it intersects with other factors, such as health and income? What can be done to address the disparities at both individual and societal levels?

5. How does the conflict perspective explain individual and institutional discrimination? How is this explanation different from those offered by the other perspectives?

6. Given the differences in drug use by race, and the different rates of arrest, conviction, and incarceration, how would a sociologist explain the differences between groups? How do these differences affect opportunities for education and employment differently for whites than for people with minority racial or ethnic identities?

7. What are the implications for policy change of Wilson's spatial mismatch theory? How would one begin to make changes and improvements if Wilson is correct about the underlying causes of higher rates of poverty among blacks?

8. What examples of color-blind racism do you see in individuals, institutions, and public policies? Think about the ways in which race is not discussed or explicitly mentioned, but that increase racial disparities and perpetuate stereotypes. How could someone challenge color-blind racism and engage across racial divides in meaningful ways?

9. How might a society solve or address problems like environmental racism and disparities within the criminal justice system? What is already being done that will improve health and income opportunities for minorities?

10. How can becoming familiar with concepts such as double consciousness, white privilege, and the myth of the model minority prompt individuals to social action?

KEY TERMS

antiracism 76

assimilation 70

bumpy-line assimilation 71

color-blind racism 76

contact hypothesis 73

costs of privilege 75

double consciousness 72

environmental racism 69

ethnicity 57

feminization of poverty 76

ideologies 56

individual discrimination 64

institutional discrimination 64

institutional racism 67

internalized racism 68

Jim Crow 66

latent function 67

manifest function 67

micropolitics 77

middleman minority 73

minority group 58

psychological wage 73

race 57

race relations cycle 69

racialization 59

racism 56

segmented assimilation 71

spatial mismatch theory 75

split labor market theory 73

stereotype threat 75

symbolic ethnicity 57

tokenistic fallacy 62

veil 72

white privilege 73

Sharpen your skills with SAGE edge at edge.sagepub.com/trevino

A personalized approach to help you accomplish your coursework goals in an easy-to-use learning environment.

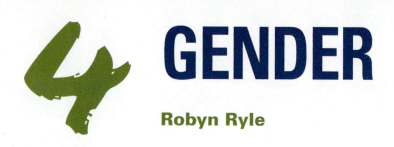

4 GENDER

Robyn Ryle

Filippo Monteforte / Staff / Getty Images

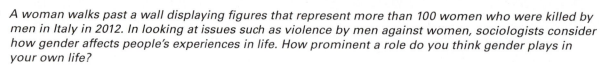

A woman walks past a wall displaying figures that represent more than 100 women who were killed by men in Italy in 2012. In looking at issues such as violence by men against women, sociologists consider how gender affects people's experiences in life. How prominent a role do you think gender plays in your own life?

Investigating Gender: My Story

Robyn Ryle

Growing up, I was that girl in your class who didn't like it when people told her what to do—the nerd who spent a lot of time at the back of the room trying to figure out how popularity worked. It's no surprise that I became a sociologist interested in gender inequality.

In my first sociology course as an undergraduate at Mills aps College in Jackson, Mississippi, I learned that all that analyzing I'd been doing in school was called sociology. As a sociology/English double major with a women's studies concentration, I was fascinated by how gender permeates all areas of social life. After getting my Ph.D. at Indiana University, I started teaching my own course on the sociology of gender.

I've been teaching that course and others at Hanover College in Indiana for the past 10 years and have transformed my teaching experiences into a textbook, *Questioning Gender: A Sociological Exploration* (2012). At Hanover, I helped institute our new gender studies major and have added Introduction to Gender Studies to my list of classes. As often as anyone will listen, I like to give talks in nonacademic settings to help people understand gender from a sociological perspective.

LEARNING OBJECTIVES

4.1 Define gender inequality.

4.2 Describe the study of gender as a social problem.

4.3 Identify gender problems on college campuses today.

4.4 Apply the functionalist, conflict, and symbolic interactionist perspectives to the problem of gender inequality.

4.5 Apply queer theory's interdisciplinary perspective to gender inequality.

4.6 Identify steps toward social change in gender inequality.

WHAT DO YOU THINK?
Questions about Gender from the General Social Survey

1. It is better for men to work and women to tend home.

   ☐ AGREE
   ☐ DISAGREE

2. Most women really want a home and kids.

   ☐ AGREE
   ☐ DISAGREE

3. Women are not suited for politics.

   ☐ AGREE
   ☐ DISAGREE

4. Are you for or against the preferential hiring of women?

   ☐ FOR
   ☐ AGAINST

5. The mother working doesn't hurt children.

   ☐ AGREE
   ☐ DISAGREE

▶▶ Turn to the end of the chapter to view the results for the total population.

SOURCE: National Opinion Research Center, University of Chicago.

EVERY NIGHT IS GIRLS' NIGHT OUT

On college campuses across the country, groups of students head out to the local bars and clubs in the evening for some well-earned relaxation and fun. They squeeze into dark booths with pitchers of beer and cheesy music playing over the sound of laughter and conversation. Everything is just as you would imagine at a bar near a college campus—except all the people at the table are women, and every night is ladies' night (Williams 2010).

If you are or have recently been a college student, this scenario probably doesn't surprise you. The ratio of women to men on campuses across the United States has reversed since the 1960s, when men outnumbered women, and has shifted further since the 1970s, when their numbers were about even (Williams 2010). Women now make up around 54% of those attending U.S. colleges and universities. According to the 2010 U.S. Census, 29.6% of women had college degrees, compared to 30.3% of men. By comparison, in 1970 only 8.1% of women had a college degree, compared to 13.5% of men (U.S. Census Bureau 2012c).

Some worry that the current gender imbalance may result in gender discrimination *against* women in college admissions. In 2009, the U.S. Commission on Civil Rights started an inquiry into discrimination against female college applicants at private liberal arts colleges (Jaschik 2009). In an op-ed piece in the *New York Times* in 2006, the dean of admissions at Kenyon College confessed to using an informal affirmative action policy in favor of men, because 55% of applications at the time were from women (Britz 2006). Other private colleges have since admitted to lowering admission standards for men in order to correct a rising gender imbalance (Allen 2010). They believe both women and men will be reluctant to attend institutions with greatly skewed gender ratios.

Is the gender imbalance at many U.S. colleges and universities a social problem? Is gender itself a social problem, or only the inequality that results from gender? Is it even possible to separate gender from gender inequality, or is inequality the inevitable result of distinguishing people as men and women?

What kinds of assumptions about gender and sexuality underpin the conversation about gender imbalance on college campuses? These are some of the questions we'll explore in this chapter, but first we need to understand exactly what we're talking about when we speak of gender.

DEFINING GENDER INEQUALITY

 4.1 Define gender inequality.

Do you wake up in the morning and think about your gender as a pressing social problem? Do you think about it much at all? If you live safely within the boundaries of what your particular society defines as "normal" for gender, you probably have the luxury of not thinking a lot about it in general, let alone as a pressing social problem. If you are a person who, in the words of Kate Bornstein (1994), is "let down" by the gender system, you probably *do* think of gender as a social problem that needs to be solved. In fact, all of us—*everyone* in society, regardless of where we are in or outside the gender hierarchy—can see gender as a social problem, and we can argue that at some point the gender system has let us down. What exactly does that mean?

First, what is **gender**? A common definition says gender is the social meaning layered on top of our sex categories. In this way of thinking, there are two discrete sex categories: you can be female or you can be male; you cannot be both. Once we are assigned a sex category, usually at birth, the way we are treated in the world and the way we think about ourselves is shaped by it. Look around a hospital nursery at all the babies with their pink or blue hats and blankets. There's nothing about the anatomy of a baby boy that requires him to wear a blue hat, but already gender has become important: in our culture at this time it tells us that male babies should wear blue and female babies pink. In other times and other places, male and female babies would wear completely different colors. It is precisely those social variations that make up gender—the social meanings we impose onto biological reality.

....
ASK YOURSELF: Can you think of other ways in which we begin to treat infants and young children differently based on sex category?
....

....
Gender: The social meanings layered on top of sex categories.

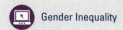

Massimo Listri / Corbis

Why do you think that many girls say pink and lavender are their favorite colors? Why is pink considered a feminine color? How do companies market products like toys and clothes differently to boys and girls?

When we say the colors associated with male and female babies vary across time and culture, we are acknowledging that gender is socially constructed. That is, like many aspects of social life, gender is a concept created and modified over time and across cultures to produce a certain account of reality. Whether it has an underlying biological reality based on sex is less important than that we *believe* in that underlying reality. If we believe gender is real, then our beliefs make it real through our actions and assumptions. When a baby is born and placed into the male sex category and a blue hat is put on his head, everyone will treat him in a particular way based on belief in the underlying reality of gender. Because of the way we treat this blue-hatted baby, he probably will, in fact, grow up to be masculine, making our belief in his gender become reality.

Supporting the argument that gender is socially constructed are the many variations in the ways different cultures understand gender. In the United States men don't generally wear skirts, but in Scotland and India they do. In the United States, once women reach puberty, we expect that certain parts of their bodies should be free of hair—usually their legs and armpits, but also their faces—and that their breasts should be covered and supported by bras. But in other parts of the world, women neither

Sexual dimorphism: The belief that there are two discrete types of people—male and female—who can be distinguished on the basis of real, objective, biological criteria.

Intersexed: Born with some range of biological conditions that make sex category ambiguous.

shave nor wear bras. These and other variations in the meanings assigned to biological sex categories convince us that gender is socially constructed.

This seems fairly straightforward, but some scholars go further and argue that not only is gender socially constructed, but biological sex is as well. From this perspective, our belief that there are two distinct types of people in the world—males and females—is just a belief, called **sexual dimorphism**, and does not represent objective reality. As evidence, scholars cite the ways in which sex has been defined differently across times and places. Today in the United States, sex assignment happens at birth and is largely in the hands of medical professionals. An infant with a penis longer than 2.5 centimeters is assigned to the male sex category, while an infant with genitalia shorter than 1.0 centimeters is assigned to the female sex category. In the gray area between 1.0 and 2.5 centimeters, doctors have to decide where to assign that infant. This is what happens to many **intersexed** individuals, those born with anatomical or genetic ambiguity about their biological sex. Their existence is important evidence for the social construction of sex, because it suggests there are not just two kinds of bodies but a continuum of different kinds (Fausto-Sterling 2000).

In ancient Greece, sex was seen as existing along a spectrum, with men at the top and women and other lesser beings, like dwarves and slaves, at the bottom. Females were viewed not as wholly different sorts of persons from males, but rather as inferior versions of males. The ancient Greeks had knowledge of external and internal anatomy, but their beliefs about sex categories led them to understand male and female anatomy differently. While we think of a penis and a vagina as two different sexual organs, the ancient Greeks saw them as the same organ; a vagina was merely an inverted penis. Ovaries and gonads were the same organ in slightly different versions. This is just one of the many ways cultures have made sense of our underlying biological reality. The wide biological variability that exists is too complex to be summarized in just two categories, suggesting that sex categories are socially constructed just as gender is.

Today, many who identify as transgender hope to expand the ways we understand both gender and sex categories. Transsexuals seek to change their biological sex categories, but increasing numbers don't want to simply go from biologically male to biologically female (or vice versa). Some have selective sex reassignment surgery, choosing perhaps to have their breasts removed but keep their female reproductive organs intact. Others elect to live as a different gender without any surgery, simply changing the way they dress and identify themselves. Some reject the attempt to live as "male" or "female" altogether, suggesting we should be free to live outside the boundaries of

🎙 The New American Man

A Fulani man from the Wodaabe subtribe makes a facial expression in Ingall, Niger. Wearing elaborate makeup, feathers, and other adornments, Fulani men perform dances and songs to attract young women seeking husbands. White eyes and teeth are signs of male attractiveness among the Wodaabe. By Western standards, do these men look feminine to you?

sex category and gender assigned by society. In these ways, transgender individuals demonstrate the fluidity of sex and gender as categories from the past and into the future.

FEMINISM, MEN, AND THE STUDY OF GENDER AS A SOCIAL PROBLEM

4.2 Describe the study of gender as a social problem.

While gender is certainly not the only social problem we can regard as socially constructed, it is unique in also being an identity to which many of us are deeply attached. What parts of your personality, behaviors, beliefs, and feelings are due to your gender, and what parts exist independent of that identity? For some theorists, as we'll discover below, every part of us and every interaction we have is touched by gender. They believe ungendering ourselves might be impossible. Would it be at all desirable?

It's easier to see gender as a social problem if we focus more specifically on gender inequality. Gender is an important source of social identity for many people, meaning it forms an important basis for how we think about ourselves as people. It is also a category that creates and sustains inequality. **Gender inequality** is the way in which the meanings assigned to sex and gender as social

categories create disparities in resources such as income, power, and status. In most—if not all—societies, those categorized as female are at a disadvantage relative to those categorized as males. There are many explanations for these inequalities, some of which we explore below. But first we should consider the relationship between gender as a concept and gender inequality.

ASK YOURSELF: Do you think it is possible to ungender ourselves? Would getting rid of gender as a social category be a good thing for society? If you believe that both sex and gender are socially constructed categories, can they take very different forms? John Stoltenberg (2006) imagines a society in which sex hormones become "individuality inducers" and sex organs like the penis and clitoris are seen as different forms of the same basic anatomy. What would gender look like in such a society, or would it exist at all?

For some, gender is a social category that makes distinctions between people, but these distinctions do not necessarily have to lead to inequality. Saying that women are more nurturing and men are less so is a distinction, but we can keep gender as a social identity and still reduce gender inequality by valuing nurturing as much as we value qualities considered masculine, like rationality and aggressiveness. Women can go on being more nurturing and men more rational; we just have to make sure we place equal value and importance on the qualities seen as masculine and feminine.

On the other hand, some argue that every time we make a distinction, an inequality is already implied. It is not just that women are seen as more nurturing than men; nurturing, if it reflects gender categories, will always be considered inferior to whatever qualities are seen as masculine. From this perspective, the whole point of gender as a social category is to distribute power by creating and sustaining inequality. Getting rid of gender inequality then requires getting rid of gender as a social category and all the distinctions it entails.

These two perspectives lead in different directions when we examine gender as a social problem. The first suggests we can address gender inequality separately from the concept of gender as a whole. Gender is not a social problem in and of itself; rather, gender inequality is. But if gender distinctions always imply gender inequality, as in the second view, then gender itself *is* the social problem. Gender and inequality go hand in hand, and if we want to reduce inequality, we must attack the problem at its root—the existence of gender. Keep these two perspectives and their implications in mind as we further explore gender as a social problem.

Gender inequality: The way in which the meanings assigned to sex and gender as social categories create disparities in resources such as income, power, and status.

 Feminists

Some leaders of the women's movement pass a torch that was carried on foot from New York City to Houston, Texas, for the 1977 National Women's Convention. Among the marchers, front, from left to right: tennis star Billie Jean King, in blue shirt and tan pants; former U.S. congresswoman Bella Abzug, wearing her trademark hat; and feminist writer Betty Friedan, in red coat. How would you compare the women's movement of the 1970s with that of today?

One sure sign that enough people in society consider something to be a social problem is the development of a social movement to solve it. Feminism is both a body of knowledge and a social movement that addresses the problem of gender inequality, seeking to end it through a wide variety of approaches If women are usually seen as the disadvantaged group, it makes sense they would be motivated to end gender inequality. Yet some of the examples discussed in this chapter suggest that men might sometimes be disadvantaged by the gender hierarchy as well.

ASK YOURSELF: Pick one of the perspectives on the relationship between gender and gender inequality described above. Imagine you are engaged in a debate to defend this perspective. What evidence might you use in support of your position? Now imagine what evidence you might use for the opposite perspective.

For example, men in the United States do not live as long on average as women, are more likely to die a violent death, and commit suicide at higher rates than do women. Is it acceptable for men to trade more power in society for shorter and more violent lives? Some men who label themselves feminists point to the ways in which the demands of masculinity damage men, even as it may benefit them in other ways. Masculinity leads men to engage in risk-taking behaviors that can put their lives and health in danger. It can make meaningful and intimate relationships with other men and women difficult by coloring these relationships with the constant need to demonstrate dominance and control. The power that comes with being at the top of the gender hierarchy seems to carry a definite price for men.

For these reasons, most scholars and activists who consider gender a social problem see it as a social problem for women *and* men. The gender system lets all of us down, though often in very different ways.

LOOKING AT GENDER ON COLLEGE CAMPUSES

 4.3 Identify gender problems on college campuses today.

There aren't many areas of our daily lives that aren't gendered in some way. You may consider a fraternity party a very gendered setting and the classroom not so much, but sociologists would argue that gender is important in both settings. In this chapter, we'll focus on just a few subjects as they relate to the world of education.

Is Getting Good Grades Girly? Masculinity and Academic Success

As the opening vignette to this chapter suggests, women seem to be doing a lot better than men when it comes to higher learning in the United States (see Figure 4.1). There are some variations in the trend; the gap between women and men is smaller for Ivy League schools, where women and men often make up about equal proportions of the student population (Williams 2010). Gender gaps in enrollment are greatest in the southern United States and lowest in some western states, such as Colorado, Nevada, and Utah (Mather and Adams 2007). Along racial and ethnic lines, the smallest gap between men and women across all racial and ethnic groups is for Asian Americans; 65% of college-age Asian American men were enrolled in college or grad school in 2010, compared to 67% of Asian American women (see Figure 4.2). Men with lower incomes also attend college at much lower rates than do men with high incomes (Jaschik 2010).

Is this gender gap in higher education a social problem? Some women, like those at the University of North Carolina, as described in a *New York Times* article, have concerns about their dating prospects as heterosexual women (Williams 2010). Men's dating prospects are considerably brighter. Women have become more aggressive in pursuing men on some campuses and, by necessity, more tolerant of men's infidelity. "If a guy is not getting what he wants, he can quickly and abruptly go on to the next one, because there are so many of us," explained one woman senior at the University of Georgia (Williams 2010). Other observers of the new gender reality on college campuses suggest the imbalance has contributed to the dominance of "hookup culture," characterized by one-night encounters rather than long-term relationships.

FIGURE 4.1 **Undergraduate Enrollment in the United States, 1970–2020 (projected)**

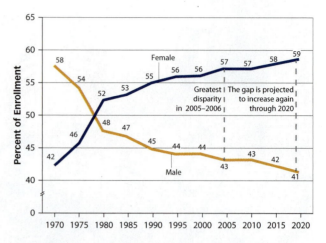

SOURCE: National Center for Education Statistics, "The Condition of Education 2011."

Though both public and private institutions face the problem of gender imbalance, it is illegal under Title IX of the Education Amendments of 1972 for public institutions to use gender in making admission decisions. When the Board of Trustees at the University of North Carolina found that the entering first-year class in 2006 would be 58% female, board members asked whether it was time to consider affirmative action for men; under current law, that would be illegal (Jaschik 2006). Private institutions are exempted from Title IX in the area of admissions, so it is legal for private colleges like Kenyon to use gender in making admission decisions. But is it right, or is it one of the ways in which gender seems to let everyone down, women *and* men?

Studies of gender and academic success suggest that it might be becoming increasingly "uncool" for boys from specific social backgrounds to do well in school. In urban settings, black and Hispanic girls are more likely than boys in those groups to go to college, to earn higher grades, and to aspire to higher-status occupations (Carter 2005; Lopez 2003; Mickelson 2003; Morris 2008). Boys in these urban neighborhoods may de-emphasize academics due to a combination of race, gender, and lack of economic and social capital that leads to a perception (often based in reality) of blocked opportunities.

Examining how gender works simultaneously with other identities such as race, social class, and sexuality is a good example of an **intersectional approach** to the study

....

Intersectional approach: A sociological approach that examines how gender as a social category intersects with other social statuses such as race, class, and sexuality.

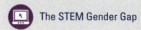 The STEM Gender Gap

FIGURE 4.2 Percentage of 18- to 24-Year-Olds Enrolled in College or Graduate School by Race/Ethnicity in the United States, 2010

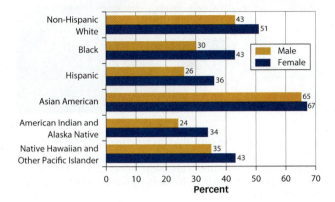

SOURCE: U.S. Census Bureau, 2010 American Community Survey.

of gender. As the research on rates of college enrollment and graduation suggest, the experience of being a man or a woman is not the same in white, middle-class neighborhoods as it is in poor, minority, inner-city areas. When we discuss gender inequality, we must take into account the differences that exist when gender intersects with other social categories.

ASK YOURSELF: Make a list of all the other social identities you occupy in addition to your gender. How do these identities affect your experience of being gendered? How might your experience of gender be different if you changed some of these other social identities?

In his study of white boys in a rural high school, Edwin W. Morris (2008) found that, like their urban counterparts, the boys felt that doing well in school is something for girls. The girls were consistently at the top of their class in all areas of academic achievement. Though many teachers and the girls themselves acknowledged that the boys were smart, the boys were largely uninterested in making the effort required to do well academically. A boy named Preston was consistently described as the "smartest kid in the school," yet his grade point average was only 3.15 (Morris 2008, 736). Preston explained the academic underperformance of boys by saying, "Well it's almost stereotypical for boys around here to not do anything and the girls to do stuff. But like everybody is trying to get the

Hegemonic masculinity: The type of gender practice that exists at the top of the hierarchy in any given place and time.

guys to keep doing their work and get As but they just sleep [laughs]! They don't listen, just sleep. The girls—they'll listen, they'll take notes, they'll do well on tests" (736). Boys who did exert more effort in this school were likely to be labeled "weird," "strange," "gay," or "pussies" by other boys, insults that reflect assumptions about gender and sexuality.

ASK YOURSELF: Why do you think white rural boys would see doing well in school as feminine? What other activities do boys and men avoid because of their association with femininity? Do women and girls avoid any activities because they are seen as masculine?

One concept that helps explain the underperformance of boys in these settings is **hegemonic masculinity**, an idea from R. W. Connell's (2005) exploration of how our dominant ideas about what it means to be a man influence the behaviors of actual men in any given society. According to Connell's theory, there is no single "male role," but rather a variety of masculinities that interact with each other in hierarchical and contested ways. Hegemonic (socially dominant) masculinity is the type of masculinity at the top of those hierarchies, and it changes across times, cultures, and subcultures. The masculinity seen as hegemonic in a rural high school is not necessarily hegemonic for adults, for American men 50 years ago, for Mexican men, or even for boys at a high school in another part of the United States. But once a particular version of masculinity becomes hegemonic, it can be used to patrol the behaviors of men or boys within that particular setting.

In the context of the rural high school Morris studied, being masculine was often defined as having common sense as opposed to "book smarts," as doing manual labor rather than office work, as being the main provider for the family, and as being a "redneck" but not a "rutter" (poor and dirty). Boys could work at getting good grades or going to college, but because of the power of hegemonic masculinity in this setting, they would pay a price for such behavior. Dynamics like these might help explain why men are becoming increasingly outnumbered by women on college campuses across the country.

Choosing a Major and Getting a Job

So far we've discovered that in some high schools, it seems uncool for boys to do well, possibly explaining why they attend college at lower rates than their female counterparts, and why some colleges and universities are lowering their standards for male students in response. If we stopped our story there, you might conclude that gender inequality as a social problem is now more about men's

Race and the Glass Escalator: Black Male Nurses

Though 95% of registered nurses are women, they are still paid 5% less than their male counterparts. In her study of men in predominantly female occupations like nursing, Christine Williams (1992) found that these men encounter a *glass escalator,* or invisible pressure to move up in their professions, sometimes in spite of their intentions. In her own study of black male nurses, Adia Harvey Wingfield (2009) found that the glass escalator may work better for white men than for African American men. Earlier research suggested that white male nurses receive a congenial welcome from their female colleagues and male supervisors; this was not the experience of the black male nurses Wingfield interviewed.

Both Williams's original study and Wingfield's research used in-depth interviews that allowed respondents to tell stories about their experiences in the nursing field. In Williams's study, 90% of the respondents were white, while Wingfield interviewed 17 male nurses who all identified as black or African American. This difference in sampling led to very different research results. *Gendered racism,* which grounds racial stereotypes, images, and beliefs in gendered ideals, caused the mostly white colleagues of black male nurses to perceive them as dangerous and threatening in a way white male nurses did not encounter.

Black male nurses also do not benefit from the automatic assumption that they are capable of and qualified for "better" work that white male nurses are granted. Finally, while patients often mistake white male nurses for doctors, a black male nurse is more likely to find himself mistaken for a janitor.

Wingfield's study demonstrates the importance of an intersectional approach to the examination of gender—that is, an approach that takes into consideration the many identities we occupy that overlap with gender and interact in complex ways. Though being a man seems to be a distinct advantage for white men, Wingfield's findings suggest that masculinity does not similarly privilege black male nurses.

▶ **THINK ABOUT IT:** What other professions can you think of in which black men would have a double-minority status?

Nursing is a profession that has historically been dominated by white women. Black male nurses are a minority within a minority in the profession. What other professions can you think of in which black men would have a double-minority status?

disadvantages than women's. Surely boys also make less money in their jobs and careers than their increasingly better-educated female counterparts. But that is not at all the case.

Women in the United States still earn 19% less than men on average (Rampell 2010). Another way of thinking about this **gender wage gap** is to say that for every dollar a man makes, his female counterpart makes about 81 cents. In global perspective, the U.S. gender wage gap is smaller than the gap in some countries and larger than that in others. In Japan and South Korea, women are paid 30% of men's earnings. The smallest gender wage gap, 9.3%, is in Belgium (Rampell 2010). Table 4.1 shows the World Economic Forum's ranking of the 10 best countries for women, measured in terms of health and wellness, educational attainment, political empowerment, and economic participation. The United States has fallen in this ranking over the past three years and is now in 22nd place.

Why do women earn less than men on average all over the world? A great deal of research has attempted to answer this question. You may even have noticed some potential answers playing out around you. Women are still more likely to major in "soft" fields like education and psychology, though business is now the most popular undergraduate major for both women and men (Goudreau 2010). Social sciences and history are among

Gender wage gap: The gap in earnings between women and men, usually expressed as a percentage or proportion of what women are paid relative to their male equivalents.

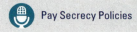

Pay Secrecy Policies

TABLE 4.1 World Economic Forum's Top Countries for Women, 2012

Rank	Country
1	Iceland
2	Finland
3	Norway
4	Sweden
5	Ireland
6	New Zealand
7	Denmark
8	Philippines
9	Nicaragua
10	Switzerland

SOURCE: Adapted from Meghan Casserly, "The Global Gender Gap Is Closing, But The US Is Still Failing Its Women," *Forbes,* October 24, 2012.

the top five majors for both men and women, but men are still more likely to major in fields like engineering and computer and information sciences, while women dominate in education, psychology, and health-related professions. You can see how these choices might explain the gender wage gap when you compare the average top salary of $132,000 in engineering to the average salaries of schoolteachers: $50,000 at the elementary level and $53,000 at the secondary level (U.S. Census Bureau 2012c; Goudreau 2010). Perhaps, then, the gender wage gap is due to the different choices women and men make as college students.

ASK YOURSELF: Think about the college majors of the people you know. Do the women and men have different majors? Do you see any evidence that the choice of major is less affected by gender now than in the past?

Choice of major is one variable social science researchers use to generate statistical models that help explain the gender wage gap. Other factors include the occupations men and women enter, their job experience, the degree of occupational segregation they encounter, the amount of information available to job seekers about high-paying jobs, and men's and women's salary expectations (Joy 2003). In current models, the choice of college major can account for only about 10% of the gender wage gap. In older studies it explained between 40% and 50%, so

changes in choice of major have had an effect in narrowing the gap. Though the debate on the exact cause of the gender wage gap is ongoing, it seems that what happens while women and men are college students is only a small part of the picture. One study suggests that even if women came to the labor market with the same educational credentials and the same labor market preferences as men, employers would still value them less; in fact, if women received the same returns on their qualifications as men do, they would make on average 25% more than they currently do (Joy 2003).

Party Rape: Sexual Assault on Campus

Though hegemonic masculinity seems to work against the academic success of many boys, when they leave high school and get jobs many of them will still make more money than the girls they sat beside in class. Gender inequality also affects women and men in their relative vulnerability to violence, influencing the distribution of power on college campuses and in other settings.

It is difficult to say for sure how frequently sexual assault happens on college campuses because of the low rate at which victims may report these crimes. One report by the U.S. Department of Justice estimates that in a given nine-month academic year, about 3% of college women will be victims of attempted or completed sexual assault on campus (Karjane, Fisher, and Cullen 2005). This statistic might not seem too frightening at first glance,

Atlantide Phototravel / Corbis

In their book *Paying for the Party: How College Maintains Inequality,* sociologists Elizabeth A. Armstrong and Laura T. Hamilton follow a group of female students at a midwestern public university, where they encounter a culture of status seeking and sororities. The researchers found that the most seductive route for students is the party scene, which is dominated by fraternities and sororities. The party scene perpetuates social hierarchies based on appearance, race, wealth, and men's perceptions of women; heavy alcohol use; and a culture of hooking up. What would you say are the positive and negative consequences of the party scene for college women?

Sex Education and Latina Youth

What are girls taught about sex before they reach college campuses? How do those lessons differ based on girls' racial, ethnic, and social class backgrounds? What assumptions reside in the messages schools send about gender and sexuality?

In her research on the sexual (mis) education of Latina youth, Lorena Garcia (2009) found important intersections among race, gender, and sexuality. Earlier research demonstrated that educators see minority youth as more like adults, as sexually precocious, and as potential teen mothers (Bettie 2003; Ferguson 2000; Fields 2007; Hyams 2006; Lopez 2003; Morris 2007; Pascoe 2007; Pérez 2006). Latinas in the Chicago public school system where Garcia conducted her research reported that sex educators made assumptions based on their Latina identity. In discussing the use of Depo-Provera as birth control, one sex educator said, "Too many Hispanic girls feel that having a baby is no big deal, but don't believe it"

(Garcia 2009, 532). Sex educators also pointed out to Latina girls that condoms were a less viable contraceptive option for them because of the machismo of their male partners.

Here is a further intersection between gender and sexuality: as in most school settings, the sex education in the schools Garcia studied was heavily *heteronormative*—that is, based on the assumption that heterosexuality is normal. When students attempted to ask questions about gay or lesbian sexuality, both teachers and other students reacted with hostility and derision.

The experiences of these Latina youth demonstrate the ways in which sex education is flawed in many

Samantha Karaffa, 17, center, checks out the sex of Helen Martinez's "baby" as Helen "feeds" the baby at Highland Park High School's teen center in New Jersey. Both girls are participating in a program at the school that teaches girls about sex, from diseases to different types of contraception and relationships.

schools, including in its emphasis on heterosexual sexuality. As an intersectional approach, Garcia's research also teaches us how the experiences of all high school girls are not the same; rather, all individuals are deeply conditioned by their particular racial, ethnic, social class, and sexual backgrounds.

▶ **THINK ABOUT IT:** Did you have a course in sex education in high school? How much of it was devoted to the issue of safe sex?

but remember that it applies to one academic year; this means that on a campus of 1,000 students, 35 women are likely to be victims of sexual assault *each academic year*. Between 80% and 90% of these assaults are perpetrated by someone the victim knows; only a small fraction are stranger rapes.

Many sexual assaults take place at fraternity parties and other settings that include alcohol, leading Armstrong, Hamilton, and Sweeney (2006) to use the term "party rape" to describe them. The party scenes that dominate many college campuses, and the ways in which female and male college students are motivated to participate, are a central part of the dynamic of sexual assault. Researchers argue that long before students ever arrive on campus, many have already been socialized into certain expectations about college life that include the party scene as a central element. Going out, drinking, and

having fun are seen as things you're supposed to do in college, as important ways for students to feel a part of the larger college community life. While the motivation to party in college is gender-neutral, however, the party scene itself is not.

In the large midwestern university where Armstrong et al. conducted their study, the dorm was coed, though the women's floor was locked to nonresidents and men could not enter the floor without a female escort. In large lecture classrooms, women found it difficult to meet or talk to men, and many complained they missed the casual, friendly contact with men they had become accustomed to in high school. The party scene, then, became the primary venue for heterosexual women to meet men, as well as to obtain the status and self-esteem that came with being seen as desirable to them. The women enjoyed dancing and kissing at parties, in part because the attention they received from men required a "skillful deployment of physical and cultural assets" (Armstrong et al. 2006, 488). These skills included wearing the right kind of outfit—"hot" but not "slutty"—and presenting the image of the "ideal" college girl with "white, even features, thin but busty, tan, long straight hair, skillfully made-up, and well-dressed in the latest youth styles" (488). The psychological benefits of being admired in the party scene were such that women with boyfriends sometimes mourned their own inability to draw such attention without making their boyfriends jealous.

Ashley Cooper / Corbis

Here is an example of how one class-privileged college student sees things, as reported by sociologists Laura T. Hamilton and Elizabeth A. Armstrong (2009, 602): "I've always looked at college as the only time in your life when you should be a hundred percent selfish. . . . I have the rest of my life to devote to a husband or kids or my job . . . but right now, it's my time."

ASK YOURSELF: The research on party rape suggests that some college women boost their self-esteem by appearing attractive and desirable to men. Do you think this is true on most college campuses? Is it true for male college students as well? If not, how do college men boost their self-esteem?

At the institutional and organizational levels, the rules of a university and those of its Greek organizations become important influences on the dynamics of party rape. For example, at the university where Armstrong et al. (2006) conducted their study, campus enforcement of state drinking laws was usually rigorous in residence halls, where the researchers observed both resident assistants and police officers patrolling for violations. Meanwhile, though the Greek system required the consent of the larger university for some of its activities, the university lacked full authority over what might take place in the fraternity houses. When deciding on party themes, fraternities often chose themes that encouraged women to wear scant, sexy clothing and put them in subordinate positions. Examples the researchers observed included "Pimps and Hos," "Victoria's Secret," "Playboy Mansion," and "CEO/Secretary Ho." Fraternities controlled who came to their parties, markedly preferred first-year women, and often turned away unaffiliated men. In fact, the ability to attract women, specifically *attractive* women, to their parties was important to the fraternities' ability to recruit new members. In these ways, both the rules of the larger university and the structure of the fraternities contributed to the incidence of party rape by funneling most of the unsupervised drinking into the Greek houses.

These individual and institutional factors come together to shape the actual interactions that create an atmosphere conducive to party rape. Ironically, the interactional production of fun is a key component of this dynamic. **Interaction routines** are patterns or norms of

Interaction routines: Patterns or norms of speech or action that individuals follow with regularity to accomplish particular tasks in interactions.

speech or action that individuals follow with regularity to accomplish particular tasks in interactions. Some of the interaction routines of the party scene at universities are gender-specific. The research suggests that women at fraternity parties are expected to wear revealing outfits; to cede control of turf, transportation, and liquor to the male fraternity members; and to be grateful to their male hosts as well as generally "nice" in ways that men are not necessarily expected to be.

This expectation of "niceness" is another way of describing an expectation of deference, that women accept their status as subordinate to men and do not challenge men's control over them. In the fraternity parties that Armstrong et al. (2006) studied, women often did not call attention to men's inappropriate behaviors because they did not want to "make a scene." Amanda, for instance, was drinking at a bar with an older male named Mike. Though she and Mike made out at the bar, Amanda made it clear this did not mean she wanted to go home with him. When she found herself stranded at the bar with no ride home, Mike promised a sober friend of his would take her. The sober friend dropped her at Mike's house instead, however, and asked whether she would be interested in a threesome. Amanda stayed up all night in fear and woke Mike early in the morning to take her home. Despite her ordeal, she deferred her own apprehension to the need not to be seen as a troublemaker. She described Mike as a "really nice guy" and exchanged telephone numbers with him.

Armstrong et al. (2006) encountered at least one instance of sexual assault in every focus group they conducted that included heterosexual women. Most of the

Gender beyond Our Borders

Holding Up Half the Sky

Mao Zedong, leader of China's communist revolution, famously said that women hold up half the sky; it was a statement about the new China's commitment to gender equality. Authors and social activists Nicholas D. Kristof and Sheryl WuDunn use Mao's expression as the title of their 2009 book *Half the Sky,* in which they chronicle the global oppression of women and suggest potential solutions to the problem of gender inequality.

While living in China, Kristof and WuDunn (who are married to each other) met Daj Manju. Daj lived with her mother, father, two brothers, and great-aunt in a wooden shack with no electricity, no running water, no radio, and virtually no possessions of any kind. The family ate meat just once a year, at the Chinese New Year. When Daj reached sixth grade, her ill parents decided the $13 yearly school fee was a waste of their money; girls didn't need to learn to read or write if they were going to spend their lives hoeing fields and darning socks. Though Daj had been a star pupil, she dropped out and resigned herself to hanging out around the school, hoping to learn something even if her parents couldn't pay.

Though Daj Manju's story may be difficult for those in the global North to hear, it is typical for many girls and women around the world. Luckily, Kristof and WuDunn were able to share Daj's story and raise money for her education. She finished high school and an accounting program that allowed her to secure a job as an accountant in a local factory. The money she sent home to her parents improved their standard of living as well. By 2006, Daj had risen to an executive position in a Taiwanese electronics company and was contemplating starting her own business (Kristof and WuDunn 2009).

From left to right, Sheryl WuDunn, Maria Shriver, and Nicholas Kristof attend an event for the Half the Sky Movement at L'Ermitage Beverly Hills Hotel in Beverly Hills, California.

Mike Windle / Getty Images

▶ **THINK ABOUT IT:** What do you think of online advocacy games like the one based on the Half the Sky movement (www.facebook.com/HalftheGame)?

women complained about the men's efforts to control their movements within the party scene and the pressure to drink they experienced. Two women who lived on the hall the researchers studied had been sexually assaulted during the first week of school, and later in the semester another was raped by a man she thought was a friend. A fourth suspected she had been drugged at a fraternity party. Given these experiences, why did the women continue to participate in the party scene? The answer is that even with such negative experiences, the party scene can also be fun for university women. Partying allows them to meet new people, experience and display belonging, and enhance their social position. Many of the women in the study were invested in the party system, and it was difficult for them to find fault with something they also enjoyed. Some responded to the victimization of others by blaming the women themselves, rather than the party scene they so valued.

If this is the reality, how can women protect themselves? In Armstrong et al.'s (2006) sample, some opted out of the party scene altogether, but this made them social misfits. Others continued to face the ongoing danger that full participation—including drinking, having fun, and feeling attractive to male college students—carries with it. Women will continue to run the risk as long as the problem of sexual assault is seen as resulting either from the decisions of individuals or from different cultural contexts, rather than as a combination of factors at many different levels. Another factor is the idea that violence against women is a "woman's" problem.

Armstrong et al.'s (2006) study shows how the threat of violence makes women's participation in the party scene at college complicated in ways that men's participation is not. Some feminist scholars argue that this is exactly why violence against women is the most important component to address in any attempt to dismantle gender inequality. They believe the threat of violence prevents women from fully participating in many areas of social life, and thus in many of the important decisions that govern their lives.

▶ Half the Sky

Gender and Education in Global Perspective

Despite the dangers some women on college campuses in the United States may face in the form of sexual assault, education is still an important avenue to a better quality of life for women and men across the globe. On average, a woman with a bachelor's degree will make $650,000 less than a man with the same educational level over the course of her lifetime (Carnevale, Rose, and Cheah 2011). A woman must earn a doctoral or professional degree in order to make more than a man with a bachelor's degree. In the developed world, better economic circumstances translate into many advantages in other areas of social life, but this relationship is even more crucial in many developing countries. The United Nations Girls' Education Initiative (2011) estimates that one in five girls in developing countries who enroll in primary school fail to finish. Because women in these countries who have received some secondary education have considerably lower mortality rates than do women who have not—in part because of their delaying marriage and childbirth—improved education for women in places like sub-Saharan Africa would result in 1.8 million fewer deaths. Girls who stay in school for seven or more years marry four years later and have two fewer children on average than do those who have less education. That educating women benefits the whole of a society is demonstrated by the fact that when 10% more girls in a country go to school, the country's gross domestic product increases on average by 3% (U.S. AID 2011) (see Figure 4.3).

Despite such benefits, there are still significant barriers to women's education around the world. In countries such as Tanzania and Ethiopia, parents of girls may consider marriage more important for their daughters than education (United Nations Girls' Education Initiative 2014). In other countries, outbreaks of violence, ongoing conflicts, and war prevent all children from attending school. Aid workers estimated that 94% of conflict-ridden Zimbabwe's schools were closed in 2009. The case of Malala Yousafzai—who gained worldwide attention and survived an assassination attempt by the Taliban—demonstrates the obstacles girls face in Pakistan when they advocate for women's education. In Benin, 13-year-old Sophia was beaten by her older brother when she refused to enter into an arranged marriage, despite the fact that it is illegal in Benin to get married before the age of 18.

FIGURE 4.3   **The Gender Gap in the Paid Workforce and Secondary Education**

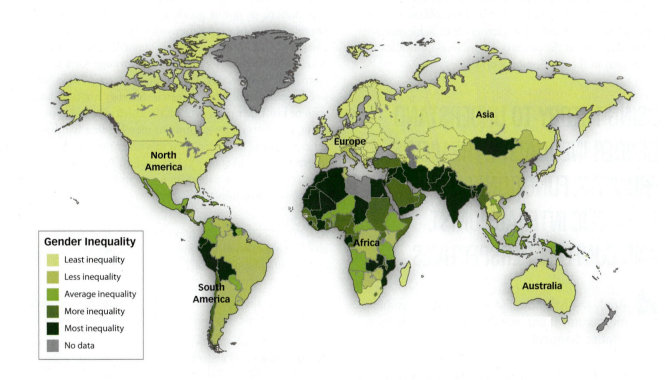

Gender Inequality
- Least inequality
- Less inequality
- Average inequality
- More inequality
- Most inequality
- No data

SOURCE: Adapted from Female/Male Inequality in Education and Employment. Princeton University QED website.

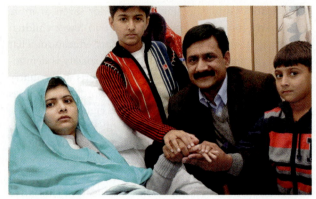

Malala Yousafzai is the Pakistani girl who was shot in the head by the Taliban in 2012 for advocating girls' education. Here she is seen with her father and her two younger brothers as she recuperates at the the Queen Elizabeth Hospital in Birmingham, England. Malala was nominated for the Nobel Peace Prize in 2013. Why do you suppose girls' education is such a threat to the Taliban?

In many countries, even girls who get to school may be subject to violence in the form of sexual assault, harassment, and exploitation. Chaos and poverty play their part as well. In the Dadaab refugee camp in Kenya, Somali girls sometimes miss school because their families cannot afford sanitary pads for them when they are menstruating (United Nations Girls' Education Initiative 2010). The Dadaab camp is home to more than 500,000 people, and it is estimated that only 48% of the children there are enrolled in school. All these factors make achieving even some education at the primary school level quite a feat for many girls in the developing world.

USING THEORY TO UNDERSTAND GENDER INEQUALITY: THE VIEWS FROM THE FUNCTIONALIST, SYMBOLIC INTERACTIONIST, AND CONFLICT PERSPECTIVES

4.4 Apply the functionalist, conflict, and symbolic interactionist perspectives to the problem of gender inequality.

Many of the theoretical perspectives through which we can view gender have been influenced by feminist scholarship and activism. Before the 1960s, sociologists

reflected the views of their time in assuming that most of the important things about social life happen among and between men. Beginning in the 1960s and 1970s, however, more women entered the field and began a serious consideration of the role of gender across many areas of social life. The gender theories that feminists and sociologists developed line up with sociology's three dominant theoretical frameworks—structural functionalism, symbolic interactionism, and conflict theory. Each focuses attention on particular aspects and dynamics of social life, giving us different views of the same social phenomenon.

Structural Functionalism

The macro-level theory of structural functionalism dates from the birth of the discipline, when scholars proposed the metaphor of society as an organism and each of its social institutions as an organ in a body. A social institution is an established pattern of behavior, group, or organization that fulfills a specific need in society. The government is a social institution that we might see as the brain of the organism; government plays a large role in setting the rules for a given society.

As applied to gender, structural functionalism takes the specific form of sex role theory. The idea of a sex role begins with the more general idea of a **social role**, a set of expectations attached to a particular status or position, such as white or black, man or woman, gay or straight. Certain expectations or norms go along with different statuses. A **sex role** is a set of expectations attached to a particular sex category. An easy way to think about this is to consider what kinds of behaviors might seem strange for a man or woman in your society. For example, in the United States one expectation of straight men is that they not hold hands with or kiss other men, even on the cheek. But in Egypt and India, it is normal to see straight men holding hands with other men, and in France, men kiss other men on the cheek in greeting. Social roles vary by society, but most cultures impose some set of expectations on individuals based on their assignment into a sex category.

ASK YOURSELF: Can you think of other examples of behaviors that are seen as appropriate for women or men in one culture and not in another?

Sex role theory fits within the structural functionalist view because it assumes that different sex roles for

Social role: A set of expectations attached to a particular status or position in society.

Sex role: The set of expectations attached to a particular sex category—male or female.

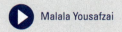
Malala Yousafzai

TABLE 4.2 Gender Inequality Index and Related Indicators for Select Countries

Country	Gender Inequality Index rank* (2011)	Maternal mortality ratio (2008)	Seats in national parliament (% female) (2011)	Population with at least secondary education (% ages 25 and older) (2010)		Labor force participation rate (%) (2009)	
				Female	Male	Female	Male
Sweden	1	5	45.0	87.9	87.1	60.6	69.2
Netherlands	2	9	37.8	86.3	89.2	59.5	72.9
Denmark	3	5	38.0	59.0	65.6	60.3	70.6
Switzerland	4	10	27.6	63.6	73.8	60.6	73.7
Finland	5	8	42.5	70.1	70.1	57.0	64.9
France	10	8	20.0	79.6	84.6	50.5	62.2
Canada	20	12	24.9	92.3	92.7	62.7	73.0
United Kingdom	34	12	21.0	68.8	67.8	55.3	69.5
China	35	38	21.3	54.8	70.4	67.4	79.7
United States	47	24	16.8	95.3	94.5	58.4	71.9
Cuba	58	53	43.2	73.9	80.4	40.9	66.9
Costa Rica	64	44	38.6	54.4	52.8	45.1	79.9
Chile	68	26	13.9	67.3	69.8	41.8	73.4
Mexico	79	85	25.5	55.8	61.9	43.2	80.6
Rwanda	82	540	50.9	7.4	8.0	86.7	85.1
South Africa	94	410	42.7	66.3	68	47.0	60.0
India	129	230	10.7	26.6	50.4	32.8	81.1
Kenya	130	530	9.8	20.1	38.6	76.4	88.1
Saudi Arabia	135	24	0	50.3	57.9	21.2	79.8
Afghanistan	141	1,400	27.6	5.8	34.0	33.1	84.5

*The Gender Inequality Index is calculated based on three dimensions (reproductive health, empowerment, and labor market) and five indicators (maternal mortality, adolescent fertility, parliamentary representation, educational attainment, and labor force participation).

SOURCE: Table 4: Gender Inequality Index and Related Indicators, United Nations Development Project, Human Development Reports.

women and men are functional for society. Functionalist sociologists such as Talcott Parsons have explained these differences in terms of instrumental versus expressive roles (Parsons and Bales 1955). Men are taught in childhood and throughout their lives to be **instrumental**, or goal- and task-oriented, while women are taught to be **expressive**, or oriented toward their interactions with

Instrumental: Oriented toward goals and tasks.

Expressive: Oriented toward interactions with other people.

other people. Theorists see this division of labor as functional for society, because women who work outside the home and men who want to stay home and take care of their children create dysfunction for society.

ASK YOURSELF: Sex role theory predicts that men will be more oriented toward the instrumental while women will be more oriented toward the expressive. Can you think of examples that support this assertion? Can you think of exceptions, or situations that contradict this assertion?

 Equality

Policy Implications of Structural Functionalism

Applied to policy, sex role theory presumes that a functional family unit is one that consists of a man who fulfills an instrumental role and a woman who occupies an expressive role. Policies that support the centrality of the nuclear family—husband, wife, and children—are thus consistent with sex role theory. For example, one of the goals of the welfare reforms passed in the United States in 1996 was to encourage the formation of two-parent families, and a 2002 welfare reform bill in the House of Representatives included $300 million for policies to promote marriage (Hu 2003). Temporary Assistance for Needy Families (TANF), which replaced Aid to Families with Dependent Children (AFDC) in 1996, requires that single women work in order to receive welfare, while married women do not have to be employed in order to receive welfare benefits. Some U.S. states have included marriage education classes as part of the training single women are required to undergo as a condition of receiving welfare benefits. Paternity establishment and child-support rules included in TANF encourage a woman receiving benefits to form some kind of relationship with the father of her children (Mink 2001). All these policies support the assumptions of sex role theory that the most functional model of a family is a father who works outside the home to support his family and a mother who takes care of the children (and the father). Feminists have criticized TANF as a policy that violates women's rights to work, to support themselves financially, and to live independent of men. Yet, acting consistently with sex role theory, many politicians see a family unit composed of a male provider, a female caregiver, and their children as the most beneficial for society.

Symbolic Interactionism

Whereas structural functionalism and sex role theory are good examples of theories at the macro level in sociology, symbolic interactionism is generally a theory that works at the micro level. It looks at the details of social interaction and group life rather than at the big picture of how larger structures in society fit together.

In the world of symbolic interactionism, everything is a symbol, including the way you wear your hair, the way you sit, your facial expressions, the words you choose, and your inflection, as well as whether you look at me or not while you speak. Crucial to understanding social life from a symbolic interactionist perspective is understanding the meanings we give to all these things, and those meanings vary. The idea of social construction is especially important, then, from a symbolic interactionist perspective.

One specific gender theory that fits within symbolic interactionism is **doing gender theory**. Doing gender draws its legacy from a specific branch of symbolic interactionism in sociology called ethnomethodology. **Ethnomethodology** is essentially the study of folkways and the meaning and operation of what at first appear to be very mundane and taken-for-granted aspects of social life. Harold Garfinkel became interested in what we might assume in relationship to gender. He studied a male-to-female transsexual named Agnes because he reasoned that the aspects of gender the rest of us take for granted would probably be more apparent to someone like Agnes, who was forced to try to pass as a gender different from the one in which she had been socialized (Garfinkel 1967). Doing gender as a theory builds on Garfinkel's work to argue that gender is not a set of internalized norms for behavior, as suggested by sex role theory. Rather, gender is an interactive performance we are all constantly staging through our interactions with others. In addition, we are all accountable to our audience—the other people with whom we are interacting.

Accountability in doing gender theory refers to whether the audience for our performance understands our actions as we have intended for them to be understood. For example, if I tell a joke, you may not laugh at it, or you may think it's a particularly bad joke. But either of those reactions still implies that the story I just told you is accountable as a joke. I meant it as a joke and you understood it as such. If I tell you a story I intended to be a joke and you stare at me blankly and wonder what the point of it was, I have failed to create an accountable joke. Doing gender as a theory assumes a deeply interactive relationship between the gender performer and the audience, because accountability is decided by both.

While sex role theory argues that gender exists internally to individuals as a set of norms and expectations, one of doing gender theory's key insights is that it is our constant performance of gender that leads us to believe that gender has some deeper underlying reality. Like a magic act, our accomplishment of gender is powerful enough to convince us there are, in fact, natural divisions of human beings into two types—male and female,

Doing gender theory: A theory of gender that claims gender is an accountable performance created and reinforced through individuals' interactions.

Ethnomethodology: A sociological approach that seeks to uncover the taken-for-granted assumptions that lie behind the basic stuff of social life and interaction.

Accountability: The ways in which people gear their actions to specific circumstances so others will correctly recognize the actions for what they are.

masculine and feminine, man and woman. But from the doing gender perspective, sex and gender consist only of our performances.

ASK YOURSELF: How does doing gender theory fit within a social constructionist perspective on gender? Based on what you know about doing gender theory, would this approach agree or disagree with sexual dimorphism?

Policy Implications of Symbolic Interactionism

If gender is a performance, how does this explain the existence of gender inequality? Those using the doing gender perspective argue that gender inequality becomes part of our performances of gender, largely through allocation. **Allocation** is simply the way decisions get made about who does what, who gets what and who does not, who gets to make plans, and who gets to give orders or take them (West and Fenstermaker 1993). The doing gender perspective assumes a widespread and deeply held belief in our society that women are both different from and inferior to men. This shapes the way in which women are held accountable for gender, especially when it comes to allocation and even in something as simple as a routine conversation.

Research has demonstrated allocation in simple conversations, each between a white middle-class man and a white middle-class woman, where the particular kind of work to be allocated is changing to a new topic when the old one runs out of steam. Two people in conversation usually change topics collaboratively, but sometimes one person does it alone. West and Garcia (1988) found that in their sample, such unilateral topic changes were always initiated by men, and from the doing gender perspective, this is an issue of allocation, controlling what two people will talk about. Men accomplish gender in conversation by changing the topic, and this seems to be especially true when women move the conversation toward topics that are not necessarily seen as consistent with ideas of masculinity (West and Garcia 1988). In this small way, men produce an accountable performance of masculinity.

If both gender and sex are largely performances and gender inequality is due to allocation, what are the policy implications of doing a gender perspective? A study of women in various occupations within the criminal justice system found that some did feel compelled by the organizational logic of institutions like law enforcement and

Allocation: The way decisions get made about who does what, who gets what and who does not, who gets to make plans, and who gets to give orders or take them.

prisons to do masculinity while on the job. These women emulated the styles of reasoning, speech, and demeanor thought to characterize men in their occupations (Martin and Jurik 1996, 218). Even those who avoided the adaptive strategy of doing masculinity felt pressured to act like men.

As a solution to gender inequality, asking women to act like men seems inadequate. Though doing gender theory emphasizes the importance of social interaction to the construction of gender, the best solutions from this theoretical perspective still lie at the level of organizations and institutions. The reason is that if one person decides not to perform his or her gender, that decision generally does not call into question the larger institutional arrangement of gender. If as a woman I stop performing an accountable version of femininity, most people will assume something is wrong with me, not with the way gender is structured in my society. Our performances of gender certainly reinforce the larger structural status quo, but we would have to change our interactions on a massive scale to significantly change the larger social structures in regard to gender.

ASK YOURSELF: Imagine situations in your own life that seem to demand different performances of gender. Are there situations in which you feel pressured to act in ways more or less consistent with your own gender? Can you identify any trends in the kinds of situations that seem to demand different types of gender performances?

Because of this relationship between social structures and interaction, the locations and contexts in which we stage our performances of gender are important. We can therefore alter our gender performances best by altering those environments. Though many women in criminal justice occupations feel pressure to do masculinity, this pressure is reduced in occupations characterized by an ethic of professionalization. Where women can project themselves as professionals, they can find ways to make femininity and competence in their jobs more compatible. Doing gender theory suggests that organizations and institutions should restructure in ways that put less pressure on women and men to perform gender.

Conflict Theory

If structural functionalism emphasizes the relatively smooth functioning of society, conflict theory draws our attention to the importance of struggles over power and resources in society. Most theories that fall under the conflict paradigm can trace their origins to Karl Marx

At a demonstration in Madrid, Spain, in support of decriminalizing abortion, a protester holds a poster with the message in English: "If I had a hammer. . . . I'd SMASH patriarchy." How can feminism smash patriarchy?

and his ideas about social class. **Socialist feminism**, for instance, translates Marx's theories about class oppression into a different context, arguing that the best way to understand gender relations is to see women as an oppressed social class.

Gender inequality, however, is different from social class inequality in that almost all women live intimately with their oppressors. The United States exhibits a high level of social class segregation; most people live, work, and socialize alongside people whose social class backgrounds are similar to their own. Social class segregation creates social inequality by concentrating resources geographically; poor neighborhoods have less money for schools, fewer amenities (like grocery stores), and fewer jobs available than do more affluent neighborhoods. Even if women are socially segregated within their own households, as happens in some countries, such as Egypt and Saudi Arabia, they still live with their male relatives. So though socialist feminists may argue that women are an oppressed social class, they are a unique kind of social class.

Radical feminism borrows from conflict theory the central idea of groups in conflict over power and resources. But rather than locating this conflict in class relationships as socialist feminists do, radical feminists see **patriarchy**, or male dominance, as the root of the problem. Patriarchal societies are designed in ways that quite explicitly favor men over women. Patriarchy can manifest in many ways, some subtle and some not so subtle. In many societies, parents prefer male children over female children and may abort female children or take other measures to increase their chances of having sons rather than daughters. More subtle forms of patriarchy include uses of language, such as the way the word *man* is often used to refer to all humanity, as in *mankind*. In general, patriarchal societies are characterized by

androcentrism, the belief that masculinity and what men do are superior to femininity and what women do.

ASK YOURSELF: What are some examples of androcentrism in your own society?

Liberal feminism posits that gender inequality is rooted in the ways institutions such as government treat men and women. When these institutions limit women's opportunities to compete with men in economic and political arenas, they create inequality. Why should women and men be provided with equal rights? Liberal feminists assert that all humans in modern societies are entitled to a set of basic rights. Thus they base their arguments regarding inequality on the *similarities* between men and women: because we are all basically the same, we all deserve the same basic rights.

Policy Implications of Conflict Theory

From a liberal feminist perspective, the best way to reduce gender inequality is to reduce the barriers that stand in the way of women's advancement. Because women and men are essentially the same, once these barriers have been removed, gender inequality will gradually disappear. But as we've seen, from the radical feminist perspective gender inequality is explained by the prevalence of patriarchy as a defining characteristic of society. Thus merely changing a few laws here and there will not rid us of gender inequality. Instead, any effort to reduce gender inequality must involve a fairly radical restructuring of society—not just government but also educational institutions, religious institutions, the family, the media, work, and so on. (This explains why radical feminism is, in fact, *radical* compared to liberal feminism.)

ASK YOURSELF: From a radical feminist perspective, patriarchy penetrates all areas of social life. Can you think of some examples that seem to support this assertion?

Socialist feminism: A version of feminist thought that employs Marxist paradigms to view women as an oppressed social class.

Radical feminism: A version of feminist thought that suggests gender is a fundamental aspect of the way society functions and serves as an integral tool for distributing power and resources among people and groups.

Patriarchy: A society characterized by male dominance.

Androcentrism: The belief that masculinity and what men do are superior to femininity and what women do.

Liberal feminism: A type of feminism that suggests men and women are essentially the same and gender inequality can be eliminated through the reduction of legal barriers to women's full participation in society.

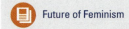 Future of Feminism

Some radical feminists argue that the first step toward ending gender inequality is for women to form their own separate institutions and organizations free of male domination. For instance, radical feminist Mary Daly famously advocated leaving Christianity behind as an institution deeply flawed by patriarchy. Other radical feminists have formed music festivals for women, women's businesses, and collectives where women could live and work apart from men.

This is not to say that radical feminists do not also support changing laws; in the 1970s, many were active in efforts to ratify the Equal Rights Amendment, which would have amended the U.S. Constitution to make any discrimination on the basis of sex illegal. But radical feminists often also engage in forms of protests and consciousness-raising activities that target institutions beyond the government. **Consciousness-raising** is a process intended to help women see the connections between their personal experiences with gender exploitation and the larger structure and politics of society—to see sexual harassment, for instance, as a fundamental and inevitable product of the patriarchal way our society is structured, part of the way men maintain control through fear and intimidation. Consciousness-raising is at the core of the popular feminist slogan "The personal is political."

Thus laws against sexual harassment and legislation aimed at protecting victims of domestic violence are part of the legacy of radical feminist organizing. It is difficult for many of us to imagine today, but as recently as the 1970s, it was not technically illegal in any U.S. state for a husband to physically assault or abuse his wife or children. This type of violence was considered strictly within the realm of the personal, and therefore not subject to public laws governing behavior. Radical feminists argued that because gender permeates all aspects of society, including the family, what happens inside the family home has very important public implications.

The laws making sexual harassment in the workplace illegal show a similar radical feminist influence because they acknowledge that merely removing legal barriers is not enough to end inequality. Many workplaces are structured in ways that make it difficult for women to occupy certain jobs; if you are the victim of constant harassment at work, just having the job does not guarantee success. Laws against sexual harassment acknowledge

that sexism is part of the status quo of some work environments, or that patriarchy is built into the very fabric of our social lives.

QUEER THEORY: AN INTERDISCIPLINARY PERSPECTIVE ON GENDER

 4.5 Apply queer theory's interdisciplinary perspective to gender inequality.

Our final theory draws on both the social constructionist aspect of doing gender theory and the society-wide approach of radical feminism. The use of the word *queer* in the name of this theory is partly political, a way of refusing and rechanneling the negative connotations this word often has. But the word also fits very well with the ideological agenda of the theory. The literal dictionary meanings of *queer* include "not usual," "eccentric," and "suspicious." A theory that is queer is therefore strange or unusual, different in some important way. It is just this type of rather eccentric and suspicious theory that queer theorists have set about to produce.

Queer theory is a hybrid perspective, and its beginnings can be traced to many different sources. Like many of the global social movements that flourished in the 1960s and 1970s, the gay and lesbian rights movement began to face internal problems in the 1980s and 1990s. For instance, lesbian feminists were sometimes at odds with gay men, who as men may benefit from systems of gender inequality. Women and men of color argued that the gay movement and its ideology reflected a white middle-class bias (Seidman 1996). Questions arose about whether it was possible for one movement to represent all lesbians and gays, given the vast differences in the two groups' experiences. Thus from the gay and lesbian rights movement and feminist movements, queer theory draws its distrust of categories of identity.

From postmodernism, queer theory borrows a distrust of grand narratives, or metanarratives (Lyotard 1984). A **metanarrative** is any attempt at a comprehensive and universal explanation of some phenomenon. Science itself is a metanarrative, as it seeks to develop theories that explain the way the universe works. The problem with metanarratives is that they inevitably leave some people at the margins or attempt to force their experiences into the grand story being told. Metanarratives as claims to knowledge have power implications for those who don't fit. If I define

Consciousness-raising: A radical feminist social movement technique designed to help women make connections between the personal and the political in their lives.

Metanarrative: An attempted comprehensive and universal explanation of some phenomenon.

what it means to be a man in a certain way and you don't fit that definition, you're not as likely to receive the privileges that go along with being defined as a man.

So what does queer theory do with all these intellectual threads? It seeks to pull the metaphorical rug out from under our feet by pointing out that there was never any clear place to stand to begin with; the rug didn't really exist anyway, and this is demonstrated in three basic features of queer theory.

First, queer theory is distrustful of categories related to sexuality—gay, straight, lesbian, bisexual, transsexual, and so on—and as a social movement it works to do away with them in their current form. The use of *queer* as a way of self-identifying among these groups represents an "aggressive impulse of generalization" and an attempt to disrupt conceptions of what is normal (Warner 1993). Categories of identity, as discussed above, are incomplete and can never successfully encompass all the diversity contained within. For example, is a male-to-female postoperative transsexual who is romantically and sexually attracted to women straight or gay? What about some women in Native American cultures who live socially as men and marry other women? Native Americans don't consider them lesbians, and whom they have sex with is much less important than the gender they are acting out (Whitehead 1981). How can a category labeled *lesbian* possibly hope to take account of all these differences? Queer theory answers that it can't. It doesn't stop there, though. Drawing on its feminist lineage, queer theory questions categories of gender as well, because all categories have these same fundamental flaws.

One solution queer theory proposes is to think of these identity categories as always open and fluid. You might think of this second feature of queer theory as suggesting that everyone can be, and in fact already is, queer. At some point all of us—straight, gay, feminine, masculine, intersexual, transgender—fail to live up perfectly to the demands placed on us by gender and are therefore hurt by this system. Heterosexual men in Anglo-European society are not supposed to show affection toward other men except in appropriate ways and venues (the slap on the butt during a sporting event), and many would argue that forbidding expressions of affection among any group of people goes against our basic human tendencies and is a form of oppression. The straight man who hugs his male friend a little too long is likely to be sanctioned in some way for not conforming perfectly to his particular category and in this way is "let down" by the gender system. The ways categories of gender and sexuality are constructed affect all of us, regardless of where we fall within those categories. None of us conform to them perfectly, and this makes all of us "queer" in some way.

....

ASK YOURSELF: Imagine, as queer theory suggests, that categories like gender, race, and sexual orientation are thought of as open and fluid. In what concrete ways would such thinking alter society? How would it matter in your own life and experiences?

....

This assumption connects to the third feature of queer theory, its ambition to "queer" many features of academic and social life that are generally considered within the bounds of normality. Queer theory aspires to be not just a theory of sexuality, or even of gender and sexuality, but also a broad and far-reaching social theory (Seidman 1996). Queer theorists believe sexuality is an important way in which knowledge and power are organized in society, and a theory of sexuality is therefore a theory of society in general. They argue that studying only gays and lesbians produces an incomplete picture of how sexuality works to produce identities such as "straight" and "gay." For that reason, queer theory is just as concerned with studying heterosexuality as it is with studying homosexuality, and with investigating how sexual practices permeate all aspects of society. Queer studies programs look at all types of literature, not just that which focuses on gays and lesbians or is written by them, arguing that sexuality is an integral part of all cultural productions. Rather than focusing strictly on the portrayal of gays and lesbians in the media, queer theory also examines the portrayal of heterosexuality. It studies science for the ways in which it is used to create many categories of difference, rather than solely for how it applies to issues of sexuality. For queer studies, the object of study is society itself, not just sexuality.

4.6 Identify steps toward social change in gender inequality.

Much progress has been made in reducing the impacts of many problems related to gender inequality. Though domestic abuse still happens, it is now illegal, and many organizations are devoted to providing support to women who are victims. The gender wage gap has not disappeared, and progress in closing it may have slowed, but it has shrunk significantly since the second wave of the women's movement began in the middle of the 20th century. Changes in wages and to laws that once gave husbands rights over the bodies of their wives are structural changes, but they would not have happened without the organized efforts of collections of individuals.

Sociology emphasizes the structural nature of social life and draws our attention to the ways in which our individual choices are limited by those larger social structural forces. But emphasizing the power of structural forces in our own lives is not the same as saying those social structures *cannot* be changed. History tells us they do change in fairly radical ways, and all of us as individuals have the choice to either contribute to the status quo or take intentional actions to change the way things are. Change may be slow and difficult, but it is always possible. Here are a few ideas for how you might contribute to social change in the area of gender inequality.

Students Active for Ending Rape (SAFER)

Many organizations work to end sexual assault in general as well as the specific type of party rape discussed in this chapter. Students Active for Ending Rape is just one example of such an organization that works at the national level. Founded by Columbia University students in 2000, SAFER empowers student-led organizations to reform often-inadequate sexual assault policies on campus. Its website (http://www.safercampus.org) provides access to a comprehensive

Microfinance loans: Small loans made at low interest rates, usually given by nongovernmental organizations to women in developing countries.

training manual, in-person workshops and training, follow-up mentoring, a database of campus sexual assault policies, and a growing online resource library. SAFER is a good resource for students who want to compare their own campuses' efforts at sexual assault prevention and procedures for victims and perpetrators with those of other schools.

Kiva: Microfinancing the Global Education of Women

At the global level, one of the most successful ways to aid women and children, and through them entire communities, is through the provision of microfinance loans. Started in Bangladesh by the Grameen Bank, **microfinance loans** are very small loans made at low interest rates, usually given by nongovernmental organizations (NGOs) to small groups of women in developing countries. The recipients of the loans use the money for basic necessities, to support tiny businesses, or to finance children's education. The amount of an individual loan is often $100 or less, which seems very small by the standards of the developed world but can sometimes make a huge difference in the lives of recipients in a poor countries. Early in the history of the microfinance movement, organizations discovered that lending money to women in a community rather than men translated more directly into gains for entire families, and eventually for the community as a whole. Research has demonstrated that giving small loans to women also increases their economic empowerment, thus helping to reduce gender inequality as part of the bargain.

Kiva is one organization that has taken the idea of microfinance to the Internet. Through the Kiva website (http://www.kiva.org), individuals anywhere in the world can become a part of the microfinance movement by making loans online in small amounts. You can choose the purpose of your loan (group loan, housing loan, or agriculture loan) and the geographic location of the borrower. Then you can track the use of your loan and its eventual repayment, and reinvest your original amount by making another loan. In this simple way, even a college student with an extra $25 can help improve the quality of life for women and children around the world.

Craig F. Walker / Denver Post via Getty Images

A woman joins a rally in downtown Denver, Colorado. The event was organized to recognize the gap that exists between the earnings of working men and those of working women. What do you think are the chances that the pay gap will close by the time you start your career?

▶▶ The WAGE Project: Closing the Gender Wage Gap

As we have learned, the significant gains in education that women have made in places like the United States have not so far eliminated the gender gap between women's earnings and those of men. The WAGE (Women Are Getting Even) Project is an initiative of the National Committee on Pay Equity, a coalition of women's and civil rights organizations seeking to eliminate sex- and race-based wage discrimination and to achieve pay equity (WAGE Project 2012). WAGE's website (http://www.wageproject.org) offers a tool for calculating job worth, information about legal options (including detailed information about laws at the federal, state, and local levels), and access to a salary negotiation coach. You can form your own WAGE club, attend a WAGE workshop, or become a trained workshop facilitator.

The site is an excellent place for you to start exploring some of the resources available for fighting wage discrimination.

▶▶ Techbridge: Encouraging Girls to Pursue Science

Techbridge is an organization that seeks to help parents, educators, and organizations encourage young girls to pursue interests that might eventually lead them to high-paying STEM (science, technology, engineering, and mathematics) jobs. The program grew out of the Chabot Space and Science Center and is located in Oakland, California. Its website (http://www.techbridgegirls .org) provides a wealth of information about how to encourage girls to get excited about science. Visit the site to start thinking about how you might help create the next generation of women scientists.

WHAT DOES AMERICA THINK?

Questions about Gender from the General Social Survey

 Turn to the beginning of the chapter to compare your answers to the total population.

1. It is better for men to work and women to tend home.

    AGREE: 31.1%

    DISAGREE: 68.9%

2. Most women really want a home and kids.

    AGREE: 47.4%

    DISAGREE: 52.6%

3. Women are not suited for politics.

    AGREE: 20%

    DISAGREE: 80%

4. Are you for or against the preferential hiring of women?

    FOR: 34.6%

    AGAINST: 65.4%

5. The mother working doesn't hurt children.

    AGREE: 72.4%

    DISAGREE: 27.6%

 ## LOOK BEHIND THE NUMBERS

Go to **edge.sagepub.com/trevino** for a breakdown of these data across time and by race, sex, age, income, and other statuses.

1. Examine the responses to the statement that "the mother working doesn't hurt children." Does education influence the responses? Explain possible reasons for this.

2. Among the respondents, 20% think that women are not suited for politics. Do you think this proportion is large or small? What impacts does that have on society?

3. Examine the data on responses to the statement that "most women really want a home and kids." What do you notice once the data are broken down by gender?

4. Examine the data on responses to the statement that "it is better for men to work and women to tend home" from 1973 to present. How would you explain the responses over time?

SOURCE: National Opinion Research Center, University of Chicago.

CHAPTER SUMMARY

 4.1 Define gender inequality.

Gender inequality is the way in which the meanings assigned to sex and gender as social categories create disparities in resources such as income, power, and status. Gender is the belief that there are two distinct types of people in the world—males and females—and that there are social meanings attached to those categories.

 4.2 Describe the study of gender as a social problem.

Gender is unique as a social problem in that it is both a source of gender inequality and an important social identity. Some argue that to make a distinction on the basis of gender is always to also assume an inequality. Others say we can keep gender as a social category without necessarily seeing women or men as better than the other. Regardless of your perspective, gender, like most social problems, is socially constructed. The particular ways in which various societies understand what gender means and how it relates to inequality vary across times and places. Some gender scholars believe sex is socially constructed as well, and that our culture affects the way we understand biological reality.

4.3 Identify gender problems on college campuses today.

Feminists and others who study gender argue that gender as a social system hurts both women and men, though often in different ways. Some boys feel pressure not to do well academically because their particular subculture defines schoolwork as feminine. However, the gender wage gap demonstrates that men still make more on average than women do around the world, even if this disparity has decreased over time. Differences between men and women in choices of college majors might be one way to explain the gender wage gap, but research suggests that women are disadvantaged in the job market by more than what they did in their college years. Sexual assault on college campuses is another way in which gender inequality manifests itself, through reducing women's sense of safety

and their free access to public areas of social life. The "party rape" phenomenon is caused in part by gendered interaction routines and norms, such as the tendency for women to defer to men.

 4.4 Apply the functionalist, conflict, and symbolic interactionist perspectives to the problem of gender inequality.

An example of structural functionalism is sex role theory, which argues that the division of men and women into gender-specific sex roles is functional for society. Doing gender theory, an example of a symbolic interactionist approach, emphasizes how we create gender through our interactional performances. Radical feminism, borrowing from conflict theory, sees patriarchy as the root of the problem of gender inequality; when a society is built on a solid foundation of male domination, the result is that men maintain power over women.

 4.5 Apply queer theory's interdisciplinary perspective to gender inequality.

Queer theory incorporates feminism, concepts based in the gay and lesbian rights movement, and postmodernist mistrust of metanarratives to question the existence and usefulness of categories in our understanding of gender and larger social life.

 4.6 Identify steps toward social change in gender inequality.

However we may understand the relationship between gender and inequality, as sociologists we know our actions contribute to and create the larger structural forces that make up society. We can choose to continue to contribute to the status quo of gender inequality and the gender system that, as Kate Bornstein says, lets all of us down at some point. Or we can make a conscious choice to help reduce gender inequality on college campuses and elsewhere around the world by becoming involved with organizations like Kiva and SAFER.

DISCUSSION QUESTIONS

1. How do sociologists understand sex and gender? How does this understanding differ from common understandings about women and men?

2. Would a model of five sexes instead of two (Fausto-Sterling 2000) result in a change to the gender inequality in society? How much gender inequality

is based on perceived biological differences between women and men and how much is based on the social construction of gender?

3. How does an individual select a major and a career? Who shapes a person's ideas about what he or she is good at or might enjoy studying? How do noncareer factors such as the need to care for family members or the desire for children play a role in this decision-making process? What about suggestions from others regarding a career path or major?

4. Feminism is offered as one path toward gender equality, and yet many women and most men are reluctant to claim the label *feminist*. Is this reluctance tied to the feminist social movement or to something else? What are the alternatives to feminism that aim at reducing gender inequality in society?

5. College campuses are sites of gender-based inequality both inside and outside the classroom. Is lowering admission standards for men an acceptable way to address the imbalance between men and women in campus populations? What if the situation were reversed and women had a harder time achieving academic equality? What role do colleges and universities play in the safety of women on campuses outside the classroom?

6. How do hegemonic masculinities shape the expectations of young men with regard to college ambitions? How do other identities such as race, ethnicity, and socioeconomic status affect the construction of masculinity and femininity? How

do these identities factor into the choices individuals make about their majors and intended careers?

7. Despite women's academic success before and during college, men still outearn women once in the workforce. What explains the disconnect between academic success and career earnings? How is the wage gap both a product of the institutional structure of education and the workplace and a product of individual choice?

8. How do specific government policies and programs support normative sex and gender roles? How have some policies and programs changed to be more gender-neutral since their inception? For examples, consider Social Security benefits, income taxes for married couples, and benefits to military spouses.

9. How does the symbolic interactionist perspective reveal the role of gender in society for individuals as well as at the institutional level? What are the specific changes that would need to be made to reduce gender inequality?

10. Why do queer theorists see sexuality as central to understanding society? Does queering work? In other words, does queer theory solve the underlying problems by exposing the limitations of sex and gender identities? What does queer theory do that is unique compared with the other perspectives?

11. What roles do individuals play in bringing about changes that can lead to greater gender equality? How much power do we have to change norms and beliefs in the face of structural inequality?

KEY TERMS

accountability 98	expressive 97	interaction routines 93	patriarchy 100
allocation 99	gender 84	intersectional approach 88	radical feminism 100
androcentrism 100	gender inequality 86	intersexed 85	sex role 96
consciousness-raising 101	gender wage gap 90	liberal feminism 100	sexual dimorphism 85
doing gender theory 98	hegemonic masculinity 89	metanarrative 101	socialist feminism 100
ethnomethodology 98	instrumental 97	microfinance loans 103	social role 96

Sharpen your skills with SAGE edge at edge.sagepub.com/trevino

A personalized approach to help you accomplish your coursework goals in an easy-to-use learning environment.

5 SEXUALITY

Rebecca F. Plante

Steven Vidler / Corbis

People's sexual lives differ in terms of where, why, how often, and with whom they have sex. Most people keep such matters to themselves and consider them to be private. Other people define themselves publicly in terms of their sexual orientation. Why do you think sexual identity is important to people?

Investigating Sexuality: My Story

Rebecca F. Plante

I went to Hampshire College in Amherst, Massachusetts, to study documentary film and photography. But all the film courses filled before I registered, and I was stuck, wondering what else I could study. After two rather aimless semesters, I saw an ad in the college newspaper: "Train to be a peer sexuality educator! Lead programs on sex, AIDS, and contraception!" I had found my calling. In dorms and classrooms I led workshops on AIDS, sexual health, sexual communication, and related topics. Before I graduated, I did internships, created newsletters on AIDS/HIV and sexuality, hosted speakers, worked for a well-known sex therapist in San Francisco, taught an upper-level class on sexuality, and took graduate courses in public health.

Studying these issues has been personally and professionally challenging. People are endlessly curious about sex and sexualities, ask many questions, and start a lot of debates. Everyone is an expert, it seems, and yet there are still so many unanswered questions about human sexualities (and genders). I've been fortunate to be able to teach and educate, research and write, and engage in activism for social change. Knowing I can be of service and help people think about their sexualities differently makes my work deeply fulfilling. Doing all this within a sociological framework has been life changing for me, along with all that peer education I started doing in college.

5.1 Identify social problems related to sexuality.

5.2 Explain how the concept of deviance relates to definitions of sexuality-related social problems.

5.3 Apply the functionalist, conflict, and symbolic interactionist perspectives to the study of sexuality-related social problems, specifically sex work and prostitution.

5.4 Apply specialized theories of sexualities.

5.5 Identify steps toward social change regarding problems related to sexuality.

WHAT DO YOU THINK?
Questions about Sexuality from the General Social Survey

1. What is your belief on having sex before marriage?
   - ☐ WRONG
   - ☐ NOT WRONG

2. Do you believe that homosexuals should have the right to marry?
   - ☐ YES
   - ☐ NO

3. What is your level of happiness with your partner?
   - ☐ VERY HAPPY
   - ☐ SOMEWHAT HAPPY
   - ☐ NOT TOO HAPPY

4. Should a homosexual be allowed to teach?
   - ☐ ALLOW
   - ☐ DO NOT ALLOW

5. Should homosexual books be allowed in the library?
   - ☐ YES
   - ☐ NO

6. Married people are happier than unmarried people.
   - ☐ AGREE
   - ☐ DISAGREE
   - ☐ NEITHER AGREE NOR DISAGREE

7. What is your opinion of sex before marriage in teens between 14 and 16 years of age?
   - ☐ ALWAYS WRONG
   - ☐ SOMETIMES WRONG
   - ☐ NOT WRONG AT ALL

8. Should sex education be taught in public schools?
   - ☐ YES
   - ☐ NO

▶▶ Turn to the end of the chapter to view the results for the total population.

SOURCE: National Opinion Research Center, University of Chicago.

FROM MOTEL TO MOTEL

The man renting the hotel room seems nervous and cocky all at once. He addresses the registration clerk brusquely—"Staying two nights. Just me and my daughter. One key." With the key he returns to his car, and to the very young woman waiting there. It's hard to tell how old she is; she could be 14, 16, or maybe even 19. Her face is deceptive—she still has what her mom called baby fat, the chubby cheeks of a much younger girl. But her body seems mature, like a woman's, with hourglass curves. When the pair finally get to the hotel room, with the door slammed shut behind them, he kisses her fully on the mouth, not at all the kiss of a father to a daughter.

"You've got a trick in an hour," he says. "Go get a shower and start getting ready."

In this case study of sex trafficking, an 11-year-old described her 29-year-old "boyfriend," a man who had transported her up and down the East Coast. He took her from motel to motel, arranging transactions with adult men who paid to engage in various sexual acts with her. She took a little money and some gifts from him; she thought he loved her. Rachel Lloyd, an activist and advocate for girls and young women who have been sexually exploited and trafficked, has heard many stories like this from a range of girls and young women. Lloyd's memoir, *Girls Like Us: Fighting for a World Where Girls Are Not for Sale, an Activist Finds Her Calling and Heals Herself* (2012), describes her work as the founder of GEMS—Girls Educational and Mentoring Services—an organization designed to help and empower 11- to 24-year-old girls and women to leave the sex industry (http://www.gems-girls.org).

By founding GEMS, Lloyd was able to blend her experiences as a survivor of commercial sexual exploitation with her undergraduate and graduate training in psychology and applied urban anthropology. She has worked with journalists, lawmakers, filmmakers, and foundations and was instrumental in the passage of New York's first-in-the-nation Safe Harbor Act for Sexually Exploited Youth, a law that ended the prosecution of trafficked children for prostitution. Lloyd's personal experiences and her understanding of the various social contexts of commercial sexual exploitation have enabled her to work toward social change in this significant sexuality-related social problem.

Commercial sexual exploitation and trafficking are issues in many countries around the world, but it is difficult to get a precise sense of exactly how many people are affected. The U.S. Department of State (2007) estimates that perhaps 12.3 million people around the world are trafficked, but this figure includes those who live as forced (nonsexual) laborers as well, and other international governmental agencies estimate the figure to be as high as 27 million people. About 80% of transnationally trafficked victims are women and girls; up to 50% are children. Estimates of the size of the problem in the United States range from 100,000 to 293,000 people (U.S. Department of State 2011). The National Human Trafficking Resource Center keeps track of phone calls to its toll-free hotline; in 2012 there were almost 21,000 callers, including people seeking information, victims of sex trafficking, and people giving tips about suspected trafficking (Polaris Project 2014).

In this chapter, we'll explore how to understand some aspects of human sexualities as social problems. It can be difficult to define *which aspects* and *which problems*. Some say social problems related to human sexuality are simply a matter of differences among moral viewpoints. Others say such problems are defined by individual experiences and psychologies. Still others say human sexuality is social and cultural, with patterns of behavior and attitudes we can easily observe and describe. Are there sexuality-related problems that appear to be *only* individual but that can actually be understood through a sociological lens, using C. Wright Mills's sociological imagination? In other words: How can we understand the public, social, and cultural aspects of sexuality-related issues and problems?

SEEING ASPECTS OF HUMAN SEXUALITIES AS SOCIAL PROBLEMS

 Identify social problems related to sexuality.

Human **sexuality** is complicated by its connections to biology and to the cultural world, with its social institutions,

Sexuality: Sexual behavior, attitudes, feelings.

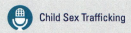
Child Sex Trafficking

customs, beliefs, and interpretations. Our social world also embraces contradictory, confusing perspectives and information. For example, we are told that "having sex"—meaning, engaging in heterosexual activities (Seidman 2003)—is "natural" and that reproduction is the key goal of these activities. We are told that people "naturally" have sexual urges, hormones, and needs that must be fulfilled, but that people should also control themselves for religious, social, or cultural reasons. These contradictions and confusion leave a lot of gray area for individual and collective interpretations.

Further, the meanings and interpretations of most of what we call "sexual" are subject to changing societal agreements about what "sex" is, who is sexual, and what our collective belief systems are (Karras 2000). Human sexualities are more than just natural urges or biological drives, such as the desire to have children. Sexualities also have specific social, cultural, and historical meanings and interpretations. In the United States, for example, many people believe it is acceptable for men and women to be sexually active premaritally, while others believe sexual activity is acceptable only after marriage (see Figure 5.1). National surveys suggest, however, that premarital sexual activity has been the norm for the past 40–50 years (Finer 2007). A considerable range of sexual behaviors and attitudes exists in the United States (and around the world).

We see even more variation if we look across time and space. Laws and religiously influenced morals have long been employed to maintain discipline, order, and control over human sexualities. By the late 1500s in England, "sexual offenders"—mostly people who had engaged in premarital intercourse—were being tied up at public whipping posts in town centers, subject to the judgment and scorn of their neighbors (Dabhoiwala 2012). English courts heard case after case of men and women who had engaged in intercourse without benefit of marriage (often leading to pregnancies and births) and imposed punishments that left the guilty to be outcasts, unemployed, homeless, or even dead. In part, Britons were worried about what they saw as the social problems associated with premarital and nonmarital intercourse: sexually transmitted diseases, crime, children born to unmarried women, and poverty. Across Europe, laws prohibited Christians from having sex with non-Christians; in Modena, Italy, in the 1500s, sex with a Muslim woman was punishable by death unless she was a prostitute, in which case the sentence was life in prison (Berkowitz 2012).

The social problems connected to sexuality seemed quite clear to these Europeans. Sexual conduct that threatened the basic structure of village life, that interfered with legally married couples, or that flouted prohibitions

against premarital and nonmarital sex was defined as problematic, as was nonreproductive sex (such as oral and anal sex and masturbation). Current conceptualizations in the United States are much less clear, however. What counts as a sexuality-related social problem? How can we differentiate between individual and social problems?

A search of news headlines for sexuality-related stories yields several contemporary social conditions, events, and patterns of behavior associated with such stories. But are the issues reported in the stories social problems? That is, recalling the definition from Chapter 1, do they negatively affect the well-being of a significant number of people (or a number of significant people)? Do enough people believe that the condition or pattern needs to be changed or ameliorated? Consider the following issues, introduced by their provocative headlines.

Issue 1, casual sex: "The Cruelty of the Hook-Up Culture" (Cheston 2013). "Hooking up" is broadly defined as "casual sexual behaviors ranging from kissing to intercourse with a partner. . . . there is no current relationship commitment and no expected future relationship commitment" (Lewis et al. 2013, 757–58). Social scientists have begun documenting the social patterns of hookups (Lambert, Kahn, and Apple 2003; Hamilton and Armstrong 2009), arguing that hooking up has replaced the dating practices of the 1940s to 1970s (Eisenberg et al. 2009).

A consequence, say some, is that young adults will not know how to develop and form long-term "posthookup" relationships such as marriages (Regnerus and Uecker 2011; Stepp 2008). Some people are especially concerned about young heterosexual women's choices

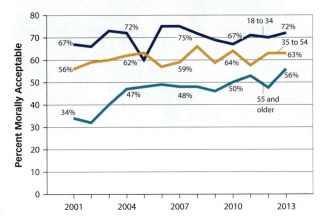

FIGURE 5.1 Perceived Moral Acceptability of Sex between an Unmarried Man and Woman by Age, 2001–2013

Swingers

At a primary school in London, England, 8- and 9-year-olds read a book titled *Let's Talk about Sex*. Do you think that sex education at this early age can have positive effects in these children's lives? How young is too young for children to learn about sex?

and behaviors (Eshbaugh and Gute 2008; Glenn and Marquardt 2001), worrying about the emotional consequences of hooking up. The "cruelty" in the headline quoted above refers to the author's perception that cultural encouragement of casual sex includes some cruel lies and misperceptions: "The entire society has bought into the idea that it isn't necessary to love someone before having sex. That, too, may be a lie, and, if so, a big one that is causing hurt and depression" (Cheston 2013). Is hooking up a social problem?

Issue 2, sexuality education: "Attacks on Sex Education Continue Nationwide" (Conklin 2012). Sexuality education in public schools has been characterized as a battle between those who want abstinence-only lessons to be taught and those who argue for comprehensive sex education (AugsJoost et al. 2014). Advocates of comprehensive sex education want students to learn about anatomy, prevention of pregnancy and sexually transmitted infections, sexual orientations, and sexual variations. They view public school–based sex education as an issue that encompasses health, morality, ethics, and human development, including sexual pleasure (Allen 2012). Sexuality educators, medical professionals, and child development specialists are concerned that inadequate and incomplete sexuality education is a societal condition that threatens the well-being of young people. For example, reduced or incomplete awareness of contraception methods can lead to unplanned and/or unintended pregnancies (Finer and Sonfield 2012). The United States leads developed countries in rates of teenage pregnancies, as well as in abortion rates (Reinberg 2011). Is poor or incomplete sexuality education a social problem?

Issue 3, sexual dysfunction: "If Sexual Dysfunction Were a Virus, 'It'd Be Pandemic': Expert" (Lin and Hensel 2013). The expert quoted in this headline is making a big claim—that sexual dysfunction is widespread enough to be problematic for millions of people. **Sexual dysfunction** is the inability to fully experience sexual responses, arousal, and/or satisfaction, with the added caveat that the person is *distressed* by what is happening. Some estimates of the global prevalence of sexual dysfunction average about 28% for men and 39% for women, higher for people over 40 (Nicolosi et al. 2004). Other estimates vary widely, but all suggest that sexual dysfunction may be the norm rather than the exception for millions of people around the world, making it a substantial pattern within human sexualities with the possibility of negatively affecting the well-being of many.

It may be hard to think of sexual dysfunction as a *social* problem, because we typically see it as a completely individual one, divulged mainly to sexual partners. Is there a way to argue that sexual dysfunction is a social problem? Who is harmed by sexual dysfunction? We will discuss two of these contemporary concerns—hooking up and teenage sexualities—as well as who might define these as sexuality-related social problems, and how we decide who is or isn't harmed by them. We'll also address some other issues that may seem indisputably problematic for society, such as sex work, prostitution, and sex trafficking.

ASK YOURSELF: What is the sociological context of sexuality in the United States? How do we tend to view sexuality? Why is it challenging to understand sexuality-based social problems? Why do we often see sexuality issues as merely individual or personal, and not as social or cultural?

LABELING THEORY

Remember that an aspect of social life may be defined as a social problem when (or if) enough people agree that it causes harm to a significant number of people (or to a number of *significant people*). The social construction of some sexuality-related conditions, patterns, and events as "problematic" requires that people have the power to define problems, to interpret them as problematic, and to enforce this view. **Deviance** is behavior that has been defined as a violation of the general or specific norms or expectations

Sexual dysfunction: The inability to fully experience sexual responses, arousal, and/or satisfaction, accompanied by distress over this inability.

Deviance: Behavior that has been defined as a violation of the general or specific norms or expectations of a culture or of powerful groups.

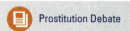

Prostitution Debate

In the 2010 movie *Easy A,* actress Emma Stone plays the character of Olive, a high school "nobody" who decides to pump up her popularity by pretending to lose her virginity. Deciding to increase her new image as a "dirty skank," Olive begins to wear more provocative clothing and, in imitation of *The Scarlet Letter,* stitches a red *A* to everything she wears. How is this an act of self-labeling on Olive's part?

of a culture or of powerful groups. A number of sexuality-based social problems are rooted in socially constructed definitions of deviance and the process of labeling.

Labeling theory (an offshoot of symbolic interactionism) is one way to explain how individuals come to understand themselves and their behavior as deviant and therefore problematic. Labeling theorists explore the ways in which a culture's particular interpretations of deviance are formalized. How do cultural expectations become official sanctions, rules, and laws? How do we internalize these expectations? In a classic work on labeling theory, sociologist Howard S. Becker (1963b, 9) states, "The *deviant is one to whom* that label has been successfully applied; *deviance is behavior* that people so label" (emphasis added).

The first requirement for labeling behavior as deviant is power. Who has the power to codify expectations and the penalties for defying those expectations? Usually it is people with the power to create laws and formal expectations, or people whose power is based on status or money. The second requirement is social interaction—the behavior must be observed or learned about. Without an audience to react, actions and behaviors in and of themselves are not deviant. They can come to be defined that way only when social construction and cultural consensus intersect. If enough people—and especially those with power—agree that an act or behavior should be called deviant, societal expectations will reflect that label.

Labeling theory: The theory that behaviors become defined as deviant when people in power socially construct deviant categories; often leads to the construction of types of deviant people.

Yet perceptions of the problematic, deviant aspects of sexualities have shifted over time. For example, writing in the late 1880s, psychiatrist Richard von Krafft-Ebing (1998) used terms that seemed to describe only a person's behavior or conduct, such as *exhibitionistic* (exposing oneself, particularly one's genitalia, to unconsenting others for sexual gratification). We then began to use language to describe, or label, a person's character or personality, such as *exhibitionist.* Instead of simply referring to patterns of conduct, we began to identify people as *extensions* of their behavior, and we identified their behavior as socially problematic and harmful to large numbers of people.

But shifting perceptions of the problematic, deviant aspects of sexualities have also had positive consequences. For example, we have seen dramatic shifts in attitudes about sexual behaviors that used to be considered problematic, such as heterosexual premarital intercourse (Smith and Son 2013). In 2012, 26.3% of U.S. adults agreed that premarital sex is "always" or "almost always wrong," according to the General Social Survey; in 1972, 45% agreed.

PATTERNS AND TRENDS IN SEXUALITY-RELATED SOCIAL PROBLEMS

5.2 Explain how the concept of deviance relates to definitions of sexuality-related social problems.

People have long been intrigued by sexual behavior. Since the publication of zoology professor Alfred Kinsey's reports on a wide range of sexual conduct in men and women (Kinsey, Pomeroy and Martin 1998; Kinsey, Pomeroy, Martin, and Gebhard 1998), we have wondered about patterns and trends.

The Case of Hooking Up

What exactly is hooking up? It is not a clearly socially defined relationship, dating, seeing someone, having a "boyfriend" or "girlfriend," or being engaged to be married. It can be somewhat committed or casual, a fling of brief duration, emotionally and physically intense, sporadic and irregular, intoxicating and drunken, shared between friends, or experienced by strangers. **Hooking up** includes

Hooking up: Something sexual happening, usually between two people, often outside the context of a socially defined relationship.

 Hookup Culture

"something sexual" happening, usually between only two people, often outside the context of a socially defined relationship. Hookups sometimes include alcohol and other drugs, and may include kissing and making out, or a range of things from touching to oral sex, penile-vaginal sex, and/or anal sex.

Analyses of random, representative samples of adolescents suggest that about 23% of teenage girls in the United States have had significant sexual experiences with people who were "just friends," whom they had just met, or with whom they had gone out "once in a while" (Manning, Longmore, and Giordano 2000) (see Figure 5.2). Smaller, nonrepresentative convenience samples gathered on college campuses suggest that between 50% and 85% of young men and women have hooked up at least once while in college (Aubrey and Smith 2013; Puentes, Knox, and Zusman 2008). Some young adults, especially on college campuses, describe hooking up in ways that suggest that it has become a normative social pattern or experience for them (Armstrong and Hamilton 2013; Allison and Risman 2014). It has become a primary way in which many

young adults explore and experience partnered sexualities. Is hooking up a *social* problem? Who believes it is problematic, and how large is the scope of the problem? Who is harmed by hooking up? Who are the "significant" people worried about the negative effects of hooking up?

Is hooking up a social pattern or condition that is harmful or negative, and, if so, to whom? Independent of their actual behavior, college students say hooking up is fun, common, low commitment, harmless, carefree, a source of status and empowerment, and a way to explore sexuality (Aubrey and Smith 2013; Kenney et al. 2013). Some researchers have studied how students make sense of and actually experience hookups (Armstrong, England, and Fogarty 2010; Wade and Heldman 2012); their findings suggest that, while hooking up can definitely be pleasurable, positive, or merely neutral ("fine"), it may also have intended and unintended consequences.

Some consequences of the "hookup culture" that may harm well-being include pressure to participate (the belief that everyone else is doing it), particularly in college or immediately after college, and emotional distress. Students in one study agreed that hookups are acceptable but also described their own experiences that led to regret, embarrassment, and disinterest in future hookups (Thomas 2010). Hookups are supposed to have no strings attached, and some "how-to" books on being more successful at casual sex and hookups teach heterosexual women that they should separate their feelings from hookups (Plante 2006).

Researchers have also observed that hooking up maintains the heterosexual gendered double standard (Hamilton and Armstrong 2009). The **double standard** is a cultural belief system in which men are expected to desire and seek sex, while women are expected to be sexual only within committed, romantic relationships. Those who hold this double standard may also believe women's sexual behavior is different from men's and should be judged differently (Allison and Risman 2013; Reid, Elliott, and Webber 2011). For instance, they may judge women negatively for seeking sex and pleasure outside relationships, while they judge men less harshly, if at all, for the same behavior (Armstrong et al. 2010).

Other consequences of hooking up may include increased exposure to sexually transmitted diseases and potential for mental health disturbances, including depression (Downing-Matibag and Geisinger 2009; Bersamin et al. 2012). A few studies suggest that those who hook up may be less aware that coercive sexual assaults and rapes are a potential outcome, in part because of previous educational efforts around "date rape" (Geisinger 2011; Arnold 2013). Because hookups are not considered "dates," it appears that participants

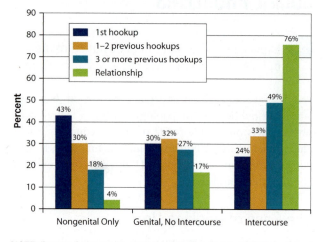

FIGURE 5.2   Percentage of College Students Engaging in Sexual Behaviors in Four Sexual Contexts

NOTE: Respondents are classified in "Nongenital Only" if they did not engage in oral sex, hand-genital stimulation, or intercourse; in "Genital, No Intercourse" if they did not engage in intercourse but engaged in oral sex or hand-genital stimulation (irrespective of who gave or who received); in "Intercourse" if they had intercourse.

SOURCE: Adapted from *Families As They Really Are,* edited by Barbara J. Risman. Copyright © 2010 W.W. Norton & Company, Inc.

Double standard: An attitude or belief that judges heterosexual women's sexual behavior more harshly and negatively than heterosexual men's sexual behavior.

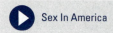

Sex In America

Sex outside Marriage

Ei Katasumata / Alamy

Many countries report that people are having "casual sex" (sex outside heterosexual marriage), there is not as much condom use as medical officials would like, morals appear to be changing—and governments and community leaders aren't convinced this is a good thing. Japan, for example, has recently pushed to improve AIDS education among sexually active teens, whose sexually oriented texts are more likely to say "let's play together" than "let's hook up" (Head 2004). Japanese public health staff and condom manufacturers are worried about the increasing rate of sexually transmitted infections, and students talk about how little formal sexuality education they get in school or elsewhere. High school student Madoka Izumi said, "I go to a girls' school, and we've never been able to learn what boys think about sex. They've taught us some of the physical sides of sex, but none of the emotional aspects, so we're not really prepared to deal with it" (quoted in Head 2004).

Researchers in East Asia have noted that Japanese college students seem more liberal than their Chinese counterparts in regard to premarital and casual sex. Only 3–4% of Japanese college students in a recent national survey said sexual activity should be delayed until marriage or engagement (JASE 2007, as cited in Farrer et al. 2012). But big changes are also afoot in China, where more than 70% of 1,013 respondents ages 20 to 39 had engaged in premarital intercourse. Approximately 15.5% of same-aged respondents had done so in 1989 (research cited in *Want China Times* 2012). This cultural change seems to be occurring despite long-standing government disapproval of youthful sexuality, which has extended to expelling students from school if they were found to have engaged in premarital intercourse (Farrer 2006). Administrators and educators feel that viewing "premarital sex . . . as merely another personal choice" (Farrer 2006, 107) clashes with the traditional Chinese social value of chastity, which they feel compelled to uphold.

In India, a large national study of more than 15,000 never-married women suggested that only 0.6%, or 97 women, had been sexually active (Narzary 2013). Long-standing cultural and sociosexual norms and attitudes make premarital sex highly taboo and problematic, not so much an individual choice as a decision nested within history and familial and cultural expectations. Virginity at marriage is highly valued in India, and premarital pregnancy is stigmatized,

Candlelight march for AIDS awareness in Kyoto, Japan. The least expensive and most confidential way for a Japanese person to get an AIDS test is at the local public health clinic (*hokenjo*). Such clinics are located in every neighborhood and urban area throughout Japan.

constructing casual and premarital sex as a major social problem there.

▶ **THINK ABOUT IT**

1. Beyond the cultural and historical context mentioned here, what else might explain the very small number of unmarried Indian women reporting that they have been sexually active?

2. Why would governments, school administrators, and educators be invested in issues that otherwise seem quite personal or individual, such as premarital sexual activity and premarital pregnancy? Why might they care about this kind of sex?

3. What do you think about China's concern about the social problem of premarital sex? Is it reasonable to think administrators or government officials could regulate sexualities? Why or why not?

can overlook the fact that the sexual activity involved may include coercion and force. Researchers have begun to explore this connection between heterosexual hook-ups and unwanted sexual activities, including fondling, oral sex, and vaginal intercourse. Structural aspects of college campuses that may facilitate coercive sexual activities include parties and social life controlled by fraternities (Flack et al. 2007).

Social systems and patterns of hooking up may have negative effects on well-being, especially for women's sexual growth and self-esteem (Regnerus and Uecker 2011; Stepp 2008). Some say that engaging in hookups can affect participants' ability to have more traditionally socially defined relationships and to be intimate in dating and marital relationships (Walsh 2014). Others worry that young adults who hook up will not want families or marriages later in life (Strawn 2013). But some research counters these concerns. The National College Health and Social Life Survey, started by sociologist Paula England, showed that 87% of (heterosexual) respondents wanted to be married or partnered in the future. And a Higher Education Research Institute (2013) study of 192,912 first-year students showed that, on average, 73.6% strongly agreed that "raising a family" was an important future goal.

We cannot know all the ways in which the social conditions surrounding hooking up affect or harm young adults, but we can easily see that some researchers and commentators are concerned about the issue. In the next section, we'll examine the always controversial issue of pornography. Is it a social problem? What is harmful or negative about it?

ASK YOURSELF: Who is harmed or negatively affected by hooking up? Have you seen examples of this on your campus? What are the larger social dynamics surrounding hooking up? Is hooking up a social problem?

Just Business? The Case of Pornography

Since earliest recorded history, people have been making pictures of sexual acts. Our human ancestors made sexual and erotic art—cave paintings, drawings, sculptures, pottery—in ancient France, Japan, China, Mexico, the South Pacific, Greece, and Rome, among other places. The word **pornography** comes from the ancient Greek word *pornographos*, or writings (*graph*) about prostitutes (*porne*, related to "harlot," a type of prostitute). Current definitions simply state that pornography is sexually explicit material intended to arouse; this is distinguished from **erotica**, literary or artistic material meant to cause sexual feelings. Pornography is also meant to be outside the bounds of culturally accepted depictions of sexualities (McNair 2013).

The invention of photography in the mid-1800s, later facilitated by the development of more portable cameras, allowed the distribution of "dirty pictures." By the 1950s, the motion picture industry was producing films depicting people engaged in various sex acts; these were watched mostly in "adult theaters" and sometimes in

Neon signs advertise strippers and adult products outside Peep Land in New York City's Times Square. For the most part, peep shows, strip shows, and porn theaters have become a thing of the past. Such entertainment and products can now be obtained on the Internet.

Viviane Moos / Corbis

private settings by small groups, mostly male. The later development of the videocassette recorder meant that more people could see pornographic movies in the privacy of their homes. Despite their long history, sexually explicit images and stories have nearly always been controversial. The 1873 Comstock Act, passed in the United States, was intended to prevent the distribution of obscene or lewd materials, particularly via the postal service (Mirkin 2009). Defining *obscene* and *lewd* was problematic, however. The way the act was worded, in addition to pornographic materials it prohibited distribution of materials referring to, explaining, or describing contraceptive devices and techniques.

Though the U.S. pornography industry is in flux, largely due to the influence of the Internet, it remains big business for entrepreneurs. Centered in Southern California, the industry was making about 11,000 films a year a decade ago; in contrast, mainstream Hollywood made about 400 features a year (Slade 2001; Paul 2004). Before Internet pornography cut into the rental market, in-store and mail rentals of pornographic videos increased 850% in only 15 years, from 79 million in 1985 to 759 million in 2001. In one year, 10 million people visited the 10 most popular cybersex websites (Cooper, McLoughlin, and Campbell 2000). From July 2009 to July 2010, about 55 million, or 13%, of the 400 million Internet searches in the Dogpile (aggregator) search engine were for something sexual or

Pornography: Sexually explicit material (video, photos, writings) intended to arouse and that may include transgressive representations of current aesthetic and cultural norms.

Erotica: Literary or artistic material meant to cause sexual feelings.

 Pornography

Steve Rhodes / Demotix / Corbis

Larry Flynt's Hustler Clubs feature female entertainers in erotic dances and poses. The clubs are found in more than a dozen U.S. cities. How is it that these clubs commit "crimes against women"?

erotic (Ogas and Gaddam 2012). It is difficult to estimate accurately how much money the "adult entertainment" industry generates; many factors may artificially inflate or deflate profit estimates, but the total could be $12 billion per year (Voss 2012; Sloan 2007).

What is the problem with pornography, and why are some people concerned about it? Researchers around the world have been studying who uses pornography and with what effects and consequences. For example, in Croatia, scholars found that "risky sexual behavior"—having sex without condoms and/or with multiple partners—was related to pornography use (Sinkovic, Stulhofer, and Bozic 2013). Some would argue that sex without condoms, sex with multiple partners, and pornography use are all major sexuality-related social problems that harm a great number of people.

In the United States, some studies have found an association between male consumers' attitudes about women and their pornography use (Hald, Malamuth, and Yuen 2010). Researchers analyzed 304 scenes from popular recent pornography films and noted that 88.2% contained physical aggression, such as spanking and slapping, and nearly half the scenes also contained verbal aggression (Bridges et al. 2010). Those studying pornography from feminist, conflict theory, and social justice perspectives argue that one significant harm of most heterosexual pornography is that it depicts the systematic domination of women (Dines and Jensen 2004).

Some researchers who have explored young adults' use of and feelings about pornography have noted a lot of ambivalence and many paradoxes. About 1,900 young Swedish men and women responded to an Internet survey about their sexual use of the Web; 5% of the women and 13% of the men reported having some problems, including feeling "addicted," feeling that their use was out of control,

and feeling disconnected from friends and partners (Ross, Månsson, and Daneback 2011). Some have tried to link pornography use with sexual addiction and compulsivity (Griffiths 2012). Sexual addiction is a controversial issue, subject to debate about its definition and parameters, along with questions about whether we can objectively assess it.

Problems related to pornography can also be the subject of intersectional analyses of race, class, gender, and sexuality. Sociologist Mireille Miller-Young (2010), who has studied the adult film industry for more than seven years, argues that racism is prominent in the industry and that all the actors are "evaluated and commodified" through the intersectional lens. She suggests that "black female bodies" in particular have been devalued in the pornographic industry, evident in black actresses' lower wages—$400–$900 for a "boy/girl" sex scene, compared to $1,000–$2,000 for white actresses (227). Miller-Young's long-term observation and interview study describes degrading comments made to black actresses, who report being judged against standards of white beauty (and always falling short) and being narrowly represented as "the exotic Other." The issues Miller-Young documents may not seem problematic, but the harm extends beyond black actresses in adult films; the industry's race-based stereotypes and salary devaluations mirror racial dynamics we can see in broader U.S. society (Brooks 2010).

Years of research suggest that the use of pornography has some discernible negative effects, particularly on heterosexual men, including the creation of "unreal expectations of women's desires and behaviors" (Tolman 2013, 87). In pornography we can see the development of sexual scripts or scenarios designed to teach men how to diminish women's resistance, as well as depictions of sexuality that include aggression and the treatment of women as objects (Vaes, Paladino, and Puvia 2011; Purcell and Zurbriggen 2013).

If pornography meets the definition of a social problem, what solutions might we generate to deal with its problematic aspects? And what about the fine line between censorship and violation of First Amendment rights? In the next section, we'll briefly explore a social condition that seems more unequivocally problematic—sex trafficking. This issue, like pornography, involves the commercialization and sale of "sex," sex acts, and sexual bodies, but a crucial distinction is that trafficking relies on force and/or coercion.

ASK YOURSELF: Is pornography a social problem? What is harmful about it? Is it less problematic for *some* consumers or in *some* contexts? Who and what are they, and why? Which social forces—such as the economy, politics, the Internet—are implicated in the construction of pornography as a social problem? How?

Global and Local: Sex Trafficking

Sex trafficking, a commercial, criminal activity that includes force, fraud, or coercion to exploit a person sexually for profit, is truly a global issue. Contrary to popular belief, trafficking does not need to include transportation from one location to another (U.S. Department of State 2011). The U.S. Department of State (2007) estimates that about 12.3 million people around the world have been trafficked, including people in the United States, Canada, and Mexico; this figure includes those who live as forced but nonsexual laborers. Other international governmental agencies estimate that the number of people trafficked could be 27 million.

In any given year, according to the United Nations Regional Information Centre for Western Europe (http://unric.org), about 2.5 million people are trafficked, including those working as forced sexual laborers. About 80% of those who are forced from one country to another are women and girls; up to 50% are children. In the United States, estimates range from 100,000 to 293,000 people per year (U.S. Department of State 2011). Human trafficking, in general, "is defined by the exploitation of victims" (Chin and Finckenauer 2012, 4).

The current dynamics of sex trafficking are rooted in the coerced movements and chosen migrations of people that began hundreds of years ago. Sex trafficking has been around for a very long time. Exploitation and coercion, particularly sexual, have deep historical roots, complicated causes, and unclear effects. In the early 1900s, for example, there were fears that white, middle-class European and North American women would be trafficked and enslaved (Saunders and Soderlund 2003; Kempadoo 2005). The 1949 United Nations Convention for the Suppression of the Traffic in Persons and of the Exploitation of the Prostitution of Others was the first legally binding international agreement to address the problem.

In recent years, headlines have proclaimed that sex trafficking is now "epidemic" in the United States—"no class and no child is immune" (Neubauer 2011). The Half the Sky Movement (2014), a U.S.-based organization devoted to combating the global oppression of women, states that "at no point in history have more people been enslaved than women currently are in the sex trade." The organization estimates that, globally, traffickers earn $27.8 billion a year.

Sex trafficking has been documented in 161 countries; its causes are quite complex and differ by region of the world and by specific countries (Segrave, Milivojevic, and Pickering 2009). Poverty is one of many variables in many global systems of trafficking (Binh 2006). Cambodian activist, author, and former sex slave Somaly Mam is an example of these complexities. Her impoverished family, members of a stigmatized and marginalized ethnic tribe, had limited economic opportunity and low status in their village. Mam (2009) has written about how her complexion was not seen as "moon" enough, not white enough. Her parents left her with a grandmother, perhaps to escape bombs dropped by the United States, or perhaps to escape the Cambodian Khmer Rouge political regime and its starvation, poverty, and injustice. Mam's grandmother sold her into sexual slavery when she was 12 years old, and she was trafficked into brothels all over Southeast Asia for the next 10 years. She eventually escaped and has since dedicated herself to helping other Cambodian girls and young women who want to leave sex slavery and trafficking. Mam's experiences illustrate some of the complex variables that enable trafficking: tribal, ethnic, and village structures; gender; war; poverty; political unrest; inequalities.

Women who have been trafficked can be reluctant to come forward because they fear they will be perceived negatively. Researchers who studied trafficking in Serbia, Thailand, and Australia found that police and government agents sometimes applied the label of "sex trafficking victim" only to women who fit certain gendered stereotypes (seeming lost, sweet, innocent) (Segrave et al. 2009). Women also report internalizing blame for having been trafficked, along with being made to feel ashamed about what has happened to them (Territo & Kirkham 2010).

Both women and men are subject to local, national, and global inequalities—financial, legal, spiritual, emotional, educational, and political (Nagel 2003; Agustín 2007). Both are trafficked, although research and policy have focused on women (and girls). On a broad scale, however, *sexual* inequalities disproportionately affect women and girls, in the form of rape (acquaintance rape, marital rape, stranger rape, and rape as a war crime), sexual assault, domestic abuse, nonconsensual genital mutilation, and childhood sexual assault (Gavey 2005). Sexual and gendered inequalities are evident in global sexual slavery, sex trafficking, **sex tourism** (in which citizens from economically developed countries travel to less economically developed countries to purchase the sexual services of local people), and **sex work** (the services

....

Sex trafficking: A commercial, criminal activity that includes force, fraud, or coercion to exploit a person sexually for profit.

Sex tourism: Travel to destinations, typically in developing countries, specifically for the purpose of buying sex from men and women there.

Sex work: Services provided by those in the commercial sex industry; the term is intended to destigmatize the work and providers of the labor (called sex workers).

Sex Slaves

provided by people who work in the commercial sex industry, including exotic dancers, prostitutes, cybersex providers, and others) (Kempadoo and Doezema 1998; Clift and Carter 2000; Pappas 2011).

Thus even a very brief historical glimpse at sex trafficking suggests that the problem is not just the coerced sexual exploitation of people, and of women particularly. Alternative perspectives on sex trafficking emphasize that sexual exploitation, in general, occurs within a complicated framework of intersecting social institutions, customs and mores, and social inequalities. This complexity is usually ignored or hidden within most historical and contemporary discussions of the problematic nature of sex trafficking. To understand the issue in some depth, we have to use the sociological imagination to see the broader contexts.

Melissa Gira Grant (2013, 2) is a writer and former sex worker who is concerned about what she calls "the sex trafficking panic." U.S. laws have recently changed to classify anyone in the sex trade who is under 18 years old as trafficked, or coerced, even if that person has never been subject to any "force, fraud, or coercion." *Deviance, social constructionism,* and *social problems* have commonalities: A consensus of powerful society members first react to an issue that has been socially constructed and given meaning. These actors further define that issue as *problematic,* and they may also define *individuals* connected to that problem as problematic, or deviant. Grant argues that "what fuels the sex trafficking panic isn't moral outrage at the lives of people forced into labor. It may be rooted in far older fears and prejudices about people who work in the sex industry" (3).

A *panic* is a "condition, episode, person or a group of persons [that] emerges to become defined as a threat to societal values and interests," usually with a moral(ized) element (Cohen 2002, 1). Thus "sex trafficking panics" or *sex panics* in general can easily be considered under an umbrella of social problems more generally. The consequences of panics may include excessive ideas about risk and harm, along with "loose definitions of sex" (Lancaster 2011, 2). The United States has a collective history that includes general discomfort with sex and sexuality.

Why might sex trafficking be an issue of concern, both to sociologists and to those outside the discipline? What broader, common cultural fears might be embedded within the discussions about trafficking? Grant (2013) and Lancaster (2011) argue that some of the fears certainly relate to more general culturally defined fears and discomfort with sexualities. Ronald Weitzer (2007), who conducts research on sex work and sex trafficking, suggests that the cultural reaction to sex trafficking has become invested with morality, and as a result we spotlight horrifying, dramatic details of victimization and inflate the significance and incidence of the problem. Organizations like Half the Sky and Rachel Lloyd's GEMS (discussed at the beginning of this chapter) have helped raise general awareness of sex trafficking, also ensuring that thousands of individual stories have been told. Although we cannot fully grasp the extent and prevalence of sex trafficking, we can see that millions of people are directly involved, millions more are affected and harmed, and solving the problem will require careful, massive, multinational efforts (McCabe and Manian 2010).

It is easy to argue that sex trafficking is in fact a significant social problem, especially for women and girls. But what about sex work and prostitution, forms of sexual commerce that are similar to trafficking but also different in terms of the dimensions of coercion, fraud, and consent? Are sex work and prostitution social problems?

ASK YOURSELF: What other kinds of sexual panics can you think of? What kinds of sexuality-related "fears and prejudices" exist? Sex trafficking has been happening for a long time. What factors and variables might explain why it is still happening?

USING THEORY TO UNDERSTAND SEX WORK AND PROSTITUTION: THE VIEWS FROM THE FUNCTIONALIST, CONFLICT, AND SYMBOLIC INTERACTIONIST PERSPECTIVES

 5.3 Apply the functionalist, conflict, and symbolic interactionist perspectives to the study of sexuality-related social problems, specifically sex work and prostitution.

Despite my misgivings about [prostitution], I was pretty sure that it was an incomplete understanding of exploitation to define it as someone getting paid for what I was willing to do for free. While men clearly benefited from the institution of prostitution, I wondered who benefited from making criminals of women charging for sex.

—Wendy Chapkis (2011, 327),
author of *Live Sex Acts:
Women Performing Erotic Labor* (1997)

 Selling Sex

Men wearing T-shirts advertising "Girls direct to you in 20 minutes" offer photo leaflets advertising call girls in Las Vegas, Nevada. Nevada is one of only two U.S. states that allow some legal prostitution. Is supplying a customer with sex in 20 minutes the sexual equivalent of fast food?

Wendy Chapkis raises a key question: Why do we consider **prostitution**—defined as having sex in exchange for something, especially money—to be exploitative and a social problem? Some prostitutes prefer the term *sex worker* and describe their activities as *sex work* in an effort to destigmatize it. Does that mean sex work may sometimes avoid being considered a social problem?

It is hard to tell exactly how large the contemporary sex work industry is. Sex work is not the same as sex trafficking, though both involve commercial sex; sex work has more potential to happen without the fraud or coercion of trafficking. Except in brothels in Nevada, prostitution is illegal in the United States, so people are not necessarily open about being employed in the industry or patronizing it. The FBI reported about 80,000 arrests for prostitution in 2006, a figure that declined to 62,700 by 2010, but most instances of sex for sale go unnoticed, so this figure cannot reflect the real incidence (Puzzanchera and Kang 2013). National data suggest that about 1 million people of all sexes and genders (or about 1% of the U.S. population) are employed in prostitution, while global data range from lows of 0.1% of the population to highs of 7.4% in countries across the world (Vandepitte et al. 2006).

Sex work happens in a variety of settings, including on the street and in parking lots, in motels and hotels, at private homes, and in brothels or multiroom buildings set up for sex work. Not all sex work is equally and fairly compensated, particularly when we consider the risks to the laborers. Those who work from their own homes via webcam, performing sex acts for paying customers who watch online, may not worry so much about sexually transmitted infections or physical violence and rape.

Those whose trade includes sex acts performed with paying customers in person may face real risks and harms. Researchers and activists who consider sex work to be a significant social problem are concerned about these kinds of risks and the wage inequalities in the system; those sex workers who work primarily on the street tend to earn the least. Other researchers and activists worry about the effects of sex work on families, relationships, and the moral framework they argue is the foundation of U.S. society.

The three primary sociological theories provide a basic framework for understanding the problematic aspects of sex work and prostitution, particularly in the United States. What are the implications and consequences of prostitution and sex work? What might they suggest about general attitudes and feelings about sexuality in the United States? We look at each theory in turn below.

Structural Functionalism

Classic work by sociologist Kingsley Davis (1937) outlined a structural functional argument for prostitution and sex work. If we accept the basic arguments of this theory, then we also accept the idea that our social structures and institutions serve particular and enduring social functions. From a structural functionalist perspective, the process of labeling and defining deviance serves the social function of clarifying broader societal norms and values.

When the sanctions and consequences for deviating are clear, we stay within legal and moral boundaries because we benefit from doing so, and because we fear the sanctions we would be subject to otherwise. A functionalist perspective would argue that the sex work industry serves important purposes in societies:

1. Clients get an outlet for a variety of sexual acts they may be unable to fulfill in other ways or in other more socially accepted relationships (such as heterosexual marriage).

2. Clients get a way to meet their sexual and emotional needs without having to be in relationships.

3. Society at large can maintain the status quo, making negative judgments and creating stigmatizing labels for those who engage in sex work (*whore, slut, rent boy*).

4. Sex work provides jobs for people who might otherwise have few options for employment.

Prostitution: The provision of sex in exchange for something, especially money. Contrast with sex work.

5. Sex work provides an outlet for same-sex sexual activities (typically between male clients and male workers).

6. Society can maintain its traditionally held beliefs about differences between heterosexual men's and women's sexualities. In this perspective, men's sexualities are seen as lusty, desiring, and needing outlets; men's purchase of sex is thus seen as fulfillment of "natural" masculine needs.

Prostitution may also serve the function of revealing and strengthening the underpinnings of the moral system operating in the United States and similar societies. An intended or **manifest consequence** of sexual morals, labeling, and deviance is that as a society we generally condemn prostitution and sex work. We may argue that "sex for sale" does not fit our cultural values, that sex itself is supposed to be meaningful, relational, safe, and even perhaps romantic. An unintended or **latent consequence** is that we then label much of our human sexualities as "good" or "bad." So "meaningless," nonrelational, "risky," and "exciting" sex might end up being defined as the job of sex workers and prostitutes.

Another unintended consequence is that our labels and judgments help maintain sexism and structural inequalities. Consider the idea that we judge heterosexual female sex workers as immoral, not respectable, and damaged because "good girls" shouldn't sell sex; recall how the double standard enables us, collectively, to argue that the function of providing heterosexual men with sexual outlets is somewhat acceptable because heterosexual men's sexualities are judged less negatively than women's (through clichés like "men have needs" and "boys will be boys"). The problem is that the double standard can lead to inequalities in laws and policies—female sex workers are arrested more often than their male clients and are given harsher sentences (Almodovar 2010).

Policy Implications of Structural Functionalism

If we accept the logic that sex work serves important social functions, such as providing an outlet for sexual practices that are otherwise negatively labeled and stigmatized, then we might be inclined to argue that we should lobby to decriminalize or legalize sex work. Scholars who have

Manifest consequence: An intended, overt, planned, and/or agreed-upon (by consensus) effect or outcome of social phenomena or individual behaviors.

Latent consequence: An unintended, covert, unplanned, and/or hidden effect or outcome of social phenomena or individual behaviors.

John Van Hasselt / Corbis

Sex workers march in the streets of Paris, France, to claim their right to exercise their profession without fear of being arrested. Some prostitutes claim that the more their work must be clandestine, the more it becomes a danger to public health and an invitation to crime. Do you agree with them?

studied the legal brothels in some counties in Nevada have suggested that legalization serves other important functions, including reduction of harm and risks and standardization of transactions (Brents and Hausbeck 2005). Harm reduction includes regulations that minimize the spread of sexually transmitted diseases and require condom use, and structures that allow privacy in sexual interactions while also protecting (women) sex workers from customers who might be physically and emotionally assaultive.

ASK YOURSELF: Consider the following: Men who purchase sex are basically behaving like men; they have needs to fulfill, and sex workers can meet those needs. Women who sell sex are not behaving like women, though, because it doesn't make sense that a woman would sell sexual services. Do you agree with this argument? Why or why not? Is it harmful that we label sex workers? Are there negative effects of this labeling?

Conflict Theory

Conflict theorists suggest that sex work, like everything else in society, is embedded in a history of struggles over the distribution of always-scarce resources. The laws that make sex work illegal are created by people with societal power and influence who have the ability to institutionalize their conceptualizations of particular morals and values. Conflict theorists would argue that sex work exists in its current forms, at least in the United States, for the following reasons:

1. Broader, persistent structural inequalities are reproduced in sex work, including racism and sexism (Carter and Giobbe 2006).

2. Women have traditionally been disadvantaged socially and occupationally.

3. Heterosexual sex work, with female workers and male clients, reproduces existing gender inequalities.

4. The "industrialization" of sex work enables male clients and procurers to benefit from purchasing and selling the workers—mostly women and young girls—who sell sex.

A conflict theorist would ask who benefits from cultural structures and attitudes about sex work, and why racial, gendered, and sexual inequalities are reproduced in the industry.

Policy Implications of the Conflict Perspective

If we accept the argument that sex work reproduces and enables inequalities, then we could suggest that the industry would change if we lobbied to legalize fair wages across the varieties of sex work (street work, outcall work, brothels). In an unregulated and mostly illegal industry, sex workers, intermediaries such as madams and pimps, and clients determine payments without regard to risk, harm, and other variables. Lever and Dolnick (2000) conducted a large-scale study of sex workers in which they compared women working the street to those who worked in motels and apartments. Nearly 70% of those on the street were black, while nearly 80% of those working indoors were white. Wages differed dramatically: on average, the price for women "on call" indoors was $200, compared to $30 for women "walking" the street. Other policy implications from the conflict perspective suggest that the only way to bring about fundamental change in the sex work industry is to create equalizing routes to economic autonomy, freedom, and self-determination in U.S. society (Snowden 2011).

Symbolic Interactionism

Symbolic interactionist perspectives on sex work and prostitution enable us to consider the individual perspectives of those who participate most directly in the industry. Interactionism is based on the concept that people understand themselves and their social worlds through interactions, adaptations, and negotiations of social cues. Interactionists would say that people develop identities and self-concepts within the context of social life and the commonly believed scripts (blueprints) for behavior and attitudes. Thus it makes sense to ask how we can understand sex workers' perspectives. Do sex workers label themselves? How do they make sense of their labor given its illegality, social judgment, double standards, and inequalities? Interactionist perspectives would also examine the symbolism, ideologies, and language around sex work (such as *whore* and *easy*). Do sex workers see themselves as stigmatized?

Researchers have found that sex workers see themselves as laborers providing a basic and necessary service that has flexible boundaries between "intimacy" and "work" (Brewis and Linstead 2000). Others have explored the way female sex workers actively construct the meaning and interpretations of their labor, from language to business rules (Williamson and Baker 2009). Sex workers describe themselves and their industry in ways that make it clear they understand the socially constructed complexity of what they do. In the introduction to her edited collection of writings by sex workers, Annie Oakley (2007, 10) asks, "What does it say about us as sexual consumers that we prefer our product to be anonymous?" Within this perspective, the social problem of sex work is its role in society—the way it is nested within sociocultural values and moral judgments about sexualities and sexual practices.

Male sex workers with male clients have been studied less frequently than female sex workers with male clients, but the research that exists suggests that some male sex workers engage in a process of self-conceptualization that mirrors what some female workers do (Smith and Grov 2011). Some see themselves as degraded by the work, others see themselves as providing an essential service to diverse customers, and some see themselves as doing a form of caregiving. From a research standpoint, though, we know very little about how male clients might fit into an interactionist framework. How do *they* see themselves? How do they make sense of their role in the sex work industry deemed so problematic by others in society? A small study of male clients in Finland suggests that some men may see themselves as participating in something that is clearly "not real" and is just fantasy or escape; as doing something "wild," socially disapproved, and therefore exciting; and as doing something that feels like a heterosexual masculine "right" (arguing that men have sexual needs they must meet) (Marttila 2003). In the United States, one sociologist reports that male clients see themselves similarly and do not seem to self-stigmatize their behavior (Monto 2010).

Policy Implications of Symbolic Interactionism

Within the symbolic interactionist framework, we see some implications we have already discussed—decriminalization

A Different Perspective on Sex Tourism

Planning a trip to Bangkok, Thailand? You might want to choose your hotel carefully, unless you prefer to stay in the middle of Bangkok's red-light district, a noisy, crowded, neon-lighted area of stores and bars and sex for sale. The district is a destination spot for international travelers who visit specifically to partake of the sexual atmosphere and buy the sexual services of a variety of girls and women.

Destinations for sex tourists are typically developing countries in the Caribbean, Latin America, Southeast Asia, and Africa. These countries enable sex tourism by helping to create places like red-light districts and by allowing (or not discouraging) the sale and purchase of sexual services. The economies of some developing countries depend on the financial gains provided by sex tourism. Sex tourism also occurs in Amsterdam's red-light district and within the United States. There is no way to know how many millions of people are connected to sex tourism as clients, procurers, and providers.

What does sex tourism have to do with intersectionality—race, class, gender, nationality, and sexualities? Sex tourism to developing countries is linked to certain societal conditions and dynamics (Enloe 1989; Chow-White 2006). Economic conditions in the host or destination countries, such as poverty and perpetually depressed economies, create the need for some people to engage in sex work in order to survive, help support their families, and meet basic living needs (Omondi 2003). White (male) travelers, typically from richer nations, need to convince themselves that the people of color who are selling sex are more available, interested, and willing than people in their home countries (Enloe 1989). Race and racism intersect with classism and stereotypes about people of color as "naturally sexual" and romantic (Jacobs 2010).

Researchers have analyzed how Asian women are portrayed in media, as "little brown fucking machine[s] powered by rice" (Shimizu 2007, 214). Interviews with male and female sex tourists in the Caribbean reveal this stereotyped belief as well—that people of color are "just doing what comes naturally" and are "naturally physical, wild, hot and sexually powerful" (O'Connell Davidson and Sanchez Taylor 1999, 47). This is "racialized sexism," combined with classism, a pattern of attitudes characterized by the stereotyped beliefs that black and brown people around the world are "naturally" more sexual, more passionate, and more desirous of "servicing" the mostly white, Western sex tourists who travel for sex.

Jack Kurtz / Zuma Press / Corbis

Ladyboy (transgender) entertainers flirt with customers and try to draw them into the Cockatoo bar in the Soi Cowboy red-light district in Bangkok, Thailand. Many of the ladyboys work in the entertainment and nightlife sectors of the Thai economy. Thailand has gained international notoriety among travelers from many countries as a sex tourism destination.

Sex tourism is problematic for several reasons, including the obvious—that is, in some countries, the sale and purchase of sex is illegal although it persists. The risk of exposure to and spread of sexually transmitted diseases is another social problem. Less obvious but real problems relate to the ways in which the practice connects discriminatory attitudes and practices—racism, sexism, nationalism, and classism—to commercialized sex.

▶ **THINK ABOUT IT**

1. Why would some people travel far from home to purchase sex, given that services are available in many local communities?

2. Can you imagine people from destination countries traveling to the United States to purchase sex? Why or why not? What bigger-picture issues apply to this practice?

Sex Tourism

and/or legalization—along with some interactionist-specific implications, such as societal stigma and negative perceptions. But it is very difficult to create policy or legislation to restructure societal interpretations and judgments. Widespread legalization or decriminalization of sex work may make certain acts "legal," but those in the industry would not instantly be free of societal stigma or negative perceptions (Harrington 2012). If prostitution were legalized, it still might not be seen as a viable career choice.

SPECIFIC THEORIES IN SEXUALITIES AND SOCIAL PROBLEMS SCHOLARSHIP

 5.4 Apply specialized theories of sexualities.

Sexual Script Theory: Condom Use

About 20 million new cases of sexually transmitted infections (STIs) are diagnosed in the United States each year, 50% of them in people ages 15–24, and health care costs associated with STIs amount to about $16 billion a year (Centers for Disease Control and Prevention 2012d). More than 1.1 million people in the United States are living with HIV infection. Almost 30,000 new infections occur each year, disproportionately affecting black men who have sex with men, who are diagnosed with about one-third of these new infections (Centers for Disease Control and Prevention 2013c) (see Figure 5.3). In the United States about 49% of the 6.7 million pregnancies each year are unintended (Alan Guttmacher Institute 2013).

While these sexual health problems are clearly negative for significant numbers of people and have significant financial and emotional costs, all can be reduced or avoided through the use of condoms. Condoms have been shown to reduce the risk of disease transmission and of unintended pregnancy (World Health Organization 2014), but it has long been challenging to convince sexually active people to use them correctly and consistently. One study of contraceptive use in a sample of more than 22,000 American men and women ages 15–44 found that only 22% of the heterosexually active women in the sample were using condoms (Jones, Mosher, and Daniels 2012).

Scholars and public health practitioners have struggled to understand this reluctance. Drawing from symbolic interactionist arguments, **sexual script theory** argues that we interpret and develop our sexualities based on sociocultural expectations, values, and attitudes. Gagnon and

FIGURE 5.3 **Estimated HIV Diagnoses in the United States by Race/Ethnicity, 2011**

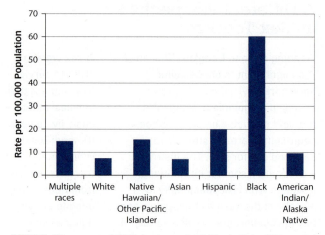

SOURCE: "Diagnoses of HIV Infection and AIDS in the United States and Dependent Areas, 2011" report, published by Centers for Disease Control and Prevention in February 2013.

Simon (1973) suggest that these influences are mapped out at the level of *culture* as well as *interpersonally* and *intrapsychically* (that is, mentally through imagery, fantasies, memories, and desires). Sexual script theory proposes that while our sexualities have biological elements, they are mostly socially constructed within the expectations developed by culture and interactions. A script theorist would ask how people create rules and expectations for condom use—how do people make condom use part of their expectations for sexual encounters? Why don't people use condoms more consistently?

Research on sexual fantasies and studies of how people describe hypothetical sexual encounters suggest that people do not often imagine these scenarios with condoms (Kimmel and Plante 2002; Alvarez and Garcia-Marques 2008). Nor do people in relationships tend to script condoms into their real encounters; many feel that proposing condom use is "not romantic" (Galligan and Terry 1993).

The belief that sex is spontaneous and mysterious may help reproduce another aspect of the gendered double standard: a (heterosexual) woman who carries even one condom (let alone more) in her purse is negatively perceived (Frankel and Curtis 2008). Women proposing the use of condoms in heterosexual encounters are subject to negotiations and gender dynamics: "While males often have the direct ability to ensure condom use even if their partners do not desire condom use, females may

Sexual script theory: The theory, developed by Gagnon and Simon in 1973, that humans create their sexualities within blueprints provided by cultural, interpersonal, and intrapsychic (mental) cues.

 HIV/AIDS

Adolescent Pregnancy and Sexualities in the Netherlands and the United States

Around 750,000 women ages 15–19 become pregnant each year in the United States (Alan Guttmacher Institute 2013). The United States has historically had a high rate of teen pregnancy compared to countries such as Sweden, France, the Netherlands, and the United Kingdom. What social conditions might help create this problem?

Until the mid-1960s, Dutch society was much like U.S. society in its sexual and moral conservatism—premarital intercourse was not condoned. Then the advent of the contraceptive pill enabled Dutch public health professionals to argue that girls should have access to affordable contraception. Dutch girls over the age of 16 may also elect to have free abortions, but the teen pregnancy and abortion rates in the Netherlands are among the lowest in the world. In the United States neither contraception nor abortion is affordable or easily and widely available; American girls are far more likely to get pregnant than are Dutch girls.

Sociologist Amy T. Schalet (2011) examined why attitudes about teen sexuality and pregnancy differ so much between the Netherlands and the United States. She interviewed 58 parents and 72 teens, matching participants on race (white), class (middle), and religiosity (moderate or secular). One of her interview questions in particular seems to symbolize the gap between Dutch and American parents: "Would you let your child spend the night with a girlfriend or boyfriend (at home)?" What would you say? What would your parents say?

Among the American parents, 9 out of 10 said, essentially, no, while 9 out of 10 of the Dutch parents said they already had or would do so, under the right circumstances, for a 16- or 17-year-old. What explains this discrepancy? For Schalet, the answer has three parts. First, the American parents cited "raging hormones," which they could not imagine their teens controlling. Second, these mothers and fathers strongly believed that sexual activity (and potential pregnancy) would be highly problematic because "boys and girls are different." They saw girls as romantics in love, willing to believe anything that lust-driven, persuasive boys might tell them. Third, the American parents believed their children needed to be independent and "on their own" *before* the parents would be comfortable knowing they were having sexual relationships.

The Dutch parents perceived their teenagers differently. They stressed "self-regulation," meaning that, with trust, education, and growth, teenagers are able to know for themselves when they are ready to be sexually active, and with whom. The Dutch parents also saw their children in less gendered terms, without the "boys against girls" framework of the American parents' narratives. They cited love, mutually respectful relationships, and context (have the teens been dating a while?) as the key components enabling their teenagers to "be ready" and responsible, and to take advantage of low-cost, easily obtainable contraception.

In the Netherlands, teenage sexuality—and, by extension, teen pregnancy—is not to be feared, dreaded, or swept under the rug. Most schools offer comprehensive sexuality education, the public health system offers medical care and constructive ways to deal with the bodily aspects of sexuality, and parents seem to trust and respect their children in these matters.

▶ **THINK ABOUT IT**

1. Would it be desirable for the United States to import some of the Dutch approach? Which aspects would you like to see in U.S. culture? Which aspects would you reject, and why?

2. What would need to change for American parents to have a more balanced view of teenagers' sexualities? Think about the big picture—systems, structures, and social institutions.

FIGURE 5.4 Birth Rates for 15–19-Year-Olds by Race and Ethnicity in the U.S., 2000–2011

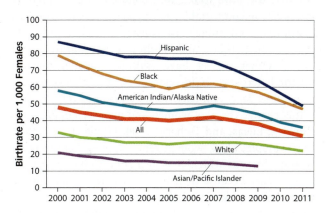

SOURCE: Hamilton BE, Martin JA, Ventura SJ. Births: Preliminary data for 2010. *National Vital Statistics Reports.* 2011;60(2):Table S-2.

be required to propose and negotiate condom use in the face of partner resistance. As a result, the gender dynamics within heterosexual relationships are especially critical in understanding and encouraging condom use and negotiation" (Broaddus, Morris, and Bryan 2010, 603).

Studies that have examined how gay men think about condom use have found that condoms are scripted as physically uncomfortable, getting in the way of intimacy, disruptive, and subject to constant renegotiation (de Zwart, van Kerkhof, and Sandfort 1998; Harawa et al. 2006). Other studies have addressed gender dynamics for heterosexuals in relation to condoms—how do things like race, ethnicity, social class, and relationship status change the way women and men see condom use (Bowleg, Lucas, and Tschann 2004; Hynie et al. 1998)? For example, black women report having heterosexual relationships in which they feel they cannot insist on condom use because their male partners do not initiate their use (Bowleg et al. 2004).

Several layers of social conditions intersect here. We may think that decisions about whether and when to use condoms are solely individual; few things seem more personal. But any one moment of sex, or any one decision about using or not using a condom, has consequences. The spread of some STIs, including HIV, is connected to the ways in which we script condom use, imbuing this seemingly individual act with symbolic significance.

ASK YOURSELF: Why do we script, or imagine, sexual acts without condoms? What values do we hold about condoms and about sex? Do we value certain sexual acts differently depending on whether they occur in a socially defined relationship such as marriage? How do we script sexualities in the United States? How might this affect condom use and perceptions of condoms?

Feminist Theory: Rape and Sexual Assault

Feminist theory is an interdisciplinary and multifaceted framework for analyzing sexuality-based social problems, including sexual assault and rape. Feminist sociological

Zuma Press Inc. / Alamy

Students at the University of California, Irvine, raise awareness about sexual violence. What policies against sexual assault and harassment does your campus have in place?

theory analyzes the connections between women's lives and persistent patterns of inequalities in a society, including sexual violence; the analyses are connected to the goal of social change and improvements in conditions for women. Feminist theorists have also explored the intersections of race, class, gender, and sexualities in sexual violence.

Rape is legally defined as forced sexual intercourse involving penetration and psychological as well as physical coercion; attempted rape includes verbal threats of rape (U.S. Bureau of Justice Statistics 2014). **Sexual assault** is a broader concept, defined as attempted or completed attacks that include unwanted sexual contact; it may include coercion or force, fondling, or verbal threats. People of all sexes and genders can experience rape and sexual assault, and offenders can be of all sexes and genders.

Historically, sexual violence was often conceptualized as a private or "marital" issue affecting only women; it was not frequently discussed as a social, public problem until the early 1970s (Chasteen 2001; Best 1999). According to a report from the U.S. Bureau of Justice Statistics, in 2009 there were more than 106,000 rapes with "female victims" in the United States, along with nearly 20,000 rapes with "male victims" (Truman and Rand 2010). Most of the female victims knew their offenders. One study found that nearly 14% of undergraduate women "were victims of at least one completed sexual assault" since starting college (Krebs et al. 2007). These figures probably grossly underestimate the actual numbers of those who have survived rape and sexual assault, particularly males. Most survivors do not report these crimes, for complex reasons including stigma, victim blaming, fear, and shame; historical and contemporary bias in law enforcement; low rates of successful prosecutions of perpetrators; and lack of awareness of what constitutes a rape or sexual assault (Grubb and Turner 2012).

Feminist theorists seek to understand the patterns of social inequalities that enable sexual violence and create classifications such as "victim" and "offender." They explore the ways in which society views sexual violence, including how we define the problem—for example, that it is bigger than just a "private" issue between two people, that "no means no," and that consent is a key variable.

Feminist theorists have also sought to raise awareness of the costs and harms of rape and sexual violence, both tangible and intangible. Consider just tangible costs. In the United States alone these are estimated to be in the billions of dollars, including lost productivity at work, fees for mental and physical health services, and costs to taxpayers for criminal justice investigations, prosecutions, and incarceration (Post et al. 2002). The intangible costs of our patterns of sexual violence include psychological effects, such as feeling powerless, depressed, and afraid, sometimes accompanied by feelings of shame, worthlessness, and the desire to commit suicide. In one recent case, a young woman was gang-raped by fellow classmates (Newton 2013). Afterward, the offenders texted friends a photo of the rape, which led to the young woman being bullied and harassed for a year; she committed suicide at just 17 years old.

Feminist theory also asks whether rape is best conceptualized as a crime of power, domination, and sexism, and therefore *not* a crime about sex or "miscommunication" ("he said, she said") (Muehlenhard, Danoff-Burg, and Powch 1996; Gavey 2005). Some feminist theorists argue that rape is a crime of power, not simply a result of "sexual miscommunication" or a problem of uncontrollable lust. This perspective clearly defines the issue as a social problem, based on patterns of institutional inequalities that may be visible in other aspects of U.S. society—for example, in familial divisions of household labor, in the gendered wage gap in employment, and even in the sexual double standard.

Another problem with sexual violence is the proliferation of **rape myths**, patterns of socially constructed attitudes and beliefs arguing, in part, that sexual violence survivors *cause* the violence and that perpetrators are justified in being violent. These myths assert, among other things, that violence is the victim's fault if she or he does not physically fight back, does not fight back early enough in the assault, wears certain (suggestive, sexual, or revealing) clothing, engages in consensual sexual contact with the offender before the assault (whether on the same day or evening or days or weeks earlier), or is intoxicated or using other drugs. Rape myths serve to reproduce and repeat prejudicial, stereotyped beliefs about those who are raped and those who rape (Grubb and Turner 2012).

Rape and sexual violence are persistent, harmful social conditions that negatively affect the well-being of millions from all social and cultural strata (Diken and Laustsen 2005). Rape is used as a systematic war crime, intended to degrade women and permanently mark or stigmatize them. Sexual violence and assaults are endemic; feminist theory provides one way to try to understand the breadth and scope of this social problem.

Rape: Forced sexual intercourse involving penetration and psychological as well as physical coercion; attempted rape includes verbal threats of rape.

Sexual assault: An attempted or completed attack that includes unwanted sexual contact; may include coercion or force, fondling, or verbal threats.

Rape myths: Assumptions about rape that tend to shift responsibility and blame to the victims.

ASK YOURSELF: What connections might exist between rape myths and social patterns of inequality? Are rape myths part of the structural, social inequalities that enable sexual violence to happen? Why or why not? How can feminist theory help us understand sexual violence against boys and men? What particular social problems surround this issue?

Identify steps toward social change regarding problems related to sexuality.

The United States has a long history of social change movements and activism in the form of collective, group efforts. Nearly every issue discussed in this chapter has been addressed by activists at least once on a widespread basis.

- Take Back the Night marches are mass public events intended to raise awareness about violence and sexual assault against women. They are held all over the world in large and small communities, in college towns and in cities.
- Margaret Sanger trained as a nurse in the early 1900s and then became an activist for birth control access and information, fighting against the Comstock laws and drawing attention to the social inequalities faced by poor, working-class, and immigrant women.
- In the early 1970s, peer sexuality education training programs sprang up on college campuses and in community centers around the country. Educators trained their peers on everything from contraception to condom use to sexual health and communication in a small but steady attempt to address and change inadequate sexuality education and broaden cultural scripting around sexual knowledge.

On college campuses right now, students are working to create change around sexuality-related social problems. You can participate.

 ## Students Respond to Global Sex Trafficking

Students have held International Justice Mission events—standing for 27 hours to represent the 27 million people who are trafficked (Matchen 2013; Smith [Janell] 2012) and starting campus anti–sex trafficking organizations (*Mount Holyoke News* 2013). At Florida International University, students created FIU 4 Freedom, an organization intended to educate the campus about U.S. and global trafficking (Edgemon 2013). The group hosted a speaker, Katariina Rosenblatt, who talked about her experiences with domestic trafficking in Florida; members also planned a Freedom Week of information and education.

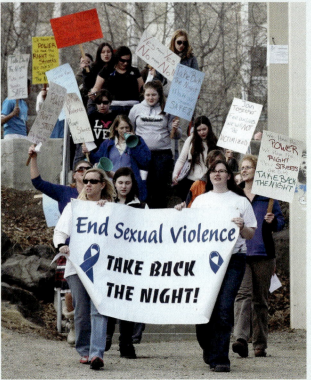

Zuma Press, Inc. / Alamy

Students at the University of Alaska, Fairbanks, march across campus during a Take Back the Night rally. The goals of such rallies are to raise awareness regarding sexual assault and to empower students to take a stand against violence and discrimination against women. Do you think that raising community awareness is an effective way to prevent future violence?

The U.S. government has even offered suggestions for change and activism on college campuses. In a post titled "20 Ways You Can Help Fight Human Trafficking," the U.S. Department of State (2014) suggests that students can raise awareness by starting clubs, studying the issue, and inviting speakers to their campuses. Students can also ask professors to teach about the issues, do research, and host conferences, symposia, or teach-ins.

 ## Men's Work: Violence Reduction

In 2010, Jared Watkins graduated from George Washington University and headed to his first job as development coordinator at the national organization Men Can Stop Rape, headquartered in Washington, D.C. Watkins had facilitated George Washington's

Campus Men of Strength club, dedicated to ending sexual violence on college campuses. The club has eight chapters across the United States, from Hawaii to D.C. The members educate themselves about sexual violence among college students—for example, about one in four college women will survive a sexual assault—and then educate others on their campuses. One student member, quoted on Men Can Stop Rape's website (http://www.mencanstoprape.org), noted that he had become much more confident about voicing his opinion when people use derogatory language to refer to women. Researchers report that men often become involved in such organizations because of personal reasons, such as knowing someone who has survived a sexual assault or rape, or they are drawn in by a charismatic male student (Piccigallo 2008). Barriers that seem to prevent men from getting involved include lack of awareness of the issues, fear about not seeming traditionally masculine, and myths about rape as a social problem. If you are a male student who might be interested in joining such a group but are hesitant, consider that even everyday acts, like talking with friends and parents about the issue, can have a powerful effect and begin to create change.

▶▶ Campus Sexual Climates and Climate Change

What is the sexual climate on your campus? Are there a variety of ways for students to learn about their sexualities—workshops, speakers, classes for credit, counseling groups, religiously affiliated groups, campus health center educational materials? Or is there just a skit or presentation for first-year students on the intersection of alcohol, drugs, and nonconsensual sex? Are there groups and organizations, as well as physical places, on your campus that seem to create unsafe spaces for women and lesbian, gay, and bisexual students? Is there overt or covert homophobia? Is there a range of ways in which students can explore the variety in contemporary sexuality and relationships, from hooking up to dating to having long-term relationships (Smiler and Plante 2013)? On most campuses, these kinds of questions do not arise, and students do not explore the campus sexual climate unless something tragic (a rape or sexual assault) happens. But there are ways to create change, as some recent examples suggest.

At Dickinson College, students asked the administration to do a self-study of sexual violence and marched to the main administration building for a three-day sit-in (Simmons 2011).

At Colgate University, students, professors, student affairs staff, counseling center staff, and coaching staff helped plan a five-week "positive sexuality" class (Lafrance, Loe, and Brown 2012). The seminar is designed to help students affirm what they want from their sexual and intimate relationships, instead of just thinking about what they don't (or shouldn't) want, such as coercive, nonconsensual sex. Students run the seminar and work on campus sexual climate issues, including studying the links between alcohol use and hooking up.

At Ithaca College, students formed Created Equal, a group committed to raising awareness about inequality-based sexuality problems, particularly for lesbian, gay, bisexual, queer, transgender, and asexual students. Recent organization president Cedrick-Michael Simmons (2012) said, "[We] work with other groups of students to understand how issues of inequality and oppression intersect in ways that we are socialized to ignore or be unaware of . . . to have those uncomfortable, personal conversations in vulnerable settings."

At Yale University, students have contributed to the administration's effort to understand the ways in which sexual assaults and rapes happen there (Hua 2013). They've also staged annual Yale Sex Weeks, with education, speakers, and events intended to foster healthy sexual self-development.

At Amherst College, there is a Facebook group called Fixing Amherst's Sexual Violence Problem, along with a diverse coalition of student activists working to change the college's policies and responses to sexual misconduct (Corey 2013).

Finally, as a response to the problems they saw in campus hookup culture, Colby College students organized a Take Back the Date week to inspire fellow students to go on dates—to converse and chat with and get to know other people, romantically or not (Rushford and Laird 2012).

WHAT DOES AMERICA THINK?

Questions about Sexuality from the General Social Survey

 Turn to the beginning of the chapter to compare your answers to the total population.

1. What is your belief on having sex before marriage?

    WRONG: 43.9%

    NOT WRONG: 56.1%

2. Do you believe that homosexuals should have the right to marry?

    YES: 49.6%

    NO: 38.6%

    NEITHER AGREE NOR DISAGREE: 11.8%

3. What is your level of happiness with your partner?

    VERY HAPPY: 61.3%

    SOMEWHAT HAPPY: 36.9%

    NOT TOO HAPPY: 1.8%

4. Should a homosexual be allowed to teach?

    ALLOW: 84.9%

    DO NOT ALLOW: 15.1%

SOURCE: National Opinion Research Center, University of Chicago.

5. Should homosexual books be allowed in the library?

    YES: 78.8%

    NO: 21.2%

6. Married people are happier than unmarried people.

    AGREE: 36.8%

    DISAGREE: 31.7%

    NEITHER AGREE NOR DISAGREE: 31.5%

7. What is your opinion of sex before marriage in teens between 14 and 16 years of age?

    ALWAYS WRONG: 68%

    SOMETIMES WRONG: 26.3%

    NOT WRONG AT ALL: 5.7%

8. Should sex education be taught in public schools?

    YES: 90.8%

    NO: 9.2%

LOOK BEHIND THE NUMBERS

Go to **edge.sagepub.com/trevino** for a breakdown of these data across time and by race, sex, age, income, and other statuses.

1. What relationship does education have with regards to the question on whether books relating to homosexuality should be allowed in the library?

2. When asked if married people are happier than unmarried, what do you predict in responses based on gender? How does the data compare to your prediction? What might explain this pattern?

3. When asked about birth control to teenagers 14 to 16 years of age, there was a very narrow difference between agree and disagree. Review the data by gender, income, and education. Did any of the variables greatly influence the participant's response?

4. Review the data for the question for level of happiness with their partner. Who responded "not too happy" for gender, education level, income level, and race?

5. When analyzing responses with regards to age, describe the pattern for the question asking about having sex before marriage. Is the pattern similar or different when asked if the respondent believes homosexuals should have the right to marry? Explain.

6. Examine the General Social Survey data regarding the belief on homosexual relations from 1973 through present. What do you notice in the responses over time? What do you predict data to look like in the next survey report?

CHAPTER SUMMARY

 5.1 Identify social problems related to sexuality.

Human sexualities are more than natural urges or drives; they are also shaped and constructed in social and historical contexts. Hence there is a considerable range of views on sexuality-related social problems in the United States. Issues like sex trafficking, hooking up, pornography, and sexual dysfunction have individual *and* sociocultural components.

 5.2 Explain how the concept of deviance relates to definitions of sexuality-related social problems.

Hooking-up behavior seems to be relatively common among college students and is not typically seen as deviant behavior among peers. Researchers ask if hooking up is harmful and, if so, who is harmed? The pornography industry is big business, with millions of Internet searches for pornographic videos and photos. Sex trafficking is a global issue involving millions of victims. Women who have been trafficked are often reluctant to call attention to their plight for fear of being labeled deviant.

5.3 Apply the functionalist, conflict, and symbolic interactionist perspectives to the study of sexuality-related social problems, specifically sex work and prostitution.

Functionalist perspectives argue that sex work serves important social functions, such as providing an outlet for expression of certain sexual practices and desires, as well as maintaining a way to label some members of society "deviant" because of their occupations. *Critical* functionalist analysis would suggest that sex work

within this framework has latent and manifest consequences, including maintenance of the heterosexual gendered double standard. Conflict theorists argue that sex work is embedded within a historical context of persistent social inequalities, pointing to the ways that race, ethnicity, class, and gender inequalities are reproduced in sex work. Interactionists suggest that we need to understand the ways in which workers and clients see themselves and make sense of these practices. The policy implications of all three perspectives include legalization, decriminalization, and destigmatization.

 5.4 Apply specialized theories of sexualities.

Sexual script theory, which we can apply to the problem of how to encourage condom use, argues that cultural, interpersonal, and intrapsychic guidelines structure the ways people make sense of their sexualities. Feminist theory is an interdisciplinary framework for analyzing sexuality-related social problems, including sexual assault and rape; it argues that rape and sexual violence are rooted in structures of inequality and the intersections of race, class, gender, and sexualities.

 5.5 Identify steps toward social change regarding problems related to sexuality.

Students have worked to raise awareness of the scope and consequences of nonconsensual sex trafficking. Some men have organized groups to educate and empower men to stop sexual violence on campuses. Still others have begun to address campus sexual climates with stakeholders and students, with an eye toward reducing problematic elements such as rapes and sexual assaults, as well as changing campus cultures that seem supportive of rape.

DISCUSSION QUESTIONS

1. In what ways are sex and sexuality socially constructed? What are some examples of how meanings differ and change over time and from place to place? What is considered normative sexual behavior in the United States?

2. How do law and religion influence sexualities? What patterns do we see with regard to sexualities

today? How are these patterns influenced by other institutions, such as education and religion?

3. What is considered deviant sexual behavior today? Who decides on the label for such behaviors? How has what is considered deviant changed over time? Is everything that is considered sexually deviant also a social problem?

4. Is hooking up equally problematic for all groups or individuals? Under what circumstances is hooking up viewed as a deviant behavior and/or a social problem?

5. How do conflict theorists approach research on pornography? What are their primary concerns? What could be done to address these concerns related to pornography?

6. From a symbolic interactionist perspective, how is sex work different from prostitution and different from sex trafficking? What role do sex workers play in defining their own experiences in the industry? How could the experiences of the workers affect policies regulating sex work?

7. What are sexual scripts? How does sexual script theory explain patterns of behavior such as gendered behavior? What about race or ethnicity? How does this theory suggest that individuals could make changes toward healthier patterns?

8. How does feminist theory describe the personal issues related to sexualities as social problems? How is this perspective different from the other theories? What does it suggest individuals can do to confront and change common rape myths?

9. What is being done on your campus to encourage discussion of sex and sexualities? Are there topics that are not covered? How effective are student or peer-led groups in changing the campus climate around sex and addressing the social problems associated with sexualities, such as violence?

10. What prompts men to get involved in efforts to reduce sexual violence and other sex-related social problems? Do women get involved for the same reasons? What can be done to ensure that men and women from all racial and ethnic groups, ages, and social classes are included in movements to make sex safer for all?

KEY TERMS

deviance 112

double standard 114

erotica 116

hooking up 113

labeling theory 113

latent consequence 121

manifest consequence 121

pornography 116

prostitution 120

rape 127

rape myths 127

sex tourism 118

sex trafficking 118

sexual assault 127

sexual dysfunction 112

sexuality 110

sexual script theory 124

sex work 118

Sharpen your skills with SAGE edge at edge.sagepub.com/trevino

A personalized approach to help you accomplish your coursework goals in an easy-to-use learning environment.

I am a Lesbi...
Bisexual...
I am Transge...
I

AGING

Duane A. Matcha

Paul Linse / Corbis

 Sociologists tell us that the populations in many countries are aging, yet most images in popular culture tend to portray the young. How do you suppose older adults, like this couple in London, England, feel when presented with images of youth all around them?

Investigating Aging: My Story

Duane A. Matcha

When I graduated from college with an undergraduate degree in social science, I had no idea what I was going to do. An ad in the local newspaper for a position as an outreach worker with the local Commission on Aging sounded interesting, so I applied, not knowing what to expect. The position was temporary, since funding was provided through a two-year state/federal grant. In those two years, however, I discovered a great deal about myself and the lives of older people.

While my job was to advocate for lower- and middle-income older persons and help them get tangible assistance, many needed only someone to talk to. Others experienced a variety of problems, ranging from illegal eviction to navigating the paperwork of a public bureaucracy. My experiences, while individually significant, also highlighted the role of the sociological imagination in addressing aging in the United States. It was not one older person but many who lacked food or meaningful human interaction. Realizing that when I provided one person with the help he or she needed others would ask for the same assistance helped me understand the difference between an individual problem and a social problem that could be addressed by public policy.

As a result of my accidental job experience, aging became the foundation of my graduate training in sociology and remains the core of my research. I've examined end-of-life decision making among older populations, the relationship between aging and health care costs, and, most recently, the way the print media portray the aging population in the United States and other countries.

LEARNING OBJECTIVES

6.1 Discuss aging as a social construct.

6.2 Discuss patterns and trends in the demographics of aging.

6.3 Apply the functionalist, symbolic interactionist, and conflict perspectives to social policy for the aging.

6.4 Apply specialized theories to the social construction of aging.

6.5 Identify steps toward social change for the aging.

WHAT DO YOU THINK?
Questions about Aging from the General Social Survey

1. Adult children are important to help elderly parents.

   ☐ AGREE
   ☐ DISAGREE

2. Who should provide help for the elderly?

   ☐ FAMILY MEMBERS
   ☐ GOVERNMENT AGENCIES
   ☐ NONPROFIT ORGANIZATIONS
   ☐ PRIVATE PROVIDERS

3. Should the aged live with their children?

   ☐ YES
   ☐ NO

4. Who should pay for help for the elderly?

   ☐ ELDERLY PEOPLE THEMSELVES OR THEIR FAMILY
   ☐ THE GOVERNMENT/ PUBLIC FUNDS

5. In the United States, do you think we're spending too much money on Social Security, too little money, or about the right amount?

   ☐ TOO MUCH
   ☐ TOO LITTLE
   ☐ ABOUT THE RIGHT AMOUNT

 Turn to the end of the chapter to view the results for the total population.

SOURCE: National Opinion Research Center, University of Chicago.

GOLDEN GIRLS HOUSE

Recently, National Public Radio reported on unmarried older persons in the United States. According to the story, one of every three older persons is unmarried, and most of the unmarried elderly are women. Who will care for them when they are unable to care for themselves? Enter Bonnie Moore, a 60-year-old divorcee living in a suburb of Washington, D.C.

After her divorce, Moore needed financial help to remain in her house. Rather than open her home to just any boarders, she decided to be more selective and take in others like her—older unmarried women. Her ad on Craigslist was headed "GOLDEN GIRLS HOUSE." Moore has been selective, bringing in women who are independent but able to get along with others in the house. As she described it, the home is "a little bit like family, a little bit like roommates, a little bit like a sorority house."

Moore wants to expand the group housing option for unmarried older women. She is developing a website and creating a guide for others who want to enjoy living situations such as hers. While there are concerns about who will care for older persons as they age, Bonnie Moore and others are attempting to provide alternative living arrangements for those who wish to remain independent as long as they can (Rovner 2013).

We begin with a brief look at the historical background of aging in the United States and then turn to a wide variety of issues and theoretical perspectives associated with the aging process. Most important, this chapter explains why aging is a socially constructed social problem and develops an alternate understanding of the older population as an integral component of the larger society, not the "problem" that has been constructed. For example, the aging population is often blamed for the rising cost of health care in the United States. In reality, older patients are responsible for a relatively small proportion of this increase.

David Mdzinarishvili / Reuters

Tsiuri Kakabadze, 80, right, performs during the Super Grandmother and Super Grandfather contest in Tbilisi, Republic of Georgia. Did you know that in the United States, May has been designated as Older Americans Month since 1963?

IS AGING A SOCIAL PROBLEM?

6.1 Discuss aging as a social construct.

Ted is a 75-year-old white male living in Sun City, Arizona. He's enjoying his life of leisure, playing golf on a daily basis and spending time with his grandchildren, who visit regularly. Ted retired 10 years ago from a management position with a multinational company. During the 40 years he worked for the company, he saved for retirement, and his company now provides him with a pension. He lives a comfortable life and has no financial concerns because he is in relatively good health and has a sufficient retirement income. His home is paid for, and he enjoys going out to eat on a regular basis. He volunteers three days a week at a local school, where he mentors at-risk children.

Diane is a 75-year-old minority female living in a working-class section of a major city. She worked at low-wage jobs most of her life and had not been able to save more than $1,000 by the time she retired 10 years ago. She receives Social Security benefits but no pension. Because of her low income, she was unable to afford a home and has lived in an apartment all her life. Her neighborhood is now in transition and becoming less safe, but she cannot move because she cannot afford the higher rent she would have to pay elsewhere. Her health is fine, but she does take a number of medications for a variety of medical conditions she developed over her lifetime.

Ted and Diane are both considered "old" because of their chronological age, but are they a social problem?

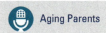 Aging Parents

Neither was considered a social problem before retirement, so why is their aging a social problem?

What do we know about aging and its consequences? The process of aging is complex and results in any number of outcomes. In other words, older people are not homogeneous. They are as diverse as any other age group. Beyond sharing a common chronological age (65 and over), older persons fit into all the social class positions members of other age groups do. They also exhibit as wide a diversity of political and religious thought as we find in the larger society. They engage in a variety of familial relationships and experience intimate discord, as do others. Thus, to understand the aging of Ted and Diane and millions of others who are 65 and older, we begin by examining how aging is socially constructed as a social problem.

The Social Construction of Aging as a Social Problem

When we think about aging, we generally think in terms of chronology. In other words, how old am I, and how does my age compare to the ages of others? While chronological age is important, it is limited as a description because it locates an individual in a single point in time. In this chapter we will use chronological age to identify segments of the larger population that fall into a category society generally classifies as "old." However, rather than focusing only on a specific chronological age, we will utilize the concept of **aging**, "a social process that is constructed from the expectations and belief systems of the structural characteristics of society" (Matcha 1997, 20).

ASK YOURSELF: How did age become, and how does it persist as, a socially constructed social *problem*?

Today, baby boomers in the United States are entering retirement age in growing numbers. By 2050, the number of people age 65 and over in the United States will essentially double from approximately 35 million today to more than 70 million (see Figure 6.1) (Federal Interagency Forum on Aging-Related Statistics 2010). This growth has fostered concern among politicians and policy makers as they try to understand the implications of such rapid demographic change. Some politicians have said the country

Aging: A social process constructed from the expectations and belief systems of the structural characteristics of society.

Welfare state: Government provision of services essential to the well-being of large or significant segments of the population that are not possible or profitable within the private sector.

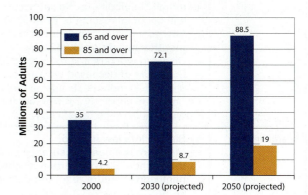

FIGURE 6.1 Increase in Numbers of U.S. Adults 65 and Over and 85 and Over, 2000–2050

SOURCE: Federal Interagency Forum on Aging-Related Statistics. Older Americans 2010: Key Indicators of Well-Being. Federal Interagency on Aging-Related Statistics. Washington, DC: U.S. Government printing Office. July 2010.

cannot afford to care for so many older people. Others have argued that government programs supporting the older population, such as Social Security and Medicare, will go broke and be unable to meet the financial and health needs of older citizens. Given the range of potential responses to these demographic changes, what is society to do?

ASK YOURSELF: If we could ensure that Social Security will remain solvent throughout this century by reducing the benefits it pays out, would you be in favor of doing so? Why or why not? Some options for protecting Social Security place the economic burden of doing so on the individual, while others place it on the larger society. Why does the choice matter?

This is not the first time older people have been thought of as a social problem. In the late 18th and early 19th centuries, earlier traditions of responsibility to older members of society gave way to norms of increased individual responsibility, and wealth inequality—believed to be relatively low during the colonial period—began increasing and creating greater generational differences at the same time (Fischer 1978). Public attitudes toward older citizens thus became increasingly negative, particularly if the elderly were not wealthy, white, and male.

The result of these changing societal attitudes was a rising level of poverty in old age and the transformation of older age into a socially constructed social problem throughout the 19th and 20th centuries. Individuals remained in the workplace because pensions, private or public, did not exist. With the emergence of **welfare state**

 Baby Boomers   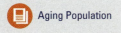 Aging Population

TABLE 6.1   Overview of Social Security, Medicare, and Medicaid

Social Security	• Signed into law in 1935. • Initially eligibility for Social Security was at age 65. Eligibility age increased to 66 in 2005 and will begin increasing to 67 in 2017. • Retired workers and dependents account for 70% of total benefits paid, with an average monthly benefit of $1,262. • Disabled workers and their dependents account for 19% of total benefits paid. • Survivors of deceased workers account for about 11% of total benefits paid. • 9 out of 10 individuals age 65 and older receive Social Security benefits. • There are currently 2.8 workers for each Social Security beneficiary. By 2033, there will be 2.1 workers for each beneficiary.

Medicare	• Signed into law in 1965.
	• Medicare is a health insurance program for the following people: those age 65 and older; those under 65 with certain disabilities; those of any age with end-stage renal disease (permanent kidney failure requiring dialysis or a kidney transplant).
	
	• **Medicare Part A (hospital insurance):**
	  ○ Helps cover inpatient care in hospitals.
	  ○ Helps cover skilled nursing facility, hospice, and home health care.
	• **Medicare Part B (medical insurance):**
	  ○ Helps cover doctors' and other health care providers' services, outpatient care, durable medical equipment, and home health care.
	  ○ Helps cover some preventive services to help maintain health and to keep certain illnesses from getting worse.
	• **Medicare Part C (also known as Medicare Advantage):**
	  ○ Offers health plan options run by Medicare-approved private insurance companies.
	  ○ Plans are ways to get the benefits and services covered under Part A and Part B.
	  ○ Most plans cover Medicare prescription drug coverage (Part D).
	  ○ Some plans may include extra benefits for extra costs.
	• **Medicare Part D (Medicare prescription drug coverage):**
	  ○ Helps cover the cost of prescription drugs.
	  ○ May help lower prescription drug costs and help protect against higher costs in the future.
	  ○ Run by Medicare-approved private insurance companies.

Medicaid	• Signed into law in 1965.
	• Medicaid is a state and federal partnership that provides coverage for people with lower incomes, older people, people with disabilities, and some families and children.
	• Each state operates a Medicaid program that provides health coverage for lower-income people, families and children, the elderly, and people with disabilities.
	• Eligibility rules differ from state to state. Beginning in 2014, most adults under age 65 with individual incomes up to about $15,000 per year qualify for Medicaid in every state.
	• Benefits covered for adults differ from state to state, but certain benefits are covered in every Medicaid program.
	• Doctors' services that are covered by Medicaid that are applicable to older citizens include the following:
	  ○ Laboratory and X-ray services
	  ○ Inpatient hospital services
	  ○ Outpatient hospital services
	  ○ Long-term care services and supports
	  ○ Medical and surgical dental services for adults
	  ○ Services provided in health clinics
	  ○ Nursing facility services for adults
	  ○ Home health care services for certain people
	  ○ Prescription drugs
	• The Affordable Care Act has expanded options for community-based care, increasing opportunities for people of all ages who have disabilities to get help with daily activities while remaining in their homes. The Medicaid program continues to move toward providing more community-based care options as alternatives to nursing homes.

SOURCES: Fact Sheet. Social Security Administration. www.ssa.gov/pressoffice/factssheet/basicfact-alt.pdf accessed June 2, 2013. Medicare Benefits. www.medicare.gov/navigation/medicare-basics/medicare-benefits/medicare-benefits-overview.aspx/accessed June 2, 2013. Medicaid. www.healthcare.gov/using-insurance/low-cost-care/medicaid/accessed June 2, 2013.

policies such as Social Security in 1935 and Medicare in 1965, however, as well as society's recognition that assistance in old age was necessary, the overall well-being of older adults improved significantly.

By the late 1980s, however, the socially constructed impression of older people changed again. This time, they were perceived as too wealthy! Terms such as "greedy geezers" conveyed an image of older people living the good life in Florida or elsewhere, playing shuffleboard while younger generations struggled to get by (Street and Cossman 2006). Currently, older adults in the United States are caught in a political vortex in which programs upon which they rely are being attacked as too expensive and no longer viable for younger generations. They are being asked to "sacrifice" for the well-being of their children and grandchildren. Efforts to frame the recent economic recession as a generational divide blame the older-age population rather than the larger structural framework of institutionalized inequality. To understand more fully how aging has been, and continues to be, socially constructed as a social problem, we next examine the role of ageism.

Ageism

Ageism is the use of a person's perceived or real chronological age as the basis for discriminatory actions. Connecting ageism to the demographic shift discussed above, Longino (2005, 81) notes that "this apocalyptic picture of the future is indeed ageist, because it objectifies people who are aging and treats them as though they are all alike. They are not people anymore; they are 'the burden.'" In the context of this commonly held view, we will explore why ageism remains a potent negative force in U.S. culture, whether among younger adults who hold stereotypical beliefs about their elders, employers who do not believe older workers can be as productive as their younger counterparts, or media outlets that promote outdated portrayals of older persons.

For example, in U.S. print advertisements, older people are generally nonexistent and are negatively stereotyped when they do appear. In newspaper articles, they are generally depicted as poor, in poor health, and needing assistance (Miller et al. 1999). The portrayal of the health and illness of Canadian seniors has been associated with the following themes: "aging as disease, individual responsibility for healthy aging, and apocalyptic demography/costs of [un]healthy aging" (Rozanova 2006, 131). A comparison of U.S. and European newspaper articles about aging found differences in the ways older persons were portrayed. For example, European newspaper

articles were more likely to suggest age-related connections with rising health care costs (Matcha and Sessing-Matcha 2007). In Ireland, Fealy et al. (2012, 99) found that "the proposition that older people might be healthy, self-reliant and capable of autonomy in the way they live their lives was largely absent" from the newspaper articles the researchers examined. In American television programs and commercials, older citizens are again nonexistent or, if visible, are portrayed in stereotypical fashion, such as being forgetful, slow, and useless (Blakeborough 2008). One study found that older people made up only 3% of characters, while children accounted for 7% and young and middle-age adults were disproportionately represented. As a result, the more hours survey respondents spent watching television, the less they understood the older-age population (Signorielli 2001). Similarly, Donlon, Ashman, and Levy (2005, 314) found that "exposure to television is a significant predictor of more negative stereotypes of aging."

We see that perhaps the most pervasive ageist attitudes are the result of an antiaging culture in the United States. This culture is framed as a way of "helping" people address the myriad problems of an aging body. Hair coloring, wrinkle creams, plastic surgery, and other aids are intended to remake the image of older individuals—again, particularly women (Hurd Clarke 2011). Ageism thus fosters the socially constructed reality that being old is a social problem.

As a result of these socially constructed images, we are less likely to have a realistic impression of older persons. Here, for example, are some common myths about aging (Kart 1994), along with the reasons each is false:

- *Myth: Senility inevitably accompanies old age.* Achieving a particular chronological age does not make a person senile, as evidenced by the many older individuals who have accomplished a great deal in later life. For instance, singers such as Bob Dylan, Mick Jagger, Paul McCartney, and David Bowie and actors Robert Redford, Samuel L. Jackson, and Betty White range in age from late 60s to early 90s, and all of them continue to perform. Older political figures include Hillary Rodham Clinton and U.S. senator John McCain.
- *Myth: Most old people are lonely and isolated from their families.* Research has demonstrated that most older individuals have at least one child living within an hour's drive, and that the amount of interaction they have with children and other family members is less important than the quality of that interaction (Fingerman 2001).
- *Myth: Most old people are in poor health.* While a small percentage of older individuals have difficulty engaging in at least one activity of daily living

....

Ageism: The use of real or perceived chronological age as a basis for discrimination.

(ADL), the rest are capable of independent living and remaining active within their communities (Ferraro 2011).

- *Myth: Old people are more likely than younger people to be victimized by crime.* While crime rates have decreased overall in the recent past, they have dropped significantly among older people, and nationally those ages 65 and over have the lowest rate of victimization (Truman, Langton, and Planty 2013). When victimized, however, older people do have a more difficult time recovering, physically, emotionally, and financially (Peguero and Lauck 2008).

- *Myth: The majority of old people live in poverty.* The majority of older adults in the United States have modest incomes that allow them to enjoy their later years. However, poverty is greater among older women, the widowed, and minority elderly. The triple threat of poverty is being female, widowed, and a member of a minority group (Federal Interagency Forum on Aging-Related Statistics 2010).

- *Myth: Old people tend to become more religious as they age.* In reality, older individuals who are religious were so in middle age and earlier (Moody and Sasser 2012). Older individuals are more likely to attend religious services than are people in other age groups, but that does not make them more religious (Hill, Burdette, and Idler 2011).

- *Myth: Older workers are less productive than younger workers.* Older workers do not experience significant declines in mental and physical abilities. They are less likely than younger persons to be in the labor market, but not because they cannot do the work. In fact, they are generally as productive as younger workers (Schulz and Binstock 2006).

- *Myth: Old people who retire usually suffer a decline in health.* In reality, if an older person suffers a decline in health after retirement, it is generally the result of a medical condition that existed before retirement (Ekerdt 2007).

- *Myth: Most old people have no interest in, or capacity for, sexual relations.* The greater the frequency of sexual activity among middle-aged adults, the greater the chance they will remain sexually active in older age. Unless there are physical problems, older men and women can remain sexually active well into their seventh and eighth decades of life (Masters and Johnson 2010).

- *Myth: Most old people end up in nursing homes and other long-term care institutions.* On any given

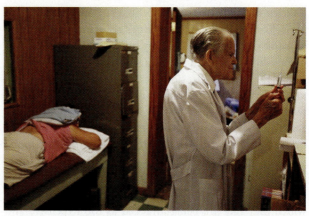

Dr. Byron Harbolt treats a patient at his clinic in Altamont, Tennessee. Harbolt, 89, who charges as little as $15 for an office visit, sees patients six days a week in the rural clinic he opened in 1960. Would you feel comfortable having a doctor who is 89 years old?

day, only about 4% of Americans ages 65 and over are in nursing homes, although the percentage among the oldest-old (age 85+) is much higher. In reality, most older U.S. adults remain in their own homes and have no need for any type of institutionalized care (Kahana, Lovegreen, and Kahana 2011).

With this more realistic view of older people in mind, we turn next to a number of patterns and trends that define current and future realities for older adults—and that perpetuate the social construction of aging as a social problem.

PATTERNS AND TRENDS

 Discuss patterns and trends in the demographics of aging.

Demographics

One hundred years ag o, the 4 million U.S. adults age 65 and over made up about 4% of the population. Today, some 40 million people in that age category represent approximately 13% of the population. By 2050, some 88 million over the age of 65 will be representing 20% of the total population. This is actually a relatively minor shift in the population pyramid compared with that in other industrialized countries. For example, in Japan and Italy those over 65 are expected soon to make up the largest percentage of the population (35% and 36%, respectively) (United Nations 2011). Figure 6.2 shows

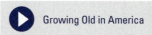 Growing Old in America   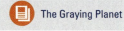 The Graying Planet

FIGURE 6.2

FIGURE 6.2 Percentage of the Population Age 65 and Over, 2010–2050

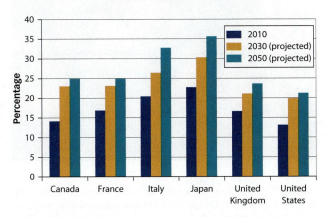

SOURCE: United Nations 2011. Population Division of the Department of Economic and Social Affairs of the United Nations Secretariat, *World Population Prospects: The 2010 Revision.*

the differences between the United States and other industrialized countries in terms of population aging.

Behind the increasing number of older people in the population are a variety of other sociodemographic factors, including decreased fertility and increased life expectancy rates. **Fertility rate** is a count of the number of children born to women during their prime fertility period. Fertility rates have decreased significantly in the United States and throughout the developed world. At the same time, people are living longer. **Life expectancy** is the average number of years a person born in a given year can expect to live. When we combine decreasing fertility rates and increasing life expectancy, we find that fewer children are being born and those who are born are living longer, resulting in a demographic shift from a younger

Fertility rate: The number of children born per 1,000 women during their prime fertility period.

Life expectancy: The average number of years a baby born in any given year can expect to live.

Sex ratio: The number of males for every 100 females in the general population or within some designated segment, such as among those age 65 and over.

Child dependency ratio: The number of children under the age of 16 per 100 adults ages 16 to 64.

Old-age dependency ratio: The number of older persons ages 65 and over for every 100 adults between the ages of 16 and 64.

Total dependency ratio: The number of children under the age of 16 and the number of older persons age 65 and over for every 100 adults ages 16 to 64.

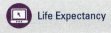
Life Expectancy

population to one that is rapidly aging. In fact, the fastest-growing segment of the population consists of those age 85 and over.

Digging deeper into the numbers, we find there are more older-age women than older-age men because women, on average, have longer life expectancy. The **sex ratio** identifies the number of men per 100 women (see Figure 6.3). These numbers are important because they measure the availability of potential mates for those who are widowed or divorced in older age. In other words, an older male has a much larger pool of eligible older women from which to select, if he is interested in a relationship, whereas an older woman finds a much smaller pool of eligible men.

Finally, the demographic shift is also changing the dependency ratio. This ratio consists of three different numbers. First is the **child dependency ratio**, which counts the number of children under age 16 for every 100 people ages 16 to 64. The **old-age dependency ratio** counts the number of older persons age 65 and over for every 100 people ages 16 to 64. Finally, the **total dependency ratio** is the number of children under 16 and the number of older persons 65 and over for every 100 persons ages 16 to 64.

The higher the total dependency ratio, the more services are necessary to provide for those identified as dependent on the larger society. The projected changes in the child and old-age dependency ratios in the United States shown in Table 6.2 are consistent with those in other developed countries. However, the overall U.S. dependency ratio is generally lower than that in most

FIGURE 6.3 Males per 100 Females in the United States by Age, 2000 and 2050

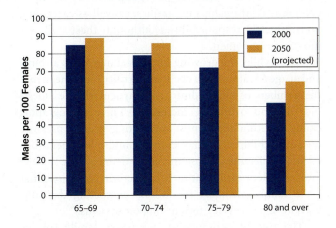

SOURCE: Kinsella, Kevin, and Victoria A. Velkoff. U.S. Census Bureau Series P95/01-1, *An Aging World: 2001,* U.S. Government Printing Office, Washington, DC, 2001.

TABLE 6.2 Child and Old-Age Dependency Ratios in the U.S., 2000 and 2050

Year	Total dependency ratio	Child dependency ratio	Old-age dependency ratio
2000	51	32	19
2050	67	31	35

SOURCE: United Nations 2011. Population Division of the Department of Economic and Social Affairs of the United Nations Secretariat, *World Population Prospects: the 2010 Revision.*

Lucy Nicholson / Reuters

Donald Smitherman, 98, kisses his wife, Marlene, at the end of a dance in Sun City, Arizona. Many older adults maintain sexual interest and activity well into their 80s and 90s. Why do you suppose media images of romance and sexual attractiveness ignore older people?

other developed countries. Demographic changes like these do not themselves make aging a social problem, but framing them as a "disaster for society" or a "tsunami of historical proportions" constructs aging as a social problem by implying that older adults are responsible for their consequences.

Next we turn to the family and the changes it is experiencing as a result of the changing demographic structure of the population.

Family

The family represents the foundation of social institutions and as such is experiencing fundamental changes (see Chapter 9). Declining fertility rates, for instance, mean families are having fewer children, making it more difficult for those children to care for older parents. On the economic front, women's increased participation in the workforce has fundamentally reshaped economic relationships in families, as well as caregiving and domestic responsibilities, although these still rest mostly with women.

Meanwhile, the growing life expectancy rates at birth and at age 65, along with declining fertility rates, mean that the numbers of older adults, and particularly the oldest-old (85 and over), are increasing. These demographic changes within the family are putting greater pressure on adult children as they care for multiple generations of family members. These increased demands are not the fault of older people, but rather structural conditions that force family members to address competing demands without the necessary formal support systems.

The role of grandparent, a primary family role, is often viewed as a welcome opportunity to provide social-emotional support to a younger generation. Increasingly, grandparents are also becoming the primary caregivers

for their grandchildren, helped by the fact that, as noted above, many live relatively close to at least one of their children.

Family relationships are also evolving in terms of sexual expectations between aging couples. The phrase "use it or lose it" has been applied to the extent to which couples engage in sexual activity in middle age (Moody and Sasser 2012). Generally speaking, men and women are capable of remaining sexually active well into their later years (Masters and Johnson 2010). While the frequency of sexual activity may decline over time, the need for intimacy remains regardless of age. Another change in family relationships is occurring as same-sex marriage becomes more widely accepted and recognized by law. As gay couples adopt children or have their own via surrogacy, their opportunities to eventually enjoy the role of grandparent increase.

ASK YOURSELF: How will changing gender roles affect the aging experience for older couples? How will they influence your image of older adults?

Elder Abuse

Elder abuse is an unfortunate reality that can take various forms—sexual, financial, physical, and emotional. Elder neglect is also common. The National Center on Elder Abuse (1999, 1) identifies the following types of abuse and neglect:

- *Physical abuse:* Use of physical force that may result in bodily injury, physical pain, or impairment

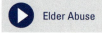 Elder Abuse   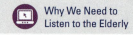 Why We Need to Listen to the Elderly

- *Sexual abuse:* Nonconsensual sexual contact of any kind with an elderly person
- *Emotional abuse:* Infliction of anguish, pain, or distress through verbal or nonverbal acts
- *Financial/material exploitation:* Illegal or improper use of an elder's funds, property, or assets
- *Neglect:* A person's refusal, or failure, to fulfill any part of his or her obligations or duties to an elderly person

Statistics reported in 2012 showed that more than half (59%) of the non-self-neglect substantiated reports of elder abuse in the United States—in other words, reports of abuse that were made by someone else and were investigated and found to be true—involved neglect, followed by physical abuse (16%), financial/material exploitation (12%), emotional abuse (7%), all other types (5%), and sexual abuse (0.04%) (Statistic Brain 2012). Whether they have been swindled out of their life savings by con artists, beaten by family members, or simply ignored because they are too much trouble for their overworked spouses, a growing number of older citizens suffer serious harm from these forms of abuse and neglect.

How common are crimes of elder abuse? In 1996 the National Center on Elder Abuse reported that 800,000 to 1.8 million older people had experienced abuse of some sort. By 2010, that number had grown to almost 6 million, or 9.5% of all adults age 60 and over (Statistic Brain 2012). Given the increased level of dependency that can occur with age, this problem will persist as the baby boom generation moves into old age.

Economics

For more than two centuries, older adults were identified as a social problem in the United States because they did not have the economic means to care for themselves. Recently, however, critics accuse them of demanding a lifestyle beyond their ability to afford. What is the economic reality? We can sum it up as "diverse." (The information provided in this section comes from the Federal Interagency Forum on Aging-Related Statistics 2010.)

The **poverty rate** is a measure of the number of people whose incomes fall below the level set by official poverty guidelines. It is calculated for the entire population and for subsections, such as by age and family size. The U.S. government established poverty guidelines in the early 1960s based on the belief that a family spends one-third

Poverty rate: A measure of the number of individuals or groups in poverty, expressed in absolute or relative terms.

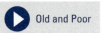
Old and Poor

Andrew Lichtenstein / Corbis

A homeless, older black man is a resident at this shelter in Jacksonville, Florida. Such a person may experience discrimination when looking for a job not only because of his race but also because of his age.

of its income on food. Each year the government calculates the cost of food for different household sizes, ranging from one person to eight, and multiplies the resulting figures by three to determine the poverty guidelines for the various household sizes. In 2013, the federal poverty line for a one-person family/household was $11,490, and for a two-person family/household it was $15,510 (U.S. Department of Health and Human Services 2013).

Compared to other age groups in the United States, those 65 and over have the lowest poverty rate. That said, as age increases, so does the likelihood of poverty (see Figure 6.4). The picture grows more complex when we also look at the profoundly influential characteristics of

FIGURE 6.4 Poverty Rate among U.S. Elderly by Age, 2010

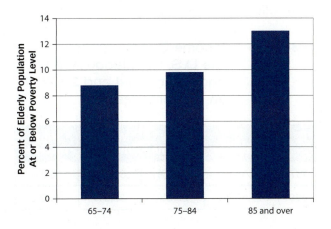

SOURCE: Federal Interagency Forum on Aging-Related Statistics. Older Americans 2010: Key Indicators of Well-Being. Federal Interagency Forum on Aging-Related Statistics. Washington, DC: U.S. Government Printing Office, July 2010.

Older Women of Color

Many older people experience increased marginalization as a result of their advanced age, and other demographic characteristics can worsen their situation. For instance, many older individuals face financial problems and rely primarily on Social Security as their main source of income. But when we take sex into account, we find that older women experience greater economic deprivation than do older men.

When an older female is a member of a racial minority, her level of economic deprivation increases even more. According to the Federal Interagency Forum on Aging-Related Statistics (2010), 12% of older women in the United States are living in poverty, compared with 7% of older men. Among older women, 9% of non-Hispanic whites are in poverty, compared with 12% of older Asian women, 27% of older black women, and 20% of older Hispanic women. In other words, the extent to which an older person is disadvantaged increases or decreases depending on additional sociodemographic characteristics such as sex, race, and ethnic heritage.

As we progress through the 21st century, the older white population in the United States will decrease from 80% of the total older population in 2010 to 58% in 2050. At the same time, the proportion of older black adults will increase from 9% to 12% in 2050. More dramatic increases will occur among older Asians (3% to 8%), Hispanics (7% to 20%), and other ethnic/racial groups (1% to 3%) (Federal Interagency Forum on Aging-Related Statistics 2010).

▶ **THINK ABOUT IT**

1. Why would being female and a member of a racial or ethnic minority group influence a person's likelihood of being economically deprived?

2. What will be the impact on society of an older population increasingly made up of racial and ethnic minority members?

---

sex, race, ethnicity, and marital status. For example, older women who live alone, regardless of race or ethnicity, are more likely than older men to live in poverty. Elderly minority women living alone experience a significantly higher poverty rate than do elderly white women living alone. In 2007, the poverty rate for older African American women living alone was 39.0%; for Hispanic older women living alone, it was 39.8%. By contrast, the poverty rate for elderly white women who were married was 4.1%.

TABLE 6.3 Income Distribution of the U.S. Population Age 65 and Over, 1974 and 2007 (in percentages)

	Poverty	Low income	Middle income	High income
1974	14.6%	34.6%	32.6%	18.2%
2007	9.7%	26.3%	33.3%	30.6%

SOURCE: Federal Interagency Forum on Aging-Related Statistics. Older Americans 2010: Key Indicators of Well-Being. Federal Interagency Forum on Aging-Related Statistics. Washington, DC: U.S. Government Printing Office. July 2010.

In Table 6.3, low income is between 100% and 199% of the poverty threshold, middle income lies between 200% and 399%, and high income is 400% or more of the poverty threshold. Over the 33-year period covered in the table, the distribution of older adults across the income brackets has skewed upward. In other words, median household income among those 65 and over increased between 1974 and 2007 from $20,838 to $29,393 (all in 2007 dollars). While seemingly impressive, this is not a significant growth rate. The data also point to the economic diversity that exists among older U.S. adults.

We can also see changes since the 1960s in the sources of income for married and nonmarried persons 65 and older. Figure 6.5 indicates how Social Security, pensions, and earnings have grown increasingly important to them over time. Some 60% of older citizens rely on Social Security as their primary source of income, which explains why any reference to reducing government funding to this program is met with concern. The data in Figure 6.6 are divided into quintiles, or fifths of the population, so we can examine differences between segments of the older-age population. While we can say that older adults are truly economically diverse, that diversity is limited.

Social Security is central to the needs of most older citizens. What can we do to ensure the long-term viability of the Social Security program? In a brief published by the National Academy of Social Insurance, Reno and Lavery (2005) reported on the economic benefits of various proposals to reduce the anticipated shortfall in Social Security benefits. According to these authors, if the earnings cap (currently about $110,000) were removed so that *all* earned income were taxed, the additional revenue generated would reduce the shortfall by 93%. Increasing the Social Security tax by 1% on individuals and employers would generate additional revenue that would cover 104% of the shortfall, effectively ensuring the well-being of Social Security through the end of the 21st century. Another option is to reduce the cost-of-living benefit that keeps Social Security in line with the inflation rate; this change would cover 111% of the expected shortfall. It would also reduce future Social Security income for middle-class recipients by as much as 46%, however. Other suggested changes would have much smaller impacts on the shortfall. They include increasing the age for full retirement from 67 to 68, lowering the yearly cost-of-living adjustments by 1%, and extending coverage to new state and local government workers. The resulting outcomes would cover 28%, 79%, and 10% of the gap, respectively.

Health

Despite efforts by some to connect rising health care costs in the United States to the increasing number of older

FIGURE 6.5 **Sources of Income for Older U.S. Adults, 1962 and 2008**

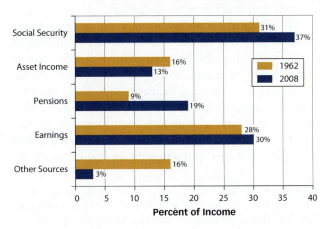

SOURCE: Federal Interagency Forum on Aging-Related Statistics. Older Americans 2010: Key Indicators of Well-Being. Federal Interagency Forum on Aging-Related Statistics. Washington, DC: U.S. Government Printing Office. July 2010.

Social Security: A federal program that provides monthly benefit payments to older workers who have participated in the workforce and paid into the system.

FIGURE 6.6 **Economic Well-Being and Source of Income in Old Age by U.S. Population Quintiles, 2010**

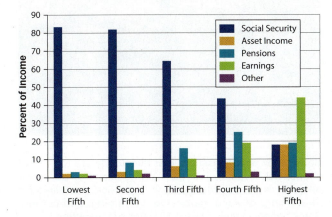

SOURCE: Interagency Forum on Aging-Related Statistics. Older Americans 2010: Key Indicators of Well-Being. Federal Interagency Forum on Aging-Related Statistics. Washington, DC: U.S. Government Printing Office. July 2010.

citizens, the relationship between the two is in fact minimal. For example, "neither the percentage of GDP that a nation spends on health care on all of its people, nor the percentage of its GDP devoted to health care strictly for the elderly, seem to be driven by the percentage of the population that is aged" (Reinhardt 2000, 73). More recently, Quesnel-Vallee, Farrah, and Jenkins (2011, 564) have noted that "population age per se is not the main driver of health care costs." The deeper question, then, is how to improve the overall health of older citizens and not blame them for higher health care costs.

Today's older adults are significantly healthier than those of 100 or even 50 years ago. One way to measure the health of a population is to examine life expectancy at birth and at age 65. In the United States, life expectancy at birth has increased from approximately 47 years at the beginning of the 20th century to about 77 years today. That increase has occurred for a number of reasons, such as improved public health, increased income, better living and working conditions, and improved medical services. At age 65, an American adult today can expect to live an additional 18.5 years on average. This is an increase of roughly 4 years since 1960 (Federal Interagency Forum on Aging-Related Statistics 2010).

Improved health is allowing more people to live longer lives, thus fueling the increase in the numbers of older persons. In particular, those surviving into oldest-old age (85 and over) are now the fastest-growing segment of the population. As people age, their utilization

Sometimes people assume that the elderly are too out of shape, sick, tired, or just plain old to exercise. But many adults ages 65 and older take part in physical activities such as walking, dancing, gardening, swimming, and cycling. Some people in their 70s and 80s even run marathons.

of health services also increases. Therefore, the growth in the oldest-old population should predict increased health care costs among this segment of the population. What we also know, however, is that only a small percentage of older individuals accounts for the majority of Medicare spending (Budrys 2012). More specifically, Medicare costs are approximately six times greater for those recipients who die than for those who do not (Hogan et al. 2001). In other words, aging is not the cause of rising health care costs—the cost of dying is.

In the United States, health care for older citizens is provided through **Medicare**, a universal health care system for those 65 and over. The Medicare insurance program, which became part of the Social Security Act in 1965 under President Lyndon B. Johnson, along with **Medicaid**, ensures access to health care services for older citizens and those living in poverty. The program has been credited with improving the overall health of older persons. However, its costs have grown significantly, and it now faces an uncertain economic and political future.

Projections currently indicate that Medicare Part A (hospital insurance) will be able to pay only 87% of hospital costs by 2024 if no changes are made to its financing mechanisms. Parts B (medical insurance) and D (prescription drug coverage), however, are not in danger (Van de Water 2013). While the economic crisis facing Medicare has been building for some time, the program and its beneficiaries have recently become political pawns in the ongoing debate regarding the role of government in everyday life. While the system could be strengthened by an increase in the Medicare tax rate, some have proposed turning it into a voucher program instead. Under such a program, an older person would receive a yearly voucher

to be used to purchase health coverage. If the person were to use up the total value of the voucher before the end of the year, he or she would have to pay for additional medical services or do without until the next year.

It is not surprising that health care has become an area of significant political debate in this country. With health care costs rising at levels well beyond the rate of inflation, efforts to control costs will continue, and in the process, the health of older citizens may be affected.

ASK YOURSELF: Should Medicare be converted to a voucher system, or should the program remain as it is? Which of these choices is in the best interests of older citizens and of the general public? How can Medicare be made more efficient and less expensive?

Political Power

Will the United States become a **gerontocracy**, a country in which the political system is run by and for older citizens at the expense of younger generations? Chances are that this will not occur. So what is the political reality for older U.S. adults?

Although older voters now enjoy a larger public presence than voters in other age groups because of their numbers, the extent to which they influence public policy is unclear. All Americans who vote can have input into their political destiny, and historically, older U.S. citizens have been more likely to vote than those in any other age group (see Table 6.4). However, older Americans are just as diverse in their political beliefs, and in their voting patterns, as Americans in other age groups.

The emergence of welfare state programs has, without a doubt, played a crucial role in improving the overall health, well-being, and financial security of older citizens in the United States and throughout the developed world. It has also, by definition, increased dependence on government programs. In recent years, some politicians have undertaken efforts to dismantle such programs, though they have proven beneficial to older persons in the United States and elsewhere, and return the services the programs

Medicare: A federal health care program for those age 65 and over. The program is divided into four parts that address health coverage for services provided by physicians and hospitals as well as prescription drug coverage.

Medicaid: A federal/state program that provides a variety of social services to those identified as eligible based on state-specific criteria.

Gerontocracy: A system in which older-age citizens have the power to run the government and dictate policies that primarily support people in their age category.

TABLE 6.4   Voting Patterns in the United States by Age, 1996–2012

	1996	2000	2004	2008	2012
Total population	54.2%	54.7%	58.3%	58.2%	56.5%
18–24 years old	32.4%	32.3%	41.9%	44.3%	38.0%
25–44 years old	49.2%	49.8%	52.2%	51.9%	49.5%
45–64 years old	64.4%	64.1%	66.6%	65%	63.4%
65 years old and over	67.0%	67.6%	68.9%	68.1%	69.7%

SOURCE: U.S. Census Bureau, Current Population Survey, November 2012 and earlier reports.

offer to the private sector. Older U.S. adults have begun to make their concerns about these efforts known through membership groups such as AARP (formerly the American Association of Retired Persons) and the more activist advocacy organization the Gray Panthers.

One of the more sensitive political issues for older voters is **generational inequity**, or the idea that they are unfairly receiving more benefits than other groups in society thanks to age-specific legislation that favors them. Programs such as Social Security and Medicare, for instance, can raise the question of fairness to other age groups. Do children receive less from the government because they do not have an advocacy group like AARP?

Social Security and Medicare do provide age-specific benefits to individuals above a certain chronological age (Kapp 1996, 2006). The problem, however, is not that older people are better at advocating for government to meet their needs, but that Congress has been unwilling to create universal support programs that provide services to *all* age groups, other than a few examples like the Americans with Disabilities Act.

Crime

As noted above, and as Figure 6.7 shows, older persons are less likely to be victims of crime in the United States

Generational inequity: A situation in which older-age members of a society receive a disproportionate share of the society's resources relative to younger members; perceptions that such inequity exists lead to calls for adjustments to ensure greater economic and social parity between generations.

than are members of other age groups (Bachman and Meloy 2008). However, research shows that older Americans believe they are *more* likely to be victimized (a finding first noted by Harris 1976). What accounts for this difference between perception and reality?

There are several possible explanations. As noted above, when older persons are victimized, they have more difficulty recovering from injuries than do younger persons, and hospitalization can be a bigger financial strain for them. Older persons are also less likely to be in the labor force, thus they may have limited ability to replenish their financial reserves after an assault. For older persons, being a victim of crime appears to be related to socioeconomic status; that is, wealthier older people have the economic means to live in areas in which they are less likely to experience victimization (Peguero and Lauck 2008). Many urban areas undergo physical and demographic transformation over a number of decades, resulting in environments that are newly daunting and sometimes difficult to navigate for older persons who have lived there for many years. Finally, the deaths of friends leave many older persons alone, without adequate bases of emotional support and assistance.

In addition to being victims, older people also commit crimes. They currently make up the fastest-growing segment of the American prison population, not because they are committing more crimes, but because of the lengthy sentences now imposed, particularly on drug offenders. When older-age persons commit crimes they tend to commit many of the same types of crimes as members of other age groups, but in far lower proportions. They are most likely to be charged with gambling, sex offenses, vagrancy, and public drunkenness (Feldmeyer and Steffensmeier 2007). Because it costs more to care for older prisoners than younger ones, researchers have begun to look closely at sentencing guidelines and at how states can imprison older inmates without increasing the overall cost of care (Matcha 2011). Again, some frame the rising costs associated with an increasingly older prison population as a social problem of aging when, in reality, the problem lies with the criminal justice system and sentencing policies.

ASK YOURSELF: Should older perpetrators of crimes be treated differently from others because of their age? Is it important to incarcerate an 80-year-old who has committed a serious crime, or should he or she experience a different type of punishment? If we treat an 80-year-old differently, what about a 75-year-old? Or a 65-year-old? Where should the chronological cutoff be for a different prison experience?

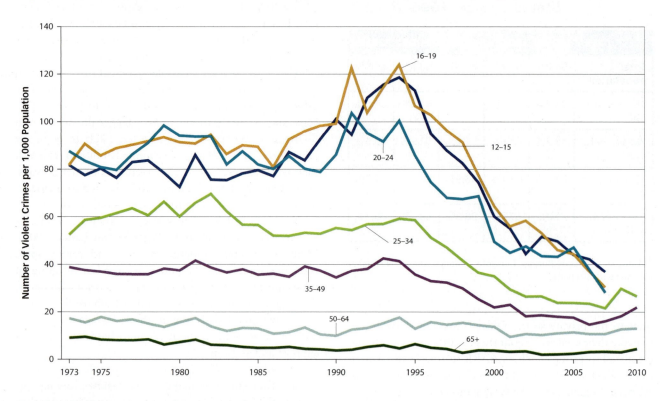

SOURCES: Rape, robbery, and assault data are from the National Crime Victimization Survey. The homicide data are collected by the FBI's Uniform Crime Reports (Supplementary Homicide Reports) from reports from law enforcement agencies. U.S. Department of Justice 2009 and 2011. Office of Justice Programs. Bureau of Justice Statistics.

Global Perspective

The demographic shift toward an older population is not confined to the United States. In fact, the United States has, and will continue to have, one of the lowest percentages of people age 65 and over in the industrialized world. By the middle of the 21st century, the percentage of older-age people in the developing world will be increasing faster than the percentage in the developed world. Tables 6.5, 6.6, and 6.7 show the changes that are expected to continue well into the middle of this century in various regions of the world.

Notice the extent to which all regions of the world will experience significant growth of their aging populations between now and 2050. In the countries of Africa, the percentage of those 65 and over will double by 2050, while in Asia and Latin America it will triple. In all regions of the world except Africa and Oceania, the old-age dependency ratio will be greater than the child dependency ratio. Similarly, the median age will be at least 40 in all regions except Africa and Oceania. These demographic changes will alter economic and social landscapes throughout the world.

Let's look more closely at Japan and Italy. Japan is the country most representative of the future of aging.

TABLE 6.5 Percentage of Population Age 65 and Over by Region, 2000 and 2050

Region	2000	2050
Africa	3.3	6.6
Asia	5.8	17.9
Europe	14.8	26.9
Latin America	5.8	19.1
Northern America	12.4	21.6
Oceania	10.2	18.4

SOURCE: Population Division of the Department of Economic and Social Affairs of the United Nations Secretariat, *World Population Prospects: The 2010 Revision.*

TABLE 6.6 Child and Old-Age Dependency Ratios by Region, 2000 and 2050

	Africa	Asia	Europe	Latin America	Northern America	Oceania
Total dependency ratio, 2000	84	57	48	60	50	55
Child	78	48	26	51	32	40
Old-age	6	9	22	9	19	15
Total dependency ratio, 2050	59	55	75	57	67	63
Child	49	27	28	27	31	33
Old-age	10	28	47	30	36	30

SOURCE: Population Division of the Department of Economic and Social Affairs of the United Nations Secretariat, *World Population Prospects: The 2010 Revision.*

Nearly 23% of its population is now 65 or over, and by 2050, that figure will be just over 35%. The government's ability to provide services in the future is in doubt because the old-age dependency ratio is expected to increase from 25 in 2000 to 70 in 2050. One reason is that life expectancy in Japan has increased steadily since the middle of the 20th century. In 2000–2005, it was 78.3 and 85.2 years for males and females, respectively. By 2050–2055, it will reach 84.5 and 91.4 years, and by the end of the 21st century it could be as high as 89 and an impressive 95.7 years.

Italy's demographics are similar to Japan's. In 2000, about 18% of the population was 65 or over; by 2050, nearly 33% will be. The old-age dependency ratio is expected to increase from 27 in 2000 to 62 in 2050 (United Nations 2011). These changes go beyond mere numbers, of course. For instance, how many aging workers are remaining in the workforce? In Japan, more than 20% of older workers are still employed, while Italy may have a problem because less than 6% of older Italians are in the workforce. Why is this low percentage a problem? Perhaps the clearest answer is the ratio of retirees who collect government benefits to workers whose taxes help pay for them. By 2050, Japan is expected to have 96 pensioners for every 100 workers. In Italy, however, there will be 155 pensioners for every 100 workers (Bongaarts 2004). Such ratios, particularly Italy's, are not sustainable because funding the pension system would take much of the workers' salary. The impact this situation will have on retiring Italians is expected to be dramatic. Both Japan and Italy will need to reevaluate their public policies and encourage greater numbers of older citizens to continue working.

Older-age populations around the world are under increasing pressure to reduce their impact on the societies in which they live. At the same time, they are being viewed as the vanguard of a new era in which changing political and economic conditions can offer them a renewed sense of purpose. It is this dichotomy that frames the lives of older persons throughout the developed world.

Before we go on to the discussion of theoretical perspectives in the next section, let's return for a moment to an earlier point and reinforce that aging is not in itself a social problem. Rather, older-age populations are diverse and are growing as a result of societal changes in family, work, and health. It is the way aging is socially constructed, in the patterns and trends reviewed above, that creates an image of aging as a social problem, of older

TABLE 6.7 Median Age by Region, 2000 and 2050

Region	2000	2050
Africa	18.6	26.4
Asia	25.9	41.0
Europe	37.6	45.7
Latin America	24.5	41.0
Northern America	35.8	40.4
Oceania	31.3	37.5

SOURCE: Population Division of the Department of Economic and Social Affairs of the United Nations Secretariat, *World Population Prospects: The 2010 Revision.*

Life Expectancy

The Challenges of Aging throughout the World

The journal *Ageing International* recently published an article titled "The Power of Global Aging" by Jason L. Powell (2010). Although Powell did not engage in original research, his article offers tremendous insight into the global impact of aging and the demographic and socioeconomic consequences of aging throughout the world.

As Powell reports, the world's population age 65 and over is expected to double between 2005 and 2030, to approximately 1 billion. The proportion of those 85 and over will increase by 151%, while only a 21% increase will be seen among those under the age of 65. The population of those 65 and over in the developing world is expected to increase by 140% between 2005 and 2030, compared with a 51% increase in the developed world.

Dividing the world into a number of geographic areas (North and South America, Asia, Europe, and Africa), Powell addresses their specific demographic changes and needs. His assessment of these and other data offers clear evidence of the dynamic quality of aging in different segments of the world population and demonstrates the need for a global understanding of this demographic shift. He sums up his argument when he notes: "While global aging represents a triumph of medical, social, and economic advances, it also presents tremendous challenges. Population aging strains social insurance and pension systems and challenges models of social support. It affects economic growth, trade, migration, disease patterns and prevalence, and fundamental assumptions about growing old" (10).

Powell acknowledges the complexity of aging within a global context, but he does not address aging as a social problem. Further, he provides evidence not only of changing family structures but also of the differences between countries' abilities to provide for expanding populations living on pensions rather than earning in the

Susana Vera / Reuters

Older people sit on a bench at a shopping center in Madrid, Spain. Many countries throughout Europe are enacting reforms to raise the retirement age in order to cut social security expenditures. Do you think that people should be expected to work past the traditional retirement age of 65?

workforce. According to Powell, these challenges offer nations the opportunity to create unique partnerships that build on their demographics, such as the relocation of elderly Japanese to Thailand, where health care costs are lower.

▶ **THINK ABOUT IT**

1. What are some concerns that might be raised by the expected doubling of the number of older persons worldwide?

2. What can we do to lessen the impact of this demographic shift?

3. What are some possible positive outcomes of the shift?

people as the driving force of change, and therefore of the aging population as the culprit in any disruption these changes bring to the broader society.

USING THEORY TO UNDERSTAND AGING: THE VIEWS FROM THE FUNCTIONALIST, CONFLICT, AND

SYMBOLIC INTERACTIONIST PERSPECTIVES

 6.3 Apply the functionalist, symbolic interactionist, and conflict perspectives to social policy for the aging.

The sociological study of aging has historically focused on finding ways to improve the lives of older

Researching Aging

Rights and Interests of Older Persons in China

What rights do you have as a young adult? Are you encouraged to participate in the daily activities around you? Do you have access to adequate food, water, and the basic necessities of life? Are there others who are willing to care for you? Think of what life would be like if your rights and interests were not protected or considered important.

Wang Zhuqing (2012) has researched how the five principles of independence, participation, care, self-fulfillment, and dignity apply to older people in China and the challenges associated with protecting the elderly's rights and interests. He found that older urban Chinese are likely to enjoy pensions and health care that allow them independence, while their rural counterparts are likely to live with and be dependent on their families. The participation of older Chinese in policy making is limited, in part by the inability of existing organizations to include them in the process. In terms of self-fulfillment, older Chinese in urban environments are interested in pursuing access to information about medicine and legal services. Opportunities for such self-fulfillment are limited in rural areas.

Zhuqing found that who cares for older Chinese is again determined by where they live. Older urban residents are generally cared for by their spouses, while older rural people are cared for by their children. Finally, Zhuqing investigated the principle of dignity by researching whether the elderly had experienced abuse. Because China does not have a firm definition of elder abuse, it is difficult to determine what percentage of older Chinese have been abused. However, Zhuqing's data indicate that older rural Chinese are more likely than their urban counterparts to experience abuse.

In addition to analyzing the data from an urban/rural perspective, Zhuqing examined them by gender. He found that older Chinese women in rural areas experience significantly greater problems relative to his five research principles than do older men. While gender differences are less significant in urban areas, they nonetheless exist.

Zhuqing's research suggests that the rights and interests of older persons

Cyclists ride past three elderly men in Beijing. China has the world's largest population of those age 60 and older. More and more of China's seniors now live by themselves.

in China are not being fully protected, particularly in rural areas and for older women. Possible solutions to this problem include a call for greater societal involvement to ensure that older persons receive the care and support they need.

▶ THINK ABOUT IT

1. Why do you think older Chinese living in rural areas are more likely than their urban counterparts to experience abuse?

2. Why do you think older women in China are less likely than older men to experience the five principles of independence, participation, care, self-fulfillment, and dignity?

3. What can Chinese society do to ensure that all older persons experience these five principles?

persons rather than on building theories. Nevertheless, theoretical frameworks have evolved and offer a range of explanations that address the aging process and its outcomes. We begin with an assessment of the primary theoretical perspectives within sociology as they apply to aging.

Structural Functionalism

Recall that structural functionalism provides a view of society in which balance and social order are central, and every action has consequences and thus a function. Manifest functions are intended, while latent functions are unintended. For example, a retirement

Owen Franken / Corbis

A first-grade student practices reading with the assistance of Edna Warf, a retired woman who volunteers as a reading tutor at Claxton Elementary School in Asheville, North Carolina. What other contributions can older citizens make to their communities?

system is a manifest function of work because it allows for the smooth transition of older workers out of the system and provides employment opportunities for younger workers. A latent function of retirement is the creation of a population with the time to engage in volunteer efforts that reduce the need for full-time paid workers.

Structural functionalism is also built around the concept of structure and the need for social institutions such as the family, education, and religion to regulate the norms and values of society. A change in one part of the system will result in reactions from other parts. For example, the ongoing demographic shift toward a larger older population is resulting in an expanded effort to provide necessary health and social services to those in need.

Policy Implications of Structural Functionalism

While functionalism has its critics, some of the policy implications of this perspective are valuable. For instance, is the retirement of older workers functional for the individual and for society? It provides a ready supply of job openings for younger workers, ensuring that they become wage earners who provide for their own economic stability and that of society rather than disengaging from society's economic well-being. The establishment of a retirement "age" also provides society with a framework of work activity to which workers are expected to adhere; not retiring "on time" is viewed as dysfunctional. Although age-defined mandatory retirement no longer exists for most U.S. workers, in fact most still leave the workforce as soon as they find it economically feasible to do so.

Conflict Theory

While functionalism is based on balance and social order, conflict theory offers a distinctively different view of society in which inherent inequality allows the dominant group to impose its norms and values on the less powerful, maintaining an economic and social advantage and igniting power struggles over the use of society's resources. While initially focused on social class differences, conflict theory has evolved and today examines any number of power issues involving race, class, sex, age, and other factors.

Conflict theory thus reflects the ongoing struggles within the aging population. Because older U.S. adults are diverse economically, politically, racially, ethnically, and religiously, they do not all reach the same outcome in life. For instance, the earliest baby boomers, known as front-enders, were born in the period 1946 through 1950. When they were eligible for the draft during the Vietnam War, the latest boomers, born from 1960 through 1964, were in preschool. Today, those early boomers are able to retire, while the youngest are vulnerable to layoffs and a bleak financial future.

As a result, conflicts have arisen between the segments of this population, and baby boomers as a whole are less able to unite behind their common needs. Exploiting this conflict, government and the private sector can win concessions on the policies and services they provide. For example, cries of the financial ruin of Social Security and the bankruptcy of Medicare drown out the economic realities, fragmenting the millions of baby boomers as they jockey for position within the public policy arena.

Policy Implications of the Conflict Perspective

If we limit conflict theory to a Marxist interpretation, then its only application is in how work affects older citizens. In other words, if what we do (work) defines who we are and what we have (or do not have) in a capitalist society, then older individuals are disadvantaged because access to work is controlled by those in the upper class, who create work to maintain their privileged position. Older citizens are thus viewed as nonproductive members of society, devalued and at the mercy of the more productive. Thus, "a Marxist view of the situation of people considered too old to be effective in the workplace places the blame for their circumstances on the general problems of capitalist society" (Cockerham 1997, 70).

Changing Demographics

Part II: Problems of Inequality

But the policy implications of conflict theory also apply to the distribution of power and resources. For example, the current debate in the United States over the proper role of government in providing services to the less fortunate is fundamentally grounded in the availability of resources: Should older citizens receive health care services through a government agency (Medicare) or through the private sector? Should workers of all ages be allowed to deposit some or all of their current Social Security funds into the stock market in an effort to grow their retirement funds at their own risk, or should the federal government control the funds and offer a safe but lower rate of return? These competing ideas and the belief systems behind them characterize the way power and resources affect the future of a growing segment of older people.

Symbolic Interactionism

Symbolic interactionism assumes that individuals in a society communicate via cultural symbols and shared meanings, and it looks at the ways we create our identities, the representations of who we believe we are in relationship to those around us. For older adults in the United States, identity is grounded in the past as well as in the present. What is an older person? Cultural symbols like white hair, wrinkles, reading glasses, and nursing homes are all components that endure as identity features. Other features are shared experiences of historical significance—such as the Great Depression, World War II, the Vietnam War, and 9/11—that connect individuals to an identity.

Policy Implications of Symbolic Interactionism

The policy implications of symbolic interactionism are significant. For years, the mass media in the United States have labeled aging adults as slow, politically conservative, overweight, hard of hearing, intellectually challenged, and overbearing toward the young. The problem with these labels is their consequences. For example, if an older person applies for a job, will the potential employer view him or her as someone who can perform the job, or as someone too slow to keep up with its demands?

Symbolic interactionism also has policy implications for efforts to address the problems older individuals experience as they attempt to adapt to changes, either social changes such as advancements in technology or changes that affect their personal lives, such as moving from environments they have known for decades into nursing homes or relinquishing car keys because they can

no longer drive without endangering themselves and others. Society compensates older individuals for changes like these by creating public policies that increase their dependence on others, such as senior transportation for those who can no longer drive. While commendable, these programs miss the larger problems of where older persons live and the lack of local services that could enable them to maintain their independence.

SPECIALIZED THEORIES ABOUT AGING

 6.4 Apply specialized theories to the social construction of aging.

Theoretical frameworks specific to the sociological study of aging have been few because of the interdisciplinary nature of aging research, its problem-solving focus, and its emphasis on the individual rather than society (Bengtson, Putney, and Johnson 2005). Beginning in the 1950s, however, several distinct theories have been developed, each of which offers a variety of explanations of the aging process. We look at them in roughly chronological order.

Disengagement Theory

Disengagement theory was developed from the Kansas City Study of Adult Life in the 1950s and became one of the first theories of aging. Originally designed to reflect the functionalist relationship between the individual and society, it suggests that the aging individual and society engage in a mutual withdrawal in the sixth decade of life, allowing the individual to begin the socialization into old age. We see the application of functionalism in disengagement theory, because this theory conceptualizes the relationship between the individual and society as one of balance and, when applied to the world of work, as one of maintaining social order between generations.

The three basic tenets of disengagement theory are that disengagement is a mutual process, that it is universal, and that it is inevitable (Cumming and Henry 1961). Further research efforts in the United States and other countries have not found support for the theory; nevertheless, it offered a beginning point from which further theoretical development has emerged.

Anita Dante searches for a job in a local newspaper's classified section at her home in Margate, Florida. After working for most of her life, Dante had planned on retiring, but her plans have changed. Dante lost most of her retirement nest egg and must now get a job to continue to support herself.

When disengagement theory was first developed, most American workers faced mandatory retirement based on age. According to the theory, people understood that after working for an organization for a number of years and growing older, they would be replaced by younger workers, and the process was generally mutually agreeable. This is only a limited example of the mutual benefit shared by the worker and society, and other problems with the theory arose.

In particular, the assumption that disengagement occurs universally in all societies is problematic, because work, the work role, and the role of older workers vary not only between but also within cultures. Finally, disengagement is not inevitable. In the current economic environment, many baby boomers will be forced to remain engaged in the workforce and in other middle-age-related roles, and, with the elimination of mandatory retirement for most occupations, others will not disengage from the workforce because they do not want to.

Activity Theory

Activity theory originated in the late 1940s and early 1950s (Cavan et al. 1949; Havighurst and Albrecht 1953), but it was not officially established until the early 1970s (Lemon, Bengtson, and Peterson 1972). Theoretically, activity theory is built on the work of symbolic interactionism.

Essentially, activity theory argues the opposite of disengagement theory by positing that as people age, they assume new roles more consistent with their current identities. As a result, they remain actively engaged in the social world and maintain their self-concepts and life satisfaction, but at levels different from before. Thus identified as aging successfully, they enjoy new sets of activities they find as satisfying as their previous ones from middle age.

On a basic level, activity theory reflects modern U.S. society and its cultural values of individualism and independence. It represents a middle-class orientation to aging and identifies it as successful. At the same time, "activity theory neglects issues of power, inequality, and conflict between age groups" (Powell 2006, 49). And, as with disengagement theory, efforts to replicate the initial work of activity theory have yielded only partial support (Longino and Kart 1982).

Political Economy of Aging

Political economy of aging is less a unified theory than a broad perspective in which factors like inequality and structural forces help us understand aging in an economic and political context. For example, this perspective's focus on the way the provisions of the welfare state are distributed within a society shows us how social and economic inequalities are perpetuated that are then manifested in old age (Quadagno and Reid 1999).

The basic tenets of the political economy of aging are as follows:

- An older person's sense of worth and power is shaped by the broader social structure.
- Labels attached to the elderly affect not only their beliefs about themselves, but also the way society creates public policies for them.
- Inequalities within society are reflected in the social policies and politics of aging. As a result, these policies enforce group-based advantages and disadvantages consistent with those in the larger society.
- Dominant political and economic ideological beliefs that reinforce advantages and disadvantages in the larger society are the basis for social policy (Estes 1991).
- This perspective thus frames the relationship between the aging population and the larger society as one in which broader social and economic inequalities dominate the creation of social policy. In addition, older-age populations experience the generally negative impact that labeling can have on their lives and opportunities.

Continuity Theory

Building on activity theory, **continuity theory** utilizes the concept of normal aging as a basis for explaining how older individuals adjust. Here, "normal aging" describes the circumstances of those who are able to live independently, provide for their economic well-being,

Continuity theory: A theory that utilizes the concept of normal aging as a basis for explaining how older individuals adjust.

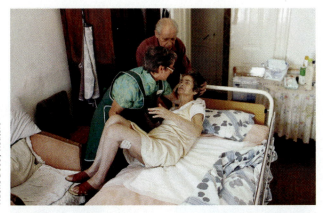

Nacho Doce / Reuters

Alzheimer's disease patient Isidora Tomaz is carried to bed by an aid worker from the Portuguese Alzheimer Association, a charity in Lisbon, Portugal. Isidora's husband, Amilcar Dos Santos, looks on. Many patients receiving care from the association live at home.

purchase nutritious foods, and meet their clothing and transportation needs. These are individuals who enjoy stability in this transitory life period as well as active involvement in the process itself. According to Atchley (1989, 183), "A central premise of continuity theory is that, in making adaptive choices, middle-aged and older adults attempt to preserve and maintain existing internal and external structures and that they prefer to accomplish this objective by using continuity (i.e., applying familiar strategies in familiar arenas of life)."

The crux of continuity theory is the existence of internal and external continuity. Inner continuity is our definition of who we are. It refers to inner qualities such as our preferences, temperament, and skills we have acquired. Atchley uses the Alzheimer's patient as an example of someone without inner continuity, because the person does not remember his or her identity, behavior patterns, or abilities. The loss of inner continuity is also problematic for others who attempt to interact with the person; they will experience lack of predictability in their interactions with the individual.

External continuity relates to our physical and social environments, roles we perform, and activities we engage in. Thus, for an older person the familiarity of his or her own home or other places where he or she spends time is important. The persistence of a particular role that a person has performed for years also provides a connection to the past as well as to the future. When external continuity is lost, the person experiences distress because surroundings are not familiar or must be experienced without access to all senses. External continuity allows an individual to cope with physical and mental changes that challenge the ability to function. If a person experiences difficulty walking or has short memory lapses, knowing the layout of his or her home enables the person to navigate hallways or stairs with less difficulty.

Finally, continuity can be too little, optimal, or too much. Too little continuity results in a lack of patterned activity, leading to unpredictability. Optimal continuity results when life adjustments are occurring at a rate consistent with the person's coping mechanisms. Too much continuity results in a lack of change, and the person feels stuck in a nonchanging environment (Atchley 1989).

SOCIAL CHANGE: WHAT CAN YOU DO?

6.5 Identify steps toward social change for the aging.

Aging continues to be socially constructed as a social problem. What can you do? In a word: everything. Utilizing the material in this chapter as a guide, become involved in changing the way aging is socially constructed from a problem to an asset. The first step is to become aware of your own ageist attitudes and behaviors. Recognizing them allows you to think about what you say and how you behave toward older individuals. You can also engage in broader activities such as those described below.

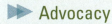 ## Advocacy

Advocacy can take many forms. If you have a grandparent or know of another older person who needs help with housing or financial support, you can become that person's advocate, going to the appropriate agencies with him or her and helping the older person receive what he or she is due. If you know of older individuals who are experiencing difficulties because they are poor, or who have a particular medical condition, you can advocate for them as a group. For example, in New York State, Tuesday is lobby day at the state capitol in Albany. Individuals meet with state legislators and attempt to convince them to write legislation that will advance the needs of the groups they are advocating for. Finally, if you are concerned about issues affecting older persons, such as potential changes to Social Security or Medicare, you could join an advocacy organization that fights for the rights of all older persons.

 ## Internships

Does your educational institution provide internships for students? If so, an internship with a local office on aging, senior center, or any other aging-related agency offers hands-on experience that can translate into exciting opportunities. You will also meet a number of great people who will be thrilled you are taking the time to provide them with the assistance they need. Often, it's the small things that make a difference. I've had students do internships in a senior center if they were interested in direct service with older adults. I have also placed students in the state office on aging if they are more interested in public policy related to aging. You might also look for internships in other organizations that advocate for older individuals, such as the Gray Panthers.

 ## Volunteering

Volunteer your time at a nursing home or wherever groups of older persons congregate. However, you should not assume that all older people want or need assistance. Generally, if they do, they will ask. Simply

Lucas Oleniuk / Toronto Star via Getty Images

Nursing homes rely on volunteers to interact with their residents. They need volunteers to provide company for residents and assist in hosting dances, card games, and bingo nights. Do you enjoy helping others? How about visiting with seniors in their residences?

assuming they need help and doing things for them can create a feeling of dependence.

Become involved with organizations that promote active and engaged aging. For example, the National Council on Aging provides information about how advocates can help the organization and, by extension, older citizens. Area Agencies on Aging, which are part of a national organization, are located in all states; the organization's local and national offices offer a wealth of information about advocacy for older persons.

 ## Service Learning

If your college or university offers a service learning component, become involved. Different from internships or volunteering, service learning provides benefits to both the student and the recipient of the services. Beyond the service provided is the learning that occurs. In other words, take what you have learned in the classroom and apply it in the broader world of aging.

WHAT DOES AMERICA THINK?

Questions about Aging from the General Social Survey

 Turn to the beginning of the chapter to compare your answers to the total population.

1. Adult children are important to help elderly parents.

    AGREE: 94%

    DISAGREE: 6%

2. Who should provide help for the elderly?

    FAMILY MEMBERS: 66%

    GOVERNMENT AGENCIES: 16.5%

    NONPROFIT ORGANIZATIONS: 8.2%

    PRIVATE PROVIDERS: 9.3%

3. Should the aged live with their children?

    YES: 61.7%

    NO: 38.3%

4. Who should pay for help for the elderly?

    ELDERLY PEOPLE THEMSELVES OR THEIR FAMILY: 54.1%

    THE GOVERNMENT/ PUBLIC FUNDS: 45.9%

5. In the United States, do you think we're spending too much money on Social Security, too little money, or about the right amount?

    TOO MUCH: 7.8%

    TOO LITTLE: 55.8%

    ABOUT THE RIGHT AMOUNT: 36.4%

LOOK BEHIND THE NUMBERS

Go to **edge.sagepub.com/trevino** for a breakdown of these data across time and by race, sex, age, income, and other statuses.

1. Examine the survey data on education level for responses to the question of who should pay for help for the elderly. Describe the relationship. Why do you think this occurred?

2. Note the interesting relationship between respondents' ages and their responses to the question about whether aged should live with their children. What explanation can you suggest for this result?

3. Questions regarding elder support and cost were added to the GSS in 2012. Why do you think they were not added previously? Why do you think they were seen as important to add to the survey in 2012?

4. Each possibility regarding the provision of care for the elderly has both benefits and shortcomings. Explain why each of the following care options is a positive choice as well as why it is a negative option: children, government agencies, nonprofits, private providers.

SOURCE: National Opinion Research Center, University of Chicago.

CHAPTER SUMMARY

 6.1 Discuss aging as a social construct.

Because aging is constructed from the expectations and beliefs of society, it has been identified as a social problem throughout U.S. history. Initially, older adults were considered a social problem because they were unable to provide for their own well-being. More recently, they have been identified as a social problem because of the cost of providing for their financial well-being and health care through taxpayer-supported government programs such as Social Security and Medicare. The construction of aging as a social problem is reinforced through the use of ageism, or the use of a person's chronological age as a basis for discrimination. We see the labeling of older citizens as a social problem on television, in newspapers and magazines, and around the Internet. As a result, societal expectations and beliefs about aging are rooted in a number of myths.

 6.2 Discuss patterns and trends in the demographics of aging.

The percentage of the population age 65 and over is increasing and will continue to increase from 20% to 35% in virtually all countries. In the United States this demographic shift may harden the socially constructed belief that aging itself is a social problem. Issues such as perceived generational inequity confront some older adults as critics believe they enjoy the fruits of a welfare state at the expense of younger generations. Others fear a growing older-age population will result in a gerontocracy, or rule by older adults. These claims have little grounding in reality, but they aid those willing to dismantle public policies aimed at assisting older persons. Smaller families place increased pressure on those caring for older members even as more people are living longer. In addition to elder abuse, older U.S. adults are also victims of crime, though at much lower rates than other age groups.

 6.3 Apply the functionalist, symbolic interactionist, and conflict perspectives to social policy for the aging.

Functionalism offers insight into issues such as work and retirement. Is the retirement role functional for society and the individual, or does it create a power imbalance whereby individuals are expected to remove themselves from the workplace even though they want to remain employed? Conflict theory offers insight into power relations and the availability of resources, both within the aging community and between older persons and the larger society. Symbolic interactionism cuts through the media-created images and offers a realistic interpretation of aging in a changing world.

 6.4 Apply specialized theories to the social construction of aging.

Several specialized theories, from disengagement to the political economy of aging, offer a variety of interpretations that allow us to understand the complexity of the aging process and the ways in which perspectives have changed from the early 1950s to the present day. These theories are interconnected with social policies of aging through the expectations placed on older citizens. For example, disengagement theory supports the idea of mandatory retirement of older workers, while the political economy of aging perspective questions how social policies control older citizens.

6.5 Identify steps toward social change for the aging.

Finally, what can you do? Become involved; become aware. Reject stereotypes of aging and volunteer, seek out an internship or service learning opportunity, or become an advocate for older persons.

DISCUSSION QUESTIONS

1. How is aging a social problem in the United States? For whom is it a social problem? How do other factors, such as crime and elder abuse, contribute to the problems associated with aging?

2. Why do sociologists use the concept of aging instead of relying on age as a determination of a problem? How does this understanding of older people in society differ from media portrayals of the same group?

3. In what ways have programs such as pensions, Social Security, and Medicare changed what old age is like from how it was a century ago? How have the changing demographics affected public opinion regarding such programs, especially among younger generations?

4. What do social scientists predict will occur in terms of shifting age demographics in the coming decades? What impacts are these changes predicted to have on younger generations today as they age?

5. Where does the conflict perspective focus our attention around work in society as it relates to aging? What problems arise for aging individuals in a society that emphasizes the value of work?

6. According to the symbolic interactionist perspective, what are the primary problems associated with aging in our society? How do race, gender, and social class play a role in these problems?

7. What do individuals do to maintain their identity as they age? How does activity theory compare with disengagement theory on the matter of identity and function later in life?

8. In what ways does continuity theory grapple with the effects of socioeconomic status and health on aging?

9. How can members of younger generations involve themselves in advocating for older persons? How effective can the actions of one person be in helping to alleviate some of the problems associated with aging in our society?

10. As the U.S. population ages, what kinds of changes do you predict for social policies? What about changes in advertising and other media? How can institutions engage in improving the image and well-being of older people?

KEY TERMS

ageism 139

aging 137

child dependency ratio 141

continuity theory 154

fertility rate 141

generational inequity 147

gerontocracy 146

life expectancy 141

Medicaid 146

Medicare 146

old-age dependency ratio 141

poverty rate 143

sex ratio 141

Social Security 145

total dependency ratio 141

welfare state 137

Sharpen your skills with SAGE edge at edge.sagepub.com/trevino

A personalized approach to help you accomplish your coursework goals in an easy-to-use learning environment.

7 EDUCATION

Ryan W. Coughlan, Alan R. Sadovnik, and Susan F. Semel

Samsul Said / Reuters

 Most Americans place great value on education. Education can help people become productive workers and informed citizens. In what ways does education get people to conform to society's expectations?

Investigating Education: Our Stories

LEARNING OBJECTIVES

7.1 Describe the social institution of education.

7.2 Discuss patterns and trends in education.

7.3 Describe the U.S. educational system and the influence of interest groups.

7.4 Apply the functionalist, symbolic interactionist, and conflict perspectives to social policy for education.

7.5 Apply specialized theories to the social institution of education.

7.6 Evaluate explanations for educational inequality.

7.7 Describe recent reforms in education.

7.8 Identify steps toward social change in education.

Ryan W. Coughlan

My mother, a public school teacher, always stressed that education can open doors. My parents' merito-cratic vision of life seemed supported by my personal experiences as I obtained scholarships first to Phillips Academy Andover, then to Harvard University, and then to graduate school at the City College of New York and Rutgers University.

Teaching in a public high school in the South Bronx, I became increasingly aware that success in school and in society is too often predetermined by advantagesand disadvantages well beyond an individual's control.My growing concern about the effects of immutable class, race, and gender identities led me to pursue my doctoral degree at Rutgers University. As a scholar, I am committed to developing a better understanding of the relationships among identity, opportunity, and achievement in order to create a more just and equitable society for all.

Alan R. Sadovnik

My parents both left Nazi Europe in 1939 and settled in New York City. Neither graduated from high school. My family was working-class, and I attended New York City public schools and Queens College of the City University of New York, where tuition was still free. Upon graduation I attended New York University on full scholarship for my doctorate in sociology and I went on to become a professor specializing in the sociology of education.

My parents made it clear to me that education is the key to success. Based on their experiences, I devel-oped a sense of social justice and a commitment to trying to ensure that all children have equal access to education and a chance for social mobility. For the past three decades, I have conducted research on education, educational inequality, and school reform.

Susan F. Semel

I was raised on the affluent Upper East Side of Manhat-tan and attended the elite Dalton School and Whea-ton College, then for women only. After completing my master's degree at Columbia University, I taught at Dalton for 25 years. Upon receiving my doctorate from Columbia, I became a professor of education at three universities and am now at the City University of New York, a beacon of opportunity for low-income and working-class students for more than 150 years.

As a professor, I immediately saw firsthand the vast differences in opportunities between students from elite independent and public schools and other students. Over the past three decades, as both a scholar and a teacher of prospective teachers, I have attempted to examine these issues and to analyze the lessons that schools like Dalton offer us for improving public education for all children.

IDRIS AND SEUN

7.1 Describe the social institution of education.

American Promise, a documentary film released in 2013, chronicles the educational experiences of two black children from kindergarten into college, revealing a number of complex issues related to race, economics, social class, and educational achievement (Dargis 2013). Both boys, Idris and Seun, begin their formal education at age 5 in an elite private school in one of Manhattan's wealthiest neighborhoods. According to the filmmakers, the boys are attending the school in response to the school administration's efforts to increase diversity among the student body, as well as their parents' desire to provide their sons with the best possible education, one they do not view as available in the district public schools in their neighborhood. As the film progresses and the boys get older, Seun leaves the private school and enters a public high school, while Idris persists at the private school despite numerous obstacles.

Throughout the film, the documentarians press the children, their parents, their teachers, and school administrators to consider the ways in which race and class affect both the day-to-day lives of Idris and Seun and the boys' life chances. From an early age, Seun and Idris are aware of differences between themselves and their predominantly white, upper-class peers at school. Simultaneously, they are aware of the differences between themselves and their predominantly black, lower- and middle-class friends in their Brooklyn neighborhood. Seun struggles to make friends at school and is unable to get classmates to visit his home in Brooklyn. While playing basketball near his house, Idris is made fun of and accused of "talking like a white boy." Both constantly appear caught in between the high-achieving world of their largely white and affluent school and their Brooklyn neighborhood.

As the boys get older and begin to struggle academically, the filmmakers move beyond a depiction of the challenges Seun and Idris face in connecting with their classmates and teachers and begin to consider the factors that contribute to the boys' relatively poor academic achievement. While the film does not offer any clear answers, it does shed light on a few key factors that contribute to some children doing better than others in school. First, both Seun and Idris have a difficult time constructing personal identities. They face pressure to adopt different sets of values from their parents, their neighborhood friends, their classmates, and school staff. Many times these values clash, making it challenging for the boys to meet everyone's expectations.

A second factor is that every child faces unique conditions independent of race and class. As Idris and Seun grow, it becomes clear that both have learning disabilities. While they both get much-needed help to manage their disabilities, these personal issues do affect their academic achievement.

A third factor that the film makes evident is that social class matters. Idris's father is a doctor and his mother is a lawyer. They live comfortably and have the resources and knowledge to support him in every way; they are more similar than Seun's family to the families at the private school, although they are not nearly as wealthy as a significant number. Seun's mom, in contrast, is a nurse who works long hours and cannot take the time to offer Seun the same level of academic support found in Idris's home. Seun's family also faces the tragic death of one of his siblings. Given that Seun's family lives with a level of economic hardship, managing this death is particularly challenging.

All these racial, circumstantial, social, and economic factors contribute to the challenges the boys encounter at school and affect their life chances. For Seun, the conditions surrounding his life lead to his family's decision to remove him from the private school and enroll him in the local public school. For Idris, intensive parental involvement aids him in persisting at the private school, but he fails to receive an acceptance letter from one of the top universities where his parents expect him to attend college, and where the majority of his classmates are admitted.

American Promise tells a poignant story, filmed over 13 years, that raises important questions about the differences between public and private schools and the ways in which students' backgrounds are related to what occurs in and outside schools. This chapter explores many of the issues illustrated by the story of Idris and Seun and focuses on the way sociological theories explain the role of schools in providing social mobility or reproducing inequality. By examining the sociological perspective on education, you will be able to analyze the roles that schools play in their societies and explain why a sociological perspective on educational problems is essential to the development of solutions to those problems.

As a nation, the United States has always placed a great deal of faith in education. Americans tend to view schools as providers of opportunities for social mobility, places that nurture and develop the hearts and minds of children, antidotes for ignorance and prejudice, and solutions to myriad social problems. Throughout this country's history, countless citizens have regarded schools as symbols of the American Dream—the idea that members of each successive generation, through hard work and initiative, could achieve more than their parents had.

This is not to say that we have not been critical of our educational system—quite the contrary! Debates concerning teaching methods, politics, curricula, racial desegregation, equality of educational opportunity, and countless other issues have always defined the educational arena. It is precisely because Americans believe so passionately in education and expect so much from their schools that the U.S. educational system has been subject to disagreements, sometimes heated.

Will and Deni Mcintyre / Corbis

The 19th-century education reformer Horace Mann once said, "A teacher who is attempting to teach without inspiring the pupil with a desire to learn is hammering on a cold iron." How does a teacher forge an educated mind in a young student?

Alternatives to Traditional Education

Once again today, education in the United States is in crisis. In the early 1970s, the American education system experienced crises related to inequalities of educational opportunity and the allegedly authoritarian and oppressive nature of schools. In the 1980s and 1990s, concerns about education shifted to the decline of standards and authority, thought to be linked to the erosion of U.S. economic superiority in the world. Today an emphasis on standards has resulted in a preoccupation with accountability, and concerns about equality of opportunity focus on achievement gaps related to race, social class, and gender.

PATTERNS AND TRENDS

 7.2 Discuss patterns and trends in education.

Based on empirical evidence, sociologists of education are more apt to ask *what is* rather than *what ought to be*. They want to know what really goes on in schools and what are the measurable effects of education on individuals and society. They are interested in collecting data, and they try to avoid abstract speculation. Without knowing *what is*, we cannot make the *ought to be* a reality.

The Achievement Gap

Since the 1960s, educational policy has focused on differences in student achievement across social classes, races, ethnicities, and genders, as revealed in countless measures such as standardized tests, attainment, and opportunity. Federal educational policy has attempted to reduce these differences, known as the **achievement gap**, beginning with the **Elementary and Secondary Education Act (ESEA)** of 1965 and continuing through the **No Child Left Behind Act (NCLB)** of 2001 and President Barack Obama's **Race to the Top (RTT)** (Cross 2004).

Figure 7.1 highlights trends in the achievement gap in reading, showing the test scores of black, Hispanic, and white high school students over the past 40 years (Aud et al. 2012). Figure 7.2 shows the gap in graduation rates between students of different races (Education Trust 2010b). With respect to investments in education, in 2006, the nation had an effective funding gap between highest- and lowest-poverty districts of $773 per student, $19,325 for a typical classroom of 25 students, and $309,200 for a typical elementary school of 400 students. These gaps vary by state; some states, such as Illinois, New York, and Pennsylvania, have large gaps, while others, including Delaware, Massachusetts, Minnesota, and New Jersey, provide more funding to high-poverty districts (Education Trust 2010b).

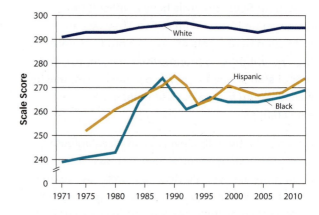

FIGURE 7.1 U.S. High School Reading Scores by Race/Ethnicity, 1971–2012

SOURCE: U.S. Department of Education, National Center for Education Statistics. (2012). The Nation's Report Card. Washington, DC.

The Crisis in Urban Education

Over the past 40 years, as central cities have become increasingly poor and populated by minorities, their schools have also come to reflect the problems associated with urban poverty. Although rural and some suburban schools share similar problems, cities' educational problems represent the nation's most serious challenge. A high proportion of urban schools are ineffective by most measures of school quality, a large percentage of urban students perform below national standards, and high school dropout rates in many large cities are over 40%.

The United States has witnessed a significant increase in the percentage of poor and minority children and youth living in the central cities of the country. In 1971, about

Achievement gap: The consistent difference in scores on student achievement tests between students of different demographic groups, including groups based on race, gender, and socioeconomic status.

Elementary and Secondary Education Act (ESEA): The primary piece of federal legislation concerning K–12 education in the United States; this act, first passed in 1965, was most dramatically revised through its reauthorization in 2001 as the No Child Left Behind Act.

No Child Left Behind Act (NCLB): U.S. federal legislation passed in 2001 as the reauthorization of the Elementary and Secondary Education Act; established a range of reforms mandating uniform standards for all students with the aim of reducing and eventually eliminating the social class and race achievement gap by 2014.

Race to the Top (RTT): Federal program established by President Obama with the goal of aiding states in meeting the various components of NCLB by offering grants to states to improve student outcomes and close achievement gaps.

 Fixing America's Education

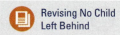 Revising No Child Left Behind

Experiencing Education

J. Anthony Lukas's *Common Ground*

Police stand guard as black students arrive at the predominantly white South Boston High School in 1974.

Recent reports by the UCLA Civil Rights Project (Flaxman 2013) and the Rutgers University–Newark Institute on Education Law and Policy (Tractenberg, Orfield, and Flaxman 2013) highlight the extreme segregation of races and social classes in New Jersey's public schools, a system in which a significant number of schools are more than 99% white and Asian or 99% black and Hispanic. The reports note the negative educational and social consequences of this situation and recommend a number of policy changes that would result in greater integration of students from different social classes and economic backgrounds. Critics have responded immediately with assertions that any attempts to require school integration will result in significant opposition.

This controversy reminds us of the school busing battles in 1970s Boston, where opposition to a federal court's order requiring the city to bus children from different neighborhoods to achieve racial balance in schools resulted in sometimes violent opposition. In his Pulitzer Prize–winning book *Common Ground* (1985), J. Anthony Lukas uses the stories of three families to illustrate how intersectionality is a complex aspect of how individuals and groups behave. Although neo-Marxist conflict theorists argue that people see the world through their economic circumstances, Lukas's portraits better support a Weberian conflict approach, in which race, ethnicity, social class, gender, and religion combine in ways that make explanations based on any one of these simplistic and often incorrect. For example, Rachel Twymon is a poor black single mother raising her family in the poor and predominantly black Roxbury section of the city;

Alice McGoff is a white Catholic working-class widow raising her family in the white Irish Catholic working-class Charlestown section; Colin Diver and his wife, Joan, are upper-middle-class white Protestants raising their family in the gentrifying South End, today one of the city's most affluent neighborhoods. Although the common ground for these parents is that they all want the best education for their children, they do not agree about what this means or about whether busing is the way to achieve it.

Rachel Twymon supports busing because she sees it as the best way to send her children to the better schools attended by white children in other parts of the city. Alice McGoff and her neighbors in Charlestown are opposed, sometimes violently, because they do not want blacks to come to their schools. The Divers support busing as a policy to improve education for all children and because, as assistant to Mayor Kevin White, Colin is responsible for implementing the policy.

Lukas demonstrates that there are few simple heroes or villains in this complicated story. The families and their neighbors, the politicians, and Judge W. Arthur Garrity Jr., who issued the decision, all are trying to improve education, but their different vantage points—based on the intersection of race, ethnicity, religion, social class, and gender—result in very different perspectives. As a working-class white woman, Alice wants to defend the cohesion of Irish Charlestown from outsiders. Although racism is a part of the reactions of the "townies," Lukas demonstrates that this is only one part of the story. Rachel, as a poor black woman, would prefer that her children attend school in Roxbury, but she believes that a school in a white neighborhood will provide them with a better education. Colin and Joan believe that working to build an integrated community in the South End is the best way to improve schools for all, but they are supportive of busing to integrate schools in segregated communities. Based on race, as whites, Alice and Colin and Joan should agree with one another; they do not. Based on social class, Rachel and Alice should agree with each other; they do not. Based on gender, Alice and Rachel should agree; they do not. Based on social class and race, Rachel and Colin and Joan should disagree; they do not.

Lukas's poignant portraits demonstrate the complicated nature of conflicts over education. Given that these types of problems remain at the forefront of educational debates today, *Common Ground* remains as timely now as it was 30 years ago.

▶ **THINK ABOUT IT:** Why do you suppose school desegregation was vehemently opposed by people living in the working-class, white ethnic areas of Boston?

FIGURE 7.2 U.S. Graduation Rates by Race/Ethnicity, 2010

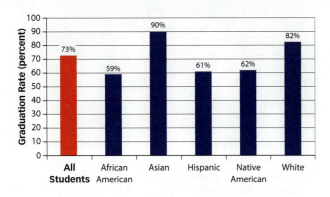

SOURCE: U.S. Department of Education, National Center for Education Statistics, Common Core of Data (CCD), "State Dropout and Completion Data File," 2009–10.

17% of the children and youth between the ages of 6 and 17 in large central cities were both poor and minority; by 1983, this figure had increased to 28%. It continued to rise throughout the 1980s, the 1990s, and into the 21st century (Anyon 1997).

Urban schools reflect social stratification and segregation. Due to the concentration of poor and minority populations in large urban areas, urban public schools have significantly higher percentages of low–socioeconomic status (SES) and minority students than neighboring suburban school districts. In 2011, more than 78% of schoolchildren in New York City were from low-income families eligible for free or subsidized lunches, and almost 86% were black, Hispanic, or Asian (Kids' Well-being Indicators Clearinghouse 2012).

Many urban public schools do not provide their students with a minimally adequate education. In 2011, only 24% of eighth-grade students in New York City performed at or above the proficient level on the **National Assessment of Educational Progress (NAEP)** mathematics test and the reading test. Furthermore, only 25% of eighth-grade students in New York City performed at or above the proficient level on the NAEP writing test, and only 13% performed at or above the proficient level on the NAEP science test. These data reflect national patterns for public schools in large urban areas (National Center for Education Statistics 2012).

The Decline of Literacy

Critics of public education in the United States have pointed to the failure of schools to teach children basic literacy skills in reading, writing, and mathematics and basic knowledge in history, literature, and the arts. Although there has been significant controversy over the value of such skills and knowledge, and whether such a decline is related to the decline in U.S. economic superiority, it is apparent that schools have become less effective in transmitting skills and knowledge. Despite some achievement increases in the 1990s, comparisons of U.S. students to students from other countries, along with other data, indicate continuing problems in literacy.

U.S. high school students have been found to perform less well than their counterparts in other industrialized nations in mathematics, science, history, and literature (Snyder and Dillow 2010). The U.S. illiteracy rate is shocking. According to the National Assessment of Adult Literacy, 30 million U.S. adults have below basic literacy levels. An additional 60 million function at a basic level and are able to perform only simple, everyday literacy activities. These literacy rates are well below those of other industrialized nations and a serious indictment of the nation's educational system.

ASK YOURSELF: What trends in U.S. education do you find most alarming? Why? What do you think are the root causes of these patterns in our education system? What does our society need to do to reverse these trends?

U.S. EDUCATION SYSTEM AND INTEREST GROUPS

7.3 Describe the U.S. educational system and the influence of interest groups.

Only a handful of social institutions interact with almost every member of U.S. society. The public education system is one of these. Because it is a massive institution, its structure is complex, and the related interest groups are varied. In this section, we provide a brief overview of the structures and interest groups that define the U.S. education system.

Structure of the System

First, we examine the U.S. elementary and secondary school system from the points of view of governance, size, degree of centralization, and student composition, to

National Assessment of Educational Progress (NAEP): A congressionally mandated set of standardized tests intended to assess the progress of a sample of U.S. students at various grade levels from all demographic groups and all parts of the country.

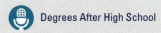 Degrees After High School

give a sense of the system's structure as a whole. Second, we compare the American system with the educational systems of several other countries in search of examples that might lead to more effective reforms for U.S. schools.

....

ASK YOURSELF: Describe your personal experience with education. In what ways do you think this experience is similar to and different from the experiences of various groups of students in the United States?

....

Governance

The U.S. Constitution states that those powers it does not explicitly identify as belonging to the federal government are retained by the individual states. Because the federal government makes no claims concerning its authority relative to education, the United States has 50 separate state school systems. This picture is made even more complex by the fact that each state also has a private school system. But this is just the beginning of the story, because most U.S. public schools are supported by revenue raised through local property taxes. This means, in effect, that the U.S. public school system is decentralized right down to the school district level. The state may mandate curricula, qualifications for teaching, and safety codes, but it is the citizens of each particular school district who implement them. Few other countries sustain such a high degree of decentralization in their school systems.

It wasn't until the civil rights movement of the 1960s that the federal government entered the educational policy field through its enforcement of students' civil rights. Its role in creating educational policy has increased since that time, particularly with the adoption of the No Child Left Behind Act and the establishment of Race to the Top funding. While decentralization remains the norm in the United States, recent efforts to standardize curricula through the national Common Core State Standards Initiative and to establish uniform reform efforts through federal education policy indicate a potential move toward a more centralized system.

....

ASK YOURSELF: Why is implementing top-down education reform such a challenge in the United States? What are the benefits and drawbacks of a decentralized education system?

....

Size and Degree of Centralization

As Figure 7.3 shows, more than 55 million youngsters are enrolled in kindergarten through the 12th grade in the United States (Aud et al. 2012). The cost of educating them is more than $650 billion annually. Figure 7.4 highlights how much the cost of educating U.S. students has increased over the past four decades.

Dropout Rate

Interestingly enough, at the same time that the school system has been growing, it has been simultaneously becoming more centralized, presumably for reasons of efficiency. For instance, in the early 1930s, there were approximately 128,000 public school districts in the United States. By the late 1980s, this number had been reduced to slightly fewer than 16,000. As a consequence of this consolidation, the average number of pupils per secondary public school rose from 195 in the early 1930s to 513 in the late 1980s (Clune, Witte, and Robert M. LaFollette Institute of Public Affairs 1990). In 2009–2010, the average number of pupils per school in the United States was 856 at the secondary level (Sable, Plotts, and Mitchell 2010). Scholars and policy makers have debated the benefits and drawbacks of both small schools and large schools. There is little consensus on the relative benefits of either, and existing research offers few definitive answers.

Interest Groups

As you can see from the discussion above, the U.S. education system is a massive and complicated institution. Another element that adds to its complexity is the range of interest groups and actors involved in it. This section considers the diversity of actors in the education system.

Students

While the student population of U.S. schools is becoming more racially and ethnically diverse, persistent residential segregation has kept schools from fully integrating.

FIGURE 7.3 U.S. K–12 School Enrollment (Public and Private), 1980–2020

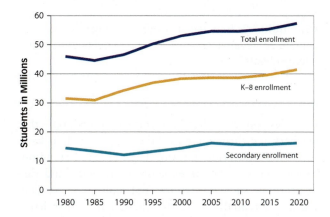

SOURCE: Snyder, Thomas D., and Dillow, Sally A. (2012). *Digest of Education Statistics 2011* (NCES 2012-001). National Center for Education Statistics, Institute of Education Sciences, U.S. Department of Education. Washington, DC.

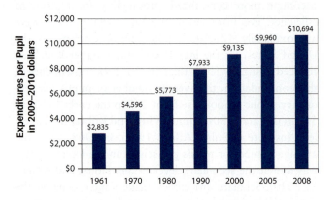

FIGURE 7.4 U.S. School Expenditures per Pupil, 1961–2008

SOURCE: Snyder, Thomas D., and Dillow, Sally A. (2012). *Digest of Education Statistics 2011* (NCES 2012-001). National Center for Education Statistics, Institute of Education Sciences, U.S. Department of Education. Washington, DC.

Ten states have almost no minority students, while many urban school districts enroll mostly minority students. In 2009 in New York City, more than 85% of the students were nonwhite; in Los Angeles, the figure was more than 91%, and in Detroit, 97% of the system's students were from minority backgrounds (Sable et al. 2010).

We can also think of student diversity in terms of gender, class, and even ability. These characteristics can affect not only the populations of schools but also educational and life outcomes. For example, we might wonder why although approximately half the students in U.S. education are female, so few of them choose to pursue technological or scientific careers. And why are students who attend schools in wealthy school districts more likely to have more curriculum options, better teachers, and access to more extracurricular activities than students in relatively poor school districts?

ASK YOURSELF: How might residential segregation affect student achievement? What are the benefits of desegregated schools?

Teachers and Teacher Unions

Countless policy makers and some scholars argue that teachers and their unions are the biggest roadblocks to successful education reform. They claim that unions protect teachers at the expense of students, and that institutions such as tenure and collective bargaining are outdated and inefficient. On the other hand, many teachers and union organizers say policy makers and administrators have made teachers and unions the scapegoats for all education problems. They note that the teaching profession is poorly respected and

undervalued, and that unions are essential to protecting teachers from policy makers, administrators, and other stakeholders. Regardless of how we feel about teachers and their unions, these groups are key players in the education system. While teacher unions are certainly not disappearing, their membership is declining. As Figure 7.5 illustrates, membership in unions is on the decline across most sectors of the economy in the United States, and teachers' unions are no exception (U.S. Bureau of Labor Statistics 2014).

One of the most important school-based factors contributing to student achievement is a high level of teacher quality. While *teacher quality* is difficult to define, characteristics such as teachers' education, experience, commitment, and innate ability all contribute. A superior education is required to equip teachers to handle the challenges of working in a classroom and to enable teachers to gain the respect afforded to other professionals.

Parents and the Community

The authority structure of the public school system is diffuse; ultimately, the people are responsible for the schools. Individuals, families, and interest groups are able to influence education by voting, by attending school district board meetings, and by paying for schools through taxes. Parents can directly hold teachers and administrators accountable by advocating for their children at personal meetings, by attending Parent–Teacher Association meetings, and by writing newspaper editorials. Business leaders worried about the quality of the future workforce and social service organizations concerned about child well-being advocate for school improvement by meeting with political leaders, supporting politicians who share their views on education, attending school board meetings, and speaking through television and print media. This democratization gives the U.S. school system a unique, egalitarian ethos.

International Comparisons

How does the U.S. system compare to other countries' education systems? This is an important question to ask, because it is through comparison that we can see the unique features of the U.S. school system and those features that it shares with other national systems. This broadening frame of reference gives us greater understanding about the relationships among educational structures, processes, and outcomes. Countries vary considerably in how they organize their school systems. Few school systems are as complex as that in the United States; for instance, most countries have a national ministry of education or department of education that is able to exert considerable influence over the entire educational

FIGURE 7.5 U.S. Trends in Union Membership, 2002–2012

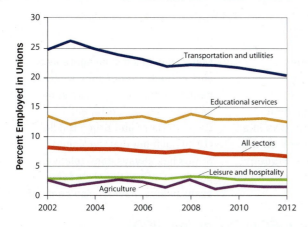

SOURCE: Bureau of Labor Statistics. 2014. "Labor Force Statistics from the Current Population Survey: Access to Historical Data for the Tables of the Union Membership News Release."

system. Educational reforms can start from the top down with relative success because the state has the authority to enforce its decisions right down to the classroom level.

Another dimension we see in comparative analysis is the relative selectivity of systems. Education in the United States is fundamentally inclusive in its purposes; most other educational systems are not as inclusive. Individuals in other systems undergo very rigorous academic rites of passage that are designed to separate the "academically talented" from the less gifted. The relative selectivity of a school system is an excellent indicator of its exclusiveness or inclusiveness. We can locate various countries' educational systems relative to each other by examining their degree of openness and the amount of authority the national governments exercise over the systems. The following descriptions of the education systems in Great Britain, Japan, and Finland highlight just a few of the many ways in which approaches to education can differ. With respect to educational inequality, there is a relationship between the amount of overall inequality in a country and the structure and processes of the country's educational system.

Great Britain

Before the 19th century, wealthy British parents hired tutors for their children, and poor children often received no schooling. The 1870 Education Act led to the beginnings of a national system of education, and a truly national system was established with the 1944 Education Act (Cookson, Sadovnik, and Semel 1992). This system, however, re-created the British class system by channeling students into different kinds of schools. Children from wealthy homes received academic training in grammar

schools, and children from working-class homes received vocational training. In short, Great Britain had a decentralized educational system that was fundamentally elitist.

The 1988 Education Reform Act attempted to move toward a more egalitarian system by establishing a national curriculum and assessment goals. Governing bodies of all secondary and many primary schools were given control over their own budgets, and parental choice was encouraged. Although teachers have been critical of the bureaucratic nature of these reforms and fewer subjects are taught, the act led to significant change. The British educational system is no longer as highly stratified as it once was, and it has eliminated the comprehensive secondary school, which offered noncollege curriculum for mostly working-class students. Nonetheless, critics argue that the 1988 act has not significantly reduced educational stratification and in some ways has worsened it (Brint 2006).

Japan

During the late 20th century, Japan's educational system produced skilled workers and highly competent managers. In fact, Japan's economic rise in the 1980s represented a serious challenge to the international economic position of the United States. The first national system of education in Japan was established in the 1880s. After World War II, compulsory education was extended from six to nine years and democratic principles of equality of opportunity were applied. The Japanese system of education is highly competitive and focused on achievement (White 1987). Both its top students and the 95% who graduate from high school excel in every measured international standard up to the age of 17.

Certainly, Japan's educational system benefits from the work ethic deeply entrenched in the nation's culture. Japanese parents have so high a regard for education that most students are exposed to two educational systems: the traditional public schools and the informal schools that act as a national system of tutorial opportunities for students during nights and weekends. This love of education has made Japan a nation of strivers, but the ethical dimensions of a moral education, which the Japanese highly value, are not always compatible with competition. Thus, the debate over education in Japan has more to do with national character than with structural reform. Reconciling achievement and competition with cooperation and mutuality will likely be the hallmark of future Japanese educational reform.

Finland

Throughout the first decade of the 21st century, Finland had some of the highest scores on the math, science, and literacy exams administered by the Program for International Student Assessment. Even more impressive is the low variation in student outcomes across racial, ethnic, and

International Tests of Student Achievement

Policy makers and scholars have increasingly used international tests of student achievement to rank the education systems of different countries. Whenever a new round of testing data is released, the media focuses on the relatively poor performance of students in the United States.

As Table 7.1 shows, of the 34 member countries of the Organization for Economic Cooperation and Development (OECD), the United States was in a three-way tie for 25th place on the Program for International Student Assessment (PISA) math test (OECD 2009).

Many view this dismal figure as a sign of the U.S. education system's decline. However, scholars such as Diane Ravitch (2013) and David Berliner and Bruce Biddle (1995) point out that the United States has always done relatively poorly on international student assessments. Ravitch also contends

TABLE 7.1   PISA Math Scores for 15-Year-Olds, OECD Countries, 2009

Rank	Country	Average Score	Rank	Country	Average Score
1	Republic of Korea	546	18	Austria	496
2	Finland	541	19	Poland	495
3	Switzerland	534	20	Sweden	494
4	Japan	529	21	Czech Republic	493
5	Canada	527	22	United Kingdom	492
6	Netherlands	526	23	Hungary	490
7	New Zealand	519	24	Luxembourg	489
8	Belgium	515	25	United States	487
9	Australia	514	25	Ireland	487
10	Germany	513	25	Portugal	487
11	Estonia	512	28	Spain	483
12	Iceland	507	28	Italy	483
13	Denmark	503	30	Greece	466
14	Slovenia	501	31	Israel	447
15	Norway	498	32	Turkey	445
16	France	497	33	Chile	421
17	Slovak Republic	497	34	Mexico	419

SOURCE: Table 7, p. 18 from Fleischman, H.L., Hopstock, P.J., Pelczar, M.P., and Shelley, B.E. (2010). *Highlights From PISA 2009: Performance of U.S. 15-Year-Old Students in Reading, Mathematics, and Science Literacy in an International Context* (NCES 2011-004). U.S. Department of Education, National Center for Education Statistics.

socioeconomic groups. Many other countries, including the United States, have large gaps between the performance of the highest-scoring and the lowest-scoring students.

How has Finland achieved such dramatic results? During the past 40 years, a major overhaul of its education system has focused on equal access to curriculum, the provision of wraparound services for students, and teacher education. Finland eliminated all forms of tracking and standardized testing and instead ensured that students attain a high level of academic success through formative evaluation and oral and narrative dialogues between teachers and students to track progress. The one standardized exam that Finland's education system does administer is a college entrance exam that consists of six to ten items designed to evaluate students' problem-solving, analysis, and writing skills (Darling-Hammond 2010).

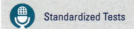 Standardized Tests

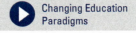 Changing Education Paradigms

that standardized test scores mask other important educational outcomes, such as critical thinking and creativity. Ravitch notes that some of the top-scoring nations are trying to emulate aspects of the U.S. education system that encourage independent thought and creativity. Unfortunately, the U.S. system seems to be moving away from these practices as it increasingly focuses on rote memorization and test-taking skills.

Another important element in an international comparison is the degree to which poverty affects student outcomes. As Figure 7.6 shows, the United States has the fourth-highest child poverty rate of all OECD nations. Berliner (2006), along with many other scholars, argues that there is a relationship between high child poverty rates and low student test scores. One piece of evidence Berliner and others use is the fact that individual U.S. states with low poverty rates, such as Massachusetts, score among the highest-achieving nations when their test results are disaggregated from those of states with high poverty rates. Like all data, international student achievement numbers must be viewed with a careful and critical eye.

▶ **THINK ABOUT IT:** How do you explain the relationship between high child poverty rates and low math scores?

FIGURE 7.6 Child Poverty Rates in OECD Nations, 2009

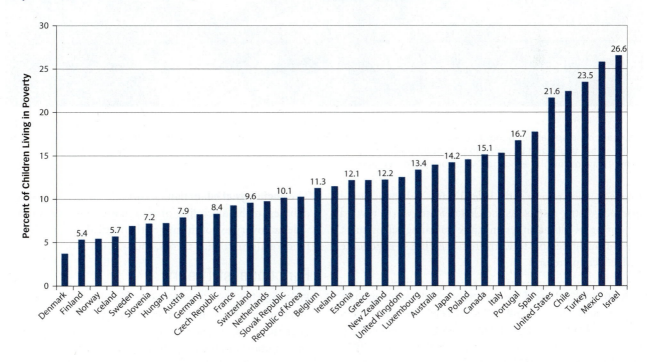

SOURCE: Organization for Economic Cooperation and Development. (2012) *OECD Income distribution questionnaire.*

Perhaps the most remarkable characteristic of the Finnish system is the way it recruits, educates, and retains classroom teachers. Only 15% of college graduates who apply for teacher education programs are admitted. They receive stipends and free tuition as they complete a three-year graduate program preparing them to be classroom teachers. Finnish teachers receive competitive wages, are treated with a high degree of professionalism, and maintain a large degree of autonomy over their teaching practices. They oversee small classes of students and are allotted significant time to collaborate with coworkers, develop curricula, and review student work. As a result they are able to develop innovative practices that meet their students' specific needs. Finnish teachers also have a high degree of work satisfaction, which has eliminated job turnover and shortages. Education reform in Finland has taken a decidedly different path

Like Japanese society in general, the Japanese system of education tends to encourage tradition, discipline, and conformity. Children are socialized to conform to group norms, which are strictly observed by members of Japanese society. What are the benefits of conformity at school? What are the drawbacks?

from education reform in the United States and has achieved markedly better results. As the United States works toward improving its education system and eliminating achievement gaps, it might be able to learn from the Finnish experience with education reform.

ASK YOURSELF: How does the structure of each country's educational system relate to the schools' role in providing social mobility or reproducing existing inequalities? Do you think that an international perspective on education is necessary? If so, why? If not, why not?

USING SOCIOLOGICAL THEORIES IN EDUCATION

7.4 Apply the functionalist, symbolic interactionist, and conflict perspectives to social policy for education.

The **sociology of education** mirrors the larger theoretical debates in the discipline of sociology. This section provides an overview of the major theoretical perspectives—functionalism, conflict theory, and symbolic interactionism.

Functionalist Theory

Functionalist sociologists view society as a kind of machine in which one part articulates with others to produce the dynamic energy required to make society work. Most important, functionalism stresses the processes that maintain social order through consensus and agreement.

Functionalist theories of school and society trace their origins to French sociologist Émile Durkheim's (1858–1917) general sociological theory. Durkheim (1977) believed that in virtually all societies, education is critical in creating the moral unity necessary for social cohesion and harmony. Functionalists tend to assume that consensus is the normal state in society and that conflict represents a breakdown of

Sociology of education: The study of how various individuals and institutions throughout society affect the education system and educational outcomes.

shared values. In a highly integrated, well-functioning society, schools socialize students with the appropriate values and sort and select them according to their abilities.

Talcott Parsons (1959) believed that education is a vital part of a modern society. He argued that education sets modern society apart from earlier periods of time because it establishes a system of **meritocracy**—a system in which it is expected that talent and hard work, rather than accidents of birth, determine the allocation of individuals to positions. Thus, in modern societies education becomes the key institution in a meritocratic selection process based on equality of opportunity for all citizens.

Policy Implications of Functionalist Theory

Functionalists believe in equality of opportunity, with education as the necessary institutional component guaranteeing a fair competition for unequal rewards. The just society, then, is one in which each member has an equal opportunity for social and economic advantages, and in which individual merit and talent replace family background as the most essential determinants of status. Education is the vehicle for ensuring that society moves toward this meritocratic system.

Functionalism thus stresses policies that promote equality of educational opportunity, seeking to provide all children with access to high-quality schools and teachers and equitable funding. However, functionalists do not believe a meritocracy should guarantee equal *outcomes,* only that the role of schooling is to provide equal *opportunity* to compete for unequal results.

ASK YOURSELF: What is the role of schools in society from a functionalist perspective? In what ways does functionalism fail to capture the role of schools in society?

Conflict Theory

Conflict theory argues that society is held together not by shared values and collective agreement alone, but by the ability of dominant groups to impose their will on subordinate groups through force, co-optation, and manipulation. Ideologies or intellectual justifications created by the powerful are designed to enhance their position by convincing everyone that inequalities are fair.

Whereas functionalists emphasize cohesion in explaining social order, conflict sociologists emphasize struggle. From a conflict point of view, schools are similar to social battlefields, where students struggle against teachers, teachers against administrators, and so on. These antagonisms, however, are

Meritocracy: A system in which personal advancement results from merit, based on knowledge and skill.

One of the main values in U.S. society is equality of opportunity. This means all members of society are eligible to compete on equal terms. Education has historically been seen as offering the opportunity for economic mobility. Do you think a child of poor or poorly educated parents is as likely to get a good education as someone born to middle-class parents with college degrees?

most often reduced due to the ability of schools to shape the ideas of the majority of students to support the system. In effect, the achievement ideology convinces both students and teachers that schools promote learning and sort and select students according to their abilities, not according to their social status. It disguises the "real" power relations within the school, which in turn reflect and correspond to power relations within the larger society (Bowles and Gintis 1976).

Karl Marx (1818–1883) is considered the founder of conflict theory. Based on Marx's critique of early capitalism, Samuel Bowles and Herbert Gintis (1976) examined the role of schooling in the United States. They argued that there is a direct correspondence between the organization of schools and the economic organization of capitalist society, and until society is fundamentally changed, there is little hope of real school reform. Other conflict sociologists of education, however, argue that traditional Marxism places too much emphasis on the independent effects of the economy and not enough on the effects of cultural, social, and political factors.

ASK YOURSELF: What should be the goal of education— training individuals for employment or for thinking? Or are these two goals compatible?

One such conflict sociologist was Max Weber (1864–1920). Like Marx, Weber was convinced that power relations between dominant and subordinate groups structure societies, but unlike Marx, he believed class differences alone cannot explain the systems of inequalities. Researchers using a Weberian perspective analyze school organizations and processes in the context of status competition and

Education Policy

organizational constraints. One of the first U.S. sociologists of education to use these concepts, Willard W. Waller (1965), argued that rational models of school organization only disguise the inherent tension that pervades the schooling process. Based on this idea, contemporary conflict theorists see schools as oppressive and view students' noncompliance with rules as a form of resistance to oppression.

Functionalists view the expansion of education as part of an ongoing expansion of democracy, meritocracy, and technology. Randall Collins (1979), in contrast, argued that the rise in the level of credentials required in a highly technological society is not a natural response to the needs of the labor market. Instead, it comes from status competition among groups battling over scarce cultural, political, and economic rewards. Collins demonstrated that educational credentials have increased far in excess of increases in occupational skills and requirements. For example, while the actual knowledge and skills of their profession have not increased dramatically, pharmacists must now complete a six-year college program leading to a doctorate rather than the apprenticeship program of the 1930s or a baccalaureate degree as was required a decade ago. Similar changes are being pressed for teachers, with little evidence to suggest that those who enter teaching with master's degrees are more effective than others.

The rise in credential requirements, according to Collins, is a result of middle-class professionals' attempts to raise their status and the stakes. As historically marginalized groups struggle to catch up, advantaged groups use professional organizations and higher credentials to increase their advantage in the competition for professional positions. Thus, for many conflict theorists, educational institutions are an instrument for perpetuating class differences, rather than a tool for promoting a democratic and meritocratic society.

Policy Implications of Conflict Theory

Conflict theorists stress the role of education in reproducing social and educational inequalities and the need to eliminate them. Like functionalists, they support policies to ensure equality of opportunity, but they go further by also supporting policies meant to reduce inequality of results in and beyond the school. Many conflict theorists contend that the roots of unequal educational outcomes lie in deeper inequalities that plague the greater society.

....

ASK YOURSELF: What is the role of schools in society from a conflict perspective? How do functionalists and conflict theorists differ in their assessment of the role of schools in helping to change societies?

....

Interactionist Theory

Interactionist theories of education are critiques of both the functionalist and the conflict perspectives, as macrosociological theories do not tell us what schools are like on an everyday level. What do students and teachers actually do? Interactionist theories attempt to "make the commonplace strange" by turning everyday, taken-for-granted behaviors and interactions on their heads. It is exactly what most people do not question that is most problematic to the interactionist.

Interactionist theory has its origins in the social psychology of early 20th-century sociologists George Herbert Mead (1863–1931) and Charles Horton Cooley (1864–1929). Mead and Cooley examined the ways in which the individual is related to society through ongoing social interactions. This school of thought, known as symbolic interactionism, views the self as socially constructed in relationship to social forces and structures, and as the product of ongoing negotiation of meanings.

Interactionist theory is usually combined with functionalism and/or conflict theory to produce a more comprehensive theory of society. One of the most influential interactionist theorists was Raymond Rist, whose research demonstrates how teacher expectations of students, based on categories such as race, class, ethnicity, and gender, affect students' perceptions of themselves and their achievement. Rist (1977) showed how labeling students based on social class resulted in the placement of low-income students in lower-ability reading groups and middle-class students in higher-ability groups, regardless of the students' actual abilities. These labels became "life sentences" with profoundly negative effects on the achievement of the low-income students, who remained in low-ability groups throughout their careers. Rist concluded that the interactional processes of the school resulted in educational inequality mirroring the larger structures of society. Combined with the findings of conflict theory, Rist's interactionist approach provides an empirical documentation of one way that schools reproduce inequality.

Policy Implications of Interactionist Theory

Interactionist theory stresses the need to base education system policies on an examination of what goes on inside schools and classrooms. For example, interactionists argue that to develop policies that will ensure equality of opportunity or reduce inequalities of results, sociological research must get inside the "black box" of schooling to understand precisely how schools reproduce inequalities (conflict theory) or increase opportunities (functionalist theory).

....

ASK YOURSELF: How does interactionist theory differ in its focus from functionalist and conflict theories? Can it complement one or both of the other theories?

....

SPECIALIZED THEORIES IN THE SOCIOLOGY OF EDUCATION

 7.5 Apply specialized theories to the social institution of education.

Among the specialized theories applied to the sociology of education are those discussed below: the code theory of Basil Bernstein, the cultural capital theory of Pierre Bourdieu, the institutional theory of John Meyer, and feminist theory.

Code Theory

British sociologist Basil Bernstein (1924–2000) drew on functionalist, conflict, and interactionist perspectives to develop his **code theory** (Bernstein 1977a, 1977b, 1990, 1996). Codes are systems that people use to understand meaning and to communicate. Bernstein (1973a, 1973b) saw differences between the communication codes of working-class and middle-class children that reflected class and power relationships in the economy, the family, and schools. For example, when asked to tell a story based on a set of photographs, working-class boys used primarily pronouns (*he, she, it*) and middle-class boys used more descriptive nouns (*the boys, a woman, a man*). Bernstein noted that in order to understand the working-class boys' stories, one would need the photographs; one would not need the photographs to understand the middle-class boys' stories. He described the language codes of the working-class boys as "restricted," that is, restricted to their own social class background and understood only by those with similar backgrounds. He described middle-class language codes as "elaborated" and understood by those with similar or different backgrounds. Working-class codes are not deficient, Bernstein argued, but rather are functionally related to individual families' occupations. Likewise, the codes of

....

Code theory: Basil Bernstein's concept that society reproduces social classes through favoring the communication codes, or manners of speaking and representing thoughts and ideas, of more powerful socioeconomic groups.

Cultural capital theory: Pierre Bourdieu's concept that a range of nonfinancial assets, such as education, physical appearance, and familiarity with various kinds of music, art, and dance, empower individuals to advance in a social group that values a particular set of these cultural assets.

Institutional theory: The concept that schools are global institutions and have developed similarly throughout the world since the 19th century as a result of processes of globalization and democratization.

the middle classes represent functional changes in society that require them to communicate with many groups. Because schools rely on middle-class codes for instruction and for organizing interactions between students and teachers, working-class children are disadvantaged.

Bernstein's study of the inner workings of the educational system showed how the schools (especially in the United Kingdom and United States) reproduce what they are ideologically committed to eradicating—social class advantages in schooling and society. Based on his work, sociologists argue that policies to reduce educational inequalities need to provide low-income students access to the dominant communication and schooling codes.

Theories of Economic, Social, and Cultural Capital

French sociologist Pierre Bourdieu (1930–2002) provides a conflict approach to understanding how education reproduces inequality (Bourdieu and Passeron 1977; Bourdieu 1977, 1984). This approach distinguishes three forms of capital—economic (wealth), social (networks and connections), and cultural (forms of knowledge, including music, art and literature)—to which different groups have unequal access. Bourdieu's **cultural capital theory** asserts that although schools appear to be neutral, they actually advantage the upper and middle classes through their symbolic representations. These classes possess more economic, social, and cultural capital, which has important exchange value in the educational and cultural marketplace. For example, economic capital can purchase better schools and services such as tutoring, social capital allows groups to use their connections to their advantage, and cultural capital is highly valued in schools and society. Thus, schooling corresponds to society's dominant interests, and upper- and middle-class forms of capital become codified in the curriculum. Unlike functionalists, Bourdieu saw these patterns as leading to class domination rather than social cohesion.

Based on Bourdieu's work, sociologists such as Annette Lareau (2003) argue that there are differences in social and cultural capital between low-income students and their higher-income counterparts. Therefore, educational policies intended to reduce inequalities need to provide low-income students with access to the dominant forms of social and cultural capital.

Institutional Theory

John W. Meyer's (1977) **institutional theory** argues that schools are global institutions and have developed similarly throughout the world since the 19th century, with mass systems of public education giving access to more and more people. At the institutional level, schools develop formal and informal rituals and processes that legitimate their existence and functions in society. Like Collins, Meyer does not believe that educational expansion is driven primarily by the needs of the labor market, but unlike Collins, he views mass schooling as springing from society's belief in a democratic civil society.

Based on Meyer's theory, David Baker and Gerald LeTendre (2005) argue that a fundamental set of beliefs has influenced the development of mass schooling, including that all children should be educated, that nations should invest in schooling, that education functions for the collective good of society, that children should receive early and ongoing schooling, that the types of cognitive skills learned in schools are good for individuals and society, and that access to schooling should not be limited based on social, economic, or racial status.

Although Meyer and colleagues believe national differences are important, they stress the commonalities among educational institutions and the worldwide belief that mass schooling is important. They believe mass universal education benefits individuals and society, and they therefore support educational policies to ensure its availability, especially in developing societies.

Feminist Theory

Feminist educators and sociologists of education have examined the ways in which schools perpetuate sexist attitudes and behaviors, as well as unequal educational outcomes based on gender. Madeleine Arnot (2002) combines feminist and Marxist theory to argue that traditional gender roles are inherently linked to capitalists' reproduction of economic inequalities.

Feminist theories support policies aimed at providing equality of opportunity for women and reducing gender-based inequalities of educational achievement. As these policies have successfully reduced or eliminated the gender gap in education—female students now outperform males in most subjects—feminists are having to grapple with the "boy problem" to ensure that both males and females perform successfully in school.

· ·

ASK YOURSELF: Which specialized theories in the sociology of education are most useful for evaluating problems with the education system in the United States, and why? How would Bernstein reform the U.S. education system? Bourdieu? Collins? What are the similarities and differences among racial, ethnic, gender, and social class inequalities in education? How are these inequalities related?

· ·

EXPLANATIONS OF EDUCATIONAL INEQUALITY

 7.6 Evaluate explanations for educational inequality.

Significant differences in educational achievement in the United States related to social class, race, gender, and other characteristics call into question the country's ideology of equality of educational opportunity. Although the data suggest there has been mobility for individuals, and that schooling has become increasingly tied to the labor market as a credentialing process, they do not support the democratic-liberal faith that schooling provides mobility for entire groups. In fact, family background remains a powerful predictor of educational achievement and attainment and economic outcomes.

How do sociologists explain these unequal outcomes? Functionalists believe the role of schools is to provide a fair and meritocratic selection process for sorting out the best and brightest individuals, regardless of family background. They expect some unequal results but believe these should come from individual differences between students, not group differences. Therefore, functionalists believe that unequal educational outcomes between groups result, in part, from unequal educational opportunities. We must understand the sources of educational inequality, eliminate barriers to educational success, and provide all groups a fair chance to compete in schools. This perspective has been the foundation of liberal educational policy in the United States since the 1960s.

Conflict theorists are not surprised by data documenting the achievement gap. They believe schools function to reproduce rather than eliminate inequality, so educational outcomes reflective of family backgrounds are fully consistent with this perspective. Nonetheless, conflict theorists, who usually fall into the more radical political category, are also eager for equality of both opportunity and results. Equality of opportunity alone is not a sufficient goal.

Despite their differences, functionalists and conflict theorists agree that understanding educational inequality is a difficult task, and that to fully grasp the problem they must employ interactionist theory. Many research studies of educational inequality use an interactionist approach based on fieldwork in order to examine what goes on in families and in schools.

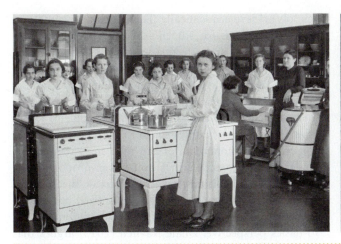

Girls attend a cooking and cleaning class at Chevy Chase High School in Bethesda, Maryland, in 1935. Boys work in a carpentry shop class at Anacostia High School in Washington, D.C., in 1939. Are there still classes in American high schools today that are largely segregated by gender?

Researchers have posed two different sets of explanations for the inequalities seen among students and in schools. **Student-centered explanations**, or *outside-school explanations*, look at factors outside the school, such as the family, the community, the culture of the group, the peer group, and the individual student. In contrast, **school-centered explanations**, or *within-school explanations*, focus on factors within the school, such as teachers and teaching methods, curriculum, ability grouping and curriculum tracking, school climate, and teacher expectations. In the following sections, we outline the major student-centered and school-centered explanations and then propose a synthesis of the two.

ASK YOURSELF: In what ways do inequalities permeate the U.S. education system? Which theory of education, functionalism or conflict theory, better explains your own experiences in education? How does interactionist theory help you understand your own educational experiences?

Student-centered explanations: Explanations of educational inequalities that focus on factors outside the school, such as the family, the community, the culture of the group, the peer group, and the individual student.

School-centered explanations: Explanations of educational inequalities that focus on factors within the school, such as teachers and teaching methods, curriculum, ability grouping and curriculum tracking, school climate, and teacher expectations.

Student-Centered Explanations

In the 1960s, sociologists suggested that economically disadvantaged students were attending inferior schools—schools that spent less money on each student, spent less money on materials and extracurricular activities, and had worse teachers. A number of research studies in the 1960s and 1970s demonstrated, however, that this conventional liberal wisdom was too simplistic and that solutions were far more complex.

In the landmark publication *Equality of Educational Opportunity* (1966), James S. Coleman and colleagues argued that differences among groups of students have a greater impact on educational performance than do school differences. Based on this work, known as the Coleman Report, educational researchers and policy makers concluded that students from lower socioeconomic backgrounds did less well in school because of characteristics of the students themselves, their families, their neighborhoods and communities, their cultures, and perhaps even their genetic makeup. These student-centered explanations became dominant in the 1960s and 1970s, and they are still highly controversial and politically charged.

Genetic Difference Theory

Some researchers have argued that deficiencies in educational performance among working-class and nonwhite students are the result of genetic differences in intelligence (Jensen 1969; Herrnstein and Murray 1994). Empirical research, however, has indicated that lower educational performance among some groups is due in part to the cultural bias of IQ test questions, the conditions under

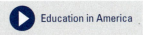
Education in America

which such tests are administered, and cultural and family differences (Hurn 1993). Ultimately, there is little or no empirical evidence to support **genetic difference theory**.

Cultural Deprivation Theory

Cultural deprivation theory suggests that working-class, poor, and nonwhite families often lack cultural resources, such as books and other educational stimuli, and thus arrive at school at a significant disadvantage (Lewis 1966). Critics argue that this explanation blames the effects of poverty on its victims instead of on the social and economic processes that produce poverty (Dougherty and Hammack 1990).

Cultural Difference Theories

Cultural difference theories agree that cultural and family differences separate white middle-class students from working-class and nonwhite students, who may indeed arrive at school without the skills and attitudes required for success. This is due not to deficiencies in their home lives, however, but rather to their being part of oppressed minority groups subject to poverty, racism, discrimination, and unequal life chances.

Clearly, the poor should not be blamed for their problems; the causes of poverty are more social and economic than cultural. Similarly, we should not deny the cultural differences related to school success and failure. The key is to move past ideology and eliminate social and educational barriers to school success for poor and nonwhite students. Perhaps more important, we must recognize that we cannot explain unequal educational achievement by looking at students and their families alone; we must also look at the schools.

....

ASK YOURSELF: Which student-centered explanation of educational inequalities do you find most compelling, and why? How do such explanations relate to your own educational experiences?

....

School-Centered Explanations

While the Coleman Report argued that between-school differences are not the key factor in explaining different student outcomes between groups, it did not say that schools have *no* effect. In fact, Coleman's later work suggested that schools do vary and may indeed make a difference (Coleman, Hoffer, and Kilgore 1982; Coleman and Hoffer 1987). In the 1980s, sociologists of education began to examine the processes within schools as well as between- and within-school differences in curriculum, pedagogy, and ability grouping.

Effective Schools Research

Research on unusually effective schools has identified characteristics that help explain why students at these schools achieve academically. These include a climate of high expectations for students by teachers and administrators, strong and effective leadership, accountability for students and teachers, monitoring of student learning, a great deal of time spent on teaching and learning, and flexibility for teachers and administrators to experiment and adapt to new situations and problems (Stedman 1987). These findings suggest that schools in lower socioeconomic communities can take steps to improve student achievement. Critics argue that proponents of the **effective schools movement** use narrow measures of academic achievement, such as standardized test scores, to define educational success from a traditional back-to-basics perspective. Diane Ravitch (2013) argues that overreliance on the use of standardized tests in reading and mathematics to measure school effectiveness has led schools to narrow their curricula and leave out important subjects such as art, music, physical education, literature, and social studies, sacrificing essential outcomes such as critical thinking. Ravitch points out that school reform that emphasizes success on standardized tests may overlook nontraditional and progressive measures of school success, such as artistic, creative, and noncognitive goals.

Between-School Differences: Curriculum and Pedagogic Practices

Conflict theorists argue that significant differences exist, in terms of culture and climate, between schools in lower socioeconomic communities and those in higher socioeconomic communities (MacLeod 2009). Of course, different life chances begin with different family backgrounds, but different school environments

....

Genetic difference theory: The discredited concept that differences in educational performance between working-class and nonwhite students and their middle- and upper-class and white counterparts are due to genetic differences in intelligence.

Cultural deprivation theory: The theory based in the concept that children from working-class and nonwhite families often lack certain cultural resources, such as books and other educational stimuli, and thus arrive at school at a significant disadvantage.

Cultural difference theories: Theories based in the concept that there are cultural and family differences between working-class and nonwhite students and white middle-class students attributable to social forces such as poverty, racism, discrimination, and unequal life chances.

Effective schools movement: A movement for school improvement based on the concept that unusually effective schools have certain characteristics (such as effective leadership, accountability, and high expectations of teachers and administrators) that help explain why their students achieve academically despite disadvantaged backgrounds

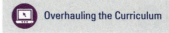 Overhauling the Curriculum

Researching Education

Evaluating the Coleman Report

In 1966, James S. Coleman and colleagues published one of the most influential studies on education ever produced, *Equality of Educational Opportunity,* commonly known as the Coleman Report. The researchers used sophisticated statistical analysis to support the argument that outside-school factors affect student achievement more than what happens in the classroom. More than 40 years after the report's publication, Geoffrey Borman and Maritza Dowling (2010) applied modern statistical tools to evaluate educational data in a similar manner. Their findings partially confirm both Coleman's original data from 1966 and his 1982 study showing that school factors matter. According to Borman and Dowling, "Going to a high-poverty school or a highly segregated African American school has a profound effect on a student's achievement outcomes, above and beyond the effect of individual poverty or minority status" (1202).

Borman and Dowling's primary findings highlight that where an individual goes to school is often related to his or her race and socioeconomic background, but the racial and socioeconomic composition of a school has a greater effect on student achievement than an individual's race and class. Borman and Dowling, like Coleman in his 1966 study, argue that race and class are predictors of academic success. However, they disagree with Coleman's 1966 argument that schools don't matter. Instead, they propose that school segregation based on race and socioeconomic status and within-school interactions dominated by middle-class values are largely responsible for gaps in student achievement. They conclude that education reform in the United States must focus on eliminating the high level of segregation that remains in the education system, and that schools must bring an end to tracking systems and biases that favor white and middle-class students. While some school districts have attempted to further desegregate schools and eliminate tracking systems, overall,

J A Giordano / Corbit Saba / Corbis

Many school buildings throughout the United States have plaster falling from their ceilings, leaky roofs, and poor indoor air quality.

American public schools remain highly segregated. Borman and Dowling's work adds to a growing body of research that demonstrates the importance of desegregation in combating the achievement gap.

▶ **THINK ABOUT IT:** Many school districts lack the funds to make costly repairs. Do you think there is a relationship between learning and the physical environment?

---

teach children to dream different sets of dreams. For conflict theorists, variations in funding, teacher quality, curriculum, pedagogy, and teacher expectations are all important. Whether they are causal factors is beside the point—that they are part of the process seems evident.

Within-School Differences: Curriculum and Ability Grouping

When different groups of students perform very differently in the same school, school characteristics may be affecting these outcomes. Ability and curriculum grouping (often referred to as **tracking**) is likely responsible to some degree. Functionalists believe tracking is an

Tracking: An educational practice in which students are divided into groups, purportedly based on their academic ability.

important means to separate students based on ability and to ensure that the "best and brightest" receive the type of education they need to prepare them for society's most essential positions. The important thing is to ensure that track placement is fair and meritocratic—that is, based on ability and hard work rather than on student characteristics such as race, ethnicity, social class, and gender.

Conflict theorists, conversely, suggest that tracking is a mechanism for separating groups, often based on their backgrounds, and for reproducing inequalities. Research shows that track placement is associated with student race and social characteristics, and that working-class and nonwhite students are more likely to be assigned to lower tracks. Grouping similar students results in unequal education for different groups, due to differences in school climate, expectations, pedagogic practices, and curriculum between tracks (Oakes 1985). Finally, it seems clear that differences in the curriculum and pedagogic practices applied to different tracks are partly responsible for the diverse academic achievement of students (Oakes, Gamoran, and Page 1992).

ASK YOURSELF: Which school-centered explanations for educational inequalities do you think are most important, and why? How do these explanations relate to your own educational experiences?

Do Schools Reproduce Inequality?

Some researchers believe that schools unfairly perpetuate social inequalities and thus confirm conflict theorists' belief that schools advantage the dominant groups in society. Other researchers believe there is insufficient evidence to support much of conflict theory in regard to school processes, and that some evidence supports the functionalist view that school selection processes are meritocratic (Hurn 1993).

We think there is evidence for some of the functionalists' hypotheses, but, on the whole, there is more support for conflict theorists' claim that schools help to reproduce inequality and help dominant groups maintain their advantages. Schools are only part of this process, and we must see them within the context of a larger set of institutional forces affecting social stratification. That is, schools do not reproduce inequality by themselves, but they are part of a process in which social inequalities are transmitted across generations.

ASK YOURSELF: What do you think are the most important factors contributing to inequalities in education? What can society do to eliminate these inequalities? Do you think schools reproduce social inequalities?

EDUCATIONAL REFORM FROM THE 1980S TO 2012

7.7 Describe recent reforms in education.

Beginning in 1983, with the National Commission on Educational Excellence's report *A Nation at Risk,* myriad stakeholders have attempted to improve the quality of U.S. schools. In the 1990s and 2000s, President Clinton's Goals 2000, President Bush's No Child Left Behind, and President Obama's Race to the Top placed the federal government at the helm of educational policy. The U.S. Department of Education has played a significant role in keeping the pressure on states and localities to improve educational outcomes and, through NCLB and RTT, has placed accountability at the forefront of reforms aimed at reducing the achievement gap.

Over the past decade, two different approaches to urban school reform have developed. The first, school-based reform, stresses the independent power of schools to eliminate the achievement gap for low-income students. The second, the societal-level approach, stresses that school-level reform is necessary but insufficient, and that societal and community-level reforms are also necessary.

School-Based Reforms

Since the 2001 adoption of the No Child Left Behind Act, the federal government has directed state and local governments to adopt a neoliberal education reform agenda focusing on school-level reform. A logical progression of the standards movement initiated in 1983 by *A Nation at Risk* and in federal legislation under Presidents George H. W. Bush (America 2000) and Bill Clinton (Goals 2000), NCLB is the most comprehensive federal legislation governing state and local education policies in U.S. history. Based on the critique that education in the United States has historically underserved low-income and minority children through curriculum tracking, poor instruction, and low-quality teachers in urban schools, NCLB mandated uniform standards for all students in order to reduce and eventually eliminate the social class and race achievement gap by 2014. To date, the law is a long way from achieving this goal.

Jason Reed / Reuters

President George W. Bush talks to fourth graders at Pierre Laclede Elementary school in St Louis, Missouri. Bush paid a visit to the school to talk about his administration's No Child Left Behind education policy.

Advocates of NCLB argued that its requirements would force states to ensure that low-income students who continue to lag far behind higher-income students will meet the same standards. Critics argued that however noble the goal of eliminating the achievement gap, NCLB did not provide sufficient funds to improve failing schools and relied on punishment, not on building school capacity (Sadovnik 2008).

Shortly after he took office in 2009, President Barack Obama established the Race to the Top, a program designed to encourage states to meet the various components of NCLB. The initial legislation provided $4.35 billion in competitive grants for states to improve student outcomes and close achievement gaps. Supporters of RTT say the grants will aid states as they work to meet the NCLB mandates, improve student outcomes, and eliminate achievement gaps.

However, the federal government now grants NCLB waivers, exempting states from certain NCLB requirements in exchange for commitments to further reform efforts. Critics of NCLB, RTT, and waivers argue that all these reform efforts will remain ineffective. They note that NCLB and RTT rely too heavily on standardized testing and the expansion of school choice through charter schools, and that these reforms have not demonstrated any significant success in improving achievement (Ravitch 2013).

Together, NCLB and RTT have driven states and local districts to focus on a range of school-based reforms over the past decade. In particular, they have led to increases in school choice, charter schools, and voucher systems; efforts to improve teacher education and teacher quality; and attempts to develop effective school models. We briefly describe each of these types of school-based reforms below.

School Choice

During the 1980s, some researchers reasoned that **magnet schools** (public schools open to students from different neighborhoods) and private schools were superior to neighborhood public schools because, as schools of choice, they reflected the desires and needs of their constituents and were thus sensitive to change (Coleman et al. 1982). By the late 1980s, **school choice** was at the forefront of the educational reform movement. Seen as nonbureaucratic, inexpensive, and egalitarian, it allowed market forces rather than educational bureaucracy to shape school policy. Currently, the two most popular varieties of school choice are charter schools and school vouchers.

Charter schools. **Charter schools** are public schools that are free of many of the regulations applied to traditional public schools, and in return they are held accountable for student performance. As public schools, charter schools are funded with tax dollars (unlike private schools, they do not charge tuition) and must be open to all students in the school districts where they are located. The admissions processes for charter schools are dictated by the laws of the individual states, but in low-income areas admission is usually based on a lottery. If a charter school fails to meet the provisions of its charter, based on student outcomes and fiscal soundness, it can lose its funding and be forced to shut its doors. While there has been significant debate about the success of charter schools compared to regular public schools, most researchers have concluded that there are excellent, average, and failing examples of each.

Davis Guggenheim's popular documentary film *Waiting for "Superman"* (2010) drew attention to charter schools by contrasting high-quality charter schools with failing traditional public schools. The film presents heartwrenching scenes of families who do not win the lottery for charter school admission. It argues that zip code should not be destiny, and that school choice is the solution to the problem of low-performing urban schools. Guggenheim is careful to note that there are excellent district public schools and teachers; however, the film provides no examples of these, or of ineffective private and charter schools or their teachers. Critics argue that although traditional public education certainly has problems, the film is simplistic, biased, and not based on research.

Vouchers. Advocates of **school vouchers** argue that school choice achieved through voucher programs that directly provide families with funds to send children to private schools (including parochial schools) will have three important educational impacts. First, vouchers will enable low-income parents to have the same choices among schools as middle-class parents and lead to increased parental satisfaction with their children's schools. Second, given that private schools,

---

Magnet schools: Publicly funded schools designed to recruit students from across entire districts by offering particular disciplinary focuses, such as arts, technology, science, or mathematics.

School choice: A school reform approach that theoretically allows market forces to shape school policies by offering parents a range of school options, including magnet schools, voucher schools, charter schools, traditional local public schools, and regular public schools.

Charter schools: Publicly funded schools that operate independent of school districts and are free of many of the regulations that apply to school districts.

School vouchers: An approach to school choice in which parents of school-age children receive government-issued vouchers of a certain monetary value that they can apply to tuition expenses at private schools.

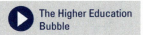 The Higher Education Bubble

like charter schools, do not have to contend with the large educational bureaucracy of urban school systems, they will provide better learning environments for low-income students and result in higher student achievement. Third, due to the competitive market effects of competition from charter and voucher schools, urban public schools will be forced to improve or close their doors. This will result in higher student achievement in the public schools that remain.

These claims about charter and private schools have stirred considerable debate. Critics argue that voucher and charter proponents make unfounded assumptions and use limited methods of analysis, and that voucher systems drain resources from public schools and cause further inequality of education. They also argue that no conclusive evidence shows that learning opportunities at charter and private schools actually lead to higher test scores.

Teacher and School Quality

What does an effective school look like? There is general agreement that it sets high standards and high expectations for students, holds teachers and administrators accountable for student performance and goals, creates a safe and orderly academic environment, employs experienced and qualified teachers who have access to high-quality professional development, hires administrators committed to education, and encourages parental and community engagement.

At the level of the classroom, course content, pedagogy, technology, and class size have impacts on student achievement. However, without effective teachers, these factors mean little. Sound instructional practices, implemented by effective teachers, are a prerequisite of school improvement (Darling-Hammond 2010).

Research reveals that the most qualified teachers possess strong academic skills, the equivalent of a major in the field in which they are teaching, at least three years' teaching experience, and participation in high-quality professional development programs (Ingersoll 2003). Because many teachers do not have these characteristics, a large share of education reform has focused on improving teacher quality. On a practical level, each state must partner with districts and schools to build an infrastructure that will help teachers develop the right skills.

As scholars and policy makers began looking at the effectiveness of teachers, teacher organizations such as the **National Education Association (NEA)** and the **American Federation of Teachers (AFT)**, fearing the scapegoating of their members, took an active role in raising the debate as an opportunity to improve the conditions under which teachers work. Over the past 20 years there have been numerous efforts to improve the quality of new teachers

U. Baumgarten via Getty Images

Fourth-grade children attend class at an elementary school in Bonn, Germany. The German education system is different in many ways from the system in the United States. In Germany, children in grades 1 through 4 attend elementary school (Grundschule), where the subjects taught are the same for all. Then, after the fourth grade, they are separated according to their academic abilities and the wishes of their families.

by improving university teacher education programs and developing alternative programs for teacher certification.

Recruiting and retaining high-quality teachers are among the most important challenges for U.S. education. NCLB's requirement that all schools have highly qualified teachers in every classroom highlighted the problem of unqualified teachers in urban schools. At the secondary school level, especially in low-income urban schools, approximately one-fifth of classes in each of the core academic subjects (math, science, English, social studies) are taught by teachers who do not hold teaching certificates in those subjects. Urban schools with high levels of minority students also typically have larger percentages of novice teachers than do other schools (National Center for Education Statistics 2008).

Since the 1990s, a number of alternatives to traditional university-based teacher education have emerged, such as **Teach for America (TFA)** and the New Teacher Project (NTP). Through these alternative certification programs, rather than enrolling in traditional multiyear university teacher education programs, high-performing

National Education Association (NEA): The largest union representing teachers in the United States.

American Federation of Teachers (AFT): One of the two largest unions representing teachers in the United States.

Teach for America (TFA): A nonprofit organization that recruits students and professionals from high-profile institutions, trains these individuals to enter the teaching profession, and places them in disadvantaged schools for a period of at least two years.

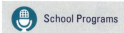
School Programs

college graduates complete a summer student teaching program and are immediately placed in teaching positions in underserved schools. Critics argue that no other profession would permit its practitioners to enter the field without training and that, because many alternative programs require only two years of service, the attrition rate is very high (Ingersoll 2004).

Recently, school reformers have stressed the role of teacher tenure, seniority-based transfers, and layoff provisions in union contracts as primary roadblocks to improving teacher quality. In *Waiting for "Superman,"* Guggenheim highlights "the dance of the lemons," a practice in which principals trade ineffective tenured teachers between schools, because it is so difficult to fire them. A number of education reformers have made efforts to halt "the dance of the lemons" and alter teacher tenure practices. As chancellor of the Washington, D.C., public schools, Michelle Rhee gained particular notoriety when she made teacher quality her major issue and engaged in heated battles with the union to overhaul the teacher contract. A number of provisions in RTT and new teacher contracts like the one in Washington, D.C., have addressed some teacher quality issues, but not without much debate and controversy.

The evidence suggests that reforms aimed at improving teacher quality and the overall effectiveness of schools have the potential to improve low-income, high-minority schools. The Education Trust (2010a) provides examples and argues that some districts (like Aldine and El Paso, Texas) and some states (Delaware, Illinois, Massachusetts, North Carolina, and Texas) have significantly reduced achievement gaps related to race, ethnicity, and social class by using some of the types of educational policies outlined in this section. However, such reforms often fail to improve consistently failing schools, and more drastic action is needed.

....

ASK YOURSELF: Which school-based reforms have the greatest potential to improve student achievement and reduce educational inequalities, and why? How might some of the school-based education reforms discussed in this section worsen problems in the U.S. education system?

....

Societal, Community, Economic, and Political Reforms

Although school-level educational reforms have demonstrated the potential to improve schools for low-income and minority children, by themselves they are limited

....

Community schools: Schools that strive to meet all the basic academic, physical, and emotional needs of students and their families while building strong, cohesive bonds among teachers, students, and students' families.

unless they also address the factors outside the schools that are responsible for educational inequalities (Anyon 2005). In addition to school-based approaches such as early childhood programs, summer programs, and after-school programs, many scholars call for economic initiatives to reduce income inequality and to create stable and affordable housing, and for the expansion of school-community clinics to provide health care and counseling (Rothstein 2010). Ultimately, school reform is necessary but insufficient to reduce achievement gaps without broader social and economic policies aimed at addressing the pernicious effects of poverty.

School Finance Reforms

Financing for schools has been a contentious issue since the establishment of public education. Following the U.S. Supreme Court's 1973 decision in *Rodriguez v. San Antonio,* which declared that there is no constitutional right to an equal education under the 14th Amendment, advocates for school finance equity have litigated at the state level. They argue that the current method of funding schools through local property taxes means affluent communities can spend significantly more on education than low-income areas, and that these spending differences contribute to the achievement gap.

In New Jersey, the case of *Abbott v. Burke* (1990–2013) resulted in the state's low-income urban districts being funded at the same level as its most affluent districts. In 1993, New York State began its own 16-year battle for equity in education. In *Campaign for Fiscal Equity (CFE) v. State of New York,* the New York Supreme Court found the state's formula for school funding to be unconstitutional, and the state was ordered to provide New York City public schools with additional funding for their annual operating budget.

Full-Service and Community Schools

Another way to attack education inequity is to educate not only the whole child but also the whole community. Full-service schools focus on meeting the educational, physical, psychological, and social needs of students and their families in a coordinated and collaborative fashion (Dryfoos, Quinn, and Barkin 2005). They serve as community centers, health clinics, and recreation facilities and provide services such as adult education, job training and placement, tutoring, after-school programs, mental health services, and drug and alcohol programs.

Specifically designed to target and improve at-risk neighborhoods, **community schools** aim to prevent problems as well as to support constituents. Community schools are frequently full-service schools, providing wraparound services to students and their families. However, community schools place a particular emphasis on building collective efficacy and developing a communal political voice that works toward justice for everyone in a neighborhood.

Notable examples of community schools that are also full-service schools are Geoffrey Canada's Harlem Children's Zone schools in New York City. Through his work as the president and CEO of Harlem Children's Zone, Canada seeks to create the conditions through which children can positively "contaminate" Harlem. Canada has stated:

> When you've got most of the kids in a neighborhood involved in high-quality programs, you begin to change the cultural context of that neighborhood. If you are surrounded by people who are always talking about going to college, you're going to end up thinking, "Hey, maybe this is something I could do, too." You can't help but get contaminated by the idea. It just seeps into your pores, and you don't even know that you've caught the virus. (quoted in Tough 2008, 125)

Canada provides programs for new parents in Harlem before their children are even born in an attempt to improve the children's academic achievement later in life. Participants of "Baby College" are recruited from every corner of Harlem to partake in the program, where instructors of color teach them how to have academic conversations with children, as well as how to provide children with a healthy home environment and acceptable forms of discipline. Baby College even purchases items for their homes that parents need and cannot afford.

Canada's formula of starting education as early as possible, along with extending the school day and offering tutoring for at-risk students, paid off in 2007 when a significant number of his middle-school students improved their state test results and their school earned an "A" on the New York City Department of Education school report card evaluation. Although supporters laud reforms such as those Canada has implemented through the Harlem Children's Zone as evidence of the positive effects on student achievement of high expectations and strong discipline, critics point to the cultural deficit model on which such reforms are based and to the highly disciplinarian processes used in these schools as problematic, while at the same time praising the impact of the schools.

To summarize, education reform in the United States from the 1980s to 2012 sought both excellence and equity, and since 2001, neoliberal policies have also stressed accountability as the key to reducing the achievement gap. Although federal, state, and local reforms have resulted in some improvement in achievement, critics point out that the U.S. educational system was never as problematic as its neoliberal critics suggested (Berliner and Biddle 1995). They suggest the real problem is that U.S. education works exceptionally well for children from higher socioeconomic backgrounds and exceptionally poorly for those from lower socioeconomic backgrounds. Despite efforts to address these inequalities, particularly in urban schools, through school choice and charter schools, the available evidence does not overwhelmingly support advocates' claims that these approaches reduce educational inequality. As the nation moves further into the new millennium, educational equity needs to be put back on the front burner of educational reform.

In her 2010 book *The Flat World and Education: How America's Commitment to Equity Will Determine Our Future,* Linda Darling-Hammond reviews education reforms around the world and outlines five key elements needed to reform U.S. education:

1. Meaningful learning goals
2. Intelligent, reciprocal accountability systems
3. Equitable and adequate resources
4. Strong professional standards and supports
5. Organization of schools for student and teacher learning

Darling-Hammond notes that our society must meet the basic needs of all children so they can focus their attention on academic work instead of on survival. She agrees with many that the U.S. education system will continue to fail its students, at great cost to society, if it does not equalize access to educational opportunity and support meaningful learning. An examination of the sociological evidence suggests that successful school improvement will require systemic reform aimed at the school, student, community, economic, and societal levels.

ASK YOURSELF: Which school-centered reforms do you think are most important to reducing educational inequalities? What are some of the challenges a district might face if it attempts to create full-service and community schools?

7.8 Identify steps toward social change in education.

A tremendous amount of work needs to be done at the school, community, and societal levels to improve our public schools and reduce achievement gaps. Individuals like you can take a number of important steps to help bring about positive change, including volunteering to be mentors or tutors in programs for disadvantaged or at-risk students at all levels. In the longer term, becoming an educator in a low-income areas is an important career choice, whether through a traditional university teacher education program or an alternative program such as TFA.

Whether or not you choose to become an educator, you can contribute to the improvement of the education system as a citizen. As philosopher of education John Dewey argued a century ago, education is a key to the development of the informed citizenry crucial to a democracy. As an educated citizen, you can support those policies aimed at reducing the achievement gaps. When others argue for policies that may exacerbate educational inequalities, you can support political leaders who promote educational policies that advocate for the strengthening of public education, including equitable school funding policies and policies aimed at aiding schools, families, and neighborhoods. By voicing your opinions and sharing your knowledge of the education system with others, you can positively shape the public discussion about education and influence the future direction of schooling in this country.

▶▶ Opportunities for Volunteering

- Volunteer through a program on your college campus.
- Become a Big Brother or Big Sister (http://www.bbbs.org).
- Tutor at a local school or community organization, such as the Boys and Girls Club (http://www.bgca.org).

▶▶ Become an Educator

- Become a licensed teacher through your university if such a program is available.
- Seek out an alternative certification program such as Teach for America (http://www.tfa.org) or the New York City Teaching Fellows Program (http://www.nyctf.org).

▶▶ Stay Informed and Engaged

- Read about changes in education policy in sources such as the Education section of the *New York Times* (http://www.nytimes.com/pages/education/index.html).
- Learn about your political leaders' views on education, thank them for upholding policies you support, and contact them when you disagree with their views and votes (http://www.usa.gov/Contact/Elected.shtml).

Martha Irvine / AP / Corbis

Monica Zheng, a student at the University of Chicago, tutors Joshua Williams, 11, as he does his homework. What do you see as some benefits of volunteering to tutor school-aged children?

WHAT DOES AMERICA THINK?

Questions about Education from the General Social Survey

 Turn to the beginning of the chapter to compare your answers to the total population.

1. What is your interest level in local school issues?

   VERY INTERESTED: 54.5%

   MODERATELY INTERESTED: 35.1%

   NOT AT ALL INTERESTED: 10.4%

2. What is your confidence level in education?

   A GREAT DEAL: 25.8%

   ONLY SOME: 57.7%

   HARDLY ANY: 16.5%

3. In the United States, do you think we're spending too much money on improving the nation's education system, too little money, or about the right amount?

   TOO MUCH: 7.9%

   ABOUT THE RIGHT AMOUNT: 17.7%

   TOO LITTLE: 74.4%

4. Do you think that sex education should be taught in public schools?

   YES: 90.8%

   NO: 9.2%

5. On the average, African Americans have worse jobs, income, and housing than white people. Do you think these differences are because most African Americans don't have the chance for the education that it takes to rise out of poverty?

   YES: 43.7%

   NO: 56.3%

 ## LOOK BEHIND THE NUMBERS

Go to **edge.sagepub.com/trevino** for a breakdown of these data across time and by race, sex, age, income, and other statuses.

1. Examine the data on income for responses to the question about level of confidence in education. Is there a pattern? Explain.

2. Do interest levels regarding local school issues vary based on gender? Have you experienced this pattern? Explain.

3. Although more than half of the respondents said that they are very interested in local school issues, only one-quarter said that they have great confidence in education. Do you think confidence in education can increase? If so, how?

4. More than 74% of the respondents think we spend too little money on improving the country's education system. Examine the data for this question in the General Social Survey from 1973 to the present. How have opinions shifted over time? Do you think this trend will continue? Why?

SOURCE: National Opinion Research Center, University of Chicago.

CHAPTER SUMMARY

 7.1 Describe the social institution of education.

As a social institution, education takes the role of teaching children the attitudes, roles, ideas, and skills they need to become adults. Its processes and outcomes differ from society to society as well as among different groups within each society.

 7.2 Discuss patterns and trends in education.

In the United States, the major patterns and trends over the past five decades include persistent achievement gaps among different groups, with white, Asian American, and affluent students performing at higher levels on standardized tests than black, Hispanic, and low-income students; the continuing crisis in urban education, with students in public schools in central cities performing at lower levels than students in suburban public schools; and the continuing crisis in overall student achievement, with the achievement scores of U.S. students consistently falling toward the bottom of international rankings.

7.3 Describe the U.S. educational system and the influence of interest groups.

The U.S. educational system is the most decentralized in the world. Whereas federal governments have a much larger role in education in other countries, in the United States education is primarily a state and local responsibility. Although the federal government has taken a larger role in the past two decades, decentralization has resulted in sometimes 50 different sets of curriculum requirements and tests. Moreover, various educational interest groups, such as parents, community organizations, teacher unions, and political leaders, lobby state and local governments and education departments to enact specific educational policies.

7.4 Apply the functionalist, symbolic interactionist, and conflict perspectives to social policy for education.

Functionalist ideals of a meritocratic education system shaped the development of the public education system in the United States and continue to mold democratic visions of education as the source of equality of opportunity. On the other hand, conflict theory highlights the ways

in which social and economic privilege define education in the United States and create marked gaps in achievement between people of different races, economic classes, and social classes. Interactionist theory guides researchers in evaluating the ways in which the relationships among students, teachers, administrators, and other community members affect schooling.

 7.5 Apply specialized theories to the social institution of education.

Code and social reproduction theorists argue that educational institutions reproduce existing social inequalities through language and through social, cultural, and economic capital (networks; art, music, and literature; and money). Institutional theorists argue that the development of mass education systems around the world has been a result of the commitment to democratic civil societies. Feminist theorists argue that schools reproduce gender inequalities for both girls and boys.

 7.6 Evaluate explanations for educational inequality.

School-centered explanations of educational inequality look at the roles of educational organization and processes, such as funding, teacher quality, and school quality, in producing unequal educational achievement by different groups. Student-centered explanations examine how factors outside schools, such as biology, families, communities, and poverty, produce unequal achievement. Although there is evidence to support parts of both kinds of explanations, the data indicate that student achievement is affected by a combination of school- and student-centered factors.

 7.7 Describe recent reforms in education.

Improving schools and reducing achievement gaps will not be easy, and sociological research highlights the need for careful and deliberate education reforms. While administrators and teachers can take many steps to improve student achievement, schools are embedded in communities that have their own sets of complex social, economic, and political issues. Education reformers must account for the role of factors outside the schools that affect student achievement.

7.8 Identify steps toward social change in education.

Everyone can take steps to improve the U.S. education system. By volunteering in underserved areas or becoming a teacher, you can directly influence students and schools. By remaining informed and pressing elected leaders to support sound education policies, you can help improve schooling through the democratic process.

DISCUSSION QUESTIONS

1. In what ways is the sociological analysis and understanding of education different from the public perception of the role education plays in a person's life chances? In what ways is the American Dream tied to education?

2. How can one explain the achievement gap for different groups? What roles do concerns such as testing, standards, and quality play in explaining the gap?

3. How are teachers' expectations of their students shaped by race, socioeconomic status, and gender? How do these expectations play into the trends in who goes into the STEM (science, technology, engineering, and mathematics) fields?

4. How can one explain the current crisis in urban education? How are the problems in urban education complicated by race, gender, and poverty?

5. How is the structure of the U.S. education system functional for, or beneficial to, society? How is it dysfunctional, or problematic? What role do private schools play in the U.S. education system?

6. According to the structural functionalist perspective, how does our federalist form of government, in which each state controls its own education system, contradict assumptions about consensus? In what ways has the move toward centralization through federal education policies alleviated these concerns?

7. From the symbolic interactionist perspective, what are the ways that education reproduces the beliefs we hold as a society about gender, race, and ethnicity? Is there a solution to the problem of education reproducing inequality and negative beliefs about some groups of people?

8. According to code theory, how does a person's use of language reflect the individual's background and allow him or her to function within that background? How can formal education work to rectify the inequalities that stem from limitations in communicating across class divides?

9. What are some possible ways to address the student-centered, or outside-school, explanations for educational inequalities? What about the school-centered explanations? Which solutions to the problem of educational inequalities are the most promising? How do programs such as Teach for America and the New Teacher Project address the different explanations for educational inequalities?

10. What role do national reform policies such as No Child Left Behind and the Race to the Top play in alleviating disparities in education? How do such policies differ in focus from school choice reforms such as vouchers and charter schools?

KEY TERMS

achievement gap 164

American Federation of Teachers (AFT) 182

charter schools 181

code theory 175

community schools 183

cultural capital theory 175

cultural deprivation theory 178

cultural difference theories 178

effective schools movement 178

Elementary and Secondary Education Act (ESEA) 164

Sharpen your skills with SAGE edge at edge.sagepub.com/trevino

A personalized approach to help you accomplish your coursework goals in an easy-to-use learning environment.

8 MEDIA

William Hoynes

Robyn Beck / Staff AFP / Getty Images

A mural decorates a work area at Facebook headquarters in Menlo Park, California. Facebook is the world's most popular social networking service, with more than a billion users worldwide. Some say that social networking forges stronger relationships because it helps people stay in touch with their friends and relatives. Others say that it causes people to be antisocial because they are not communicating face-to-face. What do you think?

Investigating Media: My Story

William Hoynes

Watching, reading, and listening to news has been my daily routine since my teenage years. In college, I learned to read the news with a critical eye, questioning journalistic quality, depth, and perspective. In graduate school at Boston College, I was an active member of the Media Research and Action Project (MRAP), codirected by William Gamson and Charlotte Ryan, working with community activists to challenge barriers to media access and promoting greater media diversity.

Working with MRAP opened a window for me onto broader questions about the ways news contributes to public understanding of political issues and current events. In the 1980s and 1990s, I began working with my colleague David Croteau, with whom I still write today, on a series of studies of the range of perspectives featured on prestigious television news programs. Our studies examining ABC's *Nightline,* PBS's *NewsHour,* and the public affairs lineup on PBS stations were published by the media watch group FAIR (Fairness & Accuracy In Reporting) and helped generate public debate about the consequences of limited political diversity on U.S. television news.

Over the past 25 years, I have worked on monitoring of the local news media in Boston and Philadelphia, activist efforts to prevent the increasing commercialization of public schools, and nationwide campaigns to maintain federal regulations limiting the size of major media conglomerates and to reform the funding and structure of public broadcasting. I continue to work with media education and media activist organizations, including the Children's Media Project in Poughkeepsie, New York, and FAIR.

LEARNING OBJECTIVES

8.1 Describe the relationship between media and social problems.

8.2 Discuss patterns and trends in media portrayals of social problems.

8.3 Describe the debate about the role of media as a potential cause of social problems.

8.4 Discuss emergent social problems associated with new media technologies.

8.5 Explain how the functionalist, conflict, and symbolic interactionist perspectives conceptualize the media–social problems relationship.

8.6 Explain how contemporary theories conceptualize the media–social problems relationship.

8.7 Identify steps toward media-related social change.

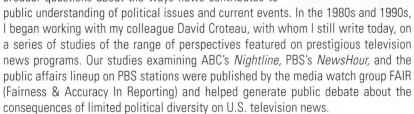

WHAT DO YOU THINK?
Questions about Media from the General Social Survey

1. What is your main source of information about events in the news?

☐ NEWSPAPERS
☐ THE INTERNET
☐ TV
☐ OTHER

2. What is your confidence level in the press?

☐ A GREAT DEAL
☐ ONLY SOME
☐ HARDLY ANY

3. How many hours do you watch TV each day?

☐ 0
☐ 1–2
☐ 3–4
☐ 5 OR MORE

4. What is your confidence level in television?

☐ A GREAT DEAL
☐ ONLY SOME
☐ HARDLY ANY

5. How often do you read the newspaper?

☐ DAILY
☐ A FEW TIMES A WEEK
☐ ONCE A WEEK
☐ LESS THAN ONCE A WEEK
☐ NEVER

Turn to the end of the chapter to view the results for the total population.

SOURCE: National Opinion Research Center, University of Chicago.

THE DRAMA OF "ROAD RAGE"

 8.1 Describe the relationship between media and social problems.

A minor traffic dispute in Carteret County, North Carolina, escalated into a dramatic confrontation in March 2013 when 40-year-old Bradley Turner jumped out of his car and threw a punch at 20-year-old William Berry, who Turner believed had cut him off. Berry and Nathan Brotzman, the 21-year-old passenger in his pickup truck, responded by punching and kicking Turner, beating him to the ground. Turner's wife stepped out of their car and handed him a pistol, which Turner pointed at Berry and Brotzman, who quickly ran away and called 911. Turner fired several shots in Berry's direction but no one was hurt.

Much of the incident was captured on cell phone video by one of Berry's neighbors, and the clip circulated widely on the Internet. Local and national news outlets—from the Greenville, North Carolina, television station WNCT and the local *Gaston Gazette* to the *New York Daily News* and Gawker—posted it. While Bradley and Christy Turner were actually charged with gun-related crimes, media reports instead highlighted the drama of "road rage."

Media play a prominent role in shaping what we define as a social problem. By calling attention to some issues, such as "road rage," they help to identify the social issues that attract our concern and action. By downplaying or neglecting other issues, they signal that, for example, the abundance of guns on the streets is not a serious social problem. Exploring the relationship between social problems and the media will help us to understand how and why some issues emerge as widely discussed social problems—and why others remain on the margins of public discussion, relegated to the category of personal trouble rather than social problem.

Sociologists have long explored the complex relationship between media and social problems. Recently, however, changes in the media environment and developments in

Do we live in a "network society" in which media networks such as Twitter, texting, and e-mail influence the social, political, economic, and cultural lives of people across the country and around the world? Some say that online media like Facebook and YouTube helped protesters launch the Tunisian Revolution of 2010 and the Egyptian Revolution of 2011. How many friends do you have who live in different countries with whom you can communicate instantly?

social problems scholarship have produced three distinct sets of questions about media and social problems.

One set focuses on media *content* and the role of media in defining issues as social problems. How, for example, do news and entertainment media portray emerging and long-standing social problems? How, if at all, do such portrayals change over time, and how do advocates shape media portrayals of specific social problems? Are new forms of digital media, including user-generated and social media, changing the way the media construct social problems?

A second set of questions looks at the potential *role* of media as a cause of, or contributor to, social problems. Does exposure to violent media imagery produce violent behavior? Do media contribute to health problems such as obesity or anorexia? And how do media influence our understanding of, and responses to, social problems?

The final set of questions about media and social problems focuses on the emergence of *new social problems* related to the development of new media technologies. For example, what are the consequences of the digital divide—that is, persistent inequality in people's access to and knowledge about new digital media? How can we understand media-related social problems such as cyberbullying and distracted driving? What new challenges do these pose for policy makers?

This chapter traces these three areas of social problems scholarship, exploring the intersection of media and social problems in the context of classic as well as more specialized theories.

PATTERNS AND TRENDS

 8.2 Discuss patterns and trends in media portrayals of social problems.

The media regularly portray social problems. Crime, for example, is a staple of local television news coverage, and print, broadcast, and online journalists routinely cover a range of issues associated with health, education, and the environment. A steady stream of Hollywood films and prime-time television programs include implicit references to school violence, homelessness, and drug abuse. Both news and entertainment media also often offer in-depth and dramatic portrayals of the causes and consequences of social problems. But what counts as a social problem?

Media and the Construction of Social Problems

The conditions that become social problems have both objective and subjective dimensions that interact. The objective dimension includes evidence of the existence, prevalence, and severity of potentially troubling issues, such as illegal drug use, gun violence, or child abuse. The subjective dimension includes collective interpretations of and public attitudes about these issues. Media are a primary arena within which the two dimensions interact, offering a prominent space where we debate and interpret the meaning and significance of incidents and trends associated with potential social problems. For example, citizens seeking to raise awareness about gun violence may offer journalists evidence of the problem—from official statistics to details of dramatic gun incidents—hoping the media will report it. Such news reports typically generate commentary, in which media become an arena for interpreting the significance of the statistics and incidents and for discussion of the appropriate ways to respond, leading to additional reporting on the debate over gun violence. Thus media help define the context within which both public policy and public opinion develop.

Only some troubling social conditions emerge as social problems earmarked for public discussion about

Moral entrepreneurs: Advocates who organize to focus broad public attention on troubling issues.

Claims making: The process whereby groups compete to have their claims about difficult social issues acknowledged, accepted, and responded to by authorities.

potential solutions. **Moral entrepreneurs** are advocates who organize to focus public attention on these issues. They do so through the process of **claims making**, whereby groups compete to have authorities acknowledge, accept, and respond to their claims about difficult social issues. Claims making, then, is at the center of the process by which some social issues are defined as social problems (Kitsuse and Spector 1973).

Media are a central and increasingly influential venue for defining troubling issues as social problems. Claims makers often use the news and online media for circulating their interpretations of social problems to policy makers and the public, jockeying for position to do so. Thus media attention is not distributed equally across issues, nor is it a simple reflection of the prevalence or severity of a given issue. Looking at examples of news coverage of crime and drugs will help us see *how* media construct social problems.

....

ASK YOURSELF: Consider news coverage of a current social problem. Can you identify the claims makers? Do reports feature various claims makers and multiple definitions of the problem or potential solutions? If so, how do you assess their competing interpretations?

....

Crime, Drugs, and Media Routines

Consider the contents of front-page headlines, lead stories on the evening news, the cable TV news crawl, and top-of-the-screen stories on news websites. Publicity—often the result of sustained media attention—is a major factor in shaping what citizens and public officials recognize as social problems requiring policy responses. However, this increased attention does not usually follow the worsening of a troubling issue. In fact, researchers have found it can occur when a social issue is stable or even improving. News coverage of crime is a classic example.

For more than half a century, the volume of news coverage of crime—that is, the number of crime stories in the major news media—has been independent of the crime rate. In other words, we should not assume that an increase in crime *news* is the result of an increase in *crime*, or that a drop in crime news reflects a decline in the crime rate. F. James Davis's (1952, 330) pioneering study of crime reporting in Colorado newspapers found "there is no consistent relationship between the amount of crime news in newspapers and the local crime rates," and this finding has been replicated in later studies (see Katz 1987).

Yet crime news remains a staple of U.S. journalism. Local television news programs and newspapers consistently report on crime and the courts, and national

 Future of TV  Perception Control

Is there an element of sensationalism in many news stories in which the messages are overdrawn? Has tabloid journalism become a major part of how serious crime is reported? Are newspapers like the Daily News, "New York's most momentous newspaper," responsible for stoking the feelings of their readers?

and online news outlets spend considerable time covering high-profile criminal cases. If the actual occurrence of crime is not the foundation of news coverage, what explains this intensity of coverage?

Research indicates that **journalists' professional routines**, the daily activities around which news reporters organize their work, are the key to understanding the consistently high level of crime coverage in the U.S. news media. Journalists know they can expect a steady stream of information from police and the courts, so they can count on crime stories to make the day-to-day work of producing news more manageable and less uncertain, just as weather and sports reports do. Crime—including stories about wayward celebrities, unusual offenses, and unfolding dramas—is a tried-and-true theme that draws the audiences that commercial and online news organizations need to earn advertising revenue.

In one classic study, sociologist Mark Fishman (1978, 533) sought to understand the roots of crime news by examining "how and why news organizations construct crime waves." Reports of a crime wave, Fishman found,

result in large part from three key journalistic practices. First, in evaluating the newsworthiness of potential stories, journalists implicitly classify events by theme—"crimes against the elderly" was the theme in Fishman's study. Events are more likely to become news—and to be featured prominently—when they fit a continuing news theme.

Second, most crime reporting relies overwhelmingly on information from authorities, especially local police, whose publicity specialists know how news organizations operate. Fishman (1978, 540) reports that "police who transmit crime dispatches to the media select incidents that they think will interest journalists," mainly the kinds of stories they have reported before, and they provide reporters with continuing examples of a currently popular theme as long as such stories exist.

Third, news organizations track their competitors, making sure they do not miss important or interesting stories their rivals are covering. The news media outlets in one city or region thus often end up reporting the same stories, reinforcing the significance of a specific theme—such as a crime wave—and further encouraging police sources to supply similar leads.

For example, understanding journalistic routines gives us insight into the way news media circulate what sociologists Orcutt and Turner (1993) call "distorted images of drug problems." The U.S. news media's focus on cocaine in 1986—highlighted by a March 17 *Newsweek* cover story, "Kids and Cocaine: An Epidemic Strikes Middle America," that identified "A Coke Plague"—relied on alarming numbers and powerful graphic representations of cocaine use to describe the crisis. These numbers and graphics, however, required significant interpretive and creative work to be consistent with a story of a cocaine crisis. Orcutt and Turner show how *Newsweek* graphically illustrated a very small one-year increase that masked a longer-term trend of relative stability in cocaine use, selectively citing survey findings in ways that were not consistent with the overall research results (see Figure 8.1a).

Reports of a growing LSD problem in the early 1990s similarly pointed to a survey showing a small increase in LSD use among high school seniors from 1989 to 1990. The reports failed to note, however, that the increase from 4.9% to 5.4% of high school seniors was not statistically significant, and that LSD use among this group had been higher in the late 1970s and early 1980s (see Figure 8.1b).

Most recently, the use of methamphetamine emerged in the first decade of the 2000s as a new national drug

---

Journalists' professional routines: The daily activities around which news reporters organize their work.

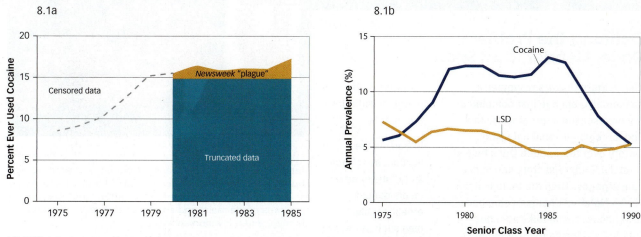

FIGURE 8.1   Cocaine and LSD Use among U.S. High School Seniors, 1975–1990

8.1a

8.1b

SOURCE: Johnston, Lloyd D., Patrick M. O'Malley, and Jerald G. Bachman. 1991. *Drug Use Among American High School Seniors, College Students and Young Adults, 1975-1990. Volume I: High School Seniors.* Rockville, MD.: National Institute on Drug Abuse.

problem. Again, news media played a prominent role in the construction of the meth crisis (Shafer 2007), with *Newsweek* using familiar language in its August 2005 cover story, "The Meth Epidemic: Inside America's New Drug Crisis."

Drug abuse is a complex social issue, and reporting can help the public understand it. But the examples noted above show that claims makers do not necessarily need to offer research data to legitimate their definitions of social problems. In fact, Deseran and Orcutt (2009, 883) argue, "if anything, there appears to be an inverse relationship between media legitimation of drug crises and empirical documentation based on drug surveys."

Sometimes news organizations are themselves the primary claims makers, and editors and reporters play a crucial role in constructing social problems. Sometimes, however, journalists are skeptical of other claims makers' efforts. During the 1996 U.S. presidential campaign, rather than running headlines about a documented marijuana crisis, news media raised critical questions about survey results and identified the primary claims makers regarding an increasing teen drug problem—President Bill Clinton and presidential candidate Bob Dole—as political actors seeking to gain media attention and sway voters (Deseran and Orcutt 2009). The debate about drugs became part of the political campaign, with reporters paying more attention to the candidates' performances

than to the "problem" of increasing marijuana use. News media, in this case, effectively deterred politicians from defining a new marijuana problem.

Media Frames and Sponsors

The way news media define social problems—that is, the common **media frames**, conventions of journalistic storytelling that situate a social problem within a broader context (Gamson 1992)—are dynamic, changing over time in response to newsworthy events and broader cultural changes. One of the most powerful factors shaping the way media frame social problems is what Gamson and Modigliani (1987) call **sponsor activities**, the advocacy and promotional work of publicizing and advancing a specific interpretation of an issue. As these researchers note, prominent media frames that define social issues "frequently have sponsors interested in promoting their careers. Sponsorship is more than merely advocacy, involving such tangible activities as speech-making, advertising, article and pamphlet writing, and the filing of legal briefs to promote a preferred package" (165).

For example, in the years after the civil rights movement, with sponsorship from civil rights organizations and several presidential administrations in the 1960s and 1970s, news media typically framed racial discrimination toward blacks as a serious problem and affirmative action as an appropriate remedial action. In later years, particularly the late 1970s and early 1980s, a network of neoconservative journals, think tanks, and organizations emerged as powerful sponsors of a very different interpretation, defining the problem as reverse discrimination,

Media frames: Conventions of journalistic storytelling that situate a social problem within a broader context.

Sponsor activities: The work of promoting and publicizing specific media frames.

🖥 Media and the Drug War

Defining the Problem: Race, Gender, and Sport

The Rutgers University women's basketball team had just completed the best season in program history, and its regional semifinal upset victory over top-seeded Duke helped propel a Cinderella story line in the sports pages. Then the team lost the NCAA National Championship game to Tennessee, and talk-radio host Don Imus referred to the women on the Rutgers team as "nappy-headed hos" on his nationally syndicated program. Over the next eight days, Imus apologized, lost his televised simulcast partner (MSNBC), and ultimately had his radio show canceled by CBS.

News coverage of Imus's derogatory remarks was far more extensive than reporting on the game. Most news media framed the incident as a story about race and racism. Undoubtedly, race was at the center: a white "shock jock" made racist remarks about a team consisting mostly of black players. However, sociologist Cheryl Cooky and her colleagues (2010) suggest that an understanding of intersectionality—in this case, the way race, gender, class, and sexuality are woven together—offers a deeper insight into the events.

In framing the incident as a "race story," major news media quoted prominent black men such as Jesse Jackson and Al Sharpton, but recognized leaders of women's organizations—and the Rutgers athletes—were far less visible; news reports mentioned black leaders or organizations more than six times as often as they mentioned female leaders or women's groups (Cooky et al. 2010, 149). And the coverage generally ignored the on-campus protests at the Rutgers Women's Center, which sought to emphasize the intersection of racism and sexism in Imus's remarks.

Cooky and her colleagues suggest that "the media's uncritical positioning of Sharpton and Jackson as the primary spokespeople racialized the controversy. Moreover, this frame silenced intersectional ways of knowing given that the quotations from Black leaders featured in the articles focused only on the racial/racist aspects of the controversy, while neglecting themes on race, gender, and sexuality in sport" (150). Journalists covered the incident as a high-profile controversy, missing the opportunity to examine its deeper meaning within the continuing problems of racism and sexism in U.S. society.

Members of the Rutgers University women's basketball team appear at a news conference in 2007. The team and school officials held the news conference after radio personality Don Imus made racist and sexist remarks about the team on his radio and television shows.

▶ **THINK ABOUT IT**

1. Why do you think news reports emphasized race rather than gender as the key issue in this story?

2. How do you think an intersectional approach would change the media's framing of this incident?

---

and this frame became increasingly prominent in the news media in the 1980s (Gamson and Modigliani 1987).

News Coverage Builds on Culturally Resonant Themes

We've seen that routine media practices, the need for audiences that drive advertising revenue, and the public's desire for dramatic and unusual stories shape media reporting on social problems. In addition, news coverage often invokes **culturally resonant themes**, widely held beliefs, values, and preferences familiar to potential audiences.

Media characterizations of food-related social problems—overweight/obesity and anorexia/bulimia—are a

Culturally resonant themes: Themes that invoke widely held beliefs, values, and preferences that are familiar to potential audiences; such themes are common in news stories of social problems.

News Reporting

prime example of portrayals rooted in deep-seated assumptions about our bodies and our eating habits, individual responsibility, and health. In the 2000s, the news media described obesity as a growing U.S. health crisis, an "epidemic." Much reporting drew on scientific research, but journalists selected, simplified, and dramatized the findings (Saguy and Almeling 2008). News coverage constructed obesity in ways that identified individuals as both the problem and the likely solution.

Media accounts typically blamed individuals' eating habits and inactivity and suggested that making better food and exercise choices would be the most productive response. They typically underplayed the social structural and genetic roots of obesity and potential policy-based responses. This individual-oriented approach to a social problem is consistent with cultural themes that value individual responsibility, as well as with long-standing stereotypes that define body weight in moral terms and overweight people as lazy and weak.

Media portrayals of anorexia and bulimia frame these eating disorders in very different terms, identifying them as legitimate eating disorders with both individual and social structural causes as well as biological, medical, psychological, and cultural foundations. Medical intervention is portrayed as a common and effective way to treat them. The volume of coverage of anorexia and bulimia remained relatively stable during the 1990s and 2000s, while news coverage of obesity, in contrast, grew dramatically as the crisis frame emerged (see Figure 8.2).

Saguy and Gruys (2010, 247) note: "In the contemporary U.S. society, where thinness is highly prized, news articles are less likely to blame individuals for being (or trying to be) *too thin* than they are to blame them for being *too fat*. This suggests that, more generally, cultural values shape how the news media assign blame and responsibility." In short, news media portrayals of social problems often invoke popular assumptions and stereotypes about their causes and consequences, and about appropriate responses.

Entertainment Media

Entertainment media play a significant role in publicizing social problems, helping identify emerging issues, and focusing attention on persistent problems. For example, according to sociologist Stephen Pfohl (1977, 320), both news media and television medical dramas helped establish child abuse as a legitimate social problem: "The proliferation of the idea of abuse by the media cannot be

....

Moral panics: Situations in which broad public fears and anxieties about particular social problems are disproportionate to the dangers of those problems.

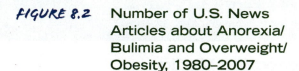

FIGURE 8.2 Number of U.S. News Articles about Anorexia/Bulimia and Overweight/Obesity, 1980–2007

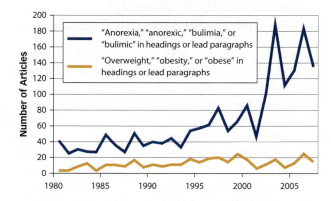

SOURCE: Saguy, Abigail C., and Kjerstin Gruys. 2010. Morality and Health: News Media Constructions of Overweight and Eating Disorders. *Social Problems* 57 (2): 231–250. Reprinted with permission from the University of California Press.

underestimated. Though its stories were sensational, its credibility went unchallenged." Two decades later, popular music helped revive concern about child abuse as a social problem. Hit songs from artists such as 10,000 Maniacs ("What's the Matter Here," 1987), Suzanne Vega ("Luka," 1987), and Pearl Jam ("Daughter," 1993) refocused national attention on the continuing problem.

The Media and Moral Panics

News media sometimes shine a dramatic spotlight on a social issue in a way that can help constitute, and inflame, a moral panic. Sociologist Stanley Cohen coined the term *moral panic* in his influential 1972 book *Folk Devils and Moral Panics*. Since then, a large research literature has explored this concept.

In **moral panics**, public fear and anxiety about particular social problems are disproportionate to the actual danger posed by those problems. In some cases, such as news coverage of the cocaine "crisis," media play an active role in promoting moral panics. In other cases, such as news reporting about child abuse, media serve more as channels for stories that fuel the panics. As Erich Goode and Nachman Ben-Yehuda (2009, 106) note, "The media are usually the vehicle that conveys the stories and claims on which moral panics are based; they are the most effective means by which indignation over a given threat is propagated because, unlike word of mouth, they reach large audiences over a brief time, often even simultaneously."

Goode and Ben-Yehuda observe that news organizations contribute to moral panics most commonly

Media Bias

Researching Media

Comparing Media Constructions of Obesity in the United States and France

Lucas Jackson / Reuters

An overweight woman sits on a chair in Times Square in New York City. In 2013, New York City mayor Michael Bloomberg launched an initiative to ban supersize sodas and limit the sizes of other sugary drinks that could be sold by restaurants, delis, movie theaters, sports stadiums, and food carts. Approximately 60% of New Yorkers opposed the measure, saying that purchasing such drinks should be a matter of individual choice. Most American see obesity as an individual problem.

If you've ever traveled outside the United States, you may have observed that news broadcasts in other countries can look quite different from U.S. news. Do American news media depictions of social problems reflect a specific national cultural context? To explore this question, sociologists Abigail C. Saguy, Kjerstin Gruys, and Shanna Gong (2010) compared American and French newspaper coverage of overweight and obesity over a 10-year period. Newspapers in both countries portrayed obesity as a social problem, but the coverage in the two framed the sources and solutions to the problem very differently.

The obesity rate in France is far lower than that in the United States, but newspapers in France were twice as likely as U.S. papers to frame obesity as a health "crisis." About half the French news stories also included discussion of other countries, while the American press focused exclusively on the United States in 95% of articles. While coverage in both countries was equally likely to highlight individual blame for increased body weight, French news was far more likely to point to social structural causes of overweight/obesity. Saguy and her

colleagues note that "an emphasis on individual blame dominates U.S. news framing, while being more equally balanced by other frames in French news reporting" (599). This difference likely reflects broader cultural differences, such as that Europeans are more likely to frame social problems in structural terms.

When it came to solving the problem of obesity, U.S. media emphasized individual solutions such as diet and exercise (56% of stories) and paid comparatively little attention to policy solutions (21%) such as the nutritional quality of school lunches. In contrast, the French press offered equal emphasis on individual and policy solutions (44% for both). In discussing dietary solutions, the American press focused primarily on low-fat, low-carbohydrate, and low-calorie diets, while the French emphasized healthy foods.

Saguy and her colleagues conclude that the distinctive national news

coverage "probably echoes general patterns in how social problems are addressed differently in each nation, with a U.S. press focusing more on individual autonomy and the French press envisaging a larger role for the state" (605).

▶ **THINK ABOUT IT**

1. Why do you think French and American news media report differently on obesity?

2. Do you think a journalistic emphasis on social structural causes of, and policy solutions to, obesity would help newspaper readers develop a deeper understanding of weight-related social problems? Why or why not?

---

through **media exaggeration**, strategies that dramatize and embellish social issues to attract an audience. Media exaggeration takes two primary forms. First, journalists pay inordinate attention to events that are uncommon or statistically unusual. Second, they overstate the extent or size of a social problem, using the language of epidemic, crisis, or plague. This kind of reporting produces

dramatic headlines and news stories that go viral, and it is one of the principal ways media can contribute to a moral panic.

Media exaggeration: Strategies of dramatizing and embellishing media stories involving social issues to attract and hold the attention of an audience.

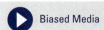 Biased Media

Media Activism and Social Problems

Much of the media reporting on social problems emerges from official government sources, but activists can intervene to try to highlight social problems in the news. Reporting of domestic violence is one example.

Beginning in the late 1990s, sociologist Charlotte Ryan began working with the Rhode Island Coalition Against Domestic Violence to improve the way local news outlets covered domestic violence issues. Leaders of the coalition knew that even sympathetic reporters often wrote stories that helped perpetuate what the leaders saw as destructive myths about domestic violence, including that it is a private family problem rather than a social problem worthy of sustained public attention. The members of the coalition sought a better understanding of how reporters gathered their information, so they could work with local journalists to improve their coverage.

Ryan examined local newspaper coverage of 12 domestic violence murders in Rhode Island from 1996 through 1999, consisting of 88 articles, most of which appeared in the first week following each murder. Her findings were striking. News stories focused primarily on the perpetrators; the victims were nearly invisible. The murders were generally portrayed as unpredictable family tragedies, and the sources quoted in news reports played key roles in defining the stories. Some, including neighbors and witnesses, emphasized the individual tragedy, and police sources focused on the details of the crime. Only when reporters turned to domestic violence experts—shelter providers, public health workers, and victims' advocates—did their stories link the murders to the problem of domestic violence. Ryan concluded: "With a few notable exceptions, the media reinforced the perception that domestic violence murders are isolated family tragedies and did not challenge common myths about domestic violence. In doing so, reporters missed opportunities to broaden the public's understanding of domestic violence, its warning signs and possibilities for prevention and community intervention" (Rhode Island Coalition Against Domestic Violence 2000, 5-4).

Ryan and the Rhode Island Coalition (2000) went on to produce a reporters' handbook about domestic violence and the law, with recommendations from survivors, that was distributed throughout the state, and a training program for survivors and advocates about how reporters work so they could become more effective news sources. The Rhode Island Coalition is now one of the principal sources in newspaper coverage of domestic violence in the state, and the coverage has changed in ways that reflect the coalition's emphasis on understanding domestic violence as a social problem, not just a private tragedy.

Claims Making in the Era of YouTube and Facebook

Just about anyone with a computer and an Internet connection can be an amateur media producer. Now, if mainstream journalists overlook an issue, advocates and claims makers can bypass traditional news outlets and create their own advocacy media to gain publicity, mobilize support, and pressure policy makers to take action. In this new media environment, claims making is more accessible to a wider range of advocates, but it is also more diffuse, with many voices competing for public attention.

....

ASK YOURSELF: What kind of social problems commentary do you see on Facebook? Do the claims draw from, and link to, traditional media? Do they point to the Facebook pages or websites of advocacy organizations? Do you think social networking sites are effective at focusing public attention on new social problems? Why or why not?

....

Digital media can democratize the process of social problem construction, opening new communication channels, additional opportunities for information sharing, and a new infrastructure for public discussion. Still, most **user-generated media content** reaches only very small networks of friends and family of the generators, and many people remain spectators, consuming content distributed largely by the major media companies that have long dominated our information environment.

DEBATING MEDIA AS A CAUSE OF SOCIAL PROBLEMS

 8.3 Describe the debate about the role of media as a potential cause of social problems.

For decades, critics have identified media as one of the fundamental *sources* of social problems, and social science researchers have debated whether, and how, media exposure might encourage behaviors and attitudes associated with social problems, including crime and delinquency, violence, unhealthy eating, and smoking. You may be familiar with some of the claims—such as that violent video games help cause school violence or that advertising is a cause of eating disorders—but you may not know how long these debates have raged or how complex the causes of social problems are.

....

User-generated media content: Publicly shared media content produced by users (often amateurs) rather than media companies.

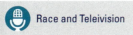 Race and Teleivision

TABLE 8.1   Nine Media Phobias

Media Phobias	
1	Undermining education and shortening kids' attention spans
2	Ruining childhood
3	Causing violence
4	Endorsing teenage sex
5	Encouraging teen pregnancy and single parenthood
6	Making children increasingly materialistic
7	Causing health problems, such as obesity and anorexia
8	Promoting substance abuse
9	Supporting racism, sexism, and homophobia

SOURCE: Sternheimer, Karen. 2010. *Connecting Social Problems and Popular Culture.* Boulder, CO: Westview Press.

In her thorough exploration of contemporary arguments that blame media for social problems, sociologist Karen Sternheimer (2010) identifies nine **media phobias**, or broad public fears about the negative impact of media, as listed in Table 8.1. Sternheimer does not discount the significance of these social problems; in fact, she argues that they warrant significant public attention. However, she finds little evidence that media are the cause of any of them: "Despite the common-sense view that media must be at least partly to blame for these social problems, the evidence suggests that there are many more important factors that create serious social problems in the United States today. Popular culture gets a lot of attention, but it is rarely a central causal factor" (2). Media are, for Sternheimer, little more than "sheep in wolf's clothing" (298) that appear to be far more powerful drivers of social problems than they really are.

ASK YOURSELF: Why do you think media are so often blamed for social problems? What do we neglect when we focus on media as the cause of social problems? How would you respond to Sternheimer's characterization of media as "sheep in wolf's clothing"?

Next we review both the claims and the counterclaims about media causing, facilitating, or worsening various social problems, to help you draw your own conclusions.

Youth and Crime: The Payne Fund Studies and Comic Books

We can conclude that exposure to media has significant influence on what we think and how we behave only if we assume that media are powerful. Public concern about media power has persisted since the early 20th century, and it often seems to intensify when new media technologies emerge. The introduction of the telephone, for example, aroused fears that the new device would threaten privacy. The development of video games and the Internet produced a new wave of concern that violent media content would produce violent children.

One of the earliest social science research efforts to study the relationship between media and social problems was the Payne Fund Studies in the 1930s. Several prominent sociologists—including social theorist Herbert Blumer and youth gang researcher Frederic Thrasher—participated in the multibook research project aimed at offering "a comprehensive study of the influence of motion pictures upon children" (Charters 1933, v).

The conclusions of the Payne Fund Studies emphasized the complexity of the relationship between movies and children. The authors noted that children learn from movies, and that the emotional responses movies evoke constitute a key component of their power. At the same time, they recognized movies' differing influence on individual children, suggesting that social context and children's experiences were a key part of the picture.

The Payne Fund authors paid particular attention to whether heavy movie attendance led children to engage in crime or other troublesome behavior. The results were decidedly mixed. In his historical review of 20th-century media effects research, McDonald (2004, 186) notes that the Payne Fund data point to a "reciprocal relationship—movies do have an effect on children, but those children who are most attracted to the worst movies tend to be those with the most problems to begin with."

Sociologist Herbert Blumer (1933) conducted the most in-depth investigation of the movies-delinquency relationship. He found movies to be a factor in the delinquent activities of only a minority of boys and girls, with an indirect effect on crime and delinquency. Still, he found, movies can exert "indirect influences disposing or leading persons to delinquency or crime," including "through the display of crime techniques and criminal patterns of behavior; by arousing desires for easy money and luxury, and by suggesting questionable methods for their achievement; by inducing a spirit of bravado, toughness, and adventurousness; by arousing intense sexual desires; and by invoking daydreaming of criminal roles" (198). Despite scholars' efforts to highlight the complex two-way relationship, the Payne Fund Studies generally affirmed public anxiety about the negative influence of movies on young people and helped

Media phobias: Fears about the negative impacts of media that lead to identifying media as the causes of persistent social problems.

A young boy reads an issue of Ha Ha Comics in New York City, 1946. Other comics on the wall behind him feature Nyota the Jungle Girl, Captain Marvel, Blondie, and Superman.

pave the way for future research on media as a cause of social problems.

Comic books, too, became a focus of concern. In the 1940s and 1950s, critics led by psychiatrist Fredric Wertham (1954) identified the reading of comic books as a cause of juvenile delinquency. Wertham argued that comic books' frequent depictions of violence, crime, and horror glamorize crime and teach criminal techniques, effectively promoting crime, delinquency, and generally antisocial behavior among youth. A U.S. Senate subcommittee on juvenile delinquency held hearings on comic books in 1954, with Wertham as a prominent witness. Other social scientists weighed in to support Wertham's critique, including C. Wright Mills (1954), who offered a glowing review of Wertham's book *Seduction of the Innocent*, which was published just a few days after the hearings.

Yet social science research findings demonstrating a relationship between comic book reading and juvenile delinquency were scant. As sociologist Frederic Thrasher (1949, 205), who had previously been involved in the Payne Fund Studies, argued, "It may be said that no

Self-regulation: A process whereby media industries propose to police themselves to stave off the imposition of government regulation.

Media Violence

acceptable evidence has been produced by Wertham or anyone else for the conclusion that the reading of comic magazines has, or has not a significant relation to delinquent behavior." Later research found little evidence of a comic book–delinquency connection, and a 1980 study concluded, "This study does not support the hypothesis that reading violent comic books leads to greater aggression among children" (Tan and Scruggs 1980, 583).

In response to the hearings and to widespread publicity, the comic book industry adopted a proactive plan of **self-regulation**, proposing to police itself to stave off government regulation. Some of the principles of the code the industry initiated appear in Table 8.2.

The Payne Fund Studies of motion pictures and Wertham's critique of comic books helped sustain the idea that media can be more than simple entertainment, that they offer genuine educational opportunities, and that government has an interest in promoting policies that support public-spirited educational forms of media (see McChesney 1996). With television rapidly emerging as the dominant form of U.S. media in the 1950s, the earlier debates about movies and comics served as backdrop to an ongoing battle over television's role, if any, in causing or worsening social problems.

Media and Violence

Violence is a foundation of contemporary television, so common that many viewers find it unremarkable. Television executives believe violence sells, that viewers—especially highly coveted young adults—are attracted to

TABLE 8.2 Select Stipulations of the 1954 Comics Code Adopted by the Comic Magazine Association of America

• Policemen, judges, government officials and respected institutions shall never be presented in such a way as to create disrespect for established authority.
• No comics shall explicitly present the unique details and methods of a crime.
• All scenes of horror, excessive bloodshed, gory or gruesome crimes, depravity, lust, sadism, masochism shall not be permitted.
• Profanity, obscenity, smut, vulgarity or words or symbols that have acquired undesirable meanings are forbidden.

SOURCE: Quoted in Hajdu, David. 2008. *The Ten-Cent Plague: The Great Comic Book Scare and How it Changed America*. New York: Farrar, Straus and Giroux.

violent programming. Why do some viewers find media violence compelling? What are the limits of its allure?

The underlying question of much research in this area is whether watching violent television promotes violent behavior, and, if so, how much. By analyzing the relationship between consuming violent entertainment and enacting real-world violence, researchers may increase understanding of, and perhaps help to alleviate, social problems associated with violence.

On the surface, questions about the influence of television violence are straightforward and intuitive. Television violence (and, more generally, media violence) is pervasive. Young people ages 8 to 18 watch, on average, more than four hours of television each day (Rideout, Foehr, and Roberts 2010) (see Table 8.3), and much popular programming includes violent images, themes, and events. In this context, it is reasonable to ask whether regular exposure to images of violence has any significant influence on viewers' behavior, attitudes, or understanding of their world.

Let's begin with the most direct question. Does television violence cause real-world violence? The answer appears to be simple common sense. How could watching heavy doses of violence on television *not* encourage people to commit acts of violence by glorifying violent behavior, suggesting that violence is rewarding, depicting violence as an acceptable way to resolve conflict, encouraging imitation, and linking violence and aggression with pleasure?

It is difficult, however, to establish a clear causal link between television violence and violent behavior. In laboratory experiments, psychologists have found that exposure to violent television images produces a short-term increase in aggressive feelings. Some lab experiments have shown that watching violent television increases postviewing aggressive behavior, such as playing aggressively with toys, and in some surveys viewers have reported an increase in aggressive behavior after watching violent television (Comstock 2008).

While many researchers accept that there is a relationship between violent television and aggression, the specific

TABLE 8.3 **TV Viewing in Hours per Day among 8- to 18-Year-Olds in the United States, 2010**

	Among all	AGE			GENDER		RACE/ETHINICITY			PARENTS' EDUCATION		
		8–10	11–14	15–18	Boy	Girl	White	Black	Hispanic	High School or Less	Some College	College +
Live TV	2:39	2:26	3:00	2:25	2:46	2:33	2:14	3:23	3:08	2:47	2:54	2:27
Time-shifted TV												
On Demand	:12	:11	:16	:09	:13	:11	:11	:21	:11	:11	:15	:12
Self-recorded (Tivo/DVR/VCR)	:09	:09	:10	:09	:10	:08	:09	:14	:07	:09	:09	:10
DVDs/Videos												
On a TV	:26	:21	:31	:24	:26	:26	:24	:27	:25	:31	:30	:22
On a computer	:06	:07	:06	:06	:07	:06	:03	:08	:11	:08	:05	:06
TV on other platforms												
Internet	:24	:16	:30	:24	:25	:23	:17	:37	:30	:25	:23	:23
iPod/Mp3 player	:16	:07	:16	:23	:18	:15	:08	:20	:29	:21	:21	:12
Cell phone	:15	:06	:15	:22	:14	:17	:09	:23	:19	:14	:19	:15
TOTAL TV CONTENT	4:29	3:41	5:03	4:22	4:40	4:18	3:36	5:54	5:21	4:46	4:55	4:07

SOURCE: *Generation M2: Media in the Lives of 8- to 18-Year-Olds* by Victoria J. Rideout, Ulla G. Foehr, and Donald F. Roberts. January 20, 2010. A Kaiser Family Foundation Study.

dynamics of that relationship remain contested. Perhaps most important, the evidence linking media violence to violent behavior—the core of the claim that violent television is a key cause of violence-related social problems—is weak. This should come as no surprise. Aggression, even aggressive play, in a laboratory setting is clearly different from real-world violent behavior. If we want to understand the potential relationship between consuming violent media and acting aggressively or violently, we need to recognize all the other factors that intervene. Children attracted to media violence, and compulsive viewers of media violence, are likely different in important respects from viewers less interested in media violence. Similarly, some children may find that televised violence—and other forms of entertainment violence—provides an arena for working through their emotions, including feelings of aggression, in the world of fantasy. And differently situated viewers may respond differently to distinct forms of television violence.

This is notoriously tricky terrain to navigate. There is good reason to be wary of television violence. It crowds out other kinds of television, and, to many viewers (and parents), it ranges from distasteful to downright scary. But this does not mean it causes violent behavior or juvenile crime. There is no simple consensus about which specific forms of television violence are most worrisome. For example, if you worry that media violence causes violent behavior, which of these kinds of violent television programs do you find most troubling?

1. A prime-time drama focused on the grisly activities of a serial killer

2. A broadcast of the *Lord of the Rings* film trilogy

3. A news program with images of graphic violence from the war in Afghanistan

4. A dramatic reality program about local law enforcement

5. An animated comedy full of ostensibly humorous family violence

Is it the sheer magnitude of the violence on display? Its goriness or casualness? The degree to which it appears to be real? The viewer's emotional connection to the perpetrators or the victims? The perpetrators' identities as authorities or criminals? Let's face it. Daily news viewers and *Lord of the Rings* fans are likely to object to different forms of television violence.

Let's return to the core question. Does watching television cause violent behavior? There is little empirical basis for an answer of yes. When one criminologist weighed in on the effects of media violence, she concluded: "The evidence suggests that there is no urgency in addressing the

THE AVENGING ANGEL RETURNS

The television series *Dexter*, which aired originally from 2006 to 2013, features the character of Dexter Morgan, a Miami blood-spatter forensics expert who moonlights as a serial killer of criminals who, he believes, have escaped justice. The drama depicts dismembered bodies and ritual killings in a "kill room" that Dexter has set up for that purpose.

media violence problem under the auspices of preventing violent crime. Even a generous reading of the literature suggests that these effects are very small by comparison with the effects of other factors" (Savage 2008, 1134).

Even if watching violent television does not cause violent crime, other potential links between televised violence and social problems merit attention. For instance, scholars have found that violent television—and other forms of media violence—can affect the way people understand and respond to violence in their communities.

Consuming a regular diet of television violence may also desensitize viewers to violence in the real world by making it ordinary, taken for granted. Communication scholar Erica Scharrer (2008, 301) summarizes how desensitization occurs "through the long-term development of emotional tolerance, in which individuals become inured through repeated exposure to violence, ultimately registering a diminished physiological response as well as a higher threshold at which to label something as violent and a greater tendency to think of violence as simply part of the everyday fabric of society."

Watching television violence may also enhance viewers' fear of violence. For example, television programs show crime and violence far more frequently than they occur in real life, and these portrayals seem to influence heavy viewers, who are more likely than others to worry about crime and violence in their own lives (Gerbner et al. 1994). During the 1990s, the volume of crime stories on television news increased dramatically, though real violent crime declined throughout the decade. In creating entertaining and emotionally engaging stories, news outlets can promote fear and anxiety and contribute to the widespread expectation that we are all in danger, contradicting the actual data on crime rates (Altheide 2002, 2009).

Sexual Politics
of Nudity on TV

George Gerbner and his colleagues (1986, 10) labeled this the "mean world" syndrome, whereby "for most viewers, television's mean and dangerous world tends to cultivate a sense of relative danger, mistrust, dependence, and—despite its supposedly 'entertaining' nature—alienation and gloom."

Of course, the relationship between media and public attitudes is complex; both media content and audience experiences matter. Local news seems especially influential in promoting fear of crime, regardless of actual local crime rates (Escholz, Chiricos, and Gertz 2003; Romer, Jamieson, and Aday 2003). Reality television programs about law enforcement also seem to promote fear of crime. Audience experiences are influential, too; one study found that local news viewing enhanced fear of crime among all kinds of viewers, but especially viewers in high-crime neighborhoods, those with recent experiences as crime victims, and those who perceived crime stories as realistic (Chiricos, Padgett, and Gertz 2000).

Scholars have asked many of the same questions about violence in video games, which sometimes occurs in highly realistic settings. The popular game *Grand Theft Auto* is a case in point. While many perceive it as a satiric commentary on violence in U.S. society, the game has attracted considerable attention because players are permitted to kill police officers and engage in other violent and criminal behaviors. Some studies have found that playing violent video games desensitizes players to real-world violence and can increase aggressive behavior (Bartholow, Sestir, and Davis 2005; Carnagey, Anderson, and Bushman 2007). However, there is no simple consensus on the effects, and other researchers argue that concerns are overstated (Ferguson 2007; Kutner and Olson 2008).

Ads, Films, and Youth Smoking

Media have also been implicated in social problems related to health, especially among youth. Tobacco advertising has long portrayed cigarette smoking as sexy, cool, mature, and independent, and most research suggests such ads are effective in promoting smoking among adolescents. One comprehensive review evaluated studies in a variety of countries, including Australia, England, India, Japan, Norway, Spain, and the United States, and the researchers conclude that tobacco ad campaigns work: "Exposure to promotion causes children to initiate tobacco use" (DiFranza et al. 2006, 1244).

Hollywood films also appear to have a significant impact on attitudes and behaviors regarding tobacco. The National Cancer Institute's in-depth review *The Role of the Media in Promoting and Reducing Tobacco Use* (2008) shows that studies using various research methods have all yielded similar findings about the influence

Joe Camel was a character used to advertise Camel cigarettes from 1987 to 1997; he appeared in magazines, billboards, and, as shown in this photo, on the side of a building in New York City. Highly recognizable, Joe Camel was presented in various entertaining situations and in bold and bright colors. The R. J. Reynolds Tobacco Company denied that the character was directed at the under-18 market. What do you think?

of smoking in the movies. High levels of exposure to on-screen smoking are associated with more positive beliefs about tobacco and higher rates of smoking. The authors conclude: "Along with the results of cross-sectional and longitudinal population-based studies, experimental research indicates that images of smoking in film can influence people's beliefs about social norms for smoking, beliefs about the function and consequences of smoking, and ultimately their personal propensity to smoke" (392).

Media are certainly not the sole, or even the primary, cause of youth tobacco use. Family members who smoke, connections to peer smokers, and various psychological traits also influence youth smoking habits. But tobacco advertisements and a steady dose of smoking images in popular culture—including those resulting from **product placement**, in which manufacturers pay for their products to be used or mentioned by film or television characters—can effectively promote smoking. By associating cigarettes with adventure, sexuality, and adult lifestyles, media help to sustain a set of cultural meanings that define smoking in terms that are attractive to some youth.

Media and Obesity

We've seen that the definition of obesity as an "epidemic" in recent years highlights the role of media in constructing social problems. At the same time, scholars and public health officials have identified media as a *contributor* to the growth in childhood obesity (Brown and

Product placement: A form of advertising in which products are used or mentioned by film or television characters.

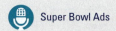
Super Bowl Ads

Bobkowski 2011): "Most large national cross-sectional studies and several longitudinal studies indicate that children who spend more time with media are more likely to be overweight than children who don't" (Kaiser Family Foundation 2004, 10). What dynamic produces the connection between media use and obesity? It is possible, for example, that children who are heavy media users are less active, and their lower levels of physical activity help cause weight gain. And the vast amount of advertising aimed at children for high-calorie, nonnutritious fast food, sugary snacks, and soda appears to have an impact on their dietary habits that leads to an increase in obesity.

Children in the early 21st century are deluged by more advertisements than were the children of any previous generation. In the 1970s, children watched an estimated 20,000 television commercials per year; by the 1990s this figure had doubled, to 40,000 a year (Kunkel 2001), and it has continued to increase in the 2000s. Today's children are also exposed to heavy advertising in other media platforms, including online, in video games, and on billboards.

Many children have a keen awareness of themselves as consumers and are often the first in their households to try new media technologies. In her study of children's consumption, *Born to Buy*, sociologist Juliet Schor (2004, 11) points out, "Children have become conduits from the consumer marketplace into the household, the link between advertisers and the family purse." As a result, children drive many forms of family consumption, often pressuring parents until they relent or using their own allowances to purchase products. Advertisers understand this process and have learned to target children accordingly.

In response to concerns about media as a factor in childhood obesity, the Walt Disney Company in 2012 instituted a requirement that foods appearing in its children's television, radio, and website programming meet strict nutritional guidelines. According to the *New York Times*, the new guidelines would lead to a change in the food items advertised to children: "Products like Capri Sun drinks and Kraft Lunchables meals—both current Disney advertisers—along with a wide range of candy, sugared cereal and fast food, will no longer be acceptable advertising material" (Barnes 2012, B1).

Disney executives were quick to point out that promoting nutrition among children is good business for a kid-oriented brand, and First Lady Michelle Obama praised Disney's commitment, encouraging other media companies to develop similar nutritional standards. With continuing research showing a link between food ads and obesity—a 2012 study found youth who recognize fast-food advertisements are more likely to be obese (American Academy of Pediatrics 2012)—pressure on media to develop new advertising guidelines is likely to grow.

Media and Eating Disorders

Sociologists and feminist scholars have long recognized that eating disorders such as anorexia and bulimia are more than just individual troubles. Defining eating disorders as a social problem leads us to consider the cultural norms that contribute to them (Hesse-Biber et al. 2006).

Many young people, disproportionately girls, desire thinner bodies. Roughly half of elementary school–age and adolescent girls in the United States are dissatisfied with their body weight (Sischo, Taylor, and Martin 2006). More than half of teenage girls and almost one-third of teenage boys "use unhealthy weight control behaviors such as skipping meals, fasting, smoking cigarettes, vomiting, and taking laxatives" (Neumark-Sztainer 2005, 5). Those who struggle with eating disorders such as anorexia nervosa (an unwillingness to eat, accompanied by a distorted sense of being overweight) or bulimia (binge eating, often accompanied by attempts to rid the body of its effects through purging) are conforming to cultural norms that encourage thinness but following extreme—and dangerous—methods to achieve an exaggeration of the culturally preferred body type.

Media play a prominent role in promoting and circulating what sociologist Sharlene Hesse-Biber (2006) calls the **cult of thinness**, which idealizes a decidedly slim body type unachievable for the vast majority of the

Two women look at a billboard showing an emaciated naked woman in Milan, Italy. The picture, used to promote the Italian women's clothing brand Nolita, appeared in double-page spreads in Italian newspapers and on city billboards to coincide with fashion week in Milan. Do you think that images like this have any effect on viewers beyond the immediate one of shock?

Cult of thinness: Idealization of a decidedly slim body type that is unachievable for the vast majority of the population.

population. While little evidence suggests that exposure to media *causes* eating disorders, media are among the central communicators of this cultural ideal (Stice and Shaw 1994), equating a slender body with beauty, intelligence, morality, and success.

Entertainment media—from prime-time television programs and Hollywood films to fashion magazines and music videos—routinely emphasize the virtues of the thin body, not always subtly. One review of research on images of the female body in contemporary visual media notes that the findings "can be easily summarized in two phrases: 'thin is normative and attractive' and 'fat is aberrant and repulsive'" (Levine and Harrison 2009, 494).

Advertising, however, may be the most consistent promoter of the ideal of the thin body. Ads for products from clothing and automobiles to beer and vacation packages typically feature slender bodies as part of the sales pitch. Advertisements about products and services associated with dieting and weight loss, exercise and fitness, and even cosmetic surgery highlight thin bodies and promote body dissatisfaction among potential consumers. In his pioneering study of the development of the emergence of consumer culture in the early 20th century, *Captains of Consciousness,* Stuart Ewen (1977) reminds us that mass advertising encourages potential customers to be dissatisfied with their bodies as a way to build demand for new consumer products. It can be difficult to escape an ad culture that consistently bombards us with reminders that we are not as thin as the bodies on billboards, in magazines, and on television—and that we can (and should!) do something to change our bodies. This idealization is so deeply embedded in our cultural fabric that we may not even recognize the ways media images celebrate the cult of thinness.

Some user-generated media content can idealize the thin body quite aggressively. A number of so-called pro-ana or pro-mia websites support women seeking to maintain an anorexic or bulimic lifestyle (Boero and Pasco 2012). Blogs, social networks, and websites offer an online community where persons with anorexia and bulimia share dieting tips, fasting strategies, purging techniques, and advice on how to hide these practices from family and friends. These sites display "thinspiration" photos showing remarkably thin women as models to inspire those who deny that their eating habits are unhealthy or in need of treatment.

Media do not simply or directly cause social problems, but the relationship between media and social problems is complex and contested. Now we turn to several examples of evolving social problems associated with new forms of media.

EMERGENT SOCIAL PROBLEMS AND NEW MEDIA TECHNOLOGY

 8.4 Discuss emergent social problems associated with new media technologies.

Digital media offer many ways to interact with friends, community, and work colleagues as well as to take courses and engage in politics. Some of the ways we use new media are also producing new kinds of social problems.

Distracted Driving

Although the combination of alcohol consumption and driving have been a cause of accidents since the development of automobiles, and U.S. states started passing laws against drunk driving in 1910, drunk driving did not emerge as a widely recognized social problem until the early 1980s, thanks to advocacy by Mothers Against Drunk Driving (MADD) and others. Just as dangerous as drunk driving is **distracted driving**, operating a motor vehicle while engaged in other attention-requiring activities (Strayer, Drews, and Crouch 2006), and the proliferation of smart phones offers increased possibilities for distracted driving.

Do you send text or e-mail messages while you drive? The National Highway Traffic Safety Administration (NHTSA) says that more than 40% of drivers between the ages of 18 and 24 report sometimes doing so. You probably know this is a hazardous activity. In fact, the NHTSA (2012a) estimates that "there are at least 3,000 deaths annually from distraction-affected crashes—crashes in which drivers lost focus on the safe control of their vehicles due to manual, visual, or cognitive distraction," and texting is among the most common ways drivers are distracted.

Individuals recognize the dangers of distracted driving. The Pew Research Center found that 44% of adults and 40% of teens report having been in a car when a driver used a cell phone in a dangerous way (Madden and Rainie 2010). With mounting evidence of its toll—3,331 people were killed in 2011 in crashes attributed to distracted driving in the United States, and 387,000 were injured—the U.S. Department of Transportation has been among the primary advocates seeking to frame distracted driving as a social problem. U.S. Secretary of Transportation Ray LaHood has

....

Distracted driving: The operation of a motor vehicle while engaged in other attention-requiring activities, such as texting or talking on the phone.

FIGURE 8.3 Cell Phone Use and Texting-while-Driving Laws, 2013

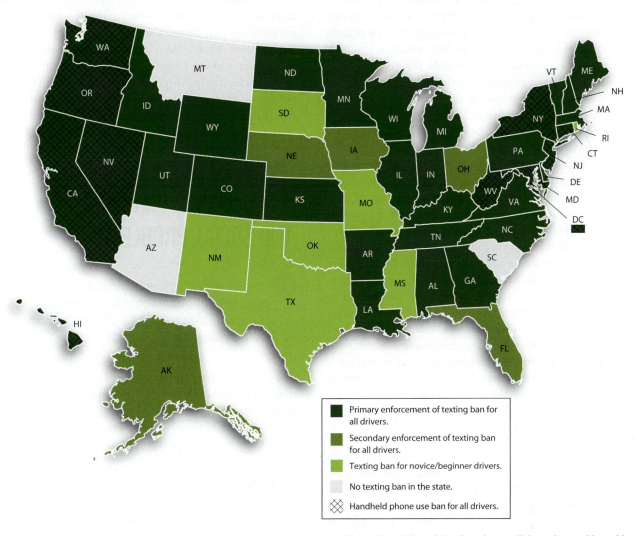

Legend:
- Primary enforcement of texting ban for all drivers.
- Secondary enforcement of texting ban for all drivers.
- Texting ban for novice/beginner drivers.
- No texting ban in the state.
- Handheld phone use ban for all drivers.

NOTE: Under secondary laws, an officer must have some other reason to stop a vehicle before citing a driver for using a cellphone. Laws without this restriction are called primary.

SOURCE: U.S. Department of Transportation, 2013, National Highway Traffic Safety Administration, *State Laws on Distracted Driving*.

called distracted driving "an epidemic of America's roadways," and the Department of Transportation has launched an information website devoted to the problem (http://www.distraction.gov).

Thanks, in part, to government efforts to define it as a serious social problem, distracted driving is becoming an issue of public concern. Many high school health classes and driver education programs now emphasize its dangers, most states have passed laws specifically outlawing texting while driving (see Figure 8.3), and the news media are full of stories about distracted driving.

Cyberbullying: Electronic forms of bullying.

ASK YOURSELF: Is distracted driving recognized as a serious problem among your network of friends? Why or why not? How do attitudes about distracted driving compare with attitudes about drunk driving?

Cyberbullying

Several high-profile cases of repeated harassment through text messages and on social networking sites, including incidents in Missouri and Massachusetts that involved teenage suicides, helped make **cyberbullying**, or electronic forms of bullying, an issue of national concern.

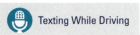

Texting While Driving

Definitions of what constitutes cyberbullying are still evolving, as are the legal issues associated with mediated and sometimes anonymous harassment and appropriate sanctions, if any. Cyberbullying usually follows a pattern of repetitive actions, such as sending hostile or insulting text messages, posting inappropriate photos to embarrass someone, and rumormongering and harassment on social networks. Two leading scholars of cyberbullying offer the following definition: "willful and repeated harm inflicted through the use of computers, cell phones, and other electronic devices" (Hinduja and Patchin 2009, 5).

The primary victims and perpetrators are teenagers. Research suggests cyberbullying "is a prevalent problem, similar to school bullying," experienced by up to one-quarter of students (Wade and Beran 2011, 45). Educators, parents, and others who work with young people have succeeded in identifying cyberbullying as an issue of public concern, and the media have helped focus public attention on the problem. The federal government includes information about reporting and preventing cyberbullying on its StopBullying.gov website, and the U.S. Centers for Disease Control and Prevention distributes information about how to protect youth from electronic aggression. Any sustained public discussion of cyberbullying will need to recognize how it is similar to traditional forms of bullying, as well as how new media technologies make it different.

The Digital Divide

Evolving media technologies offer the potential for new forms of civic engagement, more flexible work schedules, new patterns of global communication, even innovative solutions to social problems. High hopes for these possibilities, however, are tempered by the fact that all forms of media are not equally accessible to all individuals, nationally or globally. The consumption of media requires money, and the richer nations that own and produce most global media also disproportionately consume media.

In the United States, class is the primary determinant of the **digital divide**. In 2011, about 93% of U.S. households with annual incomes of at least $100,000 had high-speed Internet connections at home (see Table 8.4). In contrast, only 43% of households with annual income below $25,000 had the same access (National Telecommunications and Information Administration 2013). Inequality in Internet access intersects with other social issues. For example, the Internet offers new possibilities for communication between health care providers and their patients. However, one study of community health center patients in a low-income urban neighborhood found that a large percentage did not regularly access the Internet from home. The researchers note that these

"findings overall support the ongoing concerns about a 'digital divide' and should make clinicians in this clinic cautious about referring patients to the internet for health information" (Denizard-Thompson et al. 2011, 458).

As more people gain access to electronic media, the influence of these media will continue to grow, playing an increasingly powerful role in social life. However, persistent economic inequality will continue to create socially significant inequities in media access and use.

TRADITIONAL THEORETICAL PERSPECTIVES ON MEDIA AND SOCIAL PROBLEMS

 8.5 Explain how the functionalist, conflict, and symbolic interactionist perspectives conceptualize the media–social problems relationship.

The three traditional sociological perspectives—functionalism, conflict theory, and symbolic interactionism—are significant for the kinds of questions they direct us to consider. Let's look at how each applies to the intersection of media and social problems.

Functionalism

A functionalist approach suggests that media play the vital role of calling attention to pressing social problems, functioning as a kind of alarm system that can warn and inform the public about new and persistent social problems. From this perspective, media are a vital cultural resource, an arena for both official distribution of information about problems and public deliberation about potential solutions. For example, media have played a vital role in calling attention to problems associated with smoking, and public health officials define a robust antismoking advertising campaign as a powerful form of public education (Centers for Disease Control and Prevention 2013a). At the same time, the functionalist approach asks whether the media industry's dynamics make the

Digital divide: The gap in access to information and communication technologies between more advantaged and less advantaged groups, such as between the wealthy and poor regions of the world (the global digital divide) and between social classes within a country.

Media beyond Our Borders

The Global Digital Divide

According to the International Telecommunications Union (ITU 2013), approximately 40% of the world's population was online in 2013. However, citizens of the developed world (77%) are more than twice as likely as people in the developing world (31%) to be online. In Europe, 75% of the population has Internet access, while 61% of people in the Americas are online. In contrast, the Internet is available to just 32% in Asia and the Pacific and only 16% in Africa.

While many North Americans and Europeans can access news and information from around the globe, network with like-minded people near and far, and explore online virtual worlds, most people in the so-called global South have little or no access to basic Internet service. Instead, they live in a world where even regularly delivered electricity can be a scarce commodity. Recognizing the significance of the global digital divide, two agencies of the United Nations, the ITU and UNESCO (United Nations Educational, Scientific and Cultural Organization), established the Broadband Commission for Digital Development to try to expand global Internet access. In 2011, the commission established four goals for all countries that

members defined as "ambitious but achievable" broadband targets for 2015:

1. Establish a national strategy for making broadband a universally accessible service.

Paulo Whitaker / Reuters

Brazilian indigenous people use computers inside a tent in Cuiaba, Brazil. Who does and does not have access to computers is an important question for media sociologists. In countries such as China and Myanmar (formerly Burma) in the Far East and Iran and Saudi Arabia in the Middle East, censorship of the Internet is pervasive. Should governments limit their citizens' access to the Internet? Should there be any censorship at all?

2. Make basic broadband service affordable in developing countries, at less than 5% of average monthly income.

3. Increase the number of home Internet connections, with a target of 40% of homes in developing countries.

4. Increase global Internet use by facilitating access at work, school, and in public places, with a goal of 60% worldwide, 50% in developing countries, and at least a 15% penetration rate in the least developed countries.

The rapid development of various mobile communications technologies may offer new ways of challenging digital inequality.

Even so, achieving results will require a consistent commitment from national governments, international organizations, and the telecommunications industry, beginning with defining the global digital divide as a social problem.

▶ **THINK ABOUT IT**

1. What do you think are the social and economic consequences of the global digital divide?

2. How, if at all, do you think new forms of mobile communications technology will help reduce the global digital divide?

---

alarm system dysfunctional, calling selective attention to social problems in a way that undermines a working public information system. We might consider, for example, how the media system operates when companies that are heavy polluters are also major sources of advertising dollars for national news outlets.

ASK YOURSELF: With so much media content circulating in the digital age, do you think televised ad campaigns can effectively sound the alarm about troubling issues? Do you think graphic antismoking commercials are effective at curbing youth smoking, for example? Why or why not?

TABLE 8.4 Home Internet Connections for U.S. Households, 2011 (in percentages)

	Computer Ownership	Internet Use	Broadband Adoption
Family Income			
Income < $25,000	52	46	43
Income $25,000–$49,999	73	68	65
Income $50,000–$74,999	89	86	84
Income $75,000–$599,999	93	92	90
Income $100,000 or more	95	95	93
Householder Education			
No high school diploma	43	37	35
High school diploma	65	61	58
Some college	82	77	75
College degree or more	92	90	88
Metropolitan Status			
Rural	67	62	58
Urban	77	74	72
Householder Race and Ethnicity			
White	80	76	74
African American	62	57	55
Hispanic	63	58	56
Asian American	85	83	81
Household Type			
Households with school-age children	84	81	79
Households without school-age children	73	69	66
Householder Age			
16 to 44 years	82	79	77
45 to 64 years	79	76	73
65 years and older	56	52	49
Householder Disability Status			
Has a disability	53	48	46
Does not have a disability	79	76	73
All households	76	72	69

SOURCE: *Exploring the Digital Nation: America's Emerging Online Experience.* National Telecommunications and Information Administration.

Policy Implications of Functionalism

From a functionalist perspective, public policy should promote a media system that broadly distributes information and ideas about a wide range of social issues and promotes free expression and vigorous public debate. Public policy that protects press freedom, including in digital media and often referencing the First Amendment, is consistent with this approach. Efforts to restrict online speech—such as the Communications Decency Act of 1996 and the Child Online Protection Act of 1998, two failed efforts to restrict expression on the Internet—are likely to weaken the media system's ability to operate effectively in the collective process of defining social problems.

Conflict Theory

A conflict theory approach identifies media as a contested arena, where powerful actors seek to promote their definitions of social problems. In thinking about media and power, conflict theorists ask us to consider who owns and controls media, and how ownership patterns shape media portrayals of social problems. We should also consider how powerful actors seek to influence media representations of social issues, promoting coverage of some and downplaying others. In addition, conflict theory highlights the relationships among media, social problems, and inequality, asking how media can either reinforce or challenge social problems rooted in social and economic inequality.

Andy Rain / epa / Corbis

Demonstrators wearing masks of Prime Minister David Cameron (left) and media tycoon Rupert Murdoch (right) protest outside Parliament in London, England. The demonstrators called on the government to support the imposition of a 20% limit on how much of Britain's media any one person or company can own. Murdoch is the CEO of News Corporation, one of the largest and most influential media groups in the world. He owns a great number of media-related businesses, including Fox News and the *Wall Street Journal.*

For example, news and entertainment media offer a steady diet of dramatic stories about crime and the police, but a conflict perspective suggests that media's general inattention to the causes, consequences, and racial dynamics of mass incarceration in the United States actually reinforces social inequality. In short, from a conflict theory perspective, media are significant precisely because they are a valuable resource both for dominant groups that seek to exercise power over what we recognize as social problems and what solutions are considered legitimate and for subordinate groups that oppose or resist such definitions.

Policy Implications of Conflict Theory

With its emphasis on questions of ownership and control, a conflict theory approach suggests that media policy can effectively limit powerful actors' capacity to influence media representations of social issues. Federal regulations that prevent companies from owning both television stations and daily newspapers in the same markets, for example, are part of a larger policy agenda to promote diverse ownership and stop the trend toward media consolidation. Policies governing the operation of the Internet—including "net neutrality," the principle that Internet service providers cannot discriminate among or charge users differently for different kinds of online applications and content—spark substantial debate about media power.

Symbolic Interactionism

A symbolic interactionist approach to media and social problems says social problems emerge from "a process of collective definition" (Blumer 1971) in the news and entertainment media. Symbolic interactionist theories are generally associated with the micro-level dimensions of social life. Through interaction, in other words, individuals create a shared understanding of reality, including definitions of what constitute legitimate social problems as well as reasonable potential responses. Interactionist approaches can offer insight into how media workers—including journalists, editors, bloggers, filmmakers, and television producers—define social problems within their professional communities.

Symbolic interactionists consider, for example, how reporters learn about, discuss, and ultimately identify concussions among young athletes as a serious problem worthy of ongoing, in-depth news coverage. They also look at the way people interact with and interpret media representations of social problems, as well as how media inform public discussion about the meaning, significance of, and potential responses to long-standing and new social problems.

Policy Implications of Symbolic Interactionism

A symbolic interactionist approach has little to say about the content of specific media; instead, it looks at the policy-making process and the way policy makers collectively define media goals and possibilities. How, for example, do federal regulators interact with members of the public, with representatives of the media industry, and with media policy experts as they develop, implement, and evaluate media policies? This perspective also suggests that we should pay attention to the ways policy advocates identify media-related social problems and frame social problems to mobilize constituents and pressure policy makers.

THEORIES IN CONTEMPORARY MEDIA AND SOCIAL PROBLEMS SCHOLARSHIP

 8.6 Explain how contemporary theories conceptualize the media–social problems relationship.

While traditional theoretical perspectives offer a broad foundation for the study of social problems, the more specialized constructionist, public arenas, and agenda-setting theories help us understand the role of media in the processes of defining, disseminating, and responding to social problems.

Constructionist Approach

The most fully developed theory of social problems is the **constructionist approach** (Schneider 1985; Kitsuse and Spector 2000; Loseke and Best 2003), which highlights the process by which troubling social issues become recognized as social problems. Constructionists acknowledge a vast pool of candidate issues, only some of which gain the status of legitimate social problem. Objective measures of the prevalence, severity, or danger of a social issue are not the principal determinants of a social problem's status in the constructionist view, although advocates may invoke them. Instead, constructionists ask *how* issues become problems, and they see media as a central part of the process.

Public Arenas Model

One theoretical approach to explaining how public attention is turned toward some social problems and away from others is Hilgartner and Bosk's (1988) **public arenas model**, which offers a framework for analyzing the rise and fall in public attention to different social problems. This model assumes that public attention is limited—not all potential social problems can be the focus of public attention—and highlights media as a primary arena in which "social problems are framed and grow" (58). It identifies several key factors that influence the extent of media attention to social problems, including the "carrying capacity" of media outlets (space in newspapers, time on television, budgets for reporters), the "principles of selection" that guide decisions about media attention to social problems (including drama, novelty, powerful sponsors, and shared understandings of importance), and the patterns of feedback among media and other public arenas, such as Congress and the presidency, the courts, activist groups, religious organizations, research communities, and foundations. The public arenas model helps us to think about how, for example, the emergence of a new social problem such as an increase in the numbers of home foreclosures can squeeze other troubling issues, such as the employment and health challenges facing soldiers returning from combat deployments, out of the media spotlight and off the public agenda.

Sociologist Ray Maratea (2008) has extended the public arenas model to include the blogosphere as a venue for directing public attention to social problems, explaining how blogs, with their near-constant updating and unlimited space, run at a faster pace than traditional media and offer a larger carrying capacity than newspapers or television. Maratea recognizes that bloggers have not supplanted the traditional news media, noting, "While the Internet may indeed provide an expanded capacity to carry problem claims, bloggers must still rely on mainstream news outlets to distribute their claims to larger audiences" (156). The public arenas model offers a helpful framework for making sense of the ways various forms of online media, especially user-generated media and social media, help to focus public attention on social problems.

Agenda-Setting Theory

Media may not tell people what to think, but they can significantly influence what people think *about*. This

....

Constructionist approach: An approach to social problems theory that highlights the process whereby troubling social issues become recognized as social problems.

Public arenas model: A model that offers a framework for analyzing the rise and fall in the amount of attention the public pays to different social problems.

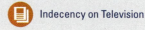 Indecency on Television

ability to direct people's attention toward certain issues is the foundation of **agenda-setting theory**, which emphasizes the role media play in influencing public understanding of social issues and social problems (McCombs 2004). Agenda setting results from patterns of news coverage of (or silence about) social issues and from the relative prominence news gives to various social problems. Early agenda-setting research demonstrated that media coverage of social issues influences public opinion more than does the issues' objective prominence (Funkhouser 1973). Experimental research later confirmed that media coverage influences audience assessments of an issue's importance (Iyengar and Kinder 2010).

....

Agenda-setting theory: A theory that emphasizes the important role media play in influencing public understanding of social issues and social problems.

Still, theorists suggest caution in making generalizations about agenda setting. One study of television news and public opinion in Germany found strong agenda-setting effects for some issues but not for others (Brosius and Kepplinger 1990). The agenda-setting role of media may be most powerful when people have no direct experience with an issue and are therefore dependent on media for basic information. Agenda-setting theory asks us to consider the process through which some social problems—for example, increasing student debt or government surveillance—become matters of broad public concern, highlighting the role of media in that process.

....

ASK YOURSELF: How, if at all, do you think media influence your understanding of which social problems are worthy of public attention?

....

SOCIAL CHANGE: WHAT CAN YOU DO?

8.7 Identify steps toward media-related social change.

Activist organizations often develop media strategies aimed at influencing, and sometimes presenting alternatives to, the narratives that circulate in the major media. Such "media activism" takes a wide variety of forms, with different organizations focused on different media-related problems, offering concerned citizens a range of different ways to get involved.

 ## Media Reform

In the early 2010s, media reform activists began seeking to restructure the U.S. media system, advocating for policies that highlight the public interest stakes in media policy, promote openness and accessibility, and emphasize the democratic role of media. Among the leading media reform organizations is Free Press (http://www.freepress.net), a national organization that "advocates for universal and affordable Internet access, diverse media ownership, vibrant public media and quality journalism." Free Press seeks to democratize the media policy-making process, engage the public in federal media policy decisions through public education

campaigns, mobilize citizens to communicate directly with elected officials, and participate in policy debates in Washington, including ongoing policy research and advocacy. Media reform activists gather every other year at the National Conference for Media Reform, which met most recently in Denver in April 2013. Students can become members of Free Press, sign up for the organization's weekly online newsletter the Media Fix, attend the National Conference for Media Reform, and take action by joining one of Free Press's timely campaigns.

 ## Media Literacy

In our media-saturated society, citizens face a daily barrage of images and messages. Advocates of media literacy argue that citizens need to be equipped with the skills and experiences that will enable them to engage critically with the media they consume and to learn the fundamentals of producing their own media. Some advocates work inside schools, others with community organizations in community centers, libraries, and local media arts organizations. Many efforts are locally focused, such as Healthy Youth Peer Education in Allentown, Pennsylvania, and the Children's Media

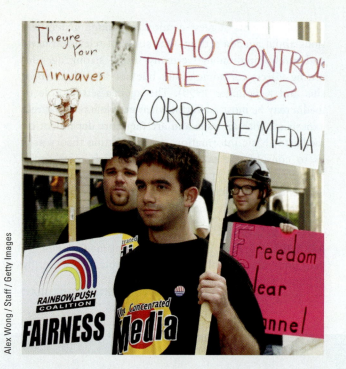

Protesters demonstrating against the Federal Communications Commission (FCC) carry signs outside FCC offices in Washington, D.C. The FCC eased regulations on media ownership, allowing broadcasters to own more television stations or combinations of newspapers, television stations, and radio stations in the same city. Do you see allowing such consolidation in the media industry as good or bad?

Project in Poughkeepsie, New York. Several national media literacy organizations try to connect media literacy activists, forging links among them so they can build strategy and share resources, and develop curricula for school and community use. Among the most prominent of these organizations are the Center for Media Literacy (http://www.medialit.org), which works to help citizens "develop critical thinking and media production skills needed to live fully in the 21st century media culture," and the National Association for Media Literacy Education (http://namle.net), which seeks to

"help individuals of all ages develop the habits of inquiry and skills of expression that they need to be critical thinkers, effective communicators and active citizens in today's world."

Media literacy groups around the United States are sponsored by schools and universities or run by community-based nonprofit organizations. You can become a media literacy activist by joining a group in your community, or by partnering with a local high school or elementary school to develop new media literacy activities. Either way, you will find valuable resources for media literacy education on the Center for Media Literacy's website, including the CML MediaLit Kit.

▶▶ Efforts to Limit Commercialism

With ads appearing almost anywhere we can imagine—from our computer screens and smart phones to inside school buses and pieces of fruit—it is increasingly difficult to identify any commercial-free zones in contemporary society. Some media activists define the omnipresence of advertising as a growing social problem in need of a sustained response. They try to protect and promote public spaces free of constant sales pitches. Commercial Alert (http://www.commercialalert.org), for example, is a national organization dedicated to limiting the reach of commercial culture, seeking to "to prevent it from exploiting children and subverting the higher values of family, community, environmental integrity and democracy." Similarly, the Campaign for Commercial Free Childhood (http://commercialfreechildhood .org) works to build a movement "to end the exploitive practice of marketing to children and promote a modern childhood shaped by what's best for kids, not corporate profits." Both organizations, which offer students various ways to get involved, are part of a growing movement to limit the presence of advertising in media and in public places.

WHAT DOES AMERICA THINK?

Questions about Media from the General Social Survey

 Turn to the beginning of the chapter to compare your answers to the total population.

1. What is your main source of information about events in the news?

   NEWSPAPERS: 12.2%

   THE INTERNET: 30.1%

   TV: 47.9%

   OTHER: 9.8%

2. What is your confidence level in the press?

   A GREAT DEAL: 9.1%

   ONLY SOME: 44.1%

   HARDLY ANY: 46.8%

3. How many hours do you watch TV each day?

   0: 6.9%

   1–2: 44.6%

   3–4: 31.5%

   5 OR MORE: 17%

4. What is your confidence level in television?

   A GREAT DEAL: 10.6%

   ONLY SOME: 48.1%

   HARDLY ANY: 41.3%

5. How often do you read the newspaper?

   DAILY: 27.1%

   A FEW TIMES A WEEK: 17.7%

   ONCE A WEEK: 15%

   LESS THAN ONCE A WEEK: 16.7%

   NEVER: 23.5%

 ## LOOK BEHIND THE NUMBERS

Go to **edge.sagepub.com/trevino** for a breakdown of these data across time and by race, sex, age, income, and other statuses.

1. Examine how responses to the question on confidence in TV break down by education level. Is there a pattern? Is the pattern similar for confidence in the press?

2. If reported confidence in the press is low, why do you think large numbers of people report reading newspapers? If confidence in TV is low, why do you think only 6% of respondents do not watch TV?

3. Do you believe that males and females receive their information about events in the news from similar sources? Explain. Examine the data; do the survey results reflect your thoughts?

4. Examine the General Social Survey data about confidence in the press from 1973 to the present. Is confidence increasing or decreasing? What do you think has influenced this change?

SOURCE: National Opinion Research Center, University of Chicago.

CHAPTER SUMMARY

8.1 Describe the relationship between media and social problems.

Media have a complex and multifaceted connection to social problems. They are embedded in the process of social problem construction, become a focus of concern as a source of social problems, and are associated with emerging social problems.

8.2 Discuss patterns and trends in media portrayals of social problems.

Media offer a prominent space where we debate and interpret the meaning and significance of incidents and trends associated with potential social problems. Journalists' professional routines and the sponsor activities of issue advocates help explain the amount of social problems coverage in the news as well as media approaches to social problems. Media sometimes contribute to moral panics by dramatizing and embellishing social issues to attract an audience.

8.3 Describe the debate about the role of media as a potential cause of social problems.

Researchers have long debated how media exposure might encourage behaviors and attitudes associated with social problems. The 1930s Payne Fund Studies found that movies were a factor in the delinquent activities of only a minority of boys and girls, with an indirect effect on crime and delinquency. While many researchers accept that there is a relationship between violent media and aggression, the specific dynamics of that relationship remain contested—and the evidence linking media violence to violent behavior is weak. Media are not the primary cause of youth tobacco use, but by associating cigarettes with adventure, sexuality, and adult lifestyles, media help to sustain a set of cultural meanings that define smoking in terms that are attractive to some youth. Media play a prominent role in idealizing a slim body type that is unachievable for the vast majority of the population. Little evidence suggests that exposure to media causes eating disorders, but media help to communicate this powerful cultural ideal. Media do not simply or directly cause social problems; the relationship between media and social problems is complex and contested.

8.4 Discuss emergent social problems associated with new media technologies.

Digital media offer us many ways to interact, and some of the ways we use new media are producing new kinds of social problems. Distracted driving, cyberbullying, and the digital divide are emerging as widely recognized social problems, generating both broad public discussion and new government policies.

8.5 Explain how the functionalist, conflict, and symbolic interactionist perspectives conceptualize the media–social problems relationship.

The three traditional sociological perspectives direct us to consider different kinds of questions about media and social problems. A functionalist approach defines media as a kind of alarm system that can warn the public about new and persistent social problems. A conflict theory approach identifies media as a contested arena, where powerful actors seek to promote their definitions of social problems. A symbolic interactionist approach to media and social problems points to the ways people create a shared understanding of reality, including definitions of what constitute legitimate social problems as well as reasonable responses.

8.6 Explain how contemporary theories conceptualize the media–social problems relationship.

Contemporary theories help us understand the role of media in the processes of defining, disseminating, and responding to social problems. The constructionist approach asks how some troubling issues become defined as social problems and sees media as a central part of the process. The public arenas model helps explain the rise and fall in public attention paid to different social problems, highlighting several key factors that influence the extent of media attention to social problems. Agenda-setting theory emphasizes how media influence public understanding of social problems, highlighting patterns of news coverage of social issues and the relative prominence news gives to various social problems.

8.7 Identify steps toward media-related social change.

Media activism takes a variety of forms, with different organizations focused on different media-related problems, offering concerned citizens a range of different ways to get involved. Media reform activists seek to restructure the U.S. media system, advocating for policies that highlight the public interest stakes in media policy, promote openness and accessibility, and emphasize the democratic role of media. Media literacy advocates work to equip citizens with the skills and experiences they need to engage critically with the media they consume and to learn the fundamentals of producing their own media. Media activists concerned about the omnipresence of advertising try to protect and promote public spaces that are free of advertisements.

DISCUSSION QUESTIONS

1. How do media shape what the public sees as a social problem? What role does the objective dimension play in the definition of issues as social problems? What about the subjective dimension?

2. How do sociologists explain the intensity of media coverage of issues such as crime and drug abuse? In what ways do those who report on these issues in the media analyze the data differently from how sociologists do so?

3. How do newer forms of media, such as YouTube, blogs, and social networking sites, shift the coverage of social problems? How do social media shift the focus of the public in defining problems?

4. In what ways is the digital divide an example of a social problem brought about by changing technology? What types of new concerns arise from the latest media technologies? Are these concerns, such as cyberbullying, significantly different from the nontechnological forms of the social problems?

5. According to the conflict perspective, what role do advertisers play in swaying news coverage, or lack of coverage, of certain problems in society?

6. How does functionalism suggest the media can be used to distribute information to society about social issues? What role do social policies that restrict speech play in the distribution of information via media?

7. What does the constructionist approach offer as an explanation for what becomes a legitimate social problem? How are interest groups able to influence the coverage of issues that are important to them in the media and construct the frameworks that society uses to understand the problems?

8. Agenda-setting theory posits that people's attention can be directed toward certain issues. How do the patterns of news coverage arise? What does it mean if an issue is omitted from coverage? Which types of issues are most likely to follow this pattern?

9. How do media contribute to the cultural meanings of smoking, body image, and the like? What can individuals do to curb the negative effects that advertising and news coverage have on society? What can individuals do to encourage more positive advertising and news coverage?

10. In what ways have laws and public policies changed in the United States to embrace and adapt to newer technologies and forms of media? What role do media play in teaching society about the social problems that emerge from newer technologies and how people can address these problems?

KEY TERMS

agenda-setting theory 213

claims making 193

constructionist approach 212

cult of thinness 205

culturally resonant themes 196

cyberbullying 207

digital divide 208

distracted driving 206

journalists' professional routines 194

media exaggeration 198

media frames 195

media phobias 200

moral entrepreneurs 193

moral panics 197

product placement 204

public arenas model 212

self-regulation 201

sponsor activities 195

user-generated media content 199

A personalized approach to help you accomplish your coursework goals in an easy-to-use learning environment.

FAMILY

Meg Wilkes Karraker

Mariana Bazo / Reuters

 Two men sit in front of a mural depicting the Simpsons in Lima, Peru. The Simpsons is seen by millions of people throughout the world. If this program were the only window into life in the United States, how do you think people in other countries would see the typical middle-class American family?

Investigating Family: My Story

Meg Wilkes Karraker

I often tell students about my father, Herbert Wilkes, born in a rural area in the South still known for staggering poverty and associated social problems. Abandoned by his father, Herbert dropped out of high school. Although he was one of the smartest and hardest-working people I have ever known, I hate to think how different his life, and perhaps my own, would have been had history not been in his favor. A decorated veteran of three wars (World War II, the Korean War, the Vietnam War), he drew the attention of a commanding officer who shepherded him on to Officer Candidate School.

My father also had the good fortune to fall in love with Mary, a home economics teacher whose family had also struggled. My mother helped my father "polish" his presentation of self to fit him for further opportunities. In exchange, she saw the world, making loving homes for my sister and me as we moved around the United States and Europe every three years.

When my father retired from the army as a lieutenant colonel, he had completed his graduate equivalency degree. Within a year he had a B.A. in sociology and then worked with the South Carolina Department of Corrections until his second retirement. My mother returned to teaching and completed her own master's degree.

During their half century of marriage, Herbert and Mary exemplified the role not only of biography but also of social structure in shaping individual opportunity. They have long inspired me in my own sociological quest to understand families and society.

LEARNING OBJECTIVES

9.1 Define the concept of family.

9.2 Discuss patterns and trends in marriage, cohabitation, and divorce.

9.3 Describe family problems related to economics, religion, and government.

9.4 Apply the functionalist, conflict, and symbolic interactionist perspectives to the concept of family.

9.5 Apply specialized theories to the family.

9.6 Identify steps toward social change to address family problems.

WHAT DO YOU THINK?
Questions about Family from the General Social Survey

1. Children are a financial burden on parents.
   - ☐ AGREE
   - ☐ DISAGREE
   - ☐ NEITHER AGREE NOR DISAGREE

2. Same-sex female couple can raise a child as well as a male-female couple.
   - ☐ AGREE
   - ☐ DISAGREE
   - ☐ NEITHER AGREE NOR DISAGREE

3. Having children increases social standing in society.
   - ☐ AGREE
   - ☐ DISAGREE
   - ☐ NEITHER AGREE NOR DISAGREE

4. Same-sex male couple can raise a child as well as a male-female couple.
   - ☐ AGREE
   - ☐ DISAGREE
   - ☐ NEITHER AGREE NOR DISAGREE

5. Single parents can raise kids as well as two.
   - ☐ AGREE
   - ☐ DISAGREE
   - ☐ NEITHER AGREE NOR DISAGREE

6. Divorce is the best solution to marital problems.
   - ☐ AGREE
   - ☐ DISAGREE
   - ☐ NEITHER AGREE NOR DISAGREE

▶▶ Turn to the end of the chapter to view the results for the total population.

SOURCE: National Opinion Research Center, University of Chicago.

A RETREAT FROM MARRIAGE AND FAMILY

9.1 Define the concept of family.

Like so many women in her deteriorating South Philadelphia neighborhood, Deena met her son's father when she was only 15 and he was 20. Three years later, Deena was living with Kevin, they were engaged to be married, and she was happily pregnant. But soon Kevin began staying out late, drinking, and cheating on her. After giving birth prematurely, Deena left Kevin and moved in with her grandmother. She has become disenchanted about what a family should be, but she has a new boyfriend, Patrick, with whom she is expecting her second child. Deena and Patrick have been together for two years and both are recently drug-free, but they still live in the old neighborhood, where the temptation to return to their old way of life hangs like a shadow over their present (Edin and Kefalas 2005).

What led Deena and Kevin to have a baby without marrying? Why has Deena repeatedly been in relationships with men who say they want to have a baby with her but who do not appear to be good potential husbands? Could Deena and Patrick set up their own household instead of living with relatives? What keeps couples such as Deena and Patrick from remaining faithful to one another? Why do their lives appear to be in such disarray? Do Deena, Kevin, Patrick, and their families serve as evidence "that American society is coming apart at the seams" (Edin and Kefalas 2005, 6), especially when it comes to families?

At first glance, Deena, who is struggling to make "promises [she] can keep" around childbearing (if not marriage), exemplifies many of the social problems facing families across U.S. society today. She has not married her children's fathers. Some would say she is too young to be having children. She became a mother before she could acquire the education and employment that would increase her chances of attaining socioeconomic stability. Some may question how parents like Deena can rear the next generation. How will they and their children contribute to the economy and other basic institutions in U.S. society?

As we shall see in this chapter, it is not only the economically disadvantaged who are in what some call a retreat from marriage and family.

Based on their research with 162 low-income single mothers in economically strapped neighborhoods in central Philadelphia and Camden, New Jersey, Kathryn Edin and Maria Kefalas (2005) conclude that we are not witnessing a rejection of the *ideal* of marriage and the American dream of family. On the contrary, the women Edin and Kefalas studied (and Edin lived among) hold extremely high expectations for marriage. In fact, they would rather forgo a risky marriage that might fail and instead hold out for a "good marriage," one characterized by sexual fidelity, happiness, and a "long list of middle-class accoutrements, like a house, a lawn, a car, a couch, a TV, and a 'nice' wedding" (108–9). When Edin and Kefalas asked Deena and Patrick (the couple in the story at the beginning of this chapter) about marriage, Patrick said, "I like to do things right though, instead of cutting corners, and doing everything half-assed. I'd rather get engaged for two years, save money, get a house, make sure . . . the baby's got a bedroom, [than get married now]" (106). Deena added, "And I get a yard with grass. [And] I want a nice wedding" (107).

We have ample evidence that economic hardship makes family formation and marital stability difficult. Katherine S. Newman and Victor Tan Chen (2007) have studied the "near poor" in the United States, the 50 million who earn between $20,000 and $40,000 per year and live just above poverty yet well below the middle class. Newman and Chen's research on this relatively invisible "missing class"

Pascal Le Segretain / Sygma / Corbis

In order to discourage divorce, in 2011 the town of Sangeorgiu de Mures in Romania passed a law making it very expensive to get a divorce. The fee was nearly 60% of an average annual salary. What expectations do you imagine this Romanian bride and groom might have of each other in their future life together?

confirms that it is not just the abjectly poor who have difficulty forming stable relationships. Among the missing class, grueling hours at low-wage jobs take a severe toll on the formation and maintenance of long-term bonds like marriage. Women cannot afford to look upon potential partners only in terms of romance, because they have bills to pay and children to feed. In other words, "money is the constant calculus underlying decisions to join and separate incomes, merge and split households" (151).

What of those who are not among the poor or the near poor? Do middle-class and better-off U.S. adults retain faith in marriage and the kind of traditional family marriage creates? Or, as some have suggested, is the family in decline across all segments of U.S. society? As we will see, people across social classes are marrying less and living in arrangements that are anything but traditional.

THE DECLINE OF THE FAMILY?

Just how extensive are these shifts in the demography of families? And do they indicate a growing disenchantment with the social institution of family? The debate over what some call the decline of the family has been raging for decades, part of the broader **culture wars** over the future direction of U.S. society as a whole. Initially, the debate focused on certain types of families, especially those living in poverty and those of particular races or ethnicities. But the second half of the 20th century also brought some striking changes in the picture of all U.S. families. The number of divorces shot up, as did the number of children born to unmarried partners. Consequently, the number of families headed by divorced or never-married women rose dramatically. Likewise, the 1960s saw the arrival of a generation that sometimes favored **cohabitation**—that is, living in an intimate relationship outside marriage.

Culture wars: Disputes over the state of American society, including the presumed decline of the family as well as "family values."

Cohabitation: Unrelated, unmarried adults in an intimate relationship sharing living quarters.

Marriage movement: Social movement that advocates traditional marriage and warns against the sexual revolution, teenage pregnancy, and same-sex marriage.

Family: (1) Two or more people related by birth, marriage, or adoption who share living quarters (U.S. Census Bureau definition), or (2) members of a social group who are in an intimate, long-term, committed relationship and who share mutual expectations of rights and responsibilities.

Household: All the related and unrelated people who share living quarters.

Taking one position in the culture wars are advocates of the **marriage movement**, who warn against the sexual revolution, teenage pregnancy, and same-sex marriage while advocating traditional marriage. Alarmed at what he saw as the collapse of the traditional family, in 1977 child psychologist James Dobson founded Focus on the Family, a Christian ministry whose mission is "nurturing and defending the God-ordained institution of the family and promoting biblical truths" (Focus on the Family 2012). Some other social scientists followed suit. In a series of provocative books and articles, sociologist David Popenoe (1988, 1993, 1996, 2004, 2009), codirector of the National Marriage Project at Rutgers University, has argued that the modern family is failing in its primary social functions: sexual regulation, procreation, and socialization of children in a stable, economically productive, and emotionally supportive unit formed by the lifelong union of a man and a woman.

ASK YOURSELF: Where do *you* stand on the culture wars around the family? Have you found the culture wars around the family nasty, even offensive? Can you suggest two or three points on which you think most people might agree when it comes to the social problems facing families today?

Family battles in the culture wars are accompanied by heated arguments around what some call "family values," often framed in terms of hot-button issues such as abortion. Yet, as we shall see later in the discussion of government policy in support of families, for all the rhetoric around family values, when it comes to a comprehensive family policy, the United States does not appear to *value families* as much as do many other developed countries (Karraker and Grochowski 2012).

Other writers, such as sociologist Judith Stacey (2011), professor of gender and sexuality studies and social and cultural analysis at New York University, see a much more complicated story than the culture wars would suggest. Stacey argues that "adaptation" describes the changing family better than "decline." Part of the debate centers on exactly how we define family, and how we understand the processes that help change family structures.

Defining the Family

Part of the answer to the question "Is the family in trouble?" depends on how we define family. The U.S. Census Bureau defines **family** as two or more people who are related to each other by birth, marriage, or adoption and who share living quarters. The Census Bureau (2012a) differentiates family from **household**, which is defined as people, related or not, who share living quarters.

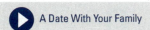 A Date With Your Family   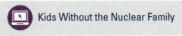 Kids Without the Nuclear Family

Feminism and Intersectionality

Feminist sociologists are among action-oriented social scientists seeking a more just world, not only around gender equity issues but also around intersections of gender with race and ethnicity, social class, sexual orientation, immigration status, (dis)ability, age, veteran status, and other social locations.

In her pioneering work *Black Feminist Thought: Knowledge, Consciousness, and the Politics of Empowerment*, Patricia Hill Collins (1990) argues that systems of oppression are bound up with the linkages among race, social class, and gender. In this chapter, we see how race and ethnicity affect the likelihood that a woman will marry or that children will grow up in a two-parent family. We also see how, although cohabitation is more common among those with lower levels of education, those with college educations (a correlate of social class) fare better economically when they do cohabit. Still other research compares professional and working-class men's ideals and practices, and (perhaps surprisingly) finds working-class men more egalitarian than their professional counterparts (Shows and Gerstel 2009). Other studies examine the challenges gay men face in being fathers in a heterosexist society (Berkowitz and Marsiglio 2007).

An intersectional approach, particularly one from a **feminist perspective**, is vital to understanding how patriarchy and sexism privilege or oppress certain social categories of women and men, relationships, and families.

▶ **THINK ABOUT IT:** Identify a pressing social problem for families and ask yourself: Can we address this problem without taking into account intersections between gender and at least one other social status? How does intersectionality

Patricia Hill Collins is Distinguished University Professor of Sociology at the University of Maryland, College Park. She has served as president of the American Sociological Association. In her book *Black Feminist Thought* she uses the concept of intersectionality to examine how race, class, gender, and sexuality are interconnected in experiences of oppression. For example, black women have the double burden of both racial and gender discrimination.

inform efforts to make a more just society for families?

In everyday life, the definition of family is not only highly contested but also socially constructed (Karraker and Grochowski 2012, 5). In research in which unmarried mothers were asked to draw pictures of their families, they first drew mothers and fathers, parents and children, and other extended kin. However, when asked to add individuals who were important to their family life but who might not fit the usual definition of family, those women added close friends and neighbors on whom they depended, individuals who might be considered **fictive kin** (Stack 1974). Finally, when asked to subtract individuals who did not fit their personal definitions of family, those women quickly excluded some persons to whom they or their children were related by blood, marriage, or adoption but who were not important to their family life. Several women excluded the mothers of their children's fathers. Even if their children's fathers were important parts of their children's lives, these mothers reported that the older women often hindered the mothers' efforts to forge good relationships with their children's fathers (Karraker and Grochowski 1998).

ASK YOURSELF: Does the U.S. Census Bureau definition of family speak to the meaning of family in the 21st century? Why or why not? (If not, offer an alternative definition.) Why is the definition of family so important?

Clearly, our definition of precisely what is *family* is shifting. On September 26, 2012, about 14.5 million television viewers tuned in to watch the season premiere

Feminist perspective: A theoretical approach that emphasizes the extent to which patriarchy and sexism undermine women (and men), relationships, and families.

Fictive kin: People to whom one is not related by blood, marriage, or adoption but on whom one nonetheless depends.

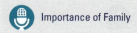
Importance of Family

The promotional poster for the first season of *Modern Family* describes the comedy series as being about "one big (straight, gay, multi-cultural, traditional) happy family." The sitcom portrays our evolving ideas of family. What is your idea of family?

of the ABC situation comedy *Modern Family*, making it the ninth most-watched show that week (Nielsen 2012). The sitcom, which debuted in 2009, received the Emmy Award for Outstanding Comedy Series for a third year in a row in 2012. The show portrays three parts of a complex, extended family: Phil Dunphy, his wife Claire, and their three children; Claire's brother Mitchell, his partner Cameron, and their adopted daughter Lily; Claire and Mitchell's father Jay Pritchett, his much younger wife Gloria, her son Manny from a previous marriage, and a baby born to Jay and Gloria.

The classic definition of family devised by cultural anthropologist George Peter Murdock (1949) more than half a century ago—characterized by common residence and the social functions of economic cooperation, sexual regulation, and child socialization—goes only so far. Another way to envision families in the 21st century is to recognize that each of us lives not just in one family but in a series of families over a lifetime. Thus we derive a definition of family not just from biology and law but also from experience with kin, friends, and others, as well as from lived experience through institutions including educational settings, faith communities, health care institutions, the media, and the workplace. Grochowski (1998) avoids the term *family* altogether, instead favoring "strategic living community," which she defines as all members of a social group who are in an intimate, long-term committed relationship. We should add to that definition the idea that family members share expectations of rights and responsibilities to one another and to the family as a whole.

PATTERNS AND TRENDS

 9.2 Discuss patterns and trends in marriage, cohabitation, and divorce.

Part of the debate around the social problems of families has to do with changes in the very structures the family assumes. In this section, we explore the ways patterns and trends in marriage, cohabitation, and divorce change family structures, and the effects of these changes on the well-being of children.

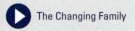 The Changing Family

Marriage

However we define it, the family is undergoing substantial demographic change, and the women described by Edin and Kefalas (2005), such as Deena in this chapter's opening vignette, are not too far from the norm. U.S. society in the 21st century is facing what we can call a growing **marriage dearth**, meaning people are dramatically less likely to be living in the state of matrimony than were comparable people a half century ago. The U.S. Census Bureau (2012a) uses four major categories for marital status: never married, married, widowed, and divorced. The Census Bureau reserves the term *married couple* for a husband and wife who share the same household but allows that, rather than being "married, spouse present," a married person might be "separated" or "married, spouse absent." Keep in mind that a person who is described as single can therefore be never married, widowed, or divorced.

Just what it means to be married varies widely across societies. For data collection purposes, the United Nations (2006a) defines marriage as "the act, ceremony, or process by which the legal relationship of husband or wife is constituted." We find the highest marriage rate in Mongolia, one of the least developed countries in the world (United Nations 2006a). In contrast, the percentage of U.S. adults 18 and older who are married not only is much lower but also has dropped steadily over the past half century. The percentage who are divorced has almost tripled, and the percentage of never marrieds has almost doubled (Cohn et al. 2011). Does societal development in some way "doom" marriage as we know it?

When we discuss the "retreat from marriage" (Edin and Kefalas 2005, 5) in the United States, however, we must recognize that the choice—some would say the privilege—to marry intersects with a wide range of other social factors. For instance, while the percentage of married people rises with age, younger people are dramatically less likely to be married today than were their counterparts 50 years ago, partly because the median age at marriage has never been higher (Cohn et al. 2011). Likewise, while whites are still more likely than either blacks or Hispanics to be married, only among whites do we see a majority who are currently married, and a slim one at that. The decline in marriage for those with less than a college education is even more striking. Only among the college educated do we find a majority currently married (Cohn et al. 2011).

Just how much of the marriage dearth is caused by extraneous "supply" factors? The **pool of eligibles**, or the supply of potential marriageable partners, is shaped by such obvious factors as age. For example, given the **marriage gradient**, or the tendency for women to marry men who are slightly older, the older a woman is, the less likely she is to find a potential husband. Black women in particular face a severely imbalanced sex ratio (Lichter, LeClere, and

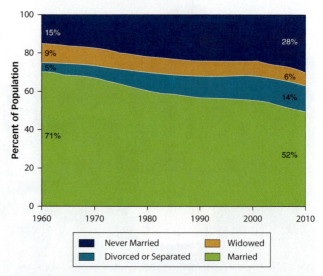

FIGURE 9.1 U.S. Marital Status, 1960–2010

SOURCE: U.S. Census Bureau. (2012). Aggregate Data 1960-2010. Washington, DC: U.S. Government Printing Office.

McLaughlin 1991; Lichter et al. 1992; South and Lloyd 1992). First, this **marriage squeeze** for black women is affected by the number of potential marriage partners. Death, imprisonment, and military enlistment rates effectively reduce the number of black men available as potential husbands. Second, higher rates of unemployment among black men reduce their perceived suitability as mates. Further, black men are more likely than black women to marry someone of another race (Crowder and Tolnay 2000). As a result, at 90 men to every 100 women, the gender ratio is more imbalanced for blacks than for any other racial or ethnic group in the United States (Spraggins 2005).

When we take all these factors into account, the race of the householder makes a great difference in the household type. As shown in Table 9.1, whites are much more likely to live in husband-wife households than are blacks. However, and in spite of their having lower median family income, Hispanic households have essentially the same percentage of husband-wife households as do whites (U.S. Census 2012c). William Julius Wilson (1987) found that, when faced with a pregnancy, white, black, and Hispanic women living in poverty on the South Side of Chicago were

....

Marriage dearth: The decline in the proportion of adult Americans who are married.

Pool of eligibles: The quantity and quality of potential partners for marriage.

Marriage gradient: The tendency for women to "marry up"—that is, to marry older men.

Marriage squeeze: The severely imbalanced sex ratio experienced by black women in regard to potential marriage partners.

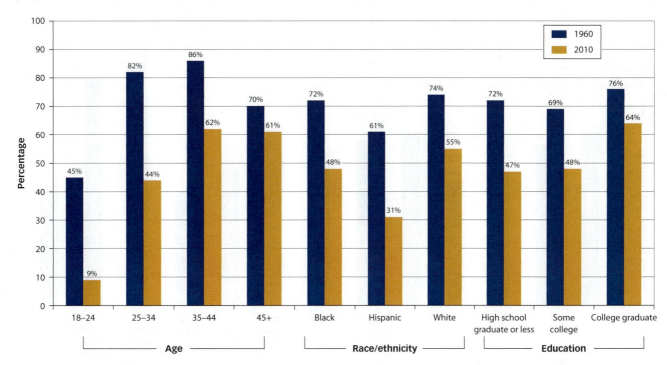

FIGURE 9.2 Percentage of U.S. Adults Currently Married, 1960 and 2010

SOURCE: Cohn, D'Vera, Jeffrey S. Passell, Wendy Wang, and Gretchen Livingston. *Barely Half of U.S. Adults Are Married: A Record Low.* December 4, 2011. Washington, DC: Pew Research Center. Reprinted with permission.

unlikely to marry the fathers of their babies unless the men were employed. Today some social policy makers would like to see marriage higher on the list of priorities for single mothers (and the fathers of their children).

ASK YOURSELF: What reasons can you think of that a single mother living in poverty should marry the father of her child if he does not have a job?

Marriage dearth aside, many in the United States are clearly not ready to give up on marriages or on families. Among those who have never been married, 61% say they wish to do so. Only 27% say they do not wish to marry, while another 12% are not sure. The proportion of high school seniors who say that having a "good marriage and family life" is "extremely important" has remained high since the 1970s, at 80% or more for girls and 69% or more for boys (National Marriage Project 2011).

Yet, as a Pew Research Center study found, "public attitudes about the institution of marriage are mixed" (Cohn et al. 2011, 2). When asked, "Is marriage becoming obsolete?" in 2011, almost four of ten U.S. adults answered yes, compared to almost three of ten in 1978 (a year when the divorce rate was at an all-time high). The percentages of affirmative responses to that statement are lowest among older white adults, those with a college degree, and the currently married (see Figure 9.3).

TABLE 9.1 Husband-Wife Households by Race and Ethnicity, 2010

Race/ethnicity of household	Percentage
White	51.2
Non-Hispanic white	51.1
Black	28.5
American Indian and Alaskan Native	40.1
Asian	59.7
Native Hawaiian and Pacific Islander	51.3
Some other race	49.6
Two or more races	41.0
Hispanic or Latino of any race	50.1
All racial and ethnic groups combined	**48.4**

SOURCE: U.S. Census Bureau, 2012b. "Households and Families: 2010." *2010 Census Briefs.* Issued April 2012.

The economic benefits of marriage are considerable. The continuously married are better off financially than those who are cohabiting, divorced and not remarried, or

FIGURE 9.3 Attitudes toward Marriage in the United States, 2010

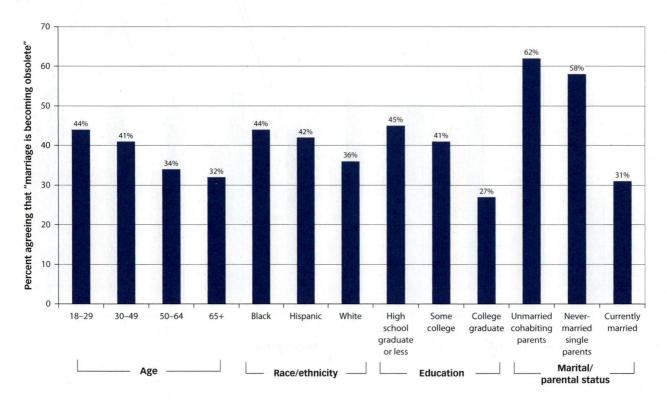

SOURCE: Cohn, D'Vera, Jeffrey S. Passell, Wendy Wang, and Gretchen Livingston. *Barely Half of U.S. Adults Are Married: A Record Low. December 4, 2011*. Washington, DC: Pew Research Center. Reprinted with permission.

never married. The reasons for these differences include economies of scale (two can live more cheaply than one), but, as the National Marriage Project (2011) notes, married couples also save and invest more in the future and act as insurance for one another in the case of illness and job loss. Married couples also receive more employment-based benefits (such as prorated health insurance) and often more help from two sets of extended families and friends. Married people, especially husbands, enjoy better health and live longer than the unmarried (Drefahl 2012).

Finally, in terms of median income, married-couple households are far better off than either female-headed households or even male-headed households (see Figure 9.4). And the families that fare best of all in economic terms? Married-couple households in which the wife is employed.

However, the positive effects of marriage may not be as great as they might seem, at least when compared to the effects of stable cohabiting relationships. Researchers have found that marriage and cohabitation have similar effects on psychological well-being, health, and social ties. Any differences tend to be small and to grow smaller the longer couples are together, whether they are married or not. What matters may not be the form of a partnership—whether the couple are married or not—but rather the duration and stability of the relationship (Musick and Bumpass 2012). This leads us to consider the dramatic rise in unmarried partnerships.

Cohabitation

As the proportion of adults who are married falls toward less than half (perhaps as soon as when this book goes to print), the prevalence of single-person households (those formed by never-married as well as divorced and widowed individuals) will very likely increase. Already, just as the number of people choosing not to marry has risen, the rate of cohabitation has increased.

The U.S. Census Bureau has been collecting data on unmarried-couple households for several decades. Today a census survey respondent can identify her- or himself as an unmarried partner in one of three ways: (1) as an unmarried partner of the householder and of the opposite sex, (2) as an unmarried partner of the householder and of the same sex, or (3) as a spouse of the householder and of the same sex (U.S. Census Bureau 2010). The number of unmarried-partner households has increased dramatically over the past half century, more than doubling in the past

Cohabitation

FIGURE 9.4　U.S. Median Income by Family Type, 2009

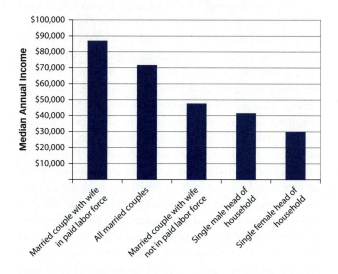

SOURCE: U.S. Census Bureau, 2012f. Statistical Abstract of the United States: 2012. Table 699. "Median Income of Families by Type of Family in Current and Constant (2009) Dollars, 1990 to 2009."

20 years alone (US. Census Bureau 2010). Today a majority of adults report having cohabited at some point in their lives (Frey and Cohn 2011).

Unmarried partners are more likely to be young, have lower levels of education and income, and be less religious than those who do not cohabit. They are also more likely to have been divorced or to have parents who were divorced, to have lived without a father in the home, or to have lived in families with high levels of marital conflict when growing up (National Marriage Project 2011).

Today, more than six of ten first marriages begin with the couple living together; 50 years ago, almost none did (Kennedy and Bumpass 2008). Does living together give a couple a chance to check out their compatibility, and thus perhaps avoid a future divorce? Any such effects related to cohabitation—and they are inconclusive—are less likely the result of the cohabitation and more likely the result of a **selection effect**. In other words, individuals who choose to cohabit may have some attitudes and characteristics that predispose them to marital instability. Research indicates that when couples enter into cohabitation after they have become engaged or have

Selection effect: In contrast to the experience effect, attitudes and characteristics that predispose an individual to a relationship outcome, such as divorce.

Crude divorce rate: The number of divorces per 1,000 population.

definite plans to marry, premarital cohabitation does not appear to be associated with the probability of later divorce. In fact, women (but not men) who cohabit after they have become engaged or have definite plans to marry may even have a lower probability of divorce than those who do not cohabit (Manning and Cohen 2012). On the other hand, couples who cohabit prior to becoming engaged may be more likely to have marital problems and to be less happy in their marriages (Rhoades, Stanley, and Markman 2009).

Again, what of the socioeconomics of cohabitation? Although cohabitation is more common among those with lower levels of education, among cohabitors with college degrees, median household income in 2009 was $106,400, slightly higher than the $101,160 among college-educated married adults. The mean household income of cohabitors without college degrees ($46,540) was significantly below that of married couples without degrees ($56,800) (Frey and Cohn 2011, 1).

ASK YOURSELF: When asked whether cohabitation is a reasonable predictor of marital success, many college students say, "Of course! Living together is a good way to test whether a more serious commitment will last." However, as the research indicates, this is hardly the case. Why do you think these attitudes persist in the face of empirical evidence to the contrary?

Divorce

In the mid-20th century, the clamor over the state of the family centered on rising rates of divorce. Since then, the percentage of U.S. adults who have been married at least once has dropped, from 85% in 1960 to 72% in 2010. Moreover, those who do marry are less likely to stay married. In the past 50 years, the proportion of American adults who are divorced or separated has almost tripled, increasing from just 5% to 14% (Cohn et al. 2011).

Worldwide, as the marriage rate has been dropping, the divorce rate has been rising (United Nations 2006a). Compared to most other developed countries, the United States has higher rates of marriage, but it also has higher rates of divorce and remarriage and more short-term cohabiting relationships (Cherlin 2004, 2009).

U.S. divorce statistics were first recorded in 1867. Data collection methods were not always reliable and have varied over the years, but the best information indicates that the **crude divorce rate**, the number of divorces per 1,000 population, increased very slowly but steadily from 1867, when very few marriages ended in divorce.

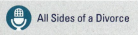
All Sides of a Divorce

TABLE 9.2 Countries with Highest Crude Divorce Rate (number of divorces per 1,000 population)

Rank	Country	Divorce rate
1	Russia	4.5
2	Gibraltar	4.2
3	Ukraine	3.8
4	Moldova	3.5
5	United States	3.4
6	Belarus	3.3
	Lithuania	3.3
7	Cuba	3.2
	Latvia	3.2
8	Czech Republic	3.1
9	Cayman Islands	3.0
10	Bermuda	2.8
	Belgium	2.8
	Estonia	2.8
	Switzerland	2.8

SOURCE: United Nations 2006b. *Demographic Yearbook.* Table 25. Divorces and Crude Divorce Rates, by Urban/Rural Residence: 2002–2006.

By 1967, 100 years later, around one-quarter of marriages ended in divorce.

Divorce rates in those years were shaped by several factors, including the stigma attached to divorce; restrictive laws that granted divorce only when the plaintiff could prove adultery, abuse, or abandonment; and, especially, limited economic opportunities for women. The Great Depression of the 1930s dampened divorce rates somewhat, because many who might have wished to could not afford the costs of obtaining divorces and living apart. Then the divorce rate resumed its slow but steady increase until World War II, spiking as the war and its effects strained family life and increased labor force participation by women, giving women the means to leave unsatisfactory marriages. That rise was followed by a decline in divorce rates during the baby boom years of the 1950s and 1960s (Plateris 1973).

The incidence of divorce again increased in the early 1960s to a high in the 1980s, before falling in the first decade of the 21st century. The more recent effects of the Great Recession on divorce are discussed later in this chapter. Research has found some cautionary evidence for a link with this economic downturn, with divorce rates higher in areas where home foreclosure rates were high. However, given the already downward trend in divorces, we should interpret such early data with caution (Cohen 2012).

The dramatic rise in divorce rates from the 1960s to the 1980s occurred at a time of remarkable social and cultural change. Women were achieving higher levels of education and greater labor force participation, making it more economically feasible for those who wanted to leave their marriages to do so. California's Family Law Act of 1969 ushered in "no-fault" divorce, now an option for terminating a marriage in all 50 states (American Bar Association, Section on Family Law 2012). The effect of allowing divorce based on "irreconcilable differences" or "irretrievable breakdown," rather than on the former adversarial criterion of wrongdoing by one party, is not easy to decipher. Early research suggested that divorce rates increased as states instituted no-fault divorce laws (see, for example, Nakonezny, Shull, and Rogers 1995), but the question remains whether the increases were caused by changes in the law or simply occurred at the same time as other significant social and cultural changes.

Approximately 20% of divorces happen in the first five years of marriage (Centers for Disease Control and Prevention 2012c). The National Marriage Project (2011) estimates the chance of any U.S. adult getting divorced at between 40% and 50% and identifies several risk factors in the first ten years of marriage, as shown in Table 9.3. Note how many risk factors are related to socioeconomic factors, either directly (annual income, education) or indirectly (age at marriage, birth of a child before marriage).

FIGURE 9.5 U.S. Divorce Rate, 1960–2009

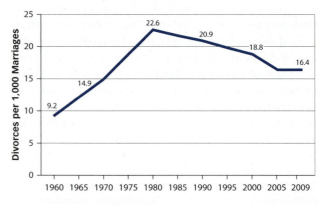

NOTE: Calculations exclude California, Georgia, Hawaii, Indiana, Louisiana, and Minnesota, which did not report data for some of the periods.
SOURCE: Centers for Disease Control and Prevention 2000, 2009; U.S. Census Bureau 2000, 2001.

TABLE 9.3 Background Characteristics and Risk of Divorce during First 10 Years of Marriage

Factor	Decrease in divorce risk (%)
Annual Income over $50,000 (versus under $25,000)	30
College (versus high school dropout)	25
Marriage at over 25 years of age (versus under 18)	24
Birth of a baby 7 months or more after marriage (versus before marriage)	24
Intact family of origin (versus divorced parents)	14
Religious affiliation (versus none)	14

SOURCE: National Marriage Project and the Institute for American Values. 2011. Social Indicators of Marital Health & Well-Being, Trends of the Past Five Decades in *The State of Our Unions: Marriage in America 2011*. Reprinted with permission.

Ironically, divorce rates are highest in some Bible Belt states (Arkansas, Oklahoma, and West Virginia), as well as in some western states (Idaho, Nevada, and Wyoming). States with the lowest rates are scattered across the Midwest (Illinois, Iowa) and the Northeast (Connecticut, Maryland, Massachusetts, New York, and Pennsylvania) (U.S. Census Bureau 2012b). Clearly, sociocultural factors such as more conservative religious traditions must be intersecting with other factors, such as early age at first marriage (a significant predictor of divorce), as well as socioeconomic and other factors.

What about the Children?

In 1960, almost nine of ten children under age 18 in the United States were living with two married parents. By 2010, only two-thirds were doing so (U.S. Census Bureau 2010). In 2010, four in ten births were to unmarried parents, and four in ten cohabiting households included at least one child. (When we are referring to a mother or father not married to the other parent, the term *unmarried parent* is more precise than *single parent*.) As revealed in the Fragile Families and Child Wellbeing Study, many unmarried parents are either living together or in a **visiting union**, meaning they live apart but are romantically involved at the time

Visiting union: Unmarried parents who are romantically involved but living apart.

of their child's birth (McLanahan 2011). Only one in ten had little or no contact when their child was born. However, most of those relationships formed during early parenthood do not last. Less than one-third of unmarried-parent couples are still together five years after their child's birth. Almost four in ten unmarried mothers form at least one new partnership, and one in seven have a child with a new partner. Fathers in these unmarried couples tend to become less engaged with their offspring over time. By the time the child is 5 years old, only half of nonresident fathers had seen the child in the last month.

The Fragile Families Study confirms that unmarried parents are much more disadvantaged than married parents (McLanahan 2011). Unmarried parents are themselves less likely to have grown up with both biological parents and are more likely to be poor and black or Hispanic. They have often begun parenting in their teens and have had children with more than one partner. They are also more likely to suffer from depression, report substance abuse, and spend time in jail. Their families are much more likely to be welfare dependent. For example, at the time the child was 5 years old, only 2% of married-parent families were receiving food stamps, compared to 33% of families in which the parents were single and not living together.

FIGURE 9.6 Relationship of Unmarried Couples at Child's Birth, 2012

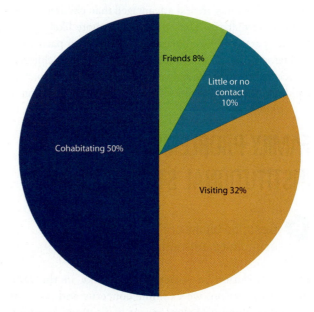

Friends 8%
Little or no contact 10%
Cohabitating 50%
Visiting 32%

SOURCE: From the Fragile Families and Child Wellbeing Study Fact Sheet, accessed at: http://www.fragilefamilies.princeton.edu/documents/FragileFamiliesandChildWellbeingStudyFactSheet.pdf

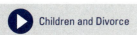
Children and Divorce

The Fragile Families and Child Wellbeing Study

Sociologists and other social scientists at Princeton University, Columbia University, and Pennsylvania State University are following almost 5,000 children born in large U.S. cities from 1998 through 2000. Approximately three-quarters of the children were born to unmarried parents. Because these families are more likely to break up and to live in poverty than other families, the investigators refer to them as "fragile families."

The Fragile Families Study addresses four important questions:

1. What are the conditions and capabilities of unmarried parents, especially fathers?

2. What is the nature of the relationship between unmarried parents?

3. How do children born into these families fare?

4. How do public policies and environmental conditions affect families and children?

Researchers interviewed both mothers and fathers when the children were born and when they were 1, 3, and 5 years old to collect data on attitudes, relationships, parenting behavior, demographic characteristics, mental and physical health, economic and employment status, neighborhood characteristics, and program participation. They also conducted in-home assessments of the children and their home environments. More information about the study, including a list of publications, is available online at http://www.fragilefamilies .princeton.edu.

▶ **THINK ABOUT IT**: The findings of the Fragile Families Study provide powerful evidence of the connections among social structure, family organization, and child well-being. But what kinds of "grades" do parents give themselves? A recent study found that two-thirds or more of black and white parents give themselves high marks for parenting, yet only a bit more than half of Hispanic parents do so (Parker and Wang 2013). What do you think accounts for this difference?

What of the children in these unions? Again, the Fragile Families Study (2012) has found that children born to unmarried parents are less advantaged than children whose parents are married. Their mothers are more likely to use harsher parenting techniques and less likely to participate in literacy activities like reading aloud. These children, especially the boys, have lower cognitive test scores than do children of married parents and exhibit more aggression.

FAMILY PROBLEMS AND THREE INSTITUTIONAL STAKEHOLDERS

 9.3 Describe family problems related to economics, religion, and government.

Every institution in society has a stake in the family. In this section, we examine concerns and interests around the family of three major institutions: economics, religion, and government. First, we focus on how the economic downturn of the Great Recession played out in families of the middle class. Second, we contemplate the roles of religion and spirituality (which are not necessarily the same thing) in family life. Third, we consider the place of government policy in regard to violence against women.

Struggles of the Middle Class: Effects of the Great Recession on Families

Socioeconomic status remains a powerful indicator of the structure and also the quality of family life. Economic hardship can reduce the chance that a couple will marry or stay married, and that a child will grow up in a two-parent family (Child Trends 2012). Social class can also shape the quality of conjugal and parent-child relationships (Hill 2012). The changes in the structure of family life described above are reshaping the economic resources available to many families. The economic downturn that began in 2008 changed the portrait of even middle-class families, determining which will retain their middle-class existence and which will fall behind.

The full verdict is not yet in on the effects of the Great Recession. How has it affected families you know? In what

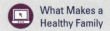
What Makes a Healthy Family

Family beyond Our Borders

Children and the Changing Family

What about the effects of changes in family structure on children worldwide? First, children appear to fare better in societies where strong bonds exist between parents. However, they do not necessarily fare better in societies in which their parents marry, or worse in societies in which their parents do not. The gap in the quality of life between children living in two-parent families and those in single-parent families is much greater in some countries (the United States, the United Kingdom, Austria) than in others (Belgium, Denmark, France, Germany, Italy, Sweden).

The difference? Germany, Italy, and Sweden all provide a universal child benefit structure that guarantees a minimum income to every child, regardless of parental situation; the United States does not (Kamerman 1996). Among economically advanced nations, the United States is at the bottom in terms of child poverty (only Romania ranks lower). In the United States, nearly a quarter of children live in households with incomes lower than 50% of the national median (Adamson 2012). So, is the problem that parents fail to marry, or that society fails to provide a safety net for struggling families, regardless of how they are structured?

The United States is not alone in experiencing dramatically shifting trends in the demography that makes up family. Are we seeing a worldwide decline in interest in family as we know it? Families composed of parents, children, and extended kin have been at the core of societies around the world, with members often living and working as a unit. This is no longer true, as more and more people around the world are choosing to forgo marriage and childbearing (Kotkin 2012).

Reasons for this global shift, while complex and variable across societies and cultures, include competitive capitalism, widespread movement away from traditional values, urbanization, and global economics. In pursuit of economic advantage, individuals are often forced to choose between family formation and career advancement. Movement away from traditional religious values (Judeo-Christian, but also Muslim, Hindu, Confucian, and Buddhist) prioritizes more secular values, including individualism and the pursuit of personal happiness and socioeconomic achievement. Urbanization suppresses both marriage and fertility rates, not only in the large urban centers of North America, Europe, and especially East Asia, but also in the fast-growing cities in developing areas of Asia, North Africa, and parts of the Middle East. Finally, a weak global economy and global fiscal crises, accompanied by a drop in the number of well-paying jobs, could dampen hope for future generations and, consequently, the desire to form families and bear children.

▶ **THINK ABOUT IT:** Do you think we will see fewer children being raised in families around the world in your lifetime? What factors worldwide do you expect to shape the answer to that question?

---

the Pew Research Center (2012) calls "the lost decade of the middle class," the Great Recession reverberates through families in the form of unemployment and underemployment, stagnant and reduced pay, and foreclosures on homes (Greenstone and Looney 2011). Today, 86% of U.S. adults consider a secure job an important part of what it takes to be middle-class, compared to 33% in 1991 who considered a white-collar job necessary to achieving middle-class status (Wang 2012). But achieving employment stability has become increasingly difficult with the rise in long-term unemployment that accompanied the Great Recession, especially among males ages 35–54 and white-collar workers (Kallberg 2012). The average monthly unemployment rate almost doubled in the years immediately before and then again after the Great Recession, to just under 10%. During the same period, median family income fell from $49,600 to $45,800.

But it was median family net worth that took the greatest hit, falling from $126,400 to $77,300 in 2010. That level had not been seen since the early 1990s, and the drop effectively did away with the accumulated prosperity of the preceding 20 years. Moreover, middle-income families lost more wealth than either the wealthiest or the poorest families (Bricker et al. 2012). Even in that presumed bastion of the middle class, the U.S. suburb, "hardship has built a stronghold" as the percentage of people living below the poverty line grew by 66% (*New York Times* 2012).

Even without the Great Recession, maintaining a middle-class family life is not easy. Dual-earner spouses strain for work-life balance (Gootman and Saint Louis

Family Challenges

Trey Green pauses for a moment while helping his wife and daughter make dinner at their home in Gilmer, Texas. Green has been home and pitching in with chores around the house since he was laid off from U.S. Steel Corporation's pipe plant. What kind of future do you think the Greens can expect with no income?

2012; Jang, Zippay, and Park 2012; Karraker and Grochowski 2012). Parents wrestle with how to manage the advantages that come with affluence, such as unlimited Internet access (Kreutzer 2012; Seltzer et al. 2012), and fret over how much is too much to give their children. They agonize over caregiving for children, elders, and grandchildren (Rogers and Welter 2012). All the while, family scholars warn that families may not be providing their members with sufficient developmental assets (Search Institute 2012).

As noted above, the divorce rate dropped during the Great Depression of the 1930s (Elder 1974), but how has the Great Recession of 2008 affected family structure? Apparently, marriage, cohabitation, and divorce rates have changed very little during the period since the economic downturn began. While divorce rates did not rise in states with high unemployment, they did so in states with high rates of home foreclosures, but only among individuals with education beyond high school (which may be an artifact of the correlation between higher education and homeownership) (Cohen 2012). However, since 2008 the percentage of young adults living with their parents has increased and fertility rates have fallen, with the steepest declines in states most affected by the recession (Morgan, Cumberworth, and Wimer 2012).

Economic distress taxes any family's **resilience**, the ability not just to bounce back from change or troubles (McCubbin, Thompson, and McCubbin 1996) but to spring forward into the future (Grochowski 2000). Have families experienced changes in their quality of life since the onset of the Great Recession? Overall negative effects on physical or mental health, as well as on access to health care, have been few, with some exceptions. Among adults

ages 25 to 44, more have reported experiencing serious psychological distress. Among black children, asthma rates have risen. Among adults, more have gone without medical care. Preliminary research does not reveal how many of these effects have been experienced by individuals whose lives have actually been touched by the Great Recession, but housing instability in particular may be related to such mental health consequences as anxiety attacks, depression, and self-ratings of health as fair to poor (Burgard 2012).

"The Family That Prays Together . . .": Religion, Spirituality, and Family Resilience in Tough Times

Religion has often been cited as a source of strength during times of economic and other hardships. I recall my mother (and grandmother) saying, "God never asks you to bear a burden greater than you can carry." In light of today's declining religious identification, how often do you now hear someone call so explicitly on a deity or religious teaching as a way to address family problems? Do such beliefs help or hinder families as they respond to economic difficulties or other troubled times?

Individuals who identify with a religion tend to form traditional marriages (Mahoney 2010). A religious orientation—that is, an integrated system of religious beliefs—seems to contribute to emotional, psychological, and social adjustment, as well as to stronger families (Stinnett and DeFrain 1985).

But religious identification is not what it used to be. Approximately 51% of all U.S. adults do not adhere to a particular faith tradition (Association of Religion Data Archives 2010). However, not belonging to a religious body or attending religious services does not preclude a person's having a sense of **spirituality**, or an underlying moral or value system. Families with religious or, more broadly, spiritual foundations express a sense of meaning and purpose on which they can draw during hard times. They also exhibit greater resilience than do families without such foundations (Karraker and Grochowski 2012). When faced with individual problems, uncertainty, or bewilderment, they may turn to their religious faith or spiritual beliefs, which may help them move from despair to adaptation, hope, and optimism. For example, one study found that parents

Resilience: The ability not just to bounce back from change or troubles but to spring forward into the future.

Spirituality: An underlying moral or value system, which may be in the absence of membership in a religious body or attendance at religious events.

Stephanie Sinclair / VII / Corbis

The Curry family prays before dinner at their home on the military base at Fort Dix, New Jersey. Do you think that this daily ritual can help bring cohesiveness to the Curry family in times of trouble?

caring for a child with HIV often described their problems in terms of spiritual metaphors and stories (Mawn 2011). Another study found that appeals to spirituality seem to ease stress and reduce crises among kidney transplant patients and their families (Tix and Frazier 1998).

Moreover, as Émile Durkheim (1915) argued in the early 20th century, religion can serve as a kind of "social glue," binding society together. Solidarity with others with whom a family shares faith or beliefs may generate powerful social networks. I found that to be the case in the small city in the midwestern United States I call Bluffton, where two-thirds of the population is Catholic. There Catholic nuns have partnered with educational, government, philanthropic, and religious institutions to ensure that the city's disadvantaged families receive the social and cultural support they need. The sisters' efforts to create a "good society" in Bluffton have included founding and funding shelters for homeless women and their children, regardless of religious identification (Karraker 2011, 2013a, 2013b).

Government efforts on behalf of families took a new "faith-based" turn in the 21st century. In 2001, the administration of President George W. Bush introduced the $300 million Faith-Based and Community Initiative to promote heterosexual marriage as a way to address poverty and reduce the dependence of unmarried mothers and their children on welfare (Berkowitz 2002). Today, the Center for Faith-Based and Neighborhood Partnerships, an office of the U.S. Department of Health and Human Services (2012), sponsors several initiatives around social problems that deeply touch families, including responsible fatherhood. (Information about these government initiatives is available online at http://www.fatherhood.gov/for-dads.)

ASK YOURSELF: Visit the website of the U.S. Department of Health and Human Services' Center for Faith-Based and Neighborhood Partnerships (http://www.hhs.gov/partnerships). If you were to apply for a grant through this office, what would you propose? What might be the pros and cons of such a faith-based initiative?

Like the culture wars around family values, discussions about what government can do about family problems are often highly contentious, and (by their very title and tradition) faith-based initiatives may take on moral, especially religious, overtones (Karraker and Grochowski 2012). Especially given current debates about abortion rights, same-sex marriage, and other charged issues, we might well be concerned about maintaining the separation of church and state.

Some faith-based programs also come up short on effectiveness. For example, Frank Furstenberg (2002, 2004), who has studied families, including teen mothers and their children, for more than three decades, offers criticisms of initiatives to promote marriage among unmarried mothers. Furstenberg found that although more than half of unmarried mothers eventually marry the fathers of their children, four in five of those marriages end within 15 years. Marriages between women and men who are not the fathers of their children have even higher rates of dissolution. Still, for all their controversy (and potential promise), partnerships between faith-based groups and government that aim to address family social problems appear to be here to stay.

Government on Behalf of Families: The Violence Against Women Act

Families appear to have fewer problems and fare best in societies that value them and make them a priority for forging civil society. Unlike most other developed nations around the world, the United States lacks a comprehensive family policy. The United States also invests less in government programs for families than does any other developed nation. For example, in the 1980s Sweden spent around 5% of its gross national product on family benefits. During the same period, the United States spent less than 2% of GNP on families. Swedish family policy embodies a commitment to equity across genders and all family forms: "inclusive, enabling, developmental, and nonmoralistic" (Ozawa 2004, 302). In contrast, U.S. family policy is a product of the high value American society has traditionally placed on individual responsibility, limited government, and the marketplace as a way to solve social problems (Danziger, Danziger, and Stern 1997).

Domestic Violence

Various groups hold a rally in support of the Violence Against Women Act on Capitol Hill in Washington, D.C. In early 2014, three American Indian tribes—the Yaqui of Arizona, the Tulalip of Washington, and the Umatilla of Oregon—were the first in the nation to exercise their inherent right to protect American Indian women from domestic violence and rape, regardless of the offenders' Indian or non-Indian status.

However, public spending on families has increased in the United States since the beginning of the 21st century (Bogenschneider and Corbett 2010), reaching the highest level in the nation's history (Moffitt 2008). Congress has enacted legislation that directly affects families in a multitude of arenas. Some of this legislation, such as the Patient Protection and Affordable Care Act (widely known as Obamacare), has been quite contentious. Other legislation, such as the Violence Against Women Act (VAWA), has a history of bipartisan support.

Domestic violence is difficult for any victim, but Native American women living on reservations have found escaping and prosecuting such violence especially difficult because of a lack of access to medical and other resources as well as the scarcity of law enforcement officers and judges on the reservations (and their lack of jurisdiction over non–Native Americans) (Childress 2013). Research has found that 46% of these women suffer rape, physical violence, and/or stalking by intimate partners, a rate much higher than that experienced by women of other races (Black et al.

2011). A recent change to VAWA allows tribal courts to try non–Native Americans who are alleged to have committed violence against Native American women on reservations.

USING THEORY TO EXPLAIN FAMILY PROBLEMS: THE VIEW FROM THE FUNCTIONALIST, CONFLICT, AND SYMBOLIC INTERACTIONIST PERSPECTIVES

 9.4 Apply the functionalist, conflict, and symbolic interactionist perspectives to the concept of family.

Philippe Laurenson / Reuters

Vincent Autin and Bruno Boileau kiss after they were married in Montpellier, France. The two men were the first same-sex couple to marry in France under a reform that has stoked some of the ugliest protests in the country in decades. The 2013 law, backed by most French and feted by gays and lesbians, makes France the 14th country to allow same-sex marriage despite heated street protests by conservatives. Do you think countries in Asia, Africa, and the Middle East will follow suit?

In July 2013, England and Wales legalized same-sex marriage (BBC News 2013a), joining Argentina, Belgium, Canada, Denmark, France, Iceland, the Netherlands, New Zealand, Norway, Portugal, South Africa, Spain, Sweden, and Uruguay (BBC News 2013b). The United States is not among those countries. In 1996, both houses of the U.S. Congress passed the **Defense of Marriage Act (DOMA)** by very large margins. DOMA defined marriage as the legal union of one man and one woman for federal and interstate purposes (Joughlin 2014; Liptak 2013). As of the time of this writing, 17 U.S. states and the District of Columbia permit same-sex couples to marry, and 33 states have laws or constitutional amendments prohibiting same-sex marriage or restricting marriage to the union of one man and one woman (Joughlin 2014).

On November 6, 2012, Minnesota voters failed to approve an amendment to the state's constitution that would have instituted a ban on same-sex marriage. The question posed in the ballot read, "Shall the Minnesota Constitution be amended to provide that only a union of one man and one woman shall be valid or recognized as a marriage in Minnesota?" The voters rejected the amendment (Helgeson 2012). To the surprise of many, just six

months later, on May 14, 2013, Governor Mark Dayton signed a bill passed by the Minnesota legislature that legalized same-sex marriages in Minnesota (Minnesota Department of Human Rights 2014).

Few issues have engendered as much public debate, personal angst, and campaign expenditures as same-sex marriage. More than $10 million was spent by both sides combined in the case of the proposed Minnesota constitutional amendment in 2012 (Mitchell 2012). Campaigns have also been launched to pass legislation that recognizes same-sex marriages. The Human Rights Campaign (HRC) is a large nonprofit organization that works "for lesbian, gay, bisexual, and transgender equal rights." HRC's Marriage Center (http://www.hrc.org/marriage-center) tracks the rapidly changing status of same-sex marriage and **civil unions**—legal arrangements that grant some or all of the provisions of marriage to same-sex couples—across the United States, state by state.

Sociological theories offer several ways to address the policy implications of banning or recognizing same-sex marriage, such as the following:

- What would be the social consequences of legalizing same-sex marriage?
- Who stands to gain and who stands to lose if same-sex marriage is legalized?
- What does the debate over same-sex marriage say about the meaning of marriage?

We next consider questions like these from the viewpoint of the functionalist, conflict, and symbolic interactionist perspectives.

Functionalism

Structural functionalism shines a macrosociological light on the family as the primary institution for economic support, emotional security, and especially childhood socialization. In this view, the family serves to maintain equilibrium in society. Writing in the mid-20th century, structural functionalists like Talcott Parsons argued that families are best organized around the instrumental and expressive needs of their members (Parsons and Bales 1955), with men traditionally serving as breadwinners for their families and women traditionally serving as what we might call C.Em.O.s (chief emotional officers). It might be tempting to think of structural functionalism only as a theory that supports the status quo. However, we can also use concepts such as manifest and latent functions and dysfunctions to understand the intended and unintended consequences of social changes facing families.

Defense of Marriage Act (DOMA): U.S. federal law, enacted in 1996, that defines marriage as the legal union of one man and one woman for federal and interstate purposes.

Civil unions: Legal provisions that grant some or all of the legal rights of marriage to unmarried couples.

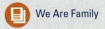 We Are Family  The Case for Same-Sex Marriage

Mercedes Santos (second from right) shares a laugh with her partner, Theresa Volpe (second from left), while playing cards with their son and daughter at their home in Chicago. Santos and Volpe are a same-sex couple raising their two biological children.

Policy Implications of Structural Functionalism

Minnesota for Marriage is a coalition of people who supported the Minnesota marriage amendment described above. The organization's website describes the traditional functions of marriage as including controlling sexuality and caring for children: "Marriage is society's mechanism for increasing the likelihood that children will be born and raised by the two people responsible for bringing them into the world—their mother and father" (Minnesota for Marriage 2012). Those who supported the Minnesota marriage amendment warned that any marital union other than that between a man and a woman would compromise the functions of that union, particularly the well-being of children (Heaney 2012).

Others, like attorney Michael Rodning Bash (2012), challenged the premise that marriage between a man and a woman is "natural." They made the argument that passage of the amendment would compromise the common good of society, children, and their parents. As Bash wrote: "It is difficult to imagine a good-faith argument that society is better off when certain children grow up with parents who are denied access to the social and legal resources and benefits that other parents and their children enjoy." Instead, opponents of the amendment asserted, social policy should be in the business of supporting parents, regardless of their sexual orientation.

What would a structural functionalist theorist say? First, although in postmodern societies like ours the family increasingly shares responsibility for the socialization of children with other institutions (day-care facilities, schools, extracurricular clubs and teams), the family remains the primary institution through which children are socialized. What appears to be in dispute is the definition of the family and, in particular, the ability of different parental configurations to socialize the next generation effectively.

Research on parenting outcomes affirms that socioeconomic conditions are a primary factor in socialization, as are quality of parenting, family climate and stability, and social networks. However, for children growing up with lesbian or gay parents, research has failed to find any negative developmental outcomes (Stacey and Biblarz 2001); any effects on academic achievement, behavior, emotional development, or self-esteem (Patterson and Hastings 2007); or any self-concept, peer relations, conduct, or gender development differences. The only differences in parenting that have been reported in research may actually favor the children of lesbian mothers. Compared with other mothers, lesbian mothers are more likely to engage in imaginative play with their children and less likely to report using corporal punishment (Goldberg and Allen 2013).

In other words, research does not support the contention that same-sex marriage is dysfunctional in terms of the socialization of children. Research conducted by the Urban Institute has estimated that same-sex couples are raising children in virtually every county (96%) in the United States (Bennett and Gates 2004). However, the same research found that same-sex couples with children are in fact disadvantaged in that they are less likely than other couples to have access to family health insurance through their employers.

Conflict Theory

Structural functionalist theory sees society as structured to ensure a stable, effective social order. Conflict theory, on the other hand, sees society as organized around competing vested interests. In the late 19th century, Karl Marx and Friedrich Engels linked the existence of social class and private property to the oppression of women in the family (see Engels 1972). A century later, Randall Collins and Scott Coltrane (1991) made a sociological argument for conflict theory as a way to examine the conflicts inevitable in day-to-day family life. Today, conflict theorists see social relationships in society, including injustices related to social class, race and ethnicity, gender, and sexual orientation, as being replicated in the family.

Policy Implications of the Conflict Perspective

Sociologist Melissa Sheridan Embser-Herbert (2012) has described the position of same-sex families in North American society and the tax and other financial, logistical, and time burdens borne by couples who cannot

Advocates for both sides chant, sing, and plead as they line the entrance to the floor of the Minnesota House of Representatives as the legislators take up the same-sex marriage bill in St. Paul, Minnesota. On May 14, 2013, Minnesota became the second state in the Midwest to legalize marriage between same-sex couples.

marry. A lesbian and an attorney, she has also outlined the heroic challenges of establishing legal custody of her son should her partner die before adoption proceedings could be completed. The organization Minnesotans United for All Families (2012) offered citizens the following rationale for opposing the marriage amendment: "This amendment violates the core Minnesotan value of treating others as we would want to be treated. It is not our place to limit the freedoms of others." From a conflict perspective, Minnesotans United made the argument that enacting a constitutional ban on same-sex marriage would oppress people like Embser-Herbert and her family while maintaining a status quo that benefits others.

Conflict theorists often see social institutions such as workplaces, schools, and religion as shoring up the claims of that status quo. Early on, the Minnesota amendment had the backing of the powerful Catholic Archdiocese of Minneapolis and Saint Paul (2010), which, two years before the amendment was to appear on the ballot, distributed to all parishioners an eight-minute DVD opposing

same-sex marriage. (Those urging Minnesotans to "vote no" on the amendment had a coalition of faith-based organizations and religious leaders on their side as well.) However, a visible number of Catholics in some neighborhoods displayed lawn signs and bumper stickers that read "Another Catholic Voting *No*."

The Public Religion Institute found that only 21% of Catholics oppose all legal recognition of same-sex unions, while 43% of Catholics support same-sex marriage and another 31% support civil unions (Jones and Cox 2011). Has some of the social solidarity the Catholic Church has enjoyed, not only with the faithful but across society on important moral issues, been challenged by the social capital expended on the Minnesota marriage amendment?

Symbolic Interactionism

Laws and constitutional amendments around same-sex marriage are about more than the structure and function of society, or even the oppression and freedom of disadvantaged groups. For an understanding of how social policy might play out in the daily lives of families and their members, we turn to microsociological theories like symbolic interactionism. Rather than focusing on macrosocial forces such as institutions and social classes, symbolic interactionism focuses on patterns of interaction among individuals. Symbolic interactionists are particularly interested in the meanings that interaction creates and the way language and other symbolic systems maintain social relationships and society. For example, some advocates of same-sex marriage rights oppose the use of the term *civil union,* arguing that it connotes more limited rights and responsibilities than the more widely accepted *same-sex marriage.*

Policy Implications of Symbolic Interactionism

Words have mattered mightily in the debates over same sex-marriage. Should we "limit" the opportunity to wed? Would matrimony be somehow "redefined" if gays were eligible to marry? Most important, what does "marriage" mean? The policy debate around who may marry provides powerful testimony about the importance of language and symbolic meanings.

Both sides in the Minnesota marriage amendment fight strongly recommended that their followers use interactional techniques to persuade others to vote their way. For example, the Minnesota for Marriage website (http://www.minnesotaformarriage.com) provided downloads aimed at helping supporters of the amendment organize house parties and print business cards and small flyers that could be personalized with supporters' contact information. The Minnesotans United for All Families website (http://mnunited.org) provided a download for a "conversation toolkit" and a way for opponents of the amendment to create their own fund-raising pages. Minnesotans United's "Family Stories" and "Gallery" were intended to create a sense that all Minnesotans, regardless of sexual orientation, share the same meaning of "family": "They believe family is about love and commitment, working together, bettering their communities, raising children, and growing old together. They believe marriage matters."

In this social media age, both sides also made heavy use of Internet communication technologies like Facebook, Twitter, Flickr, and YouTube to get their messages across to the public. Perhaps even more important, these technologies enabled supporters to connect easily with one another and with the campaign. Both Minnesota for Marriage and Minnesotans United for All Families also offered merchandise for sale on their websites, providing supporters yet another way to self-identify symbolically with their cause. Public policy campaigns will never be the same.

FOUR SPECIALIZED THEORIES BEYOND FUNCTIONALISM, CONFLICT, AND SYMBOLIC INTERACTIONISM

9.5 Apply specialized theories to the family.

Like the other social problems addressed in this book, the study of families has its own set of specialized theories, in addition to structural functionalist, conflict, and symbolic interactionist theories. This section briefly describes four such theories and applies them to family social problems: social exchange theory and sexual engagement, life course development theory and boomerang kids, family systems theory and (dis)connected families, and family ecology theory and raising families in dangerous neighborhoods.

Social Exchange Theory: Transactional Sexual Exchanges

Social exchange theory is a microsociological theory based on the idea that individuals will draw on their personal resources to maximize their rewards and minimize their costs. Furthermore, the theory suggests that we form, maintain, and dissolve social relationships based in large part on our perceptions of equity and balance in the calculus of exchange (Karraker and Grochowski 2012). In other words, we commit to and continue in long-term intimate relationships to the extent that we trust we will be treated fairly in the long run (Scanzoni 1978, 1982; Marsiglio and Scanzoni 1995).

Among the family social problems that interest sociologists is why young men and women often become sexually active before they are developmentally or socially ready to do so. Have you ever considered that sexual engagement might be driven by patterns of exchange? Nancy Luke and her colleagues (2011) in the United States and Kenya have studied premarital relationships among women in sub-Saharan Africa. They found that unmarried women who are poor are more likely to engage in **transactional sex**, the receipt of money and

Social exchange theory: A theory that posits individuals will draw on personal resources to maximize rewards and minimize costs when forming, maintaining, or dissolving relationships.

Transactional sex: The exchange of money and gifts for sexual activities.

gifts from a male partner in exchange for sexual activities, and that engaging in transactional sex decreases a young woman's power to negotiate a relationship to her advantage (such as requiring the man to use a condom). As a young woman's income increases, so does the likelihood that she will delay sex and engage in safer sexual practices

Family Life Course Development Theory: Boomerang Kids

Are you a "boomerang kid" (or do you expect you might become one in the future)? Thinking of young adults you know who have moved back in with their parents (or never left the family home), what social factors do you believe shaped their decisions? In what ways might this "new normal" of deferred adulthood affect the life course development of young adults and their parents?

Family life course development theory seeks to understand developmental processes and outcomes as families move through a series of stages across the life course. These stages are set in part by historical and social conditions and often come to be socially acceptable, as in the case of age norms for marriage and childbearing (Karraker and Grochowski 2012). For example, much recent research has examined the problem of adult children moving back in with their parents, described as "accordion families and boomerang kids" (Newman 2012) or "helicopter parents and landing pad kids" (Fingerman et al. 2012). In 2011, three in ten young adults lived with their parents. Furthermore, among those living with parents, eight in ten were satisfied with the arrangement (Parker 2012).

So, what is the social problem here? Overly dependent adult children who just will not grow up? Smothering parents who enable their children's dependency? Or social forces that are changing the very nature of the transition from child to adult? Katherine S. Newman (2012) interviewed and observed families in six developed countries: Denmark, Italy, Japan, Spain, Sweden, and the United States. Her conclusion: Global economic forces have changed cultures around the world, causing

....

Family life course development theory: A theory that examines the developmental processes and outcomes as families move through a series of normative stages across the life course.

Family systems theory: A theory that views the family as a set of subsystems defined by boundaries and striving toward social equilibrium.

the cost of living to rise along with unemployment rates. As globalization has challenged normative markers for adulthood, families have welcomed back young adults, allowing them to draw on "the bank of mom and dad" (xi) and creating a "slippery state of adulthood" (10). This may be creating a deferred crisis, as members of the younger generation are unable to establish financial and other independence, leaving them even more vulnerable as their parents age and die. In the meantime, what it means to be an adult is clearly undergoing a substantial shift worldwide.

Family Systems Theory: (Dis)connected Families

Family systems theory has received wide play among counselors, nurses, social workers, sociologists, and others who work with troubled families. This theory views the family as a series of subsystems, such as parent-child, siblings, and spouses, and proposes that a change in any part of the family system will have consequences for the other parts. Families therefore strive to maintain a sense of equilibrium (Karraker and Grochowski 2012). Scholars have examined a range of family social problems from a family systems approach, including marital conflict, parent-child conflict, and child sexual abuse. One of the most immediate problems facing family systems today is the association between media use and increasing disconnection between family members (Padilla-Walker, Coyne, and Fraser 2012).

In *Alone Together: Why We Expect More from Technology and Less from Each Other* (2011), Sherry Turkle (who is both a sociologist and a clinical psychologist) uses 15 years of research to describe how blogs, cell phones, Facebook, and other information and communication technologies have ramped up our professional productivity and enabled us to remain connected with family members when we are physically separated from them. The effects on family subsystems of these new ways of communicating, and the dissatisfaction and even anger they sometimes create, are exemplified by the case of Trey, whose brother shared the news that his wife was pregnant not with a visit or a personal call, but with a blog posted to the world. For people like Trey, Turkle notes, the new technologies have created (dis)connected families, compromising the quality of authentic interaction and relationships among partners, parents, children, and other family members, threatening connections and intimacy with the "erosion of boundaries between the real and the virtual" (xi).

Broken Families

Family Ecology Theory: Raising Children in Dangerous Neighborhoods

Families are embedded in broader natural and human-built environments (Karraker and Grochowski 2012). **Family ecology theory** helps us understand how they function and adapt within these physical, social, and other ecosystems (Bubolz and Sontag 1993). Could you construct a diagram that illustrates the social ecology of an immigrant family in the United States? How does this ecology differ from that of a family that does not have immigrant status? How do key social institutions like education, economics, government, religion, and extended and other kin create potential assets (or deficits) for immigrant families? (For in-depth information about immigrant families, see the award-winning research of Joanna Dreby 2010, 2012.)

Some of the most compelling applications of family ecology theory help us understand the importance of safe neighborhoods for families raising children. For example, research has found that mothers who perceive the neighborhoods in which they live to be dangerous spend significantly less time in outdoor activities with their children than do mothers who perceive their

Family ecology theory: A theory that views family systems as embedded in natural or human-made physical, social, and other environments.

Rebecca Cook / Reuters

A Neighborhood Watch sign posted in a neighborhood in Detroit, Michigan. Do you know the crime statistics of your neighborhood and city?

neighborhoods to be safe (Frech and Kimbro 2011). Organizations like MAD DADS (Men Against Destruction—Defending Against Drugs and Social Disorder) understand the role of the family ecosystem in raising healthy children. Founded in 1989 by a group of black fathers in Omaha, Nebraska, and now with chapters worldwide, MAD DADS (http://maddads.com) works at the local level to provide positive male role models as leaders in neighborhoods, communities, and cities, hoping to counter the effects of crime, drugs, and violence and make urban neighborhoods safer for youth and families.

SOCIAL CHANGE: WHAT CAN YOU DO?

 9.6 Identify steps toward social change to address family problems.

Recent issues of *Social Problems,* the journal of the Society for the Study of Social Problems, have included reports of cutting-edge research on family social problems, such as the effects of parental imprisonment on infant mortality (Wildeman 2012), racial/ethnic and socioeconomic inequality and cesarean births (Roth and Henley 2012), and empowerment in a battered women's shelter (Gengler 2012). But let us not neglect the power of sociology to spur change for the common good. One 20-year veteran of studying families offers a pragmatic approach to research on families and their problems. "I do what I do because I'm hoping that the knowledge we gain will make the world a better place for kids, [and] for families" (quoted in Friese and Bogenschneider 2009, 234).

Below, three undergraduate students reflect on the ways peers on their campuses have engaged in social action around three pressing family problems: affordable housing, food insecurity, and intimate partner violence. In addition, you can assess how your school or workplace stacks up against *Working Mother* magazine's "100 Best Places to Work" in terms of a culture of work-family balance.

College students volunteering with Habitat for Humanity tear shingles off a roof. College and university students from all over the United States spend their spring breaks building and repairing houses. Have you ever been involved in a service project like this?

Affordable Housing: Habitat for Humanity with the University of Minnesota

Brandon Haugrud

Like so many others in the United States, Minnesota families were devastated by the subprime mortgage crisis of 2008 that forced thousands to default on their mortgages and seek substandard housing. According to a recent study by the National Association of Realtors (2012), home foreclosures in Minnesota had fallen to nearly 2% by the end of 2012, the lowest level in more than five years and an indication that the housing market in Minnesota is slowly recovering. In the greater Twin Cities, however, more than half a million people still spend more than one-third of their net income on housing, and the problem continues to grow faster in Minnesota than in any other state. When nearly 50% of families in the Twin Cities with annual incomes under $35,000 pay more than they can afford on their housing, they are less able to afford health care, nutritious food, high-quality education, and long-term savings.

Students at the University of Minnesota, many from families that experienced home foreclosures, have partnered with Twin Cities Habitat for Humanity to eliminate poverty housing and make the dream of homeownership a reality for hardworking families. In

Food insecurity: A household's lack of access to nutritious food on a regular basis.

Intimate partner violence (IPV): Physical, sexual, or psychological/emotional harm or the threat of harm by a current or former intimate partner or spouse

addition to constructing safe, decent, affordable homes, students have become politically engaged with the Minnesota state legislature in their efforts to persuade lawmakers to support affordable-housing legislation. They also assist communities outside Minnesota, taking winter and spring break trips to build homes with other Habitat affiliates across the United States, as well as raising thousands of dollars each year for new home construction. To learn more about the work of Habitat for Humanity and its efforts to eliminate poverty housing, or to become involved with a Habitat affiliate in your community, visit http://www.habitat.org.

Food Insecurity: Lewis & Clark College's Hunger Banquet

Miriam Wilkes Karraker

What social problem could be more pressing for parents than the inability to feed their children? Almost one-third of Oregon's children experience **food insecurity**, or uncertain access to nutritious food. This is one of the highest rates in the United States. In Portland, home of Lewis & Clark College, 14% of households do not have access to nutritious food on a regular basis (Yeager 2012).

In what Barry Glassner (2012), sociologist and president of Lewis & Clark College, describes as "an impressive flip side to the absurd *Portlandia* sketch and the excess and privilege it skewers," students at Lewis & Clark presented a "hunger banquet" in 2012 to raise awareness of food insecurity. Upon arriving at the dining hall, each Lewis & Clark student received a lunch ticket. Each was then served a meal typical for a public school student based on the social class and neighborhood of a particular school. Afterward, a Feeding America Child Hunger Corps member of the Oregon Food Bank and other community partners discussed food insecurity and the social, developmental, and academic significance of food deprivation for children in the public schools. Students left the "hunger banquet" with information about how they could better serve children and families by keeping food banks well stocked and by advocating against hunger.

Intimate Partner Violence: The Clothesline Project at the University of St. Thomas

Emilee Sirek and Victoria Speake

Intimate partner violence (IPV) is "a serious, preventable public health problem that affects millions of Americans" (Centers for Disease Control and

University of Kansas students Casey Pettit (left) and Nicole Tichenor make their way along an installation of the Clothesline Project, which publicly displays T-shirts decorated by survivors of rape or domestic violence or both.

Prevention 2012b). It includes physical, sexual, and psychological/emotional harm, or the threat of such harm, by a current or former partner or spouse, and it occurs among both heterosexual and same-sex couples. IPV varies in frequency and severity and ranges from one blow to chronic, severe battering. Men and women are violent at nearly equal rates, but men make up the majority (87%) of offenders who come to the attention of the police (Melton and Sillito 2012).

The Clothesline Project (CLP) was started in 1990 to bear "witness to violence against women." Women affected by violence decorate a shirt and then hang it on a clothesline to spread community awareness of violence against women and generate support for those affected by family violence and other traumatic experiences. The colors of the shirts represent different forms of violence, from sexual abuse to political attack. Since it began on Cape Cod, Massachusetts, the CLP has crossed state and international borders, appearing in Lebanon, Germany, Namibia, and Taiwan. Friends and family members of victims and survivors of IPV can now also decorate shirts with or on behalf of their loved ones.

Students at the University of St. Thomas in St. Paul, Minnesota, have elaborated on the CLP model to engage students, faculty, and staff who may not have experienced IPV directly. All campus community members are invited to decorate or write the name of a survivor or victim on a shirt to be hung on a clothesline strung in the campus quad. This inclusive event serves as a visual reminder that everyone is connected to interpersonal violence in some way. For more information about the CLP and instructions on how to start a project on your own campus, visit http://www.clotheslineproject.org.

▶▶ The Work-Family Climate at Your School or Workplace

For more than 25 years, *Working Mother* magazine has invited companies to be recognized for "know[ing] what it takes to keep their employee moms productive and engaged both at work and home." The application for recognition asks more than 500 detailed questions about issues such as child care, flexible scheduling, and advancement programs. *Working Mother* then recognizes the "100 Best" companies for women, hourly workers, executive women, and multicultural women, as well as the best law firms and "green" companies. The Top 10 for 2012 included such well-known corporations as Bank of America, IBM, and Procter and Gamble, but the full list includes lesser-known companies as well.

How does your school or workplace measure up on indicators of quality of work-family life? Read some of the profiles of *Working Mother*'s "100 Best" at http://www.workingmother.com/best-companies/2012-working-mother-100-best-companies. Contact your human resources department for information on workplace policies, but also collect data on child care and other work-family issues from your organization's website for current or potential employees. Use social media to gather unofficial information about employee satisfaction and your organization's reputation in the community around work-family issues. You may find additional information and support if your organization has a women's center or related affinity group. When you complete your research, prepare a white paper in which you assess the status of work-family support at your organization and offer recommendations. Share it with the offices and individuals who assisted you, as well as with other leaders in the organization.

WHAT DOES AMERICA THINK?

Questions about Family from the General Social Survey

 Turn to the beginning of the chapter to compare your answers to the total population.

1. Children are a financial burden on parents.

    AGREE: 26.8%

    DISAGREE: 57.6%

    NEITHER AGREE NOR DISAGREE: 15.6%

2. Same-sex female couple can raise a child as well as a male-female couple.

    AGREE: 46.7%

    DISAGREE: 40.9%

    NEITHER AGREE NOR DISAGREE: 12.4%

3. Having children increases social standing in society.

    AGREE: 33.2%

    DISAGREE: 36.3%

    NEITHER AGREE NOR DISAGREE: 30.5%

4. Same-sex male couple can raise a child as well as a male-female couple.

    AGREE: 42.9%

    DISAGREE: 44.2%

    NEITHER AGREE NOR DISAGREE: 12.9%

5. Single parents can raise kids as well as two.

    AGREE: 48.8%

    DISAGREE: 41.7%

    NEITHER AGREE NOR DISAGREE: 9.5%

6. Divorce is the best solution to marital problems.

    AGREE: 51.5%

    DISAGREE: 33.7%

    NEITHER AGREE NOR DISAGREE: 14.8%

 ## LOOK BEHIND THE NUMBERS

Go to **edge.sagepub.com/trevino** for a breakdown of these data across time and by race, sex, age, income, and other statuses.

1. How might having children improve an individual's social standing?

2. More than half of the respondents disagreed with the statement "Children are a financial burden on parents." What are some possible reasons for their answer?

3. Examine the responses of men and women to the question about the ability of a single parent to raise a child. How would you explain the differences?

4. The questions presented in this chapter do not have a history of being asked on the General Social Survey. Why do you think they were just recently added to the GSS?

SOURCE: National Opinion Research Center, University of Chicago.

CHAPTER SUMMARY

 Define the concept of family.

Falling marriage rates, rising divorce rates, and increases in cohabitation fuel the culture wars around the family. The marriage movement asserts that the lifelong union of a man and a woman is best suited to fulfilling the traditional social functions of the family. Yet other scholars see changes in family as representing not decline, but adaptation. The U.S. Census Bureau defines family as two or more people who are related to one another by birth, marriage, or adoption and who share living quarters. A household is defined as people, related or not, who share living quarters. Beyond those definitions, the meaning of family is both contested and changing, sometimes including, for example, fictive kin. A more contemporary definition recognizes that each of us lives in a series of families over a lifetime and that family is defined not only by biology and law but also by experience with kin, friends, and others.

 Discuss patterns and trends in marriage, cohabitation, and divorce.

The United States is facing a marriage dearth. The proportion of adults who are currently married has dropped steadily over the past 50 years, to around 50%. At the same time, the percentage of adults who are divorced has almost tripled, and the percentage of those who have never married has almost doubled. The choice to marry intersects with a wide range of other social factors, including age (age at first marriage has never been higher), race and ethnicity (whites are more likely than either blacks or Hispanics to be married), and college education (a majority who are currently married hold college degrees). These patterns also reflect the available pool of eligibles and the marriage gradient, as well as the possibility of heterogamous unions. Still, a clear majority of those who have never been married say they wish to be married, although many believe marriage is becoming obsolete in spite of its advantages.

 Describe family problems related to economics, religion, and government.

The onset of the Great Recession saw family income and especially family wealth drop, the latter to the lowest level since 1990, adding to the challenges middle-class families already face. Overall, marriage, cohabitation, and divorce rates have changed very little since the economic downturn began in 2008, but circumstances like housing instability put a special strain on family resilience. Religious beliefs and practices have been linked to family resilience, but declining numbers of U.S. adults profess identification with a religious faith tradition. Although the United States lacks a comprehensive family policy, one example of government intervention on behalf of families is the Violence Against Women Act. A provision of the act is specifically targeted at aiding Native American women living on reservations, who experience higher rates of violence than do women of other races.

 Apply the functionalist, conflict, and symbolic interactionist perspectives to the concept of family.

The case of same-sex marriage effectively illustrates the three theories applied throughout this book to illuminate social policy alternatives. Structural functionalist theory calls to mind the efforts of those who wish to retain traditional marriage through passage of legislation such as the Defense of Marriage Act. Conflict theory reminds us that maintaining the status quo in the form of traditional family structures disadvantages families led by gays and lesbians in profound ways. Symbolic interactionism demonstrates the power of language in social policies affecting families, as well as the role of social media and new communication technologies in shaping public opinion around social policy.

9.5 Apply specialized theories to the family.

Social exchange theory offers an opportunity to understand why young women might engage in transactional sex. Life course development theory examines the rise of the "boomerang kids" phenomenon and the likely consequences of delayed adulthood. Family systems theory sees families as a set of systems and subsystems and explains why these systems are becoming increasingly disconnected by technology. Finally, family ecology theory reveals how parenting styles are affected by parents' perceptions of the safety of their neighborhoods.

Habitat for Humanity volunteers help provide affordable housing for families. Taking part in a "hunger banquet" can help students or members of any organization understand family food insecurity and encourage them to take action to alleviate the problem in their communities. The Clothesline Project raises awareness about intimate partner violence and promotes healing. You can conduct your own survey to assess the balance between work and family supported at your own school or workplace.

DISCUSSION QUESTIONS

1. How do we define and understand family? How is this understanding different from how we define kin? What about how we define a household? What are the primary functions of each of these—family, kin, and household—and what are our expectations of members of each group?

2. How do one's expectations of marriage and family shape one's willingness to enter into them? How have these expectations changed and how have they remained the same over time?

3. How and why have rates of marriage changed for different age groups since the start of the 20th century? What are the patterns of marriage we see in American society today? How are these patterns different from a generation or two ago? What explains the changes we see? How have these changes affected the way we define family?

4. In what ways are the patterns of marriage and family formation we see today affected by race, social class, and age? What about by level of education?

5. How do other institutions, such as the economy and religion, shape the composition of families? What about the choices individuals make regarding marriage and divorce? What about choices around childbearing, in or out of marriage?

6. How does the government support some forms of family but not others? What role does organized religion play in supporting, or not supporting, families?

7. According to structural functionalism, is expanding marriage to include more types of couples functional or dysfunctional for society? In what ways does expanding marriage maintain the normative family? How does expanding marriage threaten the normative family?

8. How might applying a different label than *marriage* to some unions affect the members of said unions? What does marriage mean today given the social and political changes that have taken place since the 1950s with regard to families, marriage, and alternatives to marriage?

9. According to social exchange theory, why are Americans so willing to marry but also to divorce? What explanations does this perspective offer for the changes to marriage and family that took place throughout the 20th century?

10. What does family ecology theory reveal about families in their social context? If family ecology theory is correct, could social action such as building more affordable homes and decreasing food insecurity have a positive impact on marriage and family? What else would need to change in order to better support families at risk for divorce or dissolution?

11. In what ways does awarding the top companies for working mothers encourage a broader change in the workplace for women, families, and all employees? Who benefits from such recognition? Are there race, class, and socioeconomic differences between the employees of such companies and those of companies that are not ranked among the best for working mothers?

KEY TERMS

civil unions 235

cohabitation 221

crude divorce rate 227

culture wars 221

Defense of Marriage
   Act (DOMA) 235

family 221

family ecology theory 240

family life course
   development
   theory 239

family systems theory 239

feminist perspective 222

fictive kin 222

food insecurity 241

household 221

intimate partner
   violence (IPV) 241

marriage dearth 224

marriage gradient 224

marriage movement 221

marriage squeeze 224

pool of eligibles 224

resilience 232

selection
   effect 227

social exchange
   theory 238

spirituality 232

transactional
   sex 238

visiting union 229

Sharpen your skills with SAGE at edge.sagepub.com/trevino

A personalized approach to help you accomplish your coursework goals in an easy-to-use learning environment.

10 WORK AND THE ECONOMY

Rudi Volti

Reuters / Shannon Stapleton

 A woman walks by a rusting mural of a huge U.S. flag painted on a wall of corrugated metal. The U.S. economy has long been the largest and strongest in the world. Do you think that the economic position of the United States has been tarnished by the financial crisis that began in 2007, the downgrading of the country's credit rating in 2013, the growing budget deficit, and the country's persistently high unemployment rate?

Investigating Work and the Economy: My Story

LEARNING OBJECTIVES

10.1 Explain the general shape of the U.S. workforce today.

10.2 Identify patterns and trends in employment and unemployment.

10.3 Discuss the role of unions and the issues of wage inequities, discrimination, and stress in the workplace.

10.4 Apply the functionalist, conflict, and symbolic interactionist perspectives to workplace issues.

10.5 Apply specialized theories to workplace issues.

10.6 Identify steps toward social change for work-related problems.

Rudi Volti

When I was a boy I was fascinated with airplanes, trains, cars, and motorcycles. But my family was anything but affluent, so many years passed before I could get a car, a very tired 1955 Chevrolet that did not take well to my efforts to improve its performance. In college my interest in mechanical devices led me to a more general consideration of technology and its interaction with the economy, culture, and society. I took this interest into my career as a college professor, where I taught a course on technology and society almost every year. These classes were the motivation for my textbook *Society and Technological Change,* now in its seventh edition. I also have a strong interest in the sociological study of work and occupations, and these two interests nicely complement each other. Of course, many forces besides technology shape the way work is structured and performed, and I have tried to account for them in *An Introduction to the Sociology of Work and Occupations,* now in its second edition. Finding connections between technological change and social change, both historical and current, is a continuing source of fascination for me.

 **WHAT DO YOU THINK?**

Questions about Work and the Economy from the General Social Survey

1. If you were to become rich, would you continue to work or stop working?

   ☐ CONTINUE TO WORK
   ☐ STOP WORKING

2. With regard to your income tax, do you think it is too high, about right, or too low?

   ☐ TOO HIGH
   ☐ ABOUT THE RIGHT AMOUNT
   ☐ TOO LOW

3. Do you think that work is most important to feel accomplished?

   ☐ MOST IMPORTANT
   ☐ NOT THE MOST IMPORTANT

4. What is your interest level in economic issues?

   ☐ VERY INTERESTED
   ☐ MODERATELY INTERESTED
   ☐ NOT INTERESTED AT ALL

5. What is your confidence level in banks and financial institutions?

   ☐ A GREAT DEAL
   ☐ ONLY SOME
   ☐ HARDLY ANY

 Turn to the end of the chapter to view the results for the total population.

SOURCE: National Opinion Research Center, University of Chicago.

FROM 500 TO 750 ENVELOPES

Lisa Weber isn't exactly a newbie at the National Envelope Company; she has been there for 28 years, having started when she was 19 years old. For many years the company paid decent wages and offered occasional perks like company picnics and holiday turkeys. These are now gone, and at the same time the pace of work has increased substantially. Today, says Ms. Weber, "It's harder for me to want to get up and go to work than it used to be. It's not something I would wish on anybody. I'm worn out. I get home and I can barely stand up" (quoted in Semuels 2013, A1).

Lisa Weber's job is the flip side of one seemingly bright spot in the Great Recession: a strong advance in worker productivity. For her, improved productivity means having gone from producing 500 envelopes per hour to 750. When she started with the firm, it was owned by a Holocaust survivor who believed benevolent treatment of employees was not only a good thing in itself but also good for business. Then e-mail came along, and with it a reduced demand for paper envelopes. The firm filed for bankruptcy in 2010 and was acquired by a private equity firm. As the new owners saw it, changes had to be made in order to return the company to solvency. Some workers were laid off permanently, while those who hung on to their jobs had to work harder. As one executive summed up the situation, "It became clear that as the market began to soften, what was in place was not a sustainable business model. . . . Sometimes you have to make dramatic changes to save the jobs that you can."

The basic elements of the National Envelope story have been repeated at thousands of other firms. Technological change has undermined the foundations of many jobs, especially those in the manufacturing sector. The survival of many firms has hinged on their ability to pare production costs to a minimum, often by reducing numbers of workers and requiring higher output from those who remain. Meanwhile, persistently high levels of unemployment have dampened workers' ability to improve their wages and avoid sharp upturns in the pace of work.

At the same time, however, technological change, globalization, and social and cultural changes are also creating new opportunities for those able to take advantage of them. The dynamic world of the early 21st century is constantly creating winners and losers; the challenge is to encourage potential winners while at the same time creating a more humane society for all. In this chapter we will examine work and unemployment against the backdrop of major technological, social, economic, and cultural changes. Along the way we will consider immigration, the trajectory of wages and salaries, labor unions, race- and gender-based discrimination, human capital, affirmative action, workplace stresses and dangers, and job satisfaction. By examining these topics we can better understand the forces that have made Lisa Weber's working life so difficult, and what, if anything, might be done to improve the working lives of men and women like her.

WORK AND THE LABOR FORCE

 10.1 Explain the general shape of the U.S. workforce today.

We begin with some basic terms. Unless they are self-employed or unpaid volunteers, workers receive **compensation** in the form of wages or salaries for their efforts. A **wage** is a sum of money paid on an hourly basis. In general, a wage earner is not as well paid as an employee who receives a **salary**, which generally is paid on a monthly or bimonthly basis. A salary provides more stable earnings, but it also may require working beyond the customary 40-hour workweek for no additional pay.

Many workers also receive a variety of **benefits** in addition to their wages or salaries. In the past, many salaried workers were entitled to pensions after they retired. "Defined benefit" plans that paid a stipulated sum of money on a regular basis have become rare in the private sector, and in their place many employers now offer "defined contribution" plans in which both the employers

....

Compensation: Salaries or wages along with benefits paid to employees. Also known as total compensation.

Wage: Payment for work done on an hourly basis.

Salary: Remuneration paid on a monthly or bimonthly basis and not directly tied to the number of hours worked.

Benefits: Noncash compensation paid to employees, such as health insurance and pension plans. Also known as fringe benefits.

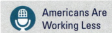 Americans Are Working Less

TABLE 10.1   The U.S. Labor Force in 2013

Total labor force over the age of 20	Men	Women	Employed men	Employed women	Unemployed men	Unemployed women
149,387,000	79,747,000	69,540,000	74,228,000	64,707,000	5,519,000	4,837,000

SOURCE: United States Department of Labor, Bureau of Labor Statistics, 2013B. Table A-1. "Employment Status of the Civilian Population by Sex and Age."

and the employees contribute to employees' retirement funds. Both employers and employees also put funds into the latter's Social Security account. Another important benefit, when it is available, is employer-provided health insurance. The United States has relied much more heavily on employers to provide health insurance than other countries do, creating a number of social and economic problems, especially for workers whose insurance is terminated when they lose their jobs. Other employer-supplied benefits may include contributions to disability insurance and perhaps financial support for employees' further education and training. Together, a wage or salary along with benefits add up to an employee's **total compensation**.

The **labor force** is conventionally defined as all persons in the civilian noninstitutional population who are either employed or unemployed but actively seeking work. In turn, the "noninstitutional population" is defined by the U.S. Department of Labor as "persons 16 years of age and older residing in the 50 states and the District of Columbia, who are not inmates of institutions (e.g., penal and mental facilities, homes for the aged), and who are not on active duty in the Armed Forces" (U.S. Bureau of Labor Statistics 2013d). The size of the labor force can change over time, substantially affecting employment and unemployment statistics.

In early 2013, the U.S. labor force looked as shown in Table 10.1. The total of 10,356,000 unemployed men and women is quite high by historical standards. We will consider its causes and consequences in this chapter.

The jobs of those who are employed fall into one of three broad sectors of the economy, known as the primary, secondary, and tertiary (or service) sectors. In 2010, about 2,937,000 workers were employed in the **primary sector**, consisting mostly of farming and mining, while 23,158,000 worked in the **secondary sector**, which includes construction and manufacturing. This leaves no fewer than 112,969,000, or more than 81% of employed workers, in the tertiary or **service sector**, a varied mix that includes health care, education, financial services, utilities, retail and wholesale trade, leisure and hospitality, transportation, and all levels of government (U.S. Census Bureau 2012d).

PATTERNS AND TRENDS

 10.2   Identify patterns and trends in employment and unemployment.

The recent shift of the majority of the labor force into the service sector has been one of the most important long-term changes in human history. Very few of us now produce tangible goods as farmers or factory workers.

People walk past clocks at Reuters Plaza in London on their way to work. Many see their jobs as the "daily grind" in which their lives are dictated by time and making money. The popular phrases "working for the weekend" and "Thank God it's Friday" connote how many people feel about their workaday worlds.

Handout / Reuters

Total compensation: Remuneration that includes a wage or salary plus benefits.

Labor force: The segment of the population either employed or actively seeking employment.

Primary sector: The sector of the economy centered on farming, fishing, and the extraction of raw materials.

Secondary sector: The sector of the economy that includes manufacturing and other activities that produce material goods.

Service sector: The sector of the economy that provides services such as education, health care, and government. Also known as the tertiary sector.

Jens Büttner / dpa / Corbis

Finding a Job

How do you get a job? How effective are formal means of finding a job such as website listings, social media, newspaper advertisements, employment agencies, university placement services, and cold calls to prospective employers?

A classic study by Mark Granovetter (1995) began with the assumption that crucial to any job search is access to information about job openings and various aspects of potential jobs. Granovetter found that "formal means" of learning about jobs often were useful but accounted for less than half of job leads. What was really crucial for the majority of successful job searches was membership in a social network that included people connected in some way to employers with openings to fill. For prospective employers, an applicant's network provided important clues. Instead of using elaborate procedures for determining a candidate's suitability, employers could simply assume that a social connection to one of their employees (or even a friend or relative of an employee) at least qualified the person for further consideration. When that employee or employee's friend was known to be competent and trustworthy, an employer would be more inclined to hire an applicant who had a connection, however tenuous, to one or the other.

Granovetter also discovered something that seems counterintuitive. We might assume that strong interpersonal ties, the sort found among kinfolk, friends, and neighbors living in close proximity, would form the core of the social networks that led to successful job placements. In fact, the opposite prevailed: *weak* ties were much more important than strong ones. Weak ties connected acquaintances rather than close friends, customers and merchants, and second-order relationships such as "a friend of my aunt Beatrice." This follows from the likelihood that our close personal relationships link people who travel in economic and social circles similar to ours. As a result, their information regarding available job opportunities is not much better than our own. In contrast, connecting with a less

---

Our livelihoods are based on the work we do as nurses, teachers, musicians, government employees, food-service workers, and employees in all the other varied occupations in the service sector.

Employment and Unemployment

Many workers lost their jobs during the course of the Great Recession, which began in late 2007, and although employment has rebounded since then, joblessness remains a serious problem, as does underemployment—that is, working part-time when a full-time job is preferred. We calculate the percentage of unemployed men and women by dividing the number of jobless people by the number of individuals in the labor force (see Figure 10.1).

We need to treat these numbers with caution, however. Far from being a stable number, the size of the labor force may vary widely. During hard economic times with high

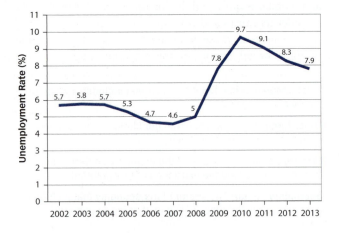

FIGURE 10.1 **Unemployment in the United States, 2002–2013**

Unemployment Rate (%)

Values: 5.7, 5.8, 5.7, 5.3, 4.7, 4.6, 5, 7.8, 9.7, 9.1, 8.3, 7.9 across years 2002–2013

SOURCE: U.S. Bureau of Labor Statistics. (2012). Labor force statistics from the *Current Population Survey.*

intimate social network considerably expands the sources of information about where work can be found. These kinds of connections can be particularly important for low-status job seekers; as subsequent research indicated, weak ties are more likely than strong ties to connect them with higher-status individuals.

To be sure, a lot has changed since Granovetter conducted his research. In particular, social networking sites and other digital media such as Twitter have become important sources of information about employment opportunities, and most prospective employers use social media to announce job openings. Job seekers have made abundant use of them, but have these media reduced the importance of personal connections? Current research says no. According to a survey conducted by the Gallup organization in 2007, the most used sources of information about available jobs were friends and family members; 74% of respondents said they made use of these sources. Only 15% said online networking tools were at least "somewhat effective" in helping them find jobs. Online job databases fared a bit better, with 25% of respondents making this assessment. In contrast, nearly 50% found friends and family were at least somewhat effective (Ott, Blacksmith, and Royal 2008). Another survey conducted by Kelly Services (2013) came to a similar conclusion, finding that only 11% of respondents had secured jobs through social media. The use of social media can even damage a person's prospects of getting a job. According to another survey, 43% of managers found information on social media sites that dissuaded them from hiring certain candidates (CareerBuilder 2013).

Perhaps we should not make too much of the limited utility of social media for finding jobs. Social media sites are relatively new, and employers and job seekers are still learning how to use them effectively. In the long run, users of social media may benefit from the fact that, as Granovetter discovered, more distant network relationships are particularly helpful when it comes to finding jobs. After all, how many of your Facebook friends are acquaintances rather than friends in the fullest sense of the word?

▶ **THINK ABOUT IT**

1. What sorts of social networks do you belong to? Which of them might be especially useful in helping you find a job?

2. Many people, especially members of minority groups, lack connections with social networks that can be useful for finding jobs. What might be done to help such job seekers expand and develop their social networks?

---

levels of unemployment, many jobless men and women will abandon their job searches and drop out of the labor force. Some may go back to school or retire earlier than planned. Many will simply join the ranks of **discouraged workers** who have quit looking for jobs and are no longer counted as unemployed. Official unemployment statistics thus may not reflect the true extent of joblessness. Paradoxically, the level of unemployment may also rise in the early months of an economic recovery as more job seekers return to the labor force.

Another group not counted as part of the labor force are those in jail or prison, whose numbers have grown substantially in recent years. At the end of 2011 there were 1,598,780 federal and state prisoners, most of whom were of working age (Carson and Sabol 2012). (For a discussion of the effects of increased levels of incarceration on official employment rates for African Americans, see Western 2006, 86–107.)

Finally, government statistics make no distinction between workers who were employed for the whole year and workers who happened to have jobs at the time they were surveyed. The unemployment rate is a snapshot, and, as such, it does not adequately capture the situations of many workers who have experienced periods of joblessness during a given year.

For these reasons, some believe the official unemployment rate may give an overly optimistic picture of employment and unemployment. On the other hand, a substantial number of workers elude the statistical net by working in the **underground economy** (also known as the shadow economy). Some work done in this sector is

Discouraged workers: Unemployed workers who have given up looking for jobs and hence are no longer counted as members of the labor force.

Underground economy: Work that is illegal or is designed to avoid the reporting of payments to government authorities such as tax collectors. Also known as the shadow economy.

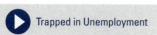 Trapped in Unemployment

clearly illegal in all or most parts of the country—drug manufacture and dealing, prostitution, bookmaking, and bootlegging, for example. A considerable amount of work also occurs in legitimate areas but is done "off the books," including repair work, gardening, and personal services performed on a cash basis to avoid sales and income taxes. Some workers are hired clandestinely so their employers can avoid making contributions to Social Security, Medicare, and other mandated programs, or because their businesses are violating health and safety codes.

By its very nature, employment in the underground economy is difficult to measure, but according to one careful study, it accounts for an average of 12% of gross national income in industrially developed economies and much more in underdeveloped ones (Schneider and Enste 2002). Including these workers in official statistics would decrease the unemployment rate by a significant margin.

The Consequences of Unemployment

Periods of high unemployment do not affect all members of the labor force in the same way. As you might expect, unemployment is negatively correlated with educational levels (Figure 10.2). Also, race and ethnicity have clear associations with employment and unemployment (Figures 10.3 and 10.4). The worst unemployment situation is that of black teenagers, who had an unemployment rate of 41.3% in 2011. Hispanic, Asian American, and white teenagers were somewhat better off at 31.1%, 25.2%, and 21.7%, respectively, but these rates are hardly cause for celebration.

FIGURE 10.2 U.S. Unemployment Rates by Educational Level, 2013

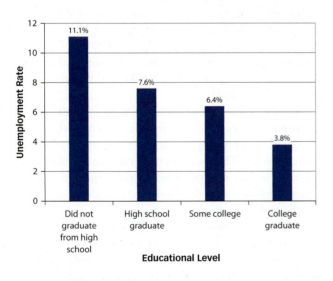

SOURCE: United States Department of Labor, Bureau of Labor Statistics, 2013A. "Employment Status of the Civilian Population 25 years and Over by Educational Attainment."

FIGURE 10.3 U.S. Unemployment by Race/Ethnicity, 2011

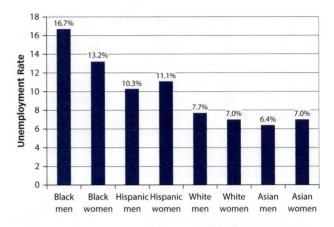

SOURCE: United States Department of Labor, Bureau of Labor Statistics, 2011. "Labor Force Characteristics by Race and Ethnicity."

The median time without a job also varies. In 2011 it was 21.4 weeks, but 43.8% of the unemployed were jobless for 27 weeks or more (U.S. Bureau of Labor Statistics 2012c, 43). Curiously, however, the length of unemployment during this period of time did not match the unemployment rates for different racial and ethnic groups (see Figure 10.5).

The economic costs of unemployment can be severe for individuals. They lose not only wages and salaries but also employer-provided health care benefits. Under

FIGURE 10.4 Unemployment Rate by Educational Attainment for Blacks and Whites 25 and Older in the United States, 2012

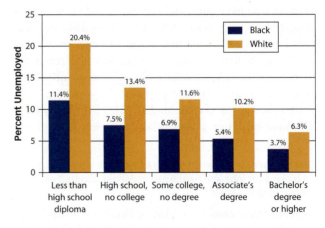

SOURCE: United States Department of Labor, Bureau of Labor Statistics, 2011. "The African-American Labor Force in the Recovery," Chart 3.

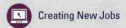
Creating New Jobs

FIGURE 10.5 Percentage of U.S. Workers Unemployed for 27 Weeks or More by Race/Ethnicity, 2011

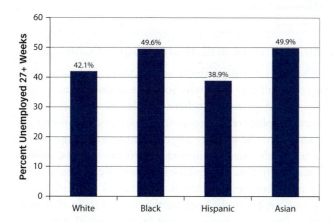

SOURCE: United States Department of Labor, Bureau of Labor Statistics, 2011. "Labor Force Characteristics by Race and Ethnicity."

these circumstances, medical problems have pushed many Americans into bankruptcy. Some can maintain their coverage by paying their former employers' shares of their insurance premiums, but this high cost adds considerably to the financial stress of unemployment.

In addition to making it more difficult to afford health care, joblessness itself can be hazardous to physical and psychological health. According to one recent study, workers between the ages of 51 and 61 who lost their jobs were twice as likely as employed workers to suffer a heart attack over the next 6 to 10 years (Bassett 2010). Another study of workers who lost their jobs during the severe recession of the early 1980s found that in the year following a job loss, the death rates of high-seniority workers increased by 50% to 100%. The consequences of unemployment also persisted for a long time; this cohort still exhibited a 10–15% higher death rate 20 years after the initial job loss (Luo 2010).

The manner in which unemployment produces these negative health consequences is not entirely clear, but unemployment does seem to be associated with poor health habits that increase the risk of diabetes and heart disease (Bassett 2010). It also seems highly likely that unemployment is accompanied by increased levels of stress, which can be the source of a multitude of physical ailments.

High unemployment levels affect the personal finances not only of the unemployed but also of those still working. Many become willing to accept lower wages, or longer

Quintile: One-fifth of anything that can be divided.

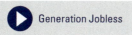
Generation Jobless

hours for the same wages, to get or keep jobs. We saw in the story that opened this chapter that many firms have boosted productivity and profits by increasing the workloads of diminished numbers of employees. According to one study, each percentage point increase in the unemployment rate lowers the incomes of families in the bottom **quintile** by 1.8%, by 1.4% in the middle quintile, and by 1% in the top quintile (Mishel, Bernstein, and Shierholz 2009, 48).

Finally, in addition to financial and health consequences, simply having been unemployed may have negative consequences that last long afterward. A study of workers unemployed during the severe recession of 1981–1982 found that two decades later their earnings were 30% less than those of workers who had remained employed during this period (*The Economist* 2010). Another study found that white men who graduated from college during the 1981–1982 recession earned 6% to 8% less for each percentage point increase in the unemployment rate than employees who graduated during more prosperous times. Their situation improved by about one-quarter of a percentage point in each following year, but 15 years after graduation their earnings were still 2.5% less than those of workers who graduated in better economic circumstances (Kahn 2009).

Jobs, Secure and Insecure

Given the many unfortunate consequences of unemployment, job security is one of the most important features a job can offer. Some occupations, notably teaching, offer the prospect of tenure in order to protect academic freedom. Tenure, however, is not ironclad; teachers and professors can lose their jobs for serious

A man rubs his eyes as he waits in a line of job seekers to attend a career fair in New York City. Long-term unemployment may lead not only to eviction and foreclosure on people's houses but also to mental stress and loss of self-esteem.

rule breaches or because their institutions have to cut staff for financial reasons. Other professions offer de facto tenure, as occurs when an attorney is made a partner in a law firm. Government workers and employees in some unionized industries and firms can be fired only after their employers have gone through formal procedures, some of them quite extensive. Employers also are prevented from firing workers for trying to organize a union or for **whistle-blowing**—that is, drawing public attention to malfeasance within the firm. Civil rights laws forbid dismissals based on race, color, gender, creed, age, or national origin. But in general, the relationship between employers and employees in the United States is governed by the doctrine of **employment at will**. This means that in most states, unless there is a specific agreement or discrimination of some sort has occurred, an employee can be summarily fired for any reason or for no reason at all (Muhl 2001).

Some of the most precariously employed are contingent workers, many of whom are "temps" placed by specialized agencies to do short-term work in offices and other work sites (see Figure 10.6). Because they do not have to give contingent workers benefits such as health insurance, some businesses make frequent use of them, while others retain them for periods of time that stretch "temporary" beyond recognition. Compared with members of the permanent workforce, temporary workers tend to be younger, less likely to be high school or college graduates, and more likely to be female, black, or Hispanic. About 40% are part-timers. The main advantage of working as a temp is flexibility, but temporary workers earn less per hour than regular employees, and most lack health insurance and pension plans. They are often given the most routine tasks and sometimes experience social isolation and poor self-image from being "just a temp" (Henson 1996).

Employment and Technological Change

What the statistics about employment and unemployment don't tell us is why jobs are abundant at certain times and scarce at others. While the business cycle, demographic trends, government policies, and even fluctuations in the weather affect the numbers, some degree of unemployment is inevitable. People may be jobless because they have moved or voluntarily left their jobs. In good economic times this frictional unemployment is not problematic because workers readily find new jobs. Even recessions may not be too painful if they are short and followed by economic expansions. This has unfortunately not been the case for the Great Recession; unemployment has stubbornly remained at a higher level than in most postrecession recoveries.

In considering the causes of present-day unemployment, it is useful to distinguish between two types of unemployment. **Cyclical unemployment** occurs during the periods of weak economic growth that seem to be inevitable features of a modern economy. Although these episodes are painful, they tend to be to be fairly short-lived and are somewhat lessened by government actions to stimulate the economy. Economic growth follows to help make up for the losses incurred. **Structural unemployment**, as its name implies, is joblessness resulting from major changes in the basic structure of the economy, such as the rise and fall of entire industries and a reordering of the occupational structure. A major cause of structural change is the introduction of new technologies, accompanied by the obsolescence of established ones. Computerization, the Internet, and smart phones have been transforming the ways we make things, communicate with one another, and send, receive, and store information. But with these benefits, has technological transformation also brought us widespread and persistent unemployment?

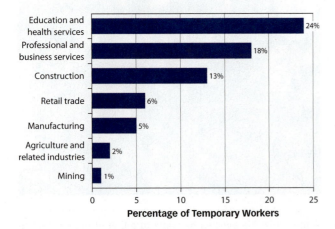

FIGURE 10.6 **Temporary Workers in Selected U.S. Industries, 2005**

Percentage of Temporary Workers

SOURCE: United States Department of Labor, Bureau of Labor Statistics, 2005. "Contingent and Alternative Employment Arrangements, February 2005."

Whistle-blowing: The act of calling attention to malfeasance in one's organization.

Employment at will: The legal practice that allows an employer to terminate a worker's employment even if no specific reason for the termination is given.

Cyclical unemployment: Unemployment caused by cyclical downturns in the economy.

Structural unemployment: Unemployment that is caused by basic changes in the economy.

The pluses and minuses of new technologies are endlessly debated. The government of Tudor England banned "engines for working of tape, lace, ribbon, and such wherein one man doth more amongst them than seven English men can do" (quoted in Thomis 1972, 14–15). Concerns about employment being destroyed by technological advance were common during the **Great Depression** of the 1930s, when a "technotax" was seriously considered for employers who replaced their workers with new equipment (Bix 2000).

The high levels of employment that followed the Great Depression should have eased these fears, but today's rapid advances in computers, robotics, expert systems, and automated processes have reignited them. On the other hand, technological advances have created new work opportunities; who was employed as a designer of Web pages before the Internet? Besides creating new jobs, technological change can create employment opportunities indirectly. A machine that reduces the cost of production puts more money in the pockets of the firm's owners or remaining workers, who then purchase more goods and services, creating more employment opportunities for workers who produce them. Cheaper production also lowers prices, resulting in higher sales and yet more production and employment opportunities. In all these cases, jobs threatened by increased productivity can be regained.

The false connection between technological change and unemployment is based on what economists call the **lump of labor fallacy**. This is the assumption that there is only so much work to be done and hence only a fixed number of jobs, so when labor-saving technologies take over some of the work, some workers necessarily lose their jobs. Some governments that subscribe to this idea have mandated a shorter workweek in the hope of creating more jobs. There are several good reasons for shortening the workweek, but creating new employment opportunities isn't one of them. There is no shortage of essential tasks to be done, now or in the future. For example, workers are needed to rectify environmental damage, rebuild crumbling infrastructure, and

Great Depression: Worldwide economic downturn in the period 1929–1941, marked by failing businesses, low or at times negative economic growth, and widespread unemployment.

Lump of labor fallacy: The notion that there is a fixed number of jobs and that unemployed individuals can find jobs only when others lose their jobs or reduce the number of hours they work.

Globalization: The process through which business firms, political authority, and cultural patterns spread throughout the world.

Today the automotive industry is highly automated, relying on robots—series of mechanical arms—in assembly lines and factories like this one in Australia. Robots are cost-effective, efficient, and safe. What do you see as the drawbacks for human workers of having robots in the factory?

bring medical services to underserved populations. The paradox of unemployment coexisting with unmet needs for workers suggests, first, that workers' skills are not matched to the kinds of jobs they require, and second, that governments and their citizens are unable or unwilling to pay for these jobs.

Should we not worry about technological advances having unfortunate consequences for work and employment? In fact, we should worry. Although technological change need not destroy *work* as a whole, it can certainly annihilate particular *jobs*. And as technological change alters the mix of jobs, it can substantially affect the distribution of income. Before we look at these issues, let us consider another force deeply affecting work and employment.

Globalization

Innovations from containerized freight traffic to e-mail to trade pacts between nations have allowed firms today to treat the whole world as a market for their products and services. Like technological advances, increasing **globalization** can lower production costs and translate into some combination of lower prices, higher wages and salaries, and greater profits. As a result, spendable income will increase, at least for some segments of the society. This in turn expands the demand for goods and services, at least some of which will be supplied by workers in the country that lost some jobs to offshore production. This is the good news, but it is not the whole story. Globalization, as well as technological change, has contributed to widening disparities in wealth and income around the world.

Globalization

Work and the Economy beyond Our Borders

The North American Free Trade Agreement

In 1965, Mexico enacted its Border Industrialization Plan, which for the most part removed tariffs for enterprises near the U.S.-Mexican border. This policy gave rise to maquiladoras, foreign-owned factories producing a wide range of industrial products along the Mexican side of the border. The number of factories expanded following the signing of the **North American Free Trade Agreement (NAFTA)** in 1994, which gradually eliminated tariff barriers between the United States, Canada, and Mexico.

Thousands of maquiladoras operate in Mexico today, many manufacturing products once made in the United States. Beyond question, U.S. workers have lost jobs due to factories relocating to Mexico and elsewhere, a form of globalization that has devastated entire communities unable to compete with workers earning roughly $2 per hour. At the same time, however, NAFTA has had some positive results. Trade between the United States and Mexico amounted to nearly half a trillion dollars in 2011. In that year the value of goods and services U.S. firms sold in Mexico came to $224 billion (Office of the U.S. Trade Representative 2013). Only Canada and China buy more U.S.-made goods. Although U.S.-Mexico trade has cost some U.S. jobs, it has also stimulated the expansion of others.

Assessing the impact of NAFTA on employment in the United States poses a number of methodological problems, but the consensus among economists is that the overall effects have been modest. Some studies show no net effect, while others indicate a net gain of a bit under a million U.S. jobs (O'Neil 2013, 96).

For Mexico and its workers, the picture is mixed. Some Mexican manufacturers closed their doors because they could not compete with foreign firms. The Mexican economy's tighter connection with the North American market has left it more vulnerable to economic slowdowns in the United States and Canada. Work in export-oriented maquiladoras, much of it done by women, is poorly compensated in comparison to work in the United States and other developed countries, but for many Mexicans it is an improvement over the widespread poverty of many parts of the country.

Despite expectations when it was enacted, NAFTA by itself has neither transformed the Mexican economy nor done much to stem the flow of undocumented immigration to the United States. Like any significant alteration in the economic status quo, it has brought significant gains to some and losses to others. Although the overall balance has been positive, those who have been adversely affected have had to make some painful adjustments.

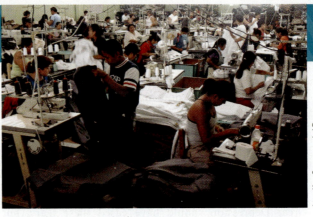

People work in a maquiladora, or garment assembly plant, in Mexico. Factories producing blue jeans have given jobs to thousands of workers, but they are pumping blue chemicals into rivers used to irrigate corn fields downstream. Locals say they do not know if the wastewater presents a long-term risk to their health, but some complain of chemical fumes that smell bad and irritate their throats.

▶ **THINK ABOUT IT**

1. Although globalized production has benefited consumers by lowering the prices of many items, it has also led to job losses in some industries. Should those who have lost their jobs due to globalization receive some sort of compensation? If so, from whom?

2. Some employees in poor countries work for miserable wages in appalling workplace conditions. How might these inequities be eliminated? What can you as a consumer do about this situation?

North American Free Trade Agreement (NAFTA): A pact initiated in 1994 to stimulate trade among the United States, Canada, and Mexico by lowering or eliminating tariff barriers.

An employee looks up from her work on a production line in the Suzhou Etron Electronics factory in Suzhou, China. China may be "the workshop of the world," but young rural migrant workers are less accepting than their parents were of life in the factories—low pay, grueling hours, and very strict workplace rules. Do you think that as its economy continues to grow, China will turn toward a service economy, with more teachers, nurses, and hairdressers than factory workers?

Chronic unemployment and underemployment are major problems in many poor countries, but jobs created by foreign firms are often dangerous, exhausting, and poorly paid. China has experienced astonishing rates of economic growth in recent years by using its huge labor supply for the production of exported goods bearing the labels of foreign firms. Many Chinese have achieved middle-class status or better as a result, but tens of millions of workers in apparel, electronics, and other labor-intensive enterprises continue to face serious workplace problems. According to one study of nine factories conducted by the nonprofit China Labor Center, workers' pay was inadequate to meet ordinary expenses, and overtime work of more than 100 hours a month was necessary to just get by. Work proceeded at a very fast pace, and rest breaks were few and far between. Workplace deaths through accident and suicide are not uncommon; some have been well publicized because they occurred at factories supplying products for Apple, Samsung, and other makers of high-tech consumer products (China Labor Watch 2013).

STAKEHOLDERS

10.3 Discuss the role of unions and the issues of wage inequities, discrimination, and stress in the workplace.

All of us have a direct interest in work and its correlates. As individual workers and as members of society as a whole, we are affected by the composition of the work-force, levels of employment and unemployment, the rise and fall of particular occupations, and the manner in which work organizations are structured. Although the money earned as a wage or salary is not the only reward for holding a job, it is hard to live a fulfilling life when unemployed or working at a minimum-wage job. Many things affect a worker's level of remuneration. Having a skill that is in high demand is one, but not the only one. As we shall see, a person's wage or salary is likely to reflect when he or she entered the labor force, prior access to education, the extent of unionization, and the extent of discriminatory behavior by employers and potential employers.

Wages and Salaries: Winners and Losers

One inescapable aspect of economic and social change in recent decades has been persistently weak growth in wages and salaries. In particular, American men ages 25 to 64 have actually seen their real wage and salary income (adjusted for inflation) decline since 1970. Women have fared better, but they started from a smaller base and have also suffered declining incomes in recent years (Greenstone 2012). One result of wage and salary stagnation is a widening income and wealth gap separating a relatively few individuals and families from the bulk of the population (see Chapter 2).

Unions and Their Decline

Income inequality in the United States has been increasing for many reasons, one of which is the steady erosion of union membership. In 1955, when the two largest union organizations merged, 37% of U.S. workers were members of labor unions (Freeman 2007, 77). By 2012, union membership had skidded to a mere 11.3% of workers (see Figure 10.7). The decline has been especially notable in the private sector, where only 6.6% of employees belong to unions. In contrast, the unionization rates for federal, state, and local government workers are 26.9%, 31.3%, and 41.7%, respectively (U.S. Bureau of Labor Statistics 2013a).

Union workers earn wages 14.1% higher than those of their nonunionized counterparts, even after education and experience, type of industry, region, and occupation are controlled for (Mishel et al. 2009, 200; Blanchflower and Bryson 2007). They also receive 15–25% more benefits, such as health insurance (Mishel et al. 2009, 123,

 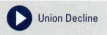 Union Decline

FIGURE 10.7 U.S. Union Membership by Sector, 1973–2011

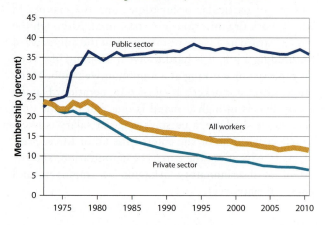

SOURCE: Adapted from Barry T. Hirsch and David A. Macpherson, "Union Membership and Coverage Database from the Current Population Survey: Note," *Industrial and Labor Relations Review,* Vol. 56, No. 2, January 2003, pp. 349–354.

202–3; Budd 2007, 165–66), as well as more workplace training and employee development.

In recent years, black and Hispanic workers have benefited from unionization more than white workers, and men more than women (Mishel et al. 2009, 200). The benefits are particularly evident among low-skilled workers (Pencavel 2007, 434). Even nonunion workers benefit when good wages are paid to dampen the appeal of unionization, such as at nonunion auto factories in the South.

The private-sector Service Employees International Union won a recent victory in organizing workers in low-paid occupations in the health care, private security, food and beverage, and hospitality industries. At the other end of the income scale, unionized pilots, upper-echelon public officials, and professional athletes have done very well as a result of union actions (Gladwell 2010). Ironically, the success of their unions has contributed to the wide income gap separating some very well-paid employees from the rest of the working population.

Is Increasing Human Capital the Answer to Wage Disparities?

The combination of technological advances and outsourcing to foreign lands has eliminated many manufacturing jobs in the United States, along with the decent wages they once paid. What is needed now is an accelerated development of **human capital**—that is, improvements in workers' skills and attitudes that will allow them to develop and effectively utilize modern workplace technologies. However, the key to earning a good income is not simply having the ability to use computers and other sophisticated equipment; what matters is being able to contribute to the development of organizational systems and processes that make the best use of these technologies (Brynjolffson and McAfee 2011, 42). Yet in recent years educational budgets have been cut and college tuition has steadily increased. It is also difficult for the United States to develop a well-educated workforce when one-fifth of the children in the nation are living in poverty.

Over a working life, college graduates, on average, earn considerably more than high school graduates (see Figure 10.8). The extent to which a college degree increases earning power depends on a number of factors, such as an individual's major (Taylor et al. 2011, 83–114), but on the whole, college is a good investment. Why is this so? Is the greater earning power of college graduates a reflection of the superior skills that college graduates bring to their jobs? Or have these workers simply passed through an educational "filter" to gain credentials attesting to their superior qualities? Does it matter what they actually learned? It is the rare prospective employer who asks for an applicant's academic transcript or even inquires about his or her grade point average. The content of most graduates' formal education is of less importance than what they are able to learn on the job.

Many firms still do a fair amount of worker training, but the benefits are not distributed equally. One study found that 35% of young college graduates received on-the-job training, but only 19% of high school graduates did (Levine 1998, 109). (The extent of employee training is notoriously difficult to determine, however. See Levine 1998, 136–37.) Race and ethnicity also affect access to these programs; one study based on the 2001–2002 California Workforce Survey found that Hispanic workers are less likely to have opportunities for training even after variables like prior education and the industries in which they work are controlled for (Yang 2007). Gender can be a factor, too. Mentorship, the process in which more experienced workers guide less experienced employees to develop their skills and abilities, is usually confined to members of the same sex; unfortunately, a connection of a sexual nature may be inferred when an older man mentors a younger woman. Since it's still the case that fewer women than men have achieved leadership positions, young women have correspondingly fewer opportunities to find mentors than do their male counterparts.

Human capital: The package of cognitive, physical, and social skills of individual workers.

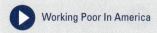

FIGURE 10.8 Earnings and Employment by Educational Attainment in the United States, 2011

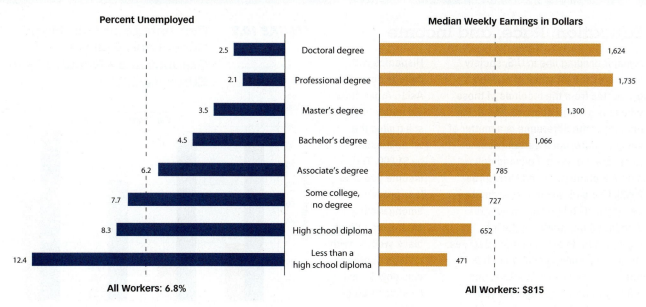

Percent Unemployed

Doctoral degree	2.5
Professional degree	2.1
Master's degree	3.5
Bachelor's degree	4.5
Associate's degree	6.2
Some college, no degree	7.7
High school diploma	8.3
Less than a high school diploma	12.4

All Workers: 6.8%

Median Weekly Earnings in Dollars

Doctoral degree	1,624
Professional degree	1,735
Master's degree	1,300
Bachelor's degree	1,066
Associate's degree	785
Some college, no degree	727
High school diploma	652
Less than a high school diploma	471

All Workers: $815

SOURCE: United States Department of Labor, Bureau of Labor Statistics. 2012. "Employment Projections: Education Pays."

Discrimination in the Workplace

Unequal access to on-the-job training programs is only one aspect of a much larger issue: lingering employment discrimination on the basis of race, ethnicity, gender, and age. Maintaining an equitable workplace is not just a matter of treating individuals fairly; it is essential that employers effectively leverage the abilities of their increasingly diverse workforces. A few decades ago the statistically typical worker in the United States was a white male. Today, white men are a minority in a diverse workforce in which women are 46.7%, blacks are 11.6%, Hispanics are 14.8%, and Asian Americans are 4.7% (Toossi 2012).

Overt discrimination is illegal. Title VII, Section 703, of the Civil Rights Act of 1964 made it a federal crime "to fail or refuse to hire or to discharge any individual" based on "such individual's race, color, religion, sex, or national origin." Similar provisions apply to employment agencies and labor unions. The passage of the Civil Rights Act and other legislation has not eliminated disparities based on race, ethnicity, and gender, however. We've seen above that unemployment rates differ substantially for racial and ethnic groups. So do incomes (Figure 10.10). In 2009 the median income for white families was $62,545. The

figures for black and Hispanic families were $38,409 and $39,730, respectively. Asian American families fared best of all at $76,027 (U.S. Census Bureau 2012e).

How much discrimination contributes to unequal outcomes in pay and employment is difficult to say. A study conducted in New York City asked closely matched groups of black, Latino, and white applicants to answer 169 newspaper want ads for low-level positions such as restaurant worker, stock clerk, mover, and telemarketer. Of these, 31.0% of white applicants were offered a job or called back for a second interview, while only 25.1% of Latinos and 15.2% of blacks received positive responses (Pager, Western, and Bonikowski 2009). White applicants had a higher rate of positive responses even when their application forms indicated they had criminal records, although the difference was not statistically significant.

ASK YOURSELF: Many believe that past and current discrimination against women and minorities requires the enactment and implementation of **affirmative action** policies and programs. Critics of affirmative action, however, note that many women and minority members come from more privileged circumstances than many white males. Would it be better, then, to use social class as a basis for affirmative action programs? If this were to be done, how would social class be defined? Is it simply a matter of income and wealth?

Affirmative action: Policies enacted by governments and private organizations to increase work and educational opportunities for women and members of certain minority groups.

Inequality and the Growth of Bad Jobs

Education, Race, and Income

A major dividing line in U.S. society separates the incomes of college graduates from the incomes of those who lack college degrees. The dollar amount of the difference is a matter of some dispute, but it certainly comes to several hundred thousand dollars over a lifetime (Day and Newburger 2002). (For a more modest estimate, see Pilon 2010.) College graduates also fare much better in the job market than do those without degrees. Attaining a college education has become massively expensive, and many graduates struggle for years to pay off the loans they incurred as students. Nor does possessing a college diploma guarantee economic success. Even so, it's clear that having a college degree considerably improves a person's odds of finding steady employment with a decent wage or salary.

Although African American and Hispanic students have made substantial strides in educational attainment in recent years, they still lag behind whites (as Figure 10.9 shows). But educational attainment is not the sole cause of income differences, as we can see by comparing the incomes of college-educated whites and minority group members (Aud, Fox, and KewalRamani 2010). In 2007, white men over 25 with college degrees had a median annual income of $65,000, an amount $15,000 greater than blacks and Hispanics with college degrees. Asian Americans did better but still trailed the white median by $1,000. The income gap was less pronounced among women; annual income of black women with college degrees was only $5,000 less than that of white women with college degrees. For college-educated Hispanic women the gap was larger at $7,000, while Asian American women actually outearned their white counterparts by $4,000.

Are these differences solely the results of prejudice and discrimination? Not all college degrees are equal, and it is possible that most white graduates went to institutions that prepared them for work better than those attended by minority graduates. Age also has to be taken into account, especially for Hispanics, who on average are younger than the workforce as a whole. Still, the income gap that separates white women and black women is smaller than the one that divides white males and black males.

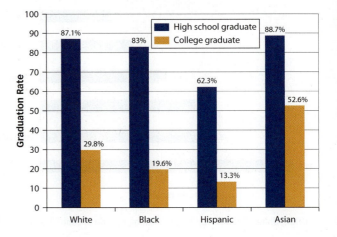

FIGURE 10.9 Percentage of U.S. High School and College Graduates by Race/Ethnicity, 2012

SOURCE: United States Bureau of the Census, 2012A. *The 2012 Statistical Abstract,* Table 229. "Educational Attainment by Race and Hispanic Origin: 1970 to 2010."

It does seem possible, then, that black men face more discrimination in the labor market than do black women.

▶ **THINK ABOUT IT**

1. Why does possession of a college degree enhance someone's ability to find a job? What are the most important job-related skills, attitudes, and habits learned in college?

2. Although having a college degree is correlated with having higher lifetime earnings, correlation does not necessarily imply causality. Is there a causal relationship in this case?

Women in the Workforce

Female employees face problems similar to those encountered by racial and ethnic minorities, but some are unique to them regardless of race and ethnicity.

Women have always worked, but until the past few decades most were not paid members of the working population. In 1947, only about one-third of adult women in the United States were employed or actively looking for work (Moen and Roehling 2005, 13–14).

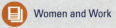
Women and Work

FIGURE 10.10 **The Gender Wage Gap by Race and Ethnicity for Full-Time U.S. Workers 16 and Older, 2011**

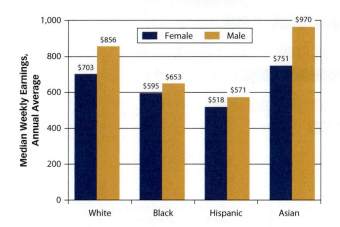

SOURCE: United States Department of Labor, Bureau of Labor Statistics 2012. "Median usual weekly earnings of full-time wage and salary workers by selected characteristics, annual averages."

Today, women's labor participation rate is only slightly below that for men (Figure 10.11), although men on average put in more hours on the job.

Much of the increase in women's labor force participation comes from white women joining the workforce; black women were already there. In 1920, for example, 33% of married and 59% of unmarried black women were in the U.S. labor force, while for white women, the figures were 7% and 45%, respectively (Reskin and Padavic 1994, 22–23). Not until the 1990s did white women's labor force participation catch up to that of black women.

Though women now participate in the labor force in numbers nearly equal to those of men, they are massively overrepresented within the ranks of secretaries, nurses, child-care workers, and receptionists. Of the hundreds of occupations tallied by the Census Bureau, just 10 account for one-third of U.S. women workers (Institute for Women's Policy Research 2011). Some observers would argue that such gender-based **occupational segregation** simply reflects the different interests and abilities of men and women. Whether these are due to inherent differences, prior socialization, or the interaction of the two has long been a matter of scholarly and popular debate. In any event, segregation by gender is problematic when it contributes to long-standing disparities in the wages and

Occupational segregation: The tendency of certain jobs to be predominantly filled on the basis of gender or according to race and ethnicity.

salaries of men and women. In 2011, full-time women workers received an average of 82 cents for every dollar earned by male workers. This actually represents an improvement over the recent past; in 1979, the ratio was 62 cents to the dollar (U.S. Bureau of Labor Statistics 2012b). Note, however, that these statistics refer to weekly earnings. Because women are more likely to be employed as part-time workers, on average they receive 77 cents for every dollar earned by men when earnings are calculated on an annual basis.

Occupations in which there are high proportions of women workers almost always have lower wages and salaries than do male-dominated occupations. The division between "men's jobs" and "women's jobs" contributes substantially to the lower average earnings of women workers; according to one calculation, it accounts for about 20% of the male-female wage gap (Figure 10.12) (Cotter, Hermson, and Vanneman 2006, 201).

Gender-based occupational segregation diminishes women's wages and salaries in several ways. One is a consequence of supply-and-demand economics. When large numbers of women are confined to a few occupations, the supply of workers there will be large relative to the demand, keeping wages and salaries low. Another is that some employers, most of whom are men, believe that by its very nature the kind of work women perform is of less value than the work done by men. Few tasks are more important than the care and education of young children, for example, but categorizing these tasks as "women's work" results in low pay for day-care workers. At the other end of the occupational spectrum, pediatric

FIGURE 10.11 **Global Employment by Gender, 1962–2010**

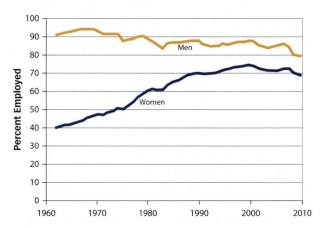

SOURCE: Based on "End of the Gender Revolution," Reeve Vanneman, Department of Sociology, University of Maryland. Author's calculations from Current Population Survey (CPS) data provided by the Integrated Public Use Microdata (IPUMS) files.

Workplace Attitudes

FIGURE 10.12 Educational Attainment and Lifetime Earnings in the United States by Gender

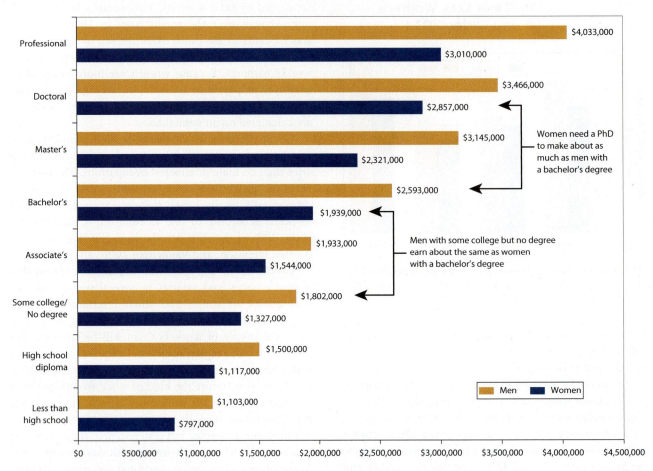

SOURCE: From *The College Payoff: Education, Occupations, and Lifetime Earnings*, Anthony P. Carnevale, Stephen J. Rose, and Ban Cheah, The Georgetown University Center on Education and Workplace. August 5, 2011. Reprinted with permission.

medicine, which has a relatively high number of female practitioners, is also one of the lowest paid medical specialties (Smith [Jacquelyn] 2012).

Women have begun to move into male-dominated occupations in significant numbers. For the period 2011–2012, 47.6% of medical school graduates were women (Jolliff et al. 2012). During the same period, the percentage of law school graduates who were women was almost identical at 47.3% (American Bar Association 2013, 4). More educational preparation for women addresses only one aspect of occupational segregation, of course, but soon we may no longer automatically associate medicine and law with male practitioners.

The income of female workers has also been undermined by another difference between women and men: the continuity of their occupational careers. The moment when employees typically arrive at the make-or-break phase

of their careers is precisely the time when many women take on the massive responsibilities of bearing and raising children. Very few men leave their jobs to be stay-at-home fathers or even cut back on their workloads to spend more time with their children. This may be an economically rational decision, given that fathers are likely to earn more than mothers. Whatever the reason, far more women than men have interrupted careers, or careers with serious role conflicts, making advancement more difficult and dampening their long-term earnings.

Women on average earn less than men for many reasons, though the gap has been narrowing in recent years. But here we must make an important qualification: between 1979 and 2010, the gap narrowed for workers lacking college degrees because men's earnings declined, not because women's earnings increased (Autor and Wasserman 2013, 11–12, 21). For college-educated women workers, the news has been mixed. Contrary to the general stagnation in wages in recent decades, these workers have enjoyed increases in pay. Even so, the male-female earnings gap has *widened* for college-educated workers because women's wages and salaries have not risen as rapidly as men's. (Keep in mind that these statements apply to the national labor force; there can be considerable deviation from general trends within regional labor markets. See McCall 2001, 123, 126.) College-educated women workers have enjoyed rising incomes, but their male counterparts have done even better (Autor and Wasserman 2013, 25).

Working May Be Hazardous to Your Health

Work is a dangerous activity for many employees. In 2009 alone, 572,000 people were victims of violent crime at work or on duty; 521 were murdered while at work (Harrell 2011). According to the U.S. Department of Labor, 4,693 workers died in 2011 as a result of work-related injuries, a rate of 3.3 deaths per 100,000 workers (U.S. Bureau of Labor Statistics 2013e). Highway accidents involving truckers and other drivers were the leading cause of job-related deaths, followed by falls, homicides, and being struck by objects. In 2009 the category encompassing agriculture, forestry, fishing, and hunting earned the dubious distinction of having the highest fatality rate, at 26.0 deaths per 100,000 full-time equivalent workers. Next came mining at 12.7 per 100,000. Other particularly dangerous sectors were transportation and warehousing (12.1 per 100,000) and construction (9.7 per 100,000). The least dangerous sector was educational and health services, with 0.7 worker fatalities per 100,000 employees (U.S. Bureau of Labor Statistics 2010a).

Workplace fatalities are rare, but on-the-job injuries are fairly common. In total, 4.14 million U.S. workers suffered nonfatal injuries on the job in 2009, or 3.9 injuries for every 100 full-time equivalent workers (U.S. Bureau of Labor Statistics 2010b). Manufacturing jobs are more dangerous than those in the service sector, with 4.3 injuries per 100 full-time equivalent workers in the former and 3.4 in the latter. There is, however, a considerable spread within the service sector. Some services, such as finance and insurance, have only 0.8 injuries per 100 workers, a sharp contrast with the 11.1 ratio for workers employed in nursing and residential care facilities, a ratio considerably higher than the one for truck

driving, which comes out to 4.6 per 100 (U.S. Bureau of Labor Statistics 2010b).

Workplace Stress

In addition to causing physical injuries and even death, a job that poses physical hazards can also induce the psychological condition known as **stress** (see Figure 10.13). Some degree of job-related stress is not necessarily a bad thing. The stress of facing a challenging set of tasks can promote a high level of performance and feelings of accomplishment. But beyond a certain point, stress becomes an overwhelmingly negative aspect of working life that has been implicated in a number of

FIGURE 10.13 **Physical and Mental Health in the Workplace**

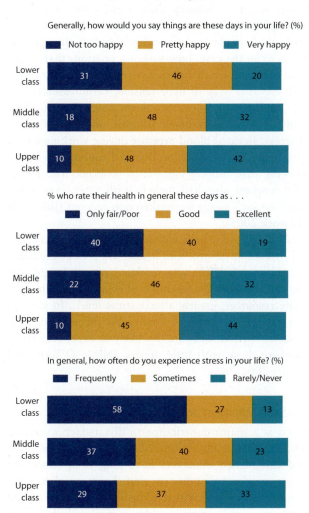

NOTE: "Does not apply" and "Don't know/Refused" responses not shown.

SOURCE: "A Third of Americans Now Say They Are in the Lower Classes" by Rich Morin and Seth Motel. September 10, 2012. Pew Research: Pew Social and Demographic Trends. Reprinted with permission.

Stress: The negative psychological and physiological effects of difficulties at work and elsewhere.

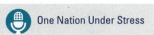 One Nation Under Stress   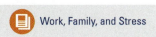 Work, Family, and Stress

physical and psychological ailments, such as depression, high blood pressure, and lower back pain, along with alcoholism and drug abuse.

Although it seems a bit counterintuitive, a monotonous job can also be quite stressful, particularly one that requires steady concentration, such as data entry or assembly-line work. Having inadequate resources is another source of stress. Anyone who has faced a deadline can attest that time is one of the most crucial resources. Power and authority also are important. A worker who is charged with implementing decisions but lacks the authority to do so will feel stress. Perhaps most important, workers have lives that extend beyond the workplace, and trying to accommodate the competing demands of work and family can be profoundly stressful.

Stressful work situations are not always offset by higher wages or salaries. Conversely, a well-paid position high in the organizational hierarchy does not necessarily result in elevated stress levels. In fact, the opposite seems to be the case. Low-wage occupations that afford little control over the work environment are associated with elevated risks of hypertension, cardiovascular disease, and mental illness (Schulman 2003, 98–100). In a study of British government officials, one key indication of stress, elevated blood pressure during working hours, was found to be more pronounced among low-status workers than among high-status workers. The lower-level workers also had higher death rates, even when variables such as age were taken into account (Job Stress Network 2005).

Although we usually characterize stress as an individual psychological problem, it also has a clear organizational dimension. The way work is structured, especially the balance between responsibilities and access to adequate resources, greatly affects stress levels. In general, workers who are able to control the demands of their working environments are less likely to experience stress than are those with little of this ability (O'Toole and Lawler 2006, 105).

Job Satisfaction and Dissatisfaction

Stress is a major contributor to dissatisfaction with a job, but hardly the only one. Sociologists, psychologists, and enlightened managers have long been concerned about working conditions that harm workers and reduce their productivity. On the whole, the majority of workers are at least reasonably satisfied with their jobs. A survey conducted by the Society for Human Resource Management (2012) found that 81% of U.S. employees were satisfied with their jobs, but only half that number reported being "very satisfied" with the core elements of their jobs: remuneration, job security, interactions with

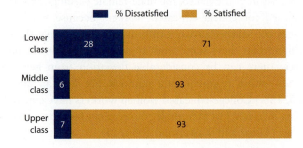

FIGURE 10.14 Job Satisfaction in the U.S. by Class

NOTE: "Don't know/Refused" responses not shown. Shares combine proportions who say they are "completely" or "mostly" satisfied.

SOURCE: "A Third of Americans Now Say They Are in the Lower Classes" by Rich Morin and Seth Motel. September 10, 2012. Pew Research: Pew Social and Demographic Trends. Reprinted with permission.

their supervisors, and opportunities to use skills and abilities (see Figure 10.14).

Workers view a high-paying job as more satisfying than one that pays badly, although one study found that men's levels of job satisfaction were lower than those of women earning equivalent incomes (Rampell 2009). In particular, job satisfaction is generally positively correlated with autonomy, the complexity and diversity of the tasks being performed, the ability to get a job done in its entirety, the perceived significance of the work being done, and the regular receipt of feedback about job performance (Hackman and Oldham 1976).

Besides the objective conditions of work, however, we must also consider the values, attitudes, and especially the expectations that workers bring to their jobs. Academics and other well-educated members of the upper-middle class who research and write about work may reflect their own responses to particular jobs, but the men and women actually doing the work may bring different sets of values and expectations. Even workers in some of the most unpleasant and low-paying jobs have expressed satisfaction with their work because, if nothing else, it is the basis of their friendship network (Bryant and Perkins 1982).

As with most other aspects of life, a person's expectations about a job affect his or her level of satisfaction with that job. Younger workers tend to have higher expectations than older workers, who have become more realistic and more resigned. This can be seen in the results of a recent Harris poll: 78% of the workers surveyed were interested in changing their careers, but only 54% of workers in their 40s expressed an interest in a career change (Boyle 2013). Differing expectations also help explain why women generally exhibit the same levels of job satisfaction as male workers, even though their jobs on the whole pay less, are less intrinsically interesting, and offer fewer opportunities

Job Satisfaction

for advancement. Rather than having lower aspirations than men, women may be comparing their job situations with those of other women (Hodson 1989).

ASK YOURSELF: What sorts of trade-offs would you make in order to have a satisfying job? Specifically, would you rather have a high-paying but not very satisfying job, or one that paid less but offered more job satisfaction? What characteristics of work and the workplace contribute to job satisfaction for you, and what characteristics detract from it?

Work in the 21st Century

In the 1950s, futurists were making bold predictions about the way automated processes would take over most of the work then being done by humans. The "age of leisure" they envisioned never came to pass, of course, although advances in production technologies went far beyond what they prophesied. Today's problem is not how to fill up vast amounts of leisure time, but how to deal with involuntary unemployment. Technological advances and globalization have profoundly influenced work, but, as noted above, a key distinction has to be made between the loss of particular *jobs* and *employment* as a whole. Immigration will affect work and employment by changing the demographic profile of the United States and other countries. Climate change, government policies, and cultural shifts will change the mix of jobs we do, who does them, and the extent to which they are rewarded. The working environment is shaped by the societies we live in, but in the final analysis, we shape society through the work we do.

USING THEORY TO EXAMINE WORK AND THE ECONOMY: THE FUNCTIONALIST, CONFLICT, AND SYMBOLIC INTERACTIONIST PERSPECTIVES

 10.4 Apply the functionalist, conflict, and symbolic interactionist perspectives to workplace issues.

Division of labor: The division of work into a multiplicity of specialized occupational roles and tasks.

Many theories are relevant to understanding work and its social context. Some have been created by sociologists, some by others. All provide useful insights, but none covers all aspects of work. Three major theoretical approaches are discussed in this section: functionalism, conflict theory, and symbolic interactionism.

Functionalism

Functionalism views society as a system of interconnected parts that support and depend on one another. The dominant theoretical approach in sociology and anthropology during the first half of the 20th century, it met with heavy criticism beginning in the late 1960s, but its influence continues today.

Functionalism has obvious relevance to the study of work. One of the fundamental characteristics of work in modern society is the **division of labor**, through which work is divided into many specialized occupational roles and tasks. To illustrate, the *Dictionary of Occupational Titles* compiled by the U.S. Bureau of the Census lists 842 separate occupational categories, encompassing 30,000 distinct job titles such as "emulsification operator," "welt trimmer," and "pickling grader" (U.S. Department of Labor 2011).

One of the first discussions of the benefits of the division of labor appears in Adam Smith's classic 1776 work *The Wealth of Nations*, in a section containing his famous presentation of pin manufacture. Smith showed that dividing pin making into several specialized tasks resulted in great improvements in productivity; where one pin maker working alone might make 20 pins a day,

Old Images / Alamy

A depiction of 17th-century pin makers. The division of labor proceeds something like this: one worker stretches the wire, another straightens it, a third cuts it, a fourth points it, a fifth grinds it at the top, and another affixes the head on the top.

10 workers performing specialized tasks could produce 48,000 pins, an average of 4,800 pins per worker.

In a single pin factory a manager can organize and coordinate the operations of a few workers, but how can this be done when a vast number of tasks are being performed in thousands of separate enterprises? Smith's answer focused on the role of market exchanges in tying together all these diverse activities. In an effective market, the providers of specialized goods and services enter into explicit and implicit contracts when engaging in mutually beneficial exchanges with the providers of other goods and services (Smith 2012).

In Smith's vision, individuals and businesses enter into these contracts out of self-interest. This is at best a partial answer, however, because it misses the crucial social dimension of marketplace exchanges. In his *Division of Labor in Society*, originally published in 1893, Émile Durkheim (1984) emphasized the role of the extralegal elements of contracts—the values and norms that make up the cultural core of society—in maintaining a durable economic and social order (Goodwin and Scimecca 2006, 121). In short, culture provides the rules governing market exchanges, without which these exchanges would not be possible.

Labor markets are populated not by socially isolated individuals but by men and women strongly influenced by preexisting social and cultural rules. Wages and salaries are not solely determined by negotiations between an employer and an employee; in many instances, they often reflect norms and values regarding the value of the work being done. In the United States, some professional baseball and football players make enormous salaries, but this is not the case in countries where baseball and football are minor sports at best. More ominously, the allocation of jobs and rates of remuneration may reflect biases and prejudices that may be part of the values and norms of some segments of the society.

Policy Implications of Functionalism

The norms and values that support discrimination on the basis of race, ethnicity, and gender were once more prevalent than they are today, but they are by no means extinct. A functionalist theorist would likely argue that lingering prejudices and discriminatory behavior hinder the effective interconnectedness of the various elements that contribute to a well-functioning society. In particular, the jobs that people hold and the work they do should be a reflection of their abilities, and not of their race, ethnicity, and gender. A society is not functioning well, for example, when a woman takes a job as a salesclerk because she is barred from studying to be a physician.

Most of today's sociologists who take a functionalist approach would not argue that a society will align itself in such a way that existing cultural values and norms will naturally result in the functionally optimal allocation of jobs and work. Rather, they would agree that it may be necessary to pass and enforce employment laws that prevent discrimination on the basis of race, ethnicity, and gender. It is to be hoped that these laws also will act as transformative forces that contribute to a shift to a set of values and norms that do not support biased behavior.

The Conflict Theory of C. Wright Mills

A number of approaches—critical theory, feminist theory, world systems theory, poststructural theory, and queer theory—can be included in the ranks of conflict theories. Here we will briefly focus on the sociological analysis of C. Wright Mills (1916–1962). Although he wrote prior to the designation of "conflict theory" as a theoretical approach, Mills's approach to sociology and the study of work resides firmly within it.

One of Mills's earliest works, *The New Men of Power*, originally published in 1948, looked at the way union officials shape the relationship between employers and employees (Mills 2001). In his later book *The Power Elite* (1956), Mills portrayed U.S. society in the 1950s as dominated by three interlinked elites: the managers of large corporations, upper-level government officials, and top military brass. In Mills's analysis, the rise of these forces threatened U.S. democracy itself. Unlike Marxists, however, he did not expect class-conscious workers to challenge this triumvirate. Absorbed in their efforts to acquire the consumer goods churned out by a booming postwar economy, members of the working class were not much inclined to dispute the prevailing distribution of power.

Nor did Mills put much hope in the political consciousness of middle-class workers, a group he analyzed in another book, *White Collar* (1951). Although their ranks had grown spectacularly during the 20th century, white-collar workers did not lean toward concentrated political action. As with the working class, this group's "usual demands are for a larger slice of a growing yield, and its conscious expectations are short-run expectations of immediate material improvements, not in any change in the system of work and life" (Mills 1951, 331). In Mills's glum summation, "the jump from numerical growth and importance of function to increased political power requires, at a minimum, political awareness and political organization. The white-collar workers do not have either to any appreciable extent" (352–53).

Mills also sought to connect what he called "private problems" and "public issues." As individuals we tend to think our problems are unique to ourselves, failing to note that they are often produced by social forces beyond our control (Mills 1959). For instance, we might view unemployment as a result of personal failings such as a lack of requisite skills or motivation. In fact, most current unemployment is the product of an economic recession brought on by reckless and even criminal activities perpetrated by a financial sector liberated from prior government oversight.

Policy Implications of Mills's Conflict Theory

Mills wrote primarily in the 1950s, and much of his work was an attack on the complacency of that postwar decade. The policy implications of his ideas are not evident when it comes to governmental actions, but they have some applicability to present-day labor unions. If unions took Mills seriously, they would remain concerned with the wages and salaries of their members, but they also would organize in support of their interests and press employers more aggressively for actions to benefit the working class and the middle class as a whole. Unions would promote specific government policies that benefit members, but they would also educate union members so they better understand how today's society is structured, and who benefits the most from that structure.

Symbolic Interactionism

Symbolic interactionism is the theoretical approach that looks into the significance of symbols in structuring society and affecting individual behavior. Anyone familiar with working environments will be at least subconsciously aware of the many symbols that distinguish workers and workplaces. Organizations as diverse as the Ford Motor Company, Goodwill, the Central Intelligence Agency, and Facebook all have their distinctive logos. The design and selection of these logos has grown into an entire industry, and organizations try to embed themselves in the consciousness of potential customers and the public at large by displaying their logos whenever and wherever possible. Logos as old as Coca-Cola's and as new as Twitter's are burned vividly into our consciousness.

The places where people work also can be rich in symbolism. Buildings are places to get work done, but they may also denote something important about organizations and the people who work for them. As architectural critics have noted, skyscrapers that loom over a city are often not justifiable in economic terms; instead they are designed and built for their symbolic value. The skyscraper used to be a distinctively U.S. construction, but today the world's tallest buildings are located in China, Malaysia, and Dubai, countries enjoying rapid

increases in wealth. As the saying goes, "If you've got it, flaunt it."

The way a building is divided and furnished also may say a lot about what goes on inside it. An office with a single occupant says one thing about that person's value to the organization, while a large, undivided work space housing many workers says something quite different. An office on the topmost floor may symbolize being at the summit of the organization's hierarchy. A corner office with a sweeping view may also denote high organizational status. The type and quality of office furnishings are often tied to employees' positions in an organization. For example, the phrase "to be called on the carpet," meaning to be called to account or castigated by a higher-up, comes from the fact that in the past low-ranking employees would be summoned to the carpeted offices of workplace superiors to be reprimanded.

Uniforms are another symbol, an obvious occupational marker. Some uniforms, such as those of police officers, denote authority. Others, like the jumpsuits worn by prisoners, convey just the opposite. At one time, many manual workers wore blue work shirts or blue coveralls, hence the term *blue collar*, still shorthand for manual work and generally low status. In contrast, in some organizations, middle- or upper-level managers are derisively known as "suits."

Three mechanics lean on a car in front of a garage in British Columbia, Canada. They wear blue shirts, jeans, and work boots as part of their working "uniform." Manual laborers like auto mechanics are often referred to as blue-collar workers.

The world contains much that we can usefully analyze from the perspective of symbolic interactionism. One symbol with obvious policy implications is the police uniform. On one hand, the policeman-as-soldier uniform strongly connotes power and authority with dark colors, a badge, and a prominently displayed sidearm and baton. Garb like this conveys the image of a powerful individual capable of bringing order and security to a harsh environment populated by dangerous people. In contrast, in community policing, an officer acts as a member of the community, working closely with residents to preserve the peace. Under these circumstances, uniforms with a less military air may better convey the intended image.

SPECIALIZED THEORIES: WEBER AND SCIENTIFIC MANAGEMENT

 10.5 Apply specialized theories to workplace issues.

Max Weber's Theoretical Approach to Bureaucracy

In the description and analysis of the organizational structures of workplaces, one term is inescapable: *bureaucracy*. Although the word has strong connotations of inefficiency, waste, coldness, and petty rules, under the right circumstances bureaucracy can be the most effective way of getting things done.

The foundation of sociological thinking about bureaucracy was built by Max Weber (1864–1920). Weber delineated the key elements of bureaucratic organization: specialized personnel, division of labor, hierarchical authority, impersonality, clearly articulated rules and regulations, and written records. In addition to presenting the major components of bureaucratic organization, Weber devoted considerable attention to the cultural values and modes of thought that gave rise to modern bureaucracies. Bureaucratic structures and processes reflected what Weber took to be the dominant cognitive orientation of modern societies: rationality. For Weber, rational thought patterns were prime elements of a historical process that he called "the disenchantment of the world." By this, he meant the ability and willingness to explain the causes of worldly events without invoking supernatural agents such as devils, ghosts, and genies. Instead, logic and empiricism are the basis for understanding why things happen as they do.

Weber saw rationality as crucial to the design and operation of modern organizations because this mode of thought provides the most effective and efficient way of attaining particular goals. However, the goals a person or organization pursues may not themselves be the result of rational thought. Rationally designed structures and processes can be used to achieve goals that defy rational comprehension; as Captain Ahab in *Moby-Dick* notes of his pursuit of the great white whale, "All my means are sane, my motive and my object mad." Equally important, rationality can serve goals that are not just irrational but unethical, immoral, and criminal as well. History has provided us with plenty of examples of rationality being used for barbaric ends, Nazi Germany being a particularly repellant case.

Bureaucracy is an inescapable element of modern life. Most of us are born in bureaucratic settings, receive our education in them, and live out our working lives in them. Many of us rely on bureaucratically organized religious bodies to assist us in our final days. For employees who work in bureaucratic settings this mode of organization has both advantages and disadvantages. Work in a bureaucratically structured organization can entail being snarled in red tape, constricted by a multiplicity of rules and regulations, and thwarted when one attempts to act in an innovative and creative manner. On the other hand, a bureaucratic structure can protect an employee from unreasonable demands made by both clients and superiors. It prevents endless rumination over what to do in a particular situation, and it adds a dose of predictability in an unpredictable world.

Whether bureaucratic organization is good or bad, effective or ineffective, depends to a great extent on the nature of the work to be done. What works in one setting may be counterproductive in another. In similar fashion, what helps workers to do their jobs effectively in one set of circumstances may block them in another. For individual workers, bureaucratic organizational structures can offer protection from capricious, unreasonable, and oppressive bosses, but it can also leave workers as little more than flesh-and-blood robots performing monotonous, routinized tasks. Which path is taken depends heavily on workers' ability to shape the rules and organizational structures that govern the way they do their work.

Scientific Management

The decades that bracketed the turn of the 20th century were marked by widespread and at times violent labor unrest. Conflicts between labor and management, capitalists and proletarians, were endemic, and some countries seemed on the brink of revolution. But to

Frederick W. Taylor (1856–1915) these conflicts were not inevitable; he believed that what was needed was a scientific approach to the management of workers.

The scion of a well-established Philadelphia family, Taylor had distinguished himself by developing improved techniques for the machining of steel and other metals. If obdurate metals could be more effectively managed through the development and use of scientific principles, thought Taylor, then surely these principles could be used for the more effective management of workers. During the latter part of the 19th century and the early 20th, he and his followers created what they called "scientific management." The fundamental assumption of scientific management was that both workers and traditional managers had failed to develop and use the most efficient production methods. Much better results would follow through the development and application of precise time-and-motion studies. When work was studied in this "scientific" manner, superfluous motions would be eliminated, and "the one best way" of doing things would prevail (Kanigel 1997).

Workers were to be completely excluded from the development of maximally efficient procedures, because it was assumed they lacked the ability to develop efficient working procedures on their own. To compensate for their complete loss of on-the-job power, workers would be rewarded through a piece-rate wage system that would ensure they received their fair share of the financial gains that came with improved production methods. As Taylor saw it, labor strife had been fueled by endless squabbles between workers and managers over how to divide a small pie. In contrast, under scientific management production would be maximized, and workers and enterprise owners would share a much larger pie.

Scientific management thinking was very influential in its heyday. Taylor was an effective publicist who claimed that the principles of scientific management were equally valid outside factory settings; they could be used to good effect for the management of schools, hospitals, and even churches. Scientific management had a wide following outside the United States; even Vladimir Lenin encouraged the application of scientific management in the newly founded Soviet Union. But as with many great ideas, its implementation failed to meet its promise. As might be expected, workers naturally objected to the rigid control of their actions, and some employers manipulated piece rates so that workers saw no improvement in their wages. Of equal or greater importance, established managers were decidedly unenthusiastic about scientific management, and many resisted the efforts of Taylor's followers to tell them how to manage their businesses. Jealously guarding their authority, they were unwilling to cede it to teams of college-educated men with stopwatches and clipboards.

Subsequent research in industrial sociology and psychology called into question one of the key assumptions of scientific management, that the main source of worker motivation is the hope of making more money. Beginning with the famous Hawthorne studies of the 1920s and 1930s, researchers came to the realization that workplaces are social systems in their own right, often with strong cultural norms. As these research projects discovered, the norms of working groups affect the speed with which workers go about their tasks and prevent the most efficient workers from outpacing fellow workers. The opportunity to earn more money is an important source of motivation, but it is not the only one.

SOCIAL CHANGE: WHAT CAN YOU DO?

 10.6 Identify steps toward social change for work-related problems.

Some social problems are not solved by massive, sweeping changes. Sometimes improvement comes through relatively small-scale actions at the local level. The first example below describes a cluster of actions that have had global consequences. The second also deals with an aspect of globalization, but one tied directly to local concerns.

▶ United Students Against Sweatshops

Bangladesh is one of the world's poorest countries. Its largest industry is garment manufacture, accounting for 80% of its export earnings and heavily dependent on extremely cheap labor, most of it done by women. Five garment factories were housed in the Rana Plaza building in Dhaka, the nation's capital. In April 2013, the building's owner and the factory managers dismissed engineers' concerns about safety even though the building had developed cracks and had begun to shake. Workers were ordered back to their jobs, and the next day the building collapsed, killing 1,127 people (Manik and Yardley 2013).

The tragedy in Bangladesh is a reminder of the sad history of the garment industry. After a fire swept through the Triangle Shirtwaist factory in New York City in 1911, killing 146 young women from Eastern European Jewish and Italian immigrant families, stronger safety laws were passed and the movement to unionize garment workers gained strength in the United States. Higher wages and safer working conditions increased production costs in a price-sensitive industry, and in the decades that followed, much of the work in the industry moved to parts of the world where wages were still low and safety was not always a prime consideration.

The ultimate responsibility for enacting and administering effective laws that protect workers necessarily rests with the countries where the factories are located. Even so, outsiders can exert a significant amount of pressure to improve the working lives of garment workers. Apparel is produced to be sold at a profit, and if a significant number of consumers decide to boycott goods produced in sweatshops, manufacturers will be strongly motivated to improve working conditions. Colleges and universities often earn

Tim Boyle / Staff / Getty Images

Demonstrators protest outside Sara Lee headquarters in Chicago. United Students Against Sweatshops protests sweatshop conditions as well as occupational injuries, low wages, and the abusive management of workers at Sara Lee's factory in Monclova, Mexico. Because of these conditions, the Monclova workers decided to organize into an independent union. Sara Lee responded by threatening to close the factory and fire the workers.

sizable revenues from the sale of apparel bearing the names and logos of their institutions, making a boycott of the manufacturers of that apparel financially painful for them.

One group committed to pressuring sweatshop employers is United Students Against Sweatshops. Activists in this organization have taken advantage of the fact that colleges and universities are major retailers of T-shirts, hoodies, caps, and other items of apparel (United Students Against Sweatshops 2014). Because students are concentrated in particular geographic locality, they are in a good position to organize themselves and pressure their institutions to require independent inspections of firms that supply merchandise carrying their schools' brands. Such efforts have produced some notable successes. In the 1990s student activism was directed at Nike's suppliers in Indonesia, who eventually raised their workers' wages by 50%. In another case, Pennsylvania State University terminated its relationship with Adidas after one of the firm's contractors abruptly shut down a factory and refused to give employees severance pay.

United Students Against Sweatshops has shown that an organized group can affect the purchasing decisions of retailers. Still, extensive changes will come about only through the combined efforts of consumers, retailers, and larger organizations such as churches and municipalities. Your campus is a place to begin.

▶▶ Pitzer College and the Day Labor Center

Day laborers are workers who station themselves in public places, often the parking lots of big-box hardware stores, in the hope of being recruited for short-term work. Their employers are typically small businesses and homeowners who need temporary workers to do semiskilled jobs such as painting, tree trimming, and moving. Day laborers are usually immigrants, and many lack documentation for legal residence in the United States. Their existence is difficult; their working conditions may be unsafe, and they have little recourse if they are taken advantage of or not paid.

Many communities have banned the solicitation of work in public places. Pomona, California, for instance, passed an ordinance that prohibited "the solicitation of or for work on any street or highway, public area or non-residential parking area." Fortunately for the men needing work in the Pomona area, in 1998 students and faculty at Pitzer College, in the adjacent town of Claremont, founded the Pomona Economic Opportunity Center (PEOC) to serve their interests. As a result of the efforts of Pitzer students and faculty, the Pomona ordinance was amended to allow day laborers a single place within the city at which to seek temporary work from prospective employers. The PEOC was then designated as this sole lawful place.

In addition to connecting workers with prospective employers, the center is a gathering site for laborers that also promotes safe and fair working conditions for them. It aids workers and their families in a multitude of ways. According to its statement of purpose, "The Center's primary goals include increasing the financial security, safety, health, civic participation and human rights of day laborers in the Pomona Valley region, along with addressing and working to change the systemic obstacles that stand in the way of achieving those goals" (Pitzer College 2013). The activities of the center include the following:

- Identifying well-paid and safe employment opportunities for day laborers
- Improving access to existing resources in the local community and building coalitions to create new resources
- Providing educational opportunities on worker and immigrant rights
- Identifying training opportunities in work and language skills
- Developing strong day laborer leaders through organizing and training

Many of the problems day laborers encounter can be traced to their lack of fluency in written and spoken English, so since 1999 the PEOC has sponsored classes in English as a second language taught by student volunteers from Pitzer and other Claremont Colleges. The instruction is not all one-way; workers affiliated with the PEOC participate in weekly lunchtime meetings with Pitzer students seeking to enhance their command of Spanish and gain a better understanding of cultures different from their own as well as the family issues and working lives of day laborers. Many communities have significant immigrant populations, and organizing informal language classes is a good way for students to strengthen ties between themselves and recent immigrants, and to benefit their communities.

WHAT DOES AMERICA THINK?

Questions about Work and the Economy from the General Social Survey

 Turn to the beginning of the chapter to compare your answers to the total population.

1. If you were to become rich, would you continue to work or stop working?

   CONTINUE TO WORK: 70%

   STOP WORKING: 30%

2. With regard to your income tax, do you think it is too high, about right, or too low?

   TOO HIGH: 50.1%

   ABOUT THE RIGHT AMOUNT: 47.6%

   TOO LOW: 2.3%

3. Do you think that work is most important to feel accomplished?

   MOST IMPORTANT: 45.8%

   NOT THE MOST IMPORTANT: 54.2%

4. What is your interest level in economic issues?

   VERY INTERESTED: 51.5%

   MODERATELY INTERESTED: 38.1%

   NOT INTERESTED AT ALL: 10.4%

5. What is your confidence level in banks and financial institutions?

   A GREAT DEAL: 11.2%

   ONLY SOME: 51.2%

   HARDLY ANY: 37.6%

LOOK BEHIND THE NUMBERS

Go to **edge.sagepub.com/trevino** for a breakdown of these data across time and by race, sex, age, income, and other statuses.

1. Examine the gender data for responses to the question regarding people's interest in working if they become rich. Is there a clear distinction between males and females? Explain. Do you find this surprising?

2. Examine the data regarding interest in economic issues as it breaks down by race. Are there clear distinctions in the responses among racial groups? What does this mean for society?

3. More than 45% of respondents reported work as the main contributing factor to feeling accomplished. What other factors might contribute to an individual's feelings of accomplishment? Which factor would you report as most important? Explain.

4. Examine responses to the General Social Survey question about confidence in banks from 1973 to the present. Confidence in banks has changed over time, but it changed significantly in 2010 and 2012. What might explain these changes?

SOURCE: National Opinion Research Center, University of Chicago.

CHAPTER SUMMARY

 10.1 Explain the general shape of the U.S. workforce today.

The labor force is conventionally defined as all persons in the civilian noninstitutional population who are either employed or unemployed but actively seeking work. At the beginning of 2014, the United States had unemployment rates that were relatively high by historic standards, while the numbers of contingent and part-time workers were on the increase.

 10.2 Identify patterns and trends in employment and unemployment.

Work is an essential activity that, like most human endeavors, has its problematic aspects. Today, the most problematic is the absence of work, often for large periods of time, for a significant portion of the labor force. Unemployment has not been spread evenly over all segments of the labor force, and some who are unemployed have become so discouraged about the prospects of finding a job that they have given up and are no longer counted as members of the labor force. As in many other arenas, race, ethnicity, and gender are important, influencing a person's likelihood of being unemployed and the duration of joblessness.

 10.3 Discuss the role of unions and the issues of wage inequities, discrimination, and stress in the workplace.

Globalization and technological change have greatly affected employment and unemployment. They have also been implicated in the widening income gap that has been a prominent feature of the U.S. economy for several decades; other causes are the decline of unionization, educational disparities, and the persistent difficulties faced by women and members of racial and ethnic minority groups. Unemployment creates many difficulties for the jobless. Some jobs are inherently dangerous, and all modes of work have their stressful elements. Yet work has the potential to bring personal satisfaction, even if the sources of job satisfaction are not always obvious.

 10.4 Apply the functionalist, conflict, and symbolic interactionist perspectives to workplace issues.

Functionalism makes evident the interconnected nature of the great variety of occupations found in a modern society and offers some ideas about what holds everything together. Conflict theorist C. Wright Mills pointed to unemployment as a public issue often mistaken for a private problem. Symbolic interactionism notes the ways in which work and occupations are suffused with symbols that give important clues about the nature of particular jobs and the workers doing them.

 10.5 Apply specialized theories to workplace issues.

Max Weber delineated the key elements of the bureaucratic organization: specialized personnel, division of labor, hierarchical authority, impersonality, clearly articulated rules and regulations, and written records. Bureaucracy is an inescapable element in modern life. Work in a bureaucratically structured organization can entail dealing with red tape and rules and regulations that may stifle creativity. On the other hand, a bureaucratic structure can protect an employee from unreasonable demands made by both clients and superiors. It prevents endless rumination over what to do in a particular situation, and it adds a dose of predictability in an unpredictable world. Scientific management, promoted by Frederick W. Taylor, had its heyday around the turn of the 20th century. Its thesis that "one best way" exists to do a particular job was an attempt to find maximum efficiency in production methods and reward workers by piece-rate wage systems. Subsequent research in industrial sociology and psychology called into question one of the key assumptions of scientific management, that the main source of worker motivation is the hope of making more money.

 10.6 Identify steps toward social change for work-related problems.

Some problematic aspects of work and unemployment seem intractable, but immobilizing despair is not a proper response. To take two examples of effective activism, United Students Against Sweatshops has challenged the use of sweatshop labor on an international scale, and at the local level Pitzer College's Pomona Economic Opportunity Center has helped immigrant workers improve their working situations as well as their lives in general.

DISCUSSION QUESTIONS

1. What does work look like in the United States today? How have technological and societal changes affected work? How are people of various ages, races, and genders affected by these changes in the workplace?

2. How is the official U.S. unemployment rate calculated? Who is not included in this number? What other ways could unemployment be measured that would be more inclusive of those currently excluded?

3. What impact does working or being unemployed have on people beyond pay? Are there ways U.S. society could ease the stress and anxiety of unemployment for people that would alleviate these concerns? How can we work to reduce stress and increase satisfaction in the workplace for employees?

4. According to the symbolic interactionist perspective, why are different values placed on different types of work and on different workplaces themselves? What are the symbols associated with the type of work you see yourself doing in the future?

5. How has union membership changed in recent decades? What explains these changes? Which types of workers benefit the most from union membership? In what ways might workers be harmed by unions?

6. Which factors are most likely to raise or lower a person's wages? How much control does an individual worker have over these factors? What is out of an employee's control when it comes to pay and advancement at work?

7. What explanations do functionalists offer for wage disparities between members of different groups who perform similar work? For the widely different wages for careers that require similar skill and/or education levels?

8. Why does Weber focus on bureaucracy? If you think about places you have worked, can you see the structure and nature of their bureaucracy? In what ways did the structure improve or hinder the functioning of these organizations?

9. How effective are U.S. consumers in advocating for the rights of garment workers in other countries? Do you expect that most people would be willing to pay more for products made by workers earning a living wage and working in safe conditions? What conditions make some groups succeed at boycotting apparel from specific companies?

KEY TERMS

affirmative action 261

benefits 250

compensation 250

cyclical unemployment 256

discouraged worker 253

division of labor 267

employment at will 256

globalization 257

Great Depression 257

human capital 260

labor force 251

lump of labor fallacy 257

North American Free Trade Agreement 258

occupational segregation 263

primary sector 251

quintile 255

salary 250

secondary sector 251

service sector 251

stress 265

structural unemployment 256

total compensation 251

underground economy 253

wage 250

whistle-blowing 256

Sharpen your skills with SAGE at edge.sagepub.com/trevino

A personalized approach to help you accomplish your coursework goals in an easy-to-use learning environment.

11 CRIME

Kathleen Currul-Dykeman
and Susan Guarino-Ghezzi

AFP / Getty Images

 Most "cop shows" on television tell stories that typically involve criminals, victims, and the police. Sociologists know that in addition to these three groups we must consider the communities in which crimes are committed. How would you depict the community in this wall painting?

Investigating Crime: Our Stories

LEARNING OBJECTIVES

11.1 Explain how crime is socially defined.

11.2 Discuss patterns and trends in crime and crime measurement.

11.3 Describe the U.S. criminal justice system and its stakeholders.

11.4 Apply the functionalist, conflict, and symbolic interactionist perspectives to the problem of crime.

11.5 Apply specialized theories of crime.

11.6 Identify steps toward social change concerning crime.

Kathleen Currul-Dykeman

As a senior in college looking to take fewer classes and get into "the field," I happened upon an internship for the first female district attorney in Massachusetts, Elizabeth Scheibel, in her Victim Witness Unit. I was surprised to find that I would be working with victims of violent crimes seeking restraining orders and help with the criminal court process. This experience molded my entire professional life. Throughout law school I worked for District Attorney John Conte, and upon passing the bar, I chose to prosecute domestic violence cases for the next five years. Later, at Northeastern University, I conducted my dissertation research on how courts handle domestic violence cases.

The social context of domestic violence spurred my passion to spread awareness of the unique challenges its victims face. Their cases are not easily won; thus few prosecutors wanted to handle them. Victims often recant, and courts do not take them very seriously. The quick dismissals that often result are a product of long-held norms and stereotypes.

Currently, I am teaching a class I created at Stonehill College in which students learn about crime victimization in the fall semester and work with crime victims in the spring semester in a practicum course. In this class, we debunk myths and stereotypes about domestic violence and educate ourselves about the barriers crime victims face.

Susan Guarino-Ghezzi

My understandings of crime began in New York City during the crime wave of the 1970s. Parents were less protective then, and I went to middle school and high school by public transportation, occasionally encountering people who acted threatening. Thus crime was never far from my mind, and by my college years, I perceived everything in relationship to crime. I pursued my obsession by going to Boston College for a Ph.D. in sociology.

Two prominent New York cases had a huge impact on me. While riding the subway, Bernhard Goetz shot a black teenager in the back after the youth robbed him of five dollars using a screwdriver as a weapon. The boy was permanently paralyzed, while Goetz became a folk hero of sorts and received a very light sentence. Later, a group of black teenagers were charged with the brutal rape of a young professional woman who had been jogging in Central Park. Police interrogators used intimidation techniques so cunning that the suspects turned on one another, each providing an account in which the others committed the rape. It was only years later, when DNA evidence implicated someone else in the crime, that the wrongly convicted young men were released.

These incidents of crime, race, and paranoia provided a social context for me as I went to graduate school and began to conduct research with juvenile offenders, judges, lawyers, and correctional workers. After working with the U.S. Department of Justice, I took a job as director of research at the Massachusetts Department of Youth Services and became an expert on what it takes to provide effective correctional programs. Later, when I started teaching, I served as consultant to several jurisdictions around the country.

1. Do you favor or oppose the death penalty for persons convicted of murder?

   ☐ *FAVOR*

   ☐ *OPPOSE*

2. In general, do you think the courts in this area deal too harshly or not harshly enough with criminals?

   ☐ *TOO HARSHLY*

   ☐ *ABOUT THE RIGHT AMOUNT*

   ☐ *NOT HARSHLY ENOUGH*

3. Would you favor or oppose a law which would require a person to obtain a police permit before he or she could buy a gun?

   ☐ *FAVOR*

   ☐ *OPPOSE*

4. In the United States, do you think we're spending too much money on law enforcement, too little money, or about the right amount?

   ☐ *TOO MUCH*

   ☐ *ABOUT THE RIGHT AMOUNT*

   ☐ *TOO LITTLE*

5. Are there any situations you can imagine in which you would approve of a policeman striking an adult male citizen?

   ☐ *YES*

   ☐ *NO*

6. Are you ever afraid to walk at night in your neighborhood?

   ☐ *YES*

   ☐ *NO*

▶▶ Turn to the end of the chapter to view the results for the total population.

SOURCE: National Opinion Research Center, University of Chicago.

IN A HOODED SWEATSHIRT

Suppose an African American friend of yours, a high school senior, is staying at a friend's house in a gated community. It's a chilly, rainy day and he's home taking care of his younger stepbrother. Bored, he decides to walk to a nearby convenience store. On his way back from the store, he notices a man following him, and, nervous, he calls his girlfriend on his cell phone. She tells him to run away, but a violent struggle between the men ensues.

This describes the case of Trayvon Martin and George Zimmerman. According to police, residents of Zimmerman's Florida neighborhood had reason to worry about crime. Home foreclosures had left many houses empty and made the neighborhood a target for thefts, so Zimmerman had formed a Neighborhood Watch group. On February 26, 2012, when he spotted Martin, a black youth in a hooded sweatshirt, he called 911. Even though the police dispatcher instructed him not to pursue Martin, he did so anyway (Blow 2012). In the confrontation that then took place, Martin was killed. Zimmerman was subsequently tried on charges of second-degree murder and manslaughter. The prosecutor in the case suggested that Martin had been racially profiled by Zimmerman, a civilian. Racial profiling occurs when police use race or ethnicity as a

Lucas Jackson / Reuters

LeTasha Brown stands with her arms around Anthony Dixon Jr. during a rally in front of the Sanford Police Department following the killing of Trayvon Martin in Sanford, Florida, in 2012. Martin was shot dead in a confrontation with George Zimmerman, a Hispanic Neighborhood Watch captain who believed the young black man looked suspicious as he walked through the gated community in a hooded sweatshirt.

factor in determining whether a particular individual is suspected of committing a crime.

Zimmerman's attorneys claimed he was defending himself against Martin and looked to Florida's controversial "stand your ground" law, which justifies an individual's using force if he or she reasonably believes it is necessary to prevent imminent death or great bodily harm. Since Martin's death, many have argued that this law needs to be repealed. However, staunch defenders of the law, including small retail businesses and the powerful National Rifle Association, will challenge any efforts to repeal. On July 13, 2013, after deliberating 16½ hours, a jury of six women, five of them white, found Zimmerman not guilty of the charges against him.

The Granger Collection

Three demonstrators at a lunch counter in Jackson, Mississippi, are smeared with ketchup, mustard, and sugar by integration opponents in 1963. Jim Crow laws mandated racial segregation in all public facilities in southern U.S. states. Until 1965 these laws prohibited blacks from using restrooms, restaurants, and drinking fountains that were intended for whites only.

CRIMES ARE SOCIALLY DEFINED

11.1 Explain how crime is socially defined.

What is crime? While it exists in all societies, there is no *single* understanding of crime as a social problem. We can best understand it from a dynamic perspective, as criminologist Richard Quinney explains in his classic book *The Social Reality of Crime* (1970). The dynamic perspective does not view crime as wrong behavior in an absolute sense. Rather, in this view, wrong behavior and enforcement of the law are social problems that are subject to change. What we define as criminal thus changes over time as individuals or groups in positions of power change. For decades in parts of the United States, for example, black citizens were prohibited from using drinking fountains designated for whites only, and from sitting at "white" lunch counters. Definitions also change when new situations emerge; for example, terrorists' threats led to the criminalization of previously permissible behaviors, such as carrying ski poles onto airplanes. In the most basic sense, crimes are nothing more than deviant behaviors that violate society's norms. Individual U.S. state legislatures are responsible for writing criminal laws that formally define what each state deems "criminal" and the possible punishments for violating those laws.

Mala in se **crimes:** Crimes that are illegal because they are bad in themselves or inherently wrong by nature.

Mala prohibita **crimes:** Crimes that are illegal because they are prohibited by law.

Crimes are grouped into two broad categories: *mala in se* and *mala prohibita*. **Mala in se crimes** are those that violate the moral conscience, such as murder, theft, and violent assault. These kinds of crimes tend to receive the most attention from politicians, civic and religious leaders, and the mainstream media. Despite support for "stand your ground" laws, for instance, there is universal consensus that murder is a problem society must control.

Mala prohibita crimes, on the other hand, are acts that may not be commonly viewed as evil, and many people might not agree they are crimes at all. Tax fraud is prohibited to protect the public welfare, but many individuals who are otherwise law-abiding have no problem with cheating on their taxes. Other *mala prohibita* crimes are gambling and use of illicit drugs. The way the law treats those accused of these crimes depends on many factors, including social and political climate, socioeconomic factors, and geographic location. While most college students probably agree that finding a designated driver is far preferable to driving while drunk, this was not the prevalent attitude before the 1980s, when Mothers Against Drunk Driving (MADD) began to organize and influence lawmakers and social norms.

ASK YOURSELF: College students and office workers often set up pools in which they fill out brackets for the NCAA Basketball Championship tournament, a socially accepted form of gambling. Can you think of other *mala prohibita* crimes your peers commonly engage in? Do you think they are acceptable behaviors? Why or why not?

▶ U.S. Criminal Justice System

Subculture Norms on Philadelphia's Streets

What makes some street criminals feel that being tough is cool? Criminologist Elijah Anderson (1999) set out to explain the criminal behaviors of people in a mostly black, poor, and violent neighborhood in Pennsylvania. He discovered that a code governed interactions between neighborhood residents and sanctioned the use of violence to resolve conflict and show "nerve." While most of the people he spoke to were more "decent" than "street," all had to know the rules of the code for self-preservation.

The primary rule was to look and act tough, rejecting mainstream customs associated with white society. Young men wore untied sneakers, pants with waistbands hanging well below the waist, and hats turned backward. While these styles were later adopted by middle-class adolescents, at first they signified antagonism toward conventional styles. The appearance of the young men gave the community a bad reputation, which also contributed to the stereotyping and demonizing of young black males. As Anderson observes:

> Many ghetto males are caught in a bind because they are espousing their particular ways of dressing and acting simply to be self-respecting among their neighborhood peers. A boy may be completely decent, but to the extent that he takes on the *presentation* of "badness" to enhance his local public image, even as a form of self-defense, he further alienates himself in the eyes of the wider society, which has denounced people like him as inclined to violate its norms, values, rules, and conventions—to threaten it. (112–13)

► **THINK ABOUT IT:** Anderson describes the way a subculture's norms encouraged young people to become alienated from society, often leading to violence and crime. How do you think community leaders could reverse these patterns and encourage positive behaviors among youth in such communities?

This mural in a black district of Philadelphia lists the names of people killed by gang violence. A west Philly neighborhood is home turf of the 60th Street Posse, also known as Six-O, which controls organized criminal activity in the area. Today's gangs tend to be smaller and less regimented than gangs of the past.

Frederic Soltan / Corbis

PATTERNS AND TRENDS

11.2 Discuss patterns and trends in crime and crime measurement.

Official Crime Measurement

Each year since 1929, the Federal Bureau of Investigation's **Uniform Crime Reports (UCR)** have provided a national overview of arrests and selected violent and property crimes reported to police, known as *Part I index crimes*. This information is useful for understanding trends in crime, since it has been collected in essentially the same way for many years. There are two exceptions. Arson was not one of the original index crimes but was added much later, in 1979. In addition, a new definition of rape took effect in 2013 that removed the requirement of "forcible" assault and the restriction that the attack must be on a woman. Table 11.1 provides the FBI's definitions of index crimes as of 2013.

Violent Crimes and Property Crimes

Reports of crimes are usually made as 911 calls or walk-in complaints. The UCR compiles reports in several categories of violent and property crimes. The FBI defines *violent crimes* as those offenses that involve force or threat of force against a person. They include murder, rape, robbery, and battery, among other things.

Uniform Crime Reports (UCR): An official source of data on crime collected by the Federal Bureau of Investigation from police departments nationwide.

TABLE 11.1 Serious Violent Crimes

Crime	Description
Murder and manslaughter	*Murder and nonnegligent manslaughter:* the willful killing of one person by another. *Manslaughter by negligence:* the killing of another person through gross negligence.
Forcible rape	Penetration, no matter how slight, of the vagina or anus of any body part or object, or oral penetration by a sex organ of another person without the consent of the victim.
Robbery	The taking or attempted taking of anything of value from the care, custody, and control of a person or persons by force or threat of force or violence and/or by putting the victim in fear.
Aggravated assault	An unlawful attack by one person upon another for the purpose of inflicting severe or aggravated bodily injury. This type of assault usually is accompanied by the use of a weapon or by means likely to produce death or great bodily harm.
Burglary (breaking and entering)	The unlawful entry of a structure to commit a felony or a theft.
Larceny-theft (except motor vehicle theft)	The unlawful taking, carrying, leading, or riding away of property from the possession or constructive possession of another.
Motor vehicle theft	The theft or attempted theft of a motor vehicle.
Arson	Any willful or malicious burning or attempt to burn, with or without intent to defraud, a dwelling house, public building, motor vehicle or aircraft, personal property of another, etc.

SOURCE: FBI Uniform Crime Report, 2012 and Criminal Justice Information Services (CJIS) Decision, Uniform Crime Reporting (UCR) Program, *Reporting Rape* in 2013.

Dark figure of crime: The amount of unreported or undiscovered crime, which calls into question the reliability of official crime statistics.

White-collar crime: Illegal acts, punishable by criminal sanctions, committed in the course of legitimate occupations or by corporations.

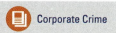 Corporate Crime

Property crimes are targeted at physical property rather than at persons. The FBI focuses on burglary, larceny, motor vehicle theft, and arson in its official data collection. Other crimes of dishonesty are also considered to be property crimes; these include embezzlement, forgery, shoplifting, and larceny.

As Table 11.2 shows, burglary and larceny are reported far more often than any of the violent crimes. But while the UCR provides the best official data for understanding crime patterns, it does not tell the whole story. In fact, because the sources of UCR data are local police agencies, which rely on citizens to report crime to them, the UCR significantly underestimates certain types of crime. The amount of unreported crimes is referred to as the **dark figure of crime**; many types of crimes are particularly likely to be unreported.

ASK YOURSELF: Crimes that take place within intimate relationships (spousal assault, child and elder abuse, date rape) are often not reported to police. Can you put yourself in the place of a victim or witness to such a crime and think of some reasons for this?

There are many reasons crimes do not come to the attention of police. Some crimes, such as intimate partner violence, are never reported because victims are too ashamed or fear repercussions from the offenders. Another common but often hidden crime is "wage law crime," a **white-collar crime** committed by employers. This form of criminal exploitation alone has been estimated to victimize more people than all forms of street crime combined (Lynch 2011). According to Kim Bobo (2009), millions of U.S. workers are having their wages stolen. She asserts that 2 to 3 million are being paid below the minimum wage, and more than 3 million are misclassified by their employers as independent contractors when they are really employees—which mean their employers are not providing benefits or paying their share of payroll taxes. Millions more aren't being paid overtime because their employers wrongly claim they are exempt from overtime laws. Several million aren't paid for their breaks or are seeing illegal deductions from their paychecks. Bobo notes: "The Economic Policy Foundation, a business-funded think tank, estimated that companies annually steal $19 billion from their employees in unpaid overtime. Labor lawyer colleagues suggest the number is far higher" (8).

ASK YOURSELF: What kinds of social problems are caused by white-collar crimes such as wage law crime? What kinds are caused by street crimes such as robbery? Do you think both types of crimes are equally serious? Why or why not?

TABLE 11.2
TABLE 11.2 Violent and Property Crimes Reported to the Police in 2009

Violent crime	
Total	**1,318,398**
Murder and nonnegligent manslaughter	15,241
Forcible rape	88,097
Robbery	408,217
Aggravated assault	806,843
Property crime	
Total	**9,320,971**
Burglary	2,199,125
Larceny-theft	6,327,230
Motor vehicle theft	794,616

SOURCE: Compiled from FBI Uniform Crime Reports 1991-2010.

Clearance Rate

The FBI also provides data on the percentage of cases that are "cleared," usually by arrests. Known as the **clearance rate**, these data indicate how successful police are in apprehending suspects. Certain types of crimes, property crimes in particular, are far less likely to result in arrests than others, such as murder and other violent offenses, as shown in Figure 11.1.

····················

ASK YOURSELF: What explanations can you give for the difference in clearance rates between violent crimes and property crimes?

····················

Arrest Profiles, Including Gender and Race

The UCR's arrest data provide us with demographic profiles of persons arrested, including gender and race. As Table 11.3 shows, men are overwhelmingly more likely than women to be arrested for crime, with certain exceptions, such as larceny-theft.

····················

ASK YOURSELF: Does it surprise you that criminal behavior is dominated by men? What might be some reasons for this?

····················

FIGURE 11.1 Clearance Rates for Violent and Property Crimes, 2009

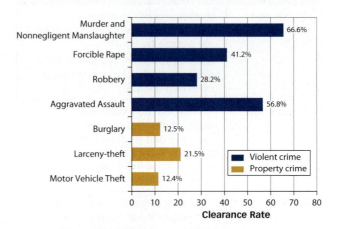

SOURCE: Compiled from FBI Uniform Crime Reports 1991–2010.

TABLE 11.3 Violent and Property Crime Arrests by Gender, 2009

Offense charged	Percentage male	Percentage female
Violent crime	81.2	18.8
Murder and nonnegligent manslaughter	89.6	10.4
Forcible rape	98.7	1.3
Robbery	88.2	11.8
Aggravated assault	78.0	22.0
Property crime	62.6	37.4
Burglary	85.1	14.9
Larceny-theft	56.3	43.7
Motor vehicle theft	82.2	17.8
Arson	83.0	17.0
Total	**74.7**	**25.3**

SOURCE: Compiled from FBI Uniform Crime Reports 1991–2010.

The male predisposition toward crime, among both offenders and victims, is well illustrated by the crime of homicide (see Figure 11.2). Two-thirds of homicides

····················

Clearance rate: The ratio of reported cases of crime to cleared cases, calculated by dividing the number of crimes that result in arrests by the total number of crimes recorded.

involve male offenders and male victims. Men are twice as likely to murder women as women are to murder men. And women murdering other women makes up only 2% of all homicides.

The UCR also looks at race. With a couple of important exceptions (murder and robbery), more white persons than black persons are arrested for each of the index crimes (see Table 11.4). We would expect this because white people make up 78% of the U.S. population, while black persons make up just 13%. But given their numbers in the population, blacks are overrepresented in arrest data for many crimes, both as offenders and as victims. For example, from 1980 through 2008, 84% of white victims were killed by whites, while 93% of black victims were killed by blacks (Cooper and Smith 2011).

ASK YOURSELF: What reasons might account for the overrepresentation of black persons found in arrest data, particularly for the crimes of murder and robbery?

Current Crime Trends

Nationwide, reported violent and property crime went down substantially between 1990 and 2009, as shown for the FBI's index crimes in Figures 11.3 and 11.4. Among violent crimes, murder declined by 47%, rape by 30.3%, and robbery by 48%. Aggravated assault went down by 38%. Of the property crimes, burglary declined by 42%, larceny-theft by 35%, and motor vehicle theft by 60%.

FIGURE 11.2 Homicide Offenders and Victims by Sex, 1980–2008

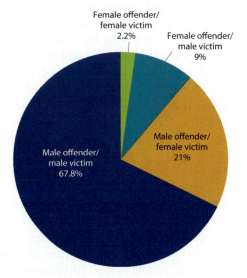

SOURCE: Data from Alexia Cooper and Erica L. Smith, *Homicide Trends in the United States, 1980–2008*. U.S. Department of Justice, Bureau of Justice Statistics, November, 2011.

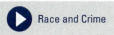
Race and Crime

TABLE 11.4 Arrests by Race, 2009

Offense charged	Percentage distribution	
	White	Black
Total crimes	**69.1**	**28.3**
Violent crime	58.7	38.9
Murder and nonnegligent manslaughter	48.7	49.3
Forcible rape	65.1	32.5
Robbery	42.8	55.5
Aggravated assault	63.5	33.9
Other assaults	65.2	32.2
Offenses against the family and children	66.6	30.8
Property crime	67.6	29.8
Burglary	66.5	31.7
Larceny-theft	68.1	29.0
Motor vehicle theft	61.1	36.3
Arson	74.8	22.8
Forgery and counterfeiting	66.7	31.7
Fraud	67.0	31.2
Embezzlement	66.0	31.7
Stolen property; buying, receiving, possessing	62.8	35.5
Vandalism	74.3	23.0
Weapons: carrying, possessing, etc.	57.4	41.0
Prostitution and commercialized vice	56.0	40.7
Sex offenses (except forcible rape and prostitution)	73.5	23.8
Drug abuse violations	65.0	33.6
Gambling	28.5	68.6
Driving under the influence	86.3	11.0
Liquor laws	84.0	11.4
Drunkenness	82.5	15.1
Disorderly conduct	63.3	34.2
Vagrancy	55.3	41.9
All other offenses (except traffic)	66.1	31.1
Suspicion	44.7	54.7
Curfew and loitering law violations	60.8	37.1
Runaways	65.7	26.7

SOURCE: Compiled from FBI Uniform Crime Reports 1991-2010.

FIGURE 11.3 Reported Violent Crime, 1990–2009

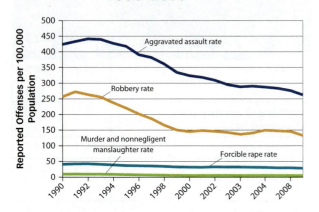

SOURCE: Compiled from FBI Uniform Crime Reports 1991–2010.

FIGURE 11.4 Reported Property Crime, 1990–2009

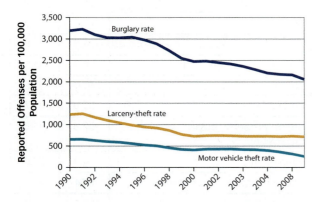

SOURCE: Compiled from FBI Uniform Crime Reports 1991–2010.

ASK YOURSELF: Between 1990 and 2009, the national rate of violent crime was halved, while property crime dropped to 60% of its previous rate, according to the National Archive of Criminal Justice Data. But almost every year since 1989, surveys of American adults have shown that they believe crime is getting worse. Why might people perceive that crime is going up when the official data show otherwise?

Global Perspective

A global view of crime allows us to better understand the variety of definitions of crime, styles of enforcement, and methods of punishment around the world, as well as the influence of globalization on crime itself. At present, however, social scientists have very poor comparative measures of crime around the globe. Trying to make cross-national comparisons about violent crime rates can be like comparing apples to oranges. Other challenges include disparities among nations' legal definitions of crimes and wide variations in enforcement of laws. For example, Haiti, Morocco, and Syria have "honor crimes" laws under which a man who kills his wife or daughter because she offended his honor, often in an adulterous situation, can present a legal defense that the killing was justified (MacKinnon 2008). The criminal justice system in India often fails to prosecute so-called dowry murders and the maiming of young brides (done so husbands can remarry for higher dowries), even though the dowry system was outlawed in 1961 (United Nations Office on Drugs and Crime 2006). The lack of worldwide consensus regarding definitions of criminal behavior extends to a host of different crimes.

Further complicating definitional differences are disparities in national data sources and the fact that data are not collected reliably in many developing countries. Even with accurate crime data, it would be very difficult to infer causation, or study relationships between social factors and crime, because there are simply too many factors to analyze. Social scientists would need a huge budget and staff, a massive database, and access to sensitive government data—so it's no wonder that studies of this nature are rarely performed.

To try to make sense of global crime patterns, the United Nations Office on Drugs and Crime (2011) took on the challenge of compiling data on several specific categories of crime from countries around the world. It found that relatively less economically and socially developed countries, and those with high income inequality, have homicide rates almost four times higher than those of more equal societies. In addition, countries in which the criminal justice systems had been strengthened over the past 15 years experienced declines in homicide rates (ChartsBin 2014).

One approach to conducting a comparative international study is to find two countries that are similar, which helps to rule out certain factors and pinpoint the degree of difference. Are you safer in England or in the United States, for example, and how would you know? U.S. conviction rates (per 1,000 population) have been observed to be six times higher for murder and three times higher for rape and robbery than the rates in England. Are more people in the United States committing murder, rape, and robbery? Or is the U.S. criminal

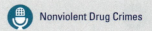

Nonviolent Drug Crimes

justice system better at catching and convicting murderers, rapists, and robbers?

To answer this question, the U.S. Department of Justice's Bureau of Justice Statistics compared the enforcement of criminal laws in the United States and England between 1981 and 1996 (Langan and Farrington 1998). The researchers found that not only murder conviction rates but also murder rates were higher in the United States than in England, and murderers were convicted accordingly. The study found the probability of rape in the two countries was about the same, but greater police professionalism in the United States led to more official recording of rapes. English laws concerning rape were also weaker during the time period of the study; they excluded marital victims, certain types of sexual intercourse, and offenders under the age of 14. Finally, when the researchers examined robbery, they found the likelihood of being a robbery victim was actually lower in the United States than in England. But the English criminal justice system was less successful at catching and convicting robbers and hence had a lower conviction rate.

Researchers have also compared criminal justice policies. For example, restorative justice models draw on the community to support the offender and ask him or her to repair the harm caused by the crime (Van Ness and Strong 2010). The concept and practice of restorative justice emerged in New Zealand in the late 1980s. Why there, and why then? The 1980s were a time of contentious debate in New Zealand about whether indigenous Maori cultural practices should play a broader part in the country's criminal justice system. The result was the Children, Young Persons and Their Families Act of 1989, which honored Maori values by permitting the victim of a crime, the offender, the families of both victim and offender, and a youth justice coordinator to meet as a way to achieve reconciliation between victim and offender and to restore social harmony and balance (MacRae and Zehr 2004). Under this system, the victim describes his or her experience of the crime, followed by a discussion by members of the group (Morris and Maxwell 2003). The offender and his or her family may express remorse and apologize to the victim. Together, participants develop plans and recommendations for reparations, such as fixing damaged property or creating opportunities for the offender to be reintegrated into the community (Karp 2001). Research has generally found positive outcomes for these practices,

Transnational crime: Crime that has effects across national borders.

including satisfaction of the offender and the victim and a reduction in future offense behaviors (Morris and Maxwell 2003; Van Ness and Strong 2010).

ASK YOURSELF: New Zealand's model of family group conference is used for most serious offenses, while the models of restorative justice found in Australia and parts of the United States apply only to nonserious offenses. What types of offenses do you believe are appropriate for restorative justice, as an alternative to formal processing by the courts? Why?

Much of what we know about crime comes from the study of patterns of crime and punishment in individual societies. Yet the fastest-growing area of crime is not confined to one country but is in fact *transnational* in scope. **Transnational crime** includes drug trafficking, cybercrime, and human trafficking, a lucrative form of modern-day slavery. The U.S. State Department estimates that 27 million people are victims of human trafficking worldwide, approximately 100,000 in the United States. A common scheme victimizes young women from "source" countries whose weak economies, natural disasters, or political oppression lead them to seek better lives elsewhere. They are lured by false job prospects to the United States, Japan, and many countries in Western Europe, but on arrival they are told they owe large debts for their transportation. They are then enslaved in brothels or forced into street prostitution.

Kacper Pempel / Reuters

In late 2013 and early 2014, millions of customers of retail stores Target and Neiman Marcus were the victims of cybercrime. Shoppers at these and other stores had their credit and debit card details stolen. It is believed that the cyberattacks were likely perpetrated by hackers living in Eastern Europe. Do events like these make you think twice before using a credit card?

Transnational Crime: An Interview with Criminologist Jay S. Albanese

In your book Transnational Crime and the 21st Century *(2011), you discuss the problem of human trafficking. What is human trafficking?* Human trafficking takes different forms, but its essence is coerced servitude. The basic elements of human trafficking are three:

- Exploitative labor (sex, manual labor, servitude)
- The harboring of victims (through recruitment, transport, or receipt)
- Coercion (accomplished through deception, force, or threats)

Is human trafficking similar to other transnational crimes? The defining feature of transnational crime is violations of law that involve more than one country in their planning, execution, or impact. These offenses are distinguished from other crimes in their multinational nature and cross-border impact, which pose unique problems in understanding causation, developing prevention strategies, and mounting effective adjudication procedures.

What different elements contribute to human trafficking as a social problem? We should not underestimate the seriousness of human trafficking as crime. Unlike most transnational crimes, which involve the buying and selling of consumable products, human trafficking entails the buying and selling of human beings who are exploited over and over again in an ongoing form of enslavement.

What is needed to combat the problem more effectively? A great deal remains to be done to better protect victims, understand the true nature and scope of trafficking enterprises, and increase the number of successful prosecutions in order to fulfill the promise of coordinated international action made by the United Nations' binding Protocol to Prevent, Suppress and Punish Trafficking in Persons, Especially Women and Children (enacted in 2003). Some progress has clearly been made, as suggested by the fact that 63% of 155 countries have passed laws against human trafficking pursuant to the U.N. Protocol. More than half of countries have developed a national action plan and an anti–human trafficking police unit. Nevertheless, progress has been slow, and we need to more effectively identify and uncover trafficking networks, protect victims, and prosecute traffickers.

Oliver Burston / Ikon Images / Corbis

Sixteen juveniles, ranging in age from 13 to 17, were forced into working as prostitutes for the 2014 Super Bowl. They were rescued in the New York City area by the FBI in the weeks before the game. Police arrested more than 45 pimps in conjunction with the international sex trafficking operation.

▶ **THINK ABOUT IT:** What are the advantages to human traffickers of carrying out their crimes transnationally? What can be done to combat human trafficking?

THE U.S. CRIMINAL JUSTICE SYSTEM AND ITS STAKEHOLDERS

11.3 Describe the U.S. criminal justice system and its stakeholders.

The U.S. criminal justice system attempts to address the social problem of crime. The system is formal, sanctioned by the laws written by state and federal legislatures, and intended to operate on behalf of its citizens. It employs **stakeholders**—including police, prosecutors, defense attorneys, and judges—who make decisions about arrests, prosecutions, and sentencing. The operation of the criminal justice system is an extremely discretionary process that can yield different versions of justice from one defendant to the next. Issues of intersectionality are present at every stage. Who is accused? What does he or

Stakeholders: All individuals who have an interest in and are affected by the workings of a given system; in the criminal justice system, stakeholders include those accused of crimes as well as those who process cases, including police, attorneys, and court and correctional staff.

she look like? What legal representation can the accused afford? What does the victim look like? The variables that affect outcomes are vast and complex.

While a system of criminal justice is essential to society, when such a system exceeds its legal boundaries new social problems are created. Boston, for example, like many American cities, implemented a controversial policy to fight gangs during the late 1980s known as "stop and frisk," which allowed police to stop and pat down any black male wearing a hooded sweatshirt, check his mouth for drugs, and even drop his pants looking for guns. The policy was eventually blocked by the Massachusetts courts as an unlawful invasion of privacy based on racial bias. Forced to find new strategies, the police realized that stop and frisk had prevented them from developing effective relationships with youths and obtaining useful information that could have helped to reduce neighborhood crimes (Guarino-Ghezzi 1994). But the practice continues in other cities.

Below, we discuss in turn the various stakeholders in the criminal justice system.

Police

The first responders to a crime scene are usually the police. They have the challenging task of entering a sometimes dangerous crime scene, investigating its circumstances, and taking the appropriate action under the law. Protecting individual liberties while conducting their investigation is paramount.

The structure of police departments in the United States is grounded in English tradition (Walker and Katz 2008) and is characterized by local control and **decentralization of power**, meaning that unless the circumstances are extreme, police hold limited power and respond to calls only within their own geographic boundaries. Decentralization of power has social implications, too, in that enforcement varies from place to place according to local traditions and norms. Police in high-crime communities might prioritize crimes differently than police in suburban communities and overlook relatively low-level offenses, such as disorderly conduct.

While the English influence is still prevalent today (Manning 2005), some aspects of policing have changed over time in the United States. During the "political era" of law enforcement history, 1840–1920, politicians and police officers worked very closely together, a practice

Decentralization of power: The distribution of functions and responsibilities of police officers to different local authorities.

Hot-spot policing: A method employed by police departments to track the ordered spatial patterns of crime by monitoring when crimes occur disproportionately in particular geographic areas and responding to those areas.

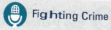 **Fighting Crime**   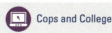 **Cops and College**

Lucy Nicholson / Reuters

Among the major responsibilities of the police are to identify criminal offenders and criminal activity and, when appropriate, to apprehend offenders and participate in later court proceedings. Police officers in Britain typically do not carry firearms, while those in the United States, such as these officers in Los Angeles, California, are usually heavily armed. Which do you think is most effective in maintaining order and controlling crime?

that sometimes led to payoffs and other corruption of the force (Cole and Smith 2008). The "professional era," 1920–1970, brought more training and education for police officers, more equal enforcement of laws, reduced political interference, merit-based employment procedures, and a focus on fighting crime. The current era, which began around 1970, has been called the "community policing era" because police work has expanded to include more proactive and community-oriented strategies. At first, police departments accomplished this by taking officers out of patrol cars and putting them on the streets, in schools, and in communities to increase cooperation and trust between private citizens and the police force (Walker and Katz 2008).

Since the 1970s many urban police departments have incorporated additional techniques, such as **hot-spot policing**, which uses cutting-edge data-mapping tools. Studies by crime scholars and police suggest that crime is not spread evenly across city neighborhoods. Instead, significant clusters, or hot spots, are the locations of half of all criminal events (Pierce 1989; Braga and Weisburd 2010). For example, New York City has had a remarkable and steady decline in crime over two decades. Police there discovered that when they mapped the locations of crimes, they could identify areas that produced the most calls. The hot spots for certain crimes also proved to be predictors of more serious crimes. For instance, clusters of robberies in particular locations tended to be followed by homicides. Many U.S. cities now use hot-spot policing. Figure 11.5 is an example of a hot-spot map showing that, in the period from January 2008 through February 2009, firearms incidents in Brockton, Massachusetts,

due to the rules and norms established by the judge and maintained by the other members of the court (Currul-Dykeman 2014).

It is the jury's responsibility to be the **finder of fact** during a jury trial. In this role, jurors identify the evidence they believe to be true beyond a reasonable doubt and render a verdict. Traditional courts in the United States operate under an adjudicative model of justice. Typical steps in the process are arraignment (in which charges against the defendant are formally announced), pretrial hearings (in which discovery of evidence is held to determine the strength of the prosecutor's case), motion hearings, and disposition (trial, plea bargain, or dismissal). Cases are dealt with individually, efficiency is the goal, and outcomes can depend on a number of factors, both legal and extralegal. Legal factors include seriousness of the crime, length of the defendant's criminal record if any, and sufficiency of evidence. Extralegal factors include the defendant's gender, race, and socioeconomic status.

Traditional courts make no attempt to deal with the larger social problems affecting the community. Efforts to overcome this limitation have recently given rise to courts of limited jurisdiction, or **specialized courts**, which can be invaluable for defendants, victims, and their communities. Rather than using a case efficiency model of justice, specialized courts make problem solving their primary goal and orient their proceedings toward social justice. Many of these courts actually try to bring about social change for defendants (e.g., to end their drug abuse), for the community (e.g., to take guns off the street), and for victims (e.g., to end the cycle of violence in which they have been trapped).

Many different types of specialized courts have been adopted across the country, and their success has been measured both quantitatively (Banks and Gottfredson 2004) and qualitatively (Currul-Dykeman 2014). Specialized courts allow judges to play a larger role in overseeing defendants' progress toward change and/or recovery. The judges gather information from specialists and advocates in the community and consider advice from community agents and partners when making decisions.

Collaboration, nontraditional roles, and the participation of private agencies are the final three distinguishing features of specialized courts (Hemmens et al. 2010). Collaboration brings people together to devise a plan that addresses the causes of the problem, rather than relying on the formal adversarial approach of making adjudications with little or no input from the community. Drug courts, for example, typically work with defendants before their cases are resolved, with the aim of helping them end their drug abuse and assisting them in finding better lives for themselves. Drug offenders who do not

have histories of violence can choose to enter substance abuse treatment programs for counseling, therapy, and education; such programs might last 12 to 18 months. Such defendants are also subject to random urine tests for the presence of drugs and are required to appear before the drug court judge. A participant who does not comply is placed back into the traditional court system, and his or her case is disposed of with probation or jail time (Hemmens et al. 2010). Drug courts have been found to be very effective at reducing substance abuse and crime (Rossman et al. 2011).

Domestic violence courts focus on offender accountability, judicial monitoring, and rehabilitation. They seek input from community service providers (civilian advocates, local hospital staff, and members of the police department) who work together to assess the likelihood that offenders might attempt to kill their victims, to identify high-risk offenders, and to help improve victim safety and services. When resources allow, prosecutors working in this model can take on reduced and specialized case loads (Welsh and Harris 2012).

Teen courts, which are generally voluntary, offer young offenders the chance to make restitution or in some other manner repair the harm they have done in return for keeping their criminal records clear. Education is a central component of teen courts, as is rehabilitation. An example of a teen court can be found in Oakland, California, where young people with histories of getting into trouble find hope at Ralph J. Bunche High School, which runs a restorative justice program for expelled students who are entering the juvenile justice system. The program encourages them to make meaningful reparations for their wrongdoings while developing empathy with each other in "talking circles."

Oakland recently expanded this program when a report by the Urban Strategies Council showed that African American boys made up 17% of the student population but 42% of all school suspensions. They were also six times more likely than their white male classmates to be suspended, often for nonviolent infractions like swearing or texting in class. Research indicates that loss of class time from suspensions and expulsions results in alienation and early involvement in the juvenile justice system.

Damon Smith was expelled from school more than 15 times before attending Bunche. He said, "You start

Finder of fact: In a criminal prosecution, the individuals assigned to determine whether the facts have been proven. This role is most often assigned to the jury.

Specialized courts: Problem-solving courts set up within local district courts to deal with social problems affecting the surrounding communities.

thinking it's cool. You think you're going to come back and catch up, but unless you're a genius you won't. It made me want to mess up even more" (quoted in Wilson 2013). Damon said that the restorative justice sessions helped him view his behavior differently and taught him how to express his emotions more appropriately.

....

ASK YOURSELF: What are some advantages of specialized courts? Can you think of any disadvantages from the defendant's point of view? Can you think of any other kinds of specialized courts that could be beneficial?

....

Corrections

If a defendant is found guilty, he or she is sentenced by the presiding judge. In some U.S. states, judges can administer whatever punishment they see fit, while in others they are restricted by policy. For example, California's "three strikes" law states that if an offender is convicted for a third serious crime, a life sentence is mandatory.

The most prominent purposes of punishment are incapacitation, rehabilitation, retribution, and deterrence. **Incapacitation** involves the loss of individual freedom and liberty. Here the offender, sentenced to jail or prison time, cannot reoffend and victimize another person in the community. However, sentencing nonviolent and minor offenders to incarceration has led to prison overcrowding (Levitt 1996). **Rehabilitation** involves helping the offender with the root cause of the criminal behavior in the hope that this will prevent it from happening again. Educational programs, mental health counseling, treatment for drug and alcohol abuse, anger management, and other behavioral therapies have all been used in this vein.

....

Incapacitation: Loss of liberty due to incarceration.

Rehabilitation: A goal of punishment that seeks to restore the offender to a more law-abiding life, free of the encumbrances that may have caused him or her to commit a crime.

Retribution: Punishment that serves no purpose except to punish and communicate to the wrongdoer that his or her behavior is not tolerated.

Deterrence: A purpose of punishment that sets out to prevent rational people from committing crimes.

General deterrence: A law or policy written to stop a person from committing a crime in the first place.

Specific deterrence: A law or policy written to stop those who break laws from offending again.

Indeterminate sentencing: Sentencing for convicted offenders in which the length of incarceration is undetermined.

Cary Wolinsky / National Geographic Society

....

Capital punishment is a form of retribution and is based on the notion of a life for a life. In 2013, 32 U.S. states had the death penalty. Methods of execution include lethal injection, electrocution, hanging, firing squad, and the gas chamber. Arizona, California, Missouri, and Wyoming still use, or could use, the gas chamber as a method of capital punishment. What are the pros and cons of using the death penalty?

Retribution involves punishment for punishment's sake. It has no additional purpose but to punish and communicate to the wrongdoer that the criminal behavior is not tolerated. Finally, **deterrence** aims either to stop crime in the first place (**general deterrence**) or to stop an offender from offending again (**specific deterrence**). For example, strict laws against drunk driving have a general deterrent effect on the public at large, while the experience of losing his or her driver's license might specifically deter an individual from driving drunk again.

....

ASK YOURSELF: Studies have shown that courts in Florida deemed African American youths to be less amenable to rehabilitation than their white counterparts who had committed the same types of crimes and had similar records. Thus African American teenagers were transferred to adult courts for processing while white teenagers were kept in the rehabilitative juvenile justice model. Why do you think this occurred?

....

Corrections in the United States has a violent past. Before 1800, U.S. and European courts alike used harsh physical punishment as the primary criminal sanction (Cole and Smith 2008). Early in the 19th century, massive penitentiaries were created in Pennsylvania and New York to make punishment less vengeful. The isolation inmates underwent was actually thought to help them.

By the end of the 1800s, it was clear penitentiaries were having neither a rehabilitative nor a deterrent effect. This realization led to open-ended or **indeterminate sentencing** (in which sentences are not definite in length),

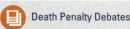 **Death Penalty Debates**    **Rehab versus Prison**

meaning that offenders remained incarcerated until they showed they could atone for their crimes and lead non-criminal lives. From the 1930s through the 1970s there was more focus on rehabilitation and less on incapacitation and retribution. The crime control model that took hold in the 1980s is punitive in nature and calls for longer prison sentences, but **recidivism** (or reoffending) remains high (Cole and Smith 2008).

Probation and parole keep offenders in the community and out of prison. **Probation** allows a convicted individual to stay in the community under certain conditions such as supervision, counseling, drug-free status, and a clean record. If an offender fails to comply, probation can be revoked, resulting in incarceration. **Parole** allows an inmate to leave prison early and finish his or her sentence within the community, also under supervision and other conditions. The transition from prison back into the community can be difficult for many, and support is not always available, a situation that often leads to new offenses.

ASK YOURSELF: Why is the transition from prison back to the community a vulnerable time for ex-inmates?

The War on Drugs that began in the 1980s produced high incarceration rates and contributed to a highly skewed distribution of inmates based on race, as shown in Figure 11.6. While drug convictions for whites doubled from 1986 through 1996, for blacks they quintupled. Today, roughly 60% of prison inmates are black or Latino. As sociologist Loïc Wacquant has observed, the racial composition of prisons today is the reverse of what is was in the 1950s, when only 30% of inmates were persons of color. Here, laws to control behaviors have led to other complex social problems. Most notably, laws against the possession of quantities of crack cocaine, favored by urban drug users, established prison terms 100 times as long as those for possession of powdered cocaine, preferred by suburban users. Such laws disproportionately incarcerated blacks for two decades, and only in 2010 were sentences reduced from 100 to 18 times longer for crack than for powder, which many feel is still too wide a disparity. This long-term practice worsened the social problems experienced by minority families with incarcerated members.

Drug laws have had especially devastating effects on women. Two-thirds of women in prison are there for nonviolent offenses, many of them drug-related crimes. In the period from 1999 through 2008, arrests of women for drug violations increased 19%, compared to 10% for men, according to the UCR. Drug laws were also

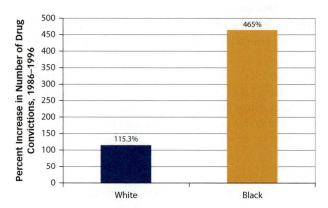

FIGURE 11.6 Increase in Drug Convictions for U.S. Whites and Blacks, 1986–1996

SOURCE: Justice Policy Institute, 2000.

largely responsible for more than doubling the number of incarcerated mothers between 1991 and 2007. Nearly two-thirds of women in U.S. prisons are mothers. At midyear 2007, approximately 65,600 women in federal and state custody reported being mothers; together, they had 147,400 minor children. Among incarcerated mothers, 77% reported that they provided most of the daily care for their children before incarceration (Glaze and Maruschak 2008).

Evidence suggests that maternal incarceration can be more damaging to a child than paternal incarceration. Courts can also terminate parental rights when children have been in foster care for 15 of the preceding 22 months. Loss of parental rights is of particular concern to mothers in prison, who are five times as likely as men to report having children placed in foster homes.

The disparate punishment of minorities and women for drug crimes relates to issues raised by the theories of crime we discuss next: economic and social disadvantages, negative environments, and opportunities to connect with both legitimate and illegitimate cultures within society.

Recidivism: The habit of reoffending.

Probation: An alternative to incarceration that offers an individual freedom if he or she can abide by the law and comply with the terms and conditions mandated by the court.

Parole: The release, under supervision, of a convicted criminal defendant after he or she has completed part of his or her sentence, based on the concept that the defendant will follow the law and become a part of society.

USING THEORY TO EXAMINE CRIME: THE VIEWS FROM THE FUNCTIONALIST, SYMBOLIC INTERACTIONIST, AND CONFLICT PERSPECTIVES

 11.4 Apply the functionalist, conflict, and symbolic interactionist perspectives to the problem of crime.

Theoretical criminologists attempt to discover why people commit crimes. Do offenders feel the strain of not being able to support themselves and use criminal means to achieve economic success? Or perhaps crime is a product of the conflict that exists within society between the powerful and the weak? Perhaps there is a problem with the very structure of our criminal justice system and the way it criminalizes offenders before they have been proven guilty. Regardless of orientation, a vast number of scientifically supported criminological theories attempt to explain the true causes of crime and question the sociolegal orientation of the courts, the laws, and the way they operate and affect society.

Functionalism

The organization of society itself can cause or contribute to crime and its patterns. Structural functionalism takes a macro view of crime and looks at how a complex social system that stresses adherence to norms and values can actually cause certain people to engage in deviant conduct classified as criminal. Émile Durkheim (1984), writing in 1893, focused mainly on anomie, or normlessness, to explain why people deviate from the norm. Broad changes in society, particularly in the roles of workers, resulted in ambiguous behavioral norms. While Durkheim studied these social phenomena as causes of suicide, criminologists have generalized his ideas to study anomie as a cause of criminal behavior.

Robert K. Merton (1938, 1968) also believed crime is a product of society. In his **strain theory**, individuals

Strain theory: A theory of crime that posits individuals commit crimes because of the strains caused by the imbalance between societally accepted goals and the individuals' inadequate means to achieve those goals.

commit crimes because they cannot succeed within the boundaries society has created for them. Merton's theory assumes that the values of American society include financial success as a universal goal. Unfortunately, many cannot achieve this goal through legal means. They may choose to respond to the resulting strain in one of five ways, or *adaptations.*

Conformists accept the means and ends of society. They do not commit crimes or engage in any deviant behavior but rather accept their position in life. They may never achieve financial success but would not dream of using illegitimate means to achieve it either. *Innovators* do not accept that they cannot achieve the goal of financial success and devise illegal ways to reach conventional goals. Within this category are white-collar criminals, burglars, and drug dealers. *Ritualists* reject the ends but accept the means of society. They do not commit crime because they are not necessarily seeking to achieve the goal of economic success. *Retreatists* such as cultists and alcoholics reject society's goals and means and remove themselves from conventional society altogether. *Rebels,* such as terrorists, reject conventional goals and replace

Handout / Reuters

Dzhokhar Tsarnaev, pictured in this FBI photo, and his brother, Tamerlan, are suspected of setting off multiple bombs near the finish line of the Boston Marathon in 2013, killing three and wounding more than 250. It is believed that, motivated by extremist Islamic beliefs, the Tsarnaev brothers mounted the terrorist attacks in response to the U.S. military presence in Iraq and Afghanistan. Do you see the brothers as "rebels" wanting to change Muslim countries by driving out Western influences?

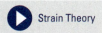 Strain Theory

them with new ones, advocating for a new system and the destruction of the current one. Note that strain theory can explain only property and premeditated crimes, and not crimes of passion such as spontaneous violence motivated by jealousy or anger.

In 1960, Richard A. Cloward and Lloyd E. Ohlin expanded Merton's theory by proposing that crime is an expression of the types of illegitimate opportunities available. Their **opportunity theory** suggests people have different access to criminal opportunities. Whether they commit crimes, and what types, depends on their opportunities. Cloward and Ohlin use the term *gang* loosely to define any group of individuals who are joined together by some criminal purpose and further delineate them by the types of activities they engage in predominantly. When individuals have no legitimate or illegitimate opportunities, some, who make up what Cloward and Ohlin call the *retreatist gang,* may retreat into the world of sex, drugs, and alcohol. Others, the *conflict gang,* become both aggressive and violent due to lack of legitimate opportunities. Finally, *criminal gangs* have both legitimate and illegitimate opportunities but engage in criminal pursuits for financial gain. Organized crime is an example of this gang type.

Travis Hirschi (1969) believed that all people are capable of committing crime and that some do not because of their close bond to conventional society. Hirschi's **social control theory** says the stronger a person's bond to society, the less likely he or she will feel "free to deviate." This bond has four elements: attachment, commitment, involvement, and belief. *Attachment* is an emotional connection to others, starting with parents and extending to other family members and teachers. When temptation appears, an individual who is strongly attached to others will remain controlled by them even though they are not physically present. Those with weak attachments have less at stake and are more likely to deviate. *Commitment* describes individuals' long-term, socially approved goals. Fear of losing that job or scholarship may cause someone to refuse to deviate. *Involvement* in conventional activities leaves less free time to deviate; those with little structured time are more likely to commit crime. Finally, when young people *believe* they should obey the rules of society, they are less likely to violate them (Hirschi 1969, 26).

ASK YOURSELF: If you got into trouble on campus, whom would you be afraid of disappointing? Does the potential for disappointing someone make you think twice about doing something prohibited?

When any of the elements of a person's bond to society are weakened, the individual's connection to society becomes unreliable, and he or she is more likely to commit crimes. Terrance Graham was only 17 when he was sentenced to life in prison without the possibility of parole. His childhood had been riddled with trouble. While his mother loved him dearly, she struggled to raise him by herself. Addicted to crack cocaine, she would disappear for weeks, leaving Terrance to care for his three younger siblings. He committed his first criminal act at 16 when he helped some other youths rob a restaurant and spent a year in a juvenile detention center as a result. Shortly after his release, he was apprehended for committing a similar crime and sentenced to life without parole for armed burglary and attempted armed robbery. In the 2010 case of *Graham v. Florida,* however, the U.S. Supreme Court held that a sentence of life without parole for a nonhomicide offense committed by someone under the age of 18 violates the U.S. Constitution's prohibition against "cruel and unusual punishment." Terrance had already served 7 years in prison when the case was decided. His life sentence was reduced to 25 years.

ASK YOURSELF: How would social control theory explain why Terrance Graham was "free to deviate"? Specifically apply the facts of his life to the elements of the social bond.

Policy Implications of Structural Functionalism

Anomie and strain theories lend themselves to broad, macro-level structural policy recommendations to alleviate the sources of the strain or normlessness that causes people to commit crimes. Programs and policies aimed at ending poverty and racism, such as affirmative action and the Job Corps, emerged from these theories as efforts to increase opportunities for those traditionally denied them because of their race and gender. Other programs aim to help parents achieve goals like flexible work options that keep them employed and earning while caring for their children (Messner and Rosenfeld 2013).

Hirschi's social control theory lends itself to more practical solutions for crime. In the absence of strong parental figures, for instance, mentoring programs might help children develop attachments with law-abiding adults that can help improve commitment. Basic afterschool recreational programs, social groups, and sports

Opportunity theory: A theory of crime that says people will chose to commit crimes based on the criminal opportunities they have.

Social control theory: A theory of crime that assumes all people are capable of committing crimes and that some are stopped by their strong bonds to society.

teams can keep young people busy, involved, and thus less free to deviate. Finally, affiliation with groups that promote positive values and respect for authority can help strengthen the final element of the bond. Boys and Girls Clubs and YMCA programs have been successful and are compatible with the goals of social control theories (Mortenson and Relin 2006).

Conflict Theory

Conflict theory stresses the inherent struggle that exists between groups within our society. The social inequities that exist among classes, races, and genders are all sources of conflict that lead to crime. In general, the weak are made to suffer at the hands of the powerful: the poor held down by the rich, ethnic minorities kept down by the white majority, and women exploited and demeaned by men. Conflict theorists also examine how the powerful write and use the laws to their own advantage and to the detriment of weaker groups. We have seen in this chapter that punishments for possession of crack cocaine, weak enforcement of wage laws, and stop-and-frisk policies all contribute to the disproportionate incarceration of people of color—and all could be explored through a conflict lens. We next explore the injustices that exist between classes and genders through the same lens.

Karl Marx was a German philosopher in the 1800s. While he said very little about crime or criminals, many conflict criminologists have used his general view of society to explain crime in a model known as **Marxist criminology**. Marx believed that limited resources and their uneven distribution among the population were the cause of much conflict within society. He described two dominant classes: the **bourgeoisie**, or the wealthy class, who own the means of production; and the **proletariat**, or the working class, who contribute their labor.

Marxist criminologists believe the struggles between classes affect crime in many ways. For instance, **bourgeoisie**

Marxist criminology: A view based on the writings of Karl Marx that sees the law as the mechanism by which the ruling class keeps the members of the surplus population in their disadvantaged position.

Bourgeoisie: In Marxist theory, the wealthy class that owns and controls the means of production and is at odds with the lower class.

Proletariat: In Marxist theory, the working class, which is at odds with the bourgeoisie.

Bourgeoisie legality: The theory that members of the upper class make the laws to serve and protect their own interests to the detriment of the lower class.

---

legality allows the members of the wealthy class—through their connections to officials and lawmakers—to write and use the law as a tool of oppression. The "deviant" behaviors of the poor are viewed as "street crimes," while similar behaviors by the ruling class are largely ignored. Further, members of the working class are excluded from many higher-paying jobs, from receiving better employee benefits, and from achieving a more comfortable lifestyle; this exclusion causes them to behave in a criminal manner.

Many of these issues are currently at play at Walmart. Although the company is ranked by *Forbes* magazine as one of the top 100 organizations to work for, most of its full-time employees with families earn $6.00 to $7.50 an hour, keeping them below the poverty line (Kim 2012). Few employees can afford the company's expensive health benefits; one-third are not eligible for benefits whatsoever. While Walmart employs many people of color nationwide, only two Hispanic women sit on its board, and only one woman holds an executive officer position in the entire company. From a conflict perspective, any crimes committed by members of the working class could be related to the stress caused by such unjust treatment.

....

ASK YOURSELF: Do you think it is a crime for corporations to impose unfavorable working conditions on employees? Why or why not?

....

Conflict theory also speaks to the U.S. economic crisis that began in 2007. As housing prices declined following reckless lending by banks, many financial institutions suffered huge losses and faced bankruptcy. The government bailed out the largest of these even as many U.S. workers faced job loss, home foreclosure, and rising food and fuel

Employees take part in a protest for better wages outside a Walmart store in Los Angeles. Can these employees use current laws to obtain higher wages? Do laws always advantage the rich?

prices. Seeing how the bourgeoisie lawmakers stepped in to serve their own class members, the Occupy Wall Street movement took flight nationwide.

....

ASK YOURSELF: Do you think Occupy Wall Street is a modern example of the proletariat rising up against the bourgeoisie? Has it been an effective approach to gaining more equality and power for "the 99%"? Explain your reasoning. Would you ever join such a movement? Why or why not?

....

Feminist criminology is often viewed as a part of the conflict perspective because it questions the inequities between the genders that permeate the criminal justice system in myriad ways. Some feminist criminologists believe that **paternalism**—that is, the practice of treating or governing women in a fatherly manner, especially by providing for their needs without giving them rights or responsibilities—explains why women are more likely than men to be victims of crimes at the hands of men they know and have relationships with (Belknap 2007). Others criticize the way the criminal justice system treats male and female offenders differently. Kathleen Daly and Meda Chesney-Lind (1988) found that female juvenile delinquents are punished more harshly than boys for minor offenses because their behaviors are contrary to beliefs about how girls should behave.

Even the laws themselves can be criticized under a feminist/conflict orientation. Did you know that for hundreds of years it was not illegal for a man to rape his wife? The marital rape exemption stated that when a woman agreed to marriage, she gave free consent to her husband to have sex with her at all times as part of the contract. Today many U.S. states have modified their rape laws to eliminate this exemption, and feminist scholars still question and challenge its existence in some states' laws.

The feminist/conflict perspective finds that other aspects of the criminal justice system have also had disproportionately negative impacts on women. For example, under marital privilege, an individual cannot be compelled to testify against his or her spouse; abusive husbands sometimes use a poor understanding of the privilege to threaten their wives with harm if they plan to testify voluntarily against the husbands. Feminist criminologists have also studied chivalry, or a tendency to overprotect women and girls. Some researchers have found that a chivalrous attitude toward women leads to leniency for female defendants in criminal cases (Mallicoat 2007), while others have found that women who violate gendered expectations are treated more harshly (MacDonald & Chesney-Lind 2001). Regardless of case outcomes, feminist criminologists find that gender is

an important variable that causes difference due to an imbalance of power between men and women.

Policy Implications of the Conflict Perspective

Policies that strive to resolve economic and social inequalities by creating better working conditions, eliminating race and gender discrimination in the workplace, providing health care for all, and offering equal opportunity in housing and education can all stem from the conflict perspective, along with the elimination of race and gender discrimination within the criminal justice system itself. Conflict theorists who have looked into the impacts of race and gender on charging and sentencing decisions have suggested that possible solutions to current inequities include an increase in the numbers of minorities and women in positions in the criminal justice system and changes in laws to eliminate criminalization of the behavior of the disenfranchised (Amster 2004; Ferrell 2013). Feminist criminologists also question the androcentric nature of the laws and continue to challenge laws that place women in a disadvantaged position relative to men (Chesney-Lind and Morash 2013).

Symbolic Interactionism

Symbolic interactionism is a microsociological theory that focuses on individuals rather than on society. This theory says the way we define and view ourselves is always changing; it depends on our interactions with others and how we think others view us. Thus when others see us or treat us as criminals, we may be more likely to see ourselves in a similar light. If we are consistently exposed to crime and the benefits of or rationalizations for it, we may learn to behave in a criminal manner, because all behavior—criminal and noncriminal—is learned.

Edwin H. Sutherland and Donald R. Cressey (1974) address this learning process in their **differential association theory**. Throughout life we have different associations with others, and we learn behavior when we interact with others. Some interactions control our behavior more strongly than others. How early in life these associations present themselves, how important they are to us, how often they occur, and how long they continue—all of these affect what we

....

Feminist criminology: A theory of crime that includes gender in its analysis.

Paternalism: The system, principle, or practice of managing or governing individuals in the manner of a father dealing with his children.

Differential association theory: A theory of crime that asserts that all behavior is learned, both criminal and noncriminal.

Fighting Stereotypes with Hate Crime Legislation

What does a victim look like? An offender? When we consider crime as the intersection of victim and offender, how often do we use racial, gender, and social class stereotypes?

Matthew Shepard was a student at the University of Wyoming in 1998. One night he met two individuals at bar who agreed to give him a ride home, but they drove him to a remote area, beat and tortured him, and finally tied him to a fence to die. Alive but in a coma, Shepard was discovered 18 hours later by a bicyclist who initially mistook him for a scarecrow. He had suffered fractures to his skull and severe brain damage, and he died without regaining consciousness.

On June 7, 1998, in Jasper, Texas, three white men (known white supremacists) tied a black man named James Byrd Jr. to the back of their pickup truck and dragged him along an asphalt road. Byrd did not die until he smashed into a pipe at the side of the road that severed his head and arm. The defendants then dumped his remains in a cemetery.

Social statuses like race, gender, and social class all factor into the development of hate crime legislation. The attack on Matthew Shepard was motivated by the defendants' perceptions of his sexual orientation, but Wyoming did not include this category in its hate crime law at the time. Texas did not have any hate crime law in place at the time of James Byrd's murder, but after his death it was finally passed.

Today 45 U.S. states have adopted some form of hate crime legislation, making it a crime to victimize a person simply because of his or her identity or beliefs. These laws allow courts to impose stiff punishments and send a message of intolerance of hate crime. Originally, only acts committed on the basis of a person's race, religion, ethnicity, or nationality were prosecuted under federal law, but in 2009 President Obama signed the Matthew Shepard and James Byrd, Jr. Hate Crimes Prevention Act, expanding the law to include crimes motivated by victims' gender, sexual orientation, gender identity, or disability.

▶ **THINK ABOUT IT:** Do you think that James Byrd Jr.'s murder was especially heinous not only because he was black but also because he was male?

Stella and James Byrd Sr. arrange flowers around the headstone of their son, James Byrd Jr., in Jasper, Texas.

Pat Sullivan / Associated Press

SOURCES: Matthew Shepard Foundation (2014) and Wong (2009).

---

learn and what we discard as unimportant. Sutherland and Cressey propose that a person becomes criminal because he or she has more criminal than noncriminal associations.

Societal reaction theory: A theory of crime that argues that people become criminals based on how others respond to their actions.

Primary deviance: In societal reaction theory, this refers to individuals' engagement in low-level offending, like speeding or experimenting with alcohol.

Secondary deviance: In societal reaction theory, this refers to individuals' engagement in more serious forms of crime after they have been labeled and treated as criminals.

Edwin M. Lemert's **societal reaction theory** (1951, 1972) explores how individuals base their self-identities on the ways others label or respond to them. Lemert believes many people engage in **primary deviance**, or low-level, nonserious offending, such as speeding or experimenting with alcohol. If they are caught, society's response will affect the way they view and handle themselves in the future. Those who are labeled delinquent, criminal, and deviant and treated poorly or ostracized are more likely to engage in more serious forms of deviance—**secondary deviance**—in the future. Those who are not caught or not labeled criminal will not start to identify as such and will discontinue deviant behavior.

Defining Hate Crimes

Sometimes it is not the actions that make a crime but rather the actor. Social context greatly influences the way we, as a society, respond to an incident. While binge drinking in college is not ideal or productive behavior, it is hardly seen as deviant, let alone criminal. However, a binge-drinking stay-at-home mom or professor would be labeled and treated much more harshly, even though a national survey found that 70% of binge-drinking episodes involve adults over 26 years old. A criminologist from the labeling perspective (a subset of symbolic interactionism) might ask: How does society decide which acts are deviant and criminal depending on the perpetrator, and not on the act alone? What impact does being labeled a drunk have on a person's future criminal choices? (For more information on this topic, see Naimi et al. 2003; Centers for Disease Control and Prevention 2012a.)

Policy Implications of Symbolic Interactionism

Policies that stem from differential association theory aim at reducing the amount of a person's exposure to criminal or delinquent individuals, such as by making sure young people have positive friends and role models (for example, through mentoring programs). Theorists such as Edwin M. Schur have called for "radical nonintervention," believing it is better not to criminalize the delinquent behaviors of juveniles. They argue that programs that divert juveniles from the formal court process and instead offer social and educational support will better assist them in avoiding a criminal life.

Symbolic interaction theories also apply to convicted criminals. By restricting their interactions with other criminals through the terms and conditions of parole, for example, we could reduce their exposure to criminal influences and encourage them to associate with law-abiding individuals within their communities. Employment, education, or community service could satisfy that need.

SPECIALIZED THEORIES ABOUT CRIME

 Apply specialized theories of crime.

Sociological theories of crime identify characteristics of societies, communities, social groups, and social processes that determine criminal behavior. According to **rational choice theory**, offenders are rational beings who exercise free will in deciding on their course of action.

Their involvement in offending includes decisions and choices, however rudimentary. For example, a friend pulls up in a car and asks you to hop in. Knowing the friend is a gang member who carries weapons, you are aware you're taking a risk, but nevertheless you jump in, only to learn he is in search of a rival gang member. If he shoots the rival while you're with him, you could be convicted as a codefendant—even though you weren't involved in the plan.

Most criminologists believe in a concept known as **bounded rationality**, which means we make choices but they are restricted by our position in life, including background, need for money or status, opportunities available, and situational factors. In our example, while most people know better than to get into a car with a gang member, some might take the risk anyway, perhaps because the friend has protected them from harm in the past and they don't want to run the more dangerous risk of saying no to him.

Rational choice theory helps explain crimes for profit, where the rewards clearly outweigh the risks. For example, art theft is one of the fastest-growing crimes globally. While it sounds relatively harmless, in fact most art thieves know nothing about art and are primarily engaged in other illicit activities, like drug trafficking. They fund these destructive endeavors through the sale of stolen art. The usual targets of art crimes—museums, churches, galleries, and private homes—are relatively unguarded, so the risk of detection and apprehension is low. The growth of art theft appears closely tied to the low risks combined with high rewards, suggesting that a rational decision process is a factor in this crime.

ASK YOURSELF: When is rational choice "bounded," and how might these bounds affect someone's decision to commit crimes? Consider a corporation's chief financial officer who steals from the corporation and the same CFO with a drug habit; a juvenile who robs a convenience store and the same juvenile with a learning disability; a woman who decides to continue living with her abuser despite repeated beatings and the same woman with a history of childhood abuse.

We saw above that disproportionate amounts of crime and disorder tend to cluster in hot spots, a fact

Rational choice theory: A theory of crime that says humans are reasoning actors who weigh costs and benefits and make rational choices to commit crimes.

Bounded rationality: The idea that an individual's thought processes are deemed to be rational even when they are constrained by low intelligence, chemical dependence, or mental illness.

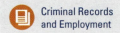 Criminal Records and Employment

the three major sociological theories do not account for. **Routine activities theory**, however, suggests that crime occurs when a motivated offender, a suitable target, and the lack of a capable guardian converge in the same place at the same time. This theory suggests we have a never-ending supply of motivated offenders ready and willing to commit crimes in the course of their routine activities, and how and when they do so largely depends on how "soft" the targets appear. If a car is unlocked on a dark and deserted street, chances are it will become a target for crime.

Policy makers are quick to respond to such a concrete theory. Installing lights, increasing police presence, and ensuring that individuals make other efforts to protect themselves and their property are easy solutions to the crime problem. Critics have argued that a weakness of routine activities theory is *crime displacement*, meaning that once potential victims alter their behavior, motivated offenders simply move on to "softer" targets.

Broken windows theory, introduced by George L. Kelling and James Q. Wilson (1982), explains how lesser crimes, untended areas, blight, graffiti, and signs of disorder increase willingness to commit minor crimes, which in turn leads to more serious crimes. The theory suggests that if a community agrees to "fix its broken windows," and the police target minor transgressions, serious crimes may be prevented.

Routine activities theory: The theory that crimes occur when motivated offenders come across suitable targets and a lack of capable guardians.

Broken windows theory: The theory that maintaining an urban environment in an orderly manner will deter both low-level and serious offending.

Social disorganization theory: A theory that links crime rates to neighborhood ecological characteristics: poverty, residential mobility, and racial heterogeneity.

Patrick Chauvel / Sygma / Corbis

Many poor neighborhoods have conditions of urban decay, with abandoned and severely neglected buildings, streets, and lots. Do you think that these physical conditions of disrepair and decrepitude ("broken windows") lead to crime? Or is it poverty and the lack of money that lead to crime?

Social disorganization theory suggests that crime occurs when community relationships and local institutions fail or are absent. Clifford R. Shaw and Henry D. McKay (1942) found that many social problems, like infant mortality and juvenile delinquency, decrease with increasing distance from the inner city. They attributed this to the poverty, residential mobility, and racial heterogeneity of inner cities. *Residential mobility* is a problem because families are not invested in where they live and are working to move out of their current situation. They have no reason to clean up their streets or form relationships with others. According to Shaw and McKay, *racial heterogeneity,* in which diverse populations live in close proximity, means people do not form community with one another due to language or cultural differences. This, too, significantly correlates to increases in crime. Shaw and McKay concluded that it is not the makeup of a community that causes crime, but the ecological conditions in which the members of the community live.

▶ **America's Poorest City Fights**

DISCUSSION QUESTIONS

1. How and why do definitions of crimes vary over time and from society to society? What additional information does one need to compare crime rates from one place to another effectively? How do societal differences factor into individuals' likelihood of arrest or prosecution for crimes?

2. How does what is defined as a crime reflect the norms of a society as a whole? For example, while murder is nearly universally illegal, why do some countries have exceptions such as "honor crimes" laws or "stand your ground" laws that allow individuals to kill others under specific circumstances?

3. Which crimes does the UCR provide data about? What further information would one need to fully understand crime in our society? How could one get the data needed to gain a fuller understanding of crime?

4. What trends can be seen in the commission of crimes by race, gender, age, and type of crime? What similarities and differences are there between crimes committed and the arrest rates for the various crimes? By race, gender, and age?

5. How has the criminal justice system changed over time? What factors have influenced the changes that have taken place at each level of the system?

6. What is meant by the assertion that there are different versions of justice? Compare how these different versions of justice play out with the police, in the courts, and in the corrections system. Are there patterns or trends with regard to which types of people encounter difficulty or ease as they navigate each component seeking justice?

7. How are the inequalities that conflict theorists focus on found in the criminal justice system? What does the feminist perspective add to this discussion about power? How do the differences that occur in sentencing for the same crimes by different people support the conflict and feminist perspectives?

8. According to rational choice theory, what explains why someone commits a crime? What role does society play in individuals' choices about engaging in criminal behavior?

9. What does social disorganization theory point to as an explanation for crime in society? How could one begin to address the problem of crime from this perspective? What would need to change at the societal level? The community level? What role can individuals play in reducing crime from this perspective?

10. What can individuals do to reduce crime in their community? Can mentoring programs effectively draw young people away from crime and toward more normative choices? How do group movements such as Take Back the Night reduce crime? What connections exist between smaller groups striving to intervene or make change and the evolution of official policies and laws over time to better define what constitutes a crime, such as with intimate partner violence, or to address problems with the corrections system, such as offering mentoring for those who are preparing to leave the system?

KEY TERMS

adjudication 290

affirmative defenses 291

bounded rationality 300

bourgeoisie 297

bourgeoisie legality 297

broken windows theory 301

clearance rate 284

dark figure of crime 283

decentralization of power 289

deterrence 293

differential association theory 298

feminist criminology 298

finder of fact 292

general deterrence 293

hot-spot policing 289

incapacitation 293

indeterminate sentencing 293

mala in se crimes 281

mala prohibita crimes 281

Marxist criminology 297

matters of law 291

opportunity theory 296

parole 294

Sharpen your skills with SAGE edge at edge.sagepub.com/trevino

A personalized approach to help you accomplish your coursework goals in an easy-to-use learning environment.

12 ALCOHOL AND OTHER DRUGS

Brian C. Kelly and Dina Perrone

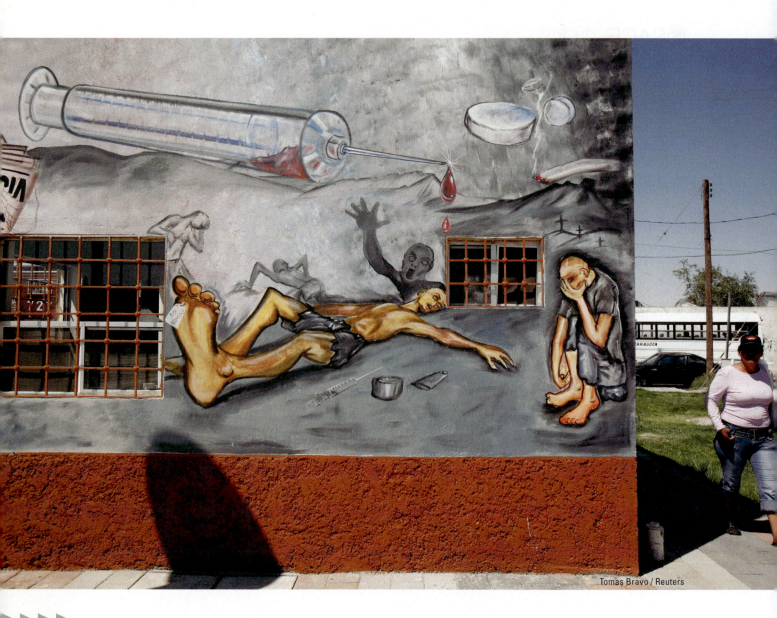

Tomas Bravo / Reuters

A woman walks by a mural depicting heroin addicts. On February 2, 2014, the actor Philip Seymour Hoffman was found dead in his Manhattan apartment with a syringe in his arm, the victim of an apparent heroin overdose. Do you think that tragedies like Hoffman's death prevent some people from ever trying heroin?

Investigating Alcohol and Other Drugs: Our Stories

Brian C. Kelly

My interest in research on drug use began while I was an undergraduate at Fordham University, when I read Philippe Bourgois's *In Search of Respect: Selling Crack in El Barrio* (1995). After receiving my M.A. and Ph.D. in sociomedical sciences from Columbia, I joined the Department of Sociology at Purdue University, where I am currently associate professor. I am also a faculty associate at the Center for HIV Educational Studies & Training in New York.

I have written extensively on drug use, sexual health, HIV/AIDS, and youth cultures and am currently conducting research on prescription drug misuse among socially active young adults, methamphetamine use and HIV risk in China, the use of ecstasy and other club drugs among young adults, drug dealers in the suburbs, and the health and well-being of adolescent girls in relationships with significantly older males. My book in progress, *Dancing with Risk: The Subcultural Logic of Clubs, Drugs, and Risk,* explores the social, structural, and subcultural factors that shape the ways youth experience and act on risk in their lives.

Dina Perrone

Messner and Rosenfeld's *Crime and the American Dream* sparked my interest in criminal justice, but my interest in drug use emerged when I became aware of racial disparities in the policing of drug offenses in New York City. How were white young adults dancing in clubs, using drugs, and evading both police detection and drug-related harms? *The High Life: Club Kids, Harm and Drug Policy* (2009) is the book I wrote about this subject.

I am an assistant professor of criminal justice at California State University–Long Beach. I earned two B.A.s from the State University of New York at Geneseo and both my M.A. and Ph.D. in criminal justice from Rutgers University–Newark. I was a NIDA-funded Behavioral Sciences Training Predoctoral Fellow at the National Development and Research Institutes, Inc.

I have written widely about my qualitative research on drug users, as well as about my experience as a female ethnographer conducting field research. I continue to study and write about patterns of use and harm among users of club drugs, *salvia divinorum,* and synthetic cannabis, with the goal of informing effective drug policy that focuses on the health of users. To that end, I am a board member of DanceSafe—a nonprofit organization that educates about and provides tools for harm reduction at primarily electronic dance music events.

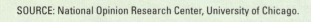

ENHANCING THE CLUBBING EXPERIENCE

In all societies, certain types of substance use are more acceptable than others, including the use of *psychoactive drugs* (which produce mood changes and distort perceptions by crossing the blood-brain barrier to affect the central nervous system). Why do some types of drug use seem normal or reasonable while others do not? Why are some people permitted these substances while others are not? The social context has a great deal to do with the answers to these questions. Let's look at club drug users for some insights into the way drug users think about their substance use within a social context.

Sociologist Dina Perrone spent 15 months with a group of young people 22 to 33 years old attending dance clubs in New York City, Miami, the Jersey Shore, and the Hamptons (in New York) and observed them using a variety of substances to enhance their experiences. Her sample of primarily white, upper-middle class, heterosexual young people preferred ecstasy (E), GHB (G), crystal methamphetamine (meth, crystal, crystal meth), ketamine (K), and marijuana. Most of the users combined these substances throughout the night to achieve the optimal "high," and they did so with few negative experiences. They were able to regulate their experiences and reduce harms.

Jack and his friends "were all really scientific about it." They "tried to take it [ecstasy] at the right moments, that way [they]'d start rolling [experiencing the high from ecstasy] as soon as the DJ was gonna start spinning. . . . [They]'d smoke joints [marijuana] and do bumps [single snorted doses] of K once the E started dying down." They called these added drugs "turbo boosters," which made them feel the effects of ecstasy even while it was starting to wear off.

In contrast, Ralph enjoyed the combination of GHB and crystal methamphetamine, since "the crystal keeps you up and keeps you goin', but the G gets you stimulated." He explained that the combination "enhances your mood and everything like that." But combining GHB with alcohol is, as Ralph stated, "very dangerous." So although Ralph and his friend Osiris liked the effects of GHB, they refrained from using it while drinking alcohol. Ralph warned, "You can't mix the two."

Most members of the sample group, like George, would never "touch certain drugs, like heroin or crack." These were just unacceptable among their peers. Some drugs were also inappropriate for dance club settings, while others were inappropriate outside these settings. For example, Mary would not use psilocybin mushrooms while at a dance club because she would "bug out too much," and Ralph would not use crystal meth at a lounge-like bar. He explained, "It just doesn't fit." These users created social norms around their drug use and learned which substances to take, when, and where in order to achieve the best experience with the least amount of consequences. Monica described how drugs can be very harmful when "given to the wrong person, at the wrong place. It's all about circumstances; it's all about environment." The environment determines the drugs used and shapes the experience of using them, while the drugs shape the experience of the environment.

For these substances users, drugs enhanced the clubbing experience. While on GHB, Osiris explained, "you don't just hear the music; you feel it. It enhances all your senses and dulls your inhibitions, which makes the club experience much more enjoyable." Using substances allowed the group to connect to the music and to their friends. As Tyler stated, "You are connected in ways that you were never connected when you were sober, with the music, with your friends that are standing around you, with everything." Drug use heightened their experience.

DRUGS IN SOCIETIES

 Discuss drug use as a social problem.

Humans have long desired to eat or drink substances that make them feel relaxed, stimulated, or euphoric. A **drug** is any substance whose properties produce psychophysiological changes when ingested. By this definition, we can consider a whole host of substances to be drugs regardless of their legality, medicinal nature, or social value. The earliest drugs, such as psychedelic mushrooms, were found naturally occurring, and humans could use their psychoactive properties with little effort. Over time, humans began to manipulate substances for

Drug: A substance that has properties that produce psychophysiological changes in the individual who ingests it.

Lloyd K. Townsend Jr. / National Geographic Creative

Many U.S. states allow the legal use of marijuana for medical purposes. The sale of marijuana for recreational use became legal in Colorado on January 1, 2014. In addition to marijuana buds, pot shops in Colorado sell marijuana-infused foods ranging from brownies and hard candies to cookies, olive oil, granola bars, chocolate truffles, and even spaghetti sauce.

psychoactive purposes—for medical, spiritual, and recreational reasons—eventually becoming increasingly scientific and ultimately giving birth to the modern pharmaceutical industry.

Drug encounters are inherently social phenomena. The experience of altered states through the use of a psychoactive substance is due not simply to the substance itself but also to the user's psychological state and the social environment in which he or she consumes the drug. Mood, expectations, and personal history influence the drug experience in conscious and subconscious ways. In other words, we learn about how to experience drugs and how to conceive of them through our social contexts and social encounters.

The social and physical contexts can also shape whether a drug encounter is positive or negative. For example, the experience of an individual using ecstasy at a rave or club will be different from the experience of a trauma victim using ecstasy during a therapeutic session. In one context, the focus is on the pleasure and exuberance the drug can produce, and in the other the drug serves as a palliative, facilitating emotional closure with difficult experiences. Indeed, the experience of a "bad trip" on LSD is often attributed more to the user's state of mind and environment than to the substance's pharmacological properties.

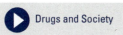 Drugs and Society    Marijuana as Revenue Source

University students on a pub crawl stand in front of a poster warning of alcohol abuse in Lincoln, England. In what ways do you think people might act differently when drinking with friends as opposed to drinking alone?

Why do people use drugs? All drugs produce psychophysiological changes that fundamentally alter the way an individual experiences the world. Some people use drugs to induce transcendent states or enhance consciousness; they seek to feel more closely connected to the spiritual realm. Others use drugs to alter their moods—to enter into a state of relaxation, induce excitement, or relieve anxiety. Some want to escape boredom or despair. Whether it is to cope with childhood trauma or with current circumstances, altering one's state with drugs serve as a psychic palliative.

Drugs, whether legal or illegal, have also long had medicinal uses precisely because of their ability to make people feel different. They not only facilitate cures; they also allow people to manage the symptoms of illness, and they play this vital role in many societies. Drugs are also a common means of enhancing social interaction. Sharing drugs can serve as a ritual for developing social intimacy.

In many cultures, drugs have contributed to artistic creativity in art, music, and literature. While using them does not directly cause artists to be profound, by altering their experience of the world, drugs can open new perspectives through which artists can channel their creative talents.

Finally, despite the wide use of psychoactive substances across societies, certain drugs in certain societies do carry taboos. Some people may want to use such drugs precisely because they are forbidden. In fact, in many subcultures, drug use may be an attempt to subvert authority.

All societies have normative patterns of drug use. While we are most familiar with laws related to psychoactive drugs, not all societies rely only on the threat of legal sanction to enforce standards of behavior in the course of psychoactive drug use. Often, members of a community "police" each other with regard to the acceptable standards of behavior within that community. In fact, all societies, even those with laws against the use of certain drugs, have informal rules and social norms governing the use of psychoactive drugs, who may use them, and how those users should behave. For example, in the United States, drinking a beer at a professional sporting event such as a baseball game is perfectly acceptable behavior for an adult. However, if the same adult were to drink a beer while attending a play performed by 8-year-olds at the local elementary school, he or she would likely face disapproval and social sanctions from others. One location is deemed socially acceptable for alcohol use by the community; the other is not.

Community norms also shape what is considered acceptable behavior for persons under the influence of a drug, which is often different from acceptable behavior for those in a sober state. For instance, while the expectation that they will be disinhibited enables drug users to act in ways typically out of bounds for sober citizens, communities typically set boundaries for permitted and expected behaviors on the part of those under the influence of psychoactive substances. The social context is important for determining the applicability of these rules. Yelling and chanting with drunken enthusiasm at a tailgate party before the big game may be socially acceptable or even encouraged, but at a holiday dinner party where wine is casually sipped, such behavior may cause a person's ejection, with no return invitation.

Drugs as a Social Problem

While drugs are often considered a social problem in U.S. society, as inanimate substances they are neither inherently good nor inherently bad. Their effects depend on the social contexts and the ways, good or bad, in which humans put them to use. Opiate drugs, for instance, can relieve excruciating pain and play an important role in reducing human suffering. However, recreational users of these substances can fall into a problematic cycle of dependence, leading to other forms of suffering and even the possibility of death from overdose. Thus, the ways in which we integrate drugs into our lives shape the impacts they have on individuals and societies, impacts that are fundamentally dependent on patterns of human behavior.

In the United States, federal efforts to control psychoactive substances began in the early 20th century, but a heightened focus on policing the use of drugs emerged in the 1970s. The resulting **War on Drugs** is popularly associated with President Ronald Reagan because of his administration's massive increase in spending toward the effort. President Richard M. Nixon first declared the War on Drugs, calling drugs "public enemy number one," channeling unprecedented resources toward drug abuse treatment programs, and addressing drug use as a

War on Drugs: The comprehensive policy first formulated by President Richard M. Nixon to address the drug problem in the 1970s.

Drug use: The ingestion of substances so as to produce changes in the body that alter the way the user experiences the world.

Drug abuse: The use of psychoactive substances in a way that creates problematic outcomes for the user.

Drug addiction: A state of dependence on a substance that produces psychophysiological changes in the user.

public health problem. For example, the National Institute on Drug Abuse—the leading government agency on the health impacts of drug use, abuse, and addiction—was founded during the Nixon administration, as was the Office of Drug Abuse Law Enforcement (ODALE), created specifically to police narcotics. ODALE became the Drug Enforcement Agency (DEA) in 1973. Public policy on drugs has since built upon the foundation of these 1970s efforts, and the issue of drugs as a social problem has become fixed in the American popular consciousness.

Today, however, the U.S. government allocates 75% of its drug-related funding to federal, state, local, and international law enforcement (Office of National Drug Control Policy 2011). In contrast, other countries around the world have reduced or even eliminated their criminal justice focus on drugs. For example, in 2001, Portugal decriminalized the possession of personal-use amounts of all drugs (including marijuana, crystal methamphetamine, and cocaine). If you are a Portuguese citizen walking down the street in Lisbon and a police search uncovers an amount of heroin small enough for personal use in your pocket, you will not be arrested. While you may think such a policy would increase drug use, a recent study found that both injection drug use and teen drug use have actually declined in Portugal (Hughes and Stevens 2010).

ASK YOURSELF: What might be some of the effects if the United States were to decriminalize simple possession of all drugs? How would such a policy shift affect the way law enforcement occurs on a day-to-day basis?

Differences among Drug Use, Drug Abuse, and Drug Addiction

How do we distinguish among drug use, drug abuse, and drug addiction? **Drug use** is simply the ingestion of substances in order to produce changes in the body or mind that alter the way the world is experienced. Any consumption of psychoactive substances (including legal drugs such as alcohol) for any purpose is considered drug use.

Drug abuse, on the other hand, is the use of psychoactive substances in a way that creates social, psychological, or physical problems for the user. All drugs can be abused, including legal ones such as alcohol, tobacco, diet pills, decongestants, and even caffeine. The fundamental distinction between drug use and drug abuse is that abuse creates harm in the life of the user. Thus, all drug abuse includes drug use; however, all drug use is not necessarily drug abuse.

Drug addiction is a state of dependence on a substance that produces psychophysiological changes in the user. This dependence can be physiological or psychological

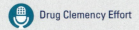 Drug Clemency Effort 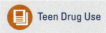 Teen Drug Use

in nature, or both, and its effects can vary considerably. For example, compared with more socioeconomically disadvantaged persons, those with sufficient resources or wealth may experience fewer problems associated with drug addiction and be less likely to be arrested, be fired from their jobs, or lose custody of their children. Table 12.1 recaps the distinctions among these terms.

ASK YOURSELF: How might wealth and fame affect a person's experiences with drugs, the criminal justice system, and family court?

To illuminate the differences among use, abuse, and addiction, let us consider the consumption of alcohol, for which there is no legal prohibition among adults. Enjoying a glass of wine or two with dinner is not considered deviant in U.S. society and is a socially sanctioned means of celebrating. This kind of alcohol consumption can be categorized as drug use.

However, consider the person who goes to happy hour on Wednesday, consumes enough beer to make himself sick, and is unable to show up for work the following day. In this instance, the user has not only brought on physical illness as a result of his drinking but has also failed to meet his responsibilities in the workplace. This is an instance of alcohol consumption leading to social and physical problems; we may consider this pattern of drinking to be alcohol abuse.

Finally, consider an individual who drinks daily, often beginning early, because he feels he needs to drink. He may be anxious about the prospect of not being able to drink, so he hides alcohol in his jacket, office, or car and takes sips while at work to be comfortable. He may go home after work to prepare another drink for himself or stop at a bar for some additional drinks on the way. He would be considered addicted to alcohol because of his dependence on it.

TABLE 12.1 Differences among Drug Use, Drug Abuse, and Drug Addiction

Term	Definition
Drug use	The ingestion of substances to produce changes in the body or mind that alter how the world is experienced
Drug abuse	The use of psychoactive substances in a way that creates social, psychological, or physical problems for the user
Drug addiction	A state of dependence on a substance that produces psychophysiological changes in the user

ADDICTION AND OTHER HARMS

 12.2 Describe the problems of addiction.

In *Righteous Dopefiend* (2009), Philippe Bourgois and Jeff Schonberg highlight the suffering often associated with addiction and the complex social, political, and institutional forces that shape addicts' lives. As illustrated by their research, the experience of addiction can be a grueling one. They describe one addict's experience of "dopesickness"—withdrawal from opiate drugs—and quote his own description:

> Felix tried to urinate into the plastic water bottle that he kept next to his blankets, but his body was shaking too hard. He stood up, but his leg muscles spasmed and he fell down the highway embankment. He had to drag himself on his hands and knees to get back up to his mattress, pausing twice to retch. . . .
>
> First I'm cold; then poof! Heat flashes, and I'm ripping the covers off. But it's cold out here, so I get like freezing, 'cause I'm covered with wet sweat. I try to spit, and all this green stuff comes out. Then I'm just squirtin' out my guts. My heart feels like it's going to stop. I can't pick up my bones. My knees hurt; my legs are locked; I can't breathe; I can't even think; I feel every nerve in my fingertips, every single one. I can't stand still. I can't lie down. (80)

Bourgois and Schonberg's graphic field notes describe the physical and psychological agony of withdrawal from opiate drugs. This suffering can be alleviated by another dose of opiates, a powerful physiological imperative that makes dependence on the drugs difficult to overcome.

The Problem of Addiction

We have seen that drug addiction can be both physiological and psychological. Physiological dependence leads the user to experience physical withdrawal symptoms in the absence of the drug, as Felix did in the description above. Not all addictions are physiological, however. Psychological dependence leads to distress or anxiety when the user is without the drug. These symptoms are not simply expressions of moral or constitutional weakness. Rather, they are very real experiences that can prevent the individual from carrying out a normal routine.

Misuse of Prescription Drugs

Prescription drug misuse—defined by Compton and Volkow (2006, S4) as "any intentional use of a medication with intoxicating properties outside of a physician's prescription for a bona fide medical condition"—has risen significantly during the past decade, particularly among youth and young adults. During 2000, an estimated 8.7 million people age 12 and older in the United States had used prescription drugs nonmedically within the previous year. By 2010, this figure had increased to 16 million (Substance Abuse and Mental Health Services Administration 2011). After marijuana use, the nonmedical use of prescription drugs is the most widespread drug issue in the United States.

Young adults ages 18–25 are the segment of the U.S. population with the highest rates of prescription drug misuse. Many are introduced to prescription drugs by means of legitimate prescriptions or through their social networks. Recent research has shown that young adults in various nightlife scenes are especially likely to misuse prescription drugs (Kelly et al. 2012b). Those in the indie rock scene

as well as those who frequent electronic dance music clubs are significantly more likely to misuse such drugs than are young adults who hang out in typical college bars (Kelly et al. 2013a). Young adults involved in hip-hop nightlife, by contrast, report the lowest prevalence of prescription drug misuse (Kelly et al. 2013a).

A key problem with prescription drug misuse is that some users may perceive the drugs to be safe because physicians prescribe them for medical problems. Yet a host of dangers arise with misuse, including the possibility of overdose, high blood pressure, drug interactions, and seizures. Because prescription drugs are still needed for legitimate treatment and care of severe or chronic conditions, however, the policies surrounding them are complex. Government cannot simply

Bruce Schreiner / AP / Corbis

Kentucky attorney general Jack Conway promotes a state-wide billboard campaign aimed at curtailing prescription drug abuse in the state. According to the Attorney General's Office, more than 1,000 people die each year in Kentucky from the abuse of powerful painkillers like oxycodone and hydrocodone. More Kentuckians die from overdoses than from traffic accidents.

make them illegal to inhibit access to those who misuse them (even though criminalization does not necessarily reduce use). The need to ensure care for patients thus makes it difficult to police the abuse of these medications.

▶ **THINK ABOUT IT**

1. Why do you think prescription drug misuse has increased so dramatically among young adults in recent years?

2. Can you think of any strategies that might help to prevent the misuse of prescription drugs?

Opiate addiction provides an illustration. The physiological properties of opiates increase the likelihood of addiction. Heroin, for instance, binds with opioid receptors in the brain to enhance endorphins and enkephalins. The body becomes physically dependent on this chemical response, such that withdrawal symptoms occur if the user reduces or stops using the drug. Withdrawal from an opiate drug can be an extremely unpleasant experience. In heavy users, symptoms may begin only hours after the previous use and typically peak within two days. As Felix's experience shows, they include cold sweats,

insomnia, bone and muscle pain, cramping, diarrhea, vomiting, nausea, and intense drug cravings. For very heavy users, sudden withdrawal may even lead to death because the symptoms are so severe.

Not everyone who uses opiates becomes addicted, and not everyone who uses them experiences withdrawal symptoms upon stopping their use. You may have used opiate pills to alleviate pain after having a wisdom tooth extracted, but when you stopped taking the pills you likely did not experience the severe symptoms that accompanied Felix's withdrawal because your body had

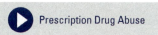
▶ Prescription Drug Abuse

A pregnant woman smokes crack in the neighborhood known as Cracolandia (Crackland) in São Paulo, Brazil. In the United States, crack is designated a Class A drug because it is thought to cause great harm. Ed Sheeran's popular song "The A Team" is about a crack-addicted prostitute. Do you think that there are as many songs that glamorize street drugs as there are that focus on their addictive effects?

not become physically habituated. Yet those who use opiate painkillers medically beyond a few days may in fact experience mild physical symptoms of withdrawal, such as aches or diarrhea, when they stop. Acclimation to such drugs builds over time. (Recall from our discussion above that drug experiences and use patterns are affected by a variety of factors.)

During 2010, an estimated 11.3 million people in the United States had a substance dependence problem in the preceding year (Substance Abuse and Mental Health Services Administration 2011). Of these, 8 million were dependent on alcohol and 4.7 million were dependent on illegal drugs (Figure 12.1). Some people suffer from both alcohol dependence and illicit drug dependence. These comorbid problems can make dependence even more difficult to treat.

Drug Treatment

Recovery from drug addiction can be a difficult and complicated process; relapse rates are high. In addition to the physiological dependence some drugs induce, addicted individuals must contend with the powerful social and psychological forces that shape drug cravings. The people, locations, and events associated with the addict's use provide powerful stimuli that provoke desires to use again. The strength of these social and environmental factors in drug addiction is a key reason the most effective treatment programs do not seek merely to cease use of the drug. Rather, they also strive to stimulate behavioral changes in the individual's wider life, attending to his or her emotional, material, and social needs and not just to the immediate physical circumstances of his or her drug addiction.

Social contexts can also encourage people to seek treatment for drug addiction. If social relationships, career, status, or self-esteem seem threatened, users may feel driven to seek out help. Other personal motivators include anxiety about the need to support a drug habit, negative physical consequences, a fear of bodily injury or death, and the user's need to improve the quality of his or her life or better care for any children.

While many suffering from drug addiction need assistance with recovery, high-quality treatment can be difficult to obtain. Uninsured individuals have limited access to some of the most basic treatments. About one-third of those who need drug treatment and do not receive it indicate that they have not entered care because they cannot afford to pay for it. Private drug treatment programs are quite expensive, and public treatment programs, particularly for individuals with special circumstances, such as women with children, often have long waiting lists. Thus, a grave paradox exists: compared with nonaddicts, addicts are both more likely to need help and less likely to have health insurance.

While many heavy drug users depend on drug treatment to move beyond their addictions, others recover in other ways. Some experience a kind of spontaneous remission, giving up drug habits without treatment in a fashion typically referred to as **natural recovery**. Natural recovery often occurs as a response to changing social conditions—the user changes residential location or finds a new job or romantic partner—and usually when the user has access to resources and support for assistance.

Drugs and Health

A significant reason that societies concern themselves with drug control is the health impact of drug consumption. We cannot fully describe here all the harms associated with the use of a wide variety of drugs. Nonetheless, although the definition of *excess* may vary from drug to drug and from individual to individual, excessive consumption is what leads to harm. For example, marijuana has been shown to have many medical benefits, including as a treatment for glaucoma and for the side effects of chemotherapy; Figure 12.2 shows the U.S. states that allow its use for

Natural recovery: A person's cessation of a drug habit without the assistance of a drug treatment program.

 Medical Marijuana   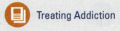 Treating Addiction

FIGURE 12.1 Past-Year Substance Dependence or Abuse among U.S. Men and Women Age 12 or Older, 2002–2010

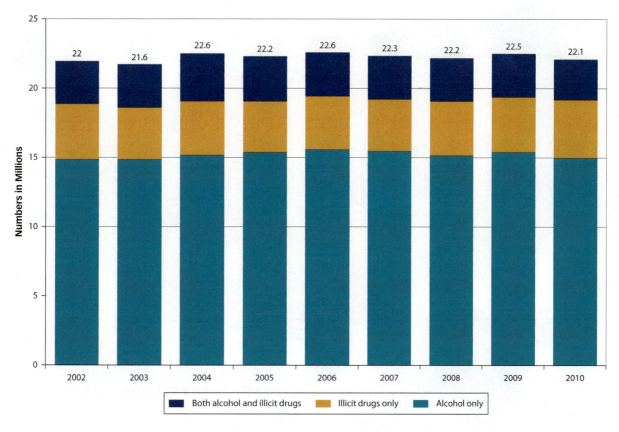

SOURCE: *Results from the 2010 National Survey on Drug Use and Health: Summary of National Findings.* Substance Abuse and Mental Health Services Administration, U.S. Department of Health and Human Services.

medical purposes, although federal law still prohibits it. However, some studies have shown that long-term, excessive marijuana use can lead to cognitive impairments. Whether a result of heavy use on one occasion or substantial use over an extended period of time, excessive consumption of any drug, regardless of legality, can create a range of problems for some individual users that include overdose, mental health problems, cognitive impairment, organ damage, infectious disease transmission, violence, and accidents.

Beyond the suffering of individual users, the health impact of drug use on society as a whole is also significant. For example, the financial cost imposed by alcohol and drug problems in the United States runs to billions of dollars per year. Most of these costs are productivity losses, particularly those related to abuse-related illness, incarceration, black market activities, and premature death. Economists have estimated that substance-using employees claim more sick days, are late to work more

often, have more job-related accidents, and file more workers' compensation insurance claims than nonusing employees. Clearly, drug and alcohol use can create costs for employers as well as for the economy more generally.

There are also societal costs. Injection drug use can facilitate the transmission of infectious diseases such as HIV and hepatitis C, affecting not only drug users but also those within their social networks; needle-borne epidemics travel faster than sexually transmitted ones. Even trace amounts of blood infected with HIV can rest within a used syringe, making its reuse highly risky. HIV and hepatitis C can also remain in blood on other injection paraphernalia, such as cookers and cottons used for heroin injection.

Many European governments have implemented innovative approaches to address the employment, health, and legal costs associated with heroin injection. Switzerland, Germany, and Spain have implemented heroin-assisted therapy programs, in which eligible heroin addicts, who

FIGURE 12.2 Medical Marijuana Laws, 2013

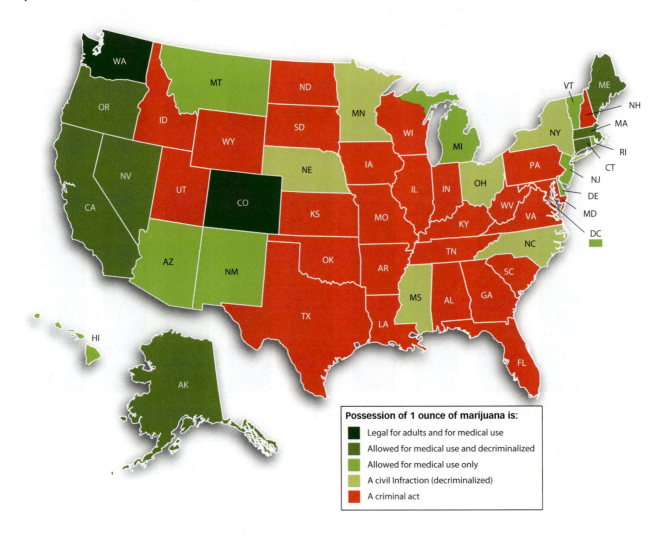

Possession of 1 ounce of marijuana is:

- Legal for adults and for medical use
- Allowed for medical use and decriminalized
- Allowed for medical use only
- A civil Infraction (decriminalized)
- A criminal act

have tried multiple times to quit using, visit clinics to receive designated doses of heroin that they inject under supervised conditions. Overall, these programs aim to minimize the social costs linked to this drug. Under such programs, HIV transmissions have declined, both drug-related and non-drug-related offending among participants has declined, and many participants have stopped heroin use because the programs provide points of entry for drug treatment and other health care services. Participants have also been able to obtain stable employment and housing (Fischer et al. 2007).

In the United States, in contrast, since the onset of the AIDS epidemic, injection drug users have accounted for almost one of every three HIV infections. Though major public health efforts have reduced infections within this population, new infections continue to emerge along the same fault lines as many other health disparities. African Americans and Hispanics are disproportionately affected by drug-related HIV exposures, for example. Policies shown to be effective elsewhere (such as **needle exchange programs**) continue to lack support among federal officials in the United States.

ASK YOURSELF: Why do you think the United States has not followed Europe's lead in addressing the social problems associated with heroin injection through harm reduction programs?

Needle exchange programs: Drug abuse harm reduction programs that provide new syringes to intravenous drug users who exchange used syringes.

Methamphetamine in China

Illicit drug use has spread quickly in China since the late 1980s, after many years of political suppression. While emerging social and economic freedoms have opened up many positive opportunities for Chinese citizens, they have also provided openings for growth in drug markets. The number of drug abusers officially documented by Chinese public security departments has increased from 70,000 in 1990 to well over 1 million today. Illicit drug use continues to escalate across the country as China modernizes. In addition to a continuing heroin problem, China has seen a surge in the consumption of other drugs, including methamphetamine, ecstasy, and ketamine during the past decade.

Methamphetamine, often in the form known as ice, is domestically produced within China. According to the United Nations Office on Drugs and Crime, among countries surveyed China had the highest number of methamphetamine seizures and has recently become one of the world's largest methamphetamine markets. Most of the recently detected drug laboratories in China produced methamphetamine, representing a significant increase over earlier years. Of registered drug users in 2004, only 1.7% used amphetamines, but that number grew to 11.1% by 2007 and has continued to increase since that time.

Chinese society has experienced rapid changes in the past generation that have benefited many people, including a newly forming urban middle class, but these changes have also introduced new social problems, such as the rise in drug use. The growth in methamphetamine use in Chinese society reflects the way changes within societies can bring negative consequences along with positive ones. Many of these results are unintended, though perhaps they

Blocks of methamphetamine confiscated by Chinese police during a crackdown on drugs are displayed. In China, crystal meth is generally called "ice" and doing meth is called "ice skating." Methamphetamine is China's second most popular drug after heroin.

are an inevitable outgrowth of rapid social change; they also highlight the extent to which the expansion of social freedoms within a society sometimes leads individuals to act in ways that are not the healthiest or most beneficial.

▶ **THINK ABOUT IT**

1. Why do you think that methamphetamine use might be growing so extensively in China?

2. How do you think rapid social change may shape drug use in China and elsewhere?

PATTERNS OF DRUG USE ACROSS SOCIAL GROUPS

12.3 Relate patterns of drug use to the life course, gender, and race/ethnicity.

Patterns of drug use differ across various groups within any society. This occurs not necessarily because of any innate characteristics of the people themselves, but because of the ways in which statuses, social norms, and societal treatment organize and define people's behaviors and interactions. Often, roles, statuses, social norms, and societal treatment apply differently to individuals depending on their characteristics, and these characteristics are understood differently within society. Various aspects of people's lives, and the expectations people have of others, shape a wide range of behaviors, including how drugs are consumed as well as who consumes them. Let's consider data from the National Survey on Drug Use and Health to see how age, gender, and race influence drug use. (To investigate other drug trends yourself, visit http://www.oas.samhsa.gov/nhsda.htm.)

 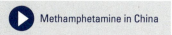 Methamphetamine in China

Drugs and the Life Course

In many societies, the use of psychoactive drugs is most prevalent among adolescents and young adults. As Figure 12.3 shows, drug use in the United States peaks during the early adulthood ages of 18 to 25. A variety of socially structured factors shape this pattern. In some instances, drug consumption may occur during the intense period of identity development expected during adolescence and early adulthood. In attempting to more clearly define their identities, young people may see risks as a challenge and sensation seeking as a part of personal growth. Thus, risk taking can contribute to self-introspection and identity formation. Young people may feel that self-exploration is a way of obtaining a broad range of life experiences before they take on enduring—and limiting—adult responsibilities. Some indicate they are doing drugs because youth is "the time to get it out of my system."

Young people also often attempt to forge independent decisions, including about drug and alcohol use, because self-sufficiency and self-reliance are bound up with their conceptions of adulthood. Decisions about drug and alcohol use may be part of these assertions of independent decision making. Drug use may be one way for them to engage in risky behaviors in an effort to distance themselves from their parents and parental values. Finally, early adulthood is distinguished by relative independence from social roles and normative expectations, a freedom that allows young people to be tremendously self-oriented and to engage in behaviors such as drug use.

Drug use, including drinking alcohol, typically declines beginning in the mid-20s as young adults assume the social roles and responsibilities of full adulthood. Note that it is changes in the social features of their lives—not physiological or cognitive changes—that enable this shift. The significant decline in drug use across young adulthood, often referred to as **maturing out**, occurs naturally, without treatment or other forms of intervention. Not only weekend pot smokers but even those engaged in heavier drug use or hard drug use can experience maturing out. This is not to say that aging is a substitute for drug treatment, but users of many substances tend to follow this pattern.

For example, in Perrone's (2009) study of club drug users in New York City, many began to reduce or stop using club drugs when they experienced increased responsibilities in their lives. Most had been using drugs such as ecstasy, ketamine, and cocaine for at least 10 years, and all used a variety of these substances at any one time to heighten their positive experiences and reduce negative ones. "Ralph" often took GHB (gamma hydroxybutyrate) for its euphoric effects and crystal methamphetamine for its stimulant effects, and when it was time to go to sleep, he would take an Ambien. But most participants in the study used only on the weekends, and when they had family or work obligations, they reduced use or did not use at all. Also, when participants later married and had children, many stopped using.

Gender and Drug Use

Age is not the only influence on drug use. We take on different roles within the family, the workplace, social circles, and other areas depending on how we understand gender within our society. Much as with any other cultural practice, the meanings and significance of drug use are viewed through the lens of our gender identities; conceptions of masculinity and femininity shape the ways drugs are used within a society.

As Figure 12.4 shows, while just over 50% of young women in the United States have ever used an illegal drug, more than 60% of young men have done so. Thus, men are more likely to become experienced with illegal drugs. Some of this difference has to do with the fact that young men are often offered greater opportunities to begin drug use within their peer networks. When we look at use in the past year, these trends hold. Less than 30% of young women have used illegal drugs in the past year, while more than 40% of young men have done so. Thus, we can see the ways in which our gender identities affect our peers, interactions, experiences, and decisions about whether to use drugs.

Maturing out: The decline and cessation of psychoactive drug use among younger people as they age into different social roles and responsibilities.

FIGURE 12.3 Illegal Drug Use in the United States by Age, 2010

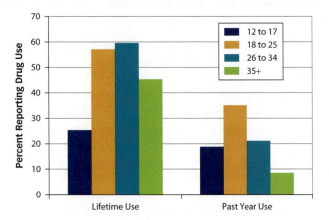

SOURCE: The National Survey on Drug Use and Health. United States Department of Health and Human Services.

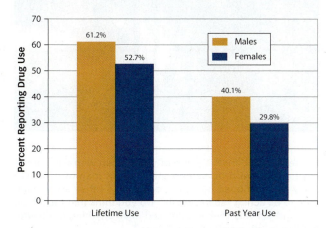

FIGURE 12.4 Illegal Drug Use among U.S. 18- to 25-Year-Olds by Gender, 2010

SOURCE: The National Survey on Drug Use and Health. United States Department of Health and Human Services.

Gender differences occur across cultures. It is believed that approximately 350 million people in China smoke tobacco, but the differences between men and women are quite stark. About 57% of men smoke, while less than 3% of women do. Smoking is highly masculinized in China and extends to social rituals. Men are often expected to offer cigarettes to other men as displays of hospitality and gestures of friendship and collegiality. Tobacco product packaging also typically displays symbols of masculinity. These socially patterned routines have led to the striking differences we observe in the gendered pattern of smoking in China.

Throughout human history, both men and women have used psychoactive drugs—though at times in different ways influenced by gender. For example, ideals of masculinity influence not only the drugs men choose to consume but also the ways they consume them. Binge drinking can be a means for men to make claims of masculinity through stamina, willingness to take risks, power, strength, and outperforming peers or winning a social competition. This is part of the reason U.S. society experiences many more deaths from alcohol poisoning among men than among women. The gender disparity in alcohol-induced fatalities is a direct result of our cultural framing of alcohol consumption as an act with gendered meanings.

Research also indicates that the pathways leading into and out of drug-using careers differ for men and women. The beginnings of many women's drug-using careers are related significantly to their relationships with men. The processes leading to drug use and termination from it can be partially explained by gender socialization. Women exit drug-using careers for family reasons and because

their using interferes with work responsibilities more often than do men. Women's stopping drug use tends to center on the personal and emotional aspects of drug experiences, while men's cessation is more directly related to external and financial factors.

Race/Ethnicity and Drug Use

Race and ethnicity are also significant influences on drug use among young adults in the United States. Throughout the nation's history of drug control, race has played a significant role in the ways drugs are used, the ways they are perceived, and the ways their use is policed. As Figure 12.5 shows, data from the 2010 National Survey on Drug Use and Health indicate that white young adults are mostly likely to have used illegal drugs. By contrast, Asian American youth have some of the lowest rates of drug use. These trends tend to hold for the use of individual drugs. For marijuana, cocaine, hallucinogens, and illegal prescription drugs, white young adults report the highest prevalence of use, while Asian young adults report the lowest. Black and Hispanic youth tend to fall between these groups. We also find these patterns in the use of legal substances such as alcohol and cigarettes.

These figures may surprise you, since you may have been led to believe that racial and ethnic minorities report more experiences with drug use than whites (see Chapters 3 and 11). Popular conceptions of drug use and drug users are shaped covertly through the news media as well as through entertainment media such as films and television. Many media depictions highlight drug use by members of

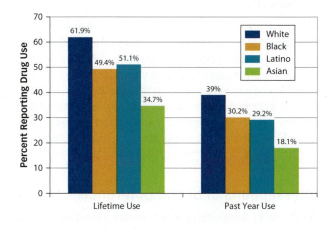

FIGURE 12.5 Prevalence of Illegal Drug Use among U.S. 18- to 25-Year-Olds by Race, 2010

SOURCE: The National Survey on Drug Use and Health. United States Department of Health and Human Services.

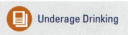 Underage Drinking

How Drug Enforcement Is Shaped by Race, Class, Age, Sexual Orientation, and Gender Identity

Can you count the number of times you have witnessed police officers canvassing the dorms and knocking down doors in search of drugs? How often have you been at a fraternity or sorority party that was raided by the police and resulted in drug convictions? How many of your university friends have been very drunk or high on marijuana in public but were never stopped and frisked by police? How many have illegally purchased prescription drugs like Adderall but have never been arrested?

Young black men living in the inner city are much more likely than students at your university to have contacts with the police in search of drugs—on their streets, at their homes, and in their cars. Even though

drugs are used illegally across the socioeconomic spectrum and among all racial groups, drug-using and drug-dealing offenders are much more accessible and visible in inner-city neighborhoods than in university dorms, fraternity houses, and middle-class homes and white communities. In addition, policing street-level drug dealing is less complex than investigating large drug operations. As a result, arrests of young, poor black men for drug offenses have risen at a much faster rate than have the arrests of others for similar offenses—even though drug use is

Police stop and frisk a group of young men who were loitering in a known drug-selling area. Young men of color are likely to be stopped by police, especially if they are considered to be acting "suspiciously." Do you think that their race, sex, and the way they are dressed have anything to do with the police being suspicious of them?

Aristide Economopoulos / Star Ledger / Corbis

not higher among black men than among white men.

One police practice in particular, known as stop and frisk, disproportionately affects people of color. In June 2012, the *New York Times* reported that in 2011 the New York Police Department (NYPD) documented 685,724 instances of stop and frisk, 87% of which involved

racial and ethnic minority groups, and exposure to these depictions can create unconscious social stereotypes and influence the ways we imagine and think about the lives of drug users.

ASK YOURSELF: How have drug users, drug addicts, and drug dealers been portrayed in the media? What messages do these representations send to viewers? To see how representations have changed over the past 75 years, you may want to spend one evening watching *Reefer Madness* and another watching *Pineapple Express* and consider how these films differ in their depictions of marijuana smokers.

Intersections of Social Difference

While race, ethnicity, gender, sexual orientation, and socioeconomic status may each influence drug use behaviors, it is the intersection of all these social differences

that shapes individuals' experiences in society. In particular, this intersection affects experiences of privilege and oppression; governs access to and experiences with the education system, housing, and peers; and influences the ways people engage with and respond to the world. A black lesbian with low socioeconomic status, for example, may experience racism, sexism, heterosexism, and classism in each stage of her life and across a variety of situations. Those who experience multiple levels of oppression are much more likely than those who do not to cope by means of substance use and even drug sales, particularly in the case of racial, sexual orientation, and gender discrimination.

In their study of black women who use drugs, Windsor, Benoit, and Dunlap (2010) found that the intersections of race, class, and gender enmeshed the women in oppressive and underprivileged conditions. Many were born to crack-addicted mothers and incarcerated fathers in neighborhoods overwhelmed with violence, guns, drugs, and

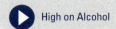

High on Alcohol

blacks or Hispanics (on average only 6% of stops lead to actual arrests). In Brownsville, Brooklyn, population 14,000, the NYPD made about 52,000 stops from January 2006 to March 2010. One young black male, Tyquan Brehon, told the *New York Times* he was stopped by police more than 60 times before he was 18 (Dressner and Martinez 2012). While race matters, females in these communities are less likely to be stopped than males, and males wearing suits are less likely to be stopped than males wearing hoodies (clothing often serves as an indicator of class position). Thus, race, gender, and social class intersect to leave poor black men highly vulnerable to stop-and-frisk procedures.

Women also experience the intersection of race, class, and gender—in terms of authorities' responses to drug use, the harms of drug use, and access to resources that can alleviate those harms.

For example, poorer women who use drugs are more likely to face scrutiny than are drug-using women with higher socioeconomic status. Pregnant white women on drugs are more likely to be perceived as in need of treatment, while pregnant black women on drugs are more likely to be perceived as criminals neglecting and abusing the fetus. Murphy and Rosenbaum's (1999) study of pregnant women on drugs found that many black women decided not to seek either prenatal care or treatment for their drug problems, to avoid arrest and loss of custody of their children.

Clearly, the intersection of race, class, age, sexual orientation, and gender identity influences the ways people use psychoactive substances, their access to resources, and their experience of harms (physical, criminal justice) associated with drug use and sales. It explains why all white people do not experience the same issues with drugs and why all

women do not face the same risks. Recognizing the intersectionality of multiple characteristics is critical to understanding the experience of substance use and substance-related harms.

▶ **THINK ABOUT IT**

1. Inner-city communities are disproportionately under the gaze of policing agencies. Should the police alter the way they approach drug problems? Should they focus more frequently on drug sales and use on college campuses?

2. If the harms associated with drug use are determined not by the drugs used but rather by the intersectionality of race, class, gender, sexual orientation, and age, how should society address the social problem of drugs?

sex. As infants they were already at a disadvantage, and the disadvantages accumulated throughout their lives. Attending their poorly funded schools was a lower priority than taking care of themselves, their mothers, and their younger siblings. Few had role models who had graduated from high school. Obtaining a job in the conventional workforce was impossible without an education, and their neighborhoods had few job opportunities that provided living wages. Most resorted to "hustling," in which they sold drugs or their bodies to buy food and clothes. At times, this led to arrest, incarceration, drug use, the loss of their children, and welfare dependence.

....

ASK YOURSELF: From childhood to adulthood, the women in Windsor et al.'s (2010) study faced disadvantages that made economically and emotionally stable lives impossible. How might such disadvantages shape the likelihood of a person's becoming dependent on drugs?

....

Your race, ethnicity, gender, sexual orientation, and socioeconomic status also affect your likes and dislikes, your friends, your high school, your neighborhood, your choice of college or university, and your employment opportunities. They influence the music to which you listen, the food you eat, the movies you like, and even the drugs with which you come into contact. It is likely that some of your classmates had access to marijuana and crack cocaine in the neighborhoods where they grew up, for instance, while others could easily find only marijuana.

Our individual characteristics and the meanings these characteristics have in society thus shape our lives in numerous ways. From influencing our access to drugs to setting normative expectations about drug use to creating stress through oppressive life conditions, features of our lives function separately and together to influence the ways we experience the world around us and the ways we behave, including our substance use.

USING THEORY TO UNDERSTAND DRUG USE: THE VIEWS FROM THE FUNCTIONALIST, CONFLICT, AND SYMBOLIC INTERACTIONIST PERSPECTIVES

Reuters / Fred Thornhill

 12.4 Apply the functionalist, symbolic interactionist, and conflict perspectives to social policy on drug use.

Fans cheer at a football game and raise their cups of beer. Fans frequently have tailgate parties during which they drink beer and grill food. Tailgating usually occurs in the parking lots of stadiums and arenas, before and sometimes after games and concerts. Is there a tailgating culture on your campus?

In this section we consider sociology's three classic theories to explore how they explain the initiation, continuation, and cessation of drug use.

Functionalism

Functionalism primarily considers how societies maintain themselves by creating a certain order for those living within them. Overall, the theory argues, the functioning of society is managed through the collective behavior of the society's members.

A living organism makes a useful analogy for society as functionalists see it. The circulatory system allows oxygen and nutrients to flow throughout the body, while internal organs perform various functions such as digestion and absorption of nutrients, minerals, and oxygen, and sensory organs such as the eyes take in the information necessary for the body to act in certain ways. If any of these functions is disrupted, it becomes more difficult for the organism to maintain its existence. According to functionalists, the collective group shares norms, institutions, and rituals that allow expectations of behavior to be passed down from one member to another, society's form and organization to be maintained, and society itself to remain stable. When individuals break social norms, for instance, they disrupt the social fabric and damage society's ability to maintain itself.

When rapid social changes are occurring, society's expectations and regulation of behavior become less clear, and anomie emerges. (Recall that anomie is a condition in which individuals feel disconnected from society and its social standards.) Individuals are more likely to break social norms when they experience anomie.

Functionalists may consider the use of certain drugs—those on which society has placed social and legal sanctions—to be an act of deviance and rejection of social norms that emerge from feelings of anomie. For example,

a young man beginning heroin use is likely to know this act breaks social norms against the drug's use. His act of deviance, according to a functionalist perspective, disrupts the established social standard and contributes to the society's instability.

On the other hand, when a drug is socially sanctioned, functionalists would argue that, rather than disrupting the social fabric, its ritualized use may contribute to community cohesion and solidarity. For example, the use of ayahuasca—a hallucinogenic brew—in ritual fashion among indigenous peoples of the Amazon provides the community with the opportunity to come together during a time of crisis, such as when a member is ill. Ayahuasca rituals are not merely permitted; they are approved by native cosmology. From a functionalist perspective, they promote community solidarity and cohesion by bringing members together for a shared purpose.

In many Western societies, alcohol is a permitted drug that serves to enhance social bonds and community cohesion in rituals from wedding toasts to tailgating to happy hour. During happy hour, coworkers are able to forge social bonds outside the workplace, collectively blow off steam related to job stress, and relax at the end of the workday. From a functionalist perspective, happy hour serves to maintain the social fabric by facilitating solidarity in a socially sanctioned forum. This behavior is seen as normative in society and, as such, contributes to its maintenance.

Policy Implications of Functionalism

According to the functionalist perspective, it remains imperative for society to create supportive communities for citizens in order to prevent the use of illegal drugs and reduce drug abuse. Fostering community cohesion and solidarity is critical in this regard, because individuals will be less likely to abuse drugs—legal and illegal—if they feel a deeper connection to the community. By reducing anomie and feelings of social dislocation, communities will be in a better position to prevent the abuse of drugs as well as the harms associated with drug use.

Local policies that encourage communities to come together are important pieces of the puzzle from the functionalist perspective. For example, the creation of public spaces, such as parks, malls, and public venues, in which members of the community feel invested facilitates social bonds, inhibiting behaviors like illegal drug use that break social norms. Policies that stimulate community participation can reduce individuals' needs to use drugs in response to social dislocation.

Efforts to build social capital—the social, material, and symbolic resources inherent within social ties—in communities also fall within functionalist policies on reducing drug abuse. For example, consider how your neighbors may act as resources to enhance your neighborhood quality of life, whether through beautifying the neighborhood, watching out for neighborhood kids, keeping an eye on your house while you're on vacation, or lending you tools. Harnessing the strength and potential of these resources allows communities to further their drug education, prevention, and intervention efforts. They can more effectively communicate information that may either inhibit the use of drugs among young people or reduce the level of harm among active drug users. By enhancing social capital, communities also more effectively position themselves to facilitate drug treatment and to accommodate those who enter recovery.

The efficient use of resources within the community helps to create an environment that better tends to the needs of those recovering from drug dependence. For example, the Office of National Drug Control Policy's Drug Free Communities Support Program provides funding for community-based efforts to reduce drug use among youth. These initiatives bring youth and adults together in community programs that inhibit drug use. Creating youth athletic leagues in resource-poor communities can provide structured activities for young people, for instance, thus reducing the likelihood they will engage in delinquent activities. Since its inception in 1997, the Drug Free Communities Support Program has provided grants to approximately 2,000 local communities in the United States.

Conflict Theory

In contrast to functionalism, conflict theory considers how conflicts between groups in society come about, often finding evidence of collective behavior that leads to the creation of social disparities and social exclusion.

Rather than examining the ways in which society maintains itself, conflict theorists consider how collective behavior creates ruptures in the social fabric. At the core of conflict theory is the issue of power.

Conflict theorists suggest that human behaviors are conditioned by the social structure of society, including its inequalities of class, gender, race, sexuality, and other dimensions of social life. Further, those in positions of power—that is, those with high status and abundant resources—act to facilitate inequality by ensuring the uneven distribution of power and resources across society. Conflicts then emerge over these inequitable allocations.

With regard to drugs, conflict theorists would argue that decisions and policies about which drugs are legal and who can access them are products of the social structure. Those in positions of power have greater ability to shape policies on drugs, often in ways that permit them to legitimate their own social position and exert social control over those less powerful. For example, sociologist Joseph R. Gusfield (1986) describes the temperance movement in the United States as an upper-class social movement and the abstinence from alcohol that accompanied it as a signifier of status. This movement occurred in the wake of immigration from Ireland and southern European nations in which the use of alcohol was a routine and normative behavior. The temperance movement was a means of articulating social distinctions between the upper class and the poor and newer immigrants within society.

Time & Life Pictures / Getty Images

Members of the Women's Christian Temperance Union (WCTU) invade a bar while customers continue drinking. In 1919, Congress ratified the 18th Amendment to the U.S. Constitution, which prohibited the manufacture, sale, and transportation of alcoholic beverages. This ushered in the era known as Prohibition (1920–1933). Prohibition ended with the repeal of the 18th Amendment; it has been called "the experiment that failed."

Prohibition in the United States

Some have also suggested that the outlawing of drugs such as heroin and cocaine during the early 20th century was tied to the emergence of the modern pharmaceutical industry, which profited from the control of these substances. The same argument has been made more recently in the debate over medical marijuana. From a conflict theory perspective, the prohibition of medical marijuana protects the revenue streams of corporate firms. (For an excellent sociological examination of medical marijuana, see *Dying to Get High: Marijuana as Medicine* [2008], by Wendy Chapkis and Richard J. Webb.)

For conflict theorists, the creation of laws governing psychoactive substances provides a means of exerting social control and policing over those who are less powerful. For example, the Beckley Foundation Drug Policy Programme's report *The Incarceration of Drug Offenders* (Bewley-Taylor, Hallam, and Allen 2009) notes that in 2005, arrests for drug possession in the United States were 4 times higher than for drug trafficking. And as we saw earlier in this chapter, young whites use illegal drugs at higher rates than black youth, yet black youth are arrested for drug crimes at rates 3.5 to 5.5 times higher that the white arrest rate (Human Rights Watch 2009). This is a stark difference (see Figures 12.6 and 12.7). A conflict theory perspective considers that these disparities occur as a means of consolidating the position of racial privilege that whites occupy.

As another example, black pregnant women and white pregnant women who use illegal drugs face similar risks to their pregnancies related to their drug use. Yet drug-using pregnant black women, who are already socially marginalized on the basis of race and class, are more likely to be

FIGURE 12.7 Illicit Drug Use among Persons Age 12 or Older, 2002–2010

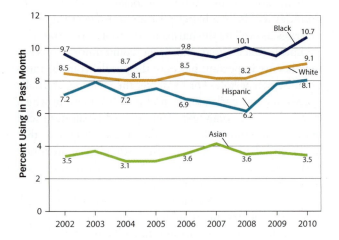

SOURCE: Substance Abuse and Mental Health Services Administration, the U.S. Department of Health and Human Services.

reported to the authorities by health care providers than are their white counterparts. In this respect, the social control exerted through drug laws extends beyond the simple act of public policing to reach the private sphere of the clinical medical encounter.

Conflict theory also describes how the social structure influences human behavior more broadly. Because everyone acts in response to the conditions of society, drug use becomes reasonable to individuals as a means of coping with marginalization and societal inequalities. Conflict theorists would argue that this explains why whites have higher rates of drug *use*, while blacks and Hispanics are more likely to experience drug *dependence*. Similar patterns emerge along social class lines. The poor are especially vulnerable to experiencing drug problems and drug harms because they also lack the resources to recover from drug dependence.

Policy Implications of Conflict Theory

Policies derived from a conflict theory perspective focus on bringing about change in the inequalities in society and, by this means, reducing the adverse impacts of drug abuse. Individuals may be less likely to use substances in abusive ways if they are not experiencing the impacts of inequality and its accompanying marginalization. Moreover, with reduced inequality, users will have greater access to resources that reduce the harms associated with drug use. For example, opening economic opportunities like jobs and developing programs that reduce poverty are important bases for policy

FIGURE 12.6 Drug Possession/Use Arrest Rates by Race, 1980–2009

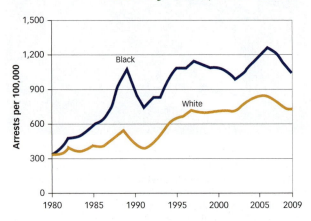

SOURCE: *Arrests in the United States, 1980–2009.* Howard N. Snyder, September 2011. U.S. Department of Justice, Office of Justice Programs. Bureau of Justice Statistics.

making according to conflict theory. By enabling all members of society to have resources beyond those that merely enable survival, societies can inhibit the abuse and harms of drugs.

As another example, early childhood intervention programs, such as the Infant Health and Development Program, the Perry Preschool Project, the Carolina Abecedarian Project, and the Chicago Child-Parent Center Program, have been shown to be very effective in reducing inequality and substance use (Pungello, Campbell, and Barnett 2006). Children who completed these programs were less likely to use substances or to be arrested and more likely to graduate from high school and earn college degrees.

Conflict theorists examine policies based not only on their intent but also on their consequences. Policies generated during the War on Drugs may appear on their face to be "race-neutral," but they have had considerable effects on racial disparities in sentencing for drug-related crimes. Mandatory minimum sentences and laws concerning school-zone enhancements, which increase the penalties for selling or using drugs near schools, tend to have their most significant influence on sentencing for crimes in inner-city neighborhoods, where racial/ethnic minorities are more likely to live.

Symbolic Interactionism

Symbolic interactionism focuses on how individuals understand themselves in relationship to society. We constantly manage our concept of self through our interactions with others in society, and we behave on the basis of the meanings we interpret from these interactions, internalizing our perceptions of the way others see us. This internalization is what George Herbert Mead (1934) referred to as the "self"; it depends on the attitudes, values, and norms we perceive during interactions.

These attitudes, values, and norms are subject to change over time on the basis of our interactions. For example, heroin users have been considered normal, sick, and criminal at different times in history. In the mid-1800s, heroin was legally purchased and commonly used recreationally by middle- and upper-class women. Their use of the drug was acceptable; hence they were normal. In the late 1890s, heroin was believed to be a miracle cure for coughs, and Bayer sold heroin-based cough syrups with directions for use by both adults and children. The users of heroin then were considered ill. When heroin was criminalized in 1914 under the Harrison Act, users became either criminals or addicts. With the shifting social and legal labels for the drug, users have reinterpreted their identities.

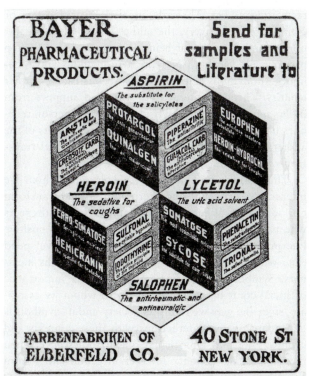

Bettmann / Corbis / AP Images

An early advertisement for Bayer Aspirin shows heroin as one of its main ingredients. In the late 19th century, cocaine was commonly used as a general tonic for sinusitis and hay fever. Sigmund Freud experimented with cocaine, and Arthur Conan Doyle's fictional detective Sherlock Holmes frequently injected himself with a 7% solution of the drug.

ASK YOURSELF: Can you think of any substances other than heroin for which the labels placed on users have shifted overtime? What might be the social impacts of such label changes?

Consider Howard S. Becker's classic study "Becoming a Marihuana User" (1963a). Becker describes the process of jazz men becoming socialized into using marijuana and learning to experience its effects in particular ways. The experiences individuals have under the influence of drugs must be interpreted, and the process of learning how to interpret the sensations and experiences of a drug high is a critical component of becoming a drug user. The subtleties and nuances of the drug's effects must be learned and understood within a particular context, and these processes unfold only in the course of interactions before, during, and after the drug is used. Certain sensations may be interpreted differently over time, and feelings that may have been uncomfortable are redefined as key components of the drug experience.

Just as becoming a drug user is a process that occurs in the course of social interaction, so is becoming a

Alcohol Advertising

recovering addict. Through interactions with peers or counselors in recovery, the addict learns the language, norms, and manners of being in recovery. The 12-step program used in both Narcotics Anonymous and Alcoholics Anonymous helps the addict reconstruct his or her identity. Through interactions with and support from others in recovery, the newly clean or sober person redefines his or her past drug-using behaviors as faults of the addiction disease. The identity of the individual transforms from "addict" to "sober."

Thus, when we change the people with whom we interact, we may shift our interpretations and transform our identities. When we spend more time with peers who use drugs and drink, we may have a more positive interpretation of those behaviors than when we spend time with family or with Narcotics Anonymous members. Symbolic interactionism stresses the importance of social context and the groups with whom we associate, since the way we interpret society and its symbols is dependent on our interactions with these contexts and groups. They play a particular role in adolescence, when the individual's primary interaction group shifts from the family to peers. Symbolic interactionism suggests that this transition facilitates the initiation into drug use among adolescents, because their primary interactions, attitudes, and perspectives about normative behaviors are changing.

Policy Implications of Symbolic Interactionism

From the perspective of symbolic interactionism, our understanding of drug use within a social context and the creation of programs that help facilitate positive identity change are key points of intervention for drug policies. Policy makers can either change the ways individuals and groups interpret behavior or change the types of people with whom at-risk individuals interact.

The symbolic interactionist perspective offers several policy options. One is to try to prevent drug use from achieving enhanced status within social networks, groups of people connected through their social ties to others. Policies affecting the meanings of drug use within these social circles may inhibit the way groups of people interact around drugs. Social marketing campaigns are often directed at shaping the ways people perceive particular drugs. For example, in response to a significant rise in methamphetamine use among gay men, a public service campaign targeted these men with the message "Buy meth, get HIV free." By linking the use of methamphetamine to HIV, the campaign highlighted the risks of drug use and associated the drug with a deadly disease.

Another approach is to shape people's interpretations of drug use in order to reduce the harms associated with particular patterns of consumption. For example, college students typically perceive that their peers drink more alcohol and more often than is actually the case. The perception of such heavy drinking as a "normal" part of college life can lead some students to overindulge. By highlighting the reality that the average college student actually drinks less, and less often, health promotion campaigns may influence students to have fewer drinks and to drink less regularly.

A similar approach, the Social Norms Program, was implemented in high schools in Rowan, New Jersey (Connell et al. 2009). There, a survey of high school students showed that many thought their friends were engaging in frequent drug use, alcohol use, and sex. However, the survey also revealed that the peers were not using drugs, drinking, or having sex as often as was perceived. Thus, the schools, with the help of researchers, implemented a social marketing campaign to educate the students about the true amount of deviance occurring among their peers. This program shifted the high schoolers' perceptions of the prevalence and acceptance of drug and alcohol use and sex.

Mentoring programs may also reduce drug use among young people by offering them the opportunity for routine interactions with good role models. Such interactions can provide positive ways for young people to interpret their lives, since the mentors display positive norms. From the symbolic interactionist perspective, through exposure to these positive norms and the development of positive interpretations of young people's lives, these programs may reduce the potential for engaging in drug use. In fact, many studies have shown that youth who participate in Big Brothers Big Sisters programs are less likely than their peers who do not to start using drugs and alcohol (see, e.g., Grossman and Tierney 1998).

Symbolic interactionists further recommend policies that remove the stigma of drug use and thus create positive drug-using or drug-recovering identities. For example, decriminalization efforts, such as the laws implemented in 14 U.S. states where possession of small amounts of marijuana is not a criminal offense, remove the criminal label from users and free them of the stigma of being criminal offenders. The Netherlands also has decriminalized marijuana. There, adults have been able to buy small quantities of marijuana in coffee shops since 1976. Yet a higher percentage of adults use marijuana in the United States, where it cannot be legally purchased, than in the Netherlands (Reinarman, Cohen, and Kaal 2004).

SPECIALIZED THEORIES ON DRINKING AND DRUGS

 12.5 Apply specialized theories to the social problems of addiction.

We now turn briefly to some of the more specialized sociological theories on drinking and drug use: social learning theory, general strain theory, self-control theory, and social disorganization theory.

Social Learning Theory

Social learning theory is related to the symbolic interactionist tradition. It assumes individuals are conditioned by their social environment to behave in particular ways and to model the behaviors of those around them. When an individual is in a social environment in which normative behaviors are routinely enacted, that individual becomes conditioned to engage in normative behavior. Similarly, in a social environment in which deviant behaviors are routinely enacted, the individual becomes conditioned to engage in acts of deviance.

From this theoretical perspective, drug use occurs when the individual has been in a social environment in which acts of deviance occur. The individual's drug use is thus a response to his or her having been conditioned toward it and is shaped directly by the social context. This is one reason scholars of adolescent deviance have been concerned with deviant peer groups. If their peers use drugs, adolescents will be more likely to use drugs. In fact, most drug users learn about drugs from friends and have friends who are drug users.

For social learning theorists, then, the process of rehabilitation from drug abuse is rooted in reconditioning the individual in an environment in which abstinence is valued and encouraged by others. This explains why Alcoholics Anonymous and Narcotics Anonymous programs have been successful in promoting abstinence for many. Through these programs, substance abusers begin to associate with others who encourage sobriety, which helps recondition their behavior.

General Strain Theory

Robert Agnew (1992) developed general strain theory from the Durkheimian tradition of functionalism. The theory suggests individuals may feel strain as a result of their experiences in society, and that strain shapes the way they behave. Strain can result from losses in individuals' social lives—whether relationship or status losses. People may also experience strain when their aspirations for status do not meet their achieved status, or when they encounter negative stimuli in their social environments, such as being bullied or physically abused. The cumulative experience of strain can lead some individuals to engage in deviant behaviors as a coping mechanism.

Drug use has been widely documented as a coping mechanism that may be induced by the cumulative experience of various forms of strain. For example, among adolescents, strain may emerge from conflicts with parents over the discrepancy between the adolescents' status claims and the parents' perception of the adolescents' status. From the perspective of strain theory, such strain may be related to initiation into drug use among teenagers. In other instances, strain stemming from personal failures to meet expected goals in school, work, or social life can lead to drug use.

Self-Control Theory

Michael R. Gottfredson and Travis Hirschi (1990) developed self-control theory, also known as a general theory of crime, as an evolutionary outgrowth of social control theories. This theory focuses on childhood socialization and parent-child relationships as determinants of behavior in later life. It suggests that children who are not socialized by being properly monitored and punished for bad behavior by their families, especially their mothers, will not develop self-control. Such children then lack the self-control needed to refrain from deviant behaviors, such as drug use. Poor parental relationships, a neglectful upbringing, and improper socialization within the family unit can increase the likelihood that an individual will engage in deviance. Thus, to prevent deviant behavior in the future, the process of socialization must occur properly at a crucial stage in a child's development.

This theoretical framework sees drug use as deriving from poor parenting, because the use of substances for pleasure is a function of the inability to delay gratification, especially when the drugs in question are illegal. Since it is rooted in poor childhood socialization, which individuals cannot change as adults, this inability to control the desire to engage in deviance is part of what makes the process of recovery from drug abuse such a difficult one.

Social Disorganization Theory

Social disorganization theory, which emerged from the Chicago School of Sociology in the early 20th century as a means of explaining social problems in urban

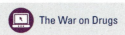 The War on Drugs

David H. Wells / Corbis

A "squatter," a person who lives in an abandoned building, sits in his squat and gets high. Crack houses are usually old, abandoned, or burned-out buildings, frequently located in run-down neighborhoods. It is in places like these that drug dealers and drug users buy, sell, produce, and use illegal drugs.

environments, is a classic theory of the influence of social ecology. According to social disorganization theory, the social environment—particularly the neighborhood environment—is a key influence on behavior. When a community is socially disorganized, primarily through concentrated poverty and residential instability, the community loses its inherent social controls, and deviant behaviors rise. Thus, the ecological characteristics of a neighborhood influence behaviors, above and beyond the individual characteristics of those living within the neighborhood.

In particular, social disorganization theorists like Sampson and Wilson (1995) describe how macro-level factors—such as deindustrialization, wage polarization, outsourcing, racism, poor housing, and discrimination—can create structurally disorganized and culturally isolated communities. Cut off from mainstream society, residents in those communities lack or have only minimal access to conventional institutions, including resources, conventional role models, and social networks that facilitate social and economic advancement. A crime-inducing landscape results, and crime, violence, and drug use become acceptable, expected, and valuable. The community then is unable to exert informal control over its members.

We can easily apply social disorganization theory to the emergence of the crack epidemic in the 1980s. During the 1970s and throughout the 1980s, entrenched poverty, erosion of community resources, and the loss of stable employment in inner-city communities encouraged the spread of crack cocaine use and allowed open-air drug markets and drug trafficking networks to flourish. Given the high degree of social disorganization, the social controls of the community were ineffective in inhibiting the use and sale of crack, and the growth of this drug problem escalated.

Social disorganization theorists warn that the policies of the War on Drugs have actually facilitated the development and maintenance of socially disorganized communities. The drug war has channeled money into the criminal justice system rather than into improving communities. Thus, police officers tend to focus efforts on particular communities (mostly those that are disorganized) where drug use and sales are visible. In these communities, arrest, conviction, and incarceration for drug offenses are more likely, and these have harmed the families, economic strength, and informal social controls of those areas. In particular, when most drug offenders return to their communities after arrest and incarceration, they do not have access to drug treatment, have fewer marketable skills, and have limited experiences in the conventional work world. As a result, they are less able to find jobs, and if they do find employment, they earn less money and are likely to quit or be fired. They are also less likely to marry. Concentrated poverty, family instability, and hence the lack of informal social control will remain part of that community, and it will continue to be disorganized.

SOCIAL CHANGE: WHAT CAN YOU DO?

12.6 Identify steps toward social change on drugs.

Drug use and responses to drug use can become social problems that affect the users and users' families, friends, and communities. It is important, then, that we all make an effort to ensure that effective, humane, and fair drug policies are implemented; that drug users and their families, friends, and communities are treated with respect and dignity; and that improving the health of drug users and their communities is paramount. You are an important asset in addressing drug use as a social problem, and in addressing the multitude of social problems that arise from both drug use and drug policy. You can educate yourself and your friends, participate in harm reduction activities, and engage in social activism to promote responsible drug policies. Here's how.

 ## Educate Yourself and Your Friends

Many misconceptions and myths persist about who uses drugs, the harms of drug use, and the effectiveness of drug policies. Educating yourself and others, however, is actually quite easy. Excellent resources are available online, and books and documentary films can also provide reliable information (see Table 12.2 for some suggestions).

Erowid is a nonprofit organization whose trusted website (http://www.erowid.org) provides up-to-date information about emerging drugs, harms of use, and legal sanctions for use. Erowid also provides a forum where users can describe their own experiences. The website organized by Students for Safe Drinking

(http://www.collegedrinking.org) will help you educate yourself about how to drink alcohol while reducing harm to yourself and your friends. Some of the tips this organization provides for students who plan to drink are (1) eat first, (2) be well hydrated, (3) plan transportation, (4) travel in pairs, (5) schedule your drinking, (6) carry condoms, (7) choose your drink, (8) alternate alcoholic drinks with nonalcoholic drinks—especially water, (9) don't let strangers pour your drinks, (10) don't do shots for each year of your age, (11) drink among friends, and (12) care for each other.

Sharing information about the effects and harms of substance use and safer ways to use substances can help support and implement drug policies that are effective, humane, and fair; that treat drug users with respect; and that improve the health of drug users and their communities. You can mobilize social networks to spread information that can reduce the harms associated with substance use and that leads others to consider how aspects of our society influence drug use. This is a great first step toward alleviating the social problems around drug use and drug policy.

TABLE 12.2 **Some Helpful Resources**

Websites	Books	Documentaries
DanceSafe http://www.dancesafe.org	Becker, Howard S. 1963. *Outsiders: Studies in the Sociology of Deviance.* New York: Free Press.	*American Drug War: The Last White Hope* (2007)
DRCNet Online Library of Drug Policy http://www.druglibrary.org	Chapkis, Wendy, and Richard J. Webb. 2008. *Dying to Get High: Marijuana as Medicine.* New York: New York University Press.	*From Heroin to Methadonia* (2006)
Drug Policy Alliance http://www.drugpolicy.org	Gusfield, Joseph R. 1986. *Symbolic Crusade: Status Politics and the American Temperance Movement,* 2nd ed. Urbana: University of Illinois Press.	*The House I Live In* (2012)
Erowid http://www.erowid.org	Musto, David F. 1999. *The American Disease: Origins of Narcotic Control,* 3rd ed. New York: Oxford University Press.	*Project Lazarus* (2009)
Harm Reduction Coalition http://www.harmreduction.org	Provine, Doris Marie. 2007. *Unequal under Law: Race in the War on Drugs.* Chicago: University of Chicago Press.	*To Do No Harm* (2003)
Students for Safe Drinking http://www.collegedrinking.org	Weil, Andrew, and Winifred Rosen. 2004. *From Chocolate to Morphine: Everything You Need to Know about Mind-Altering Drugs,* rev. ed. Boston: Houghton Mifflin.	*Worth Saving* (2004)
Students for Sensible Drug Policy http://www.ssdp.org	Zinberg, Norman E. 1984. *Drug, Set, and Setting: The Basis for Controlled Intoxicant Use.* New Haven, CT: Yale University Press.	

Participate in Harm Reduction Activities

Participating in harm reduction activities that promote safer drug-using practices and that educate others about the benefits of **harm reduction** is another way to help. You probably do not realize it, but you already participate in many harm reduction activities. You may wear a seatbelt when you get in a car, look both ways before you cross the street, and refrain from eating certain foods to avoid stomachaches. So incorporating others into your life or volunteering to help them reduce harm associated with their choices could be a natural next step.

Many organized harm reduction activities related to drug and alcohol use were actually started by young people. Students for Safe Drinking, mentioned above, is an excellent example. Another is DanceSafe, a nonprofit organization operating throughout the United States that educates and provides tools for harm reduction at raves and other dance music venues. DanceSafe also sells testing kits for ecstasy and cocaine so users can be aware of the substances that are actually contained in the drugs they plan to take. Often, users are not buying pure MDMA (the active compound in ecstasy), and the additives can be very harmful. Find your local DanceSafe chapter and volunteer.

If loud music is not your style, you can always focus your volunteer efforts on a program devoted to syringe exchange, safe crack use, or overdose prevention. Here you may be trained in street outreach, in which you provide harm reduction kits to those who enter the program and those in the surrounding streets. You may also be trained in the proper use and disposal of syringes, safe crack pipe use, and the prevention of overdose from opiates.

The resources these programs provide are invaluable in reducing the spread of hepatitis B and C, HIV, and other infectious diseases. Access to clean syringes also reduces the likelihood of abscesses, which can result in emergency room visits, and endocarditis, a potentially fatal inflammation of the lining inside the heart. Most important, overdose prevention reduces deaths and other adverse effects associated with substance abuse. By volunteering with such harm reduction programs, you can help to humanize drug users, improve their health and the health of their communities, and promote the adoption of effective and fair drug policies.

You can learn more from the Harm Reduction Coalition (http://www.harmreduction.org), which also offers training in harm reduction techniques. This organization is an excellent resource that promotes effective, humane, and fair drug policies. It seeks to humanize drug users and treat them with respect. One of its most critical efforts is to address the issues of inequality related to race, gender, sexual orientation, gender identity, and socioeconomic status that make some individuals particularly vulnerable to drug use and drug harms. Through its work, the coalition aims to enhance the dignity and health of drug users and their communities.

Engage in Social Activism to Promote Responsible Drug Policies

On a broader or macro level, you can engage in social activism to promote the adoption of responsible drug policies both in the United States and internationally. You can join your campus's chapter of Students for Sensible Drug Policy (SSDP), or, if your college or university does not have a chapter, you can start one. SSDP (http://www.ssdp.org) lobbies college administrators, local government officials, and representatives in Washington, D.C., to advocate for drug policies that do not violate individual rights and are effective in reducing drug-related harms. For example, SSDP is currently campaigning against zero-tolerance policies on campuses, student drug testing, and financial

John Moore / Staff / Getty Images

Protesters in New York City hold a candlelight vigil and a march calling for the end of the drug war. They are protesting the continued War on Drugs on both sides of the U.S.–Mexico border, which has left tens of thousands of people dead. Do you think that the War on Drugs is the answer to the drug problem?

Harm reduction: An approach to drug policy aimed at minimizing or eliminating the harms associated with drug use behaviors.

aid and higher education restrictions on drug offenders. SSDP is also working with the Amethyst Initiative to lower the legal drinking age in the United States.

The United States is one of only 9 countries where the legal drinking age is above 18 or 19 years old. The rest are Fiji, Indonesia, Iceland, Japan, Micronesia, Palau, Paraguay, and Sri Lanka. In 5 other countries, alcohol consumption is illegal for everyone. In the rest of the world, the legal drinking age is 19 or younger. In fact, 27 countries have no age minimum, and 12 set the legal drinking age at 16 or 17. SSDP and the Amethyst Initiative seek to have an educated discussion about, and advocate for, reducing the drinking age in the United States.

You can also engage in drug policy activism by working with SAFER (Safer Alternative for Enjoyable Recreation; http://www.saferchoice.org). SAFER is an educational campaign, primarily on college campuses, that aims to teach people about the harms of alcohol use versus the harms of marijuana use in order get people to think critically about the differences in the ways these substances are treated legally. SAFER has been at the forefront of changing zero-tolerance policies on college campuses where many students have been kicked out of dorms for marijuana use.

Both SAFER and SSDP work closely with the Drug Policy Alliance (DPA; http://www.drugpolicy.org), an international nonprofit organization that advocates for alternatives to the drug war and for harm reduction policies rooted in equality and compassion. DPA's executive director, Ethan Nadelmann, has been a guest on *The Colbert Report, The O'Reilly Factor,* and *Fox and Friends* to discuss the harms of the drug war and promote effective and humane drug policies. You could volunteer your time to this organization, assist in its letter-writing campaigns, or donate some money to its many causes.

WHAT DOES AMERICA THINK?

Questions about Alcohol and Other Drugs from the General Social Survey

Turn to the beginning of the chapter to compare your answers to the total population.

1. How often do you spend the evening at a bar?

   AT LEAST ONCE A WEEK: 6.7%

   AT LEAST ONCE A MONTH: 19.4%

   AT LEAST ONCE A YEAR: 24%

   NEVER: 49.9%

2. Should marijuana be made legal?

   YES: 47.5%

   NO: 52.5%

3. In the United States, do you think we're spending too much money on dealing with drug addiction, too little money, or about the right amount?

   TOO MUCH: 11.7%

   TOO LITTLE: 57.6%

   ABOUT THE RIGHT AMOUNT: 30.7%

4. In the United States, do you think we're spending too much money on dealing with drug rehabilitation, too little money, or about the right amount?

   TOO MUCH: 17.5%

   TOO LITTLE: 45.6%

   ABOUT THE RIGHT AMOUNT: 36.8%

1. What possible positive implications could the legalization of marijuana have for society? Negative implications?

2. Examine how males and females responded to the question about legalizing marijuana. Do the numbers surprise you? Explain.

3. The majority of respondents answered the questions about spending on dealing with drug addiction and drug rehabilitation by saying that too little is being spent. Do you think spending will change in the future? Why or why not?

4. As you examine the General Social Survey data from 1973 to the present, consider how responses have changed over time to the question about whether marijuana should be legal. What factors may have influenced the responses?

5. Drinking and drug use can be a sensitive subject. Do you believe that the responses given in the survey are accurate? Explain.

SOURCE: National Opinion Research Center, University of Chicago.

CHAPTER SUMMARY

 Discuss drug use as a social problem.

The use of drugs has occurred in societies over a long period of human history and for a wide range of reasons. Indeed, the use of various drugs is diverse because the effects of these substances are so wide ranging. The use of drugs can create a range of physical, psychological, and social problems, especially when social norms about such use are broken.

 Describe the problems of addiction.

Drug use can create physiological or psychological dependence on a substance. Being deprived of the drug can be a painful experience for a user, which contributes significantly toward continued use. Patterns of addiction are not evenly distributed through society but are influenced by social aspects of individuals' lives.

 Relate patterns of drug use to the life course, gender, and race/ethnicity.

Use, abuse, misuse, and addiction to drugs and alcohol occur and/or become social problems in ways that vary both within and across societies and social contexts by individual, group, culture, social norms, socioeconomic status, gender, race, age, mind-set, and setting. In the United States, whites are more likely to use illegal drugs than are blacks, and males are more likely to use drugs than are females. Young adults are the age group most likely to use drugs. Those in a lower socioeconomic stratum are more likely than those in a higher one to experience drug problems and the harms associated with drug use.

 Apply the functionalist, symbolic interactionist, and conflict perspectives to social policy on drug use.

The functionalist, conflict, and social disorganization theories focus on social structure, inequalities, and/or lack of social control as the cause of drug use, while social learning and symbolic interaction theories center their explanations of drug use on people's interactions and relationships with others.

 Apply specialized theories to the social problems of addiction.

Social learning theory explains how individuals become socialized into drug use. General strain theory assumes that individuals use drugs to cope with negative relationships. Self-control theorists argue that adverse early childhood experiences lead individuals to develop low self-control, making them unable to manage the impulse to use drugs. Social disorganization theory explains the influence of the local environment on patterns of drug use.

 Identify steps toward social change on drugs.

We challenge you to take part in programs that can help to reduce the social problem of drugs by educating yourself and your friends, participating in harm reduction activities, and engaging in social activism to promote responsible drug policies.

DISCUSSION QUESTIONS

1. How are drug use and abuse reflective of the norms of society? What criteria are used to determine if and when drug use is a social problem? Can the same drug be a problem in one group or one society but not in another? What about for one user and not for another within the same society?

2. How does the intent of the user determine if and when drug use is a problem? Where do our norms around drug use come from? How much does the setting or location of drug use factor into whether or not it is viewed as a problem?

3. What differentiates drug use from drug abuse and from drug dependence or addiction? How does society respond to each type of interaction with drugs?

4. In what ways is addiction a problem for more than just the user? What responsibilities does society have toward the person struggling with addiction? How are our responses in the United States similar to or different from responses in other societies?

5. How do social characteristics such as gender, race, and age play a role in who uses drugs in U.S. society? What are the explanations for the differences we see in drug use across gender, racial, and age groups? Why do perceived differences in groups not always align with data on differences between groups?

6. What explanations exist for the different types and frequencies of drug use by age or stage of life? How could this information be used to explain why some people continue to use drugs beyond when they are expected to stop based on norms? What are the implications for social policy and treatment if this explanation is correct?

7. According to structural functionalism, what circumstances lead to deviant drug use? What can be done to reduce drug use and abuse from this perspective?

8. How do the public policies and laws regulating drug use and sentencing reflect the power of some groups over others? Using what we know about drug use by different groups, how might a conflict theorist explain the differences in penalties for drug use? What are some potential solutions to the disparities in policies and enforcement from this perspective?

9. What are the implications of social learning theory for curbing drug use? What can be done to teach normative interaction with drugs and to reduce deviant drug use?

10. Under what circumstances does harm reduction make sense for society instead of or in addition to other solutions? What role could reducing causes of stress, such as those described by strain theory, play in reducing deviant drug use in society? How could individuals or groups reduce stresses and strains for those most at risk for deviant drug use in society?

KEY TERMS

drug 311	drug use 313	natural recovery 316	War on Drugs 313
drug abuse 313	harm reduction 332	needle exchange programs 318	
drug addiction 313	maturing out 320		

Sharpen your skills with SAGE edge at edge.sagepub.com/trevino

A personalized approach to help you accomplish your coursework goals in an easy-to-use learning environment.

13 HEALTH

Kevin White

Tony Karumba / Stinger AFP / Getty Images

A man sits in front of a mural promoting the benefits of circumcision for prevention of HIV/AIDS in Kisumu, Kenya. HIV/AIDS is a major public health concern and cause of death in many parts of Africa, and Kenya has one of the highest prevalence rates of any country outside Southern Africa. Why do you think that HIV/AIDS has been seen as both an illness and a source of social stigma?

Investigating Health: My Story

Kevin White

I was born in Edinburgh, Scotland, and migrated with my parents to Australia in 1966. Following fairly poor performance at school, I enrolled in Flinders University of South Australia, where I received a bachelor's degree in politics and psychology. After a period in the workforce—mainly washing dishes in restaurants—I returned to Flinders to earn my Ph.D. in sociology. My thesis was on the development of the medical profession in the 19th century and the political strategies it used to get a state-licensed monopoly over health care. My academic career then took me to the University of Wollongong, Victoria University of Wellington, New Zealand, and the Australian National University. Here I teach courses titled Introduction to Social Psychology, Classical Social Theory, and Qualitative Research Methods. I have authored six books, edited seven, and published more than 50 refereed papers on the history of medicine, the sociology of health and illness, and the sociology of the professions.

The vast inequalities in people's experiences of health and illness, the profound ways these inequalities affect their quality of life and death, and the fact that every person experiences sickness drive me to learn and research the area of health. I believe society places too much emphasis on the individual and biological causes of illness, and, through my work, I hope to encourage policy makers to tackle health issues through a societal rather than a solely personal framework.

LEARNING OBJECTIVES

13.1 Describe health as socially defined.

13.2 Discuss patterns and trends in health, illness, and treatment.

13.3 Describe the health care system and its stakeholders.

13.4 Apply the functionalist, conflict, and symbolic interactionist perspectives to the concept of health.

13.5 Apply specialized theories of health.

13.6 Identify steps toward social change to promote health.

WHAT DO YOU THINK?

Questions about Health from the General Social Survey

1. Do you think that the government should help pay for medical care?

☐ YES
☐ NO

2. In the United States, do you think we're spending too much money on improving and protecting the nation's health, too little money, or about the right amount?

☐ TOO MUCH
☐ TOO LITTLE
☐ ABOUT THE RIGHT AMOUNT

3. What is your confidence level in medicine?

☐ A GREAT DEAL
☐ ONLY SOME
☐ HARDLY ANY

4. What is your interest level in medical discoveries?

☐ VERY INTERESTED
☐ MODERATELY INTERESTED
☐ NOT AT ALL INTERESTED

5. Do you think that incurable patients should be allowed to die?

☐ YES
☐ NO

6. Do you think a person has the right to end his or her own life if this person has an incurable disease?

☐ YES
☐ NO

▶▶ Turn to the end of the chapter to view the results for the total population.

SOURCE: National Opinion Research Center, University of Chicago.

SUFFERING FROM DRAPETOMANIA

It is 1845 in the American South. The cotton trade is in full swing and so is slavery. Kendrick, a slave on the largest cotton plantation in Maryland, has been working in the fields in the direct sun all summer long with little water and no rest or shade. His back aches, his feet are swollen, his hands are raw, and he has a constant dry cough.

While those around him have been beaten into submissive obedience, Kendrick is different. No matter how severely he is oppressed or how regimented, repetitive, and exhausting his days are, he cannot accept his position in life. He comes to a decision. Early the next morning he will make a run for it.

It is 3:00 A.M. and the only light falls from the stars. The moon has long since gone to rest. The cool night air bathes Kendrick's sunburned skin. He feels alive and alert, as if he has been floating through a nightmare his entire life only to finally wake and feel the fresh wind of freedom just one tree line away . . .

Do you hope he makes it?

According to some 19th-century literature, Kendrick is not displaying strong resilience and an admirable will to live and be free. Rather, he is suffering from a disease. The disease, called drapetomania, was defined as the tendency for a slave to run away from his or her master (Cartwright 1851). This was a real diagnosis made by medical professionals and believed to require treatment, including the surgical removal of both big toes, so running away became a physical impossibility. Do you think this is an appropriate use of medicine in society? Could medical decisions like this be made today?

In the course of this chapter we will look at patterns and trends in health and health care, and at theories of health and health care, and ask whether the spread of sickness and disease and the social construction of sickness and disease today are so dissimilar to Kendrick's case.

The *Oxford English Dictionary* defines *illness* as a disease or period of sickness affecting the body or mind and *health* as the state of being free of illness or injury.

The front page of the French newspaper *Le Petit Journal Illustré* from October 30, 1921, shows a poor family suffering from tuberculosis as a result of living in a squalid flat in Paris. In the United States, Jacob Riis, a social reformer and photographer, documented the squalid living conditions in New York City slums in his 1890 book *How the Other Half Lives*. Riis brought attention to the spread of diseases like smallpox, typhus, and measles in the unhygienic and over-populated tenements.

So what does sociology have to do with a physical problem occurring within an individual? How can society shape an individual's experience of health and illness when these are personal, biological states within that person's own body?

We will consider several demographics of modern Western society by way of demonstrating that your social location determines your quality of life, how long you will live, and how you will die. This chapter will challenge the common definitions of illness and disease as personal experiences and show that these are not static, definite, or objective states but rather socially constructed notions.

As the literature and the example of Kendrick demonstrate, the disadvantaged, the oppressed, and the segregated in our society suffer illness at far greater rates than the wealthy. Further, it is the wealthy, using the underlying rationale of capitalism, who define what behavior falls outside the norm and therefore what behavior is categorized as illness.

WHAT IS ILLNESS?

 13.1 Describe health as socially defined.

It is common logic that illness is a physical event caused by physical factors. For example, food poisoning is the direct result of ingesting food that has become host to harmful bacteria such as *E. coli* or salmonella. The bacteria interfere with bodily functions, causing the body to react to protect the individual's physical well-being. To cure illnesses, we consult with doctors, use medications, and adopt physical strategies such as resting.

Sociologists call this taken-for-granted way of thinking about sickness and disease in our society the medical model (Engel 1981). However, this view of medicine may not account for the all-pervasive and constant dominance of medicine and health in our everyday lives. The prominence of medical television shows, healthy-eating magazines, exercise magazines, self-help books, and the like demonstrates that medicine and the treatment of health are not merely constructs that exist to help us prevent and overcome illness.

Sociologists have recognized this and ask why medicine is so present in the modern psyche. Why, when compared with other fields of scientific expertise, such as chemistry, physics, and mathematics, has medicine become so all-pervasive? What other function does it serve apart from the repair of our physical bodies?

Some sociological theorists argue that medicine has gone beyond its functional role of fixing physical bodies and is used in our everyday lives as a form of **social control**. For example, sociologists consider how diseases or sicknesses, and those who are sick or diseased, are labeled and treated. In many instances, what we call a "disease" may have very weak links to what is actually going on within the diseased person's body (Zola 1972; for recent discussion of Zola's foundational theory, see Hyde et al. 2006). Further, treatment is not simply a utilitarian method of curing illness. It incorporates wider social expectations about appropriate social behavior of both the sick person and others who interact with him or her.

Consider depression. At its most basic, depression is characterized by prolonged periods of sadness and feelings of worthlessness and has been strongly linked to lower levels of the neurotransmitter serotonin within the brain. However, a taboo still surrounds the experience of depression. Those suffering it may be labeled lazy or weak and be too embarrassed to seek help. If the medical profession links this illness directly to serotonin level and other bodily symptoms, why do we treat it differently from other physical illnesses, such as the flu or AIDS or cancer?

Social control: The ability of a strong group in society to control the actions of subordinate groups.

Social behavior itself may be labeled as diseased and sick. When we diverge from society's norms, society reins us back in to label us sick and diseased and "treat" us so we again conform. For example, recent additions and amendments to the *Diagnostic and Statistical Manual of Mental Disorders (DSM)* medicalize behaviors that traditionally were never thought to be illnesses or medical problems. The *DSM* is published by the American Psychiatric Association and provides standard criteria for the classification of mental disorders. Clinicians, insurance companies, and legal systems around the world use it extensively in diagnosis and treatment. The fifth edition of the manual, known as *DSM-5*, was published in 2013. Some of its more questionable entries include excoriation disorder (obsessive compulsive skin picking) and hoarding disorder. Further, gender-specific sexual dysfunctions have been added, and, for females, sexual desire and arousal disorders have been combined into one disorder: female sexual interest/arousal disorder (American Psychiatric Association 2013).

The medicalization of skin picking and hoarding raises the question whether this widely used manual has been drafted to aid in the diagnosis and proper treatment of medical conditions, or whether such labeling of social behaviors exceeds the realm of what should properly be medical issues. Further, the idea that a behavior in females may constitute an illness while the same or similar behavior in males does not raises serious concerns about whether the manual assists in the treatment of real medical issues or promotes social ideals of gender. The British Psychological Society (2011, 6) has recognized this concern in its response to proposed diagnoses (in *DSM-IV*) that it stated were "clearly based on social norms, with 'symptoms' that all rely on subjective judgments." The diagnoses were not value-free, but rather "reflect current normative social expectations."

This chapter does not argue that all illnesses, whether physical or mental, are social constructs. The diagnosis and subsequent treatment of many behaviors that interfere with a person's life are extremely worthwhile and important. What the chapter proposes is that the labeling of certain behaviors as illnesses may exceed the traditional functions of medicine and may reflect prevailing norms and prejudices.

ASK YOURSELF: How do depression and other mental illnesses demonstrate the setting of social standards through the medicalization of behavior? Who decides when a person is overweight? Obese? When does restricted respiratory function become asthma? Do you think a certain behavior should constitute an illness in females but not in males? Do you think the range of medical disorders has exceeded its function in diagnosing and treating medical problems? Why are certain behaviors arbitrarily labeled diseases, whereas others (for example, being a workaholic) are not?

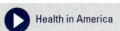 Health in America 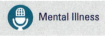 Mental Illness

The Medicalization of Attention-Deficit/Hyperactivity Disorder

The term *attention-deficit/hyperactivity disorder* did not emerge in the United States until the 1950s, when, Smith (2010, 939) asserts, "a lot was expected of the baby boom generation" and there was concern about "perceived American deficiencies in science and technology [and] education critics demanded more of students." He states that "action was taken by school guidance counsellors . . . to identify and help such underachieving children," and this "coincided with the emergence of many psychoactive drugs to treat . . . hyperactivity."

ADHD is characterized by inattention and hyperactivity and impulsivity. These symptoms must be present before the person reaches 12 years of age; occur in two or more settings; interfere with or reduce the quality of social, school, or work functioning;

and not occur during the course of some other psychotic disorder. They must occur for at least six months and include behavior inappropriate for the person's developmental level (American Psychiatric Association 2013; Centers for Disease Control and Prevention 2013b).

Of children diagnosed with ADHD in 2007 in the United States, more than 6 in 10 were taking medication for the disorder, including drugs sold under a range of trade names such as Aderall, Dexedrine, and Ritalin. These drugs act by increasing certain neurotransmitters in the frontal region of the brain—the area associated with executive functioning (Weiss 2011).

Although slightly dated, data from the 2003 National Survey of Children's Health (NSCH), analyzed by the Centers for Disease Control

and Prevention (2010b), are still instructive because they are derived from a huge number of respondents. The survey consulted 102,353 parents regarding their children's health, and the CDC analysis found that the diagnosis and treatment of ADHD had increased markedly from 2003 to 2007. The number of children ages 4 to 17 whose parents reported them as having been medically diagnosed with ADHD increased by 22% in that period, while the number whose *parents* made the diagnosis increased by 9.5% during the same years. This represents an increase of 31.5% in four years.

The standard average of all diagnosed children reported in the NSCH was 9.5%. However, analysis of the 2007 data also revealed marked differences among social groups in the prevalence of ADHD:

Characteristics of a Medicalized Society

We live in a medicalized society, one in which we explain social problems in medical terms. For example, responding to social encounters with heavy drinking is deemed a disease. Inappropriate behavior in the classroom is labeled attention-deficit/hyperactivity disorder (ADHD), or, if it includes learning difficulties, dyslexia. Research regarding the prevalence and incidence of ADHD reveals how, as societies develop over time, certain behaviors may become medicalized (see Figure 13.1).

Three general points can be made about the many possible examples of medicalized behavior:

1. Medicine sets the limits of normal behavior and defines people as sick who fall outside these limits. It sorts, labels, and treats the deviant, the nonconformist, the malingerer, and the sick. Thus the way in which medical problems are produced, conceptualized, and treated is the outcome of specific social and historical factors.

2. The way we conceptualize some social issues as medical problems has immense significance. It makes health and illness the outcome of the individual's behavioral or biological malfunctioning and independent of his or her existence in a wider social environment. For example, the drug addiction of a person of lower socioeconomic background is conceptualized as a problem with that person's will or morality, regardless of the fact that the environment in which he or she was raised was pervaded by drug use and provided no social structure of support or way out.

3. Medicalization makes these problems appear to be products of nature—of genetics, of biological dysfunction, or of innate characteristics of individuals. Thus it puts the problems safely beyond political and social interventions and solutions.

Although using medicine to categorize diseases and exert some level of social control, such as by

- Overall average: 9.5%
- Boys: 13.2%
- Girls: 5.6%
- Children covered by Medicaid: 13.6%

Furthermore, although the rates of ADHD significantly increased between 2003 and 2007, there were exceptions among the following two groups:

- Children from households where parents had less than a high school education
- Children of "other" races (not black or white)

More recent data published by the CDC and analyzed by the *New York Times* suggests that nearly 11% of school-age children in the United States have received a medical diagnosis of ADHD (Schwarz and Cohen 2013). From the data, it is estimated that 6.4 million children 4–17 years of age have

been diagnosed, representing a 16% increase since 2007 and a 41% increase since 2003.

A study conducted in Australia in 2009 considered archival data on prescriptions for stimulant medications from 1990 to 2001 and from 2001 to 2006 to identify trends in the rates of prescriptions as a whole and length of drug use among certain populations. Of particular note for this discussion, the researchers found the following:

- Patients are being prescribed these medications at younger and younger ages.
- There was geographic variation in the rate of prescriptions.
- This geographic variation was strongly correlated with and may be attributed to socioeconomic differences.

There has been an explosion in the diagnosis and treatment of ADHD.

This is not a reflection of the growth of a real underlying disease, since there are no biological markers for ADHD. Rather, the disorder is diagnosed on subjective terms by the physician, and often on evidence provided by teachers and parents. From a social problems perspective, the increase in ADHD diagnoses represents the medicalization of unacceptable behavior, particularly in boys and in white middle-class children who are underperforming at school.

▶ **THINK ABOUT IT:** Why do you think there has been a steady increase in the numbers of children diagnosed with ADHD? Why do you think boys are more than twice as likely as girls to be diagnosed with ADHD? Do you think that behavioral illnesses such as ADHD are being overdiagnosed and overmedicated? If so, why?

promoting exercise, is undeniably a benefit to society, sociologists recognize that the medicalization of society (which is in essence the current role of modern medicine) also has a dark side. The argument against it does not denounce medicine as a whole. Rather, it argues against the labeling, value-laden norms, and stigmatization associated with excess medicalization. The medicalization of society exceeds the diagnosis and treatment of physical abnormalities and extends into the labeling and control of social and behavioral abnormalities. It deems medical issues to be largely the consequences of personal choice, rather than recognizing that disease and illness occur within a framework of individual social class standing and broader governmental policies.

Three False Assumptions about Health

To distinguish the necessary functions of medicine from the overzealous, medicalizing, ones, we must think of disease as being as much a social process as a biological

product of nature. Illness and disease are the products of biology, genetic risk factors, and personal choices. However, all these factors operate within social arrangements that, when we consider health issues epidemiologically, heavily influence both who gets ill and what they get ill from.

Three flawed assumptions about disease recur constantly in our daily lives and in the media:

1. Genetics explains illness and disease to the exclusion of social factors.

2. Those who are ill experience downward social mobility.

3. People adopt lifestyle choices that make them ill.

Let us examine each of these to understand why they are misleading.

Genetics Alone Explains Disease

Genetic explanations are regularly offered for a range of conditions and illnesses, including obesity, drug

FIGURE 13.1 Children in the United States Ages 5–17 Ever Diagnosed with Attention-Deficit/Hyperactivity Disorder, 1998–2009

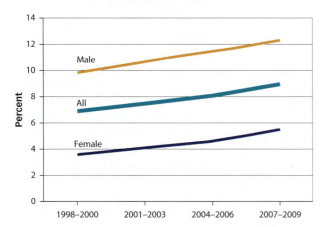

SOURCE: Centers for Disease Control and Prevention, 2013. "ADHD Throughout the Years."

addiction, and alcoholism. There is, however, no evidence for a genetic contribution to what are actually cultural practices such as drug use, nor any scientific justification for making negative moral evaluations couched in the language of medical science. The categorization of such behaviors as illnesses thus lies not in science but in a social evaluation of them.

Sociologists consider health from a perspective that is different from modern conceptions of science and medicine. Rather than view illness as an individual problem, they suggest that the patterns and incidences of illness and disease are in fact readily explainable by factors such as ethnicity, socioeconomic status, age, and gender. There is evidence that single biological risk factors do not account for the social patterning of disease.

So what does a genetic explanation achieve? Information about your own genes, now available through genetic modeling, may allow you to plan for the future, to undertake preventive measures to halt or delay the development of a disease or illness. However, this limited utility may not justify the weight that we place on genetics.

By reducing the explanation of disease to biology alone, the genetic explanation systematically excludes sociological explanations and deflects our attention from the ways in which social life shapes our experience of disease. Between the genetic predisposition for a specific disease and its occurrence actually lie the intervening variables of politics, economics, gender, and ethnicity.

Ironically, it is exactly these considerations that may determine whether a person has access to genetic modeling to predict vulnerability to some conditions, and it is these variables we must take into account in explaining who gets sick—that is, how a genetic risk is transformed into a social reality.

People Who Are Ill Experience Downward Mobility

The second false assumption is that the sick experience downward social mobility, while the healthy experience upward social mobility. As proof, some people cite what they presume to be Charles Darwin's argument about the survival of the fittest. There is no support for this argument in the literature. The sickest are certainly in the poorest sections of society, but they are ill because they are poor, not poor because they are ill. Illness and downward social mobility intersect where political, cultural, and social practices already discriminate against individuals—as in the case of single mothers, the disabled, people of color, and those with AIDS.

People Who Are Ill Have Made Poor Lifestyle Choices

The third flawed assumption is that people adopt lifestyles that make them sick—freely making bad choices about diet, smoking, and exercise, for example—and are therefore individually responsible for their conditions. However, from a social problems perspective, remember that individual lifestyles are themselves socially patterned, and that those lower down in the

Sandy Wright looks over her bag of medications at her home in Peoria, Illinois. Americans are taking record numbers of prescription drugs, over-the-counter medications, and supplements. The overprescribing of antibiotics has led to the emergence of "superbugs," or antibiotic-resistant bacteria.

The Kids Aren't All Right

A patient suffering from tuberculosis rests inside a hospital in Agartala, India. According to the World Health Organization, 22 countries, most of which are in the poorest areas of Africa and Southeast Asia, account for approximately 80% of new TB cases each year.

stratification system can make fewer choices about the foods they consume, the exercise they take, and even their smoking and drinking habits (Subramanyam et al. 2012). Research on programs targeted at individual behavior, such as the Stanford Five-City Project and the Pawtucket Heart Health Program, two large-scale studies examining the effects of lifestyle on heart disease, demonstrates that changes in lifestyle have little effect on the reduction of cardiovascular disease (Everage et al. 2013).

Common Features

For sociologists of health, these three flawed assumptions have two common features. First, they claim that when an individual becomes diseased, it is a problem of the individual's own body and unique biology. Sociologists, however, argue that the distinct patterns of health and illness that we can observe along the intersections of class, power, gender, and ethnicity demonstrate that we should not consider health and illness merely as an individual problem; rather, health and illness are heavily determined by socioeconomic location. By arguing that illness and disease are matters for societal consideration, perhaps even more than for biological consideration, sociologists show that we can understand, treat, and experience disease differently than we do. There is no pure, value-free scientific knowledge about disease. Our knowledge of health and illness, the organizations and professions that deal with health care, and our own responses to our bodily states are shaped and formed by the history of our society and our place in it.

Second, even if lifestyle behaviors were the sole cause of disease, extensive studies have shown that it is almost impossible for people to change their lifestyles on their own and in isolation from their social circumstances (Everage et al. 2013). The social factors that predispose people to adopt unhealthy lifestyles—work stress, for example—are often ignored in treatment plans that focus on immediate causes like diet, cholesterol, or drinking. Instead we need to see these risk factors in context, to understand how individuals are exposed to them and why they have limited access to resources for responding to them (Clougherty, Souza, and Cullen 2010). The lack of such resources is the fundamental cause of disease patterns. If we want to change the patterns of disease, we must change the patterns of social inequality that produce them, and not focus solely on their downstream impact on the individual.

PATTERNS AND TRENDS

 13.2 Discuss patterns and trends in health, illness, and treatment.

Now that we have examined the notion of illness as socially constructed and a means to set norms of social behavior, let us consider who suffers illness and why. What patterns and trends in illness do we find?

Who Gets Sick?

In modern Western societies it is usually assumed that health differences are biologically caused or that individual lifestyles result in people becoming sicker and dying earlier. People from lower socioeconomic backgrounds choose to smoke more, drink more, and exercise less, choices leading to biological changes that cause disease, damage health, and lead to shorter and poorer-quality lives. The argument of this chapter, however, and of sociological thought in general, is that disease is not caused by purely biological factors and individual choices. On the contrary, individual lifestyle choices are socially shaped, and to focus on them as the only explanation of disease is to ignore the social factors that shape them.

Sociologists traditionally argue that disease is shaped by broad social determinants rather than by personal choices individuals make. People from lower socioeconomic backgrounds statistically choose to drink more, smoke more, eat less healthy diets, and exercise less than their counterparts in higher socioeconomic groups. But these decisions are not made in a vacuum and should not be considered pure choices. Rather, a wide range of mediating social factors intervene between the biology of disease, individual lifestyle, and the social experience to shape and produce disease. These factors range from standards of housing and workplace conditions to emotional and psychological experiences at work and at home, to men's and women's social and gender roles, to membership in **status groups** based on ethnicity (see Figure 13.2).

Steven G. Prus (2011) conducted an analysis of social determinants of health across the United States and Canada using data obtained from the Joint Canada/United States Survey of Health. He found that sociodemographic and socioeconomic factors have substantial effects on health. Gender, country of birth, race, and education were strong predictors of a person's experience of health in the United States, and income was a stronger factor influencing health in Canada. When his statistical analysis was adjusted to account for socioeconomic status, Prus found that the influence of gender, race, and marital status on a person's experience of health was considerably weakened. This suggests that socioeconomic status may have a stronger bearing on health than these individual factors. Furthermore, psychosocial factors, behavioral risk, and health care access were very strong determinants of health in each country.

Thus we need to consider these micro factors against the background of overall patterns of inequality that exist within society. For example, is there a political commitment to reducing inequality and providing a social environment that prevents illness and disease? Are there guaranteed housing standards, access to and affordability of fresh and healthy food, and safe working conditions, as well as safe and available resources and places where people can get physical exercise, both intentionally and incidentally?

Whether they seek to promote equality by sharing wealth or adopt strictly capitalist ideals, governments directly affect the middle and lower classes' experience of health. Other social institutions also shape the experience of health within a population. For example, employers and landlords who allow substandard working and living conditions can make poor people sicker. Professional sports leagues that fail to prevent damage to players' health through injury can leave the athletes and their families with heavy burdens. Industries that promote unhealthy habits like smoking and eating junk food can harm health, as do companies and industries that pollute air, soil, and water. Even given improved living conditions and medical practices, if inequalities based on class, gender, and ethnicity are not tackled, the differences between the rich and the poor persist and widen. Disease and social inequality are intimately linked. The outcome of an unequal distribution of the political, economic, and social resources necessary for a healthy life is the **social gradient of health** (Lynch et al. 2006). Those at the top of the social system are healthier and live longer, while those at the bottom are sicker, do not live as long, and die more from preventable diseases and accidents.

....

ASK YOURSELF: Do you think it is more difficult for a person from a low socioeconomic background to make positive choices about his or her health than it is for a person from a high socioeconomic background? Why or why not?

....

FIGURE 13.2 Social Factors Affecting Health

Growing Inequality and Its Impact on Health

While our health appears to us as a personal issue, from a social problems perspective it is socially patterned: who gets sick, when we die, and what we die of are closely linked to wider patterns of inequality in society. British studies have found marked differences in health levels between occupational classes, for men and

....

Status groups: Social groups that are either negatively or positively privileged.

Social gradient of health: The consistent finding that inequality and health are related, with those at the top of the social system being healthier and living longer than those at the bottom.

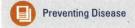

women and for all ages (Rowlingson 2011). The people at the bottom of the class system have a much higher mortality rate than those at the top. Furthermore, people in the lower classes suffer from more chronic illness, their children weigh less at birth, and they are shorter (White 2012).

There are also marked inequalities in access to health services, particularly preventive care. For example, in Southern California, researchers found that 97% of otolaryngologists (doctors specializing in treating the ear, nose, and throat) would offer an appointment to a child with commercial insurance, but only 27% would do so for a child on Medi-Cal (publicly funded health care). Of that 27%, only 19% would offer to perform a tonsillectomy; the remaining 8% would refer the child to another physician. The surgeons said they did not want to operate on those without commercial insurance due to the excessive administrative burdens (96%), low reimbursement rates (92%), and high administrative fees (87%) associated with treating Medi-Cal patients (Wang et al. 2004).

The growing inequalities of wealth and income observed within and between nations in recent years mean that inequalities of health are also widening. Income inequality in the United States—the gap between the richest and the poorest—is now greater than at any period since the 1920s. Using rigorous economic analysis, Alvaredo et al. (2013) found that the share of total annual income received by the wealthiest 1% has more than doubled, from 9% in 1976 to 20% in 2011.

It is not the extent of poverty within a society but the extent of income inequality that determines the distribution of health and illness. Countries with relatively minor differences between richest and poorest are the healthiest. Zheng and George (2012, 2179) speculate that income inequality may result in "underinvestment in human resources and social goods, while intensifying social comparisons and subsequent psychological stress and frustration . . . [and] as increasing income inequality exacerbates these disadvantageous social conditions, personal resources, especially socioeconomic status, increase in importance as tools for accessing social and health resources." Furthermore, health, like every other service, relies on profitability. When one segment of the population can afford to pay more for medical care and procedures than another, health care for those in the bottom segments becomes unaffordable.

The Gini coefficient is an index measuring the level of inequality between two values; a coefficient of zero indicates total equality between values in a data set. Karlsson et al. (2012) used the Gini coefficient to assess the impact of income inequality on health across 21 countries; their findings are represented in Figure 13.3.

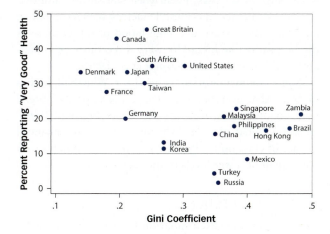

FIGURE 13.3 Relationship between Health and Income Inequality for Selected Countries, 2010

SOURCE: Karlsson et al. (2012).

The researchers found that the more an individual earns, the better his or her experience of health. Further, the degree of inequality of income within a high-income country also influences the citizen's experience of health (Hallerod and Gustafsson 2011).

Age at death and cause of death are also linked to social class. The lower social classes have significantly higher mortality rates than the upper classes. Shishehbor et al. (2006) sought to investigate the extent to which physiological characteristics account for the association between socioeconomic status and mortality. They studied 30,043 patients living in Ohio who were referred for exercise stress testing for evaluation of known or suspected coronary artery disease. The researchers collected data from 1990 through 2002 and followed up the mortality of participants until 2004, dividing them into quartiles on a four-level socioeconomic scale. They found that the lower someone's socioeconomic status, the higher the risk of death. The lowest in socioeconomic status had higher mortality in every year of the study, and the differences between quartiles grew over time. Although adjusting for other variables lessened the significance of the findings in this graph, the researchers were able to pair participants from the lowest quartile with those in the highest, largely accounting for all other variables apart from socioeconomic status. When they analyzed this comparison, they found that socioeconomic status was still strongly related to mortality rates.

In 1978, Michael G. Marmot and his colleagues published the first major study of class differences in health in Britain. His Whitehall studies found that skilled white-collar workers at the bottom of the British civil service

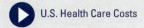 U.S. Health Care Costs   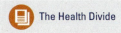 The Health Divide

hierarchy had disease rates four times those of workers at the top. Those one step below the top had disease rates twice those at the top. This finding was confirmed over a wide range of diseases. Even when statistically adjusted rates took into account lifestyle factors such as smoking, high-fat diets, obesity, and high blood pressure, those at the bottom of the hierarchy were three times as vulnerable as those at the top (Marmot et al. 1978).

Some commentators have used the Whitehall studies to argue that everyone experiences the impact of social position on health, not just the poor (Marmot 2006). However, what the data demonstrate is the nuanced impact of class on health, and its accelerating impact on individuals at lower levels of the social system.

Gender Differences

Although gender discrimination has been dramatically reduced in modernized Western societies, gender stereotypes and gender roles remain prominent. Consider the roles females usually play in advertising, television shows, and films. What characteristics and qualities do they embody? How do these compare with the ways males are presented and the roles men play?

Although the saturation of gender stereotypes in mass media appears harmless, we all internalize such stereotypes, perceiving ourselves and our health and behavior in comparison with what we see around us, including in the media. How do you think this exposure affects men's and women's experiences of health and illness? We next examine these experiences, beginning with women's.

....

ASK YOURSELF: Over the next few days, note the advertisements for painkillers that you see online and in other media. Are there differences in the ways men and women are portrayed in these ads? Are different kinds of pain relievers targeted at men and women? (See Greene and Herzberg 2010; Kempner 2006.)

....

Women's Experience of Health

The social problem of women's health is not that women are unhealthy or diseased, but that they are managed in a certain way by the medical system and, in particular, by doctors. The concept of medicalization is particularly useful for explaining women's experience in Western medicine.

Medical textbooks and journals have been criticized for their sexist attitudes (Niland and Lyons 2011), and gender-specific information is scarce or absent for various conditions such as cardiovascular disease, alcohol abuse, and pharmacology. Further, there is an underlying theme in the literature that women's health problems are aberrations of the male norms (Dijkstra, Verdonk, and Largo-Janssen 2008). For example, medical textbooks portray menopause as a medical issue, particularly as a deficiency disease (Hvas and Gannik 2008). Menopause is simply the cessation of menses in women (White 2006), but the dominant biomedical perspective explains it as a biological "hormone deficiency" that requires treatment through hormone replacement therapy (Niland and Lyons 2011). Many feminist sociologists argue that the experience of menopause has been medicalized. This is particularly apparent when we consider that in some countries menopause is celebrated as freeing women from social restrictions and reproductive pressures (Avis and Crawford 2008). In Western cultures, where aging is negatively perceived and womanhood is strongly associated with fertility, menopause is overwhelmingly conveyed as problem, conceptualized through a medical framework as requiring medical treatment (Colombo et al. 2010).

An Australian study into the detection and treatment of psychological disturbance by primary care physicians revealed that doctors were more inclined to diagnose female patients than male patients with **nonpsychotic psychological disturbance** (Horsfall 2001). Research reveals two consistent findings relating to the health of women:

1. They are diagnosed as suffering from more ill health than men are.

2. Paradoxically, they live longer than men do (see Figure 13.4).

In Australia, women's life expectancy is greater than men's (Australian Institute of Health and Welfare 2006). In the United States in 2008 women's life expectancy was 80.8 years and men's 75.7 (Miniño, Xu, and Kochanek 2010).

Several factors explain women's higher rate of medical diagnosis. For instance, between the ages of 15 and 44, women are hospitalized at a higher rate than men, largely due to childbirth. Further, women go to doctors more than men do, especially during their childbearing years when many have family planning needs and receive prenatal care (Drapeau, Boyer, and Lesage 2009). Women are also encouraged to have regular screenings for cervical cancer and breast cancer (Pap smears and mammograms, respectively).

Women are also overrepresented in health statistics as a consequence of their caretaker roles for children, for

....

Nonpsychotic psychological disturbance: A psychiatric character disorder that does not involve delusions.

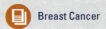
Breast Cancer

FIGURE 13.4

U.S. Life Expectancy, 1950–2050 (projected)

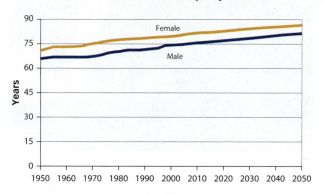

SOURCE: Reprinted with permission from Data360, http://www.data360.org/dsg.aspx?Data_Set_Group_Id=195.

other adults in the household, and for their extended families. Further, they are forced into sometimes unhealthy social roles with consequences like lower social status, longer work hours, persistently lower wages, unpaid work, greater social and emotional commitments, and fewer hours of sleep and leisure (Drapeau et al. 2009).

The final factor explaining the apparent high numbers of sick women is that women and men are socialized to experience and report their bodily sensations differently. Women are more likely to consult doctors based on how they feel, whereas men are more likely to avoid consultation with doctors unless they have physical symptoms. It is for this reason that men are less likely than women to be diagnosed as suffering from stress or depression and more likely to be diagnosed as having physical ailments (Galdas, Cheater, and Marshall 2005).

ASK YOURSELF: How do you think age and gender interact in the context of the medical encounter? Think about the types of health problems women of different ages experience. How does their health link to their gender? Do men experience the same shifts in disease profile over age? Why do you think this is so?

Men's Experience of Health

Although practices and attitudes are constantly changing, it is still not the norm for women to engage in motor sports, contact sports, reckless driving, and other displays traditionally associated with masculinity. To conform to their social role and establish their social standing, however, men engage in these and other activities that can put them in danger of serious injury and death.

Further, construction and other jobs, such as mining, that require significant manual labor continue to be dominated by men. Dangerous and sometimes unhealthy workplaces have serious consequences for men's health. Manual labor also typically exposes men to far greater levels of chemicals and other injurious substances than women are exposed to. Asbestos, a fiber commonly used in building products and insulation until the early 1990s, is now known as a carcinogen to which many men in the construction trades were exposed. And the mere fact of performing demanding physical labor for eight hours a day over many years creates stress and injuries. Table 13.1 shows the number of claims made under WorkCover South Australia, the South Australian workers' compensation system (excluding large businesses that operate outside this system) for 2002–2011, by gender. As the table shows, injured male workers far outnumbered injured females in every year.

Gender also has significant impacts on the way men understand and experience sickness and disease. Men's health, and ill health, is often framed in the context of masculinity. Traits that are dominantly linked to masculinity, such as stoicism and an emphasis on physical health rather than on emotional or mental distress, encourage men to delay visiting doctors and to underreport pain or other symptoms in medical encounters (Galdas et al. 2005).

Men delay seeking medical advice for even the most overt physical symptoms. In a review of the international literature, Kiss and Meryn (2001) found that men often fail to appear for scheduled medical checkups and

TABLE 13.1 Businesses Registered in WorkCover South Australia: Total Claims, 2002–2011

Year	Claims by males	Claims by females
2002–2003	19,038	6,753
2003–2004	18,956	6,589
2004–2005	18,508	6,474
2005–2006	17,099	6,184
2006–2007	16,512	5,758
2007–2008	15,529	5,528
2008–2009	14,459	5,357
2009–2010	13,260	5,142
2010–2011	13,785	5,062

SOURCE: WorkCover SA, Statistical Review 2010-2011. Reprinted with permission.

How Class and Ethnicity Influence Health

Class and ethnicity interact in matters of health, as in so many other social problem areas. Class position interacts with ethnic status, for instance, to produce raised blood pressure levels among many African Americans (Blascovich et al. 2001; Hajjar, Kotchen, and Kotchen 2006). The differences in sickness and death rates between African Americans and whites are not biological, not natural, and not genetic. There are instead significant differences in the treatment of members of different ethnic groups in racially defined societies. A study of the management of appendicitis revealed that, compared to Caucasian children in the United States, African American children have a much lower rate of hospitalization, higher rates of perforation of the appendix, lower rates of less invasive **laparoscopic surgery**, and longer delays in surgical management of the condition (Kokoska et al. 2007).

Similarly, disparities in treatment between members of indigenous groups and nonindigenous persons may be a result of clinical services not being culturally or geographically set up to serve indigenous communities. In other words, such services may be located far away from where indigenous populations live, and they may function to remove people from their environment and isolate them in hospitals. This is the case, for example, in Australia concerning heart disease, diabetes, and tuberculosis, diseases for which Australian Aboriginals have a mortality rate up to five times that of their non-Aboriginal counterparts. Indigenous Australian women are 10 times more likely to die from cervical cancer than nonindigenous women, and it is the number one cause of cancer deaths among indigenous women despite the fact that it is now considered one of the most easily preventable forms of cancer. The most likely reason is the low participation of indigenous women in cervical screening (Pap smear) programs because of lack of access to services (Coory et al. 2002).

In the same way, comparisons between the Native American population and the general U.S. population highlight disparities in both mental and physical health, even when factors such as location in rural versus urban areas are accounted for (Gone 2007; Baldwin et al. 2002). Maternal and infant health is another key area in which Native American populations fall behind, once again demonstrating that ethnicity, class, and gender strongly intersect to influence the incidence of illness. It is the power relationships between men and women, and between dominant and subordinate groups based on ethnicity, that determine the health and sickness of people, rather than facts of nature or biology.

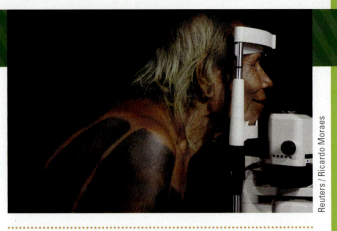

Reuters / Ricardo Moraes

The chief of the Kayapo tribe from Brazil receives ophthalmologic attention. Volunteer doctors from the Brazilian Health Expeditions built a mobile hospital to provide clinical and surgical treatments for the indigenous tribes of the Amazonian rain forest. The international medical humanitarian organization Doctors Without Borders provides medical care to people in more than 60 countries.

▶ **THINK ABOUT IT**

1. Can you see ways in which your own ethnicity has impacts on your health?

2. Is the ethnic patterning of disease the outcome of a racist society?

3. If you were asked to advise your congressional representative about strategies to improve the health of ethnic minorities, what would you suggest?

Laparoscopic surgery: A modern surgical technique in which operations are performed through small incisions (usually 0.5–1.5 cm) as opposed to the larger incisions needed in laparotomy. Also known as minimally invasive surgery, Band-Aid surgery, and keyhole surgery.

examinations. We can also infer that men are actively trying to negotiate their gender identity in the face of chronic illnesses that challenge key attributes of their masculinity—their ability to stay in control, act rationally, not complain, and "be a man." Thus men's reactions to ill health may well be to protect their socially determined sense of gender identity from threats.

ASK YOURSELF: Make a list of five character traits you think are seen as typically "masculine." How might each of these traits mediate the way in which men experience health and illness?

Socioeconomic and Occupational Differences

Sociologists have consistently demonstrated a strong correlation between socioeconomic status and health (Zheng and George 2012). The likely causes of this relationship are practical: a person in a lower socioeconomic demographic has greater exposure to stress and hardship and more limited access to valuable resources such as food, housing, health care, and medical knowledge (George 2005).

Members of lower socioeconomic groups are also more vulnerable to the worst effects of urbanism: slum dwellings, poor ventilation, garbage, and overcrowding (Craddock 2000). They are exposed to the unregulated labor market of sweatshops, home work, and piece rates. The poor pay higher cash costs, have less access to informal sources of financial assistance, such as friends and family, and depend on insecure incomes. Ironically, the poorer you are, the more it costs you to live. These features of low socioeconomic status mean that you will have a lower life expectancy, higher overall mortality rates, and higher infant mortality rates. Low socioeconomic status— the combination of unvalued work and low income—is associated with higher rates of death from the 14 major causes of death in the International Classification of Diseases (Chandola 2000). Men in unskilled manual labor are five times more likely to die prematurely than men working in professions (Chandola 2000).

At least part of the difference in the experience of health between different socioeconomic classes is their distinct experiences of work. Those in the lower or "blue-collar" working classes are often engaged in work that exposes them to harmful chemicals or dangerous machinery or practices. The World Health Organization reported in 2006 that the proportion of all cancer deaths attributable to occupational exposures in industrialized countries was

A miner works inside a coal mine near the town of Zenica in Bosnia and Herzegovina. Coal mining is one of the most dangerous jobs in the world. Not only is there a constant risk of cave-ins, but there is also the danger of coal workers' pneumoconiosis, or black lung disease, which is caused by long-term exposure to coal dust. What other occupations can you think of that may be hazardous to workers' health?

between 4% and 20% (Ivanov and Straif 2006, 1). Moreover, cancer is one of the leading causes of work-related deaths in the United States, contributing to a much higher proportion of fatalities than workplace accidents or injuries (Hämäläinen, Takala, and Saarela 2007). The stress of working conditions that combine low autonomy and high workloads in an unsupportive environment has been shown to cause up to 35% of cardiovascular mortality in the United States (Kuper et al. 2002).

In 2011 there were 4,963 fatal occupational injuries in the United States. Of these, most occurred in working-class industries and working-class occupations (see Table 13.2). In contrast, there are very few dangers in a typical office environment.

The data on work-related deaths are chastening, especially since such deaths are likely to be considerably underreported. (For example, deaths caused by vehicle crashes are not counted as work accidents, even if they occur in the course of the victims' work.) In Australia, statistics indicate that between 300 and 700 workers die each year as a result of injuries sustained at work (Australian Safety and Compensation Council 2006). An estimated 5,000 invasive cancers and 34,000 nonmelanoma skin cancers per year in Australia are caused by work-related exposure, and approximately 1.5 million people per year are exposed to known carcinogens (Fritschi and Driscoll 2006). It is increasingly recognized that the health of the individual worker does not necessarily have to be physically at risk for the impact of capitalist employment practices to make itself felt. Lack

▶ Health Care Crisis

TABLE 13.2 Fatal Occupational Injuries in the United States by Occupation and Industry, 2011

Occupation	
Management occupations	467
Protective service occupations	282
Sales and related occupations	240
Farming, fishing, and forestry occupations	261
Construction and extraction occupations	798
Installation, maintenance, and repair occupations	354
Transportation and material moving occupations	1,233
Military occupations	57
Industry	
Private Industry	4,188
Goods Producing	1,786
Agriculture, forestry, fishing, and hunting	566
Construction	738
Manufacturing	327
Service providing	2,402
Wholesale trade	190
Retail trade	268
Transportation and warehousing	749
Professional and business services	433
Leisure and hospitality	231
Government	505

SOURCE: Table modified from United States Department of Labor, Bureau of Labor Statistics, 2012. "Revisions to the 2011 Census of Fatal Occupational Injury (CFOI) Counts."

of autonomy at work, lack of control over the production process, and separation from fellow workers—the key components to Marx's account of alienation—are all now supported in empirical research as causes of disease (Benach and Muntaner 2007).

THE U.S. HEALTH CARE SYSTEM AND ITS STAKEHOLDERS

 13.3 Describe the health care system and its stakeholders.

The ways in which people seek health care, its provision, and its funding are all factors that heavily influence access to services and therefore quality and standards of health. While government policy may be the most important mediating factor in the U.S. health care system, many stakeholders influence the way the general population experiences health and illness. Next we look at government policy in the form of the Patient Protection and Affordable Care Act, widely known as Obamacare, and then at stakeholders, including private health insurers, pharmaceutical companies, members of the medical profession, and alternative practitioners.

The Government: Obamacare

The U.S. health care system stands in contrast to many others in the Western world. Health care in welfare states such as the United Kingdom, Australia, and New Zealand has traditionally been provided by the government. From a sociological perspective, these systems have been extremely beneficial. The government is responsible for the provision of health care, and taxpayers' money (with the wealthiest paying the greater portion) goes directly to benefit those in lower socioeconomic groups in the most necessary and fundamental of ways. This model is directly in line with the traditional conception of the state as the means of providing minimum standards of living for all its citizens (White 2009, ch. 4).

The United States, on the other hand, has operated under a neoliberal system of governance since its inception, with a health care sector dominated by private rather than government interests. However, whereas many countries that traditionally have operated under welfare state capitalism are now shifting toward privatization of their health care industries (a change many scholars find extremely concerning), the U.S. government has taken broad steps to move in the other direction. The Patient Protection and Affordable Care Act of 2010, upheld by the U.S. Supreme Court in 2012, does not replace Medicare, Medicaid, or private health insurance but rather supplements these models to ensure that all U.S. citizens have access to health insurance and thus

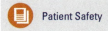 Patient Safety 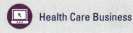 Health Care Business

Health beyond Our Borders

Health in Russia and Greece after Political and Financial Crises

The political and social upheaval that occurred in Russia following the collapse of the Soviet Union in the early 1990s and the major economic collapse in 1998 were followed by a marked decline in life expectancy across the country. Between 1987 and 1994, life expectancy of Russian adult males fell by 7.4 years, to 57.5. Female life expectancy followed a similar path, falling by 2.6 years between 1989 and 1994. These significant demographic changes were mainly due to mortality from preventable and noncommunicable factors such as cardiovascular disease, alcohol abuse, and traffic accidents (Levintova and Novotny 2004).

Greece provides a startling example of what may happen when a government drastically severs funding to health care. Following the global financial crisis that began in 2007, the government of Greece attempted to restore the country's faltering economy by adopting austerity measures that have proven controversial and, so far, ineffective.

These cost-cutting efforts have also had serious social and health effects on the country's population. The Ministry of Health was downsized by 24%, so health services were cut and many once-free services are no longer available. Meanwhile, unemployment more than tripled, from 7.2% in 2008 to 22.6% in 2012.

The cutting of publicly funded health services coupled with the huge loss of employment in the country had drastic consequences for the people's experience of health (Kondilis et al. 2013). Between 2007 and 2009 suicide rates rose by 16%, and the murder rate climbed almost 26%, with men overrepresented as victims in both cases. Deaths from infectious diseases increased by 13%, outbreaks of malaria and West Nile virus occurred, and rates of HIV infection

increased. As Kondilis et al. (2013, 973) note, "In a time of economic turmoil, rising health care needs and increasing demand for public services collide with austerity and privatization policies, exposing Greece's population health to further risks."

▶ **THINK ABOUT IT:** Have you lived in a community that was affected by sudden economic change (such as the closing of a major industry)? Can you think of any impact that change may have had on the health and well-being of community members?

Reuters / Yanni Behrakis

Prosthetics placed by people with disabilities are seen in front of the Greek parliament during a protest against new austerity measures in Athens. In 2013, Greek doctors and nurses saw their paychecks reduced by nearly a third, and the country experienced serious shortages of drugs and medical supplies. Some effects of austerity included increases in heart disease, suicides, and HIV infections. Cuts in health care have major and long-lasting effects.

---

appropriate health care. Before the passage of this law, 44 million people in the United States did not have any form of health insurance (ObamaCare Facts 2013). The new law stipulates that all U.S. citizens are to have health insurance by 2014 or pay a penalty.

In the United States, most people who have health insurance are insured through their employers; about a third are covered by the public insurance systems Medicare and Medicaid, and a smaller proportion independently purchase health insurance. Under Obamacare, all these means of obtaining health insurance have expanded to encompass more people. Companies with 50 or more employees are required to provide health insurance to their employees, for instance. Tax breaks and other incentives encourage smaller businesses to provide insurance to their employees. Medicare has not changed, but in states whose governments have cooperated, Medicaid's low-income threshold has been lowered so more people are covered. Those who do not have employer coverage or Medicaid or Medicare can shop for insurance through so-called health insurance marketplaces that make private plans easily comparable and accessible. Many people buying insurance through these marketplaces qualify for tax credits to subsidize their monthly insurance premiums.

Opponents and supporters of the Patient Protection and Affordable Care Act (Obamacare) rally on the sidewalk in front of the Supreme Court in Washington, D.C. There are pros and cons to the new health care law. Pro: Obamacare offers a number of protections not previously available and expands health care services. Con: Since many Americans work for larger employers, some employees may have the new costs involved with insuring the workforce passed on to them. Where do you stand on the issue?

The new legislation also changed the regulation of insurance companies, which now must insure everyone, including those who are already sick or have preexisting conditions. Older people will generally pay less for insurance, while many younger people will pay more. However, younger people are now able to stay on their parents' insurance plans until they are 26 years old. These sweeping reforms have met with enormous and highly organized opposition from big business, the health insurance industry, and political parties representing wealthy citizens. All these groups are to be taxed more to fund the new insurance system.

The Medical-Industrial Complex

Perhaps the second most important stakeholder in the U.S. health care system is private enterprise. Relman (1980) discusses the process by which independent hospitals and services were selected and purchased by the private sector in the 1970s and 1980s. Chains of related health care services were forged together under large corporate structures in a process he describes as a transition from a "cottage industry" to a vertically and horizontally integrated "medical-industrial complex." Horizontal integration yielded broad market share, while vertical integration enabled consumers to

be funneled upward through health networks, starting with general practitioners who referred patients to affiliated specialists, radiologists, pathologists, and hospitals.

The medical-industrial complex is a large and growing network of private corporations engaged in the business of supplying health care services to patients for profit— services that used to be provided by government, nonprofit institutions, or individual practitioners. At the base of this complex are corporate ownership of hospitals and the interlocking ownership and production of technological and diagnostic machinery, both facilitated by regulators. The popular belief that private enterprise is more efficient and effective and enables greater choice has led governments around the world to indirectly promote and actively pursue privatization policies in the health care sector. Essentially, community family doctors have been replaced by large general practitioner clinics, and state-run hospitals have been privatized.

This worldwide trend toward privatization troubles sociologists and other academics. Company directors and managers have a duty to exercise their powers in the best interests of their companies and the companies' owners, shareholders whose interests are invariably financial. On the other hand, the rationale of government spending is to allocate taxpayers' money for the

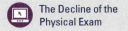

The Decline of the
Physical Exam

public good. Thus the goals of public and private enterprise are at odds in the context of health care.

Pharmaceutical Companies

Pharmaceutical companies are among the largest companies in the world. One commentator has described the U.S. pharmaceutical industry, sometimes referred to as "Big Pharma," as the "$200 billion colossus" (Angell 2005), estimating that expenditures on prescription medicines account for approximately 15% of the U.S.

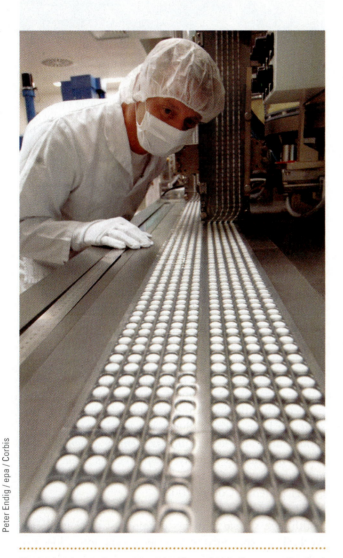

Peter Endig / epa / Corbis

Generic drugs have exactly the same pharmacological effects as their brand-name counterparts. The U.S. Food and Drug Administration requires that generic drugs be as safe and effective as brand-name drugs. And even though, on average, generic drugs cost 80–85% percent less than the equivalent brand-name products, many people still prefer the brand-name drugs. How much of this do you think is due to pharmaceutical advertising?

gross national product. Pharmaceutical companies are not only major players in the health care system; they also make up a large proportion of many Western economies in their own right.

Ironically, because they are private companies seeking to further their profits, pharmaceutical companies actually benefit from a sicker society. The more sick people in the community, the more demand for pharmaceuticals drives up their market price and profitability. Sometimes demand increases competition as new companies enter the market and drive down prices. However, the research, development, and clinical trial phases required to bring a new pharmaceutical to market incur massive costs, usually estimated to range from $802 million in 2003 to $1.3 billion or even $1.7 billion in 2009 (Collier 2009). In any event, the cost of producing a new drug effectively discourages new market entrants and thus reduces competition in the sector.

Have you ever watched a television commercial for a burger chain and suddenly felt hungry? How about an ad for cosmetics that made you feel you needed new or better makeup? Drug advertising does exactly the same thing, which explains why U.S. pharmaceutical companies are now such heavy advertisers. Pharmaceutical company spending on advertising reached $5 billion in 2006 and 2007 before slipping to $4.5 billion in 2009 (Greene and Herzberg 2010). Like private health care providers, pharmaceutical companies aim to increase their profits by increasing their market base. Advertising prescription drugs directly to consumers has many implications for the sociology of health. Superficially it increases the market base by raising awareness of health issues and encouraging people to consult their doctors if they are experiencing the symptoms noted in the ads. However, critics argue that such advertising misinforms patients, overemphasizes drug benefits, manufactures disease, and encourages the overutilization of drugs, leading to inappropriate prescribing and wasting appointment time (Ventola 2011). In fact, most countries have recognized the dangers of direct-to-consumer pharmaceutical advertising. New Zealand and the United States are the only two member countries of the Organization for Economic Cooperation and Development that allow pharmaceutical companies to advertise directly to consumers (Ventola 2011).

Of particular concern for the discussion in this chapter is the manufacturing of illness, which we have termed *medicalization*. Two major "illnesses" have been identified as heavily medicalized by the pharmaceutical industry: erectile dysfunction (Conrad 2007) and menopause (Hunter 2007). As discussed above, menopause is a natural phase in a woman's life; it is not a medical condition

Pharmaceutical Companies

requiring treatment. With respect to erectile dysfunction, only 10% of U.S. men are unable to achieve an erection (Feldman et al. 2000), and pharmaceutical advertising is said to target men experiencing what are merely normal variations in sexual performance (Shaw 2008). Pharmaceutical advertising not only encourages those experiencing symptoms to consult their doctors, but it also changes our social perceptions of what it is to be healthy and what is normal behavior or bodily function. Furthermore, medical professionals are people and are not immune to such societal shifts in norms. They are therefore also more likely to diagnose and prescribe pharmaceuticals in circumstances that may not warrant such action.

Furthermore, pharmaceutical advertising can reinforce the gendered construction of particular illnesses or conditions. One study of advertising for migraine treatments suggests that by consistently marketing these products to women, pharmaceutical companies help create the impression that migraine is a women's disorder, in turn ensuring that women are more likely than men to seek help for, and be diagnosed with, migraines (Kempner 2006).

ASK YOURSELF: Have you ever diagnosed yourself after watching a pharmaceutical advertisement? Do you think pharmaceutical advertising is shifting social conceptions of what it is to be healthy and what behaviors or bodily functions are normal or deemed illnesses? Do you think direct-to-consumer pharmaceutical advertising should be banned?

Alternative Practitioners

The most widely known therapies not supported by orthodox medicine are homeopathy, chiropractic, osteopathy, acupuncture, and herbalism. The definition of certain health care practices as "alternative" is a political and economic categorization that allows alternative practitioners to obtain state licenses to practice. In Australia, for example, chiropractic is legally recognized as a form of medicine, and in the United Kingdom homeopathy is recognized. Paradoxically, "alternative" medicine shares many of the characteristics of orthodox medicine: focusing on the individual rather than on social factors as the source of disease and increasingly depending on a wide range of preparations marketed by multinational drug companies (Barnes, Bloom, and Nahin 2008). Alternative practitioners treat conditions that orthodox medicine finds hard to deal with, such as chronic back pain. They also provide treatments for contested conditions—that is, those the medical profession does not consider diseases, such as chronic fatigue syndrome. Most people

Jianan Yu / Reuters / Stringer

A patient (table on left) receives acupuncture treatment with mashed garlic, herbs, and ignited dry moxa leaves placed on the back to treat rheumatism as another patient receives cupping treatment at a hospital in Hefei, China. In the United States, alternative forms of medicine are not typically covered by health insurance, yet many Americans spend billions of dollars every year on treatments such as yoga, acupuncture, aromatherapy, herbalism, hypnotherapy, osteopathy, and reflexology. Why do you think that is the case?

who use alternative practitioners do so in combination with orthodox practices (Barnes et al. 2008).

Patients and Patient Groups

Most patient groups take the form of self-help groups, or support groups, in which people with similar conditions come together voluntarily to share knowledge and support one another. It is the reciprocal nature of relationships in these groups that distinguishes them from patient encounters with professional physicians or the health care system. Support groups have been found particularly valuable at the psychosocial level for those suffering from chronic illness, but participation in such groups may also lead to *illness identity dependency,* in which individuals identify themselves as their disease even after successful treatment—for example, "I am a cancer patient" (Corbin 2003).

Though they are the least powerful members of the health care system, patients do most of the health care work. The experience of biological symptoms does not automatically trigger a visit to the doctor, and up to one-third of the population will ignore symptoms, self-medicate, or consult friends and family about the meaning of the experience. This consultation, called the lay referral system, highlights the powerful role that folk health knowledge still plays even in modern societies. We could say that medicine deals with disease, whereas individuals construct the meanings their symptoms have for them.

It is this lay culture that organizes the ways in which individuals perceive their symptoms, and whether or not they will approach medical professionals.

USING THEORY TO UNDERSTAND HEALTH: THE VIEWS FROM THE FUNCTIONALIST, CONFLICT, AND SYMBOLIC INTERACTIONIST PERSPECTIVES

13.4 Apply the functionalist, conflict, and symbolic interactionist perspectives to the concept of health.

We've seen that health is not merely an individual and biological function. It is significantly mediated by social factors such as race, sex, socioeconomic status, and the various influences of stakeholders. In this section we consider three of the major theoretical frameworks through which sociologists perceive issues of health and illness. We will also examine the policy implications we can derive from considering health and illness through each of these theoretical lenses.

Functionalism

The structural functionalist perspective sees society as a harmonious, balanced set of interacting institutions, like a living organism with interrelated parts. Each institution (structure) serves a particular set of social needs (functions) to ensure a stable society. For example, the religious, educational, and medical institutions of our society all interact to socialize, train, and repair individuals to ensure their smooth integration into society.

Talcott Parsons (1951), the major theorist of this position, identified a shared set of expectations between the patient and the doctor. The doctor is a highly skilled professional who applies scientific knowledge to the patient's trouble without regard to factors such as race, gender, and religion. The patient seeks out the doctor and complies with the doctor's directives so as to get better.

For Parsons, illness is not just a physiological issue; it is a deviant behavior. People adopt "the sick role" as a way of avoiding social responsibilities (Parsons 1951, 43). At the crux of Parsons's argument are the four dimensions of the sick role:

1. A sick person is excused from undertaking normal social obligations.

2. Deviant behavior through illness is viewed as being caused by nature, and thus the sick person's neglect of social obligations is not considered a personal fault or an intentional act of deviance.

3. The sick role is legitimated by the person's being socially required to seek treatment for the illness.

4. The sick person adopts an alternative role in which he or she is obliged to act in a certain manner, such as by complying with practitioners' instructions and following general social norms like resting or taking medication.

Thus Parsons argued that the sick role is a means for a person to escape arduous social responsibilities by adopting a role with different and less demanding social obligations. However, as discussed above, society no longer characterizes illness in broad terms but very often brings it home to individuals' actions and behaviors. Alan is held accountable for suffering emphysema because he chose to smoke. Julie is responsible for her poor health because she failed to eat well or exercise regularly. This shift in social conceptions of illness raises questions about whether Parsons's sick role is a valid social framework from which to consider questions of health and illness today.

Furthermore, Parsons's conception of society as a cohesive, effectively functioning set of structures is also questionable. After attaining dominance in the 20th and 21st centuries, the medical profession has recently undergone significant challenges to its authority, including technological developments, the growth of an increasingly educated public, and the rise of corporate medicine (see Table 13.3). These challenges demonstrate the transformation of medicine from what some considered to be a profession altruistically assisting those who are sick into a business model in which the sick are assisted in pursuit of profit.

So whereas medicine once undertook the responsibility for health alone, now it must share it with a wide range of other practitioners, administratively, academically, financially, and institutionally. This forced sharing has decreased the status of the medical profession and the public's trust in it. For example, the medical information available on the Internet allows patients to challenge medical diagnoses (Dent 2006) and weakens the dominance of the medical practitioner, hand in hand with the rise of the knowledgeable patient and the information revolution in health (Broom 2005). These developments have had profound effects on the doctor-patient relationship. The ability to access information (and misinformation) online can provide patients with a sense of knowledge and empowerment

 Health Reform

TABLE 13.3 Six Current Challenges to the Medical Profession

Trend	Result
Bureaucratization of medical practice	Doctors have become employees of large health care firms and have lost some of their autonomy.
Competitive threat from other health care workers	There has been a large increase in the number of allied health professionals, such as nurse practitioners and clinical psychologists, competing with the medical profession.
Globalization and the information revolution	Consumers are better informed, and via "medical tourism" patients travel to other countries for cheaper treatments.
Changing patterns of disease	Many incurable conditions are now chronic, such as type 2 diabetes. The lack of effective medical treatment has taken the shine off the "magic bullet" medicine of the mid-20th century.
Erosion of trust in the doctor-patient relationship	Patients are now much more likely to seek legal redress against their doctors.
Fragmentation of medical specialties	The once-unified medical profession is now divided into specialists and generalists with their own representative bodies.

SOURCE: Developed from McKinlay and Marceau (2002), "The End of the Golden Age of Doctoring." *International Journal of Health Services, 32*(2):379–416.

(Korp 2006), which they then bring to the medical encounter. Some studies have found that medical professionals may see better-informed patients as a challenge to their power, leading them to develop strategies to attempt to reinforce traditional patient roles (Broom 2005). Patients are affected by these changes in other ways as well. For example, the increasing fragmentation of the medical profession means that patients are now more likely to have to seek medical advice from a number of different specialists, rather than relying on a single practitioner for all their health care needs (Martin, Currie, and Finn 2009). Further, "doctor shopping" is now a more common and acceptable practice as patients seek medical practitioners who will diagnose them with the conditions they think they have.

Policy Implications of Structural Functionalism

At the heart of Parsons's structural functionalism is interpersonal trust, particularly a patient's trust in his or her doctor or health professional. Parsons argued that *value congruence,* or shared norms and values, is a key component of trust (Kehoe and Ponting 2003, 1066). Further, trust in the reliability, effectiveness, and legitimacy of "symbolic structures"—such as white coats and stethoscopes—is essential for the continuance of these structures (Parsons 1968, 155). With respect to health this means that for hospitals, primary care physicians, specialists, and nurses to function effectively, patients must trust in the ability of these structures to improve their health.

Kehoe and Ponting (2003) investigated the trust Canadians place in their health care providers, government departments, and legislative reform in the area of health. They found that Canadians are very proud of their public health care system and trust their medical and allied health workers. However, their trust in the bureaucracy is breached when hospitals are closed or there are changes to the public health system, Medicare, which "is a source of pride and part of Canadians' national identity" (1074). The researchers caution: "Given the importance of the principles of the Canada Health Act to Canadians and Canadian identity, policy makers and other stakeholders should use great caution when formulating policy that may challenge those values, if they wish to preserve trust in the present system. This might be especially true when system change is pursued for fiscal-ideological reasons" (1074). When trust in the health care system is lost, the system also loses the legitimacy that, according to structural functionalists, is critical to its operation and effectiveness.

MCT via Getty Images

According to Talcott Parsons, medical practice involves reciprocity in the doctor-patient relationship. What kind of relationship do you have with your doctor? Do you have complete confidence and trust in his or her abilities?

This analysis raises interesting questions for recent health care reforms in the United States. We might interpret the debate over the introduction of Obamacare as critically affecting U.S. citizens' trust that the government can manage the economy. However, the legislation may also reestablish those same people's trust in the legitimacy of the government as an institution that ensures minimum standards of health for all. The issue of trust in government is apparent in current U.S. political rhetoric, with President Obama constantly reiterating that the government needs to regain the trust of the people.

The policy implications from a structural functionalist perspective are paradoxical. On one hand, since those applying this framework don't critically assess medical practices, technologies, and healing processes, it would seem that to solve the social problems of the health care system we need more doctors, more hospitals, more technology, and more and better drugs. In short, structural functionalism says there is nothing wrong with the health care system that more of what we already have won't fix. On the other hand, noneconomic relationships based on trust are central to the smooth working of market economies—and these are undermined by the commodified, high-tech, corporate form U.S. medicine has developed. The structural functionalist dilemma is that it wants the social parts of society—health, housing, education—to work on market principles of competition and the laws of supply and demand at the same time that it recognizes these principles will not inspire trust.

Conflict Theory

From a conflict perspective, medicine in advanced capitalist societies is oriented toward curing disease through the application of sophisticated drugs and the use of high-cost technology. There are two major conflicts:

1. Those who suffer the most illness in modern Western societies are those who can least afford high-cost treatments and sophisticated drugs.

2. The development of costly treatments and pharmaceuticals is not the most effective way to improve health outcomes for the general population.

In the developed world today, the leading causes of mortality and of **morbidity**—the number of diagnoses of disease or other condition in a given population at a designated time, usually expressed as a rate per 100,000—are ischemic heart disease, various cancers,

Morbidity: The number of diagnoses of disease or other condition in a given population at a designated time, usually expressed as a rate per 100,000.

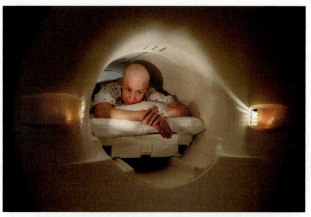

Cancer patient Deborah Charles lies inside the tube of a magnetic resonance imaging scanner during an MRI examination of her breasts at Georgetown University Hospital in Washington, D.C. Like many cancer patients, Charles spends a great deal of her time undergoing medical examinations and treatments.

mental and nervous disorders, and chronic respiratory diseases, which conflict theorists see as the result not of internally caused bodily processes but of social conditions. Further, these illnesses are not open to cure by intensive care or the use of drugs (Miniño et al. 2010). Current health standards derive less from new discoveries and technologies than from environmental health control of housing, nutrition, and water supplies prior to the 1930s. In the 1930s health standards were influenced more by factors such as sanitary water supplies, access to nutritional foods, and safe housing. The same factors are of more importance in developing countries than highly developed technological and pharmaceutical treatments.

ASK YOURSELF: Do you think environmental factors like access to clean drinking water, safe housing, and nutritious food are more important to developing countries than technological advancements, or less? Do you think the billions of dollars spent on developing pharmaceuticals and diagnostic treatments would be better spent on reducing environmental hazards, not only in developing counties but also in developed ones like the United States?

If medical and scientific advances are relatively ineffective at improving health compared to social reform, why then do society and the medical profession push forward with expensive new medical treatments, sustaining life at any cost and neglecting the social problems that cause disease and illness in the first place?

Conflict theorists explain the U.S. health care system as a central part of the capitalist economy that functions

FIGURE 13.5 **Economic Functions of the U.S. Health Care System**

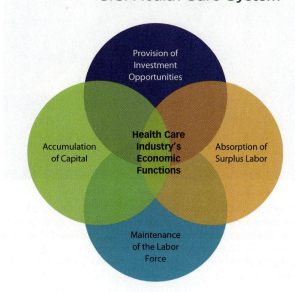

to produce profit, not to deliver health care (Waitzkin 2000). Some theorists take this further, arguing that scientific medicine equates healing with consumption. Illness and disease create a market for goods and services (namely, medicine and treatment), and therefore health care is a market. Thus satisfying the demand for health care legitimates and facilitates capitalist economic growth, despite its negative health consequences. From this perspective, the health care industry has four interrelated economic functions in capitalist society (see Figure 13.5): accumulation of capital, provision of investment opportunities, absorption of surplus labor, and maintenance of the labor force (Waitzkin 2000).

In addition, the organization of health care provides three important ideological functions (Waitzkin 2000):

1. By delivering health care, however inadequately, it legitimates the status quo, acting as an agent of social control by reducing what are basically social problems to an individual level.

2. Within its equation of hospital care and the consumption of drugs as health care, it reproduces the capitalist mode of production.

3. It reproduces the capitalist class structure both in the organization of health workers and in the consumption patterns it generates.

According to the conflict perspective, U.S. society sees health as an individual problem, to be met with individual solutions such as medication, behavioral change, and technology-based therapies. This way of looking at health and illness serves the interests of powerful groups within society, such as pharmaceutical corporations (which sell medication) and employers (for which seeing health as individual denies the role of workplace structure in causing illness). The conflict perspective highlights the role of wider social structure in causing illness; it is not the individual who is ill but the structure of society that causes illness and frames healing.

Policy Implications of the Conflict Perspective

From a conflict theory perspective, the contemporary capitalist organization of health care systematically neglects the environmental, occupational, and social production of health and disease. Hence the source of sickness and disease is the capitalist economic system itself, and only with its transformation will health be transformed. While major corporations dominate the health care system, investors seek ever-higher returns on their capital, and pharmaceutical companies seek to maximize their profits, change will not occur. The United States will continue to have the world's most expensive health care system, the most unequal access to health care, and some of the poorest health outcomes in the developed world. While conflict theorists will see President Obama's health care reforms as not going far enough, for the first time since World War II there may be a strong enough political reaction to the excesses of health care costs for a real difference to be made.

For more moderate conflict theorists, it is clear that capitalism will not be displaced any time in the near future. While Marx argued that capitalism would eventually self-destruct as worsening working conditions and wages left the working class unable to buy the products and services the ruling class was selling, he did not foresee that workers would unite to demand better treatment through unions. Although unions have been in decline for some years, Western capitalists have seen that it is far cheaper to provide safe working environments than to lose productivity and pay compensation when employees are injured and cannot work.

Symbolic Interactionism

The key to the symbolic interactionist perspective is that people construct meaning from situations and objects. As W. I. Thomas put it, "If men define situations as real, they are real in their consequences" (Thomas and Thomas 1928, 570). Thus human beings are not stimulus-response mechanisms: the way we define a situation defines the way we will act in it. What bearing does this perspective have on the way we understand health?

The Western model of health predicts that drugs should have a straightforward biochemical effect and cure the conditions at which they are targeted. Further, they should work the same way for everyone. However, sociologists have shown that this is not the case (Moerman and Jonas 2002). When a new drug is tested, the experimental group is given the drug, a control group is given a placebo (a sugar pill that is chemically inert), and a third group is given nothing. A double-blind trial is conducted in which neither the patients nor the doctors know who is getting which substance. In a study of the placebo effect in Parkinson's disease patients, the placebo was found to have a very powerful positive effect on patients' symptoms (de la Fuente-Fernández et al. 2001). This placebo effect cannot be explained by Western medicine, which separates the mind from the body (Moerman and Jonas 2002). For sociologists, however, such findings provide evidence that the way we define a situation affects what happens. In other words, if you think you've received a drug, your body will respond as if you had received it.

Policy Implications of Symbolic Interactionism

Despite its focus on the individual, symbolic interactionism can help us look at policy issues and the ways they are framed. For instance, the placebo effect seems particularly profound for people being treated with antidepressants. Most commentators now agree that the difference between an antidepressant drug and a placebo is insignificant, and 57% of trials funded by pharmaceutical companies have failed to demonstrate that antidepressant drugs had an impact, a finding that came to light only when Kirsch, Scoboria, and Moore (2002) gained access to U.S. Food and Drug Administration documents. They refer to these data as a "dirty little secret"—well-known within the pharmaceutical industry but not to the general public, doctors, or their patients.

Kirsch (2009) went on to analyze 38 published clinical trials that enrolled more than 3,000 depressed patients. He found that 75% of the antidepressant effect of drugs was also produced by placebos. "Placebos instill hope in patients by promising them relief from their distress," Kirsch wrote in his book *The Emperor's New Drugs*. "Genuine medical treatments also instill hope, and this is the placebo component of their effectiveness" (3). The clear policy implication is that a very large number of prescriptions for costly antidepressants are not needed and that costs to consumers could be significantly reduced.

SPECIALIZED THEORIES

 13.5 Apply specialized theories of health.

Social drift hypothesis: The argument that the sick, depressed, and stressed, through natural selection, move down the social system and accumulate at the bottom.

Social Drift Hypothesis

The **social drift hypothesis** suggests that the sick, depressed, and stressed move down the social system and accumulate at the bottom. Individual choices must therefore be taken into account in an explanation of how those at the bottom of the social system got there (Thoits 1995, 59). This seems to mean that individuals can be uniquely unlucky in their behaviors, and that this leads to their downward social mobility. However, from a more critical perspective, as this chapter has argued, we should see individual choices as socially patterned and recognize that social patterns do not result in drifting. Rather, they act as an undertow that systematically drags whole groups and sections of society under. A person's health is then the product of a lifetime's experience of social events. And when the impact of one set of health disadvantages sets off a descending spiral of other health disadvantages, lower social groups are not drifting—they are drowning (Pearlin et al. 2005).

Bourdieu and Physical, Social, and Cultural Capital

Pierre Bourdieu (1984) developed an innovative theory of the relationship of the body to class position in society. He saw health as socially patterned and reflected in the individual's body. Health is then a source of capital we can use to gain valued social goods—jobs, education, and social status. Bourdieu's position thus complements Marx's belief that social class as determined by the economy is central to modern societies, but he also argued that other forms of capital exist, which he labeled *cultural, social,* and *symbolic.* Possessing these forms of capital allows an individual to position him- or herself in society.

The healthy body, Bourdieu thus argued, represents a form of physical as well as symbolic capital. The well-maintained, the fit, and the not-overweight body represents claims to being a good member of society and in good social standing. Bourdieu argued that the body is inscribed with social and cultural relationships—that is, it is socially produced and not just a fact of nature. As we internalize our positions in the social hierarchy of society, so too do we learn the appropriate ways of dressing our bodies and presenting them, ways of standing and sitting and even of walking. This set of learned practices, which Bourdieu (1990) called "habitus," is culturally provided and becomes a stable way of enacting ourselves in the social world. Our bodies then form our physical capital, alongside our economic, social, and cultural capital, and "the way people treat their bodies reveals the deepest dispositions of their habitus" (Bourdieu 1984, 190).

Reuters / Phil Noble

A family eats lunch on a bench outside a fish and chips shop in Towyn, Wales. In the United States, many lower-class communities have been described as "food deserts," where affordable healthy food is not available. Many of these communities have convenience stores and fast-food restaurants that offer only high-fat, high-salt, and high-sugar products. Constant consumption of such nutrient-poor foods can lead to heart disease, obesity, and diabetes.

One good way of illustrating Bourdieu's argument is to look at patterns of eating in different classes in our society. Affluent individuals in Western societies are likely to enjoy higher-quality diets, whereas individuals of lower socioeconomic status consume high-sugar and high-fat diets that are nutrient-poor (Darmon and Drewnowski 2008). This leads to a downward social distribution of obesity, with obesity and low social class position going together. Using a Bourdieuian approach, seeing the body as socially produced and a cultural marker of social standing, Calnan and Cant (1990) have shown that food consumption is an underlying factor in this distribution of obesity. Middle-class women in their study emphasized a "balanced diet" and "everything in moderation," whereas working-class women emphasized that a meal should be "substantial" and "filling," though not necessarily nutrient-rich. So while we may think of obesity as linked to individual diet, Calnan and Cant's work demonstrates that it is the outcome of class-specific ways of relating to food. Let us look at this insight a bit further.

The interplay of physical, social, cultural, and economic capital is well illustrated in childhood obesity.

Among lower-class children, the tendency to obesity is facilitated by environments that reinforce unhealthy eating and low physical activity and that are served by fast-food outlets, poorly maintained recreational facilities, and inadequate information about diet (Cohen, Doyle, and Baum 2006). The immediate consequences include respiratory disorders, type 2 diabetes, depression, and social exclusion (Storch et al. 2007). In adulthood these individuals are then at greater risk of obesity (Freedman et al. 2005), diabetes, and cancer (Ogden et al. 2010). Thus the working-class habitus and its resulting body creates a circular effect of increasing disease in childhood leading into adulthood, thus producing the first generation in modern times to die at younger ages than their parents of preventable diseases caused by social inequalities and their impact on health.

Social Capital Theory

Émile Durkheim argued in his book *The Division of Labor in Society,* originally published in 1893, that social harmony would come about in industrial society through the formation of communities based on shared occupational interests, producing a new moral individual whose actions would be guided by a concern for the common good. Contemporary social capital theorists argue that increased concentration of population and improved communication will revitalize the idea of the common good and alleviate social conflict. In communities where there is strong social capital—neighborhood organizations, social clubs, strong sports groups, and a sense of belonging—there are also better health rates (Poortinga 2006). When communities do not generate social capital, theorists see this failure as the fault of community dysfunction.

What their approach overlooks is that economic resources and political rights are also necessary parts of a strong sense of community. Arguing that those at lower socioeconomic levels suffer poor health because they do not generate social capital suggests they are responsible for their own shortcomings and should solve them on their own. The social capital approach thus appeals to conservative, post–welfare state governments, which see it as a way of shifting responsibility for what used to be state-provided services to the local level.

13.6 Identify steps toward social change to promote health.

If most of what affects our health is a product of our social environment, it follows that changing our health means changing our social environment. Here are some ways in which you can participate in that process, starting right now.

A woman meditates at sunset on Venice Beach in California. During National Women's Health Week, women are encouraged to visit health care professionals, get active, eat healthy, pay attention to their mental health, avoid smoking, wear seat belts or bicycle helmets, and generally take care of themselves.

- *Change the menu.* Lobby for a better diet at your workplace or campus. Ask for and eat unprocessed foods—such as fresh fruits and vegetables, brown rice, and whole-grain breads—and low-fat, low-sugar, low-sodium options. Pass up sugary soft drinks in favor of water (avoid bottled water, however, because of its high environmental cost). More information about good nutrition is available at the U.S. Department of Agriculture's ChooseMyPlate website (http://www.choosemyplate.gov).

- *Find a green space.* How much open space is available to you for sports and exercise? Look for (or lobby for) accessible green space that allows activities at lunchtime and between classes, such as ball play or running. If there is no bike trail in your area, see whether you can get one designated. Many campuses now have gyms and fitness programs. See whether you can help publicize yours and increase their use. For useful information, see the Rails-to-Trails Conservancy's TrailLink website (http://www.traillink.com).

- *Reduce the number of smokers.* Start a self-help group to support people who want to quit smoking. You don't have to be a smoker to help others kick the habit. Help ensure that no-smoking rules on campus are honored. Find resources at the National Cancer Institute's Smokefree website (http://www.smokefree.gov).

- *Support responsible drinking.* Work through your student association to introduce a responsible alcohol policy and promote the use of designated drivers at social events.

- *Promote occupational health and safety.* Young workers represent about 13% of the U.S. workforce and have relatively high rates of occupational injury. Visit the National Institute for Occupational Safety and Health's website (http://www.cdc.gov/niosh) and investigate your rights at work. Know the hazards and dangers present in your workplace, educate your peers, and ensure that you and your workplace are operating in a health- and safety-conscious manner.

- *Celebrate National Women's Health Week.* National Women's Health Week is a weeklong health observance in early May, coordinated each year by the U.S. Department of Health and Human Services' Office on Women's Health. It brings together communities, businesses, government, health organizations, and other groups in an effort to promote women's health and its importance. It also empowers women to make their health a priority and encourages them to take five simple steps to improve their physical and mental health and lower their risks of certain diseases: get active, eat healthy, pay attention to mental health, avoid unhealthy behaviors like smoking, and have regular Pap smears and mammograms. For more information, see the Office of Women's Health website (http://www.aids.gov/federal-resources/federal-agencies/hhs/office-of-the-assistant-secretary-for-health/office-on-womens-health).

Reuters / Lucy Nicholson

WHAT DOES AMERICA THINK?

Questions about Health from the General Social Survey

 Turn to the beginning of the chapter to compare your answers to the total population.

1. Do you think that the government should help pay for medical care?

   YES: 69%

   NO: 31%

2. In the United States, do you think we're spending too much money on improving and protecting the nation's health, too little money, or about the right amount?

   TOO MUCH: 11.4%

   TOO LITTLE: 61.8%

   ABOUT THE RIGHT AMOUNT: 26.8%

3. What is your confidence level in medicine?

   A GREAT DEAL: 38.9%

   ONLY SOME: 50.1%

   HARDLY ANY: 11%

4. What is your interest level in medical discoveries?

   VERY INTERESTED: 60.3%

   MODERATELY INTERESTED: 34.8%

   NOT AT ALL INTERESTED: 4.9%

5. Do you think that incurable patients should be allowed to die?

   YES: 67.8%

   NO: 32.2%

6. Do you think a person has the right to end his or her own life if this person has an incurable disease?

   YES: 59%

   NO: 41%

LOOK BEHIND THE NUMBERS

Go to **edge.sagepub.com/trevino** for a breakdown of these data across time and by race, sex, age, income, and other statuses.

1. Examine the data on age for the responses to the question about interest in medical discoveries. Is there a pattern? Explain. What implications does this have on society?

2. With regard to government helping pay for medical care, which race showed the highest rate of support for government assistance? Which showed the lowest? Why do you think that is?

3. With the recently enacted requirement that all Americans have medical insurance, what changes do you expect to see in health care? Will requiring people to have medical coverage eliminate disparities in health? Explain.

4. Examine responses to the question about confidence in medicine in the General Social Survey from 1973 to the present. How has confidence in medicine changed over time? Do you think this trend will continue? Why?

SOURCE: National Opinion Research Center, University of Chicago.

CHAPTER SUMMARY

 13.1 Describe health as socially defined.

Illness and disease are social constructed notions. Medicine is pervasive in society and acts as a form of social control in our lives. Much social behavior, including hoarding and skin pricking, has been medicalized. Sociologists look to social factors to explain illness and disease.

 13.2 Discuss patterns and trends in health, illness, and treatment.

Lifestyle choices that cause disease are influenced by demographic and economic factors. The extent of social inequality determines the distribution of health and illness. Who gets sick, when we die, and what we die of are closely linked to wider patterns of inequalities of wealth and income. The social problem of women's health is not that women are unhealthy or diseased, but that they are managed in a certain way by the medical system and, in particular, by doctors. Men's health is threatened by engagement in risky activities and unsafe work conditions. Class and ethnicity also interact in matters of health.

 13.3 Describe the health care system and its stakeholders.

Unlike the United Kingdom, Australia, and New Zealand, where health care has traditionally been provided by the government, the United States has a health care system that has been dominated by the private sector. The medical-industrial complex is a large and growing network of private corporations that provide health care services to patients for profit. Pharmaceutical companies are for-profit enterprises and rely heavily on advertising prescription drugs directly to consumers. Practitioners of alternative medicine and patient groups provide health care services outside traditional medicine.

 13.4 Apply the functionalist, conflict, and symbolic interactionist perspectives to the concept of health.

In order for hospitals, primary care physicians, specialists, and nurses to deliver health care effectively, patients must have trust in their ability. Conflict theorists see the U.S. health care system, particularly the pharmaceutical industry, as having as its main goal not the delivery of health care but the generation of profit. According to the symbolic interactionist perspective, the meanings that patients give to particular drugs will largely determine the drugs' effects on them.

 13.5 Apply specialized theories of health.

The social drift hypothesis suggests that the mentally ill, through particular behaviors they engage in, are apt to experience downward social mobility. According to Bourdieu's notion of physical capital, maintaining a healthy body is symbolic of good social standing. Communities high in social capital have higher rates of health among their populations.

 13.6 Identify steps toward social change to promote health.

Take action to ensure a healthy diet in your workplace and community. Lobby for accessible green spaces in your community that allow for exercise and other forms of physical activity. Be informed about the hazards and dangers present in your workplace.

DISCUSSION QUESTIONS

1. How is illness or disease a result of social processes and not simply individual choices or biology? What does it mean that we live in a medicalized society? How does medicalizing natural processes, such as menopause, affect society?

2. How do patterns of health and illness differ between women and men? Between racial groups? Between age groups? Between social classes? What variables best explain these different patterns?

3. Who are the stakeholders in health care in the United States? Which of these are the most influential in determining health policies? What distinguishes the U.S. health care system from the systems in other industrialized nations? Do these differences constitute a social problem?

4. How do corporate ownership and for-profit status affect the delivery of health care in the United States? What problems does this model of health care delivery solve or improve?

5. According to the symbolic interactionist perspective, how does the labeling of certain kinds of health care as "alternative" affect the regulation, acceptance, and use of such therapies? What does it mean for our health care system if placebos are as effective, or nearly as effective, as some prescription drugs?

6. When you have been sick have you adopted the sick role as described by Parsons? Which groups of individuals are able, or not able, to embody this social role when sick—by gender, by race, by social class? What changes in society have undermined the model of the sick role Parsons presented?

7. Relying on the social drift hypothesis, what do the patterns of health and illness we see by race, gender, and social class mean for already disadvantaged groups? How could these patterns be disrupted or more evenly distributed throughout the population? Who is responsible for improving these patterns?

8. How does Bourdieu's theory of the healthy body as symbolic capital connect with society's images of the ideal bodies for women and men seen in media and advertising? In what ways is one's body a sign or symbol of one's social class?

9. What does our society, especially in messages conveyed through the mass media and advertising, encourage us to do to improve our health? How would a sociological approach to improving health differ from these suggestions?

10. What foods are available for purchase on your campus? Are they healthy choices? What about space for exercise—where does that exist on your campus? What is done on your campus to encourage students, faculty, and staff to make healthy choices with diet and exercise? What could be done to encourage healthier patterns for all members of your campus community?

KEY TERMS

laparoscopic surgery 348

morbidity 357

nonpsychotic psychological disturbance 346

social control 339

social drift hypothesis 359

social gradient of health 344

status groups 344

Sharpen your skills with SAGE edge at edge.sagepub.com/trevino

A personalized approach to help you accomplish your coursework goals in an easy-to-use learning environment.

14 THE ENVIRONMENT

Michael M. Bell and Katharine A. Legun

Frans Lanting / National Geographic Society

A mural featuring a sperm whale decorates a wall in a restaurant in Kaikoura, New Zealand. Sperm whales, like many other species of whales, are considered endangered due to overhunting and pollution. How is the potential extinction of different species of whales, dolphins, and porpoises an environmental problem? How is it a social problem?

Investigating the Environment: Our Stories

14.1 Explain how environmental problems are social problems.

14.2 Discuss patterns and trends in environmental issues.

14.3 Apply the functionalist, conflict, and symbolic interactionist perspectives to environmental problems and policy.

14.4 Apply specialized theories to the environment.

14.5 Identify steps toward social change concerning the environment.

Michael M. Bell

When I was 19 years old, I found myself looking over a lake high in the Talamanca Mountains of Costa Rica, accompanied by two men who had impressed me deeply: Emanuel, a sugarcane worker, and Frederico, a Cabécar Indian.

I was taking a semester off my undergraduate geology studies to work for a copper company looking to open a mine in these remote mountains, now a U.N. Biosphere Reserve and reserve for native peoples like the Cabécar. The company had hired Emanuel and Frederico to help me collect samples for lab analysis. I didn't realize it then, but I was a tool of economic, social, and ecological imperialism. And the company had conscripted my two companions in their own exploitation.

Frederico, who knew the lake well, quietly said, "There is a song for this place." He began to sing a slow, hymnlike melody in Cabécar. I didn't understand the words, and Frederico didn't try to translate them. He didn't have to. I understood its more fundamental meaning: there is a song for this whole place, this whole Earth and its inhabitants.

When I got back to school, I realized I had to try to learn that big song. I switched to environmental studies and then got a joint Ph.D. in sociology and environmental studies. I also took up an active second life as a composer and musician of grassroots and classical music. I know a bit of the big song now, I think. But I've got so, so much more to learn.

Katharine A. Legun

I was born in a resource town in Northern Canada, where my family lived in a house in the woods beside a large lake. I remember running through the woods with my brother, emerging hours later in some neighbor's backyard. I remember walking out onto the frozen lake in the winter while my mother and her friends would fly kites. At dinnertime, I would overhear conversations about too many trees being cleared on the neighbor's land, oil discovered in the forest, or too many sheep being taken by bears from our friend's farm.

We moved to the city. We still shared green spaces with neighbors, talked about the removal or placement of trees, and watched the salmon runs at the provincial park. Years later, when I took a course on the sociology of natural resources as an undergraduate, conversations about access to environmental goods and community development resonated heavily. Who would I be had my access been different?

As I learned more about changes to the environment and the governance of these resources, my interests only expanded. Whenever I move, the landscape changes, but the question in my mind stays the same: How do we make sure that access to resources is fair and fosters good relationships, while also making sure that those resources are healthy for future generations? I don't think I will ever have a good answer, but I'm amazed at the vibrant, heartfelt conversations that follow when I ask the question.

1. What is your interest level in environmental issues?

   ☐ *VERY INTERESTED*

   ☐ *MODERATELY INTERESTED*

   ☐ *NOT AT ALL INTERESTED*

2. In the United States, do you think we're spending too much money on the environment, too little money, or about the right amount?

   ☐ *TOO MUCH*

   ☐ *TOO LITTLE*

   ☐ *ABOUT THE RIGHT AMOUNT*

3. In the United States, do you think we're spending too much money on improving and protecting the environment, too little money, or about the right amount?

   ☐ *TOO MUCH*

   ☐ *TOO LITTLE*

   ☐ *ABOUT THE RIGHT AMOUNT*

4. What is your interest level in farm issues?

   ☐ *VERY INTERESTED*

   ☐ *MODERATELY INTERESTED*

   ☐ *NOT AT ALL INTERESTED*

▶▶ Turn to the end of the chapter to view the results for the total population.

SOURCE: National Opinion Research Center, University of Chicago.

EXPERIENCING THE HEAT WAVE

Gerald lived in South Chicago. He had retired from his job 5 years ago and spent much of his day in his apartment. He often went for a walk to the corner store in the morning to pick up groceries or cat food, or just to chat with Frank, who had operated the store for almost 20 years. Gerald rarely spoke to his children, except for his daughter, Janelle, who occasionally took him to the pharmacy to pick up his medication.

It had been an unusually hot July that summer of 1995. Gerald couldn't make it to the store—he could barely muster the energy to get to the fridge or pour himself a glass of water. His air conditioner had broken years ago, and he couldn't justify purchasing a new one. After falling into a deep sleep, Gerald woke up in a hospital bed, surrounded by other people who had collapsed from heat exhaustion as he had. Luckily, Frank had sent his son to check on Gerald, who found him unconscious in his favorite blue armchair.

What factors caused Gerald to experience life-threatening heat exhaustion? Is a heat wave like the one in Chicago in 1995 an environmental problem? Or is it a social problem? What social arrangements and activities precipitated the high heat-related death toll in Chicago that year? Is Gerald's experience an example of environmental inequality?

Gerald's story exemplifies the social complexity of environmental problems. We could argue that an increase in heat waves is an example of human-induced climate change and identify a broad range of possible culprits, from excessive traveling to overproduction and overconsumption. Yet Gerald also experienced the heat wave differently from others. The elderly, particularly those who take medications and live alone, are the most likely to die from heat exhaustion. Those who don't have air conditioners or access to cool spaces like movie theaters and shopping malls are also at increased risk. For some, heat waves are not such a big deal, while for others they are monumental. So how do we identify and define environmental problems when their earthly manifestations are so diverse? As we will discuss in this chapter, while many environmental problems have clearly observable effects, the perceptions of those effects and the solutions they inspire vary across populations. At times, they vary so significantly that they create conflicts between groups and spark social movements. In this sense, environmental problems are always, in part, social problems.

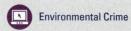

Environmental Crime

ENVIRONMENTAL PROBLEMS AS SOCIAL PROBLEMS

 14.1 Explain how environmental problems are social problems.

We often think of environmental phenomena as objectively observable within the realm of hard sciences. For example, we can identify a heat wave as the presence of unusually high temperatures several days in a row. In Chicago in 1995, for three consecutive days the heat index was around 120 degrees. Similarly, we measure pollution by sampling the air or water and determining the quantities of toxic particles it contains. We quantify biodiversity by counting the number of species in a given area. We can measure deforestation and resource depletion. The point is, these are ways to identify environmental problems and translate them into real, hard data that can clearly define the ecological dimensions of the problem (for example, see Figure 14.1). Yet how do we know these data represent environmental problems rather than just normal patterns in the natural world?

After all, the average high temperature in Las Vegas in July is around 106 degrees, but we wouldn't say that Las Vegas experiences a monthlong heat wave. Not all logging is considered an environmental problem, and many of the toxins in a test tube of tap water are naturally occurring. There is nothing necessarily bad about heat, fewer trees, or foreign substances in new landscapes or natural materials, but of course we don't talk about the environment with such neutrality. Instead, we talk about

heat waves, deforestation, and pollution. We also talk about climate change, desertification, and environmental collapse. These concepts encompass not simply events happening in the natural world but also the relationships people have with the environment and its characteristics. These relationships are all informed by our social lives.

In fact, our view of what constitutes an environmental problem has as much to do with effects on people as with events and processes in nature. Those effects are always experienced socially. They depend on how we have organized our lives and the types of information we have received from various social sources. For example, the Chicago heat wave led to high levels of illness and death. Without that human experience, those hot days would be less troubling. We commonly think of an environmental issue that is a threat to humans as an environmental problem. The *unsustainability* of a situation or process is another marker of problems in resource use and pollution. That is, if human activities are depleting or degrading resources faster than they can be renewed, the long-term effects are economic, social, and cultural stresses tied to the scarcity of those resources. While it seems the environment is nonsocial because it exists and functions without people, in practice, the only environment we know is one we can see and experience, and when those sights and experiences are unpleasant, the state of the environment becomes a problem.

We could say that an environmental problem is an ecological phenomenon that has an effect people do not want. That seems pretty straightforward, so what does a sociological perspective add? Throughout this chapter, we will discuss the ways in which the creation, identification, and experience of environmental problems are all social. They relate to our beliefs about the environment and how it influences the practices of everyday life. Even health impacts are sometimes social phenomena. For example, during the Chicago heat wave, children became ill as their school buses got mired in traffic. Two children died as a result of being stuck in a car after a trip to the movies. Using buses to get to school and driving to the movies on a hot day are social practices that influence the experience of a heat wave (Klinenberg 2002).

In short, environmental problems are *social* problems. Your experience of them is tied to where you are, who you are, and what you do. As a university student on campus, you will experience a heat wave as moderated by a cooling system. If you are a gardener, the climate index and the number of growing degree-days in a year determine what you can plant. If you are a fruit farmer, a heat wave in February can mean premature blooming and vulnerability to frost for your crop. If you are an elder whose life can be threatened by summer's extreme heat, an early heat wave may be cause for alarm.

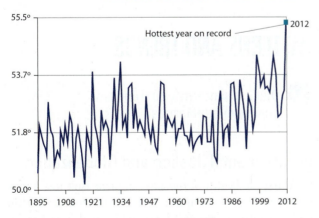

FIGURE 14.1 **Average Annual Temperature in Contiguous United States, 1895–2012**

SOURCE: Climate Central, compiled from NOAA's National Climate Data Center and Applied Climate Information System.

Air Pollution Conflict

The way you *interpret* the heat wave also has a lot to do with the social world around you. If you are engaged in conversations about climate change, you may link your daily experiences to what you know about global climate patterns. If you are majoring in plant biology, perhaps you look immediately for signs of an early spring: the grass is becoming greener sooner; daffodils are emerging from the soil too early. (One of the authors went to a grade school where the students counted the crocus and snowdrop flowers every spring. How jarring would it be to count the spring flowers in January or February instead of April?)

Experience and interpretation are not independent of each other. What you experience and the way you experience it influence the way you interpret it. Likewise, what you know can affect the way you feel. When the environment poses a threat, it can also threaten people's identities, making the experience and management of environmental problems more difficult. What some people experience as a problem may be unnoticeable or unimportant for others because their lives are organized differently. Environmental problems, for this reason, can be highly contested and difficult to resolve. We'll take up the relationship between experiences and ideas later in the chapter, but for now, the important point is that *environmental problems are also social problems*, and they have a variety of social causes and effects.

The causes of environmental problems are also social. We extract too many resources, produce too much stuff, and throw too much stuff away. We use hazardous extraction and production methods and generate toxic materials that we release into the environment. Why do we

do these things? Environmental sociologists would suggest that our society encourages us to. We economically reward industrial activities that are environmentally harmful, like cheaply producing oil or cutting down trees. Our society says it's normal to live far away from work and commute long distances in personal vehicles. We gain social status by purchasing the latest computer models and throwing the old ones away. In short, we benefit from behaving badly. We do not all benefit, however, and some of us suffer from the environmental ills of our modern lives. Some groups of people, often those already marginalized by society, are disproportionately affected by environmental problems. Much of this chapter will focus on how environmental problems are invariably related to social inequality.

It is no wonder that social organization is a focal point for social scientists interested in environmental problems. Social organization, or social structure, is the way people are divided into groups and categories and placed in a social hierarchy. This hierarchy influences people's access to economic, cultural, social, and political resources. Some scholars talk about the outcome of this hierarchy as *social inequality*, and some talk about *social stratification*, but these mean basically the same thing. These forces sometimes differentiate people based on race, ethnicity, gender, or social class. When we think about the environment specifically, these characteristics are also influential and have environment-specific implications. In particular, social organization influences *environmental rights*. These could be rights to clean air, water, and food; the right to practice a livelihood like farming or fishing; or the right to maintain traditional landscapes that play a role in people's cultural practices. In the section below we discuss environmental rights, paying attention to inequalities based on class and race. We also show why a global perspective increasingly matters in any conversation about environmental problems and environmental inequalities.

PATTERNS AND TRENDS

 14.2 Discuss patterns and trends in environmental issues.

Environmental Justice and Globalization

Ensuring the health of our environment isn't just about easing ecological disruption or threats to human health. It also requires us to consider social inequality and social equity. While we often think of social inequality as just

Reuters / Peter Andrews

Smoke billows from the chimneys of the Belchatow Power Station in Poland. The coal-fired power plant is the largest in the European Union and one of its biggest polluters. The plant released nearly 39 million tons of carbon dioxide into the atmosphere in 2011, defying EU efforts to curb emissions linked to climate change.

 Environment Faltering

Vincent van Gogh's *The Potato Eaters,* 1885 (left), and Jean Beraud's *Dinner at Les Ambassadeurs,* 1880. These two paintings present a contrast between Dutch peasants eating potatoes grown by their own manual labor and the rich enjoying themselves at the Parisian restaurant. How can you interpret these two paintings in terms of environmental justice?

the space between the rich and the poor, this description doesn't get at the unfairness or inequity of that difference. **Social equity**, on the other hand, refers to equality and takes into account the different contexts that shape opportunities, needs, and resources.

Equality can actually be quite unfair, because by applying the same rules to different people, or giving everyone the same resources, we ignore the differences that already exist in their lives. In his book *The Red Lily* (1894), the French poet Anatole France writes about the efforts the lower classes must exert to keep a prosperous country prosperous, while the benefits of living in a prosperous country, while they may be applied equally, are unfair:

> The poor must work for [the comfort of the wealthy], in presence of the majestic quality of the law which prohibits the wealthy as well as the poor from sleeping under the bridges, from begging in the streets, and from stealing bread.

This passage follows a long description of the oppression of peasants, who were being removed from their farmlands to go to war and defend France, returning landless and in the service of the wealthy population who had remained in the protected state. In the text quoted above, France is emphasizing the irony of applying the same law to the rich and the poor when clearly the poor—and not the wealthy—are compelled to seek shelter under bridges, beg in the streets, and

Social equity: Closely related to the concept of social equality, social equity stresses fairness and justice.

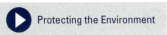 Protecting the Environment

steal their food. Moreover, the impoverishment of the poor generated the wealth and security of the rich. In such a context, equality in the law is highly inequitable.

A critical question to ask when we consider climate change, waste management, deforestation, and nuclear radiation is who benefits from the processes that create environmental problems like these, and who suffers. Often, when we are talking about social equity, we talk about justice, because it implies a broader commitment to equity and an effort to produce that equity. Justice is equity being enacted. In the context of the environment, we often talk explicitly about environmental justice. This means making sure people aren't being exploited for the benefit of others and that access to environmental resources is fair. John Rawls, in *A Theory of Justice* (1971), suggested we try to imagine what sorts of principles we would come up with for a just society if we were ignorant of where we would end up on the resulting social spectrum. Rawls believed we would arrive at two principles:

1. Each person is to have an equal right to the most extensive basic liberty compatible with a similar liberty for others.

2. Social and economic liberties are to be arranged so they are both (a) reasonably expected to be to everyone's advantage and (b) attached to positions and offices open to all.

In other words, if we were committed to a just society, we would want the best for *everyone,* not just the majority of people or the people who seem most worthy. It will always be unjust to sacrifice the well-being of some

People hold signs at the launch of Californians Against Fracking outside the downtown Los Angeles offices of California governor Jerry Brown. Californians Against Fracking is a coalition of environmental, consumer, business, health, agricultural, labor, political, and environmental justice organizations working to win a statewide ban on hydraulic fracturing, or fracking, a process in which pressurized water is used to release natural gas from deep rock formations.

for the benefit of others, or to limit the rights of some to expand the rights of others. Access to fish or timber or fertile farmland, and the right to sell the produce, is an economically important, environmentally based right. Equally vital is the right to clean air and water and the space to engage in local economic activities without a risk to health. We can also apply the standard of environmental justice to cultural rights, and to the significance of places and landscapes in the lives of community members.

Inequality can be fair only when it benefits everyone—for example, the inequality of allowing only people who are trained and certified to serve as doctors. But how do we know whether something benefits everyone? Who gets to decide? Environmental justice requires that everyone be able to participate fairly in decisions about the environment regardless of race, class, gender, or nationality, that no one coerce or force another to make an agreement, and that all stakeholders—the people who are affected by the decisions—are able to participate in the negotiation process.

The loss of environmental rights is not always unjust. If members of a minority group disproportionately lose access to a resource or are the only ones barred from disposing of waste at a waterway, the result is unjust. But some people may lose the right to use a resource because it is being overused, or because they are polluting it.

Environmental justice is increasingly complicated in the age of globalization. For example, some countries choose to have few or no environmental regulations as a strategy for attracting the subsidiary operations of wealthy transnational corporations. Because these subsidiaries are unregulated and foreign-owned, local populations suffering the environmental hazards and degradation they may create have little recourse. One outcome of this relocation of environmentally damaging production to poorer countries is the new international division of labor (Cohen 1981; Marin 2006): manufacturing jobs move to underdeveloped countries, while white-collar jobs stay in the industrialized countries.

Globalization is also transforming us culturally. As goods and industries move across national borders, cultural values transfer with them. Sociologist George Ritzer (1998) calls the resulting homogenization **McDonaldization**. He points out that the practices perfected by the McDonald's Corporation—efficiency, calculability, predictability/standardization, control, and the general culture of fast food—influence the places to which they move. Thus, Ritzer notes, human behavior is also expected to fit a rationalized model of productive activity, a model that Max Weber, writing at the beginning of the 20th century, described as a foundational element of Western European and U.S. culture (Weber 2004). Some scholars argue that the economic might of developed, industrialized countries leads to unequal trade relations and a form of economic colonialism. For example, Susan Silbey (1997) suggests that we should explicitly recognize the role of power in international trade and replace the term *globalization* with *postmodern colonialism*.

We need to be careful not to oversimplify how McDonaldization works, however. Let's use McDonald's itself as an example. The restaurants' menus are adjusted to cater to local tastes, and the company often sources locally. Just as all businesses and industries change to some extent when planted in new national ground, not all McDonald's outlets are the same. Rather than a blanket cultural transformation of local communities, the result is new places—not exactly like the culture being introduced and not exactly like the culture that came before, but what French environmental sociologist Bruno Latour calls a **hybrid**. Some scholars call this hybridization process "glocalization." It's okay for local cultures to change, they suggest; after all, even local communities are regulated by states that may have interests and values very different from their own.

Why do globalization and hybridization matter to our discussion of the environment? Because we want to know, for instance, how farms change once they are participating in more globalized markets. Are they more intensively farmed? Or are they able to reach niche markets with their regionally specialized products? What happens in forest landscapes where loggers are participating in international lumber trade? Our point here is not that globalization is without problems. Instead, it is that problems with globalization are embedded in *places*. Places surely vary in their ability to negotiate the terms of international economic participation, but they are not without power.

McDonaldization: The homogenization and rationalization that occur as culture and cultural privileges spread globally through economic expansion.

Hybrid: An entity that emerges from the combination of other entities but differs from the sum of its parts.

In the following sections, we discuss climate change, waste, and radiation to illustrate some of the issues around inequality and globalization. They are only a few among many environmental problems, and we hope you will consider the approaches discussed in this chapter when your expand your critical scope to other issues.

ASK YOURSELF: What might prevent a society from becoming just? What are some examples of environmental injustice that you have witnessed in your community? What injustices do you find particularly problematic? What do you think shapes local experiences of globalization? How do you think globalization shapes local environments?

Climate Change

Claims about the existence of climate change often rely on data provided by the U.S. Environmental Protection Agency, the Intergovernmental Panel on Climate Change, and the Goddard Institute for Space Studies. These data indicate that the warmest years around the globe have all occurred since 1998, and each decade has been a little balmier than the one before. Yet there are still cold winters and regions that seem to have gotten *colder* over the past century, indicating that the effects of the warming of Earth's atmosphere on climate are uneven and difficult to predict. However, overall trends point to a warming climate, with higher sea level and less snowpack.

The way we define climate change has a big influence on what we see when we look at the data. Parts of Georgia, Mississippi, and Alabama have experienced little

FIGURE 14.2 Global Temperature and Carbon Dioxide Concentration, 1880–2010

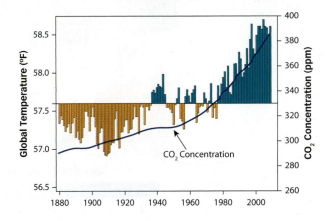

SOURCE: Global Climate Change Indicators, National Oceanic and Atmospheric Administration.

warming, and some areas have even cooled over the past century (data extracted from U.S. Environmental Protection Agency 2012a; see Figure 14.3). Areas that are warm year-round and experience less seasonal variation in climate, such as around the equator and near water, will also experience less change in surface temperature as the atmosphere warms. However, recent research has found that many of those climates that have historically experienced the least climate variability will be the most sensitive to change (Mora et al. 2013). Given that they also contain the most biodiverse regions on the planet, as well as some of the poorest populations, these regions will see much greater effects of climate change, and much sooner than other regions.

The same could be said for climate change over time. If we compare this year to last year, perhaps there is not much of a story to tell. Even over centuries there are patterns, but they do not give a full picture of the changes. Often, scientists who look at global climate change will look at *anomalies* in temperature and other aspects of weather. They take a period of time, often 1951 to 1980, and measure the degree to which current conditions diverge from the averages over those decades. For example, the graph in Figure 14.4 displays deviations from a normal temperature range, so we can see there are many more occurrences of temperatures above a normal range after 1980. While it may be generally a bit warmer than before and the winters a bit milder, it is also occasionally *much* hotter—and occasionally much wetter, drier, windier, or even colder than usual. This increase in extremes is as significant as the warming of some locations, such as the Earth's poles.

This is why scientists often object to defining the issue as "global warming" and favor the more accurate term *climate change*. Placing the emphasis on warming suggests that we should focus on heat alone, and the point, welcome to some, that winters are getting warmer too—in fact they are warming faster than summers. But if our definition of this environmental problem reminds us that greater heat in winter

FIGURE 14.3 **Rate of Temperature Change in the United States, 1901–2012**

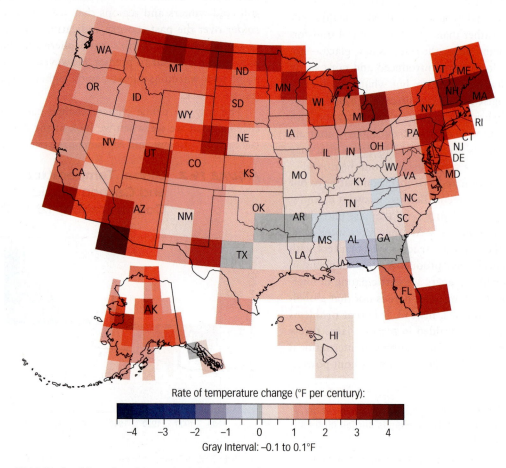

Rate of temperature change (°F per century):

−4 −3 −2 −1 0 1 2 3 4

Gray Interval: −0.1 to 0.1°F

Data source: NOAA (National Oceanic and Atmospheric Adminstration). 2013.

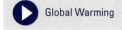
Global Warming

FIGURE 14.4 Deviations from Normal Temperatures, 1850–2010

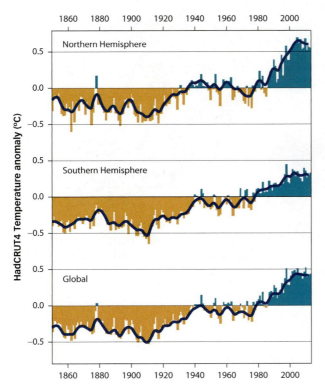

SOURCE: Climate Research Unit, University of East Anglia.

is likely to be accompanied by other effects—like stronger winter winds, bigger snowfalls, and faster evaporation of snowpack—we will consider the problem differently and act on it differently. Definitions matter hugely in social life.

One of the most profound visible aspects of climate change is the melting of polar ice. Ice melts have a number of different consequences for different people. Research has shown that Inuit living in Northern Canada already face respiratory health problems associated with warmer summers (Furgal and Seguin 2006). Moving across the ice has also become less predictable and more dangerous. For a traditionally nomadic population with strong cultural and economic roots in hunting, an increase in the risks associated with travel is highly problematic (Furgal and Seguin 2006; Laidler 2007). Climate change threatens the Inuit physically but also culturally, because many of their traditional activities now place them in danger.

As the ice melts, the sea level also rises because of thermal expansion, and as water gets warmer, it takes up more space. The Intergovernmental Panel on Climate Change's Third Assessment Report, completed in 2001, projected that sea level will rise between 0.5 and 1.4 meters by 2100. In low-lying coastal regions, even small increases in sea level can flood wetlands and leave people who live in

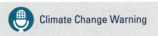

these areas at greater risk of flooding and vulnerability to storm surges (see Figure 14.5); more than a billion people could be displaced (Small and Nicholls 2003). Developing countries are likely to be the hardest hit, with sea-level rise potentially crippling Vietnam, Egypt, and the Bahamas (Dasgupta et al. 2009). Refugees fleeing endangered areas may face new or worsened conflicts with neighbors (Buhaug, Gleditsch, and Theisen 2010).

ASK YOURSELF: We've talked about Northern communities and climate change. What social and political problems may influence their resilience to the effects of global warming? Who is to blame for global warming? Does it matter? Who should take responsibility for alleviating the impacts of global warming on coastal communities? Why?

Natural Disasters

With global climate change, extreme weather events are also expected to increase (Meehl et al. 2000) (see Figure 14.6). Natural disasters have disproportionate effects on people, as we discussed in the case of the Chicago heat wave at the beginning of the chapter. More generally, the places where people live are associated with different levels of risks. Some locations are more prone than others to tornados, heat waves, or hurricanes. Often, these higher-risk areas are also associated with lower property values and may be occupied by people with lower income. These populations may also be less resilient to the effects of natural disasters, and there is evidence to suggest that their vulnerability is only increasing (Van Aalst 2006). Research has also suggested that minorities, women, and low-income populations suffer more emotional stress from natural disasters (Fothergill, Maestas, and Darlington 1999; Tierney 2007).

Hurricane Katrina is a good example of a natural disaster that was experienced differently by different people. Katrina formed over the Bahamas in 2005 and ran along the Gulf Coast from Florida to Texas. The greatest destruction occurred in New Orleans, Louisiana, where the levee system failed. Katrina was the one of the five deadliest hurricanes in U.S. history, with a death toll of more than 1,800. Just over half those deaths occurred in Louisiana, and many of those were in New Orleans. Black people in New Orleans were much more likely to die than whites, and more generally the elderly were also at higher risk (Sharkey 2007; Brunkard, Namulanda, and Ratard 2008). Income also influenced the death rate: low economic resources made it difficult for people to evacuate and relocate while the city flooded with water (Lavelle and Feagin 2006). Thus income, race, and age all influenced the magnitude of the disaster for groups of people.

FIGURE 14.5 Climate Change Vulnerability Index, 2014

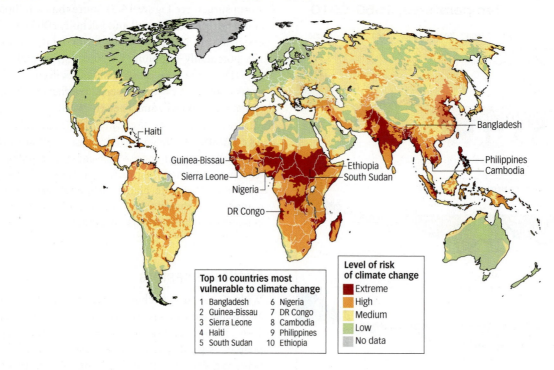

Top 10 countries most vulnerable to climate change

1 Bangladesh
2 Guinea-Bissau
3 Sierra Leone
4 Haiti
5 South Sudan
6 Nigeria
7 DR Congo
8 Cambodia
9 Philippines
10 Ethiopia

Level of risk of climate change

- Extreme
- High
- Medium
- Low
- No data

SOURCE: Maplecroft 2014. Reprinted with permission from the global risk analytics company, Maplecroft.

FIGURE 14.6 Natural Catastrophes Worldwide, 2012

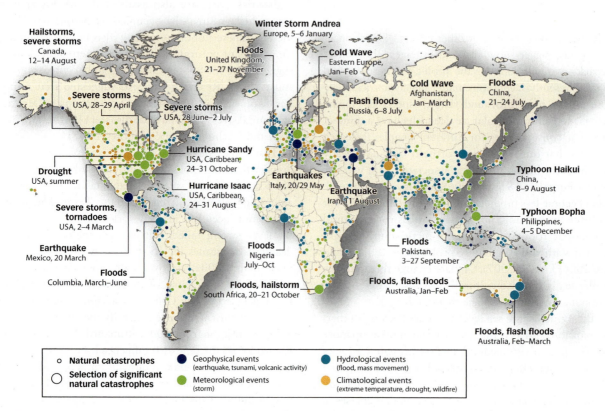

Natural catastrophes

Selection of significant natural catastrophes

Geophysical events (earthquake, tsunami, volcanic activity)

Meteorological events (storm)

Hydrological events (flood, mass movement)

Climatological events (extreme temperature, drought, wildfire)

SOURCE: Natural Catastrophes, 2012 World Map. © 2013 Münchener Rückversicherungs-Gesellschaft, Geo Risks Research, NatCatService.

Marginalization and Hurricane Katrina

Natural disasters like Hurricane Katrina do not have the same effects on everyone who experiences them. James R. Elliott and Jeremy Pais (2006) suggest that the history of race and class in New Orleans, where there are strong divisions that have not been significantly altered by migration, had a strong influence on how different residents were affected by the hurricane. They also suggest that the reasons for the differences were intersectional. That is, differences among residents in their experiences of the hurricane could not be explained purely by class, nor could they be explained entirely by race. Instead, race and class intersected to create unique experiences.

Elliott and Pais measured residents' evacuation timing, short-term recovery, stress and emotional support, and likelihood of return. They found that low-income African Americans were the most likely to have never left the city. Black workers were 3.8 times more likely to have lost their jobs, and particularly workers earning $10,000 to $20,000 a year. Low-income African Americans were also the least likely to return to their pre-Katrina communities.

Depending on their experiences, livelihoods, and resources, people experience environmental problems differently. Those who have historically been socially marginalized based on race, class, religion, or gender may feel these events more profoundly, in part because they receive the least social protection

and meet more barriers to recovery resources. Understanding how those experiences of marginalization intersect, as in the case of Hurricane Katrina, helps us understand the social dimensions of environmental problems so that we can generate sound and just solutions.

▶ **THINK ABOUT IT**

1. How does intersectionality relate to justice?

2. What policy recommendations might you make to encourage a fair and just recovery for New Orleans?

3. What does an intersectional approach say about other environmental problems, such as climate change?

Waste

The disposal of human waste is a social problem and a problem of social justice (see Figure 14.7). While everyone produces waste, nobody wants to have to deal with it. In much of the world, intricate systems have been built to whisk away refuse, quickly and effortlessly, never to be seen again. For the most part, we wash our hands, literally and figuratively, of our everyday pollution.

Clearly, waste does not simply evaporate but instead gets deposited in particular locations. While technologies for containing and treating landfills have improved, such facilities often remain unwelcome additions to local neighborhoods. Many adopt the NIMBY (not-in-my-backyard) approach, whereby people who may not be opposed to the establishment of landfills are opposed to having them located near their own homes and businesses (Camacho 1998; Cole and Foster 2001; Saha and Mohai 2005). The health effects of living near a landfill or incinerator are unclear, but there is evidence that low birth weight, birth defects, and some types of cancer are more common among populations that live near such facilities (Porta et al. 2009; Elliott et al. 2009; Goldberg

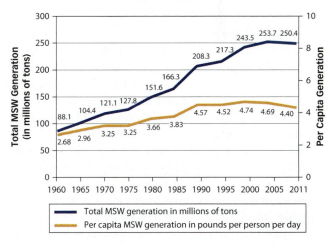

FIGURE 14.7 Municipal Solid Waste (MSW) Generation Rates, 1960–2011

SOURCE: Municipal Solid Waste, United States Environmental Protection Agency.

et al. 1999). Health effects aside, the presence of a landfill does seem to consistently decrease the value of nearby residential property (Ready 2005).

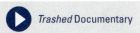

Trashed Documentary

Waste in a Global Context

As electronics become cheaper and more available to consumers, the waste generated in their production and disposal also becomes an increasing problem.

Electronic waste is highly toxic and difficult to recycle (Schmidt 2002). As a result, nations like the United States often ship their electronic waste to China, India, or Pakistan to be recycled or dumped (SVTC 2002). Alastair Iles (2004) has discussed the ways that technology flows, in which electronics are designed in one location, produced in another, and dumped in another, raise questions of environmental justice.

Thousands are employed in the disposal of electronics, and while there may be financial benefits, the health and environmental costs are huge. Not only are there risks associated with handling the e-waste, but spills and pollution from disposal and recycling can contaminate the groundwater and air, causing a bevy of illnesses for those who occupy nearby areas. These areas, Iles suggests, suffer disproportionate ills from the electronics industry, while the benefits are enjoyed to a much greater extent in other parts of the globe.

Computer manufacturers have an obligation to develop greener technologies to alleviate the problems associated with disposal. On the other hand, we should also reconsider any trade agreements and development programs that make it difficult for under-developed countries and regions to negotiate healthier and more environmentally friendly working conditions.

Workers sort electronic scrap on a conveyor belt at a recycling plant in Zurich, Switzerland. Parts from old computers and other electronic devices may contain contaminants such as lead, cadmium, beryllium, barium, and other heavy metals that can cause serious health and pollution problems. What do you do with your discarded computers and cell phones?

Reuters / Arnd Wiegmann

▶ **THINK ABOUT IT**

1. Who benefits from the global trade of hazardous waste?

2. How might electronic waste disposal differ if it couldn't be conducted across national borders?

Research has also shown that waste sites are more likely to emerge in less wealthy communities. Often, these are minority communities. Mohai and Saha (2007) found that, in the United States in 1990, more than 40% of people living within a mile of a disposal site were persons of color. The minority population in 1990 was only a quarter of the U.S. total, meaning that disposal sites were disproportionately placed in those neighborhoods. Mohai and Saha contend that the disproportionately high numbers of waste sites in Hispanic and African American communities may result from a number of economic, sociopolitical, and racial factors. Firms may locate waste management plants in areas where the cost of land is low, and these areas tend to be occupied by the economically disadvantaged, who are disproportionately people of color. Once a plant has been built, the more affluent may move away from the area. From a sociopolitical perspective, wealthy communities may have more political clout to influence the placement of waste management sites.

Lastly, Mohai and Saha suggest, racial factors may influence the placement of sites. Waste management firms may see minority neighborhoods as the least likely to resist the development of such sites and therefore as easy targets. We might therefore conclude that the placement of waste management systems exemplifies environmental racism, in which environmental degradation is more pronounced in places occupied or utilized by minority communities.

Radiation

We've seen above that globalization makes it difficult to identify the stakeholders in environmental decisions, particularly given the scope and longevity of the outcomes. What happens in one part of the globe often has far-reaching consequences. The effects of the disaster that took place at the nuclear power plant in Chernobyl, Ukraine, in 1986, for example, were not contained to the city, region, or state that surrounded it. All over Europe,

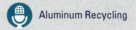
Aluminum Recycling

FIGURE 14.8 Radiation from Chernobyl

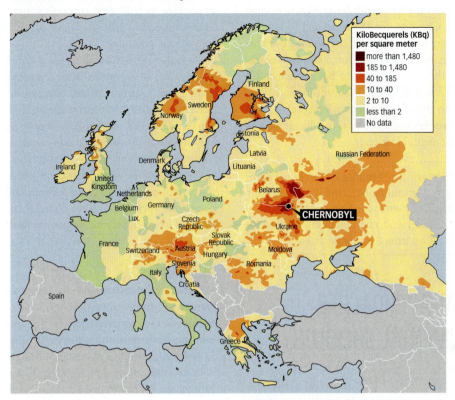

SOURCE: UNEP/GRID-Arendal, European Environment Agency; *AMAP Assessment Report: Arctic Pollution Issues,* Arctic Monitoring and Assessment Programme (AMAP), 1998, Oslo; European Monitoring and Evaluation Programme (MEP); Co-operative programme for monitoring and evaluation of the long-range transmission of air pollutants in Europe, 1999. Adapted from *Le Monde Diplomatique, July 2000.*

people experienced the consequences of radioactive fallout. Some have estimated the total premature deaths globally resulting from the Chernobyl disaster to be as high as 985,000 (Yablokov et al. 2009) (see Figure 14.8). But still, some groups have suffered the effects more than others.

The population that experienced the highest radioactivity from Chernobyl in Norway were the Saami, a minority group of reindeer herders (Mehli et al. 2000). Most of their exposure was through the consumption of reindeer meat contaminated when the animals grazed in areas that received fallout. This exposure created a threat to the Saamis' health and to their economic well-being. The Norwegian government introduced a range of measures to try to reduce their health risk, including restricting the slaughter of reindeer for food to particular times of the year and moving the reindeer to less contaminated areas. The Saami were also prevented from selling any contaminated meat and encouraged to reduce their own consumption.

These measures of protection were highly disruptive to the Saami and came with significant social and economic consequences. Not only were their traditional grazing and slaughtering practices disrupted, but their cultural identities as herders with traditional knowledge and a unique relationship to nature were challenged. An environmental

justice framework would suggest that they should have been protected from the unequal burden of contamination that they faced, but also that they should have been able to maintain access to the resources that are economically and culturally so important for them.

The Chernobyl disaster was a profound environmental event that captured international attention, but thinking of it as an isolated catastrophe may mask the ways in which nuclear risks can be more local, ever present, and disproportionate. The testing of nuclear weapons, for example, is not random but often happens in more sparsely populated, less fertile areas. While it makes more sense rationally to test in Nevada rather than New York State, the result is that those occupying certain types of landscapes suffer the brunt of the hazards associated with testing, while the security benefits supposedly accrue to everyone. Yet little is known about the health impacts experienced by those exposed to radiation from weapons testing. Some see this lack of research on exposed populations as unjust.

Wing (2010) suggests that the low level of political power, wealth, and education of local populations may have inhibited the development of research programs. Moreover, he suggests that employees at different nuclear weapons testing sites were tested for radiation exposure to varying degrees, depending on their race and gender. Research on employee records from the Savannah River Site, a nuclear reservation in South Carolina, for 1951 to 1999 found that female employees were less likely to receive testing, decreasing their access to financial compensation, and black workers had a significantly higher chance of having detectable levels of radiation (Angelon-Gaetz, Richardson, and Wing 2010). Research into the effects of environmental ills and the monitoring of people's exposure to those ills are part of any vision of environmental justice.

. . . .

ASK YOURSELF: What are the benefits of nuclear power and nuclear weapons production? Who benefits from nuclear power and nuclear weapons testing? Who should be responsible for testing and compensating people for health problems resulting from these industries?

. . . .

THEORETICAL APPROACHES IN ENVIRONMENTAL SOCIOLOGY

 14.3 Apply the functionalist, conflict, and symbolic interactionist perspectives to environmental problems and policy.

Environmental problems like climate change, waste disposal, and nuclear radiation are actually abstract, social concepts, and the experiences associated with them are rarely immediate and direct. Consider climate change: We cannot see carbon dioxide rising to the sky and getting trapped in the atmosphere and then immediately feel the temperature rise. In a sense, there are no direct effects—only **indicators** that we place within a larger context of meaning. This is true not only of climate change but also of anything we seek to understand. Scientists may have the most precise, detailed, sophisticated, and extensive technologies with which to make observations, but what are these observations of?

The numbers on a digital thermometer go up, but does that indicate higher temperatures? Or is it changing electrical pulses passing through a series of tiny diodes that result in different patterns of light? Perhaps it's both (or, if the thermometer is broken, maybe neither). All perceptions require conceptions. The tools we use may be technical and oriented toward developing an objective assessment, but they are also cultural and social, in the sense that they are developed by and used by specific groups of people in the pursuit of their interests. This does not necessarily make scientific claims any less valid. On the contrary, the culture of scientific production overall is highly specialized,

laborious, and laudable. We are merely suggesting that everything gets filtered through some social and cultural lens, whether the lens of climate science or the lens of local knowledge practices.

Social scientists use different theoretical lenses to try to make sense of the world too. A phenomenon like climate change has a particular meaning among climatologists and perhaps a slightly different meaning to Inuit living in Northern Canada, while sociologists may be more concerned with the process of meaning making and what those different meanings say about social structures and the distribution of power among the different stakeholders. We will deal with a few popular sociological lenses next and discuss how environmental sociologists have honed them in ways that work particularly well for environmental problems.

Functionalism

Structural functionalism focuses on the macro-level structures and processes that shape society. In environmental sociology, a structural functionalist perspective directs our attention to the organization of society and how it might create environmental problems. We might also consider how environmental problems themselves reproduce types of social organization.

Our society is organized in ways that encourage some behaviors while making others more difficult. For instance, it is easy to engage in the types of activities that have higher environmental costs, and in some cases avoiding those activities will put you at a disadvantage. The paving of roads and expansion of highways enable speedy movement between suburbs and cities by way of motor vehicles. Unless you live in a fairly dense city with excellent public transportation, driving your own car may best enable you to accept a better job, arrive at that job on time, and significantly reduce your daily commute. In such circumstances, even people with environmentally friendly attitudes may find it hard to put their beliefs into practice (Kollmuss and Agyeman 2002).

We have become too dependent on environmentally bad behaviors in our everyday lives, building a world in which those behaviors are easier and more rewarding than environmentally considerate behaviors (Stern 1992; Stern, Dietz, and Kalof 1993; Stern, Dietz, and Guagnano 1995). It is simply too much work to avoid driving, or too expensive to buy local fresh produce, or too harmful for our careers to forgo the latest gadgets, even if we are perfectly aware of the problems those actions create. We do too well at being environmental villains.

. . . .

Indicators: Observable changes in social and ecological behaviors that are used to indirectly measure other changes that are less visible.

The PS10 solar power plant near Seville, Spain, was designed to produce 11 megawatts of electricity from the sun's rays, collected by more than 600 giant movable mirrors. The mirrors concentrate the sun's rays onto the top of a 300-foot tower, where the resulting heat produces steam to drive a turbine.

Policy Implications of Structural Functionalism

If we adopt a structural functionalist perspective, we need to focus on reorganizing society to make bad environmental behaviors less appealing and more inconvenient, perhaps by raising the economic costs associated with them, or we could make good practices cheaper and more convenient. A third strategy is simply to make bad practices much less harmful.

We've basically described the ecological modernization (EM) perspective. **Ecological modernization theory** suggests that we can find solutions to our environmental problems by altering our current economic system to encourage good environmental behaviors. Competition, management, and taxes can reduce our inclinations to use the environment for free. The production of green technology will follow, as efficiency and better use of resources become driving forces in research and development. Rather than rejecting modernization, as some environmental sociologists do, we should solve problems by modernizing further (Mol and Spaargaren 2000). We can keep our standard of living and engage in the same types of activities with a much smaller environmental impact.

Perhaps the greatest benefit of the EM approach is that it does not ask for big changes to people's lifestyles or challenge the cultural practices people enjoy. It does not require any radical economic restructuring. The changes are subtle and organic and can occur without any real notice or discomfort. The government can offer incentives

Ecological modernization theory: The theory that society can become environmentally sustainable through the development of greener technologies and government regulations.

Solar Power

for green changes too. The "cash for clunkers" program, or Car Allowance Rebate System (CARS), was an EM-style program introduced in 2009 in the United States to subsidize the purchase of high-efficiency vehicles when the buyers traded in old low-efficiency vehicles. Fuel is expensive, and people are willing to pay more for a clean environmental conscience, so high-efficiency technology is being developed and refined, and cars that utilize it are increasingly accessible and affordable.

Ecological modernization theory has its critics, however. Some challenges invoke the idea of social inequality. Many countries now switching to green technology have undergone industrialization processes that were far from environmentally friendly, such as Western Europe, the United States, and Australia. If other countries undertake similar economic development, the environmental impacts will be significant and potentially disastrous. Yet the economic disadvantages in these countries, and their need for economic growth and infrastructure development, make it difficult for them to gain access to expensive new green technologies. Critics question whether EM theory is appropriate outside industrialized nations, where the need for environmentally sound economic development is greatest.

Some argue that current levels of consumption are unsustainable, even if we switch to green technologies. More efficient cars still aren't carbon-neutral. An increase in green consumerism may not actually reduce environmental impacts. For example, rather than forgoing disposable food containers, we may use them more if they are compostable, recyclable, or made from organic materials. Critics are particularly skeptical of green technologies given capitalist societies' need to continue growing.

Many of these critiques are aimed at the technological and market-based aspects of EM and the faith it places in green consumers. Skeptics are even more critical of corporate greenwashing, the practice in which organizations advertise themselves as green when their actions are not. For example, "clean" coal technology and oil-drilling innovations might reduce the environmental impacts of the coal and oil industries, but these will never be green industries, given that they are highly polluting in their production and consumption. Ecological modernization cannot guarantee that companies' ecological politics are anything but a thin veneer.

But EM also sees a big role for government. While globalization has long been seen as unfriendly to environmental conservation, Sonnenfeld and Mol (2002) suggest that the right types of global governance could make globalization positive for the environment (see also Mol 2003). Governments could set a baseline gas mileage for all new cars, for example, so that auto companies would be forced to produce high-efficiency vehicles.

Conflict Theory

Conflict theory is often associated with Karl Marx and his understanding of society's structure as being tied to the distribution of materials and resources. For the conflict theorist in environmental sociology, materials are pulled from the environment and used to generate profit, essentially without being paid for. Our economic system rewards companies for producing more and reducing costs, which encourages them to exploit the environment.

From the conflict perspective, we could think of the environment as engaged in a type of labor: it generates goods, such as wood and steel, and services, such as waste disposal. We could also consider how the desire to accumulate capital and wealth leads to an attempt to reduce both human and environmental labor costs while expanding production and increasing inequality and environmental degradation. The free labor of the environment then simply participates in the class conflict inherent in capitalist production. Why is environmental labor free?

First, the environment produces goods but has no ability to negotiate prices for those goods. There may even be ecological value in not selling: an apple left unpicked can feed insects, attract wildlife, and fertilize the ground when it falls. But without price negotiation, most environmental products are treated as free because they cannot be withheld. We may have to negotiate access to water, soil, trees, and fish, but once we do, we can treat them as 100% ours.

Second, many environmental consequences of human activities are shared and do not fall specifically on the individuals who caused the problems. Once carbon dioxide (CO_2) is in the air, there is no way to contain it and attach it to the exact producer who put it there. To make matters worse, CO_2 may interact with other pollutants to produce further negative consequences—for example, climate change that combines with habitat loss to undermine the reproductive abilities of wildlife. How do we tie these compounded costs back to an individual?

A third reason environmental labor is free is that many actions don't show their environmental consequences for many years, sometimes centuries. Even if we know exactly what those consequences are, and even if they would directly affect the person responsible for them, it is easy to put off future suffering for immediate gains.

Some say it is impossible to fully predict the future outcomes of our present actions. The world is too complicated, and we haven't been studying the environment long enough to know.

The absence of environmental costs in the economy feeds what environmental sociologists call a **treadmill of production** (ToP) (Schnaiberg and Gould 1994; Pellow, Schnaiberg, and Weinberg 2000; Schnaiberg, Pellow, and Weinberg 2002). Rather than solving environmental problems, ToP theorists say, ecological modernization is more likely to perpetuate them by supporting a fundamentally unsustainable economic system. Under capitalism there will always be pressure for economic growth and the increased use of environmental resources. Even greener consumption will encourage production to expand and propel environmental degradation at an increasing rate as competition forces firms to cut their costs of labor and other inputs. What we need is a different economic system. We need to get off the treadmill of production.

Sometimes reducing the costs of inputs can be good for the environment. Technology that makes resource extraction more efficient, for example, means less waste in the extraction process. We can reduce the costs of getting rid of waste by producing less waste in the first place, and the less energy used to produce energy, the better. These are all possible positive aspects of pushing firms to reduce costs through ecological modernization.

Unfortunately, there is still a problem, as the ToP perspective illuminates. First, even if we reduce costs through technology and efficiency, we still cannot reduce the environmental impact to zero. Second, competition in capitalism is so fierce that even if technology improves the efficient use of resources, firms will still be compelled to find the cheapest supply sources, which often means locating factories where energy is cheap, getting resources from places where the land and labor for extraction are cheap, and finding waste sites that are cheap. Third, the treadmill is always accelerating: if firms get more from their resources, they won't necessarily use less but instead might expand production. If a firm can use half the amount of energy to make the same number of cars, for example, why not double the number made and sell them for less, expanding market share and putting pressure on competitors before they can catch up? The ToP perspective suggests that the capitalist economy is organized to promote cost cutting and expansion, so the environmental benefits of new technology will always be limited.

Treadmill of production: A theory that describes the ways that production is constantly accelerating without moving forward.

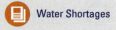

Water Shortages

Reuters / Kathryn Hansen / NASA

Climate change is causing the Arctic to warm more quickly than the rest of the world, causing a dramatic loss of Arctic sea ice. The primary role that sea ice plays in global climate is its ability to reflect the sun's radiation efficiently. As sea ice is lost, more sunlight is absorbed into the newly open ocean, shifting the ocean surface from highly reflective to one that absorbs most of the sun's energy. What meaning do you suppose the average person would give to all this?

Policy Implications of the Conflict Perspective

Conflict theory suggests that we must deal with the problems of consumption, competition, labor, and environmental degradation simultaneously, by addressing the capitalist economic system. One solution is to legislate labor and environmental protections. After all, if the treadmill of production is propelled by competition, legislation that has similar effects on all firms will curb inequality and the overuse of resources while still allowing firms to compete in other areas. Yet because firms exist in particular locations, and because local governments want to protect their tax bases and constituents' jobs by keeping them there, legislation that might harm or curtail particular firms is a tough sell. Globalization has also significantly curbed governments' ability to resolve environmental abuses and labor exploitation through governance because, as we've seen, companies can now operate in many places where they are not closely regulated.

For conflict theorists, the plight of the environment is closely tied to the plight of labor. One of the only ways to resolve environmental problems from a conflict theory perspective is to drastically reduce inequality among people, both within and between nations, while developing a strong environmentally protective state. Reducing inequality would change the nature of competition by reducing producers' ability to find cheaper labor and laxer environmental regulations. For example, if the people working in e-waste plants in China had a higher standard of living and stronger local government, they could demand a higher wage for such dangerous work,

and environmental protections could drive the cost of disposal up. The result may be a higher price for electronics or a stronger incentive to make their disposal greener.

ASK YOURSELF: From a conflict theory perspective, fostering equality will help resolve environmental problems, but this might take a while to achieve. What should we do in the meantime? What would happen if we just factored environmental labor into production costs? What problems could arise from decreasing inequality and increasing production costs?

Symbolic Interactionism

We've seen that people often attach different meanings to environmental problems depending on who they are and what they want to accomplish. Symbolic interactionist theorists might say that every environmental problem is really a conflict over the meanings different groups attach to a phenomenon, and these meanings are associated with different outcomes. For example, consider the bulk movement of undesirable materials to a new site miles away. When is this called waste management and constructed as an environmental problem? Some might say it is a very efficient way of dealing with the by-products of a healthy economic life. The disposal of waste becomes an environmental problem when it is seen as a threat to our health, our sense of justice, or our visions of a beautiful landscape and functioning ecosystem.

Environmental sociologists often rely on the social constructionist perspective rather than on symbolic interactionism, but the two are closely related. Social constructionism highlights the ways we give environmental materials meanings through social interactions, even though we often think those meanings are inherent in the things themselves. That is, socialization gives us conceptual tools with which to see the world, and the way we see it therefore depends on the shape and character of those tools. We have no means to grasp what is happening in a pure, unmediated way, because we make sense of the world through knowledge we generate and share socially.

Climate change is the perfect example. The concept of climate change is not something anyone comes up with in a vacuum. Even scientists who can observe CO_2 levels in the atmosphere use technologies developed for that purpose by others and shared by others. They talk to other people about their findings and publish in journals where dialogues between scientists occur. The average person confronted with some hotter days, higher sea level, or odd species behavior probably wouldn't think, "Ah, it's carbon dioxide trapped in the atmosphere. It must be global warming." The concept of global warming is necessary for us to know what we are seeing and interpret it and give it meaning. Hotter days become much more ominous when the concept of global warming is available to us.

In fact, we do not just absorb all the concepts around us that help make sense of the environment. Instead, we focus on those that resonate with us and that are shared by our friends, family members, and society. Knowledge is not something we pick up as we encounter it; rather, what we take to be knowledge gains credence through our identification with those who extend it to us. In short, gaining knowledge is an active process of culture, closely bound up in our sense of identity, which we can call the *cultivation of knowledge* (Bell 2004).

For example, we use a common language when trying to describe an idea like global warming, and that language develops more depth and becomes more meaningful the more we use it. Even if you don't believe that global warming is taking place, you know people like you find the idea important and compelling, so you pay attention to it. If you are a student at a university, those conversations may be shaped by campus culture and discussions of research and science. If you are a city planner, the concept of global warming might be ripe with future scenarios and adaptations that relate to things like sea level and water supplies. If you are a manufacturer, public discussion about global warming may seem accusatory and uninformed about business practices, or it may make people feel on edge. The way people build environmental knowledge depends on the social foundations they are building from. The result can be a clash of visions in which people are not simply debating global warming but are defending their identities.

In her work on logging on the northwest coast of Canada, for example, anthropologist Terre Satterfield (2002) suggests that debates about logging are about much more than trees and environmental preservation; they are about the identities of local groups and their claims to legitimacy in the area. Whose forest is it? Who should decide what the forest means and does? Is it a sacred place? A cultural, recreational space? Or is the forest a productive space that can feed families? These contested values were so hotly debated in the community Satterfield studied that elementary school children were divided into those who perceived logging as a part of their own positive cultural heritage and those who demonized it.

The theory of **frame analysis** is associated with social interactionism and social constructionism because it focuses on the meanings people give to elements in the environment. Frame analysis suggests that people present issues in ways that elicit particular types of responses. For example, fishermen frame a river with deformed fish as contaminated and threatened by economic interests, while the oil company upriver frames the river as healthy and an economic resource for oil production. If the public accepts the fishermen's frame, it not only produces a tangible outcome—such as new legislation about acceptable levels of contaminants—but also signals that the fishermen's knowledge is valid and that the fishermen have more right to fish than the oil company has to pump oil. If the oil company's frame becomes more widely accepted instead, its legitimacy on the river is validated and its rights are confirmed.

At its crudest, framing is about the framer's ability to convince people to see things the same way as the framer so they will form the same opinions. That skill is determined by the communicator's use of what Snow and Benford (1988) call **frame alignment**, or the presentation of information in a way that is congruent with or complementary to the knowledge the frame recipient already has.

Framing that serves political interests isn't always bad. If people are concerned about an environmental problem because it threatens their well-being, they will use frames for their own benefit. Some argue that it is in fact impossible to avoid framing, because we are always presenting information from our own standpoints and seeking agreement. Without framing, it would be difficult for scientists to communicate ideas like global warming to the public or to get the public to support efforts to resolve environmental issues. People generally like information that fits with what they already know, and they don't like information that challenges their perceptions of the world. Psychologists call the clashing of incongruent information **cognitive dissonance**. Rather than hold on to contradictory information, people will often reject it. To some degree, environmental activists need to frame ideas in particular ways so that others can hear and consider those ideas. No environmental battle is won without some rhetoric.

Policy Implications of Symbolic Interactionism

If the meanings we attribute to the environment are products of social interaction, does that make them less real? If social constructions and frames are political and integral to the process of environmental claims making, should we then remain critical and skeptical of all environmental problems? Even if we accept that the meanings people give to environmental problems are generally self-interested, we do not necessarily have to become cynics. Instead, we could consider the types of representations particular constructions and frames enable, and to what extent they include a variety of voices and encourage conversation as opposed to silence. For example, one

....

Frame analysis: A sociological approach that focuses on the presentation of information and ideas in ways that are intended to elicit particular understanding and responses.

Frame alignment: A situation in which multiple frames work together to enhance the efficacy of each.

Cognitive dissonance: The discomfort of holding conflicting beliefs or values.

way to evaluate and accept frames with a critical eye is to consider the processes through which they are made and the flexibility and inclusiveness of their boundaries. Frame analysis is useful for directing attention to the interests embedded in a frame and the interests the frame advances. These interests are not necessarily bad. Indeed, social justice is all about responding to interests—the interests of those whose legitimate concerns have been neglected or actively suppressed.

We could make this observation about symbolic interactionism more generally. If environmental problems are at least partly about conflicts between social groups and threats to the identities of their members, we can reach resolution only when we recognize and legitimate different perspectives. For example, suppose people downstream from an industrial production facility begin feeling sick. They notice fewer birds migrating to the shore, and the grasses that normally grow in the water in the spring aren't there anymore. The managers at the production facility have had the water tested recently, and they suggest the residents are merely upset because their company had to let some people go in response to the recession. To resolve the problem, we need to make sure all parties, both the community members and the managers of the facility, have the resources to perform the necessary research and to test and vocalize their concerns. The solutions to environmental problems lie as much in the processes taken to address them as in the outcomes.

ASK YOURSELF: Do some motivations make a frame seem more legitimate? Do some motivations invalidate a frame? From a symbolic interactionist perspective, what factors may prevent environmental problems from being resolved? Who do you think has the right to participate in discussions about global warming, waste management, or radiation? What about other environmental problems?

SPECIALIZED THEORIES IN ENVIRONMENTAL SOCIOLOGY

 14.4 Apply specialized theories to the environment.

We look next at two specialized theories within environmental sociology that tie some of the other perspectives together: risk society and ecological dialogue. Risk society emphasizes the ways in which conflicts between groups of people are increasingly tied to the groups' different perceptions of risk. Ecological dialogue considers how the meanings people give to environmental problems are constantly being renegotiated by the types of direct

Drivers stand on vehicles following a large car accident on a highway on the outskirts of Saltillo, Mexico. Icy roads were blamed for the 30-car pileup. We live in a "risk society." Do you ever think about how many risks you take on a daily basis, from crossing the street to eating food that may be contaminated?

material experiences more commonly associated with ecological modernization or the treadmill of production. In these two theories, our social experiences and environmental experiences are very explicitly intertwined.

Risk Society

Leaving the house in the morning is risky. Driving to work is certainly risky, and even heading to work on foot requires navigating some dangerous situations. Then again, staying home can be risky, too, depriving you of exercise and reducing your exposure to fresh air and sunlight. Some basic risks are unavoidable. Our choices of which risks to take are influenced by our culture, the benefits associated with the risks, and the costs of avoiding them.

For example, many people live far from where they work. They could live closer, but the housing near work is too expensive. They could work at home, but they don't have the money or time to set up their own businesses. It's easier to take the job in the city and live in the suburbs. But that means driving, and risking becoming one of the 2 million people injured and 35,000 killed every year in traffic accidents in the United States (U.S. Census Bureau 2012g). Driving to work may be a known risk, but it's one we perceive as normal and acceptable. As public transportation networks grow, bicycle lanes spread, and housing prices near business areas decline, the risk of driving may begin to seem too great and the rewards too low. Some may decide it is now unacceptable and leave the car at home or get rid of it altogether. Others may decide they enjoy their space and the drive to work so much that they will continue to take the chance.

Bettmann / Corbis

Beachgoers are sprayed with DDT as a new machine for distributing the insecticide is tested for the first time. In the 1940s and 1950s, many American neighborhoods were sprayed with DDT to suppress gypsy moths, mosquitoes, beetles, and other insects. Children would sometimes run into the spray as the DDT trucks went by. Today, thousands of migrant farmworkers (many of whom are undocumented) are injured by pesticide poisoning.

Many of the risks to which we are exposed are more complicated and less predictable, and much less visible, than that of driving to work. Take, for example, the use of DDT. DDT (dichlorodiphenyltrichloroethane) is an insecticide best known for its use in agriculture. During the middle of the 20th century, however, when it was thought that humans were not affected by it, DDT was also sprayed over towns to kill mosquitoes and used to exterminate mammals, like bats, and invertebrates, like sea crustaceans. Adults and children were doused with DDT to get rid of lice.

In the 1950s and 1960s, concern about the effects of DDT began to mount. It reached a pinnacle in 1962 with the publication of Rachel Carson's book *Silent Spring*. Carson was a marine biologist and conservationist who had seen the effects of DDT in birds (the title of her book is meant to conjure up a vision of a spring without birdsong). As it happens, when DDT builds up in a female bird's system, the shells of the eggs she lays become paper thin, and successful reproduction is unlikely. Carson suggested that pesticides like DDT hurt not only mammals and birds but humans as well. She was right. If people ingest enough DDT, they develop nausea and tremors and can even die, but there are also more subtle effects, like low birth weight in children born to women with high DDT levels. Evidence also links DDT to diabetes and cancer.

DDT is still sometimes used overseas to fight malaria because it is so effective at killing mosquitoes—although even where malaria rates are extremely high, there is much concern that the benefits aren't high enough to justify its use (Paull 2007). Yet an assessment of the risk of using DDT is not a simple, straightforward calculation. It is contested and socially situated. The U.S. Department of Agriculture deems DDT to be moderately toxic, and most people have some DDT stored in their bodies. Even when Carson published her book and evidence against DDT was mounting, some scientists were extremely critical of her blanket condemnation and the public frenzy that resulted. Dr. Robert White-Stevens, a former biochemist and spokesman for the chemical industry, suggested at the time, "If man were to follow the teachings of Miss Carson, we would return to the Dark Ages, and the insects and diseases and vermin would once again inherit the earth" (quoted in McLaughlin 1998). DDT is not all bad, some would say. It's bad only when it's used thoughtlessly and excessively. If we know more about the risks, we can use it better and without major impacts on the ecosystem. After all, even *nutmeg* is toxic at some level.

Of course, nutmeg and DDT are not the same thing. The trick is to make more educated decisions about what we are using and to what effect. To modernize and develop, some risk is necessary, because otherwise we would be constrained to the knowledge we already have and the practices already in place. At least some technology we have now is better than what we had in the 1950s, and we can produce some things with much less environmental impact than before. Certainly, we have undergone some level of ecological modernization. Those changes would have been impossible, however, if we had insisted that there be no possibility of unforeseen effects. So we blunder ahead, but in the best case we do so only after considering what the consequences might be and with our eyes open for what we may have missed. Increasingly, modernization is accompanied by anxiety and caution, and the sense that projects should be undertaken only after scientific testing and due consideration. While still committed to the advancement of living standards and the refinement of human practices, societies are increasingly driven by what Ulrich Beck (1992; Beck, Giddens, and Lash 1994) calls **reflexive modernization**, that is, modernization that is increasingly *reflective* about what it is doing. No longer confident that all technological changes will necessarily be for the best, we debate and investigate and insist on those open eyes.

Beck (1992) suggests that this form of modernization is part of what he calls the **risk society**. His overarching thesis is that risks are everywhere and play an

Reflexive modernization: A form of economic development focused on revising current systems of production and making careful assessment of future outcomes of projects and decisions.

Risk society: A society stratified by the ability to avoid risk.

Researching the Environment

The Work of Riley E. Dunlap and Aaron M. McCright

What people notice and how they think about what they've experienced depends on how it fits with what they already know and the frameworks they've developed to process information. We all have sociocultural lenses through which we peer to see the world. Along these lines, Riley E. Dunlap and Aaron M. McCright have worked at analyzing those social and demographic characteristics that correlate to attitudes about climate change.

Self-identified liberals are more likely than self-identified conservatives to be concerned about climate change (Dunlap and McCright 2008). While we could not say that all liberals are green activists and all conservatives are nonbelievers, the pattern is significantly strong. Nor does the research mean that being a Democrat makes a person believe the climate is changing, or that being a Republican makes a person disagree. On the other hand, Dunlap and McCright (2010) have found increasing polarization between Democrats and Republicans on the issue of climate change (see also McCright and Dunlap 2003, 2010).

In recent work, McCright (2011) found that some systems of thought or general orientations predispose people to be more or less likely to

believe that climate change is taking place. Those more critical of industrial capitalism are more likely to believe, whereas defenders of industrial capitalism are more likely to challenge the existence of climate change. Those who practice reflexive modernization, who look for ways to critique and refine industry, differ from those who advocate for industrial expansion. It makes sense: if your interests lie in changing industry, you're looking for problems and see them readily. If you are more oriented to expansion, you may be more hesitant to rework the past and present.

One of the problems faced by climate science is that when the news media report on it, they want to appear to be evenhanded and unbiased, and the resulting coverage doesn't accurately reflect the relative weight of the arguments. Instead, the news media treat both perspectives as equally valid. Moreover, they often focus on disagreement and controversy to make stories more compelling, making it seem that there is much more dissent about the existence of

At a Tea Party rally held in Racine, Wisconsin, a child holds up a placard suggesting that global warming is as real as unicorns.

climate change than there actually is. McCright (2011) suggests that this presentation of divisive information can polarize people into different climate change camps. It doesn't help that media outlets themselves are often polarized into two camps: those that are more conservative and critical of climate change claims (such as Fox News) and those that are more liberal and concerned about climate change (such as MSNBC). Increasingly, the worlds that political groups occupy are isolated from one another. As a result, the disagreement in public opinion exceeds the disagreement in the scientific community, increasing both the challenge to and the need for ecological dialogue.

▶ **THINK ABOUT IT:** Why do you suppose that liberals tend to be concerned about global warming while conservatives tend to deny it exists?

increasing role in shaping society. The ability to avoid risk exposure creates a new way in which people are divided into social groups, replacing old systems that differentiated them by their access to money and other economic resources. Whereas conflict used to arise over the distribution of goods, with everyone wanting more, it now arises over dodging bads and wanting less. According to Beck,

"The driving force in the class society can be summarized in the phrase: *I am hungry!* The movement set in motion by the risk society, on the other hand, is expressed in the statement: *I am afraid!*" (49). Our fear is spurred by our inability to predict the future and our lack of assurance that the government can and will protect society. If risk is about a subjective evaluation of whether the benefits of some activity are worth the potential future costs, leaving it up to the government seems foolhardy. We have lost faith in what Beck calls the **risk contract**, or the implicit understanding that government will enact rules to make sure that people will be protected as society bounds progressively forward.

Governments still have rules about acceptable levels of risk, but people in the risk society are less likely to place their faith in these figures. New scientific studies often find that what we knew before was wrong, and different people can draw different conclusions and even significantly different facts from the same phenomena. The industry scientists say one thing, while those employed by the environmentalists say another. Sometimes it seems there's science to back up any claim, and all you need to be right are some really deep pockets.

Even if our science were flawless, there is still the problem of averages. What we consider to be an acceptable level of risk is based on average exposure, but some people are much more exposed or susceptible than others. For example, young children drink large volumes of apple juice, and apples have relatively high levels of trace pesticides due to the difficulty of producing the crop. Environmental sociologist John Wargo (2009) points out that because of their faster rate of development and new-cell formation, children are more likely than adults to form flawed cells that will become cancerous. Assuming that the government has factored in social and physical differences like these when setting acceptable levels of pesticides could be dangerous, especially as cultural practices change. On the other hand, rejecting the role of government is also wrong. Information about risk levels may not be easily available, and the burden of negotiating those risks shouldn't fall entirely on the shoulders of the individual.

ASK YOURSELF: If a group's cultural practices expose group members to unsafe levels of risk, is anyone at fault? What can or should be done to protect people in these circumstances?

Beck has said that risk is the great class equalizer in this age of global environmental problems. Critics argue that he takes this point too far, however. To some degree, risks do confront everyone, but air pollution, for instance, tends to settle in lower elevations, commonly poorer neighborhoods. Waterborne illnesses disproportionately afflict those with lower socioeconomic status. The farmworkers who apply pesticides are typically poor and can't afford expensive organic food. Radiation from nuclear weapons testing conducted many years ago in sparsely populated Nevada has shown up all along the East Coast of the United States (Beck and Bennett 2002), yet various forms of cancer disproportionately affect people in Nevada and Utah. Environmental risks do have impacts on everyone, to some degree, but they certainly seem to come down more heavily on some—and some, generally the wealthy, are better positioned to avoid the worst consequences. Perhaps this is one reason surveys usually show that the socially advantaged are the least concerned about environmental problems.

Ecological Dialogue

In the structural functionalist and conflict theory approaches, we largely assume that environmental problems have an objective, scientific grounding. This is called **realism** in environmental sociology, and it is often contrasted with social constructionism. In practice, however, the distinction between realism and constructionism can be a little fuzzy. Many theories that claim to be realist creep into social constructionism, and much social constructionism depends on the existence of material realities. But realists argue that we can separate ecological problems from human relationships and social organization, whereas constructionists claim that environmental problems are human problems and are impossible for us to parse out from human relations and experience in any sort of objective way. Theoretically, it sounds fairly straightforward. Practically, it becomes much more difficult to be clearly planted on one side or the other. Instead, sociologists often travel between the two when trying to think through environmental problems.

Perhaps we should look at environmental problems using an **ecological dialogue** approach (Bell and Lowe 2000; Bell 2012), in which the material and the ideal interact and inform each other, together creating the world in which we live. That interplay between things and thoughts never generates a static product. It is constantly in flux with conflict, collaboration, and creativity.

The ecological dialogue approach assumes that the world we experience is not a complete or stable thing that we can pin down and know definitely and conclusively. There has not been, and will not be, a historical moment when we fully know the world. But there are moments when we can know it *better*—and not better merely in the positivist sense of more accurately, but with greater depth and richness. We can know the world better by seeing it

Risk contract: The implicit understanding that government will enact rules to make sure people are protected as society bounds progressively forward.

Realism: The point of view that the world is directly knowable.

Ecological dialogue: An approach to the environment and society that focuses on the interactions between aspects of human environmental relationships.

 Plastic

in multiple ways and engaging with it experientially and intellectually. How poorly would we know the world if we didn't think about what we saw and felt? How poorly would we know the world if we only read about it and talked about it with others? We can see redwood trees and know them. We can read about redwood trees and know them. How much better do we know them when we've read about the ancient forests and marveled about these arboreal giants with friends, having also stood amid them, touched their bark, and looked up, trying to imagine how they taper off, 300 feet up in the air? How much better do we know them after a lifetime of reading, seeing, touching, smelling, thinking, and talking, all these things

playing together in our bodies and minds? Practically, the line between the material tree and our ideal tree is unclear, although sometimes it makes sense for analytic purposes to make a momentary distinction.

When we think about environmental problems as an ecological dialogue, we also open ourselves to learning from others and their experiences—whether those others are human or nonhuman, alive today or rocks with 4.5 billion years of history. When we bring them together into dialogue, they push us to create new information that may be more complicated and uncomfortable, but also more nuanced and better able to help us consider such varied and dynamic global environmental issues as climate change.

SOCIAL CHANGE: WHAT CAN YOU DO?

 Identify steps toward social change concerning the environment.

If we are on an ever-accelerating treadmill of production that makes ecological modernization ever harder to attain, it seems that small environmentalist actions might keep the treadmill going longer. For example, driving a hybrid car only modestly contributes to curbing global warming. After all, such a car is still using gasoline. Maybe buying a hybrid even supports the present car-based transportation system. The environmentalist who just bought a hybrid will now be less inclined to put up with the inconvenience of a poor bus system, thus denying the bus system the additional ridership it needs to fund better service. Does buying a hybrid then make larger, society-level changes less likely to happen?

We don't think so—one of us owns a hybrid and we both frequently use the bus! We like to think of the problem as the social equivalent of how landscapes change. We rarely see the hills and valleys of the land change much in our own lifetimes, but geology tells us that, over time, they change enormously. Geology also tells us that the really noticeable and important changes take place in short, dramatic moments: through floods, earthquakes, and eruptions that cause the bonds of rock and soil to slip and slide in great masses of movement, until the land is almost unrecognizable. So it is with social change. We may desire a landslide in the order of things, but without the preparation provided by countless cultural and political raindrops on the soil and rock of social life,

Claire Culpepper (left) and Anne Elisabeth Alders sort through cans for recycling at the Habitat for Humanity Re-Store in Nacogdoches, Texas. Recycling is the third component of the "reduce, reuse, and recycle" approach to waste management.

nothing would move. *For things to change, we need both the rain and the landslide.* Few of us will experience the landslide, but we can all be part of the rain.

So what can you do to get fired up about an environmental problem as large as climate change? Ask questions, and think through them thoughtfully, acknowledging that the questions you choose predispose you to a particular type of answer. That's okay. Sometimes we need to limit our vision to focus and gain some depth and detail. But keep in mind that your answer is probably not *the* answer. There will never be an end to the conversation, unless we withdraw from participation, and that doesn't help anyone. While it may be valuable to see one aspect of a problem clearly, we also need to engage in conversations, be they heated disagreements or wholehearted camaraderie, or perhaps some of both. Sometimes the rain is stormy.

Environmental problems may seem to have relatively straightforward technical solutions. Stop CO_2 emissions, stop climate change. Stop using paper, plastics, electronics, and manufacturing chemical compounds like pesticides, and the problem of waste disposal virtually disappears. Make the globe a nuclear-free zone, stop the problem of radiation. What we've tried to illustrate is that environmental problems are social, and even solutions that seem technically straightforward are socially very messy. While different perspectives may have slightly different policy implications, they all suggest that some attention to social justice is important. Along these lines, we have tried to emphasize that we are engaging in an ecological dialogue, and encouraging that dialogue to be more representative and vibrant is a fundamental part of any solution.

So, whether people in your community are discussing oil drilling, logging, toxic waste, bicycle lanes, or just access to resources for marginalized groups, learn about the issue and get involved, however you can. It doesn't matter whether you agree with everyone who's voicing their opinions. It's great if you don't agree, so you can add something new to the conversation. Be sure you respect the different contexts people come from and think about what they might know that you don't, and vice versa. You'll leave those conversations better equipped to take a critical look at how you've organized your life and consider whether there is anything you might be able revise to be more environmentally friendly and more environmentally just. Try to find an ethical way to dispose of that old computer. Ride a bike to work, and if your city isn't bike-friendly, participate in the growing movement to lobby local governments for better bike lanes. Attend a political rally for rights to clean water. These efforts might seem small, but aggregated among those of other people engaging in similar actions, they can be raindrops in a landslide.

WHAT DOES AMERICA THINK?

Questions about Environment from the General Social Survey

 Turn to the beginning of the chapter to compare your answers to the total population.

1. **What is your interest level in environmental issues?**

   VERY INTERESTED: 47.1%

   MODERATELY INTERESTED: 43.4%

   NOT AT ALL INTERESTED: 9.5%

2. In the United States, do you think we're spending too much money on the environment, too little money, or about the right amount?

   TOO MUCH: 13.1%

   TOO LITTLE: 55%

   ABOUT THE RIGHT AMOUNT: 31.9%

3. In the United States, do you think we're spending too much money on improving and protecting the environment, too little money, or about the right amount?

   TOO MUCH: 10.9%

   TOO LITTLE: 57.6%

   ABOUT THE RIGHT AMOUNT: 31.5%

4. What is your interest level in farm issues?

   VERY INTERESTED: 23.9%

   MODERATELY INTERESTED: 49.7%

   NOT AT ALL INTERESTED: 26.4%

LOOK BEHIND THE NUMBERS

Go to **edge.sagepub.com/trevino** for a breakdown of these data across time and by race, sex, age, income, and other statuses.

1. Examine the data for interest level in the environment broken down by age, gender, race, income level, and education level. Do any of the variables appear to influence responses? Explain possible reasons for each finding, or explain why you believe that no variable was influential.

2. When reviewing the data on age for responses to the question about spending money to improve the environment, what pattern do you notice? Does this concern you? Explain.

3. Describe the relationship between willingness to spend money on the environment and age. What implications might this have for society? What changes might this lead to in the future?

4. Examine the General Social Survey data from 1974 through the present for the question about interest in farm issues. Is such interest increasing, remaining the same, or decreasing? Does this concern you? Explain.

SOURCE: National Opinion Research Center, University of Chicago.

CHAPTER SUMMARY

 Explain how environmental problems are social problems.

Environmental problems occur in the natural world, but they are experienced and interpreted by people who exist in the social world. What we see as problems depends on who we are, where we live, and how we interact with the environment in our daily lives. The solutions we dream up depend on the way we envision ourselves in the environment in the future.

 Discuss patterns and trends in environmental issues.

Environmental justice and globalization are major trends influencing the way we think of patterns in environmental problems. Environmental justice entices us to look at fairness in the distribution of environmental hazards and bounties, while globalization draws our attention to the scope of modern environmental problems and their geographic and political complexity. Climate change, waste management, natural disasters, and radiation are all issues that bring attention to questions of fairness and the global qualities of environmental problems.

 Apply the functionalist, conflict, and symbolic interactionist perspectives to environmental problems and policy.

A functionalist perspective shows us how society has organized everyday life in ways that create environmental problems, so we can recognize how reorganizing life and building more efficient technologies can alleviate the negative effects of human action. Conflict theory suggests that our economy is going to continue to exploit the environment as competition puts pressure on industry to produce more while reducing environmental costs, so a fundamental economic reorganization of society is the only way to truly resolve our environmental problems. Symbolic interactionists consider how people identify environmental problems and give them meanings in ways that relate to identity, access to resources, and what people hold to be culturally valuable.

 Apply specialized theories to the environment.

According to risk theory, people are increasingly concerned with avoiding environmental risks. Moreover, society is organized hierarchically according to levels of safety or hazard, so wealth is less determinant of class position than the ability to avoid harm. The ecological dialogue suggests that the environmental world is never fully knowable, but that we can gain more knowledge about the environment through interaction. We will never be able to see perfectly what happens in an ecosystem, so that we can predict with perfect accuracy how it will behave under certain conditions, but we can gain a better understanding by experiencing nature and sharing those experiences through dialogue.

 14.5 Identify steps toward social change concerning the environment.

One of the biggest challenges to solving environmental problems is that we all have personal relationships with the environment, and ways of seeing the environment, that are culturally, socially, and economically important to us. In order to think critically about our own practices, we need to engage in open conversations with others about their environmental experiences and beliefs. Environmental problems can also seem global and insurmountable. Yet we can make small changes to our everyday practices that add up over time, and across our communities, so the effects can be significant. For example, using environmentally friendly transportation, reducing waste, and sourcing more environmentally just products seem like good places to start, as long as the conversations about the bigger issues continue.

DISCUSSION QUESTIONS

1. How does one determine if an environmental concern is a social problem? Does it matter if the problem has its roots in human activity, or can it be a result of natural causes? In what ways does the interpretation of environmental issues determine if a set of concerns constitutes a social problem?

2. In what ways does one's identity—age, race, socioeconomic status, and gender especially—affect how one experiences environmental problems firsthand? Which individuals and groups bear the responsibility for alleviating the effects of environmental problems? What influences the extent to which the stakeholders are also the decision makers in the communities most affected by environmental hazards?

3. What impact has globalization had on the environment? How do other variables, such as the relative wealth and power of a country, affect the distribution of environmental risk and harm?

4. Does naming the environmental issue "*climate change* rather *global warming* have an impact on the meanings attached to the issue? What is the evidence to support or refute climate change as a social problem? Who is affected by changes in temperature, ocean levels, and weather patterns around the world?

5. According to the structural functionalist perspective, what would need to change in order to bring about positive changes to the environment? Who is responsible for the environmental problems we face as a society based on this perspective? What sorts of technological and social changes would reduce the environmental harm humans are causing?

6. According to the conflict perspective, how effective are attempts to legislate solutions to environmental issues? What obstacles exist that make effective legislation difficult? How do the meanings we associate with environmental concerns play a role in the traction that potential legislation gets from constituents?

7. According to the risk society perspective, what changes in the social structure would positively or negatively affect the environment? How is risk avoidance correlated with socioeconomic status when it comes to choices such as where to live and what to eat? How do people determine their own acceptable levels of risk in regard to all the various environmental concerns they potentially encounter?

8. What does one gain from viewing environmental social problems from the ecological dialogue approach that is not seen from other perspectives? Which experts from other fields would be most helpful to those trying to better understand environmental problems from a sociological perspective?

9. How much impact do the actions of individuals have on environmental problems? What choices made by individuals are likely to have the greatest impact over time? What sort of data or evidence will determine when our society has improved the impact we are having on the environment?

10. How can one encourage not only local and individual changes to benefit the environment but also societal and global improvements? What role do governments and international organizations play in reducing environmental harm around the world and not just in their own backyards?

KEY TERMS

cognitive dissonance 384

ecological dialogue 388

ecological modernization theory 381

frame alignment 384

frame analysis 383

hybrid 373

indicators 380

McDonaldization 373

realism 388

reflexive modernization 386

risk contract 388

risk society 386

social equity 371

treadmill of production 382

Sharpen your skills with SAGE edge at edge.sagepub.com/trevino

A personalized approach to help you accomplish your coursework goals in an easy-to-use learning environment.

15 SCIENCE AND TECHNOLOGY

Wenda K. Bauchspies

Mark Wilson / Staff / Getty Images

A boy looks at a mural depicting an astronaut walking on the moon at the Smithsonian Air and Space Museum in Washington, D.C. The first moon landing, on July 20, 1969, was a great achievement accomplished through innovations in science and technology. Neil Armstrong, the first man to set foot on the surface of the moon, famously proclaimed, "That's one small step for a man, one giant leap for mankind." What do you think will be the next giant leap in science and technology that will help solve social problems?

Investigating Science and Technology: My Story

Wenda K. Bauchspies

After teaching high school physics for several years, I joined the Peace Corps and spent many hours talking with Togolese middle school teachers about the realities of teaching science in their schools. The conversations echoed those I'd had with colleagues at home, but what I wasn't prepared for was the need to negotiate our different scientific and technological understandings. These negotiations led me to ask, How do science and technology travel? What happens when science or technology is adopted? Is science gendered in Togo as in the United States?

Twenty years later I am still exploring how science and technology travel, teaching and studying the way the social (rather than the physical) world works from the nexus of science, technology, and society. My early research explored where Togolese women are in science education. Like women from industrialized nations, they enter science with the help of their social networks, and in particular the support of male relatives, such as fathers or uncles, who encourage them.

LEARNING OBJECTIVES

15.1 Identify social problems related to science and technology.

15.2 Describe how science and technology are socially defined.

15.3 Discuss patterns and trends in science and technology.

15.4 Identify the stakeholders in science and technology.

15.5 Apply the functionalist, conflict, and symbolic interactionist perspectives to science and technology issues.

15.6 Apply specialized theories to science and technology issues.

15.7 Identify steps toward social change regarding science and technology.

 ## WHAT DO YOU THINK?

Questions about Science and Technology from the General Social Survey

1. **What is your interest level in scientific discoveries?**
   - ☐ VERY INTERESTED
   - ☐ MODERATELY INTERESTED
   - ☐ NOT AT ALL INTERESTED

2. **What is your confidence level in the scientific community?**
   - ☐ A GREAT DEAL
   - ☐ ONLY SOME
   - ☐ HARDLY ANY

3. **Does science make our way of life change too fast?**
   - ☐ YES
   - ☐ NO

4. **Do the benefits of scientific research outweigh harmful results?**
   - ☐ YES
   - ☐ NO

5. **Scientific research is necessary and should be supported by the federal government.**
   - ☐ AGREE
   - ☐ DISAGREE

6. **What is your interest level in technologies?**
   - ☐ VERY INTERESTED
   - ☐ MODERATELY INTERESTED
   - ☐ NOT AT ALL INTERESTED

7. **Do you use the home Internet through a mobile device?**
   - ☐ YES
   - ☐ NO

▶▶ Turn to the end of the chapter to view the results for the total population.

SOURCE: National Opinion Research Center, University of Chicago.

DATA-MINING TECHNOLOGY

In the summer of 2013, a 30-year-old American computer specialist was proclaimed a hero, a patriot, and a whistle-blower by some and a dissident and traitor by others. Edward J. Snowden, a former employee of the Central Intelligence Agency (CIA) and a former contractor for the National Security Agency (NSA), had leaked classified information to the British newspaper the *Guardian* regarding top-secret mass surveillance of civilians' phone calls and e-mails by the U.S. and British governments.

How would you label Snowden's actions? The U.S. government immediately charged him with espionage and theft. Snowden was quoted as saying that the extent of the government's mass data collection was far greater than the public knew. The documents he revealed contradicted what James Clapper, U.S. director of national intelligence, had recently told a congressional hearing—that the NSA was *not* collecting such forms of information about American citizens.

Snowden's actions became a catalyst for worldwide discussions about mass surveillance versus secrecy and national security versus individual privacy in a post-9/11 world. Is using a portable digital device to store sensitive documents a safe or dangerous practice? Do we need stricter policies and new technologies to ensure that top-secret information stays top-secret? Are U.S.-based hosting and other Web service companies losing business to overseas competitors? If so, does that pose a danger to U.S. security? Has Snowden's leak damaged the U.S. government's espionage capabilities and left the nation at higher risk of terrorism? Or are governments in fact going too far and endangering the privacy of their citizens? In tandem with these questions, sociologists are asking how the incorporation of surveillance technologies into everyday life is redefining social inequality, social relations, and the concepts of public versus private space. Technology is at the center of a new social problem: the shifting balance between privacy and security.

We use cell phones, computers, and other devices to communicate, shop, bank, and do business online.

Former intelligence contractor Edward J. Snowden poses for a photo during an interview in an undisclosed location in Moscow, Russia. Snowden, who exposed extensive details of global electronic surveillance by the National Security Agency, was given temporary asylum by Russia, allowing him to evade prosecution by authorities in the United States. Do you consider him a traitor or a patriot? An idealist or an opportunist?

New communication technologies such as Skype, Viber, and Tango have been assumed to offer more privacy than landlines that could be wiretapped. But are they? What technologies are being data-mined? How and by whom? What is public and what is private on the Internet? Are physically mailed and e-mailed documents equally private and secure? Google, Facebook, and Amazon freely engage in sophisticated consumer surveillance and data mining to boost their bottom lines. Their collection and analysis of consumer data is part of the **big data** revolution. That is, using technological advances in digitization, inexpensive memory, massive processing power, and advanced analytics, corporations are now able to aggregate large quantities of digital data to tailor services, advertising, and products to particular consumers. Civil and medical institutions are using big data too, to sift hospital statistics on infections, mortality rates, durations of patient stays, and health care providers, hoping to make hospitals safer and improve medical outcomes.

However, identity thieves, insurance companies, prospective employers, and opponents of individuals or nations may also be using big data, compiling consumers' personal information, passwords, bank account information, or medical histories intending to

Big data: The large quantities of digital data produced by digital societies, including data from cell phones, keystrokes, and GPS units.

cause harm. For example, identity fraud is on the rise, with the number of global victims topping 1 million a day, causing the loss of more than $110 billion annually worldwide. In 2013 there were 12.6 million U.S. victims of identity fraud, or approximately 1 victim every three seconds (Javelin Strategy & Research, 2013). Have you or has someone you know been a victim of identity fraud? Do you know where your data are?

....

ASK YOURSELF: Can governments use surveillance to increase security while still respecting civil liberties such as the right to privacy? What trade-offs between privacy and safety shape public and private security and surveillance activities? How does our usual assumption that the Internet is secure shape our social relationships there?

....

Science and technology play a prominent role in shaping what we define as a social problem. By exploring the relationship between social problems and science and technology, this chapter will help you understand how and why some technology issues emerge as widely discussed social problems while others remain in the category of purely technological or scientific problems.

HACKING AND CYBERCRIME AROUND THE WORLD

 15.1 Identify social problems related to science and technology.

"I'm a computer hacker. I haven't hurt anyone," says a young male being questioned by a detective in a TV show. In fact, more than 75% of hacking worldwide is done by men between the ages of 18 and 30, most likely living in California, Florida, New York, or Texas (United Nations Office on Drugs and Crime 2013; Internet Crime Complaint Center 2011) (see Figure 15.1). The original hackers were members of the MIT Tech Model Railroad Club who tinkered with the circuitry of model railroads in the 1950s. Some of them discovered that the toy whistles of the train engines could fool the telephone system and allow them to make long-distance calls for free. Here we see the origin of the term *hacking* as we know it—tinkering with a technology to gain an advantage, still the core practice of hacking today.

A *white-hat hacker* hacks to protect companies and help identify individuals engaged in cybercrime. A *black-hat*

FIGURE 15.1 Top 10 Countries for Hackers, 2010

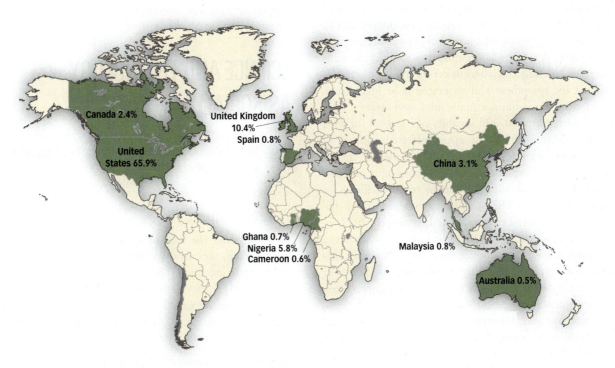

NOTE: Percentages indicate global share of individual perpetrators per country.
SOURCE: Internet Crime Complaint Center (2011, 11). NW3C, Inc., d/b/a the National White Collar Crime Center. All rights reserved.

 Data Mining   Cybercrime

hacker, in contrast, aims to break into company computers to steal data or vandalize computer networks or websites. A hacker can also be a "hacktivist"—someone who steals or manipulates data to make a political or social statement. Aaron Swartz believed that information on the Internet should be available to all for free, so he downloaded 4.8 million academic articles from a subscription-only service in the United States. Though he acted for political reasons rather than for financial gain, he was charged with wire and computer fraud. Whether it is done for political, financial, or personal gain, hacking is on the increase worldwide. Approximately 3% of the hackers worldwide are based in China, where the government places major restrictions on citizens' Internet access and online communication. In China, hacking offers some individuals a chance to tinker with the Internet in order to gain freedom of expression, autonomy, and empowerment, while other Chinese hackers have attacked government and corporate websites and networks around the world, hitting organizations such as the U.S. Federal Election Commission, Google, and Microsoft.

About 6 in 10 global Internet users have been touched by cybercrimes such as identity theft, computer viruses, or online fraud. Are you one of them? Globally there are 14 cybervictims every second (Norton 2012). Your chance of being a victim of cybercrime depends on your geographic location, your Internet habits, and your Internet technologies. The theft of real property is a long-familiar social problem, whereas the theft or manipulation of electronic data has become one of the top four economic crimes of the early 21st century (PricewaterhouseCoopers 2011). New forms of cyberespionage and cyberwarfare are also proliferating. A nonprofit organization called Spamhaus in London identified Cyberbunker in the Netherlands as a host for spammers and requested it be blacklisted. In response, Spamhaus e-mails and webservers were flooded with traffic at 300 gigabits per second for over a week in March 2013. The attack affected millions of Internet users by slowing down global Internet traffic. Another form of espionage that is becoming a problem worldwide is the stealing of human resource files as a means of terrorism. The human resource records of the Nigerian secret service were hacked in August 2012 by Boko Haram, an anti-Western group known for attacking Christians, schools, and police stations in Nigeria. This attack illustrates the growing capabilities of the cyber arsenal available to groups or nations wanting to employ new forms of warfare or espionage.

As we have seen throughout this book, to understand social problems sociologists ask questions about who, why, how, and what. In cybercrime or hacking, the "who" can be anyone from a local employee to a customer to a stranger halfway around the world, acting alone or in a group. The "why" is motivated by economic gain, espionage, activism,

terrorism, or warfare. The "how" is the use of knowledge and skills to manipulate software and to take advantage of Internet behaviors. The "what" is as dynamic as the Internet, ranging from an individual being scammed out of money to sensitive data being stolen and sold. Hacking thus attempts to modify an existing sociotechnical system like the Internet by introducing new social practices and technologies. A **sociotechnical system** is a system that includes material artifacts, human skills, and social practices defined by social norms within an organizational pattern to obtain or address a goal or objective.

Social problems like cybercrime and hacking are unique because of the role technology plays in them. That is, without the Internet and electronic hardware and software, there would be no cybercrime. However, not all cyberthreats come from criminals or black-hat hackers. They can also originate from the unintended consequence of software upgrades or defective equipment. Regardless of their origins, cyberthreats are defined by the skill levels, motivations, and abilities of the actors.

ASK YOURSELF: Consider the information displayed in Figure 15.1. Why might the United States, the United Kingdom, and Nigeria be hot spots for hackers? What do the other seven top locations for hacking have in common with the these three countries that might explain why they all support hackers in large numbers? Is there a correlation with tinkering to gain advantage? What social factors support or suppress Internet hacking?

SCIENCE AND TECHNOLOGY AS SOCIALLY DEFINED

 15.2 Describe how science and technology are socially defined.

What Is Science?

To understand the role of science in a social problem like hacking, we begin by defining it. The term *science* can refer to particular fields of study, such as biology, physics, or geology. Science is a method of collecting and verifying observed facts. It is the entire societal institution of gathering, reproducing, and maintaining

Sociotechnical system: A system that includes material artifacts, human skills, and social practices defined by social norms within an organizational pattern to obtain or address a goal or objective.

knowledge, and it includes actors, material culture, and resources. Robert K. Merton (1942), the first sociologist of science, called it a "deceptively inclusive word" because it is all of these. For our purposes, **science** is the accumulation of knowledge by specific methods within a particular culture that certifies, applies, and governs what is named science.

Science as a form of knowledge plays an active role in what becomes a social problem. The Love Canal neighborhood in Niagara Falls, New York, was the home of Hooker Chemical before that company's property was sold for suburban development in the 1950s. The area was known to have puddles of oil and other chemicals that children often played in. In 1976, journalists reported that the community was suffering an unusual number of miscarriages, birth defects, and other health problems, and that toxic chemicals were present in the soil and water. Local authorities denied there was a problem, ignoring local activists' complaints of strange odors and documentation of residents' birth defects. Scientists were divided, and studies were inconclusive about whether chemicals caused the reported illnesses. Studies by the U.S. Environmental Protection Agency (EPA) found harm to residents' chromosomes, while other studies found little direct evidence of harm.

What we consider knowledge and who knows it often defines social problems. Science is a social problem gatekeeper because it designates what knowledge has authority and when. In the case of Love Canal, only scientists were believed when they labeled the community safe, while the concerns of local parents were brushed aside. Eventually both science and parental knowledge came into alignment when in 1978 President Jimmy Carter named Love Canal the site of a federal health emergency. Science has the power to determine what knowledge is relevant, and when, and how other knowledge is interpreted within and outside social problems.

In December 1984 a gas leak in Bhopal, India, became one of the world's worst industrial disasters, killing more than 2,200 people outright and exposing 500,000 others to a toxic cloud. Today the Indian government argues that there is no contamination at the site, and that documented birth defects are unrelated to the disaster. Studies of local groundwater and the breast milk of residents show the continued presence of toxic chemicals above typical levels in the community. As a result, environmental scientists, the environmental advocacy group Greenpeace, and

Science: The accumulation of knowledge by specific methods within a particular culture that certifies, applies, and governs what is named science.

Technology: An artifact that is composed of social practices, social institutions, and systems that create and constrain it.

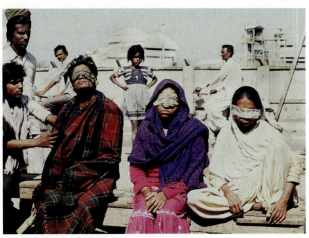

AFP / Getty Images

A 1984 photo shows victims who lost their eyesight after a poison gas leak from a Union Carbide pesticide plant in Bhopal, India. The gas leak was the world's worst industrial disaster, claiming more than 2,850 lives. Other industrial disasters include the partial nuclear meltdown at the Three Mile Island nuclear station in Pennsylvania in 1979; the nuclear meltdown at the Chernobyl nuclear power plant in Ukraine in 1986; the *Exxon Valdez* oil spill off the coast of Alaska in 1989; the *Deepwater Horizon* (or BP) oil spill in the Gulf of Mexico in 2010; the fire at the Ali Enterprises garment factory in Karachi, Pakistan, in 2012; and the Elk River chemical spill in West Virginia in 2014.

local community members are asking for renewed efforts to clean up the site and its contaminated groundwater. While science as a form of knowledge plays an active role in defining how governments, corporations, and communities respond to and accept responsibility for social problems, in the absence of a long-term health study of those exposed to the gas at Bhopal, science is unable to offer an opinion.

ASK YOURSELF: In the case of Love Canal, the truth won out. Does the truth always win out? Does the moment before science identifies the "truth" augment or diminish social problems?

What Is Technology?

We often think of technology as consisting of material objects like computers, handheld electronic devices, and other machines. But a broader and more useful definition identifies technology as the means to serve a need, work efficiently, make a profit, or offer a service. Thus technology, like science, has multiple meanings. It can be a computer, but it can also be a complex whole consisting of the knowledge, methods, and materials needed to make and use a computer. More formally, **technology** is an artifact that is defined by social practices, social institutions, and social relationships.

Consider a slaughterhouse at the beginning of the 20th century in the midwestern United States, and think about how, as a technology, it was defined and constrained by wider social practices. Male butchers gained income and status in the slaughterhouse and in their community because of their skill with the knife. After World War I, black men entered knife work and gained stature as well. Women were a small minority in the meatpacking industry and were paid less than men through the 1960s. Within this minority a hierarchy based on race defined the activity, technology, and location of "women's work." After men cut up the meat, certain parts were sent down a chute to the women's work areas for processing. Black women were given the least desirable women's jobs in the offal part of the slaughterhouse, though they could still earn more doing the lowest-paid work there than they could working as maids elsewhere. Native-born white women were considered temporary workers who earned the same as black women. However, they did clean work in the packing department, where visitors were shown the modern business of meatpacking. Eastern European women did the work that required the most training and skill because they were long-term dependable workers. Societal notions about race and gender structured what men and women did in the slaughterhouse, what technologies they used, and where they used them (Horowitz 1997).

ASK YOURSELF: Make a list of technologies in your home. Does everyone in the household use the same technologies, and in the same manner? How do people of different genders and races use technologies differently or similarly?

What Is Techn oscience?

Where is the boundary between science and technology? To answer this question, we return to the topic of hacking. Early hackers were a few individuals with high-level computer skills and techniques. An early hacker action made a political statement with the WANK worm, which declared "Worms Against Nuclear Killers" when it infected computers at NASA and the U.S. Department of Energy. Such malware, or software intended to disrupt computer operations, was a type of "science" because the knowledge to wield it was maintained and produced by a small group of people. Today, malware tool kits are readily available and make participation in cybercrimes and hacking easier. They have become a technology.

In its history hacking has sometimes behaved as a "science" and sometimes as a "technology." **Technoscience** includes all supporters, detractors, and social relationships that define the categories of science and technology.

A technoscientific analysis can help capture the "messiness" around the boundaries of each term by exploring how hacking is both a science and a technology simultaneously. For example, technoscience would address how a computer infected with a virus could turn an unwitting computer user into a hacker, or how the skills and knowledge of computer science become a means for espionage between nations.

Science as a Social Problem

Traditional images of science portrayed it as a truth-seeking activity that used quantitative assessments and expert knowledge to arrive at facts, until we began to question the facts of science. For example, society recognized that the atom bomb was a military marvel as well as a device of horrific destruction. Industrialization brought labor-saving devices into the factory and the home while also polluting environments with chemical by-products. These complications prompt us to ask the question: Is science a social problem?

To frame science as a social problem, we must understand it as a human endeavor rather than as a method that creates rationality, objectivity, and purity. As long as science offers us certainty, authority, and answers, we will see it as a solution. When it creates uncertainty, risk, and danger, we identify and study science as a social problem.

ASK YOURSELF: Identify a social problem that involves science, such as stem cell research or climate change. Describe how science could be the problem or the solution in regard to that issue.

Technology as a Social Problem

Modern Times, a film written and directed by Charlie Chaplin in 1936, examines the idea of technology as a social problem. The film asks whether technology has gotten too big and made humans its servants, simply parts of the machine. With the entrance of industrialization, workers' skills and knowledge become obsolete next to the machine. This deskilling of workers shifts control from them to a centralized authority.

Lewis Mumford, one of the founders of technology studies, wrote about the changes the increased mechanization of human labor brought to society and suggested that the way we use technology may threaten what it means to

Technoscience: A concept that encompasses the boundary between science and technology and includes all supporters, detractors, and social relations that work to eventually close the division between the categories of science and technology.

 Technology and the Workforce

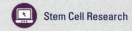 Stem Cell Research

Electrosensitivity in Sweden

Have you ever wondered about the impact of wireless networks on your health? In 2000, the Swedish government set a goal to cover 99.98% of Sweden with a 3G telecommunications network by the end of 2003. Due to problems in obtaining building permits, the implementation of work on the network was delayed. Meanwhile, local protests focused on the locations of towers and the potential health risks posed by the transmitters' radiation.

Among the major stakeholders in these protests were people who suffer from electrosensitivity, experiencing headaches, nausea, and skin abrasions as the result of exposure to electromagnetic fields (EMFs). (Several countries host associations of electrosensitives, who may call themselves "victims of EMFs" or "ElectroSensitive.") Electrosensitivity is controversial because there is no scientific explanation for symptoms associated with proximity to electronic equipment. In the absence of accepted scientific evidence, knowledge is often contested between various stakeholders. In this case, Swedish citizens were calling for stricter regulations because the long-term effects of radiation were unknown. Local authorities and industry stated that 3G radiation

is harmless and attributed public concerns to media scaremongering. The public deliberations on Sweden's 3G network soon became polarized, pitting scientific facts against individuals' experiences as policy makers interpreted protests as challenges to scientific expertise and economic policies.

Through interviews and participant observation, social scientist Linda Soneryd (2007) studied how Swedish citizens developed an understanding of the risks and uncertainties related to 3G radiation and EMFs. She found that their conclusions were based on their understanding of science, their interactions with authorities, and their use of technologies. Many told Soneryd that they had measured EMFs in their homes, changed their routines to decrease exposure, and observed changes in their health according to the presence or use of electronics. Others described their work in technology-based careers and the experiences of colleagues and family members with electrosensitivity in health care facilities and workplaces.

In 2004 and 2005, the Swedish Radiation Protection Authority sponsored "Transparency Forums for Mobile Phones Communication" as a response to the public protests. At these events, various actors

discussed electrosensitivity and what was known and unknown about it. At times the discussions were heated and polarized, and some speakers changed their positions in the process. All participants responded to established norms of authority to express and justify themselves using the dominant scientific and technical discourse. This limited the discussion to radiation and risk and excluded other conversations that would have introduced a greater focus on ethical issues and pragmatic solutions.

Soneryd's work illustrates the importance of public deliberations regarding new technologies by showing how various actors and interests come together to articulate viewpoints and engage in dialogues. She found that community deliberations depend on reference points and facts to stabilize the conversation, in order for opposing perspectives to find common ground in addressing the social problem of a new technology.

▶ **THINK ABOUT IT:** Why do you think there has been public protest against EMFs in Sweden when the scientific evidence regarding harm from EMFs is inconclusive, insufficient, or absent? What other citizens around the globe are protesting or not protesting EMFs, and why?

be human. Mumford argued that technology is an integral part of civilization that reflects the entire society. A society where everyone visits the well daily to obtain water develops social interactions that are different from those of a society where members use water in isolation, inside rooms devoted to water usage. Mumford criticized the machine-dominated culture for altering community engagement, individual autonomy, and quality of life. In other words, he foresaw the possibility of technology being a social problem that dehumanizes humanity. The introduction of household water sources decreased community solidarity in communities that formerly depended on limited numbers of common wells, even as it decreased physical labor and improved water quality.

The most famous scene from the 1936 film *Modern Times* shows Charlie Chaplin working on the gears of a giant machine. Other films in which technology is seen as controlling humans include *2001: A Space Odyssey,* in which the HAL 9000 computer takes over a spacecraft with two astronauts in it; *Westworld,* in which a malfunctioning android terrorizes vacationers at a futuristic Western-themed amusement park; and *I, Robot,* in which an evolved supercomputer programs robots to kill humans. Can you think of other films and novels with similar themes?

In his later work, Mumford (1967) wrote of the **megamachine**, a new social order composed of humans and technology that is dominated by technological rather than human needs. Megamachines alter human **social organization**, the pattern of relationships among individuals and groups. Could they become reality?

In South Korea, 90% of households have broadband, and 66% of the population have smart phones. More than 2.55 million South Koreans are using their Internet devices longer than eight hours a day. More than half the nation plays online games regularly. Teachers report that children ages 5 to 9 are animated when using smart phones and distracted and nervous without them. One young girl said she gets nervous when she has less than 20% power on her device. This intense engagement with the Internet is a megamachine, in which humans and technology are creating a new social organization and people may be spending more time with machines than with other people. Government officials, health care practitioners, and teachers have called this social problem "Internet addiction" and ask whether it might become an illness (Lee 2012). Educators are responding by introducing curriculum to teach elementary school children about safe and healthy uses of connectivity.

ASK YOURSELF: Identify a megamachine and describe how it is altering social organization. Is it creating new social problems?

PATTERNS AND TRENDS

 15.3 Discuss patterns and trends in science and technology.

If we view science and technology as a social problem, the trends and patterns that emerge illustrate a connection between modern science, "personal troubles," and "public issues" that is often overlooked when we view science, technology, and society separately. C. Wright Mills (1961, 16) described this connection between science and society as a **science machine** that is built by a community of individuals who share a common culture. He suggested that once we see the science machine driving science, we can begin to understand its connections and relationships to society and its problems.

Values and Doing Science

For decades modern science has been sampling our blood and studying our genes to evaluate our health, identify our predispositions for certain illnesses, and prescribe treatments. We assign to science the power to discover the truth about our health. This power is reinforced by the success of science in developing new vaccines, insecticides, and drugs to solve social problems. However, what happens when an illness moves through a population faster than science can find an answer? The science's protocol is to do research in the laboratory. When a solution is suspected, it is tested carefully in a controlled environment until guidelines are established to protect people from unintended consequences. Once the efficacy of the science has been established, the solution is introduced to the general public.

What happens when there isn't sufficient time to go through the established protocols? In response to social scientific problems such as HIV/AIDS, activists have suggested the need to implement **crisis science**, or triage science, when there is no time to follow time-consuming research protocols. The goal of crisis science is to respond

Megamachine: A new social order composed of humans and technology that is dominated by technological rather than human needs.

Social organization: The pattern of relationships between individuals and groups.

Science machine: A connection between science and society that is built by a community of individuals who share a common culture.

Crisis science: Medical science that works in tandem with Mode 1 science and has the freedom to respond to crises and the needs of patients faster than traditional science.

quickly and produce results quickly, allowing individuals to participate in studies that may be risky and soliciting community participation in the research (Hood 2003). Crisis science works in tandem with the normal protocols of science while simultaneously engaging activists and patients in the coproduction of knowledge through experimental procedures of drug testing. This occurred in the case of AIDS research (Epstein 1995).

Another response of the scientific community to social problems is the development of **science shops**, facilities hosted by universities where citizens can participate in science, ask scientific questions, and become part of the scientific process. Science shops began in the Netherlands in the 1980s as a bottom-up strategy for bringing the social needs of communities into universities' scientific research agendas. They can now be found at universities around the globe from Europe to South Korea, demonstrating how science is being redefined by the organizations that create it.

Reform movements that typically address health or social problems, such as advocacy for nutritional cancer therapies and environmental change, have also generated their own research (by the Gerson Research Organization and the World Wide Fund for Nature, for instance). They have conducted peer-reviewed research and in some cases provide alternative theories to engage with mainstream science (Hess 1999, 2009). Thus science is being redefined by social problems to include more active roles for actors typically excluded from the production of knowledge.

When we analyze social problems and science simultaneously, our view of science changes from certainty, facts, and objectivity to uncertainty, conflicting values, high stakes, and urgent decisions (Ravetz 2005). By broadening the products of science from ones that offer certainty, objectivity, and established knowledge to ones that recognize the risks of the unknown, we redefine our understanding of science to acknowledge the complexities rather than to eliminate them. By recognizing human values, risks, and uncertainties, science engages with social problems to find new solutions.

Science shops: Facilities hosted by universities where citizens can participate in science, ask scientific questions, and become part of the scientific process.

Mode 1: A type of scientific discovery or knowledge production done by scientists in universities through the application of experimental science within distinct disciplines.

Mode 2: A type of scientific discovery or knowledge production that is done by experts and nonexperts working together in transdisciplinary environments to create applications that are socially responsible.

Today corporations, citizens, governments, and nonprofit organizations are interested in the knowledge, technologies, and patents of a newly interdisciplinary science. The shift in what science is, who it serves, and how it does what it does is summarized in Table 15.1, which distinguishes the traits of classic scientific discovery as **Mode 1** and socially responsible and application-oriented science as **Mode 2**.

ASK YOURSELF: What are the advantages and disadvantages of applying Mode 1, Mode 2, and crisis science to the solution of social problems?

Technology and Values

One of the responses to threats of terrorism in the United States was the development of an all-body scanner to be used in airports as a quick and efficient means of searching for concealed weapons. Two types of three-dimensional millimeter-wave machines were developed: "naked" machines and "blob" machines. The naked machines showed graphic naked images of the human body and anything concealed under the clothing. The blob machines displayed sexless avatars with baseball caps that indicated where on the body something was hidden. Public response to the naked machines was negative enough for the Obama administration to order that they be retrofitted as blob machines.

This is a case in which a technological solution to one social problem, security, spurred a new social problem by

TABLE 15.1 Traits of Mode 1 and Mode 2 Forms of Knowledge Production

Traits	Mode 1	Mode 2
Audience	Academic	Wider society
Context	Disciplinary	Transdisciplinary
Organization	Hierarchical	Egalitarian
Priority	Academic freedom	Social responsibility
Evaluation	Peer review	Social relevance
Validation	Scientific certainty	Acknowledges uncertainty
Planning	Long-term and linear	Exploratory

SOURCE: Gross (2010, 26). *Ignorance and Surprise: Science, Society, and Ecological Design.* Cambridge, MA: MIT Press.

 3D Printing

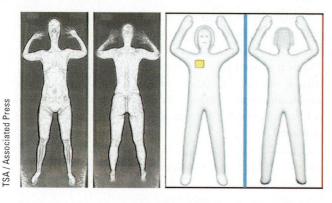

These two sets of images show details of what Transportation Security Administration (TSA) officers see on computer monitors when passengers pass through airport body scanners. At left are two images created using backscatter advanced image X-ray technology ("naked" machines). At right are images from scanners using millimeter wave technology ("blob" machines), which produce cartoonlike outlines rather than the more naked images of passengers produced by X-ray scanners. Which of the two technologies do you think is most effective?

invading privacy. The technological solution that solved the social problem of body scanning embraced the value of protecting privacy as well as security (Rosen and Wittes 2011).

The example of the naked and blob machines demonstrates that there may be several technological solutions to a social problem. The technological solution that meets the most needs of all the actors will be the ideal solution. Unfortunately, this ideal technological solution doesn't always get designed or implemented. However, by identifying different actors in social problems and their needs, we can begin to design technology that is more inclusive of multiple needs.

Science Constructs and Solves a Social Problem

Chagas disease affects roughly 18 million people in Latin America. The *Trypanosoma cruzi* parasite is transmitted to humans by an insect called the vinchuca that nests in walls and roofs made of adobe. Once infected, a person may not show external signs of the disease, but his or her nervous, digestive, and circulatory systems are being attacked by the parasite. If a patient is treated early, the parasite can be controlled or killed; however, if left untreated the disease is fatal—it is the fourth leading cause of death in Latin America. The World Health Organization (WHO) considers Chagas disease a neglected disease that others have called a disease of poverty.

In 1909 Carlos Chagas, a physician, discovered the disease in Brazil while working on urban epidemics for the Manguinhos Serum Therapy Institute, an internationally recognized center of experimental science. However, the disease that was named for him was not immediately recognized as a social problem in Latin America and did not draw the attention of scientists and public health administrators. In the 1930s Salvador Mazza, an Argentinean epidemiologist working on Chagas disease, carefully researched acute cases to document the symptoms and identified traces of parasites in the blood of infected patients. Mazza's commitment to documenting evidence of infection of the parasite contributed to the recognition of Chagas disease by national public health departments and the Pan American Health Organization.

In the 1940s and 1950s Chagas disease gained recognition as a chronic ailment and a social problem. Scientists shifted from studying individual patients to studying the disease in the general population. These larger-scales studies led to statistical analyses that estimated the number of people afflicted. Public health officials could then mobilize to fight the problem through hygiene education and improved access to health care. In addition, a new insecticide, gammexane, was found to eliminate vinchucas, and massive fumigation of housing was implemented by the El Salvadoran Ministry of Health.

By the 1970s, the *T. cruzi* parasite had become the focus of study, instead of the person infected with Chagas disease. Researchers studies the physiology of the parasite and its insect host in order to find a means to attack the parasite and create a vaccine against it. A vaccine would solve the social problem and replace fumigation and education as a first defense. Though no vaccine was discovered, the study of *T. cruzi* became an important biological model that legitimated Latin American scientists in the eyes of the international scientific community. Today the primary strategy for addressing Chagas disease is to control and attack the parasite (Kreimer and Zabala 2007).

Different social actors choose different facts and frameworks from which to approach and understand the social problem of Chagas disease. For the infected patient, Chagas is the cause of illness. For the scientific community and public health officials, knowledge of Chagas and its environment, host, and parasite helped identify a potential social problem, construct the social problem, and offer solutions. Science's role as authority remained constant even as solutions and constructions of the social problem changed.

Technological Fixes

In the United States and other Western cultures, people generally associate technological improvements with progress. In the late 18th century, science and technology were seen as instruments of societal transformation and began to symbolize progress. Today the ideal of **technocracy**, a system in which science and technology provide rationality, expertise, and logic and create a better world, is still widely considered desirable. This technocratic view of progress sees technology as a means to fix social problems.

For example, we use radar to deter speeding on the highways by monitoring automobiles and identifying those in violation of the speed limit. Drivers still speed, of course, and some buy radar detectors and occasionally get tickets. Their **technological fix** uses technology to solve a problem that is nontechnical and ignores the social components of the problem. In other words, when we use technology to solve a social problem like speeding, we may create another like the use of radar detectors. Or our solution may isolate the problem from the social context, such as ignoring the fact that the average speed of cars traveling on a particular highway is always 10 miles per hour over the speed limit.

ASK YOURSELF: What social problems does birth control address? Explain why birth control is or is not a technological fix. What values shape your answer to this question?

Industrialized Science Creates Social Problems

Science was once done by educated European male elites such as Galileo, Newton, and Kepler. Today it is the primary activity of a broad range of experts in academia, industry, and government. We have moved from an era of little science to big science, with the number of researchers growing steadily throughout the 20th century (see Figure 15.2). Science itself is now an industry. With the rise of **industrialized science**, in which science is done on a large scale for profit, new social problems are emerging (Ravetz 1971). With industry pursuing genomics, robotics, and nanotechnology for profit, for instance, the possibilities for intervention in and manipulation of human life and our environment are raising new questions.

In rich countries around the world, backbreaking labor and repetitive physical work have already been taken over by machines in an example of technology making life easier for many. With the help of robotics, more types of human labor could become unnecessary and alter

Technocracy: A means of governing that is guided by rationality, expertise, and logic.

Technological fix: The use of technology to solve a social problem that is nontechnical. In fixing the problem it creates another, because the underlying social issue is still present and has been isolated from the social context.

Industrialized science: Science that is done on the large scale for profit.

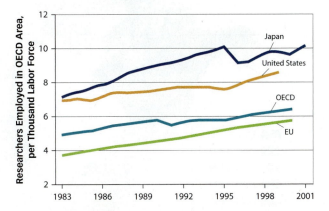

FIGURE 15.2 Total Numbers of Researchers Employed around the Globe, 1983–2001

SOURCE: Organization for Economic Cooperation and Development, Main Science and Technology Indicators. Reprinted with permission.

what humans do. What types of work will everyone do in a robotic world? We depend on our livelihoods to define who we are in society and where we fit. What will define the social order in a robotic world?

We now can create genetically modified organisms (GMOs) for food production, though some safety issues about manipulating genes in the food we eat remain unresolved. Nanotechnology offers similar engineering possibilities, such as genomics to modify our bodies and our world. Will we bioengineer ourselves to eliminate genetic propensities or vulnerabilities to disease? Who will be eligible, and what engineered traits will be desirable? Industrialized science may be offering us a "brave new world," or it may re-create our current world with social problems even more complex than those we already face. The problem is that we don't know what the outcomes will be. One solution is to redirect science to focus on safety, health, environment, and ethics rather than on industrialized goals (Ravetz 2005). This focus would ensure that science's agenda stays in tune with and responsive to social problems.

ASK YOURSELF: What will science look like in 50 years, and why? Will today's social problems alter the way science is done tomorrow? Why or why not?

Social Problems within Science

Worldwide there are more than 7 million scientists and engineers (see Figure 15.3), approximately 62% of them in industrialized nations. We know from Chapter 4 that

FIGURE 15.3 Number of R&D Researchers per Million People, 2006–2012

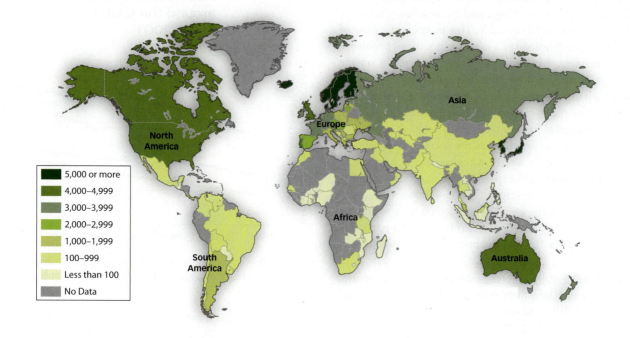

Legend:
- 5,000 or more
- 4,000–4,999
- 3,000–3,999
- 2,000–2,999
- 1,000–1,999
- 100–999
- Less than 100
- No Data

Map labels: North America, South America, Europe, Africa, Asia, Australia

SOURCE: United Nations Educational, Scientific, and Cultural Organization (UNESCO) Institute for Statistics: Catalog Sources: World Development Indicators. Reprinted with permission.

women are a minority within science. Looking at science from a global perspective, we can see that another minority consists of people from developing countries. Thus a social problem within science is the dearth of diversity in the science, technology, engineering, and math (STEM) workforce. Greater diversity in who does science will help science to fulfill its promise of creating a shared future beneficial to all.

However, some of the same obstacles that have prevented women from entering science also prevent citizens of developing countries from becoming scientists. Scarcity of role models and lack of access to education and resources are all potential obstacles to developing scientific capacity. Removing these can enrich the culture of science and expand its abilities to respond to social problems.

The Global Young Academy (GYA; http://www.globalyoungacademy.net) is an organization of early-career scientists from more than 55 countries who are mobilizing to improve the effectiveness of science to benefit all. At a recent meeting, GYA members emphasized the need for multidisciplinary and internationally connected research to address issues of sustainability that both developed and developing communities must face. In particular, societal trust and communication within and outside science were highlighted as obstacles to effective science. A common concern among

those working in resource-poor regions or on the periphery of science is access to global scientific networks. Science depends on strong networks to enable scientists to contribute to scientific discussions and global policy decisions.

ASK YOURSELF: Consider the data displayed in Figure 15.3. What types of social problems would science be addressing if more scientists were working in the Global South?

SCIENCE, TECHNOLOGY, AND THEIR STAKEHOLDERS

 15.4 Identify the stakeholders in science and technology.

One of the roles of science in modern society is to be the authority or voice of truth about the natural world. Science and technology validate programs and policies that tell us what we should eat, how we should treat illness, and what is best for our safety. They do this by providing knowledge and techniques that let us describe

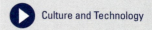
Culture and Technology

What Does It Mean to Be a Black Woman in Science?

Minority groups in the United States are underrepresented within the science and engineering professions compared to their proportions in the general population. Of all scientists and engineers in the United States, 2% are black women, compared to 51% who are white men (see Figure 15.4).

While all students need to be encouraged in scientific pursuits by parents, teachers, and mentors, minority students may receive less parental and school support to study science than their nonminority peers. High schools that serve minority populations often have limited offerings in math and science, lacking classes in subjects like analytical geometry, precalculus, and calculus that provide the foundation for majoring in science in college. A white male can always find a peer who shares his interests because he is in the majority, while minority students may have fewer peers to discuss and explore science or engineering with. Students who form study groups and complete their homework together are generally more successful than isolated students.

One black scientist described her shock at being overlooked by her peers and teachers, not because she is black but because she is a woman. Black women in science encounter not only racism but also sexism in the scientific culture. As students they may fail to be elected to student science organizations, may find their male lab partners (whether black or white) dismantling the labs they set up and redoing them, or may be advised to take freshman physics when male peers are taking junior-level quantum mechanics.

The culture of science is aware that minority women are rare in science and that many potential scientists are exiting the pathway before achieving their goal. Supplementary educational programs, efforts to change cultural norms, and mentoring are strategies that can change scientific culture and create a more welcoming community for minorities and women.

▶ **THINK ABOUT IT:** What stereotypes might the following individuals encounter: A Hispanic man working in a laboratory? An Asian woman directing a laboratory? A black woman giving a scientific presentation? A white homosexual man running for president of a scientific association?

FIGURE 15.4 Scientists and Engineers Working in Science and Engineering Occupations in the United States, 2010

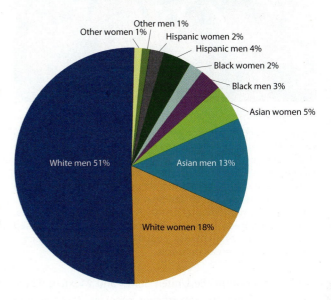

SOURCE: National Science Foundation.

---

problems with certainty and prescribe solutions with accuracy. For example, when we are ill and visit a doctor, we expect that he or she will diagnose our illness with certainty and prescribe the correct treatment.

In this section we will look at how different social actors or stakeholders use science and technology in specific and deliberate ways to frame, respond to, and solve social problems. Typical stakeholders of science and technology include the experts (scientists, engineers, and technicians), the funders (government, nonprofit organizations, and corporations), the producers (universities, corporations, and professional societies), and the consumers (average citizens, groups, and entire communities).

Social problems involving science and technology often take the form of complex controversies among scientific, medical, or technical experts. The social, political, and economic implications of these disagreements affect stakeholder groups unequally. Let us look at one example of

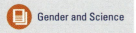
Gender and Science

An activist with the nongovernmental environmental organization Greenpeace holds up a corn cob during a demonstration outside the Ministry of Agriculture in Mexico City. Greenpeace opposes all form of genetic engineering, not only of plants but also of animals and microorganisms. The organization sees genetic engineering as a potential threat to human and environmental health. According to Greenpeace, scientific progress on molecular biology should not be used to turn the environment into a giant genetic experiment conducted by commercial interests.

corn production in the United States and Mexico, where the stakeholders are government agencies, farmers, and consumers in both countries.

In 2003, approximately 5% of total arable land worldwide was planted with transgenic crops. *Transgenic crops* are grown from seed that has had genes artificially inserted (rather than acquired through pollination) in order to increase yields, raise pest or disease resistance, or improve tolerance of heat, cold, or drought. The majority of transgenic crops grown today are herbicide-tolerant soybeans, insect-resistant cotton, and maize that is either herbicide-tolerant or insect-resistant. Of these crops, 90% are grown in the United States and Argentina, with Canada and China producing most of the remaining 10%. Concerns about the widespread adoption of transgenic crops include the potential for damage to human health, destruction of the environment, and disruptions to farming practices and food production.

Different governments have taken different stances on transgenic crops that reflect cultural, economic, and political factors. In the United States three federal agencies—the Department of Agriculture, the Environmental Protection Agency, and the Food and Drug Administration—ensure the safety of transgenic crops. There are no sexually compatible wild relatives for transgenic maize to pollinate in the United States, thus the primary concern of the U.S. government is the biosafety of humans and the environment, not the spread of transgenic maize into the local maize germplasm.

Mexico welcomes the importation of U.S. transgenic maize for food consumption. However, it has banned the planting of transgenic maize in its own soil since 1998 in order to keep the locally bred maize free of GMOs. Maize was first domesticated in Mexico several thousand years ago, and its wild ancestor still grows there. Thus the primary concern of the Mexican government is to maintain the genetic diversity of the landraces of maize in Mexico that are open-pollinated and bred by local farmers. **Landraces** are local varieties of seeds that have been domesticated by communities over time and have adapted to local cultural and environmental needs.

The Mexican government's interest in controlling transgenic maize is to preserve genetic diversity, while the U.S. government's concern centers on ensuring food and environmental safety. Thus similar types of stakeholders may have different interpretations or approaches to the same social problem. If transgenic crops become a social problem in the United States, it will likely focus on the safety of the crop for humans or the potential destruction of habitats for insects like the monarch butterfly. In Mexico the social problem will be preventing the flow of genes from transgenic crops to wild ancestors of maize and farmer-bred landraces of maize. Or it might be maintaining the traditional breeding practices of Mexican farmers if transgenic crops are introduced.

U.S. farmers prefer high-yielding maize and buy the first-generation hybrids yearly. Typically they do not save seeds for replanting from year to year, and their primary goal is the production of crops. Transgenic crops and large-scale farmers are both part of an industrial agricultural system.

In contrast, Mexican farmers produce maize and conserve landraces that have often been handed down through their families for generations. These traditional farmers develop new plant varieties, process their crops, and consume what they grow. They select and grow different varieties of maize based on cropping systems, local environmental conditions, and consumer preferences for color, texture, cookability, and shelf life. Mexican farmers trade seeds with relatives and neighbors in exchanges that reflect and reinforce their social relationships (Snow 2005).

One common concern among most of the stakeholders involved with transgenic crops is the safety of the crops for human consumption. Risks associated with these crops include allergic reactions to food and antibiotic resistance. Only two transgenic crops, of all that have been studied, have been found to cause allergies. One was never

Landraces: Local varieties of seeds that have been domesticated by communities over time and have adapted to local cultural and environmental needs.

developed further, and the safety of the other, StarLink corn, is still being debated by scientists. Research continues, but it is commonly believed that GMOs cause no greater risk of allergy than conventional foods. In the laboratory stage, transgenic crops are given antibiotic resistance markers that become part of the final product. Another concern is thus about the risk that a horizontal transfer of these drugs could lead to antibiotic resistance in humans. This too is believed to be highly unlikely, though the potential risk is there.

Little scientific evidence to date indicates that transgenic crops are riskier than conventionally bred crops. However, Zimbabwe refused to import GMO corn in 2010 because of concerns about its safety for the population and the purity of future crops.

The creation of transgenic crops is an expensive but powerful technology that industry has been quick to patent for profit. In the United States, the ability to secure intellectual property rights on living organisms and biological processes has helped the seed industry—once a regional business that supported a broad range of genetic diversity—to consolidate and become big business. Today the industry is dominated by only a few companies. In traditional agriculture, seed stock was a public good that individuals traded for the community's benefit. The entrance of transgenic crops into traditional agricultural communities threatens contamination of the seed stock, reduction of genetic diversity, and the pursuit of legal action by patent holders against smallholder farmers (Gepts 2005).

Transgenic crops that are insect-resistant are designed to address particular pests in particular regions. However, these pests and nontarget pests are different in other locations, so the introduction of a transgenic crop to a new area may cause unintended harm in the new ecosystem. For example, the monarch butterfly is susceptible to the *Bacillus thuringiensis* (Bt) toxin used in transgenic crops. Studies indicate there is minimal effect on the monarch in the short term, but further investigation is needed to measure any long-term effects. Other insects may be affected by the introduction of transgenic crops in ways we have yet to identify. Thus insects are additional potential stakeholders in the debate surrounding transgenic crops.

Science is an active stakeholder in this debate. However, within science there are different sorts of stakeholders among the individual scientists, critics, scientific publishers, and agribusiness. In 2001, two biologists, David Quist and Ignacio Chapela, documented the presence of transgenic genes in maize landraces in Mexico. Their paper, published in the science journal *Nature*, created a controversy in science and highlighted a social problem in agricultural biotechnology. Critics asked how the transgenes came to be there. It is a normal part of science for new theories to be challenged, but in this case

the critique was used to obscure the primary finding that transgenes were present in Mexican landraces of maize. The challengers' research was funded in part by an agriculture biotech firm involved in transgenic crop production. Their financial and political ties to industry raised questions about their motives for critiquing the findings of Quist and Chapela, who themselves were critics of the university-industry alliance.

Uncharacteristically, the editors of *Nature* disowned the original report by Quist and Chapela in a response that reflected the interests of the publication's sponsors. The controversy highlighted "the intensity of the marriage of science to corporations" in the field of agricultural biotechnology (Worthy et al. 2005,143). In 2005, the area in Mexico where Quist and Chapela had discovered transgenic genes was retested. Such genes were no longer present in the landraces of maize.

ASK YOURSELF: In regard to the debate around transgenic crops, what happens when a stakeholder is both a farmer and a consumer? Or a scientist and a consumer? What if a farmer is a stockholder in an agriculture biotech firm, or a scientist is funded by a biotechnology company? How do individuals with multiple roles in relation to transgenic crops negotiate conflicting values?

USING THEORY TO EXAMINE SCIENCE AND TECHNOLOGY: THE VIEWS FROM THE FUNCTIONALIST, CONFLICT, AND SYMBOLIC INTERACTIONIST PERSPECTIVES

 15.5 Apply the functionalist, conflict, and symbolic interactionist perspectives to science and technology issues.

Social scientists have long used the traditional three sociological perspectives—functionalism, conflict theory, and symbolic interactionism—to suggest alternative points of view from which to assess social problems. Contemporary scholarship on science, technology, and social problems uses these theories in conjunction with feminist theory, science and technology studies, and cultural studies to extend the analysis, definition, and content of social problems research.

Functionalism

A structural functionalist approach to science and social problems illustrates the positive and negative functions of social structures. One social problem within science is that top scientists receive the lion's share of scientific credit. A structural functionalist explanation for this would cite **cumulative advantage**, which multiplies the advantage for those who have resources and limits the capacity of those without. Cumulative advantage explains why graduate students who attend top-tier American research universities such as Harvard, Stanford, and MIT are more likely to become prominent scientists than those who attend nonresearch universities. At a top-tier research university students have access to active scientists and their scientific networks. These resources provide students with a cumulative advantage over their peers who lack such access.

Another example of cumulative advantage is the accumulation of cultural capital—that is, social assets that promote social mobility, such as a parent's educational background. Doctoral students are more likely to have a parent with an advanced degree (43%) than a parent with only some college (12%) (National Science Foundation 2013). Cumulative advantage helps explain the absence from science of individuals from a wide variety of backgrounds, socioeconomic levels, and educational institutions. Lack of diversity reinforces the preexisting scientific social networks, which means most scientists train at the same institutions with comparable cultural capital from the same recognized scientific leaders. This sameness in turn stabilizes the scientific culture by ensuring that similar questions are asked and studied by similar people.

A structural functionalist position may also help researchers pose questions about what role science or technology is playing in the creation of a social problem. That is, researchers might trace what knowledge is defining a social problem and how it is being applied in order to describe the relationship between science and the social problem. Or they might focus on a technology (such as the automobile) and ask how individuals and communities are using it in order to understand the role of the technology in social problems (such as traffic accidents or poor air quality).

Policy Implications of Structural Functionalism

Public policy can use a structural functionalist perspective to recognize what role science or technology plays in a social problem. When science is the authority that names a social problem, policy makers can ask for opposing scientific views or views outside the realm of scientific expertise. Historically, the absent voice in social problems has been the lay perspective. Remember the story of Love Canal, in which local residents were not believed about the high levels of illness in their community? A structural functionalist perspective applied to policy can ensure that lay perspectives and other previously unheard voices are heard and considered along with scientific ones.

We can ask a similar question about technologies associated with social problems. People use automobiles to travel for work, play, and everyday needs. The use of this technology contributes to poor air quality for all, but not everyone uses cars. If we identify who uses cars for what, as well as when and where cars are not used and why, we can begin to identify economic, cultural, and historical factors that may not have been visible before. These invisible aspects—such as nondrivers depending on friends who drive or people choosing to live close to shops and work—offer clues to solving social problems related to air quality. By including technology's role in a social problem, structural functional analysis helps to broaden the potential solution sets by revealing interests and factors that may have been invisible.

Conflict Theory

A conflict theory approach studies aspects of social problems that are contested within the scientific culture. For example, the use of male subjects in the majority of clinical trials in the United States was identified as a social problem in the late 1980s. The social problem was addressed by the 1993 National Institutes of Health Revitalization Act, which mandated the inclusion of previously underrepresented groups in clinical trials. As a result, BiDil was licensed as an antihypertension drug specifically for African Americans. BiDil symbolizes a shift in biomedicine from a universal model of medicine to one that focuses on niches or specific social groups. Some within the scientific community see this as a potential new social problem, while others believe it has solved one. A conflict perspective can help identify scientific controversies and show how they shape the framing or solving of social problems by science (Epstein 2007).

Conflict theory can also expose the social relationships defined by material and social conditions within social problems. For example, the unpaid labor of housewives emerged as a social problem in the 1960s, at the same time that industrialized nations were adopting household technologies. Since 1972, the proportion of households with washing machines in the United Kingdom has increased

Cumulative advantage: A position that multiplies advantages for those who have them and limits the capacity for those without resources.

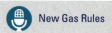 New Gas Rules

from 66% to 96%. Washing machines made washing clothes less physically demanding and raised household expectations about cleanliness and the number of clothes needed. In other words, the new domestic technologies of the home industrial revolution altered the way laundry was done. Before machines, women helped each other (or hired help) on wash day and washed fewer clothes. With washing machines in their homes, women were washing more clothes and doing it alone (Cowan 1983).

Cash is required to buy a washing machine, rather than labor to trade, as women had previously traded with others on wash day. If households were to participate in the formal economy, they needed more cash to buy items such as washing machines. The need for cash highlighted that women's household labor was unpaid and that their domestic responsibilities prevented them from joining the labor market to bring cash into the household. By using conflict theory to look at the material and social conditions of women's activities in the home, we can describe the social and technological changes that contribute to the social problem.

Policy Implications of the Conflict Perspective

When we merge conflict theory with science and technology studies, issues of inequality, power, and control are highlighted. By considering how material power is played out through technology, or how science can reinforce inequality, we can reframe social problem definitions and solutions and perhaps develop policies more responsive to changes in society. For example, General Motors, Daimler, Audi, Nissan, and BMW are planning to sell autonomous (self-driving) cars by 2020, predicting that traffic accidents and fatalities will decrease or be eliminated. Driving rules may stay the same with autonomous cars, or new policies may be adopted. Conflict theory would suggest that we consider access and control—who sets boundaries for the autonomous car and how? Will anyone be able to operate an autonomous car? Who will be responsible if there is an accident? These are just a few of the questions conflict theory might ask about technological changes that require new policies.

Symbolic Interactionism

A symbolic interactionism approach to science, technology, and social problems studies interaction, negotiation, and meaning making at local sites in order to interpret how humans behave in solving social problems. By studying the meanings and practices attached to a technology by different actors, for instance, scholars have documented how that technology becomes the right tool for the task.

Cervical cancer was identified as a women's health problem in the United States in the early 1940s. One solution to this social problem was the development of a technology to screen for cervical cancer. The Pap smear became the "right tool" for cancer screening because it was shaped by various practices, from cost juggling and hiring low-wage lab workers to negotiating local disagreements between clinicians and laboratories about test results. For all the women whose cancer was successfully detected and treated, the Pap smear *was* the right tool. However, it was the wrong tool for the underpaid female cytotechnologists and the women whose screenings resulted in false negatives or false positives. With symbolic interactionism, we can illustrate the diverse ways technologies are used and applied, as well as the involvement of social organizations, actors, and diverse agendas in social problems (Casper and Clarke 1998; Wajcman 2000).

Policy Implications of Symbolic Interactionism

A symbolic interactionist approach can help identify the interaction and negotiation of the actors engaged in defining or solving social problems, as well as the meaning making that is shaping the problem. If policy makers assume science is normal and providing them with facts, truth, and objectivity, they will use it very differently than if they recognize its postnormal attributes of being risky, uncertain, and shaped by different interests. Mode 1 science and Mode 2 science will inform very different types of policies to solve the same social problem. If we assume nanotechnology is safe because of Mode 1 science, we will readily buy and use sunscreen that relies on nanotechnology or approve it for general use in the population. A Mode 2 science perspective would encourage us to ask: What are the risks? Who is most at risk or least at risk? What is unknown about this technology and how might we address it?

....

ASK YOURSELF: Pick a technology currently being used to solve a social problem. Identify the different actors and interests that would argue the technology is the right one or the wrong one for this social problem.

....

SPECIALIZED THEORIES

 Apply specialized theories to science and technology issues.

Traditional theoretical perspectives offer a broad foundation for the study of social problems. Contemporary scholarship on the relationships among science, technology, and social problems builds upon traditional views to develop more specialized theoretical approaches. These in turn help us identify the sociocultural contexts in which science and technology interact and affect social problems.

Social Construction of Science

When scholars focus on science as a social institution they study the biographies, methods, and experiments of scientists. Biographies of scientists tell us about their social networks, education, and experiences; we can use this information to explain and describe the development of scientific knowledge. Knowing what scientists do and how they do it also contributes to our understanding of the emergence of ideas, facts, and questions in science. This information helps sociologists to identify the social facts of science. Émile Durkheim (1982) describes **social facts**, the ways of thinking, acting, and feeling that are external to and exert pressure on the individual. Social facts like methods and findings allow us to understand science as a social institution and describe its beliefs, tendencies, and practices. The social facts of science highlight how science is socially constructed. In other words, science is produced by people within social networks and a scientific culture.

We believe social facts are stable and objective, but they change. For example, one ethnographer of science studying diabetes research in Mexican populations at the U.S.-Mexican border documented how changing social categories of race have resulted in nonstandard categorization in the laboratory. Identification of blood samples taken in the same region over 10 years included terms as different as "MexAm," "Hispanic," and "Texas" (Montoya 2011), illustrating a shift in labels, one of the variables under study. Here the social facts, represented by labels identifying the samples, document the changing forms of categorization based on heritage, illustrating that science and the authority of science are built upon categories that are socially dependent and change through time.

In 1991, roughly 20% of Americans of African descent preferred to be categorized as black rather than African American. By 2007, 23% preferred to be called African American and 13% preferred black. In both years, 61% said that the choice of term didn't matter (Newport 2007). These changes over time reflect a cultural ambiguity about how individuals label themselves and are labeled by others.

The existence of social facts in science helps social scientists to uncover the role of science within social problems. When we analyze science as a human endeavor, we can begin to understand the multiple roles science plays in social problems.

ASK YOURSELF: In labeling samples according to race, is it better to use the label the individual uses or the generic label used by the society at that particular time? (Remember that race is a socially constructed label.) What is the impact on science of using labels based on social norms?

Social Construction of Technology

New technologies often create new social problems. In 1898 a woman bicyclist was refused service in an English pub because she was wearing knickerbockers (baggy trousers) when the norm was for women to wear long skirts. That norm made it difficult for women to ride bicycles until both bicycle designs and clothing styles began to change.

The social construction of technology is a theory that analyzes social problems associated with technology. It begins with the perspective of users as agents of technological change in order to understand how human actions and values shape technology. For example, when a new

The Granger Collection

A racing meet of the League of American Wheelmen, 1890. High-wheeler bicycles (also called "bone shakers" and "penny-farthings") were considered unsafe due to the high risk of a headlong fall when the brakes were applied. Mounting a high-wheeler was particularly difficult.

Social facts: The ways of thinking, acting, and feeling that are external to the individual and exert pressure on the individual.

Science and Technology beyond Our Borders

Nuclear Power

France is the world's largest net exporter of electricity, because electricity from nuclear power, which provides 75% of France's own electricity needs, has low production costs. Areva, the third-largest uranium producer in the world, is a French public multinational conglomerate based in Paris and the strategic partner in uranium for Niger, the fourth-ranking producer of the metal.

Areva has been operating in Niger for more than 40 years and will soon be opening the Imouraren mine there, which is expected to produce 5,000 tons of uranium per year for 35 years. In addition to its investment in the mine of 1.2 billion euros (about $1.6 billion), Areva will also spend 6 million euros (about $8 million) per year on health care, education, training, transport, and access to water and energy for the local people (World Nuclear Association 2013). Niger is one of the poorest countries in the world; most of its people live on less than a dollar a day. Is this a human success story about how France has solved a major social problem by providing electricity to its citizens while also improving the lives of citizens in another country?

In the past decade, allegations have arisen of contaminated scrap metals finding their way into Niger's local housing construction, kitchen utensils, and tools. It is suspected that radioactive waste has been used in road construction. Increased respiratory problems from blown radioactive dust are afflicting people living in the region near the mine. Radioactivity has been reported at more than 100 times the level recommended by international standards. Wells have been contaminated and depleted. Areva denies culpability and maintains that it has ensured the highest levels of safety in its operations. Is this a story of failure caused by corporate greed, government corruption, and poor implementation?

The way we see this situation will play a major role in determining what type of social problem it is, and for whom. France and Areva have the science and technology to build and the ability to define this as a success story. Their expertise and access to resources facilitates their ability to negotiate with another country that lacks the means to mine and use its uranium for its own people. It is the citizens of that country who may define the mine as a failure because they do not have the ability to make informed decisions about their health, livelihoods, and energy choices in light of corporate and nation-state actions.

▶ **THINK ABOUT IT:** What are the roles and responsibilities of citizen groups, corporations, and nation-states in resolving a social problem like nuclear power?

France, which is about the size of Texas, has more than 20 active nuclear power plants, one of which is the Tricastin plant shown in this photo. Tricastin is run by the French public multinational industrial conglomerate Areva. The plant has four reactors that convert uranium from mines into fuel. In 2013, Greenpeace activists breached the Tricastin site, calling for its closure. In 2013 there were 65 nuclear power plants operating in the United States.

Matthieu Colim / Hemis / Corbis

---

technology such as the bicycle is introduced, different groups assign different meanings to the technology. Male users of high-wheeler bicycles used them for sport, and the bicycles came to symbolize "machismo." Female users and elderly men wanted bikes for transport and labeled the high-wheeler "unsafe." These identities of macho and unsafe

Interpretive flexibility: The ability of the development path to respond to different users' needs.

influenced the bicycle's development paths. Ultimately, the safety bicycle was developed and came to dominate other designs due to its **interpretive flexibility**, or ability of the development path to respond to different users' needs. By studying the ways different user groups define and label an emerging social problem connected to a new technology, the social construction of technology highlights the way technological change responds to cultural influences and the way a technology develops into a working artifact.

Actor-Network Theory

In the 1970s, science and technology scholars began studying laboratories using social science research methods that included participant observation, discourse analysis, and interviews (Latour and Woolgar 1979; Knorr-Cetina 1981; Lynch 1985). This new line of research represented a shift away from studying the products of science to studying the *production* of science. By focusing on actors, technology, material culture, and shared practices, scholars began to document the "constructed" aspect of science through their ethnographies of laboratories.

Their analyses using actor-network theory revealed how scientific facts are constructed in laboratories through social networks, communication technologies, and shared interests. This approach to studying the laboratory illustrated the mundane processes, social ordering, and social organization required to produce a scientific fact. Scientific knowledge is negotiated between scientists in laboratories and funders, suppliers, governments, investors, and clients outside the laboratories. Actor-network theory also places nonhuman actors, such as microscopes and laboratory benches, into studies of science, acknowledging that these nonhuman actors define and regulate the context or place of science. Actor-network theory studies the heterogeneous networks of human and nonhuman actors in order to identify the material and social actions and forces of science and technology (Callon, Law, and Rip 1986; Latour 1987; Law 1991).

SOCIAL CHANGE: WHAT CAN YOU DO?

15.7 Identify steps toward social change regarding science and technology.

In order to ensure that science and technology contribute to beneficial solutions and do not create or reinforce social problems, all interested stakeholders—including you—must perform certain roles. By engaging in community service opportunities, you can have a direct impact on the ways in which science and technology are developed, applied, and integrated into society. A few opportunities for you to get involved are described below.

Join or start a chapter of Engineers Without Borders on your campus (http://www.ewb-usa.org). The goal of EWB is to provide clean water, power, and sanitation to communities in need. Students and professionals from all disciplines, including public health, anthropology, geology, business, communications, and engineering, apply a holistic approach to community development and community projects requiring an element of engineering design. Individuals gain leadership experiences, apply technical and management skills, and help communities create solutions they can sustain for the long term.

The U.S. Environmental Protection Agency's Office of Water encourages all citizens to learn about their water resources and supports volunteer monitoring because of its many benefits. Participants in the EPA Volunteer Monitoring Program build awareness of pollution

South Dakota State University engineering student Rebecca Hofmeister samples water at a trough in Bolivia. SDSU's student chapter of Engineers Without Borders gathered information about the local water system in order to construct and install treatment units for disinfection. The goal is to improve drinking water safety and sanitation for residents of the Carmen Pampa community in Bolivia.

problems, become trained in pollution prevention, help clean up problem sites, provide data on waters that may otherwise be unassessed, and increase the amount of information on water quality available to decision makers at all levels of government. The data resulting from volunteer monitoring are used for delineating and characterizing watersheds, screening for water quality problems, and measuring baseline conditions and trends. For more information, see the EPA's website at http://water.epa.gov/type/watersheds/monitoring/vol.cfm.

Become active in your school's sustainable campus initiative program, or if one doesn't exist, create one. Such a program identifies a social problem on campus that has or could have a scientific or technological component. At the University of Utah, for example, every student pays a small fee into the Sustainable Campus Initiative Fund, which pays for sustainable projects or businesses on campus. All students are eligible to submit project proposals; to be funded, a project must have a positive environmental impact, encourage earth-conscious habits, and incorporate economic, social, and scientific factors. For more on the University of Utah initiative, see http://sustainability.utah.edu/get-involved/students/sustainable-campus-fund.php.

Join or start an interdisciplinary student organization on your campus to tackle a social problem. At Cornell University, students are composting, turning lights out, eliminating carbon emissions, and identifying and discussing social problems. One interdisciplinary campus group is called Design, Engineering, Education, and Development; its members work with developing communities to improve equity and sustainability. Another group designs and builds resilient structures for ecological, social, and economical sustainability. Some Cornell undergraduates have collaborated to establish an accessible, sustainable, and free bike-share program on campus. For more information, visit http://www.sustainablecampus.cornell.edu/getinvolved/studentorgs.cfm.

Conduct a "no-impact project" alone, as a class, or as a family for one week to see what a difference no-impact living can have on your quality of life. Keep a journal of the impact of modern technology and "conveniences" on your life, emotions, relationships, time, and money. At the end of the week identify one change you will retain in your life to minimize your impact on the environment. Two students at Drake University turned their no-impact project into a campus-wide effort that banned bottled-water sales on campus. For more information, see the No Impact Project website at http://noimpactproject.org.

WHAT DOES AMERICA THINK?

Questions about Science and Technology from the General Social Survey

Turn to the beginning of the chapter to compare your answers to the total population.

1. What is your interest level in scientific discoveries?

   VERY INTERESTED: 41.4%

   MODERATELY INTERESTED: 43.6%

   NOT AT ALL INTERESTED: 15%

2. What is your confidence level in the scientific community?

   A GREAT DEAL: 41.9%

   ONLY SOME: 50.8%

   HARDLY ANY: 7.3%

3. Does science make our way of life change too fast?

   YES: 42.4%

   NO: 57.6%

4. Do the benefits of scientific research outweigh harmful results?

   YES: 89.1%

   NO: 10.9%

5. Scientific research is necessary and should be supported by the federal government.

   AGREE: 85.9%

   DISAGREE: 14.1%

6. What is your interest level in technologies?

   VERY INTERESTED: 42.6%

   MODERATELY INTERESTED: 46%

   NOT AT ALL INTERESTED: 11.4%

7. Do you use the home Internet through a mobile device?

   YES: 23.4%

   NO: 76.6%

Go to **edge.sagepub.com/trevino** for a breakdown of these data across time and by race, sex, age, income, and other statuses.

1. Examine the data on education for responses to the questions concerning interest level in scientific discoveries and interest level in technologies. Does education influence the interest levels? Explain possible reasons for this.

2. Only 23.4% of respondents reported using home Internet through mobile devices. Do you predict this figure will increase, stay about the same, or decrease? What social changes will that be likely to create?

3. Examine the data on gender for responses to the question about whether the benefits of scientific research outweigh harmful results. Do the results surprise you? Explain.

4. Examine the General Social Survey data about confidence in the scientific community from 1973 to the present. Is confidence increasing, staying about the same, or decreasing? Why do you think that is?

SOURCE: National Opinion Research Center, University of Chicago.

CHAPTER SUMMARY

 15.1 Identify social problems related to science and technology.

Science and technology scholars ask questions about the incorporation of science and technology into society; how science and technology are redefining social inequality, social relationships, and public/private space; and how and why some issues emerge as widely discussed social problems while others are relegated to the category of technological or scientific problems.

 15.2 Describe how science and technology are socially defined.

Science as a form of knowledge plays an active role in defining how governments, corporations, and communities respond to and accept responsibility for social problems. Technology is embedded as an artifact in social practices, social institutions, and systems that are part of emerging social problems and their solutions. By analyzing science and technology as technoscience, we can broaden our analysis of them to raise new questions about social problems, science, and technology. Science plays an active role in social problems, sometimes as part of the authority that solves them and sometimes as a factor creating the culture and the social problem. Science can be a social problem or it can have its own social problems. Our cultural beliefs about technology and progress can define what is and is not a social problem. Technology too can be a social problem or part of the solution.

 15.3 Discuss patterns and trends in science and technology.

By viewing science and technology as social problems, we can identify trends and patterns illustrating that the way we do science, and the values that shape science, change over time, that technologies we use are shaped by values, and that we use technologies to fix social problems. In addition, the way we use science to solve social problems is dynamic; science as a social institution can have social problems.

 15.4 Identify the stakeholders in science and technology.

Stakeholders use science and technology in specific and deliberate ways to frame, respond to, and solve social problems. They shape the way science is done, what science is done, and where it is applied. Stakeholders of science and technology may include individuals, nonhumans, interest groups, and social institutions.

15.5 Apply the functionalist, conflict, and symbolic interactionist perspectives to science and technology issues.

Structural functionalism, symbolic interactionism, and conflict theory are important theories in the analysis of science, technology, and social problems. Structural functionalism explains that one reason eminent scientists receive most of the credit in their fields is that, because they have access to resources like elite education and cultural capital, their advantages are compounded; conversely, those without these resources are not as likely to get credit. Conflict theory shows how scientific controversies can help to frame or solve social problems. By studying the meanings and practices that different people give to a particular technology, symbolic interactionists can demonstrate how that technology can benefit them.

 15.6 Apply specialized theories to science and technology issues.

Specialized theories such as social construction of science, social construction of technology, and actor-network theory are used to describe, interpret, and troubleshoot science, technology, and social problems.

 15.7 Identify steps toward social change regarding science and technology.

You can take several actions to ensure that science and technology contribute to beneficial solutions and do not create problematic situations. Some of these actions include joining or starting a chapter of Engineers Without Borders on your campus; becoming active in your university's sustainable campus initiative program, or, if one doesn't exist, creating one; and conducting a "no-impact project" to see what difference no-impact living has on your quality of life.

DISCUSSION QUESTIONS

1. How do sociologists define science? Technology? In what ways do these definitions differ from how these two terms might otherwise be defined? What is the significance of the different definitions for the purpose of our studies?

2. Are the crimes associated with technology new crimes altogether or newer versions of old crimes? What are the differences between cybercrimes and their nontechnological counterparts? Are the targets of the two kinds of crimes similar or different?

3. What role does science play in determining what constitutes a social problem? How is science influenced by other social forces in making this determination?

4. Who does science? How has the answer to this question changed over the past century? Who uses technology? How has the answer to this question changed over the past century? In what ways does the "who" of science and technology constitute a social problem?

5. How do the various stakeholders involved in science and technology have different

amounts of power? How are disputes between the various stakeholders resolved?

6. According to the symbolic interactionist perspective, what role does science play in policy making in the United States? For example, from this perspective, how important is it for the United States to adopt a policy that requires labeling of GMOs in foods?

7. How does conflict theory interpret technological advances for society? What questions does a conflict theorist ask of new technologies and their consequences? For example, what questions would a conflict theorist raise about smart phones as they relate to, or potentially solve, social problems?

8. What changes can be seen within science and technology from the social constructionism perspective? How do these changes in labels and meanings have an impact on the validity of science over time?

9. How significant is modern technology in your own daily life? What would it be like for you to go one hour during a typical day without using any modern technology? What problems would arise as a result of your nonparticipation? What benefits

could arise? What changes might an individual make to maximize the benefits of reducing the use of technology while minimizing negative consequences?

10. What strategies are most effective at increasing access to technology for marginalized groups?

Are there any modern technologies so vital to social participation that they should be available to everyone? What strategies could help to increase the numbers of women, minorities, and people from the global periphery who do science? Who should be responsible for such efforts, both domestically and globally?

KEY TERMS

big data 396	landraces 408	science machine 402	technocracy 405
crisis science 402	megamachine 402	science shops 403	technological fix 405
cumulative advantage 410	Mode 1 403	social facts 412	technology 399
industrialized science 405	Mode 2 403	social organization 402	technoscience 400
interpretive flexibility 413	science 399	sociotechnical system 398	

Sharpen your skills with SAGE edge at edge.sagepub.com/trevino

A personalized approach to help you accomplish your coursework goals in an easy-to-use learning environment.

16 WAR AND TERRORISM

Paul Joseph

Reuters / Brian Snyder

The paint peels off a mural depicting the Twin Towers in flames after the September 11, 2001, terrorist attacks in New York City. The United States responded to the attacks by launching the Global War on Terror and invading Afghanistan. Do you think that people have forgotten the significance of what happened on 9/11, as this neglected mural suggests?

Investigating War and Terrorism: My Story

Paul Joseph

While a graduate student in sociology at the University of California, Berkeley, I took a seminar on the *Pentagon Papers,* a collection of documents leaked to the press by Daniel Ellsberg and Tony Russo, Pentagon employees who had turned against the Vietnam War. Eventually I wrote my Ph.D. dissertation on the events of March 1968, one of the most critical months in the history of the war. It was based on documents found in the *Pentagon Papers,* but also on memoirs and interviews with many officials in President Lyndon B. Johnson's administration, including William Bundy, Dean Rusk, Admiral Ulysses Grant Sharp, and Paul Warnke. I started to teach at Tufts University and then expanded the dissertation into a book on the Vietnam War titled *Cracks in the Empire.* In other research, I have continued to explore the impact of domestic politics—including business interests, public opinion, and peace movements—on Washington decision making.

My latest book, *Are Americans Becoming More Peaceful?,* argues that a majority of the U.S. public are becoming more sensitive to the costs of war. As a simple illustration, polls indicate that a majority registered their disapproval of the conduct of the war in Iraq more quickly than during the Vietnam conflict. I testified on this work before a special congressional hearing conducted by Representative Maxine Waters (D-CA).

My current project concerns Human Terrain Teams—social scientists who provide cultural information to military commanders. The vignette that opens this chapter is drawn from that project.

LEARNING OBJECTIVES

16.1 Describe war as a social concept.

16.2 Discuss patterns and trends in the incidence and costs of war.

16.3 Describe the future of war.

16.4 Apply the functionalist, symbolic interactionist, and conflict perspectives to war.

16.5 Apply the two-society thesis to the relationship between the U.S. military and U.S. society.

16.6 Discuss the Global War on Terror.

16.7 Identify steps toward social change to foster peace.

WHAT DO YOU THINK?
Questions about War and Terrorism from the General Social Survey

1. Do you expect the United States to be in a world war in the next 10 years?

   ☐ *YES*
   ☐ *NO*

2. What is your confidence level in Congress?

   ☐ *A GREAT DEAL*
   ☐ *ONLY SOME*
   ☐ *HARDLY ANY*

3. What is your interest level in international issues?

   ☐ *VERY INTERESTED*
   ☐ *MODERATELY INTERESTED*
   ☐ *NOT AT ALL INTERESTED*

4. What is your interest level in military policy?

   ☐ *VERY INTERESTED*
   ☐ *MODERATELY INTERESTED*
   ☐ *NOT AT ALL INTERESTED*

5. In the United States, do you think we're spending too much money on military, armaments, and defense, too little money, or about the right amount?

   ☐ *TOO MUCH*
   ☐ *TOO LITTLE*
   ☐ *ABOUT THE RIGHT AMOUNT*

▶▶ Turn to the end of the chapter to view the results for the total population.

SOURCE: National Opinion Research Center, University of Chicago.

DOING RESEARCH FOR THE MILITARY

Paula Loyd, a Wellesley-educated anthropologist working with the U.S. military, was in the midst of an interview with a group of Afghan villagers. The subject was the price of cooking fuel, an indicator of Taliban influence in the region. The higher the price, the more control the insurgents were exercising over supply chains. A stranger approached and chatted for a few minutes. Then, just as the troops guarding Loyd turned away, the man suddenly emptied a container of oil on the young woman, threw a lighted match, and set her on fire. Severely burned, she was evacuated to a hospital in Houston, Texas. The perpetrator was detained and placed in handcuffs, and when the full extent of Loyd's injuries became known, he was shot and killed by Don Ayala, a member of Loyd's team. Loyd died two months later.

Paula Loyd was a member of the Human Terrain System (HTS), a relatively new Pentagon program that attaches small teams of social scientists to combat brigades. The scientists' purpose is to provide cultural information that will improve the military commanders' understanding of the local population. HTS has proven to be extremely controversial. Two other social scientists have been killed and several wounded, and the program has raised a deep debate over the ethics of social science research carried out for the military in combat zones. The American Anthropological Association (AAA) has declared that HTS violates its professional code of conduct, which stipulates that confidentiality must be preserved, that research subjects must give informed consent before participating, and that care must be taken to ensure they are not harmed. "You can't really do anthropology in a group of people with guns," said Sally Engle Merry, Loyd's senior thesis adviser at Wellesley, who has served on the board of the AAA (quoted in Stockman 2009).

We can best understand the emergence of the Human Terrain System and its goal of providing cultural information in the context of the rise of counterinsurgency and the Pentagon's recognition that waging war has become ever more complex. Conflict is taking place not on isolated battlefields, but within societies and in the midst of civilians. Learning more about local social conditions, power structures, grievances, kinship networks, and tribal and religious identities is a necessary step in making the military more effective. In theory, social science will enable the military to become more intelligent and discriminating in its use of force.

Loyd's death raises other issues, too: the impact of war on civilians; the role of private contractors such as BAE Systems, the company that recruited her and Ayala; and the absence of an adequate legal process to review the execution of prisoners. Another issue involves gender. Paula Loyd was not part of the regular army, but almost 15% of the U.S. armed forces are women, up from only 2% when the all-volunteer force was introduced in 1973. Over that time, women have served in a widening range of roles, including working with men in armed patrols and on dangerous search operations. We will explore these and other issues in this chapter, but we begin with a closer look at the concept of war itself.

WAR AS A SOCIAL CONCEPT

 16.1 Describe war as a social concept.

We can define **war** as organized, collective fighting between at least one political unit that seeks political or economic control over a territory or other important resource and another political unit or social group. This definition expands the traditional focus on state-to-state war (the military of one government against the military of another fought over a specific territory) by including war waged by substate units, as well as the possibility that a distinct political, religious, ethnic, or racial group might become the target. War is "organized and collective," which sets it off from more individual, sporadic, and spontaneous acts of violence. It is "political" because the fighting units use violence deliberately in the search of a particular outcome, such as control over a governing structure, control over a valuable natural resource, or suppression of a population that is regarded as oppositional.

In the past, war was conventionally seen as organized violence carried out between national states and across national borders. Other forms of organized violence also existed, such as the wars conducted against the native

....

War: Organized, collective fighting involving at least one political unit that seeks political or economic control over a territory or other important resource against another political unit or social group.

populations of the Americas, but the decolonization process that began following the end of World War II in 1945 brought new recognition that parties in conflict do not have to be states, war is usually not formally declared, and fighting may be carried out solely within rather than across the borders. For example, colonial powers such as the French in Vietnam and Algeria and the Portuguese in Africa fought against substate groups seeking national liberation to retain parts of their empires. They often enlisted local elites, who in turn recruited soldiers from the local population, creating elements of civil war as well.

Wars also take the form of *campaigns of ethnic cleansing,* such as in the former Yugoslavia in the early 1990s; *genocide,* such as in Rwanda in 1994; and *violent political repression,* such as the so-called Dirty War carried out against those opposed to military rule in Argentina, or against Buddhist monks in Myanmar (the former Burma). The scale of this sometimes catastrophic killing is one important reason to include these actions in our definition of war. In Cambodia, over the last half of the 1970s, as much as 25% of the population was decimated, as Cambodians were either executed by the Khmer Rouge, an ultraleft political group that had seized power, or died in a famine aggravated by the destruction of agricultural production during the Indochina War. In all these cases, states waged wars against their own populations.

In globalized intrastate wars, organized violence is less political and more economic because the motive is to control valuable resources. These resources include diamonds (Sierra Leone), the production and distribution of drugs (Colombia and Mexico), timber (East Timor), oil (the Niger Delta), and valuable minerals and ore such as coltan, used in the manufacture of electronic products (Democratic Republic of the Congo). Sometimes called "resource wars," these conflicts differ from classic war in several ways: (1) they include multiple types of fighting units, such as paramilitary forces, mercenaries, self-defense units, militaries from other countries, and even peacekeeping forces; (2) they frequently target civilians, often by employing sexual violence; (3) they often conscript child soldiers; and (4) they establish connections between in-country actors, such as local warlords and traders in the valuable commodity, and international players such as corporations, banking interests, and global agencies such as the United Nations. In many respects, resource wars are similar to organized crime but on a larger scale.

ASK YOURSELF: What wars are being fought as you read this chapter? Who are the fighting parties? Are they armies controlled by states, or other types of combatants?

War is a social concept because it involves culture, politics, and economics, the features of human society examined throughout this textbook. While no doubt

 Terrorism and Privilege

Khmer Rouge guerrillas at a base camp in Cambodia, 1981. Their radical communist leader, Pol Pot, set up a totalitarian regime that oversaw an extremely brutal attempt to establish a classless agrarian society. While attempting to engineer this society, Pol Pot orchestrated a campaign of genocide that lasted from 1975 to 1979, in which approximately 25% of the Cambodian population died from execution, starvation, disease, or overwork.

some elements of human nature are expressed in war, sociologists try to understand this form of activity not by examining genes or biology but instead by describing the social relationships contained within it. Situating war in social life does not imply approval, any more than our social understandings of crime and racism imply support for those behaviors. War can also be said to be "social" because it has important impacts on society: there are physical casualties, of course, but also effects on nationalism, psychology, patterns of inequality, issues concerning race and ethnicity, economic performance, technology, and the environment. In these respects, war can be said to have a "long tail," or a social legacy that continues to influence social life long after the fighting itself has subsided.

PATTERNS AND TRENDS

16.2 Discuss patterns and trends in the incidence and costs of war.

As a "social activity," war contains several patterns and new trends that are important to understand, especially if we want to reduce if not eliminate its occurrence. Among the most important questions is whether fewer wars are being fought now than a generation ago. Another is whether wars are becoming less deadly, as measured by the number of battlefield deaths. Are we, as some commentators have suggested, winning the "war against war" (Goldstein 2011; Pinker 2011)?

Incidence of War

It does appear that wars waged between states are declining in number (Human Security Report Project 2011, 2012). The **democratic theory of peace** proposes that political democracies are less likely to wage war, at least with each other, so as more nations become democratic, the chances of peace triumphing over armed conflict are becoming better. Europe has become a zone of peace, the probability of war between Latin American countries is remote, and it appears that many East and South Asian nations, at least those advancing toward democracy, will not go to war with each other either.

Democracies do fight wars. The United States, France, and the United Kingdom have all engaged in several armed conflicts. But democracies are less likely to fight each other because they have too much to lose from disrupting their mutually beneficial trade and commerce. The "McDonald's theory of conflict resolution" suggests that countries where McDonald's fast-food restaurants have been established do not fight each other (Friedman 2005). The theory is not fully supported by evidence, however. In 1999, during the war with Serbia over Kosovo, the United States and other countries in the North Atlantic Treaty Organization (NATO), all possessing McDonald's, bombed Belgrade, which also had several McDonald's outlets. But in general, participation in advanced consumer societies does seem to reduce significantly, if not quite eliminate, the likelihood of countries going to war with other prosperous countries. The dark blue section in Figure 16.1 represents interstate war; note how it has declined, especially since the end of the Cold War in 1989.

What other features of democracy might make us optimistic about the future of war? Leaders are more likely to believe negotiation and diplomacy will work because the leaders of other countries think so as well. Citizens see war as a measure of last resort; they are less likely to cherish martial values or welcome combat as an opportunity to test their bravery and heroism. War is expensive, financially and in human terms, and is to be avoided, especially when countries are facing others whose populations feel much the same way. If these features of democratic systems are real, and as many countries lurch, however unevenly, in the direction of democracy, then over time the incidence of interstate war will continue to decline.

Similar predictions apply to politically motivated civil wars. The European colonial systems of the 19th century have been almost entirely dismantled; the green section in Figure 16.1 reveals that colonial wars ended after 1973. Former colonies now enjoy at least formal political sovereignty. They may suffer different forms of subordination, including high levels of poverty, poor governance, and inadequate education and health care—conditions often called "structural

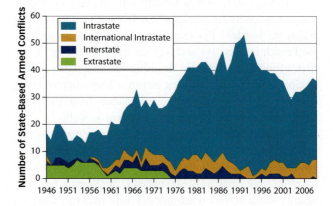

FIGURE 16.1 Trends in State-Based Conflicts by Type, 1946–2009

"State-based conflicts" are those in which the warring parties include a state and one of more nonstate armed groups. Extrastate—or anti-colonial—conflicts ended by 1975, while interstate conflicts became rare in the 2000s. As a result of this shift, all conflicts in 2009 were intrastate, though nearly a quarter were internationalized.

NOTE: This figure is a "stacked graph," meaning that the number of conflicts in each category is indicated by the depth of the band of color. The top line shows the total number of conflicts of all types in each year.

SOURCE: Human Security Report Project, *Human Security Report 2012: Sexual Violence, Education, and War: Beyond the Mainstream Narrative* (Vancouver: Human Security Press, 2012), p. 158. Reprinted with permission.

violence" and "neocolonialism"—but they no longer need to engage in direct violence to achieve independence.

We find a similar pattern in Figure 16.2, which captures the rate of battle deaths in state-based conflicts between 1946 and 2009. There are three peaks of casualties, one around 1950 and the Korean War, another in the late 1960s and early 1970s marking the most intense fighting in Vietnam, and finally a third, an extremely bloody war between Iran and Iraq in the early 1980s. Since then the rate of deaths from state-based conflicts has declined significantly.

With the end of the Cold War, neither the United States nor the former Soviet Union needs to wage "proxy wars" through allies. For example, one important feature of the Vietnam War was Moscow's support for North Vietnam and U.S. support for South Vietnam. Several African conflicts were fought with the two superpowers lurking in the background. The United States and (now) Russia may continue their shadow dance on many fronts, but for now the pattern of fighting via subordinate partners appears to be over. The United Nations, now free of the constraints of the Cold War, has been able to play a more

Democratic theory of peace: The theory that political democracies are less likely than nondemocracies to wage war with each other.

FIGURE 16.2 Reported Battle Deaths from State-Based Conflicts, 1946–2009

SOURCE: Human Security Report Project, *Human Security Report 2012: Sexual Violence, Education, and War: Beyond the Mainstream Narrative* (Vancouver: Human Security Press, 2012), p. 210. Reprinted with permission.

active peacekeeping role. That too has reduced violence, even if the record is imperfect.

Unfortunately, wars between states and battlefield deaths are not the only measures of the future of war. We look at civilian casualties next.

Civilian Casualties

During World War I, the combatants often deployed their forces in trenches relatively close to each other. The defenses were usually much stronger than any offensive, and the consequences were usually tragic. At the Battle of the Somme, the British took nearly 60,000 casualties on the first day. Despite appalling losses on all sides, civilians were relatively protected. Noncombatants made up less than 10% of the war's total losses.

About two decades later, on April 26, 1937, the German air force, supporting General Franco during the Spanish Civil War, deliberately targeted the market areas of the Basque village of Guernica to make a point about the costs it was willing to impose on civilians. Bombing civilians was not entirely new, but Guernica was a turning point (Tanaka and Young 2009). Pablo Picasso's famous painting of the event, showing human bodies in anguish, the distorted faces of bulls and horses, broken parts, and missing pieces, gave us a different understanding of the impact of war.

World War II was devastating to the militaries on all sides, but even more civilians than soldiers died. The Soviet Union lost 25 million people, 75% of them civilians. German bombers attacked London and other cities in England, and British and U.S. bombers struck German cities. Kurt Vonnegut's famous novel *Slaughterhouse-Five* grapples with the firebombing of the German city of Dresden, where

40,000 inhabitants were killed. Japanese occupation in the Pacific was responsible for the deaths of millions. Toward the end of the war, U.S. incendiary bombing set many Japanese cities on fire, including Tokyo, where 100,000 people died in one night. The technology employed in the atomic bombs used on Hiroshima and Nagasaki was new, but the targeting of civilians on a mass scale was not.

The United States lost approximately 58,000 soldiers during the Vietnam War. About 1 million Vietnamese, counting government forces from both North and South and revolutionary forces, also died. Yet another million Vietnamese civilians were killed (some sources put the figure closer to 2 million).

In the post-Vietnam era, the ratio of military to civilian deaths has often been entirely reversed. In many globalized intrastate wars, noncombatant deaths have reached 90%, the exact inverse ratio of World War I. In Bosnia, the militaries on both sides even colluded to target civilians and thereby intensify the pace of ethnic cleansing (Andreas 2008). Civilians have suffered by far the largest losses in armed conflicts in East Timor, Sierra Leone, and Colombia, with catastrophic results. Conflict in south-central Somalia was made more devastating by extremist militants' decision to ban the delivery of humanitarian assistance. An estimated 258,000 people died between October 2010 and April 2012, including 133,000 children under the age of 5 (Food Security and Nutrition Analysis Unit—Somalia 2013). Due to the intersection of fighting and disruption of normal social life, conflict in the Democratic Republic of the Congo may have taken an extraordinarily high toll of 5 million people (International Rescue Committee 2012).

These figures counter our relative optimism about the future of interstate war. National armies, particularly from democracies, may be less likely to engage each other, but other forms of war continue, and a true accounting recognizes the loss of noncombatants as well as those in uniform. As of the end of 2012, the United States had lost 4,486 soldiers in Iraq and 2,174 in Afghanistan (Coalition Casualty Count 2014). These are significant, painful losses to their families and friends, and to the country as a whole. At least 125,000 civilians have also died in Iraq; the actual number is probably considerably higher (Iraq Body Count 2014). In Afghanistan, the United Nations Mission for the Protection of Civilians in Armed Conflict places the number of noncombatant dead at 14,728 for the six years from 2007 through 2012.

Economic Costs of War and War Preparation

The United States spends almost as much on its military as the rest of the world combined. In other words, the budget of the U.S. Department of Defense equals the combined total of the military budgets of all Washington's allies,

 Munich Olympics

Pablo Picasso's *Guernica,* 1937. Picasso created this painting to bring the world's attention to the atrocities committed against the defenseless civilian population of the little Basque village of Guernica in northern Spain. *Guernica* has become a powerful antiwar symbol. The gratuitous horrors of modern war and the suffering it inflicts on individuals, particularly innocent civilians, are depicted in the painting through tortured images of people, animals, and buildings wrenched by violence and chaos.

including NATO, Japan, and South Korea, *plus* the combined total of the military budgets of all potential enemies, including China, Russia, North Korea, and Iran (Stockholm International Peace Research Institute 2013).

In fiscal year 2012, the official U.S. defense budget came to $562 billion. The true figure is significantly larger. That year, the United States allocated an additional $115 billion for military operations in Iraq and Afghanistan; funding those two wars has required an annual budget "supplemental" whose cumulative total, now more than a trillion dollars, is not part of the official budget. Additional military expenditures by the Department of Homeland Security, the State Department, Veterans Administration, NASA, and the Department of Energy (for the production of nuclear warheads) bring annual U.S. military spending near a trillion dollars, significantly more than the annual federal deficit.

During World War II, U.S. military spending accounted for an astonishing 40% of the gross domestic product (GDP). The country finally escaped the Great Depression not through President Roosevelt's New Deal but through the huge stimulus provided to the automobile industry by orders for tanks, trucks, and jeeps; to the steel industry for naval ships; to clothing manufactures for uniforms, boots, and the like; and to the new aircraft industry for fighter planes and bombers. Military spending later fell from that unique high point but remained significant as the Cold War set in, reaching 8% to 10% of GDP as the

government maintained a sizable army, navy, and air force; garrisoned troops in Germany; established military bases in the Pacific; and developed and deployed nuclear weapons. Expenditures on the Vietnam War became so large that many argued they were actually undermining U.S. strength. National debt increased, as did inflation, and the U.S. dollar declined in value. Research and development for civilian manufacturing dropped in priority, and innovation fell relative to Europe and Japan. Many were reminded of President Dwight D. Eisenhower's warning, made in a speech given on April 16, 1953, that "every gun that is made, every warship launched, every rocket fired signifies, in the final sense, a theft from those who hunger and are not fed, those who are cold and not clothed."

Not until the end of the Cold War and the transformation of the Soviet Union did the United States reap a "peace dividend." During President Bill Clinton's administration military spending declined, especially relative to the size of the overall economy, reaching a low point of 3.5% of GDP in 1999.

After the terrorist attacks on New York City and Washington, D.C., on September 11, 2001, however, budget increases over the next decade for the Global War on Terror and the new wars in Afghanistan and Iraq doubled U.S. defense spending. Yet the uncertain outcomes of both wars, and debate over federal spending in general, have renewed the question of whether military spending should be reduced.

Experiencing War and Terrorism

Who Serves in the U.S. Armed Forces?

The Vietnam War was called the "working-class war" because U.S. college students who were drafted were able to defer their military service. Since they were more likely to be from middle and upper income brackets, deferment created a bias in which those located in the lower brackets were more likely to be drafted, fight, and die. After Vietnam, the Pentagon moved to an all-volunteer force. How has this decision affected the composition of the current U.S. military?

The clearest change is in the sex distribution of the armed forces. Since 1973, the proportion of female soldiers has moved from only 2% to approximately 15%. This shift carries profound implications, which we explore later in this chapter.

Yet there continues to be substantial class patterning in the armed forces. As before, the middle and top income brackets are significantly underrepresented. For example, in 2007, during the height of the war in Iraq, census districts with mean incomes between $30,000 and $60,000 contributed significantly more than their share of active-duty army recruits. Districts with higher incomes contributed significantly fewer than we would expect if soldiers were drawn evenly from the whole population. Districts with average incomes over $120,000 contributed only one-third their "fair share"

(National Priorities Project 2008).

However, contrary to many impressions, the military does not draw from the lowest levels of society either. Discipline, teamwork, and basic education skills are highly valued in the modern force. The Pentagon's goal is for 80% of recruits to have high school diplomas. Except during the worst years in Iraq, it has met that goal. (During that time, to meet pressing needs, the way was eased for the recruitment of individuals with felony records, histories of drug use, problematic character backgrounds, and lack of the educational requirement.)

Historically, African Americans have been overrepresented in the post–World War II military. There they have been able to achieve success and social mobility—often more so than in civilian society. On the other hand, the wars in Iraq and Afghanistan have not been very popular in the black community, and the proportion of the military that is African American, while still higher than average, has declined somewhat. Meanwhile, Latinos have steadily increased their representation.

Cadets at the United States Military Academy (West Point) march during formation. Cadets who graduate from West Point are commissioned as second lieutenants in the U.S. Army. In 2013 the demographic profile of cadets attending West Point was as follows: male, 84%; female, 16%; white, 71.89%; Hispanic, 9.06%; and black, 6.88%.

Geographically, the military is disproportionately drawn from rural areas, the South, and the Mountain States. The Midwest, major cities, and the two coasts are underrepresented. In 1968, ROTC training programs had 123 units in the East and 147 in the South. Six years later, there were 180 branches in the South and only 93 in the East (Nelson 2010). Due to recent base consolidations and closings, only 10 states serve as home to 70% of those in uniform.

▶ THINK ABOUT IT

1. Do you think each income class in the United States should contribute its "fair share" to the military? Why or why not?

2. Since World War II, blacks have been overrepresented in the U.S. military. Why has their proportion declined during the past decade while the proportion of Latinos has increased?

Psychological Costs of War

As early as Homer's *Iliad*, humans have recognized that no one returns from war unchanged. Political authorities and military leaders have generally underplayed the psychological damage of war to avoid negative impacts on recruitment and public opinion. Early in World War II, political and military leaders expected that "real men" would be relatively immune from the effects of war and that conventional heterosexual masculinity would protect

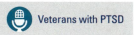 Veterans with PTSD

TABLE 16.1 Trade-Offs for Costs of War

Military expenditures	Comparable domestic priorities
Taxpayers in Fort Lauderdale, Florida, will pay $10 million as their share of the F-35 Joint Strike Fighter Jet.	Those funds are sufficient to pay the salaries of 160 elementary school teachers for one year.
Taxpayers in Denver, Colorado, will pay $48.57 million for nuclear weapons and associated costs.	Those funds are sufficient to pay for 6,123 university scholarships for one year.
Taxpayers in Burlington, Vermont, will pay $59.76 million for their share of overall Department of Defense expenditures.	Those funds are sufficient to enable 11,565 low-income people to receive health care for one year.

NOTE: All data are projected for FY 2014.

SOURCE: www.costofwar.com; nationalpriorities.org.

against combat's psychological effects. Unfortunately, the intensity of fighting soon demonstrated the consequences of exposure to violence.

Post-traumatic stress disorder (PTSD) is a specific set of symptoms associated with the aftermath of exposure to traumatic experiences. These include flashbacks, sleep disturbances, extreme sensitivity to noise, disturbing dreams, and poor concentration. Those with PTSD are also more likely to suffer alcohol and drug abuse, family problems, and suicide. The term did not become official until after the end of the Vietnam War, when a determined group of veterans, advocates, and medical professionals lobbied to include it in the *Diagnostic and Statistical Manual of Mental Disorders* (Scott 1990) so soldiers could become eligible to receive treatment from the Veterans Administration.

Measuring the incidence of PTSD and other psychological consequences of war is very difficult, in part because symptoms may not appear for months or even years. A RAND Corporation study conducted during the early part of the Iraq War found between one-sixth and one-third of veterans experiencing PTSD, depression, or other significant psychological trauma (Tanielian and Jaycox 2008). The consequences are significant. Approximately 2.5 million have served in Iraq and Afghanistan, of whom 400,000 to 800,000 have or will have significant psychological wounds. Less than half will seek professional help for their conditions, however. Many fear being stigmatized, while others are immersed in a culture that emphasizes self-reliance and individual response to

adversity. If treatment were extended to all in need, the cost would be approximately $1 trillion over 40 years, about equal to the direct cost of the Iraq and Afghanistan wars themselves (Stiglitz and Bilmes 2008).

THE FUTURE OF WAR

 16.3 Describe the future of war.

Drones

Unmanned vehicles, or drones, are among the more innovative—and controversial—instruments of war. Drones constitute a key component of the so-called revolution in military affairs that applies new digital technologies to enhance the accuracy and effectiveness of weapons. Drones have become key counterterrorism instruments; their enhanced surveillance capacity makes it possible for users to track and destroy targets in real time.

The military use of drones increased dramatically during the first years of President Barack Obama's administration, especially in northwest Pakistan but also in Afghanistan, Yemen, and Africa, most notably Somalia. Drones appear to offer an effective and less expensive substitute for ground forces. Also, the drone program over Pakistan is run by the Central Intelligence Agency and is not officially acknowledged by the government. It is thereby possible for the CIA to use lethal force covertly, while the government of Pakistan can deny it is allowing a foreign power to wage war on its territory.

But there are also social problems associated with drone use. Using official numbers, the ratio of militant to civilian deaths has improved over the relatively short life of the program (see Table 16.2). For example, civilians accounted for roughly 50% of deaths from drone strikes between 2004 and 2007, but less than 5% between 2010 and 2012 (New America Foundation 2013). Yet the rules for defining "militant" and "civilian" remain contentious; some reports indicate that all armed men under age 40 in the vicinity are counted as "militant." Since virtually all men in northwest Pakistan are armed, lower reported deaths may not actually prove noncombatants are being protected. Drone operations sometimes employ a "double-tap" strategy, in which a target is hit with a missile and then struck again when others come to help or investigate. Regardless of the actual number of fatalities, the widespread impression that

Post-traumatic stress disorder (PTSD): A mental health condition triggered by a terrifying event. Symptoms include flashbacks, nightmares, and severe anxiety, as well as thoughts about the event that cannot be controlled.

 Trusting Foreign Terrorism Intelligence

 U.S. Foreign Policy

TABLE 16.2 Annual Drone Casualties in Pakistan by Category, 2004–2012 (in percentages)

Year	Militant	Civilian	Unknown
2004-7	35–43	54–61	9–10
2008	80–84	8–10	16–21
2009	69–70	11–19	12–19
2010	94	2–3	5–6
2011	80	1–15	8–18
2012	89	2	9
Total	**78–81**	**10**	**9–13**

SOURCE: New America Foundation.

drones do kill many innocent people undermines U.S. credibility among Pakistan's population.

Nor are the rules of engagement that govern the drone program transparent. At least four U.S. citizens have been assassinated by drones, and some point out that these individuals were not granted the legal "due process" the Constitution guarantees. The Obama administration has said that it conducts an extensive review before selecting any target, and the president himself signs off on any attack on an American (Becker and Shane 2012). Since 2011, the overall number of drone attacks has actually dropped, although reports of devastating consequences, such as in Miram Shah, in northwest Pakistan, persist (Walsh and Mehsud 2013).

Drones also have considerable "second-order effects," or indirect impacts, on local populations. Even where killings are largely limited to militants, the constant buzzing of hovering drones and the unpredictable threat of attack have limited normal social functions like weddings and funerals, religious gatherings, schools, and bazaars. Agriculture may also be disrupted, with significant economic impact. Surviving militants may blame locals for providing intelligence to guide the strikes and may take revenge (Stanford Law School/NYU Law School 2012). When people leave targeted areas, they contribute to the flow of refugees to already overcrowded urban areas. The use of drones can also become a grievance point that enables opposition fighters to recruit new members (Sluka 2011).

Finally, drone operators are not immune to psychological fallout from being agents of violence. Though physically safe on military bases in the United States, these pilots can suffer the effects of PTSD. All the pieces—civilian casualties, the hidden chain of command, second-order effects, and psychological toll on all sides—speak to the need for a more sociologically grounded interpretation of the use of drones rather than one limited to conventional military measures.

Women in Combat Roles

In January 2013, Defense Secretary Leon Panetta and the Joint Chiefs of Staff announced the end of the ban on women serving in combat roles in the U.S. Army. Nearly 15% of the 1.4 million active-duty military are female, and more than 255,000 women have deployed to Iraq or Afghanistan over the past decade. Before 1973, women in the U.S. military served mostly as nurses or clerks; now they serve on surface ships, pilot helicopters and fighter jets, and are deployed overseas as cooks, mechanics, drivers, military police, and intelligence officers. The Pentagon recently revised regulations to allow women to be permanently assigned to battalions—ground forces of approximately 800 soldiers—where they can be frontline medics and radio operators. There are even plans for an all-female submarine crew.

Many of these changes have placed more women in harm's way. In fact, the new policies only formalize what was already happening in Iraq and Afghanistan. Women have demonstrated bravery under fire, been captured, won medals, and served in many difficult circumstances. Although their casualty rate remains lower than that of men, more than 800 women have been wounded or killed in Iraq and Afghanistan.

The movement of women into combat roles, phasing in over several years, will continue a controversy that has

Reuters / Finbarr O'Reilly

U.S. Marine and Female Engagement Team leader Sergeant Sheena Adams (left) and Hospital Corpsman Shannon Crowley sit in an armored vehicle before heading out on an operation from their base in Afghanistan. Female marines create relationships with Afghan women to gain their trust and bring them better health care and education. The Female Engagement Teams gain access to the 51% of the Afghan population that male marines cannot.

been brewing for more than a decade. For example, a commander can still make a case for an exception, preserving the traditional all-male fighting unit.

The social construction of gender is one of the key sociological questions in the end of the ban on women in combat. Historically, masculine traits have been considered crucial for the proper training and performance of soldiers, especially those directly engaged in fighting. Will the presence of women constitute a "social problem" in the front lines? Must warriors always be male?

Some suggest the warrior role requires a hypermasculine culture (Titunik 2008; Leatherman 2011; Wood 2006). **Hypermasculinity** is an intensification of traits typically associated with stereotypical male behavior: physical strength, aggressiveness, assertiveness, risk taking, virility, and an appreciation for danger and adventure. Military training, and the goal of strengthening bonding within small units, may also rest on shared male identity. Songs ("This is my rifle, this is my gun; this one is for fighting, this one is for fun"), shaved heads, a steady stream of references to intimate body parts, and a major role for sexual innuendo consolidate this identity. Masculinity may be as crucial for group performance as competence in handling weapons. Women may still face opposition in taking combat roles, but not because they are physically weaker. The "problem" is that their presence may rupture male solidarity.

Another sociological perspective concentrates on professionalism rather than masculinity. In this view, the military is a complex institution in which male warrior traits are not as important for success as are the skills and attitudes that create group cohesion. With bare chest and bulging muscles, hefting a huge heavy machine gun and exuding anger with every step, Sylvester Stallone's Rambo character may have done well at the box office, but he does not embody the teamwork, discipline, obedience, and service considered more important to fulfilling most military missions. In the not-so-distant past, women were excluded from serving on police patrols, performing complex surgery, long-distance running, and arguing legal cases in court. Many believed that women were physically incapable of performing these activities properly. But women have gained widespread acceptance in these and other activities because they are able to carry out their functional roles. Biological sex has not disappeared, but it has become much less important than task or functional training. While some style differences may remain between the sexes, women have shown their ability to achieve and contribute on par with men.

Those who favor continuing the ban on women in combat often invoke more traditional perspectives on gender relations. For example, women have limited upper-body strength and would be unable to carry heavy

Female marine recruit Kylieanne Fortin goes through close combat training at the U.S. Marine Corps training depot in Parris Island, South Carolina. Marine Corps boot camp, with its combination of strict discipline and exhaustive physical training, is considered the most rigorous of all U.S. armed forces recruit training. The first three women ever to graduate from the infantry training course completed the program in November 2013.

loads or drag wounded comrades to safety. Moreover, their presence encourages distractions that compromise morale and interfere with the bonding necessary for an effective fighting force. During the 2012 presidential campaign, Republican candidate Rick Santorum argued, "When you have men and women together in combat, I think men have emotions when you see a woman in harm's way. I think it is something that's natural. It's very much in our culture to be protective." While still chief of staff of the U.S. Air Force, General Merrill McPeak testified to the Senate Armed Services Committee, then considering allowing women to fly combat aircraft, that he would choose a less qualified male pilot over a more qualified female because, "even though logic tells us that women can [conduct combat operations] as well as men, I have a very traditional attitude about wives and mothers and daughters being ordered to kill people" (quoted in McSally 2011). The Center for Military Readiness, based in Washington, D.C., is one organization that is particularly vociferous in defending the exclusion of women from combat.

Those favoring an end to the combat ban focus on more fluid construction of gender roles, with new possibilities for women. For example, technology may be more important to the contemporary soldier than strength.

Hypermasculinity: An intensification of traits normally associated with stereotypical male behavior: physical strength, aggressiveness, assertiveness, risk taking, and appreciation for danger and adventure.

Scott Olson / Getty Images

Many standard-issue weapons are relatively light, making it possible even for children to use them. All recruits could be required to meet standards of strength, speed, and endurance that apply evenly to women and men. Men might have an easier time meeting the marks, but some women would qualify while some men would fail. Furthermore, the distinction between combat and noncombat positions has already been blurred. Early in Operation Iraqi Freedom, Private First Class Jessica Lynch and two other female soldiers, Lori Piestewa and Shoshana Johnson, were captured and suffered injuries. All three were members of the 507th Maintenance Company. Lynch and Piestewa were unit supply specialists; Johnson prepared meals. All were clearly in harm's way.

Ending the combat ban would simply enable the rules to catch up with reality. Female soldiers have been "colocated" with combat teams and participated in patrols for many years, primarily because they are better able than male soldiers to avoid offending cultural sensitivities when local women need to be searched. In the Marine Corps, Female Engagement Teams serve on the front lines in Afghanistan. Cultural Support Teams have deployed with the Special Forces. Public opinion polls show most U.S. adults generally agree with lifting the ban (*New York Times* 2009).

Finally, eligibility for full combat will be necessary for women if they are to achieve full equality in the armed forces. Without that opportunity they will always be considered second-class citizens and held back unfairly. A final, crucial argument is that ending the combat ban may be necessary to reduce sexual violence and harassment in the armed forces and service academies.

Globalized Intrastate Wars

The number of state-based wars per year has declined. However, this comparatively bright note is balanced by the emergence of another type of conflict, globalized intrastate war. What are the features of this type of conflict?

The most important goal of such a war is control of the flow of valuable natural resources. **Globalized intrastate wars** are fought largely for economic gain rather than for political outcomes. Indeed, it sometimes appears that combatants are uninterested in managing the state for any particular purpose (Kaldor 2012).

Globalized intrastate wars engage many types of fighting units. Paramilitary forces play a major role, with warlords operating largely in their own self-interest and sometimes abducting and enlisting children to fight. Foreign mercenaries, private military contractors, and international forces, sometimes backed by the United Nations, may also engage. Deliberate expulsion of civilians in ethnic cleansing campaigns allows the warlords to tighten control over territory. Civilians bear the brunt of these conflicts, with tens and even hundreds of thousands of deaths and high levels of sexual violence.

International agencies, other nations, nongovernmental organizations, and private donors may provide humanitarian assistance to vulnerable populations, often instead of undertaking riskier efforts to reduce fighting in the first place. Unfortunately, humanitarian aid can become an additional lootable resource that, despite donors' good intentions, fuels the conflict and makes the war self-financing. During the war in Bosnia, both Serb militia and local Bosnian criminal gangs kept threats of violence high enough to maintain a flow of humanitarian assistance to besieged Sarajevo, some of which was shunted off to black markets, but not high enough to invite direct intervention by Europe and the United States (Andreas 2008). Presumed enemies actually engaged in a peculiar type of cooperation because each had an interest in keeping assistance coming in. Civilian aid officials and nongovernmental organizations may have to make a pact with the devil in which they allow some aid to enter the black market in return for ensuring that some can be used for its intended purpose. The U.S. military paid contractors to transport supplies across Afghanistan, but the social networks included criminal groups, Afghan power brokers, and subcontractors with links to insurgents. This endemic form of corruption has been called "threat financing": U.S. taxpayers funded development efforts in Afghanistan but inadvertently gave support to the Taliban.

> **Globalized intrastate wars:** Organized violence used to control territory containing valuable resources, often fought by paramilitary forces, often targeting civilians, often containing high levels of sexual violence, and often using child soldiers.

USING THEORY TO EXAMINE WAR AND TERRORISM: THE VIEWS FROM THE FUNCTIONALIST, CONFLICT, AND SYMBOLIC INTERACTIONIST PERSPECTIVES

 16.4 Apply the functionalist, symbolic interactionist, and conflict perspectives to war.

Sexual Violence in the Military

Under pressure from different constituencies and after years of complaints about avoiding the problem, the U.S. Department of Defense now issues an annual report on sexual assault in the military. The edition for fiscal year 2012 chronicles a 46% increase in sexual assault reports, the number of which rose to 3,553 in the period October 2012 to June 2013 (U.S. Department of Defense 2012). These reports certainly undercount the actual number of assaults. The Pentagon estimates that 26,000 members of the military, men as well as women, were sexually assaulted during the period.

Equally controversial are the actions being taken to respond to this epidemic. The military has introduced hotlines, mandatory online training, zero-tolerance policies, workshops, and specialized units charged with reducing sexual violence. These steps may have an effect, but advocacy groups outside the military and many soldiers themselves claim the problem has actually worsened over the past decade.

Because some commanders have set aside convictions on sexual assault charges and even forced victims to continue working alongside perpetrators, Senator Kirsten Gillibrand (D-NY) has championed legislation that would remove military commanders from the process of deciding whether sexual misconduct cases should go to military trial. An analysis of 2,039 rape and sexual assault allegations in the U.S. military in the period 2009–2010 found that only 551 of these cases had gone to courts-martial. Of these, 147 resulted in convictions on the original charges.

Shelli Hanks (far right), sister-in-law of Kimberly Hanks, speaks during a protest outside the U.S. Air Force base in Tucson, Arizona. The protesters rallied to denounce the air force's decision to transfer Lieutenant Colonel James Wilkerson to Arizona after his conviction on sexual assault charges was overturned by a commander. Kimberly Hanks, a civilian employee who works with service members, accused Wilkerson of sexually assaulting her.

▶ **THINK ABOUT IT**

1. Why do you think sexual assault occurs at a higher rate in the military than in civilian life?

2. What can be done about the problem of underreporting of such assaults?

3. What would you do to reduce the level of sexual assault within the military?

Political scientists and international relations theorists have long studied war. Nonetheless, sociology has much to contribute. All the major theories—functionalism, symbolic interactionism, and conflict theory—address the sociological relationships found in war, each through distinct approaches.

Functionalism

The structural functionalist approach takes a macro view and looks at the relationships between particular phenomena, such as crime or health, and the overall organization of society. Its tendency is to focus on social order. "Structures" can be said to be "functional" when they strengthen the capacity of society to hold itself together.

Given its devastation, war may seem an odd contributor to the stability and functioning of society. And its dysfunctions usually do outweigh the benefits. Even in trying to understand the functions of war, we must not forget the multiple tragedies that always accompany human beings' use of violence against other human beings.

The U.S. experience during World War II illustrates the structural functionalist perspective. The entire country was mobilized behind the war effort. Every medically eligible male served in the armed forces, intelligence, administration, or government. The economy was largely driven by the war, women flowed into the workforce to replace men fighting overseas, and the participation of minorities improved on the past record of discrimination. Though blacks fought in segregated units led by white officers, their service made it more difficult for them to accept the racial status quo after the war. Japanese Americans were herded into detention centers, a shameful practice that violated their rights as U.S.

It's Our Fight Too!

American World War II–era recruitment poster for women workers. "Rosie the Riveter" was the iconic image representing American women working in factories during the war. The equivalent image of women working for the war effort in Canada was "Ronnie, the Bren Gun Girl," and in Britain it was the painting *Ruby Loftus Screwing a Breech Ring*.

citizens. But many young men from these camps ended up in Europe fighting for their country. This experience helped lay the groundwork for the expansion of citizenship rights after the war. Finally, women demonstrated that they could build tanks, construct aircraft, and forge steel. Though the effects were not immediate—men came home to reclaim these jobs—the experience helped women prepare for new postwar opportunities to work outside the home.

World War II also helped the United States finally emerge from the Great Depression. Some technical innovations of the war, such as radar and improvements in aircraft engines, were applied in the postwar civilian sector. And lower spending on consumption during the war and the resulting savings helped create the groundwork for a postwar period of prosperity, including the expansion of homeownership and the purchase of automobiles. Still,

Military-industrial complex: The relationships among government, the Pentagon, and defense contractors that promote the acquisition of weapons systems and a militarized foreign policy.

▶ Women and the Military

we can be excused for hoping there might be a better way to achieve such benefits.

Policy Implications of Structural Functionalism

The most important policy implication of the structural functionalist perspective is that war, or at least preparation for war, might be necessary to defend a society against outside threats. Supporters of nuclear deterrence would argue that during the Cold War, the mutual threat of the United States and Soviet Union to destroy each other with atomic weapons did maintain a certain kind of peace between them. In this view, the capacity to wage war—even extreme war—contributed to each side's national security. Many would argue instead, however, that peace can be achieved without the threat of nuclear annihilation.

The production and control of atomic weapons imply a strong concentration of power, calling attention to Max Weber's (1958) definition of the state as the organization that holds the only legitimate means of violence. For Weber, the emergence of the nation-state was useful because force could now be centralized in a single organization governed by norms or rules that most people found acceptable. Moreover, the use of that force was increasingly professionalized, meaning it was more carefully regulated and subject to political authority. In this way of thinking, a country can live with nuclear weapons when the public believes the weapons are carefully controlled and an elaborate decision-making structure ensures that they will be used only as a last resort. The weapons' force might be deadly, but, if properly managed, the possession of such weapons might lead to actual violence being replaced by carefully regulated threats that are never carried out.

Structural functionalists take a similar stance toward the armed forces as a whole: lethal force can be used, but only under clearly defined circumstances and with the approval of civilian leaders. Ultimately, the raison d'être of the military is to keep the country safe. Maintaining the security of society by means of its military certainly falls short of a nonviolent ideal, but it is preferable to the existence of numerous armed substate actors, all using or threatening violence to achieve private interests.

Conflict Theory

Conflict theory focuses on power structures and the domestic and international inequalities that drive the war system. One of the most important concepts conflict theorists employ is the idea of the **military-industrial complex**, or the relationships among government forces, the Pentagon, and defense contractors that promote the acquisition of weapons systems and a militarized foreign policy.

In his January 17, 1961, farewell address to the nation, President Dwight D. Eisenhower warned of

> an immense military establishment and a large arms industry [that] is new in the American experience. The total influence— economic, political, even spiritual—is felt in every city, every statehouse, every office of the federal government. . . . In the councils of government, we must guard against the acquisition of unwarranted influence, whether sought or unsought, by the military-industrial complex. The potential for the disastrous rise of misplaced power exists, and will persist.

This remarkable statement came from an individual who was not only president of the United States but also the former commanding general of Allied forces in Europe and the head of the D-Day invasion of Normandy. With Eisenhower's speech, the term *military-industrial complex* entered the national vocabulary.

Sociologically, the military-industrial complex contains a series of distinct features. These include a strong compatibility of interest among top Pentagon officials, defense contractors, and members of Congress (a series of ties that has also been called the "iron triangle") (Adams 1981). This common interest results in the purchase of expensive weapons systems that are often unneeded or that underperform (Hartung 2011). The military-industrial complex is guided by self-interest rather than policy. For example, the military continues to invest in the acquisition of large tanks, weapons of a method of conducting war that is largely obsolete. Members of Congress often support weapons procurement programs that benefit their districts, regardless of whether the programs contribute to national security. Even liberals, generally doves with respect to war policy, vote to retain military bases that are no longer useful, or armaments the military itself may oppose, in order to benefit their local constituencies. Counterinsurgency capabilities such as language skills, intelligence gathering, and social science–based cultural knowledge, including the Human Terrain Teams described in this chapter's opening vignette, do appear in the Department of Defense budget, but they receive less support than expensive heavy-weapons hardware.

Ideology plays an important role in the military-industrial complex, especially a view of the world that C. Wright Mills (1956) called the "military definition of reality." According to Mills, most civilian and military leaders in the United States see the world as an unsettled, competitive, often hostile arena in which military prowess

is the best option for securing national interests and maintaining U.S. status as the most powerful nation in the world. According to the Constitution and formal regulations, the U.S. military is under civilian control. Civilians, however, share the military mind-set regarding the importance of projecting power, ensuring that nonmilitary options such as diplomacy receive less attention and lower policy priorities. Military leaders and their values thus play a significant role in Washington's policies, not conspiring against civilians, but working alongside and often supported by them.

Mills is unusual among conflict theorists because he regarded the military as a source of power in its own right. He was certainly aware of corporate power, but unlike conventional Marxists, who call attention to property rights and market forces, Mills identified power as rooted in the control of large-scale, bureaucratically structured organizations, be they big business, the executive branch of government, or the military itself. Mills thought the Cold War had degraded the capacity of the United States to engage in productive diplomacy with other nations. Though he wrote more than 50 years ago, his ideas remain influential.

Policy Implications of the Conflict Perspective

One policy implication of the thesis that the military-industrial complex holds considerable influence is that the United States is more war-prone than most Americans believe. The chance that it will fight other democracies is

As fellow troopers aid wounded soldiers, the first sergeant of A Company, 101st Airborne Division, guides a medevac helicopter through the jungle foliage to pick up soldiers who suffered casualties during a five-day patrol during the Vietnam War, 1968. Military and civilian casualties and losses on both sides of the conflict were massive.

Art Greenspon / Associated Press

fairly remote, yet Washington has certainly established a belligerent record, especially since the end of World War II. During the Cold War, the Pentagon fought major wars in Korea and Vietnam as well as numerous smaller conflicts. Defense spending averaged 8% to 10% of GDP. And the country provided military aid and training to many repressive regimes, such as those of Mobutu in Zaire, Pinochet in Chile, and Sukarno in Indonesia. According to conflict theorists, the war system proved expensive at home and shrank the possibilities for democratic reform abroad.

Ideology has operated in the post–Cold War era as well. In 2002, President George W. Bush endorsed an internal government report titled *National Security Strategy of the United States of America,* which outlined a strategy of preventive war in which the United States would have to "act against emerging threats before they are fully formed." The document declared the nation's right to "dissuade potential adversaries from pursuing a military buildup in the hopes of surpassing, or equaling, the power of the United States." Simple deterrence, or preventing war by threatening retaliation, was thought less likely to work. The conclusion called for "anticipatory action to defend ourselves—even if uncertainty remains as to the time and place of the enemy's attack. To forestall or prevent such hostile acts by our adversaries, the United States will, if necessary, act preemptively." In this controversial statement—the authors of which were civilians—diplomacy, negotiation, and multilateral cooperation with allies take a backseat.

Conflict theorists also note profiteering in the recent wars in Iraq and Afghanistan, especially because new policies relied more heavily on private military contractors such as Halliburton and Blackwater. While humanitarian aid and development projects existed, both wars saw strategies that relied more on "hard power" military options. The Global War on Terror (discussed below) also favors a militarized approach to security rather than a combination of policing, building a broader range of allies, and conflict resolution. Meanwhile, the illegal "rendition" of terror suspects to foreign prisons, abuse and torture conducted by the United States itself, negative images of the detention center at Guantanamo Bay, and the use of drones have provided robust recruitment incentives for the very insurgents the United States is trying to defeat. Conflict theorists say these policies are counterproductive for most U.S. citizens but reflect the priorities of the country's power elite.

....

Authorization: Enemy-making behavior facilitated by leaders that absolves individuals of the responsibility to make personal moral choices.

Symbolic Interactionism

Symbolic interaction theorists try to understand how individuals acquire the meanings and understandings that govern their interactions with other individuals and social groups. Human beings do not automatically act out directives from authorities or dominant structures. They interpret the surrounding circumstances and then play out these interpretations. They may even change the script depending on time, place, and key engagements with other people. Social interaction is a bottom-up rather than a top-down approach to social life.

Symbolic interactionism is a very human perspective because it examines the constant exchange, dialogue, and communication that guide social life. We could not get through the day without utilizing a huge toolbox of social skills that enable us to peacefully coordinate our actions with our families, neighbors, and coworkers. Even when we disagree with them or consider them different, strange, or possibly threatening, we usually do not want to kill them. Many people believe we are condemned to competition, even conflict and violence, by our genetic makeup. It would be far more accurate to say our biology "condemns" us to cooperation (Fry 2006; United Nations Educational, Scientific and Cultural Organization 1986).

But if we are predominantly cooperative, how can we also engage in torture, rape, killing, and other destructive acts, at times on a stupefying scale? The Rwanda genocide, the bombing of civilians by both sides in World War II, rape camps in Bosnia, and the use of child soldiers all serve as social alarm bells. Humans do carry the potential to do great harm. What does symbolic interactionism tell us about this more tragic side of social behavior?

Several factors must come together for humans to exercise violence on a horrific scale. Three in particular mark the passage from acceptance of others to violent killing: authorization, routinization, and dehumanization (Fellman 1998; Gamson 1995; Kelman and Hamilton 1989). Fortunately, the combination of these three is rare.

Under **authorization**, leaders define a situation so that individuals are absolved of responsibility for making personal moral choices. People act badly because an authority has given them approval to do so. Hutu militia butchered Tutsi during the Rwanda genocide believing their leaders had been given approval for these actions. Those who dropped the atomic bombs on civilians in Hiroshima and Nagasaki did not have to think about the consequences because they were following orders from the president and the military chain of command. Japanese soldiers killed hundreds of thousands of civilians in

Muslim American Terrorism

The Granger Collection

An old woman and children on their way to the gas chambers at the Auschwitz concentration camp in Poland, 1944. The "Final Solution" was the systematic effort by the Nazi bureaucracy to exterminate the Jews of Europe during World War II by gassing, shooting, and other means. Can you think of other examples of systematic killing that are rational, efficient, and devoid of emotion?

Nanjing because they believed they were authorized by the highest military officers (Chang 1997).

Under **routinization**, actions become organized by well-established procedures so there is no opportunity for raising moral questions. Individuals act badly because they believe in a routine that determines how they are to behave; they no longer have to make deliberate decisions. For example, those who ran the Nazi death camps followed closely prescribed procedures governing how many people they were to kill on each shift, how they were to administer the gas, how hot they were to make each oven, and how they were to dispose of the bodies.

Under **dehumanization**, attitudes reflect perceptions that the targets are less than human. People act badly because they see only objects, animals, or vicious enemies, not human beings. For example, the terrible medical experiments the Japanese conducted on prisoners of war during World War II were carried out on what they called *maruta*, or wooden logs. The Nazi regime portrayed Jews as rats or other vermin. During the 1994 genocide in Rwanda, Hutu hate propaganda referred to Tutsis as *inyenzi*, or cockroaches.

In all these cases, the scale of enemy making intensified. Leaders gave their approval, perpetrators were given instructions and mechanisms to follow, and those killed no longer counted as human beings. All moral decision making was suspended. The symbolic interactionist perspective helps us understand how these meanings, no matter how heinous, can be acquired—and, fortunately, how unusual they are.

Policy Implications of Symbolic Interactionism

One striking sociological finding is that it is actually very difficult to get human beings to kill each other, even in the midst of war. It can be done, obviously—we have just reviewed several dismaying examples. But we cannot assume soldiers will kill just because they have been given orders to do so. Killing is, sociologically speaking, extremely problematic.

One of the earliest applications of sociological studies to the battlefield found that complexity and contradiction were the rule rather than devotion to duty as defined by superior officers. During World War II, less than 25% of combat soldiers could be counted on to fire their weapons at the enemy. Everyone else fired in the air, refused to shoot, or huddled near the ground. Lieutenant Colonel Robert Cole described the behavior of his soldiers under attack in 1944: "Not one man in twenty-five voluntarily used his weapon. . . . they fired only while I watched them or while some other soldier stood over them" (quoted in Malesevic 2010, 74). Almost all the actual fighting was carried out by a relatively small number of combatants.

Firing ratios improved during the Vietnam War and among frontline soldiers in Iraq and Afghanistan. This rise in efficiency rested on findings of other studies that in the heat of battle, soldiers fight not for abstractions such as "democracy" or "freedom," or even to protect the homeland from attack. Instead, they fight because they are loyal to the people in their immediate unit. Training therefore now focuses on deepening the micro-level solidarity of small fighting units; comradeship, mutual respect, and not letting others down are the key motivations. Left to themselves, individuals generally do not kill efficiently; only through close attention to social organization and the creation of new norms forged in the intensity of small-group interaction do soldiers perform as their leaders desire.

SPECIALIZED THEORY: THE TWO-SOCIETY THESIS

 16.5 Apply the two-society thesis to the relationship between the U.S. military and U.S. society.

Routinization: The organizing and structuring of enemy-making behavior so thoroughly that there is no opportunity for raising moral questions.

Dehumanization: Enemy-making behavior that makes the other side appear to be less than human; eliminates the need to raise moral questions.

The Network of U.S. Foreign Military Bases

The United States has established an enormous number of military bases throughout the world (see Figure 16.3). Some are large: approximately 48,000 soldiers are currently stationed in Germany, 11,000 in Italy, and 51,000 in Japan. Others are relatively small and contain only small contingents of advisers. One growing subcategory is bases connected to the use of drones, especially in Africa and the Middle East. The total number of overseas U.S. bases is more than 1,000. The Pentagon places the annual cost of maintaining these bases at $22.1 billion, but others offer estimates as high as $170 billion (Vine 2012).

Some bases are legacies of the Cold War whose original purpose was to ring the Soviet Union in a "forward strategy," so war could be fought as close to Soviet territory as possible. Military bases also provide opportunities to influence countries through their significant impact on local economies. Base commanders and in-country military leaders establish working relationships that can be more important than conventional diplomatic connections.

At times, U.S. military personnel on foreign bases have become embroiled in sex scandals with locals and have committed violence against women and girls living nearby. Okinawa, islands south of Japan and the site of several important U.S. military bases, was the scene of the 1995 rape and murder of a young girl by several U.S. servicemen. The local population's reaction led to the election of political leaders hostile to the continued presence of American soldiers, sailors, and marines and forced dramatic restructuring of the bases themselves.

Other kinds of incidents can turn local opinion against U.S. military bases as well. In Italy, the severing of a gondola cable by the tail of a U.S. jet flying below its permitted altitude led to a dozen deaths. Other criminal acts have included murder in Afghanistan, more incidents of rape in Japan, and environmental spoilage in the Philippines. The United States has also tortured prisoners at bases in Iraq, Afghanistan, and Guantanamo Bay, and in CIA secret prisons (Shane 2013b). In almost all these cases adjudication, where it has occurred at all, has taken place in the United States. Structural functionalists might argue that the bases are a vital component of U.S. defense; conflict theorists might suggest they are better understood as agents of influence and control.

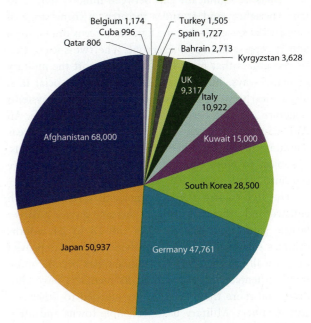

FIGURE 16.3 U.S. Soldiers Stationed at Foreign Military Bases

Belgium 1,174
Cuba 996
Qatar 806
Turkey 1,505
Spain 1,727
Bahrain 2,713
Kyrgyzstan 3,628
UK 9,317
Italy 10,922
Kuwait 15,000
South Korea 28,500
Germany 47,761
Japan 50,937
Afghanistan 68,000

SOURCE: Department of Defense, September 30, 2012.

▶ **THINK ABOUT IT**

1. How would you regard the presence of a foreign military base on the outskirts of your town? Would the fact that your government has approved this base affect your views?

2. Do you think U.S. staff on foreign bases should be governed by the local legal process, or by U.S. procedures? Why?

The political and social turmoil surrounding the Vietnam conflict in the 1960s, especially opposition to the draft, fundamentally altered the U.S. military's enlistment policy. In 1973, the Pentagon ended the draft and established an all-volunteer force (AVF). Conscription still exists in theory; young men must register with the Selective Service System, but few expect they will be forced to serve. Entering the military is an option to choose—or not.

International Affairs

One important result of an AVF is that the military may become a society within a society. This relationship between the civilian and military sectors might become a social problem if the two sectors exhibit differences in members' social backgrounds, cultural values, and political beliefs. A significant gap between military and civilian experiences and attitudes threatens a cornerstone of democratic society—that the fighting force is drawn from and is representative of everyone. The two-society thesis recognizes that most U.S. adults support the military in many ways. But beneath that important social fact, disparities between classes, cultures, and belief systems structure a divide between military and civilian life. An AVF may actually be easier to commit to fighting, whereas a military in which soldiers are drafted, despite problems, is subject to more constraints before those soldiers are sent into battle.

The two-society thesis assumes that soldiers, both enlisted and officers, will make military service a career lasting significantly longer than the 18 to 24 months draftees served. Pay scales and benefits have improved dramatically in the AVF. The military has become more family-oriented; more than half its members have children, and more than 100,000 are married to other service members. Military bases resemble towns and often provide schools, recreational and medical facilities, and subsidized shopping. During times of considerable economic uncertainty in the civilian sector, these features attract volunteers to become absorbed into the military's thinking, perspective, and attitudes. One study of marines returning home after boot camp found them repulsed by "the physical unfitness of civilians, by the uncouth behavior they witnessed, and by what they saw as pervasive selfishness and consumerism" (Ricks, quoted in Rahbek-Clemmensen et al. 2012, 672).

Yet a very small proportion of U.S. citizens serve in the armed forces. During the long-running wars in Iraq and Afghanistan, more than 2.5 million soldiers have deployed to combat theaters. That is a large number—but significantly less than 1% of the population. During the Cold War, the percentage of veterans in Congress was higher than the percentage in the country as a whole. Now, less than a quarter of Americans have served in the military. At the beginning of the 2003 war with Iraq, among 535 members of Congress, only one had a child deployed to Iraq. Among the general public, the proportion who know someone who has served in the military has also declined (Parker 2011). These concentrations seem to have influenced political and social views on different topics.

Members of the military are significantly more conservative than the rest of the population. One large-scale

A recruit responds to a motivational speech being made by his commanding officer before graduation from boot camp at the U.S. Marine Corps recruit depot in Parris Island, South Carolina. The French sociologist Émile Durkheim used the term "collective effervescence" to describe the shared emotional excitement or "electricity" that is created in a group when people come together and participate in an activity that serves to unify them.

survey found 63.9% of leaders in the armed forces identifying as Republicans, compared with only 30.3% of civilian nonveteran leaders. About two-thirds of military leaders called themselves "somewhat conservative" or "very conservative," compared with less than a third of civilian nonveteran leaders (Feaver and Kohn 2001). Meanwhile, less than 5% of the military elite identified as "very liberal" or "somewhat liberal," compared with 37.5% of civilian leaders.

Serving in the military is also a distinct experience. While flying a fighter jet for the air force is very different from fixing a tank in the army, important commonalities make military culture in all branches substantially different from civilian life. These include the following (Burk 2008):

- *Cohesion:* the emotional bond of shared identity and camaraderie among soldiers in their local unit
- *Esprit de corps:* the pride soldiers take in the effectiveness and importance of their organization
- *Discipline:* the commitment soldiers make to conform to rules, command, instruction, and drill
- *Etiquette:* the elaborate prescriptions that guide interpersonal interactions, especially between individuals of different ranks
- *Ceremonies:* the rituals that mark events and convey the distinct experiences and expectations of soldiers as different from civilians.

Beyond these cultural elements, it is not difficult to imagine how the combination of overseas deployment, exposure to hazard, the possibility of killing, and the possibility of being killed all can create a sense of personal commitment and national service quite different from what we find in civilian occupations. Not everyone in the military is a warrior; the so-called tooth-to-tail ratio, which compares those trained to fight on the ground with those who provide support, is only 10%. Even among those deployed to Iraq and Afghanistan, significantly less than half have engaged in actual fighting. Nonetheless, the warrior mentality continues to play a major role in the self-conception of the military. As Burk (2008) notes, "Warfighting still determines the central beliefs, values, and complex symbolic formations that define military culture." And Army veteran Matt Gallagher, who served in Iraq, has observed, "A lot of guys feel that they're part of a warrior caste, separate and distinct from society" (quoted in Thompson 2011).

The end of the draft, longer time in service, a distinct set of political and social views, and unique features of the military experience support the two-society thesis. Is there any counterevidence?

In 1993, President Clinton modified the standing policy of excluding gays and lesbians from the military by adopting a policy of "don't ask, don't tell" (DADT). This may have eased some homophobic practices, but many gays and lesbians continued to be expelled from the armed forces once their identities became known. DADT also put the military at odds with civilian society, which has been moving, however unevenly, toward greater inclusion and the extension of more civil rights to gays and lesbians. In response to the establishment of DADT, some universities and colleges barred ROTC programs from their campuses, in part because any policy that required homosexuals to "stay in the closet" violated their non-discrimination charters. However, over the past decade a remarkable sea change has occurred within the military, driven largely by generational changes in the larger society. Younger soldiers, marines, and junior officers moving up the ranks are not nearly so fixed in their views as their elders. Many in the military recognized that dismissing gays and lesbians, particularly when skilled, capable people were in demand, was self-destructive. A seminal article describing the negative impact of DADT on military efficacy was published in *Joint Forces Quarterly*, the main journal of the Joint Chiefs of Staff (Prakash 2009). In 2012, following a congressional debate and extensive preparation within the armed forces, President Obama ended DADT. As in many other militaries around the world, gays and lesbians can now serve openly in the U.S. armed forces. Discrimination has not ended, and backlash still occurs, but in their general movement toward greater equality, the military and civilian worlds now appear more alike than different.

ASK YOURSELF: Should a democratic society rely on an all-volunteer force, or should military service be evenly distributed across the population through a draft? If the draft were reintroduced in the United States, should women be eligible as well as men? Has the adoption of the AVF made it easier for the United States to engage in war? Why or why not?

TERRORISM

 Discuss the Global War on Terror.

Definition Issues

The U.S. State Department defines **terrorism** as "violence perpetrated for political reasons by subnational groups or secret state agents, often directed at noncombatant targets, and usually intended to influence an audience." Kidnapping, bombing, seizure of public buildings, and assassinations are intended to induce fear, often because witnesses feel the targets of these acts do not deserve the violence they suffer. There is a random element, too; anyone could become a victim. In sociological terms, terrorism is a dramatic taboo.

The hijacking of passenger airliners on September 11, 2001, and the subsequent attacks on the World Trade Center in New York City and the Pentagon in Washington, D.C., fit this definition of terrorism and dominate public perceptions and political debate. The April 15, 2013, bombings near the finish line of the Boston Marathon provide another example. Responses to terrorist acts often include moral outrage at the loss of civilian lives, anger at the violation of normal rules regarding public safety, desire for revenge, and, at times, gloating by perpetrators. These emotions heighten the already significant tension surrounding such acts.

Terrorism can be *international* in the sense that the attacking party is based in one part of the world and organizes violence so that perpetrators and weapons cross

Terrorism: Violence perpetrated for political reasons by subnational groups or secret state agents, often directed at noncombatant targets, and usually intended to influence an audience.

 America Remembers 9/11   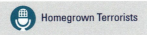 Homegrown Terrorists

Only part of the outer shell of the South Tower was left standing as a result of the 9/11 terrorist attacks on the World Trade Center in New York City. Terrorists crashed two passenger airliners into the Twin Towers, killing 2,752 people, including all 157 passengers (including the hijackers) and crew aboard the two planes.

borders. Terrorism can also be *domestic,* or "homegrown," when attackers and target are within a single country, even if inspiration may come from outside sources. The 9/11 al-Qaeda attacks in the United States were certainly international. The 2005 bombings in the London subway system are considered domestic because they were carried out by people who had lived in the United Kingdom for many years, although they received at least some guidance from abroad. Other examples of domestic terrorism in the United States include a nail bombing during the 1996 Summer Olympic Games in Atlanta, Georgia, the destruction of a federal building in Oklahoma City in 1995, and attacks on and killing of medical professionals who provide abortions.

In addition, we must consider *repressive state terrorism,* which is the employment of systematic violence against political opposition within national borders, and

state-sponsored terrorism, in which a government provides material support, weapons, and training to subnational units in another country so they can attack the government or civilians in that country. In both cases, the violence undermines democratic processes and holds the wrong people responsible for presumed grievances.

There are many examples of repressive state terrorism. The Communist Party in China and the Soviet Union under Stalin killed millions of political opponents, both real and presumed. Other examples include the "disappearances" carried out by Argentina's military junta in the early 1970s and the mass execution of Cambodians by the Khmer Rouge in the late 1970s. During the 1980s, South Africa and several Central American states organized death squads to repress social movements within their own borders. Saddam Hussein's ruthless control of Iraq qualifies as well.

Labeling the actions of a state or organization "terrorist" can be controversial. The U.S. State Department considers Hezbollah, a complex political organization that includes both fighting units and welfare providers, operates in Lebanon, and has fought Israel, to be a terrorist organization. The United States also criticizes Iran for providing military and monetary support to Hezbollah. During the 1980s, the South African government labeled the African National Congress (ANC) a "terrorist" group when it sabotaged power lines and carried out other acts of violence against property. Yet, from their own standpoint, the members of the ANC were "freedom fighters" engaged in a just struggle to overthrow the authoritarian apartheid system. As the Truth and Reconciliation Commission later documented, it was the government's brutal repression of antiapartheid activists that was fully "terrorist." Other examples are the Irish Republican Army and its struggle against British occupation, and Jewish settlers in Palestine who "cleansed" key villages before the formal creation of the state of Israel. Finally, militant U.S. environmentalists have been labeled "ecoterrorists" for driving large metal spikes into trees to wreck the machinery used in harvesting old-growth forests. These activists consider their acts a "just" method of protecting a valuable natural heritage against callous profit making by timber companies.

The U.S. government has participated in terrorism. In the past, the Pentagon trained military officers from Central and South America in repressive techniques aimed at suppressing local social movements. Washington has also supplied military equipment and other support to governments that have systematically violated human rights—the Saigon regime during the Vietnam War, Saddam Hussein's government in Iraq in the 1980s, and the regime of Augusto Pinochet in Chile, which overthrew the democratically elected government of Salvador Allende. Any government that possesses nuclear weapons might be considered guilty of state "terrorism" because it seeks a political outcome, deterrence of war, by threatening extreme violence against civilian noncombatants in another country. It might achieve stability, but only by creating a "balance of terror."

One final form is *cyberterrorism,* the use of the Internet to disrupt rival computer networks with the goal of spreading alarm and panic. Fortunately, this practice has not yet emerged on a significant scale, although governments and private companies have expended considerable effort to defend against it. Several examples of *cyberwar* have also taken place, most notably the introduction of the Stuxnet worm into the computer systems of Iran's nuclear facilities. Finally, we recognize *cyberespionage,* such as the efforts of China's government to hack into the computer networks of the Pentagon, energy labs, and defense contractors. China's intelligence services have broken into Google accounts in an effort to identify individuals the Federal Bureau of Investigation is keeping under surveillance in the United States. China has also infiltrated the computer systems of human rights organizations critical of Chinese government policies. For its part, the United States has conducted cyberespionage against China—and even against some of its NATO allies in Europe.

Weighing the Risks of Terrorism

No matter the definition, terrorism is a political act that threatens the lives of innocent people. Protection against this risk is necessary, yet security measures can themselves create problems. Currently, the United States spends $70 billion annually on programs administered by the Department of Homeland Security. Funds are allocated to security systems at airports and other transportation systems, to many levels of police and federal agencies, to new surveillance technologies, to cooperation with foreign governments, and to counterterrorist intelligence operations. From the social problems perspective, are these commitments the best way to allocate scarce resources? The goal is to save lives. Is this the most efficient way to spend money to accomplish that goal?

I write in the aftermath of the bombings at the site of the Boston Marathon. Three of my students were injured and many more at my university were psychologically affected. A friend of another of my students died in the bombing. Friends live four houses away from where Dzhokhar Tsarnaev, the younger of the two brothers who placed the explosives, was finally captured. I have participated in four Boston Marathons myself and have a deep attachment to the event. So I appreciate the depth of anger Americans felt at the targeting of one of the country's most compelling public festivals. For me, the bombings struck close to home.

Runners continue to run toward the finish line of the Boston Marathon as an explosion erupts near the end of the race on April 15, 2013. Two simultaneous explosions ripped through the crowd, killing 3 people and injuring 264 others on a day when tens of thousands of people had lined the streets to watch the world-famous race. Do you think that the installation of more security cameras might deter similar incidents in the future?

And yet the risk of a U.S. citizen's becoming a victim of a terrorist attack at home is relatively low; victims number fewer than 10 a year since September 11, 2001. In comparison, about 50 people in the United States are murdered, 85 take their own lives, and 120 die in traffic accidents *every day* (Schneier 2010). We can reduce the deaths, injuries, and other costs of many of those problems and others considered in this volume more effectively than we can reduce those from terrorism. Gun control would significantly cut the number of homicides; about 70% of murders are committed with guns. A relatively modest increase in public mental health programs would lower the suicide rate, as would legislation making it harder for mentally unstable individuals to acquire handguns. Requiring ignition devices in automobiles that make it impossible for people to start their cars when drunk would reduce the number of fatal motor vehicle accidents, about half of which involve alcohol.

Such measures are controversial. Initiating them would cost money, although far less than is currently spent on combatting the terrorist threat. But the government's monitoring of private telephone conversations and other forms of communication in the name of counterterrorism is, from a civil liberties view, also controversial. The sociological perspective makes two points when it comes to policy alternatives: first, the way we prioritize social problems has important consequences for society, and second, the way we respond to social problems—how much money we spend, which remedies we follow and which we ignore—creates an agenda. Does a militarized approach receive greater support? Or is social reform favored?

U.S. citizens are made physically more secure by counterterrorist expenditures. The clear physical threat posed by terrorism presents itself differently than the more abstract dangers of a possible automobile accident, generalized social stress, and victimization by a storm or other natural disaster. The risks of terrorism cannot be ignored. I travel on airplanes and like to feel safe when I do so. But it is also clear that concentrating more effort on programs that address other social problems would save more lives.

The Global War on Terror

After the September 11, 2001, attacks, the Bush administration established a distinct framework for response. President Bush called for a Global War on Terror (GWOT) that would integrate a series of military, political, legal, intelligence, and policy measures, with a focus largely on militant Islamic groups such as al-Qaeda and other jihadist organizations. Under the new doctrine, countries that harbor or sponsor terrorists would be considered enemies, and the United States pledged to conduct preemptive strikes against those that even seemed like they might begin to organize attacks. Internationally, the two most visible features of the GWOT were military interventions in Afghanistan and Iraq, both undertaken in the name of pursuing terrorists in their home territory—even if the evidence did not always support this claim.

The GWOT also included several important pieces of legislation and executive findings. After 9/11 the definition of "enemy combatant" was broadened to include any person who engages in hostile acts against the United States as designated by the commander in chief. Hundreds of individuals—some dangerous, some not, some captured on battlefields in Iraq and Afghanistan, others from various sites in Europe, the Middle East, and South Asia—were incarcerated at Guantanamo Bay, a navy base and detention center on the island of Cuba. These prisoners entered a legal limbo in which they were neither tried for specific acts nor provided a process through which they could eventually be released. All were interrogated in the search for further information by means that violated the Geneva Convention regarding the treatment of prisoners. Detainees were isolated from each other, sometimes deprived of sleep, and subjected to pain and different humiliations in an effort to break their will.

At home, the Bush administration and Congress passed the Patriot Act of 2001, which significantly increased the capacities of law enforcement and intelligence-gathering agencies. Phone records could now be more easily accessed. The Internet, including private e-mail exchanges, could be monitored more aggressively. And many medical, employment, and financial records could be reviewed with less

judicial oversight. For example, the National Security Agency (NSA) now uses a key-word search to screen all international phone calls. More surveillance cameras have been installed, although the United States lags behind Great Britain in this regard. Such cameras played a key role in law enforcement's identification of the perpetrators of the Boston Marathon bombings.

Other important domestic measures created under the Department of Homeland Security include the closer tracking of noncitizens within the United States and new requirements that they register and report to immigration authorities. Authorities can more easily detain and deport individuals suspected of engaging in terrorism-related activities. And the secretary of the Treasury has expanded authority to regulate financial transactions, particularly those of foreign individuals and other economic units.

Limitations of the Global War on Terror

The Global War on Terror has been credited with helping to prevent several attacks on U.S. soil. After the Boston Marathon bombings in April 2013, the *New York Times* argued that during the previous decade, the "United States was strikingly free of terrorist attacks, in part because of far more aggressive law enforcement tactics" (Shane 2013a). Examples include a 2001 shoe-bomb plot that would have brought down a civilian airliner, a planned 2007 attack against Fort Dix, New Jersey, and a 2010 plot to bomb Times Square in New York City. (In the case of the 2001 shoe-bomb incident, it could also be claimed that vigilant fellow passengers actually prevented Richard Reid from setting off explosives in the soles of his sneakers.) Perhaps the GWOT's best claim to success lies in deterrence: despite these incidents and the Boston Marathon bombings, the number of international terrorist acts carried out on U.S. home territory remains relatively small. At the same time, the GWOT has raised many questions, including the possibility that some of its measures violate U.S. law and norms, and that some are actually self-defeating.

The American Civil Liberties Union has challenged many sections of the Patriot Act as infringing on civil liberties in general and on the First Amendment in particular. The government's right to search an individual's library records, book purchases, and business and private finances without disclosing that the person is being investigated is also a breach of the right to due process. Some city police departments, especially New York's, have carried out widespread surveillance on Muslim Americans, paying informants to photograph prayer sessions in mosques, recording the names of those signing protest petitions, and reporting Muslims who volunteer to feed poor families. The NYPD has used plainclothes detectives to eavesdrop

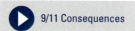 9/11 Consequences

on ordinary conversations and, under an organizational entity called the Demographics Unit, has cataloged Muslim businesses engaged in normal commerce. Using a strategy called "create and capture," New York and other municipalities have used undercover agents to coax young men into discussions about terrorism and then into the margins of terrorist activities. In the decade after 9/11, the FBI and Department of Justice convicted approximately 150 men in these sting operations. Most had little to no connection with international terrorist networks. Indeed, most of the questionable behavior appears to have been generated by contact with the law enforcement agencies themselves (Goldman and Apuzzo 2013).

Activities undertaken in the name of counterterrorism have acquired a life of their own. Undercover NYPD officers have attended meetings of liberal political organizations and kept intelligence files on activists who planned protests having no connection with terrorism. The police department's infiltration of activist organizations immediately before the 2004 Republican National Convention continued in the years that followed. An officer in the intelligence unit even traveled to New Orleans, where the People's Summit had gathered to oppose U.S. trade policies with Canada and Mexico (Goldman and Apuzzo 2013). In these respects, counterterrorism efforts have contributed to a deepening of "the surveillance society."

Many other GWOT programs have shortcomings and even negative feedback loops that undermine their original purpose of helping control terrorism. U.S. military interventions in Iraq and Afghanistan have heightened unfavorable views of the United States in the Middle East, precisely where Washington is trying to increase its influence, as have reports of conditions at Guantanamo Bay. Prisoners have been subjected to aggressive interrogation practices, including physical assaults, insults such as desecration of the Koran, and questionable practices such as sexual touching by female interrogators and smearing of faux menstrual blood on prisoners' bodies to create embarrassment and humiliation. Despite President Obama's original vow to close Guantanamo, some

members of Congress, Democrats included, have blocked every effort. In 2013, a number of prisoners there went on a hunger strike. In some countries, the detention center at Guantanamo Bay has become a symbolic martyr site that encourages still more opposition to the United States.

Suspects have also been captured by foreign intelligence operators abroad with the assistance of U.S. agents and then "rendered" to facilities in other countries for waterboarding and other forms of torture. At Abu Ghraib in Iraq and Bagram in Afghanistan, prisoners have died from abusive treatment while under custody. These incidents have received some attention in the U.S. media but have secured a much higher profile abroad, especially in the countries considered most likely to harbor terrorist networks.

Counterterrorist drone attacks also contain self-defeating features. They are extremely unpopular in Pakistan, and President Obama's ambassador to Pakistan, Cameron Munter, has "wondered whether the pace of the drone war might be undercutting relations with an important ally for the quick fix of killing midlevel terrorists" (Coll 2013).

In April 2007, the British government announced that it would no longer employ the term "War on Terror." Lady Eliza Manningham-Buller, the former director of MI5, the British intelligence service, stated her preference for the change, calling the 9/11 attacks "a crime, not an act of war" (Norton-Taylor 2011). In May 2013, President Obama also called for a new, more precise focus on terrorist networks rather than a broad-based "war." The United States must redefine its efforts, Obama argued, "as a series of persistent, targeted efforts to dismantle specific networks of violent extremists that threaten America" (quoted in Baker 2013).

Like any effort to grapple with a specific social problem, the shift from "war" to a more focused "targeting of networks" will shift resources, produce new agendas for some organizations, end missions for others, and call for a different language to discuss the problem. One of the most challenging issues, especially for public perceptions, is that whatever it is called, we cannot, in all probability, reduce terrorism to zero.

16.7 Identify steps toward social change to foster peace.

 ## Join a Peace Movement

In his famous military-industrial complex speech, President Eisenhower argued, "Only an alert and knowledgeable citizenry can compel the proper meshing of the huge industrial and military machinery of defense with our peaceful methods of goals, so that security and liberty may prosper together." Eisenhower was not an antiwar activist, but many citizens have felt that not only informed public opinion but also popular mobilization is necessary in order for peace to win out over war. Identify a student or community antiwar organization, determine what its strategy is, what kinds of public events it holds, and how it attempts to exert influence. (Examples include United for Peace and Justice, Peace Now, and the Women's International League for Peace and Freedom, although not all may be active in your particular area.) Where has it been successful, and where might it need to follow a different strategy? Do you feel motivated to help?

 ## Help Provide Direct Assistance to War Victims

Many organizations provide assistance to the victims of war, like the International Red Cross and the United Nations Children's Emergency Fund (UNICEF). Others focus on particular aspects of war; examples include Save Our Children for child soldiers and Survivors Corps for those injured by antipersonnel land mines. Still other organizations offer aid along particular themes, such as helping refugees who have fled war-torn areas, women who have become widows, or persons suffering the aftermath of sexual violence. The Duvet Project (http://www.zcommunications.org/in-kabul-widows-and-orphans-move-up-by-kathy-kelly), organized by Afghan Peace Volunteers, pays women a living wage to sew wool-filled duvets and

Antiwar protesters demonstrate on Hollywood Boulevard in Los Angeles. Prior to the Iraq War, on the weekend of February 15–16, 2003, a series of coordinated antiwar protests were held in more than 600 cities around the world, with millions of people taking part. The U.S.-led invasion of Iraq occurred a month later. How effective do you think antiwar protests are?

delivers them to families. Many of these organizations could do more with more money. With some friends, do some research and identify a program that carries out effective work on a particular issue. Is it possible for your group to raise some money for this organization?

 ## Promote Civilian-Military Dialogue

In general, the U.S. public respects the nation's armed forces. Yet most Americans do not have much contact with the military, and many students are poorly informed about its internal structure. Intersections is a nongovernmental organization that promotes peace, justice, and reconciliation. One of its most important activities is facilitating a series of veteran-civilian dialogues. Some campuses also have local clubs that attempt to create bridges between the military and civilian communities. An example is ALLIES (the Alliance Linking Leaders in Education and the Services) at Tufts University, dedicated to improving civilian-military relations through joint education, research, and training. Can you help create a similar dialogue group on your campus?

WHAT DOES AMERICA THINK?

Questions about War and Terrorism from the General Social Survey

 Turn to the beginning of the chapter to compare your answers to the total population.

1. Do you expect the United States to be in a world war in the next 10 years?

    YES: 51.3%

    NO: 48.7%

2. What is your confidence level in Congress?

    A GREAT DEAL: 6.7%

    ONLY SOME: 43.9%

    HARDLY ANY: 49.4%

3. What is your interest level in international issues?

    VERY INTERESTED: 22.3%

    MODERATELY INTERESTED: 46.3%

    NOT AT ALL INTERESTED: 31.4%

4. What is your interest level in military policy?

    VERY INTERESTED: 40.1%

    MODERATELY INTERESTED: 45.3%

    NOT AT ALL INTERESTED: 14.6%

5. In the United States, do you think we're spending too much money on military, armaments, and defense, too little money, or about the right amount?

    TOO MUCH: 33.3%

    TOO LITTLE: 25.1%

    ABOUT THE RIGHT AMOUNT: 41.6%

LOOK BEHIND THE NUMBERS

Go to **edge.sagepub.com/trevino** for a breakdown of these data across time and by race, sex, age, income, and other statuses.

1. Only 6.7% of survey respondents said that they have a great deal of confidence in Congress. From your own experience, why do people not have a great deal of confidence in Congress? Do you think that is an issue for U.S. society?

2. Examine the data on respondents' level of education for the question about the possibility of the United States being in a world war in the next 10 years. Why do you think this pattern might be occurring?

3. For the question about military spending, responses were split among the three possible answers. Why do you think there was such a variance?

4. Examine the General Social Survey data for the question about military spending from 1973 to the present. You'll see there is a stark change in 1980 but a return to numbers similar to previous years in 1982. What do you think occurred at this time? What does this say about U.S. society?

SOURCE: National Opinion Research Center, University of Chicago.

CHAPTER SUMMARY

 16.1 Describe war as a social concept.

Sociologically, war is an organized, collective activity of political units against other political units. It may or may not be carried out by states. War often has costs even greater than the numbers killed or wounded on the battlefield.

16.2 Discuss patterns and trends in the incidence and costs of war.

War between nations seems to be declining. At the same time, new types of globalized intrastate conflict are increasing. These wars carry high costs for civilians, who are often targeted in campaigns of ethnic cleansing. The economic and psychological burdens of war—and even preparing for war—are significant.

16.3 Describe the future of war.

The future of war is paradoxical. Wars are likely to be fought with high-tech weapons such as drones that promise to make conflict more precise and discriminating. These promises are not always met. At the same time, many contemporary wars are extremely bloody and include the targeting of civilians. They do not even promise to be more precise. In the U.S. armed forces, women may move into more direct combat roles.

 16.4 Apply the functionalist, symbolic interactionist, and conflict perspectives to war.

In the structural functionalist view, some technical innovations of World War II, such as radar and improvements in aircraft engines, were usefully applied in the postwar civilian sector. Lower spending on consumption during the war and the resulting savings helped create the groundwork for a postwar period of prosperity. One policy implication of this view is that war, or preparation for war, might be necessary to defend a society against outside threats. Conflict theorists employ the idea of the military-industrial complex, or the relationships among government forces, the Pentagon, and defense contractors that promote the acquisition of weapons systems and a militarized foreign policy. One policy implication of this idea is that the United States is more war-prone than most Americans believe. Symbolic interactionists identify three factors that must come together for violence to be exercised on a horrific scale: authorization, routinization, and dehumanization. Because studies have found that soldiers fight not for abstractions such as "democracy" and "freedom" but rather out of loyalty to the people in their immediate units, training now focuses on deepening comradeship, mutual respect, and not letting others down.

 16.5 Apply the two-society thesis to the relationship between the U.S. military and U.S. society.

The two-society thesis proposes that the all-volunteer force has reduced the proportion of U.S. citizens with military experience and has widened the social gap between those who have served and those who remain in civilian occupations.

 16.6 Discuss the Global War on Terror.

The Global War on Terror has had some successes, notably deterrence, but it has also raised questions about the extent of government surveillance, and some programs have shortcomings; the use of drones, for instance, has become extremely unpopular. President Obama has sought to reframe the war on terror as "a series of persistent, targeted efforts to dismantle specific networks of violent extremists that threaten America."

 16.7 Identify steps toward social change to foster peace.

You might consider engaging in antiwar activity, trying to reduce the impact of war on its victims, or stimulating military-civilian dialogue on your campus.

DISCUSSION QUESTIONS

1. In what ways does the sociological definition expand or change the definition of war? What are the pros and cons of such an expanded definition?

2. What attributes of war make it a social problem? What differences exist between war as a conflict over control of a territory and war as a conflict over control of a resource? Do these differences change the nature of the social problem?

3. How has war changed in the past century? Do we fight fewer wars or more wars? Do we engage in war differently? Has war become less deadly? What explains the changes?

4. Describe the social and economic costs of war. What could be done with the money saved if our nation engaged in fewer military conflicts? How are the costs of war, including the psychological costs, distributed throughout the population?

5. How are newer technologies changing the way we wage war? Does the shift in the means of war change the ways in which war is a social problem? Which problems arise as a result of these changes? And which are improved or solved as a result of the changes?

6. What are some of the changes to war as a result of women in the military and specifically in combat? How does the movement of women into combat roles intersect not only with our social construction of gender but also with other aspects of identity, such as race and social class?

7. Which of the major theoretical perspectives best addresses your own understandings of war? How does this perspective align, or not, with popular explanations such as those offered by media? Which of the perspectives most challenges your view of war?

8. According to the symbolic interactionist perspective, what are the mechanisms by which humans can be compelled to kill or hurt other humans? How do these mechanisms connect to concerns about returning veterans as they reenter civilian life?

9. What support is there for the two-society thesis described in this chapter? What sorts of differences might one expect to see between soldiers in an all-volunteer force and those who make decisions about military funding and operations, such as our elected officials? What are the benefits and problems associated with these two societies, military and civilian?

10. Are peace movements suited to address the contemporary forms of war, including the Global War on Terror, or are they primarily aimed at more traditional forms of war? What prompts people to join movements for peace? In what ways can a person engage in both peace activism and support for those who have served in the military, and what are the challenges to doing both?

KEY TERMS

authorization 435

dehumanization 436

democratic theory of peace 424

globalized intrastate wars 431

hypermasculinity 430

military-industrial complex 433

post-traumatic stress disorder 428

routinization 436

terrorism 439

war 422

Sharpen your skills with SAGE edge at edge.sagepub.com/trevino

A personalized approach to help you accomplish your coursework goals in an easy-to-use learning environment.

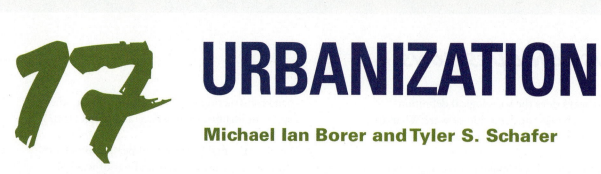

17 URBANIZATION

Michael Ian Borer and Tyler S. Schafer

Bill Hatcher / National Geographic Creative

A woman walks her bicycle in front of a mural depicting numerous similar-looking black-and-white buildings. C. Wright Mills once told his readers to sociologically consider the public issues of the metropolis— "the horrible, beautiful, ugly, magnificent sprawl of the great city." What do you think of Mills's description?

Investigating Urbanization: Our Stories

LEARNING OBJECTIVES

17.1 Explain social problems that uniquely arise from urbanization and city growth.

17.2 Discuss patterns and trends in urbanization and city growth.

17.3 Apply the functionalist, conflict, and symbolic interactionist perspectives to problems that arise from urbanization and city growth.

17.4 Apply specialized theories to urbanization and city growth.

17.5 Identify steps toward social change regarding urbanization and city growth.

Michael Ian Borer

My relationship to cities began before I was even born. My grandparents fled the Nazis and arrived almost miraculously in New York City. "The City"—as we in the suburbs referred to it—was consistently a part of my life. I visited museums and green spaces. I went to baseball games with my grandfather, who adopted the Dodgers and then the Mets. I ate food from various ethnic enclaves and rode trains above- and belowground. I shuffled through busy streets avoiding eye contact with passersby. I was offered drugs and sex for sale of all varieties. Even as a kid from the 'burbs, I grew up urban. In many ways, today we've all become urban in some way.

Even at a young age, I grappled with questions about social order. How could so many people from so many different places moving so quickly from one place to the next be so physically close yet so culturally far from one another? How do they get along under such conditions? The existential burden of these questions stayed with me through college, then graduate school, and remains a key motivator for my research as a professional sociologist traveling to cities across the United States and the world. Now, as a sociologist living in and studying Las Vegas, I find my early questions have led to other questions. Sometimes I have to remind myself that often the best answers are questions.

Tyler S. Schafer

Given my roots, you might assume I should have become a rural sociologist. I grew up in a small mid-Missouri town ringed with farmland in every direction. A few times a year my dad and I would hit the road to catch a St. Louis Cardinals game, and I would ask questions about the city and he would tell stories the whole way. The Arch, the massive animated Anheuser-Busch neon sign, and the bustling baseball stadium were such a contrast to the stimuli I encountered in my daily life. What I found more intriguing, however, were the people zipping along the interstate and highways. Where were they coming from? Where were they going? What were the stories of the old men playing saxophones on the street corners? What kinds of lives were the boys and girls my age in the city living?

Moving to Las Vegas for graduate school was quite a shift. It has been fascinating for me to watch Las Vegans establish institutions many older cities take for granted. Las Vegas and the Southwest have also encouraged me to think more about the relationship between cities and the natural environment. What happens here may serve as a bellwether for other cities. No doubt, my explorations as an urban sociologist in Las Vegas have provided me with research questions I will pursue for the rest of my career.

URBANIZATION AND CITY GROWTH IN GLITTER GULCH

The urban sociologist Robert E. Park famously described cities as social laboratories. For sociologists interested in a range of issues from the environmental to the cultural, Las Vegas—with its extreme climate and its extreme adult amusements and copycat architecture—is an ideal subject. This city provides us with a fascinating, and at times unsettling, laboratory for exploring issues of urbanization. At once lauded as a testament to the ability of humans to dominate and control nature through technology, decried as the modern-day Gomorrah, and celebrated as one of the nation's leading tourist destinations, it is rife with complexity, contradiction, and calculated awe.

Las Vegas grabbed headlines across the globe in the 1990s as it experienced unprecedented growth, its population jumping from about 800,000 in 1980 to approximately 2 million in 2007. At the peak of its boom, in 2006, U.S. Census Bureau demographers estimated the city was adding more than 8,000 new residents per month. When the housing bubble burst and the recession began in 2008, Las Vegas earned the not-so-coveted title of "Foreclosure Capital of the World." This brief hiccup in the city's population surge provides an opportunity for the city to assess the quality of the growth, diagnose growing pains, and try to prepare for another projected boom in population.

The growing pains, it turns out, have been numerous. The flood of new residents coincided with an ongoing drought, now 14 years long, that has drastically strained the city's water supply. The increased population of children put stress on an already low-performing public school system, while health care, public transit, community centers, public parks, bike lanes, and state universities took major hits in funding due to a weak state budget and a governor who put private interests ahead of public ones. Were these developments inevitable?

URBANIZATION, GROWTH, AND SOCIAL PROBLEMS

17.1 Explain social problems that uniquely arise from urbanization and city growth.

While we may take cities for granted, as simply the backdrop against which modern life unfolds, they are by no means new. Humans have been building cities for thousands of years. What is relatively new, however, is the centrality of cities to human life.

Urbanization is the process by which cities, suburbs, and metropolitan areas develop and grow over time. Migrations from rural communities to dense urban ones call for new forms of **social order** and social control; because these both solve and create social problems, growth is *not* value-neutral. What happens to working-class and poor underclass residents of neighborhoods that are demolished and replaced with highways, malls, and luxury condominiums? What happens to families who rely on social services that have been eliminated due to changes in tax structures that help some city dwellers but not all? What happens to the air that city dwellers breathe when factories move in or cars are the only means of transportation? In a city with a heterogeneous population, there will be winners and losers. The political, economic, and cultural structures of a **city** often dictate who ends up on which side. Those structures, and the processes that put them in motion, are at the heart of the social problems that result from urbanization and population growth.

In 1800, a mere 3% of the world's population lived in cities. In 2007, that figure was 50%. By 2050 it is estimated that more than 75% of the world's population will be living in metropolitan areas. This boom in urbanization will not be evenly distributed across the globe. As Table 17.1 indicates, over the past few decades the percentage of people living in cities in less developed regions of the world—for example, parts of Africa, Asia, the

....

Urbanization: The movement of populations from rural to urban areas; the growth and development, and redevelopment, of cities.

Social order: The conformity of individuals to explicit and implicit social rules of behavior.

City: A relatively large, dense, and heterogeneously populated place or settlement.

TABLE 17.1 Percentage of Urban and Rural Population in More and Less Developed Regions of the World, 1950–2050

Area	1950	2011	2050
More developed regions			
Total population in billions	0.81	1.24	1.31
Percentage urban	54.5	77.7	85.9
Less developed regions			
Total population in billions	1.72	5.73	7.99
Percentage urban	17.6	46.5	64.1

SOURCE: Data derived from *World Population Prospects: The 2011 Revision.* Population Division of Economic and Social Affairs of the United Nations Secretariat.

Caribbean, and Latin America—has approached that of more developed countries in North America and Europe and is growing at a faster pace, a trend expected to continue indefinitely into the future.

At the time same, however, the rural populations in less developed regions will remain much larger (see Figure 17.1). This boom in both metro and rural populations will have a major impact on how cities grow in developing regions, and on their ability to accommodate the needs of city dwellers. If these regions follow the path of urbanization that developed areas have, their increasing populations will require them to solve growth-related problems much more quickly and broadly.

The United States has also witnessed a shift to cities. In 1860, 20% of the U.S. population resided in urban areas. Forty years later that number had doubled to 40%. Today more than 250 million people in the United States—more than 75% of the population—live in cities. Figure 17.2 illustrates the drop in U.S. rural populations and accompanying urbanization, which occurred under conditions of slower population growth than in less developed regions. As you can see, even if cities are an old phenomenon, their role in human life has changed dramatically in recent history.

While many social problems, such as poverty, unemployment, and inequality, occur *in* cities, in this chapter we address those that arise *because of* urbanization and city

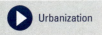
Urbanization

FIGURE 17.1 **Urban and Rural Populations by Development Group, 1950–2050 (estimated)**

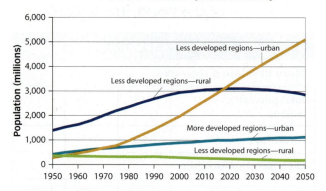

SOURCE: *World Population Prospects: The 2011 Revision: Highlights.* Population Division of Economic and Social Affairs of the United Nations Secretariat.

growth. In a rapidly urbanizing world it is critical that we learn from past successes and failures in city building and management in order to better understand the massive urbanization occurring now in places like China, India, and throughout the African continent.

Although cities today look markedly different from those of the late 19th and early 20th centuries, the time at which sociology firmly took root as a discipline, many of the social dynamics in cities at that time have persisted. The early urban sociologists were primarily concerned with the ways city life would differ from the rural traditions many of them held dear. Much like the current shift from national economies to increasingly global ones, the shift from rural, traditional human settlements to increasingly urban, industrial ones generated a great deal of fear and anxiety in urban analysts. One of their primary concerns was the manner and extent to which social relations and communal forms that dominated traditional societies would be reproduced in urban settings.

German sociologist Ferdinand Tönnies was interested in identifying the consequences of mass urbanization and the relational forms emerging in the new urban social order. In his famous text *Gemeinschaft und Gesellschaft,* originally published in 1887, Tönnies (1957) outlines two basic organizing principles of social relationships and institutions. He associates these "ideal types" loosely with towns and cities and understands them as stages in the evolution of human society. The first stage is **gemeinschaft**, or "communal association." This is the traditional, rural settlement with a homogeneous population in which everyone knows all the other residents and their biographies. Relationships are intimate and enduring, and interactions are guided by a mutual interest in the common good of the village. Because kinship, community, and religion unite

individuals, the shared traditions and culture of the village, in addition to religious beliefs, function as the main instruments of social control.

At the other end of the continuum, or the next stage in human social development, is **gesellschaft**, or "societal association." This is the modern city in which "rational self-interest" or individualism eclipses community interests. Relationships are no longer steeped in sentiment but instead are primarily associational and based on calculating, economic exchanges. Given the heterogeneous populations of emerging cities, residents no longer share language, religion, and traditions, and behavior and interaction are governed by external forces like the evolving criminal justice system. For Tönnies, the process of urbanization was inseparable from the parallel process of **industrialization**. Together these forces erode social bonds and weaken the family unit, which he saw as a vital component of a healthy society.

FIGURE 17.2 **Proportion of Urban and Rural Residents in the United States, 1950–2050 (projected)**

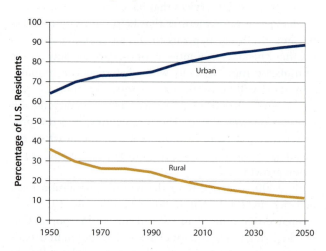

SOURCE: *2011 United Nations World Urbanization Prospects Report.* Country Profile: United States. Population Division of Economic and Social Affairs of the United Nations Secretariat.

Gemeinschaft: Communal association, or a sense of close-knit community relations based on shared traditions and values.

Gesellschaft: Societal association, or a sense of relationships typified by impersonal bureaucracies and contractual arrangements rather than informal ones based on kinship and family ties.

Industrialization: A process that leads to a significant increase in the proportion of a population engaged in specialized factory work and nonagricultural occupations; increases the number of people living near factories and relying on mechanically produced goods and services.

Rapid Urbanization

Pieter Brueghel the Younger's *Peasants Merrymaking outside the Swan Inn in a Village Street*, 1630. This scene, depicting 17th-century Flemish village life, illustrates what Ferdinand Tönnies called the gemeinschaft type of community. These rural peasants have personal interactions that give them a feeling of togetherness, and their behavior is regulated by common social traditions.

Although Tönnies understood this evolutionary process as a necessary development in human organization, he was largely pessimistic about the likelihood of communal associations materializing in cities. His view of city life has persisted in some form for more than a century in urban studies. Though communities do exist in cities, sometimes those bonds can be very fragile. When cities undergo large development or redevelopment, neighborhoods and social networks can be torn apart as residents are dispersed throughout or driven from the city.

Georg Simmel was interested more in social psychological adaptations to the heterogeneity of urban life than he was in social cohesion. His starting point was that people in cities must interact with strangers, living physically close to one another yet emotionally and culturally distant. Simmel (1971, 325) argued that the large size and dense concentration of strangers in cities leads urbanites to develop a new kind of defense mechanism against the potential sensory overload, the "swift and continuous shift of external and internal stimuli," of cities. City dwellers develop relational forms that are reserved and "intellectualistic," as opposed to sentimental and tradition based, as in small towns or villages. Simmel noted:

> Thus the metropolitan type—which naturally takes on a thousand individual modifications—creates a protective organ for itself against the profound disruption with which the fluctuations and discontinuities of the

external milieu threaten it. Instead of reacting emotionally, the metropolitan type reacts primarily in a rational manner, thus creating a mental predominance through the intensification of consciousness, which in turn is caused by it. (326)

This "protective organ" and intellectualistic mental state of urban dwellers is manifested most clearly in a "blasé attitude," a general indifference to the bombardment of stimuli. Simmel argued that urbanites would experience a sort of paralysis if they addressed all the stimuli they encounter. Nothing would get done.

For those who can adapt to diminished traditional social bonds and indifferent, rational interactional styles, the city provides spaces and opportunities for heightened individuality and creativity. Others, however, do not handle the shift as well and are overcome with feelings of alienation. As Simmel (1971, 334) stated, "Under certain circumstances, one never feels as lonely and as deserted as in this metropolitan crush of persons." For Simmel, then, cities do not guarantee but rather provide the *potential for* increases in individuality and creativity.

Not all our current social problems produced by cities were identified in classic sociology, however. Advancements in transportation have made it possible not only for more people to access or own vehicles but also for cities to spread farther into their hinterlands, taking up increasingly large amounts of space. Early urbanists could not imagine the massive surge in energy consumption that would be required to power innumerable lightbulbs and air conditioners—two things very familiar to us from living in Las Vegas. As Chapter 14 points out, environmental problems produce social effects.

ASK YOURSELF: Why would a shift from rural, small-town settlements to urban, big-city settlements cause fear in both observers of social life and those living through those changes? What problems might emerge from rapid population growth in cities? Are the concerns of early urban observers similar to or different from those of observers, commentators, politicians, reformers, and others today?

PATTERNS AND TRENDS

 17.2 Discuss patterns and trends in urbanization and city growth.

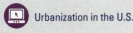 Urbanization in the U.S.

Heterogeneity, Strangers, and Community

If we are to focus on social problems that arise uniquely from urbanization, we must address the effects of increased *heterogeneity* that come with the growth of the city and its rising centrality in the human experience. Unlike the moral homogeneity of village life, where everyone shares similar values, beliefs, rituals, traditions, symbols, and languages, cities are cultural crucibles, and their social control and social institutions have to incorporate the complex constellations of city residents' interests.

Urban heterogeneity also means a population of **biographical strangers**. People in cities regularly spend most of their time near, around, or with people they do not know who come from somewhere else, and interactions with strangers become the dominant form of social relations. How is any semblance of social order possible? Much has been written about the *perceived* threat of "strange" black men by both male and female whites (Anderson 1990). The power differential that allows some to define others as "strange," along with the legal ramifications of such labeling, is a social problem.

Conflict can emerge from the diversity of cultures present in cities (Zukin 1995). City dwellers—especially newcomers and outsiders—also are **cultural strangers**. That is, they do not know or share each other's values, customs, and views about what passes for acceptable behavior, especially about what is allowed when they are in public and cannot avoid each other.

Historically, cities have served as immigrant "gateways" into the United States. Of the 24 million people who arrived during the classic era of U.S. immigration (1880–1930), 19 million came between 1900 and 1930; of these, 80% were from Europe (Massey 1995; Waters and Jiménez 2005). They came from Italy, Poland, Hungary, Lithuania,

Czechoslovakia, and Russia and faced irresistible pressure to downplay their ethnicity, to "acculturate" or "assimilate." Ethnic identities were feared as threats to national unity.

Quotas in the 1920s, World War I, the Great Depression, and World War II limited the numbers of arrivals, but a "new regime" in immigration began in the 1970s and has persisted through today (Massey 1995). The postwar boom brought a growing need for labor, and many immigrants from Latin American countries filled these positions. A steady flow of new immigrants is projected, blurring the boundaries between cohorts of arrivals (Massey 1995; Waters and Jiménez 2005). This continuous flow from Latin America, the Caribbean, and Asia is unlike the episodic bursts of the classic era and will change the nature of assimilation, and thus cities, in the United States (Massey 1995).

Immigrant ethnicity is affected not only by differences in the sequencing and duration of the immigrant flow but also by the locations from which immigrants come. Asians and Latinos are now the largest racial and ethnic minority populations in the United States, displacing blacks in the lead (Alba and Nee 2003). Immigrants who arrive in these flows come from similar cultures and speak similar languages. They experience less pressure to assimilate since more people speak their native languages and adhere to their native traditions, and there are more native cultural ties for newer immigrants to latch onto (Massey 1995).

Compared with earlier immigrants, members of this continuous and more homogeneous flow of immigrants will have vastly different assimilation experiences, including the proliferation of foreign-language or cultural communities (Massey 1995), or "immigrant enclaves" (Portes and Manning 1986). Such communities used to be part of a temporary stage in an immigrant group's assimilation process. Now they are taking on more permanent and enduring forms in cities, though they are often the first to be bulldozed if they are not deemed profitable as "tourist spectacles" or "ethnic theme parks" (Krase 2012). Think about this the next time you enter one of these neighborhoods. Is the ethnic identity of the residents being presented authentically, or is it more like what you might find at Disney's Epcot Center?

Another shift is an emphasis on multiculturalism, which encompasses a trend toward enacting policy that embraces and protects culturally diverse practices and behaviors in public schools, workplaces, and public spaces. Although cultural diversity may be increasingly protected by law, racial and ethnic prejudice and discrimination persist in cities. Since current immigrant groups are able to hold on to

So close and yet so far. These commuters on a New York City subway car sit only inches from each other but are also strangers to each other. Have you ever felt lonely in a crowded city?

Stefano Amantini / Atlantide Phototravel / Corbis

Biographical strangers: Individuals who do not know each other on a personal basis or who have never met.

Cultural strangers: Individuals who are from different symbolic worlds or cultures.

Smart Cities

Italian neighborhood with street market, Mulberry Street, New York City, circa 1900. Urban sociologists have long been interested in the ethnic enclaves of cities. In *The Ghetto* (1928), Louis Wirth examined Jewish immigrant colonies in big cities like Chicago. In *The Urban Villagers* (1962), Herbert J. Gans wrote about the Italian American working-class community in Boston's West End. Have you ever visited Chinatown in San Francisco, Little Italy in Boston, or Little Havana in Miami?

cultural elements of their native countries, however, it may be more accurate to describe the United States as a "salad bowl," in which different racial and ethnic groups mix together but hold their original "flavors," than as a "melting pot" in which they combine to forge new patterns of behavior. Diverse groups can exist separately while still participating in political and economic life. Moreover, there is growing consensus that preserving cultural differences is not only possible but also important.

Migration within the country's borders has also produced anxiety in U.S. cities throughout history. In the decades following the emancipation of black slaves, factories began to proliferate in northeastern and midwestern cities as industrialization took hold, creating massive labor demands in cities like Chicago, Detroit, Cleveland, Pittsburgh, and New York. When World War I broke out and men were drafted to fight, many factories recruited black laborers from the South. At around the same time, the boll weevil—an insect native to Central America that feeds on cotton buds and flowers—migrated into the U.S. South and decimated the crops of many growers. This combination of push and pull factors led to a massive relocation of black

individuals and families from southern towns and cities to growing cities of the Northeast and Midwest. Conflict arose between newly arrived blacks and some white ethnic groups with whom they competed for jobs.

On the heels of the Great Depression, President Franklin D. Roosevelt developed a plan for helping people rebound economically by promoting homeownership as a means for attaining and growing wealth through assets. To encourage people to buy homes, he implemented a program to back loans for home buyers through the Federal Housing Administration (FHA). These federally backed loans had fixed interest rates and could be paid off in lower payments over a longer period of time than previously available. Roosevelt was hesitant to approve all loans, however, so he told banks to approve loans for homes only in certain parts of U.S. cities. In a practice later known as redlining, he literally took a red pen and drew lines around neighborhoods he arbitrarily deemed "too risky" for loans. These were neighborhoods that had primarily black residents or were integrated. Over the next 40 years, 90% of the loans approved through the FHA program went to white home buyers. Not only did this contribute to massive accumulations of white wealth while denying such growth to black residents; it started a process of intense **segregation** in U.S. cities that persists to this day (see Figure 17.3).

Segregation: The practice of physically separating the occupants of some social statuses from the occupants of others.

FIGURE 17.3 Concentration of Whites, Blacks, and Hispanics in Chicago, 2008

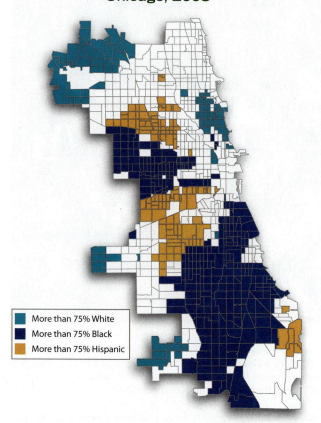

- ■ More than 75% White
- ■ More than 75% Black
- ■ More than 75% Hispanic

SOURCE: From "Chicago Is America's Most Segregated City," *The Chicago Tribune,* January 21, 2009. Data from the Center for Governmental Studies, Northern Illinois University.

Although de jure, or legal, racial segregation has been outlawed in the United States since the 1960s, de facto, or in practice, segregation persists. Social justice organizations routinely conduct experiments to see whether landlords, real estate agents, and banks discriminate against prospective homeowners or renters on the basis of race and consistently find that they do (Massey and Denton 1993; Massey and Lundy 2001; Oliver and Shapiro 1995; Roscigno, Karafin, and Tester 2009; Turner et al. 2002; Yinger 1995). In large part these practices stem from a deep anxiety about heterogeneity in cities.

Segregation does not simply result from anxiety about heterogeneity, however; it also worsens anxiety. Researchers who have studied black ghettos argue that residents must adapt to conditions of joblessness, drug use, welfare dependency, teenage childbearing, police unresponsiveness, and hopelessness. This often results in the evolution of attitudes and behaviors that are at odds with or opposed to dominant, mainstream ones (Anderson 1999; Massey and Denton 1993). Severe racial and class isolation have produced language patterns among black

ghetto residents so distinct from Standard American English they function as a barriers to occupational and educational success (Massey and Denton 1993).

Racial and ethnic diversity thus contribute to the heterogeneity in cities, but so too can ideological and moral differences, as well as the mere *possibility* of difference. Heterogeneity in cities is about more than the color of someone's skin or the country of his or her birth. Lyn H. Lofland (1998, 3) describes the connection between strangers and city life: "The city, because of its size, is the locus of a peculiar social situation: the people to be found within its boundaries at any given moment know nothing personally about the vast *majority* of others with whom they share this space."

Interacting with the "Other" on a daily basis is a social problem reserved almost exclusively for cities. Urban scholars and reformers continue to be deeply troubled by the question of how to generate consensus among diverse strangers around a shared meaningful way of life that could bring continuity and predictability to a chaotic and overstimulating environment. Today, as more of the world moves to cities, migration patterns bring increasingly diverse populations together, and we become a more global society, we still grapple with questions about how to form meaningful or at least effective ties with others.

The term *globalization* refers to the often uneven development of social, political, and economic relationships that stretch worldwide. The accelerated flow of capital across international borders is the defining attribute of globalization. In our increasingly global economy, some cities fare better than others, and the most successful are those with financial institutions critical for the functioning of the global economy, advanced telecommunication infrastructure, and a good business climate (low real estate, payroll, revenue, and other taxes) (Friedmann 1986). These become central organizing nodes of the global economy and are known as *global cities* (Sassen 2001). As central locations within the global economy, global cities attract people from the cities' poorer outskirts as well as from developing countries. Thus multiculturalism is as much a part of globalization as is the flow of capital (Sassen 2001), and the social problems of heterogeneity are now a global phenomenon. People will need to adapt swiftly in order to relate to and interact with one another in cities in more and less developed regions.

ASK YOURSELF: Although the specific contexts have changed over time, the same general issue of heterogeneity in cities continues to puzzle urban scholars. How do we create order among such a diversity of biographies, moral orders, and interests? If diversity is generally accepted as a positive attribute, why does it create social problems in cities as populations increase? Who benefits from worldwide urbanization, and who doesn't?

Heterogeneity in Global Cities

Some migrants who move to global cities are highly educated and highly paid corporate professionals, but many are low-skilled workers who end up in service jobs or the "informal" economies of these booming cities (Friedmann 1986; Sassen 2001). The wealth gap between transnational elites and low-skilled workers in global cities is widening rapidly. Accordingly, the populations of global cities are becoming more culturally diverse and income distributions more inequitable, producing more heterogeneity and interest groups with vastly different priorities. People are therefore learning new ways to interact with others in new urbanized areas.

For example, rapid urbanization in China has compelled people to change the ways they think about and treat each other. In the presence of so many new people they do not know personally and whose origins and social classes are unknown, formerly polite interactions with neighbors have been replaced by "indifference." "Neighborhood obligations," Jankowiak (2010, 267) observes, "have been discarded in favor of other forms of connectivity," including ties based on school affiliation, "work contacts, association with places of origin, friendship bonds, and close family relationships." Secret societies, guilds, and "common ethnic and/or religious affiliation" have also become more important.

According to Jankowiak, "Taken together, ethnicity, religion, and native place associations serve as essential bases for the formation of social connection or kinship ties" in contemporary China (260–61).

Urban "kinship" ties have become more elaborate. "Individuals who are outside the formal (e.g., bilateral or patrilineal) genealogical systems are frequently transformed from casual friends into close quasi-kin," Jankowiak notes (262). Bilateral grandparent ties also became more important as China's one-child policy took hold and more working parents needed help with child-rearing duties. However, the emerging "bilateral multigenerational family is a fragile institution" (265–66).

▶ **THINK ABOUT IT**

1. In what ways do people act alike or differently in cities across the world?

2. Have you seen any changes in your city or town similar to those happening in China?

Urbanization and the Natural Environment

One basic component of cities is that they contain immense numbers of people. These people, in turn, consume large amounts of resources like water and energy, so as cities grow, the provision of resources and, by extension, resource scarcity become serious concerns for city planners and governments. The ways in which these concerns are addressed have impacts on the environment. In this section we will describe some of the social problems that arise as cities grow in both physical size and population, including resource scarcity, carbon dioxide emissions and climate change, and suburban sprawl and the destruction of natural ecosystems.

The intersection of urban and environmental sociology has only recently garnered the attention it deserves. Some of these issues cannot be addressed by traditional theories from urban sociology like structural functionalism, conflict theory, and symbolic interactionism, so we address them more comprehensively in the section on specialized theories below.

Water Scarcity

Humans cannot survive without water. Water also irrigates the farmlands where their growing food demands are met. Cultural practices like green lawns—which were brought across the Atlantic from England and then into desert climates like the U.S. Southwest—require water to maintain. Water cleans urbanites' bodies, clothes, dishes, and cars, fills their swimming pools and hot tubs, and animates their decorative fountains. As cities grow, they put increasing strains on their water supplies. Although water is a renewable resource, it is also finite. As urban areas add to their populations or otherwise increase their demand for water, they must confront the possibility of exhausting their supply or locate alternate sources.

The infamous Owens Valley water grab in California is one example of how cities meet rising demands for water. In the early 20th century, Los Angeles mayor Frederick Eaton envisioned a much larger metropolitan area than existed then. He identified water availability as a crucial barrier to growth and appointed his friend William Mulholland as the new superintendent of Los Angeles Department of Water

 Megacities    California Drought

A siphon of the Los Angeles–Owens River Aqueduct in Southern California, photographed shortly after its construction, circa 1910. As metropolitan areas and their populations grow, they require more and more resources such as land and water. The appropriation of land and the diversion of water frequently cause major social conflicts.

and Power to help relieve this perceived shortage. The two partners identified the Owens Valley, about 200 miles north, as a potential source of additional water for Los Angeles because of the abundant runoff the area received from the snowcapped Sierra Nevada mountain range. At the same time, however, the U.S. Bureau of Land Management (BLM) was attempting to construct irrigation systems to divert the same snowmelt water to farmers in the Owens Valley. Through a series of shady practices, including soliciting advice from individuals inside the BLM on how to acquire land rights, posing as cattle ranchers interested in overpaying for land with water access, faking water shortages and droughts, and lying about how Owens Valley water would be used, Eaton and Mulholland got their water. From 1908 to 1913 Mulholland oversaw the construction of a massive aqueduct to move water from the Owens Valley to Los Angeles, and on November 5, 1913, at the ceremony for its completion, he famously stated of the water, "There it is. Take it."

The Owens Valley water was used to irrigate the San Fernando Valley, which soon became a part of Los Angeles. Developers bought land in the Valley and began to increase demands for water. Los Angeles drew most of the rest of its water from the Colorado River, but the

amount was limited, so Mulholland increased the amount coming from the Owens Valley.

The Owens Valley farmers attempted to organize in order to use the remaining water as efficiently as possible, but Mulholland managed to purchase more water rights out from under them, and eventually the thirst from the San Fernando Valley dried up the Owens Valley water supply. The farmers rebelled and even dynamited portions of the aqueduct, but an economic collapse in the Owens Valley weakened their resistance, and in later years Los Angeles bought more water rights in the area. Farming in the Owens Valley was a thing of the past.

Water shortages, real or perceived, produce social relationships characterized by anxiety, resentment, hostility, and competition. The farmers of the Owens Valley could not stand up against the demand from Los Angeles. A similar situation is unfolding in our home state of Nevada. Southern Nevada is proposing a pipeline to move groundwater (water naturally accumulated over many years in underground aquifers) from central and eastern Nevada to augment its existing water resources. The proposal has sparked a heated debate, with southern Nevadans arguing for the need to diversify the sources from which they draw their water and to ensure the region can support projected population growth. The project is strongly opposed by many other Nevadans, including rural residents, ranchers, Native American tribes, the Mormon Church, conservationists, and outdoor enthusiasts.

The water war between central and southern Nevada is but one side effect of a much larger resource shortage in the U.S. Southwest today, the result of a combination of massive population growth, urbanization, and climate change. The Colorado River quenches the thirst of 40 million people in seven states, and that number is rapidly rising. The river serves 22 Native American tribes, 7 national wildlife refuges, and 11 national parks (Deneen 2013), in addition to irrigating more than 4 million acres of farmland (Kenworthy 2013). As it flows, it passes through an area experiencing its worst drought on record. The drought has brought a steady decline in water levels at Lake Mead—the lake from which Las Vegas draws 90% of its water supply and that also serves cities and agriculture in California and Arizona. A white "bathtub ring" of mineral deposits is visible on the rocks around the lake, a reminder of where the lake's water level used to be.

Despite aggressive conservation efforts that have reduced per capita water demands by more than 29% (Southern Nevada Water Authority 2009), hydrologists predict there is a 50% chance Lake Mead will go dry if drought conditions persist, the climate changes as predicted, and future demand is not further curtailed (Scripps Institution of Oceanography 2008). Unfortunately for Las Vegas, the amount of water the city is allowed to draw from Lake Mead was set in 1922 when the population of Clark County, which today includes the Las Vegas Metropolitan Area, was a mere 5,000. Las Vegas thus gets 4% of the total water allotted to the Lower Basin states; California gets 58.7% and Arizona 37.3%. No one could have predicted the hyperbolic growth the area experienced at the beginning of the 21st century.

Other Sunbelt cities, like Phoenix and Los Angeles, experienced massive population growth during the same period. As the Colorado River's flow dwindles under drought conditions and climate change, the region faces serious social conflicts over how to deal with shortages. If the water levels get so low that guaranteed allotments can no longer be met, how will reductions be divided up among the states that draw from the river?

In 1968, after much debate, the Central Arizona Project (CAP), an aqueduct more than 300 miles long from Lake Havasu to Phoenix and eventually Tucson, was approved for construction. The project was a massive one, since it had to pump water over and through mountain ranges to deliver it to Arizonans. A major stipulation of the deal, called the California Guarantee, was that California would be guaranteed its full allotment for the year before Arizona got a drop. Congress accepted California's demands, altering the playing field for any future water debates in the event of severe shortage. If drought conditions persist and climate changes as predicted, states will have to cut their use of Colorado River water. But because of the California Guarantee, the cuts will not be shared across the board (Reisner 1986). Arizona will have to sacrifice before California. This is but one example of the social struggles associated with resource shortages that stem from the processes of urbanization and city growth. These scenarios play out in urbanizing and growing regions across the globe.

The breakneck pace of urbanization in many parts of the world has created unprecedented challenges for providing clean water to booming populations. According to the United Nations (2010), 141 million urban residents worldwide lack access to clean drinking water. Cities in Ghana, Africa, have experienced rapid urbanization and slum development that has not been matched by development of water distribution infrastructure, resulting in lack of access to water in many parts of the cities, disease related to unsanitary sewer systems, and massive water waste due to faulty pipes and illegal connections. Cities in Peru, Nicaragua, and Egypt also face water shortages due to increased demands from urbanization, worsened by weak infrastructure (United Nations 2010). Among city dwellers globally, from 2000 to 2008 there was a 20% decrease in access to clean tap water (United Nations Human Settlement Programme 2011).

Greenhouse Gas Emissions

In 2011 the United Nations Human Settlement Programme reported that while cities occupy only 2% of land globally,

The early-morning brown haze that hangs over Cape Town, South Africa, is the product of smoke and fumes from fires, factories, and automobiles. As long ago as the 14th century, the Arab sociologist Ibn Khaldun (1332–1406) noted that air pollution was caused by overcrowding and recommended that urban areas preserve open, empty spaces so that the wind could carry away the fetid air.

they are responsible for emitting up to 70% of all harmful greenhouse gases (GHG). This relationship is complicated, however. Most of the urbanization occurring across the globe is now taking place in low- to middle-income nations, and this trend is predicted to continue well into the future. In these regions many households have incomes so low they hardly contribute to GHG levels (Satterthwaite 2009). However, in more developed countries with some of the slowest urban population growth, GHG emission levels are much higher per person and have been growing at a much faster pace (Satterthwaite 2009). The reason is that consumption patterns are more influential on greenhouse gas emissions than raw numbers of people.

Increasingly, researchers are suggesting that cities are not actually as bad as may have been thought in terms of GHG emissions. For instance, per capita GHG emission rates are often *lower* in cities than the average rates for the countries in which they are located (Dodman 2009). Some also argue that the share of global GHG emissions commonly attributed to cities has been grossly overstated (Satterthwaite 2009). This view tries to separate per capita GHG emissions from those produced in cities' outskirts in activities like agriculture, deforestation, and energy production. However, these activities occur only to meet the demands of residents in nearby cities. Recall that in the United States, more than 75% of the population resides in cities. Nonurban activities are overwhelmingly serving urban populations and should not be considered rural.

The Erasing of Ecosystems and Bulldozing of Biodiversity

Skylines notwithstanding, cities have tended to grow outward as opposed to upward. As the population and economy grow, so does the amount of physical space a city takes up. A variety of environmental and social problems are associated with sprawl, but here we have space to

Natural Gas Pollution

consider only those with direct impacts on the social well-being of urban residents.

First, **urban sprawl** contributes to the GHG emission spikes mentioned above. Public transit has generally not grown with the geographic expansion of cities. Instead, sprawl assumes a reliance on personal automobiles. Further, in neighborhoods built on the edges of existing cities homes are clustered together, businesses are clustered together, and office parks are clustered together, dramatically increasing both the time spent and the distance traveled in daily commutes and producing massive spikes in GHG emissions from cars. According to the U.S. Environmental Protection Agency (2012b), transportation has become the second-leading contributor to GHG emissions in the United States, accounting for approximately 27% since 1990. In sprawling cities, not only are there more cars on the road, but they are traveling farther and more frequently.

In addition to polluting, urban sprawl affects the natural ecosystems just outside city boundaries. For instance, despite being much smaller than trees and often perceived as less attractive, many species of desert flora absorb GHGs such as carbon dioxide. When city growth destroys certain types of plants, it intensifies the effects of the GHGs it produces by reducing nature's ability to absorb those GHGs.

Other ecosystems that ring cities serve as defenses against natural hazards like floods and fires. A trend in urban planning and landscape architecture in the early 20th century was to urge cities to adopt "hazard zoning" that would preserve natural settings like floodplains, fire-prone foothills, arroyos, and washes that could naturally prevent disasters (Davis 2003). Cities all too often pave and build over such natural areas, rendering their inhabitants more vulnerable and requiring additional resources to combat disasters and repair damage. Still other natural ecosystems in and around cities, like wetlands, help naturally purify water before it reaches aquifers that supply water to city residents. Destroying these ecosystems requires cities to invest in infrastructure to accomplish a task that was occurring naturally. Finally, although much of the population growth and urbanization in the next few decades will occur in places with low GHG emission levels, the growth of cities in these regions will threaten more than 200 species of animals, posing serious problems for biodiversity (Seto, Güneralp, and Hutyra 2012).

ASK YOURSELF: How do urbanization and population growth create environmental problems? Who is responsible for the environmental problems produced by cities—city officials? Businesses located in cities? The people who live, work, and play in cities? Are cities and the problems connected to them inevitable, so that the only solution is to get rid of cities? If so, then where will the millions of displaced people live?

THEORETICAL PERSPECTIVES IN URBAN SOCIOLOGY

 17.3 Apply the functionalist, conflict, and symbolic interactionist perspectives to problems that arise from urbanization and city growth.

Structural Functionalism

Herbert Spencer coined the phrase "survival of the fittest" in an attempt to incorporate Charles Darwin's ideas about natural selection into his theory of functionalism. Spencer put forth an "evolutionary" theory of societal change that suggested development is automatically and intrinsically positive. That is, social life is automatically better in the future than it was in the past due to natural processes of growth and adaptation.

Building on Spencer's basic ideas, the urban ecologists of the Chicago School of Sociology wanted to understand the natural forces behind the city's growth and diverse population. They used the term *natural* to draw an analogy between people and plants. They believed the city was a "superorganism" where competition for space was won by the "fittest." Though they dismissed other factors, like wealth and feelings, they felt understanding the natural laws of urbanization would allow them to better account for and fix persistent social problems associated with dense and heterogeneous populations.

Beginning with Roderick D. McKenzie and then Ernest W. Burgess and Amos H. Hawley, urban ecologists promoted the view that life in a human **community** functions like life in other biological communities. Like other organisms, human beings must adapt to their surroundings and fend off potential dangers. The most successful communities and people will take over the "best" areas of the city and have a higher survival rate. Chicago ecologists also noted the ways urban dwellers cooperate for the sake of mutual survival and defense against successive "invasions" of newcomers and migrants. The researchers' focus on natural competition and cooperation suggested that the city's spatial structure is a result of natural processes beyond the reach of human participation and engineering.

One of the most enduring legacies of the Chicago School ecologists is the model they constructed to depict

Urban sprawl: The unplanned and unregulated growth of urban areas into surrounding areas.

Community: A usually positive (though not necessarily so) form of sustained social cohesion, interaction, and organization that exists between the larger society and individuals who have similar characteristics or attributes (e.g., ethnicity, geography, beliefs).

 Vacant Lots

the biological processes that created the city of Chicago and the divisions within it. Ernest W. Burgess's (1925) *concentric-zone model* showed how patterns of land use reflected successive phases of invasion and occupation. The outcome was a series of concentric circles or zones, with the **central business district (CBD)** placed firmly in the center (see Figure 17.4). This was the hub of the city's economic activity and had the highest land values. Moving outward, the CBD was surrounded by a "zone of transition" perpetually under threat of invasion by businesses and industries with growing commercial interests. Those who could leave this vulnerable area did, but those who could not afford to move were forced to stay, forming a marginal population of immigrants, criminals, and the mentally ill in an area known for poverty and vice. This is where the Jewish ghetto, Little Sicily, Chinatown, and parts of the Black Belt were located.

The next zone was for the assimilated and upwardly mobile, such as the children of immigrants. Burgess called this the "zone of working-men's homes." The second-generation immigrants and factory laborers who lived there weren't poor, but neither were they wealthy enough to own land or their own apartments. The "residential zone," instead, was populated by the middle class, mostly white-collar employees and small-business owners and managers. They lived in newer, or at least renovated, apartments and single-family homes. Crime rates were significantly lower in this zone than in the working class's natural area, which in turn was less crime-ridden than the "zone of transition" just outside the CBD. The zone farthest away was the suburbs, the "commuters' zone," filled with residents who depended on the city for their jobs but were successful enough to live in the safer periphery of the city.

With artistic license to deal with Lake Michigan (which cut the zones in half down a north-south line), Burgess's model was a pretty accurate description of the residential segregation of Chicago. But it was intended to do more than describe Chicago; the goal was to show the social patterns one could expect to find in all industrial cities. Because Burgess painted in broad strokes, his model was open to criticisms that led others—including his own colleagues—to offer modified layouts of the city.

Homer Hoyt's (1939) *sector model* is based on the idea that cities' growth patterns depend on the cities' main lines of transportation. Transport corridors produce patterns of intense competition for land and real estate around them. Instead of concentric zones, in Hoyt's model "the city was pictured more like a starfish or a spoked

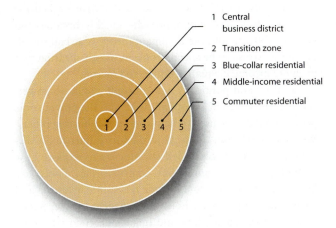

FIGURE 17.4 Concentric-Zone Model of the City

1 Central business district
2 Transition zone
3 Blue-collar residential
4 Middle-income residential
5 Commuter residential

wheel" (Karp, Stone, and Yoels 1991, 55). Chauncy Harris and Edward Ullman disagreed with both Burgess and Hoyt. Their *multiple-nuclei model* de-emphasizes the CBD in favor of a decentralized vision of the city, with several nuclei in areas with specific concentrations of specialized activities and facilities like manufacturing, shopping, and education.

One of the major problems with the Chicago School's ethnographic and ecological studies is their lack of attention to culture as a productive force. The researchers often assumed culture to be only reactionary, while larger natural forces in the competition for land shaped human relations. But if human agency isn't part of a model of urban life, then how can social reform be possible? The conflict-oriented urban political economists try to answer this question by focusing on the political and economic interests of powerful players, as we see next.

Conflict Theory

In the late 1960s and early 1970s, social and political unrest in urban areas grew, in part, from increased racial polarization and restrictive government policies. Urban scholars were prompted to find new ways to understand these emerging realities of city life (Walton 1993, 302; Kleniewski 1997, 35). They drew upon Max Weber's writings and the rediscovered ideas of Karl Marx (and to a lesser extent Friedrich Engels) to explain what the Chicago School's theories could not. Developed under a few different names, this newly emerging perspective was tied together by few basic assumptions that directly challenged the Chicago School's approach (Kleniewski 1997, 37).

Of particular importance is the idea that a city's form and growth are not the result of "natural processes" but come from decisions made by people and organizations that control wealth and other key resources. Powerful decision

Central business district (CBD): The commercial, office, transportation, and cultural center of a city; land values in the CBD are usually among the highest in the city.

makers, rather than some abstract evolutionary principles, are thus responsible for the conditions of cities. Due to its emphasis on powerful actors, this perspective—called the *urban political economy* approach—quickly became, and perhaps still remains, the dominant theory of urban sociology for addressing the social problems of urbanization that promote income inequality, crime, and racism.

Wealthy and politically active people are more powerful than the Chicago School allowed, and the power some people yield can be used to help some while hurting others. Weber's ideas about the ways key actors influence the distribution of social goods led sociologists to explore how individuals and organizations control urban assets and land markets. Such actors include real estate investors and agents, urban planners, housing managers, police, policy makers, mortgage lenders, and financiers. Theorists argue that these actors can determine which social groups and populations gain access to particular property markets.

In one of the first books to adopt this new perspective and address these issues, *Whose City? And Other Essays on Sociology and Planning,* R. E. Pahl (1970, 221) states:

> A truly urban sociology should be concerned with the social and spatial constraints on access to scarce urban resources and facilities as dependent variables and managers or controllers of the urban system, which I take as the independent variable.

Human agency is intricately connected to conflicts over the distribution of resources that, in turn, influence urban forms and social arrangements. Solidarity and cooperation are impossible because the city forces people to view others only as cogs within the urban "growth machine" (Logan and Molotch 1987; Gottdiener and Feagin 1988), in which cities depend on capitalism for growth and sustenance.

The "new" urban sociology, then, sought to explain cities as part of a larger story about class conflict, capital accumulation, and ideological control. Urban theorists directly inspired by Marxian theories—like David Harvey, Manuel Castells, and Henri Lefebvre—transformed general theories about the "evil and avaricious capitalist system" (Harvey 1973, 133) into explanations about the struggle for urban space.

Harvey (1973) argues that the continual **redevelopment** of certain areas of cities—not the areas with the most need—is driven by profit-motivated capitalists without interference from, and sometimes with the help of, local and federal governments. According to Harvey, this tends to benefit affluent whites and hurts poor African Americans and other minorities who have trouble obtaining loans to buy houses. From this vantage point, Harvey stresses the role of the **built environment** as commodity and as a source of profit and loss:

> Under capitalism there is a perpetual struggle in which capital builds a physical landscape appropriate to its own condition at a particular moment in time, only to have to destroy it, usually in the course of a crisis, at a subsequent point in time. The temporal and geographical ebb and flow of investment in the built environment can be understood only in the terms of such a process. The effects of the internal contradictions of capitalism, when projected into the specific context of fixed and immobile investment in the built environment, are thus writ large in the historical geography of the landscape that results. (124)

Investment and disinvestment by the power elite divides upper-class and working-class residential areas to avoid confrontation between them. This residential segregation, in turn, creates an unevenly developed environment with high and low land values that benefit the capitalist class at the expense of the underclass.

From the urban political economy perspective, the city is a profit-making machine fed by the reconstruction and redevelopment of the built environment wherever revenue can be generated. Manuel Castells (1977) connects Marxist theories to the city by interpreting the dual roles of the city as a unit of production (similar to Harvey's ideas) and a locus of social reproduction. Uneven and unequal social relations are reproduced by individuals' consumption of goods like food and clothing and their collective consumption of services like housing and other social services (health care, education, recreation). Castells argues that the state is a tool for the wealthy. Therefore, cities are organized so the state provides the minimal social services and facilities needed to reproduce and maintain a flexible, somewhat educated, and mostly healthy workforce at the lowest cost possible. This includes providing government-subsidized housing, often cheaply and poorly built.

Castells (2000, 293) stresses that the spatial form of the city reproduces the contradictions of capitalism Marx outlined long ago for cities that exhibit great disparities in wealth: "Spatial transformation must be understood in the broader context of social transformation: space does

Redevelopment: The rebuilding of parts of a city; sometimes large areas are completely demolished before being rebuilt, sometimes older buildings are preserved or updated.

Built environment: The human-constructed physical and material objects that make up the city, like buildings, streets, and sidewalks.

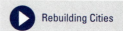 Rebuilding Cities

The low-income neighborhood known as Boca la Caja in Panama City, Panama, is adjacent to an area of expensive real estate that includes the Trump World Tower (left). Boca la Caja faces many social problems as a result of Panama City's rapid growth and urbanization: crime, poor waste management, social and economic isolation, poor infrastructure, and organizational disorder.

not reflect society, it expresses it, it is a fundamental dimension of society." He criticizes the Chicago School as well as other scholars who have unrealistically approached the city as a distinct ecology independent of the larger capitalist system.

Castells's structural take on cities is intended to correct the idea that urban spaces are shaped by the knowledge and actions of those who live, work, and play in them. Along with other Marxist-oriented theorists, however, Castells put himself at the other extreme, where the spatial forms of the city are determined by forces outside the control of everyday people. A new generation of urban scholars he influenced set out to study the processes and effects of the most dominant institutions that shape cities: economics and politics. Their operating assumption is that cities are products of the forces of capitalism and are therefore influenced by and a part of the global political economy. This claim has led to much research on world-systems theory (Wallerstein 1979; Smith and Timberlake 1995), globalization (Short 2004), and global cities (Sassen 2001, 2002, 2010).

Symbolic Interactionism

Influenced by symbolic interactionist writings on everyday life in cities (Karp et al. 1991; Lofland 1998), and by cultural sociology's imperative to analyze "meaning making," the urban culturalist perspective focuses on the practices and processes of culture and community building in cities. Urban culturalists explicitly investigate the symbolic relationships between people and places and the ways that places are given meaning and value. They view the development and redevelopment of the urban built environment as a means for understanding cultural values, ideas, and practices (Monti 1990; Bridger 1996; Lofland 1998; Borer 2008). Their overarching goal is to understand the ways in which people contribute, in varying degrees and with varying reasons, to the social life of the city. They view the city, therefore, as a collective accomplishment regardless of the social problems that exist within it.

The urban culturalist perspective is place based, but it is not city based. That is, it does not view one city as the

 Gentrification

Perceptions of Disorder

After we recognize that heterogeneity is a social problem caused by urbanization and population growth, we then also need to recognize that the individuals in cities, and elsewhere, are themselves heterogeneous. That is, all people's identities are made up of different attributes, such as gender, race, social class, occupation, religion, age, and marital status. It is imperative that we be aware, however, that people experience urban social problems differently depending on the configurations of attributes that make up their identities. Because urbanization is a worldwide phenomenon, all people are affected by it, though not *equally* affected.

Concerned about the role of heterogeneity on perceptions of social order and disorder in urban neighborhoods, Robert J. Sampson and Stephen W. Raudenbush (2004) studied the cues and clues that trigger such perceptions. Do people react only to observable signs like broken windows or graffiti on walls, or do they "see" disorder based on factors such as race, ethnicity, and social class? Sampson and Raudenbush found that the latter—the racial, ethnic, and class-based composition of the neighborhood—was much more influential on perceptions of disorder among blacks, whites, and Latinos than supposedly objective measures. The sight of poor black males was the key trigger for *all* populations.

Sampson and Raudenbush argue that disorder is not just about race, but about the socially constructed and historically biased associations among race, gender, and disorder across populations. Thus policies to fix social problems through urban redevelopment that rely solely on "beautifying" neighborhoods or increasing police presence are insufficient. A better, yet much more difficult, approach is to undo the stigma attached to poor minorities that is "due to social psychological processes of implicit bias and statistical discrimination as played out in the current (and historically durable) racialized context of cities in the United States" (337). Changing the way people think has proven to be much harder, though it can be more effective, than removing graffiti or abandoned cars.

▶ **THINK ABOUT IT**

1. How does an intersectional approach help us make sense of the ways people understand social problems in their neighborhoods?

2. What are the most important social attributes to consider when you are attempting to understand others' respective identities, and your own?

absolute example of 21st-century **urbanism** in the way that Los Angeles, as well as Miami (Nijman 2000) and New York (Halle and Beveridge 2011), have been presented by contemporary scholars. City-based theories are problematic because they don't allow comparisons between cities (or between cities, suburbs, and towns). Also, as Robert A. Beauregard (2011, 199) argues, they favor particular cities and schools where scholars reside, tend to be exclusionary, and reduce the utility of urban studies:

> In addition, by fueling radical uniqueness, a proliferation of city-based theories diminishes what cities have in common and often denies that an "ordinary" city can add value to urban theory. Instead the claim is that some cities have theoretical value and other cities do not. The latter receive theory; the former create it. Thus, what is needed is not an acceptance of city-based urban theories but a critical spirit that fosters skepticism.

Most urban sociologists begin with a social problem or phenomenon, then seek out places in the city or cities they're investigating where it happens. The urban culturalist perspective prompts scholars to begin with a place and ask an open and inductive question: What happens or happened here? This method provides opportunities for researchers to build new ideas and theories from the ground up, instead of making and then testing assumptions. This does not mean researchers shouldn't be aware of past theories or research on the areas and populations they are studying.

Even while allowing "local knowledge" to play a central role, urban culturalists still bring certain theories and "sensitizing concepts" with them into the field. They have

Urbanism: The ways of life or cultures of people in cities; the myths, symbols, and rituals of urbanites.

contributed to and continue to cultivate six key areas of inquiry: (1) images and representations of the city; (2) urban community and civic culture; (3) place-based myths, narratives, and collective memories; (4) sentiment and meaning of and for places; (5) urban identities and lifestyles; and (6) interaction places and practices. These can form a comparative framework for studying the similarities and distinctions between types of places and the people who use and inhabit them.

Urban culturalists have been particularly adept at investigating issues that arise from cities' heterogeneous populations. Norton E. Long (1958), a political scientist interested in the ways cultural practices influence the social lives of cities, characterized the city as an "ecology of games." He contended that while each social grouping or "game" has different rules and roles for its "players," no game within the city is so isolated that it does not come into contact with another or, for that matter, does not need to come into contact with another. In contrast with Robert E. Park's understanding of the city as a mosaic whose social worlds do not interpenetrate, Long argued that often proximity is enough to foster at least weak civic bonds between presumably incompatible interest groups. As he described it: "Sharing a common territorial field and collaborating for different and particular ends in the achievement of overall social functions, the players in one game make use of the players in another and are, in turn, made use of by them" (255). Interdependence is necessary between specialized occupations and lifestyles.

While the games have their own places to be played, they also occur in places people commonly share, often referred to as **third places**. Ray Oldenburg (1999, 16) defines third places as "public places that host the regular, voluntary, informal, and happily anticipated gatherings of individuals beyond the realms of home and work." Coffee shops, pubs, and other small businesses (Oldenburg 1999; Milligan 1998; Borer and Monti 2006; Macgregor 2010) provide settings for the "games" played by businessmen and -women (the owners, managers, and employees), patrons (playing leisure "games"), and other groups who use the sites for gatherings and for displaying information for various causes, retail opportunities, and local events.

Because individuals utilize many different places within their city, they learn and are capable of playing by the rules for multiple "games." The rules are usually a hodgepodge of liberal and conservative values. As Monti's (1999) historical analysis of civic culture in U.S. cities shows, liberal and conservative thinkers see the world very differently, in theory. But people reconcile

Shen Hong / Xinhua Press / Corbis

Federal-style row houses line Beacon Street in Boston's tony Beacon Hill neighborhood. Through the years, Beacon Hill has been home to many wealthy and influential people, such as Oliver Wendell Holmes Sr., who, in 1860, coined the term "Boston Brahmins" to refer to the city's upper-class citizens.

these different and seemingly irreconcilable points of view in their everyday routines. The civic culture of U.S. cities, and of cities around the world, is a hybrid culture made up of individuals and groups that think and act in a variety of liberal and conservative ways.

Even though communities are collective accomplishments, not everyone plays an equal role in making the decisions or follows the rules exactly the same way all the time. Urban dwellers can change their ways of thinking and acting, but only within tolerable limits. This hybrid mixing is at the heart of what Monti calls the "paradoxical community." Because the cultural influence of cities stretches beyond their physical borders, the same kinds of "paradoxical community" practices can be found in suburbs and small towns (see Macgregor 2010).

Paradoxical or not, communities in cities are packed with meaning and emotional attachments. In 1945, Walter Firey published a study on the sentimental value attached to certain areas in Boston and the way land had been used throughout the city. His "Sentiment and Symbolism as Ecological Variables" showed that large areas of land were not only reserved for noneconomic uses but also left undeveloped because they had been collectively endowed with symbolic meaning. These areas could not be fitted into a model based on concentric circles, zones, or nuclei. Boston's "sacred sites," the parks, cemeteries, and 48-acre area in the center of the city that formed the original "commons," had never been developed (140). Furthermore, Beacon Hill, an upper-class residential neighborhood near the center of the city, was not taken over by the CBD and maintains its privileged position inside the city.

Beacon Hill survives not merely because the people who live there share a common ecological space with

---

Third places: Locations that serve social needs beyond work and home life (e.g., local coffee shops).

rational economic functions. Rather, its existence derives from cultural values, the sentiment residents attach to their territory. According to Firey (1945, 144), people could have lived in less expensive districts with an "equally accessible location and even superior housing conditions. There is thus a noneconomic aspect to land use on Beacon Hill, one which is in some respects actually diseconomic in its consequences." "Sentiment" and "symbolism," which mean everything from social prestige to ethnic or racial prejudice, are ecological factors that influence spatial distribution and patterns of development and redevelopment. Firey's study has had lasting impact by showing how cultural factors affect political agendas related to land-use decisions (Maines and Bridger 1992; Borer 2008, 2010).

ASK YOURSELF: Which of the schools of thought discussed here align with your way of thinking about cities? Which are best suited for addressing the social problems that arise from urbanization and population growth? Theorists have described the city as an organism, a growth machine, an ecology of games. What term or metaphor would you use to describe the city?

SPECIALIZED THEORIES IN URBAN SOCIOLOGY

 Apply specialized theories to urbanization and city growth.

Historically, sociology has been hesitant to embrace the natural environment as a topic of study, partly because early researchers wanted to differentiate their discipline from the other social sciences. Specialized modern theories redress that oversight.

Urban Sustainability

The concept of sustainability has taken a central place in most recent discussions of development, industry, and urban planning. It has its roots in a 1987 report by the United Nations World Commission on Environment and Development titled *Our Common Future*. This document, commonly known as the Brundtland Report (for Gro Harlem Brundtland, who chaired the commission), defined sustainable development as "development that meets the needs of the present without compromising the ability of future generations to meet their own needs." One major goal of the commission was to position environmental concerns as a central factor in global development planning.

FIGURE 17.5 The Three Components of Urban Sustainability

In 1992 the United Nations convened the Earth Summit, which produced Agenda 21, an action plan for implementing sustainable development at the local, national, and international levels. While the Brundtland Report emphasized the need to protect the natural environment for the sake of ecological systems and resources critical for economic and social life, Agenda 21 emphasized the importance of social issues in the sustainability puzzle (Colantonio 2007). This triad of environmental protection, economic growth, and social justice, also known as the "triple bottom line" (Elkington 1994, 1997) or the "three pillars" model of sustainability, has also been adopted by many cities as the guiding principle for achieving urban sustainability (see Figure 17.5).

The increased concern for urban sustainability represents an effort to address the social and environmental problems produced by urban growth guided simply by a desire to grow the economy. This theoretical foundation for urban growth not only addresses environmental problems in a way traditional sociological theories have not but also bridges environmental problems and social problems, understanding that they are intricately related.

Sustainability asks that we consider the long-term viability of our current actions. How long before we run up against economic, environmental, and/or social limits? How can and should we manage healthy nature–society relationships now and in the future? How can we foster and maintain healthy social and economic well-being, cultural diversity, and equity across diverse populations? This is a perspective in which we consider how the decisions we make within each of these three domains affect the others.

Economic and environmental sustainability are relatively straightforward notions if we refer back to the idea of meeting "the needs of the present without compromising

The Effects of Sustained Population Growth on Community Relations: The Las Vegas Metropolitan Area Social Survey

The population growth rates in Las Vegas were among the highest in the United States at the end of the 20th century. The Las Vegas metropolitan area grew about 83% between 1990 and 2000 and continued at this rapid pace until about 2010. In 2009 a team of sociologists administered surveys and conducted focus group interviews in neighborhoods throughout the Las Vegas Valley to assess residents' knowledge and attitudes about economic, social, and environmental issues in the city (Futrell et al. 2010). The questions probed residents' knowledge about the environment and trust in environmental information as well as their perceptions about their responsibility for environmental issues and their willingness to pay to address these issues. The researchers also asked questions about migration and residential mobility, neighborhood and social bonds, and quality of life. Finally, they probed residents' economic problems, job satisfaction, and employment history.

Of the study's respondents, only 8% were born in Las Vegas, while 75% were born in other U.S. states and 16% in other countries. On average, they had lived in their homes for 12.1 years; 64% had moved from other Las Vegas Valley homes, while 34% came from outside the state. The high rate of recent arrivals was accompanied by a weak sense of belonging to both the city and the neighborhood. Those born in Las Vegas or other parts of Nevada were much more likely to feel attached to the city than those from other states or countries, and the longer they had lived in their homes the more likely they were to report attachment. More respondents felt a sense of belonging to Nevada and Las Vegas than felt a sense of belonging to their neighborhoods.

These patterns suggest potentially low levels of social capital among those who were part of the city's population boom. The data support this. Among respondents 41% reported visiting their neighbors "almost never" and 63% reported

"almost never doing or receiving favors for neighbors." Focus group respondents overwhelmingly reported weak bonds among neighbors and feeling as though most people in their neighborhoods were strangers. At the same time, most reported yearning for more community bonds.

These findings imply that unmanaged rapid urbanization or population growth poses problems for creating community. The slow development of social capital and bonds to city and neighborhood suggests that as cities grow, they must take quality-of-life issues seriously and facilitate the creation and maintenance of institutions and amenities that can support community development.

▶ **THINK ABOUT IT:** What can residents of cities in flux do to create a strong sense of belonging in their neighborhoods?

---

the ability of future generations to meet their own needs." Economic sustainability, then, suggests that we not engage in risky financial practices that could destabilize the economy and that we ensure the existence of decent-paying jobs for future generations. Common goals are low unemployment rates, diversified economies, and labor force stability. Similarly, environmental sustainability asks that we practice environmental stewardship and avoid practices and policies that could jeopardize the health of natural resources like water, soil, and air. What about social sustainability, though?

The social dimension is focused on creating and maintaining healthy, sustainable communities. A diversity of issues gets folded into the notion of healthy communities, including trust, cohesion, community identification, cultural and community diversity, pride, sense of place,

security, and high quality of life, which also tend to translate into feelings of personal and collective responsibility for future generations (Colantonio 2007; Colantonio and Dixon 2011). An interest in social sustainability and in healthy communities centers on urban dwellers' basic needs and social well-being, social capital, equity, and social and cultural dynamism (Colantonio 2007). These are critical elements for fulfilling individuals' needs for belonging and attachment in cities characterized by immense heterogeneity and mutual strangeness.

"Just" Sustainability

Critics have argued, however, that the three major dimensions of the triple bottom line are prioritized unequally

(Agyeman, Bullard, and Evans 2002; Campbell 1996; Colantonio and Dixon 2011; Drakakis-Smith 1995; Littig and Grießler 2005) because the priorities of the interest groups behind the various pillars diverge (Campbell 1996). Left unmediated, these priorities must vie for attention among planners, politicians, activists, and the public. For example, the ideal of sustainability emerged partly in response to the broad conflict of "human versus nature." That is, urban planning has tended to promote city building at the cost of the natural environment (Campbell 1996), which ultimately threatens cities' persistence into the future. Similarly, efforts to grow a local economy in a capitalist city urge corporations and large businesses to keep wages low. While in the short term this increases profits, it also threatens to destabilize the labor force by pushing workers into poverty. Just like natural resources, human resources (labor) must not be exploited or they will not continue to deliver into the future (Campbell 1996). Finally, the most complicated conflict in balancing the three pillars of sustainability is created by the need to ensure both social equity *and* environmental protection. If environmental protection entails more tempered economic growth, how do we create greater economic opportunities, and by extension social capital and high quality of life, for those at the bottom of the socio-economic ladder? This conflict expresses the difficulty of addressing social sustainability in a way that also treats environmental and economic sustainability.

In theory, social sustainability is understood as vital to be preserved and stabilized for future generations in order to protect the achievements of human civilization (Littig and Grießler 2005). In practice, however, the social dimension, especially the emphasis on equity, has been largely marginalized. Accordingly, Agyeman et al. (2002, 78) have developed the concept of "just" sustainability,

which they define as "the need to ensure a better quality of life for all, now and into the future, in a just and equitable manner, whilst living within the limits of supporting ecosystems." This reworking of the economic, environmental, and social triad of sustainability emphasizes the need to extend the quality of life and social capital elements of social sustainability to communities of color and low-income populations (Alkon and Agyeman 2011). It takes seriously the imperative to build sustainable communities for *all* people (Agyeman and Evans 2003). Moreover, research suggests that those living in low-income and racially segregated communities face serious barriers to social capital, social mobility (the ability to climb the social class ladder), and quality-of-life resources like access to good schools, high-quality health care, reliable transportation, and political representation (Massey and Denton 1993).

....

ASK YOURSELF: In what ways do or could the different types of sustainability complement each other? In what ways do or could they contradict each other? What do you think are the most important practices and principles for building sustainable cities?

....

Creating sustainable communities in cities helps establish a collective will to preserve the communities and the cities. This attachment to place and foundation for the establishment of shared goals and visions can serve as the social and cultural buttress for growth plans that meaningfully incorporate environmental stewardship. When communities are invested in one another and in the environment, policies and practices like New Urbanism, "smart" growth, and civic engagement in general become much more potent.

SOCIAL CHANGE: WHAT CAN YOU DO?

 17.5 Identify steps toward social change regarding urbanization and city growth.

Urban and town planners today are much more likely to talk about the ways in which given projects affect not just the economic vibrancy of particular areas but also the environment and social justice or equity. How much "social engineering" can be accomplished through

better or more socially responsive kinds of planning is another issue that has gained a lot of attention among professionals. Contemporary experts have begun to cool, perhaps prematurely, to the idea that spreading "middle-class culture" will succeed in unifying a diverse urban population (Monti 2013). At the same time, ironically, they still believe bringing more low-income and minority people to live and work in the suburbs is a good thing to do according to the "contact hypothesis," which suggests that less desirable people or places can be improved by being exposed to more desirable people or places.

More modest and scaled-down visions of what might be accomplished with better designed urban and suburban places appear in planned New Urbanist developments like Celebration and Seaside, both in Florida. (You might recognize Seaside as the setting for Jim Carey's film *The Truman Show*.) These places were supposed to manufacture a sense of community by bringing residents together a lot more often through the integration of private residential space with carefully designed public space (Talen 2000,173). We can think of **New Urbanism** as a response to urban and suburban sprawl, both of which cater to people moving in cars rather than on foot. Walking or riding a train with others instead is supposed to help foster better physical and social health.

This approach has been successful, up to a point. It turns out that people will hang out more in attractive, well-designed spaces and are more likely to "bump into each other" when they can walk to a shopping area or workplace that's within a couple of blocks of where they live. At the same time, building a town or neighborhood with such principles in mind doesn't guarantee that everyone living there is going to get along or pledge undying loyalty to the place (Frantz and Collins 1999).

The connection between creating a new place or improving an older one and fixing the people who live, work, or play there simply isn't as straightforward as reformers, policy makers, and planners would have us think. That shouldn't stop them from trying to make better places. It also shouldn't stop you from helping make your city, suburb, or town better. But where do you start?

··

New Urbanism: An approach to designing cities, towns, and neighborhoods aimed at reducing traffic and sprawl and increasing social interactions.

There are a few things that you can do provided you have the means, desire, and gusto. Remember, however, that since urbanization and population growth are *social* problems, individual actions are only a small first step to larger changes and reforms.

First, try to break up the everyday monotony of traveling from home to school or work and back by shaking up your daily routine. If you're in a car, take some streets you haven't been on before. Maybe park the car, get out, and walk around to see who's there and what they're doing. Second, if you're making one of these stops, try to do it in an ethnic enclave. Stop at a restaurant or food truck and take in the local delicacies. Eating foods from other ethnicities is a first step toward breaking the barrier between populations and making the "Other" less strange.

Third, in your own neighborhood, get to know those around you by spending more time in the front of your house or apartment rather than inside or in the backyard. Creating a "front porch" culture is one of the primary tools New Urbanist planners use to help foster connections between neighbor and neighbor *and* between neighbor and passerby. Fourth, be mindful of the ways city life and its built environment infringe on the natural environment. If water is an issue, use less. If air pollution is an issue, reduce the amount you drive. Take public transportation when you can. You'll be helping the environment and you might even rub elbows and chat with some fellow responsible citizens you wouldn't have met otherwise.

··

ASK YOURSELF: Urban planners and policy makers often assume that fixing the physical "face" of a city—the way it looks—will make the city "better." Do you think there are connections between the way a city looks and the actions and activities of the people who live and work there? Besides making changes to your own behavior, what things can you do to fix the social problems that affect people you know and people you don't in your city or town?

··

WHAT DOES AMERICA THINK?

Questions about Urbanization from the General Social Survey

 Turn to the beginning of the chapter to compare your answers to the total population.

1. In the United States, do you think we're spending too much money on highways and bridges, too little money, or about the right amount?

TOO MUCH: 12.9%

TOO LITTLE: 44.1%

ABOUT THE RIGHT AMOUNT: 43%

2. In the United States, do you think we're spending too much money on mass transportation, too little money, or about the right amount?

TOO MUCH: 11.1%

TOO LITTLE: 40.1%

ABOUT THE RIGHT AMOUNT: 48.8%

3. In the United States, do you think we're spending too much money on assistance to big cities, too little money, or about the right amount?

TOO MUCH: 40.1%

TOO LITTLE: 17.4%

ABOUT THE RIGHT AMOUNT: 42.5%

4. In the United States, do you think we're spending too much money on solving problems of big cities, too little money, or about the right amount?

TOO MUCH: 17.8%

TOO LITTLE: 43.7%

ABOUT THE RIGHT AMOUNT: 38.5%

 ## LOOK BEHIND THE NUMBERS

Go to **edge.sagepub.com/trevino** for a breakdown of these data across time and by race, sex, age, income, and other statuses.

1. Examine the data on race for responses to the questions about assistance to big cities and solving problems of big cities. What possible explanations can you give for why blacks are the largest group answering "too little" on both questions?

2. When you read the question about solving the problems of big cities, what problems came to mind?

3. Examine the General Social Survey data from 1973 to the present on responses to the question about solving the problems of big cities. How would you describe the pattern of responses? What explanations might you offer for this pattern?

CHAPTER SUMMARY

 17.1 Explain social problems that uniquely arise from urbanization and city growth.

Cities are the biggest things that humans have ever built together, but that doesn't mean that people who live in cities are all the same. In fact, people who live in cities are often quite different from their neighbors. While diversity is generally a favorable quality for healthy communities, it takes a lot of work for people of diverse backgrounds to find common ground and work together. Without some degree of trust and tolerance, social order is threatened, as is the ability of city dwellers to address important social issues like environmental degradation, education reform, and residential segregation.

 17.2 Discuss patterns and trends in urbanization and city growth.

As the world becomes increasingly urban, many people fear that individuals will become further alienated from their neighbors, and, consequently, the general social fabric of societies will forever be frayed and unraveled. This fear is reinforced by rising income inequalities and health disparities within and between cities as well as the impacts that cities are having on the lands they are built upon and near.

 17.3 Apply the functionalist, conflict, and symbolic interactionist perspectives to problems that arise from urbanization and city growth.

A functionalist perspective or urban ecological approach shows us how cities and their respective populations develop out of natural processes of adaptation, competition, and succession. Recognizing how these processes work can help alleviate the negative effects of urbanization and population growth. A conflict theory or urban political economy approach would suggest that people in cities are always competing for scarce resources and that those who can accumulate more and more of those resources will continue to exploit those who don't have many or any resources. A fundamental restructuring of the economy is, therefore, the only way to truly fix urban problems. A symbolic interactionist or urban culturalist perspective uncovers how people make sense of the cities they live, work, and play in and how that influences how they interact with others and the city's built environment. By identifying the things and practices that people hold to be culturally valuable, we can gain a better understanding of what they see as the most important problems.

 17.4 Apply specialized theories to urbanization and city growth.

The increased concerns for urban sustainability in recent years represent an effort to address the social and environmental problems produced by urban growth guided simply by a desire to grow the economy. Such a theoretical foundation for urban growth not only addresses environmental problems in a way traditional sociological theories have not but also bridges environmental problems and social problems, understanding that they are intricately related. Thinking about urban sustainability as a combination of environmental, economic, and social factors is a necessary way to address cities' most pressing problems. "Just" sustainability attempts to meet "the need to ensure a better quality of life for all, now and into the future, in a just and equitable manner, whilst living within the limits of supporting ecosystems" (Agyeman et al. 2002, 78).

 17.5 Identify steps toward social change regarding urbanization and city growth.

No redevelopment scheme, no matter how successful it may be in terms of making nicer buildings and more public space for people to share, can guarantee that everyone who ends up living in the rebuilt area will behave wonderfully all the time and get along. As an approach to rebuilding inner cities, however, comparatively modest size and modestly scaled social expectations for the people living and working in these places holds more promise than massive urban clearance and bulldozing projects have ever delivered. And it is in the hands of those who are civically engaged and work hard to know others across the city's symbolic boundaries to moderate and negotiate the extent of expectations.

DISCUSSION QUESTIONS

1. How have changes in the size and nature of urban populations both caused and solved social problems? What determines the extent to which change leads to problems when it comes to understanding cities?

2. Which aspects of cities did the early sociologists find appealing to study? In what ways have our interests shifted since these early studies?

3. How do concepts such as gemeinschaft and gesellschaft help one better understand problems we see today around urbanization? How does urbanization as a social problem interact and intersect with other social problems, such as those having to do with the environment and with race and ethnicity?

4. What are the patterns of immigration we see over time in cities? What role does the city itself play in the arrival of new immigrants? What are the issues around immigration and cities that concern sociologists?

5. Compare the concentric-zone model with the other models of understanding cities. What does one learn from these different models? What is missed when we examine cities from these perspectives?

6. What role does culture play in our study of cities? How do the people who live in a city define the city? How do these varying definitions interact and conflict with one another in the heterogeneous city?

7. In what ways do the specialized theories in urban sociology respond to previous theorists' reluctance to consider the natural environment? How does this concern for the environment shift the focus within urban sociology?

8. How does "just" sustainability shift the priorities of development? What value might such a construct have for those who are most vulnerable and/or least privileged in urban areas? What are the costs to those with more privilege?

9. What do you think about the appeal of New Urbanist developments like Celebration, Florida? Have you ever visited such a place? Would you want to live in a planned community? What does such a community have to offer residents? Could the same benefits be created in existing cities?

10. In terms of social change, how important are individual actions such as eating in new places or spending time getting to know one's neighbors? How are these individual actions connected to larger goals for social change?

KEY TERMS

biographical strangers 454

built environment 462

central business
    district (CBD) 461

city 451

community 460

cultural strangers 454

gemeinschaft 452

gesellschaft 452

industrialization 452

New Urbanism 469

redevelopment 462

segregation 455

social order 451

third places 465

urbanism 464

urbanization 451

urban sprawl 460

Sharpen your skills with SAGE edge at edge.sagepub.com/trevino

A personalized approach to help you accomplish your coursework goals in an easy-to-use learning environment.

Absolute measure of poverty: A threshold or line (usually based on income) at or below which individuals or groups are identified as living in poverty.

Accountability: The ways in which people gear their actions to specific circumstances so others will correctly recognize the actions for what they are.

Achievement gap: The consistent difference in scores on student achievement tests between students of different demographic groups, including groups based on race, gender, and socioeconomic status.

Adjudication: The process in which a final judicial decision or sentence is made in a criminal case.

Affirmative action: Policies enacted by governments and private organizations to increase work and educational opportunities for women and members of certain minority groups.

Affirmative defenses: Legal defenses in which new facts or sets of facts operate to defeat claims even if the facts supporting the claims are true.

Ageism: The use of real or perceived chronological age as a basis for discrimination.

Agenda-setting theory: A theory that emphasizes the important role media play in influencing public understanding of social issues and social problems.

Aging: A social process constructed from the expectations and belief systems of the structural characteristics of society.

Alienation: The separation of workers from their human nature in the capitalist production process—that is, the separation between the labor to make something and the object itself.

Allocation: The way decisions get made about who does what, who gets what and who gets to make plans, and who gets to give orders or take them.

Altruistic suicide: Suicide that occurs as a result of too much social integration.

American Federation of Teachers (AFT): One of the two largest unions representing teachers in the United States.

Androcentrism: The belief that masculinity and what men do are superior to femininity and what women do.

Anomic suicide: Suicide that occurs as a result of too little social regulation.

Anomie: A state of normlessness in society.

Antiracism: The active struggle against racism in everyday life (micro) and/or institutionally (macro).

Assimilation: The act of literally "becoming like" the dominant group of the host society; in its purest sense, when assimilation is complete an immigrant would be indistinguishable from the dominant group in society.

Authorization: Enemy-making behavior facilitated by leaders that absolves individuals of the responsibility to make personal moral choices.

Benefits: Noncash compensation paid to employees, such as health insurance and pension plans. Also known as fringe benefits.

Big data: The large quantities of digital data produced by digital societies, including data from cell phones, keystrokes, and GPS units.

Biographical strangers: Individuals who do not know each other on a personal basis or who have never met.

Bounded rationality: The idea that an individual's thought processes are deemed to be rational even when they are constrained by low intelligence, chemical dependence, or mental illness.

Bourgeoisie: In Marxist theory, the wealthy class that owns and controls the means of production and is at odds with the lower class.

Bourgeoisie legality: The theory that members of the upper class make the laws to serve and protect their own interests to the detriment of the lower class.

Broken windows theory: The theory that maintaining an urban environment in an orderly manner will deter both low-level and serious offending.

Built environment: The human-constructed physical and material objects that make up the city, like buildings, streets, and sidewalks.

Bumpy-line assimilation: A modification of early 20th-century assimilation theory that challenges the traditional linear one-way progression; instead, immigrants can become full participating members of the host society while still retaining certain ties to their nationalities of origin (incorporates notion of "thick" versus "thin" ties).

Capitalism: An economic system that includes the ownership of private property, the making of financial profit, and the hiring of workers.

Capitalists: The economically dominant class that privately owns and controls human labor, raw materials, land, tools, machinery, technologies, and factories.

Central business district (CBD): The commercial, office, transportation, and cultural center of a city; land values in the CBD are usually among the highest in the city.

Charter schools: Publicly funded schools that operate independent of school districts and are free of many of the regulations that apply to school districts.

Child dependency ratio: The number of children under the age of 16 per 100 adults ages 16 to 64.

City: A relatively large, dense, and heterogeneously populated place or settlement.

Civil unions: Legal provisions that grant some or all of the legal rights of marriage to unmarried couples.

Claims making: The process whereby groups compete to have their claims about difficult social issues acknowledged, accepted, and responded to by authorities.

Class: A person's social position relative to the economic sector.

Clearance rate: The ratio of reported cases of crime to cleared cases, calculated by dividing the number of crimes that result in arrests by the total number of crimes recorded.

Code theory: Basil Bernstein's concept that society reproduces social classes through favoring the communication codes, or manners of speaking and representing thoughts and ideas, of more powerful socioeconomic groups.

Cognitive dissonance: The discomfort of holding conflicting beliefs or values.

Cohabitation: Unrelated (unmarried) adults in an intimate relationship sharing living quarters.

Cohort: Within a population, a group of individuals of similar age who share a particular experience.

Color-blind racism: A type of racism that avoids overt arguments of biological superiority/inferiority and instead uses ideologies that do not always mention race specifically.

Community: A usually positive (though not necessarily so) form of sustained social cohesion, interaction, and organization that exists between the larger society and individuals who have similar characteristics or attributes (e.g., ethnicity, geography, beliefs).

Community schools: Schools that strive to meet all the basic academic, physical, and emotional needs of students and their families while building strong, cohesive bonds among teachers, students, and students' families.

Compensation: Salaries or wages along with benefits paid to employees. Also known as total compensation.

Concepts: Ideas that sociologists have about some aspect of the social world.

Conflict theory: The sociological theory that focuses on dissent, coercion, and antagonism in society.

Consciousness-raising: A radical feminist social movement technique designed to help women make connections between the personal and the political in their lives.

Constructionist approach: An approach to social problems theory that highlights the process whereby troubling social issues become recognized as social problems.

Contact hypothesis: The prediction that persons with greater degrees of cross-racial contact will have lower levels of racial prejudice than those with less contact.

Continuity theory: A theory that utilizes the concept of normal aging as a basis for explaining how older individuals adjust.

Costs of privilege: Experiences that members of the majority group may miss out on due to racial isolation and limited worldviews.

Crisis science: Medical science that works in tandem with Mode 1 science and has the freedom to respond to crises and the needs of patients faster than traditional science.

Crude divorce rate: The number of divorces per 1,000 population.

Cult of thinness: Idealization of a decidedly slim body type that is unachievable for the vast majority of the population.

Cultural capital theory: Pierre Bourdieu's concept that a range of nonfinancial assets, such as education, physical appearance, and familiarity with various kinds of music, art, and dance, empower individuals to advance in a social group that values a particular set of these cultural assets.

Cultural deprivation theory: A theory based in the concept that children from working-class and nonwhite families often lack certain cultural resources, such as books and other educational stimuli, and thus arrive at school at a significant disadvantage.

Cultural difference theories: Theories based in the concept that there are cultural and family differences between working-class and nonwhite students and white middle-class students attributable to social forces such as poverty, racism, discrimination, and unequal life chances.

Culturally resonant themes: Themes that invoke widely held beliefs, values, and preferences that are familiar to potential audiences; such themes are common in news stories of social problems.

Cultural strangers: Individuals who are from different symbolic worlds or cultures.

Culture: A style of life.

Culture of poverty thesis: The idea that living in poverty leads to the acquisition of certain values and beliefs that perpetuate remaining in poverty.

Culture of service: A style of life that includes various forms of civic engagement, community service, and volunteerism intended to help alleviate social problems.

Culture wars: Disputes over the state of American society, including the presumed decline of the family as well as "family values."

Cumulative advantage: A position that multiplies advantages for those who have them and limits the capacity for those without resources.

Cyberbullying: Electronic forms of bullying.

Cyclical unemployment: Unemployment caused by cyclical downturns in the economy.

Dark figure of crime: The amount of unreported or undiscovered crime, which calls into question the reliability of official crime statistics.

Data sources: Collections of information.

Decentralization of power: The distribution of functions and responsibilities of police officers to different local authorities.

Defense of Marriage Act (DOMA): U.S. federal law, enacted in 1996, that defines marriage as the legal union of one man and one woman for federal and interstate purposes.

Dehumanization: Enemy-making behavior that makes the other side appear to be less than human; eliminates the need to raise moral questions.

Democratic theory of peace: The theory that political democracies are less likely than nondemocracies to wage war with each other.

Demographic factors: Social characteristics of a population, in particular those of race, age, and gender.

Deterrence: A purpose of punishment that sets out to prevent rational people from committing crimes.

Deviance: Behavior that has been defined as a violation of the general or specific norms or expectations of a culture or of powerful groups.

Dialectical materialism: The contradictions in an existing economic and social order that create a push for change, which eventually leads to new economic conditions and social relations.

Differential association theory: A theory of crime that asserts that all behavior is learned, both criminal and noncriminal.

Digital divide: The gap in access to information and communication technologies between more advantaged and less advantaged groups, such as between the wealthy and poor regions of the world (the global digital divide) and between social classes within a country.

Discouraged workers: Unemployed workers who have given up looking for jobs and hence are no longer counted as members of the labor force.

Distracted driving: The operation of a motor vehicle while engaged in other attention-requiring activities, such as texting or talking on the phone.

Distributive justice: Relative equality in how social and economic resources are distributed in a society.

Division of labor: The division of work into a multiplicity of specialized occupational roles and tasks.

Doing gender theory: A theory of gender that claims gender is an accountable performance created and reinforced through individuals' interactions.

Double consciousness: African Americans' ability to see themselves both as active agents with full humanity and as they are seen through the eyes of whites who view them as inferior and problematic.

Double standard: An attitude or belief that judges heterosexual women's sexual behavior more harshly and negatively than heterosexual men's sexual behavior.

Drug: A substance that has properties that produce psychophysiological changes in the individual who ingests it.

Drug abuse: The use of psychoactive substances in a way that creates problematic outcomes for the user.

Drug addiction: A state of dependence on a substance that produces psychophysiological changes in the user.

Drug use: The ingestion of substances so as to produce changes in the body that alter the way the user experiences the world.

Dysfunctions: Negative consequences of social structures or social institutions.

Ecological dialogue: An approach to the environment and society that focuses on the interactions between aspects of human environmental relationships.

Ecological modernization theory: The theory that society can become environmentally sustainable through the development of greener technologies and government regulations.

Effective schools movement: A movement for school improvement based on the concept that unusually effective schools have certain characteristics (such as effective leadership, accountability, and high expectations of teachers and administrators) that help explain why their students achieve academically despite disadvantaged backgrounds.

Egoistic suicide: Suicide that occurs as a result of too little social integration.

Elementary and Secondary Education Act (ESEA): The primary piece of federal legislation concerning K–12 education in the United States; this act, first passed in 1965, was most dramatically revised through its reauthorization in 2001 as the No Child Left Behind Act.

Employment at will: The legal practice that allows an employer to terminate a worker's employment even if no specific reason for the termination is given.

Environmental racism: The process by which the dominant race in society is shielded from the most toxic/harmful environmental threats, while such health risks/hazards are located closest to

neighborhoods where minority groups reside.

Erotica: Literary or artistic material meant to cause sexual feelings.

Ethnicity: Cultural background, often tied to nationality of origin and/or the culture practiced by the individual and his or her family of origin.

Ethnomethodology: A sociological approach that seeks to uncover the taken-for-granted assumptions that lie behind the basic stuff of social life and interaction.

Expressive: Oriented toward interactions with other people.

Extreme poverty neighborhoods: Areas (usually based on census tracts) that have poverty rates of 40% or more.

Family: (1) Two or more people related by birth, marriage, or adoption who share living quarters (U.S. Census Bureau definition), or (2) members of a social group who are in an intimate, long-term, committed relationship and who share mutual expectations of rights and responsibilities.

Family ecology theory: A theory that views family systems as embedded in natural or human-made physical, social, and other environments.

Family life course development theory: A theory that examines the developmental processes and outcomes as families move through a series of normative stages across the life course.

Family systems theory: A theory that views the family as a set of subsystems defined by boundaries and striving toward social equilibrium.

Fatalistic suicide: Suicide that occurs as a result of too much social regulation.

Feminist criminology: A theory of crime that includes gender in its analysis.

Feminist perspective: A theoretical approach that emphasizes the extent to which patriarchy and sexism undermine women (and men), relationships, and families.

Feminization of poverty: The trend of poverty being concentrated disproportionately in female-headed single-parent families.

Fertility rate: The number of children born per 1,000 women during their prime fertility period.

Fictive kin: People to whom one is not related by blood, marriage, or adoption but on whom one nonetheless depends.

Finder of fact: In a criminal prosecution, the individuals assigned to determine whether the facts have been proven. This role is most often assigned to the jury.

Food insecurity: A household's lack of access to nutritious food on a regular basis.

Frame alignment: A situation in which multiple frames work together to enhance the efficacy of each.

Frame analysis: A sociological approach that focuses on the presentation of information and ideas in ways that are intended to elicit particular understanding and responses.

Functionalist theory: The hypothesis that societies are complex systems whose parts work together to maintain cohesion and stability.

Functions: Positive consequences of social structures or social institutions.

Gemeinschaft: Communal association, or a sense of close-knit community relations based on shared traditions and values.

Gender: The social meanings layered on top of sex categories.

Gender inequality: The way in which the meanings assigned to sex and gender as social categories create disparities in resources such as income, power, and status.

Gender wage gap: The gap in earnings between women and men, usually expressed as a percentage or proportion of what women are paid relative to their male equivalents.

General deterrence: A law or policy written to stop a person from committing a crime in the first place.

Generational inequity: A situation in which older-age members of a society receive a disproportionate share of the society's resources relative to younger members; perceptions that such inequity exists lead to calls for adjustments to ensure greater economic and social parity between generations.

Genetic difference theory: The discredited concept that differences in educational performance between working-class and nonwhite students and their middle- and upper-class and white counterparts are due to genetic differences in intelligence.

Gerontocracy: A system in which older-age citizens have the power to run the government and dictate policies that primarily support people in their age category.

Gesellschaft: Societal association, or a sense of relationships typified by impersonal bureaucracies and contractual arrangements rather than informal ones based on kinship and family ties.

Globalization: The process through which business firms, political authority, and cultural patterns spread throughout the world.

Globalized intrastate wars: Organized violence used to control territory containing valuable resources, often fought by paramilitary forces, often targeting civilians, often containing high levels of sexual violence, and often using child soldiers.

Global perspective: A viewpoint from which we compare our own society to other societies around the world.

Great Depression: Worldwide economic downturn in the period 1929–1941, marked by failing businesses, low or at times negative economic growth, and widespread unemployment.

Harm reduction: An approach to drug policy aimed at minimizing or eliminating the harms associated with drug use behaviors.

Hegemonic masculinity: The type of gender practice that exists at the top of the hierarchy in any given place and time.

Hooking up: Something sexual happening, usually between two people, often outside the context of a socially defined relationship.

Hot-spot policing: A method employed by police departments to track the ordered spatial patterns of crime by monitoring when crimes occur disproportionately in particular geographic areas and responding to those areas.

Household: All the related and unrelated people who share living quarters.

Human capital: The package of cognitive, physical, and social skills of individual workers.

Hybrid: An entity that emerges from the combination of other entities but differs from the sum of its parts.

Hypermasculinity: An intensification of traits normally associated with stereotypical male behavior: physical strength, aggressiveness, assertiveness, risk taking, and appreciation for danger and adventure.

Ideologies: Belief systems that serve to rationalize/justify existing social arrangements.

Incapacitation: Loss of liberty due to incarceration.

Income: Money that comes into a family or household from a variety of sources, such as earnings, unemployment compensation, workers' compensation, Social Security, pension or retirement income, interest, and dividends.

Indeterminate sentencing: Sentencing for convicted offenders in which the length of incarceration is undetermined.

Indicators: Observable changes in social and ecological behaviors that are used to indirectly measure other changes that are less visible.

Individual discrimination: Discrimination in which actors carry out their own intentions to exclude based on race, as opposed to being explicitly supported in doing so or directed to do so by an organization.

Industrialization: A process that leads to a significant increase in the proportion of a population engaged in specialized factory work and nonagricultural occupations; increases the number of people living near factories and relying on mechanically produced goods and services.

Industrialized science: Science that is done on the large scale for profit.

Inequality: Differences between individuals or groups in the quantities of scarce resources they possess.

Institutional discrimination: Discrimination based in policies often written without overt racial language that nonetheless have disproportionately negative impacts on people of color.

Institutional racism: Policies and practices embedded in social institutions that consistently and disproportionately favor members of the dominant/majority group while systematically excluding/disadvantaging people of color.

Institutional theory: The concept that schools are global institutions and have developed similarly throughout the world since the 19th century as a result of processes of globalization and democratization.

Instrumental: Oriented toward goals and tasks.

Interaction routines: Patterns or norms of speech or action that individuals follow with regularity to accomplish particular tasks in interactions.

Interest groups: Organized associations of people mobilized into action because of their membership in those associations.

Internalized racism: Feelings that occur in people of color when they buy into racist ideology that characterizes their own group as inferior—for example, when they believe that they themselves and/or other members of their group are not deserving of prestigious positions in society, or they assume that members of their group are prone to exhibiting stereotypical behaviors.

Interpretive flexibility: The ability of the development path to respond to different users' needs.

Intersectional approach: A sociological approach that examines how gender as a social category intersects with other social statuses such as race, class, and sexuality.

Intersectionality: The ways in which several demographic factors—especially social class, race, ethnicity, and gender—combine to affect people's experiences.

Intersexed: Born with some range of biological conditions that make sex category ambiguous.

Interviewing: A method of data collection in which the researcher asks respondents a series of questions.

Intimate partner violence (IPV): Physical, sexual, or psychological/emotional harm or the threat of harm by a current or former intimate partner or spouse.

Jim Crow: The system of racialized segregation that existed in the United States from the Emancipation Proclamation of 1865 to the landmark civil rights legislation of the late 1960s. During this era, legal segregation was enforced by both law enforcement and white terror perpetrated by groups such as the Ku Klux Klan.

Journalists' professional routines: The daily activities around which news reporters organize their work.

Labeling theory: The theory that behaviors become defined as deviant when people in power socially construct deviant categories; often leads to the construction of types of deviant people.

Labor force: The segment of the population either employed or actively seeking employment.

Landraces: Local varieties of seeds that have been domesticated by communities over time and have adapted to local cultural and environmental needs.

Laparoscopic surgery: A modern surgical technique in which operations are performed through small incisions (usually 0.5–1.5 cm) as opposed to the larger incisions needed in laparotomy. Also known as minimally invasive surgery, Band-Aid surgery, and keyhole surgery.

Latent consequence: An unintended, covert, unplanned, and/or hidden effect or outcome of social phenomena or individual behaviors.

Latent function: An unintentional or unanticipated positive outcome of social institutions or policies.

Legislation: Enacted laws that make some condition or pattern of behavior legal or illegal.

Liberal feminism: A type of feminism that suggests men and women are essentially the same and gender inequality can be eliminated through the reduction of legal barriers to women's full participation in society.

Life expectancy: The average number of years a baby born in any given year can expect to live.

Looking-glass self: The idea that we see ourselves as we think others see us.

Lump of labor fallacy: The notion that there is a fixed number of jobs and that unemployed individuals can find jobs only when others lose their jobs or reduce the number of hours they work.

Magnet schools: Publicly funded schools designed to recruit students from across entire districts by offering particular disciplinary focuses, such as arts, technology, science, or mathematics.

***Mala in se* crimes:** Crimes that are illegal because they are bad in themselves or inherently wrong by nature.

***Mala prohibita* crimes:** Crimes that are illegal because they are prohibited by law.

Manifest consequence: An intended, overt, planned, and/or agreed-upon (by consensus) effect or outcome of social phenomena or individual behaviors.

Manifest function: The intended positive outcome of social institutions or policies; the reason they were designed or created.

Marriage dearth: The decline in the proportion of adult Americans who are married.

Marriage gradient: The tendency for women to "marry up"—that is, to marry older men.

Marriage movement: Social movement that advocates traditional marriage and warns against the sexual revolution, teenage pregnancy, and same-sex marriage.

Marriage squeeze: The severely imbalanced sex ratio experienced by black women in regard to potential marriage partners.

Marxist criminology: A view based on the writings of Karl Marx that sees the law as the mechanism by which the ruling class keeps the members of the surplus population in their disadvantaged position.

Matters of law: The legal process issues that arise during court proceedings and that are in the exclusive jurisdiction of a judge to resolve.

Maturing out: The decline and cessation of psychoactive drug use among younger people as they age into different social roles and responsibilities.

McDonaldization: The homogenization and rationalization that occur as culture and cultural privileges spread globally through economic expansion.

Media exaggeration: Strategies of dramatizing and embellishing media stories involving social issues to attract and hold the attention of an audience.

Media frames: Conventions of journalistic storytelling that situate a social problem within a broader context.

Media phobias: Fears about the negative impacts of media that lead to identifying media as the causes of persistent social problems.

Medicaid: A federal/state program that provides a variety of social services to those identified as eligible based on state-specific criteria.

Medicare: A federal health care program for those age 65 and over. The program is divided into four parts that address health coverage for services provided by physicians and hospitals as well as prescription drug coverage.

Megamachine: A new social order composed of humans and technology that is dominated by technological rather than human needs.

Meritocracy: A system in which personal advancement results from merit, based on knowledge and skill.

Metanarrative: An attempted comprehensive and universal explanation of some phenomenon.

Microfinance loans: Small loans made at low interest rates, usually given by nongovernmental organizations to women in developing countries.

Micropolitics: An individual's use of his or her own personal sphere of influence to affect social change.

Middleman minority: A racial group that is not in the majority but is held up by the majority as a "positive" example of a minority and is used by those in power to pit minority groups against each other.

Military-industrial complex: The relationships among government, the Pentagon, and defense contractors that promote the acquisition of weapons systems and a militarized foreign policy.

Mind: The internal conversations we have within ourselves.

Minority group: A group that does not hold a sizable share of power and resources in a society; often the share of such resources is disproportionately small relative to the group's numerical presence in the overall population, and the group has a history of being systemically excluded from those resources.

Mode 1: A type of scientific discovery or knowledge production done by scientists in universities through the application of experimental science within distinct disciplines.

Mode 2: A type of scientific discovery or knowledge production that is done by experts and nonexperts working together in transdisciplinary environments to create applications that are socially responsible.

Moral entrepreneurs: Advocates who organize to focus broad public attention on troubling issues.

Moral panics: Situations in which broad public fears and anxieties about particular social problems are disproportionate to the dangers of those problems.

Morbidity: The number of diagnoses of disease or other condition in a given population at a designated time, usually expressed as a rate per 100,000.

National Assessment of Educational Progress (NAEP): A congressionally mandated set of standardized tests intended to assess the progress of a sample of U.S. students at various grade levels from all demographic groups and all parts of the country.

National Education Association (NEA): The largest union representing teachers in the United States.

Natural recovery: A person's cessation of a drug habit without the assistance of a drug treatment program.

Needle exchange programs: Drug abuse harm reduction programs that provide new syringes to intravenous drug users who exchange used syringes.

New Urbanism: An approach to designing cities, towns, and neighborhoods aimed at reducing traffic and sprawl and increasing social interactions.

No Child Left Behind Act (NCLB): U.S. federal legislation passed in 2001 as the reauthorization of the Elementary and Secondary Education Act; established a range of reforms mandating uniform standards for all students with the aim of reducing and eventually eliminating the social class and race achievement gap by 2014.

Nonpsychotic psychological disturbance: A psychiatric character disorder that does not involve delusions.

Norms: Social rules.

North American Free Trade Agreement (NAFTA): A pact initiated in 1994 to stimulate trade among the United States, Canada, and Mexico by lowering or eliminating tariff barriers.

Objective aspect of social problems: Those empirical conditions or facts that point to the concreteness of social problems "out there."

Occupational segregation: The tendency of certain jobs to be predominantly filled on the basis of gender or according to race and ethnicity.

Old-age dependency ratio: The number of older persons ages 65 and over for every 100 adults between the ages of 16 and 64.

Opportunity theory: A theory of crime that says people will chose to commit crimes based on the criminal opportunities they have.

Paradigms: Theoretical perspectives.

Parole: The release, under supervision, of a convicted criminal defendant after he or she has completed part of his or her sentence, based on the concept that the defendant will follow the law and become a part of society.

Participant observation: A research method that includes observing and studying people in their everyday settings.

Paternalism: The system, principle, or practice of managing or governing individuals in the manner of a father dealing with his children.

Patriarchy: A society characterized by male dominance.

Personal Responsibility and Work Opportunity Reconciliation Act (PRWORA): U.S. federal legislation passed in 1996 that eliminated Assistance for Families with Dependent Children (AFDC) and established Temporary Assistance for Needy Families (TANF). Also known as welfare reform.

Pool of eligibles: The quantity and quality of potential partners for marriage.

Pornography: Sexually explicit material (video, photos, writings) intended to arouse and that may include transgressive representations of current aesthetic and cultural norms.

Post-traumatic stress disorder (PTSD): A mental health condition triggered by a terrifying event. Symptoms include flashbacks, nightmares, and severe anxiety, as well as thoughts about the event that cannot be controlled.

Poverty: Deficiencies in necessary material goods or desirable qualities, including economic, social, political, and cultural.

Poverty guidelines: A simplified version of the U.S. Census Bureau poverty thresholds, which take into account only family size; the poverty guidelines are used to set the federal poverty level (FPL).

Poverty rate: A measure of the number of individuals or groups in poverty, expressed in absolute or relative terms.

Poverty thresholds: Measures of poverty used by the U.S. Census Bureau that take into account family size, number of children, and their ages.

Power: The aspect of social structure related to political affiliations and connections.

Presumption of innocence: The principle that a criminal defendant is innocent until proven guilty, placing the burden on the government to establish proof of guilt beyond a reasonable doubt.

Primary deviance: In societal reaction theory, this refers to individuals' engagement in low-level offending, like speeding or experimenting with alcohol.

Primary sector: The sector of the economy centered on farming, fishing, and the extraction of raw materials.

Probation: An alternative to incarceration that offers an individual freedom if he or she can abide by the law and comply with the terms and conditions mandated by the court.

Product placement: A form of advertising in which products are used or mentioned by film or television characters.

Proletariat: In Marxist theory, the working class, which is at odds with the bourgeoisie.

Prostitution: The provision of sex in exchange for something, especially money. Contrast with sex work.

Psychological wage: Feelings of racial superiority accorded to poor/working-class whites in the absence of actual monetary compensation for labor.

Public arenas model: A model that offers a framework for analyzing the rise and fall in the amount of attention the public pays to different social problems.

Quantitative research: Research that studies social problems through statistical analysis.

Quintile: One-fifth of anything that can be divided.

Race: A socially and politically constructed category of persons that is often created with certain physical traits (e.g., skin color, eye color, eye shape, hair texture) in mind but can also incorporate religion, culture, nationality, and social class, depending on the time, place, and political/economic structure of the society.

Race relations cycle: A pathway of incorporation into a host society that immigrants follow; includes four stages: contact, competition, accommodation, and eventual assimilation.

Race to the Top (RTT): Federal program established by President Obama with the goal of aiding states in meeting the various components of NCLB by offering grants to states to improve student outcomes and close achievement gaps.

Racialization: The process by which a society incorporates and clearly demarcates individuals who fit a certain profile into a particular racial group.

Racism: A system that advantages the dominant racial group in a society.

Radical feminism: A version of feminist thought that suggests gender is a fundamental aspect of the way society functions and serves as an integral tool for distributing power and resources among people and groups.

Rape: Forced sexual intercourse involving penetration and psychological as well as physical coercion; attempted rape includes verbal threats of rape.

Rape myths: Assumptions about rape that tend to shift responsibility and blame to the victims.

Rational choice theory: A theory of crime that says humans are reasoning actors who weigh costs and benefits and make rational choices to commit crimes.

Realism: The point of view that the world is directly knowable.

Recidivism: The habit of reoffending.

Redevelopment: The rebuilding of parts of a city; sometimes large areas are completely demolished before being rebuilt, sometimes older buildings are preserved or updated.

Reflexive modernization: A form of economic development focused on revising current systems of production and making careful assessment of future outcomes of projects and decisions.

Rehabilitation: A goal of punishment that seeks to restore the offender to a more law-abiding life, free of the encumbrances that may have caused him or her to commit a crime.

Relative measure of poverty: A measure that looks at individuals or groups relative to the rest of their community or society rather than setting an absolute line.

Research methods: Techniques for obtaining information.

Resilience: The ability not just to bounce back from change or troubles but to spring forward into the future.

Retribution: Punishment that serves no purpose except to punish and communicate to the wrongdoer that his or her behavior is not tolerated.

Risk contract: The implicit understanding that government will enact rules to make sure people are protected as society bounds progressively forward.

Risk society: A society stratified by the ability to avoid risk.

Routine activities theory: The theory that crimes occur when motivated offenders come across suitable targets and a lack of capable guardians.

Routinization: The organizing and structuring of enemy-making behavior so thoroughly that there is no opportunity for raising moral questions.

Salary: Remuneration paid on a monthly or bimonthly basis and not directly tied to the number of hours worked.

School-centered explanations: Explanations of educational inequalities that focus on factors within the school, such as teachers and teaching methods, curriculum, ability grouping and curriculum tracking, school climate, and teacher expectations.

School choice: A school reform approach that theoretically allows market forces to shape school policies by offering parents a range of school options, including magnet schools, voucher schools, charter schools, traditional local public schools, and regular public schools.

School vouchers: An approach to school choice in which parents of school-age children receive government-issued vouchers of a certain monetary value that they can apply to tuition expenses at private schools.

Science: The accumulation of knowledge by specific methods within a particular culture that certifies, applies, and governs what is named science.

Science machine: A connection between science and society that is built by a community of individuals who share a common culture.

Science shops: Facilities hosted by universities where citizens can participate in science, ask scientific questions, and become part of the scientific process.

Secondary deviance: In societal reaction theory, this refers to individuals' engagement in more serious forms of crime after they have been labeled and treated as criminals.

Secondary sector: The sector of the economy that includes manufacturing and other activities that produce material goods.

Segmented assimilation: A theory acknowledging different segments of the host society into which an immigrant can assimilate (not just the white middle class).

Segregation: The practice of physically separating the occupants of some social statuses from the occupants of others.

Selection effect: In contrast to the experience effect, attitudes and characteristics that predispose an individual to a relationship outcome, such as divorce.

Self-fulfilling prophecy: The social process whereby a false definition of a situation brings about behavior that makes the false definition "come true."

Self-made myth: The belief that anyone can rise from humble beginnings to become wealthy and successful simply by applying him- or herself.

Self-regulation: A process whereby media industries propose to police themselves to stave off the imposition of government regulation.

Service sector: The sector of the economy that provides services such as education, health care, and government. Also known as the tertiary sector.

Service sociology: A socially responsible and mission-oriented sociology of action and alleviation.

Settlement houses: Neighborhood centers that provide services to poor immigrants.

Sex ratio: The number of males for every 100 females in the general population or within some designated segment, such as among those age 65 and over.

Sex role: The set of expectations attached to a particular sex category— male or female.

Sex tourism: Travel to destinations, typically in developing countries, specifically for the purpose of buying sex from men and women there.

Sex trafficking: A commercial, criminal activity that includes force, fraud, or coercion to exploit a person sexually for profit.

Sexual assault: An attempted or completed attack that includes unwanted sexual contact; may include coercion or force, fondling, or verbal threats.

Sexual dimorphism: The belief that there are two discrete types of people—male and female—who can be distinguished on the basis of real, objective, biological criteria.

Sexual dysfunction: The inability to fully experience sexual responses, arousal, and/or satisfaction, accompanied by distress over this inability.

Sexuality: Sexual behavior, attitudes, feelings.

Sexual script theory: The theory, developed by Gagnon and Simon in 1973, that humans create their sexualities within blueprints provided by cultural, interpersonal, and intrapsychic (mental) cues.

Sex work: Services provided by those in the commercial sex industry; the term is intended to destigmatize the work and providers of the labor (called sex workers).

Social class: A category of people whose experiences in life are determined by the amount of income and wealth they own and control.

Social constructionism: The social process by which people define a social problem into existence.

Social control: The ability of a strong group in society to control the actions of subordinate groups.

Social control theory: A theory of crime that assumes all people are capable of committing crimes and that some are stopped by their strong bonds to society.

Social disorganization theory: A theory that links crime rates to neighborhood ecological characteristics: poverty, residential mobility, and racial heterogeneity.

Social drift hypothesis: The argument that the sick, depressed, and stressed, through natural selection, move down the social system and accumulate at the bottom.

Social empathy: The insights individuals have about other people's lives that allow them to understand the circumstances and realities of other people's living conditions.

Social equity: Closely related to the concept of social equality, social equity stresses fairness and justice.

Social exchange theory: A theory that posits individuals will draw on personal resources to maximize rewards and minimize costs when forming, maintaining, or dissolving relationships.

Social facts: The ways of thinking, acting, and feeling that are external to the individual and exert pressure on the individual.

Social gradient of health: The consistent finding that inequality and health are related, with those at the top of the social system being healthier and living longer than those at the bottom.

Social inclusion: A sense of belonging to or membership in a group or a society.

Social institutions: Any set of persons, such as a family, economy, government, or religion, cooperating for the purpose of organizing stable patterns of human activity.

Social integration: The unity or cohesiveness of society.

Social interaction: The communication that occurs between two or more people.

Socialist feminism: A version of feminist thought that employs Marxist paradigms to view women as an oppressed social class.

Social mobility: Upward or downward movement in social position by groups or individuals over time.

Social movements: The collective efforts of people to realize social change in order to solve social problems.

Social order: The conformity of individuals to explicit and implicit social rules of behavior.

Social organization: The pattern of relationships between individuals and groups.

Social policy: A more or less clearly articulated and usually written set of strategies for addressing a social problem.

Social problem: A social condition, event, or pattern of behavior that negatively affects the well-being of a significant number of people (or a number of significant people) who believe that the condition, event, or pattern needs to be changed or ameliorated.

Social regulation: The control society has over the behavior of its members.

Social revolution: A total and complete transformation in the social structure of society.

Social role: A set of expectations attached to a particular status or position in society.

Social safety net: Public programs intended to help those who are most vulnerable in a society.

Social Security: A federal program that provides monthly benefit payments to older workers who have participated in the workforce and paid into the system.

Social self: A process by which people are able to see themselves in relationship to others.

Social structure: The pattern of interrelated social institutions.

Societal reaction theory: A theory of crime that argues that people become criminals based on how others respond to their actions.

Socioeconomic status (SES): A conceptualization of social class in terms of a continuum or index based on social and economic factors.

Sociological imagination: A form of self-consciousness that allows us to go beyond our immediate environments of family, neighborhood, and work and understand the major structural transformations that have occurred and are occurring.

Sociology: The study of social behavior and human society.

Sociology of education: The study of how various individuals and institutions throughout society affect the education system and educational outcomes.

Sociotechnical system: A system that includes material artifacts, human skills, and social practices defined by social norms within an organizational pattern to obtain or address a goal or objective.

Spatial mismatch theory: The theory that the movement of jobs away from central cities in the postindustrial era left many African Americans without employment.

Specialized courts: Problem-solving courts set up within local district courts to deal with social problems affecting the surrounding communities.

Specific deterrence: A law or policy written to stop those who break laws from offending again.

Spirituality: An underlying moral or value system, which may be in the absence of membership in a religious body or attendance at religious events.

Split labor market theory: The theory that white elites encourage divisions between working-class whites and blacks so that little unity can form between the two groups, preventing their coordinated revolt against exploitation.

Sponsor activities: The work of promoting and publicizing specific media frames.

Stakeholders: All individuals who have an interest in and are affected by the workings of a given system; in the criminal justice system, stakeholders include those accused of crimes as well as those who process cases, including police, attorneys, and court and correctional staff.

Status: Social position, revolving around characteristics such as education, prestige, and religious affiliation.

Status groups: Social groups that are either negatively or positively privileged.

Stereotype threat: The tendency of individuals to perform better or worse on standardized tests depending on what they have been told about their group's abilities.

Strain theory: A theory of crime that posits individuals commit crimes because of the strains caused by the imbalance between societally accepted goals and the individuals' inadequate means to achieve those goals.

Stress: The negative psychological and physiological effects of difficulties at work and elsewhere.

Structural functionalism (or functionalism): The sociological theory that considers how various social phenomena function, or work in a positive way, to maintain unity and order in society.

Structural unemployment: Unemployment that is caused by basic changes in the economy.

Student-centered explanations: Explanations of educational inequalities that focus on factors outside the school, such as the family, the community, the culture of the group, the peer group, and the individual student.

Subjective aspect of social problems: The process by which people define social problems.

Supplemental Nutrition Assistance Program (SNAP): Federal program that provides low-income Americans with subsidies for food purchases; formerly known as the food stamp program.

Survey: A research method that asks respondents to answer questions on a written questionnaire.

Symbolic ethnicity: An ethnicity that is not particularly salient in an individual's daily life and becomes relevant only at certain symbolic times or events.

Symbolic interactionism: The sociological perspective that sees society as the product of symbols (words, gestures, objects) given meaning by people in their interactions with each other.

Symbols: Words, gestures, and objects to which people give meaning.

Teach for America (TFA): A nonprofit organization that recruits students and professionals from high-profile institutions, trains these individuals to enter the teaching profession, and places them in disadvantaged schools for a period of at least two years.

Technocracy: A means of governing that is guided by rationality, expertise, and logic.

Technological fix: The use of technology to solve a social problem that is nontechnical. In fixing the problem it creates another, because the underlying social issue is still present and has been isolated from the social context.

Technology: An artifact that is composed of social practices, social institutions, and systems that create and constrain it.

Technoscience: A concept that encompasses the boundary between science and technology and includes all supporters, detractors, and social relations that work to eventually close the division between the categories of science and technology.

Terrorism: Violence perpetrated for political reasons by subnational groups or secret state agents, often directed at noncombatant targets, and usually intended to influence an audience.

Theory: A collection of related concepts.

Third places: Locations that serve social needs beyond work and home life (e.g., local coffee shops).

Tokenistic fallacy: The common misunderstanding that when a small number of persons from a minority group become successful in a society there must no longer be racism in that society.

Total compensation: Remuneration that includes a wage or salary plus benefits.

Total dependency ratio: The number of children under the age of 16 and the number of older persons age 65 and over for every 100 adults ages 16 to 64.

Tracking: An educational practice in which students are divided into groups, purportedly based on their academic ability.

Transactional sex: The exchange of money and gifts for sexual activities.

Transnational crime: Crime that has effects across national borders.

Treadmill of production: A theory that describes the ways that production is constantly accelerating without moving forward.

Underground economy: Work that is illegal or is designed to avoid the reporting of payments to government authorities such as tax collectors. Also known as the shadow economy.

Uniform Crime Reports (UCR): An official source of data on crime collected by the Federal Bureau of Investigation from police departments nationwide.

Urbanism: The ways of life or cultures of people in cities; the myths, symbols, and rituals of urbanites.

Urbanization: The movement of populations from rural to urban areas; the growth and development, and redevelopment, of cities.

Urban sprawl: The unplanned and unregulated growth of urban areas into surrounding areas.

User-generated media content: Publicly shared media content produced by users (often amateurs) rather than media companies.

Values: Social beliefs.

Veil: A metaphor for the physical and psychic separation between the dominant/majority group and subordinate/minority groups.

Visiting union: Unmarried parents who are romantically involved but living apart.

Wage: Payment for work done on an hourly basis.

War: Organized, collective fighting involving at least one political unit that seeks political or economic control over a territory or other important resource against another political unit or social group.

War on Drugs: The comprehensive policy first formulated by President Richard M. Nixon to address the drug problem in the 1970s.

Wealth: Assets (or possessions) or net worth (the difference between the value of assets and the amount of debt for an individual, family, or household).

Welfare state: Government provision of services essential to the well-being of large or significant segments of the population that are not possible or profitable within the private sector.

Whistle-blowing: The act of calling attention to malfeasance in one's organization.

White-collar crime: Illegal acts, punishable by criminal sanctions, committed in the course of legitimate occupations or by corporations.

White privilege: The often unseen or unacknowledged benefits that members of the majority group receive in a society unequally structured by race.

Workers: Those who own no property and must work for the capitalists in order to support themselves and their families financially.

REFERENCES

Abramovitz, Mimi. 2000. *Under Attack, Fighting Back: Women and Welfare in the United States.* New York: Monthly Review Press.

Abramovitz, Mimi, and Sandra Morgen. 2006. *Taxes Are a Woman's Issue: Reframing the Debate.* New York: Feminist Press at the City University of New York.

Adams, Gordon. 1981. *The Politics of Defense Contracting: The Iron Triangle.* New York. Council on Economic Priorities.

Adamson, Peter. 2012. *Measuring Child Poverty: New League Tables of Child Poverty in the World's Richest Countries.* Innocenti Research Centre, Report Card 10. Florence, Italy: UNICEF. http://www.unicef-irc.org/publications/pdf/rc10_eng.pdf.

Adelman, Larry. 2003. *Race: The Power of an Illusion.* DVD. San Francisco: California Newsreel.

Agnew, Robert. 1992. "Foundation for a General Strain Theory of Crime and Delinquency." *Criminology* 30(1): 47–88.

Agustín, Laura María. 2007. *Sex at the Margins: Migration, Labour Markets and the Rescue Industry.* London: Zed Books.

Agyeman, Julian, Robert D. Bullard, and Bob Evans. 2002. "Exploring the Nexus: Bringing Together Sustainability, Environmental Justice, and Equity." *Space and Polity* 6 (1): 77–90.

Agyeman, Julian, and Tom Evans. 2003. "Toward Just Sustainability in Urban Communities: Building Equity Rights with Sustainable Solutions." *Annals of the American Academy of Political and Social Science* 590: 35–53.

Alan Guttmacher Institute. 2013. "Facts on American Teens' Sexual and Reproductive Health." http://www.guttmacher.org/pubs/FB-ATSRH.html.

Alba, Richard, and Victor Nee. 2003. *Remaking the American Mainstream: Assimilation and Contemporary Immigration.* Cambridge, MA: Harvard University Press.

Albanese, Jay S. 2011. *Transnational Crime and the 21st Century: Criminal Enterprise, Corruption, and Opportunity.* New York: Oxford University Press.

Alexander, Michelle. 2012. *The New Jim Crow: Mass Incarceration in the Age of Colorblindness.* New York: New Press.

Aliverdinia, Akbar, and William Alex Pridemore. 2009. "Women's Fatalistic Suicide in Iran: A Partial Test of Durkheim in an Islamic Republic." *Violence against Women* 15 (3): 307–20.

Alkon, Alison Hope, and Julian Agyeman, eds. 2011. *Cultivating Food Justice: Race, Class, and Sustainability.* Cambridge: MIT Press.

Allan, Kenneth. 2011. *The Social Lens: An Invitation to Social and Sociological Theory,* 2nd ed. Thousand Oaks, CA: Pine Forge Press.

Allen, Charlotte. 2010. "The Quiet Preference for Men in Admissions." Minding the Campus, Manhattan Institute, June 7. http://www.mindingthecampus.com/originals/2010/06/the_quiet_preference_for_men_i.html.

Allen, Louisa. 2012. "Pleasure's Perils? Critically Reflecting on Pleasure's Inclusion in Sexuality Education." *Sexualities* 15 (3–4): 455–71.

Allison, Rachel, and Barbara J. Risman. 2013. "A Double Standard for 'Hooking Up': How Far Have We Come toward Gender Equality?" *Social Science Research* 42 (5): 1191–1206.

———. 2014. "'It Goes Hand in Hand with the Parties': Race, Class, and Residence in College Student Negotiations of Hooking Up." *Sociological Perspectives* 57 (1): 102–23.

Allport, Gordon. 1954. *The Nature of Prejudice.* Cambridge, MA: Addison-Wesley.

Almodovar, Norma Jean. 2010. "The Consequences of Arbitrary and Selective Enforcement of Prostitution Laws." *Wagadu: A Journal of Transnational Women's and Gender Studies* 8: 241–57.

Altheide, David L. 2002. *Creating Fear: News and the Construction of Crisis.* Piscataway, NJ: Aldine Transaction.

———. 2009. "Moral Panic: From Sociological Concept to Public Discourse." *Crime, Media, Culture* 5 (1): 79–99.

Alvaredo, Facundo, Anthony B. Atkinson, Thomas Piketty, and Emmanuel Saez. 2013. "The Top 1 Percent in International and Historical Perspective." *Journal of Economic Perspectives* 27 (3): 3–20.

Alvarez, Maria João, and Leonel Garcia-Marques. 2008. "Condom Inclusion in Cognitive Representations of Sexual Encounters." *Journal of Sex Research* 45 (4): 358–70.

American Academy of Pediatrics. 2012. "Familiarity with Television Fast-Food Ads Linked to Obesity." April 29. http://www.aap.org/en-us/about-the-aap/aap-press-room/pages/Familiarity-With-Television-Fast-Food-Ads-Linked-to-Obesity.aspx.

American Bar Association. 2013. *A Current Glance at Women in the Law, February 2013.* Chicago: ABA, Commission on Women in the Profession. http://www.americanbar.org/content/dam/aba/marketing/women/current_glance_statistics_feb2013.authcheckdam.pdf.

American Bar Association, Section of Family Law. 2012. "Family Law in the Fifty States: Case Digests." *Family Law Quarterly* 45. http://www.americanbar.org/content/dam/aba/publications/family_law_quarterly/v0145/4win12_chart4_divorce.authcheckdam.pdf.

American Psychiatric Association. 2013. *Highlights of Changes from DSM-IV-TR to DSM-5.* Arlington, VA: American Psychiatric Association. http://www.dsm5

.org/Documents/changes%20from%20dsm-iv-tr%20 to%20dsm-5.pdf.

Amster, Randall. 2004. *Street People and the Contested Realms of Public Space.* El Paso, TX: LFB Scholarly Publishing.

Anderson, Elijah. 1990. *Streetwise: Race, Class, and Change in an Urban Community.* Chicago: University of Chicago Press.

———. 1999. *Code of the Street: Decency, Violence, and the Moral Life of the Inner City.* New York: W. W. Norton.

Andreas, Peter. 2008. *Blue Helmets and Black Markets: The Business of Survival in the Siege of Sarajevo.* Ithaca, NY: Cornell University Press.

Angell, Marcia. 2005. *The Truth about Drug Companies: How They Deceive Us and What to Do about It.* New York: Random House.

Angelon-Gaetz, Kim A., David B. Richardson, and Steve Wing. 2010. "Inequalities in the Nuclear Age: Impact of Race and Gender on Radiation Exposure at the Savannah River Site (1951–1999)." *New Solutions* 20 (2): 195–210.

Anyon, Jean. 1997. *Ghetto Schooling: A Political Economy of Urban Educational Reform.* New York: Teachers College Press.

———. 2005. *Radical Possibilities: Public Policy, Urban Education, and a New Social Movement.* New York: Routledge.

Archdiocese of Minneapolis and Saint Paul. 2010. *Preserving Marriage in Minnesota.* DVD. Minneapolis and Saint Paul, Office of the Archbishop (John C. Nienstedt).

Armstrong, Elizabeth A., Paula England, and Alison C. K. Fogarty. 2010. "Orgasm in College Hookups and Relationships." In *Families as They Really Are,* edited by Barbara Risman, 362–77. New York: W. W. Norton.

Armstrong, Elizabeth A., and Laura T. Hamilton. 2013. *Paying for the Party: How College Maintains Inequality.* Cambridge, MA: Harvard University Press.

Armstrong, Elizabeth A., Laura Hamilton, and Brian Sweeney. 2006. "Sexual Assault on Campus: A Multilevel, Integrative Approach to Party Rape." *Social Problems* 53 (4): 483–99.

Arnold, Ryan. 2013. "Persistent Rape Culture at Amherst College." AC Voice, April 24. http://acvoice .com/2013/04/24/persistent-rape-culture-at-amherst-college.

Arnot, Madeleine. 2002. *Reproducing Gender: Selected Critical Essays on Educational Theory and Feminist Politics.* London: Falmer.

Associated Press. 2003. "Racial Profiling Study: Police Stop Minorities More Often than Whites." *Brainerd Dispatch,* September 24.

Association of Religion Data Archives. 2010. "U.S. Membership Report." http://thearda.com/rcms2010/r/u/ rcms2010_99_US_name_2010.asp.

Atchley, Robert C. 1989. "A Continuity Theory of Normal Aging." *Gerontologist* 29 (2): 183–90.

Aubrey, Jennifer Stevens, and Siobhan E. Smith. 2013. "Development and Validation of the Endorsement of the Hookup Culture Index." *Journal of Sex Research* 50 (5): 435–48.

Aud, Susan, Mary Ellen Fox, and Angelina KewalRamani. 2010. *Status and Trends in the Education of Racial and Ethnic Groups.* U.S. Department of Education, National Center for Education Statistics, NCES 2010-015. Washington, DC: Government Printing Office. http:// nces.ed.gov/pubs2010/2010015.pdf.

Aud, Susan, William Hussar, Frank Johnson, Grace Kena, Erin Roth, Eileen Manning, Xiaolei Wang, and Jijun Zhang. 2012. *The Condition of Education 2012.* U.S. Department of Education, National Center for Education Statistics, NCES 2012-045. Washington, DC: Government Printing Office. http://nces.ed.gov/ pubs2012/2012045.pdf.

AugsJoost, Brett, Petra Jerman, Julianna Deardorff, Kim Harley, and Norman A. Constantine. 2014. "Factors Associated with Parent Support for Condom Education and Availability." *Health Education and Behavior* 41 (2): 207–15.

Australian Institute of Health and Welfare. 2006. *Australia's Health 2006: The Tenth Biennial Health Report of the Australian Institute of Health and Welfare.* AIHW Cat. No. AUS 73. Canberra: Australian Institute of Health and Welfare.

Australian Safety and Compensation Council. 2006. *Estimating the Number of Work Related Traumatic Injury Fatalities in Australia 2003–04.* Canberra: Commonwealth of Australia.

Autor, David, and Melanie Wasserman. 2013. *Wayward Sons: The Emerging Gender Gap in Labor Markets and Education.* Washington, DC: Third Way. http:// economics.mit.edu/files/8754.

Avis, Nancy E., and Sybil Crawford. 2008. "Cultural Differences in Symptoms and Attitudes toward Menopause. *Menopause Management* 17(3): 8–13.

Bachman, Ronet, and Michelle Meloy. 2008. "The Epidemiology of Violence against the Elderly: Implications for Primary and Secondary Prevention." *Journal of Contemporary Criminal Justice* 24 (2): 186–97.

Baker, David, and Gerald K. LeTendre. 2005. *National Differences, Global Similarities: World Culture and the Future of Schooling.* Stanford, CA: Stanford Social Sciences.

Baker, Peter. 2013. "Pivoting from a War Footing, Obama Acts to Curtail Drones." *New York Times,* May 23, 1.

Baldwin, Laura-Mae, David C. Grossman, Susan Casey, Walter Hollow, Jonathan R. Sugarman, William L. Freeman, and L. Gary Hart. 2002. "Perinatal and Infant Health among Rural and Urban American Indians/Alaska Natives." *American Journal of Public Health* 92 (9): 1491–97.

Banks, Duren, and Denise C. Gottfredson. 2004. "Participation in Drug Treatment Court and Time to Rearrest." *Justice Quarterly* 21 (3): 637–58.

Barnes, Brooks. 2012. "Promoting Nutrition: Disney to Restrict Junk-Food Ads." *New York Times,* June 5, B1.

Barnes, Patricia M., Barbara Bloom, and Richard L. Nahin. 2008. *Complementary and Alternative Medicine Use among Adults and Children: United States, 2007.* National Health Statistics Reports 12 (December 10). Hyattsville, MD: National Center for Health Statistics. http://www.cdc.gov/nchs/data/nhsr/nhsr012.pdf.

Bartholow, Bruce D., Marc A. Sestir, and Edward B. Davis. 2005. "Correlates and Consequences of Exposure to Video Game Violence: Hostile Personality, Empathy, and Aggressive Behavior." *Personality and Social Psychology Bulletin* 31 (11): 1573–86.

Bash, Michael Rodning. 2012. "Avoid This Concept in Defining Marriage: 'Natural.'" *Star Tribune,* November 2. http://www.startribune.com/opinion/commentaries/177031211.html.

Bassett, Laura. 2010. "Study: Longterm Unemployment Has Disastrous Effects on Health and Longevity." Huffington Post, November 5. http://www.huffingtonpost.com/2010/11/05/study-longtermunemployme_n_779743.html.

BBC News. 2013a. "Same-Sex Marriage Becomes Law in England and Wales." July 17. http://www.bbc.com/news/uk-politics-23338279.

———. 2013b. "Same-Sex Marriage: French Parliament Approves New Law." April 23. http://www.bbc.com/news/world-europe-22261494.

Beauregard, Robert A. 2011. "Radical Uniqueness and the Flight of Urban Theory." In *The City, Revisited: Urban Theory from Chicago, Los Angeles, and New York,* edited by Dennis R. Judd and Dick Simpson, 186–202. Minneapolis: University of Minnesota Press.

Beck, Harold L., and Burton G. Bennett. 2002. "Historical Overview of Atmospheric Nuclear Weapons Testing and Estimates of Fallout in the Continental United States." *Health Physics* 82 (5): 591–608.

Beck, Ulrich. 1992. *Risk Society: Towards a New Modernity.* London: Sage.

Beck, Ulrich, Anthony Giddens, and Scott Lash. 1994. *Reflexive Modernization: Politics, Tradition and Aesthetics in the Modern Social Order.* Cambridge: Polity Press.

Becker, Howard S. 1963a. "Becoming a Marihuana User." In *Outsiders: Studies in the Sociology of Deviance,* 41–58. New York: Macmillan.

———. 1963b. *Outsiders: Studies in the Sociology of Deviance.* New York: Macmillan.

Becker, Jo, and Scott Shane. 2012. "Secret 'Kill List' Proves a Test of Obama's Principles and Will." *New York Times,* May 29.

Beckett, Katherine, Kris Nyrop, Lori Pfingst, and Melissa Bowen. 2005. "Drug Use, Drug Possession Arrests, and the Question of Race: Lessons from Seattle." *Social Problems* 52 (3): 419–41.

Belknap, Joanne. 2007. "Culturally Focused Batterer Counseling." *Criminology & Public Policy* 6 (2): 337–40.

Bell, Michael Mayerfeld. 2004. *Farming for Us All: Practical Agriculture and the Cultivation of Sustainability.* University Park: Pennsylvania State University Press.

———. 2012. *An Invitation to Environmental Sociology,* 4th ed. Thousand Oaks, CA: Pine Forge Press.

Bell, Michael Mayerfeld, and Philip Lowe. 2000. "Regulated Freedoms: The Market and the State, Agriculture and the Environment." *Journal of Rural Studies* 16 (3): 285–94.

Benach, Joan, and Carles Muntaner. 2007. "Precarious Employment and Health: Developing a Research Agenda." *Journal of Epidemiology and Community Health* 61: 276–77.

Bengtson, Vern L., Norella M. Putney, and Malcolm L. Johnson. 2005. "The Problem of Theory in Gerontology Today." In *The Cambridge Handbook of Age and Ageing,* edited by Malcolm L. Johnson, 3–20. Cambridge: Cambridge University Press.

Bennett, Lisa, and Gary J. Gates. 2004. *The Cost of Marriage Inequality to Children and Their Same-Sex Parents.* Washington, DC: Human Rights Campaign.

Berkowitz, Bill. 2002. "The Mullahs of Marriage." *The Nation,* May 14. Retrieved July 9, 2010 (www.thenation.com/article/mullahs-marriage).

Berkowitz, Dan, and William Marsiglio. 2007. "Gay Men: Negotiating Procreative, Father, and Family Identities." *Journal of Marriage and Family* 69: 366–81.

Berkowitz, Eric. 2012. *Sex and Punishment: Four Thousand Years of Judging Desire.* Berkeley, CA: Counterpoint Press.

Berliner, David C. 2006. "Our Impoverished View of Educational Research." *Teachers College Record* 108 (6): 949–95.

Berliner, David C., and Bruce J. Biddle. 1995. *The Manufactured Crisis: Myths, Fraud, and the Attack* on *America's Public Schools.* Reading, MA: Addison-Wesley.

Bernstein, Basil. 1973a. *Class, Codes and Control.* Vol. 1, *Theoretical Studies towards a Sociology of Language.* London: Routledge & Kegan Paul. First published 1971.

———. 1973b. *Class, Codes and Control.* Vol. 2, *Applied Studies towards a Sociology of Language.* London: Routledge & Kegan Paul. First published 1971.

———. 1977a. "Class and Pedagogies: Visible and Invisible" (rev. ed.). In *Class, Codes and Control.* Vol. 3, *Towards a Theory of Educational Transmissions,* 116–56. London: Routledge & Kegan Paul.

———. 1977b. *Class, Codes and Control.* Vol. 3, *Towards a Theory of Educational Transmissions.* London: Routledge & Kegan Paul. First published 1975.

———. 1990. "Social Class and Pedagogic Practice." In *Class, Codes and Control.* Vol. 4, *The Structuring of Pedagogic Discourse,* 63–93. London: Routledge.

———. 1996. *Pedagogy, Symbolic Control and Identity: Theory, Research, Critique.* London: Taylor & Francis.

Bersamin, Melina M., Mallie J. Paschall, Robert F. Saltz, and Byron L. Zamboanga. 2012. "Young Adults and Casual Sex: The Relevance of College Drinking Settings." *Journal of Sex Research* 49 (2–3): 274–81.

Bertrand, Marianne, and Sendhil Mullainathan. 2004. "Are Emily and Greg More Employable than Lakisha and Jamal? A Field Experiment on Labor Market Discrimination." *American Economic Review* 94 (4): 991–1013.

Best, Joel. 1999. *Random Violence: How We Talk about New Crimes and New Victims.* Berkeley: University of California Press.

Bettie, Julie. 2003. *Women without Class: Girls, Race, and Identity.* Berkeley: University of California Press.

Bewley-Taylor, Dave, Chris Hallam, and Rob Allen. 2009. *The Incarceration of Drug Offenders: An Overview.* London: Beckley Foundation Drug Policy Programme.

Binh, Vu Ngoc. 2006. "Trafficking of Women and Children in Vietnam: Current Issues and Problems." In *Trafficking and the Global Sex Industry,* edited by Karen Beeks and Delila Amir, 33–43. Lanham, MD: Lexington Books.

Bix, Amy Sue. 2000. *Inventing Ourselves Out of Jobs? America's Debate over Technological Unemployment, 1929–1981.* Baltimore: Johns Hopkins University Press.

Black, Michele C., Kathleen C. Basile, Matthew J. Breiding, Sharon G. Smith, Mikel L. Walters, Melissa T. Merrick, Jieru Chen, and Mark R. Stevens. 2011. *The National Intimate Partner and Sexual Violence Survey (NISVS): 2010 Summary Report.* Atlanta, GA: National Center for Injury Prevention and Control, Centers for Disease Control and Prevention. http://www.cdc.gov/ViolencePrevention/pdf/NISVS_Report2010-a.pdf.

Blakeborough, Darren. 2008. "'Old People Are Useless': Representations of Aging on *The Simpsons.*" *Canadian Journal on Aging* 27 (1): 57–67.

Blanchflower, David G., and Alex Bryson. 2007 "What Effect Do Unions Have on Wages Now and Would Freeman and Medoff Be Surprised?" In *What Do Unions Do? A Twenty-Year Perspective,* edited by James T. Bennett and Bruce E. Kaufman, 79–113. New Brunswick, NJ: Transaction.

Blascovich, Jim, Steven J. Spencer, Diane Quinn, and Claude Steele. 2001. "African Americans and High Blood Pressure: The Role of Stereotype Threat." *Psychological Science* 12 (3): 225–29.

Blauner, Bob. 1996. "Talking Past Each Other: Black and White Languages of Race." In *The Meaning of Difference: American Constructions of Race, Sex and Gender, Social Class, and Sexual Orientation,* edited by Karen E. Rosenblum and Toni-Michelle C. Travis, 167–76. New York: McGraw-Hill.

Blow, Charles M. 2012. "The Curious Case of Trayvon Martin." *New York Times,* March 16. http://www.nytimes.com/2012/03/17/opinion/blow-the-curious-case-of-trayvon-martin.html.

Blumer, Herbert. 1933. *Movies, Delinquency, and Crime.* New York: Macmillan.

———. 1971. "Social Problems as Collective Behavior." *Social Problems* 18: 298–306.

Bobo, Kim. 2009. *Wage Theft in America: Why Millions of Working Americans Are Not Getting Paid—and What We Can Do about It.* New York: New Press.

Boero, Natalie, and C. J. Pascoe. 2012. "Pro-anorexia Communities and Online Interaction: Bringing the Pro-ana Body Online." *Body & Society* 18 (2): 27–57.

Bogenschneider, Karen, and Thomas J. Corbett. 2010. "Becoming a Field of Inquiry and a Subfield of Social Policy." *Journal of Marriage and Family* 72: 783–803.

Bonacich, Edna. 1972. "A Theory of Ethnic Antagonism: The Split Labor Market." *American Sociological Review* 37: 547–59.

Bonacich, Edna, and John Modell. 1980. *The Economic Basis of Ethnic Solidarity: Small Business in the Japanese American Community.* Berkeley: University of California Press.

Bonczar, Thomas P. 2003. *Prevalence of Imprisonment in the U.S. Population, 1974–2001.* U.S. Bureau of Justice Statistics, NCJ 197976. Washington, DC: U.S. Department of Justice. http://www.bjs.gov/content/pub/pdf/piusp01.pdf.

Bongaarts, John. 2004. "Population Aging and the Rising Cost of Public Pensions." *Population and Development Review* 30 (1): 1–23.

Bonilla-Silva, Eduardo. 2001. *White Supremacy and Racism in the Post–Civil Rights Era.* Boulder, CO: Lynne Rienner.

———. 2010. *Racism without Racists: Color-Blind Racism and the Persistence of Racial Inequality in America,* 3rd ed. Boulder, CO: Rowman & Littlefield.

Borer, Michael Ian. 2008. *Faithful to Fenway: Believing in Boston, Baseball, and America's Most Beloved Ballpark.* New York: New York University Press.

———. 2010. "From Collective Memory to Collective Imagination: Time, Place, and Urban Redevelopment." *Symbolic Interaction* 33 (1): 96–114.

Borer, Michael Ian, and Daniel J. Monti Jr. 2006. "Community, Commerce, and Consumption: Businesses as Civic Associations." In *Varieties of Urban Experience: The American City and the Practice of Culture,* edited by Michael Ian Borer. Lanham, MD: University Press of America.

Borman, Geoffrey, and Maritza Dowling. 2010. "Schools and Inequality: A Multilevel Analysis of Coleman's Equality of Educational Opportunity Data." *Teachers College Record* 112 (5): 1201–46.

Bornstein, Kate. 1994. *Gender Outlaw: On Men, Women, and the Rest of Us.* New York: Vintage Books.

Bourdieu, Pierre. 1977. *Outline of a Theory of Practice.* Cambridge: Cambridge University Press.

———. 1984. *Distinction: A Social Critique of the Judgment of Taste.* Cambridge, MA: Harvard University Press.

———. 1990. *The Logic of Practice.* Cambridge: Polity.

Bourdieu, Pierre, and Jean-Claude Passeron. 1977. *Reproduction in Education, Society and Culture.* London: Sage.

Bourgois, Philippe. 1995. *In Search of Respect: Selling Crack in El Barrio.* Cambridge: Cambridge University Press.

Bourgois, Philippe, and Jeff Schonberg. 2009. *Righteous Dopefiend.* Berkeley: University of California Press.

Bowleg, Lisa, Kenya J. Lucas, and Jeanne M. Tschann. 2004. "'The Ball Was Always in His Court': An Exploratory Analysis of Relationship Scripts, Sexual Scripts, and Condom Use among African American Women." *Psychology of Women Quarterly* 28 (1): 70–82.

Bowles, Samuel, and Herbert Gintis. 1976. *Schooling in Capitalist America: Educational Reform and the Contradictions of Economic Life.* New York: Basic Books.

Boyle, Justin. 2013. "Millions of Americans Looking to Change Careers, Study Shows." Degree360, July 15. http://www.onlinedegrees.com/degree360/workplace/millions-of-americans-looking-to-change-careers.html.

Braga, Anthony A., and David L. Weisburd. 2010. *Policing Problem Places: Crime Hot Spots and Effective Prevention.* New York: Oxford University Press.

Brents, Barbara G., and Kathryn Hausbeck. 2005. "Violence and Legalized Brothel Prostitution in Nevada: Examining Safety, Risk, and Prostitution Policy." *Journal of Interpersonal Violence* 20 (3): 270–95.

Breslau, Daniel. 2007. "The American Spencerians: Theorizing a New Science." In *Sociology in America: A History,* edited by Craig Calhoun, 39–62. Chicago: University of Chicago Press.

Brewis, Joanna, and Stephen Linstead. 2000. "'The Worst Thing Is the Screwing': Consumption and the Management of Identity in Sex Work." *Gender, Work & Organization* 7 (2): 84–97.

Bricker, Jesse, Arthur B. Kennickell, Kevin B. Moore, and John Sabelhaus. 2012. "Changes in U.S. Family Finances from 2007 to 2010: Evidence from the Survey of Consumer Finances." *Federal Reserve Bulletin* 98 (2): 1–80. http://www.federalreserve.gov/pubs/bulletin/2012/pdf/scf12.pdf.

Bridger, Jeffrey C. 1996. "Community Imagery and the Built Environment." *Sociological Quarterly* 37 (3): 353–74.

Bridges, Ana J., Robert Wosnitzer, Erica Scharrer, Chyng Sun, and Rachael Liberman. 2010. "Aggression and Sexual Behavior in Best-Selling Pornography Videos: A Content Analysis Update." *Violence against Women* 16 (10): 1065–85.

Brint, Steven G. 2006. *Schools and Societies,* 2nd ed. Stanford, CA: Stanford University Press.

British Psychological Society. 2011. "Response to the American Psychiatric Association: DSM-5 Development." http://apps.bps.org.uk/_publicationfiles/consultation-responses/DSM-5%202011%20-%20BPS%20response.pdf.

Britz, Jennifer Delahunty. 2006. "To All the Girls I've Rejected." *New York Times,* March 23. http://www.nytimes.com/2006/03/23/opinion/23britz.html?_r=1.

Broaddus, Michelle R., Heather Morris, and Angela D. Bryan. 2010. "'It's Not What You Said, It's How You Said It': Perceptions of Condom Proposers by Gender and Strategy." *Sex Roles* 62 (9–10): 603–14.

Brooks, Siobhan. 2010. "Hypersexualization and the Dark Body: Race and Inequality among Black and Latina Women in the Exotic Dance Industry." *Sexuality Research and Social Policy* 7 (2): 70–80.

Broom, Alex. 2005. "Medical Specialists' Accounts of the Impact of the Internet on the Doctor/Patient Relationship." *Health* 9 (3): 319–38.

Brosius, Hans-Bernd, and Hans Mathias Kepplinger. 1990. "The Agenda Setting Function of Television News: Static and Dynamic Views." *Communication Research* 17 (2): 183–211.

Brown, Jane D., and Piotr S. Bobkowski. 2011. "Older and Newer Media: Patterns of Use and Effects on Adolescents' Health and Well-Being." *Journal of Research on Adolescence* 21 (1): 95–113.

Brunkard, Joan, Gonza Namulanda, and Raoult Ratard. 2008. "Hurricane Katrina Deaths, Louisiana, 2005." *Disaster Medicine and Public Health Preparedness* 2 (4): 215–23.

Bryant, Clifton D., and Kenneth B. Perkins. 1982. "Containing Work Disaffection: The Poultry Processing Worker." In *Varieties of Work,* edited by Phyllis L. Stewart and Muriel G. Cantor, 199–212. Beverly Hills, CA: Sage.

Brynjolffson, Erik, and Andrew McAfee. 2011. *Race against the Machine.* Lexington, MA: Digital Frontier Press.

Bubolz, Margaret M., and M. Suzanne Sontag. 1993. "Human Ecology Theory." In *Sourcebook of Family Theories and Methods: A Contextual Approach,* edited by Pauline G. Boss, William J. Doherty, Ralph LaRossa, Walter R. Schumm, and Suzanne K. Steinmetz, 419–48. New York: Plenum.

Budd, John W. 2007. "The Effect of Unions on Non-wage Compensation: Monopoly Power, Collective Voice, and Facilitation." In *What Do Unions Do? A Twenty-Year Perspective,* edited by James T. Bennett and Bruce E. Kaufman. New Brunswick, NJ: Transaction.

Budrys, Grace. 2012. *Our Unsystematic Health Care System,* 3rd ed. Lanham, MD: Rowman & Littlefield.

Buhaug, Halvard, Nils Petter Gleditsch, and Ole Magnus Theisen. 2010. "Implications of Climate Change for Armed Conflict." In *Social Dimensions of Climate Change: Equity and Vulnerability in a Warming World,* edited by Robin Mearns and Andrew Norton, 75–102. Washington, DC: World Bank.

Bullard, Robert. 2000. *Dumping in Dixie: Race, Class, and Environmental Quality.* Boulder, CO: Westview Press.

Burgard, Sarah. 2012. "Is the Recession Making Us Sick?" *Pathways* (Fall): 19–23.

Burgess, Ernest W. 1925. "The Growth of the City: An Introduction to a Research Project." In *The City,* by Robert E. Park, Ernest W. Burgess, and Roderick D. McKenzie, 47–62. Chicago: University of Chicago Press.

Burk, James. 2008. "Military Culture." In *Encyclopedia of Violence, Peace, and Conflict,* edited by Lester Kurtz. Oxford: Elsevier Science and Technology.

Calhoun, Craig. 2007. "Sociology in America: An Introduction." In *Sociology in America: A History,* edited by Craig Calhoun, 1–38. Chicago: University of Chicago Press.

Callon, Michel, John Law, and Arie Rip. 1986. *Mapping the Dynamics of Science and Technology: Sociology of Science in the Real World.* Basingstoke, England: Macmillan.

Calnan, Michael, and Sarah Cant. 1990. "The Social Organisation of Food Consumption: A Comparison of Middle Class and Working Class Households." *International Journal of Sociology and Social Policy* 10 (2): 53–79.

Camacho, David E., ed. 1998. *Environmental Injustices, Political Struggles: Race, Class, and the Environment.* Durham, NC: Duke University Press.

Campbell, Scott. 1996. "Green Cities, Growing Cities, Just Cities? Urban Planning and the Contradictions of Sustainable Development. *Journal of the American Planning Association* 62 (3): 296–312.

CareerBuilder. 2013. "More Employers Finding Reasons Not to Hire Candidates on Social Media, Finds CareerBuilder Survey." June 27. http://www.career builder.com/share/aboutus/pressreleasesdetail.aspx?sd =6%2F26%2F2013&id=pr766&ed=12%2F31%2F2013.

Carnagey, Nicholas L., Craig A. Anderson, and Brad J. Bushman. 2007. "The Effect of Video Game Violence on Physiological Desensitization to Real-Life Violence." *Journal of Experimental Social Psychology* 43 (3): 489–96.

Carnevale, Anthony P., Stephen J. Rose, and Ban Cheah. 2011. *The College Payoff: Education, Occupations, Lifetime Earnings.* Washington, DC: Georgetown University Center on Education and the Workforce.

Carson, E. Ann, and William J. Sabol. 2012. *Prisoners in 2011.* Bureau of Justice Statistics Bulletin NCJ 239808, December. Washington, DC: U.S. Department of Justice. http://www.bjs.gov/content/pub/pdf/p11.pdf.

Carson, Rachel. 1962. *Silent Spring.* Boston: Houghton Mifflin.

Carter, Prudence L. 2005. *Keepin' It Real: School Success beyond Black and White.* New York: Oxford University Press.

Carter, Vednita, and Evelyn Giobbe. 2006. "Duet: Prostitution, Racism, and Feminist Discourse." In *Prostitution and Pornography: Philosophical Debate about the Sex Industry,* edited by Jessica Spector, 17–39. Stanford, CA: Stanford University Press.

Cartwright, Samuel. 1851. "Report on the Diseases and Physical Peculiarities of the Negro Race." *New Orleans Medical and Surgical Journal* (May): 691–715.

Casper, Monica J., and Adele E. Clarke. 1998. "Making the Pap Smear into the 'Right Tool' for the Job: Cervical Cancer Screening in the USA, circa 1940–95." *Social Studies of Science* 28 (2): 255–90.

Castells, Manuel. 1977. *The Urban Question: A Marxist Approach.* Cambridge: MIT Press.

———. 2000. *The Information Age: Economy, Society, and Culture.* Oxford: Blackwell.

Cavan, Ruth S., E. W. Burgess, Robert J. Havighurst, and Herbert Goldhamer. 1949. *Personal Adjustment in Old Age.* Chicago. Science Research Associates.

Centers for Disease Control and Prevention. 2001. *Births, Marriages, Divorces, and Deaths: Provisional Data for January–December 2000.* National Vital Statistics Reports 49, no. 6. Hyattsville, MD: National Center for

Health Statistics. http://www.cdc.gov/nchs/data/nvsr/nvsr49/nvsr49_06.pdf.

———. 2010a. *Births, Marriages, Divorces, and Deaths: Provisional Data for 2009.* National Vital Statistics Reports 58, no. 25. Hyattsville, MD: National Center for Health Statistics. http://www.cdc.gov/nchs/data/nvsr/nvsr58/nvsr58_25.pdf.

———. 2010b. "Increasing Prevalence of Parent-Reported Attention-Deficit/Hyperactivity Disorder among Children—United States, 2003 and 2007." *Morbidity and Mortality Weekly Report,* November 12, 1439–43. http://www.cdc.gov/mmwr/preview/mmwrhtml/mm5944a3.htm.

———. 2011. "CDC Health Disparities and Inequalities Report—United States, 2011." *Morbidity and Mortality Weekly Report,* Supplement, January 11.

———. 2012a. "Binge Drinking: Nationwide Problem, Local Solutions." *Vital Signs,* January. http://www.cdc.gov/vitalsigns/pdf/2012-01-vitalsigns.pdf.

———. 2012b. "Intimate Partner Violence: Definitions." Accessed December 31. http://www.cdc.gov/ViolencePrevention/intimatepartnerviolence/definitions.html.

———. 2012c. "Marriage and Divorce." Accessed November 25. http://www.cdc.gov/nchs/fastats/divorce.htm.

———. 2012d. "STD Trends in the United States: 2011 National Data for Chlamydia, Gonorrhea, and Syphilis." Fact sheet. http://www.cdc.gov/STD/stats11/trends-2011.pdf.

———. 2013a. "Antismoking Messages and Intention to Quit—17 Countries, 2008–2011." *Morbidity and Mortality Weekly Report,* May 31, 417–22. http://www.cdc.gov/mmwr/pdf/wk/mm6221.pdf.

———. 2013b. "Attention-Deficit/Hyperactivity Disorder: Symptoms and Diagnosis." Accessed October 10. http://www.cdc.gov/ncbddd/adhd/diagnosis.html.

———. 2013c. "HIV in the United States: At a Glance." http://www.cdc.gov/hiv/statistics/basics/ataglance.html.

Cervantes, Mario. 2014. "Scientists and Engineers: Crisis, What Crisis?" OECD Observer, accessed April 24. http://www.oecdobserver.org/news/archivestory.php/aid/1160/Scientists_and_engineers.html.

Chambliss, William J. 1999. *Power, Politics, and Crime.* Boulder, CO: Westview Press.

Chandola, Tarani. 2000. "Social Class Differences in Mortality Using the New UK National Statistics Socio-economic Classification." *Social Science & Medicine* 50 (5): 641–49.

Chang, Iris. 1997. *The Rape of Nanking: The Forgotten Holocaust of World War II.* New York. Basic Books.

Chapkis, Wendy. 1997. *Live Sex Acts: Women Performing Erotic Labor.* New York: Routledge.

———. 2011. "Sex Workers" (interview). In *Introducing the New Sexuality Studies,* 2nd ed., edited by Steven Seidman, Nancy Fischer, and Chet Meeks, 327–33. New York: Routledge.

Chapkis, Wendy, and Richard J. Webb. 2008. *Dying to Get High: Marijuana as Medicine.* New York: New York University Press.

Charters, W. W. 1933. *Motion Pictures and Youth: A Summary.* New York: Macmillan.

ChartsBin. 2014. "Current Worldwide Homicide/Murder Rate." Accessed April 17. http://chartsbin.com/view/1454#.UA650iTrKAA.mailto.

Chasteen, Amy L. 2001. "Constructing Rape: Feminism, Change, and Women's Everyday Understanding of Sexual Assault." *Sociological Spectrum* 21 (2): 101–40.

Cherlin, Andrew J. 2004. "The Deinstitutionalization of American Marriage." *Journal of Marriage and Family* 66: 848–61.

———. 2009. *The Marriage-Go-Round: The State of Marriage and the Family in America Today.* New York: Alfred A. Knopf.

Chesney-Lind, Meda, and Merry Morash. 2013. "Transformative Feminist Criminology: A Critical Re-thinking of a Discipline." *Critical Criminology* 21 (3): 287–304.

Cheston, Duke. 2013. "The Cruelty of the Hook-Up Culture." John William Pope Center for Higher Education Policy, March 7. http://www.popecenter.org/commentaries/article.html?id=2816.

Childress, Sarah. 2013. "Will the Violence Against Women Act Close a Tribal Justice 'Loophole'?" *Frontline,* PBS, February 4.

Child Trends. 2012. "Percent of Non-marital Births to All Women, 1940–2009." http://www.childtrends.org/index.cfm.

Chin, Ko-Lin, and James O. Finckenauer. 2012. *Selling Sex Overseas: Chinese Women and the Realities of Prostitution and Global Sex Trafficking.* New York: New York University Press.

China Labor Watch. 2013. Home page. Accessed October 17. http://www.chinalaborwatch.org.

Chiricos, Ted, Kathy Padgett, and Marc Gertz. 2000. "Fear, TV News, and the Reality of Crime." *Criminology* 38 (3): 755–85.

Chitose, Yoshimi. 2005. "Transitions into and out of Poverty: A Comparison between Immigrant and Native Children." *Journal of Poverty* 9 (2): 63–88.

Chou, Rosalind S., and Joe R. Feagin. 2008. *The Myth of the Model Minority: Asian Americans Facing Racism.* Boulder, CO: Paradigm.

Chow-White, Peter. 2006. "Race, Gender and Sex on the Net: Semantic Networks of Selling and Storytelling Sex Tourism." *Media, Culture and Society* 28 (6): 883–905.

Christy-McMullin, Kameri, Yvette Murphy, Marcia Shobe, Shikkiah Jordan, Lauren Barefield, and Erika Gergerich. 2010. "Second-Generation Individual Development Account Research: Preliminary Findings." *Journal of Evidence-Based Social Work* 7 (3): 251–66.

Clift, Stephen, and Simon Carter, eds. 2000. *Tourism and Sex: Culture, Commerce, and Coercion.* New York: Pinter.

Clougherty, Jane E., Kerry Souza, and Mark R. Cullen. 2010. "Work and Its Role in Shaping the Social Gradient of Disease." *Annals of the New York Academy of Sciences* 1186: 102–24.

Cloward, Richard A., and Lloyd E. Ohlin. 1960. *Delinquency and Opportunity: A Theory of Delinquent Gangs.* Glencoe, IL: Free Press.

Clune, William H., John F. Witte, and Robert M. LaFollette Institute of Public Affairs. 1990. *Choice and Control in American Education.* London: Falmer.

Coalition Casualty Count. 2014. Accessed April 24. http://icasualties.org.

Cockerham, William C. 1997. *This Aging Society,* 2nd ed. Upper Saddle River, NJ: Prentice Hall.

Cohen, Philip N. 2012. "Recession and Divorce in the United States: Economic Conditions and the Odds of Divorce, 2008–2010." Maryland Population Research Center Working Paper. http://papers.ccpr.ucla.edu/papers/PWP-MPRC-2012-008/PWP-MPRC-2012-008.pdf.

Cohen, R. B. 1981. "The New International Division of Labor, Multinational Corporations, and Urban Hierarchy." In *Urbanization and Urban Planning in Capitalist Society,* edited by Michael Dear and Allen J. Scott, 287–315. London: Methuen.

Cohen, Sheldon, William J. Doyle, and Andrew Baum. 2006. "Socioeconomic Status Is Associated with Stress Hormones." *Psychosomatic Medicine* 68 (3): 414–20.

Cohen, Stanley. 2002. *Folk Devils and Moral Panics: The Creation of the Mods and Rockers,* 3rd ed. London: Routledge.

Cohn, D'Vera, Jeffrey S. Passell, Wendy Wang, and Gretchen Livingston. 2011. "Barely Half of U.S. Adults Are Married—A Record Low." Pew Research Center, Social and Demographic Trends, December 14. http://www.pewsocialtrends.org/files/2011/12/Marriage-Decline.pdf.

Colantonio, Andrea. 2007. "Social Sustainability: An Exploratory Analysis of Its Definition, Assessment Methods, Metrics and Tools." 2007/01: EIBURS Working Paper Series, Oxford Institute for Sustainable Development—International Land Markets Group, Oxford Brookes University.

Colantonio, Andrea, and Tim Dixon. 2011. *Urban Regeneration and Social Sustainability: Best Practice from European Cities.* Hoboken, NJ: Wiley-Blackwell.

Cole, George F., and Christopher E. Smith. 2008. *Criminal Justice in America,* 5th ed. Belmont, CA: Thomson Higher Education.

Cole, Luke W., and Sheila R. Foster. 2001. *From the Ground Up: Environmental Racism and the Rise of the Environmental Justice Movement.* New York: New York University Press.

Coleman, James S., et al., for the U.S. Office of Education, National Center for Education Statistics. 1966. *Equality of Educational Opportunity.* Washington, DC: Government Printing Office.

Coleman, James S., and Thomas Hoffer. 1987. *Public and Private High Schools: The Impact of Communities.* New York: Basic Books.

Coleman, James S., Thomas Hoffer, and Sally Kilgore. 1982. *High School Achievement: Public, Catholic, and Private Schools Compared.* New York: Basic Books.

Coles, Robert. 1993. *The Call of Service: A Witness to Idealism.* Boston: Houghton Mifflin.

Coll, Steve. 2013. "Remote Control." *New Yorker,* May 6, 77.

Collier, Roger. 2009. "Rapidly Rising Clinical Trial Costs Worry Researchers." *Canadian Medical Association Journal* 180 (3): 277–78.

Collins, Chuck. 2012. *99 to 1: How Wealth Inequality Is Wrecking the World and What We Can Do about It.* San Francisco: Berrett-Koehler.

Collins, Patricia Hill. 1990. *Black Feminist Thought: Knowledge, Consciousness, and the Politics of Empowerment.* Boston: Unwin Hyman.

———. 2008. *Black Feminist Thought: Knowledge, Consciousness, and the Politics of Empowerment,* 2nd ed. New York: Routledge.

Collins, Randall. 1979. *The Credential Society: An Historical Sociology of Education and Stratification.* New York: Academic Press.

Collins, Randall, and Scott Coltrane. 1991. *Sociology of Marriage and the Family: Gender, Love, and Property.* Chicago: Nelson-Hall.

Colombo, Cinzia, Paola Mosconi, Maria Grazia Buratti, Alessandro Liberati, Serena Donati, Alfonso Mele, and Roberto Satolli. 2010. "Press Coverage of Hormone Replacement Therapy and Menopause." *European Journal of Obstetrics & Gynecology and Reproductive Biology* 153 (1): 56–61.

Compton, Wilson M., and Nora D. Volkow. 2006. "Abuse of Prescription Drugs and the Risk of Addiction." *Drug & Alcohol Dependence* 83 (1) Suppl. 1: S4–7.

Comstock, George. 2008. "A Sociological Perspective on Television Violence and Aggression." *American Behavioral Scientist* 51 (8): 1184–1211.

Conklin, Kurt. 2012. "Attacks on Sex Education Continue Nationwide." Reproductive Health Reality Check,

October 9. http://rhrealitycheck.org/article/2012/10/09/school-controversies-in-sex-education.

Conley, Dalton. 1999. *Being Black, Living in the Red: Race, Wealth, and Social Policy in America.* Berkeley: University of California Press.

Connell, Nadine M., Pamela M. Negro, Allison N. Pearce, Dawn M. Reilly, and B. A. Fera. 2009. *New Jersey Department of Education and Rowan University Social Norms Project: Report for the 2008–2009 School Year.* Report to the New Jersey Department of Education. Trenton: State of New Jersey.

Connell, R. W. 2005. *Masculinities,* 2nd ed. Berkeley: University of California Press.

Conrad, Peter. 2007. *The Medicalization of Society: On the Transformation of Human Conditions into Treatable Disorders.* Baltimore: Johns Hopkins University Press.

Cookson, Peter W., Jr., Alan R. Sadovnik, and Susan F. Semel, eds. 1992. *International Handbook of Educational Reform.* New York: Greenwood Press.

Cooky, Cheryl, Faye L. Wachs, Michael Messner, and Shari Dworkin. 2010. "It's Not about the Game: Don Imus, Race, Class, Gender and Sexuality in Contemporary Media." *Sociology of Sport Journal* 27: 139–59.

Cooley, Charles Horton. 1902. *Human Nature and the Social Order.* New York: Charles Scribner's Sons.

Cooper, Al, Irene P. McLoughlin, and Kevin M. Campbell. 2000. "Sexuality in Cyberspace: Update for the 21st Century." *CyberPsychology and Behavior* 3 (4): 521–36.

Cooper, Alexia, and Erica L. Smith. 2011. *Homicide Trends in the United States, 1980-2008: Annual Rates for 2009 and 2010.* Patterns and Trends, November, NCJ 236018. Washington, DC: U.S. Department of Justice. http://www.bjs.gov/content/pub/pdf/htus8008.pdf.

Coory, Michael D., Jennifer M. Muller, Nathan A. M. Dunn, and Patricia S. Fagan. 2002. "Participation in Cervical Cancer Screening by Women in Rural and Remote Aboriginal and Torres Strait Islander Communities in Queensland." *Medical Journal of Australia* 177 (10): 544–47.

Corbin, Juliet M. 2003. "The Body in Health and Illness." *Qualitative Health Research* 13 (2): 256–67.

Corey, Ethan. 2013. "Students Protest Lenient Sexual Misconduct Sanctions." *Amherst Student,* May 1. http://amherststudent.amherst.edu/?q=article/2013/05/01/students-protest-lenient-sexual-misconduct-sanctions.

Corporation for National and Community Service. 2011. "Volunteering in America." Accessed September 8. http://www.volunteeringinamerica.gov/national.

———. 2013. "Volunteering and Civic Life in America." Accessed November 13. http://www.volunteeringinamerica.gov/national.

Costantini, Cristina. 2012. "Bilingual Border Cities Challenge Movement to Make English the Official Language." Huffington Post, February 2. http://www.huffingtonpost.com/2012/02/02/english-official-language-border-bilingual_n_1249307.html.

Cotter, David, Joan Hermson, and Reeve Vanneman. 2006. "Gender and Inequality at Work." In *Working in America: Continuity, Conflict, and Change,* 3rd ed., edited by Amy Wharton. New York: McGraw-Hill.

Cowan, Ruth Schwartz. 1983. *More Work for Mother: The Ironies of Household Technology from the Open Hearth to the Microwave.* New York: Basic Books.

Craddock, Susan. 2000. *City of Plagues: Disease, Poverty, and Deviance in San Francisco.* Minneapolis: University of Minnesota Press.

Cross, Christopher. 2004. *Political Education: National Policy Comes of Age.* New York: Teachers College Press.

Crowder, Kyle D., and Stewart E. Tolnay. 2000. "A New Marriage Squeeze for Black Women: The Role of Racial Intermarriage by Black Men." *Journal of Marriage and the Family* 62: 792–807.

Cumming, Elaine, and William E. Henry. 1961. *Growing Old.* New York: Basic Books.

Currul-Dykeman, Kathleen Erin. 2014. *Domestic Violence Case Processing: A Serious Crime or a Waste of Precious Time?* El Paso, TX: LFB Scholarly Publishing.

Dabhoiwala, Faramerz. 2012. *The Origins of Sex: A History of the First Sexual Revolution.* Oxford: Oxford University Press.

Dahrendorf, Ralf. 1959. *Class and Class Conflict in Industrial Society.* Stanford, CA: Stanford University Press.

Daly, Kathleen, and Meda Chesney-Lind. 1988. "Feminism and Criminology." *Justice Quarterly* 5 (4): 497–538.

Danziger, Sheldon, Sandra Danziger, and Jonathan Stern. 1997. "The American Paradox: High Income and High Child Poverty." In *Child Poverty and Deprivation in the Industrialized Countries, 1945–1995,* edited by Giovanni Andrea Cornia and Sheldon Danziger, 181–209. Oxford: Clarendon Press.

Dargis, Manohla. 2013. "Two Boys' Schooling, for 13 Years of It: 'American Promise,' a Documentary on Dalton Students." *New York Times,* October 17.

Darling-Hammond, Linda. 2010. *The Flat World and Education: How America's Commitment to Equity Will Determine Our Future.* New York: Teachers College Press.

Darmon, Nicole, and Adam Drewnowski. 2008. "Does Social Class Predict Diet Quality?" *American Journal of Clinical Nutrition* 87 (5): 1107–17.

Dasgupta, Susmita, Benoit Laplante, Craig Meisner, David Wheeler, and Jianping Yan. 2009. "The Impact of Sea

Level Rise on Developing Countries: A Comparative Analysis." *Climatic Change* 93 (3–4): 379–88.

Davis, F. James. 1952. "Crime News in Colorado Newspapers." *American Journal of Sociology* 57 (4): 325–30.

Davis, Kingsley. 1937. "The Sociology of Prostitution." *American Sociological Review* 2: 744–55.

Davis, Kingsley, and Wilbert E. Moore. 1945. "Some Principles of Stratification." *American Sociological Review* 10: 242–49.

Davis, Mike. 2003. *Dead Cities, and Other Tales.* New York: New Press.

Day, Jennifer Cheeseman, and Eric C. Newburger. 2002. *The Big Payoff: Educational Attainment and Synthetic Estimates of Work-Life Earnings.* U.S. Census Bureau, Current Population Reports P23-210. Washington, DC: Government Printing Office. http://www.census.gov/prod/2002pubs/p23-210.pdf.

de la Fuente-Fernández, R., T. J. Ruth, V. Sossi, M. Schulzer, D. B. Calne, and A. J. Stoessl. 2001. "Expectation and Dopamine Release: Mechanism of the Placebo Effect in Parkinson's Disease." *Science* 293(5532): 1164–66.

DeNavas-Walt, Carmen, Bernadette D. Proctor, and Jessica C. Smith. 2011. *Income, Poverty, and Health Insurance Coverage in the United States: 2010.* U.S. Census Bureau, Current Population Reports P60-239. Washington, DC: Government Printing Office. https://www.census.gov/prod/2011pubs/p60-239.pdf.

———. 2012. *Income, Poverty, and Health Insurance Coverage in the United States: 2011.* U.S. Census Bureau, Current Population Reports P60-243. Washington, DC: Government Printing Office. https://www.census.gov/prod/2012pubs/p60-243.pdf.

———. 2013. *Income, Poverty, and Health Insurance Coverage in the United States: 2012.* U.S. Census Bureau, Current Population Reports P60-245. Washington, DC: Government Printing Office. https://www.census.gov/prod/2013pubs/p60-245.pdf.

Deneen, Sally. 2013. "Feds Slash Colorado River Release to Historic Lows." National Geographic Daily News, August 16. http://news.nationalgeographic.com/news/2013/08/130816-colorado-river-drought-lake-powell-mead-water-scarcity.

Denizard-Thompson, Nancy M., Kirsten B. Feiereisel, Sheila F. Stevens, David P. Miller, and James L. Wofford. 2011. "The Digital Divide at an Urban Community Health Center: Implications for Quality Improvement and Health Care Access." *Journal of Community Health* 36: 456–60.

Dent, Mike. 2006. "Disciplining the Medical Profession? Implications of Patient Choice for Medical Dominance." *Health Sociology Review* 15: 458–68.

Deseran, Travis A., and James D. Orcutt. 2009. "The Deconstruction of a Drug Crisis: Media Coverage of Drug Issues during the 1996 Presidential Campaign." *Journal of Drug Issues* 39: 871–91.

Desmond, Matthew, and Mustafa Emirbayer. 2010. *Racial Domination, Racial Progress: The Sociology of Race in America.* New York: McGraw-Hill.

de Zwart, Onno, Marty P. N. van Kerkhof, and Theo G. M. Sandfort. 1998. "Anal Sex and Gay Men." *Journal of Psychology and Human Sexuality* 10 (3–4): 89–102.

DiFranza, Joseph R., Robert J. Wellman, James D. Sargent, Michael Weitzman, Bethany J. Hipple, and Jonathan P. Winickoff. 2006. "Tobacco Promotion and the Initiation of Tobacco Use: Assessing the Evidence for Causality." *Pediatrics* 117 (6): 1237–48.

Dijkstra, A. F., P. Verdonk, and A. L. Lagro-Janssen. 2008. "Gender Bias in Medical Textbooks: Examples from Coronary Heart Disease, Depression, Alcohol Abuse and Pharmacology." *Medical Education* 42 (10): 1021–28.

Diken, Bulent, and Carsten Bagge Laustsen. 2005. "Becoming Abject: Rape as a Weapon of War." *Body & Society* 11 (1): 111–28.

Dines, Gail, and Robert Jensen. 2004. "Pornography and Media: Toward a More Critical Analysis." In *Sexualities: Identities, Behaviors, and Society,* edited by Michael S. Kimmel and Rebecca F. Plante, 369–79. New York: Oxford University Press.

DiNitto, Diana M., with Linda K. Cummins. 2005. *Social Welfare: Politics and Public Policy,* 6th ed. Boston: Allyn & Bacon.

Dodman, David. 2009. "Blaming Cities for Climate Change? An Analysis of Urban Greenhouse Gas Emissions Inventories." *Environment & Urbanization* 21 (1): 185–210.

Donlon, Margie M., Ori Ashman, and Becca R. Levy. 2005. "Re-vision of Older Television Characters: A Stereotype-Awareness Intervention." *Journal of Social Issues* 61 (2): 307–19.

Dougherty, Kevin J., and Floyd M. Hammack, eds. 1990. *Education and Society: A Reader.* San Diego, CA: Harcourt Brace Jovanovich.

Downing-Matibag, Teresa M., and Brandi Geisinger. 2009. "Hooking Up and Sexual Risk Taking among College Students: A Health Belief Model Perspective." *Qualitative Health Research* 19 (9): 1196–1209.

Drakakis-Smith, David. 1995. "Third World Cities: Sustainable Urban Development, 1." *Urban Studies* 32 (4–5): 659–77.

Drapeau, Aline, Richard Boyer, and Alain Lesage. 2009. "The Influence of Social Anchorage on the Gender Difference in the Use of Mental Health Services." *Journal of Behavioral Health Services & Research* 36 (3): 372–84.

Dreby, Joanna. 2010. *Divided by Borders: Mexican Migrants and Their Children.* Berkeley: University of California Press.

———. 2012. "The Burden of Deportation on Children in Mexican Immigrant Families." *Journal of Marriage and Family* 74: 829–45.

Drefahl, Steven. 2012. "Do the Married Really Live Longer? The Role of Cohabitation and Socioeconomic Status." *Journal of Marriage and Family* 74: 462–75.

Dressner, Julie, and Edwin Martinez. 2012. "The Scars of Stop-and-Frisk." *New York Times,* June 12. http://www.nytimes.com/2012/06/12/opinion/the-scars-of-stop-and-frisk.html.

Dryfoos, Joy G., Jane Quinn, and Carol Barkin. 2005. *Community Schools in Action: Lessons from a Decade of Practice.* Oxford: Oxford University Press.

Du Bois, W. E. B. 1995. *The Philadelphia Negro: A Social Study.* Philadelphia: University of Pennsylvania Press. First published 1899.

———. 2003. *Darkwater: Voices from within the Veil.* Amherst, NY: Humanity Books. First published 1920.

Dunlap, Riley E., and Aaron M. McCright. 2008. "A Widening Gap: Republican and Democratic Views on Climate Change." *Environment* 50 (5): 26–35.

———. 2010. "Climate Change Denial: Sources, Actors and Strategies." In *The Routledge Handbook of Climate Change and Society,* edited by Constance Lever-Tracy, 240–59. New York: Routledge.

Durkheim, Émile. 1915. *The Elementary Forms of Religious Life.* London: Allen & Unwin.

———. 1977. *The Evolution of Educational Thought: Lectures on the Formation and Development of Secondary Education in France.* London: Routledge & Kegan Paul.

———. 1979. *Suicide: A Study in Sociology.* New York: Free Press. First published 1897.

———. 1982. *The Rules of Sociological Method.* Edited by Steven Lukes; translated by W. D. Halls. New York: Free Press. First published 1895.

———. 1984. *The Division of Labor in Society.* Translated by W. D. Halls. New York: Free Press. First published 1893.

The Economist. 2010. "Something's Not Working." April 29. http://www.economist.com/node/16010303.

Edgemon, Erin. 2013. "College Students Fight Human Trafficking." United Methodist Church, January 11. http://www.umc.org/news-and-media/college-students-fight-human-trafficking.

Edin, Kathryn, and Maria Kefalas. 2005. *Promises I Can Keep: Why Poor Women Put Motherhood before Marriage.* Berkeley: University of California Press.

Education Trust. 2010a. "Achievement in America: How Are We Doing? What Comes Next?" http://www.edtrust.org/dc/resources.

———. 2010b. *Education Watch: Achievement Gap Summary Tables.* Washington DC: Education Trust.

Eisenberg, Marla E., Dianne M. Ackard, Michael D. Resnick, and Dianne Neumark-Sztainer. 2009. "Casual Sex and Psychological Health among Young Adults: Is Having 'Friends-with-Benefits' Emotionally Damaging?" *Perspectives on Sexual and Reproductive Health* 41: 231–37.

Eisenhower, Dwight D. 1961. "Farewell Address." Dwight D. Eisenhower Presidential Library. http://www.eisenhower.archives.gov/research/online_documents/farewell_address.html.

Ekerdt, David J. 2007. "Work, Health, and Retirement." In *Encyclopedia of Health and Aging,* edited by Kyriakos S. Markides. Thousand Oaks, CA: Sage.

Elder, Glen H. 1974. *Children of the Great Depression: Social Change in Life Experience.* Chicago: University of Chicago Press.

Elkington, John. 1994. "Towards the Sustainable Corporation: Win-Win-Win Business Strategies for Sustainable Development." *California Management Review* 36 (2): 90–100.

———. 1997. *Cannibals with Forks: The Triple Bottom Line of 21st Century Business.* Oxford: Capstone.

Elliott, James R., and Jeremy Pais. 2006. "Race, Class, and Hurricane Katrina: Social Differences in Human Responses to Disaster." *Social Science Research* 35 (2): 295–321.

Elliott, P., S. Richardson, J. J. Abellan, A. Thomson, C. de Hoog, L. Jarup, and D. J. Briggs. 2009. "Geographic Density of Landfill Sites and Risk of Congenital Anomalies in England." *Occupational and Environmental Medicine* 66 (2): 81–89.

Embser-Herbert, Melissa Sheridan. 2012. "On Being a (Lesbian) Family in North American Society." In *Families with Futures: Family Studies into the Twenty-First Century,* edited by Meg Wilkes Karraker and Janet R. Grochowski, 33–34. London: Routledge.

Engel, George L. 1981. "The Need for a New Medical Model: A Challenge for Biomedicine." In *Concepts of Health and Disease: Interdisciplinary Perspectives,* edited by Arthur L. Caplan, H. Tristram Englehardt Jr., and James J. McCartney. Reading, MA: Addison-Wesley.

Engels, Friedrich. 1972. *The Origin of the Family, Private Property, and the State.* Atlanta, GA: Pathfinder. First published 1884.

Enloe, Cynthia. 1989. *Bananas, Beaches and Bases: Making Feminist Sense of International Politics.* London: Pandora Press.

Ennis, Sharon R., Merarys Ríos-Vargas, and Nora G. Albert. 2011. *The Hispanic Population: 2010.* U.S. Census Bureau, Census Brief C2010BR-04. Washington, DC: Government Printing Office. http://www.census.gov/prod/cen2010/briefs/c2010br-04.pdf.

Enten, Harry J. 2012. "How US Rules on Former Felons Voting Can Swing Presidential Elections." *Guardian,* July 3.

Epstein, Steven. 1995. "The Construction of Lay Expertise: AIDS Activism and the Forging of Credibility in the Reform of Clinical Trials." *Science, Technology, & Human Values* 20: 408–37.

———. 2007. *Inclusion: The Politics of Difference in Medical Research.* Chicago: University of Chicago Press.

Ermisch, John, Markus Jantti, and Timothy M. Smeeding, eds. 2012. *From Parents to Children: The Intergenerational Transmission of Advantage.* New York: Russell Sage.

Escholz, Sarah, Ted Chiricos, and Marc Gertz. 2003. "Television and Fear of Crime: Program Types, Audience Traits, and the Mediating Effect of Perceived Neighborhood Racial Composition." *Social Problems* 50 (3): 395–415.

Eshbaugh, Elaine M., and Gary Gute. 2008. "Hookups and Sexual Regret among College Women." *Journal of Social Psychology* 148 (1): 77–89.

Estes, Carroll L. 1991. "The New Political Economy of Aging: Introduction and Critique." In *Critical Perspectives on Aging: The Political and Moral Economy of Growing Old,* edited by Meredith Minkler and Carroll L. Estes, 19–36. Amityville, NY: Baywood.

Everage, Nicholas J., Crystal D. Linkletter, Annie Gjelsvik, Stephen T. McGarvey, and Eric B. Loucks. 2013. "Implementation of Permutation Testing to Determine Clustering of Social and Behavioral Risk Factors for Coronary Heart Disease, National Health and Nutrition Examination Survey 2001–2004." *Annals of Epidemiology* 23(7): 381–87.

Ewen, Stuart. 1977. *Captains of Consciousness: Advertising and the Social Roots of Consumer Culture.* New York: McGraw-Hill.

Farrer, James. 2006. "Sexual Citizenship and the Politics of Sexual Story-Telling among Chinese Youth." In *Sex and Sexuality in China,* edited by Elaine Jeffreys, 102–23. London: Routledge.

Farrer, James, Gefei Suo, Haruka Tsuchiya, and Zhongxin Su. 2012. "Re-embedding Sexual Meanings: A Qualitative Comparison of the Premarital Sexual Scripts of Chinese and Japanese Young Adults." *Sexuality & Culture* 16 (3): 263–86.

Fausto-Sterling, Anne. 2000. *Sexing the Body: Gender Politics and the Construction of Sexuality.* New York: Basic Books.

Feagin, Joe R. 2000. *Racist America: Roots, Current Realities, Future Reparations.* New York: Routledge.

Feagin, Joe R., and Clairece Booher Feagin. 2008. *Racial and Ethnic Relations,* 8th ed. Upper Saddle River, NJ: Prentice Hall.

Feagin, Joe R., and Melvin P. Sikes. 1994. *Living with Racism: The Black Middle-Class Experience.* Boston: Beacon Press.

Fealy, Gerard, Martin McNamara, Margaret Pearl Treacy, and Imogen Lyons. 2012. "Constructing Ageing and Age Identities: A Case Study of Newspaper Discourses." *Ageing & Society* 32: 85–102.

Feaver, Peter D., and Richard H. Kohn, eds. 2001. *Soldiers and Civilians: The Civil-Military Gap and American National Security.* Cambridge: MIT Press.

Federal Bureau of Investigation. 2013a. "Crime in the United States: Offense and Population Percent Distribution by Region, 2012." Uniform Crime Reports. http://www.fbi.gov/about-us/cjis/ucr/crime-in-the-u.s/2012/crime-in-theu.s.2012/tables/3tabledatadecover viewpdf/table_3_crime_in_the_united_states_offense_ and_population_distribution_by_region_2012.xls.

———. 2013b. "Crime in the United States: Offenses Known to Law Enforcement by State by City, 2012." Uniform Crime Reports. http://www.fbi.gov/about-us/cjis/ucr/crime-in-the-u.s/2012/crime-in-the-u.s.-2012/tables/8tabledatadecpdf/table_8_offenses_known_to_ law_enforcement_by_state_by_city_2012.xls/view.

Federal Interagency Forum on Aging-Related Statistics. 2010. *Older Americans 2010: Key Indicators of Well-Being.* Washington, DC: Government Printing Office.

Feeney, Floyd, and Patrick G. Jackson. 1990–1991. "Public Defenders, Assigned Counsel, Retained Counsel: Does the Type of Criminal Defense Counsel Matter?" *Rutgers Law Journal* 22: 361–456.

Feldman, H. A., C. B. Johannes, C. A. Derby, K. P. Kleinman, B. A. Mohr, A. B. Araujo, and J. B. McKinlay. 2000. "Erectile Dysfunction and Coronary Risk Factors: Prospective Results from the Massachusetts Male Aging Study." *Preventive Medicine* 30 (4): 328–38.

Feldmeyer, Ben, and Darrell Steffensmeier. 2007. "Elder Crime: Patterns and Current Trends, 1980–2004." *Research on Aging* 29 (4): 297–322.

Fellman, Gordon. 1998. *Rambo and the Dalai Lama: The Compulsion to Win and Its Threat to Human Survival.* Albany: State University of New York Press.

Ferguson, Ann Arnett. 2000. *Bad Boys: Public Schools in the Making of Black Masculinity.* Ann Arbor: University of Michigan Press.

Ferguson, Christopher John. 2007. "The Good, the Bad and the Ugly: A Meta-analytic Review of Positive and Negative Effects of Violent Video Games." *Psychiatric Quarterly* 78: 309–16.

Fernandez-Kelly, M. Patricia, and Richard Schauffler. 1994. "Divided Fates: Immigrant Children in a Restructured Economy." *International Migration Review* 28: 662–89.

Ferraro, Kenneth F. 2011. "Health and Aging: Early Origins, Persistent Inequalities?" In *Handbook of Sociology of Aging,* edited by Richard A. Settersten Jr. and Jacqueline L. Angel, 465–75. New York: Springer.

Ferrell, Jeff. 2013. "Cultural Criminology and the Politics of Meaning." *Critical Criminology* 21 (3): 257–71.

Fields, Jessica. 2007. "Knowing Girls: Gender and Learning in School-Based Sexuality Education." In *Sexual Inequalities and Social Justice,* edited by Niels Teunis and Gilbert H. Herdt, 66–85. Berkeley: University of California Press.

Finer, Lawrence B. 2007. "Trends in Premarital Sex in the United States, 1954–2003." *Public Health Reports* 122 (1): 73–78.

Finer, Lawrence B., and Adam Sonfield. 2012. "The Evidence Mounts on the Benefits of Preventing Unintended Pregnancy." *Contraception* 87 (2): 126–27.

Fingerman, Karen L. 2001. "A Distant Closeness: Intimacy between Parents and Their Children in Later life." *Generations* 25 (2): 26–33.

Fingerman, Karen L., Yen-Pi Cheng, Eric D. Wesselmann, Steven Zarit, Frank Furstenberg, and Kira S. Birditt. 2012. "Helicopter Parents and Landing Pad Kids: Intense Parental Support of Grown Children." *Journal of Marriage and Family* 74: 880–96.

Firey, Walter. 1945. "Sentiment and Symbolism as Ecological Variables." *American Sociological Review* 10: 140–48.

Fischer, Benedikt, Eugenia Oviedo-Joekes, Peter Blanken, Christian Haasan, Jürgen Rehm, Martin T. Schecter, John Strang, and Wim van den Brink. 2007. "Heroin-Assisted Treatment (HAT) a Decade Later: A Brief Update on Science and Politics." *Journal of Urban Health* 84 (4): 552–62.

Fischer, D. H. 1978. *Growing Old in America.* New York: Oxford University Press.

Fishman, Mark. 1978. "Crime Waves as Ideology." *Social Problems* 25 (5): 531–43.

Flack, William F., Jr., Kimberly A. Daubman, Marcia L. Caron, Jenica A. Asadorian, Nicole R. D'Aureli, Shannon N. Gigliotti, et al. 2007. "Risk Factors and Consequences of Unwanted Sex among University Students: Hooking Up, Alcohol, and Stress Response." *Journal of Interpersonal Violence* 22 (2): 139–57.

Flaxman, Greg, with John Kucsera, Gary Orfield, Jennifer Ayscue, and Genevieve Siegel-Hawley. 2013. *A Status Quo of Segregation: Racial and Economic Imbalance in New Jersey Schools, 1989–2010.* Los Angeles: Civil Rights Project, UCLA. http://civilrightsproject.ucla .edu/research/k-12-education/integration-and-diver sity/a-status-quo-of-segregation-racial-and-economic-imbalance-in-new-jersey-schools-1989-2010/Norflet_ NJ_Final_101013_POSTb.pdf.

Focus on the Family. 2012. "Mission Statement." Accessed October 22. http://www.focusonthefamily.com/about_ us/guiding-principles.aspx.

Food Security and Nutrition Analysis Unit—Somalia. 2013. "Study Suggests 258,000 Somalis Died Due to Severe Food Insecurity and Famine." Press release, May 2. http://www.fsnau.org/in-focus/technical-release-study-suggests-258000-somalis-died-due-severe-food-insecurity-and-famine-.

Fothergill, Alice, Enrique G. Maestas, and JoAnne D. Darlington. 1999. "Race, Ethnicity and Disasters in the United States: A Review of the Literature." *Disasters* 23 (2): 156–73.

Fragile Families and Child Wellbeing Study. 2012. "Fact Sheet." http://www.fragilefamilies.princeton.edu/ documents/ FragileFamiliesandChildWellbeingStudyFactSheet.pdf.

Frankel, Arthur, and Debra A. Curtis. 2008. "What's in a Purse? Maybe a Woman's Reputation." *Sex Roles* 59: 615–22.

Frankenberg, Ruth. 1993. *White Women, Race Matters: The Social Construction of Whiteness.* Minneapolis: University of Minnesota Press.

Frantz, Douglas, and Catherine Collins. 1999. *Celebration, U.S.A.: Living in Disney's Brave New Town.* New York: Henry Holt.

Frech, Adrianne, and Rachel Tolbert Kimbro. 2011. "Maternal Mental Health, Neighborhood Characteristics, and Time Investments in Children." *Journal of Marriage and Family* 73: 605–20.

Freedman, D. S., L. K. Khan, M. K. Serdula, W. H. Dietz, S. R. Srinivasan, and G. S. Berenson. 2005. "The Relation of Childhood BMI to Adult Adiposity: The Bogalusa Heart Study." *Pediatrics* 115 (1): 22–27.

Freeman, Richard B. 2007. *America Works: Critical Thoughts on the Exceptional U.S. Labor Market.* New York: Russell Sage Foundation.

Frey, Richard, and D'Vera Cohn. 2011. "Living Together: The Economics of Cohabitation." Pew Research Center, Social and Demographic Trends, June 27. http://www .pewsocialtrends.org/files/2011/06/pew-social-trends-cohabitation-06-2011.pdf.

Friedman, Thomas. 2005. *The World Is Flat: A Brief History of the Twenty-First Century.* New York: Picador.

Friedmann, John. 1986. "The World City Hypothesis." *Development and Change* 17 (1): 69–83.

Friese, Bettina, and Karen Bogenschneider. 2009. "The Voice of Experience: How Social Scientists Communicate Family Research to Policymakers." *Family Relations* 58 (2): 229–43.

Fritschi, L., and T. Driscoll. 2006. "Cancer Due to Occupation in Australia." *Australian and New Zealand Journal of Public Health* 30 (3): 213–19.

Fry, Douglas. 2006. *The Human Potential for Peace.* New York: Oxford University Press.

Fry, Richard. 2013. "A Rising Share of Young Adults Live in Their Parents' Home." Pew Research Center, Social and Demographic Trends, August 1. http://www.pewsocialtrends.org/2013/08/01/a-rising-share-of-young-adults-live-in-their-parents-home.

Funkhouser, G. Ray. 1973. "The Issues of the Sixties: An Exploratory Study in the Dynamics of Public Opinion." *Public Opinion Quarterly* 66: 942–48, 959.

Furgal, Christopher, and Jacinthe Seguin. 2006. "Climate Change, Health, and Vulnerability in Canadian Northern Aboriginal Communities." *Environmental Health Perspectives* 114 (12): 1964–70.

Furstenberg, Frank R. 2002. "What a Good Marriage Can't Do." *New York Times,* August 13. http://www.nytimes.com/2002/08/13/opinion/what-a-good-marriage-can-t-do.html.

———. 2004. "Values, Policy, and the Family." In *The Future of the Family,* edited by Daniel P. Moynihan, Timothy M. Smeeding, and Lee Rainwater, 267–75. New York: Russell Sage Foundation.

Futrell, Robert, Christie Batson, Barbara G. Brents, Andrea Dassopoulos, Chrissy Nicholas, Mark J. Salvaggio, and Candace Griffith. 2010. *City of Las Vegas Your City Your Way Initiative: Final Report.* Las Vegas, NV: Las Vegas Metropolitan Area Research Team. http://www.lasvegasnevada.gov/files/Your_City_Your_Way_Final_Report.pdf.

Gagnon, John H., and William Simon. 1973. *Sexual Conduct: The Social Sources of Human Sexuality.* Chicago: Aldine.

Galdas, Paul M., Francine Cheater, and Paul Marshall. 2005. "Men and Health Help-Seeking Behaviour: Literature Review." *Journal of Advanced Nursing* 49 (6): 616–23.

Gallagher, Charles A. 2003a. "Miscounting Race: Explaining Whites' Misperceptions of Racial Group Size." *Sociological Perspectives* 46 (3): 381–96.

———. 2003b. "Playing the White Ethnic Card: Using Ethnic Identity to Deny Contemporary Racism." In *White Out: The Continuing Significance of Racism,* edited by Ashley W. Doane and Eduardo Bonilla-Silva, 145–58. New York: Routledge.

Galligan, Roslyn F., and Deborah J. Terry. 1993. "Romantic Ideals, Fear of Negative Implications, and the Practice of Safe Sex." *Journal of Applied Social Psychology* 23 (20): 1685–1711.

Gamson, William A. 1992. *Talking Politics.* New York: Cambridge University Press.

———. 1995. "Hiroshima, the Holocaust, and the Politics of Exclusion: 1994 Presidential Address." *American Sociological Review* 60 (1): 1–20.

Gamson, William A., and Andre Modigliani. 1987. "The Changing Culture of Affirmative Action." *Research in Political Sociology* 3: 137–77.

Gans, Herbert J. 1971. "The Uses of Poverty: The Poor Pay All." *Social Policy* (July/August): 20–24.

———. 1979. "Symbolic Ethnicity: The Future of Ethnic Groups and Cultures in America." *Ethnic and Racial Studies* 2 (1): 1–20.

———. 1992. "Comment: Ethnic Invention and Acculturation: A Bumpy Line Approach." *Journal of American Ethnic History* 12 (1): 42–52.

Garcia, Lorena. 2009. "'Now Why Do You Want to Know about That?': Heteronormativity, Sexism, and Racism in the Sexual (Mis)education of Latina Youth." *Gender & Society* 23 (4): 520–41.

Garfinkel, Harold. 1967. *Studies in Ethnomethodology.* Englewood Cliffs, NJ: Prentice-Hall.

Gavey, Nicola. 2005. *Just Sex? The Cultural Scaffolding of Rape.* New York: Routledge.

Geisinger, Brandi N. 2011. "Critical Feminist Theory, Rape, and Hooking Up." Master's thesis, Iowa State University.

Gengler, Amanda M. 2012. "Defying (Dis)Empowerment in a Battered Women's Shelter: Moral Rhetorics, Intersectionality, and Processes of Control and Resistance." *Social Problems* 59: 501–21.

George, Linda K. 2005. "Socioeconomic Status and Health across the Life Course: Progress and Prospects." *Journal of Gerontology: Social Sciences* 60B: 135–39.

Gepts, Paul. 2005. "Introduction of Transgenic Crops in Centers of Origin and Domestication." In *Controversies in Science and Technology: From Maize to Menopause,* edited by Daniel Lee Kleinman, Abby J. Kinchy, and Jo Handelsman, 119–134. Madison: University of Wisconsin Press.

Gerbner, George, Larry Gross, Michael Morgan, and Nancy Signorielli. 1994. "Growing Up with Television: The Cultivation Perspective." In *Media Effects: Advances in Theory and Research,* edited by Jennings Bryant and Dolf Zillmann, 17–41. Hillsdale, NJ: Lawrence Erlbaum.

Gerbner, George, Larry Gross, Nancy Signorielli, and Michael Morgan. 1986. "Television's Mean World: Violence Profile No. 14-15." Unpublished paper, Annenberg School of Communications, University of Pennsylvania.

Geronimus, Arline T., Margaret Hicken, Danya Keene, and John Bound. 2006. "'Weathering' and Age Patterns of Allostatic Load Scores among Blacks and Whites in the United States." *American Journal of Public Health* 96: 826–33.

Gladwell, Malcolm. 2010. "Talent Grab: Why Do We Pay Our Stars So Much Money?" *New Yorker,* October 11, 85–93.

Glassner, Barry. 2012. "Organic Food for Thought on Campuses." *Chronicle of Higher Education,* March 11. http://chronicle.com/article/Organic-Food-for-Thought-on/131119.

Glaze, Lauren E., and Laura M. Maruschak. 2008. "Parents in Prison and Their Minor Children." U.S. Department of Justice, Bureau of Justice Statistics, Special Report, NCJ 222984, August. http://www.bjs.gov/content/pub/pdf/pptmc.pdf.

Glazer, Sarah. 2010. "Europe's Immigration Turmoil: Is Europe Becoming Intolerant of Foreigners?" *CQ Global Researcher* 4 (12): 289–320.

Glenn, Norval, and Elizabeth Marquardt. 2001. *Hooking Up, Hanging Out, and Hoping for Mr. Right: College Women on Dating and Mating Today.* New York: Institute for American Values.

Goldberg, Abbie E., and Katherine R. Allen, eds. 2013. *LGBT-Parent Families.* Heidelberg, Germany: Springer.

Goldberg, Mark S., Jack Siemiatyck, Ron DeWar, Marie Désy, and Hélène Riberdy. 1999. "Risk of Developing Cancer Relative to Living Near a Municipal Solid Waste Landfill Site in Montreal, Quebec, Canada." *Archives of Environmental Health* 54 (4): 291–96.

Goldman, Adam, and Matt Apuzzo. 2013. "NYPD Linked Mosques to Terror." *New York Times,* August 29.

Goldstein, Joshua. 2011. *Winning the War on War.* New York: Penguin Books.

Gone, Joseph P. 2007. "'We Never Was Happy Living Like a Whiteman': Mental Health Disparities and the Postcolonial Predicament in American Indian Communities." *American Journal of Community Psychology* 40 (3/4): 290–300.

Goode, Erich, and Nachman Ben-Yehuda. 2009. *Moral Panics: The Social Construction of Deviance,* 2nd ed. Malden, MA: Wiley-Blackwell.

Goodwin, Glenn A., and Joseph Scimecca. 2006. *Classical Sociological Theory: Rediscovering the Promise of Sociology.* Belmont, CA: Thomson Higher Education.

Gootman, Elissa, and Catherine Saint Louis. 2012. "Maternity Leave? It's More Like a Pause." *New York Times,* July 20. http://www.nytimes.com/2012/07/22/fashion/for-executive-women-is-maternity-leave-necessary.html?_r=1&agewanted=all.

Gordon, Milton. 1964. *Assimilation in American Life: The Role of Race, Religion, and National Origins.* New York: Oxford University Press.

Gottdiener, Mark, and Joe R. Feagin. 1988. "The Paradigm Shift in Urban Sociology." *Urban Affairs Review* 24 (2): 163–87.

Gottfredson, Michael R., and Travis Hirschi. 1990. *A General Theory of Crime.* Stanford, CA: Stanford University Press.

Goudreau, Jenna. 2010. "Most Popular College Majors for Women." *Forbes,* August 10. http://www.forbes.com/2010/08/10/most-popular-college-degrees-for-women-forbes-woman-leadership-education-business.html?boxes=Homepagechannels.

Granovetter, Mark, 1995. *Getting a Job: A Study of Contacts and Careers,* 2nd ed. Chicago: University of Chicago Press.

Grant, Melissa Gira. 2013. "Unpacking the Sex Trafficking Panic." *Contemporary Sexuality* 47 (2): 2–6.

Graves, Joseph L., Jr. 2004. *The Race Myth: Why We Pretend Race Exists in America.* New York: Dutton.

Greene, Jeremy A., and David Herzberg. 2010. "Hidden in Plain Sight: Marketing Prescription Drugs to Consumers in the Twentieth Century." *American Journal of Public Health* 100 (5): 793–803.

Greenstone, Michael. 2012. "The Uncomfortable Truth about American Wages." *New York Times,* Economix blog, October 22. http://economix.blogs.nytimes.com/2012/10/22/the-uncomfortable-truth-about-american-wages.

Greenstone, Michael, and Adam Looney. 2011. "The Great Recession May Be Over, but American Families Are Working Harder than Ever." Brookings Institution, Hamilton Project blog, July 8. http://www.brookings.edu/blogs/jobs/posts/2011/07/08-jobs-greenstone-looney.

Griffiths, Mark D. 2012. "Sex Addiction: a Review of Empirical Research." *Addiction Research and Theory* 20 (2): 111–24.

Grochowski, Janet R. 1998. "Strategic Living Communities: Families for the Future." *Futurics: Quarterly Journal of Futures Research* 21: 24–29.

———. 2000. "Families as Strategic Living Communities." Paper presented at the annual meetings of the American Academy of Health Behavior, Santa Fe, New Mexico, September.

Gross, Matthias. 2010. *Ignorance and Surprise: Science, Society, and Ecological Design.* Cambridge: MIT Press.

Grossman, Jean Baldwin, and Eileen M. Garry. 1997. *Mentoring: A Proven Delinquency Prevention Strategy.* OJJDP Juvenile Justice Bulletin, April. Washington, DC: U.S. Department of Justice. https://www.ncjrs.gov/pdffiles/164834.pdf.

Grossman, Jean Baldwin, and Joseph P. Tierney. 1998. "Does Mentoring Work? An Impact Study of the Big Brothers Big Sisters Program." *Evaluation Review* 22 (3): 403–26.

Grubb, Amy, and Emily Turner. 2012. "Attribution of Blame in Rape Cases: A Review of the Impact of Rape Myth Acceptance, Gender Role Conformity, and Substance Use on Victim Blaming." *Aggression & Violent Behavior* 17 (5): 443–52.

Guarino-Ghezzi, Susan. 1994. "Reintegrative Police Surveillance of Juvenile Offenders: Forging an Urban Model." *Crime & Delinquency* 40 (2): 131–53.

Guerino, Paul, Paige M. Harrison, and William J. Sabol. 2011. *Prisoners in 2010.* U.S. Bureau of Justice Statistics, NCJ 236096. Washington, DC: U.S. Department of Justice. http://www.bjs.gov/content/pub/pdf/p10.pdf.

Gusfield, Joseph R. 1986. *Symbolic Crusade: Status Politics and the American Temperance Movement,* 2nd ed. Urbana: University of Illinois Press.

Hacker, Andrew. 2003. *Two Nations: Black and White, Separate, Hostile, Unequal.* New York: Scribner.

Hackman, J. Richard, and Greg R. Oldham. 1976. "Motivation through the Design of Work: Test of a Theory." *Organizational Behavior and Human Performance* 16: 250–79.

Hajdu, David. 2008. *The Ten-Cent Plague: The Great Comic Book Scare and How It Changed America.* New York: Farrar, Straus and Giroux.

Hajjar, Ihab, Jane Morley Kotchen, and Theodore A. Kotchen. 2006. "Hypertension: Trends in Prevalence, Incidence, and Control." *Annual Review of Public Health* 27: 465–90.

Hald, Gert M., Neil Malamuth, and Carlin Yuen. 2010. "Pornography and Attitudes Supporting Violence against Women: Revisiting the Relationship in Nonexperimental Studies." *Aggressive Behavior* 36 (1): 14–20.

Half the Sky Movement. 2014. "Sex Trafficking and Forced Prostitution." Accessed March 25. http://www .halftheskymovement.org/campaigns/sex-trafficking.

Halle, David, and Andrew A. Beveridge. 2011. "The Rise and Decline of the L.A. and New York Schools." In *The City, Revisited: Urban Theory from Chicago, Los Angeles, and New York,* edited by Dennis R. Judd and Dick Simpson, 137–68. Minneapolis: University of Minnesota Press.

Hallerod, Björn, and Jan-Eric Gustafsson. 2011. "A Longitudinal Analysis of the Relationship between Changes in Socio-economic Status and Changes in Health." *Social Science & Medicine* 72 (1): 116–23.

Hämäläinen, P., J. Takala, and K. L. Saarela. 2007. "Global Estimates of Fatal Work-Related Diseases." *American Journal of Industrial Medicine* 50 (1): 28–41.

Hamilton, Laura, and Elizabeth A. Armstrong. 2009. "Gendered Sexuality in Young Adulthood: Double Binds and Flawed Options." *Gender & Society* 23 (5): 589–616.

Hansen, Randall. 2012. *The Centrality of Employment in Immigrant Integration in Europe.* Washington, DC: Migration Policy Institute.

Harawa, Nina, John Williams, Hema Ramamurthi, and Trista Bingham. 2006. "Perceptions towards Condom Use, Sexual Activity, and HIV Disclosure among HIV-Positive African American Men Who Have Sex with Men: Implications for Heterosexual Transmission." *Journal of Urban Health* 83 (4): 682–94.

Harrell, Erika. 2011. "Workplace Violence, 1993–2009: National Crime Victimization Survey and the Census of Fatal Occupational Injuries." U.S. Department of Justice, Bureau of Justice Statistics, Special Report, NCJ 233231, March. http://bjs.gov/content/pub/pdf/wv09.pdf.

Harrington, Carol. 2012. "Prostitution Policy Models and Feminist Knowledge Politics in New Zealand and Sweden." *Sexuality Research and Social Policy* 9 (4): 337–49.

Harrington, Michael. 1962. *The Other America.* New York: Macmillan.

Harris, Louis. 1976. *The Myth and Reality of Aging in America.* Washington, DC: National Council on the Aging.

Hartung, William. 2011. *Prophets of War: Lockheed Martin and the Making of the Military-Industrial Complex.* New York. Nation Books.

Harvey, David. 1973. *Social Justice and the City.* Athens: University of Georgia Press.

Hassan, Riaz. 2011. *Suicide Bombings.* New York: Routledge.

Head, Jonathan. 2004. "Japan's AIDS Time Bomb." BBC News, July 13. http://news.bbc.co.uk/2/hi/asia-pacific/3890689.stm.

Healey, Joseph F. 2009. *Race, Ethnicity, Gender, and Class: The Sociology of Group Conflict and Change,* 5th ed. Thousand Oaks, CA: Pine Forge Press.

Heaney, Stephen J. 2012. "Marriage Vote: For the Children." *Star Tribune,* October 16. http://www.startribune.com/opinion/commentaries/174479341.html.

Helgeson, Baird. 2012. "Same-Sex Marriage Ban Defeated." *Star Tribune,* November 6. http://www.startribune.com/politics/statelocal/177544631.html?refer=y.

Hemmens, Craig, David C. Brody, and Cassia C. Spohn. 2010. *Criminal Courts: A Contemporary Perspective.* Thousand Oaks, CA: Sage.

Henson, Kevin. 1996. *Just a Temp.* Philadelphia: Temple University Press.

Herrnstein, Richard J., and Charles Murray. 1994. *The Bell Curve: Intelligence and Class Structure in American Life.* New York: Free Press.

Hess, David J. 1999. *Evaluating Alternative Cancer Therapies.* New Brunswick, NJ: Rutgers University Press.

———. 2009. "The Potentials and Limitations of Civil Society Research: Getting Undone Science Done." *Sociological Inquiry* 79 (3): 306–27.

Hesse-Biber, Sharlene N. 2006. *The Cult of Thinness.* New York: Oxford University Press.

Hesse-Biber, Sharlene N., Patricia Leavy, Courtney E. Quinn, and Julia Zoino. 2006. "The Mass Marketing of

Disordered Eating and Eating Disorders: The Social Psychology of Women, Thinness and Culture." *Women's Studies International Forum* 29 (2): 208–24.

Higher Education Research Institute. 2013. "CIRP Freshman Survey Results for 2013." http://heri.ucla.edu.

Hilgartner, Stephen, and Charles L. Bosk. 1988. "The Rise and Fall of Social Problems: A Public Arenas Model." *American Journal of Sociology* 94 (1): 53–78.

Hill, Shirley A. 2012. *Families: A Social Class Perspective.* Thousand Oaks, CA: Sage.

Hill, Terrence D., Amy M. Burdette, and Ellen L. Idler. 2011. "Religious Involvement, Health Status, and Mortality Risk." In *Handbook of Sociology of Aging,* edited by Richard A. Settersten Jr. and Jacqueline L. Angel, 533–46. New York: Springer.

Hinduja, Sameer, and Justin W. Patchin. 2009. *Bullying beyond the Schoolyard: Preventing and Responding to Cyberbullying.* Thousand Oaks, CA: Sage.

Hirschi, Travis. 1969. *Causes of Delinquency.* Berkeley: University of California Press.

Hirvonen, Lalaina H. 2008. "Intergenerational Earnings Mobility among Daughters and Sons: Evidence from Sweden and a Comparison with the United States." *Journal of Economics and Sociology* 67: 777–826.

Hodson, Randy. 1989. "Gender Differences in Job Satisfaction: Why Aren't Women More Dissatisfied?" *Sociological Quarterly* 30 (3): 385–99.

Hogan, Christopher, June Lunney, Jon Gabel, and Joanne Lynn. 2001. "Medicare Beneficiaries' Costs of Care in the Last Year of Life." *Health Affairs* 20 (4): 188–95.

Hood, Robert. 2003. "AIDS, Crisis, and Activist Science." In *Science and Other Cultures: Issues in Philosophies of Science and Technology,* edited by Robert Figueroa and Sandra Harding, 15–25. New York: Routledge.

Horowitz, Roger. 1997. "'Where Men Will Not Work': Gender, Power, Space, and the Sexual Division of Labor in America's Meatpacking Industry, 1890–1990." *Technology and Culture* 38 (1): 187–213.

Horsfall, Jan. 2001. "Gender and Mental Illness: An Australian Overview." *Mental Health Nursing* 22 (4): 421–38.

Hoyt, Homer. 1939. *The Structure and Growth of Residential Neighborhoods in American Cities.* Atlanta, GA: Federal Highway Administration.

Hu, Wei-Yin. 2003. "Marriage and Economic Incentives: Evidence from a Welfare Experiment." *Journal of Human Resources* 38 (4): 942–63.

Hua, Cynthia. 2013. "2012–'13 Sexual Climate Assessment Released." *Yale Daily News,* May 15. http://yaledaily news.com/crosscampus/2013/05/15/2012–13-sexual-climate-assessment-released.

Hughes, Caitlin Elizabeth, and Alex Stevens. 2010. "What Can We Learn from the Portuguese Decriminalization of Illicit Drugs?" *British Journal of Criminology* 50 (6): 999–1022.

Human Rights Watch. 2009. *Decades of Disparity: Drug Arrests and Race in the United States.* New York: Human Rights Watch.

Human Security Report Project. 2011. *Human Security Report 2009/2010: The Causes of Peace and the Shrinking Costs of War.* New York: Oxford University Press.

———. 2012. *Human Security Report 2012: Sexual Violence, Education, and War: Beyond the Mainstream Narrative.* Vancouver: Human Security Press.

Humes, Karen R., Nicholas A. Jones, and Roberto R. Ramirez. 2011. *Overview of Race and Hispanic Origin: 2010.* U.S. Census Bureau, Census Brief C2010BR-02. Washington, DC: Government Printing Office. http://www.census.gov/prod/cen2010/briefs/c2010br-02.pdf.

Hunter, Myra. 2007. "Bio-psycho-socio-cultural Perspectives on Menopause." *Best Practice & Research: Clinical Obstetrics & Gynaecology* 21 (2): 261–74.

Hurd Clarke, Laura. 2011. *Facing Age: Women Growing Older in Anti-aging Culture.* Lanham, MD: Rowman & Littlefield.

Hurn, Christopher J. 1993. *The Limits and Possibilities of Schooling: An Introduction to the Sociology of Education,* 3rd ed. Boston: Allyn & Bacon.

Hvas, Lotte, and Dorte Effersøe Gannik. 2008. "Discourses on Menopause—Part 1: Menopause Described in Texts Addressed to Danish Women 1996–2004." *Health* 12 (2): 157–75.

Hyams, Melissa. 2006. "*La Escuela*: Young Latina Women Negotiating Identities in School." In *Latina Girls: Voices of Adolescent Strength in the United States,* edited by Jill Denner and Bianca L. Guzmán, 93–108. New York: New York University Press.

Hyde, Abbey, Margaret P. Treacy, Anne P. Scott, Padraig MacNeela, Michelle Butler, Jonathan Drennan, Kate Irving, and Anne Byrne. 2006. "Social Regulation, Medicalisation, and the Nurse's Role: Insights from an Analysis of Nursing Documentation." *International Journal of Nursing Studies* 43 (6): 735–44.

Hynie, Michaela, John E. Lydon, Sylvana Cote, and Seth Wiener. 1998. "Relational Sexual Scripts and Women's Condom Use: The Importance of Internalized Norms." *Journal of Sex Research* 35 (4): 370–80.

Iles, Alastair. 2004. "Mapping Environmental Justice In Technology Flows: Computer Waste Impacts in Asia." *Global Environmental Politics* 4(4), 76–106.

Ingersoll, Richard. 2003. *Who Controls Teachers' Work? Power and Accountability in America's Schools.* Cambridge, MA: Harvard University Press.

———. 2004. "Why Some Schools Have More Underqualified Teachers than Others." In *Brookings Papers on Education Policy,* edited by Diane Ravitch. Washington, DC: Brookings Institution Press.

Institute for Women's Policy Research. 2011. "The Gender Wage Gap: 2010." Fact Sheet, IWPR C350, September. http://www.Iwpr.org.

International Rescue Committee. 2012. "DRC Study Shows Congo's Neglected Crisis Leaves 5.4 Million Dead." http://www.rescue.org/news/irc-study-shows-congos-neglected-crisis-leaves-54-million-dead-peace-deal-n-kivu-increased-aid—4331.

International Telecommunications Union. 2013. *The World in 2013: ICT Facts and Figures.* Geneva: International Telecommunications Union. http://www.itu.int/en/ITU-D/Statistics/Documents/facts/ICTFactsFigures2013-e.pdf.

Internet Crime Complaint Center. 2011. *2010 Internet Crime Report.* Washington, DC: National White Collar Crime Center. http://www.ic3.gov/media/annualreport/2010_ic3report.pdf.

Iraq Body Count. 2014. Accessed March 25. http://www.iraqbodycount.org.

Ivanov, Ivan D., and Kurt Straif. 2006. "Prevention of Occupational Cancer." *World Health Organization GOHNET Newsletter* 11: 1–4.

Iyengar, Shanto, and Donald R. Kinder. 2010. *News That Matters: Television and American Opinion,* updated ed. Chicago: University of Chicago Press.

Jackman, Mary, and Marie Crane. 1986. "Some of My Best Friends Are Black: Interracial Friendships and Whites' Racial Attitudes." *Public Opinion Quarterly* 50: 459–86.

Jacobs, Jessica. 2010. *Sex, Tourism and the Postcolonial Encounter: Landscapes of Longing in Egypt.* Farnham, England: Ashgate.

Jang, Soo Jung, Allison Zippay, and Rhokeum Park. 2012. "Family Roles as Moderators of the Relationship between Schedule Flexibility and Stress." *Journal of Marriage and Family* 74: 897–912.

Jankowiak, William. 2010. "Neighbors and Kin in Chinese Cities." In *Urban Life: Readings in the Anthropology of the City,* 5th ed., edited by George Gmelch, Robert V. Kemper, and Walter P. Zenner, 256–68. Long Grove, IL: Waveland Press.

Jaschik, Scott. 2006. "Affirmative Action for Men." Inside Higher Ed, March 27. http://www.insidehighered.com/news/2006/03/27/admit.

———. 2009. "Probe of Extra Help for Men." Inside Higher Ed, November 2. http://www.insidehighered.com/news/2009/11/02/admit.

———. 2010. "Gender Gap Stops Growing." Inside Higher Ed, January 26. http://www.insidehighered.com/news/2010/01/26/gender.

Javelin Strategy & Research. 2013. *2013 Identity Fraud Report: Data Breaches Becoming a Treasure Trove for Fraudsters.* Pleasanton, CA: Javelin Strategy & Research. https://www.javelinstrategy.com.

Jensen, Arthur R. 1969. "How Much Can We Boost IQ and Scholastic Achievement?" *Harvard Educational Review* 39 (1): 1–123.

Job Stress Network. 2005. "The Whitehall Study." Accessed November 1. http://www.workhealth.org/projects/pwhitew.html.

Jolliff, Lauren, Jennifer Leadley, Elizabeth Coakley, and Rae Anne Sloan. 2012. "Table 1. Medical Students, Selected Years, 1965–2012." In *Women in U.S. Academic Medicine and Science: Statistics and Benchmarking Report 2011–2012.* Washington, DC: Association of American Medical Colleges. https://www.aamc.org/members/gwims/statistics.

Jones, Jo, William Mosher, and Kimberly Daniels. 2012. *Current Contraceptive Use in the United States, 2006–2010, and Changes in Patterns of Use since 1995.* National Health Statistics Reports 60 (October 18). Hyattsville, MD: National Center for Health Statistics. http://www.cdc.gov/nchs/data/nhsr/nhsr060.pdf.

Jones, Robert P., and Daniel Cox. 2011. *Catholic Attitudes on Gay and Lesbian Issues.* Washington, DC: Public Religion Research Institute. http://publicreligion.org/site/wp-content/uploads/2011/06/Catholics-and-LGBT-Issues-Survey-Report.pdf.

Joughlin, Charlie. 2014. "Today: Tenth Circuit to Hear Argument in Utah Marriage Case." Human Rights Campaign, HRC Blog, April 10. http://www.hrc.org/blog/entry/today-tenth-circuit-to-hear-argument-in-utah-marriage-case.

Joy, Lois. 2003. "Salaries of Recent Male and Female College Graduates: Educational and Labor Market Effects." *Industrial and Labor Relations Review* 56 (4): 606–21.

Kahana, Eva, Loren Lovegreen, and Boaz Kahana. 2011. "Long-Term Care: Tradition and Innovation." In *Handbook of Sociology of Aging,* edited by Richard A. Settersten Jr. and Jacqueline L. Angel, 583–602. New York: Springer.

Kahn, Lisa. 2009. "The Curse of the Class of 2009." *Wall Street Journal,* May9. http://online.wsj.com/article/SB124181970915002009.html.

Kailin, Julie. 2002. *Antiracist Education: From Theory to Practice.* Boulder, CO: Rowman & Littlefield.

Kaiser Family Foundation. 2004. *The Role of Media in Childhood Obesity.* Issue Brief, February. Menlo Park, CA: Henry J. Kaiser Family Foundation.

Kaldor, Mary. 2012. *New and Old Wars: Organized Violence in a Global Era,* 3rd ed. Stanford, CA: Stanford University Press.

Kallberg, Arne L. 2012. "The Social Contract in an Era of Precarious Work." *Pathways* (Fall): 3–6.

Kamerman, Sheila B. 1996. "Child and Family Policies: An International Overview." In *Children, Families, and*

Investigating Social Problems

Government: Preparing for the Twenty-First Century, edited by Edward F. Zigler, Sharon Lynn Kagan, and Nancy W. Hall, 31–48. New York: Cambridge University Press.

Kanigel, Robert. 1997. *The One Best Way: Frederick Winslow Taylor and the Enigma of Efficiency.* New York: Viking Press.

Kansas State University. 2012. "Racial and Gender Profiling Can Affect Outcome of Traffic Stops." ScienceDaily, June 12. http://www.sciencedaily.com/releases/2012/06/120621130716.htm.

Kapp, Marshall B. 1996. "Aging and the Law." In *Handbook of Aging and the Social Sciences,* 4th ed., edited by Robert H. Binstock and Linda K. George, 467–79. San Diego, CA: Academic Press.

———. 2006. "Aging and the Law." In *Handbook of Aging and the Social Sciences,* 6th ed., edited by Robert H. Binstock and Linda K. George, 419–35. San Diego, CA: Academic Press.

Karger, Howard Jacob, and David Stoesz. 2006. *American Social Welfare Policy: A Pluralist Approach,* 5th ed. Boston: Pearson/Allyn & Bacon.

Karjane, Heather M., Bonnie S. Fisher, and Francis T. Cullen. 2005. *Sexual Assault on Campus: What Colleges and Universities Are Doing about It.* Washington, DC: National Institute of Justice. https://www.ncjrs.gov/pdffiles1/nij/205521.pdf.

Karlsson, Martin, Therese Nilsson, Carl Hampus Lyttkens, and George Leeson. 2012. "Income Inequality and Health: Importance of a Cross-Country Perspective." *Social Science & Medicine* 70 (6): 875–85.

Karp, David A. 1996. *Speaking of Sadness: Depression, Disconnection, and the Meanings of Illness.* New York: Oxford University Press.

Karp, David A., Gregory P. Stone, and William C. Yoels. 1991. *Being Urban: A Sociology of City Life,* 2nd ed. Westport, CT: Praeger.

Karp, David R. 2001. "Harm and Repair: Observing Restorative Justice in Vermont." *Justice Quarterly* 18 (4): 727–57.

Karraker, Meg Wilkes. 2011. "Religious, Civic, and Interpersonal Capital: Catholic Sisters in One Community's Response to Migrant Families." *Forum on Public Policy* 2011 (2). http://forumonpublicpolicy.com/vol2011.no2/archivevol2011.no2/karraker.pdf.

———. 2013a. *Diversity and the Common Good: Civil Society, Religion, and Catholic Sisters in a Small City.* Lanham, MD: Lexington Books.

———. 2013b. *Global Families,* 2nd ed. Thousand Oaks, CA: Sage.

Karraker, Meg Wilkes, and Janet R. Grochowski. 1998. "Dual Vision Research for a Postmodern Perspective on Single Mothers' Families." Paper presented at the annual meeting of Sociologists of Minnesota, Minneapolis, October.

———. 2012. *Families with Futures: Family Studies into the Twenty-First Century,* 2nd ed. London: Routledge.

Karras, Ruth Mazo. 2000. "Active/Passion, Acts/Passions: Greek and Roman Sexualities." *American Historical Review* 105 (4): 1250–66.

Kart, Cary S. 1994. *The Realities of Aging: An Introduction to Gerontology,* 4ed. Boston: Allyn & Bacon.

Katz, Jack. 1987. "What Makes Crime 'News'?" *Media, Culture and Society* 9: 47–75.

Kehoe, Susan M., and J. Rick Ponting. 2003. "Value Importance and Value Congruence as Determinants of Trust in Health Policy Actors." *Social Science & Medicine* 57 (6): 1065–75.

Kelling, George L., and James Q. Wilson. 1982. "Broken Windows: The Police and Neighborhood Safety." *Atlantic Monthly,* March, 29–38.

Kelly, Brian C., Brooke E. Wells, Amy LeClair, Daniel Tracy, Jeffrey T. Parsons, and Sarit A. Golub. 2013a. "Prescription Drug Misuse among Young Adults: Looking across Youth Cultures." *Drug and Alcohol Review* 32 (3): 288–94.

———. 2013b. "Prevalence and Correlates of Prescription Drug Misuse among Socially Active Young Adults." *International Journal of Drug Policy* 25: 265–76.

Kelly Services. 2013. "Job Searches Go Viral as Individuals Embrace Social Media." Press release, November 20. http://ir.kellyservices.com/releasedetail.cfm?ReleaseID=808643.

Kelman, Herbert C., and V. Lee Hamilton. 1989. *Crimes of Obedience: Toward a Social Psychology of Authority and Responsibility.* New Haven, CT: Yale University Press.

Kempadoo, Kamala. 2005. "From Moral Panic to Global Justice: Changing Perspectives on Trafficking." In *Trafficking and Prostitution Reconsidered: New Perspectives on Migration, Sex Work, and Human Rights,* edited by Kamala Kempadoo with Jyoti Sanghera and Bandana Pattanaik. Boulder, CO: Paradigm.

Kempadoo, Kamala, and Jo Doezema. 1998. *Global Sex Workers: Rights, Resistance, and Redefinition.* New York: Routledge.

Kempner, Joanna. 2006. "Gendering the Migraine Market: Do Representations of Illness Matter?" *Social Science & Medicine* 63 (8): 1986–97.

Kennedy, David M. 2011. "Whither Streetwork? The Place of Outreach Workers in Community Violence Prevention." *Criminology & Public Policy* 10 (4): 1045–51.

Kennedy, Sheila, and Larry Bumpass. 2008. "Cohabitation and Children's Living Arrangements: New Estimates from the United States." *Demographic Research* 19: 1663–92.

Kenney, Shannon R., Vandana Thadani, Tehniat Ghaidarov, and Joseph W. LaBrie. 2013. "First-Year College Women's Motivations for Hooking Up: A Mixed-Methods Examination of Normative Peer Perceptions and Personal Hookup Participation." *International Journal of Sexual Health* 25 (3): 212–24.

Kenworthy, Tom. 2013. "How Two Reservoirs Have Become Billboards for What Climate Change Is Doing to the American West." ThinkProgress, August 12. http://thinkprogress.org/climate/2013/08/12/2439931/reservoir-billboards-southwest/#.

Khan, Shamus Rahman. 2011. *Privilege: The Making of an Adolescent Elite at St. Paul's School.* Princeton, NJ: Princeton University Press.

Kids' Well-Being Indicators Clearinghouse. 2012. http://www.nyskwic.org.

Kilty, Keith M. 2009. "'Greed Is Good': The Idle Rich, the Working Poor, and Personal Responsibility." In *Family Poverty in Diverse Contexts,* edited by C. Anne Broussard and Alfred L. Joseph, 11–25. New York: Routledge.

Kilty, Keith M., and Thomas M. Meenaghan. 1977. "Drinking Status, Labeling, and Social Rejection." *Journal of Social Psychology* 102 (1): 93–104.

Kim, Susanna. 2012. "Pressure on SEC to Implement Rule Disclosing CEO to Median Worker Pay." ABC News, March 13. http://abcnews.go.com/Business/sec-pressured-implement-ceo-worker-pay-disclosure-walmarts/story?id=15886752.

Kimmel, Michael S., and Rebecca F. Plante. 2002. "The Gender of Desire: The Sexual Fantasies of Women and Men." *Advances in Gender Research* 6: 55–78.

Kinsey, Alfred C., Wardell B. Pomeroy, and Clyde E. Martin. 1998. *Sexual Behavior in the Human Male.* Bloomington: Indiana University Press. First published 1948.

Kinsey, Alfred C., Wardell B. Pomeroy, Clyde E. Martin, and Paul H. Gebhard. 1998. *Sexual Behavior in the Human Female.* Bloomington: Indiana University Press. First published 1953.

Kirsch, Irving. 2009. *The Emperor's New Drugs: Exploding the Antidepressant Myth.* London: Bodley Head.

Kirsch, Irving, Alan Scoboria, and Thomas J. Moore. 2002. "Antidepressants and Placebos: Secrets, Revelations, and Unanswered Questions." *Prevention & Treatment* 5 (1). doi:10.1037/1522–3736.5.1.533r.

Kiss, Alexander, and Siegfried Meryn. 2001. "Effects of Sex and Gender on Psychosocial Aspects of Prostate and Breast Cancer." *British Medical Journal* 323 (7320): 1055–58.

Kitsuse, John I., and Malcolm Spector. 1973. "Toward a Sociology of Social Problems: Social Conditions, Value-Judgments, and Social Problems." *Social Problems* 20 (4): 407–19.

———. 2000. *Constructing Social Problems.* New Brunswick, NJ: Transaction.

Kleniewski, Nancy. 1997. *Cities, Change, and Conflict: A Political Economy of Urban Life.* Belmont, CA: Wadsworth.

Klinenberg, Eric. 2002. *Heat Wave: A Social Autopsy of Disaster in Chicago.* Chicago: University of Chicago Press.

Kneebone, Elizabeth, Carey Nadeau, and Alan Berube. 2011. *The Re-emergence of Concentrated Poverty: Metropolitan Trends in the 2000s.* New York: Metropolitan Policy Program, Brookings Institution. http://www.brookings.edu/~/media/research/files/papers/2011/11/03%20poverty%20kneebone%20nadeau%20berube/1103_poverty_kneebone_nadeau_berube.pdf.

Knorr-Cetina, Karen. 1981. *The Manufacture of Knowledge: An Essay on the Constructivist and Contextual Nature of Science.* Oxford: Pergamon Press.

Kokoska, E., T. Bird, J. Robbins, S. Smith, S. Corsi, and B. Campbell. 2007. "Racial Disparities in the Management of Pediatric Appendicitis." *Journal of Surgical Research* 130 (2): 83–88.

Kollmuss, Anja, and Julian Agyeman. 2002. "Mind the Gap: Why Do People Act Environmentally and What Are the Barriers to Pro-Environmental Behavior?" *Environmental Education Research* 8 (3): 239–60.

Kondilis, Elias, Stathis Giannakopoulos, Magda Gavana, Ioanna Ierodiakonou, Howard Waitzkin, and Alexis Benos. 2013. "Economic Crisis, Restrictive Policies, and the Populations' Health and Health Care: The Greek Case." *American Journal of Public Health* 103 (6): 973–79.

Korgen, Kathleen. 2002. *Crossing the Racial Divide: Close Friendships between Black and White Americans.* Westport, CT: Praeger.

Korp, Peter. 2006. "Health on the Internet: Implications for Health Promotion." *Health Education Research* 21 (1): 78–86.

Kotkin, Joel. 2012. *The Rise of Post-familialism: Humanity's Future?* Singapore: Soh Tze Min (Civil Service College).

Krafft-Ebing, Richard von. 1998. *Psychopathia Sexualis.* New York: Arcade. First published 1886.

Krase, Jerome. 2012. *Seeing Cities Change: Local Culture and Class.* Burlington, VT: Ashgate.

Krebs, Christopher P., Christine H. Lindquist, Tara D. Warner, Bonnie S. Fisher, and Sandra L. Martin. 2007. "Campus Sexual Assault (CSA) Study: Final Report." Prepared for the National Institute of Justice. https://www.ncjrs.gov/pdffiles1/nij/grants/221153.pdf.

Kreimer, Pablo, and Juan Pablo Zabala. 2007. "Chagas Disease in Argentina: Reciprocal Construction of Social and Scientific Problems." *Science Technology & Society* 12 (1): 49–72.

Kreutzer, Laura. 2012. "A Cellphone Mom Struggles to Keep in Touch." *Wall Street Journal,* April 20. http://online.wsj.com/article/SB1000142405270230429930457734963205565796.html?reflink=wsj_redirect.

Krieger, Nancy, and Stephen Sidney. 1996. "Racial Discrimination and Blood Pressure: The CARDIA Study of Young Black and White Adults." *American Journal of Public Health* 86: 1370–78.

Kristof, Nicholas D., and Sheryl WuDunn. 2009. *Half the Sky: Turning Oppression into Opportunity for Women Worldwide.* New York: Alfred A. Knopf.

Kunkel, Dale. 2001. "Children and Television Advertising." In *Handbook of Children and the Media,* edited by Dorothy G. Singer and Jerome L. Singer, 375–94. Thousand Oaks, CA: Sage.

Kuper, Hannah, Archana Singh-Manoux, Johannes Siegrist, and Michael G. Marmot. 2002. "When Reciprocity Fails: Effort-Reward Imbalance in Relation to Coronary Heart Disease and Health Functioning within the Whitehall II Study." *Occupational Environmental Medicine* 59: 777–84.

Kutner, Lawrence, and Cheryl Olson. 2008. *Grand Theft Childhood: The Surprising Truth about Violent Video Games and What Parents Can Do.* New York: Simon & Schuster.

Lafrance, Dawn E., Meika Loe, and Scott C. Brown. 2012. "'Yes Means Yes': A New Approach to Sexual Assault Prevention and Positive Sexuality Promotion." *American Journal of Sexuality Education* 7 (4): 445–60.

Laidler, Gita Joan. 2007. "Ice, through Inuit Eyes: Characterizing the Importance of Sea Ice Processes, Use, and Change around Three Nunavut Communities." Doctoral dissertation, University of Toronto.

Lambert, Tracy A., Arnold S. Kahn, and Kevin J. Apple. 2003. "Pluralistic Ignorance and Hooking Up." *Journal of Sex Research* 40: 129–34.

Lancaster, Roger N. 2011. *Sex Panic and the Punitive State.* Berkeley: University of California Press.

Langan, Patrick A., and David P. Farrington. 1998. *Crime and Justice in the United States and in England and Wales, 1981–96.* NCJ 169284. Washington, DC: U.S. Department of Justice, Bureau of Justice Statistics.

Lareau, Annette. 2003. *Unequal Childhoods: Class, Race, and Family Life.* Berkeley: University of California Press.

Latour, Bruno. 1987. *Science in Action: How to Follow Scientists and Engineers through Society.* Cambridge, MA: Harvard University Press.

Latour, Bruno, and Steve Woolgar. 1979. *Laboratory Life: The Social Construction of Scientific Facts.* Beverly Hills, CA: Sage.

Lavelle, Kristen, and Joe R. Feagin. 2006. "Hurricane Katrina: The Race and Class Debate." *Monthly Review* 58 (3): 52–66.

Law, John. 1991. *A Sociology of Monsters: Essays on Power, Technology, and Domination.* London: Routledge.

Leatherman, Janie L. 2011. *Sexual Violence and Armed Conflict.* Cambridge: Polity Press.

Lee, James. 2012. *U.S. Naturalizations: 2011.* Annual Flow Report. Washington, DC: Office of Immigration Statistics, U.S. Department of Homeland Security. http://www.dhs.gov/xlibrary/assets/statistics/publications/natz_fr_2011.pdf.

Lee, Sharon M. 1993. "Racial Classifications in the U.S. Census: 1890 to 1990." *Ethnic and Racial Studies* 16 (1): 75–94.

Lee, Youkyung. 2012. "South Korea: 160,000 Kids between Age 5 and 9 Are Internet-Addicted." Huffington Post, November 28 (updated January 27, 2013). http://www.huffingtonpost.com/2012/11/28/south-korea-internet-addicted_n_2202371.html.

Lemert, Edwin M. 1951. *Social Pathology: A Systematic Approach to the Theory of Sociopathic Behavior.* New York: McGraw-Hill.

———. 1972. *Human Deviance, Social Problems, and Social Control.* Englewood Cliffs, NJ: Prentice-Hall.

Lemon, Bruce W., Vern L. Bengtson, and James A. Peterson. 1972. "An Exploration of the Activity Theory of Aging: Activity Types and Life Satisfaction among In-Movers to a Retirement Community." *Journal of Gerontology* 27 (4): 511–23.

Lenski, Gerhard E. 1966. *Power and Privilege: A Theory of Social Stratification.* New York: McGraw-Hill.

Lever, Janet, and Deanne Dolnick. 2000. "Clients and Call Girls: Seeking Sex and Intimacy." In *Sex for Sale: Prostitution, Pornography, and the Sex Industry,* edited by Ronald Weitzer, 85–101. New York: Routledge.

Levine, David I. 1998. *Working in the Twenty-First Century: Policies for Economic Growth through Training, Opportunity, and Education.* Armonk, NY: M. E. Sharpe.

Levine, Michael P., and Kristen Harrison. 2009. "Effects of Media on Eating Disorders and Body Image." In *Media Effects: Advances in Theory and Research,* 3rd ed., edited by Jennings Bryant and Mary Beth Oliver, 490–516. New York: Routledge.

Levintova, Marya, and Thomas Novotny. 2004. "Noncommunicable Disease Mortality in the Russian Federation: From Legislation to Policy." *Bulletin of the World Health Organization* 82 (11): 875–80.

Levitt, Steven D. 1996. "The Effect of Prison Population Size on Crime Rates: Evidence from Prison Overcrowding Litigation." *Quarterly Journal of Economics* 111 (2): 319–51.

Lewis, Melissa A., David C. Atkins, Jessica A. Blayney, David V. Dent, and Debra L. Kaysen. 2013. "What Is Hooking Up? Examining Definitions of Hooking Up in Relations to Behavior and Normative Perceptions." *Journal of Sex Research* 50 (8): 757–66.

Lewis, Oscar. 1966. "The Culture of Poverty." *Scientific American,* October, 19–25.

———. 1969. "Culture of Poverty." In *On Understanding Poverty: Perspectives from the Social Sciences,* edited by Daniel Patrick Moynihan, 187–220. New York: Basic Books.

Lichter, Daniel T., Felicia B. LeClere, and Diane K. McLaughlin. 1991. "Local Marriage Markets and the Marital Behavior of Black and White Women." *American Journal of Sociology* 96: 843–67.

Lichter, Daniel T., Diane K. McLaughlin, George Kephart, and David J. Landry. 1992. "Race and the Retreat from Marriage: A Shortage of Marriageable Men?" *American Sociological Review* 57: 781–99.

Lin, Daisy, and Bruce Hensel. 2013. "If Sexual Dysfunction Were a Virus, 'It'd Be Pandemic': Expert." NBC News, Los Angeles. http://www.nbclosangeles.com/news/local/Couples-Sexual-Problems-Health-ED-207639941.html.

Liptak, Adam. 2013. "Supreme Court Bolsters Gay Marriage with Two Major Rulings." *New York Times,* June 26. http://www.nytimes.com/2013/06/27/us/politics/supreme-court-gay-marriage.html.

Littig, Beate, and Erich Grießler. 2005. "Social Sustainability: A Catchword between Political Pragmatism and Social Theory." *International Journal of Sustainable Development* 8 (1/2): 65–79.

Lloyd, Rachel. 2012. *Girls Like Us: Fighting for a World Where Girls Are Not for Sale, an Activist Finds Her Calling and Heals Herself.* New York: HarperPerennial.

Lofland, Lyn H. 1998. *The Public Realm: Exploring the City's Quintessential Social Territory.* New York: Aldine de Gruyter.

Lofquist, Daphne, Terry Lugaila, Martin O'Connell, and Sarah Feliz. 2012. *Households and Families: 2010.* U.S. Census Bureau, Census Brief C2010BR-14. Washington, DC: Government Printing Office. http://www.census.gov/prod/cen2010/briefs/c2010br-14.pdf.

Logan, John R., and Harvey L. Molotch. 1987. *Urban Fortunes: The Political Economy of Place.* Berkeley: University of California Press.

Lombe, Margaret, and Michael Sherraden. 2008. "Effects of Participating in an Asset-Building Intervention on Social Inclusion." *Journal of Poverty* 12 (3): 284–305.

Long, Norton E. 1958. "The Local Community as an Ecology of Games." *American Journal of Sociology* 64 (3): 251–61.

Longino, Charles F., Jr. 2005. "The Future of Ageism: Baby Boomers at the Doorstep." *Generations* 29 (3): 79–83.

Longino, Charles F., Jr., and Cary S. Kart. 1982. "Explicating Activity Theory: A Formal Replication." *Journal of Gerontology* 37 (6): 713–22.

Lopez, Nancy. 2003. *Hopeful Girls, Troubled Boys: Race and Gender Disparity in Urban Education.* New York: Routledge.

Loseke, Donileen R., and Joel Best, eds. 2003. *Social Problems: Constructionist Readings.* New York: Aldine de Gruyter.

Lui, Meizhu, Barbara Robles, Betsy Leondar-Wright, Rose Brewer, and Rebecca Adamson, with United for a Fair Economy. 2006. *The Color of Wealth: The Story behind the U.S. Racial Wealth Divide.* New York: New Press.

Lukas, J. Anthony. 1985. *Common Ground: A Turbulent Decade in the Lives of Three American Families.* New York: Alfred A. Knopf.

Luke, Nancy, Rachel E. Goldberg, Blessing U. Mberu, and Eliya M. Zulu. 2011. "Social Exchange and Sexual Behavior in Young Women's Premarital Relationships in Kenya." *Journal of Marriage and Family* 73: 1048–64.

Luo, Michael. 2010. "At Closing Plant, Ordeal Included Heart Attacks." *New York Times,* November 24. http://www.nytimes.com/2010/02/25/us/25stress.html.

Lynch, John, George Davey Smith, Sam Harper, and Kathleen Bainbridge. 2006. "Explaining the Social Gradient in Coronary Heart Disease: Comparing Relative and Absolute Risk Approaches." *Journal of Epidemiology and Community Health* 60: 436–41.

Lynch, Michael. 1985. *Art and Artifact in Laboratory Science: A Study of Shop Work and Shop Talk in a Research Laboratory.* London: Routledge & Kegan Paul.

Lynch, Michael J. 2011. Review of *Wage Theft in America (Why Millions of Working Americans Are Not Getting Paid—and What We Can Do About It),* by Kim Bobo. *Contemporary Justice Review* 14 (2): 255–58.

Lyotard, Jean-François. 1984. *The Postmodern Condition: A Report on Knowledge.* Translated by Geoff Bennington and Brian Massumi. Minneapolis: University of Minnesota Press.

Macartney, Suzanne, Alemayehu Bishaw, and Kayla Fontenot. 2013. *Poverty Rates for Selected Detailed Race and Hispanic Groups by State and Place: 2007–2011.* U.S. Census Bureau, American Community Survey Brief 11-17. Washington, DC: Government Printing Office. http://www.census.gov/prod/2013pubs/acsbr11-17.pdf.

MacDonald, John M., and Meda Chesney-Lind. 2001. "Gender Bias and Juvenile Justice Revisited: A Multiyear Analysis." *Crime & Delinquency* 47 (2): 173–95.

Macgregor, Lyn C. 2010. *Habits of the Heartland: Small-Town Life in Modern America.* Ithaca, NY: Cornell University Press.

MacKinnon, Catharine A. 2008. "The ICTR's Legacy on Sexual Violence." *New England Journal of International and Comparative Law* 14 (2): 211–20.

MacLeod, Jay. 2009. *Ain't No Makin' It: Aspirations and Attainment in a Low-Income Neighborhood,* 3rd ed. Boulder, CO: Westview Press.

MacRae, Allan, and Howard Zehr. 2004. *The Little Book of Family Group Conferences: New Zealand Style.* Intercourse, PA: Good Books.

Madden, Mary, and Lee Rainie. 2010. "Adults and Cell Phone Distractions." Pew Research Center, Internet Project, June 18. http://pewinternet.org/Reports/2010/Cell-Phone-Distractions.aspx.

Maher, Timothy. 1998. "Environmental Oppression: Who Is Targeted for Exposure?" *Journal of Black Studies* 28: 357–67.

Mahoney, Annette. 2010. "Religion in Families, 1999–2000: A Relational Spirituality Framework." *Journal of Marriage and Family* 72: 805–27.

Maines, David R., and Jeffrey C. Bridger. 1992. "Narratives, Community, and Land Use Decisions." *Social Science Journal* 29 (4): 363–80.

Malesevic, Sinisa. 2010. *The Sociology of War and Violence.* Cambridge: Cambridge University Press.

Mallicoat, Stacy L. 2007. "Gendered Justice: Attributional Differences between Males and Females in the Juvenile Courts." *Feminist Criminology* 2 (1): 4–30.

Mam, Somaly. 2009. *The Road of Lost Innocence: The True Story of a Cambodian Heroine.* New York: Spiegel & Grau.

Manik, Julfikar Ali, and Jim Yardley. 2013. "Building Collapse in Bangladesh Leaves Scores Dead." *New York Times,* April 24. http://www.nytimes.com/2013/04/25/world/asia/bangladesh-building-collapse.html?_r=0.

Manning, Peter K. 2005. "The Study of Policing." *Police Quarterly* 8 (1): 23–43.

Manning, Wendy D., and Jessica A. Cohen. 2012. "Premarital Cohabitation and Marital Dissolution: An Examination of Recent Marriages." *Journal of Marriage and Family* 74: 377–87.

Manning, Wendy D., Monica Longmore, and Peggy Giordano. 2000. "The Relationship Context of Contraceptive Use at First Intercourse." *Family Planning Perspectives* 32: 104–10.

Maratea, Ray. 2008. "The e-Rise and Fall of Social Problems: The Blogosphere as a Public Arena." *Social Problems* 55 (1): 139–60.

Marin, Dalia. 2006. "A New International Division of Labor in Europe: Outsourcing and Offshoring to Eastern Europe." *Journal of the European Economic Association* 4 (2–3): 612–22.

Marmot, Michael G. 2006. "Health in an Unequal World." *The Lancet* 368: 2081–84.

Marmot, Michael G., Geoffrey Rose, Martin J. Shipley, and Peter J. Hamilton. 1978. "Employment Grade and Coronary Heart Disease in British Civil Servants." *Journal of Epidemiology and Community Health* 32: 244–49.

Marr, Chuck, and B. Chye-Ching Huang. 2012. *Misconceptions and Realities about Who Pays Taxes.* Washington, DC: Center on Budget and Policy Priorities. http://www.cbpp.org/files/5-26-11tax.pdf.

Marsiglio, William, and John H. Scanzoni. 1995. *Families and Friendships: Applying the Sociological Imagination.* New York: HarperCollins.

Martin, Andrew, and Andrew W. Lehren. 2012. "A Generation Hobbled by the Soaring Cost of College." *New York Times,* May 12. http://www.nytimes.com/2012/05/13/business/student-loans-weighing-down-a-generation-with-heavy-debt.html?pagewanted=all&_r=0.

Martin, Graham P., Graeme Currie, and Rachael Finn. 2009. "Reconfiguring or Reproducing Intra-professional Boundaries? Specialist Expertise, Generalist Knowledge and the 'Modernization' of the Medical Workforce." *Social Science & Medicine* 68 (7): 1191–98.

Martin, Susan Ehrlich, and Nancy C. Jurik. 1996. *Doing Justice, Doing Gender: Women in Law and Criminal Justice Occupations.* Thousand Oaks, CA: Sage.

Marttila, Anne-Maria. 2003. "Consuming Sex: Finnish Male Clients and Russian and Baltic Prostitution." Paper presented at the European Feminist Research Conference "Gender and Power in the New Europe," Lund University, Sweden.

Massey, Douglas S. 1995. "The New Immigration and Ethnicity in the United States." *Population and Development Review* 21: 631–52.

Massey, Douglas S., and Nancy A. Denton. 1993. *American Apartheid: Segregation and the Making of the Underclass.* Cambridge, MA: Harvard University Press.

Massey, Douglas S., and Garvey Lundy. 2001. "Use of Black English and Racial Discrimination in Urban Housing Markets: New Methods and Findings." *Urban Affairs Review* 36 (4): 452–69.

Masters, William, and Virginia Johnson. 2010. *Human Sexual Response.* New York: Ishi Press.

Matcha, Duane A. 1997. *The Sociology of Aging: A Social Problems Perspective.* Boston: Allyn & Bacon.

———. 2011. "Crime, the Law, and Aging." In *Handbook of Sociology of Aging,* edited by Richard A. Settersten Jr. and Jacqueline L. Angel, 431–44. New York: Springer.

Matcha, Duane A., and Bonita A. Sessing-Matcha. 2007. "A Comparison of American and European Newspaper Coverage of the Elderly." *Hallym International Journal of Aging* 9 (2): 77–88.

Matchen, Quiche. 2013. "IJM Stands for 27 Hours against Sex Trafficking." WKU Herald, March 26. http://wkuherald.com/news/campus_life/article_1fe4f982-9592-11e2-ba36-001a4bcf6878.html.

Mather, Mark, and Dia Adams. 2007. "The Crossover in Male-Female College Enrollment Rates." Population Reference Bureau, February. http://www.prb.org/Articles/2007/CrossoverinFemaleMaleCollegeEnrollmentRates.aspx.

Matthew Shepard Foundation. 2014. "Matthew's Story." Accessed April 17. http://www.matthewshepard.org.

Mawn, Barbara Ellen. 2011. "Children's Voices: Living with HIV." *American Journal of Maternal and Child Nursing* 36: 368–72.

McCabe, Kimberly A., and Sabita Manian, eds. 2010. *Sex Trafficking: A Global Perspective.* Lanham, MD: Lexington Books.

McCall, Leslie. 2001. *Complex Inequality: Gender, Class, and Race in the New Economy.* New York: Routledge.

McChesney, Robert W. 1996. "The Payne Fund and Radio Broadcasting, 1928–1935." In *Children and the Movies: Media Influence and the Payne Fund Controversy,* edited by Garth S. Jowett, Ian C. Jarvie, and Kathryn H. Fuller, 303–35. New York: Cambridge University Press.

McCombs, Maxwell E. 2004. *Setting the Agenda: The Mass Media and Public Opinion.* Cambridge, MA: Polity Press.

McCright, Aaron M. 2011. "Political Orientation Moderates Americans' Beliefs and Concern about Climate Change." *Climatic Change* 104 (2): 243–53.

McCright, Aaron M., and Riley E. Dunlap. 2003. "Defeating Kyoto: The Conservative Movement's Impact on U.S. Climate Change Policy." *Social Problems* 50 (3): 348–73.

———. 2010. "Anti-reflexivity: The American Conservative Movement's Success in Undermining Climate Science and Policy." *Theory, Culture & Society* 27 (2–3): 100–133.

McCubbin, Hamilton, Anne Thompson, and Marilyn McCubbin. 1996. *Family Assessment: Resiliency, Coping, and Adaptation.* Madison: University of Wisconsin Press.

McDonald, Daniel G. 2004. "Twentieth-Century Media Effects Research." In *The Sage Handbook of Media Studies,* edited by John D. H. Downing, 183–200. Thousand Oaks, CA: Sage.

McIntosh, Peggy. 2001. "White Privilege and Male Privilege: A Persona Account of Coming to See Correspondences through Work in Women's Studies." In *Race, Class, and Gender: An Anthology,* 4th ed., edited by Margaret L. Anderson and Patricia Hill Collins. Belmont, CA: Wadsworth.

McKinlay, John B., and Lisa D. Marceau. 2002. "The End of the Golden Age of Doctoring." *International Journal of Health Services* 32 (2): 379–416.

McLanahan, Sara 2011. "Family Instability and Complexity after a Nonmarital Birth: Outcomes for Children in Fragile Families." In *Social Class and Changing Families in an Unequal America,* edited by Marcia J. Carlson and Paula England, 108–33. Palo Alto, CA: Stanford University Press.

McLaughlin, Dorothy. 1998. "*Silent Spring* Revisited." *Frontline,* PBS. http://www.pbs.org/wgbh/pages/frontline/shows/nature/disrupt/sspring.html.

McNair, Brian. 2013. *Porno? Chic! How Pornography Changed the World and Made It a Better Place.* London: Routledge.

McSally, Martha E. 2011. "Defending America in Mixed Company: Gender in the U.S. Armed Forces." *Daedalus* 140 (3): 148–64.

Mead, George Herbert. 1934. *Mind, Self, and Society.* Chicago: University of Chicago Press.

Meehl, Gerald A., Francis Zwiers, Jenni Evans, Thomas Knutson, Linda Mearns, and Peter Whetton. 2000. "Trends in Extreme Weather and Climate Events: Issues Related to Modeling Extremes in Projections of Future Climate Change." *Bulletin of the American Meteorological Society* 81 (3): 427–36.

Mehli, H., L. Skuterud, A. Mosdøl, and A. Tønnessen. 2000. "The Impact of Chernobyl Fallout on the Southern Saami Reindeer Herders of Norway in 1996." *Health Physics* 79 (6): 682–90.

Melton, Heather C., and Carry Lafeve Sillito. 2012. "The Role of Gender in Officially Reported Intimate Partner Abuse." *Journal of Interpersonal Violence* 27: 1090–1111.

Merton, Robert K. 1938. "Social Structure and Anomie." *American Sociological Review* 3(5): 672–82.

———. 1942. *The Sociology of Science: Theoretical and Empirical Investigations.* Chicago: University of Chicago Press.

———. 1968. *Social Theory and Social Structure.* New York: Simon & Schuster.

Messner, Steven F., and Richard Rosenfeld. 2013. *Crime and the American Dream,* 5th ed. Belmont, CA: Wadsworth.

Meyer, John W. 1977. "The Effects of Education as an Institution." *American Journal of Sociology* 85: 55–77.

Mickelson, Roslyn Arlin. 2003. "Gender, Bourdieu, and the Anomaly of Women's Achievement Redux." *Sociology of Education* 76 (4): 373–75.

Miller, Brian, and Mike Lapham. 2012. *The Self-Made Myth: And the Truth about How Government Helps Individuals and Businesses Succeed.* San Francisco: Berrett-Koehler.

Miller, Patricia N., Darryl W. Miller, Eithen M. McKibbin, and Gregory L. Pettys. 1999. "Stereotypes of the Elderly in Magazine Advertisements 1956–1996." *International Journal of Aging and Human Development* 49 (4): 319–37.

Miller-Young, Mireille. 2010. "Putting Hypersexuality to Work: Black Women and Illicit Eroticism in Pornography." *Sexualities* 13 (2): 219–35.

Milligan, Melinda J. 1998. "Interactional Past and Potential: The Social Construction of Place Attachment." *Symbolic Interaction* 21 (1): 1–33.

Mills, C. Wright. 1951. *White Collar: The American Middle Class.* London: Oxford University Press.

———. 1954. "Nothing to Laugh At." *New York Times,* April 25, BR20.

———. 1956. *The Power Elite.* New York: Oxford University Press.

———. 1959. *The Sociological Imagination.* New York: Oxford University Press.

———. 1961. *The Sociological Imagination.* New York: Grove Press.

———. 2000. *The Power Elite,* 2nd ed. New York: Oxford University Press.

———. 2001. *The New Men of Power: America's Labor Leaders.* Champaign: University of Illinois Press. First published 1948.

Miniño, Arialdi M., Jiaquan Xu, and Kennet D. Kochanek. 2010. *Deaths: Preliminary Data for 2008.* National Vital Statistics Reports 59, no 2. Hyattsville, MD: National Center for Health Statistics. http://www.cdc.gov/nchs/data/nvsr/nvsr59/nvsr59_02.pdf.

Mink, Gwendolyn. 2001. "Violating Women: Rights Abuses in the Welfare Police State." *Annals of the American Academy of Political and Social Science* 577 (September): 79–93.

Minnesota Department of Human Rights. 2014. "Minnesota's New Same-Sex Marriage Law." Accessed April 17. http://www.mn.gov/mdhr/public_affairs/samesex_marriage.html.

Minnesota for Marriage. 2012. "Why Preserving Marriage Matters." Accessed November 24. http://www.minnesotaformarriage.com/why.

Minnesotans United for All Families. 2012. "Fact Sheet." http://mnunited.org/wp-content/uploads/2012/07/8VoteNoFacts.pdf.

Mirkin, Harris. 2009. "The Social, Political, and Legal Construction of the Concept of Child Pornography." *Journal of Homosexuality* 56 (2): 233–67.

Mishel, Lawrence, Jared Bernstein, and Heidi Shierholz. 2009. *The State of Working America, 2008–2009.* Ithaca, NY: Cornell University Press.

Mishel, Lawrence, Josh Bivens, Elise Gould, and Heidi Shierholz. 2013. *The State of Working America,* 12th ed. Ithaca, NY: Cornell University Press.

Mitchell, Corey. 2012. "Both Sides in Marriage Battle Rake in Millions." *Star Tribune,* September 27. http://www.startribune.com/politics/statelocal/171442411.html.

Moen, Phyllis, and Patricia Roehling. 2005. *The Career Mystique: Cracks in the American Dream.* Lanham, MD: Rowman & Littlefield.

Moerman, Daniel E., and Wayne B. Jonas. 2002. "Deconstructing the Placebo Effect and Finding the Meaning Response." *Annals of Internal Medicine* 136 (6): 471–76.

Moffitt, Robert. 2008. "A Primer on U.S. Welfare Reform." *University of Wisconsin Institute for Research on Poverty Focus* 26 (1): 15–25.

Mohai, Paul, and Robin Saha. 2007. "Racial Inequality in the Distribution of Hazardous Waste: A National-Level Reassessment." *Social Problems* 54 (3): 343–70.

Mol, Arthur P. J. 2003. *Globalization and Environmental Reform: The Ecological Modernization of the Global Economy.* Cambridge: MIT Press.

Mol, Arthur P. J., and Gert Spaargaren. 2000. "Ecological Modernisation Theory in Debate: A Review." *Environmental Politics* 9 (1): 17–49.

Monti, Daniel J. 1990. *Race, Redevelopment, and the New Company Town.* Albany: State University of New York Press.

———. 1999. *The American City: A Social and Cultural History.* Malden, MA: Blackwell.

———. 2013. *Engaging Strangers: Civil Rites, Civic Capitalism, and Public Order in an American City.* Lanham, MD: Fairleigh Dickinson University Press.

Monto, Martin A. 2010. "Prostitutes' Customers: Motives and Misconceptions." In *Sex for Sale: Prostitution, Pornography, and the Sex Industry,* 2nd ed., edited by Ronald Weitzer, 233–54. New York: Routledge.

Montoya, Michael J. 2011. *Making the Mexican Diabetic: Race, Science, and the Genetics of Inequality.* Berkley: University of California Press.

Moody, Harry R., and Jennifer R. Sasser. 2012. *Aging: Concepts and Controversies,* 7th ed. Thousand Oaks, CA: Sage.

Mora, Camilo, Abby G. Frazier, Ryan J. Longman, Rachel S. Dacks, Maya M. Walton, Eric J. Tong, Joseph J. Sanchez, et al. 2013. "The Projected Timing of Climate Departure from Recent Variability." *Nature* 502 (7470): 183–87.

Morgan, S. Philip, Erin Cumberworth, and Christopher Wimer. 2012. "Sheltering the Storm: American Families in the Great Recession." *Pathways* (Fall): 24–27.

Morin, Rich. 2012. "Rising Share of Americans See Conflict between Rich and Poor." Pew Research Center, Social and Demographic Trends, January 11. http://pew research.org/pubs/2167/rich-poor-social-conflict-class.

Morin, Rich, and Seth Motel. 2012. "A Third of Americans Now Say They Are in the Lower Classes." Pew Research Center, Social and Demographic Trends, September 10. http://www.pewsocialtrends.org/files/2012/09/the-lower-classes-final.pdf.

Morris, Allison, and Gabrielle Maxwell. 2003. "Restorative Justice in New Zealand." In *Restorative Justice and Criminal Justice: Competing or Reconcilable Paradigms,* edited by Andrew von Hirsch, Julian Roberts, Anthony E. Bottoms, Kent Roach, and Mara Schiff, 257–72. Portland, OR: Hart.

Morris, Edward W. 2007. "'Ladies' or 'Loudies'? Perceptions and Experiences of Black Girls in Classrooms." *Youth & Society* 38 (4): 490–515.

———. 2008. "'Rednecks,' 'Rutters,' and 'Rithmetic: Social Class, Masculinity, and Schooling in a Rural Context." *Gender & Society* 22 (6): 728–51.

Mortenson, Greg, and David Oliver Relin. 2006. *Three Cups of Tea: One Man's Mission to Promote Peace—One School at a Time.* New York: Penguin Books.

Mount Holyoke News. 2013. "Students Found Anti–Sex Trafficking Club on Campus." April 18. http:// mountholyokenews.org/2013/04/18/students-found-anti-sex-trafficking-club-on-campus.

Mudde, Cas. 2012. *The Relationship between Immigration and Nativism in Europe and North America.* Washington, DC: Migration Policy Institute.

Muehlenhard, Charlene L., Sharon Danoff-Burg, and Irene G. Powch. 1996. "Is Rape Sex or Violence? Conceptual Issues and Implications." In *Sex, Power, Conflict: Evolutionary and Feminist Perspectives,* edited by David M. Buss and Neil M. Malamuth, 119–37. New York: Oxford University Press.

Muhl, Charles J. 2001. "The Employment-at-Will Doctrine: Three Major Exceptions." *Monthly Labor Review,* January, 3–11. http://www.bls.gov/opub/mlr/2001/01/art1full.pdf.

Mumford, Lewis. 1967. *The Myth of the Machine.* New York: Harcourt, Brace & World.

Murdock, George Peter. 1949. *Social Structure.* New York: Macmillan.

Murphy, Sheigla, and Marsha Rosenbaum. 1999. *Pregnant Women on Drugs: Combating Stereotypes and Stigma.* New Brunswick, NJ: Rutgers University Press.

Murray, Charles. 2012. *Coming Apart: The State of White America 1960–2010.* New York: Crown Forum.

Murray, Christopher J. L., Sandeep C. Kalkarni, Catherine Michaud, Niels Tomijima, Maria T. Bulzacchelli, Terrell J. Iandiorio, and Majid Ezzati. 2006. "Eight Americas: Investigating Mortality Disparities across Races, Counties, and Race-Counties in the United States." *Public Library of Science Medicine* 3 (9): 1513–24.

Musick, Kelly, and Larry Bumpass. 2012. "Reexamining the Case for Marriage: Union Formation and Changes in Well-Being." *Journal of Marriage and Family* 74: 1–18.

Musto, David F. 1999. *The American Disease: Origins of Narcotic Control,* 3rd ed. New York: Oxford University Press.

Nagel, Joane. 2003. *Race, Ethnicity, and Sexuality: Intimate Intersections, Forbidden Frontiers.* New York: Oxford University Press.

Naimi, Timothy S., Robert D. Brewer, Ali Mokdad, Denny Clark, Mary K. Serdula, and James S. Marks. 2003. "Binge Drinking among US Adults." *Journal of the American Medical Association* 289 (1): 70–75.

Nakonezny, Paul A., Robert D. Shull, and Joseph Lee Rogers. 1995. "The Effect of No-Fault Divorce Law on the Divorce Rate across the 50 States and Its Relation to Income, Education, and Religiosity." *Journal of Marriage and the Family* 57: 477–88.

Narzary, Pralip Kumar. 2013. "Sexual Exposure and Awareness of Emergency Contraceptive Pills among Never Married." *Journal of Social and Development Sciences* 4 (4): 164–73.

National Association of Realtors. 2012. *Minneapolis–St. Paul–Bloomington Area Local Market Report, Second Quarter 2012.* Chicago: National Association of Realtors. http://www.realtor.org/sites/default/files/reports/2012/local-market-reports-2012-q2/local-market-reports-2012-q2-mn-minneapolis.pdf.

National Cancer Institute. 2008. *The Role of the Media in Promoting and Reducing Tobacco Use.* Tobacco Control Monograph 19, NIH 07-6242. Bethesda, MD: U.S. Department of Health and Human Services, National Institutes of Health.

National Center for Education Statistics. 2008. "Schools and Staffing Survey." http://nces.ed.gov/surveys/sass.

———. 2012. "Trial Urban District Assessment." Nation's Report Card, National Assessment of Educational Progress. http://nationsreportcard.gov/tuda.asp.

National Center on Elder Abuse. 1999. *Types of Elder Abuse in Domestic Settings.* Elder Abuse Information Series, No. 1. Washington, DC: National Center on Elder Abuse.

National Highway Traffic Safety Administration. 2012a. *Blueprint for Ending Distracted Driving.* DOT HS 811 629. Washington, DC: U.S. Department of Transportation. http://www.distraction.gov/download/campaign-materials/8747-811629-060712-v5-Opt1-Web-tag.pdf.

———. 2012b. *Traffic Safety Facts: 2010 Data.* DOT HS 811 630. Washington, DC: U.S. Department of Transportation. http://www-nrd.nhtsa.dot.gov/Pubs/811630.pdf.

National Institute on Drug Abuse. 2013. "Abuse of Prescription (Rx) Drugs Affects Young Adults Most." http://www.drugabuse.gov/related-topics/trends-statistics/infographics/abuse-prescription-rx-drugs-affects-young-adults-most.

National Marriage Project. 2011. *Social Indicators of Marital Health and Well-Being: Trends of the Past Five Decades.* Charlottesville, VA: National Marriage Project. http://www.stateofourunions.org/2011/social_indicators.php.

National Priorities Project. 2008. http://nationalpriorities.org.

National Science Foundation. 2013. "Table 34. Highest Educational Attainment of Either Parent of Doctorate Recipients: Selected Years, 1982–2012." http://www.nsf.gov/statistics/sed/2012/pdf/tab34.pdf.

National Telecommunications and Information Administration. 2013. *Exploring the Digital Nation: America's Emerging Online Experience.* Washington, DC: U.S. Department of Commerce. http://www.ntia.doc.gov/files/ntia/publications/exploring_the_digital_nation_-_americas_emerging_online_experience.pdf.

NBC News. 2011. "Are Immigration Laws Blocking Economic Potential?" *NBC Nightly News,* March 3.

Nelson, Michael. 2010. "Warrior Nation." *Chronicle Review,* October 29, B6–7.

Neubauer, Chuck. 2011. "Sex Trafficking in the U.S. Called 'Epidemic': 'No Class and No Child Is Immune.'" *Washington Times,* April 23. http://www.washingtontimes.com/news/2011/apr/23/sex-trafficking-us-called-epidemic/?page=all.

Neumark-Sztainer, Dianne. 2005. *I'm, Like, So Fat!* New York: Guilford Press.

New America Foundation. 2013. "Drone Wars Pakistan: Analysis." http://natsec.newamerica.net/drones/pakistan/analysis.

Newman, Katherine S. 2012. *Accordion Families: Boomerang Kids, Anxious Parents, and the Private Toll of Global Competition.* Boston: Beacon Press.

Newman, Katherine S., and Victor Tan Chen. 2007. *The Missing Class: Portraits of the Near Poor in America.* Boston: Beacon Press.

Newport, Frank. 2007. "Black or African American? 'African American' Slightly Preferred among Those Who Have a Preference." Gallup, September 28. http://www.gallup.com/poll/28816/black-african-american.aspx.

Newton, Paula. 2013. "Canadian Teen Commits Suicide after Alleged Rape, Bullying." CNN, April 10. http://www.cnn.com/2013/04/10/justice/canada-teen-suicide/index.html.

New York Times. 2009. "Support for Women on the Battlefield." *New York Times*/CBS News Poll, August 16. http://www.nytimes.com/imagepages/2009/08/16/us/16women_poll_ready.html.

———. 2012. "Struggling in the Suburbs." July 7. http://www.nytimes.com/2012/07/08/opinion/sunday/struggling-in-the-suburbs.html.

Nickols, Sharon Y., and Robert B. Nielsen. 2011. "'So Many People Are Struggling': Developing Social Empathy through a Poverty Simulation." *Journal of Poverty* 15 (1): 22–42.

Nicolosi, Alfredo, Edward O. Laumann, Dale B. Glasser, Edson D. Moreira, Anthony Paik, and Clive Gingell. 2004. "Sexual Behavior and Sexual Dysfunctions after Age 40: The Global Study of Sexual Attitudes and Behaviors." *Urology* 64 (5): 991–97.

Nielsen. 2012. "Television: Prime Broadcast Network TV—United States." Accessed October 22. http://www.nielsen.com/us/en/insights/top10s/television.html.

Nijman, Jan. 2000. "The Paradigmatic City." *Annals of the Association of American Geographers* 90 (1): 135–45.

Niland, Patricia, and Antonia C. Lyons. 2011. "Uncertainty in Medicine: Meanings of Menopause and Hormone Replacement Therapy in Medical Textbooks." *Social Science & Medicine* 73 (8): 1238–45.

Norton. 2012. *Cybercrime Report 2012.* Sunnyvale, CA: Symantec Corporation. http://us.norton.com/cybercrimereport/promo.

Norton-Taylor, Richard. 2011. "MI5 Former Chief Decries 'War on Terror.'" *Guardian,* September 2.

Oakes, Jeannie. 1985. *Keeping Track: How Schools Structure Inequality.* New Haven, CT: Yale University Press.

Oakes, Jeannie, Adam Gamoran, and Reba N. Page. 1992. "Curriculum Differentiation: Opportunities, Outcomes, and Meanings." In *Handbook of Research on Curriculum,* edited by Philip W. Jackson, 570–608. New York: Macmillan.

Oakley, Annie. 2007. "Introduction." In *Working Sex: Sex Workers Write about a Changing Industry,* edited by Annie Oakley, 7–13. Emeryville, CA: Seal Press.

ObamaCare Facts. 2013. "ObamaCare 2013: What 2013 Means for ObamaCare and Health Care Reform." http://www.obamacarefacts.com/obamacare-2013.php.

O'Brien, Eileen. 2008. *The Racial Middle: Latinos and Asian Americans Living beyond the Racial Divide.* New York: New York University Press.

O'Brien, Eileen, and Kathleen Korgen. 2007. "It's the Message, Not the Messenger: The Declining Significance of Black-White Contact." *Sociological Inquiry* 77: 356–82.

O'Connell Davidson, Julia, and Jacqueline Sanchez Taylor. 1999. "Fantasy Islands: Exploring the Demand for Sex Tourism." In *Sun, Sex, and Gold: Tourism and Sex Work* in the Caribbean, edited by Kamala Kempadoo, 37–54. Lanham, MD: Rowman & Littlefield.

Office of National Drug Control Policy. 2011. *National Drug Control Strategy: 2011*. Washington, DC: Executive Office of the President. http://www.whitehouse.gov/sites/default/files/ondcp/ndcs2011.pdf.

Office of the U.S. Trade Representative. 2013. "Mexico." Accessed April 27. http://www.ustr.gov/countries-regions/americas/mexico.

Ogas, Ogi, and Sai Gaddam. 2012. *A Billion Wicked Thoughts: What the Internet Tells Us about Sexual Relationships*. New York: Plume.

Ogden, Cynthia L., Margaret D. Carroll, Lester R. Curtin, et al. 2010. "Prevalence of High Body Mass Index in US Children and Adolescents, 2007–2008." *Journal of the American Medical Association* 303 (3): 242–49.

Oldenburg, Ray. 1999. *The Great Good Place: Cafés, Coffee Shops, Bookstores, Bars, Hair Salons and Other Hangouts at the Heart of a Community*. New York: Da Capo Press.

Oliver, Melvin L., and Thomas M. Shapiro. 1995. *Black Wealth/White Wealth: A New Perspective on Racial Inequality*. New York: Routledge.

Omondi, Rose Kisia. 2003. "Gender and the Political Economy of Sex Tourism in Kenya's Coastal Resorts." Paper prepared for the international symposium/doctoral course "Feminist Perspective on Global Economic and Political Systems and Women's Struggle for Global Justice," Tromsø, Norway.

O'Neil, Shannon K. 2013. *Two Countries Indivisible: Mexico, the United States, and the Road Ahead*. Oxford: Oxford University Press.

Orcutt, James D., and J. Blake Turner. 1993. "Shocking Numbers and Graphic Accounts: Quantified Images of Drug Problems in the Print Media." *Social Problems* 40 (2): 190–206.

Organization for Economic Cooperation and Development, Program for International Student Assessment. 2009. "Mathematics, Age 15 OECD Scores."

O'Toole, James O., and Edward Lawler III. 2006. *The New American Workplace*. New York: Palgrave Macmillan.

Ott, Bryant, Nikki Blacksmith, and Ken Royal. 2008. "Job Seekers: Personal Connections Still Matter." Gallup Business Journal, May 8. http://businessjournal.gallup.com/content/106957/personal-connections-still-matter.aspx.

Ozawa, Martha N. 2004. "Social Welfare Spending on Family Benefits in the United States and Sweden: A Comparative Study." *Family Relations* 53 (3): 301–9.

Padilla-Walker, Laura M., Sarah M. Coyne, and Ashley M. Fraser. 2012. "Getting a High-Speed Family Connection: Associations between Family Media Use and Family Connection." *Family Relations* 61: 426–40.

Pager, Devah. 2003. "Blacks and Ex-Cons Need Not Apply." *Contexts* 2 (4): 58–59.

Pager, Devah, Bruce Western, and Bart Bonikowski. 2009. "Discrimination in a Low-Wage Labor Market: A Field Experiment." *American Sociological Review* 74 (5): 777–99.

Pahl, R. E. 1970. *Whose City? And Other Essays on Sociology and Planning*. London: Longmans.

Papademetriou, Demetrios G. 2012. *Rethinking National Identity in the Age of Migration*. Council Statement from the 7th Plenary Meeting of the Transatlantic Council on Migration. Washington, DC: Migration Policy Institute.

Pappas, Chris. 2011. "Sex Sells, but What Else Does It Do? The American Porn Industry." In *Introducing the New Sexuality Studies*, 2nd ed., edited by Steven Seidman, Nancy Fischer, and Chet Meeks, 320–26. New York: Routledge.

Park, Robert E., and Ernest W. Burgess. 1924. *Introduction to the Science of Sociology*. Chicago: University of Chicago Press.

Park, Robert E., Ernest Burgess, and Roderick D. McKenzie. 1925. *The City*. Chicago: University of Chicago Press.

Parker, Kim. 2011. "The Military-Civilian Gap: Fewer Family Connections." Pew Research Center, Social and Demographic Trends, November 23. http://www.pewsocialtrends.org/2011/11/23/the-military-civilian-gap-fewer-family-connections.

———. 2012. "The Boomerang Generation: Feeling OK about Living with Mom and Dad." Pew Research Center, Social and Demographic Trends, March 15. http://www.pewsocialtrends.org/files/2012/03/PewSocialTrends-2012-BoomerangGeneration.pdf.

Parker, Kim, and Wendy Wang. 2013. *Modern Parenthood: Roles of Moms and Dads Converge as They Balance Work and Family*. Washington, DC: Pew Research Center. http://www.pewsocialtrends.org/files/2013/03/FINAL_modern_parenthood_03-2013.pdf.

Parsons, Talcott. 1951. *The Social System*. New York: Free Press.

———. 1959. "The School Class as a Social System." *Harvard Educational Review* 29: 297–318.

———. 1968. "On the Concept of Value-Commitments." *Social Inquiry* 38: 135–60.

Parsons, Talcott, and Robert F. Bales. 1955. *Family, Socialization and Interaction Process*. New York: Free Press.

Pascoe, C. J. 2007. *Dude, You're a Fag: Masculinity and Sexuality in High School*. Berkeley: University of California Press.

Patterson, Charlotte J., and Paul D. Hastings. 2007. "Socialization in the Context of Family Diversity." In *Handbook of Socialization: Theory and Research,* edited by Joan E. Grusec and Paul D. Hastings, 328–51. New York: Guilford.

Paul, Pamela. 2004. "The Porn Factor." *Time,* January 19, 99–100.

Paull, John. 2007. "Toxic Colonialism." *New Scientist,* November 3, 25.

Pearlin, Leonard I., Scott Schieman, Elena M. Fazio, and Stephen C. Meersman. 2005. "Stress, Health and the Life Course: Some Conceptual Perspectives." *Journal of Health and Social Behavior* 46 (2): 205–19.

Peguero, Anthony A., and Amanda M. Lauck. 2008. "Older Adults and Their Vulnerabilities to the Exposure of Violence." *Sociology Compass* 2 (1): 62–73.

Pellow, David N., Allan Schnaiberg, and Adam S. Weinberg. 2000. "Putting the Ecological Modernisation Thesis to the Test: The Promises and Performances of Urban Recycling." In *Ecological Modernisation around the World: Perspectives and Critical Debates,* edited by Arthur P. J. Mol and David A. Sonnenfeld, 109–37. London: Frank Cass.

Pencavel, John. 2007. "Unionism Viewed Internationally." In *What Do Unions Do? A Twenty-Year Perspective,* edited by James T. Bennett and Bruce E. Kaufman. New Brunswick, NJ: Transaction.

Pérez, Gina M. 2006. "How a Scholarship Girl Becomes a Soldier: The Militarization of Latina/o Youth in Chicago Public Schools. *Identities: Global Studies in Culture and Power* 13: 53–72.

Perrone, Dina. 2009. *The High Life: Club Kids, Harm and Drug Policy.* Boulder, CO: Lynne Rienner.

Pettit, Becky, and Bruce Western. 2004. "Mass Imprisonment and the Life Course: Race and Class Inequality in U.S. Incarceration." *American Sociological Review* 69: 151–69.

Pew Research Center. 2012. *The Lost Decade of the Middle Class: Fewer, Poorer, Gloomier.* Washington, DC: Pew Research Center. http://www.pewsocialtrends.org/files/2012/08/pew-social-trends-lost-decade-of-the-middle-class.pdf.

Pfohl, Stephen J. 1977. "The 'Discovery' of Child Abuse." *Social Problems* 24 (3): 310–23.

Piccigallo, Jacqueline. 2008. "Men against Rape: Male Activists' Views towards Campus-Based Sexual Assault and Acquaintance Rape." Master's thesis, University of Delaware.

Pierce, Richard J., Jr. 1989. "Public Utility Regulatory Takings: Should the Judiciary Attempt to Police the Political Institutions?" *Georgetown Law Journal* 77: 2031–77.

Pilon, Mary. 2010. "What's a Degree Really Worth?" *Wall Street Journal,* February 2. http://online.wsj.com/article/SB10001424052748703822404575019082819966538.html.

Pincus, Fred L. 2011. *Understanding Diversity,* 2nd ed. Boulder, CO: Lynne Rienner.

Pinker, Steven. 2011. *The Better Angels of Our Nature: Why Violence Has Declined.* New York: Viking Press.

Pitzer College, Community Engagement Center. 2013. "Pomona Economic Opportunity Center." Accessed June 7. http://www.pitzer.edu/offices/cec/partners/PEOC.asp.

Piven, Frances Fox. 2006. *Challenging Authority: How Ordinary People Change America.* Lanham, MD: Rowman & Littlefield.

Piven, Frances Fox, and Richard A. Cloward. 1993. *Regulating the Poor: The Functions of Public Welfare,* updated ed. New York: Vintage.

Plante, Rebecca F. 2006. "Hooking it Up: Sex in the Bedroom." In *Sexualities in Context: A Social Perspective.* Boulder, CO: Westview Press.

Plateris, Alexander. 1973. *100 Years of Marriage and Divorce Statistics: United States, 1867–1967.* U.S. Department of Health, Education, and Welfare, DHEW Publication (HRA) 74-1902. Washington, DC: Government Printing Office. http://www.cdc.gov/nchs/data/series/sr_21/sr21_024.pdf.

Polaris Project. 2014. "Sex Trafficking." Accessed March 31. http://www.polarisproject.org/resources/resources-by-topic/sex-trafficking.

Poortinga, Wouter. 2006. "Social Relations or Social Capital? Individual and Community Health Effects of Bonding Social Capital." *Social Science & Medicine* 63 (1): 255–70.

Popenoe, David. 1988. *Disturbing the Nest: Family Change and Decline in Modern Societies.* Piscataway, NJ: Aldine Transaction.

———. 1993. "American Family Decline, 1960–1990: A Review and Appraisal." *Journal of Marriage and the Family* 55: 527–42.

———, ed. 1996. *Promises to Keep: Decline and Renewal of Marriage in America.* Lanham, MD: Rowman & Littlefield.

———. 2004. *War over the Family.* Piscataway, NJ: Transaction.

———. 2009. *Families without Fathers: Fathers, Marriage, and Children in Modern Society.* Piscataway, NJ: Transaction.

Porta, Daniela, Simona Milani, Antonio Lazzarino, Carlo A. Perucci, and Francesco Forastiere. 2009. "Systematic Review of Epidemiological Studies on Health Effects Associated with Management of Solid Waste." *Environmental Health* 8: 60.

Portes, Alejandro, and Robert D. Manning. 1986. "The Immigrant Enclave: Theory and Empirical Examples." In *Competitive Ethnic Relations,* edited by Susan Olzak and Joane Nagel, 47–68. New York: Academic Press.

Portes, Alejandro, and Rubén G. Rumbaut. 2006. *Immigrant America: A Portrait,* 3rd ed. Berkeley: University of California Press.

Post, Lori A., Nancy J. Mezey, Christopher Maxwell, and Wilma Novalés Wibert. 2002. "The Rape Tax: Tangible and Intangible Costs of Sexual Violence." *Journal of Interpersonal Violence* 17 (7): 773–82.

Powell, Jason L. 2006. *Social Theory and Aging.* Lanham, MD: Rowman & Littlefield.

———. 2010. "The Power of Global Aging." *Ageing International* 35: 1–14.

Prakash, Om. 2009. "The Efficacy of 'Don't Ask, Don't Tell.'" *Joint Forces Quarterly* 55 (4): 88–94.

Preston, Julia A. 2011. "After a False Dawn, Anxiety for Illegal Immigrant Students." *New York Times,* February 8.

PricewaterhouseCoopers. 2011. *Cybercrime: Protecting against the Growing Threat: Global Economic Crime Survey.* London: PricewaterhouseCoopers. http://www.pwc.com/en_GX/gx/economic-crime-survey/assets/GECS_GLOBAL_REPORT.pdf.

Provine, Doris Marie. 2007. *Unequal under the Law: Race in the War on Drugs.* Chicago: University of Chicago Press.

Prus, Steven G. 2011. "Comparing Social Determinants of Self-Rated Health across the United States and Canada." *Social Science & Medicine* 73 (1): 50–59.

Puentes, Jennifer, David Knox, and Marty E. Zusman. 2008. "Participants in 'Friends with Benefits' Relationships." *College Student Journal* 42 (1): 176–80.

Pungello, Elizabeth P., Frances A. Campbell, and W. Steven Barnett. 2006. "Poverty and Early Childhood Educational Intervention." University of North Carolina Center on Poverty, Work and Opportunity, Policy Brief Series, December 13.

Purcell, Natalie J., and Eileen L. Zurbriggen. 2013. "The Sexualization of Girls and Gendered Violence: Mapping the Connections." In *The Sexualization of Girls and Girlhood: Causes, Consequences, and Resistance,* edited by Eileen L. Zurbriggen and Tomi-Ann Roberts, 149–65. New York: Oxford University Press.

Puzzanchera, C., and W. Kang. 2013. "Easy Access to FBI Arrest Statistics 1994–2010." National Center for Juvenile Justice, Office of Juvenile Justice and Delinquency Prevention. http://www.ojjdp.gov/ojstatbb/ezaucr.

Quadagno, Jill, and Jennifer Reid. 1999. "The Political Economy Perspective in Aging." In *Handbook of Theories of Aging,* edited by Vern L. Bengtson and K. Warner Schaie, 344–58. New York: Springer.

Quesnel-Vallee, Amélie, Jean-Simon Farrah, and Tania Jenkins. 2011. "Population Aging, Health Systems, and Equity: Shared Challenges for the United States and Canada." In *Handbook of Sociology of Aging,* edited by Richard A. Settersten Jr. and Jacqueline L. Angel, 563–81. New York: Springer.

Quinney, Richard. 1970. *The Social Reality of Crime.* Boston: Little, Brown.

Rahbek-Clemmensen, Jon, Emerald M. Archer, John Barr, Aaron Belkin, Mario Guerrero, Cameron Hall, and Katie E. O. Swain. 2012. "Conceptualizing the Civil-Military Gap: A Research Note." *Armed Forces and Society* 38 (4): 669–78.

Rampell, Catherine. 2009. "Money, Gender, and Job Satisfaction." *New York Times,* Economix blog, November 18. http://economix.blogs.nytimes.com/2009/11/18/money-gender-and-job-satisfaction.

———. 2010. "The Gender Wage Gap, around the World." *New York Times,* Economix blog, March 9. http://economix.blogs.nytimes.com/2010/03/09/the-gender-wage-gap-around-the-world.

Ravetz, Jerome R. 1971. *Scientific Knowledge and Its Social Problems.* Oxford: Clarendon Press.

———. 2005. *The No-Nonsense Guide to Science.* Toronto: Between the Lines.

Ravitch, Diane. 2013. *Reign of Error: The Hoax of the Privatization Movement and the Danger to America's Public Schools.* New York: Alfred A. Knopf.

Rawls, John. 1971. *A Theory of Justice.* Cambridge, MA: Belknap Press.

Ready, Richard C. 2005. *Do Landfills Always Depress Nearby Property Values?* Rural Development Paper 27. University Park, PA: Northeast Regional Center for Rural Development. http://aese.psu.edu/nercrd/publications/rdp/rdp27.pdf.

Regnerus, Mark and Jeremy Uecker. 2011. *Premarital Sex in America: How Young Americans Meet, Mate, and Think about Marrying.* New York: Oxford University Press.

Reid, Julie A., Sinikka Elliott, and Gretchen R. Webber. 2011. "Casual Hookups to Formal Dates: Refining the Boundaries of the Sexual Double Standard." *Gender & Society* 25 (5): 545–68.

Reiman, Jeffrey. 2001. *The Rich Get Richer and the Poor Get Prison: Ideology, Class, and Criminal Justice,* 6th ed. Boston: Allyn & Bacon.

Reinarman, Craig, Peter D. A. Cohen, and Hendrien L. Kaal. 2004. "The Limited Relevance of Drug Policy: Cannabis in Amsterdam and in San Francisco." *American Journal of Public Health* 94 (5): 836–42.

Reinberg, Steve. 2011. "U.S. Teen Birth Rate Hits Record Low, but American Young People Are Still Having Babies at Rates Higher than Other Rich Nations, CDC Says." *U.S. News & World Report,* April 5. http://health.usnews .com/health-news/family-health/brain-and-behavior/ articles/2011/04/05/us-teen-birth-rate-hits-record-low.

Reinhardt, Uwe. 2000. "Health Care for the Aging Baby Boom: Lessons from Abroad." *Journal of Economic Perspectives* 14 (2): 71–83.

Reisner, Marc. 1986. *Cadillac Desert: The American West and Its Disappearing Water.* New York: Penguin Books.

Relman, Arnold S. 1980. "The New Medical-Industrial Complex." *New England Journal of Medicine* 303: 963–70.

Reno, Virginia P., and Joni Lavery. 2005. *Options to Balance Social Security Funds over the Next 75 Years.* Social Security Brief 18, February. Washington, DC: National Academy of Social Insurance.

Reskin, Barbara, and Irene Padavic. 1994. *Women and Men at Work.* Thousand Oaks, CA: Pine Forge Press.

Rhoades, Galena K., Scott M. Stanley, and Howard J. Markman. 2009. "The Pre-engagement Cohabitation Effect: A Replication and Extension of Previous Findings." *Journal of Family Psychology* 23: 107–11.

Rhode Island Coalition Against Domestic Violence. 2000. *Domestic Violence: A Handbook for Journalists.* Warwick: Rhode Island Coalition Against Domestic Violence.

Rideout, Victoria J., Ulla G. Foehr, and Donald F. Roberts. 2010. *Generation M2: Media in the Lives of 8- to 18-Year-Olds.* Menlo Park, CA: Henry J. Kaiser Family Foundation.

Riley, Kevin M. 2010. "Suicide and the Economy." Paper available through Academia.edu. https://www.academia .edu/1963339/Suicide_and_the_Economy.

Rist, Raymond. 1977. *The Urban School: A Factory for Failure.* Cambridge: MIT Press.

Ritzer, George. 1998. *The McDonaldization Thesis.* London: Sage.

Robinson, Jennifer. 2003. "Social Classes in U.S., Britain, and Canada." Gallup, August 5. http://www.gallup.com/ poll/8998/Social-Classes-US-Britain-Canada.aspx.

Roediger, David R. 1991. *The Wages of Whiteness: Race and the Making of the American Working Class.* New York: Verso.

Rogers, Chrissie, and Susie Welter. 2012. *Critical Approaches to Care: Understanding Caring Relations, Identities, and Cultures.* London: Routledge.

Romer, Daniel, Kathleen Hall Jamieson, and Sean Aday. 2003. "Television News and the Cultivation of Fear of Crime." *Journal of Communication* 53 (1): 88–104.

Romero, Mary. 2011. "Keeping Citizenship Rights White: Arizona's Racial Profiling Practices in Immigration Law Enforcement." *Law Journal for Social Justice* 1 (1): 97–113.

Roscigno, Vincent J., Diana L. Karafin, and Griff Tester. 2009. "The Complexities and Processes of Racial Housing Discrimination." *Social Problems* 56 (1): 49–69.

Rosen, Jeffrey, and Benjamin Wittes. 2011. *Constitution 3.0: Freedom and Technological Change.* Washington, DC: Brookings Institution Press.

Ross, M. W., S. A. Månsson, and K. Daneback. 2012. "Prevalence, Severity, and Correlates of Problematic Sexual Internet Use in Swedish Men and Women." *Archives of Sexual Behavior* 41 (2): 459–66.

Rossman, Shelli B., Janine M. Zweig, Dana Kralstein, Kelli Henry, P. Mitchell Downey, and Christine Lindquist. 2011. *The Multi-site Adult Drug Court Evaluation: The Drug Court Experience,* vol. 3. Washington, DC: Urban Institute.

Roth, Louise Marie, and Megan M. Henley. 2012. "Unequal Motherhood: Racial-Ethnic and Socioeconomic Disparities in Cesarean Sections in the United States." *Social Problems* 59: 207–27.

Rothstein, Richard. 2010. "How to Fix Our Schools: It's More Complicated, and More Work, than the Klein-Rhee 'Manifesto' Wants You to Believe." *Education Digest* 76 (6): 32–37.

Rovner, Julie. 2013. "Boomer Housemates Have More Fun." Your Health, NPR, May 22.

Rowlingson, Karen. 2011. *Does Income Inequality Cause Health and Social Problems?* London: Joseph Rowntree Foundation.

Royster, Deirdre A. 2003. *Race and the Invisible Hand: How White Networks Exclude Black Men from Blue-Collar Jobs.* Berkeley: University of California Press.

Rozanova, Julia. 2006. "Newspaper Portrayals of Health and Illness among Canadian Seniors: Who Ages Healthily and at What Cost?" *International Journal of Ageing and Later Life* 1 (2): 111–39.

Rumburger, Russell W., and Katherine A. Larson. 1998. "Toward Explaining Differences in Educational Achievement among Mexican American Language-Minority Students." *Sociology of Education* 71: 68–92.

Rushford, Carly, and Courtney Laird. 2012. "Join the Movement: Take Back the Date." *Colby Echo,* November 7. http://www.thecolbyecho.com/opinion/join-the-movement-take-back-the-date.

Ryan, William. 1976. *Blaming the Victim,* rev. ed. New York: Vintage.

Ryle, Robyn. 2012. *Questioning Gender: A Sociological Exploration.* Thousand Oaks, CA: Pine Forge Press.

Sable, Jennifer, Chris Plotts, and Lindsey Mitchell. 2010. *Characteristics of the 100 Largest Public Elementary and Secondary School Districts in the United States: 2008–09.* U.S. Department of Education, National Center for Education Statistics, NCES 2011-301. Washington,

DC: Government Printing Office. http://nces.ed.gov/pubs2011/2011301.pdf.

Sadovnik, Alan R. 2008. *No Child Left Behind and the Reduction of the Achievement Gap: Sociological Perspectives on Federal Educational Policy.* New York: Routledge.

Saguy, Abigail C., and Rene Almeling. 2008. "Fat in the Fire? Science, the News Media, and the 'Obesity Epidemic.'" *Sociological Forum* 23 (1): 53–83.

Saguy, Abigail C., and Kjerstin Gruys. 2010. "Morality and Health: News Media Constructions of Overweight and Eating Disorders." *Social Problems* 57 (2): 231–50.

Saguy, Abigail C., Kjerstin Gruys, and Shanna Gong. 2010. "Social Problem Construction and National Context: News Reporting on 'Overweight' and 'Obesity' in the United States and France." *Social Problems* 57 (4): 586–610.

Saha, Robin, and Paul Mohai. 2005. "Historical Context and Hazardous Waste Facility Siting: Understanding Temporal Patterns in Michigan." *Social Problems* 52: 618–48.

Sampson, Robert J., and Stephen W. Raudenbush. 2004. "Seeing Disorder: Neighborhood Stigma and the Social Construction of 'Broken Windows.'" *Social Psychology Quarterly* 67 (4): 319–42.

Sampson, Robert J., and William Julius Wilson. 1995. "Toward a Theory of Race, Crime, and Urban Inequality." In *Crime and Inequality,* edited by John Hagan and Ruth D. Peterson, 37–54. Stanford, CA: Stanford University Press.

Sassen, Saskia. 2001. *The Global City: New York, London, Tokyo,* 2nd ed. Princeton, NJ: Princeton University Press.

———. 2002. *Global Networks, Linked Cities.* New York: Routledge.

———. 2010. *Cities in a World Economy.* Thousand Oaks, CA: Pine Forge Press.

Satterfield, Terre. 2002. *Anatomy of a Conflict: Identity, Knowledge, and Emotion in Old-Growth Forests.* Vancouver: UBC Press.

Satterthwaite, David. 2009. "The Implications of Population Growth and Urbanization for Climate Change." *Environment & Urbanization* 21 (2): 545–67.

Saunders, Penelope, and Gretchen Soderlund. 2003. "Threat or Opportunity? Sexuality, Gender and the Ebb and Flow of Trafficking as Discourse." *Canadian Woman Studies* 22 (3–4): 16–24.

Savage, Joanne. 2008. "The Role of Exposure to Media Violence in the Etiology of Violent Behavior: A Criminologist Weighs In." *American Behavioral Scientist* 51 (8): 1123–36.

Scanzoni, John H. 1978. *Sex Roles, Women's Work, and Marital Conflict: A Study of Family Change.* Lexington, MA: Lexington Books.

———. 1982. *Sexual Bargaining: Power Politics in the America Marriage,* 2nd ed. Chicago: University of Chicago Press.

Schalet, Amy T. 2011. *Not under My Roof: Parents, Teens, and the Culture of Sex.* Chicago: University of Chicago Press.

Scharrer, Erica. 2008. "Media Exposure and Sensitivity to Violence in News Reports." *Journalism and Mass Communication Quarterly* 85 (2): 291–310.

Schmidt, Charles W. 2002. "e-Junk Explosion." *Environmental Health Perspectives* 110 (4): 188–94.

Schmitt, John, and Heather Boushey. 2010. *The College Conundrum: Why the Benefits of a College Education May Not Be So Clear, Especially to Men.* Washington, DC: Center for American Progress. http://www.americanprogress.org/issues/labor/report/2010/12/03/8765/the-college-conundrum.

Schnaiberg, Allan, and Kenneth Alan Gould. 1994. *Environment and Society: The Enduring Conflict.* New York: St. Martin's Press.

Schnaiberg, Allan, David N. Pellow, and Adam S. Weinberg. 2002. "The Treadmill of Production and the Environmental State." In *The Environmental State under Pressure,* edited by Arthur P. J. Mol and Frederick H. Buttel, 15–32. London: Elsevier Science.

Schneider, Friedrich, and Dominik H. Enste. 2002. *The Shadow Economy: An International Survey.* Cambridge: Cambridge University Press.

Schneider, Joseph W. 1985. "Social Problems Theory: The Constructionist View." *Annual Review of Sociology* 11: 209–29.

Schneier, Bruce. 2010. "The Comparative Risk of Terrorism." *Wall Street Journal,* January 12.

Schor, Juliet. 2004. *Born to Buy: The Commercialized Child and the New Consumer Culture.* New York: Scribner.

Schulman, Beth. 2003. *The Betrayal of Work: How Low-Wage Jobs Fail 30 Million Americans and Their Families.* New York: New Press.

Schulz, James H., and Robert H. Binstock. 2006. *Aging Nation: The Economics and Politics of Growing Older in America.* Baltimore: Johns Hopkins University Press.

Schwarz, Alan, and Sarah Cohen. 2013. "A.D.H.D. Seen in 11% of U.S. Children as Diagnoses Rise." *New York Times,* March 31, 2013.

Scott, Wilbur. 1990. "PTSD in DSM-III: A Case in the Politics of Diagnosis and Disease." *Social Problems* 37 (3): 294–310.

Scripps Institution of Oceanography. 2008. "Lake Mead Could Be Dry by 2021." February 12. https://scripps.ucsd.edu/news/2487.

Search Institute. 2012. *Family Assets.* Minneapolis, MN: Search Institute.

Segal, Elizabeth A. 2006. "Welfare as We *Should* Know It: Social Empathy and Welfare Reform." In *The Promise of*

Welfare Reform: Political Rhetoric and the Reality of Poverty in the Twenty-First Century, edited by Keith M. Kilty and Elizabeth A. Segal, 265–74. New York: Haworth.

———. 2007. "Social Empathy: A New Paradigm to Address Poverty." *Journal of Poverty* 11 (3): 65–81.

Segal, Elizabeth A., and Keith M. Kilty. 2003. "Political Promises for Welfare Reform." *Journal of Poverty* 7 (1/2): 51–67.

Segrave, Marie, Sanja Milivojevic, and Sharon Pickering. 2009. *Sex Trafficking: International Context and Response.* New York: Taylor & Francis.

Seidman, Steven. 1996. "Introduction." In *Queer Theory/Sociology,* edited by Steven Seidman, 1–29. Malden, MA: Blackwell.

———. 2003. *The Social Construction of Sexuality.* New York: W. W. Norton.

Seltzer, Leslie J., Ashley R. Prososki, Toni E. Ziegler, and Seth D. Pollak. 2012. "Instant Messages vs. Speech: Hormones and Why We Still Need to Hear Each Other." *Evolution and Human Behavior* 33: 42–45.

Semuels, Alana. 2013. "Efficient and Exhausted." *Los Angeles Times,* April 7.

Seto, Karen C., Burak Güneralp, and Lucy R. Hutyra. 2012. "Global Forecasts of Urban Expansion to 2030 and Direct Impacts on Biodiversity and Carbon Pools." *Proceedings of the National Academy of Sciences of the United States of America* 109 (40): 16083–88.

Shaefer, H. Luke, and Kathryn Edin. 2012. "Extreme Poverty in the United States, 1996 to 2011." National Poverty Center, Policy Brief 28, February. http://www.npc.umich.edu/publications/policy_briefs/brief28/policybrief28.pdf.

Shafer, Jack. 2007. "Meth Madness at Newsweek." *Slate,* January 31, http://www.slate.com/articles/news_and_politics/press_box/2005/08/meth_madness_at_newsweek.html.

Shane, Scott. 2013a. "Bombings End Decade of Strikingly Few Successful Terrorism Attacks in U.S." *New York Times,* April 16.

———. 2013b. "U.S. Engaged in Torture After 9/11, Review Concludes." *New York Times,* April 16.

Shapiro, Thomas M., Tatjana Meschede, and Laura Sullivan. 2010. *The Racial Wealth Gap Increases Fourfold.* Research and Policy Brief, May. Waltham, MA: Institute on Assets and Social Policy. http://www.insightcced.org/uploads/CRWG/IASP-Racial-Wealth-Gap-Brief-May2010.pdf.

Sharkey, Patrick. 2007. "Survival and Death in New Orleans: An Empirical Look at the Human Impact of Katrina." *Journal of Black Studies* 37 (4): 482–501.

Shaw, Amy. 2008. "Direct-to-Consumer Advertising (DTC) of Pharmaceuticals." ProQuest Discovery Guide. http://165.215.193.14/discoveryguides/direct/review.pdf.

Shaw, Clifford R., and Henry D. McKay. 1942. *Juvenile Delinquency and Urban Areas.* Chicago: University of Chicago Press.

Shimizu, Celene Parreñas. 2007. *The Hypersexuality of Race: Performing Asian/American Women on Screen and Scene.* Stanford, CA: Stanford University Press.

Shishehbor, M. H., D. Litaker, C. E. Pothier, and M. S. Lauer. 2006. "Association of Socioeconomic Status with Functional Capacity, Heart Rate Recovery, and All-Cause Mortality." *Journal of the American Medical Association* 295 (7): 784–92.

Short, John Rennie. 2004. *Global Metropolitan: Globalizing Cities in a Capitalist World.* New York: Routledge.

Shows, Carla, and Naomi Gerstel. 2009. "Fathering, Class, and Gender: A Comparison of Physicians and Emergency Medical Technicians." *Gender & Society* 23: 161–87.

Signorielli, Nancy. 2001. "Aging on Television: The Picture in the Nineties." *Generations* 25 (3): 34–38.

Silicon Valley Toxics Coalition (SVTC). 2002. *Exporting Harm: The High-Tech Trashing of Asia.* February 25, 2002. http://svtc.org/wp-content/uploads/technotrash.pdf

Silbey, Susan. 1997. "Let Them Eat Cake: Globalization, Postmodern Colonialism, and the Possibilities of Justice." *Law and Society Review* 31: 207–35.

Silva, Jennifer M. 2013. *Coming Up Short: Working-Class Adulthood in an Age of Uncertainty.* New York: Oxford University Press.

Simmel, Georg. 1971. *On Individuality and Social Forms.* Edited by Donald N. Levine. Chicago: University of Chicago Press.

Simmons, Cedrick-Michael. 2012. "Campus Involvement: Created Equal." E-portfolio. http://eportfolios.ithaca.edu/csimmon1/campusinvolvement/createdequal.

Simmons, Michelle. 2011. "Student Activists Push for Change." *Dickinson Magazine,* Spring. http://www.dickinson.edu/news-and-events/publications/dickinson-magazine/2011-spring/Student-Activists-Push-for-Change.

Sinkovic, Matija, Aleksandar Stulhofer, and Jasmina Bozic. 2013. "Revisiting the Association between Pornography Use and Risky Sexual Behaviors: The Role of Early Exposure to Pornography and Sexual Sensation Seeking." *Journal of Sex Research* 50 (7): 633–41.

Sischo, Lacey, John Taylor, and Patricia Yancey Martin. 2006. "Carrying the Weight of Self-Derogation? Disordered Eating Practices as Social Deviance in Young Adults." *Deviant Behavior* 27 (1): 1–30.

Slade, Joseph W. 2001. *Pornography and Sexual Representation: A Reference Guide.* Westport, CT: Greenwood Press.

Sloan, Paul. 2007. "Getting in the Skin Game." CNN, February 13. http://money.cnn.com/magazines/business2/business2_archive/2006/11/01/8392016.

Sluka, Jeffrey. 2011. "Death from Above: UAVs and Losing Hearts and Minds." *Military Review,* May–June, 70–76.

Small, Albion W. 1903. "What Is a Sociologist?" *American Journal of Sociology* 8 (4): 468–77.

Small, Christopher, and Robert J. Nicholls. 2003. "A Global Analysis of Human Settlement in Coastal Zones." *Journal of Coastal Research* 19 (3): 584–99.

Smiler, Andrew P., and Rebecca F. Plante. 2013. "Let's Talk about Sex on Campus." *Chronicle of Higher Education,* May 20. http://chronicle.com/article/Lets-Talk-About-Sex-on-Campus/139353.

Smith, Adam. 2012. *An Inquiry into the Nature and Causes of the Wealth of Nations.* Chicago: University of Chicago Press. First published 1776.

Smith, David A., and Michael Timberlake. 1995. "Cities in Global Matrices: Toward Mapping the World-System's City System." In *World Cities in a World-System,* edited by Paul L. Knox and Peter J. Taylor. New York: Cambridge University Press.

Smith, Janell. 2012. "Students Stand in Quad for 27 Hours to Fight Sex Trafficking." *Daily Tar Heel,* November 18. http://www.dailytarheel.com/article/2012/11/50a9a6e7064f4.

Smith, Jacquelyn. 2012. "The Best- and Worst-Paying Jobs for Doctors." *Forbes,* July 20. http://www.forbes.com/sites/jacquelynsmith/2012/07/20/the-best-and-worst-paying-jobs-for-doctors-2.

Smith, Matthew. 2010. "Do Adults Have ADHD? A History Lesson." *British Medical Journal* 340: 939–40.

Smith, Michael D., and Christian Grov. 2011. *In the Company of Men: Inside the Lives of Male Prostitutes.* Santa Barbara, CA: Praeger.

Smith, Tom W., and Jaesok Son. 2013. *Trends in Public Attitudes about Sexual Morality.* Chicago: National Opinion Research Center. http://www.norc.org/PDFs/sexmoralfinal_06-21_FINAL.PDF.

Snow, Allison A. 2005. "Genetic Modification and Gene Flow: An Overview." In *Controversies in Science and Technology: From Maize to Menopause,* edited by Daniel Lee Kleinman, Abby J. Kinchy, and Jo Handelsman, 107–18. Madison: University of Wisconsin Press.

Snow, David A., and Robert D. Benford. 1988. "Ideology, Frame Resonance, and Participant Mobilization." *International Social Movement Research* 1 (1): 197–217.

Snowden, Carisa R. 2011. *Choices Women Make: Agency in Domestic Violence, Assisted Reproduction, and Sex Work.* Minneapolis: University of Minnesota Press.

Snyder, Thomas D., and Sally A. Dillow. 2010. *Digest of Education Statistics 2009.* U.S. Department of Education, National Center for Education Statistics, NCES 2010-013. Washington, DC: Government Printing Office. http://nces.ed.gov/pubs2010/2010013.pdf.

Society for Human Resource Management. 2012. *2012 Employee Job Satisfaction and Engagement.* Alexandria, VA: Society for Human Resource Management. http://www.shrm.org/LegalIssues/StateandLocalResources/StateandLocalStatutesandRegulations/Documents/12-0537%202012_JobSatisfaction_FNL_online.pdf.

Soneryd, Linda. 2007. "Deliberations on the Unknown, the Unsensed, and the Unsayable? Public Protests and the Development of Third-Generation Mobile Phones in Sweden." *Science, Technology, & Human Values* 32 (3): 287–314.

Sonnenfeld, David A., and Arthur P. J. Mol. 2002. "Globalization and the Transformation of Environmental Governance: An Introduction." *American Behavioral Scientist* 45 (9): 1318–39.

South, Scott J., and Kim M. Lloyd. 1992. "Marriage Opportunities and Family Formation: Further Implications of Imbalanced Sex Ratios." *Journal of Marriage and the Family* 54: 440–51.

Southern Nevada Water Authority. 2009. "Water Resource Plan." http://www.snwa.com/assets/pdf/wr_plan.pdf.

Spector, Malcolm, and John I. Kitsuse. 1987. *Constructing Social Problems.* New York: Aldine de Gruyter.

Spraggins, Reneé E. 2005. *We the People: Women and Men in the United States.* Census 2000 Special Report, CENSR-20. Washington, DC: U.S. Department of Commerce. https://www.census.gov/prod/2005pubs/censr-20.pdf.

Stacey, Judith. 2011. *Unhitched: Love, Marriage, and Family Values from West Hollywood to Western China.* New York: New York University Press.

Stacey, Judith, and Timothy J. Biblarz. 2001. "(How) Does the Sexual Orientation of Parents Matter?" *American Sociological Review* 66 (2): 159–83.

Stack, Carol. 1974. *All Our Kin: Strategies for Survival in a Black Community.* New York: Harper & Row.

Stanford Law School/NYU Law School. 2012. "Living under Drones: Death, Injury, and Trauma to Civilians from US Drone Practices in Pakistan." September. http://livingunderdrones.org.

Statistic Brain. 2012. "Elderly Abuse Statistics." http://www.statisticbrain.com/elderly-abuse-statistics.

Stedman, Lawrence C. 1987. "It's Time We Changed the Effective Schools Formula." *Phi Delta Kappan* 69 (3): 215–24.

Steele, Claude M. 1997. "A Threat in the Air: How Stereotypes Shape Intellectual Identity and Performance." *American Psychologist* 52: 613–29.

Steele, Claude M., and Joshua Aronson. 1995. "Stereotype Threat and the Intellectual Test Performance of African Americans." *Journal of Personality and Social Psychology* 69: 797–811.

Stepp, Laura Sessions. 2008. *Unhooked: How Young Women Pursue Sex, Delay Love and Lose at Both.* New York: Riverhead Trade.

Stern, Paul C. 1992. "Psychological Dimensions of Global Environmental Change." *Annual Review of Psychology* 43 (1): 269–302.

Stern, Paul C., Thomas Dietz, and Gregory A. Guagnano. 1995. "The New Ecological Paradigm in Social-Psychological Context." *Environment & Behavior* 27 (6): 723–43.

Stern, Paul C., Thomas Dietz, and Linda Kalof. 1993. "Value Orientations, Gender, and Environmental Concern." *Environment & Behavior* 25 (5): 322–48.

Sternheimer, Karen. 2010. *Connecting Social Problems and Popular Culture.* Boulder, CO: Westview Press.

Stice, Eric, and Heather E. Shaw. 1994. "Adverse Effects of the Media Portrayed Thin-Ideal on Women and Linkages to Bulimic Symptomatology." *Journal of Social and Clinical Psychology* 13: 288–308.

Stiglitz, Joseph E. 2013. "Student Debt and the Crushing of the American Dream." *New York Times,* May 12. http://opinionator.blogs.nytimes.com/2013/05/12/student-debt-and-the-crushing-of-the-american-dream.

Stiglitz, Joseph E., and Linda J. Bilmes. 2008. *The Three Trillion Dollar War: The True Cost of the Iraq Conflict.* New York. W. W. Norton.

Stinnett, Nick, and John DeFrain. 1985. *Secrets of Strong Families.* Boston: Little, Brown.

Stockholm International Peace Research Institute. 2013. "Military Expenditure." http://www.sipri.org/research/armaments/milex.

Stockman, Farah. 2009. "Anthropologist's War Death Reverberates." *Boston Globe,* February 12.

Stoltenberg, John. 2006. "How Men Have (a) Sex." In *Reconstructing Gender: A Multicultural Approach,* 4th ed., edited by Estelle Disch, 264–74. Boston: McGraw-Hill.

Storch, Eric A., Vanessa A. Milsom, Ninoska DeBraganza, Adam B. Lewin, Gary R. Geffken, and Janet H. Silverstein. 2007) "Peer Victimization, Psychosocial Adjustment, and Physical Activity in Overweight and At-Risk-for-Overweight Youth." *Journal of Pediatric Psychology* 32 (1): 80–89.

Strawn, Kirsten. 2013. "Hooking Up: Destroying Intimacy." The Faith Coach, February 20. http://thefaithcoach.wordpress.com/2013/02/20/hooking-up-destroying-intimacy-1.

Strayer, David L., Frank A. Drews, and Dennis J. Crouch. 2006. "A Comparison of the Cell Phone Driver and the Drunk Driver." *Human Factors* 48 (2): 381–91.

Street, Debra, and Jeralynn Sittig Cossman. 2006. "Greatest Generation or Greedy Geezers? Social Spending Preferences and the Elderly." *Social Problems* 53 (1): 75–96.

Subramanyam, M. A., A. V. Diez-Roux, D. A. Hickson, D. F. Sapong, M. Sims, H. A. Taylor Jr., D. R. Williams, and S. B. Wyatt. 2012. "Subjective Social Status and Psychosocial and Metabolic Risk Factors for Cardiovascular Disease among African Americans in the Jackson Heart Study." *Social Science & Medicine* 74 (8): 1146–54.

Substance Abuse and Mental Health Services Administration. 2011. *Results from the 2010 National Survey on Drug Use and Health: Summary of National Findings.* NSDUH Series H-41, HHS Publication (SMA) 11-4658. Rockville, MD: Substance Abuse and Mental Health Services Administration.

Sullivan, Susan Crawford. 2011. *Living Faith: Everyday Religion and Mothers in Poverty.* Chicago: University of Chicago Press.

Sutherland, Edwin H., and Donald R. Cressey. 1974. *Criminology,* 9th ed. Philadelphia: Lippincott.

Talen, Emily. 2010. "The Problem with Community Planning." *Journal of Planning Literature* 15 (2): 171–83.

Tan, Alexis S., and Kermit Joseph Scruggs. 1980. "Does Exposure to Comic Book Violence Lead to Aggression in Children?" *Journalism Quarterly* 57 (4): 579–83.

Tanaka, Yuki, and Marilyn Young, eds. 2009. *Bombing Civilians: A Twentieth-Century History.* New York: New Press.

Tanielian, Terri, and Lisa H. Jaycox, eds. 2008. *Invisible Wounds of War: Psychological and Cognitive Injuries, Their Consequences, and Services to Assist Recovery.* Santa Monica, CA: RAND Center for Military Health Policy Research.

Tatum, Beverly Daniel. 2003. *"Why Are All the Black Kids Sitting Together in the Cafeteria?" and Other Conversations about Race: A Psychologist Explains the Development of Racial Identity.* New York: Basic Books.

Taylor, Paul, Kim Parker, Richard Fry, D'Vera Cohn, Wendy Wang, Gabriel Velasco, and Daniel Dockterman. 2011. *Is College Worth It? College Presidents, Public Assess Value, Quality and Mission of Higher Education.* Washington, DC: Pew Research Center. http://www.pewsocialtrends.org/files/2011/05/Is-College-Worth-It.pdf.

Tepper, Steven J. 2011. *Not Here, Not Now, Not That! Protest over Art and Culture in America.* Chicago: University of Chicago Press.

Territo, Leonard, and George Kirkham. 2010. *International Sex Trafficking of Women and Children: Understanding the Global Epidemic.* New York: Looseleaf Law.

Thoits, Peggy A. 1995. "Stress, Coping, and Social Support Processes: Where Are We? What Next?" *Journal of Health and Social Behavior* 35 (extra issue): 53–79.

Thomas, Anna Lind. 2010. "Hooking Up on Campus: Cognitive Dissonance and Sexual Regret among College Students." Master's thesis, University of California, Chico.

Thomas, William I., and Dorothy S. Thomas. 1928. *The Child in America: Behavior Problems and Programs.* New York: Alfred A. Knopf.

Thomis, Malcolm I. 1972. *The Luddites: Machine-Breaking in Regency England.* New York: Schocken.

Thompson, Mark. 2011. "The Other 1%." *Time,* November 21. http://content.time.com/time/magazine/article/0,9171,2099152,00.html.

Thrasher, Frederic. 1949. "The Comics and Delinquency: Cause or Scapegoat." *Journal of Educational Sociology* 23 (4): 195–205.

Tierney, Kathleen J. 2007. "From the Margins to the Mainstream? Disaster Research at the Crossroads." *Annual Review of Sociology* 33: 503–25.

Titunik, Regina F. 2008. "The Myth of the Macho Military." *Polity* 40 (2): 137–63.

Tix, Andrew P., and Patricia A. Frazier. 1998. "The Use of Religious Coping during Stressful Life Events: Main Effects, Moderation, and Mediation." *Journal of Consulting and Clinical Psychology* 66: 411–22.

Tolman, Deborah. 2013. "It's Bad for Us Too: How the Sexualization of Girls Impacts the Sexuality of Boys, Men, and Women." In *The Sexualization of Girls and Girlhood: Causes, Consequences, and Resistance,* edited by Eileen L. Zurbriggen and Tomi-Ann Roberts, 84–106. New York: Oxford University Press.

Tönnies, Ferdinand. 1957. *Community and Society.* Translated and edited by Charles P. Loomis. Lansing: Michigan State University Press.

Toossi, Mitra. 2012. "Labor Force Projections to 20: A More Slowly Growing Workforce." *Monthly Labor Review,* January, 43–64. http://www.bls.gov/opub/mlr/2012/01/art3full.pdf.

Torry, Jack, and Jessica Wehrman. 2013. "Sen. Brown Backs Bill to Increase Social Security Benefits." *Columbus Dispatch,* November 6. http://www.dispatch.com/content/stories/local/2013/11/05/brown-backs-bill-to-increase-social-security-benefits.html.

Tough, Paul. 2008. *Whatever It Takes: Geoffrey Canada's Quest to Change Harlem and America.* Boston: Houghton Mifflin.

Tractenberg, Paul, Gary Orfield, and Greg Flaxman. 2013. *New Jersey's Apartheid and Intensely Segregated Urban Schools: Powerful Evidence of an Inefficient and Unconstitutional State Education System.* Newark, NJ: Institute on Education Law and Policy, Rutgers University. http://ielp.rutgers.edu/docs/IELP%20final%20report%20on%20apartheid%20schools%2020101013.pdf.

Treviño, A. Javier. 2011. "Teaching and Learning Service Sociology." *Teaching/Learning Matters* (newsletter of the American Sociological Association's Section on Teaching and Learning in Sociology) 40 (1): 4–6.

———. 2012. "The Challenge of Service Sociology." *Social Problems* 59 (1): 2–20.

———. 2013. "On the Facilitating Actions of Service Sociology." *Journal of Applied Social Science* 7 (1): 95–109.

Treviño, A. Javier, and Karen M. McCormack. 2014. *Service Sociology and Academic Engagement in Social Problems.* Burlington, VT: Ashgate.

Truman, Jennifer L., Lynn Langton, and Michael Planty. 2013. *Criminal Victimization, 2012.* Bureau of Justice Statistics Bulletin NCJ 243389, October. Washington, DC: U.S. Department of Justice. http://www.bjs.gov/content/pub/pdf/cv12.pdf.

Truman, Jennifer L., and Michael R. Rand. 2010. *Criminal Victimization, 2009.* Bureau of Justice Statistics Bulletin NCJ 231327, October. Washington, DC: U.S. Department of Justice. http://www.bjs.gov/content/pub/pdf/cv09.pdf.

Turkle, Sherry. 2011. *Alone Together: Why We Expect More from Technology and Less from Each Other.* New York: Basic.

Turner, Margery Austin, Stephen L. Ross, George C. Galster, and John Yinger. 2002. *Discrimination in Metropolitan Housing Markets: National Results from Phase I HDS 2000.* Washington, DC: Urban Institute, Metropolitan Housing and Communities Policy Center. http://www.urban.org/uploadedPDF/410821_Phase1_Report.pdf.

Tyson, Karolyn. 2011. *Integration Interrupted: Tracking, Black Students, and Acting White after Brown.* New York: Oxford University Press.

Uchida, Craig D. 2010. "The Development of American Police: An Historical Overview." In *Critical Issues in Policing: Contemporary Readings,* 6th ed., edited by Roger G. Dunham and Geoffrey P. Alpert, 17–36. Long Grove, IL: Waveland Press.

United Nations. 2006a. "Table 23. Marriages and Crude Marriage Rates, by Urban/Rural Residence: 2002–2006." In *Demographic Yearbook.* New York: United Nations. http://unstats.un.org/unsd/demographic/products/dyb/dyb2006/Table23.pdf.

———. 2006b. "Table 25. Divorces and Crude Divorce Rates, by Urban/Rural Residence: 2002–2006." In *Demographic Yearbook.* New York: United Nations. http://unstats.un.org/unsd/demographic/products/dyb/dyb2006/Table25.pdf.

———. 2009. "International Migrant Stock: The 2008 Revision." http://esa.un.org/migration/index.asp?panel=1.

———. 2010. "Water and Urbanisation." Media brief. http://www.un.org/waterforlifedecade/swm_cities_zaragoza_2010/pdf/03_water_and_urbanisation.pdf.

———. 2011. *World Population Prospects: The 2010 Revision,* 2 vols. Department of Economic and Social Affairs, Population Division. New York: United Nations.

United Nations Educational, Scientific and Cultural Organization. 1986. Seville Statement on Violence. http://www.unesco.org/cpp/uk/declarations/seville.pdf.

United Nations Girls' Education Initiative. 2010. "Lacking Sanitary Pads, Girls Miss School in Dadaab Refugee Camp." October 13. http://www.ungei.org/news/kenya_2922.html.

———. 2011. "UN Girls' Education Initiative Reaffirms the Need for Education to Be Central to Improving the Lives of Women and Girls." March 7. http://www.ungei.org/infobycountry/247_3065.html.

———. 2014. "Empowering Adolescent Girls in Ethiopia and Tanzania." Accessed March 25. http://www.ungei.org/tanzania_3072.html.

United Nations Human Settlements Programme. 2011. "Hot Cities: Battle-Ground for Climate Change." http://mirror.unhabitat.org/downloads/docs/E_Hot_Cities.pdf.

United Nations Office on Drugs and Crime. 2006. *2006 Global Study on Ending Violence against Women.* Vienna: United Nations Office on Drugs and Crime.

———. 2011. *2011 Global Study on Homicide: Trends, Context, Data.* Vienna: United Nations Office on Drugs and Crime.

———. 2013. *Comprehensive Study on Cybercrime* (Draft, February). Vienna: United Nations Office on Drugs and Crime. http://www.unodc.org/documents/organized-crime/UNODC_CCPCJ_EG.4_2013/CYBERCRIME_STUDY_210213.pdf.

United Students Against Sweatshops. 2014. "Garment Worker Solidarity." Accessed April 16. http://usas.org/campaigns/garment-worker-solidarity.

U.S. AID. 2011. "Why Invest in Women?" http://50.usaid.gov/infographic-why-invest-in-women/usaid-women.

U.S. Bureau of Justice Statistics. 2005. *State Court Sentencing of Convicted Felons.* Washington, DC: U.S. Department of Justice.

———. 2014. "Rape and Sexual Assault." Accessed March 25. http://www.bjs.gov/index.cfm?ty=tpandtid=317.

U.S. Bureau of Labor Statistics. 2010a. "National Census of Fatal Occupational Injuries in 2009 (Preliminary Results)." Press release, August 19. http://www.bls.gov/news.release/pdf/cfoi.pdf.

———. 2010b. "Workplace Injuries and Illnesses—2009." Press release, October 21. http://www.bls.gov/news.release/archives/osh_10212010.pdf.

———. 2012a. "Employment Status of the Civilian Population by Race, Sex, and Age." Accessed June 12. http://www.bls.gov/news.release/empsit.t02.htm.

———. 2012b. *Highlights of Women's Earnings in 2011.* Report 1038. Washington, DC: U.S. Department of Labor. http://www.bls.gov/cps/cpswom2011.pdf.

———. 2012c. *Labor Force Characteristics by Race and Ethnicity, 2011.* Report 1036. Washington, DC: U.S. Department of Labor. http://www.bls.gov/cps/cpsrace2011.pdf.

———. 2012d. "Labor Force Statistics from the Current Population Survey: Labor Force, Employment, and Unemployment Statistics by Age Group, 2012." http://www.bls.gov/cps/cpsaat03.pdf.

———. 2013a. "The Editor's Desk: Union Membership Declines in 2012." January 24. http://www.bls.gov/opub/ted/2013/ted_20130124.htm.

———. 2013b. "Employment Status of the Civilian Population by Sex and Age." Accessed April 8. http://www.bls.gov/news.release/empsit.t01.htm.

———. 2013c. "Employment Status of the Civilian Population 25 Years and Over by Educational Attainment." Accessed April 9. http://www.bls.gov/news.release/empsit.t04.htm.

———. 2013d. "Frequently Asked Questions." Accessed March 8. http://www.bls.gov/dolfaq/bls_ques23.htm.

———. 2013e. "Number of Fatal Work Injuries, 1992–2011." http://www.bls.gov/iif/oshwc/cfoi/cfch0010.pdf.

———. 2014. "Labor Force Statistics from the Current Population Survey: Access to Historical Data for the Tables of the Union Membership News Release." Accessed March 26. http://www.bls.gov/cps/cpslutabs.htm.

U.S. Census Bureau. 2010. "Table UC3. Opposite Sex Unmarried Couples by Presence of Biological Children under 18, and Age, Earnings, Education, and Race and Hispanic Origin of Both Partners: 2010." http://www.census.gov/population/www/socdemo/hh-fam/cps2010.html.

———. 2012a. "About Families and Living Arrangements." Accessed October 19. http://www.census.gov/hhes/families/about.

———. 2012b. "Table 133. Marriages and Divorces: Number and Rate by State, 1990–2009." In *Statistical Abstract of the United States: 2012.* Washington, DC: Government Printing Office. http://www.census.gov/compendia/statab/2012/tables/12s0133.pdf.

———. 2012c. "Table 229. Educational Attainment by Race and Hispanic Origin: 1970 to 2010." In *Statistical Abstract of the United States: 2012.* Washington, DC: Government Printing Office. http://www.census.gov/compendia/statab/2012/tables/12s0230.pdf.

———. 2012d. "Table 620. Employment by Industry: 2000 to 2012." In *Statistical Abstract of the United States: 2012.* Washington, DC: Government Printing Office.

http://www.census.gov/compendia/statab/2012/tables/12s0620.pdf.

———. 2012e. "Table 697. Money Income of Families—Median Income by Race and Hispanic Origin in Current and Constant (2009) Dollars: 1990 to 2009." In *Statistical Abstract of the United States: 2012.* Washington, DC: Government Printing Office. http://www.census.gov/compendia/statab/2012/tables/12s0697.pdf.

———. 2012f. "Table 699. Median Income of Families by Type of Family in Current and Constant (2009) Dollars, 1990 to 2009." In *Statistical Abstract of the United States: 2012.* Washington, DC: Government Printing Office. http://www.census.gov/compendia/statab/2012/tables/12s0699.pdf.

———. 2012g. "Table 1106. Motor Vehicle Occupants and Nonoccupants Killed and Injured: 1980 to 2009." In *Statistical Abstract of the United States: 2012.* Washington, DC: Government Printing Office. http://www.census.gov/compendia/statab/2012/tables/12s1106.pdf.

U.S. Department of Defense. 2012. *Department of Defense Annual Report on Sexual Assault in the Military: Fiscal Year 2012.* Washington, DC: U.S. Department of Defense. http://s3.documentcloud.org/documents/697934/pentagon-report-on-sexual-assault-in-2012.pdf.

U.S. Department of Health and Human Services. 2012. "The Center for Faith-based and Neighborhood Partnerships." Accessed November 26. http://www.hhs.gov/partnerships/index.html.

———. 2013. "2013 Poverty Guidelines." http://aspe.hhs.gov/poverty/13poverty.cfm.

U.S. Department of Labor. 2011. *Dictionary of Occupational Titles.* Washington, DC: Government Printing Office. http://www.occupationalinfo.org.

U.S. Department of State. 2007. "Trafficking in Persons Report 2007." http://www.state.gov/j/tip/rls/tiprpt/2007/index.htm.

———. 2011. "Trafficking in Persons Report 2011." http://www.state.gov/j/tip/rls/tiprpt/2011/index.htm.

———. 2014. "20 Ways You Can Help Fight Human Trafficking." Accessed March 31. http://www.state.gov/j/tip/id/help.

U.S. Environmental Protection Agency. 2012a. "Climate Change." Accessed May 31. http://www.epa.gov/climatechange.

———. 2012b. "Climate Change Indicators in the United States." http://www.epa.gov/climatechange/science/indicators/ghg/us-ghg-emissions.html.

U.S. Equal Employment Opportunity Commission. 2009. "Title VII of the Civil Rights Act of 1964." http://www.eeoc.gov/laws/statutes/titlevii.cfm.

Vaes, Jeroen, Paola Paladino, and Elisa Puvia. 2011. "Are Sexualized Women Complete Human Beings? Why Men and Women Dehumanize Sexually Objectified Women." *European Journal of Psychology* 41 (6): 774–85.

Van Aalst, Maarten K. 2006. "The Impacts of Climate Change on the Risk of Natural Disasters." *Disasters* 30 (1): 5–18.

Vandepitte, J., R. Lyerla, G. Dallabetta, F. Crabbé, M. Alary, and A. Buvé. 2006. "Estimates of the Number of Female Sex Workers in Different Regions of the World." *Sexually Transmitted Diseases* 82 (3): 18–25.

Van de Water, Paul N. 2013. "Medicare Is Not 'Bankrupt': Health Reform Has Improved Program's Financing." Center on Budget and Policy Priorities, June 3. http://www.cbpp.org/cms/?fa=view&id=3532.

Van Hook, Jennifer, Susan I. Brown, and Maxwell Ndigume Kwenda. 2004. "A Decomposition of Trends in Poverty among Children of Immigrants." *Demography* 41 (4): 649–70.

Van Ness, Daniel W., and Karen Heetderks Strong. 2010. *Restoring Justice: An introduction to Restorative Justice,* 4th ed. New Providence, NJ: LexisNexis.

Van Orden, Kimberly, and Yeates Conwell. 2011. "Suicides in Late Life." *Current Psychiatry Reports* 13 (3): 234–41.

Vasquez, Jessica M. 2011. *Mexican Americans across Generations: Immigrant Families, Racial Realities.* New York: New York University Press.

Ventola, C. Lee. 2011. "Direct-to-Consumer Pharmaceutical Advertising: Therapeutic or Toxic?" *Pharmacy and Therapeutics* 36 (10): 669–74, 681–84.

Vine, David. 2012. "Tomgram: The True Costs of Empire." December 11. http://www.tomdispatch.com/post/175627/tomgram%3A_david_vine,_the_true_costs_of_empire.

Voss, Georgina. 2012. "Treating It as a Normal Business': Researching the Pornography Industry." *Sexualities* 15 (3–4): 391–410.

Waddan, Alex. 2010. "The US Safety Net, Inequality, and the Great Recession." *Journal of Poverty and Social Justice* 18 (3): 243–54.

Wade, Ann, and Tanya Beran. 2011. "Cyberbullying: The New Era of Bullying." *Canadian Journal of Social Psychology* 26 (1): 44–61.

Wade, Lisa, and Caroline Heldman. 2012. "Hooking Up and Opting Out: Negotiating Sex in the First Year of College." In *Sex for Life: From Virginity to Viagra, How Sexuality Changes throughout Our Lives,* edited by Laura M. Carpenter and John DeLamater, 128–45. New York: New York University Press.

WAGE Project. 2012. "WAGE (Women Are Getting Even)." Accessed July 12. http://www.wageproject.org/index.php.

Waitzkin, Howard. 2000. *The Second Sickness: Contradictions of Capitalist Health Care.* Lanham, MD: Rowman & Littlefield.

Wajcman, Judy. 2000. "Reflections on Gender and Technology Studies: In What State Is the Art?" *Social Studies of Science* 30 (3): 447–64.

Walker, Samuel, and Charles M. Katz. 2008. *The Police in America: An Introduction,* 6th ed. Boston: McGraw-Hill.

Waller, Willard. 1965. *The Sociology of Teaching.* New York: John Wiley.

Wallerstein, Immanuel. 1979. *The Capitalist World-Economy.* Cambridge: Cambridge University Press.

Walsh, Declan, and Ihsanullah Tipu Mehsud. 2013. "Civilian Deaths in Drone Strikes Cited in Report." *New York Times,* October 22, 1.

Walsh, Susan. 2014. Hooking Up Smart home page. Accessed March 28. http://www.hookingupsmart.com.

Walton, John. 1993. "Urban Sociology: The Contribution and Limits of Political Economy." *Annual Review of Sociology* 19: 301–20.

Wang, E. C., M. C. Choe, J. G. Meara, and J. A. Koempel. 2004. "Inequality of Access to Surgical Specialty Health Care: Why Children with Government-Funded Insurance Have Less Access than Those with Private Insurance in Southern California." *Pediatrics* 114 (5): e584-90.

Wang, Wendy. 2012. "Public Says a Secure Job Is the Ticket to the Middle Class." Pew Research Center, Social and Demographic Trends. http://www.pewsocialtrends.org/files/2012/08/Job-report-final.pdf.

Want China Times. 2012. "Over 70% of Chinese Have Had Pre-marital Sex: Survey." April 10. http://www.wantchinatimes.com/news-subclass-cnt.aspx?id=20120410000035andcid=1103.

Ward, Lester F. 1902. "Contemporary Sociology." *American Journal of Sociology* 7 (4): 475–500.

Wargo, John. 2009. *Green Intelligence: Creating Environments That Protect Human Health.* New Haven, CT: Yale University Press.

Warner, Michael. 1993. "Introduction." In *Fear of a Queer Planet: Queer Politics and Social Theory,* edited by Michael Warner, vi–xxxvi. Minneapolis: University of Minnesota Press.

Waters, Mary C. 1999. *Black Identities: West Indian Immigrant Dreams and American Realities.* Cambridge, MA: Harvard University Press.

Waters, Mary C., and Tomás R. Jiménez. 2005. "Assessing Immigrant Assimilation: New Empirical and Theoretical Challenges." *Annual Review of Sociology* 31: 105–25.

Watkins, S. Craig. 2005. *Hip Hop Matters: Politics, Pop Culture, and the Struggle for the Soul of a Movement.* Boston: Beacon Press.

Weber, Max. 1958. *From Max Weber: Essays in Sociology.* Edited by H. H. Gerth and C. Wright Mills. New York. Oxford University Press.

———. 2004. *The Protestant Ethic and the Spirit of Capitalism.* New York: Oxford University Press. First published 1904–1905.

Weil, Andrew, and Winifred Rosen. 2004. *From Chocolate to Morphine: Everything You Need to Know about Mind-Altering Drugs,* rev. ed. Boston: Houghton Mifflin.

Weiss, Nicholas. 2011. "Assessment and Treatment of ADHD in Adults." *Psychiatric Annals* 41 (1): 23–31.

Weitzer, Ronald. 2007. "The Social Construction of Sex Trafficking: Ideology and Institutionalization of a Moral Crusade." *Politics and Society* 35 (3): 447–75.

Welsh, Wayne N., and Phillip W. Harris. 2012. *Criminal Justice Policy and Planning,* 4th ed. Waltham, MA: Elsevier.

Wertham, Fredric. 1954. *Seduction of the Innocent.* New York: Rinehart.

West, Candace, and Sarah Fenstermaker. 1993. "Power, Inequality and the Accomplishment of Gender: An Ethnomethodological View." In *Theory on Gender, Feminism on Theory,* edited by Paula England, 151–74. New York: Aldine de Gruyter.

West, Candace, and Angela Garcia. 1988. "Conversational Shift Work: A Study of Topical Transition between Women and Men." *Social Problems* 35: 551–75.

Western, Bruce. 2006. *Punishment and Inequality in America.* New York: Russell Sage Foundation.

White, Kevin. 2006. *The Sage Dictionary of Health and Society.* Thousand Oaks, CA: Sage.

———. 2009. *An Introduction to the Sociology of Health and Illness.* Thousand Oaks, CA: Sage.

———. 2012. 'The Body, Social Inequality and Health." In *The Routledge Handbook of Body Studies,* edited by Bryan S. Turner, 264–74. London: Routledge.

White, Merry I. 1987. *The Japanese Educational Challenge: A Commitment to Children.* New York: Free Press.

Whitehead, Harriet. 1981. "The Bow and the Burden Strap: A New Look at Institutionalized Homosexuality in Native North America." In *Sexual Meanings: The Cultural Construction of Gender and Sexuality,* edited by Sherry B. Ortner and Harriet Whitehead, 80–115. Cambridge: Cambridge University Press.

Wildeman, Christopher. 2012. "Imprisonment and Infant Mortality." *Social Problems* 59: 228–57.

Williams, Alex. 2010. "The New Math on Campus." *New York Times,* February 5.

Williams, Christine L. 1992. "The Glass Escalator: Hidden Advantages for Men in the 'Female' Professions." *Social Problems* 39 (3): 253–67.

Williams, David R., and Michelle Sternthall. 2010. "Understanding Racial-Ethnic Disparities in Health: Sociological Contributions." *Journal of Health and Social Behavior* 51 (S): S15–27.

Williamson, Celia, and Lynda M. Baker. 2009. "Women in Street-Based Prostitution: A Typology of Their Work Styles." *Qualitative Social Work* 8 (1): 27–44.

Wilson, Jim. 2013. "Restorative Justice Programs Take Root in Schools." *New York Times,* April 3.

Wilson, William Julius. 1978. *The Declining Significance of Race: Blacks and Changing American Institutions.* Chicago: University of Chicago Press.

———. 1987. *The Truly Disadvantaged: The Inner City, the Underclass, and Public Policy.* Chicago: University of Chicago Press.

———. 1996. *When Work Disappears: The World of the New Urban Poor.* New York: Alfred A. Knopf.

———. 2009. *More than Just Race: Being Black and Poor in the Inner City.* New York: W. W. Norton.

Windsor, Liliane Cambraia, Ellen Benoit, and Eloise Dunlap. 2010. "Dimensions of Oppression in the Lives of Impoverished Black Women Who Use Drugs." *Journal of Black Studies* 41 (1): 21–39.

Wing, Steve. 2010. "Ethics for Environmental Health Research: The Case of the U.S. Nuclear Weapons Industry." *New Solutions* 20 (2): 179–87.

Wingfield, Adia Harvey. 2009. "Racializing the Glass Escalator: Reconsidering Men's Experiences with Women's Work." *Gender & Society* 23 (1): 5–26.

Wise, Tim. 2008. *White Like Me: Reflections on Race from a Privileged Son.* New York: Soft Skull Press.

Wong, Kristina. 2009. "Obama on Hate Crimes Legislation Signing: 'The Bells of Freedom Ring Out a Little Louder.'" ABC News, October 28. http://abcnews.go.com/blogs/politics/2009/10/obama-on-hate-crimes-legislation-signing-the-bells-of-freedom-ring-out-a-little-louder.

Wood, Jean Elisabeth. 2006. "Variation in Sexual Violence during War." *Politics and Society* 34: 307–42.

World Commission on Environment and Development. 1987. *Our Common Future.* Oxford: Oxford University Press.

World Health Organization. 2014. "Condoms for HIV Prevention." Accessed March 31. http://www.who.int/hiv/topics/condoms/en.

World Nuclear Association. 2013. "Uranium in Niger." http://world-nuclear.org/info/Country-Profiles/Countries-G-N/Niger/#.UbTSnutYg8Y.

Worthy, Kenneth A., Richard C. Strohman, Paul R. Billings, and the Berkeley Biotechnology Working Group. 2005.

"Agricultural Biotechnology Science Compromised: The Case of Quist and Chapela." In *Controversies in Science and Technology: From Maize to Menopause,* edited by Daniel Lee Kleinman, Abby J. Kinchy, and Jo Handelsman, 135–49. Madison: University of Wisconsin Press.

Yablokov, Alexy V., Vassily B. Nesterenko, and Alexy V. Nesterenko. 2009. "Chernobyl: Consequences of the Catastrophe for People and the Environment." *Annals of the New York Academy of Sciences* 1181 (December).

Yamato, Gloria. 2001. "Something about the Subject Makes It Hard to Name." In *Race, Class, and Gender: An Anthology,* 4th ed., edited by Margaret L. Anderson and Patricia Hill Collins, 90–94. Belmont, CA: Wadsworth.

Yancey, George. 2003. *Who Is White? Latinos, Asians, and the New Black/Nonblack Divide.* Boulder, CO: Lynne Rienner.

Yang, Song. 2007. "Racial Disparities in Training, Pay-Raise Attainment, and Income." *Research in Social Stratification and Mobility* 25 (4): 323–35.

Yeager, Angela. 2012. "Survey: Health Care Providers Not Checking for Family Food Insecurity, Barriers Still Exist." Oregon State University Extension Service, July 10. http://extension.oregonstate.edu/news/release/2012/07/survey-health-care-providers-not-checking-family-food-insecurity-barriers-still-exis.

Yetman, Norman. 1999. *Majority and Minority: The Dynamic of Race and Ethnicity in American Life.* Boston: Allyn & Bacon.

Yinger, John. 1995. *Closed Doors, Opportunities Lost: The Continuing Costs of Housing Discrimination.* New York: Russell Sage Foundation.

Zheng, Hui, and Linda K. George. 2012. "Rising U.S. Income Inequality and the Changing Gradient of Socioeconomic Status on Physical Functioning and Activity Limitations, 1984–2007." *Social Science & Medicine* 75 (12): 2170–82.

Zhuqing, Wang. 2012. "A Study of the Rights and Interests of the Older Persons in China." *Ageing International* 37: 386–413.

Zola, Irving Kenneth. 1972. "Medicine as an Institution of Social Control." *American Sociological Review* 20 (4): 487–504.

Zukin, Sharon. 1995. *The Cultures of Cities.* Malden, MA: Blackwell.

INDEX

interpretive flexibility and, 413
landraces and, 408, 409
malware and, 400
megamachine concept and, 402
minorities in science/engineering and, 406, 407, 407 (figure)
Mode 1 knowledge and, 403, 403 (table)
Mode 2 knowledge and, 403, 403 (table)
nanotechnology and, 405
niche medicine, development of, 410
nuclear risk and, 378–380, 379 (figure), 390, 399, 413
research & development personnel and, 405, 406 (figure)
science machine and, 402
science shops and, 403
science, social problems and, 400, 407–409, 410
science, socially defined field of, 398–399
social change initiatives and, 414–415
social construction of, 412–413
social facts and, 412
social organization and, 402
sociotechnical systems and, 398
stakeholders in, 406-409, 407 (figure), 409, 411
structural functionalism theory and, 410
sustainability initiatives and, 415
symbolic interactionism and, 411
technocracy and, 405
technological developments, societal values and, 403–404
technological fixes and, 404–405
technology, social problems and, 400–402, 407–409, 410, 411
technology, socially defined field of, 399–400
technoscience and, 400
transgenic crops and, 408–409
wireless networks, electrosensitivity and, 401
within-science social problems and, 405–406
Scientific management, 270–271
Scoboria, A., 359
Sector model of cities, 461
Segal, E. A., 27, 46
Segmented assimilation, 71
Segregation, 19, 66, 69, 165, 166, 167–168, 263, 455, 455–456, 456 (figure), 462
Selection effect, 227
Selective Service System, 437
Self:
depression and, 18
labeling process and, 16
looking-glass self and, 16
social self and, 16
Self-control theory, 329
Self-fulfilling prophecy, 16

Self-made myth, 34–35, 36
Semel, S. F., 161
September 11, 2001 terrorist attacks, 21, 290, 420, 439, 440, 441, 442, 443
Service economy, 5, 21, 251–252
See also Culture of service; Work; Workers
Service Employees International Union (SEIU), 260
Service learning opportunities, 156
Service sociology, 3, 20–21
Settlement houses, 20, 21
Sex education, 92
Sex ratio, 141, 141 (figure)
Sex role theory, 96-97, 98
Sex tourism, 118, 123
Sex trafficking, 110, 117, 118–119, 128
Sex Trafficking Opposition Project (STOP), 303
Sex work, 118–119, 120
conflict theory and, 121–122
decriminalization/legalization of, 121, 122, 124
latent consequence of sexual morals and, 121
male client perspective on, 122
manifest consequence of sexual morals and, 121
rationales for, 121–122
sex worker perspective on, 122
sexism/structural inequalities, maintenance of, 121, 122
sexual double standard and, 121
societal purposes of, 120–121
structural functionalism theory and, 120–121
symbolic interactionism theory and, 122, 124
See also Prostitution; Sex tourism; Sex trafficking; Sexualities
Sexual assault, 82, 91–94, 115, 126-129, 432, 435, 437, 444
Sexual dimorphism, 85
Sexual dysfunction, 112
Sexual harassment, 101
Sexual orientation, 34, 70, 85–86, 92, 108
Sexual script theory, 124, 126
Sexualities, 110–111
collective belief systems/morals and, 111, 111 (figure), 119, 121
college campus sexual assault and, 91–94, 115, 129
commercialization of sex and, 117–119
Comstock laws and, 128
condom use and, 124, 126
continuum of, 85
deviance and, 112–113
erotica and, 116
extra-marital sexual activity and, 113–116, 114 (figure)

feminist theory and, 126-127
hookup culture and, 88, 111–112, 113–116, 114 (figure)
intersexed individuals and, 85
labeling theory and, 112–113
latent consequence of sexual morals and, 121
manifest consequence of sexual morals and, 121
peer sexuality education programs and, 128
pornography industry and, 116-117
prostitution and, 111, 120
sex assignment and, 85
sex education programs and, 92, 112, 128
sex roles and, 96
sex tourism and, 118, 123
sex trafficking and, 110, 117, 118–119, 128
sexual dimorphism and, 85
sexual double standard and, 114, 121
sexual dysfunction and, 112
sexual script theory and, 124, 126
social change initiatives and, 128–129
teen pregnancy and, 92, 112, 125, 125 (figure)
transsexual individuals and, 85–86
See also Gender; Queer theory; Rape; Sex work; Sexual assault; Sexual orientation
Sexually transmitted infections (STIs), 124, 124 (figure), 126
Shadow economy, 253–254
Shaefer, H. L., 32
Shaw, C. R., 301
Shepard, M., 299
Shishehbor, M. H., 345
Shull, R. D., 228
Silva, J. M., 4, 5
Simmel, G., 453
Simmons, C. -M., 129
Simon, W., 124
Slavery, 34, 70, 118, 338
Small, A. W., 21
Smith, A., 267, 268
Smith, M., 340
Smokefree website, 361
Snow, D. A., 384
Snowden, E. J., 396
Social capital, 325, 359, 360
Social class, 5, 34
capitalists and, 14
class, concept of, 35–36
class warfare and, 34, 44
classless egalitarianism and, 34–35, 37
code theory and, 175
colonialism and, 34
conflict theory and, 44–45
functionalist theory and, 40, 42